NETWORK+
Guide To Networks

Tamara Dean

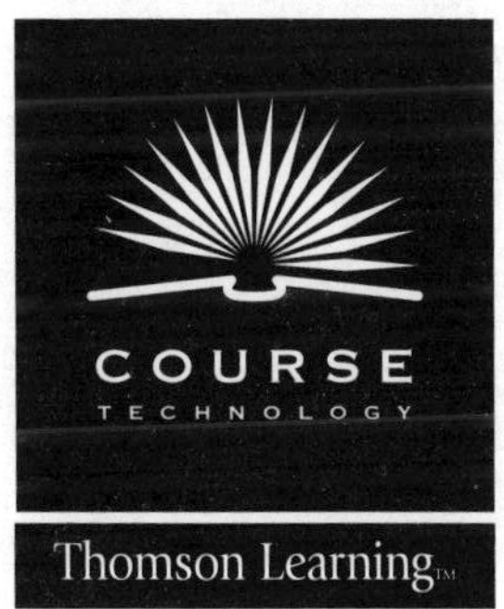

ONE MAIN STREET, CAMBRIDGE, MA 02142

Australia • Canada • Denmark • Japan • Mexico • New Zealand • Philippines
Puerto Rico • Singapore • South Africa • Spain • United Kingdom • United States

Network+ Guide to Networks is published by Course Technology.

Associate Publisher:	Kristen Duerr
Senior Acquisitions:	Stephen Solomon
Product Manager:	David George
Production Editor:	Megan Cap-Renzi
Developmental Editor:	Ann Shaffer
Quality Assurance Manager:	John Bosco
Associate Product Manager:	Laura Hildebrand
Manufacturing:	Denise Sandler
Composition Designer:	GEX, Inc.
Text Designer:	GEX, Inc.
Cover Designer:	Efrat Reis
Marketing Manager:	Susan Ogar

Disclaimer

Course Technology reserves the right to revise this publication and make changes from time to time in its content without notice.

The Web addresses in this book are subject to change from time to time as necessary without notice.

For more information, contact Course Technology, One Main Street, Cambridge, MA 02142; or find us on the World Wide Web at *www.course.com*.

For permission to use material from this text or product, contact us by

- Web: www.thomsonrights.com
- Phone: 1-800-730-2214
- Fax: 1-800-730-2215

ISBN 0-7600-1145-1

Printed in Canada

5 WC 02 01 00

CONTENTS AT A GLANCE

TABLE OF CONTENTS

PREFACE

Knowing how to install, configure, and troubleshoot a computer network is a highly marketable and exciting skill. This book covers a wide range of material about networking, from assessments of careers in networking to discussions of local area networks, wide area networks, protocols, topologies, transmission media, and security. It not only introduces a variety of concepts, but also provides in-depth examinations of the most significant aspects of networking, such as the TCP/IP protocol suite. In addition to explaining concepts, each chapter includes several real-world examples of networking issues from a professional's standpoint, making the book a practical learning tool.

The material in this book addresses all of the objectives for CompTIA's Network+ certification. Individual chapters discuss the following topics:

Chapters 1, 2, and 3 provide an introduction to networking fundamentals, including networking standards organizations, the OSI Model, and networking protocols.

Chapter 4 builds on the fundamentals introduced in earlier chapters by explaining the variety of logical and physical architectures used in local area networks.

Chapters 5 and 6 discuss the physical parts of a network, including wiring, network interface cards, hubs, routers, bridges, and switches. In Chapter 6, you will find several photos portraying typical networking equipment.

Chapter 7 expands on your knowledge of local area networks by examining wide area networking topologies and transmission methods.

Chapters 8, 9, and 10 introduce the most popular network operating systems: Windows NT, NetWare, and UNIX.

Chapter 11 provides a detailed examination of the components and uses of the TCP/IP protocol suite, the most popular protocol in use on contemporary networks.

Chapters 12 and 13 approach the tasks of troubleshooting and maintaining networks in a logical, practical manner. Once you have learned how networks operate and how to create them, you will need to know how to fix and maintain them.

Chapters 14 and 15 consider how to keep the network safe in the face of dangers such as power flaws, hardware or software failures, and security breaches. In Chapter 15, you will also learn how to implement an enterprise-wide security policy.

Chapter 16 brings together all of your knowledge about networking by tackling a network implementation project. This chapter includes tips on project planning specifically for technical endeavors.

The three appendices at the end of this book serve as references for the networking professional. Appendix A provides an exhaustive list of software and hardware resources related to networking. Appendix B expands on what you learned about networking hardware by providing pictures of a typical networking professional's tools. Appendix C gives examples of forms that you can use while planning, installing, and troubleshooting your network.

The Intended Audience

This book is intended to serve the needs of professionals who are interested in mastering broad, vendor-independent networking concepts. In particular, it will help those professionals who are seeking to pass the Computing Technology Industry Association's Network+ certification exam. For more information on Network+ certification, visit CompTIA's web site at www.comptia.org. The text and pedagogical features are designed to provide a truly interactive learning experience, preparing you for the challenges of the highly dynamic networking industry. In addition to the information presented in the text, each chapter includes Hands-on Projects that take you through various tasks in a step-by-step fashion. Each chapter also contains a running case study that places you in the role of problem solver, requiring you to use concepts presented in the chapter so as to achieve a successful solution.

Features

To aid you in fully understanding networking concepts, this book includes many features designed to enhance your learning experience.

- **Chapter Objectives.** Each chapter begins with a detailed list of the concepts to be mastered within that chapter. This list provides you with both a quick reference to the chapter's contents and a useful study aid.
- **Illustrations and Tables.** Numerous illustrations of server screens and components help you visualize common setup steps, theories, and concepts. In addition, the many tables included provide details and comparisons of both practical and theoretical information.
- **Hands-on Projects.** Although it is important to understand the theory behind networking technology, nothing can improve upon real-world experience. To this end, along with theoretical explanations, each chapter provides numerous Hands-on Projects aimed at providing you with practical implementation experience.
- **Chapter Summaries.** Each chapter's text is followed by a summary of the concepts introduced in that chapter. These summaries provide a helpful way to recap and revisit the ideas covered in each chapter.
- **Review Questions.** The end-of-chapter assessment begins with a set of review questions that reinforce the ideas introduced in each chapter. Answering these questions will ensure that you have mastered the important concepts.
- **Case Projects.** Located at the end of each chapter are several cases. In these extensive exercises, you implement the skills and knowledge gained in the chapter through real design and implementation scenarios.

TEXT AND GRAPHIC CONVENTIONS

Wherever appropriate, additional information and exercises have been added to this book to help you better understand the topic at hand. Icons throughout the text alert you to additional materials. The icons used in this textbook are described below.

The Note icon signals that additional helpful material related to the subject being described is available.

Each hands-on activity in this book is preceded by the Hands-On icon and a description of the exercise that follows.

Tips based on the authors' experience provide extra information about how to attack a problem or what to do to in certain real-world situations.

The cautions warn you about potential mistakes or problems so you can prevent or avoid them.

Case project icons mark the running case projects, which are more involved, scenario-based assignments. In these extensive case examples, you are asked to implement independently what you have learned.

INSTRUCTOR'S MATERIALS

The following additional materials are available when this book is used in a classroom setting. All of the supplements available with this book are provided to the instructor on a single CD-ROM.

Electronic Instructor's Manual. The Instructor's Manual that accompanies this textbook includes the following items:

- Additional instructional material to assist in class preparation, including suggestions for lecture topics, suggested lab activities, tips on setting up a lab for the hands-on assignments, and alternative lab setup ideas in situations where lab resources are limited.
- Solutions to all end-of-chapter materials, including the Project and Case assignments.

Course Test Manager 1.3. Designed by Course Technology, this cutting-edge Windows-based testing software helps instructors design and administer tests and pretests. In addition to generating tests that can be printed and administered, this full-featured program has an online testing component that allows students to take tests at the computer and have their exams automatically graded.

PowerPoint presentations. This book comes with a set of Microsoft PowerPoint slides for each chapter. These slides are meant to be used as a teaching aid for classroom presentations, to be made available to students on the network for chapter review, or to be printed for classroom distribution. Instructors are also at liberty to add their own slides for other topics introduced.

MeasureUp™ Test Prep Software. Bound into the back of this book is a CD-ROM containing MeasureUp's exam preparation software. Each CD-ROM includes a test engine and fifty sample exam questions, simulating the Network+ exam. For more information about MeasureUp, visit their Web site at www. measureup.com.

ACKNOWLEDGMENTS

I could not have completed this book without the help of many friends, fellow networking professionals, and Course Technology staff. Thanks go to Kristen Duerr, associate publisher, for her enthusiasm and assistance in launching the book. Stephen Solomon, acquisitions editor, and Jennifer Normandin and Dave George, product managers at Course Technology, have all made significant contributions in transforming this book from a mere idea into a weighty product. I am deeply grateful to Ann Shaffer, developmental editor and friend, for suggesting that I write a book on networking, for being a constant cheerleader, and most of all, for steering my writing to greater clarity and specificity. Megan Cap-Renzi, production editor, and Jill Hobbs, copy editor, fabulously minded the details and polished the final drafts for production. Credit also goes to all of the quality assurance and technical reviewers who checked my work at every step, helping to make the book more accurate.

Thanks to all of my colleagues at Berbee Information Networks, in particular those who helped with technical material—Jim Berbee, Tom Callaci, Peyton Engel, Dan Geisler, David Klann, Katie McCullough, Tom Pendergast, Jerry Steinhauer, and Craig Weinhold—and those who sustained me with their good humor—Ken Bywaters, Gill Engel, Nancy Gibson, Jackie Ramin, Dale Schuster, and Scott Severson. I am especially grateful to Jim Berbee and Karen Walsh, without whom I would not have the experience that enabled me to write this book. Thanks also to Paul and Janet Dean, scientists and teachers both, for their encouragement, pedagogical advice, and technical bent. Finally, thanks to Rick, whose contribution was and continues to be inexpressible and immeasurable.

CHAPTER 1

AN INTRODUCTION TO NETWORKING

After reading this chapter and completing the exercises, you will be able to:

- List the advantages of networked computing relative to standalone computing
- Identify the elements of a network
- Describe several specific uses for a network
- Identify some of the certifications available to networking professionals
- Identify the kinds of nontechnical, or "soft," skills that will help you succeed as a networking professional

ON THE JOB

I never intended to be a networking professional. In high school my greatest love was reading, so I decided to study literature in college. I only used computers for writing term papers and e-mail. When I graduated from college, I don't think I even knew what a network was. With an English degree, I tried to find interesting jobs, and occasionally I did, but usually I wound up as a temp answering phones and typing all day.

One of the more interesting temporary jobs I had was at a pharmaceutical company, setting up laptop computers for their sales force. I installed software, tested the software, then shipped the machines to their owners. Soon I became fascinated with the hardware inside the machines and performed small repairs such as swapping out memory chips or fixing a keyboard connector. After I learned about PCs, I became more and more curious about the network: for example, how the laptop users picked up their e-mail while they were travelling. And before I knew it, I was supporting these users and troubleshooting the network problems that affected them. Because there was no one else around to help them, I had to learn quickly and without much formal training.

Since that time I've taken classes to fill in what I couldn't learn on the job. I've also met a lot of networking professionals who, like me, never intended to be in this field. In fact, very few of my colleagues have computer science degrees: some studied Music, Film, Microbiology, Russian, Meteorology, Math, Accounting, Mechanical Engineering, and the list goes on. We're all proof that you may wind up doing something entirely different from what you planned, but that you may enjoy it more than you imagined.

Lisa Stefanik
Abbotsford Information Networks

Loosely defined, a **network** is a group of computers and other devices (such as printers) that are connected by some type of transmission media, usually wire or cable. The variations on the hardware, software, transmission media, and design of networks, however, are nearly infinite. Networks may consist of two computers connected by a cable in a home office or several thousand computers connected across the world via a combination of cable, phone lines, and satellite links. In addition to connecting personal computers, networks may link together mainframe computers, modems, CD-ROMs, printers, plotters, fax machines, and phone systems. They may communicate through copper wires, fiber-optic cable, radio waves, infrared, or satellite links.

All networks offer advantages relative to using a **standalone computer** (a personal computer that uses programs and data only from its local disks). Most importantly, networks enable multiple users to share devices and data that, collectively, are referred to as the networks' **resources**. For any organization, sharing devices saves money. For example, rather than buying 20 printers for 20 staff members, you can buy one printer and have those 20 staff members share it over a network. Sharing devices also saves time. For example, it's faster for co-workers to share data over a network than to copy data to a disk and transport it from one computer to another—an outdated method commonly referred to as **sneakernet** (presumably because people wore sneakers when walking from computer to computer). Before networks, transferring data via floppy disks (illustrated in Figure 1-1) was the only possible way to share data.

Figure 1-1 Data sharing before the advent of networks

Another advantage to networks is that they allow you to manage, or administer, hardware and software on multiple computers from one central location. Imagine you work in the Information Technology (IT) department of a multinational insurance company and must verify that each of 5000 insurance agents across the world uses the same version of WordPerfect. Without a network you could never keep up! Networks, along with network management software, allow you to manage computers in your office or around the world from one computer. The computer on which you are actually working is referred to as the **local computer**. The computer that you are controlling or working on via the network is referred to as the **remote computer**. Because they allow you to share devices and administer computers centrally, networks increase productivity. It's not surprising, then, that most businesses depend on their networks to stay competitive.

The simplest form of a network—and one still used today—connects a handful of computers through one cable and uses peer-to-peer communication. **Peer-to-peer communication** enables computers to talk directly to other computers on a single segment of cable and share devices such as printers or CD-ROM drives. No computer in a peer-to-peer network has more authority than another, and every computer can use resources from every other computer. Most computers in a peer-to-peer network are general-purpose personal computers that are not designed to handle heavy processing loads. Peer-to-peer networks are simple to configure, but not very flexible or secure. Also, they are not practical for connecting more than a handful of computers, because they do not necessarily centralize resources. For example, if your computer is part of a peer-to-peer network that includes five other computers, and each computer user stores his or her spreadsheets and word-processing files on his or her own hard disk, whenever your colleagues want to edit your files, they must attach to your machine on the network. If one colleague saves a changed version of one of your spreadsheets on her hard disk, you'll find it difficult to keep track of which version is the most current. As you can imagine, the more computers you add to a peer-to-peer network, the more difficult it becomes to find and track resources. Peer-to-peer networks are most often used in small offices where technical expertise is scarce. Figure 1-2 shows an example of a peer-to-peer network.

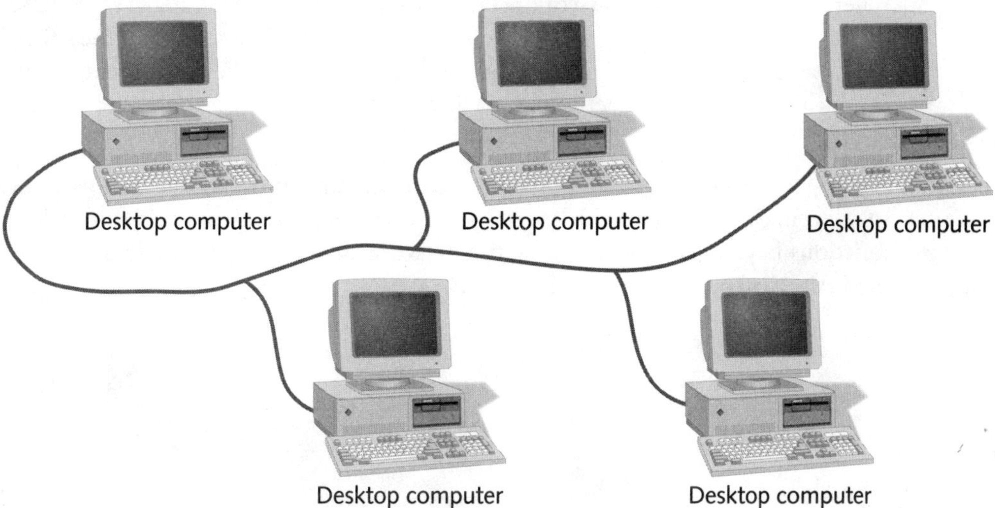

Figure 1-2 A simple peer-to-peer network

One way to establish a peer-to-peer network is using Windows 95 or Windows 98 file-sharing controls. Peer-to-peer networks do not require a special network operating system such as Windows NT Server or Novell NetWare. Instead, each user on this type of network can modify the properties of his or her desktop operating system to allow others to read and edit files on that particular computer's hard disk. Because access depends on many different users, it typically isn't uniform and may not be secure.

The peer-to-peer network is a very simple example of a local area network. As its name suggests, a **local area network (LAN)** is a network of computers and other devices that is confined to a relatively small space, such as one building or even one office. Small LANs became popular in businesses in the early 1980s. Today's LANs are typically larger and more complex than the peer-to-peer network in the previous example.

LANs involving many computers are usually server-based. On a **server-based network**, special computers, known as **file servers**, process data for and facilitate communication between the other computers on the network, which are known as **clients**. Clients usually take the form of desktop computers, known as **workstations**. A file server functions something like a librarian, who allows and helps the public to deposit and withdraw (literary) resources while protecting those materials from theft or damage.

Likewise, the file server's main job is to allow clients to share resources. To function as a file server, a computer must be running a network operating system, such as Microsoft Windows

NT or Novell NetWare. (By contrast, a standalone computer, or a client computer, uses a somewhat simpler operating system, such as Windows 98.) A **network operating system (NOS)** is special system software designed to manage data and other resources on a server for a number of clients. Network operating systems also provide the ability to manage network security, network users and groups, protocols, and networked applications.

Client/server architecture is the term used for the networking model in which clients (typically desktop PCs) use a central file server to share applications and data. Every computer on a client/server network is either a client or a server. Clients on a network can still run applications from and save data to their local hard disk; a server, on the other hand, offers the option of using shared applications and data. Typically, clients on a client/server network do not communicate directly with each other, but rather use the server as an intermediate step in communications.

Usually, file servers are more powerful computers than those found on a user's desktop. They may even be equipped with special hardware designed to provide network management functions beyond that provided by the network operating system. Figure 1-3 depicts a simple LAN that incorporates a file server.

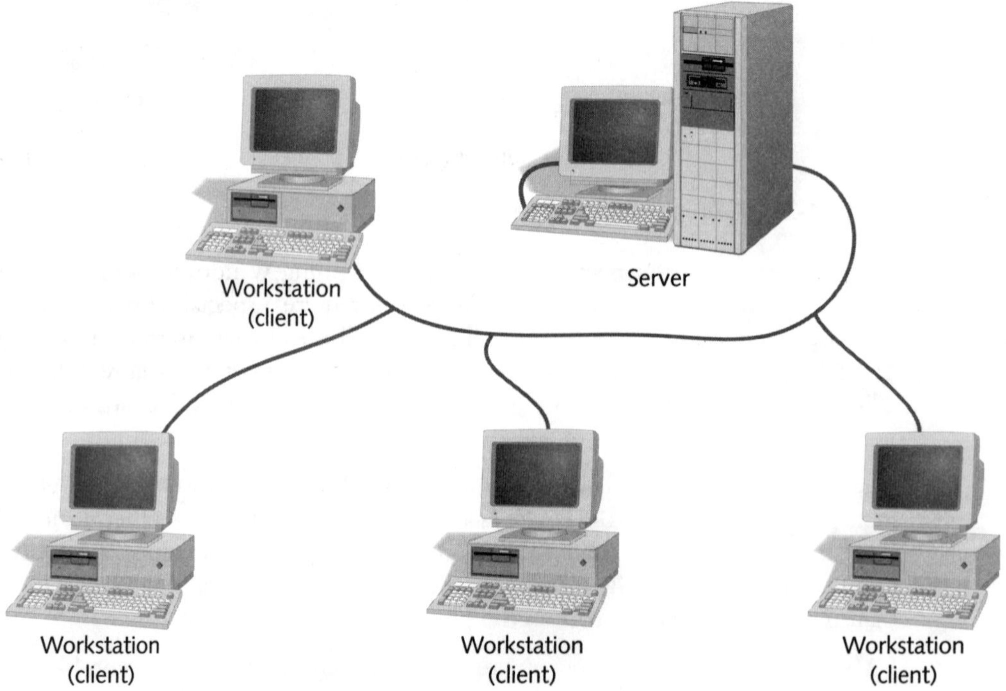

Figure 1-3 LAN with a file server

Networks are usually more complex than the simple LAN example in Figure 1-3. Often separate LANs are interconnected and rely on several file servers running many different applications and managing resources other than data. For example, a single network may connect 15 file servers, 200 printers, 3 fax machines, 5 CD-ROM devices, 2 mainframes, and 7 scanners. Figure 1-4 depicts a more complex network.

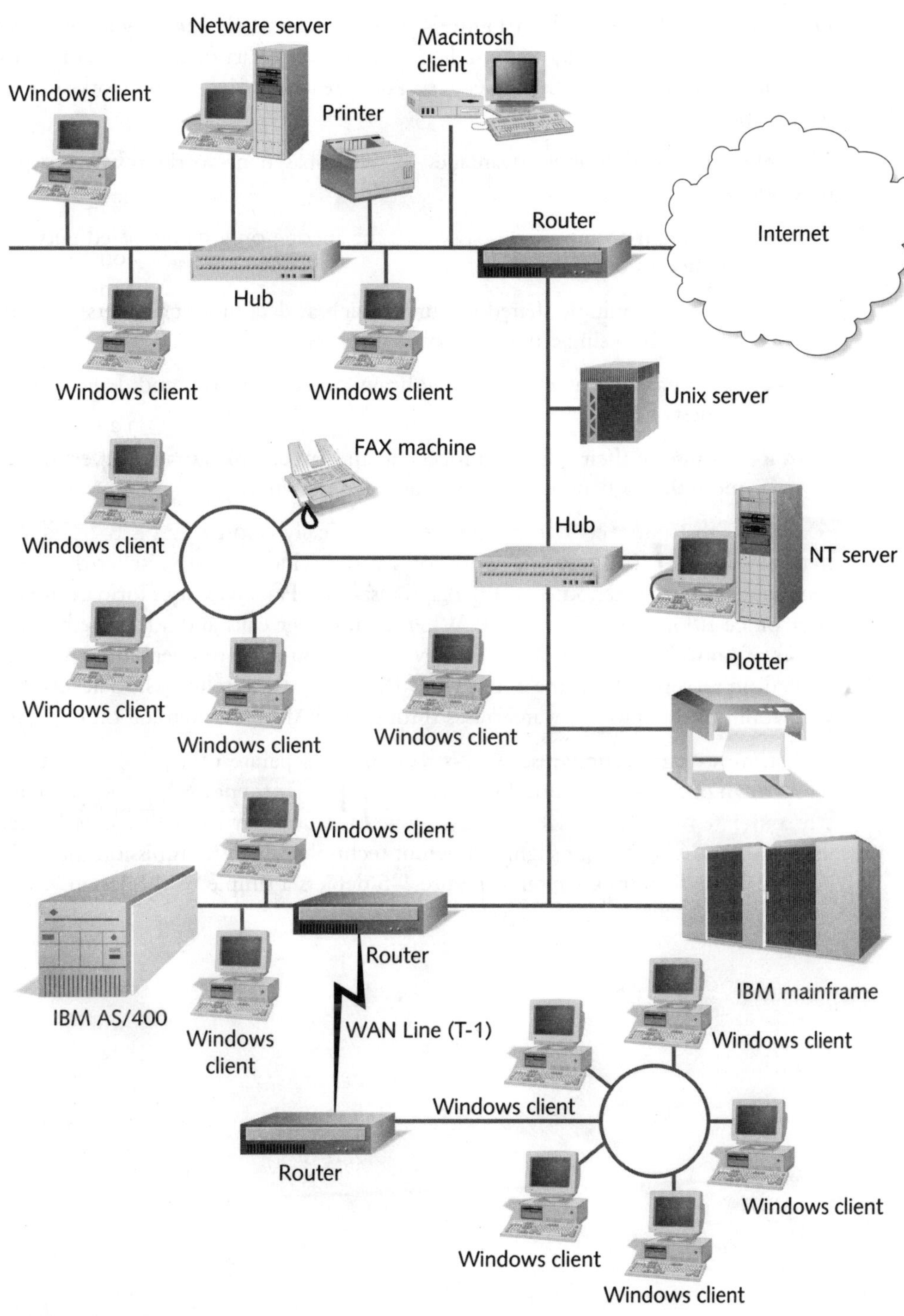

Figure 1-4 An example of a complex network

Don't worry if the network in Figure 1-4 looks overwhelming to you right now. As you progress through this book, you will learn about every part of this diagram. In the process, you will learn to integrate these pieces so as to create a variety of networks that are reliable, secure, and manageable.

The following list describes advantages of server-based networks relative to peer-to-peer networks:

- User login accounts and passwords for anyone on a server-based network can be assigned in one place.
- Access to multiple shared resources (such as data files or printers) can be centrally granted, by a single user or groups of users.
- Servers are optimized to handle heavy processing loads and dedicated to handling requests from clients.
- Because of their efficient processing and larger disk storage, servers can connect more than a handful of computers on a network.

A network that connects two or more geographically distinct LANs is called a **wide area network (WAN)**. Imagine you work for a nationwide software reseller that keeps its software inventory in warehouses in Topeka, Kansas, and Panama City, Florida. Suppose also that your office is located in New York. When a customer calls and asks whether you have 70 copies of Lotus Notes available to ship overnight, you need to check the inventory database located on servers at both the Topeka and Panama City warehouses. To access these servers, you would connect to the warehouses through a WAN link, then log on to their servers.

In fact, most organizations use WANs to connect separate offices, whether the offices are across town or across the world from each other. The **Internet** is an example of a very intricate and extensive WAN that spans the globe. Because they carry data over longer distances than LANs, WANs require slightly different technology and transmission media. WANs will be covered in detail in Chapter 7. Figure 1-5 depicts a simple WAN design.

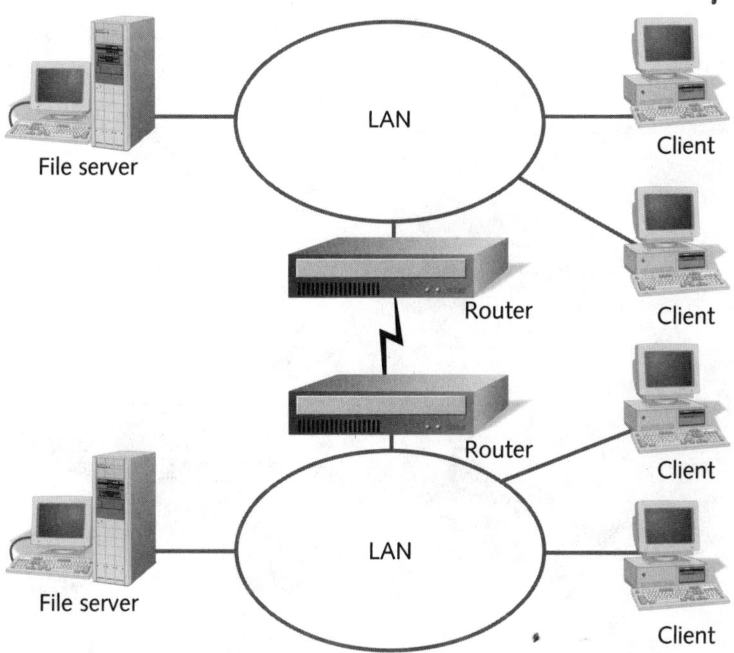

Figure 1-5 A simple WAN

ELEMENTS COMMON TO ALL SERVER-BASED NETWORKS

You have learned that networks—no matter how simple or how complex—provide some benefits over standalone computers. They also share terminology and common building blocks, some of which you've already encountered. The following list provides a more complete rundown of basic elements common to all server-based networks. You will learn more about these topics throughout this book.

- *Client.* A computer on the network that requests resources or services from another computer on a network. In some cases, a client could also act as a server. The term "client" may also refer to the human **user** of a client workstation.
- *Server.* A computer on the network that manages shared resources. Servers usually have more processing power, memory, and hard disk space than clients. They run network operating software that can manage not only data, but also users, groups, security, and applications on the network.
- *Workstation.* A desktop computer, which may or may not be connected to a network. Most clients are workstation computers.
- *Network interface card (NIC).* The device that enables a workstation to connect to the network and communicate with other computers. Several companies (such as 3Com, IBM, Intel, SMC, and Xircom) manufacture NICs, which come with a

variety of specifications that are tailored to the requirements of the workstation and the network. Figure 1-6 shows a typical workstation NIC.

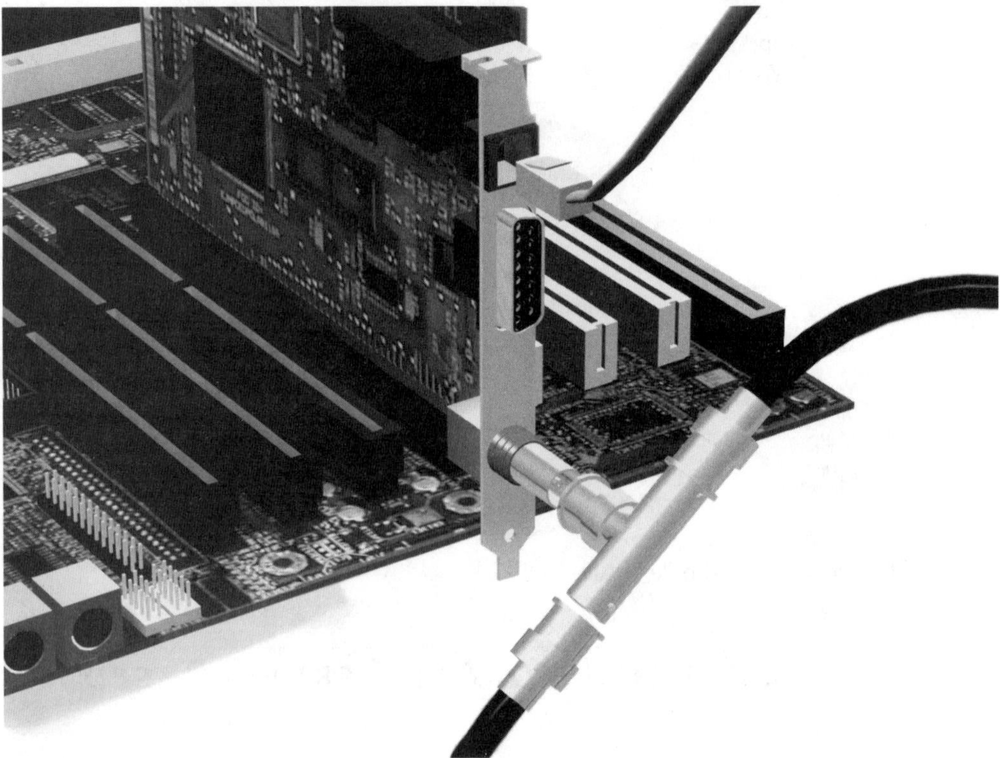

Figure 1-6 A network interface card (NIC)

Because different PCs and network types require different kinds of network interface cards, you cannot assume that a NIC that works in one workstation will work in another.

- *Network operating system (NOS).* The software that runs on a file server and enables the server to manage data, users, groups, security, applications, and other networking functions. The most popular network operating systems are Microsoft's Windows NT, Novell's NetWare, and UNIX.
- *Host.* A server that manages shared resources.
- *Node.* Any client, server, or other device on a network that is identified by a unique identifying number, known as its network address.

- *Topology*. The physical layout of a computer network. Topologies vary according to the needs of the organization and available hardware and expertise. Networks are usually arranged in a ring, bus, or star formation; hybrid combinations of these patterns are also possible. Figure 1-7 illustrates the most common network topologies, which you must understand to design and troubleshoot networks. (You will learn about topologies in detail in Chapter 5.)

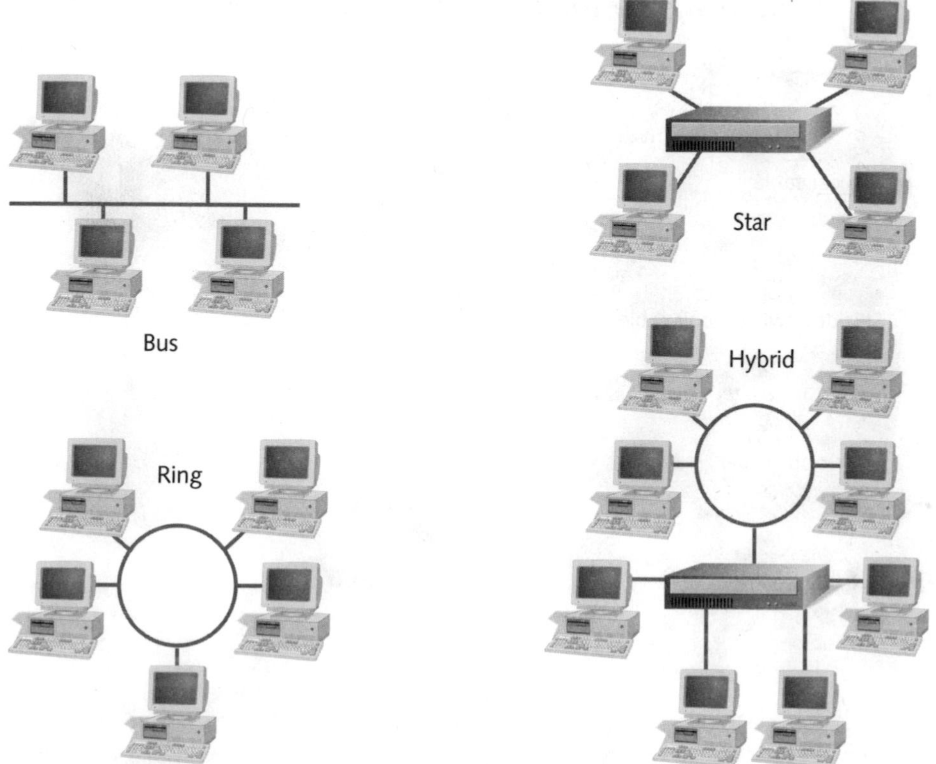

Figure 1-7 Commonly used network topologies

- *Protocol*. The rules that the network uses to transfer data. Protocols ensure that data are transferred whole, in sequence, and without error from one node on the network to another. To effectively maintain and manage a network, you must have a thorough understanding of network protocols. You will learn about network protocols in Chapter 3.
- *Data packets*. The distinct units of data that are transmitted from one computer on a network to another. Data packets are also known as datagrams, protocol data units (PDU), frames, or cells. You will learn more about data packets in Chapters 2 and 3.
- *Addressing*. The scheme for assigning a unique identifying number to every workstation and device on the network. The type of addressing used depends

on the network's protocols and network operating system. It is important that each computer on a network have a unique **address** so that data can be transmitted reliably to and from that computer. You will learn more about network addressing in Chapters 2 and 3.

- *Transmission media.* The means through which data are transmitted and received. Transmission media may be physical, such as wire or cable, or atmospheric (wireless), such as radio waves. You will learn more about transmission media in Chapter 4. Figure 1-8 shows several examples of transmission media.

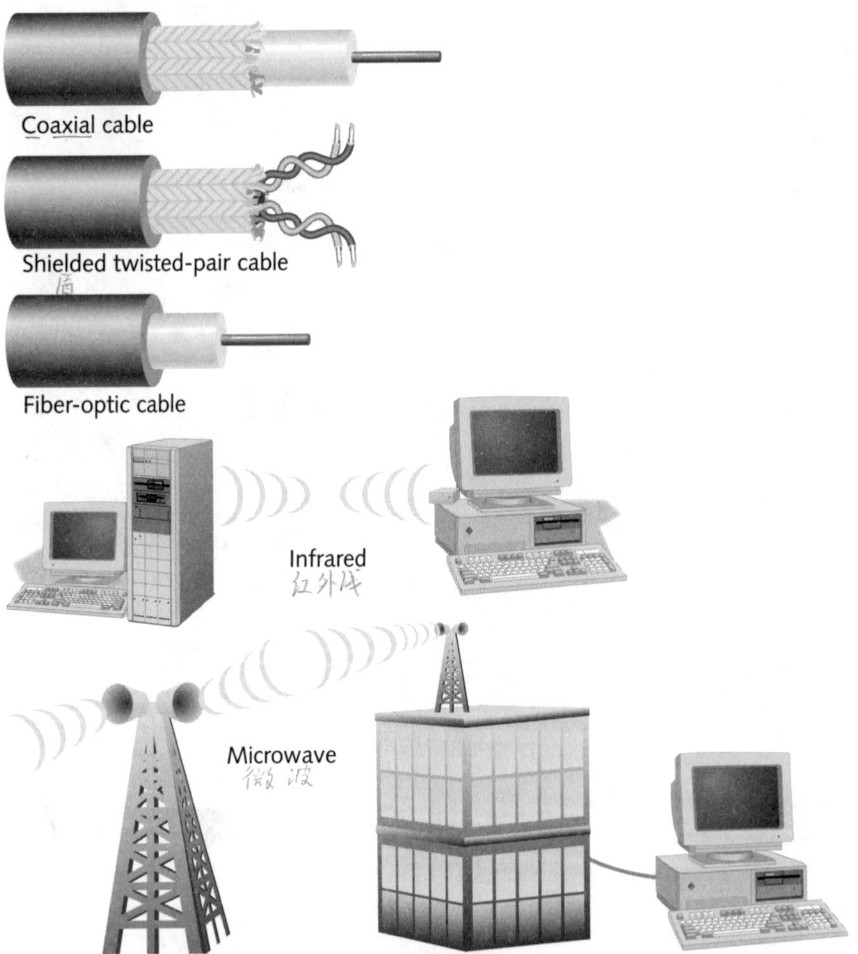

Figure 1-8 Examples of network transmission media

Now that you are familiar with basic network terminology, you are ready to appreciate the many uses of computer networks.

How Networks Are Used

The features provided by a network are usually referred to as **services**. Any network manager will tell you that the network service with the highest visibility is e-mail. If your company's e-mail system fails, users will notice within minutes—and they will not be shy about informing you of the failure. Although e-mail may be the most visible network service, other services are just as vital. Printing, file sharing, Internet access, remote dial-in capabilities, mainframe communication, and management services are all critical business functions provided through networks. In large organizations, separate servers may be dedicated to performing each of these functions. In offices with only a few users and little network traffic, one server may perform all functions.

File and Print Services

File services refer to the capability of a file server to share data files, applications (such as word-processing programs or spreadsheets), and disk storage space. File services accounted for the first use of networks and remain the foundation of networking today, for a number of reasons. As mentioned earlier, it's easier and faster to store shared data at a central location than to copy files to a disk and then pass the disks around. Data stored at a central location are also more secure because, as the network administrator, you can take charge of backing up this data, rather than relying on individual users to make their own copies. In addition, using a file server to run applications for multiple users requires that fewer copies of the application be purchased and results in less maintenance work for the network administrator.

Using print services to share printers across a network also saves time and money. A high-capacity printer costs thousands of dollars, but can simultaneously print jobs for an entire department, thereby eliminating the need to buy a desktop printer for each worker. With one printer, less time is spent on maintenance and management. If a shared printer fails, the network administrator can diagnose the problem from a workstation anywhere on the network using the network operating system's printer control functions. Often, the administrator can solve the problem without even visiting the printer.

Communications Services

A network's communications services allow remote users to connect to the network (usually through a phone line and modem). (The term **remote user** refers to a person working on a computer in a different geographical location from the LAN's server.) Less frequently, communications services allow network users to connect to machines outside the network. Network operating systems such as Windows NT and NetWare include built-in communications services. In Windows NT, the communications software is known as Remote Access Server (RAS). In NetWare, it is called Network Access Server (NAS). Both enable users to dial into a **communications server**, or the server running these communications services, then log in to the network and take advantage of any network features, just as if they were logged in to a workstation in the server's home office.

Businesses and other organizations commonly use communications services to provide LAN access for workers at home, workers on the road, and workers at small satellite offices where WAN connections are not cost-effective. In addition, they may use communications services to allow staff from other organizations (such as a software or hardware vendor) to help diagnose a network problem. For example, suppose you work for a clothing manufacturer that uses embroidery software to sew insignias on shirts and hats. You are an expert on networking, but less adept with the automated embroidery software. When the software causes problems, you turn to the software vendor for help. If that software company is located in Australia, however, it's much easier and cheaper to allow the vendor's technician to dial in to your network through a communications server and remotely diagnose the software than to fly the technician to your office.

Communications servers are also referred to as "access servers." It's important to remember that communications servers—no matter which platform (hardware or operating system software) they run on—allow external users to use network resources and devices just as if they were logged in to a workstation in the office. From a remote location, users can print files to shared printers, log in to IBM mainframe hosts, retrieve mail from an internal messaging system, or run queries on internal databases. Because they can be accessed by the world outside the local network, communications servers necessitate strict security measures.

Mail Services

Mail services coordinate the storage and transfer of e-mail between users on a network. Users depend on e-mail for fast, convenient communication both within and outside the organization. In addition to sending, receiving, and storing mail, however, mail services can include intelligent e-mail routing capabilities (for example, forwarding a message to a supervisor automatically if a technical support representative has not opened that message within 15 minutes of receiving it), notification, scheduling, document management, and gateways to other mail servers. (A **gateway** is a combination of software and hardware that enables two different kinds of networks to exchange data.) Mail services can run on several kinds of systems; they may be connected to the Internet or may be isolated within an organization. Examples of mail services software include Microsoft's Exchange Server, NetWare's GroupWise, and Lotus's cc:Mail. Mail services are the most visible networking functions to users. As a result, their client interfaces (that is, the part of the software with which the user interacts) are usually well developed and easy to use. Also, because of their heavy use, mail services require a significant commitment of technical support and administration resources.

Internet Services

Gone are the days when businesses could remain competitive by using isolated local area networks. Today, global communication and data exchange is essential. The Internet, as the most far-reaching network in the world, has become a necessary tool. You have probably connected to the Internet already without knowing or caring about all of the services running behind the scenes. Once you establish a connection, your workstation and its accompanying servers must run standard protocols to use the Internet's features. **Internet services** include World Wide Web servers and browsers, file transfer capabilities, Internet addressing schemes, security filters, and a means for directly logging into other computers on the Internet. Internet services are a broad category of network functions; reflecting their growing importance, entire books have been devoted to them. You will learn more about Internet services in Chapter 11.

MANAGEMENT SERVICES

When networks were small, they could be managed easily by a single network administrator and the network operating system's internal functions. For instance, suppose a user called to report a problem logging on to the network. The administrator diagnosed the problem as an addressing conflict (that is, two workstations having the same network address). In a very small network, the conflicting workstations might be located right around the corner from each other, and one address could be changed quickly. In another example, if a manager needed to report the number of copies of Lotus 1-2-3 in use in a certain department, the network administrator could probably get the desired information by just walking through the department and checking the various workstations.

As networks grow larger and more complex, however, they become more difficult to manage. To keep track of a large network, you need to employ special network management services. Network **management services** centrally administer and simplify complicated management tasks on the network, such as making sure that no more than 20 workstations are using WordPerfect at one time. Some organizations dedicate a number of servers to network management functions, with each server performing only one or two unique services.

Numerous services fall under the category of network management. Some of the most important services include the following:

- *Traffic monitoring and control.* Determining how much **traffic** (that is, data transmission and processing activity), is taking place on a network or network segment and notifying administrators when a segment becomes overloaded. A **segment** is a part of a LAN that is logically separated from other parts of the LAN and that shares a fixed amount of traffic capacity. In general, the larger the network, the more critical it is to monitor traffic.
- *Load balancing.* Distributing processing activity evenly across a network so that no single device becomes overwhelmed. Load balancing is especially important for networks where it's difficult to predict the number of requests that will be issued to a server, as is the case with Web servers.
- *Hardware diagnosis and failure alert.* Determining when a network component fails and automatically notifying the network administrator through e-mail or paging.
- *Asset management.* Collecting and storing data on the number and types of software and hardware assets (or resources) in an organization's network. The data collection process, in which each network client is examined electronically, takes place automatically. In the past, these data were typically gathered manually from paper records and typed into spreadsheet form.

- *License tracking.* Determining how many copies of a single application are currently in use on the network. This information is important for legal reasons, as the concern over illegal software copying and excessive usage grows.
- *Security auditing.* Evaluating what security measures are currently in force and notifying the network administrator if a security breach occurs.
- *Software distribution.* Automatically transferring a data file or program from the server to a client on the network. Software distribution can be initiated from either the server or the client. Several options are available when distributing software, such as warning users about updates, writing changes to a workstation's system files, and restarting the workstation after the update.
- *Address management.* Centrally managing a finite number of network addresses for an entire LAN. Usually this task can be accomplished without touching the client workstations.
- *Backup and restoration of data.* Copying (or **backing up**) critical data files to a secure storage area and then **restoring** (or retrieving) data if the original files are lost or deleted. Often backups are performed according to a formulaic schedule. Backup and data restoration services provide centralized management of data backup on multiple servers and on-demand restoration of files and directories.

Network management services will be covered in depth in Chapters 12 through 13 of this book. For now, it is enough to be aware of the variety of services and the importance of this growing area of networking.

Becoming a Networking Professional

Examine the classified ad section of any newspaper, and you will probably find more ads for computer professionals than any other kind of skilled worker. Of course, the level of expertise required for each of these jobs differs. Some companies simply need "warm bodies" to ensure that a mainframe's tape backup doesn't fail during the night; other companies are looking for people to plan their information technology strategies. Needless to say, the more varied your skills, the better your chances for landing a lucrative and interesting job in networking. To prepare yourself to enter this job market, you should master a number of general networking skills. Only then should you pick a few areas that interest you and study those specialties. Hone your communication and teamwork skills, and stay abreast of emerging technologies. Consider the tremendous advantages of attaining professional certification and getting to know others in your field. The following sections offer suggestions on how to approach a career in networking.

Mastering the Technical Challenges

Although computer networking is a varied field, some general technical skills will serve you well no matter which specialty you choose. Because you are already interested in computers, you probably enjoy an aptitude for logical and analytical thinking. Some additional skills you will want to acquire are as follows:

- Installing, configuring, and troubleshooting network file server software
- Installing, configuring, and troubleshooting network file server hardware
- Installing, configuring, and troubleshooting network client software
- Installing, configuring, and troubleshooting network client hardware
- Understanding the characteristics of different transmission media
- Understanding network design
- Understanding network protocols
- Understanding how users interact with the network

Because you can expand your networking knowledge in almost any direction, you should pay attention to the general skills that interest you most, then pick one or two of those areas and concentrate on them. If you try to become a specialist in everything at once, you are likely to become frustrated. Some specialty areas that are currently in high demand for networking professionals include the following:

- Network security
- Internet and intranet design
- Network management
- Voice/data integration
- Remote and mobile computing
- Data integrity and fault tolerance
- In-depth knowledge of Microsoft networking products
- In-depth knowledge of NetWare networking products
- In-depth knowledge of router configuration and management

Determine what method of learning works best for you. A small classroom with an experienced instructor and a hands-on projects lab is an excellent learning environment, because there you can ask questions and learn by doing. Many colleges offer courses or continuing education on networking topics. You may also want to enroll in training at a computer training center. These training centers can be found in every metropolitan area and even many small towns. If you are pursuing certification, make sure the training center you choose is authorized to provide training for that certification. Most computer training centers also operate a Web site that provides information on their course schedule, fees, and qualifications. Some of these sites even offer online class registration.

Another great way to improve your technical skills is by gaining practical experience. There is no substitute for hands-on experience when it comes to networking hardware and software skills. If you don't already work in an Information Technology department, try to find a position that puts you in that environment, even if it isn't your dream job. Volunteer a few hours a week if necessary. Once you are surrounded with other information technology professionals and encounter real-life situations, you will have the opportunity to expand your skills by practicing and asking questions of more experienced staff. On the Web, you can find a number of searchable online job boards and recruiter sites. The placement office at your local college or university can also connect you with job opportunities.

If you already work in an Information Technology department, you should pay close attention to the technical issues and trends, experiment, and ask lots of questions.

If your organization offers a mentoring program, participate in it. If not, find an unofficial mentor among your experienced colleagues who is willing to spend extra time explaining technical details to you. Chances are, your colleague will be honored to be chosen and eager to help.

DEVELOPING YOUR "SOFT SKILLS"

Knowing how to configure a router or install Windows NT will serve you well, but without advanced soft skills, you cannot excel in the networking field. The term "**soft skills**" refers to those skills that are not easily measurable, such as customer relations, oral and written communications, dependability, teamwork, and leadership abilities. Some of these soft skills might appear to be advantages in any profession, but they are especially important when you must work in teams, in challenging technical circumstances and under tight deadlines—characteristics that apply to most networking projects. For this reason, soft skills merit closer examination.

- *Customer relations.* Perhaps one of the most important "soft skills," customer relations involve an ability to listen to customers' frustrations and desires and then empathize, respond, and guide customers to their goals without acting arrogant. Bear in mind that some of your customers will not appreciate or enjoy technology as much as you do, and they will value your patience as you help them. The better your customer relations, the more respected and in demand you will be as a network professional.
- *Oral and written communications.* You may understand the most complicated technical details about a network, but if you cannot communicate them to colleagues and clients, the significance of your knowledge is diminished. Imagine that you are a networking consultant who is competing with another firm to overhaul a metropolitan school district's network, a project that could generate $10 million in business for your company. You may have designed the best solution and have it clearly mapped out in your head, but your plan is useless if you can't convey it. The members of the school board will accept whichever proposal makes the most sense to them—that is, the proposal whose suggestions and justifications are plainly communicated.
- *Dependability.* This characteristic will help you in any career. However, in the field of networking, where breakdowns or glitches can occur at any time of day or

night and only a limited number of individuals have the expertise to fix them, being dependable is critical. Your career will benefit when you are the one who is available to address a problem, even if you don't always know the answer immediately.

- *Teamwork.* Individual computer professionals often have strong preferences for a certain type of hardware or software. And some technical people like to think that they have all of the answers. For these and other reasons, teamwork in Information Technology departments is often lacking. To be the best networking professional in your department, you must be open to new ideas, encourage cooperation among your colleagues, and allow others to help you and make suggestions.
- *Leadership abilities.* As a networking professional, you will sometimes need to make difficult or unpopular decisions under pressure. You may need to persuade opinionated colleagues to try a new product, tell a group of angry users that what they want is not possible, or manage a project with nearly impossible budgetary and time restrictions. In all of these situations, you will benefit from having strong leadership skills.

Once your career in networking begins, you will discover which soft skills you already possess and which ones you need to cultivate. The important thing is that you realize the importance of these attributes and are willing to devote the time necessary to develop them.

PURSUING CERTIFICATION

Certification is the process of mastering material pertaining to a particular hardware system, operating system, programming language, or other program, then proving your mastery by passing a series of exams. Certification programs are developed and administered either by a manufacturer or a professional organization such as the **Computing Technology Industry Association** (**CompTIA**). You can pursue a number of different certifications, depending on your specialty interest. For example, if you want to become a PC technician, you should attain **A+** certification. If you want to specialize in Microsoft product support and development, you should pursue **Microsoft Certified Systems Engineer** (**MCSE**) certification. If you want to specialize in Novell networking product support and administration, you should pursue **Certified NetWare Engineer (CNE)** certification. If you want to prove a mastery of many aspects of networking, you should choose to become Net+ certified. **Net+** is a professional certification established by CompTIA that verifies broad, vendor-independent networking technology skills such as an understanding of protocols, topologies, networking hardware, and network troubleshooting. The material in this book addresses the knowledge objectives to qualify for Net+ certification.

Certification is a popular career development tool for job seekers and a measure of an employee's qualifications for employers. Following are a list of benefits you can expect after becoming certified:

- *Better salary.* Professionals with certification can usually ask for higher salaries than those who aren't certified. Employers will also want to retain certified employees, especially if they helped pay for their training, and will offer incentives to keep certified professionals at the company.
- *Greater opportunities.* Certification may qualify you for additional degrees or more advanced technical positions.
- *Professional respect.* Once you have proved your skills with a product or system, your colleagues and clients will have great respect for your ability to solve problems with that system or product. They will therefore feel confident asking you for help.
- *Access to better support.* Many manufacturers reward certified professionals with less expensive, more detailed, and more direct access to their technical support.

One potential drawback of some certifications is the number of people attaining them—so many that they now have less value. Currently, hundreds of thousands of networking professionals have acquired the MCSE certification. When only tens of thousands of people had MCSEs, employers were willing to pay substantially higher salaries to workers with that certification. However, now that so many people are cramming for the MCSE exams and passing with little hands-on experience, MCSEs cannot demand the same respect. Other kinds of certifications, such as Cisco's Certified Internetworking Engineer program, require candidates to pass lab exams. These kinds of certifications, because they cannot be faked, remain very highly respected.

FINDING A JOB IN NETWORKING

With the proper credentials and demonstrated technical knowledge, you will qualify for a multitude of positions in networking. For this reason, you can and must be selective when searching for a job. Following are some ways to research your possibilities:

- *Search the Web.* Because your job will deal directly with technology, it makes sense that you should use technology to find it. Companies in the computer industry recruit intensively on the Web, either through searchable job databases or through links on their company Web sites. Unlike firms in other industries, these companies typically do not mind (and might prefer) receiving résumés and letters through e-mail. Most job database Web sites do not charge for their services or require you to register with them. Table 1-1 lists a few of these Web sites, some of which are devoted exclusively to posting information technology positions. The table provides just a sample of the best-known job databases on the Web; you could probably find hundreds more.

Table 1-1 Web sites with job databases

Web Site Location	Description and Emphasis
http://www.informationweek.com/career/bestjobs.htm	InformationWeek's "Best Jobs": an IT career site with links to job searches, career advice, salary surveys, and training sites
http://www.jobengine.com/	JobEngine: a searchable site for IT job seekers and employers sponsored by Ziff Davis's Web division
http://www.cweb.com/	Career Web: a searchable site for job seekers and employers from across the United States and from many different industries
http://www.monster.com/	The Monster Board: a searchable site for job seekers and employers from around the world and from many different industries
http://www.ajb.dni.us/	America's Job Bank: a searchable site for job seekers and employers from around the world and from many different industries
http://www.careermosaic.com/	Career Mosaic: a searchable site for job seekers and employers from around the world and from many different industries
http://www.ups.purdue.edu/Student/jobsites.htm	Purdue University's Job Search Resources: a list of links to numerous searchable job databases and other career resources

- *Read the paper.* An obvious place to look for jobs is the classified ad section of your local newspaper. Papers with large distributions often devote a section of their classified ads to careers in computing. Highlight the ads that sound interesting to you, even if you don't have all of the qualifications cited by the employer. In some ads, employers will list every skill they could possibly want a new hire to have, but they don't truly expect one person to have all of them.

- *Visit a career center.* Regardless of whether you are a registered university or college student, you can use career center services to find a list of job openings in your area. Companies that are hiring pay much attention to the collegiate career centers because of the number of job seekers served by these centers. Visit the college or university campus nearest you and search through its career center listings.

- *Network.* Find like-minded professionals with whom you can discuss job possibilities. You may meet these individuals through training classes, conferences, professional organizations, or career fairs. Let them know that you're looking for a job and specify exactly what kind of job you want. If they can't suggest any leads for you, ask these people if they have other colleagues who might.

- *Attend career fairs.* Most metropolitan areas host career fairs for job seekers in the information technology field, and some large companies host their own job fairs. Even if you aren't sure you want to work for any of the companies represented at a job fair, attend the job fair to research the market. You can find out which skills are in high demand in your area and which types of companies are hiring the most networking professionals. You can also meet other people in your field who may offer valuable advice based on their employment experience.

JOINING PROFESSIONAL ASSOCIATIONS

At some point in your life, you have probably belonged to a club or organization. You know, therefore, that the benefits of joining can vary, depending on many factors. In the best case, joining an organization can connect you with people who have similar interests, provide new opportunities for learning, allow you to access specialized information, and give you more tangible assets such as free goods. Specifically, a networking professional organization might offer its own journal, technical workshops and conferences, free software, pre-release software, and access to expensive hardware labs. Some associations even offer health insurance benefits to their members.

Several prominent professional organizations exist in the field of networking. Because the field has grown so quickly and because so many areas in which to specialize exist, however, no single professional organization stands out as the most advantageous or highly respected. You will have to decide whether an organization is appropriate for you. Among other things, you will want to consider the organization's number of members, membership benefits, membership dues, technical emphasis, and whether it hosts a local chapter. You may also want to find a professional association that caters to your demographic group (such as Women in Technology International, if you are female). Table 1-2 lists a number of professional organizations and their Web sites.

Table 1-2 Web sites of networking organizations

Professional Organization	Emphasis	Web Site
Network Professional Association	All disciplines, all groups	http://www.npa.org
Association for Computing Machinery (ACM)	All disciplines, all groups	http://www.acm.org
IEEE Computer Society	Advanced computing, all groups	http://www.computer.org
Network Professional's Guild	Beginning computing, all groups	http://netproguild.com/
Network and Systems Professionals Association	All disciplines, all groups	http://www.naspa.net/
Society of Computer Professionals	All disciplines, college graduates with at least two years of experience	http://www.comprof.com/
Enterprise Networking Association	Enterprise networking, all groups	http://www.enanet.org/
Chinese Information and Networking Association	All disciplines, Chinese Americans	http://www.cina.org/
Women in Technology International	All disciplines, women	http://www.witi.com

Chapter Summary

- A network is a group of computers and other devices that are connected by some type of transmission media, usually wire or cable.
- Networks may consist of two computers connected by a cable in a home office or several thousand computers connected across the world. In addition to connecting personal computers, they may incorporate mainframe computers, modems, CD-ROMs, printers, plotters, fax machines, or phone systems. Computers on a network may communicate through cables, wires, radio waves, infrared, or satellite links.
- All networks provide advantages relative to the use of a standalone personal computer. Most importantly, networks enable multiple users to share devices and data. They also allow for centralized administration of hardware and software.
- The simplest form of a network still used today connects a handful of computers through one cable and uses peer-to-peer communication. Peer-to-peer communication enables computers to talk directly to other computers on a single segment of cable, without any computer having more authority than another.
- A local area network (LAN) is a network of computers and other devices that is confined to a relatively small space, such as one building or even one office. A peer-to-peer network is a simple example of a LAN. More complex LANs are server-based and rely on a central file server to manage resources.

- A network that connects two or more geographically distinct LANs is called a wide area network (WAN).
- All server-based networks share some common elements, including clients, servers, workstations, transmission media, protocols, addressing, topology, network interface cards, data packets, network operating systems, hosts, and nodes.
- The physical layout of a computer network is called a topology. Topologies are usually arranged in a ring, bus, or star formation; hybrid combinations of these patterns are also possible. You must understand topologies to design and troubleshoot networks.
- Network protocols are the rules that the network uses to transfer data. Protocols ensure that data are transferred whole, in sequence, and without error from one node on the network to another. To effectively maintain and manage a network, you must have a thorough understanding of network protocols.
- Although e-mail is the most visible network service, networks also provide services for printing, file sharing, Internet access, remote dial-in capabilities, mainframe communication, and management services.
- File and print services provide the foundation for networking. They enable multiple users to share data, applications, storage areas, and printers.
- Networks use communications services to allow remote users to connect to the network (usually through a phone line and modem) or network users to connect to machines outside the network. Communications servers are also called "access servers."
- Mail services allow users on a network to exchange and store e-mail. Many mail packages also provide routing, scheduling, notification, document management, and gateways to other mail systems.
- Internet services such as World Wide Web servers and browsers, file transfer capabilities, addressing schemes, and security filters enable organizations to connect to and use the global Internet.
- Network management services centrally administer and simplify complicated management tasks on the network. Some organizations dedicate a number of servers to network management functions, with each server performing only one or two unique services.
- Networking professionals are currently in great demand. The more varied your skills, the better your chances for landing a lucrative and interesting job in networking. To prepare yourself, you should master a number of broad networking skills. Only then should you pick a few areas that interest you and study those specialties. Hone your communication and teamwork skills, and stay abreast of emerging technologies. Consider the tremendous advantages of attaining professional certification and get to know members of your field.
- Certification is the process of mastering material pertaining to a particular hardware system, operating system, programming language, or other software program, then proving your mastery by passing a series of exams. The benefits of certification include a better salary, more job opportunities, greater professional respect, and better access to technical support.

- To excel in the field of networking, you should hone your soft skills, such as leadership abilities, written and oral communication, a professional attitude, dependability, and customer relations.
- With the proper credentials, you can easily find a job in networking. To find the *best* job, you should perform research using the newspaper classified ads, searchable job databases on the Web, networking with colleagues, a nearby college career center, and career fairs.
- Joining an association for networking professionals can connect you with like-minded people, give you access to workshops and other educational materials, allow you to receive discounted or free software, and maybe even provide insurance benefits. Before joining an association, make sure its emphasis is appropriate for you and that you will be able to use its membership benefits.

Key Terms

- **A+** — Professional certification established by CompTIA that verifies knowledge about PC operation, repair, and management.
- **address** — A number that uniquely identifies each workstation and device on a network. Without unique addresses, computers on the network could not reliably communicate.
- **address management** — Centrally administering a finite number of network addresses for an entire LAN. Usually this task can be accomplished without touching the client workstations.
- **addressing** — The scheme for assigning a unique identifying number to every workstation and device on the network. The type of addressing used on a network depends on its protocols and network operating system.
- **asset management** — Collecting and storing data on the number and types of software and hardware assets in an organization's network. The data collection is automated by electronically examining each network client from a server.
- **backup** — The process of copying critical data files to a secure storage area. Often backups are performed according to a formulaic schedule.
- **certification** — The process of mastering material pertaining to a particular hardware system, operating system, programming language, or other software program, then proving your mastery by passing a series of exams.
- **Certified Network Engineer (CNE)** — Professional certification established by Novell that demonstrates an in-depth understanding of Novell's networking software, including NetWare.
- **client** — A computer on the network that requests resources or services from another computer on a network. In some cases, a client could also act as a server. The term "client" may also refer to the user of a client workstation.

- **client/server architecture** — The model of networking in which clients (typically desktop PCs) use a central file server to share applications and data.
- **communications server** — A server that runs communications services such as Windows NT's RAS or NetWare's NAS, also known as an "access server."
- **Computing Technology Industry Association (CompTIA)** — An association of computer resellers, manufacturers, and training companies that sets industry-wide standards for computer professionals. CompTIA established and sponsors the A+ and Network+ (Net+) certifications.
- **data packet** — A discreet unit of information sent from one computer on a network to another.
- **file server** — A computer that runs the network operating system and enables workstations connected to the network to share resources.
- **file services** — The function of a file server that allows users to share data files, applications, and storage areas.
- **gateway** — A combination of hardware and software that enables two different kinds of networks to exchange data.
- **host** — A type of computer that enables resource sharing by other computers on the same network.
- **Internet** — A complex WAN that connects LANs around the globe.
- **Internet services** — Services that enable a network to communicate with the Internet, including World Wide Web servers and browsers, file transfer capabilities, Internet addressing schemes, security filters, and a means for directly logging in to other computers.
- **license tracking** — Determining how many copies of a single application are currently in use on the network.
- **load balancing** — Distributing processing activity evenly across a network so that no single device is overwhelmed.
- **local area network (LAN)** — A network of computers and other devices that is confined to a relatively small space, such as one building or even one office.
- **local computer** — The computer on which you are actually working (as opposed to a remote computer).
- **mail services** — Network services that manage the storage and transfer of e-mail between users on a network. In addition to sending, receiving, and storing mail, mail services can include intelligent e-mail routing capabilities, notification, scheduling, indexing, document libraries, and gateways to other mail servers.
- **management services** — Network services that centrally administer and simplify complicated management tasks on the network. Examples of management services include license tracking, security auditing, asset management, addressing management, software distribution, traffic monitoring, load balancing, and hardware diagnosis.

- **Microsoft Certified Systems Engineer (MCSE)** — A professional certification established by Microsoft that demonstrates in-depth knowledge about Microsoft's products, including Windows 98 and Windows NT.
- **network** — A group of computers and other devices (such as printers) that are connected by some type of transmission media, usually wire or cable.
- **Network+ (Net+)** — Professional certification established by CompTIA that verifies broad networking technology skills such as an understanding of protocols, topologies, networking hardware, and network troubleshooting.
- **network interface card (NIC)** — The device that enables a workstation to connect to the network and communicate with other computers. NICs are manufactured by several different companies and come with a variety of specifications that are tailored to the workstation's and the network's requirements.
- **network operating system (NOS)** — The software that runs on a file server and enables the server to manage data, users, groups, security, applications, and other networking functions. The most popular network operating systems are Microsoft's Windows NT and Novell's NetWare.
- **node** — Any computer or other device connected to a network.
- **peer-to-peer communication** — A simple means of networking computers using a single cable. In peer-to-peer communication, no single computer has more authority than another and each computer can share files with other computers.
- **print services** — The network service that allows printers to be shared by several users on a network.
- **protocol** — The rules that the network uses to transfer data. Protocols ensure that data are transferred whole, in sequence, and without error from one node on the network to another.
- **remote computer** — The computer that you are controlling or working on via a network connection.
- **remote user** — A person working on a computer in a different geographical location from the LAN's server.
- **resources** — The devices and data provided by a computer, whether standalone or shared.
- **restore** — The process of retrieving files from a backup if the original files are lost or deleted.
- **security auditing** — Evaluating security measures currently in place on a network and notifying the network administrator if a security breach occurs.
- **segment** — A part of a LAN that is separated from other parts of the LAN and that shares a fixed amount of traffic capacity.

- **server** — A computer on the network that manages shared resources. Servers usually have more processing power, memory, and hard disk space than clients. They run network operating software that can manage not only data, but also users, groups, security, and applications on the network.
- **server-based network** — A network that uses special computers, known as file servers, to process data for and facilitate communication between the other computers on the network.
- **services** — The features provided by a network.
- **sneakernet** — The only means of exchanging data without using a network. Sneakernet requires that data be copied from a computer to a floppy disk, carried (presumably by someone wearing sneakers) to another computer, then copied from the floppy disk onto the second computer.
- **soft skills** — Skills such as customer relations, leadership ability, and dependability, which are not easily measured, but are nevertheless important in a networking career.
- **software distribution** — The process of automatically transferring a data file or program from the server to a client on the network.
- **standalone computer** — A computer that uses programs and data only from its local disks and that is not connected to a network.
- **topology** — The physical layout of a computer network.
- **traffic** — The data transmission and processing activity taking place on a computer network at any given time.
- **traffic monitoring** — Determining how much processing activity is taking place on a network or network segment and notifying administrators when a segment becomes overloaded.
- **transmission media** — The means through which data are transmitted and received. Transmission media may be physical, such as wire or cable, or atmospheric (wireless), such as radio waves.
- **user** — A person who uses a computer.
- **wide area network (WAN)** — A network that spans a large distance and connects two or more LANs.
- **workstation** — A computer that typically runs a desktop operating system and connects to a network.

Review Questions

1. What resources do networks *not* enable workstations to share?

   a. data

   b. passwords

c. printers
d. fax machines

2. All server-based networks:
   a. allow multiple users to share applications
   b. allow multiple users to access each other's workstations
   c. allow multiple users to share floppy disks
   d. allow multiple users to share modems
3. What is the simplest form of a network still in use today?
   a. server-based networking
   b. thin client networking
   c. host-to-host networking
   d. peer-to-peer networking
4. Servers usually possess the same amount of memory and hard disk capacity as workstations. True or False?
5. What is the primary function of a file server on a network?
   a. It routes traffic between two or more LAN segments.
   b. It monitors how many people are logged on to a wide area network.
   c. It supplies error messages when unauthorized users try to access the network.
   d. It manages shared resources such as spreadsheet and word-processing files.
6. LANs and WANs differ not only in their geographical scope, but also in:
   a. the transmission media they use
   b. the services they can offer
   c. the amount of traffic they can support
   d. the protocols they can use
7. Any two computers can use the same network interface card to connect to the network. True or False?
8. Why is it important to make sure that each workstation on a network has a unique network address?
   a. to enable users to move from one workstation to another and still find their data
   b. to enable the workstation to communicate with the server and other networked workstations
   c. to enable the workstation to request priority processing from the file server
   d. to enable the user to identify his or her machine to technical support representatives
9. A shared HP Laserjet 6P could be considered a network node. True or False?
10. Which of the following is not a network topology?

a. star

b. bus

c. cube

d. ring

11. Which of the following is not true about peer-to-peer networks?

a. They are typically very secure.

b. They are typically inexpensive.

c. They are typically easy to set up.

d. They do not depend on a file server.

12. In addition to message storage and transfer, what additional function might a mail server provide?

a. mail text search and replace

b. address book creation

c. mail gateways to other systems

d. mail attachment conversion

13. Which of the following could not be considered a network management service?

a. automated software distribution

b. license tracking

c. traffic control

d. dial-up access authentication

14. Security is a concern when using communications servers on a network because:

a. communications servers enable computers to dial into a network, thereby opening the network up to the outside world

b. communications servers have poor password enforcement capabilities, so they rely on users to choose good passwords

c. communications servers cannot accept encrypted data transfers, requiring users to transmit plain text to and from the network

d. communications servers are difficult to understand and support, so many networks are using them incorrectly and perhaps insecurely

15. Which of the following services does not belong to the Internet services group of networked functions?

a. World Wide Web browser service

b. file transfer service

c. Internet addressing services

d. load balancing traffic on multiple Internet connections

16. One function that network protocols serve is to ensure that data are delivered in the correct sequence. True or False?
17. Name three specialties within the networking field that are in high demand.
18. Soft skills are probably not necessary in which of the following on-the-job scenarios?
    a. An angry customer fumes at you because you inform him that you do not have access to his mail account and cannot look up a message he sent three weeks ago.
    b. The server on which you're working continually hangs up while rebooting, and you can't find a bootable floppy disk.
    c. One of your software suppliers insists she never received an order that you faxed to her twice in the last week, and you need the software now.
    d. For several hours one morning, your network had problems that prevented any users from logging on, and now your supervisor is asking you why you didn't fix the problem sooner.
19. Some benefits of pursuing professional certification might include:
    a. a better-paying job
    b. faster access to technical support
    c. never having to attend additional training courses
    d. more respect from technical colleagues
20. To find the best possible job in networking, what sources would you investigate?

Hands-On Projects

Project 1-1

During your career in networking, you will frequently need to interpret network diagrams, if not design them yourself. This exercise is the first of several in this book that give you practice in drawing network diagrams.

On a separate piece of paper, draw a simple diagram of a network composed of 12 clients, 2 shared printers, 2 file servers, and a mainframe host. This network should use the bus topology.

After you have drawn a simple network based on the bus topology, try drawing the same type of network with a ring topology.

PROJECT 1-2

Even before you are ready to look for a job in networking, you should be familiar with the kinds of employers who are looking for information systems professionals and the skills that they desire. The more research you do, the better prepared you will be when you begin job hunting in earnest. This exercise will familiarize you with searching job databases on the Web. To complete this project you need a computer with access to the Internet.

The steps in this project matched the Web sites mentioned at the time this book was published. If you notice discrepancies, look for similar links and follow the same general steps.

1. Access the Internet and go to http://www.monster.com/
2. From The Monster Board's home page, click **Search Job**.
3. Ignore the Location Search and Category Search options, and scroll down to the Keyword Search text box. Type **network administrator**, then click the **Search Jobs** button. How many jobs were returned by the search?
4. Click the first 15 job postings, one after the other, to display the job descriptions. On a separate piece of paper, note how many require or recommend each technical proficiency listed below.
   - NetWare
   - Windows NT
   - Macintosh
   - UNIX
   - TCP/IP
   - Internet Services
   - Bridges, routers, or gateways
   - Network security
   - Printers
   - WANs
5. For each proficiency, calculate the percentage of jobs that require it.
6. How many of the position descriptions mention A+, Net+, MCSE, CCIE, or CNE certification?
7. Return to the job search page, verify that "network administrator" still appears in the Keyword text box, then use the Location Search list box to select the metropolitan areas in your state. How many jobs did the search return? Which areas have the most job openings?
8. Return to the search page. In the Keyword text box replace "network administrator" with "manager," deselect any locations in the Location Search list box, select **Information Technology** in the Category Search list box, then click the **Search Jobs** button.
9. How many jobs did the search return?
10. Examine the first 15 jobs. On a separate piece of paper, note the number of these jobs that require the "soft skills" listed below.

- Leadership
- Oral/written communication
- Customer relations
- Teamwork
- Supervision
- Motivation (of yourself and others)

11. Continue to search The Monster Board, choosing keywords or categories for specialty areas of networking that appeal to you. Some examples might be network security, voice/data integration, or router configuration.
12. As you read the job descriptions, jot down terms and skills that are new to you, then look up their definitions in the glossary of this text.

PROJECT 1-3

If you intend to pursue the Net+ certification, you should familiarize yourself with the Net+ exam objectives. Although these objectives are mentioned in the pertinent chapters of this book and summarized in Appendix A, you can learn more about them at the CompTIA (Computing Technology Industry Association) organization's Web site. In this exercise, you will explore CompTIA's Web site.

1. Access the Internet and go to http://www.comptia.org
2. Click **Certifications** to view information about the different computer certifications that CompTIA sponsors.
3. Click Network+ to view more information about the Net+ certification. What kind of prior experience does CompTIA suggest for those aspiring to obtain Net+ certification?
4. From the navigational bar at the top of the page, click **Examination Blueprint**.
5. Among other things, this page describes how different skills are weighted in the Net+ exam. For example, questions about networking technology security account for approximately 6% of all exam questions. What percentage of the exam questions pertains to TCP/IP fundamentals? What percentage of the exam questions pertains to troubleshooting the network?
6. From the navigational bar at the top of the page, click **Benefits**.
7. One feature of the Net+ examination is its company-neutral approach, meaning that it does not focus solely on any one vendor's networking products. How might this neutrality benefit your networking career?

CASE PROJECTS

1. You have been asked by Thrift Towne, a local charity retail organization, to install a network in its downtown office. It currently has four PCs running Windows 95, with the following specifications:
   - 486/25 MHz processor, 80 MB hard drive, 8 MB RAM

- 486/66 MHz processor, 120 MB hard drive, 16 MB RAM
- Pentium 75 MHz processor, 500 MB hard drive, 16 MB RAM
- Pentium 133 MHz processor, 1 GB hard drive, 32 MB RAM

Thrift Towne's owners are not very concerned about security, because the network will share only inventory information (their customers remain anonymous and are not tracked). Thrift Towne uses volunteers to run its stores, and the volunteers are not technical experts. In addition, Thrift Towne doesn't have much money to spend on this project. The owners have asked for a simple, inexpensive solution. What type of network would you recommend and why? What role (or roles) would you assign to each of the four workstations and any other equipment you recommend? What type of upgrades might the workstations require to make your solution work?

2. Your work at Thrift Towne was so successful that you are asked to provide networking advice to a chain of ice cream stores called Scoops. Scoops already has a server-based network. The server that holds the company's inventory, ordering, sales, time tracking, and employee information and provides an Internet connection is located at their store across the street from Thrift Towne. Three other Scoops stores in town connect to a modem on the central server through dial-in phone lines. Scoops is having problems with heavy traffic and slow server response at 8:00 A.M. and 3:00 P.M. each day. They don't exactly know where the traffic originates or what type of traffic it is. They also don't know whether the two heavy traffic times every day warrant a change in their connection methods. What kind of services do you suggest will help them assess their traffic situation and provide answers about possible network expansion? What types of things can they find out? What other kinds of services might they also use, given their network configuration?
3. The owners of Thrift Towne and Scoops were so impressed with your networking abilities that they recommended you apply for a network administrator position at the City. You applied for the job and got an interview. Although you think the interview was successful, the City's Director of Planning unfortunately didn't offer you the job because he didn't think you were qualified. In particular, he wanted you to have more hands-on experience with enterprise-wide networks. What can you do to gain that experience to make sure you don't miss another great opportunity?

CHAPTER 2

NETWORKING STANDARDS AND THE OSI MODEL

After reading this chapter and completing the exercises, you will be able to:

- Identify organizations that set standards for networking
- Explain the layers of the OSI Model
- Describe specific networking services within each layer of the OSI Model
- Explain how two systems communicate through the OSI Model
- Discuss the structure and purpose of data frames
- Describe the two types of addressing contained in the OSI Model

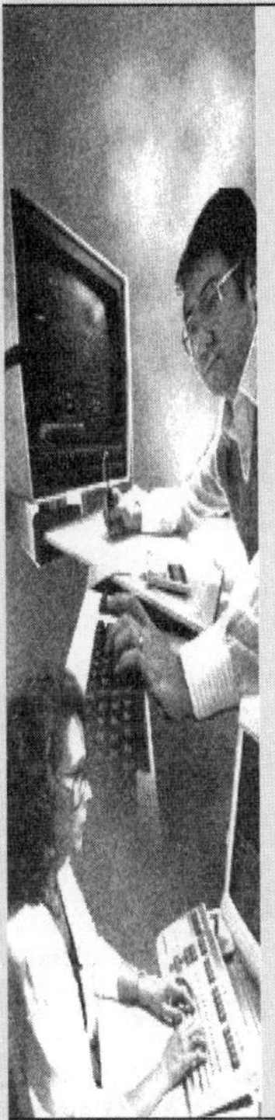

ON THE JOB

When I first heard about the OSI Model, I had already been working as a networking technician for a few months. I thought I knew all about NICs and cabling, but I didn't know the OSI layer to which they belonged. When someone tried to teach me about the OSI Model, I thought it was baloney. The more I learned, however, the more I realized I didn't understand. For example, once a colleague and I tried to figure out why a networked printer wasn't printing. He insisted that it was a "Layer 3 problem." I didn't know what he meant, so I couldn't agree or disagree. From the symptoms, I thought that the printer was probably experiencing an addressing conflict with another device. The printer worked for a while, but after we restarted it, the network didn't recognize it. I didn't know whether this error was a Layer 3 problem; not wanting to sound foolish, I didn't say anything at all. Luckily, an addressing conflict is exactly what my colleague meant by a "Layer 3 problem," and he quickly fixed the problem.

You can be sure that I quietly figured out what "Layer 3" meant shortly after that incident. Since then, I've noticed that an increasing number of people refer to networking hardware, applications, or problems by the OSI Model layer involved. For instance, one networking hardware manufacturer's slogan is "Providing solutions for Layers 1–3." The company doesn't even have to mention the OSI Model, because anyone involved in networking understands the message.

These days we take for granted that servers and clients from different hardware manufacturers, such as Compaq, IBM, Dell, and Hewlett-Packard, will work together. Before the OSI Model, no standard existed, which meant that computing professionals could not assume any kind of compatibility between different manufacturers' hardware and software. Believe it or not, the OSI Model has made our lives easier.

Andy Zimmerman
MedTech Data Systems

When trying to grasp a new theoretical concept, it often helps to form a picture of that concept in your mind. In the field of chemistry, for example, even though you can't see a water molecule, you can represent it with a simple drawing of two hydrogen atoms and one oxygen atom. Similarly, in the field of networking, even though you can't see the communication that occurs between two nodes on a network, you can use a model to depict how the communication takes place. The model commonly used to describe network communications is called the Open Systems Interconnection (OSI) Model.

In this chapter, you will learn about the standards organizations that have helped create the various models (such as the OSI Model) used in networking. Next, you'll be introduced to the seven layers of the OSI Model and learn how they interact. You will then take a closer look at what goes on in each layer. Finally, you will learn to apply those details to a practical networking environment. Granted, learning the OSI Model is not the most exciting part of becoming a networking expert. Unless you understand it thoroughly, however, you will never become an expert.

NETWORKING STANDARDS ORGANIZATIONS

Standards are documented agreements containing technical specifications or other precise criteria that stipulate how a particular product or service should be designed or performed. Many different industries use standards to ensure that products, processes, and services suit their purpose. For example, when plastics manufacturers test their products for flexibility, the tests must adhere to strict American National Standards Institute (ANSI) specifications so that the results can be accurately compared with other manufacturers' results. If manufacturers didn't use the same ANSI test, one company might test flexibility by pulling on the plastic, while one might test flexibility by poking it. The flexibility numbers that each manufacturer obtained, even for the same type of plastic, would then be completely different, and consumers could not compare the two products' flexibility.

Because of the wide variety of hardware and software in use today, standards are especially important in the world of networking. Without standards, you could not design a network because one piece of hardware might not work properly with another. Likewise, one software program might not be able to communicate with another. For example, if one manufacturer designed a network cable with a 1-centimeter-wide plug and another company manufactured a wall plate with a 0.8-centimeter-wide opening, you would not be able to insert the cable into the wall plate.

Because the computer industry grew so quickly out of several technical traditions, many different organizations evolved to oversee its standards. In some cases, a few organizations are responsible for a single aspect of networking. For example, both ANSI and ITU are involved in setting standards for Integrated Services Digital Network (ISDN) communications. While ANSI prescribes the kind of hardware that the consumer needs to accept an ISDN connection, ITU prescribes how the ISDN link will ensure that data arrive in the correct sequence, among other things. A complete list of the standards that regulate computers and networking would fill an encyclopedia. At a minimum, you should be familiar with the handful of significant groups that set the standards referenced by manuals, articles, and books. These groups are responsible for establishing the future of networking.

ANSI

ANSI (American National Standards Institute) is an organization composed of more than 1000 representatives from industry and government who together determine standards for the electronics industry in addition to other fields, such as chemical and nuclear engineering, health and safety, and construction. ANSI also represents the United States in setting international standards. This organization does not dictate that manufacturers comply with its standards, but requests them to comply voluntarily. Of course, manufacturers and developers benefit from compliance, because compliance assures potential customers that the systems are reliable and can be integrated with an existing infrastructure. New electronic equipment and methods must undergo rigorous testing to prove they are worthy of ANSI's approval.

An example of an ANSI standard is ANSI T1.240-1998, "Telecommunications—Operations, Administration, Maintenance, and Provisioning (OAM&P)—Generic Network Information Model for Interfaces between Operations Systems and Network Elements." You can purchase ANSI standards documents online from ANSI's Web site (http://www.ansi.org) or find them at a university or public library. You need not read complete ANSI standards to be a competent networking professional, but you should understand the breadth and significance of ANSI's influence.

EIA

EIA (Electronics Industry Alliance) is a trade organization composed of representatives from electronics manufacturing firms across the United States. EIA began as the Radio Manufacturers Association (RMA) in 1924; over time, it evolved to include manufacturers of televisions, semiconductors, computers, and networking devices. This group not only sets standards for its members, but also helps write ANSI standards and lobbies for legislation favorable to the growth of the computer and electronics industry.

EIA is divided into several subgroups: the Telecommunications Industry Association (TIA); the Consumer Electronics Manufacturers Association (CEMA); the Electronic Components, Assemblies, Equipment & Supplies Association (ECA); the Joint Electron Device Engineering Council (JEDEC); the Solid State Technology Association; the Government Division; and the Electronic Information Group (EIG). In addition to lobbying and setting standards, each specialized group sponsors conferences, exhibitions, and forums in its area of interest. You can find out more about EIA from its Web site: http://www.eia.org.

IEEE

The **IEEE (Institute of Electrical and Electronic Engineers)**, or "I-triple-E," is an international society composed of engineering professionals. Its goals are to promote development and education in the electrical engineering and computer science fields. To this end, IEEE hosts numerous symposia, conferences, and local chapter meetings and publishes papers designed to educate members on technological advances. It also maintains a standards board that establishes its own standards for the electronics and computer industry and contributes to the work of other standards-setting bodies, such as ANSI.

IEEE technical papers and standards are highly respected in the networking profession. Among other places, you will find references to IEEE standards in the manuals that accompany network interface cards. Following are just a few examples of IEEE standards: "Information Technology Year 2000 Test Methods," "Virtual Bridged Local Area Networks," and "Software Project Management Plans." Hundreds more are currently in use. You can order these documents online from IEEE's Web site (http://www.ieee.org) or find them in a university or public library.

ISO

ISO (International Organization for Standardization) is a collection of standards organizations representing 130 countries; its headquarters is located in Geneva, Switzerland. ISO's goal is to establish international technological standards to facilitate global exchange of information and barrier-free trade. Given the organization's full name, you might assume it should be called "IOS," but "ISO" is not meant to be an acronym. In fact, "iso" is the Greek word for "equal." Using this term conveys the organization's dedication to standards.

ISO's authority is not limited to the information-processing and communications industry, but also applies to the fields of textiles, packaging, distribution of goods, energy production and utilization, shipbuilding, and banking and financial services. The universal agreements on screw threads, bank cards, and even the names for currencies are all products of ISO's work. In fact, only about 500 of ISO's nearly 12,000 standards apply to computer-related products and functions. International electronics and electrical engineering standards are separately established by the International Electrotechnical Commission (IEC), a similar international standards body. All of ISO's information technology standards are designed in tandem with the IEC. You can find out more about ISO at its Web page: http://www.iso.ch.

ITU

The **ITU (International Telecommunication Union)** is a specialized United Nations agency that regulates international telecommunications, including radio and TV frequencies, satellite and telephony specifications, networking infrastructure, and tariffs applied to global communications. It also provides developing countries with technical expertise and equipment to advance those nations' technological bases.

The ITU was founded in Paris in 1865. It became part of the United Nations in 1947 and relocated to Geneva, Switzerland. Its standards arm contains members from 188 countries and publishes detailed policy and standards documents that can be found on its Web site: http://www.itu.ch. Typically, ITU's documents pertain more to global telecommunications issues than to industry technical specifications. Some examples of ITU documents are "Communications for Rural and Remote Areas," "Telecommunication Support for the Protection of the Environment," and "The International Frequency List."

The ITU used to be called the CCITT, or Consultative Committee on International Telegraph and Telephony. You may still see references to CCITT standards in manuals and texts.

THE OSI MODEL

In the early 1980s, ISO began work on a universal set of specifications that would enable computer platforms across the world to communicate openly. The organization created a helpful model for understanding and developing computer-to-computer communications. This model, called the **Open Systems Interconnection (OSI) Model**, divides networking architecture into seven layers: Physical, Data Link, Network, Transport, Session, Presentation, and Application. Each layer has its own set of functions and interacts with the layers directly above and below it. At the top, the application layer interacts with the software you use (such as a word-processing or spreadsheet program). At the bottom of the OSI Model are the networking cables and connectors that carry signals. Generally speaking, every layer in between the top and bottom layers ensures that data are delivered in a readable, error-free, and properly sequenced format.

The combination of a network's building blocks is often described as its "architecture." The use of the term "architecture" in the networking field reflects the fact that, like a building, a network contains many distinct but integrated elements: the cabling, servers, protocols, clients, applications, NICs, and so on. A professional involved in network design is sometimes called a **network architect**.

The OSI Model is a theoretical representation of what happens between two nodes on a network. It does not prescribe the type of hardware or software that should support each layer. Everything you will learn about networking can be associated with a layer of this model, however, so you should know not only the names of the layers, but also their functions and the way in which the layers interact. Figure 2-1 depicts the OSI Model and its layers.

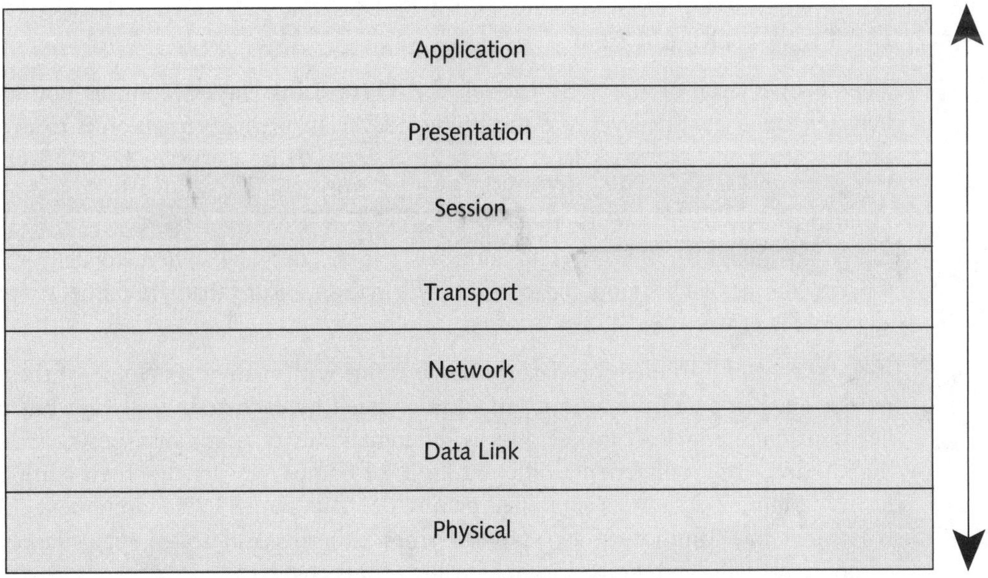

Application
Presentation
Session
Transport
Network
Data Link
Physical

Figure 2-1 The OSI Model

Networking professionals typically devise their own mnemonics for remembering the seven layers of the OSI Model. One strategy is to make a sentence using words that begin with the same first letter of each layer, starting with the Physical layer and ending with the Application layer. For example, you might choose to remember the phrase "Phil Donahue Never Televises Sick People Anymore." If the mnemonic phrase you create is quirky or unexpected, you'll probably remember it more easily.

Physical Layer

The **Physical layer** is the lowest, or first, layer of the OSI Model. This layer contains the physical networking medium, such as cabling, connectors, and repeaters. Protocols at the Physical layer generate and detect voltage so as to transmit and receive signals carrying data. When you install a NIC in your desktop PC, you are establishing the foundation that allows the computer to be networked. In other words, you are providing a Physical layer. The Physical layer sets the data transmission rate and monitors data error rates, though it does not provide error correction services. Physical network problems, such as a severed wire, affect the Physical layer. Similarly, if you insert a NIC but fail to seat it deeply enough in the computer's circuit board, your computer will experience network problems at the Physical layer.

The IEEE has set standards for protocols used at the Physical layer. In particular, the IEEE 802 standards specify how data is handled by Ethernet and Token Ring networks (see Chapter 3). The terms "layer 1 protocols" and "Physical layer protocols" refer to the standards that dictate how the electrical signals are amplified and transmitted over the wire. You will find references to Physical layer devices (such as NICs and hubs) and their operation in Chapters 4 and 6.

Data Link Layer

The second layer of the OSI Model, the **Data Link layer**, controls communications between the Network layer and the Physical layer. Its primary function is to divide data it receives from the Network layer into distinct frames that can then be transmitted by the Physical layer. A **frame** is a structured package for moving data that includes not only the raw data, or "payload," but also the sender's and receiver's network addresses, and error checking and control information. The addresses tell the network where to deliver the frame, whereas the error checking and control information ensure that the frame arrives without any problems.

It may be helpful to envision data frames as trains with many cars. Some of these cars may not be necessary, and the amount of cargo carried by each train will vary, but every train needs an engine and a caboose. Just as different kinds of trains may position their cars in slightly different arrangements, different kinds of frames may arrange their components differently. Figure 2-2 shows a simplified picture of a data frame. Each component of this frame is essential and common to all types of frames. Ethernet and Token Ring frames and their components will be described in detail later in this chapter.

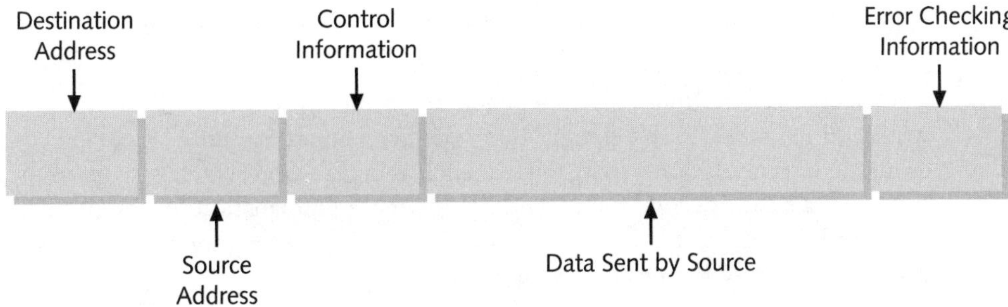

Figure 2-2 A simplified data frame

To fully understand the concept of the function of the Data Link layer, pretend for a moment that computers communicate as humans do. You might be in a large classroom full of noisy students and need to ask the teacher a question. Your teacher's name is Ms. Jones. To get your message through, you might say, "Ms. Jones? Can you explain more about the effects of railroads on commerce in the mid-nineteenth century?" In this example, you are the sender (in a busy network) and you have addressed your recipient, Ms. Jones, just as the Data Link layer addresses another computer on the network. In addition, you have formatted your thought as a question, just as the Data Link layer formats data into frames that can be interpreted by receiving computers.

What happens if the room is so noisy that Ms. Jones hears only part of your question? For example, she might receive "on commerce in the late-nineteenth century?" This kind of error can happen in network communications as well (because of electrical interference or wiring problems). The Data Link layer's job is to find out that information has been dropped and ask the first computer to retransmit its message—just as in a classroom setting Ms. Jones might say, "I didn't hear you. Can you repeat the question?" The Data Link layer accomplishes this task through a process called error checking. Later in this chapter, you will learn more about error checking.

In general, the sender's Data Link layer waits for acknowledgment from the receiver that data was received correctly. If the sender does not get this acknowledgment, its Data Link layer gives instruction to retransmit the information. The Data Link layer does not try to figure out what went wrong in the transmission. Similarly, as in a busy classroom, Ms. Jones will probably say, "Pardon me?" rather than, "It sounds as if you might have a question about railroads, and I heard only the last part of it, which dealt with commerce, so I assume you are asking about commerce and railroads; is that correct?" Obviously, the former method is more efficient for both the sender and the receiver.

Another communications mishap that might occur in a noisy classroom or on a busy network is a glut of communication requests. For example, at the end of class, 20 people might ask Ms. Jones 20 different questions at once. Of course, she can't pay attention to all of them simultaneously. She will probably say, "One person at a time, please," then point to one student who asked a question. This situation is analogous to what the Data Link layer does for the Physical layer. One node on a network (a server, for example) may receive multiple requests that include many frames of data each. The Data Link layer controls the flow of this information, allowing the NIC to process data without error.

The Data Link layer functions independently of the type of Physical layer used by the network and its nodes. It also doesn't care whether you are running WordPerfect or Excel or using the Internet. Connectivity devices, such as bridges and switches, work in the Data Link layer, because they decode frames and use the frame information to transmit data to its correct recipient. Ethernet is an example of a Data Link layer technology. Chapters 3 and 6 both discuss elements of the Data Link layer.

NETWORK LAYER

The primary function of the **Network layer,** the third layer in the OSI Model, is to translate network addresses into their physical counterparts and decide how to route data from the sender to the receiver. For example, a computer might have a network address of 10.34.99.12 (if it's using the TCP/IP protocol) and a physical address of 0060973E97F3. In the classroom example, this addressing scheme is like saying that "Ms. Jones" and "U.S. citizen with Social Security number 123-45-6789" are the same person. Even though there may be other people named "Ms. Jones" in the United States, only one person has the Social Security number 123-45-6789. Within the confines of your classroom, however, there is only one Ms. Jones, so you can be certain the correct person will respond when you say, "Ms. Jones?"

The Network layer determines the best path from point A on one network to point B on another network by factoring in delivery priorities, network congestion, quality of service, and cost of alternative routes. Because the Network layer handles routing, **routers**—the devices that connect network segments and intelligently direct data—belong in the Network layer. In networking, the term "to **route**" means to intelligently direct data based on addressing, patterns of usage, and availability. Chapter 6 explains routers and their functions in detail.

The Network layer protocols also compensate for disparities in the capabilities of the devices they are transmitting data to, through, and from. To accomplish this task, they employ segmentation and reassembly of packets. **Segmentation** refers to the process of decreasing the size of the data units when moving data from a network segment that can handle larger data units to a network segment that can handle only smaller data units. This process is just like the process of breaking down words into recognizable syllables that a small child uses when learning to read. **Reassembly** is the process of reconstructing the segmented data units. To continue the reading analogy, when a child understands the separate syllables, he can combine them into a word—that is, reassemble the parts into a whole.

The segmentation that takes place in the Network layer of the OSI Model has nothing to do with network segmentation, which was introduced in Chapter 1 and will be described in more detail in Chapters 5 and 10. Segmentation in the Network layer refers to a reduction in the size of the data frames, while network segmentation refers to the separation of a network into smaller logical or physical pieces.

TRANSPORT LAYER

The **Transport layer** is primarily responsible for ensuring that data are transferred from point A to point B (which may or may not be on the same network segment) reliably, in the correct sequence, and without errors. The Transport layer may be considered the most important layer in the OSI Model because without it, data could not be verified or interpreted by their recipients. Transport protocols also handle **flow control**, or the method of gauging the appropriate rate of transmission based on how fast the recipient can accept data.

In addition, Transport layer services break arbitrarily long packets into the maximum size that the type of network in use can handle. For example, Ethernet networks cannot accept packets larger than 1500 bytes. When the sending node's Transport layer services divide its data into smaller pieces, they assign a sequence number to each piece, so that the data can be reassembled in the correct order by the receiving node's Transport layer services. This process is called **sequencing**.

To understand how sequencing works, consider the classroom example again. Suppose you asked the question, "Ms. Jones? How did poor farming techniques contribute to the Dust Bowl?" but that the words arrived at Ms. Jones's ear as "poor farming techniques Ms. Jones? how did to the Dust Bowl? contribute." On a network, the Transport layer would recognize this disorder and rearrange the data pieces so that they make sense. In addition, the Transport layer sends an **acknowledgment (ACK)** to notify the sender that data were received correctly. If the data contained errors, the Transport layer would request that the sender retransmit the data. Also, if the data weren't acknowledged within a given time period, the sender's Transport layer would consider the data lost and retransmit them.

One service that works in the Transport layer is TCP (Transmission Control Protocol) of the TCP/IP protocol suite. Another Transport layer service is SPX (Sequence Packet Exchange) of the IPX/SPX protocol suite. You will learn more about these and other Transport layer services in Chapter 3.

SESSION LAYER

The **Session layer** is responsible for establishing and maintaining communication between two nodes on the network. The term **session** refers to a connection for data exchange between two parties; it is most often used in the context of terminal and mainframe communications, in which the **terminal** is a device with little (if any) of its own processing or disk capacity that depends on a host to supply it with applications and data processing services. Among the Session layer's functions are establishing and keeping alive the communications link for the duration of the session, synchronizing the dialog between the two nodes, determining whether communications have been cut off, and, if so, figuring out where to restart transmission. Often you will hear the Session layer called the "traffic cop" of network communications. When you dial your Internet service provider (ISP) to connect to the Internet, the Session layer services at your ISP's server, and on your PC client, negotiate the connection. If your phone line is accidentally pulled out of the wall jack, the Session layer on your end will detect the loss of a connection and initiate attempts to reconnect.

The Session layer also sets the terms of communication by deciding which node will communicate first and how long a node can communicate. In this sense, the Session layer acts as a judge in a debate competition. For example, if you were a member of a debate team and had two minutes to state your opening argument, the judge might signal you after one and a half minutes that you have only 30 seconds remaining. If you tried to interrupt a member of the opposing debate team, he would tell you to wait your turn. Finally, the Session layer monitors the identification of session participants, ensuring that only the authorized nodes can access the session.

Presentation Layer

The **Presentation layer** serves as a translator between the application and the network. At the Presentation layer, data become formatted in a schema that the network can understand; this format varies with the type of network used. The Presentation layer also manages data encryption and decryption, such as the scrambling of system passwords. For example, if you look up your bank account status on the Internet, you are using a secure connection, and your account data will be encrypted before they are transmitted. On your end of the network, the Presentation layer will decrypt the data as they are received. In addition, Presentation layer protocols code and decode graphics and file format information.

Application Layer

The top, or seventh, layer of the OSI Model is the Application layer. The **Application layer** provides interfaces to the software that enable programs to use network services. The term "Application layer" does not refer to a particular application, such as Microsoft Word, running on the network. Instead, some of the services provided by the Application layer include file transfer, file management, and message handling for electronic mail. For example, if you are running Microsoft Word on a network and choose to open a file, your request for that data is transferred to the network by the Application layer.

You may have heard the term "API." An **API (application program interface)** is a routine (a set of instructions) that allows a program to interact with the operating system. APIs belong to the Application layer of the OSI Model. Programmers use APIs to establish links between their code and the operating system. An example of an API used in a network environment is **Microsoft Message Queueing (MSMQ)**. MSMQ stores messages sent between nodes in queues and then forwards them to their destinations based on when the link to the recipient becomes available. As a result, programs can run independently of whether the data's destination is connected to the network when the messages are sent.

APPLYING THE OSI MODEL

Now that you have been introduced to the seven layers of the OSI Model, you can take a closer look at exactly how the layers interact. For reference, Table 2-1 summarizes the functions of the seven OSI Model layers.

Table 2-1 Actions for Each Layer of the OSI Reference Model

OSI Layer	Function
Application	Transfers information from program to program
Presentation	Handles text formatting and displays code conversion
Session	Establishes, maintains, and coordinates communication
Transport	Ensures accurate delivery of data
Network	Determines transport routes and handles the transfer of messages
Data Link	Codes, addresses, and transmits information
Physical	Manages hardware connections

COMMUNICATION BETWEEN TWO SYSTEMS

An exemplary process to trace through the OSI Model layers is the retrieval of a message file from the server. Once you log in to the network and start your mail program, you can choose to pick up your mail. At that point, the Application layer recognizes your choice and formulates a request for data from a remote node (in this case, the mail server). The Application layer transfers the request to the Presentation layer.

The Presentation layer first determines whether and how it should format or encrypt the data request received from the Application layer. After it has made that determination, it adds any translation or codes required to implement that formatting and then passes your request on to the Session layer.

The Session layer picks up your formatted request and assigns a data token to it. A **token** is a special control frame that indicates to the rest of the network that you have the right to transmit data. (Remember that the Session layer acts as the "traffic cop" for communications between nodes.) The Session layer then passes your data to the Transport layer.

At the Transport layer, your data and the control information it has accumulated thus far are broken down into manageable chunks of data and prepared to be packaged in frames at the Data Link layer. If the data is too large to fit in one frame, the Transport layer subdivides it into several smaller blocks and assigns sequence identifiers to each block. This layer then passes the data blocks, one at a time, to the Network layer.

The Network layer adds addressing information to the data it receives from the Transport layer, so that subsequent layers will know the source and the destination of the data. It then passes the data blocks, with their addressing identifications, to the Data Link layer.

At the Data Link layer, the data blocks are packaged into individual frames. As you have learned, a frame is a structured format for transmitting small blocks of data. Using frames reduces the possibility of lost data or errors on the network, because each frame has its own built-in error check. This error checking algorithm, also known as the **Frame Check Sequence (FCS)**, is inserted at the end of the frame by the Data Link layer. In addition, the Data Link layer adds a header to the frame that incorporates destination and source addresses assigned by the Network layer. (Frame types and specifications are discussed in more detail in the next section.) The Data Link layer then passes the frames to the Physical layer.

Finally, your request for your mail message hits the NIC at the Physical layer. The Physical layer does not interpret the frame or add information to the frame; it simply delivers the data to the cabling and across the network. Once the data arrives at the Physical layer of the remote system, the mail server's Data Link layer begins to unravel your request, reversing the process just described, until it responds to your request with its own transmission, beginning from its Application layer. Figure 2-3 shows how data is transferred from your system to the server, then back to your system through the OSI Model.

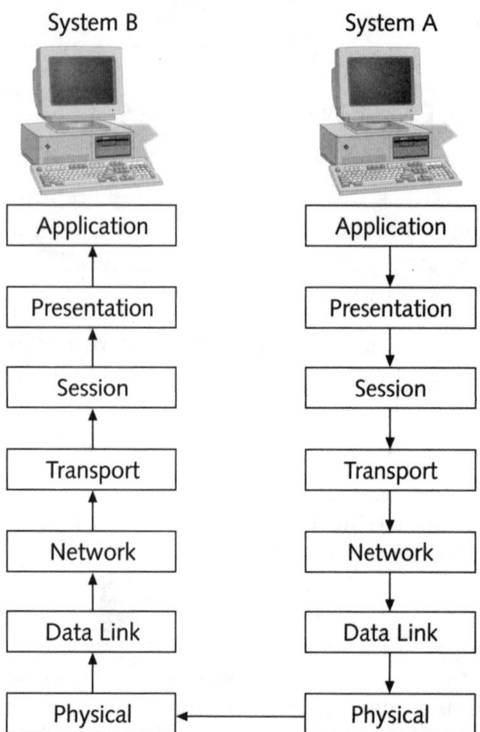

Figure 2-3 Data transfer between two systems

In the preceding example, you learned that every successive layer in the OSI Model—beginning with the Application layer and ending with the Physical layer—adds some control, formatting, or addressing information to the data it handles. The receiving system then interprets and uses the added information as it reverses the process, passing data from the

Physical layer back up to the Application layer. Between your initial software request and the network cable, your blocks of data grow larger as they accumulate more handling information. Figure 2-4 depicts the transformation of data as it travels through the OSI Model layers.

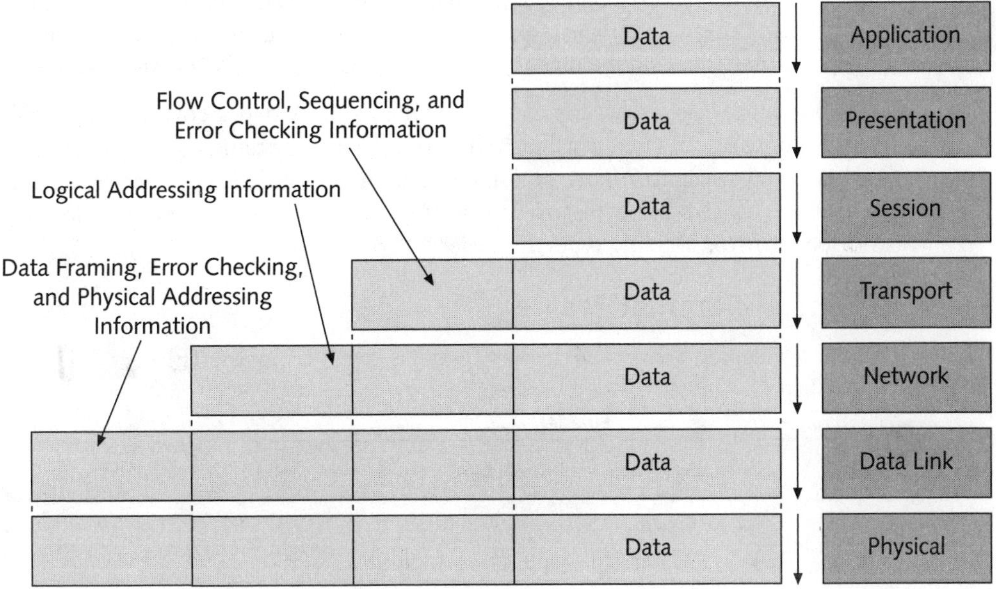

Figure 2-4 Data transformed through the OSI Model

FRAME SPECIFICATIONS

Figure 2-2 introduced the basic structure of a data frame. In reality, frames are composed of several smaller components, or fields. The characteristics of these components depend on the type of network on which the frames run and on the standards that they must follow. The two major categories of frame types, Ethernet and Token Ring, correspond to the two most commonly used network technologies.

Ethernet is a networking technology originally developed at Xerox in 1970 and improved by Digital Equipment Corporation, Intel, and Xerox. Today, four types of Ethernet technology are used on LANs, with each type being governed by a set of IEEE standards. Ethernet LANs can transmit data at different rates and on a multitude of networking media. Ethernet is covered in detail in Chapter 5.

Token Ring is a networking technology developed by IBM in the 1980s. It relies upon direct links between nodes and a ring topology, passing around tokens that allow nodes to transmit data. Token Ring technology will be discussed in detail in Chapter 5.

Each frame type is unique and will not interact with different frame types on the network, because routers cannot support more than one frame type per physical interface. You can, however, work with multiple protocols on a network while using only one frame type. For example, you can run both IPX/SPX and TCP/IP on an Ethernet network. Although you can conceivably transmit both Token Ring and Ethernet frames on a network, Ethernet interfaces cannot interpret Token Ring frames, and vice versa. Normally, LANs use *either* Ethernet or Token Ring. On the other hand, many LANs run both TCP/IP *and* IPX/SPX.

It's important to know what frame type (or types) your network environment requires. You will use this information when installing network operating systems, configuring servers and client workstations, installing NICs, troubleshooting network problems and purchasing network equipment. It's also important to know what constitutes the frame. The following sections describe two typical frame types, Ethernet 802.3 and Token Ring 802.5.

A Typical Ethernet Frame

Figure 2-5 depicts a typical Ethernet frame as specified by the IEEE **802.3** standard.

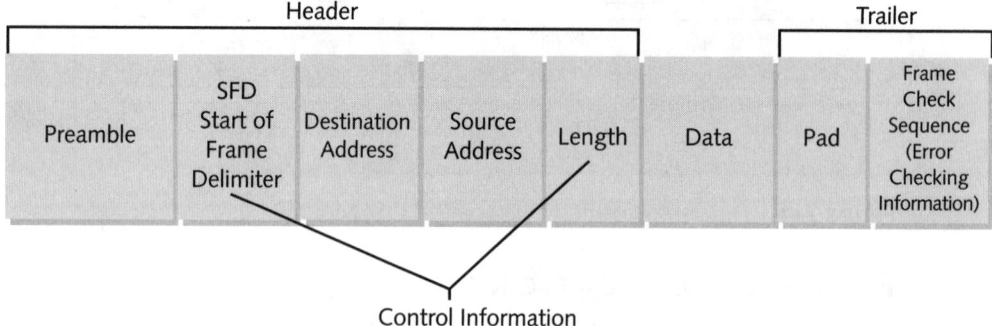

Figure 2-5 Ethernet frame as specified by the IEEE 802.3 standard

The components of the Ethernet 802.3 frame are described in the following list:

- *Preamble*—Marks the beginning of the entire frame, providing a signal that essentially announces to the network that data is en route. Because this field is part of the communications process, a preamble typically isn't included when calculating the size of a frame.
- *Start of Frame Delimiter (SFD)*—Indicates the beginning of the addressing frame.
- *Destination Address*—Contains the destination node address.
- *Source Address*—Contains the address of the originating node.
- *Length (LEN)*—Indicates the length of the packet.
- *Data*—Contains the data, or segmented part of that data, transmitted from the originating node.

- *Pad*—Used to increase the size of the frame to its minimum size requirement of 46 bytes.
- *Frame Check Sequence (FCS)*—Provides an algorithm to determine whether the data were received correctly. The most commonly used algorithm is called **Cyclic Redundancy Check (CRC)**, so you may also see this field called "CRC."

2

Chapter 5 provides more detail on this type of Ethernet frame. Chapter 5 also covers the other three Ethernet frame types.

A Typical Token Ring Frame

Figure 2-6 depicts a typical Token Ring frame, which is specified in the IEEE **802.5** standard. Note that some of its characteristics match those of the Ethernet frame, but significant differences arise in how the control information is handled.

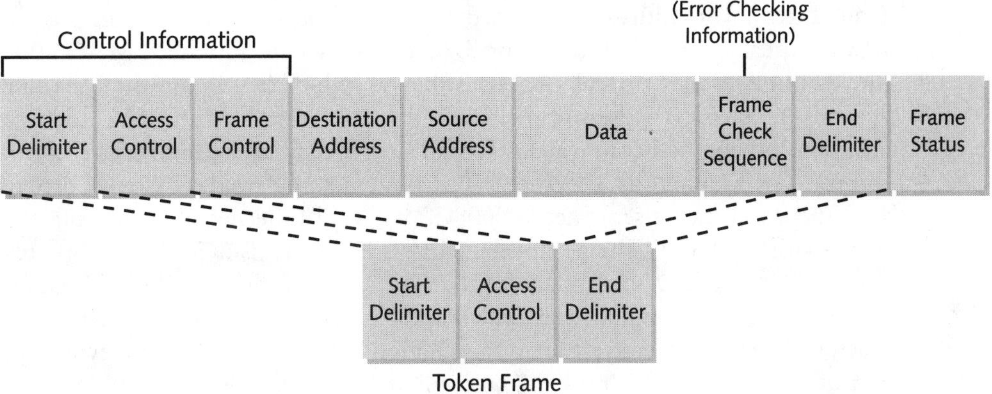

Figure 2-6 A typical Token Ring frame

The following list describes the components of the typical Token Ring frame:

- *Start Delimiter (SD)*—Signifies the beginning of the packet. It is one of three fields that compose the Token Ring frame.
- *Access Control (AC)*—Contains information about the priority of the frame. It is the second of three fields that compose the Token Ring frame.
- *Frame Control (FC)*—Defines the type of frame; used in the Frame Check Sequence.
- *Destination Address*—Contains the destination node address.
- *Source Address*—Contains the address of the originating node.
- *Data*—Contains the data transmitted from the originating node. May also contain routing and management information.

- *Frame Check Sequence (FCS)*—Used to check the integrity of the frame.
- *End Delimiter (ED)*—Indicates the end of the frame. It is the third field that composes the Token Ring frame.
- *Frame Status (FS)*—Indicates whether the destination node recognized and correctly copied the frame, or whether the destination node was not available.

Token Ring networks and frame types will be covered in more detail in Chapter 5.

Addressing Through the Layers

In Chapter 1, you learned that addressing is a system for assigning unique identification numbers to each node on a network. In this chapter, you learned that addressing is interpreted at the network layer of the OSI Model. In fact, each node on a network can be identified by two types of addresses: Network layer addresses and Data Link layer addresses.

Data Link layer addresses are fixed numbers associated with the networking hardware; they are usually assigned at the factory. These addresses are also called **MAC addresses**, after the **Media Access Control (MAC) sublayer**, which lies within the Data Link layer and appends the physical address of the destination to the data frame. MAC addresses are guaranteed to be unique because industry standards specify which numbers each manufacturer can use. For example, all Ethernet NICs manufactured by the 3Com Corporation begin with the six-character sequence "00608C," while all Ethernet NICs manufactured by Intel begin with "00AA00." The part of the MAC address that is unique to a particular vendor is called the **Block ID**. Some manufacturers have several different Block IDs. The remaining six characters in the sequence are added at the factory, based on the NIC's model and manufacture date, and collectively form the **Device ID**. An example of a Device ID assigned by a manufacturer might be 005499. The combination of the Block ID and Device ID result in a unique MAC address of 00608C005499. Networks rely upon unique MAC addressing to transmit data to their correct destination.

Data Link layer—or MAC—addresses are also called physical addresses or hardware addresses.

Network layer addresses, which reside at the network level of the OSI Model, follow a hierarchical addressing scheme and can be assigned through operating system software. They are hierarchical because they contain subsets of data that incrementally narrow down the location of a node, just as your home address is hierarchical because it provides a country, state, zip code, city, street, house number, and person's name. Network Layer addresses, therefore, are more useful to internetworking devices such as routers, because they make sorting data more logical. Network layer address formats differ depending on which protocols the network uses. Chapter 3 covers the addressing rules for the different protocols.

Network layer addresses are also called logical addresses or virtual addresses.

IEEE Networking Specifications

2

In addition to frame types, the IEEE networking specifications apply to connectivity, networking media, error checking algorithms, encryption, emerging technologies, and more. All of these specifications fall under the IEEE's "Project 802," an effort to standardize physical elements of a network. IEEE developed these standards before the OSI Model was standardized by ISO, but IEEE's 802 standards can be applied to the layers of the OSI Model. Table 2-2 describes the IEEE 802 specifications. You should be familiar with the topics that each standard covers.

Table 2-2 IEEE 802 Standards

Standard	Name	Explanation
802.1	Internetworking	Covers routing, bridging, and internetwork communications
802.2	Logical Link Control	Relates to error and flow control over data frames
802.3	Ethernet LAN	Covers all forms of Ethernet media and interfaces
802.4	Token Bus LAN	Covers all forms of Token Bus media and interfaces
802.5	Token Ring LAN	Covers all forms of Token Ring media and interfaces
802.6	Metropolitan Area Network (MAN)	Covers MAN technologies, addressing, and services
802.7	Broadband Technical Advisory Group	Covers broadband networking media, interfaces, and other equipment
802.8	Fiber-Optic Technical Advisory Group	Covers use of fiber-optic media and technologies for various networking types
802.9	Integrated Voice/Data Networks	Covers integration of voice and data traffic over a single network medium
802.10	Network Security	Covers network access controls, encryption, certification, and other security topics
802.11	Wireless Networks	Standards for wireless networking for many different broadcast frequencies and usage techniques
802.12	High-Speed Networking	Covers a variety of 100Mbps-plus technologies, including 100BASEVG-AnyLAN

To accommodate shared access for multiple network nodes (as opposed to simple point-to-point communication), the IEEE expanded the OSI Model by separating the Data Link layer into two sublayers: the Logical Link Control (LLC) sublayer and the Media Access Control (MAC) sublayer. The **LLC**, the upper sublayer in the Data Link layer, provides a common interface and supplies reliability and flow control services. The **MAC**, the lower sublayer of the Data Link layer, actually appends the physical address of the destination computer onto the data frame. IEEE's specifications for Ethernet and Token Ring technology (found in Table 2-2) apply to the MAC sublayer of the Data Link layer. Figure 2-7 shows how the IEEE subdivided the Data Link layer.

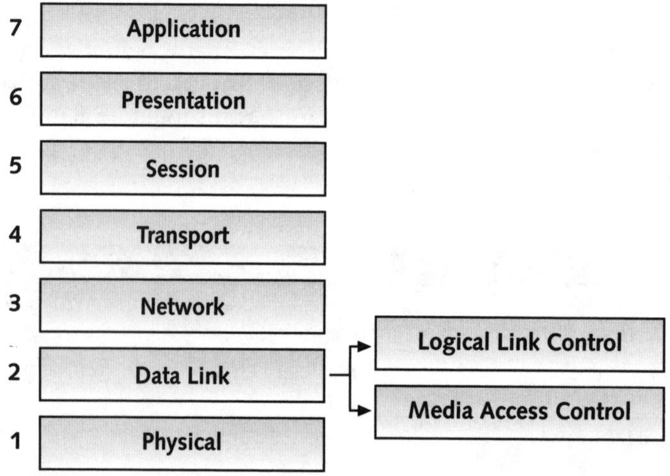

Figure 2-7 The Logical Link Control and Media Access Control sublayers

CHAPTER SUMMARY

- Standards are documented agreements containing technical specifications or other precise criteria that are used as guidelines to ensure that materials, products, processes, and services suit their purpose. Without standards, you could not design a network because your hardware would not fit together and your programs could not communicate with each other.

- A complete compilation of standards that apply to the networking and computer industries would fill an encyclopedia. Some of the significant standards organizations are ANSI (American National Standards Institute), EIA (Electronic Industries Association), IEEE (Institute of Electrical and Electronic Engineers), ISO (International Organization for Standardization), and ITU (International Telecommunications Union, formerly called the CCITT).

- In the early 1980s, ISO began work on a universal set of specifications that would enable computer platforms across the world to communicate openly. The result was a helpful model for understanding and developing computer-to-computer communication. This model, called the Open Systems Interconnection (OSI) Model, divides networking architecture into seven layers: Physical, Data Link, Network, Transport, Session, Presentation, and Application. Each layer has its own set of functions and interacts with the layers directly above and below it.

- The Physical layer is the lowest, or first, layer of the OSI Model. It contains the physical networking medium, such as cabling, connectors, and repeaters. Protocols at the Physical layer generate and detect voltage so as to transmit and receive signals carrying data. The Physical layer sets the data transmission rate and monitors data error rates, though it does not provide error correction.
- The second layer of the OSI Model, the Data Link layer, bridges the networking media with the abstract software and data streams. Its primary function is to divide data it receives from the Network layer into frames that can then be transmitted by the Physical layer. Connectivity devices such as bridges and switches work in the Data Link layer, because they decode frames and use the frame information to transmit data to its correct recipient.
- The Network layer, the third OSI Model layer, manages addressing and routing data based on addressing, patterns of usage, and availability. Routers belong to the Network layer because they use this information to intelligently direct data from sender to receiver. The Network layer is also responsible for segmentation and reassembly of packets.
- The Transport layer is primarily responsible for ensuring that data are transferred from point A to point B (which may or may not be on the same network segment) reliably and without errors. For example, the Transport layer ensures that data are sent and received in the same order, or sequence. It also establishes the level of packet error checking.
- The Session layer establishes and maintains communication between two nodes on the network. It can be considered the "traffic cop" of network communications. The term "session" refers to a connection for data exchange between two parties; it is most often used in the context of terminal and mainframe communications.
- The Presentation layer, the sixth OSI Model layer, serves as a translator between the application and the network. At the Presentation layer, data are formatted in a schema that the network can understand; this format varies with the type of network used. The Presentation layer also manages data encryption and decryption, such as the scrambling of system passwords.
- The top, or seventh, layer of the OSI Model is the Application layer. It provides interfaces to the software that enable it to use network services. Some of the services provided by the Application layer include file transfer, file management, and message handling for electronic mail.
- A data request from a software program is received by the Application layer services and is transferred down through the layers of the OSI Model until it reaches the Physical layer, or the network cable. At that point, data are sent to their destination over the wire, and the Physical layer services at the destination send it back up through the layers of the OSI Model until it reaches the Application layer.
- Data frames, also known simply as "frames," are small blocks of data with control, addressing, and handling information attached to them. Frames are composed of several smaller components. The characteristics of these components depend on the type of network on which the frames run and the standards that they must follow. The two major categories of frame types, Ethernet and Token Ring, correspond to the two most commonly used network technologies.

- Each node on a network can be identified by two types of addresses: Network layer addresses and Data Link layer addresses. Data Link Layer addresses are hardwired into the networking device, and are also called physical, MAC, or hardware addresses. Network layer addresses, also called logical or virtual addresses, are assigned to devices through operating software. These logical addresses are composed of hierarchical information, so they can be easily interpreted by routers and used to direct data to their destinations.
- In addition to frame types, the IEEE networking specifications apply to connectivity, networking media, error checking algorithms, encryption, emerging technologies, and more. All of these specifications fall under the IEEE's Project 802, an effort to standardize the elements of networking.
- The IEEE expanded the OSI Model by separating the Data Link layer into two sublayers: the Logical Link Control (LLC) sublayer and the Medium Access Control (MAC) sublayer. The LLC, the upper sublayer in the Data Link layer, provides a common interface and supplies reliability and flow control services. The MAC, the lower sublayer of the Data Link layer, actually appends the physical address of the destination computer onto the data frame.

KEY TERMS

- **802.3** — The IEEE standard for Ethernet networking devices and data handling.
- **802.5** — The IEEE standard for Token Ring networking devices and data handling.
- **ACK (acknowledgment)** — A response generated at the Transport layer of the OSI Model that confirms to a sender that its frame was received.
- **ANSI (American National Standards Institute)** — An organization composed of more than 1000 representatives from industry and government who together determine standards for the electronics industry in addition to other fields, such as chemical and nuclear engineering, health and safety, and construction.
- **API (application programming interface)** — A routine (or set of instructions) that allows a program to interact with the operating system. APIs belong to the Application layer of the OSI Model.
- **Application layer** — The seventh layer of the OSI Model. The Application layer provides interfaces to the software that enable programs to use network services.
- **Block ID** — The first set of six characters that make up the MAC address and that are unique to a particular vendor.
- **CRC (Cyclic Redundancy Check)** — An algorithm used to verify the accuracy of data contained in a data frame.
- **Data Link layer** — The second layer in the OSI Model. The Data Link layer bridges the networking media with the Network layer. Its primary function is to divide the data it receives from the Network layer into frames that can then be transmitted by the Physical layer.

- **Data Link layer address** — See MAC address.
- **Device ID** — The second set of six characters that make up a network device's MAC address. The Device ID, which is added at the factory, is based on the device's model and manufacture date.
- **EIA (Electronics Industry Alliance)** — A trade organization composed of representatives from electronics manufacturing firms across the United States.
- **Ethernet** — A networking technology originally developed at Xerox in 1970 and improved by Digital Equipment Corporation, Intel, and Xerox. Today, four types of Ethernet technology are used on LANs, with each type being governed by a set of IEEE standards.
- **flow control** — A method of gauging the appropriate rate of data transmission based on how fast the recipient can accept data.
- **frame** — A package for data that includes not only the raw data, or "payload," but also the sender's and receiver's network addresses and control information.
- **Frame Check Sequence (FCS)** — The field in a frame responsible for ensuring that data carried by the frame arrives intact. It uses an algorithm, such as CRC, to accomplish this verification.
- **IEEE (Institute of Electrical and Electronic Engineers)** — An international society composed of engineering professionals. Its goals are to promote development and education in the electrical engineering and computer science fields.
- **ISO (International Organization for Standardization)** — A collection of standards organizations representing 130 countries with headquarters located in Geneva, Switzerland. Its goal is to establish international technological standards to facilitate the global exchange of information and barrier-free trade.
- **ITU (International Telecommunications Union)** — A United Nations agency that regulates international telecommunications, including radio and TV frequencies, satellite and telephony specifications, networking infrastructure, and tariffs applied to global communication. It also provides developing countries with technical expertise and equipment to advance these nations' technological bases.
- **Logical Link Control (LLC) sublayer** — The upper sublayer in the Data Link layer. The LLC provides a common interface and supplies reliability and flow control services.
- **MAC address** — A number that uniquely identifies a network node. The manufacturer hard-codes the MAC address on the NIC. This address is composed of the block ID and device ID.
- **Media Access Control (MAC) sublayer** — The lower sublayer of the Data Link layer. The MAC appends the physical address of the destination computer onto the frame.
- **Microsoft Message Queueing (MSMQ)** — An API used in a network environment. MSMQ stores messages sent between nodes in queues then forwards them to their destination based on when the link to the recipient is available.

- **network architect** — A professional who designs networks, performing tasks that range from choosing basic components (such as cabling type) to figuring out how to make those components work together (by, for example, choosing the correct protocols).
- **Network layer** — The third layer in the OSI Model. The **Network layer** translates network addresses into their physical counterparts and decides how to route data from the sender to the receiver.
- **Network layer addresses** — Addresses that reside at the Network level of the OSI Model, follow a hierarchical addressing scheme, and can be assigned through operating system software.
- **Open Systems Interconnection (OSI) Model** — A model for understanding and developing computer-to-computer communication developed in the 1980s by ISO. It divides networking architecture into seven layers: Physical, Data Link, Network, Transport, Session, Presentation, and Application.
- **Physical layer** — The lowest, or first, layer of the OSI Model. The Physical layer contains the physical networking media, such as cabling and connectors.
- **Presentation layer** — The sixth layer of the OSI Model. The Presentation layer serves as a translator between the application and the network. Here data are formatted in a schema that the network can understand, with the format varying according to the type of network used. The Presentation layer also manages data encryption and decryption, such as the scrambling of system passwords.
- **reassembly** — The process of reconstructing data units that have been segmented.
- **route** — To direct data between networks based on addressing, patterns of usage, and availability of network segments.
- **routers** — Devices that connect network segments and intelligently direct data based on information contained in the data frame.
- **segmentation** — The process of decreasing the size of data units when moving data from a network segment that can handle larger data units to a network segment that can handle only smaller data units.
- **sequencing** — The process of assigning a placeholder to each piece of a data block to allow the receiving node's Transport layer to reassemble the data in the correct order.
- **session** — A connection for data exchange between two parties. The term "session" is most often used in the context of terminal and mainframe communications.
- **Session layer** — The fifth layer in the OSI Model. The Session layer establishes and maintains communication between two nodes on the network. It can be considered the "traffic cop" for network communications.
- **standards** — Documented agreements containing technical specifications or other precise criteria that are used as guidelines to ensure that materials, products, processes, and services suit their intended purpose.
- **terminal** — A device with little (if any) of its own processing or disk capacity that depends on a host to supply it with applications and data-processing services.

- **token** — A special control frame that indicates to the rest of the network that a particular node has the right to transmit data.
- **Token Ring** — A networking technology developed by IBM in the 1980s. It relies upon direct links between nodes and a ring topology, using tokens to allow nodes to transmit data.
- **Transport layer** — The fourth layer of the OSI Model. The Transport layer is primarily responsible for ensuring that data are transferred from point A to point B (which may or may not be on the same network segment) reliably and without errors.

Review Questions

1. Which international standards organization is part of the United Nations?
   a. IEEE
   b. ITU
   c. ISO
   d. ANSI
2. What does "ISO" stand for?
   a. Institute for Standards Organization
   b. International Standards Organization
   c. International Organization for Standardization
   d. International Statisticians Organization
3. Which organization represents the United States in ISO?
   a. ANSI
   b. ITU
   c. IEEE
   d. EIA
4. Which technology is standardized in the IEEE 802.5 specification?
   a. network security
   b. Token Ring LANs
   c. wireless networks
   d. Ethernet LANs
5. Which technology is standardized in the IEEE 802.3 specification?
   a. network security
   b. Token Ring LANs
   c. wireless networks
   d. Ethernet LANs

6. Which layer of the OSI Model provides file transfer services?
   - a. Application layer
   - b. Data Link layer
   - c. Transport layer
   - d. Presentation layer
7. Netscape is an example of a program that runs in the Application layer. True or False?
8. Which layer of the OSI Model establishes the rules of communication between two nodes?
   - a. Transport layer
   - b. Session layer
   - c. Data Link layer
   - d. Presentation layer
9. In which layer of the OSI Model do switches and bridges belong?
   - a. Data Link layer
   - b. Transport layer
   - c. Network layer
   - d. Session layer
10. In which layer of the OSI Model do routers belong?
    - a. Data Link layer
    - b. Transport layer
    - c. Network layer
    - d. Physical layer
11. In which layer of the OSI Model do NICs belong?
    - a. Data Link layer
    - b. Transport layer
    - c. Network layer
    - d. Physical layer
12. Which standards organization developed the OSI Model?
    - a. IEEE
    - b. ITU
    - c. OSI
    - d. ISO
13. Under what circumstances would the Network layer use segmentation?
    - a. when too many data frames are flooding into a receiving node's NIC
    - b. when the network is transmitting too many incorrect frames

c. when the destination node cannot accept the size of the data blocks transmitted by the source node

d. when the source node requests that data blocks be segmented for faster processing

14. Generating and detecting voltage so as to transmit and receive signals carrying data is the responsibility of which OSI Model layer?

a. Transport layer

b. Session layer

c. Presentation layer

d. Physical layer

15. Flow control is the process of making sure data frames are received in the correct order. True or False?

16. What is the purpose of a token in a token-passing network?

a. It indicates to the rest of the network that one node has the right to transmit data.

b. It indicates to the rest of the network that one node is busy and cannot receive traffic.

c. It indicates to the rest of the network that a broadcast message is about to be sent.

d. It indicates to the rest of the network that one node is causing transmission errors for the rest of the network.

17. If you use a password to log in to your Microsoft Exchange program, which layer of the OSI Model would decode your password?

a. Application layer

b. Session layer

c. Presentation layer

d. Network layer

18. Which layer of the OSI Model handles error checking and retransmission of bad data?

a. Transport layer

b. Network layer

c. Session layer

d. Physical layer

19. What are the differences between MAC addresses and Network layer addresses?

20. One frame type will not interact with another frame type on the network. True or False?

21. Which of the following types of addresses follow a hierarchical format?

a. Physical layer addresses

b. MAC addresses

c. Network layer addresses

d. Data Link layer addresses

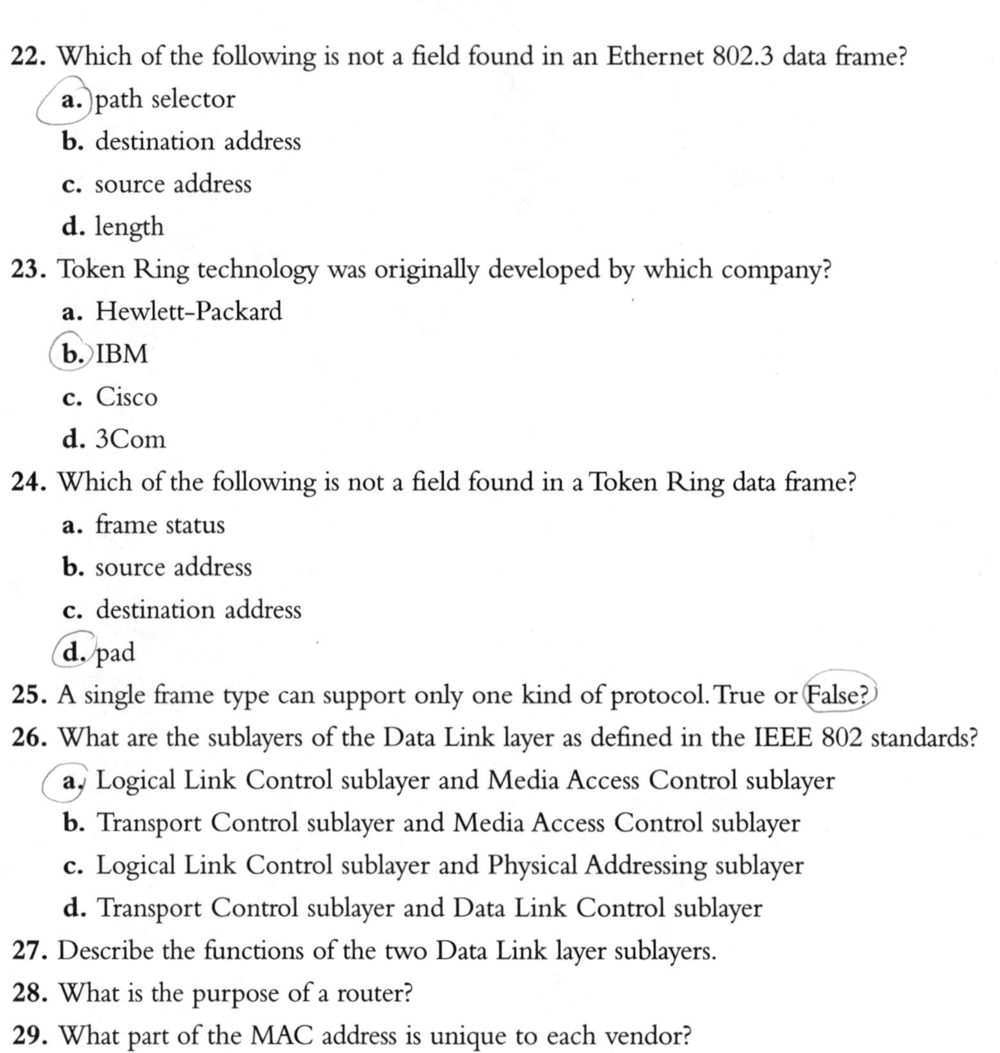

22. Which of the following is not a field found in an Ethernet 802.3 data frame?
    - **a.** path selector
    - **b.** destination address
    - **c.** source address
    - **d.** length
23. Token Ring technology was originally developed by which company?
    - **a.** Hewlett-Packard
    - **b.** IBM
    - **c.** Cisco
    - **d.** 3Com
24. Which of the following is not a field found in a Token Ring data frame?
    - **a.** frame status
    - **b.** source address
    - **c.** destination address
    - **d.** pad
25. A single frame type can support only one kind of protocol. True or False?
26. What are the sublayers of the Data Link layer as defined in the IEEE 802 standards?
    - **a.** Logical Link Control sublayer and Media Access Control sublayer
    - **b.** Transport Control sublayer and Media Access Control sublayer
    - **c.** Logical Link Control sublayer and Physical Addressing sublayer
    - **d.** Transport Control sublayer and Data Link Control sublayer
27. Describe the functions of the two Data Link layer sublayers.
28. What is the purpose of a router?
29. What part of the MAC address is unique to each vendor?
    - **a.** The destination ID
    - **b.** The Block ID
    - **c.** The physical node ID
    - **d.** The segment ID
30. IEEE has standardized four Ethernet frame types. True or False?

Hands-on Projects

Project 2-1

To better understand the impact IEEE has on networking standards, it is helpful to look at some of the specifications developed by IEEE. This exercise will guide you through the process of searching for IEEE specifications on the Web. To complete this project, you need a computer with access to the Internet.

1. Access the Internet and go to http://standards.ieee.org.
2. On the Standards page, click the **Standards Information** link.
3. Under the heading "Information about IEEE Standards," click the **Abstracts** link.
4. Type **ethernet** in the Search text box, then click **Search**!
5. Note how many abstracts your search returned. For those abstracts that give designation numbers, note the numbers as well.

Project 2-2

When supporting computers on a network, you will often need to change the network properties on client workstations. You may perform this task when you first set up a machine or later, if it is having problems or if the network specifications have changed. This exercise introduces you to the process of finding and changing network properties on a client workstation. You will need to be familiar with this process not only to be a successful networking professional, but also to qualify for Net+ certification.

This project requires a desktop computer client running Windows 95 and both the TCP/IP and IPX/SPX protocols connected to a Windows NT server running on an Ethernet network. (You will learn more about the TCP/IP and IPX/SPX protocols in Chapter 3.)

1. On the Windows 95 computer, right-click the **Network Neighborhood** icon, then click **Properties** in the shortcut menu. The Network Properties dialog box opens.
2. Click the **Configuration** tab, if necessary.
3. Scroll down the list of installed services until you find the IPX/SPX-compatible protocol, then double-click this service to see its properties.
4. Click the **Advanced** tab.
5. In the list of properties, highlight **Frame Type**.
6. The frame type value appears to the right of the properties list. What is your current frame type value?

7. Change the frame type value to "Ethernet SNAP," then click OK to save your change.
8. Click **OK** again to continue.
9. When prompted to restart your computer, click **Yes**.
10. Note what happens after you restart your computer and try to connect to the network. Do you have trouble making a connection, or does the network accept your login ID and password? Why or why not?
11. To ensure that your workstation will function properly on the network once again, you should restore your original frame type settings. To do so, repeat Steps 1 through 5. In the Frame type properties list, select the original frame type you noted in Step 6.
12. Click **OK** to save your change, then click **OK** to continue.
13. When prompted to restart your computer, click **Yes**.

PROJECT 2-3

You will need to know how to find and interpret MAC addresses when supporting networks. In this exercise, you will discover two ways of finding your computer's MAC address, also known as its physical address, or sometimes, its adapter address. For this exercise you will need a workstation running the Windows 95 operating system and the TCP/IP protocols connected to a Windows NT server. You will also need a screwdriver that fits the workstation's cover screws.

1. On the Windows 95 computer, click **Start**, then click **Run**. The Run dialog box opens. Now you can run a program that, in addition to displaying your TCP/IP properties, provides information about your MAC address.
2. In the Open text box, type **winipcfg**.
3. Click **OK**.
4. The IP Configuration window opens. Make sure that your network adapter is listed in the drop down box at the top. Note the "Adapter Address," also known as the MAC address, of your NIC.
5. Click **OK** to close the IP Configuration window.
6. Log off the network and shut down your workstation.
7. Use the screwdriver to remove the screws that secure the workstation's housing. Ask your instructor for help if you can't find the correct screws. Usually there are three to five screws. In some cases, a computer housing may use no screws.
8. Remove the cover from the rest of the CPU.
9. With the computer open, remove the screw that holds the NIC in place. Gently remove the NIC from its place in the computer's motherboard.

10. In most cases, a NIC's MAC address is printed on a small white sticker attached to the NIC; alternatively, it may be stamped directly on the NIC itself. Find the MAC address and compare it to the one you discovered in Step 4.
11. Reinsert the NIC into its slot so that it is secure and replace the screw that holds it in.
12. Replace the computer's cover and the screws that fasten it to the CPU.

CASE PROJECTS

1. You are a networking professional who works in a college computer lab. The computers run only the TCP/IP protocol on an Ethernet network, and all computers use 3Com NICs. Many beginning computer science students use this lab for homework; you help them access the network and troubleshoot problems with their connections on a daily basis. One day a student begins tampering with his computer; when he restarts the computer, it alerts him that it can't find the network. In a step-by-step fashion, explain the approach you take to find and fix the problem.
2. The same student is curious about how a Web site appears on his computer screen. On a separate piece of paper, draw and explain the process that occurs between a client and a server when requesting a Web page, using the OSI Model as a reference. Explain to the student why each step is important and how it contributes to data arriving in the correct place without errors.
3. The student appreciates the time you spent explaining what happens to the data as it moves through the OSI Model layers, but he wonders why he should ever care about the OSI Model or data frames. He says he wants to become a network architect and concern himself with routers, switches, and cabling. The student indicates that he doesn't care about the little details like packets. In response, draw a picture of an Ethernet data frame and identify its fields. Describe how these fields can impact a network's design and networking in general.

CHAPTER 3

NETWORK PROTOCOLS

After reading this chapter and completing the exercises, you will be able to:

- Identify the characteristics of TCP/IP, IPX/SPX, NetBIOS, and AppleTalk
- Understand the position of network protocols in the OSI Model
- Identify the core protocols of each protocol suite and its functions
- Understand each protocol's addressing scheme
- Install protocols on Windows 95 and Windows NT clients

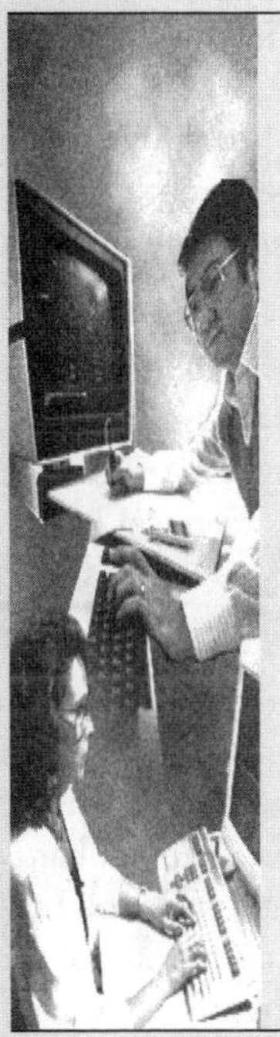

ON THE JOB

As a member of the Y2K team (a group of technical staff devoted to testing applications and systems to ensure that they will work properly in the year 2000), I am responsible for the setup and configuration of Y2K-compliant communication software. The Ontario Government is moving from an antiquated DOS-based information management system on a VAX server to Microsoft Outlook 98 on a Windows NT/95 network.

I recently performed a routine MS Outlook setup for a prominent user. Upon installation, when I made attempts to connect the client to the domain server, the system repeatedly crashed. Since this was a routine installation that goes smoothly 99% of the time, I knew there was something very wrong. Network communication problems are often caused by human error (such as typing a password incorrectly), but neither my client, nor myself was able to access the system. This was a sign of a protocol conflict.

Because our network has grown and changed so rapidly, we often run into communication problems between servers and workstations. Upon viewing the workstation's TCP/IP properties, I found that while the workstation was assigned a static IP address, a particular application was configured to use DHCP for WINS resolution. Within five minutes, I got the PC connected to the domain, simply by reconfiguring the system's protocols.

Now I can check for this conflict as a proactive measure. Thanks to my knowledge and experience with protocols, I can give my clients the best service possible.

Lisa Comeau
Ontario Ministry of Health

As you learned in Chapter 1, a **protocol** is a rule that governs how networks communicate. Protocols define the standards for communication between network devices. Without protocols, devices could not interpret the signals sent by other devices, and data would go nowhere. Unfortunately, you cannot turn on a file server, add some clients, and expect the protocols to work their magic. Instead, you must first understand which protocol suits your network environment. Then you must install and configure protocols on file servers and clients and test your configuration.

In this chapter, you will learn about the most commonly used networking protocols, their components, and their functions. This chapter is not an exhaustive study of protocols, but rather a practical guide to applying them. At the end of the chapter, you will have the opportunity to read about some realistic networking scenarios pertaining to protocols and devise your own solutions. As protocols form the foundation of network communications, you must fully understand them to manage a network effectively.

INTRODUCTION TO PROTOCOLS

In Chapter 2, you learned about the tasks associated with each layer of the OSI Model. These tasks are actually carried out by network protocols. In the networking industry, the term "protocol" is often used to refer to a group, or suite, of individual protocols that work together. The protocols within a suite are assigned different tasks, such as data translation, data handling, error checking, and addressing; they correspond to different layers of the OSI Model. In the sections that follow, you will learn about the four major networking protocol suites—TCP/IP, IPX/SPX, NetBIOS, and AppleTalk—and see how their components correspond to the layers of the OSI Model. You must understand these protocols to qualify for Net+ certification. Pay particular attention to the TCP/IP discussions, because the Net+ certification exam emphasizes TCP/IP knowledge.

The protocol (or protocol suite) you use will depend on many factors, including the existing network operating environment, your organization's technical expertise, and your network's security and speed requirements. Protocols vary according to their speed, transmission efficiency, utilization of resources, ease of setup, compatibility, and ability to travel between one LAN segment and another. Protocols that can span more than one LAN segment are **routable**, because they carry Network layer and addressing information that can be interpreted by a router. Not all protocols are routable, however.

In addition to the size of the network, you will need to consider its interconnection requirements, data security needs, and the technical expertise of personnel who manage the network. Most networks use more than one kind of protocol because they have a mixed hardware or software infrastructure, so it is not only important to know about each protocol, but also to understand how they work together. A network that uses more than one protocol is called a **multiprotocol network**. Multiprotocol networks are common in businesses whose LANs are well established and have evolved from legacy systems to newer, more efficient networks. You will undoubtedly encounter networks that simultaneously run two or more protocols.

As you read about the most commonly used protocols in this chapter, keep in mind that you may occasionally encounter additional protocols (such as SNA or DLC) on a network. The more flexible and robust protocols described in this chapter are gradually replacing these older protocols. TCP/IP is by far the most commonly used of the major protocols, followed by IPS/SPX, NetBIOS and NetBEUI, and finally AppleTalk. In the next section, you'll begin by learning about the most popular of the four—TCP/IP.

Transmission Control Protocol/Internet Protocol (TCP/IP)

TCP/IP is not simply one protocol, but rather a suite of small, specialized protocols—including TCP, IP, UDP, ARP, ICMP, and others—called **subprotocols**. Most network administrators refer to the entire group as "TCP/IP," or sometimes simply "IP." TCP/IP's roots lie with the U.S. Department of Defense, which developed the precursor to TCP/IP for its Advanced Research Projects Agency network (ARPAnet) in the late 1960s. Thanks to its low cost and its ability to communicate between a multitude of dissimilar platforms, TCP/IP has grown extremely popular. It is a de facto standard on the Internet and is fast becoming the protocol of choice on LANs. Some recently released network operating systems (such as NetWare 5.0) use TCP/IP as their default protocol.

One of the greatest advantages to using TCP/IP relates to its status as a routable protocol, which means that it carries network addressing information that can be interpreted by routers. TCP/IP is also a flexible protocol, running on any combination of network operating systems or network media. Because of its flexibility, however, TCP/IP may require significant configuration.

TCP/IP is a broad topic with numerous theoretical, historical, and practical aspects. Because it is such an important protocol, it is covered in even more detail in Chapter 11. If you want to become an expert on TCP/IP, you should invest in a book or study guide solely devoted to this suite of protocols.

TCP/IP Compared to the OSI Model

The TCP/IP suite of protocols can be divided into four layers that roughly correspond to the seven layers of the OSI Model, as depicted in Figure 3-1 and described following.

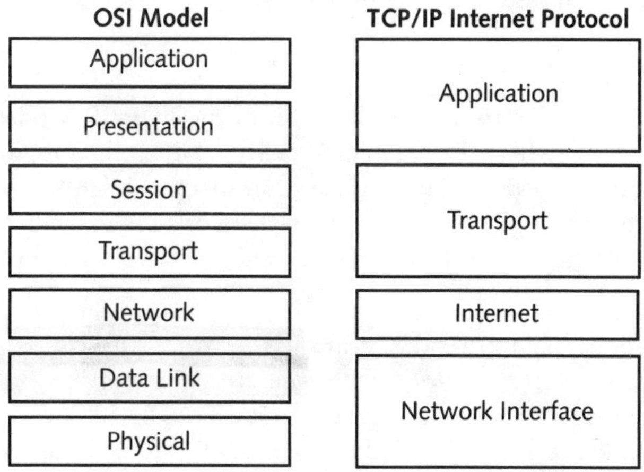

Figure 3-1 TCP/IP compared to the OSI Model

- *Application layer*—Roughly equivalent to the Application and Presentation layers of the OSI Model. Applications gain access to the network through this layer, via protocols such as Winsock API, File Transfer Protocol (FTP), Trivial File Transfer Protocol (TFTP), Hypertext Transfer Protocol (HTTP), Simple Mail Transfer Protocol (SMTP), and Dynamic Host Configuration Protocol (DHCP).
- *Transport layer*—Roughly corresponds to the Session and Transport layers of the OSI Model. This layer holds the Transmission Control Protocol (TCP) and User Datagram Protocol (UDP), which provide flow control, error checking, and sequencing. All service requests use one of these protocols.
- *Internet layer*—Equivalent to the Network layer of the OSI Model. This layer holds the Internet Protocol (IP), Internet Control Message Protocol (ICMP), Internet Group Message Protocol (IGMP), and Address Resolution Protocol (ARP). These protocols handle message routing and host address resolution.
- *Network Interface layer*—Roughly equivalent to the Data Link and Physical layers of the OSI Model. This layer handles the formatting of data and transmission to the network wire.

The TCP/IP Core Protocols

The subprotocols of the TCP/IP suite, or **TCP/IP core protocols**, are designed to operate in the Transport or Network layers of the OSI Model, where they provide communications between hosts on a network. They also provide services to the protocols in the Application layer, which is the highest level of the four-layer model. As you might guess, TCP and IP are the most significant core protocols in the TCP/IP suite.

In addition to the subprotocols discussed following, the TCP/IP suite features **routing protocols**, protocols that assist routers in efficiently managing information flow. Because understanding routing protocols depends on knowing how routers work, the discussion of routing protocols will be deferred until Chapter 6.

Internet Protocol (IP)

The **Internet Protocol (IP)** belongs to the Internet layer of the TCP/IP Model and provides information about how and where data should be delivered. IP is the subprotocol that enables TCP/IP to **internetwork**—that is, to traverse more than one LAN segment and more than one type of network through a router. In an internetwork, the individual networks that are joined together are called subnetworks, or **subnets**. Using subnets is an important part of TCP/IP networking.

The IP portion of a data frame is called an **IP datagram**. The IP datagram acts as an envelope for data and contains information necessary for routers to transfer data between subnets. The length of the IP datagram including its header and data cannot exceed 65,535 bytes. The components of an IP datagram header are described following and depicted in Figure 3-2.

- *Version*—Identifies the version number of the protocol. The receiving workstation looks at this field first to determine whether it can read the incoming data. If it cannot, it will reject the packet. Rejection rarely occurs, however, because most

TCP/IP networks use IP version 4 (IPv4). A more sophisticated IP version, called IP version 6 (IPv6), has been developed and will be implemented in coming years. IPv6 will be backward-compatible so that it can accommodate IPv4 transmissions.

- *Internet header length (IHL)*—Identifies the length of the IP header in 32-bit groupings. The most common header length comprises four groupings, or 20 octets. This field is important because it indicates to the receiving node where data will begin (immediately after the header ends).
- *Type of service (ToS)*—Tells IP how to process the incoming datagram by indicating the data's speed, priority, or reliability.
- *Total length*—Identifies the total length of the IP datagram, including the header and data, in bytes.
- *Identification*—Identifies the message to which a datagram belongs and enables the receiving node to reassemble fragmented, or segmented, messages. This field and the following two fields, flags and fragment offset, assist in segmentation and reassembly of packets.
- *Flags: don't fragment (DF) or more fragments (MF)*—Indicates whether a message is fragmented and, if it is fragmented, whether the datagram is the last in the fragment.
- *Fragment offset*—Identifies where the datagram fragment belongs in the incoming set of fragments.
- *Time to live (TTL)*—Indicates the maximum time, in seconds, that a datagram can remain on the network before it is discarded. TTL also corresponds to number of router hops that a datagram can go through; each time a datagram passes through a machine, another second is taken off its TTL, regardless of whether the machine took a whole second to process the data.
- *Protocol*—Identifies the type of transport layer protocol that will receive the datagram (for example, TCP or UDP).
- *Header checksum*—Determines whether the IP header has been corrupted.
- *Source address*—Identifies the full IP address of the source node.
- *Destination IP address*—Indicates the full IP address of the destination node.
- *Options*—May contain optional routing and timing information.
- *Padding*—Contains filler information to ensure that the header is a multiple of 32 bits. The size of this field may vary.
- *Data*—Includes the data originally sent by the source node, plus TCP information.

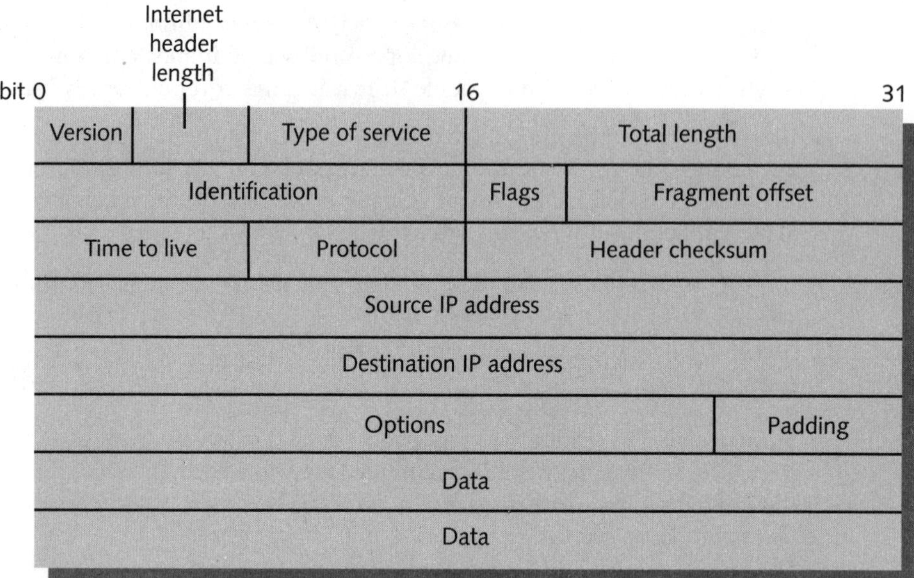

Figure 3-2 Components of an IP datagram

IP is an unreliable, **connectionless** protocol, which means that it does not guarantee delivery of data. Higher-level protocols of the TCP/IP suite, however, can use IP information to ensure that data packets are delivered to the right addresses. Note that the IP datagram does contain one checksum component, the header checksum, which verifies only the integrity of the routing information in the IP header. If the checksum accompanying the message does not have the proper value when the packet is received, then the packet is presumed to be corrupt and is discarded; at that point, a new packet is sent.

Transport Control Protocol (TCP)

The **Transport Control Protocol (TCP)** belongs to the Transport layer of the TCP/IP suite and provides reliable data delivery services. TCP is a **connection-oriented** subprotocol, which means that a connection must be established between communicating nodes before this protocol will transmit data. TCP sits on top of the IP subprotocol and compensates for IP's reliability deficiencies by providing checksum, flow control, and sequencing information. If an application relied only on IP to transmit data, IP would send packets indiscriminately, without checking whether the destination node is offline, for example, or whether the data becomes corrupt during transmission. TCP, on the other hand, contains several components that ensure data reliability. The fields of the **TCP segment**, the entity that becomes encapsulated by the IP datagram, are described following. Figure 3-3 depicts a TCP segment and its fields.

- *Source port*—Indicates the port number at the source node. A **port** is the address on a host where an application makes itself available to incoming data. One example of a port is port 80, which is typically used to accept Web page requests. You will learn more about ports in Chapter 11.

- *Destination port*—Indicates the port number at the destination node.
- *Sequence number*—Identifies the data segment's position in the stream of data segments already sent.
- *Acknowledgment number (ACK)*—Confirms receipt of the data via a return message to the sender.
- *TCP header length*—Indicates the length of the TCP header.
- *Codes*—Includes flags that signal special conditions—for example, if a message is urgent, or if the source node wants to request a connection or terminate a connection.
- *Sliding-window size*—Indicates how many blocks of data the receiving machine can accept.
- *Checksum*—Allows the receiving node to determine whether the TCP segment became corrupted during transmission.
- *Urgent pointer*—Can indicate a location in the data where urgent data resides.
- *Options*—Used to specify special options.
- *Padding*—Contains filler information to ensure that the size of the TCP header is a multiple of 32 bits.
- *Data*—Contains data originally sent by the source node.

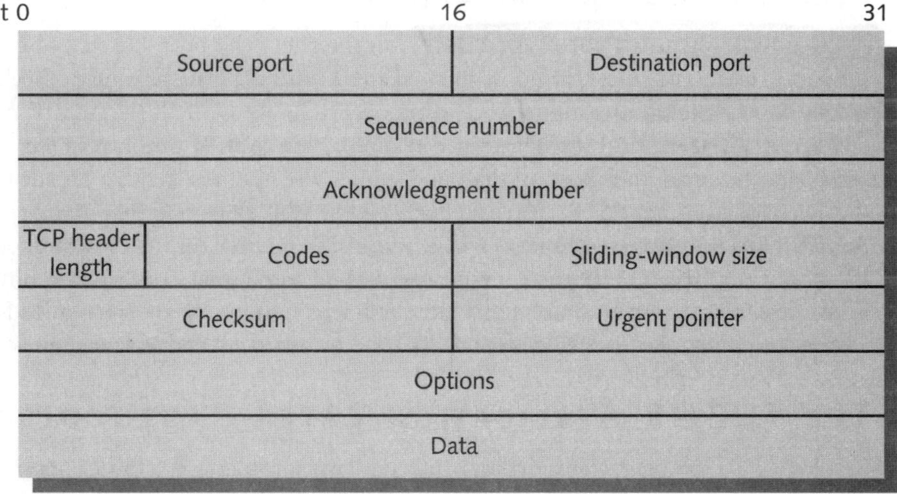

Figure 3-3 A TCP segment

User Datagram Protocol (UDP)

The **User Datagram Protocol (UDP)**, like TCP, sits in the Transport layer, between the Internet layer and the Application layer of the TCP/IP model. Unlike TCP, however, UDP is a connectionless transport service. UDP offers no assurance that packets will be received in the correct sequence. In fact, this protocol does not guarantee that the packets will be received at all. Furthermore, it provides no error checking or sequence numbering. Nevertheless, UDP's lack of sophistication makes it more efficient than TCP and renders it useful in situations where data must be transferred quickly, such as live audio or video transmissions over the Internet. In these cases, TCP—with its acknowledgments, checksums, and flow control mechanisms—would add too much overhead to the transmission and bog it down. In contrast to TCP's 10 fields, the UDP header contains only four fields: source port, destination port, length, and checksum.

Internet Control Message Protocol (ICMP)

Whereas IP ensures that packets reach the correct destination, **Internet Control Message Protocol (ICMP)** notifies the sender when something goes wrong in the transmission process and the packets are not delivered. ICMP sits between IP and TCP in the Internet layer of the TCP/IP model and does not provide error control. Instead, it simply reports which networks are unreachable and which packets have been discarded because the allotted time for their delivery (their TTL) expired. ICMP is used by diagnostic utilities such as PING and TRACERT, which are described in Chapter 11.

Address Resolution Protocol (ARP)

Address Resolution Protocol (ARP) is an Internet layer protocol that obtains the MAC (physical) address of a host, or node, then creates a local database that maps the MAC address to the host's IP (logical) address. ARP works very closely with IP, because IP must have the address of a destination host before it can direct data to it. If one host needs to know the MAC address of another host on the same subnet, the first host sends a broadcast message to the network through ARP that essentially says, "Will the computer with the IP address AA.BB.CC.DD please send me its MAC address?" The host on the local subnet that has the IP address AA.BB.CC.DD then broadcasts an ARP reply that contains the physical address of the destination host. To make ARP more efficient, computers save recognized IP-to-MAC address mappings in a cache, so they don't have to broadcast redundant requests.

The TCP/IP Application Layer Protocols

In addition to the core Transport and Internet layer protocols, TCP/IP encompasses several Application layer protocols. These protocols work over TCP or UDP and IP, translating user requests into a format the network can read. The following list describes the most commonly used Application layer protocols:

- *Telnet*—A terminal emulation protocol used to log on to remote hosts using the TCP/IP protocol suite. Often Telnet is used to connect two dissimilar systems (such as PCs and UNIX machines). Through Telnet, you can control a remote host over LANs and WANs such as the Internet. For example, network managers can use Telnet to log on to their company's routers from home and modify the router's configuration.

- *File Transfer Protocol (FTP)*—A protocol used to send and receive files via TCP/IP. FTP is a client/server protocol in which the host running the FTP server portion accepts commands from another host running the FTP client portion. It comes with a set of very simple commands that make up its user interface.
- *Simple Mail Transfer Protocol (SMTP)*—The protocol responsible for moving messages from one e-mail server to another over the Internet and other TCP/IP-based networks. SMTP uses a simple request-and-response mechanism to move messages and relies upon more sophisticated protocols, such as the Post Office Protocol (POP), to keep track of storing and forwarding messages.
- *Simple Network Management Protocol (SNMP)*—A communication protocol used to manage devices on a TCP/IP network. To use SNMP, each device on the network runs an agent that collects information about that device. SNMP transports the collected information to a central database. All standard network management programs use SNMP.

You will learn about more Application layer TCP/IP protocols in Chapter 11.

Addressing in TCP/IP

As you learned in Chapter 1, each node on a network must have a unique identifying number called an address. You have also learned that networks recognize two kinds of addresses: logical and physical (or MAC) addresses. MAC addresses are burned into a device's network interface card and are therefore unchangeable, but logical addresses depend on rules set by the protocol standards. In the TCP/IP protocol suite, IP is the core protocol responsible for logical addressing. For this reason, addresses on TCP/IP networks are sometimes called "**IP addresses**." IP addresses are assigned and used according to very specific parameters.

Each IP address is a unique 32-bit number, divided into four groups of **octets**, or 8-bit bytes, that are separated by periods. An example of a valid IP address is 144.92.43.178. An IP address contains two types of information: network and host. The first octet identifies the network class. Three types of network classes exist: Class A, Class B, and Class C. Table 3-1 summarizes the three commonly used classes of TCP/IP networks.

Table 3-1 Commonly used TCP/IP classes

Network Class	Beginning Octet	Number of Networks	Host Addresses per Network
A	1–126	126	16,777,214
B	128–191	>16,000	65,534
C	192–223	>2,000,000	254

Although 8 bits have 256 possible combinations, only the numbers 1 through 254 can be used to identify networks and hosts. The numbers 0 and 255 are reserved for **broadcasts**, or transmissions to all stations on a network.

All nodes on a Class A network share the first octet of their IP numbers, a number between 1 and 126. Nodes on a Class B network share the first two octets, and their IP addresses begin with a number between 128 and 191. Class C network IP numbers share the first three octets, with their first octet being a number between 192 and 223. For example, nodes with the following IP addresses may belong to the same Class A network: 23.78.110.109, 23.164.32.97, 23.48.112.43, and 23.108.37.22. Nodes with the following IP addresses may belong to the same Class B network: 168.34.88.29, 168.34.55.41, 168.34.73.49, and 168.34.205.113. Nodes with the following addresses may belong to the same Class C network: 204.139.118.7, 204.139.118.54, 204.139.118.14, and 204.139.118.31.

Because only 126 Class A networks are available on the Internet, most Class A networks have already been reserved by large corporations or governments. In addition, some IP addresses are reserved for network functions, like broadcasts, and cannot be assigned to machines or devices. Notice that 127 is not a valid first octet for any IP number. The range of addresses beginning with 127 is reserved for loopback information, with the IP address 127.0.0.1 being called a **loopback address**. When you try to contact this IP number, you are actually communicating with your own machine. This address can prove useful when you must troubleshoot problems with a workstation's TCP/IP communications. If you receive a positive response from the loopback test, you know that the TCP/IP protocols are installed and in use on your workstation.

A company can request a class of network addresses from **InterNIC** (also known as *Network Solutions*), the current Internet naming authority, or an Internet service provider (ISP), which will either request network addresses from InterNIC on the company's behalf or lease some of its already-reserved IP addresses to the company.

For example, suppose that you decide to go into business for yourself, selling high-quality, homemade jams and jellies on the Internet. You name your company "Jan's Jams," and you hire five staff members who will work on your office network in your shop. You would like each staff person to have his or her own address to use when communicating with the Internet. You also think that your products will be so successful that you might add five or more new staff members in the coming year. To obtain addresses for all existing staff and allow for growth, you can register with InterNIC for a group of 16 addresses. It will probably be much quicker, however, to lease these addresses from an ISP that has already reserved them from InterNIC.

Alternatively, if the network is behind a firewall, administrators can make up their own IP addressing scheme without adhering to InterNIC standards. A **firewall** is a special kind of router that secures a network from outside penetration via the Internet; it is commonly used to protect businesses with a presence on the Web. (You will learn more about firewalls and other network security measures in Chapter 15.) For example, you could use a firewall to protect the Jan's Jams network from security breaches related to e-commerce transactions on its Web site. A firewall isolates the network from the Internet at large. As a result, valid IP addresses aren't required within the network. If your office machines aren't really using valid IP addresses, however, how will your staff get through the firewall and onto the Internet? When staff members request access to machines outside your office LAN, they must be assigned valid Internet IP addresses at the firewall.

Isolating a network behind a firewall and then using your own address scheme provide useful management benefits. (For example, if you ran a large LAN, you could assign all machines on the third floor of an office building addresses, beginning with 10.3.) In addition, this scheme allows an organization to use more IP addresses than it could if it assigned InterNIC-sanctioned numbers to each machine.

A secondary number, known as a subnet mask, is also assigned as part of the TCP/IP configuration process. A subnet mask allows large networks to be subdivided into smaller subnetworks known as subnets. The subnet mask identifies to the network software which addresses appear on the same local network and which addresses need to be contacted through a router. Subnetting is a complex, but highly useful aspect of TCP/IP networking. Chapter 11 explains subnetting in more detail.

Recall from Chapter 1 that a host is any machine on a network that enables resource sharing. All individual computers connected through a TCP/IP network can be called **hosts**. This idea represents a slightly different interpretation of the term "host," because not all computers on a TCP/IP network will probably facilitate resource sharing (though theoretically, they could).

IP address data are sent across the network in binary form, with each of the four octets consisting of eight bits. For example, the IP address 131.127.3.22 is the same as the binary number 10000011 01111111 00000011 00010110. Converting from the dotted decimal notation to binary number is a simple process when you use a scientific calculator, such as the one available with the Windows 95 or Windows 98 operating system.

To convert the first octet (131) of the IP address above to a binary number:

1. On a Windows 95 computer, click **Start**, point to **Programs**, point to **Accessories**, then click **Calculator**.
2. Click **View**, then click **Scientific**. Make sure that the **Dec option button** is selected.
3. Type **131**, then click the **Bin option button**. The binary equivalent of the number 131, 10000011, appears in the display window.

You can reverse this process to convert a binary number to a decimal number.

Every host on a network must have a unique number, as duplicate addresses will cause problems on a network. If you add a host to a network and its IP address is already in use by another host on the subnet, an error message will be generated on the new client and its TCP/IP services will be disabled. The existing host may also receive an error message, but can continue to function normally.

You may assign IP addresses manually, by modifying the client workstation's TCP/IP properties. A manually assigned IP address is called a **static IP address** because it does not change automatically. It changes only when you reconfigure the client's TCP/IP properties. Alternatively, you can have IP addresses assigned automatically through the **Dynamic Host Configuration Protocol (DHCP) protocol**, an Application layer protocol in the TCP/IP suite. Most networks provide the capability of dynamically assigning IP addresses.

You must take care to avoid assigning duplicate addresses. For example, suppose you spend an afternoon manually assigning IP addresses to 50 Windows 98 machines in a computer lab. After the forty-eighth machine, you feel tired and mistakenly give the same IP address, 198.5.77.207, to machines 49 and 50. The next day, a student uses computer 49 to pick up her e-mail. A few minutes later, a student turns on computer 50. When he tries to connect to the network, he receives an error message effectively saying that "IP address 198.5.77.207 is being used by 08-AF-82-01-44-CE," where 08-AF-82-01-44-CE is the MAC address of computer 49. The student at computer 50 cannot proceed until either computer 49 is shut down or changes its IP address or until he changes the IP address of computer 50.

Using a DHCP server to assign IP addresses can almost completely eliminate duplicate-addressing problems. (DHCP is described in detail in Chapter 11.) You can envision DHCP as a kind of resource manager for IP addresses. To understand how it works, think of how a health club might hand out towels. When you arrive at the club, the person at the desk hands you a towel. You don't care which towel it is, because all towels are the same. You use the towel while you're at the club, then return it when you no longer need it. While you have possession of the towel, no one else can use it. Once you return the towel, it will be returned to the group of towels that the person behind the desk might hand out to other health club members.

Both Windows NT and Windows 95 workstations allow users to view their current IP addresses. To view your current IP information on a Windows 95 workstation connected to a network:

1. Click **Start**, then click **Run**. The Run dialog box opens.
2. Type **winipcfg** in the Open text box.
3. Click **OK**. An IP configuration window containing four numbers appears. The IP address appears second in the list of numbers.
4. To view more information about your network addressing, click the **More Info** button at the lower-right corner of the IP configuration window. A larger IP configuration window appears, as shown in Figure 3-4. Some examples of additional information you can find are the host name, DNS server and DHCP server address.

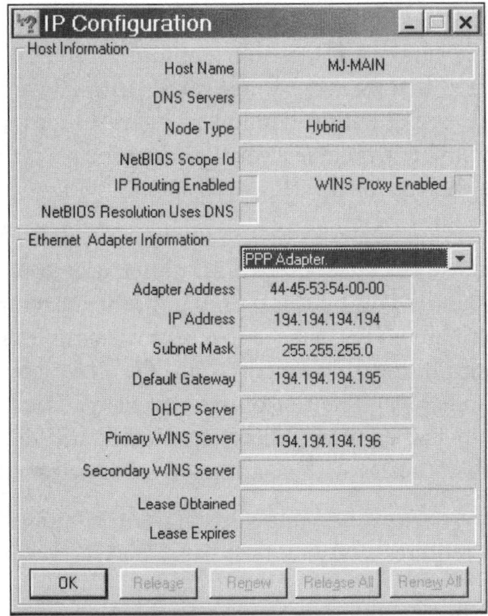

Figure 3-4 An example of an IP configuration window

5. Click **OK** to close the IP configuration window.

To view your current IP address from a workstation running Windows NT:

1. Click **Start**, point to **Programs**, then click **MS-DOS Prompt**. The Command Prompt window opens.
2. At the DOS prompt, type **ipconfig/all**. Your workstation's IP address information is displayed, similar to the information shown in Figure 3-5.

```
Command Prompt
(C) Copyright 1985-1996 Microsoft Corp.

C:\>ipconfig /all

Windows NT IP Configuration

        Host Name . . . . . . . . . : rpstax
        DNS Servers . . . . . . . . :
        Node Type . . . . . . . . . : Hybrid
        NetBIOS Scope ID. . . . . . :
        IP Routing Enabled. . . . . : No
        WINS Proxy Enabled. . . . . : No
        NetBIOS Resolution Uses DNS : No

Ethernet adapter LNEPCI21:

        Description . . . . . . . . : Novell 2000 Adapter.
        Physical Address. . . . . . : 00-20-78-11-DB-D9
        DHCP Enabled. . . . . . . . : No
        IP Address. . . . . . . . . : 131.107.3.5
        Subnet Mask . . . . . . . . : 255.255.0.0
        Default Gateway . . . . . . : 131.107.3.1
        Primary WINS Server . . . . : 131.107.3.5

C:\>_
```

Figure 3-5 IP address information on a Windows NT workstation

In addition to using IP addresses, TCP/IP networks use names for networks and hosts, so as to make them more easily identifiable to humans. Each host (computer on a TCP/IP network) requires a host name. Each network must have a network name, also known as a **domain name**. If, while viewing the IP configuration window on your Windows 95 workstation, you click the More Info button, you would see your workstation's host name and domain name in the very first field at the top of the IP configuration window, under the Host Information section.

For example, your host name might be student1.sacc.tec.ca.us. Other users on a TCP/IP network, such as the Internet, would identify you by this name, and other machines would associate your IP address with this host name. The first section of this example host name, "student1," is a field the network administrator configures on the computer (see the Installing Protocols section later in this chapter). The rest of the host name, "sacc.tec.ca.us," is the network's domain name. Domain names must follow strict rules and depend on a domain name server to resolve network addresses with the domain name assigned to them.

Chapter 11 covers TCP/IP naming services in more detail. For now, it is enough to know that every node on a TCP/IP network requires a unique host name plus a domain name to communicate over the Internet.

IPX/SPX

Internetwork Packet Exchange/Sequenced Packet Exchange (IPX/SPX) is a protocol originally developed by Xerox, then modified and adopted by Novell in the 1980s for its NetWare network operating system. IPX/SPX is required to ensure the interoperability of LANs running NetWare versions 3.2 and lower and can be used with LANs running higher versions of the NetWare operating system. Other network operating systems, such as Windows NT, and workstation operating systems, such as Windows 95, can use IPX/SPX to internetwork with Novell NetWare systems. In the Windows NT network operating system, IPX/SPX is called NWLink.

IPX/SPX, like TCP/IP, is a combination of protocols that reside at different layers of the OSI Model. Also like TCP/IP, IPX/SPX carries network addressing information, so it is routable.

IPX/SPX Compared to the OSI Model

IPX/SPX contains a number of subprotocols that belong to different layers of the OSI Model. It does not contain as many subprotocols as TCP/IP, however. For this reason, it is not typically assigned its own model of communications. The IPX/SPX subprotocols roughly correspond to the OSI Model as shown in Figure 3-6. Notice that IPX corresponds to the Network layer of the OSI Model and SPX corresponds to the Transport layer. Later in this chapter, you will be introduced to the higher-level IPX/SPX protocols, including NCP, SAP, and RIP.

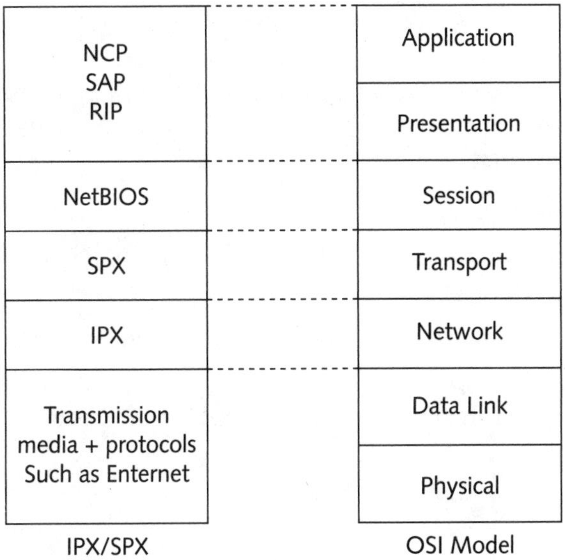

IPX/SPX	OSI Model
NCP SAP RIP	Application Presentation
NetBIOS	Session
SPX	Transport
IPX	Network
Transmission media + protocols Such as Enternet	Data Link Physical

Figure 3-6 IPX/SPX compared to the OSI Model

IPX/SPX Core Protocols

The core protocols of IPX/SPX provide services at the Transport and Network layers of the OSI Model. As you might guess, the most important subprotocols are IPX and SPX. These and other core protocols are explained following.

IPX

Internetwork Packet Exchange (IPX) operates at the Network layer of the OSI Model and provides routing and internetwork services, similar to IP in the TCP/IP suite. Like IP, IPX also uses datagrams to transport data. IPX is a connectionless service because it does not require a session to be established before it transmits, and it does not guarantee that data will be delivered in sequence or without errors. In summary, it is an efficient subprotocol with limited capabilities. All IPX/SPX communication relies upon IPX, however, and upper-layer protocols handle the functions that IPX cannot perform. The elements of an IPX datagram are described in the following list, and its structure is illustrated in Figure 3-7.

- *Checksum*—Provides integrity checking for the IPX datagram, or packet.
- *Packet length*—Identifies the length of the complete IPX packet in bytes.
- *Transport control*—Tracks the number of routers that a packet has passed through (similar to the TTL parameter in IP). IPX/SPX packets are discarded by the sixteenth router they encounter.
- *Packet type*—Defines the service offered or required by the packet.
- *Destination Network*—Indicates the network address of the destination network.

- *Destination node address*—Indicates the node address of the destination node (that is, its MAC address).
- *Destination socket*—Refers to the process address on the destination node. A **socket** is a logical address assigned to a specific process running on a computer. Some sockets are reserved for operating system functions.
- *Source network*—Indicates the network address of the source network.
- *Source node address*—Indicates the node address of the source node, equivalent to its MAC address.
- *Source socket*—Indicates the socket address of the process running on the source node.
- *Data*—Contains data originally sent by the source and the SPX packet.

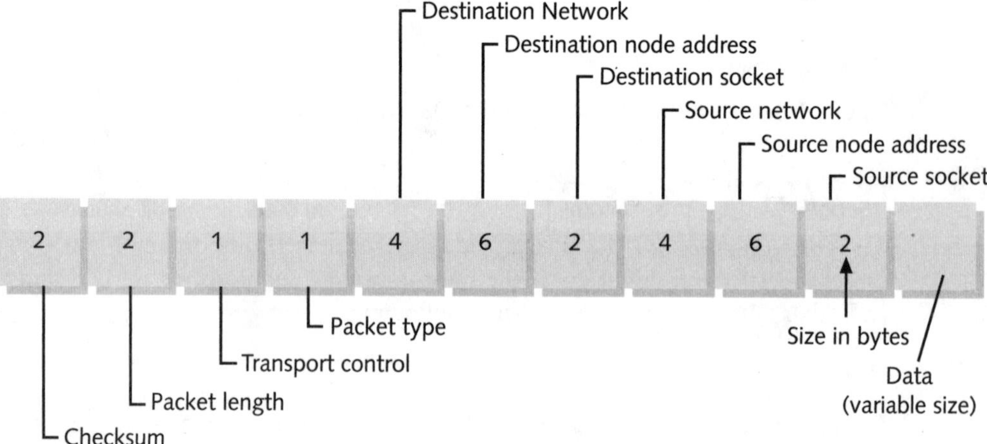

Figure 3-7 Components of an IPX datagram

SPX

Sequence Packet Exchange (SPX) belongs to the Transport layer of the OSI Model. It works in tandem with IPX to ensure that data are received whole, in sequence, and error free. SPX, like TCP in the TCP/IP suite, is a connection-oriented protocol and therefore must verify that a session has been established with the destination node before it will transmit data. It can detect whether a packet was not received in its entirety. If it discovers a packet has been lost or corrupted, SPX will resend the packet.

The SPX information is enveloped by IPX. That is, its fields sit inside the data field of the IPX datagram, as depicted in Figure 3-8.

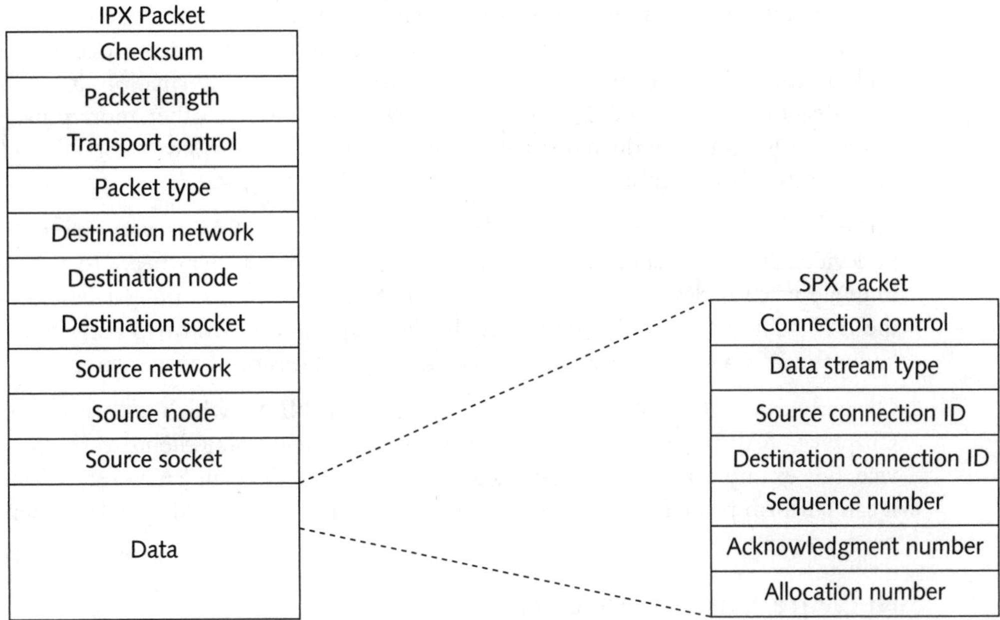

Figure 3-8 SPX packet encapsulated by an IPX packet

The SPX packet, like the TCP segment, contains a number of fields to ensure data reliability. An SPX packet consists of a 42-byte header followed by 0 to 534 bytes of data. An SPX packet can be as small as 42 bytes (the size of its header) or as large as 576 bytes. The following list describes each field in an SPX packet and its function:

- *Connection control*—Indicates whether the packet is a system or application packet.
- *Data stream type*—Indicates the type of data found in the packet—for example, whether the packet is the beginning or the end of a data stream.
- *Source connection ID*—Identifies the source node.
- *Destination connection ID*—Identifies the destination node.
- *Sequence number*—Indicates the number of packets exchanged in one direction on the connection.
- *Acknowledgment number*—Identifies the sequence number of the next packet that an SPX connection expects to receive.
- *Allocation number*—Used to manage flow control between communicating applications.

Service Advertising Protocol (SAP)

The **Service Advertising Protocol (SAP)** works in the Application, Presentation, and Session layers of the OSI Model and runs directly over IPX. NetWare servers and routers use SAP to advertise to the entire network which services they can provide. For example, a server that functions as a print server might use SAP to effectively announce to every node on the network, "I'm available to help you print." By default, SAP broadcasts occur every 60 seconds. Because SAP uses the broadcast mode to transmit its information, it may generate a great deal of unnecessary traffic on the network, slowing down other, more important transmissions. One way to reduce this traffic is to increase the time between SAP broadcasts from 60 seconds to a few minutes.

Once devices have advertised their availability through SAP, SAP servers maintain a database of device names correlated with their IPX addresses. When a client needs to request a service from a particular device, the client queries the SAP database and the database then provides the IPX address for the desired device. In this way, the protocol frees users from having to know the IPX addresses of other servers and workstations on their network.

On networks that use NetWare Directory Services (NDS), which is discussed in detail in Chapter 9, SAP may not be necessary because NDS will point clients to the necessary service. For example, rather than having a server advertise through SAP every 60 seconds that it can perform printer services, NDS can point clients directly to that server when the client needs to print.

NetWare Core Protocol (NCP)

The **NetWare Core Protocol (NCP)** handles requests for services, such as printing and file access, between clients and servers. NCP works over IPX and within the Presentation and Session layers of the OSI Model. In essence, NCP acts as a translator between the workstation's operating system and the NetWare operating system. It uses a request-and-response mechanism to accomplish its translation; that is, once a client asks it to request a service, it notifies the server that a request is pending. NCP then waits for the server to acknowledge the request before it allows the workstation to transmit data. Although this exchange results in high reliability, it also generates extra traffic and may add to congestion on networks, such as WANs, that use routers.

Addressing in IPX/SPX

Maintaining network addresses for computers running IPX/SPX is easier than maintaining addresses for TCP/IP networks, because IPX/SPX networks primarily rely on the MAC address for each workstation (although addressing for IPX/SPX servers can be somewhat more complex). Just as with TCP/IP networks, IPX/SPX networks require that each node on a network be assigned a unique address to avoid communication conflicts. Because IPX is the component of the protocol that handles addressing, addresses on an IPX/SPX network are called **IPX addresses**. IPX addresses contain two parts: the network address (also known as the **external network number**) and the node address.

The network administrator establishes a network address when installing the NetWare operating system software on a server. The network address must be an 8-bit hexadecimal address, which means that each of its bits can have a value of either 0–9 or A–F. An example of a valid network address is 000008A2. The network address then becomes the first part of the IPX address on all nodes that use the particular server as their primary server.

The address 00000000 is a null value and cannot be used as a network address. The address FFFFFFFF is a broadcast address and also cannot be assigned as a network address.

The second part of an IPX address, the node address, is equal to the network device's MAC address. Because every network interface card should have a unique MAC address, no possibility of duplicating IPX addresses exists under this system. In addition, the use of MAC addresses means that you need not configure addresses for the IPX/SPX protocol on each client workstation. Instead, they are already defined by the NIC. Adding a MAC address to the network address example used previously, a complete IPX address for a workstation on the network might be 000008A2:0060973E97F3.

Imagine you are the administrator for a building's NetWare 3.11 network with one server and 40 connected workstations, plus five printers. Your network is connected to six other networks on a large corporate campus. A colleague alerts you that one of the Accounting department's four workstations is generating excessive error messages. You need to determine the malfunctioning workstation's IPX address so as to disconnect it from the server. Because you installed the network originally, you know that your network address is 0000AAAA. The workstation's address must therefore begin with 0000AAAA (addresses for workstations coming from networks elsewhere on campus will begin with a different sequence). You also know that the Accounting department's computers contain NICs manufactured by Compaq. You look up the manufacturer's Ethernet code (the first part of the MAC address) and find that it is 00805F. In the list of currently attached workstations, you find only one IPX address that matches the pattern beginning with 0000AAAA:00805F—a machine with the full address of 0000AAAA: 00805F059822. You can correctly assume that it is the faulty Accounting workstation.

In addition to the network and node addresses, processes running on IPX-enabled workstations are identified by socket addresses. When a process needs to communicate on the network, it requests that a socket number be assigned to it. Any packets addressed to that socket are passed on to the corresponding process. This approach enables nodes to route communications between their own sockets. An example of a socket address is 456h; Novell has reserved this particular socket for its diagnostics process. Socket addresses are appended to IPX addresses, so an example of a complete IPX address for a socket would be 000008A2:0060973E97F3:456h.

To view your Windows 95, Windows 98, or Windows NT workstation's IPX address while connected to a NetWare server running version 4.0 or higher:

1. Click **Start**, point to **Programs**, then click **MS-DOS Prompt**.
2. Change directories to a drive letter you have mapped to the network (for example, typing the command F: will work on most networks.)
3. At the DOS prompt, type **nlist XXXXX /a** where "XXXXX" is your NetWare logon ID. The **nlist** command in NetWare is a listing command, while **user** defines the kind of information that you want to list and the **/a** parameter indicates that you want to see the address for the specified user. As a result of this command, you see the user ID you specified along with its corresponding IPX address.

To view your Windows 95 or Windows NT workstation's IPX address while connected to a NetWare server running a version lower than 4.0:

1. Click **Start**, point to **Programs**, then click **MS-DOS Prompt**.
2. At the DOS prompt, type **userlist user=XXXXX /a** where XXXXX is your NetWare logon ID. In NetWare versions lower than 4.0, the userlist command performs the same function as the nlist command in NetWare versions 4.0 and higher. You see the user ID you specified along with its corresponding IPX address.

NetBIOS and NetBEUI

NetBIOS (Network Basic Input Output System) is a protocol originally designed by IBM to provide Transport and Session layer services for applications running on small, homogenous networks. Microsoft adopted IBM's NetBIOS as its foundation protocol, initially for networks using LAN Manager or Windows for Workgroups, but then added an Application layer component on top of NetBIOS called the **NetBIOS Enhanced User Interface** (**NetBEUI**; pronounced, "net-bóo-ee"). NetBEUI is a fast and efficient protocol that consumes few network resources, provides excellent error correction, and requires little configuration. It can support only 254 connections, however, and does not allow for good security. Furthermore, because NetBEUI lacks a Network layer (addressing information), it is nonroutable. (If necessary, NetBEUI can be encapsulated by other protocols, then routed, but the preferred method would be to migrate a NetBEUI network to a network running TCP/IP.) Thus, this protocol is not suitable for large networks. Today NetBEUI is most commonly used in small Microsoft-based networks to integrate legacy, peer-to-peer networks. In newer Microsoft-based networks, TCP/IP has become the protocol of choice because it is more flexible and scalable than NetBEUI.

NetBIOS and NetBEUI Compared to the OSI Model

Because neither NetBIOS nor NetBEUI provides services at all layers of the OSI Model, both are commonly paired with other protocol suites, such as IPX/SPX or TCP/IP when placed in the OSI Model. Figure 3-9 shows how NetBIOS and NetBEUI fit into the OSI Model.

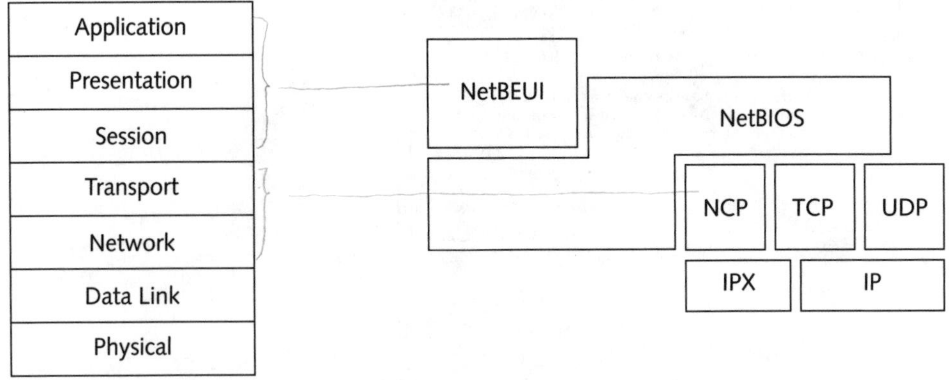

Figure 3-9 NetBIOS/NetBEUI compared to the OSI Model

NetBIOS Addressing

You have learned that NetBIOS does not contain a Network layer and therefore cannot be routed. To transmit data between network nodes, however, NetBIOS needs to reach each workstation. For this reason, network administrators must assign a NetBIOS name to each workstation. The NetBIOS name can consist of any combination of 16 or fewer alphanumeric characters (the only exception is that you cannot begin a NetBIOS name with an asterisk). Once NetBIOS has found a workstation's NetBIOS name, it will discover the workstation's MAC address and then use this address in further communications with the workstation. For example, a valid NetBIOS name is MY_COMPUTER. You might use NetBIOS names when troubleshooting problems on a NetBIOS network.

If you are running both TCP/IP and NetBIOS on your network, you should make the NetBIOS name identical to the TCP/IP host name.

To view your workstation's NetBIOS name:

1. Right-click the Network Neighborhood icon, then click **Properties**. The Network window opens.
2. Click the **Identification** tab. As shown in Figure 3-10, the first text box in the Identification tab is your computer name. Your computer name is the same as your NetBIOS name.

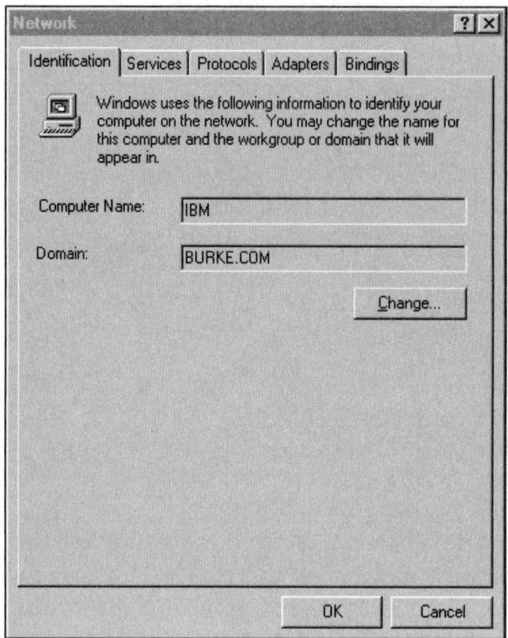

Figure 3-10 The Identification tab in Network properties

AppleTalk

Businesses and institutions involved in art or education, such as advertising agencies, elementary schools, and graphic designers, often use Apple Macintosh computers. **AppleTalk** is the protocol suite used to interconnect Macintosh computers. Although AppleTalk was originally designed to support peer-to-peer networking among Macintoshes, it can now be routed between network segments and integrated with NetWare- or Microsoft-based networks.

An AppleTalk network is separated into logical groups of computers called **AppleTalk zones**. Each network can contain multiple zones, but each node can belong to only one zone. AppleTalk zones enable users to share file and printer resources on one another's Macintoshes. Zone names are not subject to the same strict naming conventions that TCP/IP and IPX/SPX networks must follow. Instead, zone names typically describe a department or other group of users who share files. An example of a zone name is "Sales and Marketing."

Although Apple has improved AppleTalk's ability to use different network models and span network segments, it remains unsuited to large LANs or WANs. Even Apple has begun supporting the TCP/IP protocol to integrate Macintoshes with other networks, including the Internet.

3

AppleTalk Compared to the OSI Model

AppleTalk is a complete protocol suite containing services that fit into each layer of the OSI Model, as depicted in Figure 3-11.

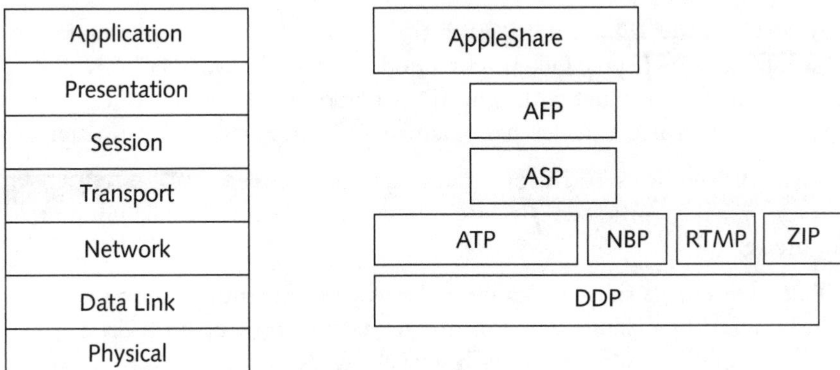

Figure 3-11 The AppleTalk protocol compared to the OSI Model

The AppleTalk subprotocols that are significant for node-to-node communications are described following:

- *AppleShare*—Provides file sharing services, print queueing services, password access to files or folders, and user accounting information.
- *AppleTalk Filing Protocol (AFP)*—Provides transparent access to files on both local and remote systems.
- *AppleTalk Session Protocol (ASP)*—Establishes and maintains connections between nodes and servers.
- *AppleTalk Transaction Protocol (ATP)*—Ensures reliable delivery of data by checking connections between nodes, checking packet sequence, and retransmitting any data packets that become lost.
- *Name Binding Protocol (NBP)*—Translates human-readable node names into numeric AppleTalk addresses.
- *Routing Table Maintenance Protocol (RTMP)*—Maintains a routing table of AppleTalk zones and their networks, and uses ZIP to manage data in the routing table.
- *Zone Information Protocol (ZIP)*—Updates zone information maps that tie zones to their networks for routing purposes.
- *Datagram Delivery Protocol (DDP)*—Assigns an AppleTalk node's address upon start-up and manages addressing for communications between AppleTalk nodes.

Addressing in AppleTalk

You have learned that AppleTalk uses zones and that zone names can be plain words or numbers with no restrictions. In addition to zone names, AppleTalk uses node IDs and network numbers to identify computers on a network.

An **AppleTalk node ID** is a unique 8-bit or 16-bit number that identifies a computer on an AppleTalk network. AppleTalk assigns a node ID to each workstation when the workstation first connects to the network. The ID is randomly chosen from a group of currently available addresses. Once a device has obtained an address, it stores it for later use.

An **AppleTalk network number** is a unique 16-bit number that identifies the network to which a node is connected. Its use allows nodes from several different networks to communicate.

AppleTalk addressing is simple because it allows you to identify a group of shared addresses from the server. When clients attach to that server they pick up an address, thus eliminating the need to configure addresses on each separate workstation.

Installing Protocols

The protocols you install will depend on which operating system you are running. This section describes how to install the most commonly used protocols on Windows 95 and Windows NT client workstations. Chapters 7 and 8 discuss installing and configuring protocols on the two most commonly used network operating systems, NetWare and Windows NT, respectively.

Installation is merely the first step to making protocols work. After they are installed, you must bind them to the NICs and services they will run on or with. **Binding** is the process of assigning one network component to work with another. Once you install a protocol on a Windows NT or Windows 95 workstation, it binds itself automatically to the NICs and services it finds on the computer. For the bindings to take effect, however, you must reboot the workstation. For optimal network performance, you should install and bind only those protocols that you absolutely need. For example, a Windows NT server will attempt to use bound protocols in the order in which they appear in the protocol listing until it finds the correct one for the response at hand. This approach wastes processing time, making it more efficient to bind only the protocols you need.

Installing Protocols on a Windows NT Workstation

The following exercise shows you how to install the NWLink (IPX/SPX) protocol on a Windows NT workstation. The process of installing other protocols on a Windows NT workstation is almost identical.

1. Insert the Windows NT installation CD-ROM.
2. Log on to the workstation as an Administrator.

3. Right-click the **Network Neighborhood** icon, then click **Properties**. The Network dialog box opens.
4. Click the **Protocols** tab.
5. Click **Add**. The Select Network Protocol dialog box opens.
6. In the list of network protocols, click **NWLink IPX/SPX Compatible Transport**, then click **OK**. The Windows NT Setup dialog box opens, asking for the location of the Windows NT installation files.
7. Type the appropriate path to the installation files (typically the I386 directory on the installation CD-ROM), then click **Continue**.
8. Click **OK**. You are prompted to restart your workstation to allow for the changes to take effect.
9. Click **Yes** to restart your workstation.
10. To verify that the protocol was installed, log on to the workstation as an Administrator again.
11. Right-click the **Network Neighborhood** icon, then click **Properties**. The Network dialog box opens.
12. Click the **Protocols** tab.
13. Verify that NWLink (IPX/SPX) Protocol appears in the list of installed protocols.
14. Click **Cancel** to close the Network dialog box.

On a Windows NT workstation, you can install any other protocol in the same manner as you installed the NWLink (IPX/SPX) protocol. Although the IPX/SPX protocol requires no further configuration, usually you must configure the AppleTalk and TCP/IP protocols after installing them. Chapter 11 covers TCP/IP configuration in detail.

Installing Protocols on a Windows 95 Workstation

The following exercise shows you how to install the TCP/IP protocol on a Windows 95 workstation (it assumes that you did not choose to install this protocol when you first installed the operating system; Windows 98 installations include the TCP/IP protocol by default).

1. Right-click the **Network Neighborhood** icon, then click **Properties**.
2. Verify that the **Configuration** tab is selected.
3. Click **Add**. The Select Network Component Type window opens.
4. Double-click **Protocol**. The Select Network Protocol window opens.
5. In the list of manufacturers, click **Microsoft**.

6. In the list of protocols, click **TCP/IP**.
7. Click **OK**.
8. If TCP/IP is not already installed on your workstation, you will be prompted to restart your workstation to allow the changes to take effect. Click **Yes** to restart your workstation.
9. To verify that the protocol was installed, right-click the **Network Neighborhood** icon, then click **Properties**.
10. Verify that the **Configuration** tab is selected. One of the items in the list of services, clients, and protocols should be TCP/IP.
11. Click **Cancel** to close the Network properties window.

You can add other protocols to your Windows 95 workstation in the same manner. Although usually you do not need to configure IPX/SPX or NetBEUI after installation, you must configure TCP/IP unless you are using DHCP. Chapter 11 covers TCP/IP configuration in detail.

It is possible to bind multiple protocols to the same network adapter. In fact, this is necessary on networks that use more than one type of protocol. In addition, a workstation may have multiple NICs, in which case several different protocols might be bound to each NIC. What's more, the same protocol may be configured differently on different NICs. For example, let's say you managed a NetWare server that contained two NICs and provided both TCP/IP and IPX/SPX communications to many clients. After installing the TCP/IP protocol on the server, you would need to configure TCP/IP separately for each NIC using the network operating system's protocol configuration utility. Similarly, you would need to configure IPX/SPX separately for each NIC. If you did not configure the protocols for each NIC separately, clients would not know which NIC to address when sending and receiving information to and from the server.

CHAPTER SUMMARY

- Protocols define the standards for communication between nodes on a network. The term *protocol*, in networking, can refer to a group, or suite, of individual protocols that work together to accomplish data translation, data handling, error checking, and addressing.
- Protocols vary by speed, transmission efficiency, utilization of resources, ease of setup, compatibility, and ability to travel between one LAN segment and another. Protocols that can span more than one LAN segment are routable, because they carry Network layer and addressing information that can be interpreted by a router.
- The most commonly used protocols are TCP/IP, IPX/SPX, NetBIOS, and AppleTalk. You may also find other, outdated protocols in use, such as SNA and DLC.
- A network that uses more than one protocol is called a multiprotocol network. Multiprotocol networks are common in businesses with well-established LANs that have evolved from a legacy system to a newer, more efficient one.

- TCP/IP is fast becoming the most popular network protocol because of its low cost and its ability to communicate between a multitude of dissimilar platforms. It is a de facto standard on the Internet and is commonly the protocol of choice on LANs. TCP/IP is routable and flexible.
- The TCP/IP suite of protocols can be divided into four layers that roughly correspond to the seven layers of the OSI model: the Application layer, the Transport layer, the Internet layer, and the Network Interface layer.
- The TCP/IP core protocols operate in the Transport or Network layers of the OSI Model, where they provide communications between hosts on a network. The most significant core protocols in the TCP/IP suite are IP and TCP.
- The Internet Protocol (IP) belongs to the Internet layer of the TCP/IP Model and provides information about how and where data should be delivered. IP is the subprotocol that enables TCP/IP to internetwork—that is, to traverse more than one LAN segment and more than one type of network through a router.
- The Transport Control Protocol (TCP) belongs to the Transport layer of the TCP/IP suite and provides reliable data delivery services. TCP is a connection-oriented subprotocol, which means that it requires a connection to be established between communicating nodes before it will transmit data. TCP sits on top of the IP subprotocol and compensates for IP's reliability deficiencies with its checksum, flow control, and sequencing information.
- The User Datagram Protocol (UDP), like TCP, sits in the Transport layer, between the Internet layer and the Application layer of the TCP/IP model. Unlike TCP, however, UDP is a connectionless transport service. It offers no error checking and no assurance that packets will be received in the correct sequence. UDP's lack of sophistication actually makes it more efficient than TCP and useful in situations where data must be transferred quickly, such as live audio or video transmissions over the Internet.
- Internet Control Message Protocol (ICMP), another TCP/IP core protocol, notifies the sender that something has gone wrong in the transmission process and that packets were not delivered. ICMP sits between IP and TCP in the Internet layer of the TCP/IP model and reports which networks are unreachable and which packets have been discarded because the allotted time for their delivery has expired.
- The Address Resolution Protocol (ARP) belongs to the Internet layer of the TCP/IP Model. It obtains the MAC (physical) address of a host, or node, then creates a local database that maps the MAC address to the host's IP (logical) address.
- The TCP/IP suite includes a number of useful Application layer protocols, such as Telnet, FTP, SMTP, and SNMP.
- Each IP address is a unique 32-bit number, divided into four groups of octets that are separated by periods. An example of a valid IP address is 144.92.43.178. An IP address contains two types of information: network and host.

- All nodes on a Class A network share the first octet of their IP numbers, a number between 1 and 126. Nodes on a Class B network share the first two octets, and all their IP addresses begin with a number between 128 and 191. Class C network IP numbers share the first three octets, with their first octet being a number between 192 and 223.
- The range of addresses beginning with 127 is reserved for loopback information. The IP address 127.0.0.1 is called a loopback address. When you try to contact this IP number, you actually communicate with your own machine. This address is useful for troubleshooting problems with a workstation's TCP/IP communications.
- Every host on a network must have a unique number, as duplicate addresses will cause problems. If a host is added to a network and its IP address is already assigned to another host on the subnet, an error message will be generated on the new client and its TCP/IP services will be disabled. The existing host may also receive an error message, but can continue to function normally.
- Although you may assign IP addresses manually, you must take care to avoid assigning duplicate addresses. IP addresses assigned manually are called static IP addresses. Most networks provide the capability of dynamically assigning IP addresses through the Dynamic Host Configuration Protocol (DHCP) protocol, an Application layer protocol in the TCP/IP suite. Using a DHCP server to assign IP addresses can nearly eliminate duplicate-addressing problems.
- Internetwork Packet Exchange/Sequenced Packet Exchange (IPX/SPX) is a protocol originally developed by Xerox, then modified and adopted by Novell in the 1980s for its NetWare network operating system. IPX/SPX is required for interoperability with LANs running NetWare versions 3.2 and lower; it can also be used with LANs running higher versions of the NetWare operating system. IPX/SPX, like TCP/IP, is a suite of protocols that reside at different layers of the OSI Model. Also like TCP/IP, IPX/SPX carries network addressing information, so it is routable.
- The core protocols of IPX/SPX provide services at the Transport and Network layers of the OSI Model. Its most important subprotocols are IPX and SPX.
- Internetwork Packet Exchange (IPX) operates at the Network layer of the OSI Model and provides routing and internetwork services, similar to IP in the TCP/IP suite. IPX uses datagrams to transport data. This protocol is a connectionless service because it does not require a session to be established before it transmits data, and it does not guarantee that data will be delivered in sequence or without errors. It is an efficient subprotocol with limited capabilities.
- Sequence Packet Exchange (SPX) belongs to the Transport layer of the OSI Model. It works in tandem with IPX to ensure that data are received whole, in sequence, and error free. SPX is a connection-oriented protocol and therefore must verify that a session has been established with the destination node before it will transmit data. It can detect whether a packet was not received in its entirety; if it discovers that a packet has been lost or corrupted, SPX will resend the packet.

- The Service Advertising Protocol (SAP) works in the Application, Presentation, Session, and Transport layers of the OSI Model and runs directly over IPX. NetWare servers and routers use SAP to advertise to the entire network which services they can provide.
- The NetWare Core Protocol (NCP) handles requests for services, such as printing and file access, between clients and servers. NCP works over IPX and within the Presentation and Session layers of the OSI Model. It acts as a translator between the workstation's operating system and the NetWare operating system.

- Because IPX is the component of the protocol that handles addressing, addresses on an IPX/SPX network are called IPX addresses. IPX addresses contain two parts: the network address and the node address. The network address must be an 8-bit hexadecimal address, which means that each of its bits can have a value of either 0–9 or A–F. The second part of an IPX address, the node address, is equal to the network device's MAC address.
- NetBIOS (Network Basic Input Output System) is a protocol originally designed by IBM to provide Transport and Session layer services for applications running on small, homogenous networks.
- Microsoft adopted IBM's NetBIOS as its foundation protocol, initially for networks using LAN Manager or Windows for Workgroups, but then added an Application layer component on top of NetBIOS called the NetBIOS Enhanced User Interface (NetBEUI). NetBEUI is a fast and efficient protocol that consumes few network resources, provides excellent error correction, and requires little configuration. It can support only 254 connections, however, and does not allow for good security. Furthermore, because NetBEUI lacks a Network layer, it is nonroutable and therefore not suitable for large networks.
- To transmit data between network nodes, NetBIOS needs to know how to reach each workstation. For this reason, network administrators must assign a NetBIOS name to each workstation. The NetBIOS name can be any combination of 16 or fewer alphanumeric characters (although you cannot begin a NetBIOS name with an asterisk). Once NetBIOS has found a workstation's NetBIOS name, it will discover the workstation's MAC address and then use this address in further communications with the workstation.
- AppleTalk is the protocol suite used to interconnect Macintosh computers. Although AppleTalk was originally designed to support peer-to-peer networking among Macintoshes, it can now be routed between network segments and integrated with NetWare- or Microsoft-based networks.
- An AppleTalk network is separated into logical groups of computers called AppleTalk zones. Each network can contain multiple zones, but each node can belong to only one zone. AppleTalk zones enable users to share file and printer resources on one another's Macintoshes. Zone names typically describe a department or other group of users who share files.
- Although Apple has improved AppleTalk's ability to use different network models and span network segments, it remains unsuited to large LANs or WANs. Even Apple has begun supporting the TCP/IP protocol to integrate Macintoshes with other networks, including the Internet.

- In addition to zone names, AppleTalk uses node IDs and network numbers to identify computers on a network. An AppleTalk node ID is a unique 8- or 16-bit number that identifies a computer on an AppleTalk network. AppleTalk assigns a node ID to each workstation when the workstation connects to the network. An AppleTalk network number is a unique 16-bit number that identifies the network to which a node is connected. AppleTalk addressing can be managed centrally from the server.
- Although some protocols, such as NetBIOS, require no configuration after they are installed, more complex protocols, such as TCP/IP, do require configuration.

KEY TERMS

- **Address Resolution Protocol (ARP)** — A core protocol in the TCP/IP suite that belongs in the Internet layer. It obtains the MAC (physical) address of a host, or node, and then creates a local database that maps the MAC address to the host's IP (logical) address.
- **AppleTalk** — The protocol suite used to interconnect Macintosh computers. Although AppleTalk was originally designed to support peer-to-peer networking among Macintoshes, it can now be routed between network segments and integrated with NetWare- or Microsoft-based networks.
- **AppleTalk network number** — A unique 16-bit number that identifies the network to which an AppleTalk node is connected.
- **AppleTalk node ID** — A unique 8-bit or 16-bit (if you are using extended networking, in which a network can have multiple addresses and support multiple zones) number that identifies a computer on an AppleTalk network.
- **AppleTalk zone** — Logical groups of computers defined on an AppleTalk network.
- **binding** — The process of assigning one network component to work with another.
- **broadcast** — A transmission to all stations on a network.
- **connection-oriented** — A feature of some protocols that requires the establishment of a connection between communicating nodes before the protocol will transmit data.
- **connectionless** — A feature of some protocols that allows the protocol to service a request without requiring a verified session and without guaranteeing delivery of data.
- **domain name** — The symbolic name that identifies an Internet domain. Usually, a domain name is associated with a company or other type of organization, such as a university or military unit.
- **Dynamic Host Configuration Protocol (DHCP) protocol** — An Application layer protocol in the TCP/IP suite that manages the dynamic distribution of IP addresses on a network. Using a DHCP to assign IP addresses can nearly eliminate duplicate-addressing problems.
- **external network number** — Another term for the network address portion of an IPX/SPX address.

- **File Transfer Protocol (FTP)** — An Application layer protocol used to send and receive files via TCP/IP.
- **firewall** — A specialized device (typically a router, but possibly only a PC running special software) that selectively filters or blocks traffic between networks. A firewall may be strictly hardware-based, or it may involve a combination of hardware and software.
- **host** — A computer connected to a network that uses the TCP/IP protocol.
- **Internet Control Message Protocol (ICMP)** — A core protocol in the TCP/IP suite that notifies the sender that something has gone wrong in the transmission process and that packets were not delivered.
- **Internet Protocol (IP)** — A core protocol in the TCP/IP suite that belongs to the Internet layer of the TCP/IP model and provides information about how and where data should be delivered. IP is the subprotocol that enables TCP/IP to internetwork.
- **internetwork** — To traverse more than one LAN segment and more than one type of network through a router.
- **Internetwork Packet Exchange (IPX)** — A core protocol of the IPX/SPX suite that operates at the Network layer of the OSI Model and provides routing and internetwork services, similar to IP in the TCP/IP suite.
- **Internetwork Packet Exchange/Sequenced Packet Exchange (IPX/SPX)** — A protocol originally developed by Xerox, then modified and adopted by Novell in the 1980s for the NetWare network operating system.
- **InterNIC** — The authority for Internet IP addressing and domain name registration. Also known as *Network Solutions*.
- **IP address** — A logical address used in TCP/IP networking. This unique 32-bit number is divided into four groups of octets, or 8-bit bytes, that are separated by periods.
- **IP datagram** — The IP portion of a TCP/IP frame that acts as an envelope for data, holding information necessary for routers to transfer data between subnets.
- **IPX address** — An address assigned to a device on an IPX/SPX network.
- **loopback address** — An IP address reserved for communicating from a node to itself (used mostly for testing purposes). The value of the loopback address is always 127.0.0.1.
- **multiprotocol network** — A network that uses more than one protocol.
- **NetBEUI (NetBIOS Enhanced User Interface)** — Microsoft's adaptation of IBM's NetBIOS protocol. NetBEUI expands on NetBIOS by adding an Application layer component. NetBEUI is a fast and efficient protocol that consumes few network resources, provides excellent error correction and requires little configuration.

- **NetWare Core Protocol (NCP)** — One of the core protocols of the IPX/SPX suite. NCP handles requests for services, such as printing and file access, between clients and servers.
- **octet** — One of the four 8-bit bytes that are separated by periods and together make up an IP address.
- **port** — The address on a host where an application makes itself available to incoming data.
- **protocol** — The rules a network uses to transfer data. Protocols ensure that data is transferred whole, in sequence, and without error from one node on the network to another.
- **routable** — Protocols that can span more than one LAN segment because they carry Network layer and addressing information that can be interpreted by a router.
- **routing protocols** — Protocols that assist routers in efficiently managing information flow.
- **Sequence Packet Exchange (SPX)** — One of the core protocols in the IPX/SPX suite. SPX belongs to the Transport layer of the OSI Model and works in tandem with IPX to ensure that data are received whole, in sequence, and error free.
- **Service Advertising Protocol (SAP)** — A core protocol in the IPX/SPX suite that works in the Application, Presentation, Session, and Transport layers of the OSI Model and runs directly over IPX. NetWare servers and routers use SAP to advertise to the entire network which services they can provide.
- **Simple Mail Transfer Protocol (SMTP)** — The protocol responsible for moving messages from one e-mail server to another over the Internet and other TCP/IP-based networks.
- **Simple Network Management Protocol (SNMP)** — A communication protocol used to manage devices on a TCP/IP network.
- **socket** — A logical address assigned to a specific process running on a computer. Some sockets are reserved for operating system functions.
- **static IP address** — An IP address that is manually assigned to a device.
- **subnets** — In an internetwork, the individual networks that are joined together by routers.
- **subprotocols** — Small, specialized protocols that work together and belong to a protocol suite.
- **TCP segment** — The portion of a TCP/IP packet that holds TCP data fields and becomes encapsulated by the IP datagram.
- **TCP/IP core protocols** — The subprotocols of the TCP/IP suite.
- **Telnet** — A terminal emulation protocol used to log on to remote hosts using the TCP/IP protocol. Telnet resides in the Application layer of the TCP/IP suite.

- **Transport Control Protocol (TCP)** — A core protocol of the TCP/IP suite. TCP belongs to the Transport layer and provides reliable data delivery services.
- **User Datagram Protocol (UDP)** — A core protocol in the TCP/IP suite that sits in the Transport layer, between the Internet layer and the Application layer of the TCP/IP model. UDP is a connectionless transport service.

Review Questions

1. What characteristics make a protocol routable?
   a. MAC sublayer addresses that can be interpreted by a server
   b. Network layer and addressing information that can be interpreted by a router
   c. Logical Link sublayer address information that can be interpreted by a hub
   d. Transport layer flow control information that can be interpreted by a router
2. Which layer in the TCP/IP model of network communications roughly corresponds to the Physical and Data Link layers of the OSI Model?
   a. Network Interface layer
   b. Internet layer
   c. Transport layer
   d. Application layer
3. To which layer of the TCP/IP model does the IP protocol belong?
   a. Network Interface layer
   b. Internet layer
   c. Transport layer
   d. Application layer
4. To which layer of the TCP/IP model does the TCP protocol belong?
   a. Network Interface layer
   b. Internet layer
   c. Transport layer
   d. Application layer
5. What is the function of ARP?
   a. to acknowledge that a data frame was received
   b. to obtain the IP address of a host, then map that IP address to a registered domain name
   c. to measure the number of dropped packets in a single transmission
   d. to obtain the MAC address of a host, and then map the MAC address to the host's IP address

6. Which TCP/IP utility might you use to connect to a UNIX host from your PC over the network?
   a. SNMP
   b. SMTP
   c. Telnet
   d. hup
7. What does SMTP stand for?
   a. Simple Mail Transfer Protocol
   b. Simple Message Transport Protocol
   c. Simple Media Transfer Protocol
   d. Simple Message Tracking Protocol
8. Which version of IP are most TCP/IP networks currently using?
   a. 3.0
   b. 4.0
   c. 5.0
   d. 6.0
9. Why might an application be better served by UDP than TCP?
10. What is an octet?
    a. an 8-bit control frame
    b. 8-byte segments that are separated by commas
    c. 8-bit bytes that are separated by periods
    d. an 8-byte address that is used in subnetting
11. Which technique is used to break large TCP/IP-based networks into smaller logical segments?
    a. subnetting
    b. subclassing
    c. reverse lookups
    d. domain transfers
12. On which Class network would you find the workstation that uses the following IP address: 193.12.176.55?
    a. A
    b. B
    c. C
    d. D

13. Which of the following is the loopback address?
    a. 1.1.1.1
    b. 255.255.255.0
    c. 1.0.1.0
    d. 127.0.0.1
14. Which of the following is an alternative to configuring each workstation on a network with its own IP address?
    a. DHCP
    b. SNMP
    c. RARP
    d. TFTP
15. What kind of network operating system requires IPX/SPX?
    a. Windows NT Server
    b. UNIX
    c. NetWare version 3.2 or lower
    d. NetWare versions higher than 3.2
16. Which IPX/SPX core protocol provides data reliability services?
    a. IPX
    b. SPX
    c. NCP
    d. SAP
17. The node address portion of an IPX/SPX address is equivalent to what other address?
    a. MAC address
    b. IP address
    c. Data Link layer address
    d. Network address
18. What function is performed by the time to live (in IP) and the transport control (in IPX) fields?
19. Which of the following is not a valid network address for a NetWare server?
    a. F290F45A
    b. AAAAAAAA
    c. 23AK80A3
    d. 01010101

20. Why wouldn't you want to use NetBIOS for Internet connections?
    - a. It's not routable.
    - b. It's not secure.
    - c. It's not reliable.
    - d. Both a and b.
21. Why are hosts on a TCP/IP network assigned host names?
22. All workstations on networks connected to the Internet must register their individual IP addresses with InterNIC. True or False?
23. Macintosh computers can be integrated with Microsoft-based networks. True or False?
24. On a Windows 95 workstation, how would you find your computer's NetBIOS name?
    - a. Click Start, click Run, and type winipcfg.
    - b. Double-click My Computer, double-click Control Panel, and double-click System.
    - c. Double-click My Computer, click General, and note the computer identification text.
    - d. Right-click the Network Neighborhood icon, click Properties, click the Identification tab, and note the computer name.
25. Which AppleTalk protocol ensures reliable data delivery?
    - a. NCP
    - b. ZIP
    - c. DDP
    - d. ATP
26. What is a logically defined group of workstations called on an AppleTalk network?
    - a. an AppleTalk zone
    - b. an AppleTalk domain
    - c. an AppleTalk segment
    - d. an AppleTalk universe
27. On a Windows NT workstation, after you install the NWLink (IPX/SPX) protocol, you need not configure it so as to use it. True or False?
28. On a Windows 95 workstation, what is the default setting for the IP address in the TCP/IP protocol properties?
    - a. Obtain IP address automatically
    - b. Specify an IP address
    - c. Enable NetBIOS over TCP/IP
    - d. Enable WINS resolution

29. What information does the winipcfg command (run from a Windows 95 or Windows 98 workstation) give you?

30. How many protocols can you install on a single Windows 95 workstation?

    a. 2

    b. 3

    c. 4

    d. as many as you want

Hands-on Projects

You can detect protocols and test their effects through a variety of ways. The Hands-on Projects that follow add to what you have learned about protocols thus far, and form the basis for protocol troubleshooting and more in-depth analysis of the TCP/IP protocol in Chapter 11.

Project 3-1

This project requires a workstation running Windows 95 that has the TCP/IP protocol installed and that is connected to a Windows NT server with Internet access. It introduces the PING (Packet Internet Groper) utility, which can be used to verify that TCP/IP is running, configured correctly, and communicating with the network. A ping test is typically the first thing network professionals try when troubleshooting a TCP/IP connection problem. The process of sending out a signal is known as pinging. You can ping either an IP address or a host name. (You will learn more about PING and other diagnostic TCP/IP utilities in Chapter 11.)

1. Click **Start**, point to **Programs**, then click **MS-DOS Prompt**.

2. At the DOS prompt, type **PING 127.0.0.1**. (Remember that 127.0.0.1 is the loopback address.) If your workstation is properly connected to the network, you should see a screen that contains five lines. The first line will read "Pinging 127.0.0.1 with 32 bytes of data." Following that you will see four lines that begin "Reply from 127.0.0.1." If you do not see four positive reply lines, or if you see four lines with the words "Request timed out," check the syntax of your ping command. If you typed the command correctly, check the status of your TCP/IP protocol. Is it installed and bound to your NIC? To reinstall TCP/IP, follow the steps mentioned earlier in this chapter for installing protocols.

3. At the end of each of the four reply lines, a TTL value appears. What is the value of the TTL and what does this number represent? Because you received these replies to your loopback ping test, you know that your TCP/IP services are installed correctly and bound to your NIC. The loopback test, however, doesn't indicate whether your TCP/IP services are operating correctly to grant you access to the network. In the next step, you will try a ping test that can help you determine whether your TCP/IP services are operating successfully.

4. At the DOS prompt, type **PING** http://www.yahoo.com.
5. What was the response? If you received a "Request timed out" message, why might you have received it? If you received a valid response, with four lines of replies, note the TTL. Why does it differ from the TTL observed when you pinged the loopback address?
6. Type **exit** at the MS DOS prompt to close the window.

PROJECT 3-2

This project requires a workstation that is connected to a Windows NT network running Windows 95 with the TCP/IP protocol installed and a static IP address assigned to the workstation. In this project, you will unbind and rebind a protocol to a NIC. As you have learned, protocols are normally bound to the NIC by default after they're installed. Sometimes, due to tampering or technical difficulties, they may become unbound. One indication of an unbound protocol comes when you cannot perform a successful loopback ping test, but you can see that the TCP/IP protocol is installed. Unless the protocol is bound to the NIC, the NIC cannot use that protocol to communicate with any devices on the network, even if the protocol is present.

1. Right-click the **Network Neighborhood** icon, then click **Properties**.
2. Verify that the **Configuration** tab is selected.
3. On a separate piece of paper, write down all the network components that you currently have installed. Components may include network services, clients, or protocols—for example, TCP/IP or an Ethernet adapter.
4. Select your network interface card from the list of components, then click the **Properties** button. The adapter's property window opens.
5. Click the **Bindings** tab. Protocols listed with a checked box next to them are bound to the NIC. Which protocols are bound to your NIC? In the next step, you will unbind the TCP/IP protocol from your NIC to test what happens when a protocol is installed, yet not bound to the primary adapter.
6. Click the check box next to the TCP/IP protocol listing to unbind the TCP/IP protocol, then click **OK**.
7. Click **OK** again to save your changes. You are prompted to restart your workstation to allow the changes to take effect.
8. Click **Yes** to restart your workstation.
9. When your workstation restarts, do you see any error messages? If so, write them on a separate piece of paper, then choose to ignore the errors and continue the start-up process.
10. Try pinging the loopback address as you did in Project 3-1. How did your workstation respond?

11. Right-click the **Network Neighborhood** icon, then choose **Properties**. Verify that the **Configuration** tab is selected.
12. Write down all networking components currently installed on your system. This list should differ from the list you created in Step 3. What's missing? In the next step, you will reinstall the TCP/IP protocol to once again bind it to the NIC. (Note: If you have more than one NIC installed in your workstation, the TCP/IP protocol should remain bound to adapters other than the one you selected in Step 4. Reinstalling TCP/IP will not harm or change the bindings of other adapters or other protocols, but it is the quickest way to reestablish a binding that has either been manually removed or somehow lost.)
13. Click **Add**. The Select Network Component Type window opens.
14. Double-click **Protocol**. The Select Network Protocol window appears.
15. In the list of manufacturers, click **Microsoft**.
16. In the list of protocols, click **TCP/IP** and click **OK**.
17. Click **OK** to install TCP/IP. You are prompted to restart your workstation to allow the changes to take effect.
18. Click **Yes** to restart your workstation. In the next step, you will verify that the TCP/IP protocol is once again bound to your NIC, and you will find out whether your TCP/IP properties for that NIC have changed after unbinding and rebinding the protocol.
19. Right-click the **Network Neighborhood** icon, then click **Properties**.
20. Verify that the **Configuration** tab is selected.
21. Double-click the TCP/IP protocol that is now bound to your NIC to view its properties. The TCP/IP Properties dialog box appears.
22. Click the **IP Address** tab. What is your IP address? Has it changed? How might this feature be useful?
23. Click **OK** to close the TCP/IP Properties dialog box.
24. Click **OK** to close the Network properties dialog box.

PROJECT 3-3

In this project, you will exercise your knowledge about data frames and datagrams. Because these structures form the basis of all networking, it's important that you be able to visualize and understand their components. You will need a pencil and paper to complete this project.

1. Pretend that you are a device on a network with the MAC address of 0573AC and you want to send 8 bytes of data to another device on the network that has the MAC address 22A0F3. You are on an Ethernet network with a network address of 00002020. Draw a picture of the IPX/SPX datagram that will carry your data. Name the parts of the datagram and fill in the values that you can (for example, addresses, size, and packet type).

2. Pretend that you are the same device as in Step 1 sending 8 bytes of data to the same second device on the same network; this time, however, you're sending the information with the TCP/IP protocol. Your IP address is 209.122.38.7 and the second device's IP address is 209.122.38.9. Draw a picture of the IPX/SPX datagram that will carry your data. Name the parts of the datagram and fill in the values that you can (for example, addresses, length, and protocol type).

CASE PROJECTS

1. As a consultant for the First National Bank of Monroe, you have been asked to solve problems on the bank's network. According to the bank manager, since Monday, at the beginning of each day two of the 16 tellers have been unable to log on to the network. Two other tellers occasionally experience problems at the beginning of the day, but not if they get to work before everyone else. They receive an error that says something like "another machine is using that name." When you arrive at the bank, the college intern who has been setting up the machines tells you that he is using a program called Ghost to clone all PCs from a single disk image. In other words, an exact copy of one machine's software, operating system, and its properties has been copied to all of the computers. All of the PCs are brand new, are running Windows 98, and use the same hardware and software. First National Bank's network consists of two Windows NT servers and runs both TCP/IP and NetBIOS/NetBEUI protocols. It uses DHCP to allocate TCP/IP addresses. What might be preventing the two tellers from logging on to the network in the morning?
2. First National Bank's president congratulates you on quickly solving the problem. She then shares the information that she's about to make an offer to buy Monroe's other bank, Metropolitan Savings. She's worried that the two banks' networks won't integrate easily. She isn't sure what kinds of servers or workstations are used by the other bank, but Metropolitan Savings' manager mentioned something about a UNIX system. What can you tell her about integrating the two systems? What protocols would you recommend that she use or continue to use to facilitate the integration process?
3. Six months later, First National Bank has successfully consolidated the networks at its original location and at its new acquisition. Business is booming, and the bank is investigating the possibility of allowing customers to check their account balances from the Web. Bank personnel, however, have no experience with the Internet. In fact, the bank's president tells you the bank doesn't even have a connection to the Internet at this time. She understands that she needs to obtain IP addresses for all of her machines. But, she says, they are already using IP addresses internally and they work well without having to pay InterNIC for new IP addresses. Would you recommend leaving the bank's IP addressing as is or changing it? How do you suggest that the bank obtain Internet access? What concerns would you bring up with regard to allowing customers access to their account information off the Web? How might Internet access affect the bank's internal LAN?

CHAPTER 4

NETWORKING MEDIA

After reading this chapter and completing the exercises, you will be able to:

- Explain concepts related to data transmission and noise
- Describe the physical characteristics of coaxial cable, STP, UTP, and fiber-optic media
- Explain the benefits and limitations of different networking media
- Identify the best practices for cabling buildings and work areas
- Describe methods of transmitting data through the atmosphere
- Identify the network media best suited to specific LAN environments

ON THE JOB

I was once asked to test the quality of various network monitoring software packages. Our test lab had all the latest new equipment to mimic the client's LAN: managed stacks of 100 MHz hubs, powerful Intel-based servers with RAID subsystems, and nicely configured workstations. We also had the best surge arrestors available and an excellent UPS system.

Installation of the operating systems went well, but the results from the various management programs were unreliable. It soon became apparent that the lab contained bad hardware; the logs of traffic on the server NICs showed too many errors for a busy LAN—let alone an isolated test LAN. Internal diagnostics programs said that the cards were okay. When I generated as much traffic as I could through the new hubs, using a laptop with a new NIC, I found no errors.

What was next? I had checked the system's entire Physical layer—except for the LAN's wires. When testing the hubs, I had used the new cable that came with my new NIC. I visually double-checked the termination patterns to verify that I had a proper TIA-568 CAT5 cable. A continuity test also showed the cables to be correct.

Finally, I decided to reterminate the cable ends. As soon as I snipped off the ends and exposed the wires, it became apparent that the cable was CAT3 at best! In fact, our company was color-coding cables, using one color for one purpose. It had ordered several large spools from the same vendor—but the vendor did not check the wire before shipping it. The green twisted-pair cable used for my project was not stamped with a CAT5 verification and was not of the same quality as the other cable in the shipment.

Quality cable is as critical as quality memory or RAID subsystems. Termination of cable can be poorly done, however, leading to intermittent, difficult-to-trace problems. As little as 1 inch of untwist at cable ends can reduce the capacity of a wire set from 150 MHz to 30 MHz! In my case, a CAT5 test on a high-quality cable tester would have detected the cable problem. I've learned my lesson. When odd problems arise on high speed connections, I head for our company's sophisticated cable and fiber tester.

Tom Callaci
Berbee Information Networks

Just as highways and streets provide the foundation for automobile travel, networking media provide the physical foundation of data transmission. As you know, networking media reside at the lowest layer of the OSI Model. The first networks transmitted data over thick, heavy coaxial cables. Today, most networking media resemble telephone cords, with their flexible outsides and twisted copper wire inside. Because networks now demand more speed, versatility, and reliability, however, networking media are changing. Modern networks may incorporate not only copper wiring, but also fiber-optic cables, infrared, radio waves, and possibly other media.

Before you can fully understand network communications, you must understand how data are transmitted. You should also be familiar with the characteristics of various networking media. Although network users take data transmission for granted, giving little thought to how their e-mail messages or files move from point A to point B, you need to understand this process thoroughly. This chapter elucidates the details of data transmission. You'll learn what it takes to make data transmission dependable and how to correct some common transmission problems.

DATA TRANSMISSION

Information can be transmitted via one of two methods: analog or digital. Both methods use voltage to generate their signals.

Analog signals use variable voltage to create continuous waves, resulting in an inexact transmission. To understand this concept, think of two tin cans connected by a wire. When you speak into one of the tin cans, you produce analog sound waves that vibrate over the wire until they reach the tin can at the other end. These sound waves are merely approximations of your voice, and they are significantly affected by the quality of the wire. For example, if you try the tin can experiment with a pure copper wire with no twists or bends in it, your voice will arrive at the other end sounding clearer than if you use an unfolded coat hanger. Regardless of which medium you use, however, the sound waves will experience distortion while they traverse the wire, arriving at the second tin can at least a little muddled.

Figure 4-1 shows a small portion of an analog signal. Notice how the **amplitude**, or the signal's strength, varies over time.

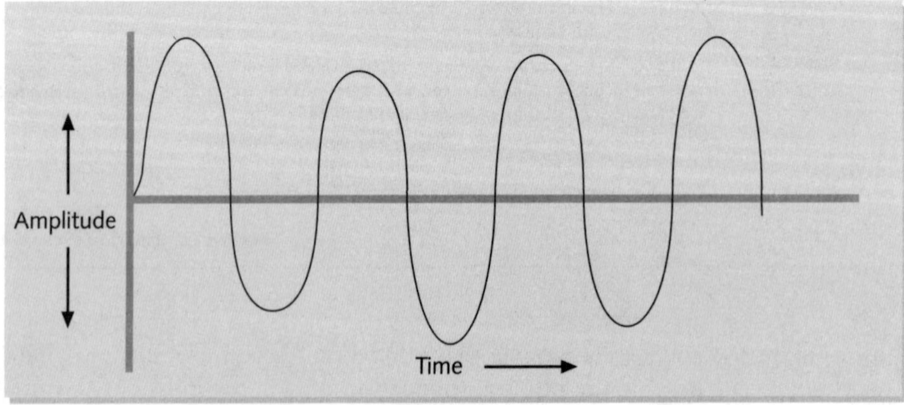

Figure 4-1 An example of an analog signal

To determine the frequency of the signal depicted in Figure 4-1, count how many times the amplitude cycles between its peak and lowest values over time. For example, if the total time represented by the x-axis in Figure 4-1 equaled 1 second, the frequency of that wave would be 3.5 cycles per second, or 3.5 Hz.

Now contrast the analog signal to a digital signal, as shown in Figure 4-2. **Digital** signals are composed of precise voltages that create pulses with values of either 1 or 0. As in any **binary** system, these 1s and 0s combine to encode information. (You learned about binary numbers in Chapter 3's discussion of TCP/IP addressing.) Every pulse in the digital signal is called a binary digit, or **bit**. A bit can have only one of two possible values: 1 or 0. Eight bits together form a **byte**. One byte carries one piece of information. For example, the byte "01111001" means "121" on a digital network. As you learned in Chapter 3, in the case of TCP/IP addressing, a byte is also known as an octet.

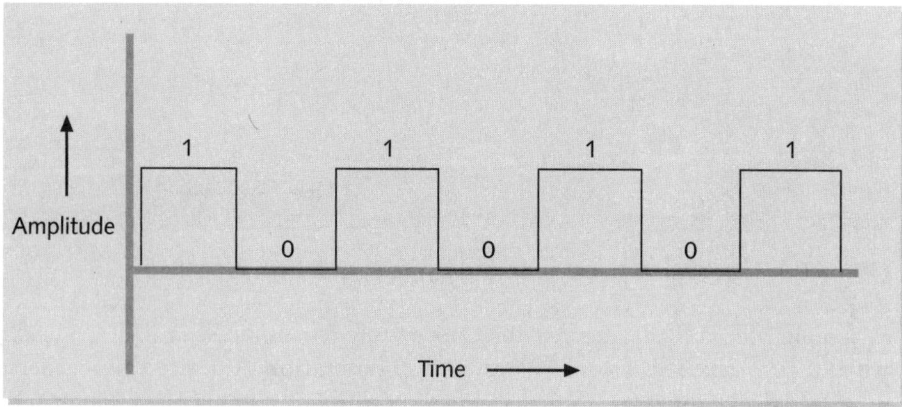

Figure 4-2 An example of a digital signal

Whereas an analog signal's amplitude essentially measures the strength of the signal, **frequency** is the number of times that a signal's amplitude changes over a fixed period of time; it is usually expressed in cycles per second, or **Hertz (Hz)**. One benefit to analog signals is that, because they are more variable than digital signals, they can convey greater subtleties. For example, think of the difference between your voice and the digital voice of an automated teller machine or a digital answering machine. These digital voices have a poorer quality than your own voice—that is, they sound "like machines." They can't convey the subtle changes in inflection that you expect in a human voice.

Networks, however, are not concerned with subtleties. Analog signals are not optimal for data transmission because they are more prone to errors than data signals. **Noise**, or unwanted interference from other sources, affects them profoundly. You may be familiar with this phenomenon if you have talked on a cellular phone and heard someone else's conversation in the background; the other conversation is an example of noise. Static on the line is also noise.

Noise on the line distorts signals. When it affects analog signals, this distortion can result in the incorrect transmission of data, just as if static on the phone line prevented you from hearing the person on the other end of the line.

Another drawback to analog transmission is that it **attenuates**, or loses its strength as it travels farther away from its source. This characteristic is not so bad by itself, because digital transmission attenuates as well. To compensate for attenuation, both analog and digital signals are repeated so that they can travel farther. The problem with analog signals is that when they are repeated, they become amplified, and the accompanying noise they have accumulated is amplified as well. This indiscriminate amplification causes the analog signal to become progressively worse. Figure 4-3 shows an analog signal distorted by noise and then amplified.

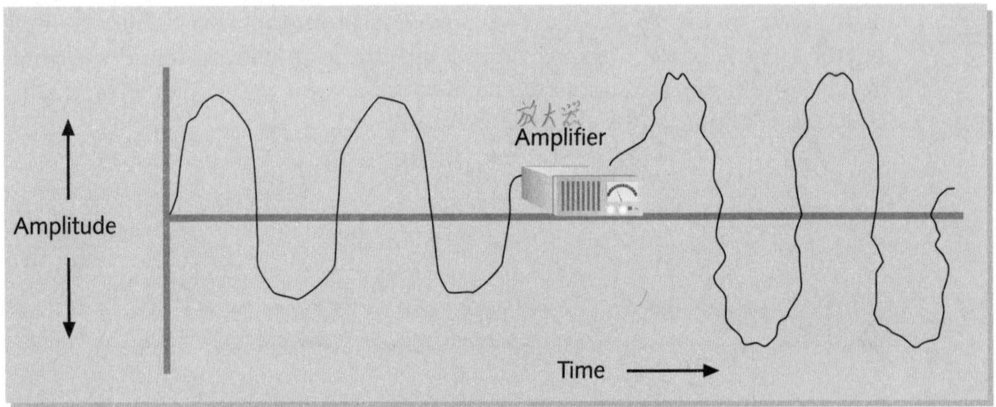

Figure 4-3 An analog signal distorted by noise and then amplified

When digital signals are repeated, they are actually retransmitted in their original, pure form, without any noise. This process is known as **regeneration**. A device that regenerates a digital signal is called a **repeater**. (You will learn more about repeaters in Chapter 6.) Figure 4-4 shows a digital signal distorted by noise and then regenerated by a repeater.

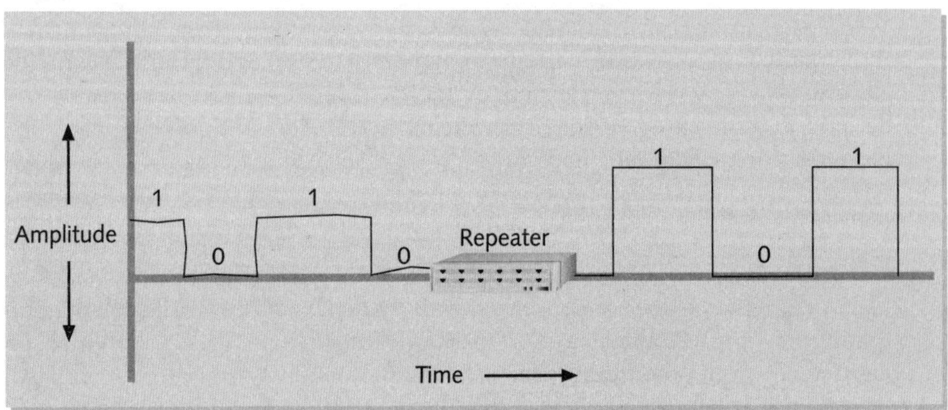

Figure 4-4 A digital signal distorted by noise and then repeated

Most networks rely exclusively on digital transmissions. One situation in which you are likely to employ analog signals to transmit data is when you use a modem to connect two systems. The modem may transmit signals in analog over the phone lines, but the signals must be converted into digital signals by the modem at the receiving computer. The word **modem** reflects this device's function as a **mod**ulator/**dem**odulator—that is, it modulates analog signals into digital signals at the transmitting end, then demodulates digital signals into analog signals at the receiving end. (You will learn more about modem communications in Chapter 7.)

Because a network has to send and receive only a pattern of 1s and 0s, represented by precise pulses, digital transmission is more reliable than analog transmission, which relies on variable waves. In addition, noise affects digital transmission less severely. As shown in Figure 4-4, a digital signal distorted by noise can still be interpreted as a pattern of 1s and 0s. On the other hand, digital transmission requires many pulses to transmit the same amount of information that an analog signal can transmit with a single wave.

For example, you might convey the word "one" with a single wave in analog format; in digital format, however, the same message would require 8 bits (00000001), or 8 separate pulses. Nevertheless, the high reliability of digital transmission makes this extra signaling worthwhile. In the end, digital transmission is more efficient than analog transmission, because it causes fewer errors and therefore requires less overhead to compensate for errors.

Although some digitized voices sound like machines, other digitized audio signals, such as those on a CD recording, sound perfectly realistic. Such high-quality digital audio uses many more bytes of information to create a signal. The more information, the more precise the signal. When a digitized voice contains enough information, the human ear cannot distinguish between it and an analog (live) voice.

Media Characteristics

When deciding which kind of transmission media to use, you must match your networking needs with the characteristics of the media. This section describes the characteristics that pertain to all means of data transmission. Later, you will learn how to choose the appropriate media for your network.

Generally speaking, you must consider five characteristics when choosing a data transfer media (listed here roughly in order of significance): throughput and bandwidth; cost; size and scalability; connectors; and noise immunity. Of course, every networking situation varies; what is significant for one organization may not matter to another. You need to decide what aspect is most important to your organization.

Throughput and Bandwidth

Perhaps the most significant factor in choosing a transmission medium is throughput. **Throughput** is the amount of data that the medium can transmit during a given period of time. Throughput is usually measured in megabits (1,000,000 bits) per second, or Mbps. It may also be called **capacity**.

The physical nature of every transmission media determines its potential throughput. For example, the laws of physics limit how fast electricity can travel over copper wire, just as they limit how much water can travel through a one-inch-diameter hose. If you try to direct more water through the one-inch-diameter hose than it can handle, you will wind up with water splashing back at you or a ruptured hose. Similarly, if you try to push more data through a copper wire than it can handle, the result will be lost data and data errors. Noise and devices connected to the transmission media can further limit throughput. A noisy circuit spends more time compensating for the noise and therefore has fewer resources available for transmitting data.

Often, the term "bandwidth" is used interchangeably with throughput. Strictly speaking, **bandwidth** is a measure of the difference between the highest and lowest frequencies that a media can transmit. This range of frequencies, which is expressed in Hz, is directly related to throughput. For example, if the FCC told you that you could transmit a radio signal between 870 and 880 MHz, your allotted bandwidth would be 10 MHz. The higher the bandwidth, the higher the throughput, as shown in Figure 4-5. This situation arises because higher frequencies can transmit more data in a given period of time than lower frequencies. Later in this chapter, you will discover the throughput characteristics of the most common networking media.

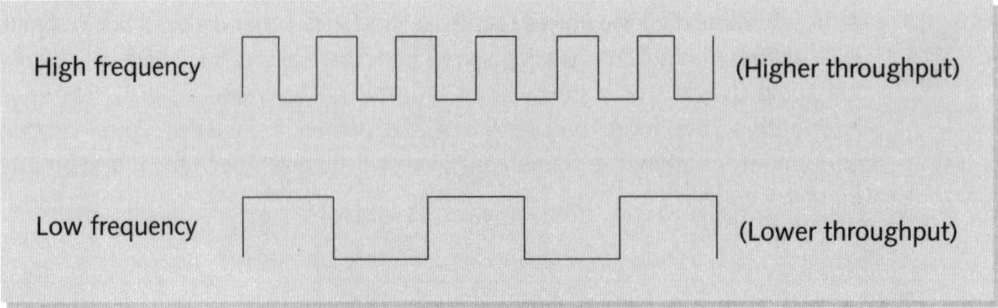

Figure 4-5 A comparison of two digital frequencies

COST

The cost implications for different kinds of transmission media are difficult to pinpoint. Not only do they depend on the hardware that already exists in an environment, but they also depend on your location. The following variables can all influence the final cost of implementing a certain type of media:

- *Cost of installation*—Can you install the media yourself, or must you hire contractors to do it? Will you need to move walls or build new conduits or closets? Will you need to lease lines from a service provider?
- *Cost of new infrastructure versus reusing existing infrastructure*—Can you use existing wiring? In some cases, for example, installing all new Category 5 UTP wiring may not pay off if you can use existing Category 3 UTP wiring. If you replace only part of your infrastructure, will it easily integrate with the existing media?

- *Cost of maintenance and support*—Reuse of an existing cabling infrastructure does not save any money if it is in constant need of repair or enhancement. Also, if you use an unfamiliar media type, it may cost more to hire a technician to service it. Will you be able to service the media yourself, or must you hire contractors to service it?
- *Cost of a lower transmission rate affecting productivity*—If you save money by reusing existing slower lines, are you incurring costs by reducing productivity? In other words, are you making staff wait longer to save and print reports or exchange e-mail?
- *Cost of obsolescence*—Are you choosing media that may become passing fads, requiring rapid replacement? Will you be able to find reasonably priced connectivity hardware that will be compatible with your chosen media for years to come?

Size and Scalability

Three specifications determine the size and scalability of networking media: maximum nodes per segment, maximum segment length, and maximum network length. In cabling, each of these specifications is based on a physical characteristic of the wire. The maximum number of nodes per segment depends on the **attenuation**, the amount of signal loss over a given distance. Each addition of a device to a network segment adds slightly to the signal's attenuation. To ensure a clear, strong signal, you must limit the number of nodes that can exist on a segment.

The length of a network segment is also limited because of attenuation. After a certain distance, a signal loses so much strength that it cannot be accurately interpreted. Before this deterioration occurs, a repeater on the network must retransmit and amplify the signal. The maximum distance that a signal can travel and still be accurately interpreted equals the maximum segment length. Beyond this length, data loss is apt to occur. As with the maximum number of nodes per segment, maximum segment length varies between different cabling types.

In an ideal world, networks could transmit data instantaneously between sender and receiver, no matter how far apart the two were. Unfortunately, we don't live in an ideal world, and every network is subjected to a delay between the transmission of a signal and its eventual receipt. For example, when you press a key on your computer to save a file to the network, the file's data must travel through your NIC, the network wire, through a hub or possibly a switch or router, more cabling, and the server's NIC before it lands on the server's hard disk. Although electrons travel rapidly, they still have to travel, and a brief delay takes place between the moment you press the key and the moment the server accepts the data. This delay is called **latency**.

The length of the cable involved affects latency, as does the existence of any intervening connectivity device, such as a router. The effects of latency become a problem only when a receiving node is expecting some type of communication, such as the rest of a data stream it has begun to accept. If that node does not receive the rest of the data stream, it assumes that no more data is coming. This assumption causes transmission errors on a network.

When you connect multiple network segments, you increase the latency in the network. To constrain the latency and avoid its associated errors, each type of cabling is rated for a maximum number of connected network segments.

Connectors

Connectors are the pieces of hardware that connect the wire to the network device, be it a file server, workstation, switch, or printer. Every networking medium requires a specific kind of connector. The type of connectors you use will affect the cost of installing and maintaining the network, the ease of adding new segments or nodes to the network, and the technical expertise required to maintain the network. For example, connectors used with UTP wiring (which look like large telephone wire connectors) are much simpler to insert and replace than are the connectors used with coaxial cabling. UTP wiring connectors are also less expensive and can be used for a variety of cabling designs. You will learn more about the connectors required by different media later in this chapter.

Noise Immunity

As mentioned earlier, noise can distort data signals. The extent to which noise affects a signal depends partly on the transmission media. Some types of media are more susceptible to noise than others.

Whatever the medium, two types of noise can affect its data transmission: **electromagnetic interference (EMI)** and **radio frequency interference (RFI)**. Both EMI and RFI are waves that emanate from electrical devices or cables carrying electricity. Motors, power lines, televisions, copiers, fluorescent lights, and other sources of electrical activity can cause both EMI and RFI. RFI may also be caused by strong broadcast signals from radio or TV towers.

Either way, you can take measures to limit noise's impact on your network. For example, you should install cabling well away from powerful electromagnetic forces. If your environment still leaves your network susceptible, you should choose a type of transmission media that limits the amount of noise affecting the signal. Cabling may attain noise immunity through shielding, thickness, or anti-noise algorithms. If shielded cabling still doesn't ward off interference, you may need to use a metal **conduit**, or pipeline, to contain and further protect the cabling.

Network Cabling

Now that you understand the characteristics that will help you decide on an appropriate transmission medium, you need to learn more about how the most popular networking medium—cabling—works. To qualify for Net+ certification, you must know the characteristics of each type of cabling, how to install and design a network with each type, and how to provide for future network growth with each cabling option.

The following sections detail the types of cabling you are likely to find in a modern networking environment. The last section also describes good practice for cabling buildings, work areas, and data closets.

BASEBAND AND BROADBAND TRANSMISSION

Baseband is a transmission form in which digital signals are sent through direct current (DC) pulses applied to the wire. This direct current requires exclusive use of the wire's capacity. As a result, baseband systems can transmit only one signal, or one channel, at a time. Every device on a baseband system shares the same channel. When one node is transmitting data on a baseband system, all other nodes on the network must wait for that transmission to end before they can send data. Baseband transmission supports bidirectional signal flow, which means that computers can both send and receive information on the same length of wire.

Baseband transmission is susceptible to attenuation. That is, a digital signal loses strength as it travels farther from its source. To compensate for the signal loss, baseband systems use repeaters to regenerate and amplify the signal, enabling data to travel beyond the maximum segment length of the cabling. Baseband systems are typically inexpensive and simple to install.

Ethernet is an example of a baseband system found on many business LANs. In Ethernet (which is described in detail in Chapter 5), each device on a network can transmit over the wire—but only one device at a time. For example, if you want to save a file to the server, your NIC submits your request to use the wire; if no other device is using the wire to transmit data at that time, your workstation can go ahead. If the wire is in use, you must wait and try again later. Of course, this retrying process happens so quickly that you, as the user, may not even notice the wait.

The terms "wire" and "cable" are used synonymously in some situations. Strictly speaking, however, "wire" is a subset of "cabling," because the "cabling" category may also include fiber-optic cable, which is almost never called "wire." The exact meaning of the term "wire" depends on context. For example, if you said, in a somewhat casual way, "We had 6 Gigs of data go over the wire last night," you would be referring to whatever transmission media helped carry the data—whether fiber, radio waves, coax, or UTP.

Broadband is a form of transmission in which signals are modulated as radio frequency (RF) analog pulses that use different frequency ranges. Unlike baseband, broadband technology does not involve digital pulses. Nevertheless, the use of multiple frequencies enables a broadband system to access several channels and therefore carry much more data than a baseband system.

As you may know, broadband transmission is used to bring cable TV to your home. Your cable TV connection can carry at least 25 times as much data as a typical baseband system (like Ethernet) carries, including many different broadcast frequencies (channels). In broadband systems, signals travel in only one direction. Therefore, broadband cabling must provide a separate wire for both transmission and receipt of data. (Because most TV cable provides only one wire, it cannot be used for transmitting data out of your home without some modification. In Chapter 7, you will learn more about using cable to provide Internet access.) Broadband transmission is generally more expensive than baseband transmission because of the extra hardware involved. On the other hand, broadband systems can span longer distances than baseband.

As you have learned, analog signals, such as broadband signals, are susceptible to attenuation. For this reason, a broadband system uses amplifiers to boost the signal before it becomes so faint that it cannot be interpreted. The amplification is similar to the boost provided by the repeaters on baseband networks. Fewer amplifiers are required on a broadband system, however, than the number of repeaters required on a baseband system. The reason for this discrepancy is that broadband can span longer distances before the signal loses its strength.

In the field of networking, some terms have more than one meaning, depending on their context. "Broadband" is one of those terms. The "broadband" described in this chapter is the transmission system that carries RF signals across multiple channels on a coaxial cable, as used by cable TV. This definition was the original meaning of broadband. In the discussion of WANs in Chapter 7, the term "broadband" refers to networks that use digital signaling and have very high transmission rates, such as Asynchronous Transfer Mode (ATM) networks.

Coaxial Cable

Coaxial cable, called "coax" for short, was the foundation for Ethernet networks in the 1980s and remained a popular transmission medium for many years. Over time, however, twisted-pair cabling has replaced coax in most modern LANs. Coaxial cable consists of a central copper core surrounded by an insulator, a braided metal shielding called **braiding**, and an outer cover called the **sheath** or jacket. Figure 4-6 depicts a typical coaxial cable. The copper core carries the electromagnetic signal, and the braided metal shielding acts as both a shield against noise and a ground for the signal. The insulator layer usually consists of a ceramic or plastic material such as polyvinyl chloride (PVC) or Teflon. It protects the copper core from the metal shielding, because if the two made contact, the wire would short-circuit. The jacket, which protects the cable from physical damage, is usually manufactured from a flexible, fire-resistant plastic.

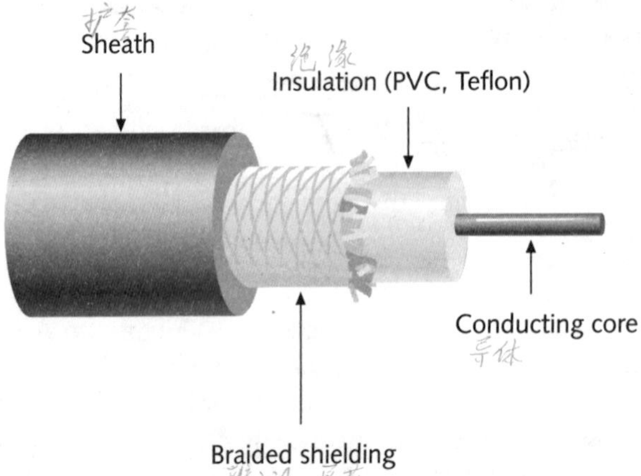

Figure 4-6 Coaxial cable

Because of its insulation and protective braiding, coaxial cable has a high resistance to interference from noise. It can also carry signals farther than twisted-pair cabling before amplification of the signals becomes necessary, although not as far as fiber-optic cabling. On the other hand, coaxial cable is more expensive than twisted-pair cable and generally supports lower throughput. Coaxial cable also requires each end of its segments to be terminated with a resistor. This type of cabling comes in many specifications, although you are likely to see only two or three types of coax in use today. In any case, each of the many varieties have been assigned a Radio Government (RG) specification number.

The significant differences between the cable types lie in the materials used for their center cores, which in turn influence their impedance (or the resistance that contributes to controlling the signal, as expressed in ohms), throughput, and typical usage. Table 4-1 lists the specifications for several types of coaxial cable. The two with which you should be familiar are RG-58 A/U (Thinnet) and RG-62 (Thicknet).

RG-59 is the coaxial cabling specification used for cable TV transmission. Because of its different impedance requirements, you cannot use this type of cabling for data networks, even though it might fit with your connectors.

Table 4-1 Types of Coaxial Cable

Designation	Type	Impedance	Description
RG-58/U	Thinwire	50 ohms	Solid copper core
RG-58 A/U	Thinwire	50 ohms	Stranded copper core
RG-58 C/U	Thinwire	50 ohms	Military version of RG-58 A/U
RG-59	CATV	75 ohms	Broadband cable, used for cable TV
RG-8	Thickwire	50 ohms	Solid core; approximately 0.4-inch diameter
RG-11	Thickwire	50 ohms	Standard core; approximately 0.4-inch diameter
RG-62	Baseband	90 ohms	Used for ARCnet and IBM 3270 terminals

Thicknet (10Base5)

Thicknet cabling, also called thickwire Ethernet, is a rigid coaxial cable approximately 1 cm thick used for the original Ethernet networks. Because it is often covered with a yellow sheath, Thicknet is sometimes called "yellow Ethernet" or "yellow garden hose." IEEE designates Thicknet as **10Base5** Ethernet. The "10" represents its throughput of 10 Mbps, the "Base" stands for baseband transmission, and the "5" represents the maximum segment length of a Thicknet cable, which is 500 m. You will almost never find Thicknet on new networks, but you may find it on older networks, where it is used to connect one data closet to another as part of the network backbone. Thicknet's characteristics are summarized following.

- *Throughput*—According to the IEEE 802.3 standard, Thicknet transmits data at a maximum rate of 10 Mbps, although it may be possible to use Thicknet cable on networks that transmit data at 100 Mbps. It uses baseband transmission.
- *Cost*—Thicknet is less expensive than fiber-optic cable, but more expensive than other types of coaxial cabling, such as Thinnet.

- *Connector*—Thicknet requires a combination of a vampire tap (a connector that pierces a hole in the wire) to connect to a transceiver, plus a drop cable to connect network devices. Figure 4-7 depicts Thicknet network connectivity.

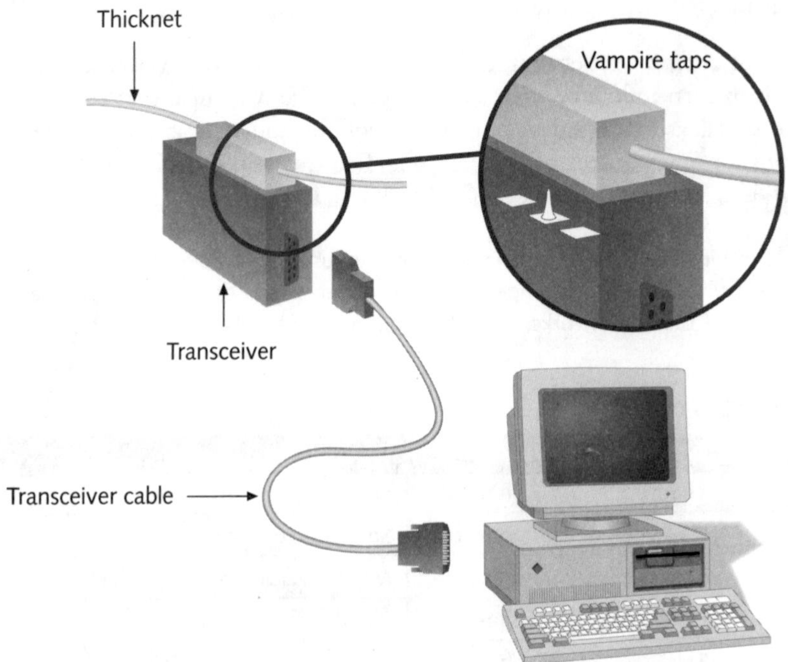

Figure 4-7 Thicknet cable transceiver with detail of a vampire tap piercing the core

- *Noise immunity*—Because of its wide diameter and excellent shielding, Thicknet has the highest resistance to noise of any of the commonly used network cabling options.
- *Size and scalability*—Because Thicknet has high resistance to noise, it allows data to travel for longer distances than other types of cabling. Its maximum segment length is 500 m, or approximately 1640 feet. Thicknet can accommodate a maximum of 100 nodes per segment. Its total maximum network length is 1500 m. To minimize the possibility of interference between stations, you should separate network devices by at least 2.5 m.

Thicknet is rarely used on modern networks because of its significant disadvantages. First, this type of cable is difficult to manage. Its rigidity makes it hard to handle and install. Second, it does not allow for network advances because high-speed data transmission cannot run on Thicknet. Although it is less expensive and more resistant to noise than many of the currently popular transmission media, Thicknet is essentially an obsolete technology.

Thinnet (10Base2)

Thinnet, also known as thin Ethernet, was the most popular medium for Ethernet LANs in the 1980s. Like Thicknet, Thinnet is rarely used on modern networks, although you may encounter it on networks installed in the 1980s or on newer small office or home office LANs. IEEE has designated Thinnet as 10Base2 Ethernet, with the "10" representing its data transmission rate of 10 Mbps, the "Base" representing the fact that it uses baseband transmission, and the "2" representing its maximum segment length of 185 (or roughly 200) m. Because of its black sheath, Thinnet may also be called "black Ethernet." Thinnet's cable diameter is approximately 0.64 cm, which makes it more flexible and easier to handle and install than Thicknet. More of Thinnet's characteristics are listed following.

- *Throughput*—Thinnet can transmit data at a maximum rate of 10 Mbps. It uses baseband transmission.
- *Cost*—Thinnet is less expensive than Thicknet and fiber-optic cable, but more expensive than twisted-pair wiring. Prefabricated cables are available for approximately $1/foot. For this reason, Thinnet is sometimes called "cheapnet."
- *Size and scalability*—Thinnet allows a maximum of 185 m per network segment. This length is less than that available with Thicknet, because Thinnet's resistance to noise is not as strong. For the same reason, Thinnet can accommodate a maximum of only 30 nodes per segment. Its total maximum network length is slightly more than 550 m. To minimize interference, devices on a Thinnet network should be separated by at least 0.5 m.
- *Connector*—Thinnet connects the wire to network devices with BNC T connectors, as shown in Figure 4-8. A BNC connector with three open ends attaches to the Ethernet interface card at the base of the "T" and to the Thinnet cable at its two sides so as to allow the signal in and out of the NIC. The origin of the acronym "BNC" is somewhat muddy, but probably stands for British Naval Connector. BNC barrel connectors (with only two open ends) are used to join two Thinnet cable segments together, as shown in Figure 4-8.

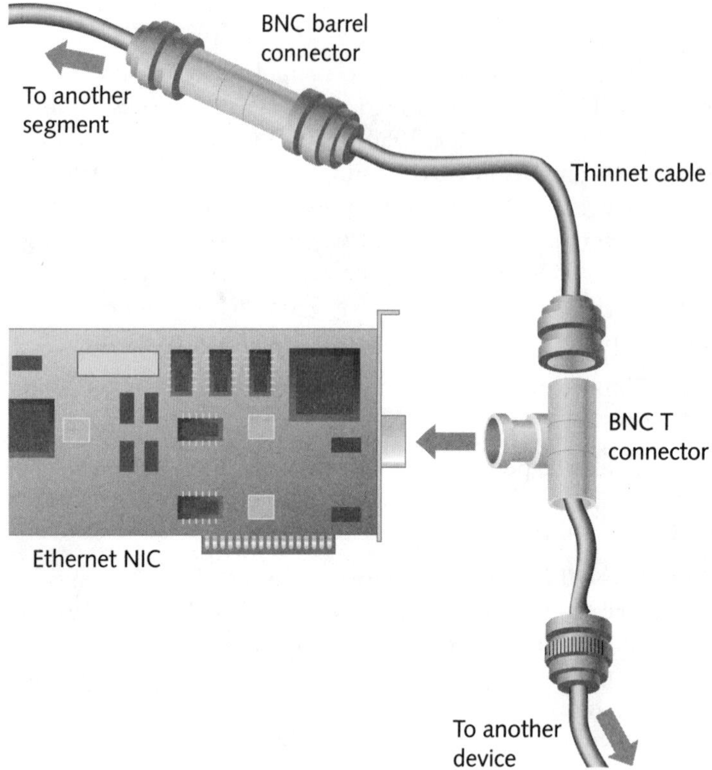

Figure 4-8 Thinnet BNC connectors

- *Noise immunity*—Because of its insulation and shielding, Thinnet is more resistant to noise than twisted-pair wiring. It is not as resistant as Thicknet, however.

Thinnet is occasionally used on modern networks, but more often you will see it on networks installed in the 1980s. Its major advantages are its very low cost and relative ease of use. Because twisted-pair wiring can carry more data and has come down in price, Thinnet has become almost obsolete.

Both Thicknet and Thinnet coaxial cable rely on the bus topology (described in detail in Chapter 5). Networks using the bus topology must be terminated at both ends. Without terminators, signals on a bus network would travel endlessly between the two ends of the network, a phenomenon known as **signal bounce**. You will learn more about topologies and signal bounce in Chapter 5. Figure 4-9 depicts a typical coaxial cable network using a bus topology.

Thicknet and Thinnet cable both require 50-ohm resistors terminating either end of the network. These cables must also be grounded at one end. If you ground a coaxial network at both ends or not at all, you will experience intermittent data transmission errors.

Bus topologies are best suited to small office or home office LANs, because, although they are easy and inexpensive to set up, they do not scale well. Also, they are not very fault-tolerant. A break in a bus topology affects all devices on the network—not just the device to which it is directly connected. For this reason, bus networks are difficult to troubleshoot.

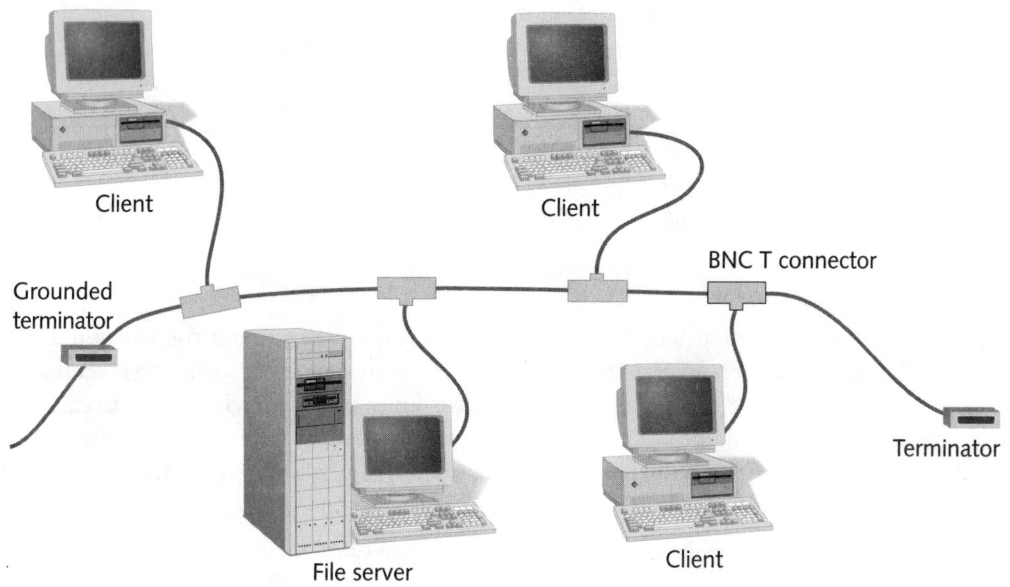

Figure 4-9 A typical coaxial network using a bus topology

Twisted-Pair Cable

Twisted-pair (TP) cable is similar to telephone wiring and consists of color-coded pairs of insulated copper wires, each with a diameter of 0.4 to 0.8 mm, twisted around each other and encased in plastic coating, as shown in Figure 4-10. One wire in a pair carries signal information; the second wire in the pair is grounded and absorbs interference. The twists in the wire help to reduce the effects of crosstalk. **Crosstalk**, which is measured in decibels (dB), occurs when signals traveling on nearby wire pairs infringe on another pair's signal. If you envision the wire pairs in a single cable as couples in an elevator, you can imagine how one couple speaking very loudly might impair the other couple's ability to converse. Another form of crosstalk, called **alien crosstalk**, can occur when signals from adjacent cables interfere with another cable's transmission. Alien crosstalk becomes a real threat when network administrators bundle more cables into smaller conduits.

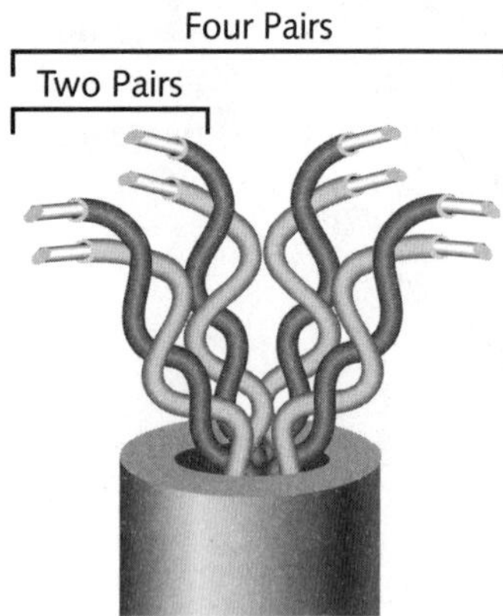

Figure 4-10 Twisted-pair cable

The more twists per inch in a pair of wires, the more resistant the pair will be to all forms of noise. Higher-quality, more expensive twisted-pair cable contains more twists per foot. The number of twists per meter or foot is known as the **twist ratio**. Because twisting the wire pairs more tightly requires more cable, however, a high twist ratio can result in greater attenuation. For optimal performance, cable manufacturers must strike a balance between crosstalk and attenuation reduction.

Because twisted-pair is used in such a wide variety of environments and for a variety of purposes, it comes in hundreds of different designs. These designs vary in their twist ratio, the number of wire pairs that they contain, the grade of copper used, the type of shielding (if any), and the materials used for shielding, among other things. A twisted-pair cable may contain from 1 to 4200 wire pairs. Early network cables incorporated two wire pairs: one pair dedicated to sending data and one pair dedicated to receiving data. Modern networks typically use cables containing two or four wire pairs, with more than one wire pair both sending and transmitting data simultaneously.

In 1991, two standards organizations, TIA (Telecommunications Industry Association) and EIA (Electronic Industry Association), finalized their specifications for twisted-pair wiring in a standard called TIA/EIA 568. Since then, both groups have continually revised the international standards for new and modified transmission media. Their standards now cover cabling media, design, and installation specifications. The TIA/EIA 568 standard divides twisted-pair wiring into several categories. Thus you will hear twisted-pair referred to as CAT (category) 1, 2, 3, 4, or 5, and soon CAT6 will become available. All of these cables fall under the TIA/EIA 568 standard. LANs frequently use CAT3 or CAT5 wiring.

Twisted-pair cable is the most common form of cabling found on LANs today. It is relatively inexpensive, flexible, and easy to install, and it can span a significant distance before requiring a repeater (though not as far as coax). Twisted-pair cable easily accommodates several different topologies, although it is most often implemented in star or star-hybrid topologies. Furthermore, twisted-pair can handle the faster networking transmission rates currently being employed. Due to its wide acceptance, it will probably be updated to handle the even faster rates that will emerge in the future. One drawback to twisted-pair is that, because of its flexibility, it is more prone to physical damage than coaxial cable. This problem is a minor factor given its many benefits over coax. All twisted-pair cable falls into one of two categories, shielded twisted-pair (STP) or unshielded twisted-pair (UTP).

Shielded Twisted-Pair (STP)

As the name implies, **shielded twisted-pair (STP)** cable consists of twisted wire pairs that are not only individually insulated, but also surrounded by a shielding made of a metallic substance such as foil. Some STP uses a braided metal shielding. The shielding acts as an antenna, converting the noise into current (assuming that the wire is properly grounded). This current induces an equal, yet opposite current in the twisted pairs it surrounds. The noise on the shielding mirrors the noise on the twisted pairs, allowing the two to cancel each other out. The effectiveness of STP's shield depends on the level and type of environmental noise, the thickness and material used for the shield, the grounding mechanism, and the symmetry and consistency of the shielding. Figure 4-11 depicts an STP cable.

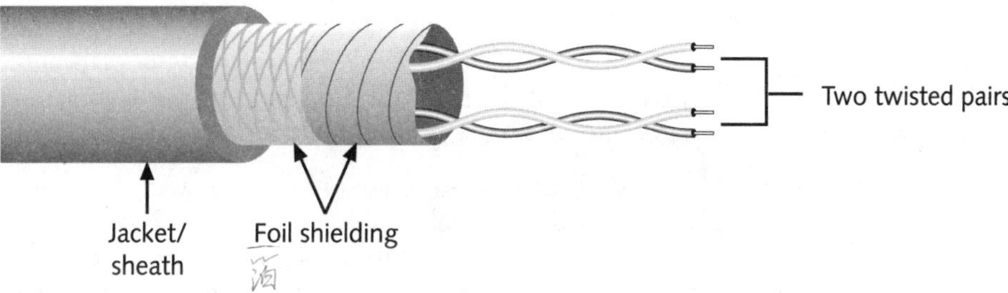

Figure 4-11 STP cable

Unshielded Twisted-Pair (UTP)

Unshielded twisted-pair (UTP) cabling consists of one or more insulated wire pairs encased in a plastic sheath. As its name implies, UTP does not contain additional shielding for the twisted pairs. As a result, UTP is both less expensive and less resistant to noise than STP. Figure 4-12 depicts a typical UTP cable. IEEE has designated UTP cabling as 10BaseT, with the "10" representing its minimum transmission rate of 10 Mbps, "Base" representing the fact that it carries signals in the baseband method, and "T" representing UTP.

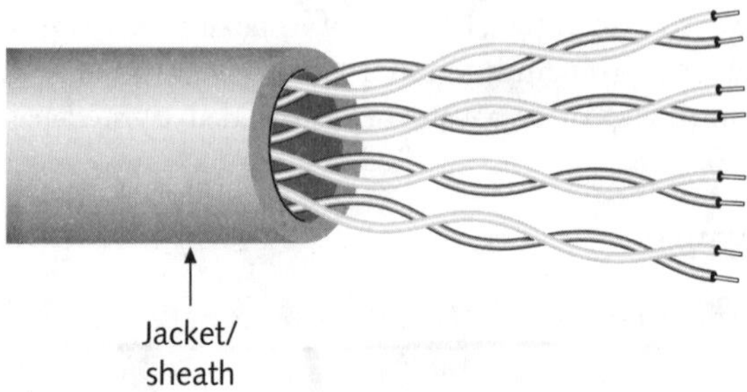

Figure 4-12 UTP cable

Earlier, you learned that the TIA/EIA consortium designated standards for twisted-pair wiring. To manage network cabling, you need to be familiar with the standards that may be used on modern networks, particularly CAT3 and CAT5.

- *Category 1 (CAT1)*—A form of UTP that contains two wire pairs. CAT1 is suitable for voice communications but not for data. At most, it can carry only 20 kilobits per second (Kbps) of data.
- *Category 2 (CAT2)*—A form of UTP that contains four wire pairs and can carry up to 4 Mbps of data. CAT2 is rarely found on modern networks, however, because most systems require higher throughput.
- *Category 3 (CAT3)*—A form of UTP that contains four wire pairs and can carry up to 10 Mbps of data with a possible bandwidth of 16 MHz. CAT3 has typically been used for 10 Mbps Ethernet or 4 Mbps Token Ring networks. Network administrators are gradually replacing CAT3 cabling with CAT5 to accommodate higher throughput, although CAT3 remains less expensive than CAT5.
- *Category 4 (CAT4)*—A form of UTP that contains four wire pairs and can support up to 16 Mbps throughput. CAT4 may be used for 16 Mbps Token Ring or 10 Mbps Ethernet networks. It is guaranteed for signals as high as 20 MHz and provides more protection against crosstalk and attenuation than CAT1, CAT2, or CAT3.
- *Category 5 (CAT5)*—The most popular form of UTP for new network installations and upgrades to Fast Ethernet. CAT5 contains four wire pairs and supports up to 100 Mbps throughput and a 100 MHz signal rate. In addition to 100 Mbps Ethernet, CAT5 wiring can support other fast networking technologies, such as Asynchronous Transfer Mode (ATM). Figure 4-13 depicts a typical CAT5 UTP cable with its twisted pairs untwisted, allowing you to see their matched color coding. For example, the wire that is colored solid orange is twisted around the wire that is part orange and part white to form the pair responsible for transmitting data.
- *Enhanced CAT5*—A higher-grade version of CAT5 wiring that contains high-quality copper, offers a high twist ratio, and uses advanced methods for reducing crosstalk. Enhanced CAT5 can support a signaling rate as high as 200 MHz, double the capability of regular CAT5.

- *Category 6 (CAT6)*—A twisted-pair cable that contains four wire pairs, each wrapped in foil insulation. Additional foil insulation covers the bundle of wire pairs, and a fire-resistant plastic sheath covers the second foil layer. The foil insulation provides excellent resistance to crosstalk and enables CAT6 to support at least six times the throughput supported by regular CAT5. Because it is new and because most network technologies cannot exploit its superlative capacity, CAT6 is rarely encountered in today's networks.

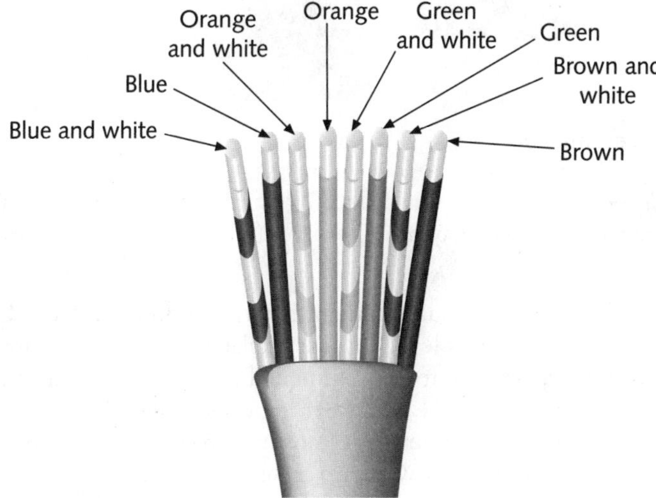

Figure 4-13 A CAT5 UTP cable

STP and UTP share several characteristics. The following list highlights their similarities and differences.

- *Throughput*—STP and UTP can transmit data at 10 Mbps. CAT5 UTP and, under some circumstances, CAT3 UTP can carry data at 100 Mbps. High-quality CAT5 UTP may also be able to transmit data at 1000 Mbps, or 1 gigabit per second.
- *Cost*—STP and UTP vary in cost, depending on the grade of copper used, the category rating, and any enhancements. Typically, STP is more expensive than UTP. High-grade UTP, however, can be very expensive. For example, enhanced CAT5 costs 20% more per foot than regular CAT5 cabling. The new CAT6 cabling is even more expensive than enhanced CAT5.
- *Connector*—STP and UTP use RJ-45 connectors and data jacks, which look similar to telephone connectors and jacks. Figure 4-14 shows a close-up of an RJ-45 connector for a cable containing four wire pairs. The section on "Installing Cable" later in this chapter describes the use of RJ-45 connectors and data jacks in more detail.

Figure 4-14 An RJ-45 connector

- *Noise immunity*—Because of its shielding, STP is more noise-resistant than UTP is. On the other hand, UTP may use filtering and balancing techniques to offset the effects of noise.
- *Size and scalability*—The maximum segment length for both STP and UTP is 100 m, or 328 feet. This span is less than that available with coaxial cable because twisted-pair is more susceptible to environmental noise. Twisted-pair can accommodate a maximum of only 1024 nodes per logical segment. Its maximum overall network length depends on the network transmission method used. See the discussion of Ethernet technology in Chapter 5 for more details.

Fiber-Optic Cable

Fiber optic cable, or simply *fiber*, contains one or several glass fibers in its **core**. Data are transmitted via pulsing light sent from a laser or light-emitting diode (LED) through the central fibers. Outside the fibers, a layer of glass called **cladding** acts as a mirror, reflecting light back to the core in patterns that vary depending on the transmission mode. This reflection allows the fiber to bend around corners without diminishing the integrity of the light-based signal. Outside the cladding, a layer of plastic and a braiding of Kevlar (an advanced polymeric fiber) protect the inner core. Finally, a plastic jacket covers the braiding. Figure 4-15 shows the different layers of a fiber-optic cable.

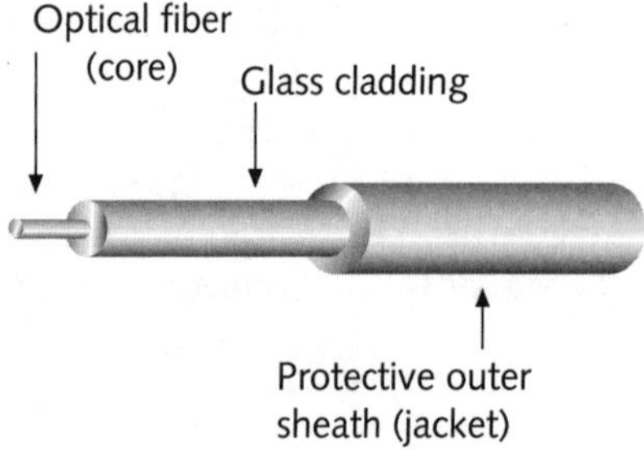

Figure 4-15 A fiber-optic cable

Like twisted-pair cable, fiber comes in a number of different types. Fiber cable variations fall into two categories: single-mode and multimode. **Single-mode fiber** carries a single frequency of light so as to transmit data from one end of the cable to the other end. Data can be transmitted more rapidly and for longer distances on single-mode fiber, but the fiber costs too much to be considered for use on typical data networks. **Multimode fiber**, in contrast, carries several frequencies of light simultaneously over a single fiber or over multiple fibers. This type of fiber-optic system is more typically used by data networks. Figure 4-16 graphically depicts the differences between single-mode and multimode fiber.

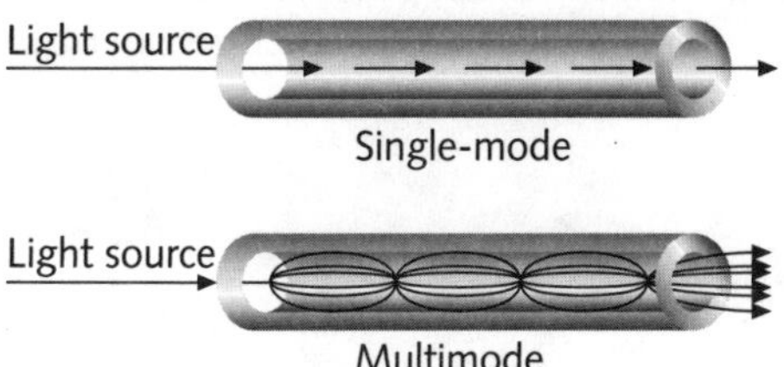

Figure 4-16 Single-mode and multimode fiber-optic cables

On networks, fiber is currently used primarily as a backbone cable. Experts predict, however, that it will replace UTP as the primary means of bringing data to the desktop within the next decade. Fiber-optic cable provides the benefits of nearly unlimited throughput, very high resistance to noise, and excellent security. Because fiber does not conduct electricity like copper wire, it does not emit a current. As a result, the signals it carries stay within the fiber and cannot easily be picked up except at the destination node. Copper, on the other hand, generates a signal that can be monitored by taps into the network. Fiber can also carry signals for longer distances than can coax or twisted-pair cable. Its overall network length benefits from not depending on repeaters or amplifiers. In addition, fiber is widely accepted by the high-speed networking industry.

The most significant drawback to the use of fiber is its high cost. Another disadvantage is that fiber can transmit data in only one direction at a time; to overcome this drawback, each cable must contain two strands—one to send data and one to receive it. Finally, unlike copper wiring, fiber is difficult to splice. Fiber's characteristics are summarized following.

- *Throughput*—Fiber has proved reliable in transmitting data at rates as high as 1 gigabit per second. With further improvements expected, fiber will probably surpass that limit in the future. Fiber's amazing throughput is partly due to the physics of light traveling over glass. Unlike electrical pulses traveling over copper, the light experiences virtually no resistance and therefore can be reliably transmitted at faster rates than electrical pulses. In fact, a pure glass strand can accept up to 1 billion laser light pulses per second. Because of its high cost, however, fiber is currently found almost exclusively on backbone lengths. Nevertheless, its high throughput capability also makes it suitable for applications that generate a great deal of traffic, such as video or audio conferencing.

- *Cost*—Fiber is the most expensive type of cable. The cost of running fiber to every desktop is currently prohibitive; consequently, fiber is typically used only for long-distance transmission or network backbones that must bear extraordinary amounts of traffic. Not only is the cable itself more expensive than metal cabling, but fiber-optic NICs and hubs can cost as much as five times more than NICs and hubs designed for UTP networks. In addition, hiring skilled fiber cable installers costs more than hiring twisted-pair cable installers.
- *Connector*—Fiber cabling may use any of several different types of connectors. Figure 4-17 shows a popular connector type, called an SMA connector. Splicing fiber is a difficult and unforgiving task, so you should purchase fiber cabling with the connectors pre-installed.

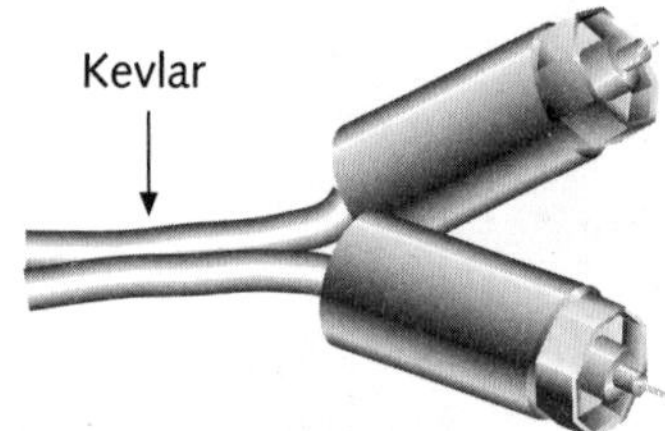

Figure 4-17 An SMA fiber connector

- *Noise immunity*—Fiber is immune to both EMI and RFI. Its impressive noise resistance is one reason why fiber can span such long distances before it requires repeaters to regenerate its signal.
- *Size and scalability*—Network segments made from fiber can span 100 m. Overall network lengths vary depending on the type of fiber-optic cable used. For multimode fiber, TIA/EIA recommends a segment limit of 2 km. For single-mode fiber, the limit is 3 km.

Like twisted-pair and coaxial cabling, fiber-optic cabling comes in a number of different varieties, depending on its intended use and the manufacturer. For example, one type of fiber-optic cabling, the D series, is used for underground conduits to high-volume telecommunications carriers (such as AT&T or MCI). This cable may contain as many as 1000 fibers and be heavily sheathed to prevent damage caused by rodents gnawing on it. At the other end of the spectrum, fiber-optic patch cables for use on LANs may contain only two strands of fiber and be pliable enough to easily bend around corners.

Cable Design and Management

For a long time, organizations took their **cable plant**—the hardware that makes up the enterprise-wide cabling system—for granted. Because increasing traffic demands and business's increasing reliance on networks, however, organizations must now actively manage their physical infrastructure. Proactive cable design and management make moves and expansion smoother and limit productivity losses due to Physical layer problems. Although it doesn't get as much attention as asset management or security concerns, cable management is a significant element of a sound network management strategy.

In 1991, TIA/EIA released their joint 568 Commercial Building Wiring Standard, also known as **structured cabling**, for uniform, enterprise-wide, multivendor cabling systems. Structured cabling suggests how networking media can best be installed to maximize performance and minimize upkeep. It is based on a hierarchical design that divides cabling into six subsystems, described in the following list. You should be familiar with the principles of structured cabling before you attempt to design, install, or troubleshoot an organization's cable plant. Figure 4-18 illustrates how the six subsystems fit together.

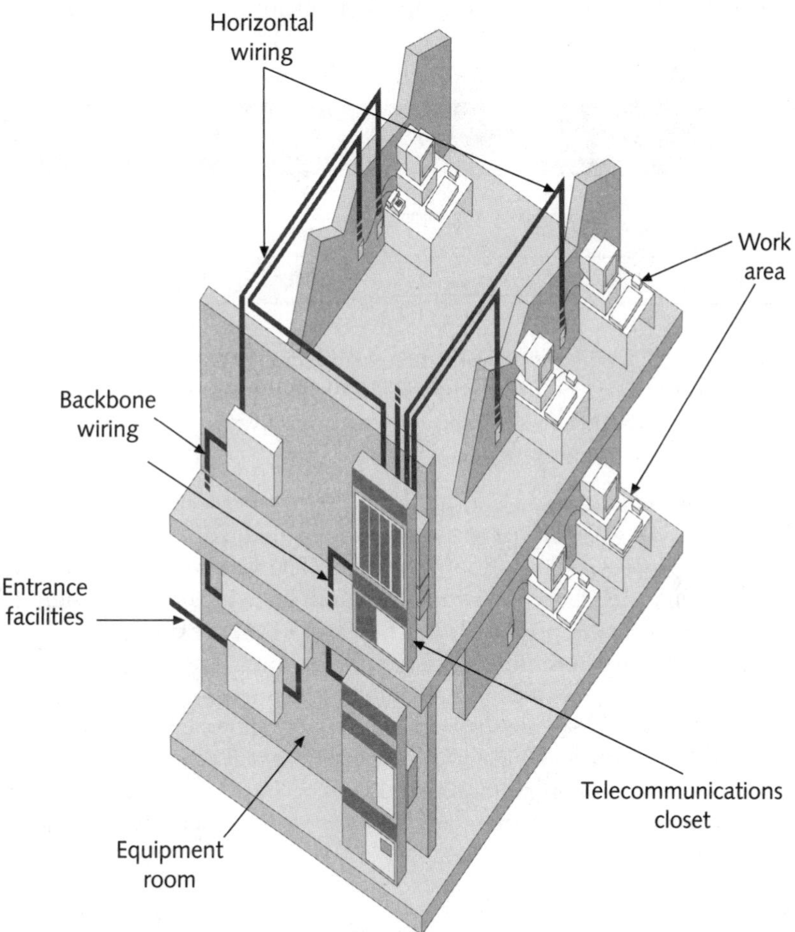

Figure 4-18 TIA/EIA structured cabling subsystems

- *Entrance facilities*—The point at which a building's internal cabling plant begins. The entrance facility separates LANs from WANs and designates where the telecommunications service carrier (whether it's a local phone company, dedicated, or long-distance carrier) accepts responsibility for the (external) wire.
- *Backbone wiring*—A **backbone** is essentially a network of networks. Backbone wiring provides interconnection between telecommunications closets, equipment rooms, and entrance facilities. On a campus-wide network, the backbone includes not only vertical connectors between floors, or **risers**, and cabling between equipment rooms, but also cabling between buildings. You will learn more about backbone topology and design in Chapter 5. The TIA/EIA standard designates distance limitations for backbones of varying cable types, as specified in Table 4-2. On modern networks, backbones are usually composed of fiber-optic or UTP cable. The cross connect is the central connection point for the backbone wiring.

Table 4-2 TIA/EIA Specifications for Backbone Cabling

Cable Type	Cross Connects to Telco Room	Equipment Room to Telco Room	Cross connects to Equipment Room
UTP	800 m (voice specification)	500 m	300 m
Single-mode fiber	3000 m	500 m	1500 m
Multimode fiber	2000 m	500 m	1500 m

- *Equipment room*—The location where significant networking hardware, such as servers and mainframe hosts, resides. Cabling to equipment rooms usually connects telecommunications closets. On a campus-wide network, each building may have its own equipment room.
- *Telecommunications closet*—A "telco room" that contains connectivity for groups of workstations in its area, plus cross connections to equipment rooms. Large organizations may have several telco rooms per floor. Telecommunications closets typically house patch panels, punch-down blocks, hubs or switches, and possibly other connectivity hardware. A **punch-down block** is a panel of data receptors into which horizontal cabling from the workstations is inserted. If used, a **patch panel** is a wall-mounted panel of data receptors into which cross-connect patch cables from the punch-down block are inserted. Figure 4-19 shows examples of a punch-down block and a patch panel. Finally, patch cables connect the patch panel to the hub or switch. Because telecommunications closets are usually small, enclosed spaces, good cooling and ventilation systems are important to maintaining a constant temperature in telco rooms.

Figure 4-19 Patch panel (left) and punch-down block (right)

- *Horizontal wiring*—Wiring that connects workstations to the telecommunications closet in their area. TIA/EIA recognizes three possible cabling types for horizontal wiring: STP, UTP, or fiber-optic. The maximum allowable distance for horizontal wiring is 100 m. This span includes 90 m to connect a data jack on the wall to the telecommunications closet plus a maximum of 10 m to connect a workstation to the data jack on the wall. Figure 4-20 depicts a horizontal wiring configuration.

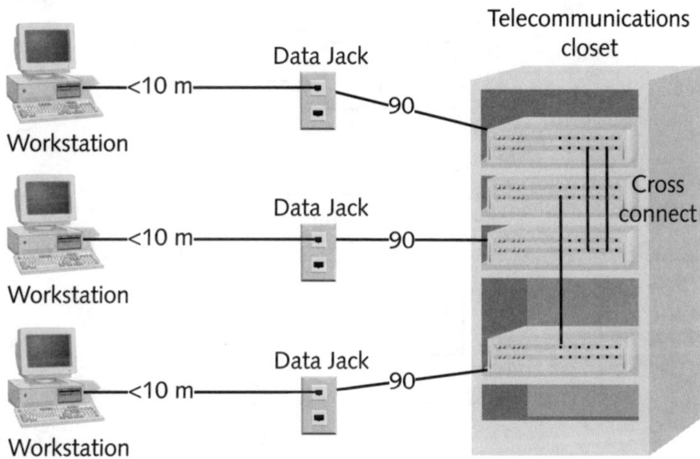

Figure 4-20 Horizontal wiring

- *Work area*—An area that encompasses all patch cables and horizontal wiring necessary to connect workstations, printers, and other network devices from their NICs to the telecommunications closet. A **patch cable** is a relatively short section (usually between 3 and 50 feet long) of twisted-pair cabling with connectors on both ends that connects network devices to data outlets. The TIA/EIA standard calls for each wall jack to contain at least one voice and one data outlet, as pictured in Figure 4-21. Realistically, you will encounter a variety of wall jacks. For example, in a student computer lab lacking phones, a wall jack with a combination of voice and data outlets is unnecessary.

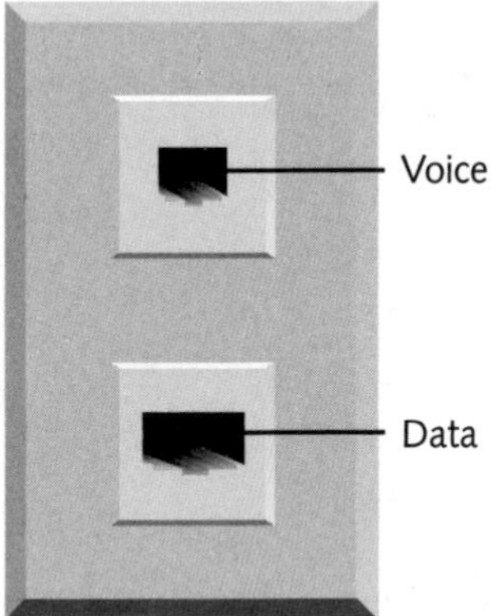

Figure 4-21 A standard TIA/EIA wall jack

Figure 4-22 depicts an example of a possible structured cabling hierarchy. The TIA/EIA standard dictates that a single hierarchy contain no more than two levels of cross-connection wiring.

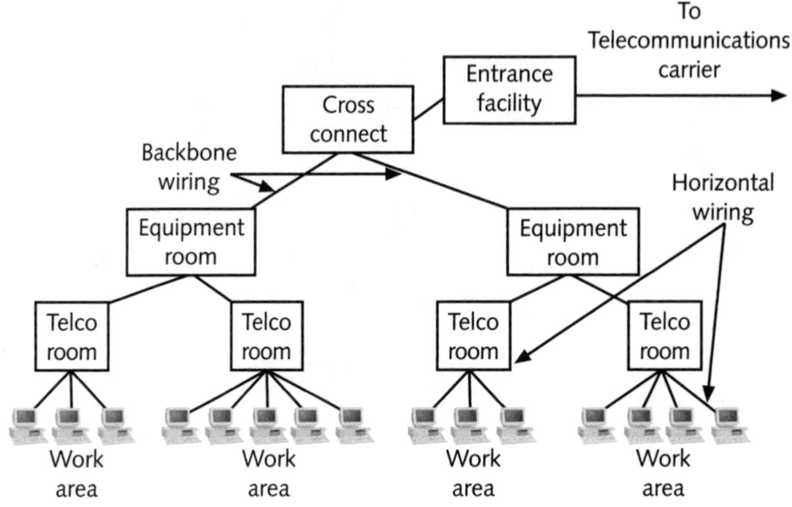

Figure 4-22 A structured cabling hierarchy

Adhering to standard cabling hierarchies is only part of a smart cable management strategy. You or your network manager should also specify standards for the types of cable used by your organization and maintain a list of approved cabling vendors. Keep a supply room stocked with spare parts so that you can easily and quickly replace defective parts.

Create documentation for your cabling plant, including the locations, lengths, and grades of installed cable. Label every data jack, punch-down block, and connector. Use color-coded cables for different purposes (cables can be purchased in a variety of sheath colors). For example, you might want to use pink for patch cables, green for horizontal wiring, and gray for vertical (backbone) wiring. Keep your documentation in a centrally accessible location and be certain to update it as you change the network. The more you document, the easier it will be to move or add cable segments.

Finally, plan for how your cabling plant will lend itself to growth. For example, if your organization is rapidly expanding, consider replacing your backbone with fiber and leave plenty of space in your telecommunications closets for more racks.

As you will most likely work with twisted-pair cable, the next section explains how to install this type of cabling from the server to the desktop.

INSTALLING CABLE

So far, you have read about the variety of cables used in networking and the limitations inherent in each. You may worry that with hundreds of varieties of cable, choosing the correct one and making it work with your network is next to impossible. The good news is that if you follow both the manufacturers' installation guidelines and the TIA/EIA standards, you are almost guaranteed success. Many network problems can be traced to poor cable installation techniques. For example, if an installer does not crimp twisted-pair wires in the correct position in an RJ-45 connector, the cable will fail to transmit or receive data (or both—in which case, the cable will not function at all). Installing the wrong grade of cable can either cause your network to fail or render it more susceptible to damage (for example, using typical, inexpensive twisted-pair cable in areas that might be susceptible to fire damage).

With networks moving to faster transmission speeds, adhering to installation guidelines is a more critical concern than ever. A Category 5 UTP segment that flawlessly transmits data at 10 Mbps may suffer data loss when pushed to 100 Mbps. In addition, some cable manufacturers will not honor warranties if their cables were improperly installed. This section outlines the most common method of installing UTP cable and points out cabling mistakes that can lead to network instability.

In the previous section, you learned about the six subsystems of the TIA/EIA structured cabling standard. A typical UTP network uses a modular setup to distinguish between cables at each subsystem. Figure 4-23 provides an overview of a modular cabling installation.

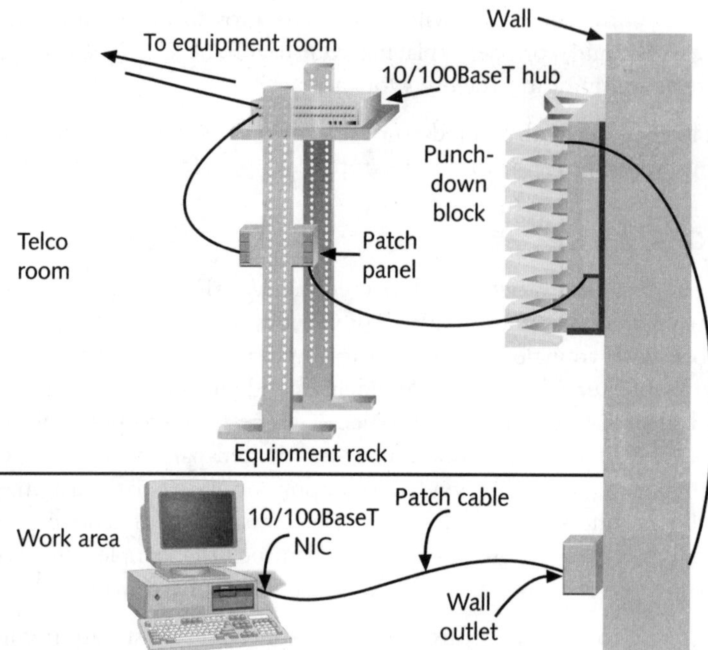

Figure 4-23 A typical UTP cabling installation

In this example, patch cables connect network devices (such as a workstation) to the wall jacks. Longer cables connect wire from the wall jack to a punch-down block in the telecommunications closet. From the punch-down block, patch cables bring the connection into a patch panel. From the patch panel, more patch cables connect to the hub or switch, which in turn connects to the equipment room or to the backbone, depending on the scale of the network. All of these sections of cable make network moves and additions easier. Believe it or not, they also keep the telecommunications closet organized.

Although you will probably never have to make your own patch cables, you may have to repair one in a pinch. Table 4-3 explains how the pins in an RJ-45 connector correspond to the wires in a UTP cable. This method of UTP coding follows the TIA/EIA wiring standard. Two different (but similar) coding schemes have been established by AT&T and IEEE, and it typically doesn't matter which scheme you choose. Nevertheless, you should ensure that you cable all wiring on your LAN according to one standard, to avoid confusion and potential transmission errors. In Project 4-2 at the end of this chapter, you will have the opportunity to create your own patch cable following these guidelines. Be advised, however, that any imperfection in how you fasten the wires in the connector will prevent the cable from working.

Table 4-3 Pin Numbers and Color Codes for an RJ-45 Connector

Pin Number	Use	Color
1	Transmit +	White and green
2	Transmit –	Green
3	Receive +	White and orange
4	Not used	Blue
5	Not used	White and blue
6	Receive –	Orange
7	Not used	White and brown
8	Not used	Brown

The art of proper cabling could fill an entire book. If you plan to specialize in cable installation, design, or maintenance, you should invest in a reference dedicated to this topic. As a network professional, you will likely occasionally add new cables to a room or telecommunications closet, repair defective cable ends, or install a data outlet. Following are some cable installation tips that will help prevent Physical layer failures:

- Do not untwist twisted-pair cables more than one-half inch before inserting them into the punch-down block.
- Do not strip off more than 1 inch of insulation from the copper wire in twisted-pair cables.
- Pay attention to the bend radius limitations for the type of cable you are installing. **Bend radius** is the radius of the maximum arc into which you can loop a cable before you will impair data transmission. Generally, a cable's bend radius is less than four times the diameter of the cable. Be careful not to exceed it.
- Test each segment of cabling as you install it with a cable tester. This practice will prevent you from later having to track down errors in multiple, long stretches of cable. You will have the opportunity to use a cable tester in the Hands-on Projects at the end of this chapter.
- Use only cable ties to cinch groups of cables together. In addition, do not cinch cables so tightly that you squeeze their outer covering. This practice will undoubtedly lead to difficult-to-diagnose data errors.
- Avoid laying cable across the floor where it might sustain damage from rolling chairs or foot traffic. If you must take this tack, cover the cable with a cable protector.
- Install cable at least 3 feet away from fluorescent lights or other sources of EMI.
- Always leave slack in cable runs. Stringing cable too tightly risks connectivity and data transmission problems.

- If you run cable in the **plenum**, the area above the ceiling tile or below the subflooring, make sure the cable sheath is plenum-rated. A plenum-rated cable is more fire-resistant than other cables.
- Pay attention to grounding requirements and follow them religiously.

Do not lay cable where animals or children can access it. Cases of squirrels or rabbits chewing through UTP are more common than you might think.

ATMOSPHERIC TRANSMISSION MEDIA

The atmosphere provides an intangible means of transporting data over networks. For decades, radio and TV stations have used the atmosphere to transport information via analog signals. The atmosphere is also capable of carrying digital signals. Networks that transmit signals through the atmosphere are known as **wireless** networks. Wireless LANs typically use infrared or radio frequency (RF) signaling. These transmission media are suited to very specialized network environments. For example, inventory control personnel who drive through large warehouses to record inventory data benefit from the mobility of wireless networking. In addition to infrared and RF transmission, microwave and satellite links can be used to transport data through the atmosphere. These methods, which can span longer distances, apply to WAN communications and are discussed in detail in Chapter 7.

INFRARED TRANSMISSION

Infrared networks use infrared light signals to transmit data through space, not unlike the way a television remote control sends signals across the room. Networks may use two types of infrared transmission: direct or indirect.

Direct infrared transmission depends on the transmitter and receiver remaining within the line of sight of each other. Just as you cannot switch TV channels with your remote control from behind a wall, so you cannot transmit data through direct infrared between two computers that don't have a clear atmospheric path between them. This "line of sight" limitation prevents widespread use of direct infrared in modern networking environments. On the other hand, the same requirement makes direct infrared more secure than many other transmission methods. When signals are limited to a specific pathway, they become difficult to intercept.

Currently, direct infrared transmission is most often used for communications between devices in the same room. For example, wireless printer connections use direct infrared transmission, as do some synchronizing features of palmtop PCs. Infrared ports are almost standard on business desktop PCs.

In **indirect infrared transmission**, signals bounce off walls, ceilings, and any other objects in their path. Because indirect infrared signals are not confined to a specific pathway, this means of transmitting data is not very secure.

Infrared pathways can carry data at rates that rival fiber-optic cable's throughput. Infrared has been proven to function at 100 Mbps, but could probably carry even more traffic. It can span distances up to 1000 m, which is nearly as far as multimode fiber.

RF TRANSMISSION

Radio frequency (RF) transmission relies on signals broadcast over specific frequencies, in the same manner as radio and TV broadcasts. At certain frequencies, RF can penetrate walls, making it the best wireless solution for networks that must transmit data through or around walls, ceilings, and other obstacles. This same characteristic permits easy interception of most types of RF transmissions. Therefore, RF should not be used in environments where data security is important.

In addition, RF is very susceptible to interference and therefore would not be a good medium for EMI-saturated locations such as factory floors. Because RF signals can easily interfere with each other, frequencies must be licensed from the Federal Communications Commission (FCC). Neither the frequency nor the geographic location where the frequency is transmitted can be altered without violating the terms of the license. Makers of RF computer and networking components must therefore obtain licenses for specific frequencies in different geographic locations. The licensing procedure ensures that nearby systems will not operate at the same frequencies and interfere with each other's signals.

The two most common RF technologies are **narrowband**, which concentrates significant RF energy at a single frequency, and **spread spectrum**, which uses a lower-level signal distributed over several frequencies simultaneously. Although narrowband RF can be easily intercepted and is therefore not suited for sensitive data transfer, spread spectrum RF is quite secure. Both types of RF offer a moderate throughput, ranging as high as 10 Mbps.

The U.S. Navy uses spread spectrum RF networking in a most intriguing way. Its ships travel in groups and communicate with each other across the water using RF and satellite network links. Because their transmissions must remain secure, they use spread spectrum RF rather than narrowband RF.

CHOOSING THE RIGHT TRANSMISSION MEDIUM

Now that you have read about the characteristics, benefits, and disadvantages to all types of network transmission media, you need to consider how to evaluate them in terms of realistic network environments. The following list summarizes the majority of environmental factors you must take into account and suggests appropriate transmission media for the various conditions. Most environments will contain a combination of these factors; you must therefore weigh the significance of each against the cost of your optimal solution.

- *Areas of high EMI or RFI*—If the environment houses a number of electrical power sources, you will want to use the most noise-resistant medium possible. Thick Ethernet and fiber-optic cable are the most noise-resistant media currently available.

- *Corners and small spaces*—If the environment requires that cable bend around tight corners or through small spaces, you should use the most flexible medium possible. STP and UTP are both very flexible.
- *Distance*—If the environment requires long stretches of transmission, you might want to consider fiber-optic or wireless media. You can use twisted-pair and coaxial media, but they are more susceptible to attenuation and interference and will require the use of repeaters.
- *Security*—If your organization is concerned about wire taps, you will want to choose the transmission media with the highest security. Fiber-optic and direct infrared media are both excellent choices for this environment.
- *Existing infrastructure*—If you are adding cable to an existing cable plant, you will need to consider how it will interact with existing cabling and connectivity hardware. The media you choose should be tailored to your organization's previously installed equipment.
- *Growth*—Find out how your organization plans to expand its network and consider future applications, traffic, and geographic expansion when designing its cable plant. In this instance, the medium you choose should be tailored to your organization's needs.

CHAPTER SUMMARY

- Information can be transmitted via two methods: analog or digital. Analog signals are continuous waves that result in variable and inexact transmission. Digital signals are based on electrical or light pulses that represent information encoded in binary form.
- Noise is interference that distorts an analog or digital signal. It may be caused by electrical sources, such as power lines, fluorescent lights, copiers, and microwave ovens, or by broadcast signals.
- Analog and digital signals both suffer attenuation, or loss of signal as they travel farther from their sources. To compensate, analog signals are amplified and digital signals are regenerated through repeaters. Digital signals can be regenerated without any noise they might have accumulated; analog signals, on the other hand, are amplified along with the accompanying noise.
- Throughput is the amount of data that the medium can transmit during a given period of time. Throughput is usually measured in megabits (1,000,000 bits) per second, or Mbps. The physical nature of every transmission media determines its potential throughput.
- The costs of different transmission media vary depending on many factors. When considering cost, you must calculate not only the cost of the physical medium, but also the cost of installation, connectivity hardware, maintenance, obsolescence, and productivity gained or lost as a result of a medium's capacity.

- Three specifications dictate the size and scalability of networking media: maximum nodes per segment, maximum segment length, and maximum network length. In cabling, each of these specifications is determined by a physical characteristic of the wire.
- The length of a network segment is limited because of attenuation. After a certain distance, a signal loses so much strength that it cannot be accurately interpreted. Before this deterioration occurs, a repeater on the network must retransmit and amplify the signal. The maximum distance that a signal can travel and still be accurately interpreted equals the maximum segment length.
- Every network is susceptible to a delay between the transmission of a signal and its receipt. This delay is called latency. The length of the cable contributes to latency, as does the presence of any intervening connectivity device, such as a router.
- Connectors are the pieces of hardware that connect the wire to the network device, be it a file server, workstation, switch, or printer. Every networking medium requires a specific kind of connector.
- You will typically work with various types of cabling as transmission media, rather than atmospheric media. Cabling transmits data by conducting electromagnetic waves over a metal wire.
- Coaxial cable consists of a central copper core surrounded by a ceramic or plastic insulator, a braided metal shielding called braiding, and an outer plastic cover called the sheath. The copper core carries the electromagnetic signal, and the braiding acts as both a shield against noise and a ground for the signal. The insulator layer protects the copper core from the metal shielding. The sheath protects the cable from physical damage.
- Baseband is a form of transmission in which digital signals are sent through direct current pulses applied to the wire. This direct current requires exclusive use of the wire's capacity, so baseband systems can transmit only one signal, or one channel, at a time. Broadband, on the other hand, uses modulated analog frequencies to transmit multiple signals over the same wire.
- Thicknet cabling, also called thickwire Ethernet, is a rigid coaxial cable approximately 1 cm thick that was used for the original Ethernet networks. IEEE has designated Thicknet as 10Base5 Ethernet. The "10" represents its throughput of 10Mbps, the "Base" stands for baseband transmission, and the "5" represents the maximum segment length of a Thicknet cable, 500 m.
- Thinnet, also known as Thin Ethernet, was the most popular medium for Ethernet LANs in the 1980s, but is rarely used on modern networks. IEEE has designated Thinnet as 10Base2 Ethernet. The "10" represents its data transmission rate of 10 Mbps, "Base" represents the fact that it uses baseband transmission, and the "2" represents its maximum segment length of 185 m (roughly 200 m). Thinnet is easier to handle and install than Thicknet, but provides less resistance to noise.
- Both Thicknet and Thinnet coaxial cable rely on the bus topology and must be terminated at both ends with a resistor to prevent signal bounce. Thicknet and Thinnet cable must also be grounded at one end.

- Twisted-pair cable consists of color-coded pairs of insulated copper wires, each with a diameter of 0.4 to 0.8 mm, twisted around each other and encased in plastic coating. One wire in the wire pair carries signal information, and the second wire in the pair is grounded and absorbs interference. The twists in the wire help to reduce the effects of crosstalk.
- The more twists per inch in a pair of wires, the more resistant the cable will be to all forms of noise. Higher-quality, more expensive twisted-pair cable contains more twists per foot. The number of twists per meter or foot is known as the twist ratio.
- Shielded twisted-pair (STP) cable consists of twisted wire pairs that are not only individually insulated, but also surrounded by a shielding made of a metallic substance such as foil. The shielding acts as an antenna, converting the noise into current. This current induces an equal, yet opposite current in the twisted pairs it surrounds. The noise on the shielding mirrors the noise on the twisted pairs, and the two cancel each other out.
- Unshielded twisted-pair (UTP) cabling consists of one or more insulated wire pairs encased in a plastic sheath. As its name suggests, UTP does not contain additional shielding for the twisted pairs. As a result, UTP is both less expensive and less resistant to noise than STP.
- UTP comes in a variety of specifications, including CAT1 through CAT6, as specified by the TIA/EIA 568 standard. You will probably encounter CAT3 or CAT5 on contemporary LANs.
- CAT3 is a form of UTP that contains four wire pairs and can carry data at a rate as high as 10 Mbps with a possible bandwidth of 16 MHz. CAT3 has typically been used for 10 Mbps Ethernet or 4 Mbps Token Ring networks. Network administrators are gradually replacing CAT3 cabling with CAT5 to accommodate higher throughput, even though CAT3 is less expensive than CAT5.
- CAT5 is the most popular form of UTP for new network installations and upgrades to Fast Ethernet. It contains four wire pairs and supports up to 100 Mbps throughput and a 100 MHz signal rate. In addition to 100 Mbps Ethernet, CAT5 wiring can support other fast networking technologies, such as Asynchronous Transfer Mode.
- The maximum segment length for both STP and UTP is 100 m, or 328 feet. This distance is less than coaxial cable, because twisted-pair cable is more susceptible to environmental noise. Twisted-pair cable can accommodate a maximum of only 1024 nodes per logical segment. Its maximum overall network length depends on the network transmission method used.
- Fiber-optic cable contains one or several glass fibers in its core. Data are transmitted via pulsing light sent from a laser or light-emitting diode through the central fiber(s). Outside the fiber(s), a layer of glass called cladding acts as a mirror, reflecting light back to the core in different patterns that vary depending on the transmission mode. Outside the cladding, a layer of plastic and a braiding of Kevlar protect the inner core. A plastic jacket covers the braiding.

- Fiber cable variations fall into two categories: single-mode and multimode. Single-mode fiber carries a single frequency of light to transmit data from one end of the cable to the other end. Data can be transmitted more rapidly and for longer distances on single-mode fiber, but this type of fiber costs too much to be considered for use on data networks. Multimode fiber carries several frequencies of light simultaneously over a single fiber or over multiple fibers.
- On today's networks, fiber is used primarily as a backbone cable. Experts predict that, within the next decade, it will replace UTP as the primary means of bringing data to the desktop. Fiber-optic cable provides the benefits of nearly unlimited throughput, very high resistance to noise, and excellent security.
- In 1991, TIA/EIA released their joint 568 Commercial Building Wiring Standard, also known as structured cabling, for uniform, enterprise-wide, multivendor cabling systems. Structured cabling suggests how cabling can best be installed to maximize performance and minimize upkeep. It is based on a hierarchical design that divides cabling into six subsystems: entrance facility, backbone (vertical) wiring, equipment room, telecommunications closet, horizontal wiring, and work area.
- You can take several measures to better manage your organization's cable plant. For example, you should record the types, locations, and lengths of major cabling. You should also keep a list of preferred vendors for cable, keep plenty of spare patch cables and RJ-45 connectors on hand, label every connector and outlet, and plan for growth.
- The best practice for installing cable is to follow the TIA/EIA 568 specifications and manufacturer's recommendations. Be careful not to exceed a cable's bend radius, untwist wire pairs more than one-half inch, or remove more than 1 inch of insulation from copper wire. Install plenum-rated cable in ceilings and floors, and run cabling far from where it might suffer physical damage.
- Wireless LANs can use either radio frequency (RF) or infrared transmission. Wireless transmission is typically used in very specialized applications, often to facilitate mobile computing.
- Infrared transmission comes in two main flavors: indirect infrared and direct infrared. Indirect infrared signals bounce off ceilings, walls, and any other obstacles between the sender and receiver. Direct infrared signals require that the sender and receiver establish an unobstructed path through the air.
- RF transmission also comes in two flavors: narrowband and spread spectrum. Narrowband RF uses a single frequency and can be easily intercepted and decoded. Spread spectrum RF distributes the signals over several frequencies and is difficult to intercept.
- To determine what transmission media is right for a particular networking environment, you must consider the organization's required throughput, cabling distance, noise resistance, security, flexibility, and plans for growth.

Key Terms

- **10Base2** — see *Thinnet.*
- **10Base5** — see *Thicknet.*
- **alien crosstalk** — A type of interference that occurs when signals from adjacent cables interfere with another cable's transmission.
- **amplitude** — A measure of a signal's strength.
- **analog** — A signal that uses variable voltage to create continuous waves, resulting in an inexact transmission.
- **attenuate** — To lose signal strength as a transmission travels farther away from its source.
- **attenuation** — The amount of signal loss over a given distance.
- **backbone** — A network of networks. Backbone wiring provides interconnection between telecommunications closets, equipment rooms, and entrance facilities.
- **bandwidth** — A measure of the difference between the highest and lowest frequencies that a media can transmit.
- **baseband** — A form of transmission in which digital signals are sent through direct current pulses applied to the wire. This direct current requires exclusive use of the wire's capacity, so baseband systems can transmit only one signal, or one channel, at a time. Every device on a baseband system shares a single channel.
- **bend radius** — The radius of the maximum arc into which you can loop a cable before you will cause data transmission errors. Generally, a cable's bend radius is less than four times the diameter of the cable.
- **binary** — A system founded on using 1s and 0s to encode information.
- **bit** — Short for binary digit. A bit equals a single pulse in the digital encoding system. It may have only one of two values: 0 or 1.
- **braiding** — A braided metal shielding used to insulate some types of coaxial cable.
- **broadband** — A form of transmission in which signals are modulated as radio frequency analog pulses that use different frequency ranges. Unlike baseband, broadband technology does not use binary encoding. The use of multiple frequencies enables a broadband system to use several channels and therefore carry much more data than a baseband system.
- **byte** — Eight bits of information. In a digital signaling system, one byte carries one piece of information.
- **cable plant** — The hardware that constitutes the enterprise-wide cabling system.
- **capacity** — see *throughput.*

- **Category 1 (CAT1)** — A form of UTP that contains two wire pairs. CAT1 is suitable for voice communications, but not for data. At most, it can carry only 20 Kbps of data.
- **Category 2 (CAT2)** — A form of UTP that contains four wire pairs and can carry up to 4 Mbps of data. CAT2 is rarely found on modern networks, because most require higher throughput.
- **Category 3 (CAT3)** — A form of UTP that contains four wire pairs and can carry up to 10 Mbps with a possible bandwidth of 16MHz. CAT3 has typically been used for 10 Mbps Ethernet or 4 Mbps Token Ring networks. Network administrators are gradually replacing CAT3 cabling with CAT5 to accommodate higher throughput. CAT3 is less expensive than CAT5.
- **Category 4 (CAT4)** — A form of UTP that contains four wire pairs and can support up to 16 Mbps throughput. CAT4 may be used for 16 Mbps Token Ring or 10 Mbps Ethernet networks. It is guaranteed for data transmission up to 20 MHz and provides more protection against crosstalk and attenuation than CAT1, CAT2, or CAT3.
- **Category 5 (CAT5)** — The most popular form of UTP for new network installations and upgrades to Fast Ethernet. CAT5 contains four wire pairs and supports up to 100 Mbps throughput and a 100 MHz signal rate. In addition to 100 Mbps Ethernet, CAT5 wiring can support other fast networking technologies, such as Asynchronous Transfer Mode (ATM) and Fiber Distributed Data Interface (FDDI).
- **Category 6 (CAT6)** — A twisted-pair cable that contains four wire pairs, each wrapped in foil insulation. Additional foil insulation covers the bundle of wire pairs, and a fire-resistant plastic sheath covers the second foil layer. The foil insulation provides excellent resistance to crosstalk and enables CAT6 to support at least six times the throughput supported by regular CAT5.
- **cladding** — The glass shield around the fiber core of a fiber-optic cable. Cladding acts as a mirror, reflecting light back to the core in patterns that vary depending on the transmission mode. This reflection allows fiber to bend around corners without losing the integrity of the light-based signal.
- **coaxial cable** — A type of cable that consists of a central copper core surrounded by an insulator, a braided metal shielding, called braiding, and an outer cover, called the sheath or jacket. Coaxial cable, called "coax" for short, was the foundation for Ethernet networks in the 1980s and remained a popular transmission medium for many years.
- **conduit** — Pipeline used to contain and protect the cabling. Conduit is usually made from metal.
- **connectors** — The pieces of hardware that connect the wire to the network device, be it a file server, workstation, switch, or printer.
- **core** — The central component of a fiber-optic cable that consists of one or several pure glass fibers.
- **crosstalk** — A type of interference caused by signals traveling on nearby wire pairs infringing on another pair's signal.

- **digital** — As opposed to analog signals, digital signals are composed of pulses that can have a value of only 1 or 0.
- **direct infrared transmission** — A type of infrared transmission that depends on the transmitter and receiver being within the line of sight of each other.
- **electromagnetic interference (EMI)** — A type of interference that may be caused by motors, power lines, televisions, copiers, fluorescent lights, or other sources of electrical activity.
- **enhanced CAT5** — A higher-grade version of CAT5 wiring that contains high-quality copper, offers a high twist ratio, and uses advanced methods for reducing crosstalk. Enhanced CAT5 can support a signaling rate of up to 200 MHz, double the capability of regular CAT5.
- **fiber-optic cable** — A form of cable that contains one or several glass fibers in its core. Data are transmitted via pulsing light sent from a laser or light-emitting diode through the central fiber(s). Outside the fiber(s), a layer of glass called cladding acts as a mirror, reflecting light back to the core in patterns that vary depending on the transmission mode. Outside the cladding, a layer of plastic and a braiding of Kevlar protect the inner core. A plastic jacket covers the braiding
- **frequency** — The number of times that a signal's amplitude changes over a fixed period of time, expressed in cycles per second, or Hertz (Hz).
- **Hertz (Hz)** — A measure of frequency equivalent to the number of amplitude cycles per second.
- **indirect infrared transmission** — A type of infrared transmission in which signals bounce off walls, ceilings, and any other objects in their path. Because indirect infrared signals are not confined to a specific pathway, this means of transmitting data is not very secure.
- **infrared** — A type of data transmission that uses infrared light signals to transmit data through space, similar to the way a television remote control sends signals across the room. Networks may use two types of infrared transmission: direct or indirect.
- **latency** — The delay between the transmission of a signal and its receipt.
- **modem** — A device that modulates analog signals into digital signals at the transmitting end for transmission over telephone lines, and demodulates digital signals into analog signals at the receiving end.
- **multimode fiber** — A type of fiber-optic cable that carries several frequencies of light simultaneously over a single fiber or over multiple fibers. It is the type of fiber-optic system typically used by data networks. Multimode fiber is less expensive than single-mode fiber.
- **narrowband** — A type of radio frequency transmission in which signals travel over a single frequency. The same method is used by radio and TV broadcasting stations, and signals can be easily intercepted and decoded.

- **noise** — Unwanted signals, or interference, from sources near network cabling, such as electrical motors, power lines and radar.
- **patch cable** — A relatively short section (usually between 3 and 50 feet) of twisted-pair cabling with connectors on both ends that connects network devices to data outlets.
- **patch panel** — A wall-mounted panel of data receptors into which cross-connect patch cables from the punch-down block are inserted.
- **plenum** — The area above the ceiling tile or below the subfloor in a building.
- **punch-down block** — A panel of data receptors into which horizontal cabling from the workstations is inserted.
- **radio frequency (RF)** — A type of transmission that relies on signals broadcast over specific frequencies, in the same manner as radio and TV broadcasts. RF may use narrowband or spread spectrum technology.
- **radio frequency interference (RFI)** — A kind of interference that may be generated by motors, power lines, televisions, copiers, fluorescent lights, or broadcast signals from radio or TV towers.
- **regeneration** — The process of retransmitting a digital signal. Regeneration, unlike amplification, repeats the pure signal, with none of the noise it has accumulated.
- **repeater** — A device used to regenerate a signal.
- **risers** — The backbone cabling that provides vertical connections between floors of a building.
- **sheath** — The outer cover, or jacket, of a cable.
- **shielded twisted-pair (STP)** — A type of cable containing twisted wire pairs that are not only individually insulated, but also surrounded by a shielding made of a metallic substance such as foil. The shielding acts as an antenna, converting the noise into current (assuming that the wire is properly grounded). This current induces an equal, yet opposite current in the twisted pairs it surrounds. The noise on the shielding mirrors the noise on the twisted pairs, and the two cancel each other out.
- **signal bounce** — A phenomenon caused by improper termination on a bus network in which signals travel endlessly between the two ends of the network, preventing new signals from getting through.
- **single-mode fiber** — A type of fiber-optic cable that carries a single frequency of light to transmit data from one end of the cable to the other end. Data can be transmitted faster and for longer distances on single-mode fiber than on multimode fiber. Single-mode fiber is extremely expensive.
- **spread spectrum** — A type of radio frequency transmission that uses lower-level signals distributed over several frequencies simultaneously. Spread spectrum RF is more secure than narrowband RF.
- **structured cabling** — A method for uniform, enterprise-wide, multivendor cabling systems specified by the TIA/EIA 568 Commercial Building Wiring Standard. Structured cabling is based on a hierarchical design using a high-speed backbone.

- **Thicknet** — A type of coaxial cable, also known as thickwire Ethernet, that is a rigid cable approximately 1 cm thick. Thicknet was used for the original Ethernet networks. Because it is often covered with a yellow sheath, Thicknet is also called "yellow Ethernet." IEEE has designated Thicknet as 10Base5 Ethernet, with the "10" representing its throughput of 10 Mbps, the "Base" standing for baseband transmission, and the "5" representing the maximum segment length of a Thicknet cable, 500 m.
- **Thinnet** — A type of coaxial cable, also known as Thin Ethernet, that was the most popular medium for Ethernet LANs in the 1980s. Like Thicknet, Thinnet is rarely used on modern networks. IEEE has designated Thinnet as 10Base2 Ethernet, with the "10" representing its data transmission rate of 10 Mbps, the "Base" representing the fact that it uses baseband transmission, and the "2" roughly representing its maximum segment length of 185 m.
- **throughput** — The amount of data that a medium can transmit during a given period of time. Throughput is usually measured in megabits (1,000,000 bits) per second, or Mbps. The physical nature of every transmission media determines its potential throughput.
- **twist ratio** — The number of twists per meter or foot in a twisted-pair cable.
- **twisted-pair (TP)** — A type of cable similar to telephone wiring that consists of color-coded pairs of insulated copper wires, each with a diameter of 0.4 to 0.8 mm, twisted around each other and encased in plastic coating.
- **unshielded twisted-pair (UTP)** — A type of cabling that consists of one or more insulated wire pairs encased in a plastic sheath. As its name implies, UTP does not contain additional shielding for the twisted pairs. As a result, UTP is both less expensive and less resistant to noise than STP.
- **wireless** — Networks that transmit signals through the atmosphere via infrared or RF signaling.

Review Questions

1. When they become faint, analog signals are regenerated while digital signals are amplified. True or False?
2. What is the origin of the word "modem?"
   a. modifier/demodifier
   b. modulator/demodulator
   c. modulator/decoder
   d. moderator/demoderator

3. How does the number of devices attached to a network affect attenuation?
   a. The fewer devices on a network, the more attenuation.
   b. The more devices on a network, the less the attenuation.
   c. The more devices on a network, the more the attenuation.
   d. Both a and b.

4. How does noise affect a digital signal?
   a. Noise enhances a digital signal.
   b. Noise weakens a digital signal.
   c. Noise increases the frequency of a digital signal.
   d. Noise distorts the signal.
5. How does noise on a wire affect throughput?
   a. The more noise, the lower the throughput.
   b. The less noise, the lower the throughput.
   c. Noise does not affect throughput.
   d. Noise impairs throughput only at high frequencies.
6. Which of the following would not be a source of EMI?
   a. fluorescent lighting
   b. a microwave
   c. a loud gong
   d. a cord that carries electricity to a printer
7. When determining the cost of a cabling system, what—besides the cost of the wire—must you bear in mind?
8. What is the term that refers to the outer covering of a cable?
   a. cladding
   b. insulation
   c. sheath
   d. braiding
9. Which of the following would not contribute to latency on a network?
   a. a NIC in a PC
   b. CAT5 wiring
   c. a router
   d. a patch cable that is too short

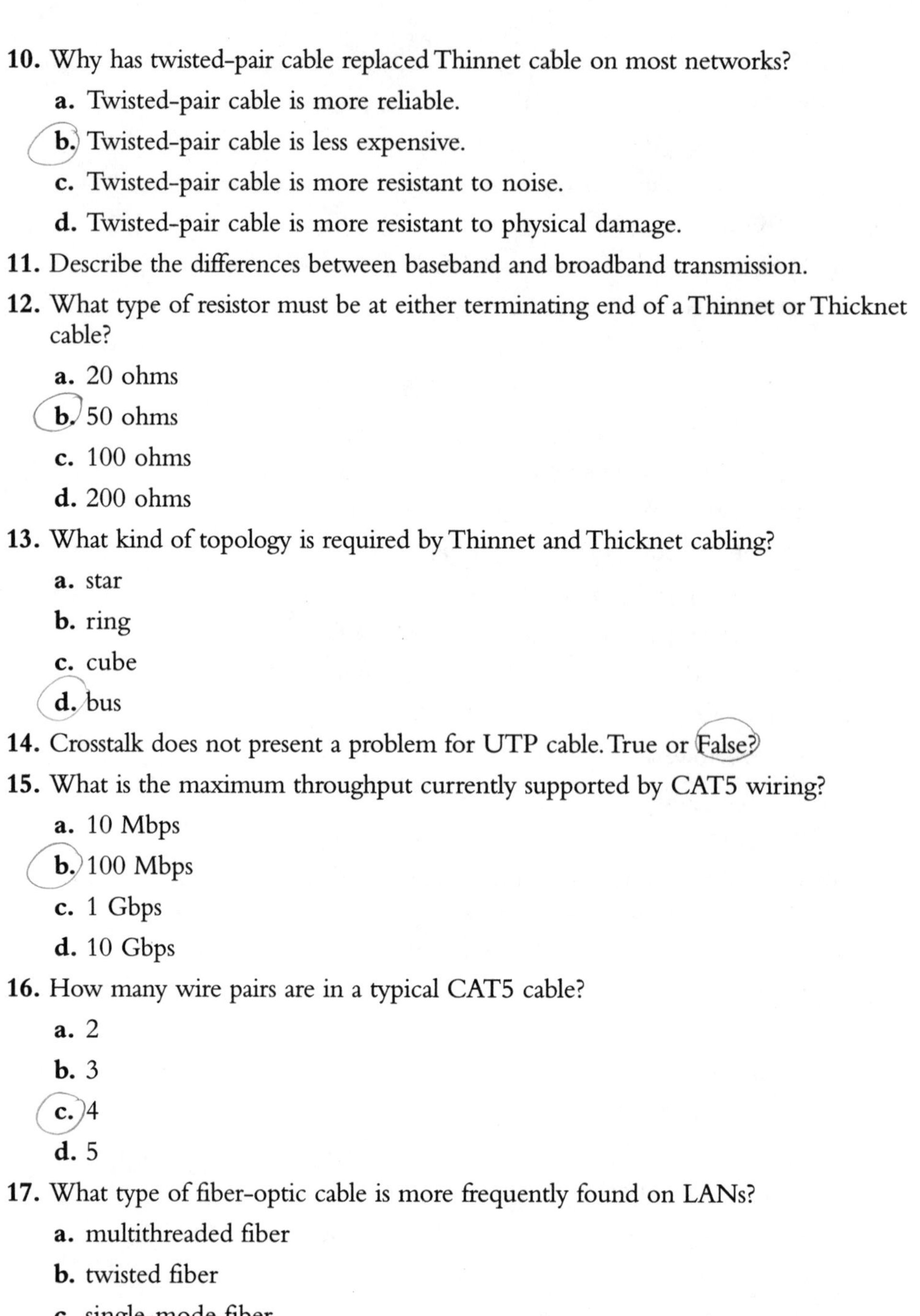

10. Why has twisted-pair cable replaced Thinnet cable on most networks?
    - a. Twisted-pair cable is more reliable.
    - b. Twisted-pair cable is less expensive.
    - c. Twisted-pair cable is more resistant to noise.
    - d. Twisted-pair cable is more resistant to physical damage.
11. Describe the differences between baseband and broadband transmission.
12. What type of resistor must be at either terminating end of a Thinnet or Thicknet cable?
    - a. 20 ohms
    - b. 50 ohms
    - c. 100 ohms
    - d. 200 ohms
13. What kind of topology is required by Thinnet and Thicknet cabling?
    - a. star
    - b. ring
    - c. cube
    - d. bus
14. Crosstalk does not present a problem for UTP cable. True or False?
15. What is the maximum throughput currently supported by CAT5 wiring?
    - a. 10 Mbps
    - b. 100 Mbps
    - c. 1 Gbps
    - d. 10 Gbps
16. How many wire pairs are in a typical CAT5 cable?
    - a. 2
    - b. 3
    - c. 4
    - d. 5
17. What type of fiber-optic cable is more frequently found on LANs?
    - a. multithreaded fiber
    - b. twisted fiber
    - c. single-mode fiber
    - d. multimode fiber

18. Why is fiber-optic cable more secure than copper-based wiring?
    a. It does not carry current and is therefore more difficult to tap.
    b. It is more difficult to cut.
    c. It can withstand higher pressure.
    d. It does not service multiple transmissions simultaneously.

19. Which of the following is a drawback to using fiber-optic cable for LANs?
    a. It is expensive.
    b. It cannot handle high bandwidth transmissions.
    c. It can carry transmissions using only the TCP/IP protocol.
    d. It is a poorly understood technology and therefore difficult to support.
20. What is the maximum allowable distance for a horizontal wiring subsystem?
    a. 10 m
    b. 100 m
    c. 200 m
    d. 500 m
21. In what subsystem of a structured cabling design are patch cables used?
    a. in the horizontal wiring
    b. in the work area
    c. in the backbone wiring
    d. in the entrance facilities
22. What part of the TIA/EIA structured cabling recommendations provides connectivity to a telecommunications service provider?
    a. work area
    b. horizontal wiring
    c. telecommunications closet
    d. entrance facilities
23. Why might you need plenum-rated cable?
    a. to guard wiring from excessive heat and fire damage
    b. to guard wiring from excessive EMI noise
    c. to guard wiring from excessive moisture
    d. to guard wiring from physical damage

24. In general, what type of cabling can sustain the most bending without impairing transmission?

    a. Thinnet

    b. Thicknet

    c. STP

    d. UTP

25. What is the *maximum* amount of insulation you should strip from copper wires before inserting them into connectors?

    a. ¼ of an inch

    b. ½ of an inch

    c. 1 inch

    d. 2 inches

26. What is the *maximum* amount you should untwist twisted-pair wires before inserting them into connectors?

    a. ¼ of an inch

    b. ½ of an inch

    c. 1 inch

    d. 2 inches

27. What are the two main types of infrared transmission, and how do they differ?

28. Radio frequency transmissions can be easily intercepted. True or False?

29. What kind of transmission media would you recommend for video conferencing between two buildings that are across the street from each other?

    a. fiber-optic cable

    b. CAT5 UTP

    c. Thinnet

    d. Thicknet

30. Which government agency in the United States allocates radio frequencies?

    a. FTA

    b. FCC

    c. FTC

    d. FAA

HANDS-ON PROJECTS

PROJECT 4-1

One of the characteristics that you must consider when choosing the right type of cable for your network is its bend radius. Bending a cable may affect its ability to transmit data. When you bend a cable past its maximum bend radius, data errors may occur. In this exercise, you will attempt to impair the transmission of data over a Thinnet coaxial cable by bending it past its maximum bend radius.

For this project, you will need a Windows 95 or Windows 98 workstation connected to a Windows NT or NetWare server via Thinnet coaxial cable. You will also need a compass and a tape measure. In the first five steps of this project, you will create a continuously looping batch file, called "dirtest.bat," that performs a directory listing on one directory on the server. The purpose of this batch file is to generate a steady flow of traffic between the server and your workstation.

1. At the Windows 95 or Windows 98 workstation, click **Start**, point to **Programs**, point to **Accessories**, and the click **Notepad**. The Notepad window opens.
2. Type **dir /s**
3. Click **File** on the menu bar, then click **Save**. The Save As dialog box opens.
4. Save the file as **dirtest.bat** in the root directory of the C: drive.
5. Close Notepad.
6. At the Windows 95 or Windows 98 workstation, click **Start**, click **Programs**, then click **MS DOS Prompt**.
7. At the DOS prompt, type **dirtest**. The batch file runs. You should see a directory listing continually scrolling down the screen.
8. While watching the DOS window, take a 4-foot section of the coaxial cable in your hands and slowly bend it as if you were trying to create a circle. At what point does the traffic between the workstation and the server slow down? At what point does it stop, if ever?
9. Using the compass, measure the bend radius of the cable when you notice that the transmission begins to slow down, and again when you notice that it stops.

PROJECT 4-2

You may sometimes need to create your own patch cables or install a new connector on an existing cable. In this exercise, you will practice putting an RJ-45 connector on a twisted-pair cable, and then use the cable to connect a workstation to the network. The process of inserting wires into the connector is called crimping, and it is a skill that requires practice—so don't be discouraged if the first cable you create doesn't reliably transmit and receive data.

For this project, you will need a crimp tool, a wire stripper, a wire cutter, a 5-foot length of CAT5 UTP, two RJ-45 connectors, and a simple client/server network system (for example, a Windows 95 or Windows 98 workstation connected to a Windows NT server) that you have verified works with a reliable twisted-pair cable.

1. Using the wire cutter, make a clean cut at both ends of the UTP cable.
2. Using the wire stripper, remove the sheath off 1 inch (or less) of one end of the UTP cable, being careful to not damage the insulation on the twisted pairs inside.
3. Separate the four wire pairs slightly while keeping each pair twisted around the other.
4. Using the wire stripper or a penknife (but not your teeth), remove approximately ⅜ of an inch of insulation from each of the eight wires. You will have to untwist the wire pairs to accomplish this task, but do not separate the wires in each pair more than ½ inch from each other.
5. Using a crimping tool, connect the wires in the RJ-45 connector, matching their color to their correct pin number as described in Table 4-3.
6. Repeat Steps 1 through 4 for the other end of the UTP segment.
7. Use your newly created patch panel to connect your workstation to the network. Can you log in? Can you open a file?
8. If you cannot communicate reliably with the network, try the process again from Step 1. Although you *could* try to remove and reinsert the wires in the connector, this method usually doesn't work. Continue until you can reliably log into the server from your workstation using your newly made cable.

PROJECT 4-3

In this exercise, you will have the opportunity to use an atmospheric transmission medium, infrared signaling. Recall that infrared is a line-of-sight medium, meaning that it depends on a direct path between two devices that are trying to communicate.

For this project, you will need a workstation running Windows 95 or Windows 98 and a printer with an infrared port. Your first step is to make sure that the printer drivers are correctly installed on the workstation.

1. Install and configure drivers for the infrared ports on each device.
2. Place the workstation and the printer on the same table, approximately 2 feet apart, with their infrared ports facing each other. Ensure that the workstation recognizes the printer.
3. Print a document using the infrared port.
4. Now turn the printer 180 degrees so that its infrared port faces away from the workstation. Attempt to print the same document. Are you successful?
5. Experiment with moving the devices farther and farther away from each other, while their infrared ports have a direct and clear path between them. At what distance does communication break down?

CASE PROJECTS

1. You have been asked to design the entire cabling system for a footwear manufacturer's new central warehouse. The company already has three buildings on two city blocks, and the warehouse will be its fourth building. Currently, the buildings run on separate networks, but the company would like to be able to exchange data among them. In addition, the Marketing department would like to hold video conferences with the Sales department in the next building. The Marketing personnel have heard about a high-speed transmission technology called Asynchronous Transfer Mode (ATM), and think they might want to implement it within the next two years. In the warehouse, 50 shipping and packing personnel will be riding up and down the aisles on forklifts pulling inventory off the shelves. What kind of transmission media would you recommend for the different departments of the footwear company and why?
2. Now the footwear company is experiencing data transmission problems in the Quality Control department, which is located in one corner of the research building. Because only part of a floor is affected, you head for the telecommunications closets in that building. What will you look for?
3. Thanks to your fast thinking, the footwear company was able to keep its quality control tasks on track. It has just one more problem: The company has a secret project under way at a warehouse across the street, which is disguised as an antique mall. The project is highly sensitive and its existence cannot be divulged, even to current staff. The footwear company executives will not allow any new construction or cabling that might raise suspicion. Nevertheless, they need a way to transmit data to and from the warehouse. What do you suggest?

CHAPTER 5

NETWORK ARCHITECTURE

After reading this chapter and completing the exercises, you will be able to:

- Describe the basic and hybrid LAN topologies
- Describe a variety of enterprise-wide and WAN topologies
- Explain the benefits and uses of different topologies
- Discuss several versions of the Ethernet transport system
- Explain the structure and functioning of the Token Ring network transport system

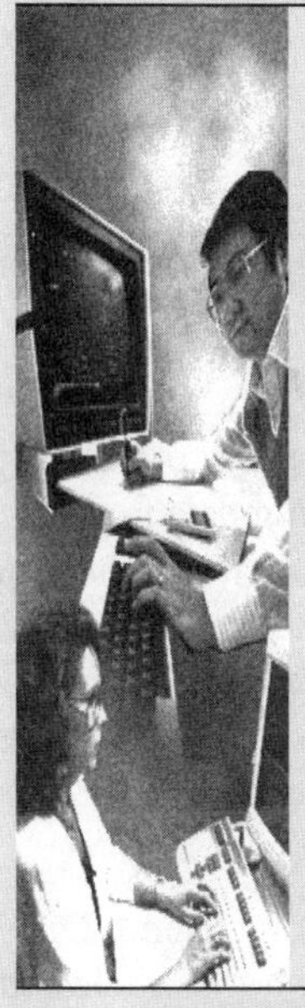

ON THE JOB

If there is one important lesson to be learned with Ethernet-based networks, it is that proper termination is a *must*. When all nodes on the network are properly terminated, you have a stable network. If a terminator is missing, you can have an extremely hard-to-track problem.

Once, at a company where I was employed as a programmer, I noticed the hardware guys wandering around, trying to track down a problem with the network (it was an Ethernet network running NetBIOS in a 10Base2 bus topology.) Being the curious type, I asked what was wrong, and what the symptoms were. The troubleshooters explained that the system had been working fine earlier in the day, but in the afternoon the system became "flaky": there were sporadic failures in reading and writing data over the network, and programs began giving unexpected and non-reproducible error messages.

I remembered that this "flaky network" problem had come up at another company I had worked for, so I asked if they had checked the network terminations. Sure enough: after lunch, someone had removed a computer from an unoccupied cubicle, but hadn't bothered to put a line terminator on the network connection. When a terminator was installed, the system "magically" worked fine again.

Jim Cooper
Systems Developer

Just as an architect of a house must decide where to place walls and doors, where to install electrical and plumbing systems, and how to manage traffic patterns through rooms to make a house more livable, a network architect must consider many factors, both seen and unseen, when designing a network. This chapter introduces the elements of network architecture, a subject you need to understand thoroughly before considering the fundamentals of network design in Chapters 6 and 7.

This chapter describes the basic layouts of LANs and WANs, the advantages and disadvantages of each layout, and the optimal application for each layout. It also covers the two most commonly used transport systems: Ethernet and Token Ring. Once you master the fundamentals of network architecture, you will have all the tools necessary to design a network as elegant as the Taj Mahal.

Simple LAN Topologies

A **physical topology** is a drawing that illustrates the physical layout of a network. It depicts a network in broad scope; that is, it does not specify devices, connectivity methods, or addresses on the network. Physical topologies are classified as being one of three fundamental geometric shapes: bus, ring, and star. These shapes can be mixed to create hybrid topologies. Before you design a network, you need to understand physical topologies, because they can affect which logical topology you use (for example, Ethernet or Token Ring), how your building is cabled, and what kind of network media you use. You must also understand a network's physical topology to troubleshoot its problems or change its infrastructure.

This chapter builds on the terms and concepts discussed in Chapters 2, 3, and 4. If you do not have a clear understanding of the material covered in those chapters, take time to review them now.

Bus

A **bus topology** consists of a single cable connecting all nodes on a network without intervening connectivity devices. Figure 5-1 depicts a typical bus topology.

The single cable is called the **bus** and can support only one channel; as a result, every node shares the bus's total capacity. A bus topology can be considered a peer-to-peer topology, because every device on the network shares the responsibility for getting data from one point to another. Because of the single channel limitation, however, the more nodes on a bus network, the slower the network will transmit and deliver data. Each node on a bus network passively listens for data directed to it. When one node wants to transmit data to another node, it broadcasts an alert to the entire network, informing all nodes that a transmission is being sent; the destination node then picks up the transmission. Nodes between the sending and receiving nodes ignore the message.

For example, suppose that you want to send an instant message to your friend, Diane, who works across the hall, asking whether she wants to have lunch with you. You click the send button after typing your message, and the data stream that contains your message is sent to your NIC. Your NIC then broadcasts a message across the shared wire that essentially says, "I have a message for Diane's computer." The broadcast passes by every NIC between your computer and Diane's computer until Diane's computer recognizes that the message is meant for it and responds by accepting the data.

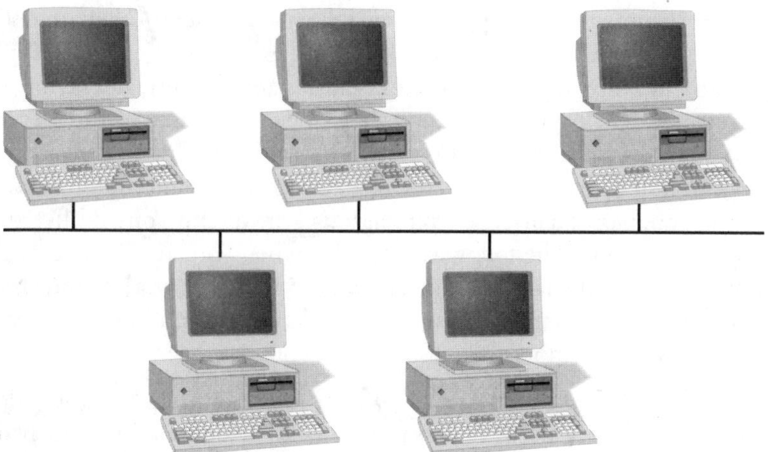

Figure 5-1 A bus topology network

At the ends of each bus network are 50-ohm resistors known as **terminators.** The terminators stop signals after they have reached their destination. Without these devices, signals on a bus network would travel endlessly between the two ends of the network—a phenomenon known as **signal bounce**—and new signals could not get through. To understand this concept, imagine that you and a partner standing at opposite sides of a canyon are yelling to each other. When you call out, your words echo; when your partner replies, his words also echo. Now imagine that the echoes never die away. After a short while you could not continue conversing because all of the sound waves generated previously would still be bouncing around, creating too much noise for you to hear anything else. On a network, terminators halt the transmission of the old signals. Figure 5-2 depicts a terminated bus network.

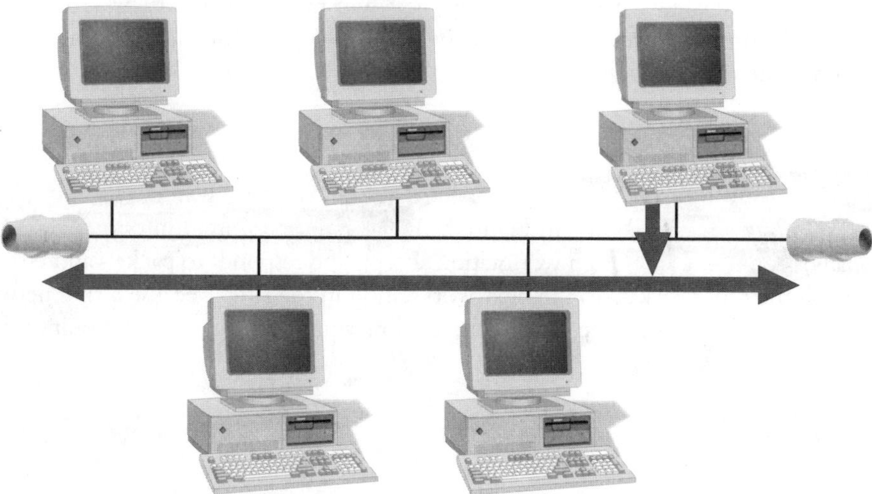

Figure 5-2 A terminated bus network

Although networks based on a bus topology are inexpensive to set up, they do not scale well. As you add more nodes, the network's performance degrades. For example, suppose a bus network in your small office supports two workstations and a server, and saving a file to the server takes 2 seconds. During that time, your NIC first announces to the server, and then announces to the other workstation on the network, that it has data to deliver to the server; when the announcement reaches the server, the server accepts the transmission. Suppose, however, that your business experiences tremendous growth and you add five more workstations during one weekend. The following Monday, when you attempt to save a file to the server, the save process might take 5 seconds, because the new workstations must also be informed of the intended transmission. As this example illustrates, a bus topology would not be practical for a network of more than 200 workstations.

Bus networks are also difficult to troubleshoot, because it is a challenge to identify fault locations. To understand why, think of the game called "telephone," in which one person whispers a phrase into the ear of the next person, who whispers the phrase into the ear of another person, and so on, until the final person in line repeats the phrase aloud. The vast majority of the time, the phrase recited by the last person bears little resemblance to the original phrase. Indeed, when the game ends, it's hard to determine precisely where in the chain the individual errors cropped up. Similarly, errors may occur at any intermediate point on a bus network, but at the receiving end it's possible to tell only that an error occurred. Finding the source of the error can prove very difficult, because you cannot retrace the data's progress from one node to the next; that is, the nodes don't "remember" the data after they pass it on. (In the telephone game analogy, this situation would be similar to every person in the line forgetting the phrase after he or she passed it on—a situation that would make it impossible to trace the evolution of the phrase as it moves from one person to the next.)

A final disadvantage to bus networks is that they are not very fault-tolerant, because a break or a defect in the bus affects the entire network. As a result, and because of the other disadvantages associated with this topology, you will rarely see a network run on a pure bus topology. You may, however, encounter hybrid topologies that include a bus component, as discussed later in this chapter.

RING

In a **ring topology**, each node is connected to the two nearest nodes so that the entire network forms a circle, as shown in Figure 5-3. Data are transmitted in one direction (unidirectionally) around the ring. Each workstation accepts and responds to packets addressed to it, then forwards the other packets to the next workstation in the ring. Because a ring network has no "ends," and because data stop at their destination, ring networks do not require terminators.

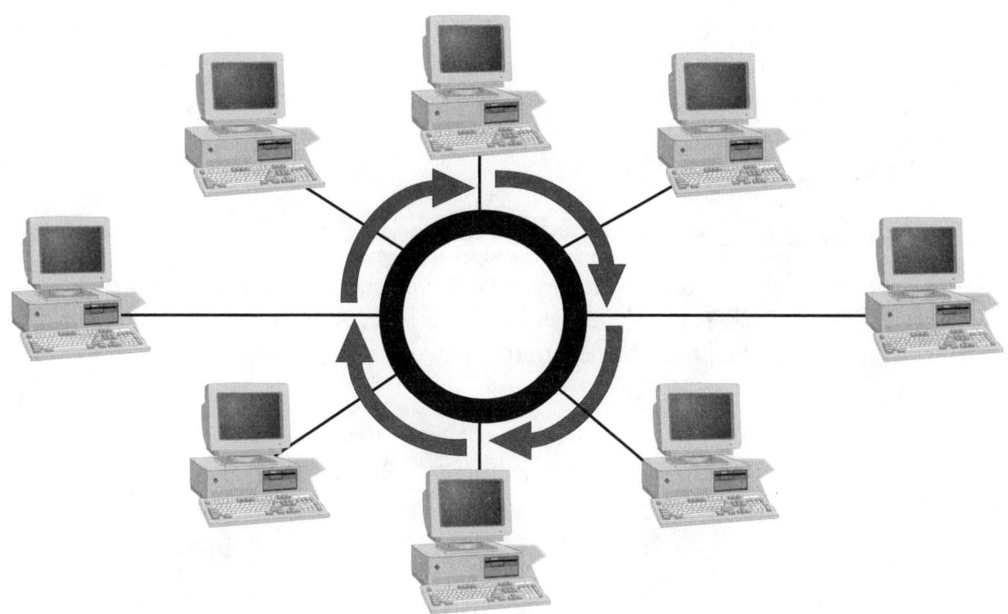

Figure 5-3 A typical ring network

One method for passing data on a ring network is token passing. In **token passing**, a 3-byte packet, called a token, is transmitted from one node to another around the ring. If a computer on the ring has information to transmit, it picks up the token packet, adds control and data information plus the destination node's address to transform the token into a data frame, and then passes the token on to the next node. The transformed token, now in the form of a frame, circulates around the network until it reaches its intended destination. The destination node picks it up and returns an acknowledgment message to the originating node. After the originating node receives the acknowledgment, it releases a new free token and sends it down the ring. This approach ensures that only one workstation transmits data at any given time. Because each workstation participates in sending the token around the ring, this architecture is known as an **active topology**. Each workstation acts as a **repeater**, a device that regenerates signals, for the transmission.

The drawback of a simple ring topology is that a single malfunctioning workstation can disable the network. For example, suppose that you and five colleagues share a pure ring topology LAN in your small office. You decide to send an instant message to Thad, who works three offices away, telling him that you accidentally received a package addressed to him. Between your office and Thad's office are two other offices, and two other workstations on the ring. Your instant message must pass through the two intervening workstations' NICs before it reaches Thad's computer. If one of these workstations has a malfunctioning NIC, your message will never reach Thad.

In addition, just as in a bus topology, the more workstations that must participate in token passing, the slower the response time. Consequently, pure ring topologies are not very flexible or scalable.

Contemporary LANs rarely use pure ring topologies. A variation of the ring topology, known as a star-wired ring, is popular for some types of networks, such as Token Ring networks. Star-wired rings and Token Ring technology will be discussed later in this chapter.

STAR

In a **star topology,** every node on the network is connected through a central device, such as a hub. Figure 5-4 depicts a typical star topology. Any single physical wire on a star network connects only two devices (for example, a workstation and a hub), so a cabling problem will affect two nodes at most. Devices such as workstations or printers transmit data to the hub, which then retransmits the data to the network segment containing the destination node.

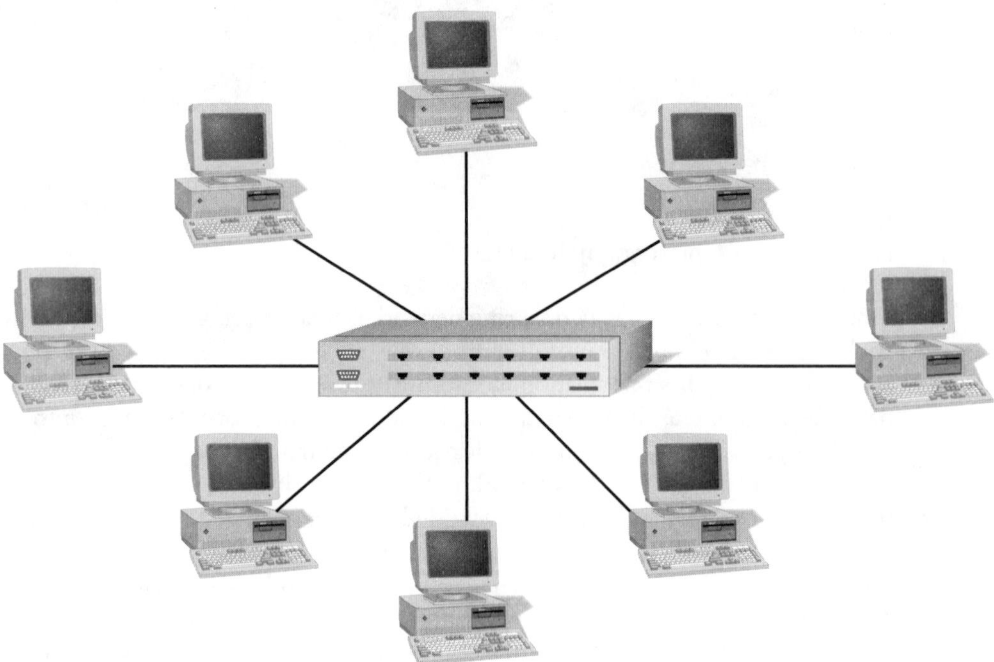

Figure 5-4 A typical star topology network

Star topologies require slightly more cabling and configuration than ring or bus networks. A single malfunctioning cable or workstation cannot disable star networks, but a hub failure can take down a LAN segment.

Because of their use of a centralized connection point, star topologies can easily be moved, isolated, or interconnected with other networks; they are therefore scalable. For this reason, the star topology has become the most popular fundamental architecture used in contemporary LANs. Many network administrators have replaced their old bus or ring networks with star networks in recent years. Single star networks are commonly interconnected with other networks through hubs and switches to form more complex topologies. Modern Ethernet networks, for example, use a star topology.

Hybrid LAN Topologies

Except in very small networks, you will rarely encounter a network that follows a strict bus, ring, or star topology. Simple topologies are too restrictive, particularly if the LAN must accommodate a large number of devices. More likely, you will work with a complex combination of these topologies, known as a **hybrid topology**. Several kinds of hybrid topologies are explained in the following sections.

Star-Wired Ring

The **star-wired ring topology** uses the physical layout of a star in conjunction with the token ring–passing data transmission method. In Figure 5-5, which depicts such an architecture, the solid lines represent a physical connection and the dotted lines represent the flow of data. Data are sent around the star in a circular pattern. This hybrid topology benefits from the fault tolerance of the star topology (data transmission does not depend on each workstation to act as a repeater) and the reliability of token passing. Modern Token Ring networks, as specified in IEEE 802.5, use this hybrid topology.

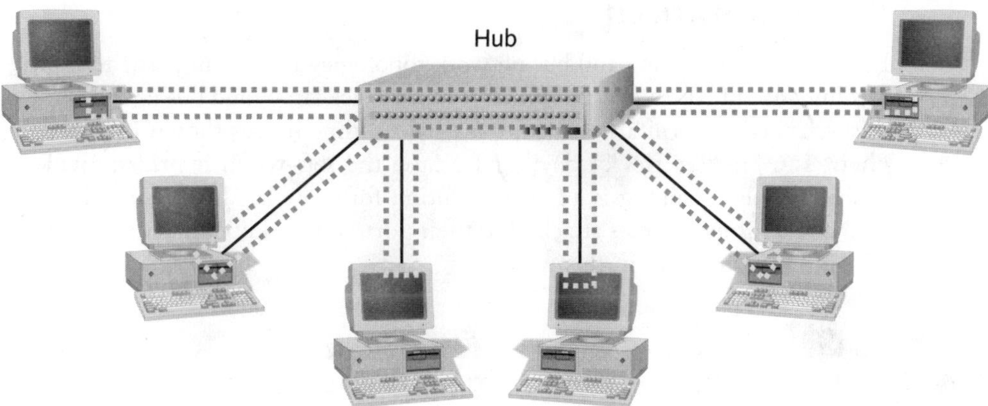

Figure 5-5 A star-wired ring topology network

Star-Wired Bus

Another popular hybrid topology combines the star and bus formations. In a **star-wired bus topology**, groups of workstations are star-connected to hubs and then networked via a single bus, as shown in Figure 5-6. With this design, you can cover longer distances and easily interconnect or isolate different network segments. One drawback is that this option is more expensive than using either the star or especially the bus topology alone. The star-wired bus topology commonly forms the basis for Ethernet and Fast Ethernet networks.

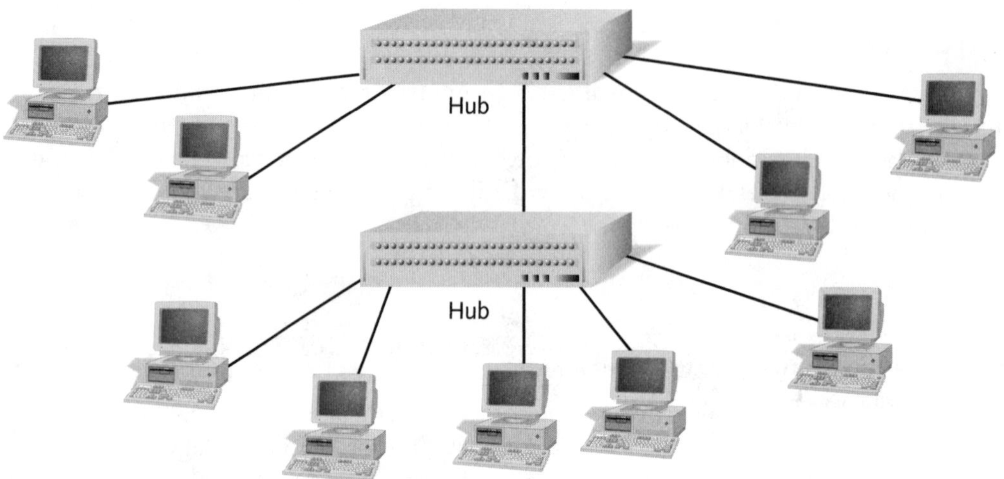

Figure 5-6 A star-wired bus network topology

DAISY-CHAINED

Even the star-wired ring and bus network topologies are too simplistic to represent a typical medium-sized LAN. Nevertheless, hubs that service star-wired bus or ring topologies can be daisy-chained to form a more complex hybrid topology, as shown in Figure 5-7. A **daisy chain** is a linked series of devices. Because the star-wired hybrids provide for modular additions, daisy chaining is a logical solution for growth. Also, because hubs can be easily connected through cables attached to their ports, little additional cost is required to expand a LAN's infrastructure in this way.

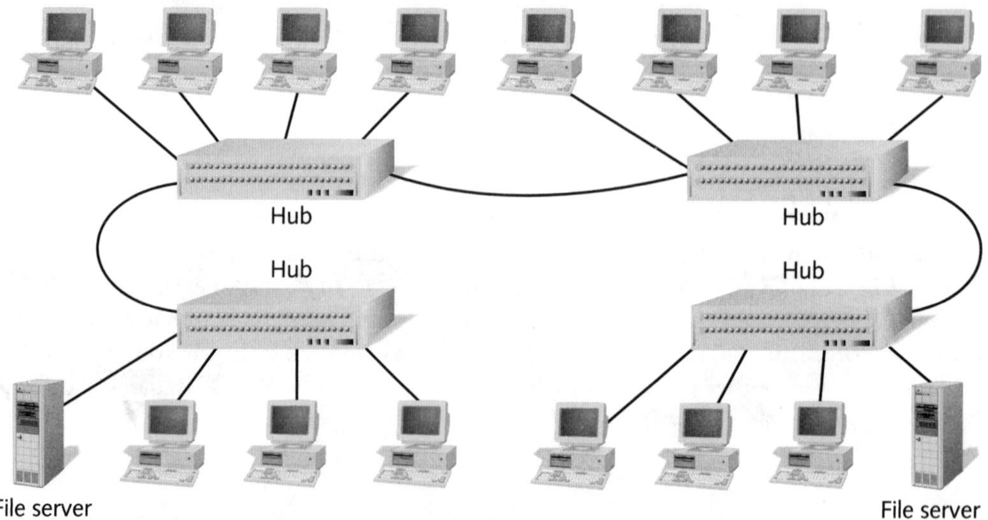

Figure 5-7 Daisy-chained star-wired bus topology

Daisy-chaining simple topologies can present hazards. For example, IEEE specifications such as the Ethernet 802.3 standard dictate the maximum number of hubs that may be connected in sequence to maintain transmission integrity. Using more hubs than the standard suggests will adversely affect the functionality of a LAN. Among other things, if you extend a LAN beyond its recommended size, intermittent and unpredictable data transmission errors will result. In addition, if you daisy-chain a topology with limited bandwidth, you risk overloading the channel and generating more data errors.

HIERARCHICAL

None of the topologies discussed previously distinguishes between the functions or priorities of the various workgroups. For example, a server that contains a payroll database and serves 50 clients may be attached to the same hub as a workstation that is used only twice each week for data processing. Although both devices are connected to the same hub, they perform vastly different functions. Accordingly, you should assign the payroll server a higher priority for network access. For example, you need to ensure that the payroll server almost never loses network connectivity as a result of a device failure on the network. Thus, you might choose to connect the payroll server directly to the backbone using a more expensive, fault-tolerant hub. The less important, data processing workstation could be connected to a small, inexpensive hub that is connected to a better hub, which is in turn connected to the backbone. This arrangement minimizes the possibility for the payroll server losing connectivity but increases the possibility of the data processing workstation losing connectivity.

There are many reasons for separating devices in a hierarchy. You may want to separate hubs, switches, and routers for reasons related to security, cost, scalability, network addressing, bandwidth, or reliability. In addition, there are many ways to separate devices and workgroups, leading to many variations on the hierarchical topology. You can consider the hierarchical topology as similar to an organizational chart in a company, where groups are divided by function, and different personnel belong to different levels in the organizational chart.

One possible way to group devices on a network is to divide them into layers. A layer is simply a logical division between devices on a network. A hierarchical hybrid topology uses layers to separate devices based on their priority or function. A hierarchical topology may have any number of layers and may connect different types of simple topologies. For example, Figure 5-8 depicts a hierarchical ring topology with three layers. The top layer services the network's backbone, while the second layer provides direct connectivity for the file server ring and intermediate connectivity to the third layer. The third layer then services multiple workgroups, such as Administration, Sales, and IT.

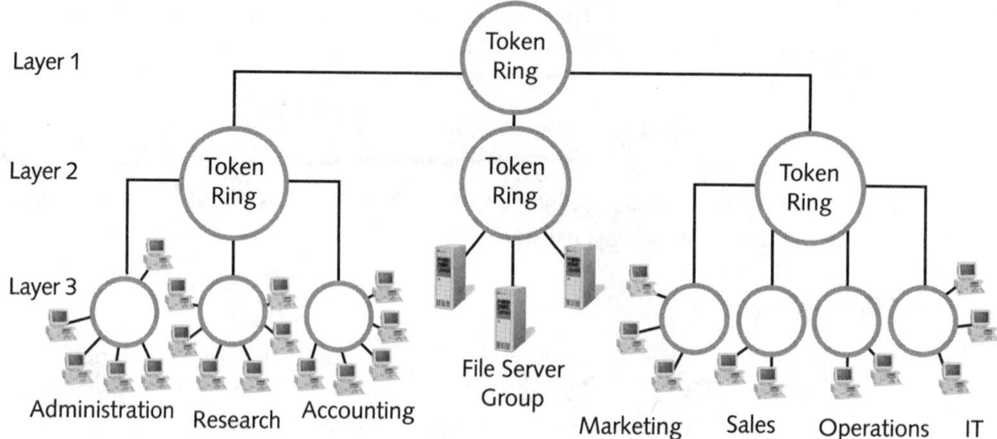

Figure 5-8 Hierarchical ring topology

Arranging topologies in a hierarchy offers several advantages: the ability to segregate bandwidth among different groups, ease in adding or isolating different network groups, and the flexibility to interconnect different network types. For these reasons, hierarchical topologies underlie high-speed LAN and WAN designs.

ENTERPRISE-WIDE TOPOLOGIES

In networking, the term **enterprise** refers to an entire organization, including its local and remote offices, a mixture of computer systems, and a number of departments. Enterprise-wide computing must therefore take into account the breadth and diversity of a large organization's computer needs. Enterprise-wide networks expand on the simple and hybrid LAN topologies. As a result, their topologies require more interconnection devices and more robust data transmission environments than simple LAN topologies can provide. An enterprise-wide network may use or form part of a WAN, but an enterprise-wide network connects only one organization's resources. A WAN (for example, the Internet) may connect resources from many different organizations.

As with LAN topologies, a number of variations on the basic enterprise-wide topologies exist. This section describes some popular methods of arranging these larger networks.

BACKBONE NETWORKS

As noted earlier, a network backbone is the cabling that connects the hubs, switches, and routers on a network. Backbones usually are capable of more throughput than the cabling that connects workstations to hubs. This added capacity is necessary because backbones carry more traffic than any other cabling in the network. For example, an increasing number of businesses are implementing fiber-optic backbone but continue to use CAT5 wiring for the cabling from hubs to workstations. Although even the simplest LAN technically has a backbone, enterprise-wide backbones are more complex and more difficult to plan. The backbone is the most significant building block of these networks.

Serial Backbone

A **serial backbone** is the simplest kind of backbone. It consists of two or more hubs connected to each other by a single cable. Serial backbone networks are identical to the daisy-chained networks discussed in the Hybrid LAN Topologies section. As mentioned earlier, they are not suitable for large networks or long distances. Although the serial backbone topology could be used for enterprise-wide networks, it is rarely implemented for that purpose.

Distributed Backbone

A **distributed backbone** consists of a number of hubs connected to a series of central hubs or routers in a hierarchy, as shown in Figure 5-9. In Figure 5-9, the cross-hatched lines represent the backbone. This kind of topology allows for simple expansion and limited capital outlay for growth, because more layers of hubs can be added to existing layers. For example, suppose that you are the network administrator for a small publisher's office. You might begin your network with a distributed backbone consisting of two hubs that supply connectivity to your 20 users, 10 on each hub. When your company hires more staff, you can connect another hub to one of the existing hubs, and use the new hub to connect the new staff to the network.

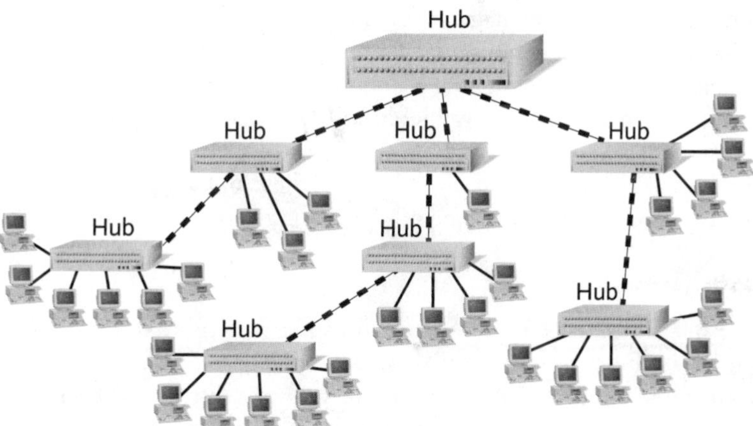

Figure 5-9 A simple distributed backbone network

A more complicated distributed backbone connects multiple LANs or LAN segments using routers, as shown in Figure 5-10. In this example, the routers form the highest layer of the backbone to connect the LANs.

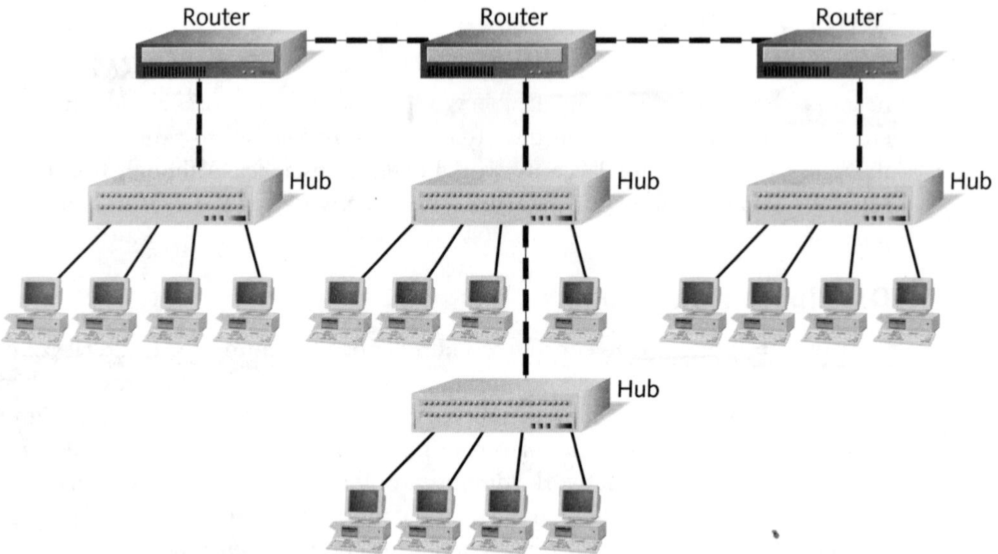

Figure 5-10 A distributed backbone connecting multiple LANS

A distributed backbone also provides network administrators with the ability to segregate workgroups and therefore manage them more easily. It adapts well to an enterprise-wide network confined to a single building, where layers of hubs can be assigned according to the floor or department. When designing a network with a distributed backbone, however, you must consider the maximum allowable distance between nodes and the server dictated by the network media. Another possible problem in this design relates to the central point of failure, the hub at the uppermost layer. Despite these potential drawbacks, implementing a distributed backbone network can be relatively simple, quick, and inexpensive.

Collapsed Backbone

The **collapsed backbone** topology uses a router or switch as the single central connection point for multiple subnetworks, as shown in Figure 5-11. Contrast Figure 5-11 with Figure 5-10, where multiple LANs are connected via a distributed backbone. In a collapsed backbone, a single router or switch is the highest layer of the backbone. The router or switch that makes up the collapsed backbone must contain multiprocessors to handle the heavy traffic going through it. The dangers of using this arrangement relate to the fact that a failure in the central router or switch can bring down the entire network. In addition, because routers cannot move traffic as quickly as hubs, using a router may slow data transmission. (You will learn more about hubs and routers in Chapter 6.)

Nevertheless, a collapsed backbone topology offers substantial advantages. Most significantly, this arrangement allows you to interconnect different types of subnetworks. You can also centrally manage maintenance and troubleshooting chores.

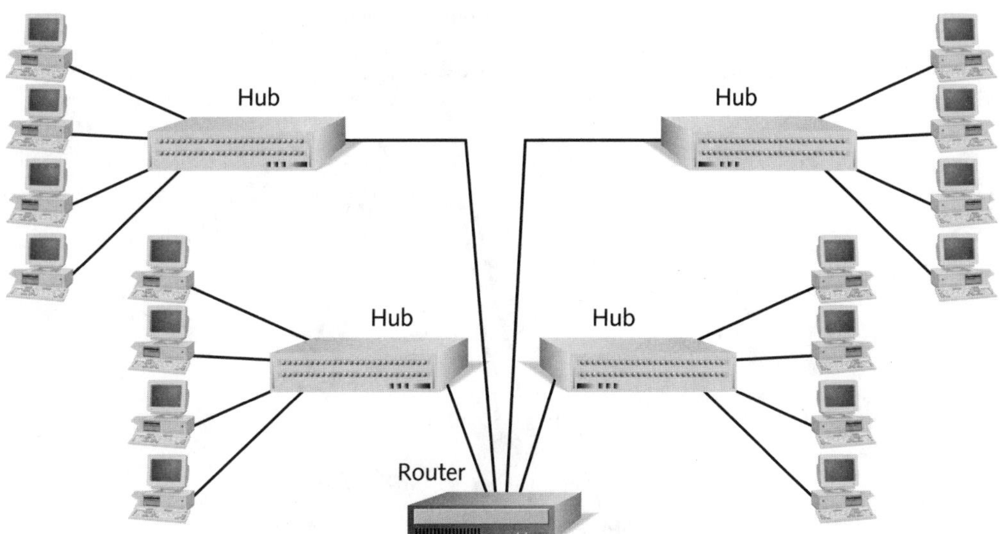

Figure 5-11 A collapsed backbone network

Parallel Backbone

A **parallel backbone** is the most robust enterprise-wide topology. This variation of the collapsed backbone arrangement consists of more than one connection from the central router or switch to each network segment. Figure 5-12 depicts a simple parallel backbone topology. The most significant advantage of using a parallel backbone is that its redundant links assure network connectivity to any area of the enterprise. Parallel backbones are more expensive than other enterprise-wide topologies, but they make up for the additional cost by offering increased performance.

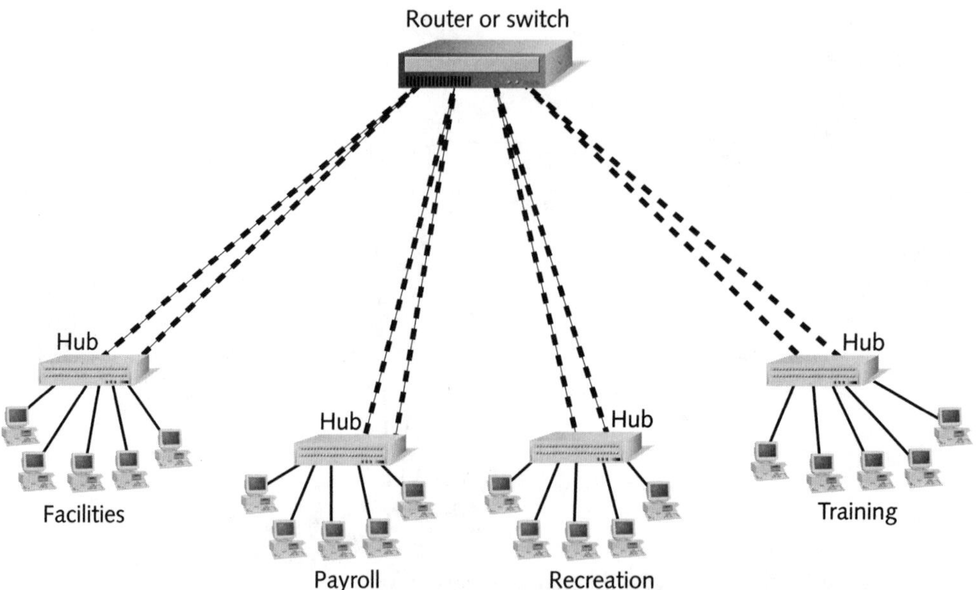

Figure 5-12 A parallel backbone network

As a network administrator, you might choose to implement parallel links to only some of the most critical devices on your network. For example, if the first and second hubs in Figure 5-12 connected your Facilities and Payroll departments to the rest of the network, and your organization could never afford to lose connectivity with those departments, you might keep the parallel structure in place. If the third and fourth hubs in Figure 5-12 connected your organization's Recreation and Training departments to the network, you might decide that parallel links were unnecessary for these departments. By selectively implementing the parallel structure, you can lower connectivity costs and leave available additional ports on the connectivity devices.

MESH NETWORKS

In a **mesh network**, routers are interconnected with other routers with at least two pathways connecting each router, as depicted in Figure 5-13. The mesh network is more complex than the backbone networks discussed previously. In fact, it typically contains several different backbone networks. Indeed, the term "mesh network" is a general topology term that can apply to many different arrangements of workgroups and interconnection devices.

Although a simple LAN can be a mesh network, most often this topology is employed for enterprise-wide networks and WANs. The Internet is an example of a mesh WAN.

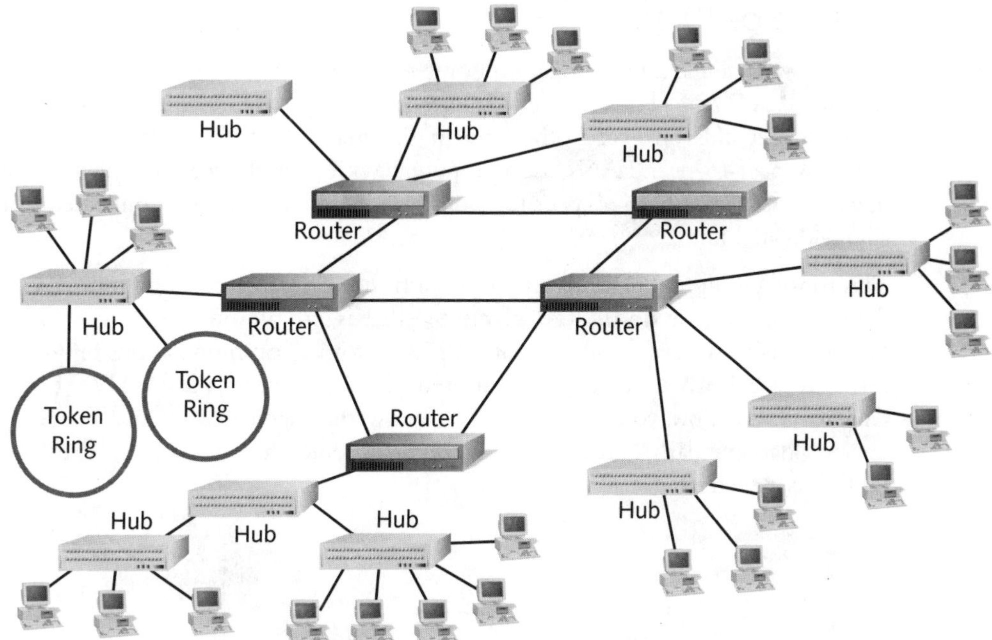

Figure 5-13 An example of a mesh network

WAN Topologies

A **wide area network (WAN)** is a network connecting geographically distinct locations, which may or may not belong to the same organization. WAN topologies use both LAN and enterprise-wide topologies as building blocks, but add more complexity because of the distance they must cover, the larger number of users they serve, and the heavy traffic they often handle. For example, although a simple ring topology may suffice for a small office with 10 users, it does not scale well and therefore cannot serve 1000 users. The particular WAN topology you choose will depend on the number of sites you must connect, the distance between the sites, and any existing infrastructure.

WAN topologies also differ from LAN topologies in the type and extent of interconnectivity devices they use (for example, routers and switches). This difference is directly related to the fact that networking protocols are handled differently on local network segments than they are on segments involving longer distances. For example, a LAN might carry NetBEUI, IPX/SPX, and TCP/IP traffic over a single segment. Because WANs depend on routers to interconnect LANs, and because NetBEUI is not a routable protocol, however, a WAN link will carry only IPX/SPX and/or TCP/IP traffic. WAN networking technologies, such as ATM, DSL, FDDI, and Frame Relay, are discussed in detail in Chapter 7.

Peer-to-Peer

A WAN with single interconnection points for each location is arranged in a **peer-to-peer topology**. A WAN peer-to-peer topology is similar to a LAN peer-to-peer model in that each site depends on every other site in the network to transmit and receive its traffic. Whereas peer-to-peer LANs use computers with shared access connected with cabling, however, the WAN peer-to-peer topology uses different locations connected through (usually) dedicated lines.

This topology often represents the best solution for organizations with only a few sites and the capability to use **dedicated circuits**—that is, continuous physical or logical connections between two access points that are leased from a communications provider, such as an ISP. You will learn more about dedicated circuits, such as T1 or ISDN connections, in Chapter 7. For now, you simply need to know that dedicated circuits make it possible to transmit data regularly and reliably. Figure 5-14 depicts a peer-to-peer WAN using T1 and ISDN's connections.

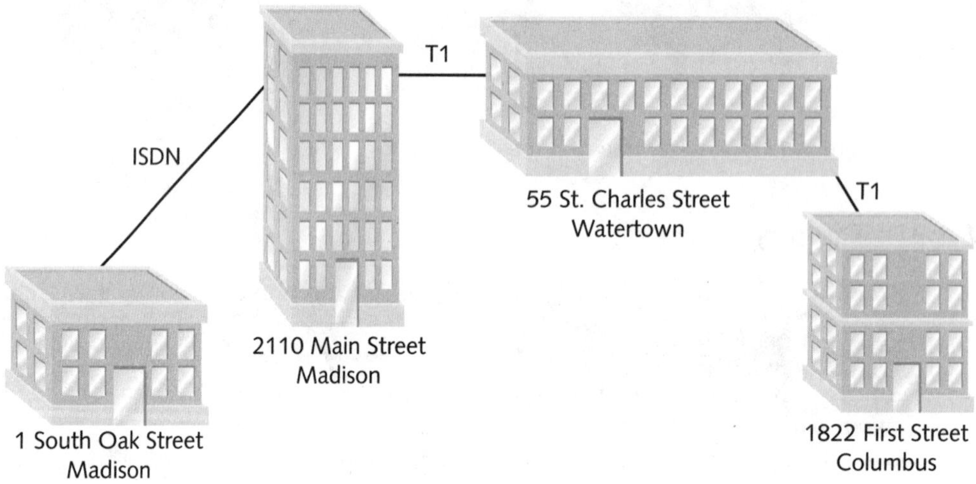

Figure 5-14 A peer-to-peer WAN

Peer-to-peer WAN topologies are suitable for only small WANs. Because all sites must participate in carrying traffic, this model does not scale well. The addition of more sites can cause performance to suffer. Also, a single failure on a peer-to-peer WAN can take down communications between all sites.

Ring

In a **ring WAN topology**, each site is connected to two other sites so that the entire WAN forms a ring pattern, as shown in Figure 5-15. This architecture is similar to the ring LAN topology, except that a ring WAN topology connects locations rather than local nodes. The advantages of a ring WAN over a peer-to-peer WAN are two-fold: a single cable problem will not affect the entire network and routers at any site can redirect data transmissions based on traffic patterns. On the other hand, expanding ring-configured WANs is difficult and expensive. For these reasons, WANs that use the ring topology are only practical for connecting fewer than four or five locations.

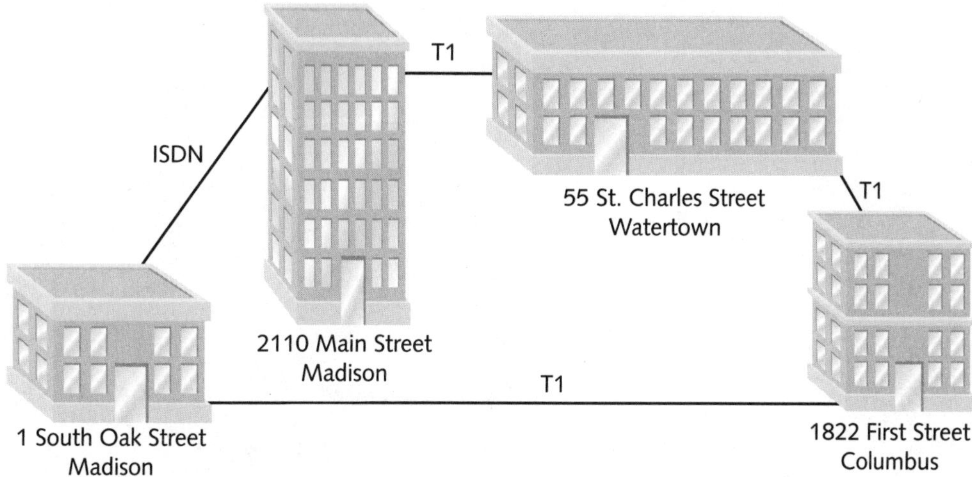

Figure 5-15 A ring-configured WAN

5

STAR

The **star WAN topology** mimics the arrangement of a star LAN. A single site acts as the central connection point for several other points, as shown in Figure 5-16. This arrangement provides separate routes for data to traverse between any two sites. As a result, star WANs are more reliable than the peer-to-peer or ring WANs. As a general rule, reliability increases with the number of potential routes data can follow. For example, if the T1 link between the Oak Street and Main Street locations fails, the Watertown and Columbus locations can still communicate with the Main Street location because they use different routes. In a peer-to-peer or ring topology, however, a single failure would halt all traffic between all sites.

Another advantage of a star WAN is that when all of its dedicated circuits are functioning, a star WAN provides shorter data paths between any two sites.

Extending a star WAN is easy, and this expansion costs less than extending a peer-to-peer or ring WAN. For example, if the organization that uses the star WAN pictured in Figure 5-16 wanted to add a Maple Street, Madison, location to its topology, it could simply lease a new dedicated circuit from the Main Street office to its Maple Street office. None of the other offices would be affected by the change. If the organization were using a peer-to-peer or ring WAN topology, however, two separate dedicated connections would be required to incorporate the new location into the network.

As with star LAN topologies, the greatest drawback of a star WAN is that a failure at the central connection point can bring down the entire WAN. In Figure 5-16, for example, if the Main Street office suffered a catastrophic fire, the entire WAN would fail.

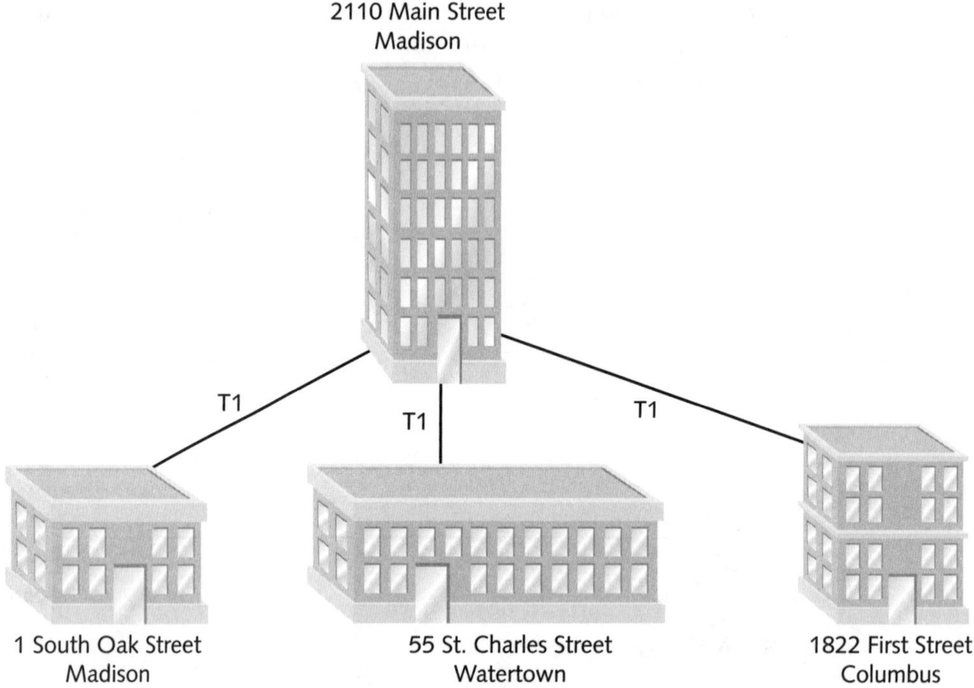

Figure 5-16 A star-configured WAN

MESH

Like an enterprise-wide mesh, a **mesh WAN topology** incorporates many directly interconnected nodes—in this case, geographical locations. Because every site is interconnected, data can travel directly from its origin to its destination. If one connection suffers a problem, routers can redirect data easily and quickly. Mesh WANs represent the most fault-tolerant WAN configuration because they provide multiple routes for data to follow between any two points. For example, if the Madison office in Figure 5-17 suffered a catastrophic fire, the Dubuque office could still send and transmit data to and from the Detroit office by going directly to the Detroit office. If both the Madison and Detroit offices failed, the Dubuque and Indianapolis offices could still communicate.

One drawback to a mesh WAN is the cost; connecting every node on a network to every other entails leasing a large number of dedicated circuits. With larger WANs, the expense can become enormous. To reduce costs, you might choose to implement a partial mesh, in which critical WAN nodes are directly interconnected and secondary nodes are connected through star or ring topologies, as shown in Figure 5-17. Partial-mesh WANs are more practical, and therefore more common in today's business world, than full-mesh WANs.

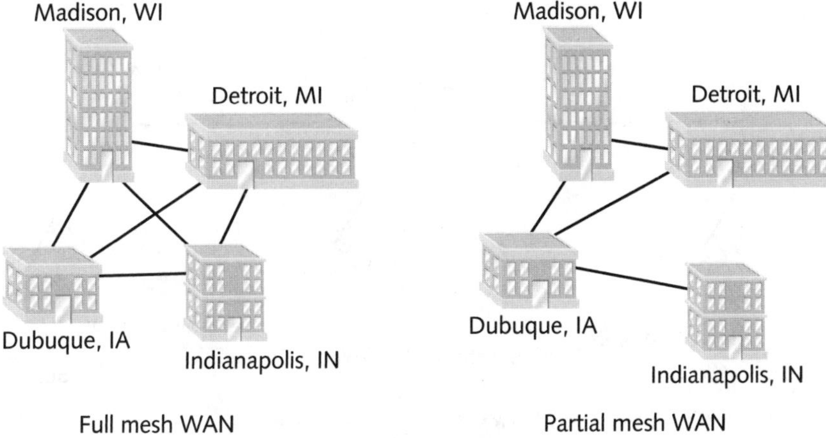

Figure 5-17 Full-mesh and partial-mesh WANs

TIERED

Tiered WAN topologies are similar to the hierarchical hybrid topologies used with LANs. In a **tiered WAN topology**, WAN sites connected in star or ring formations are interconnected at different levels, with the interconnection points being organized into layers. Figure 5-18 depicts a tiered WAN. In this example, the Madison, Detroit, and New York offices form the upper tier, and the Dubuque, Indianapolis, Toronto, Toledo, Washington, and Boston offices form the lower tier. If the Detroit office suffers a failure, the Toronto and Toledo offices cannot communicate with any other nodes on the WAN. Similarly, the Dubuque and Indianapolis offices depend on the Madison office for their WAN connectivity, just as the Washington and Boston offices depend on the New York office for their connectivity.

Variations on this topology abound. Indeed, flexibility makes the tiered approach quite practical. A network architect can determine the best placement of top-level routers based on traffic patterns or critical data paths. In addition, tiered systems allow for easy expansion and inclusion of redundant links to support growth. On the other hand, their enormous flexibility means that creation of tiered WANs requires careful consideration of geography, usage patterns, and growth potential.

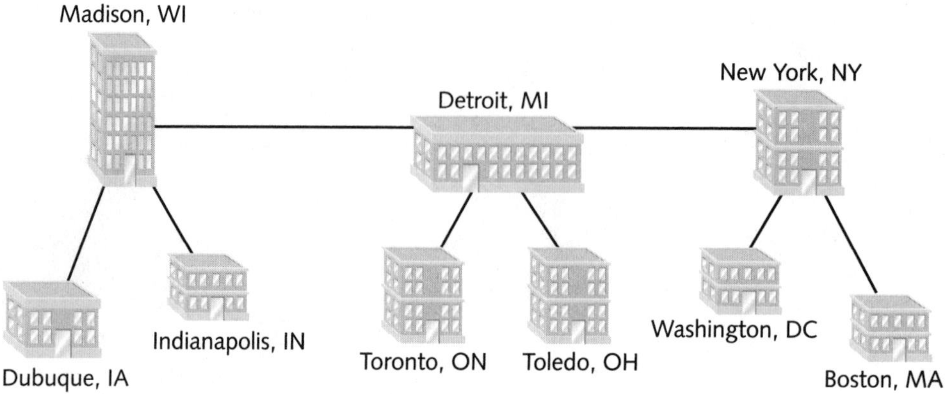

Figure 5-18 A tiered WAN topology

NETWORK TRANSPORT SYSTEMS

A **network transport system** is sometimes referred to as the network's **logical topology** because it describes the network's logical interconnection between nodes, rather than its physical interconnection. The network transport system depends on electrical pulses carried by the Physical layer of the OSI Model. In contrast, a physical topology applies to the configuration of a network's cabling, which resides *below* the Physical layer of the OSI Model.

The two most popular network transport systems are Ethernet and Token Ring. In Chapter 2, in learning how data are transformed through the OSI Model layers, you were introduced to Ethernet and Token Ring technologies. These technologies have been standardized by the IEEE, an organization you also learned about in Chapter 2. This section explains both Ethernet and Token Ring systems in more detail, paying special attention to their place in network designs. Each network transport system not only has its own set of data transmission rules, but also imposes unique requirements on the networking media and physical topology.

SWITCHING

Before you can understand specific network transport systems, such as Ethernet and Token Ring, you must be familiar with the concept of switching. **Switching** is a component of a network's logical topology that determines how connections are created between nodes. You will learn more about switches, the hardware that manages network switching, in Chapter 6. For now, you should be aware of the three methods for switching: circuit switching, message switching, and packet switching. Every network transport system relies on one of these switching mechanisms.

Circuit Switching

In **circuit switching**, a connection is established between two network nodes before they begin transmitting data. Bandwidth is dedicated to this connection and remains available until the users terminate communication between the two nodes. While the nodes remain connected, all data follow the same path initially selected by the switch. When you place a telephone call, for example, your call goes through a circuit switched connection.

Because circuit switching monopolizes its piece of bandwidth while the two stations remain connected, it is not an economical technology. Some network applications that cannot tolerate the time delay it takes to reorganize data packets, such as live audio or video conferencing, benefit from such a dedicated path, however. Circuit switching is used by the following networking technologies: Asynchronous Transfer Mode (ATM), dial-up, ISDN, and T1. These technologies will be discussed in more detail in Chapter 7.

Message Switching

Message switching establishes a connection between two devices, transfers the information to the second device, and then breaks the connection. The information is stored and forwarded from the second device once a connection between that device and a third device on the path is established. This "store and forward" routine continues until the message reaches its destination. All information follows the same physical path; unlike with circuit switching, however, the connection is not continuously maintained. E-mail systems use message switching. Message switching requires that each device in a data's path have sufficient memory and processing power to accept and store the information before passing it to the next node. None of the LAN or WAN network models discussed in this chapter uses message switching.

Packet Switching

A third method for connecting nodes on a network is packet switching. **Packet switching** breaks data into packets before they are transported. Packets can travel any path on the network to their destinations, because each packet contains the destination address and sequencing information. Consequently, packets can attempt to find the fastest circuit available at any instant.

To understand this technology, imagine that you organized a field trip for 50 colleagues to the National Air and Space Museum in Washington, DC. You gave the museum's precise address to your colleagues and told them to leave precisely at 7:00 A.M. from your office building across town. You did not tell your co-workers which route to take. Naturally, each person will want to take the fastest route to the museum. Some might choose the subway, others might hail a taxicab, and still others might choose to drive their own cars. No matter which transportation method your colleagues choose, you will all arrive at the museum and reassemble as a group. This analogy illustrates how packets travel in a packet switched network.

The destination node on a packet switched network reassembles the packets based on their control information. Because of the time it takes to reassemble the packets into a message, packet switching is not suited to live audio or video transmission. Nevertheless, it is a fast and efficient mechanism for transporting typical network data, such as word-processing or spreadsheet files. The greatest advantage to packet switching lies in the fact that it does not waste bandwidth by holding a connection open until a message reaches its destination, as circuit switching does. And unlike message switching, it does not require devices in the data's path to process any information. Examples of packet-switched networks include: Ethernet, FDDI, and Frame Relay. The Internet is an example of a packet-switched WAN.

SHARED ETHERNET

As you learned in Chapter 2, Ethernet is a networking transport method originally developed by Xerox in the 1970s and later improved by Xerox, Digital Equipment Corporation (DEC), and Intel. This flexible technology can run on a variety of network media and offers excellent throughput at a reasonable cost. Ethernet is, by far, the most popular logical topology for LANs today, and its popularity continues to grow.

Ethernet has evolved through many variations, and continues to improve. As a result of this history, it supports many different versions and speeds—so many, in fact, that you will probably find the many variations a little confusing. The following sections introduce the most common types of Ethernet systems in use today, their benefits and limitations, and some characteristics shared by all Ethernet networks.

CSMA/CD

Ethernet follows a set of communication rules called **Carrier Sense Multiple Access with Collision Detection (CSMA/CD).** All Ethernet networks, independent of their speed or frame type, use CSMA/CD. To understand Ethernet, you should first examine CSMA/CD. Defining the function of each CSMA/CD component will help. The term "Carrier Sense" refers to the fact that Ethernet NICs listen on the network and wait until they detect that no other nodes are transmitting data before they begin to transmit. The term "Multiple Access" refers to the fact that several Ethernet nodes can be connected to a network and can monitor traffic at the same time. Any node can transmit data when it determines that the line is free. If two nodes have detected a free circuit and begin to transmit simultaneously, a data collision will occur. In this event, the network performs the collision detection routine. If a station's NIC determines that its data has been involved in a collision, it will first propagate the collision throughout the network (in a process known as **jamming**), ensuring that no other station attempts to transmit; after propagating the collision, the NIC will remain silent for a period of time. (This period of time depends on software and hardware settings for the station's NIC, but a typical waiting period is 9 microseconds.) After waiting, the node will retransmit its data once it determines that the line is again available.

On heavily trafficked networks, collisions are not uncommon. Not surprisingly, the more nodes transmitting data on a network, the more collisions will take place (although a collision rate greater than 1% of all traffic is unusual and may point to a problematic NIC on the network). When an Ethernet network grows to include a particularly large number of nodes, you may see performance suffer as a result of collisions. This "critical mass" number depends on the type and volume of data that the network regularly transmits. Collisions can corrupt data or truncate data frames, so it is important that the network detect and compensate for them. Figure 5-19 depicts the CSMA/CD process.

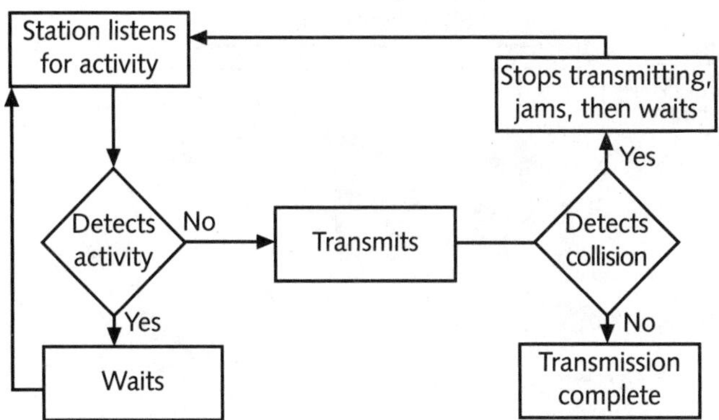

Figure 5-19 CSMA/CD process

Collisions play a role in the Ethernet cabling distance limitations. For example, if the distance between two nodes connected to the same bus exceeds 2500 meters, data propagation delays will occur and prevent CSMA/CD's collision detection routine from operating accurately.

Ethernet Versions

As mentioned earlier, Ethernet comes in a variety of implementations. Each Ethernet version follows a slightly different IEEE 802.3 specification that outlines its speed, topology, and cabling characteristics. The following section describes the most common Ethernet Physical layer varieties, as well as their benefits and limitations.

Some of the material in this section reiterates what you learned about transmission media in Chapter 4. If you do not recall characteristics of the transmission media, such as security, maximum segment length, and relative cost, that were covered in Chapter 4, you should review that material now.

10Base2 Recall from Chapter 4 that **10Base2** is an Ethernet adaptation that, according to IEEE 802.3 standards, uses thin coaxial cable and a simple bus topology, as shown in Figure 5-20. 10Base2 is also called Thinnet or Thin Ethernet. When 10Base2 was developed, the only alternative for Ethernet networks was to use thick coaxial cable. By contrast, the thin cable offered more flexibility and easier installation. The "10Base" part of its name refers to its network speed, which is 10 megabits per second. As you learned in Chapter 4, **Megabits per second (Mbps)** is a measure of how much data a network can optimally transmit, based on its physical characteristics.

In Ethernet technology, the most common network speeds are 10 Mbps and 100 Mbps. Actual data transfer rates on a network will vary, just as you might average 25 miles per gallon (mpg) driving your car to work and back, even though the manufacturer rates the car's gas mileage at 30 mpg. The 10 Mbps specification limits the use of 10Base2 Ethernet, as more networks are moving to faster speeds.

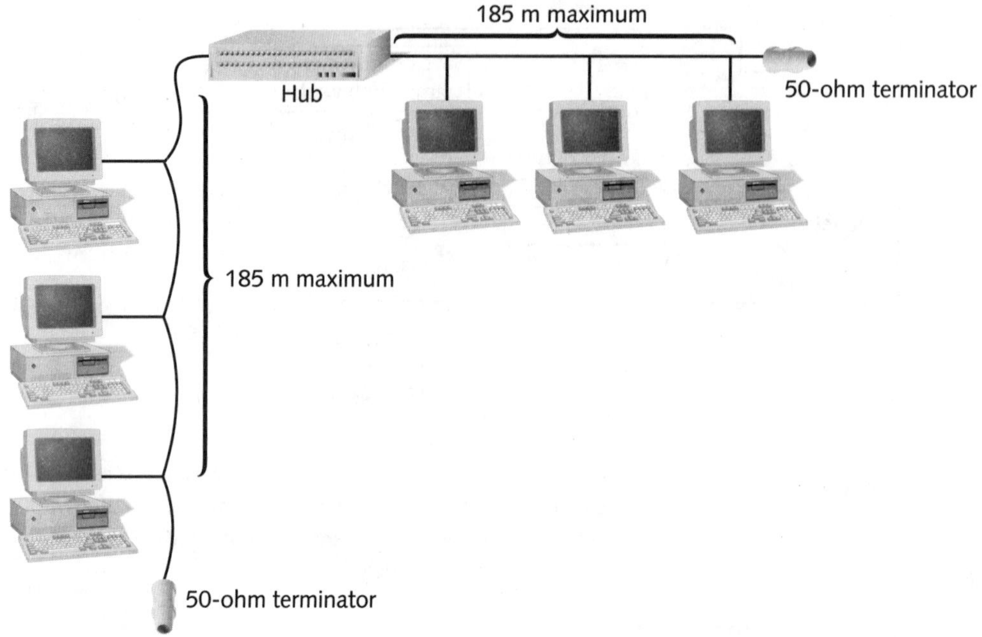

Figure 5-20 A 10Base2 Ethernet network

Typical of a bus topology, 10Base2 networks are terminated with 50-ohm resistors at either end to prevent signal bounce. As you learned in Chapter 4, the maximum length of one Ethernet 10Base2 segment is 185 meters (607 feet). The 10Base2 specification was developed to support a maximum of 30 nodes per segment, each of which is connected to the bus by a BNC T connector. **BNC T connectors** attach to the BNC connector on a network interface card specially designed for 10Base2 networks. Multiple Thinnet segments can be connected with repeaters. A complete Ethernet network can include as many as four repeaters that connect a maximum of five network segments.

Considering its size and speed limits, 10Base2 is not well suited to large LANs. The primary advantages to using 10Base2 are its low cost and ease of installation. For these reasons, you may encounter Thinnet networks in small offices or computer labs, but probably not in enterprise-wide networks.

10Base5 As you will recall from Chapter 4, **10Base5** was the original cabling standard for Ethernet and uses thick, rather than thin, coaxial cable. It is also known as Thicknet or Thick Ethernet. Like 10Base2, Thicknet uses a bus topology with 50-ohm resistors at either end and can carry data at speeds of 10 Mbps. The "5" in 10Base5 refers to its maximum distance of 500 meters, although 10Base5 segments—like 10Base2 segments—can be connected through repeaters to include a maximum of five network segments in a complete Ethernet network. Although it can traverse longer distances than Thinnet, Thicknet is more expensive to implement. 10Base5 is rarely used today because of its thick, inflexible cable and cumbersome connectivity devices. You may never have to work with a 10Base5 network, but you should nevertheless be familiar with its characteristics.

10BaseT 10BaseT is the most ubiquitous Ethernet cabling specification in use today. **10BaseT** employs twisted-pair cabling (the source of the letter "T" in its name) and a star topology to transmit data at 10 Mbps. You should be familiar with **twisted-pair cable** after reading Chapter 4. The twisted-pair cable used by 10BaseT networks is unshielded twisted-pair, a type of wiring that includes Category 3, 4, and 5 cables. Unshielded twisted-pair is the same kind of wiring used for telephone connections; for this reason, 10BaseT networks historically fit well into an organization's existing physical infrastructure. In addition, twisted-pair cabling can support newer, faster technologies, so it increases the scalability of a network.

One possible disadvantage to using unshielded twisted-pair cabling is its sensitivity to electromagnetic interference caused by signals from nearby sources such as electric motors, power lines, and radar. 10BaseT technology compensates for interference through noise balancing and filtering techniques on the wire. For this reason, it is important to install 10BaseT network wiring strictly according to IEEE specifications and to avoid installing Ethernet wiring in telephone closets or next to large electrical devices such as air conditioners.

Nodes on a 10BaseT Ethernet network connect to a central hub or repeater in a star fashion. As is typical of a star topology, a single network cable connects only two devices. This characteristic makes 10BaseT networks more fault-tolerant than 10Base2 or 10Base5, both of which use the bus topology. It also means that 10BaseT networks are easier to troubleshoot because you can isolate problems more readily when every device has a separate connection to the LAN. Figure 5-21 depicts a small 10BaseT Ethernet network.

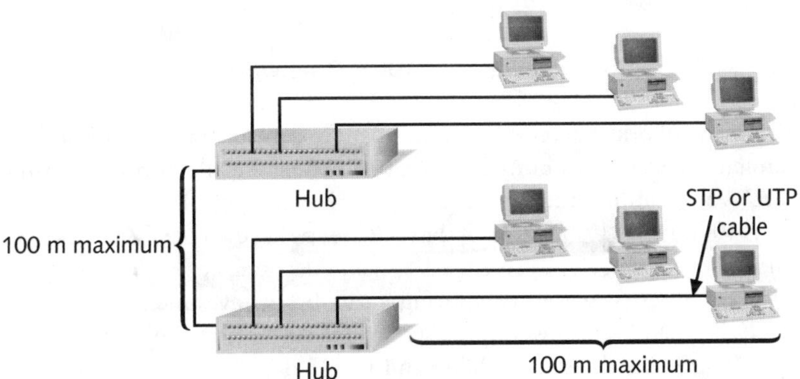

Figure 5-21 A 10BaseT Ethernet network

Each node on a 10BaseT network uses RJ-45 connectors to connect the network cable with the NIC at the workstation end and to connect the cable with the hub at the network end. As discussed in Chapter 4, you are most likely to encounter these types of Ethernet connectors on a modern LAN.

10BaseT, like 10Base2 and 10Base5, is also subject to a distance limitation. The maximum distance that a 10BaseT segment can traverse is 100 meters. To go beyond that distance, Ethernet star segments must be connected by additional hubs or switches to form a hybrid star-bus or hierarchical topology. As with 10Base2 and 10Base5, this arrangement can connect a maximum of five sequential network segments. Figure 5-22 illustrates how Ethernet 10BaseT segments can be interconnected to form an enterprise-wide Ethernet network.

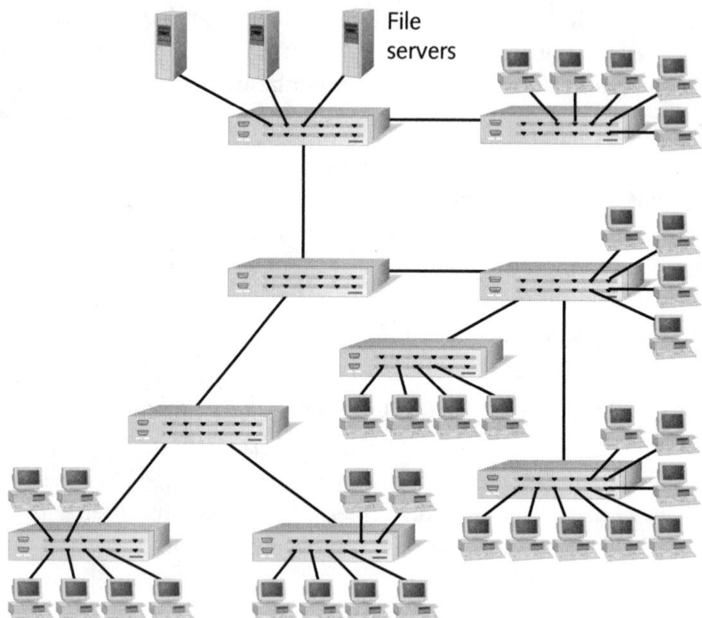

Figure 5-22 An enterprise-wide Ethernet 10BaseT network

100BaseT As networks become larger and handle heavier traffic, Ethernet's longstanding 10 Mbps limitation becomes a bottleneck that detrimentally affects response time. The need for faster LANs that can use the same infrastructure as the popular 10BaseT technology has been met by 100BaseT, also known as **Fast Ethernet**. **100BaseT**, specified in the IEEE 802.3u standard, enables LANs to run at a 100 Mbps data transfer rate, a tenfold increase from that provided by 10BaseT, without requiring a significant investment in new infrastructure. 100BaseT uses baseband transmission in a star-wired bus or hierarchical hybrid topology, just like 10BaseT. It also uses the same cabling and RJ-45 data connectors. Therefore, 100BaseT upgrades are easy and inexpensive to accomplish for an organization that currently uses the popular 10BaseT technology.

As with 10BaseT, the length between an end node and the hub for 100BaseT networks cannot exceed 100 meters. Another limitation of 100BaseT technology is that, although it uses CSMA/CD like the other Ethernet versions, data travel so quickly that NICs can't always keep up with the collision detection and retransmission routines. In CSMA/CD, when a collision occurs, the NIC has a small amount of time to both detect and compensate for the error. Because of the speed employed on a 100BaseT network, the window of time for the NIC to accomplish these routines is further reduced. To minimize undetected collisions, 100BaseT buses can practically support a maximum of three network segments connected with two hubs. This shorter path reduces the highest potential propagation delay between nodes.

As with other Ethernet technologies, the actual data transmission rate on a 100BaseT network will vary, depending on the processing power of the server, the bus, the NIC, and the connectivity devices. In fact, because of the small size of the average Ethernet packet, it is not possible to achieve even true 100 Mbps throughput. Installing a 100BaseT network, however, ensures that the groundwork is laid for future Ethernet improvements.

Two 100BaseT specifications—100BaseT4 and 100BaseTX—are competing for popularity as organizations move to 100 Mbps technology. The difference between these technologies relates primarily to the way they achieve the 100 Mbps transmission rate, which affects their cabling requirements.

100BaseTX—the version you are most likely to encounter—achieves its speed by sending the signal 10 times faster and condensing the time between digital pulses as well as the time a station must wait and listen in CSMA/CD. It requires Category 5 unshielded twisted-pair cabling.

100BaseT4 achieves its speed by breaking the 100 Mbps data stream into three streams of 33 Mbps each. These three streams are sent over three pairs of unshielded twisted-pair wiring. The fourth pair is used for collision detection. 100BaseT4 can use lower-cost Category 3 wiring. Because 100BaseT4 technology uses all four wire pairs for unidirectional signaling, it cannot support **full duplexing**, an enhancement that allows simultaneous two-way transmission between nodes while eliminating collisions. Full duplexing can potentially double the bandwidth of a 100BaseT network to 200 Mbps. 100BaseTX can support full duplexing, which is one reason it is more popular than 100BaseT4.

You cannot mix 100BaseTX and 100BaseT4 on a single network segment. For example, if you purchase a hub designed for 100BaseTX transmission, you cannot use NICs designed for 100BaseT4 transmission to connect to that hub.

100BaseVG A cousin of Ethernet that also supports the 100 Mbps data transmission rate is **100BaseVG**, also called 100VG AnyLAN. The "VG" stands for "voice grade." 100BaseVG, which was originally developed by Hewlett-Packard and AT&T, is now governed by IEEE standard 802.12; the Ethernet versions discussed earlier are governed by IEEE standard 802.3.

One difference between 100BaseVG and 100BaseT is that 100BaseVG does not use CSMA/CD, but rather an access method called demand priority. In **demand priority**, each device on a star or hierarchical network sends a request to transmit to the central hub, which grants the requests one at a time. The hub examines incoming data packets, determines the location of the destination node, and forwards the packets to that destination. Because demand priority runs on a star topology, no workstations except the source and destination can "see" the data. Data travel from one device to the hub, then to another device. The hub acts as a central transfer point. Figure 5-23 contrasts CSMA/CD with demand priority techniques.

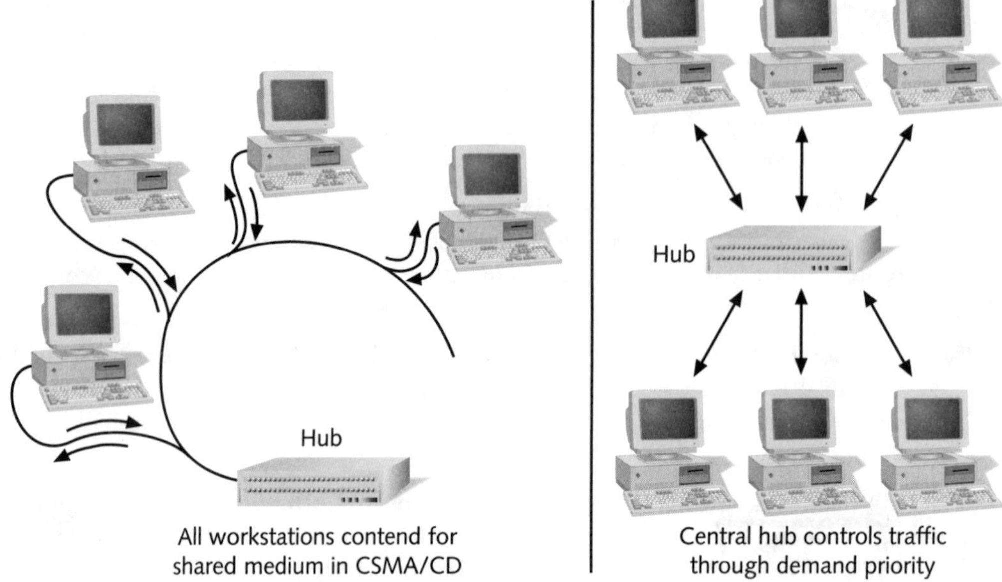
Hub
All workstations contend for shared medium in CSMA/CD
Hub
Central hub controls traffic through demand priority

Figure 5-23 CSMA/CD versus demand priority

Because the hub determines which nodes transmit and when, data collisions do not happen in demand priority. Without the collision detection and correction that occur in CSMA/CD, data travel unimpeded. Another advantage to using 100BaseVG is that, because data do not pass by each node on the network, they remain secure; packets transmitted from one workstation cannot be trapped and decoded by any workstation on the network except for the destination. In addition, 100BaseVG enables the hub to prioritize transmission requests. If multiple requests arrive at the hub simultaneously, the hub services the highest-priority request first. This approach allows 100BaseVG to better serve networks that carry audio, video, or other time-sensitive data (explaining the "voice grade" specification). NIC drivers compatible with the 100BaseVG priority assignment scheme must be in place to take advantage of this feature.

Like 100BaseT4, 100BaseVG uses all four wire pairs in the twisted-pair cable; it can, however, use the same cabling that 10BaseT networks employ. 100BaseVG requires an **intelligent hub**—that is, a hub that can manage transmissions by dictating which nodes send and receive data at every instant—rather than a hub that simply regenerates signals. Many of today's Ethernet networks do not have intelligent hubs.

Another disadvantage of 100BaseVG is that the time the hub takes to process each request reduces the network's overall performance, so that it cannot usually match the speed of a 100BaseT network. Also, 100BaseVG cannot take advantage of full duplexing, which can potentially double a network's bandwidth. For these reasons, 100BaseVG is not widely implemented.

SWITCHED ETHERNET

Traditional Ethernet LANs (shared Ethernet) supply a fixed amount of bandwidth that must be shared by all devices on a segment. Stations cannot send and receive data simultaneously, nor can they transmit a signal when another station on their segment is sending or receiving data. The limiting device in this case comprises the hub or repeater, which merely amplifies and retransmits a signal. In contrast, a **switch** is a device that can separate a network segment into smaller segments, with each segment being independent of the others and supporting its own traffic. **Switched Ethernet** is a newer Ethernet model that enables multiple nodes to simultaneously transmit and receive data and individually take advantage of more bandwidth because they are assigned separate logical network segments through switching. Figure 5-24 shows how switches can isolate network segments. You will learn more about switches in Chapter 6.

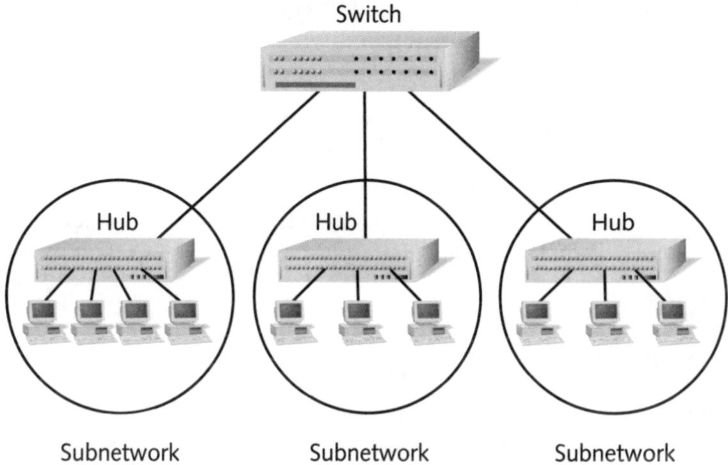

Figure 5-24 A switched Ethernet network

Using switched Ethernet increases the effective bandwidth of a network segment because fewer workstations must vie for the same time on the wire. In fact, applying switches to a 10 Mbps Ethernet LAN can increase its effective data transmission rate to 100 Mbps. For organizations with existing 10BaseT infrastructure, switches offer an inexpensive way to add bandwidth. Switches can be placed strategically on an organization's network to balance traffic loads and reduce congestion.

Note, however, that switches are not always the best answer to heavy traffic and a need for greater speeds. In a case where an enterprise-wise Ethernet LAN is generally overtaxed, you should consider upgrading the network's design or infrastructure.

As you would probably guess, the evolution of Ethernet will not stop with the development of switched Ethernet and the 100 Mbps standard. Through its 802.3z project, IEEE is currently finalizing the specifications for an Ethernet version that runs at 1000 Mbps, called **1 Gigabit Ethernet**.

IEEE intends to provide a standard that can use some existing infrastructure from 10BaseT or 100BaseT networks, thereby facilitating the transition to 1 Gigabit Ethernet. Although 1 Gigabit Ethernet can technically run over unshielded twisted-pair (UTP) cable, it performs much better over fiber. Running over UTP, 1 Gigabit Ethernet's distance limitation is approximately 80 feet, a very impractical requirement for any sizable LAN. In contrast, a segment of 1 Gigabit Ethernet running on fiber can span a maximum of 3 kilometers. IEEE is working to exceed the UTP limitation; this goal could be achieved by using an even higher grade of copper wire than is commonly available today.

The 1 Gigabit technology will compete directly with other fast networking solutions such as Asynchronous Transfer Mode (ATM), which is covered in Chapter 7 of this book. You will most likely encounter 1 Gigabit Ethernet as part of a network's backbone. It is well suited to connecting multiple buildings on a single campus, for example. Currently, this scheme would not be appropriate for connecting workstations to hubs, for example, because workstations' NICs and CPUs could not process data fast enough to make the cost worthwhile. In the near future, however, PCs will be equipped with adequate hardware and processing power to take advantage of 1 Gigabit Ethernet.

Like 100BaseT technology, 1 Gigabit Ethernet will include several variations suited to different purposes. Currently, IEEE has identified three versions: 1000BaseCX, 1000BaseSX, and 1000BaseLX. To learn more about 1 Gigabit Ethernet, connect to the Gigabit Ethernet Alliance's Web site at http://www.gigabit-ethernet.org/. The Gigabit Ethernet Alliance is a consortium of organizations championing the development and use of this emerging technology.

ETHERNET FRAME TYPES

Chapter 2 introduced you to data frames, the packages that carry higher-layer data and control information that enables data to reach their destinations without errors and in the correct sequence. The Ethernet data frame discussed in Chapter 2 is an example of a typical Ethernet data frame. In fact, networks may use one (or a combination) of four kinds of Ethernet data frames: Ethernet 802.2, Ethernet 802.3, Ethernet II, and Ethernet SNAP.

Each frame type differs slightly in the way it codes and decodes packets of data from one NIC to another. All frame types have four fields in common: the source address, the destination address, a data field, and an error checking field. On contemporary LANs, you will most likely encounter Ethernet 802.2 or Ethernet 802.3 frame types.

Ethernet frame types do not depend on the Ethernet version used by a network. Whereas the version (10Base2 versus 10BaseT, for example) depends on the Physical layer, frame types follow Network and Data Link layer specifications. In fact, frame types have little relation to the topology or cabling characteristics of the network.

Ethernet frame sizes vary. Each frame contains a 14-byte header and a 4-byte Frame Check Sequence field. These two fields add 18 bytes to the frame size. The data portion of the frame may contain from 46 to 1500 bytes of information (if less than 46 bytes of data are carried, the network pads out the data portion until it totals 46 bytes). Thus the minimum Ethernet frame size is 18 + 46, or 64, bytes and the maximum Ethernet frame size is 18 + 1500, or 1518, bytes. Because of the overhead present in each frame and the time required to enact CSMA/CD, the use of larger frame sizes on a network generally results in faster throughput. To some extent, you cannot control frame sizes. You can, however, minimize the number of broadcast frames on your network, as broadcast frames tend to be very small.

Ethernet 802.2

Ethernet 802.2 is the default frame type for versions 4.x and higher of the Novell Netware network operating system. It supports the IPX/SPX protocol. The defining characteristics of its data portion are the source and destination service access points that belong to the Logical Link Control layer, a sublayer of the Data Link layer. Figure 5-25 depicts an Ethernet 802.2 frame.

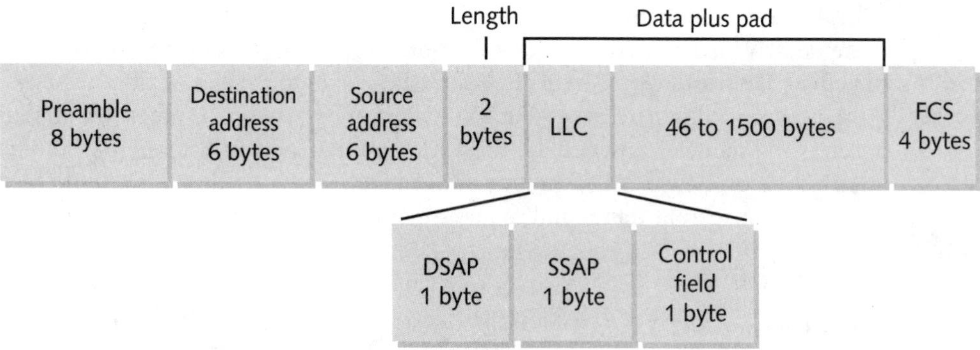

Figure 5-25 An Ethernet 802.2 frame

Like other Ethernet frame types, an Ethernet 802.2 frame contains an 8-byte preamble. This preamble signals the receiving node that data are incoming and indicates when the data flow is about to begin. Preambles are not included when you calculate a frame's total size.

The Destination Address and Source Address fields in an Ethernet 802.2 frame are each 6 bytes long. As you might guess, the destination address identifies the recipient of the data frame, and the source address identifies the network node that originally sent the data. Recall from Chapter 3 that any network device can be identified by its logical address (protocol-dependent) or its physical address (hardware-dependent). The physical address is also called the Medium Access Control (MAC) address. Because MAC addresses are hard-coded into the node's NIC, and each manufacturer uses a different identifying code, no two devices should ever have the same address. The Source Address and Destination Address fields of an Ethernet 802.2 frame use the MAC address to identify where data originated and where it should be delivered. The same is true for all Ethernet frame types.

Ethernet 802.2 frames also include a field 2 bytes long that identifies the length of the data field. The data field in an 802.2 frame contains not only the data transmitted by the source node, but also Logical Link Control (LLC) layer information whose purpose is to distinguish among multiple clients on a network. It may also include padding, if the LLC and data information do not total at least 46 bytes. The length field, however, does not care about the padding. It will report only the length of LLC plus data information.

The LLC information comprises three fields: Destination Service Access Point (DSAP), Source Service Access Point (SSAP), and a control field. Each of these fields is 1 byte long, making the total LLC field 3 bytes long. A **Service Access Point (SAP)** identifies a node or internal process that uses the LLC protocol. Each process between a source and destination node on the network may have a unique SAP. The control field identifies the kind of LLC connection that must be established, from unacknowledged (connectionless) to fully acknowledged (connection-oriented).

The data field of the Ethernet 802.2 frame is the easiest field to understand. It contains the data sent by the originating node, before the packet was passed down from the top layer of the OSI Model.

The **Frame Check Sequence (FCS)** field ensures that the data are received just as they were sent. When the source node transmits the data, it performs an algorithm called a **Cyclical Redundancy Check (CRC)**. CRC takes the values of all of the preceding fields in the frame and generates a unique 4-byte number, the FCS. When the destination node receives the frame, it unscrambles the FCS via CRC and makes sure that the frame's fields match their original form. If this comparison fails, the receiving node assumes that the frame has been damaged in transit and requests that the source node retransmit the data.

Ethernet 802.3

The **Ethernet 802.3** frame type is the original NetWare frame type and the default frame type for networks running NetWare versions lower than 3.12. It supports only the IPX/SPX protocol. Ethernet 802.3 is sometimes also called 802.3 "raw," because its data portion contains no control bits. Its fields match those of Ethernet 802.2, minus the Logical Link Control layer information. Figure 5-26 depicts an Ethernet 802.3 frame.

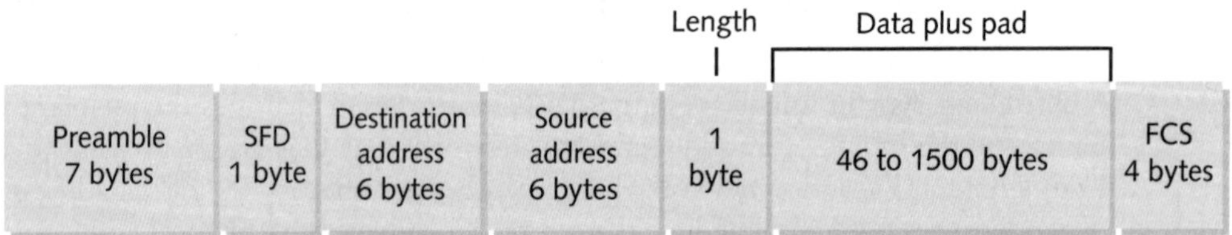

Figure 5-26 An Ethernet 802.3 frame

In an Ethernet 802.3 frame, the preamble is actually 7 bytes—the preamble can contain an additional field called the Start of Frame Delimiter (SFD). The SFD identifies where the data field begins.

Ethernet II

Ethernet II was the original Ethernet frame type developed by DEC, Intel, and Xerox, before the IEEE began to standardize Ethernet. The Ethernet II frame is similar to the Ethernet 802.3 frame, in that it lacks LLC information. Ethernet II frames contain a 2-byte type field, however, whereas the Ethernet 802.2 and 802.3 frames contain a 2-byte length field. This type field identifies the upper-layer protocol contained in the frame. For example, IPX uses a type field of 8137. IP uses a type field of 0800. This field enables Ethernet II to support Novell IPX/SPX, TCP/IP, and AppleTalk protocols, and it compensates for the lack of LLC information. Figure 5-27 depicts an Ethernet II frame.

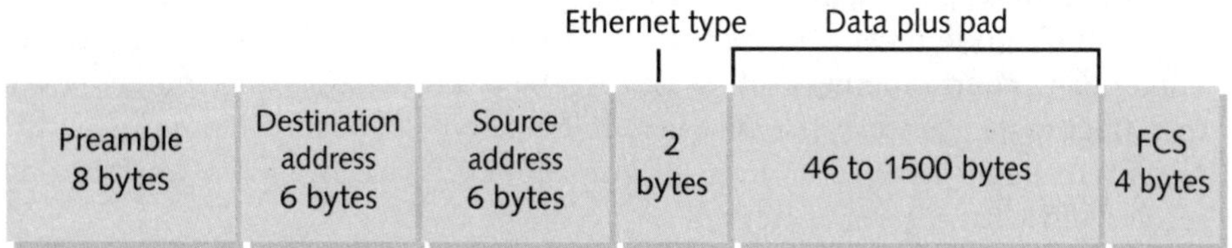

Figure 5-27 An Ethernet II frame

Ethernet SNAP

Ethernet SNAP is an adaptation of Ethernet 802.2 and Ethernet II. "SNAP" stands for Sub-Network Access Protocol. The SNAP portion of the frame is what Ethernet SNAP borrowed from Ethernet 802.2—the three LLC fields (DSAP, SSAP, and the control field). The Ethernet SNAP frame, however, contains an additional field: the Organization ID (OUI), a method of identifying the type of network on which the frame is running. In addition, Ethernet SNAP frames carry Ethernet type information, just as an Ethernet II frame does. Ethernet SNAP is compatible with IPX/SPX, TCP/IP, and AppleTalk protocols, but it is rarely used. Figure 5-28 depicts an Ethernet SNAP frame.

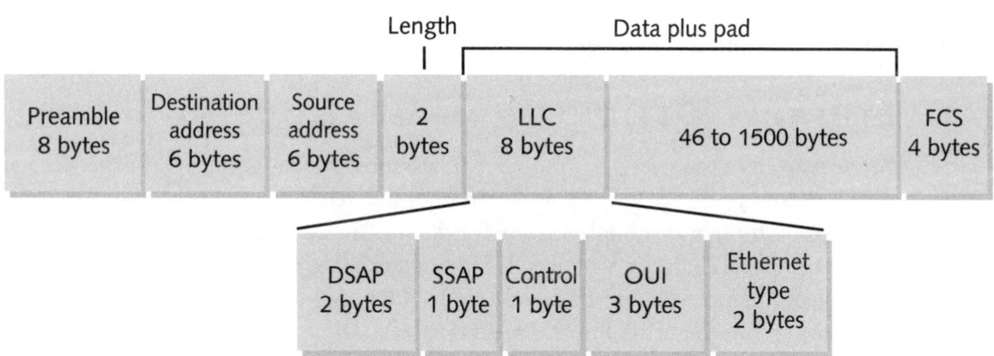

Figure 5-28 An Ethernet SNAP frame

Understanding Frame Types

You might wonder why you should learn about frame types, which represent the underlying structure of data signals. It's a good question, and the answer relates to problem solving in networks. As a professional networker, you may need to capture data and analyze frames when troubleshooting with a protocol analyzer. When analyzing the frames, you can actually decode the data in every field, if you know what the fields are.

Learning about frame types is analogous to learning a foreign language, with the frame type being the language's syntax. Just as you might know the Japanese word for "go," but not know how to use it in a sentence, you may know all about the IPX/SPX protocol, but not how devices handle it. (Chapter 12 covers this kind of troubleshooting in more detail.)

A good knowledge of frame types will help you in many areas of your networking career. For example, to improve a network's performance, you might need to identify the kinds of frames that traverse the network. When working with bridges and routers, you might have to configure the device to handle a certain frame type. Probably the most common problem relating to frame types arises from incompatibility between what a workstation expects to receive and what the server transmits.

As you learned in Chapter 2, you may use multiple frame types on a network, but you cannot expect interoperability between the frame types. For example, in a mixed environment of NetWare 3.11 and NetWare 4.11 servers, your network will probably support both Ethernet 802.3 and Ethernet 802.2 frames. A workstation connecting to the NetWare 3.11 server might be configured to use the Ethernet 802.3 frame while a workstation connecting to the NetWare 4.11 server might use Ethernet 802.2.

Modern networks simplify the issue of frame type specification by allowing you to instruct a NIC, through the device driver software, to automatically sense what types of frames are running on a network and set themselves to that specification. This feature, called **autosense**, is generally available on all NICs manufactured in the last few years. Workstations, networked printers, and servers added to an existing network can all take advantage of autosense. Even if you use autosense, you should nevertheless know what frame types are running on your network so that you can troubleshoot connectivity problems. As easy as it is to configure, the autosense feature is not infallible.

Ethernet Design Considerations

More than any other network model, you are most apt to work on an Ethernet network. You may be asked to design one from scratch, consult with clients on how to expand or improve a current system, or troubleshoot one for design flaws. As you've seen in this chapter, Ethernet comes in several different varieties. It's important to understand the differences between each version and frame type and their limitations. Table 5-1 summarizes the characteristics of each Ethernet version described in the preceding sections.

Table 5-1 Characteristics of different Ethernet versions

Standard	Speed (Mbps)	Maximum Distance (m)	Physical Media (typical)	Topology (typical)
10Base2	10	185	Thin coaxial cable	Bus
10Base5	10	500	Thick coaxial cable	Bus
10BaseT	10	100	Unshielded twisted-pair	Star-wired bus
100BaseTX	100	100	Unshielded twisted-pair	Star-wired bus
100BaseT4	100	100	Unshielded twisted-pair	Star-wired bus
100BaseVG	100	100	Unshielded twisted-pair	Star-wired bus
1 Gigabit	1000	500	Multimode fiber	Various
1 Gigabit	1000	3000	Single-mode fiber	Various

Some networks may use more than one type of physical media. For instance, 100BaseTX could run on fiber, even though the minimum standard is unshielded twisted-pair cabling. 1 Gigabit Ethernet could run on unshielded twisted-pair, albeit with severe distance limitations, so fiber is recommended.

In addition to the limitations mentioned earlier, Ethernet networks can support a maximum of only 1024 addressable nodes on a logical network. Thus, if you have a campus with 3000 users, hundreds of networked printers, and scores of other devices, you must strategically create smaller logical networks. Even if you had 1000 users and *could* put them on the same logical network, you wouldn't, because doing so would result in poor performance and impossible management. Instead, you should subdivide the users and their peripherals into workgroups according to their needs or geographic locations. Chapter 15 describes the process of evaluating user and organizational requirements when designing a network.

Token Ring

Now that you have learned about the many forms of Ethernet, you are ready to learn about Token Ring, a less common, but still important network transport model. As you learned in Chapter 2, Token Ring is a network transport system first developed by IBM in the 1980s. In the early 1990s, the Token Ring architecture competed strongly with Ethernet to be the most popular networking technology. Since that time, Ethernet has improved its economics, speed, and reliability, leaving Token Ring behind. Because IBM developed Token Ring, some IBM-centric IS departments continue to use it. Many other network managers have changed their former Token Ring networks into Ethernet networks.

Token Ring networks are generally more expensive to implement than Ethernet networks. Proponents of the Token Ring technology argue that, although some of its connectivity hardware is more expensive, its reliability results in less downtime and lower network management costs than Ethernet provides. On a practical level, Token Ring has probably lost the battle for superiority because of its limited speed. Token Ring networks currently run at either 4 or 16 Mbps. Faster Token Ring technology is being developed, but may arrive too late to win many converts.

Token Ring networks use the token passing routine and a star-ring hybrid physical topology. Recall from the discussion of the ring topology earlier in this chapter that a token designates which station on the ring can transmit information on the wire. On a Token Ring network, one workstation, called the active monitor, acts as the controller for token passing. Specifically, the **active monitor** maintains the timing for ring passing, monitors token and frame transmission, detects lost tokens, and corrects errors when a timing error or other disruption occurs. Only one workstation on the ring can act as the active monitor at any given time.

In token passing, a 3-byte token circulates around the network. When a station has something to send, it picks up the token, changes it to a frame, and then adds the header, information, and trailer fields. The header includes the address of the destination node. All nodes read the frame as it traverses the ring to determine whether they are the intended recipient of the message. If they are, they pick up the data, then retransmit the frame to the next station on the ring. When the frame finally reaches the originating station, the originating workstation reissues a free token that can then be used by another station. The token passing control scheme ensures high data reliability (no collisions) and an efficient use of bandwidth. It also does not impose distance limitations on the length of a LAN segment, unlike CSMA/CD. On the other hand, token ring passing generates extra network traffic.

The Token Ring architecture is often mistakenly described as a pure ring topology. In fact, it uses a star-ring hybrid topology in which data circulate in a ring fashion, but the physical layout of the network is a star.

IEEE standard 802.5 describes the specifications for Token Ring technology. Token Ring networks transmit data at either 4 Mbps or 16 Mbps over shielded or unshielded twisted-pair wiring. You may have as many as 260 addressable stations on a Token Ring network that uses shielded twisted-pair or as many as 72 addressable stations on one that uses unshielded twisted-pair. All Token Ring connections rely on an NIC that taps into the network through a **Multistation Access Unit (MAU)**, Token Ring's equivalent of a hub. NICs can be designed to run specifically on 4 or 16 Mbps networks or they can be designed to accommodate both data transmission rates. In the star-ring hybrid topology, the MAU completes the ring internally with Ring In and Ring Out ports at either end of the unit. In addition, MAUs typically provide eight ports for workstation connections. You can easily expand a Token Ring network by connecting multiple MAUs through by their Ring In and Ring Out ports, as shown in Figure 5-29. Unused ports on a MAU, including Ring In and Ring Out ports, have self-shorting data connectors that internally close the loop.

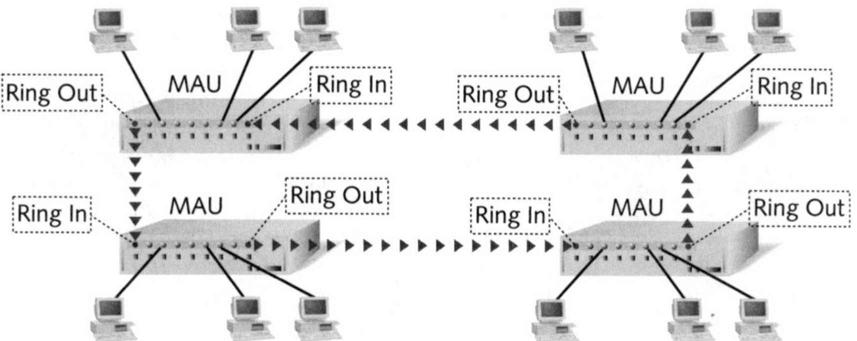

Figure 5-29 Interconnected Token Ring MAUs

The self-shorting feature of Token Ring MAU ports makes Token Ring highly fault-tolerant. For example, if you discover a problematic NIC on the network, you can remove that workstation's cable from the MAU and the MAU's port will close the ring internally. Similarly, if you discover a faulty MAU, you can remove it from the ring by disconnecting its Ring In and Ring Out cables from its adjacent MAUs and connect the two good MAUs to each other to close the loop.

Token Ring Switching

Like Ethernet networks, Token Ring networks can take advantage of switching to better utilize limited bandwidth. Token Ring switching products are typically more expensive and more difficult to manage than Ethernet switches, although they perform essentially the same function. A Token Ring switch can subdivide a large network ring into several smaller network rings. For example, if a 16 Mbps Token Ring network supports 40 users, each workstation has access to approximately 0.4 Mbps. Installing a Token Ring switch that is configured to subdivide the network into four logical subnetworks provides each workstation with approximately 1.6 Mbps (under optimal physical conditions). Thus switching effectively quadruples the bandwidth in this example.

Remember, however, that Token Ring technology does not allow collisions. For this reason, the bandwidth available to each user does not quickly degrade as more users are added; contrast this characteristic to the performance hit Ethernet takes when more users connect to a single segment.

Token Ring Frames

Token Ring networks may use one of two types of frames: the IEEE 802.5 or the IBM Token Ring frame. The only difference between the two types is that the IBM Token Ring frame adds 2 to 16 octets of routing information that only IBM applications use. Figure 5-30 shows the IBM version of a Token Ring frame.

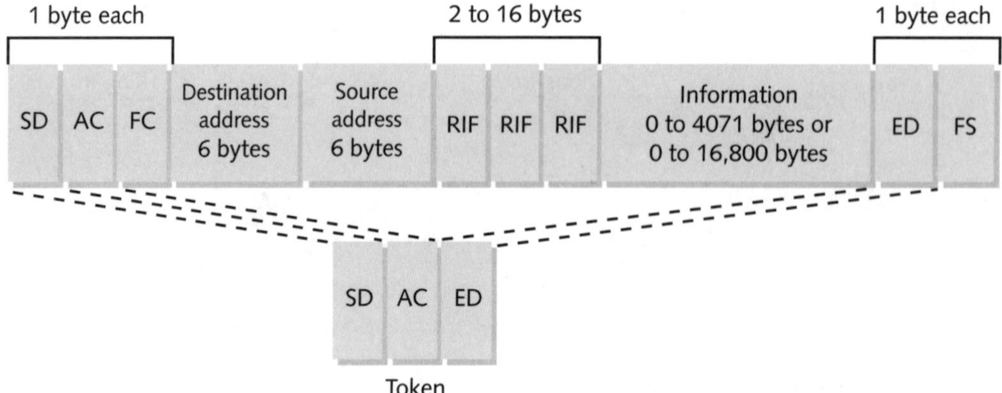

Figure 5-30 An IBM Token Ring frame

Every Token Ring frame includes Starting Delimiter (SD), Access Control (AC), and Ending Delimiter (ED) fields. These three fields of 1 octet each make up the token. Remember that the token is not a frame, but rather is transformed into a frame after a workstation picks it up. The Access Control byte of the token equals 0 bytes if the token is available and 1 if the token is part of a frame currently carrying data, thus signaling that it is not free.

Token Ring frames, just like Ethernet frames, contain destination address and source address fields. As with Ethernet, Token Ring addresses use the MAC address of the device. The destination address is the MAC address of the workstation that will receive the data. The source address is the MAC address of the workstation that transmitted the data. On Token Ring networks, you may also encounter manually administered addresses, a result of limitations in IBM's early host equipment. Manually assigning network addresses is not a good policy, however. By doing so, you create more work for network administrators and increase the potential for errors.

IBM Token Ring frames use the 2 to 16 octets of routing information mentioned earlier with a routing protocol called Source Route Bridging. Source route bridges analyze the information to determine the best path for data transmission between two nodes. You will learn more about source route bridges in Chapter 6.

Both IEEE 802.5 and IBM Token Ring frames contain an information field. Depending on the speed of the Token Ring network, this field can contain from 0 to more than 4000 bytes (for a 4 Mbps network) or from 0 to more than 16,000 bytes (for a 16 Mbps network). Altogether, the maximum frame size for a 4 Mbps network is 4094 bytes; for a 16 Mbps network, it is 17,800 bytes. Notice how much larger the Token Ring frames are than Ethernet frames. As you have learned, larger frame sizes result in more efficient data transmission.

After the data field, each Token Ring frame possesses a Frame Check Sequence (FCS). As in Ethernet networks, Token Ring frames use a CRC algorithm to ensure that the data received matches the data sent. The FCS contains the results of this algorithm. In addition, Token Ring frames use a Frame Status (FS) to provide low-level acknowledgment that the frame was received whole.

DESIGN CONSIDERATIONS FOR TOKEN RING NETWORKS

If you work on Token Ring networks, you will most likely use a long-established LAN rather than a newly implemented one. In this case, your design considerations will apply to expansion and improvement of an existing infrastructure. Bear in mind these characteristics of Token Ring networks:

- **Cabling**—Token Ring networks can use shielded or unshielded twisted-pair cabling.
- **Connectivity devices**—Token Ring NICs, switches, hubs, routers, and bridges are generally more expensive than comparable Ethernet equipment.
- **Number of stations**—The number of allowable stations on a Token Ring network is limited, depending on its cabling. You may attach 260 addressable stations on a Token Ring network that uses shielded twisted-pair, or as many as 72 addressable stations on one that uses unshielded twisted-pair.
- **Speed**—Token ring networks can run at either 4 Mbps or 16 Mbps. Faster Token Ring technology remains in the development stage.
- **Scalability**—You can easily daisy-chain Token Ring MAUs to expand the network. Nodes are also easily added to a network due to its star layout.
- **Topology**—Token Ring networks use a star-wired ring hybrid topology, which is highly fault-tolerant.

CHAPTER SUMMARY

- A physical topology is a drawing that represents the basic physical layout of a network; it does not specify devices, connectivity methods, or addresses on the network. Physical topologies are categorized into three fundamental geometric shapes: bus, ring, and star.
- A bus topology consists of a single cable connecting all nodes on a network without intervening connectivity devices. At either end of a bus network, 50-ohm resistors (terminators) stop signals after they have reached their destination. Without terminators, signals on a bus network would travel endlessly between the two ends of the network, a phenomenon known as signal bounce.
- In a ring topology, each node is connected to the two nearest nodes so that the entire network forms a circle. Data are transmitted unidirectionally around the ring. Each workstation accepts and responds to packets addressed to it, then forwards the other packets to the next workstation in the ring.
- In a star topology, every node on the network is connected through a central device, such as a hub. Any single physical wire on a star network connects only two devices, so a cabling problem will affect only two nodes. Nodes transmit data to the hub, which then retransmits the information to the rest of the network segment where the destination node can pick it up.

- Except for home office networks, few LANs use the simple physical topologies in their pure form. More often, LANs employ a hybrid of more than one simple physical topology.
- The star-wired ring topology is a network that uses the physical layout of a star and the token-passing data transmission method. Data are sent around the star in a circular pattern. Modern Token Ring networks, as specified in IEEE 802.5, use this hybrid topology.
- In a star-wired bus topology, groups of workstations star-connected to hubs are networked via a single bus. This design allows you to cover longer distances and easily interconnect or isolate different network segments, although it is more expensive than using either the star or bus topology alone. The star-wired bus topology commonly forms the basis for Ethernet and Fast Ethernet networks.
- Hubs that service star-wired bus or star-wired ring topologies can be daisy-chained to form a more complex hybrid topology.
- A hierarchical hybrid topology can designate hubs at different layers to perform different functions.
- The cabling that connects each hub, or different level of the hierarchy, is called the backbone. A backbone is sometimes called "a network of networks." Backbones usually transmit data at faster speeds than does the cabling that connects each workstation, because they handle the largest loads.
- A serial backbone is the simplest kind of backbone. It consists of two or more hubs connected to each other by a single cable.
- A distributed backbone consists of a number of hubs connected to a series of central hubs or routers in a hierarchy.
- The collapsed backbone topology uses a router or switch as the single central connection point for multiple subnetworks.
- A parallel backbone is the most robust enterprise-wide topology. It is a variation of the collapsed backbone arrangement that consists of more than one connection from the central router or switch to each network segment.
- In a mesh network, routers are interconnected with other routers so that at least two pathways connect each node.
- WAN topologies use the LAN and enterprise-wide topologies as building blocks, but add more complexity because of the distance they must cover, the higher number of users they serve, and heavier traffic they often handle. The WAN topology you choose will depend on the number of sites you must connect, the distance between the sites, and any existing infrastructure.
- Dedicated circuits are continuous physical or logical connections between two access points that are leased from a communications provider, such as an ISP or local phone company.

- A WAN with single interconnection points for each location is arranged in a peer-to-peer topology. This topology often represents the best solution for organizations with only a few sites and access to dedicated circuits.
- The star topology in a WAN mimics the arrangement of a star LAN. A single site acts as the central connection point for several other points. This arrangement provides several routes for data to follow between any two sites and is therefore more reliable than the peer-to-peer or ring WANs.
- In WAN ring topology, each site is connected to two other sites so that the entire WAN forms a ring pattern. This architecture is similar to the LAN ring topology, except that a WAN ring topology connects locations rather than local nodes.
- As with an enterprise-wide mesh, a mesh WAN topology consists of many directly interconnected nodes—in this case, locations. Mesh WANs are the most fault-tolerant WAN configuration. Connecting every node on a network is very expensive, however, because of the number of dedicated circuits involved.
- Tiered WAN topologies are similar to the hierarchical hybrid topologies used with LANs. In a tiered topology, WAN sites connected in star or ring formations are interconnected at different levels, with the interconnection points being organized into layers. Tiered systems allow for easy expansion and inclusion of redundant links to support growth.
- Network transport systems encompass a set of rules specifying which data are packaged and transmitted over network media. They are sometimes referred to as the network's logical topology. The two most popular network transport systems are Ethernet and Token Ring.
- Switching is a component of a network's logical topology that manages filtering and forwarding of packets between nodes on the network. Every network relies on one of three types of switching: circuit switching, message switching, or packet switching.
- Ethernet is a networking technology originally developed by Xerox in the 1970s and improved by Xerox, Digital Equipment Corporation, and Intel. This flexible technology can run on a variety of network media and offers excellent throughput at a reasonable cost. Ethernet is by far the most popular logical topology for LANs today, and its popularity continues to grow.
- Ethernet follows a set of communication rules called Carrier Sense Multiple Access with Collision Detection (CSMA/CD). All Ethernet networks, independent of their speed or frame type, use CSMA/CD.
- On heavily trafficked Ethernet networks, collisions are not uncommon. The more nodes that are transmitting data on a network, the more collisions that will take place. When an Ethernet network grows to a particular number of nodes, performance may suffer as a result of collisions.
- Ethernet comes in a variety of implementations. Each Ethernet version follows a slightly different IEEE 802.3 specification that outlines its speed, topology, and cabling characteristics.

- 10Base2 is an Ethernet adaptation that, according to IEEE 802.3 standards, uses thin coaxial cable and a simple bus topology. It is also called Thinnet or Thin Ethernet. 10Base2 uses baseband transmission, can carry data at a rate of 10 Mbps, and has a maximum distance limitation for the cabling between nodes and hubs of 185 meters. It is not suited to large LANs. The primary advantages to using 10Base2 are its low cost and ease of installation.
- 10Base5 is the original cabling standard for Ethernet and uses thick coaxial cable. It is also known as Thicknet or Thick Ethernet. Like 10Base2, Thicknet uses a bus topology and can carry data at speeds of only 10 Mbps. The "5" in 10Base5 refers to its maximum cabling distance of 500 meters. Thicknet is more expensive than Thinnet and is rarely used today because of its thick, inflexible cable and cumbersome connectivity devices, in addition to its size and speed limits.
- 10BaseT is the most ubiquitous Ethernet cabling specification today. It uses twisted-pair cabling and a star topology to transmit data at 10 Mbps. Its maximum segment length is 100 meters.
- The actual transmission rate on an Ethernet network will vary and will likely be less than its rating, either 10 Mbps or 100 Mbps.
- 100BaseT, also called Fast Ethernet and specified in the IEEE 802.3u standard, enables LANs to provide a 100 Mbps data transfer rate, a tenfold increase from what 10BaseT provides, without requiring significant investment in new infrastructure. 100BaseT uses baseband transmission in a star-wired bus or hierarchical hybrid topology, just like 10BaseT.
- Two 100BaseT specifications—100BaseT4 and 100BaseTX—are competing for popularity as organizations move to 100 Mbps technology. The difference between these technologies lies primarily in the way they achieve the 100 Mbps transmission rate, which affects their cabling requirements. Both 100BaseT technologies use CSMA/CD, unshielded twisted-pair cabling, and a star-wired bus or hierarchical topology.
- A variation of Ethernet that also supports the 100 Mbps data transmission rate is 100BaseVG, also called 100VG AnyLAN (where the "VG" stands for "voice grade"). 100BaseVG does not use CSMA/CD, but rather a transmission technique called demand priority in which each device on a star or hierarchical network sends a request to transmit to the central hub, which grants the requests one at a time.
- 1 Gigabit Ethernet is an emerging 1000 Mbps Ethernet technology defined by IEEE 802.3z specifications.
- A switch is a device that can separate a network segment into smaller segments, each independent of the other and supporting its own traffic. The use of switched Ethernet increases the effective bandwidth of a network segment because fewer workstations vie for the same time on the wire.
- Networks may use one (or a combination) of four kinds of Ethernet data frames: Ethernet II, Ethernet SNAP, Ethernet 802.2, and Ethernet 802.3. Each frame type differs slightly in the way it codes and decodes packets of data from one NIC to another. All frame types have the following fields in common: a source address, a destination

address, a data field, and an error checking field. On contemporary LANs, you will most likely encounter Ethernet 802.2 or Ethernet 802.3 frame types.

- Token Ring networks currently run at either 4 or 16 Mbps, as specified by IEEE 802.5. Faster Token Ring technology is being developed, but will arrive too late to be widely adopted. Token Ring is generally more expensive to implement than Ethernet, but offers high reliability and fault tolerance.
- Token Ring networks use the token-passing routine and a star-ring hybrid physical topology. Workstations connect to the network through Multistation Access Units (MAUs). Token Ring networks may use shielded or unshielded twisted-pair cabling.

KEY TERMS

- **1 Gigabit Ethernet** — A new version of high-speed Ethernet specified by IEEE's 802.3z project. 1 Gigabit Ethernet runs at 1000 Mbps and usually relies on fiber-optic cable, although it can run on short segments of unshielded twisted-pair wiring.
- **10Base2** — An Ethernet adaptation that, according to IEEE 802.3 standards, uses thin coaxial cable and a simple bus topology. 10Base2 is also called Thinnet or Thin Ethernet. Its name derives from the fact that it can transmit data at 10 Mbps (thus the "10Base") and its maximum segment length is 185, or approximately 200, meters (thus the "2").
- **10Base5** — The original cabling standard for Ethernet; it uses a bus topology and thick coaxial cable. It is also known as Thicknet or Thick Ethernet. Its name derives from the fact that it can transmit data at 10 Mbps (thus the "10Base") and its maximum segment length is 500 meters (thus the "5").
- **10BaseT** — An Ethernet version that uses twisted-pair cabling and a star-bus or hierarchical hybrid topology to transmit data at 10 Mbps. Its name derives from the fact that it can transmit data at 10 Mbps (thus the "10Base") and it requires twisted-pair wiring (thus the "T").
- **100BaseT** — An Ethernet version specified in the IEEE 802.3u standard that enables LANs to run a 100 Mbps data transfer rate, without requiring significant investment in new infrastructure. 100BaseT uses baseband transmission in a star-bus or hierarchical hybrid topology, like 10BaseT. Also like 10BaseT, the "T" in 100BaseT refers to the fact that it uses twisted-pair cabling.
- **100BaseT4** — A type of 100BaseT technology that achieves its speed by breaking the 100 Mbps data stream into three streams of 33 Mbps each. These three streams are sent over three pairs of unshielded twisted-pair wiring. The fourth pair is used for collision detection. 100BaseT4 uses lower-cost Category 3 wiring.
- **100BaseTX** — A type of 100BaseT technology that achieves its speed by sending the signal 10 times faster and condensing the time between digital pulses and the time a station is required to wait and listen in CSMA/CD. It requires Category 5 unshielded twisted-pair cabling.

- **100BaseVG** — A network transport model that can transmit data at 100 Mbps. Unlike Ethernet, 100BaseVG uses a demand priority access method rather than CSMA/CD. Like 100BaseTX, 100BaseVG uses all four wire pairs in a twisted-pair cable. The "VG" in its name refers to the fact that it can be used for "voice grade" communications (i.e., to carry audio or video signals).
- **active monitor** — On a Token Ring network, the workstation that maintains timing for token passing, monitors token and frame transmission, detects lost tokens, and corrects problems when a timing error or other disruption occurs. Only one workstation on the ring can act as the active monitor at any given time.
- **active topology** — A topology in which each workstation participates in transmitting data over the network.
- **autosense** — A feature of modern NICs that enables a NIC to automatically sense what types of frames are running on a network and set itself to that specification.
- **backbone** — The cabling that connects each connectivity device, or the different levels of a hierarchy of connectivity devices.
- **BNC T connectors** — Connectors used by nodes on a Thinnet (Ethernet 10Base2) cabling technology to tap into the network.
- **bus** — The single cable connecting all devices in a bus topology.
- **bus topology** — A topology in which a single cable connects all nodes on a network without intervening connectivity devices.
- **Carrier Sense Multiple Access with Collision Detection (CSMA/CD)** — Rules for communication used by shared Ethernet networks. In CSMA/CD each node waits its turn before transmitting data, to avoid interfering with other nodes' transmissions.
- **circuit switching** — A type of switching in which a connection is established between two network nodes before they begin transmitting data. Bandwidth is dedicated to this connection and remains available until users terminate the communication between the two nodes.
- **collapsed backbone** — A type of enterprise-wide backbone that uses a router or switch as the single central connection point for multiple subnetworks.
- **Cyclical Redundancy Check (CRC)** — An algorithm used by the FCS field in Ethernet frames. CRC takes the values of all preceding fields in the frame and generates a unique 4-byte number, the FCS. When the destination node receives the frame, it unscrambles the FCS via CRC and makes sure that the frame's fields match their original organization. If this comparison fails, the receiving node assumes that the frame has been damaged in transit and requests the source node retransmit the data.
- **daisy-chain** — A linked series of devices.
- **dedicated circuits** — Continuous physical or logical connections between two access points that are leased from a communications provider, such as an ISP or local phone company.

- **demand priority** — A method for data transmission used by 100BaseVG Ethernet networks. Each device on a star or hierarchical network sends a request to transmit to the central hub, which grants the requests one at a time. The hub examines incoming data packets, determines the destination node, and forwards the packets to that destination. Because demand priority runs on a star topology, no workstations except the source and destination can "see" the data. Data travel from one device to the hub, then to another device.
- **distributed backbone** — A type of enterprise-wide backbone that consists of a number of hubs connected to a series of central hubs or routers in a hierarchy.

- **enterprise** — An entire organization, including local and remote offices, a mixture of computer systems, and a number of departments. Enterprise-wide computing takes into account the breadth and diversity of a large organization's computer needs.
- **Ethernet 802.2** — The default frame type for Novell's IntraNetware network operating system. It supports the IPX/SPX protocol. The defining characteristics of its data portion are the source and destination service access points that belong to the Logical Link Control layer, a sublayer of the Data Link layer.
- **Ethernet 802.3** — The original NetWare Ethernet frame type and the default frame type for networks running NetWare versions lower than 3.12. It supports only the IPX/SPX protocol. Ethernet 802.3 is sometimes called 802.3 "raw," because its data portion contains no control bits.
- **Ethernet II** — The original Ethernet frame type developed by Digital, Intel, and Xerox, before the IEEE began to standardize Ethernet. Ethernet II lacks Logical Link Control layer information but contains a 2-byte type field to identify the upper-layer protocol contained in the frame.
- **Ethernet SNAP** — An adaptation of Ethernet 802.2 and Ethernet II. SNAP stands for Sub-Network Access Protocol. The SNAP portion of the frame contains the three Logical Link Control fields (DSAP, SSAP, and control). An additional field, the Organization ID (OUI), provides a method of identifying the type of network on which the frame is running. In addition, Ethernet SNAP frames carry Ethernet type information, just as an Ethernet II frame does.
- **Fast Ethernet** — See 100BaseT.
- **Frame Check Sequence (FCS)** — A field located at the end of an Ethernet frame that ensures data are received just as they were sent.
- **full duplexing** — An enhancement that allows simultaneous two-way transmission between nodes on a network while eliminating collisions. Full duplexing can potentially double a network's bandwidth.
- **hierarchical hybrid topology** — A network topology that uses layers to separate devices by their priority or function.
- **hybrid topology** — A complex combination of the simple physical topologies.

- **intelligent hub** — A hub that, rather than simply regenerating signals, can manage transmissions by dictating which nodes can send and receive data at every instant.
- **jamming** — The process by which a station's NIC will first propagate a collision throughout the network so no other station attempts to transmit; after propagating the collision, the NIC will remain silent for a period of time.
- **LAN topology** — The physical layout of a local area network (LAN).
- **layer** — A logical division between devices on a network.
- **logical topology** — The data transmission characteristics of a network design, such as its network transport model.
- **Megabits per second (Mbps)** — A measure of how much data a network can optimally transmit, based on its physical characteristics.
- **mesh network** — An enterprise-wide topology in which routers are interconnected with other routers so that at least two pathways connect each node.
- **mesh WAN topology** — A WAN topology that consists of many directly interconnected locations forming a complex mesh.
- **message switching** — A type of switching in which a connection is established between two devices in the connection path; one device transfers data to the second device, then breaks the connection. The information is stored and forwarded from the second device once a connection between that device and a third device on the path is established.
- **Multistation Access Unit (MAU)** — A device on a Token Ring network that regenerates signals; equivalent to a hub.
- **network transport systems** — A set of rules specifying which data are packaged and transmitted over network media.
- **packet switching** — A type of switching in which data are broken into packets before they are transported. In packet switching, packets can travel any path on the network to their destination, because each packet contains a destination address and sequencing information.
- **parallel backbone** — The most robust enterprise-wide topology. This variation on the collapsed backbone arrangement consists of more than one connection from the central router or switch to each network segment.
- **peer-to-peer topology** — A WAN with single interconnection points for each location.
- **physical topology** — The physical layout of a network. A physical topology depicts a network in broad scope; it does not specify devices, connectivity methods, or addresses on the network. Physical topologies are categorized into three fundamental geometric shapes: bus, ring, and star. These shapes can be mixed to create hybrid topologies.
- **repeater** — A device that regenerates and amplifies signals.

- **ring topology** — A network layout in which each node is connected to the two nearest nodes so that the entire network forms a circle. Data are transmitted unidirectionally around the ring. Each workstation accepts and responds to packets addressed to it, then forwards the other packets to the next workstation in the ring.
- **ring WAN topology** — A WAN topology in which each site is connected to two other sites so that the entire WAN forms a ring pattern. This architecture is similar to the LAN ring topology, except a WAN ring topology connects locations rather than local nodes.
- **serial backbone** — The simplest kind of backbone, consisting of two or more hubs connected to each other by a single cable.
- **Service Access Point (SAP)** — A feature of Ethernet networks that identifies a node or internal process that uses the LLC protocol. Each process between a source and destination node on the network may have a unique SAP.
- **signal bounce** — A phenomenon in which signals travel endlessly between the two ends of a bus network. Using 50-ohm resistors at either end of the network prevents signal bounce.
- **star topology** — A physical topology in which every node on the network is connected through a central device, such as a hub. Any single physical wire on a star network connects only two devices, so a cabling problem will affect only two nodes. Nodes transmit data to the hub, which then retransmits the data to the rest of the network segment where the destination node can pick it up.
- **star WAN topology** — A WAN topology that mimics the arrangement of star LANs. A single site acts as the central connection point for several other locations.
- **star-wired bus topology** — A hybrid topology in which groups of workstations are connected in a star fashion to hubs that are networked via a single bus.
- **star-wired ring topology** — A hybrid topology that uses the physical layout of a star and the token-passing data transmission method.
- **switch** — The hardware that manages network switching; used to separate a network segment into smaller segments, with each segment being independent of the others, and supporting its own traffic.
- **Switched Ethernet** — A newer Ethernet model that enables multiple nodes to simultaneously transmit and receive data and individually take advantage of more bandwidth because they are assigned separate logical network segments through switching.
- **switching** — A component of a network's logical topology that manages how packets are filtered and forwarded between nodes on the network.
- **terminator** — A resistor at the end of a bus network used to stop signals after they have reached their destination.
- **tiered WAN topology** — A WAN topology in which sites are connected in star or ring formations and interconnected at different levels with the interconnection points organized into layers.

- **token passing** — A means of data transmission in which a 3-byte packet, called a token, is passed around the network in a round-robin fashion.
- **twisted-pair cable** — The least expensive LAN cabling, consisting of four sets of two insulated wires twisted around each other. The two insulated wires form the "pair." One wire in each pair carries signal information, and the other is grounded and absorbs interference.
- **WAN topology** — The physical layout of a WAN.
- **wide area network (WAN)** — A network connecting geographically distinct locations, which may or may not belong to the same organization.

REVIEW QUESTIONS

1. Under what circumstance might you use a simple bus topology?
   - **a.** when you have many users on a LAN
   - **b.** when your LAN services multiple locations
   - **c.** when you have few users on a LAN
   - **d.** when you use hubs to separate workstation groups
2. What kind of topology is susceptible to signal bounce?
   - **a.** peer-to-peer
   - **b.** bus
   - **c.** ring
   - **d.** tree
3. What are the primary advantages of using a star topology over a ring or bus topology?
4. Most modern networks with more than a few nodes use a hybrid topology. True or False?
5. Why might you want to use a hierarchical topology?
   - **a.** to differentiate levels of connectivity devices and workstation groups
   - **b.** to enable multiprotocol routing between LAN segments
   - **c.** to account for signal bounce between two LAN segments
   - **d.** to ensure greater reliability for critical network connections
6. What logical topology, or network transport model, relies most often on a star-wired bus topology?
   - **a.** Ethernet
   - **b.** full mesh
   - **c.** partial mesh
   - **d.** Token Ring

7. How do workstations in a ring topology negotiate their data transmissions?
   a. by using CSMA/CD Ethernet
   b. by using RARP
   c. by using demand priority
   d. by using tokens
8. Which of the following is a potential problem with daisy-chaining hubs?
   a. exceeding maximum segment length
   b. exceeding maximum number of workstations per hub
   c. exceeding maximum collision rate
   d. exceeding maximum transmission rate
9. Which of the following is *not* an advantage to using a distributed backbone?
   a. better scalability
   b. improved reliability
   c. less expense
   d. easier workgroup management
10. What type of network backbone has the simplest structure?
    a. distributed
    b. collapsed
    c. parallel
    d. serial
11. What type of network backbone is the most reliable?
    a. distributed
    b. collapsed
    c. parallel
    d. serial
12. The Internet is an example of what kind of WAN topology?
    a. peer-to-peer
    b. ring
    c. mesh
    d. tiered
13. Which of the following is another term for "network transport model" (for example, Ethernet)?
    a. logical topology
    b. physical topology
    c. access method
    d. transmission algorithm

14. Why is packet switching more efficient than circuit switching?
    - a. In packet switching, two communicating nodes establish a channel first, then begin transmitting, thus ensuring a reliable connection and eliminating the need to retransmit.
    - b. In packet switching, packets can take the quickest route between nodes and arrive independent of when other packets in their data stream arrive.
    - c. In packet switching, data are sent to an intermediate node and reassembled before being transmitted, en masse, to the destination node.
    - d. In packet switching, packets are synchronized according to a timing mechanism in the switch.
15. Describe the steps a workstation takes when it participates in CSMA/CD.
16. What is one consequence of excessive data collisions on a network?
    - a. asynchronous communication
    - b. inability to log on to the server
    - c. poor performance
    - d. inability for routers to handle multiple protocols
17. How do 10Base2 and 10Base5 Ethernet networks differ?
    - a. 10Base2 uses coaxial cabling while 10Base5 uses twisted-pair.
    - b. 10Base2 uses CSMA/CD and 10Base5 uses demand priority.
    - c. 10Base2 uses a bus topology and 10Base5 uses a ring topology.
    - d. 10Base2 uses thin coaxial cabling and 10Base5 uses thick coaxial cabling.
18. What type of connectors do 10BaseT networks use at the end of their data cables?
    - a. BNC T connectors
    - b. RJ-11 connectors
    - c. RJ-45 connectors
    - d. SMA connectors
19. What type of cabling is typically used for 1 Gigabit Ethernet?
    - a. fiber-optic
    - b. unshielded twisted-pair
    - c. thick coaxial
    - d. shielded twisted-pair
20. What is unusual about 100BaseVG?
    - a. It uses a demand priority access method.
    - b. It relies on packet switching.
    - c. It can support only TCP/IP traffic.
    - d. It can support only IPX/SPX traffic.

21. Switching essentially breaks up a single network segment into multiple, smaller network segments. True or False?

22. What fields do all Ethernet frame types have in common?

23. What is the purpose of the pad field in an Ethernet frame?
   - a. to ensure that the frame and data arrive without error
   - b. to ensure that the frame arrives in sequence
   - c. to indicate the length of the frame
   - d. to ensure that the data portion of the frame totals at least 46 bytes

24. What is the purpose of a Frame Check Sequence field in an Ethernet frame?
   - a. to ensure that data are received without errors at the destination node
   - b. to ensure that the frame's length stays constant through transmission
   - c. to ensure that the frame is synchronized with other frames in its data stream
   - d. to ensure that the frame arrives at the proper destination address

25. NIC device drivers come with what feature that reduces the need for you to worry about frame types?
   - a. autodetect
   - b. autonegotiate
   - c. autosense
   - d. autorespond

26. What are the minimum and maximum sizes for an Ethernet frame?
   - a. 46 and 64 bytes
   - b. 64 and 1518 bytes
   - c. 64 and 1600 bytes
   - d. 46 and 128 bytes

27. What is the name of a hub used on a Token Ring network?
   - a. Multistation Access Unit
   - b. Multiple Carrier Control Unit
   - c. Multinode Access Station
   - d. Media Access Control Unit

28. Which of the following is a disadvantage to using Token Ring networks?
   - a. They are less fault-tolerant than Ethernet.
   - b. They are slower than Ethernet.
   - c. They are less reliable than Ethernet.
   - d. They are more expensive to implement than Ethernet.

29. Modern Token Ring networks may transmit data at either 4, 16, 32, or 64 Mbps. True or False?

30. Which of the following IEEE standards describes Token Ring networks?
    a. IEEE 802.2
    b. IEEE 802.3
    c. IEEE 802.4
    d. IEEE 802.5

HANDS-ON PROJECTS

PROJECT 5-1

In this exercise, you will create a simple star-wired bus network, one of the most typical forms of an Ethernet network. This project requires two Ethernet 10 Mbps hubs, containing at least four ports each, six patch cables, four workstations, and one file server, all with 10 Mbps NICs (installed and correctly configured). The workstations may run Windows 95, Windows 98, or Windows NT and should have TCP/IP installed. They should be able to log on to the server (using any user ID).

1. Make sure all that hubs, workstations, and the server are plugged in.
2. Connect the two hubs to each other by inserting one end of a patch cable in one hub's link port and the other end of the patch cable in the second hub's link port. Turn on both hubs.
3. Using another patch cable, connect one of the workstations to another port in the first hub. In the same manner, connect the server to the first hub, then turn on the workstation and server. Notice what happens to the lights on the hub when the workstation and server start up.
4. Repeat Step 3, but connect two different workstations to the second hub and then turn on the workstations.
5. Log on to the server from one of the four workstations. If you can see the server's resources, you have successfully created a star-wired bus Ethernet network, where the two hubs form the network's backbone. If you cannot log on to the server, check the cable connections from your workstations to the hub, between the hubs, and between the hub and the server.

PROJECT 5-2

In this exercise, you will use Windows NT Network Monitor (an optional tool for Windows NT Server that analyzes traffic) to view different data frames traveling to and from a server's NIC. You will also review the fields within those data frames. This project requires Windows NT Network Monitor installed on a Windows NT 4.0 server that is running IPX/SPX and TCP/IP with at least two clients attached and logged in. The clients may be Windows 95, Windows 98, or Windows NT workstations.

1. On the Windows NT server, click **Start**, point to **Programs**, point to **Administrative Tools (common)**, then click **Network Monitor**. The Network Monitor window opens. (Maximize the Network Monitor screen if it does not open automatically.) In the next step, you will begin the capture process to gather data that can later be analyzed.
2. Click **Capture** on the menu bar, then click **Start** to begin capturing network traffic information. In the next step, you will generate traffic to and from the server by accessing its shared resources.
3. From one of the workstations that is logged into the server, open a file on the server (for example, a spreadsheet or word-processing document).
4. From another workstation that is logged into the server, view the contents of the **Network Neighborhood** folder.
5. Now that you have generated traffic to and from the server, return to the server to stop capturing data. In the Network Monitor menu bar, click **Capture**, then click **Stop**.
6. In the Network Monitor menu bar, click **Capture**, then click **Display Captured Data**.
7. Double-click on any packet in the list to divide the window into three panes, as shown in Figure 5-31. The top pane displays the list of captured frames, the middle frame gives the header and delivery details, and the bottom pane shows a hexadecimal/ASCII representation of the frames' content.

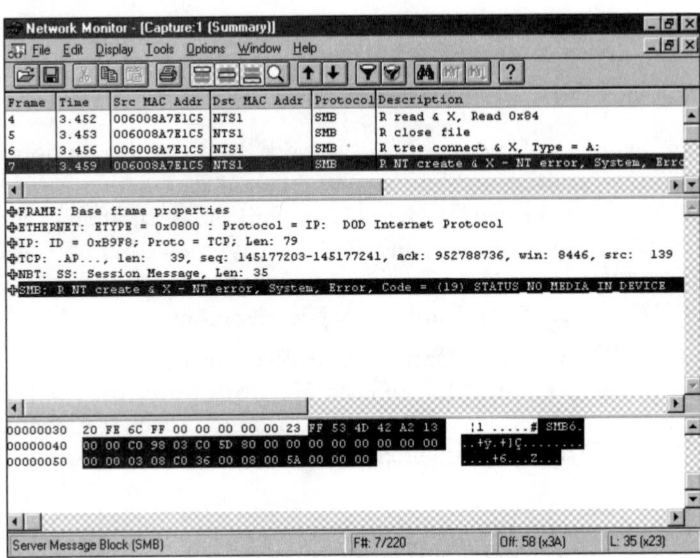

Figure 5-31 Windows NT Network Monitor window

8. In the middle pane, find the frame's protocol type, length, and source address information. View the other frame fields, too.
9. In the top pane, choose to view a frame that has a different kind of protocol listed in its protocol column than the frame you just viewed. Browse through its fields to find its protocol type, length, and source address information.
10. To close Network Monitor, click **File**, then click **Exit**. Do not save the information you have captured.

PROJECT 5-3

In this exercise, you will survey organizations in your area to determine which network transport model, cabling types, and transmission speeds are used on their LANs. From this information, you can determine the most popular networking design approaches. You may also be able to tell what approaches will grow in popularity and which ones will become obsolete.

1. Identify five businesses, schools, or civic organizations in your area that use networking technology—for example, an insurance company, a utility company, a local school district, a chain of retail stores, an architectural firm, or an ISP.
2. For each organization, find contact information for its manager of the Information Technology department.

3. Call the IT department manager and ask him or her the following questions:
   - Does your network use Ethernet, Token Ring, or both?
   - What transmission speed does your network use?
   - On what type of backbone does your network rely?
   - What type of wiring does your network use? Do you use the same type of wiring for the backbone as you do for connecting workstations?
   - Do you use WAN technologies? If so, in what kind of a topology are your separate locations arranged?
   - If you had all the money you wanted in your budget, what type of upgrades would you make to your network?
   - If you had money enough to make only one of these upgrades, which one would it be?
4. Compile the answers from all five managers. Which network transport method is most popular? Which transmission speed? Which type of backbone? How do the economics of each networking approach affect the manager's decisions regarding wiring and logical topology? Compare your results with results of others in your group.

CASE PROJECTS

1. You have been asked to design a LAN for a very successful CPA firm with five departments in one building and a total of 560 employees. Currently, the firm has no networked computers, and it is open to any suggestions you can offer. The firm does have a few requirements, however. It wants to make sure that it can easily expand its LAN in the future without exorbitant costs and moving a lot of equipment. The firm also wants to make sure that every department has very fast access to the LAN, and, of course, it wants the LAN to remain up at all times. It has already decided to use the NetWare 5.0 network operating system. What kind of LAN will you design for this company?
2. AstroTech Components, a company that manufactures parts for the aeronautics industry, is having trouble with a network segment in one of its plants and has asked you for help. According to the network administrator, the plant was added into the existing Ethernet 10BaseT network two weeks ago. Since then, the users have been complaining of intermittent lockups, GPFs, and disconnections. During your visit, she shows you the very organized telecommunications closet. Then, the network administrator escorts you to the production floor, where she points out the 20 Windows 95 machines that the supervisors use to enter numbers into a database from their desks in the production area. The supervisors try to explain their problems in detail, but you and the network administrator can barely hear above the roar of stamping machines. You begin to walk away when you notice that the network cabling is strung along the outside of support posts between stamping machines. When you reach her office, what suggestions do you make to the network administrator to fix the problem?

3. Because you solved AstroTech's plant dilemma so quickly, the network administrator has time to ask you more questions. In particular, she is concerned about the CAD/CAM workgroup. The users in this group fought for months to get new machines. Now that her technicians finally installed the more powerful workstations, however, the users can't access the network. You ask what kind of network they are on, and the network administrator says that this group was upgraded to 100BaseT, along with two other groups, just yesterday, because these users needed the extra speed. When you ask whether all users are affected, she says that everyone—even the department vice president, who has full rights to the network—is prevented from logging on. You suspect that the CAD/CAM users' network access is the problem. What steps do you take next?
4. The network administrator understands everything you've explained so far, and although it will cost a little more, she's glad you solved the company's CAD/CAM workgroup problem. Now she asks about the Finance department, which is experiencing problems logging on. These personnel are running on Windows 95 workstations connected to a 10BaseT bus Ethernet segment. The problem happens about half the time. Once they're logged in, these users occasionally experience other problems, but they haven't recorded any of the error messages. For a long time, the network administrator thought that Finance staff members were just forgetting their passwords, but her technicians have verified that the connectivity problem is real. She admits that the wiring closet for the Finance area is a mess, because the department doubled in size when the company bought out its main competitor, Solstice, Inc., a few months ago. What do you think might be causing the problem?
5. Before you leave, the network administrator asks your opinion about upgrading the rest of the company to 100BaseT from 10BaseT. Although her technicians have told her that this move is necessary, she is concerned about the costs associated with replacing wiring, NICs, switches, and hubs. As it is, she has to purchase 500 new desktop PCs this year. The network administrator has heard about 1 Gigabit Ethernet and wonders whether it would be better to wait for that architecture. What considerations do you point out that might help her with her decision?

CHAPTER 6

NETWORKING HARDWARE

After reading this chapter and completing the exercises, you will be able to:

- Identify the functions of LAN connectivity hardware
- Install and configure a network interface card (NIC)
- Identify problems associated with connectivity hardware
- Describe the factors involved in choosing a NIC, hub, switch, or router
- Describe the uses of repeaters, hubs, bridges, switches, and gateways
- Describe the function of routing protocols

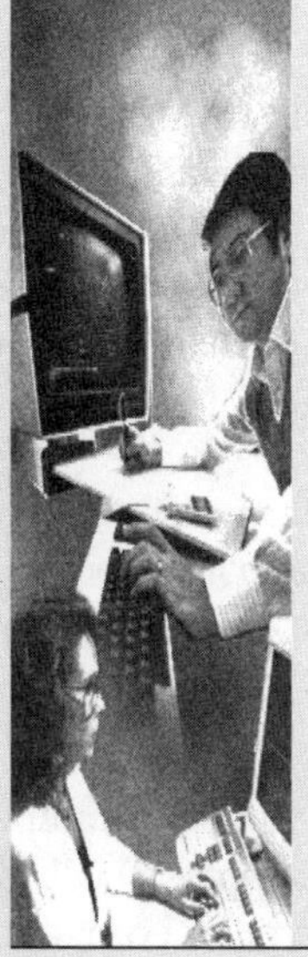

ON THE JOB

As a network architect, I was asked to investigate why a large insurance company was experiencing performance degradation between campus buildings. This company was planning to expand their staff, but felt they needed to solve the network problem before adding any more users. The link between the buildings was fiber-optic cable, which should have provided plenty of capacity for mainframe data from one building to quickly reach the screens of claims processors at another building.

Realizing that wiring wasn't the problem, I looked at the connectivity hardware on the network. This network relied on a single router and 10 hubs for over two hundred users. The router was software-based and ran on a Novell server (as opposed to a hardware-based router). Software-based routers are never as efficient as hardware-based routers; that was probably one bottleneck. In addition, having a network comprised of hubs and routers meant that all bandwidth was being shared by the devices. To cut down congestion, I replaced the router with a switch.

That replacement solved the performance problem. Now, instead of waiting 3 seconds for a screen to refresh, the insurance company employees get a new screen instantly after pressing the Enter key.

Carrie McClelland
ARK Consulting

In Chapter 5, you learned how data are transmitted over cable or through the atmosphere. Now you need to know how data arrive at their destination. The process of transmitting data is analogous to the means by which the U.S. Postal Service delivers mail, where mail trucks, airplanes, and delivery staff serve as the transmission media that move information from place to place. Machines and personnel at the post office interpret addresses on the envelopes and either deliver the mail to a transfer point or to your home. Inefficiencies in mail delivery, such as letters being misdirected to the wrong transfer point, frustrate both the sender and the receiver of the mail and increase the overall cost of delivery.

In data networks, the task of directing information to the correct destination in as efficient a manner as possible is handled by hubs, routers, bridges, and switches. In this chapter, you will learn about these devices and their roles in managing data traffic. Whereas earlier chapters focused on the Physical layer of the OSI Model, this chapter delves into the Data Link and Network layers. It introduces the concepts involved in moving data from place to place, including issues related to switching and routing protocols. It also provides pictures of the hardware—repeaters, hubs, switches, bridges, and routers—that make data transfer possible. (It's important for you to have an accurate mental image of this equipment because, in a cluttered telecommunications closet, it may prove difficult to identify the hardware underneath the wiring.) In addition, you will learn all about network interface cards, the workstation's link to the network and often the source of many connectivity problems.

NETWORK INTERFACE CARDS (NICS)

In Chapter 1, you learned that NICs are connectivity devices that enable a workstation, server, printer or other node to receive and transmit data over the network media. NICs are sometimes called **network adapters**. They belong to the Physical layer of the OSI Model because they transmit data signals but do not analyze the data from higher layers. In some cases, NICs may perform rudimentary interpretation of the data they carry rather than simply passing signals to the CPU to interpret.

Advances in NIC technology are making this hardware smarter than ever. Not only do all NICs read addressing information so as to deliver data to its proper destination (and, in the case of Ethernet networks, to detect collisions), but many can also perform prioritization, network management, buffering, and traffic filtering functions.

Network interface cards come in a variety of types depending on the network transport system (Ethernet versus Token Ring), network transmission speed (for example, 10 Mbps versus 100 Mbps), connector interfaces (for example, BNC versus RJ-45), type of compatible system board or device, and, of course, manufacturer. Popular NIC manufacturers include 3Com, Adaptec, IBM, Intel, Linksys, Olicom, SMC, and Western Digital, just to name a few. In fact, during your networking career, you may run into NICs made by at least a dozen manufacturers.

As you learn about installing, configuring, and troubleshooting NICs, you should concentrate first on generalities, then move on to special situations. Because NICs are common to every networking device and every network, knowing all about them may prove to be the most useful tool you have at your disposal.

TYPES OF NICS

Before you order or install a NIC in a network device, you need to know the type of interface required by the device. For a desktop or tower PC, the NIC must match its bus. A **bus** is the circuit used by the system board to transmit data to components.

The capacity of a bus is defined principally by the width of its data path (expressed in bits) and its speed (expressed in MHz). A data path on a bus equals the number of data bits that it can transmit in parallel at any given time. In the earliest PCs, buses had an 8-bit data path. Later, manufacturers expanded buses to handle 16 bits of data, then 32 bits. Most new Pentium computers use buses capable of exchanging 64 bits of data. As the number of bits of data that a bus can handle increases, so too does the speed of the device attached to the bus.

In addition to the amount of data that can travel through their circuits, buses differ by type. The following list describes PC bus types you may encounter. (If you have already completed coursework for the A+ certification, this material will look familiar.)

- *Industry Standard Architecture (ISA)*—The original PC bus, developed in the early 1980s to support an 8-bit and later 16-bit data transfer capability. 8-bit ISA (pronounced "ice-uh") bus connectors contain one long row of pins, and 16-bit ISA bus connectors add another, shorter row, for a second 8 bits, as shown in Figure 6-1. ISA buses cannot support 100 Mbps throughput; because of this limitation, they are typically not used for NICs in new PCs, although they may still be found in "economy" PCs. ISA buses may connect serial devices, such as mice or modems, in new PCs.

- *MicroChannel Architecture (MCA)*—IBM's proprietary 32-bit bus for personal computers, introduced in 1987 and later replaced by the standardized EISA and PCI buses. Unless you are in an IBM-centric environment with older PS/2 or AIX equipment, you probably won't be concerned with MCA devices. Figure 6-1 shows an MCA NIC.

- *Extended Industry Standard Architecture (EISA)*—A 32-bit bus that is compatible with older ISA devices because it shares the same length and pin configuration as the ISA bus, as shown in Figure 6-1, but that uses a deeper, two-layered slot connector for a second 16 bits to achieve faster throughput. The EISA (pronounced "ees-uh") bus was introduced in the late 1980s to compete with IBM's MCA bus.

- *Peripheral Component Interconnect (PCI)*—A 32- or 64-bit bus introduced in the 1990s that has become the NIC connection type used for nearly all of today's new PCs. It's characterized by a shorter connector length than ISA, MCA or EISA cards, but offers a much faster data transmission capability. Figure 6-1 shows a typical PCI network adapter. Currently, 128-bit PCI buses are under development.

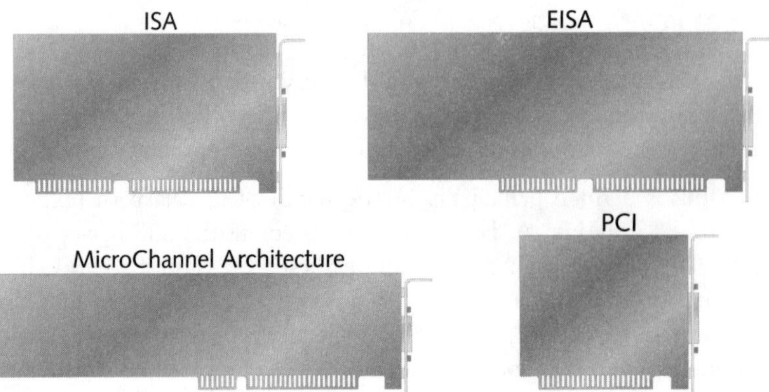

Figure 6-1 The four primary bus architectures

You can easily determine what type of bus your PC uses by reading the documentation that came with the computer. This information should appear either on the purchase order or in the very beginning of the booklet that lists the computer's specifications. Someday, however, you may need to replace a NIC on a PC whose documentation is missing. To verify what type of bus a PC uses, look inside the PC case. (Later in this chapter, you will learn how to safely open a computer case, check the computer's bus, and install a NIC.) Most PCs have at least two different types of bus connections on the same board, as illustrated in Figure 6-2.

If a system board supports more than one kind of bus, refer to the NIC and PC manufacturers' guidelines for information on the preferred type of NIC to install. If possible, you should choose a NIC that matches the most modern bus on the system board. For example, if a PC supports both ISA and PCI, attempt to use a PCI NIC and bus. Although you may be able to use the older bus and NIC types without any adverse effects, some NICs (such as 3Com's products) will not work in an older bus if a faster, newer bus is available on the system board.

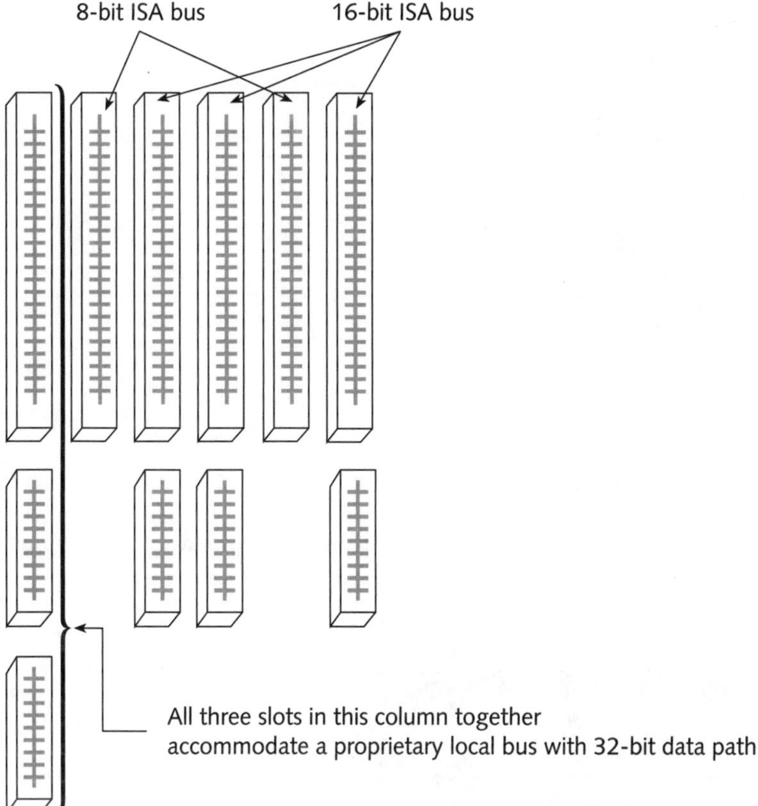

Figure 6-2 Three kinds of bus connections on the same board

NICs may connect to interfaces other than a PC's bus. For laptop computers, Personal Computer Memory Card International Association (PCMCIA) slots may be used to connect NICs; in older models, parallel ports may serve the same function. **PCMCIA** (also called **PC card**) interfaces were developed in the early 1990s to provide a standard interface for connecting any type of device to a portable computer. PCMCIA slots may hold modem cards, NICs, external hard disk cards, or CD-ROM cards. Most often, they are used for NICs or modems; in fact, some PCMCIA cards contain both devices. You may also hear PCMCIA NICs called "credit card adapters" because they are approximately the same size as a credit card. Figure 6-3 depicts a typical PCMCIA NIC.

Figure 6-3 A typical PCMCIA NIC

Parallel port NICs are rarely used on modern laptops, but you may encounter them on older laptops. These specialized devices can be difficult to obtain or support. One popular parallel port NIC manufacturer is Xircom. Figure 6-4 depicts a typical parallel port NIC.

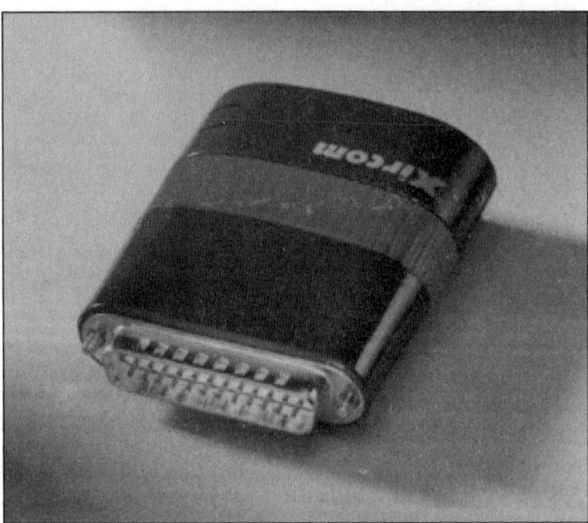

Figure 6-4 A parallel port NIC

In addition to NICs that connect with network cabling, you can employ NICs designed for wireless transmission. Typically, a wireless NIC uses an antenna to exchange signals with a base station transceiver or other wireless NIC adapter. This type of connectivity suits environments where cabling cannot be installed, or clients who need to move about while staying connected to the network. For example, library assistants who walk through stacks of books and record inventory data in the library's central database using handheld PCs. Because wireless NICs are unique products serving a niche market, companies other than those that provide bus-adapter or PCMCIA NICs usually manufacture them. Wireless connectivity manufacturers include Alcatel, AMP, ComStar, Lucent, Proxim, RadioLAN, and Raytheon. Figure 6-5 depicts a wireless NIC and transceiver.

Figure 6-5 A wireless NIC and transceiver

Devices other than PCs use specialized NICs as well. Printer NICs, for example, come in a variety of styles suited to different applications. By far, the most popular printer NIC is Hewlett-Packard's JetDirect card. Printer NICs often provide processing and support for all seven OSI Model layers (making them even more complex than PC NICs) so as to handle print server functions. Figure 6-6 depicts a typical Ethernet NIC for a networked printer.

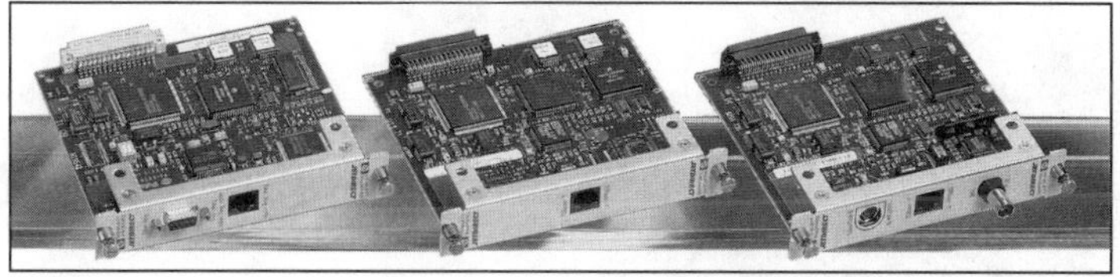

Figure 6-6 Ethernet NICs for printers

As mentioned earlier, NICs also vary by the type of network transport model they support (Ethernet or Token Ring), and their connector types. Figure 6-7 shows a variety of NICs that might be used on Ethernet networks, and Figure 6-8 shows a variety of NICs for use on Token Ring networks. Notice that some NICs provide only one type of cabling connector, while others provide two or even three types of connectors.

Figure 6-7 A variety of Ethernet NICs

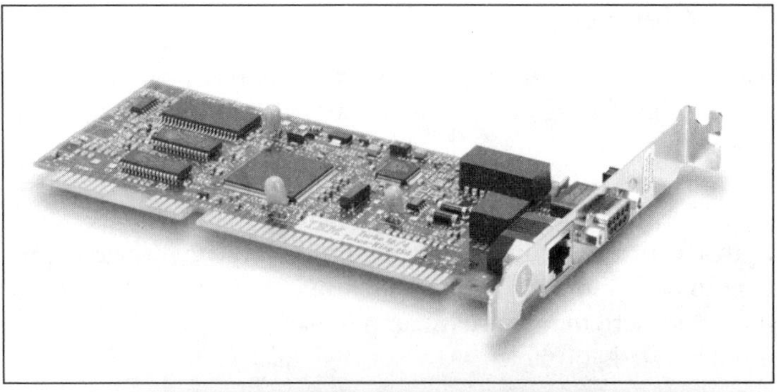

Figure 6-8 A variety of Token Ring NICs

INSTALLING NICs

Installing a NIC requires three steps: installing the hardware, configuring the software, and configuring the **firmware,** which is a combination of hardware and software. The hardware component of firmware is a read-only memory (ROM) chip that stores data established at the factory. The ROM may be changed by configuration utilities that come with a NIC. Because its data can be erased or changed, this particular type of ROM is called **erasable programmable read-only memory (EPROM)**.

A NIC's firmware contains information about its transmission speed capabilities, its preferred Interrupt Request Line (discussed later in this chapter) input/output (I/O) port address, and duplexing capabilities, among other things. In many cases, especially if you are using Windows 95 or Windows 98 plug-and-play technology, you will not have to change the NIC's firmware.

The following sections explain the process of installing a NIC in more detail.

Installing NIC Hardware

As with any hardware installation, you should first read the manufacturer's documentation that accompanies the NIC hardware. The following steps generally apply to any kind of bus-adapter NIC installation.

To install a bus-adapter NIC:

1. Make sure that your toolkit includes a Phillips-head screwdriver, a ground strap, and a ground mat to protect the internal components from electrostatic discharge. Also, make sure that you have ample space in which to work, whether it be on the floor, a desk, or table.
2. Turn off the computer's power switch. In addition to endangering you, opening a PC while it's turned on can damage its internal circuitry.
3. Attach the ground strap to your wrist and make sure that it's connected to the ground strap underneath the computer.
4. Open the computer's case. Computer cases are attached in several different ways. Most new computers use four or six Phillips-head screws to attach the housing to the back panel, although some might not use any. Remove all necessary screws and slide the computer's case off.
5. Select a slot on the computer's system board where you will insert the NIC. Make sure that the slot matches the type of NIC, and, if the PC contains more than one type of slot, use the most modern type (for example, PCI). Remove the metal slot cover for that slot from the back of the PC. Some slot covers are attached with Phillips-head screws; others are merely metal parts with perforated edges that you can punch out with your fingers.
6. Insert the NIC by lining up its slot connector with the slot, rocking it into place, and pressing it firmly into the slot. If you have correctly inserted the NIC, you should not be able to wiggle it from side to side. If you can wiggle it, press it in farther. A loose NIC will cause connectivity problems. Figure 6-9 depicts a properly inserted NIC.

Figure 6-9 A properly inserted NIC

7. The metal bracket at the end of the NIC should now be positioned where the metal slot cover was located before you removed the slot cover. Attach the bracket with a Phillips-head screw into the back of the computer cover to secure the NIC in place.
8. Make sure that you have not loosened any cables or cards inside the PC or left any screws or debris inside the computer.
9. Replace the cover on the computer and reinsert the screws that you removed in Step 4.
10. Plug in the computer and turn it on. Proceed to configure the NIC's software, as discussed later in this chapter.

Installing a PCMCIA NIC is much easier than installing a bus-adapter NIC. In general, you can simply turn off the machine, insert the PCMCIA card into the PCMCIA slot, as shown in Figure 6-10, then turn on the computer. Most modern operating systems (such as Windows 98) allow you to insert and remove the PCMCIA adapter without restarting the machine. Make sure that the PCMCIA card is firmly inserted. If you can wiggle it, you need to push it in farther.

Figure 6-10 Installing a PCMCIA NIC

The same process applies to installing parallel port NICs. Turn off the computer, attach the parallel port NIC, then turn the computer back on. Make sure that the parallel port NIC is securely connected to the parallel port by tightening the screws on either side of the device.

On servers and other high-powered computers, you may need to install multiple NICs. For the hardware installation, you can simply repeat the installation process for the first NIC, choosing a different slot. The trick to using multiple NICs on one machine lies in correctly configuring the software for each NIC. Simple NIC configuration is covered in the following section. The exact steps involved in configuring NICs on servers will depend on the server's networking operating system. Chapters 8 and 9 will describe the NIC configuration process for servers using the Windows NT Server and NetWare network operating systems.

Installing and Configuring NIC Software

Even if your computer runs Windows 95 or 98 with plug-and-play technology, you must ensure that the correct device driver is installed for the NIC and that it is configured properly. This section describes how to install and configure NIC software on a Windows 95 desktop operating system. For other operating systems, the process will be similar. Regardless of which operating system you use, you should first refer to the NIC's documentation, because your situation may vary. Read the NIC documentation carefully before installing the relevant drivers. Performing a DOS or Windows 3.1 installation on a Windows 95 computer, for example, may cause problems.

Installing and configuring a NIC in a computer running Windows 95 is usually easier than installing one on a DOS or Windows 3.1 machine (although not always). The following steps describe a typical NIC software installation from a Windows 95 interface. For this process, you will need access to the Windows 95 CAB files (via either a Windows 95 CD or a drive mapping to the files on a network or hard disk) and the floppy disk that came with the NIC.

If you do not have the floppy disk that shipped with the NIC, you can download the NIC software from the manufacturer's Web site. If you choose this option, make sure that you get the appropriate drivers for your operating system and NIC type. Also, make sure that the drivers you download are the most current version (sometimes called "shipping drivers") and not beta-level (unsupported) drivers.

1. Physically install the NIC, and then restart the PC.
2. As long as you haven't disabled the plug-and-play technology, Windows 95 should automatically detect the new hardware. Upon detecting the NIC, it will prompt you to choose the appropriate drivers, as shown in Figure 6-11. (Windows 95 may automatically recognize the hardware and attempt to install its own drivers. In this case, you can skip to Step 6.)

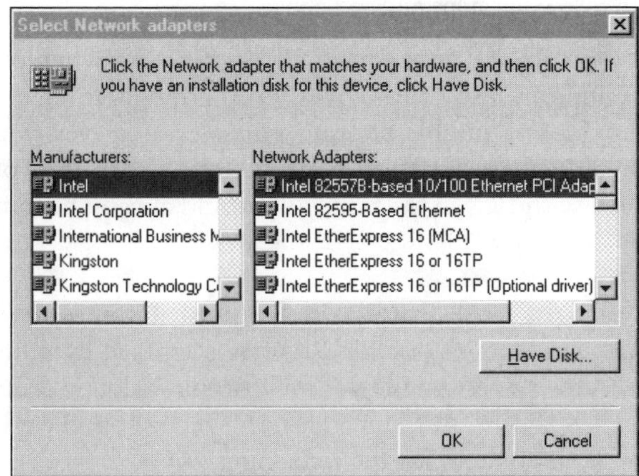

Figure 6-11 Windows 95 prompt for hardware drivers

3. At this point, you may insert the Windows 95 installation CD-ROM, if the standard drivers will be used. To make certain that you install the correct drivers, however, it's best to choose **Have Disk**, and insert the disk that came with the NIC into your floppy drive.
4. After you click Have Disk, Windows 95 asks for the location of the drivers. Type the path or browse to the floppy drive (usually A: or B:) where the Windows 95 drivers are located. The drivers will probably appear in a subdirectory on the disk, as most NICs ship with a single disk that contains DOS, Windows 95, and other platform-specific drivers. Once you type the correct path, click **OK**.

5. If the disk sent with the NIC contains drivers for more than one type of NIC, you will be asked to select the precise model you are using. After making your choice, click **OK**.
6. The driver files for the NIC will be installed onto your hard disk and their specifications written to the Registry. In the process, you may be asked for the location of the Windows 95 CAB files. If so, insert the Windows 95 installation CD. When prompted, direct the installation program to that drive (usually D: or E:), then click **OK**.
7. Once the NIC drivers have been successfully installed, you will be prompted to restart your PC. Confirm that you want to restart it by clicking **Yes**.

The preceding steps will work in most situations. Because every situation is different, however, you should always read the manufacturer's documentation and follow its installation instructions. Some manufacturers supply setup programs that automatically install and register NIC software once you run them, thereby eliminating the need to follow the steps outlined above.

The next sections describe the variable settings you should understand when configuring NICs. Depending on your computer's use of resources, NIC configuration may or may not be necessary after installation. For troubleshooting purposes, however, you need to understand how to view and adjust these variables. If you completed coursework for the A+ certification or have worked with PCs in the past, you should already be familiar with these variables.

IRQ (Interrupt Request Line) An **IRQ** (**Interrupt Request Line**) is the means by which a device can request attention from the CPU. IRQs are identified by numbers from 0 to 15. Some computer devices reserve IRQ numbers; for example, a floppy disk controller claims IRQ 6 and a keyboard takes IRQ 1. Additional devices such as sound cards, graphics cards, modems, and NICs must then contend for the remaining IRQs.

If two devices choose the same IRQ, resource conflicts and performance problems will result. For example, if a keyboard uses IRQ 1 and you configure the NIC to use IRQ 1 as well, the computer's CPU will not know whether the data received through IRQ 1 comes from the computer or the NIC; thus the CPU will be unable to follow the instructions of either device.

If IRQ conflicts occur, you must manually set a device's IRQ rather than accepting the default suggested by the operating system or BIOS. Keep in mind that the BIOS will attempt to assign free IRQs. Typically, it will assign IRQs 10, 11, 12 or 13 to NICs, as other devices do usually not take these numbers. The BIOS can be wrong, however.

When two devices attempt to use the same IRQ, any of the following problems may occur:

- The computer may lock up or "hang" either upon starting or when the operating system is loading.
- The computer may run much slower than usual.

- Although the computer's NIC may work properly, other devices—such as serial or parallel ports—may stop working.
- Video or sound card problems may occur. For example, after Windows 95 loads, you may see an error message indicating that the video settings are incorrect or your sound card may stop working.
- The computer may fail to connect to the network (as evidenced by an error message after you attempt to log on to a server).
- The computer may experience intermittent data errors during transmission.
- In Windows NT, a blue screen full of error messages may appear and prevent the operating system from loading.

To view IRQ settings on computers running Windows 95:

1. Right-click the **My Computer** icon. A shortcut menu opens.
2. Click **Properties**. The System Properties dialog box opens.
3. Click the **Device Manager** tab.
4. Double-click the **Computer** icon. The Computer Properties dialog box opens.
5. With the **View Resources** tab and **Interrupt Request** setting selected by default, you can scroll through the list of IRQ settings for your computer, as shown in Figure 6-12.

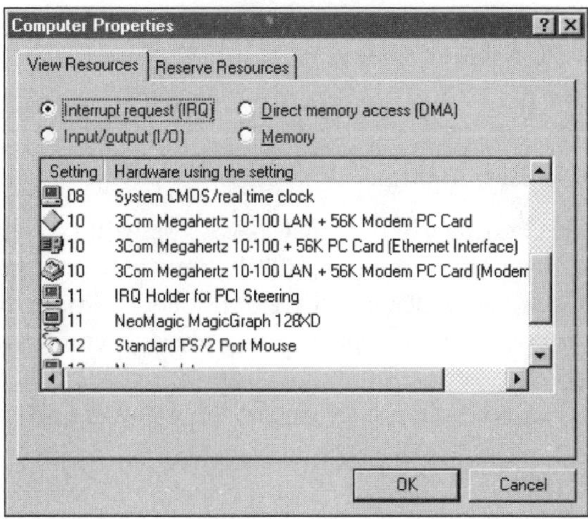

Figure 6-12 Computer resource settings in Windows 95

To view IRQ settings on computers running Windows NT:

1. Click **Start**, point to **Programs**, point to **Administrative Tools**, then click **Windows NT Diagnostics**. The Windows NT Diagnostics dialog box opens.
2. Click the **Resources** tab. The Resources window opens.

3. Click **IRQ**. The list of assigned IRQs appears.
4. View the IRQ settings for each device on the computer, as pictured in Figure 6-13.

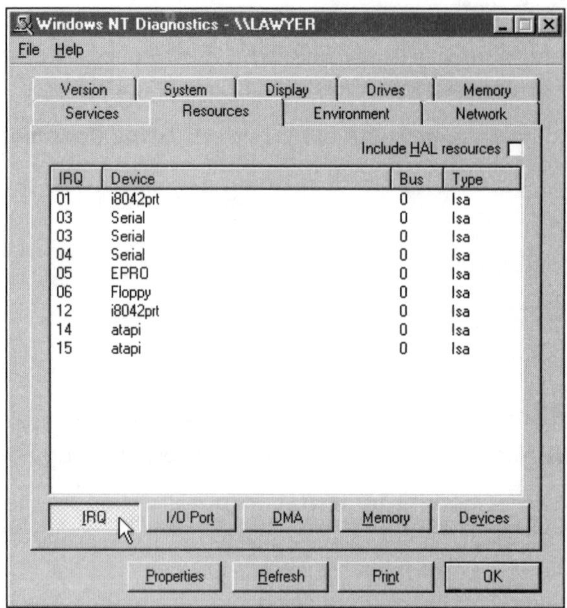

Figure 6-13 IRQ settings displayed in Window NT Diagnostics

You can also view IRQ settings in the computer's CMOS utility. The **complementary metal oxide conductor (CMOS)** is firmware attached to the system board that controls the configuration of a computer's devices, among other things.

Although you can usually modify IRQ settings in the CMOS, whether you can change them from the operating system software depends on the type of NIC involved. For example, on a PCI NIC, which requires a PCI bus controller, the PCI controller's settings will dictate whether this type of modification is possible. The default setting prevents you from changing the NIC's IRQ from the operating system; if you attempt to make this change, the Resources tab in the PCI NIC's Properties dialog box will display one of the following messages:

- For Windows NT: "Cannot configure the software component"
- For Windows 95: "This resource setting cannot be modified."

Thus, if you need to alter the IRQ for a PCI NIC, you should make the change in the CMOS. Different system board manufacturers use different keystrokes to invoke the CMOS setup program when the computer starts. You may need to press Del, Shift-F1, F10, Ctrl-Shift-Enter, or another key(s) to access the CMOS settings. The required keystroke or combination of keystrokes should appear on the screen when the computer starts. Once you are in the CMOS setup program, follow the menu selections until you find the network adapter IRQ setting, change it, then save your changes and restart the computer.

Sometimes you cannot access a computer's CMOS setup utility. In this case, you *may* be able to resolve an IRQ conflict by physically moving the NIC from its present slot to another slot, by physically resetting dip switches on the NIC, or by using a special setup program that is shipped with the NIC. You could also try temporarily disabling or removing conflicting devices such as video cards, infrared ports, or modems. Alternatively, you may need to update the BIOS on the workstation. A **BIOS (basic input/output system)** is another piece of firmware on the system board that controls communication with devices such as monitors, keyboards, and NICs. If nothing else works, you may need to install a different type or model of NIC.

Memory Range The **memory range** indicates, in hexadecimal notation, the area of memory that the NIC and CPU will use for exchanging, or buffering, data. As with IRQs, some memory ranges are reserved for specific devices—most notably, the system board. Reserved address ranges can never be selected for new devices.

NICs typically use a memory range in the high memory area, which in hexadecimal notation equates to the A0000–FFFFF range. As you work with NICs, you will notice that some manufacturers prefer certain ranges. For example, a 3Com PCMCIA adapter might, by default, choose a range of C8000–C9FFF. An IBM Token Ring adapter might choose a range of D8000–D9FFF.

Memory range settings are less likely to cause resource conflicts than IRQ settings, mainly because more memory ranges are available than IRQs exist. Nevertheless, you may run into situations when you need to change a NIC's memory address. In such an instance, you may or may not be able to change the memory range from the operating system. Refer to the manufacturer's guidelines for instructions.

Base I/O Port The **base I/O port** setting specifies, in hexadecimal notation, which area of memory will act as a channel for moving data between the NIC and the CPU. Like its IRQ, a device's base I/O port cannot be used by any other device. Most NICs use two memory ranges for this channel, and the base I/O port settings identify the beginning of each range. Although a NIC's base I/O port will vary depending on the manufacturer, some popular addresses (in hexadecimal notation) are 300 (which means that the range is 300–30F), 310, 280, or 2F8.

You will probably not need to change a NIC's base I/O port. If you do, bear in mind that, as with IRQ settings, base I/O port settings for PCI cards generally must be changed in the computer's CMOS setup utility.

Changing NIC Firmware

As mentioned earlier, firmware comprises the combination of an EPROM chip on the NIC and the data it holds. When you change the firmware, you are actually writing to the EPROM chip on the NIC. You are not writing to the computer's hard disk. Although most configurable settings can be changed in the operating system or NIC setup software, you may encounter complex networking problems that require a change to firmware settings.

To change a NIC's firmware, you will need a bootable floppy disk (DOS version 6.0 or higher) containing the configuration or DOS install utility that shipped with the NIC. If you don't have the utility, you can usually download it from the manufacturer's Web site. To run the utility, you must start the computer with this floppy disk inserted. The NIC configuration utility may not run if an operating system or memory management program is already running.

Each configuration utility will differ slightly, but all should allow you to view the IRQ, I/O port, base memory, and node address. Some may allow you to change settings such as the NIC's CPU utilization, its ability to handle full duplexing, or its capability to be used with only 10BaseT or 100BaseT media, for example. The changeable settings will vary depending on the manufacturer. Again, read the manufacturer's documentation to find out the details for your hardware.

NIC configuration utilities also allow you to perform diagnostics—tests of the NIC's physical components and connectivity. One connectivity test, called a loopback test, requires you to install a loopback plug into the NIC's media connector. A **loopback plug** is a connector that plugs into a port, such as a serial or parallel port, and crosses over the transmit line to the receive line so that outgoing signals can be redirected back into the computer for testing. Connectivity tests should not be performed on a live network. If a NIC fails its connectivity tests, it is probably configured incorrectly. If a NIC fails a physical component test, it may need to be replaced.

Choosing the Right NIC

You should consider several factors when choosing a NIC for your workstation. Of course, the most critical factor is compatibility with your existing system. You will need to determine whether your workstation requires an ISA, EISA, MCA or PCI card in addition to choosing a NIC that matches your network's media, connector types, transmission speed, and network model. You also need to ensure that drivers available for that NIC will work with your operating system.

Beyond these considerations, however, you should examine more subtle differences, such as those that affect network performance. Table 6-1 lists some features available on NICs that specifically influence performance and ease of use. As you review this table, keep in mind that performance is especially important if the NIC will be installed in a server.

Table 6-1 NIC Characteristics

NIC Feature	Function	Benefit
Automatic speed selection	Enables NICs to automatically sense and adapt to a network's speed and mode (half or full duplex)	Aids in configuration and performance
One or more on-board NIC CPUs	Allows a card to perform some data processing independently of the PC's CPU	Improves performance
Direct Memory Access (DMA)	Enables a card to directly transfer data to the computer's memory	Improves performance
Diagnostic LEDs (lights on the NIC)	Indicate traffic, connectivity, and sometimes speed	Aids in troubleshooting
Dual channels	Effectively create two NICs in one slot	Improves performance; suited to servers
Load balancing	Allows the NIC's processor to determine when to switch traffic between internal cards	Improves performance for heavily trafficked networks; suited to servers
"Look Ahead" transmit and receive	Allows the NIC's processor to begin processing data before it has received the entire packet	Improves performance
Management capabilities (SNMP)	Allows the NIC to perform its own monitoring and troubleshooting, usually through installed application software	Aids in troubleshooting, can find a problem before it becomes dire
Power management capabilities	Allows a NIC to participate in the computer's power-saving measures; found on PCMCIA adapters	Increases life of the battery for laptop computers
RAM buffering	Provides additional memory on the NIC, which in turn provides more space for data buffering	Improves performance
Upgradable (flash) ROM	Allows for on-board chip memory to be upgraded	May improve ease of use and performance

More Information About NICs

The quality of the printed documentation that you receive from a manufacturer about its NICs may vary. What's more, this documentation may not apply to the different kinds of computers or networking environments you are using. To find out more about the type of NIC you are installing or troubleshooting, you can visit the manufacturer's Web site. See Appendix A, "Resources for More Information on Networking Software and Hardware," for information on how to contact NIC manufacturers and obtain support.

REPEATERS

As you'll recall from Chapter 4, the telecommunications closet is the area containing the connectivity equipment (usually for a whole floor of a building). Within the telecommunications closet, horizontal cabling from the workstations attaches to punch-down blocks, patch panels, hubs, switches, routers, and/or bridges. In addition, telecommunications closets may house repeaters. **Repeaters** are the connectivity devices that perform the regeneration and amplification of an analog or digital signal. (As you learned in Chapter 4, signals subject to attenuation must be amplified and regenerated to enable them to travel longer distances.)

Repeaters belong to the Physical layer of the OSI Model and therefore have no means to interpret the data they retransmit. For example, they cannot improve or correct a bad or erroneous signal; they merely repeat it. They repeat noise along with the signal. In this sense, they are not "intelligent" devices.

A repeater is limited not only in function, but also in scope. A repeater contains one input port and one output port, as shown in Figure 6-14, so it is capable of receiving and repeating only the data stream. Furthermore, repeaters are suited only to bus topology networks. The advantage to using a repeater is that it allows you to extend a network inexpensively.

For example, suppose that you need to connect a single PC located in a school's gymnasium to the rest of the network, that the nearest data jack is 220 meters away, and that you are using 10Base2 Ethernet, which limits the maximum cable length to 185 meters. In this instance, you could use a repeater to add 185 meters to the existing 185-meter limitation and connect the gymnasium workstation to the network. Bear in mind that the overall network distance limitations still apply. Because the entire network cannot exceed 1000 meters, you cannot use more than five repeaters in sequence to extend the cabling's reach.

Figure 6-14 A repeater

HUBS

At its most primitive, a **hub** is a multiport repeater containing one port that connects to a network's backbone and multiple ports that connect to a group of workstations. Hubs typically support a star or hybrid topology on an Ethernet network. On Token Ring networks, hubs are called Multistation Access Units (MAUs). As you learned in Chapter 5, MAUs internally complete the ring topology using their Ring In and Ring Out ports.

In addition to connecting Macintosh and PC workstations, hubs can connect print servers, switches, file servers, or other devices to a network. They can support a variety of different media and data transmission speeds. Some hubs also allow for multiple media connector types or multiple data transmission speeds. As you can imagine, the number of different hubs commercially available is huge. By classifying hubs into categories according to their uses and features, however, you will quickly get the lay of the land and soon learn to understand any hub. Figure 6-15 details the various elements of a hub, some of which are optional. The elements shared by most hubs are described below.

6

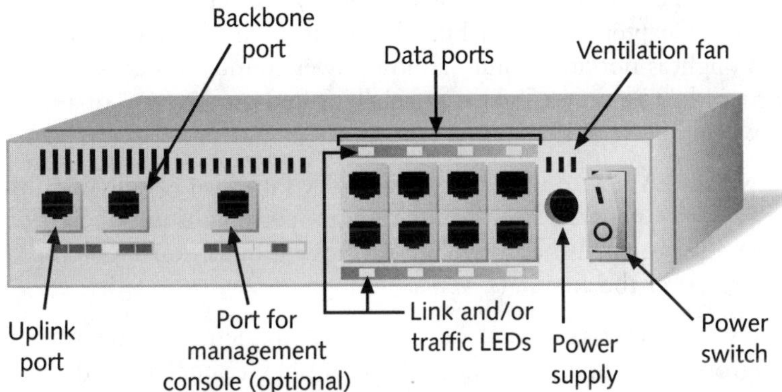

Figure 6-15 Detailed diagram of a hub

- *Ports*—Receptacles where patch cables connect workstations or other devices to the hub. The type of receptacle (RJ-45 versus BNC, for example) will depend on your network technology. The number of ports on a hub generally ranges from 4 to 24. This number does not include the uplink port, described below.
- *Uplink port*—The receptacle used to connect one hub to another hub in a daisy-chain or hierarchical fashion. An uplink port may look like any other port, but it should be used only to interconnect hubs.
- *Port for management console*—A receptacle used to connect a console (such as a laptop PC) that enables you to view the hub's management information, such as the traffic load or number of collisions. Not all hubs provide management information, so not all have a management console port.
- *Backbone port*—The receptacle used to connect a hub to the network's backbone. For 10BaseT networks, this type of connection is often made with short lengths of Thinnet coaxial cabling.

- *Link LED*—The light on a port that indicates whether it is in use. If a connection is live, this light should be solid green. If you think that the connection is live but the light is not on, you need to check connections, transmission speed settings, and power supplies for both the NIC and hub.
- *Traffic (transmit or receive) LED*—The light on a port that indicates that traffic is passing through the port. Under normal data traffic situations, this light should blink. Some hubs include separate LEDs for transmission and receipt of data; others do not even have traffic LEDs for their ports. If they exist, traffic LEDs are normally found adjacent to link LEDs beside each data port.
- *Collision LED (Ethernet hubs only)*—The light that indicates how many collisions are occurring. The hub may include one light for the entire hub or individual lights for each port. If this light is continuously lit, a node is experiencing dire connectivity or traffic problems and may need to be disconnected. Because only Ethernet hubs have collision LEDs, Figure 6-15 does not show one.
- *Power supply*—The device that provides power to the hub. Every hub has its own power supply (for this reason, you will want to connect critical hubs to a UPS, as explained in Chapter 14). Every hub also has its own power-on light. If the power-on light is not lit, the hub has lost power. Some hubs contain surge-resistant power supplies. The power light is normally found on the front of a hub, and so is not shown in Figure 6-15.
- *Ventilation fan*—A device used to cool a device's internal circuitry. Hubs, like other electronics, generate heat. To function properly, hubs must cool their circuitry with a ventilation fan. When installing or moving hubs, you should be careful not to block or cover the air-intake vents.

Placement of hubs in a network design can vary. The simplest structure would employ a standalone workgroup hub that is connected to another connectivity device such as a switch or router. Most networks use several hubs to serve different workgroups, thereby benefiting from multiple potential failure points and possibly switching and data management. Figure 6-16 indicates how hubs fit into the overall network design.

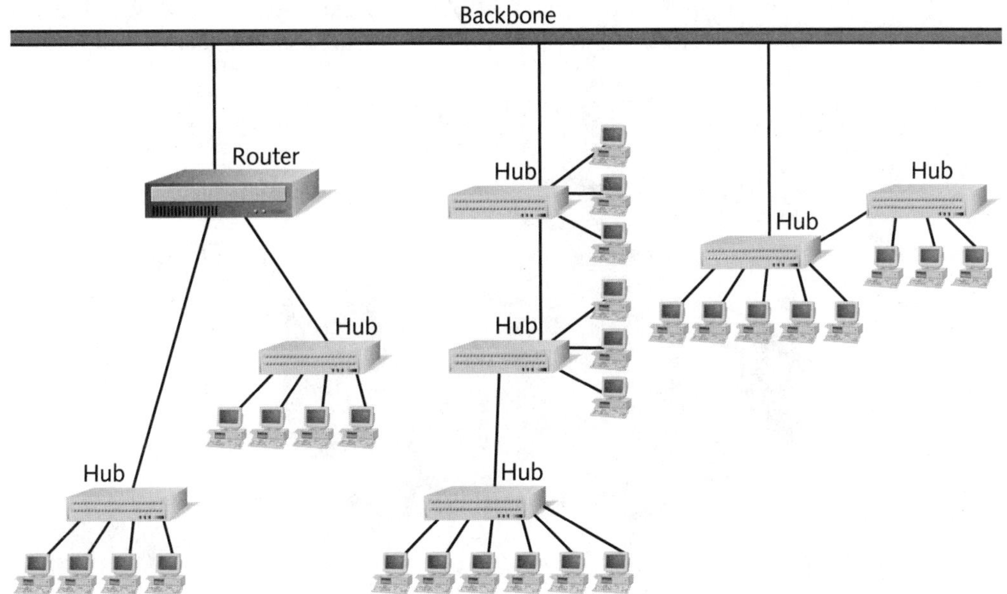

Figure 6-16 Hubs in a network design

Many hubs—known as **passive hubs**—do nothing but repeat signals. Like NICs, however, some hubs possess internal processing capabilities. For example, they may permit remote management, filter data, or provide diagnostic information about the network. Hubs that can perform any of these functions are known as **intelligent hubs**.

Technological advances are making hubs more capable and more vital in network management. The following sections introduce the different types of hubs, their functions, advantages, and disadvantages. Hubs represent a significant element in network design, configuration, and troubleshooting. To prepare for the Net+ certification exam, you should pay close attention to the material in the following sections.

Standalone Hubs

Standalone hubs, as their name implies, are hubs that serve a workgroup of computers that are isolated from the rest of the network. They may be connected to another hub by a coaxial, fiber-optic, or twisted-pair cable; however, they are typically not connected in a hierarchical or daisy-chain fashion. Standalone hubs are best suited to small, independent departments, home offices, or test lab environments. They can be passive or intelligent, and they are simple to install and connect for a small group of users.

Standalone hubs do not follow one design, nor do they contain a standard number of ports (though they usually contain 4, 8, 12, or 24 ports). A small, standalone hub that contains only 4 ports (primarily used for a small or home offices) may be called a "hubby," "hublet," or a "mini-hub." On the other hand, standalone hubs can provide as many as 200 connection ports. The disadvantage to using a single hub for so many connections is that you introduce a single point of failure on the network. In general, a large network would include multiple hubs (or other connectivity devices). Figure 6-17 depicts a variety of standalone hubs.

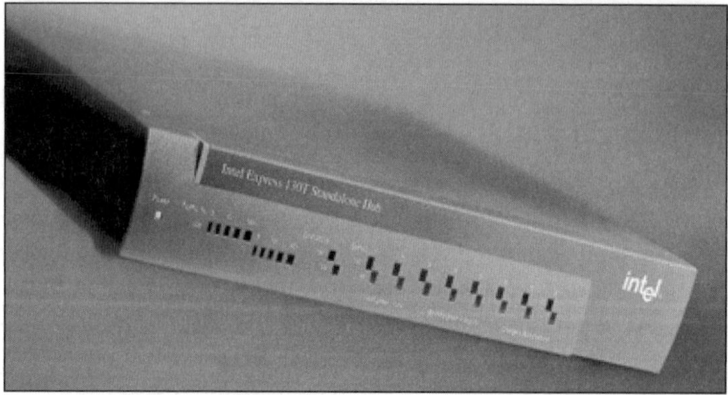

Figure 6-17 Standalone hubs

STACKABLE HUBS

Stackable hubs resemble standalone hubs, but they are physically designed to be linked with other hubs in a single telecommunications closet. Stackable hubs linked together logically represent one large hub to the network. A great benefit to using stackable hubs is that your network or workgroup does not depend on a single hub that introduces a single point of failure.

Models vary in the maximum number that can be stacked. For instance, some hub manufacturers restrict the number of their stacked hubs to five; others can be stacked eight units high.

Although many stackable hubs use Ethernet uplink ports, some use a proprietary high-speed cabling system to link the hubs together for better inter-hub performance. This setup often creates incompatibilities between the bus cabling of different product lines, even when those products come from the same manufacturer. Hubs that use standard Ethernet uplink ports can usually be interconnected with other product lines. As a general rule, although stacked hubs do not have to be made by the same manufacturer to work together properly, it is always preferable to interconnect hardware that is known to be compatible right out of the box.

Like standalone hubs, stackable hubs may support a number of different media connectors and transmission speeds and may come with or without special processing features. The number of ports they provide also varies, although you will most often see 6, 12, or 24 ports on a stackable hub. Figure 6-18 depicts a variety of stackable hubs, and Figure 6-19 shows a rack-mounted stackable hub system, such as you might find in a telecommunications closet.

Figure 6-18 Stackable Hubs

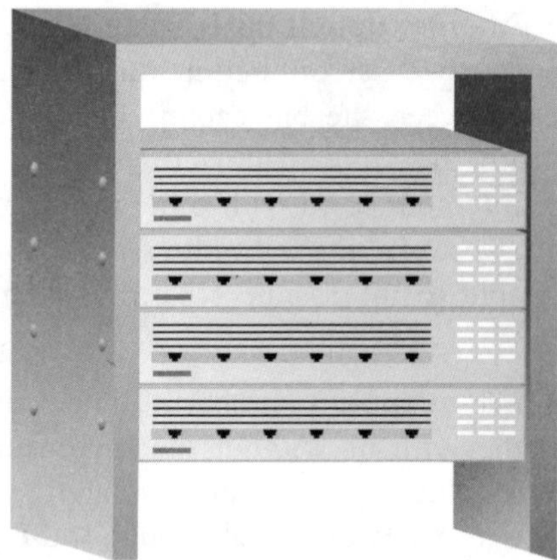

Figure 6-19 Rack-mounted stackable hubs

Modular Hubs

Modular hubs provide a number of interface options within one chassis, making them more flexible than either stackable or standalone hubs. Similar to a PC, a modular hub contains a system board and slots into which you can insert different adapters. These adapters may connect the modular hub to other types of hubs, routers, WAN links, or Token Ring or Ethernet network backbones. They may also connect the modular hub to management workstations or redundant components, such as an extra power supply. Because you can attach redundant components to modular hubs, they offer the highest reliability of any type of hub. Another benefit to modular hubs is that they allow for a network's future growth by providing expansion slots for additional devices. In addition, they can accommodate many types of devices. In other words, you can customize a modular hub to your network's needs. On the downside, modular hubs are the most expensive type of hub, and for a small network they may be overkill. Modular hubs are nearly always intelligent hubs.

Intelligent Hubs

Earlier in this chapter, you learned that an intelligent hub can process data, monitor traffic, and provide troubleshooting information, among other things. Intelligent hubs are also called **managed hubs**, because they can be managed from anywhere on the network. Remember that standalone, stackable, or modular hubs may all contain processing capabilities and therefore be considered intelligent.

The advantage of intelligent hubs derives from their ability to analyze data. A network administrator can store the information generated by intelligent hubs in a MIB. A **MIB (management information base)** is a collection of data used by management programs (which may be part of the network operating system or third-party programs) to analyze network performance and problems. Novell's ManageWise is one example of a program that relies on MIBs. From such a program, the network administrator can view the network layout in graphical form, disconnect problem nodes, set alarms to go off when certain events occur, identify nodes that may be generating unnecessary traffic, or find out information (such as IP addresses) about remote nodes. Using this tool, the network administrator can also track historical data about network traffic patterns—for example, to determine where more connectivity equipment is needed.

Although you might be tempted to assume that intelligent hubs are your best solution in every situation, they have their disadvantages. For example, an intelligent hub will report every time a port detects a lost connection. In fact, lost connections happen hundreds of times each day—when a formerly connected workstation is restarted, for example. This event, its trivial nature notwithstanding, is recorded in the MIB, along with hundreds of other inconsequential events. When the MIB includes so many inconsequential events, network administrators may find it difficult to determe which errors are critical and which can be ignored. In addition, intelligent hubs are significantly more expensive than passive hubs. For a routine networking environment with limited staff, intelligent hubs might be more trouble than they are worth.

Installing a Hub

As with NICs, the best way to ensure that you install a hub properly is to follow the manufacturer's guidelines. Most of the time, hubs are simple to install—arguably even simpler than connecting workstations to the network.

First, plug the hub in and turn it on. Make sure that the hub's power light goes on. Most hubs will perform self-tests when turned on, and blinking lights will indicate that these tests are in progress. When the tests are completed (as indicated by a steady, lit power light on most hubs), attach the hub to the network by connecting a patch cable from it to the backbone or to an intermediate switch or router. Next, connect patch cables from the patch panel or workstations into the hub's receptacles, as shown in Figure 6-20. Once the workstation connects to the network through the newly installed hub, check to verify that the link and traffic lights act as they should, according to the hub's documentation.

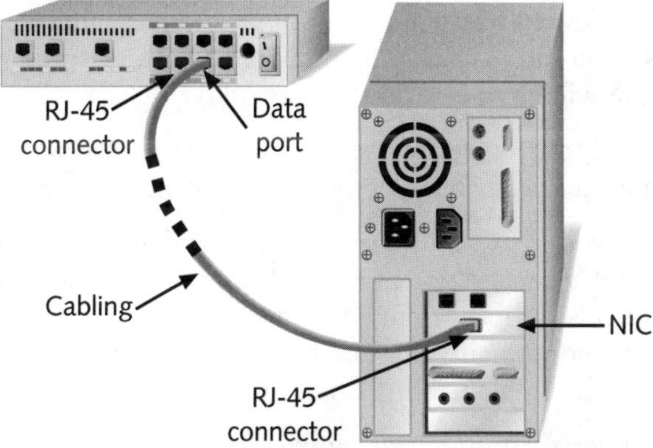

Figure 6-20 Connecting a workstation to a hub

In addition, you will probably need to configure the hub's firmware and, in the case of intelligent hubs, its software as well. For example, you will need to assign an IP address to the hub. Refer to the instructions that came with your hub to find out how to configure its firmware and software.

If you are installing a stackable hub, or a rack-mounted hub, you will need to use the screws and clamps that came with the hub to secure it to the rack or connect it to the other hubs. In the case of a stackable hub, you must connect it with its proprietary cabling or through its uplink port. Again, the best approach is to read the instructions that came with the hub.

Choosing the Right Hub

Any one of thousands of hubs might work on your network. So how do you decide which is right for you? First, narrow your list of options to hubs that match your network model, transmission speed, and media type. Then examine the following list of variables and decide which enhancements are necessary for your network and how much you can afford.

- *Performance*—If performance is your concern, you may want to use switches, rather than hubs, to subdivide a current LAN segment into several, smaller segments. You may also want to upgrade part of your network to a faster transmission technology (for example, 10BaseT to 100BaseTX). To support this transition, you may need a hub that can handle traffic at *either* 10 Mbps or 100 Mbps. Because of the way in which hubs work, you should avoid mixing hubs that can handle only speeds of 10 Mbps with hubs that can handle speeds of 100 Mbps, because all 100 Mbps devices will be slowed down by the presence of even a single 10 Mbps device. Switches (discussed later in this chapter) do support mixing of speeds.
- *Cost*—If your budget is tight, and your environment does not demand the flexibility, reliability, or security of more sophisticated hubs, a passive standalone or a few passive stackable hubs might be your answer.
- *Size and growth*—You need to determine how many devices will connect to each hub in each telecommunications closet. If one segment consists of only 10 connections now but you know its size will double in six months, purchase a hub with at least 24 ports. (You must balance the number of hubs with the number of points of failure you are willing to risk on the network.)
- *Security*—If your network carries sensitive data, you should probably consider using more sophisticated connectivity equipment like switches, routers, or firewalls.
- *Management benefits*—If you manage a huge enterprise-wide network containing many different types of devices and potential problems, you will want to purchase an intelligent hub, which is capable of providing management information to your network management program. This purchase will require more planning and technical expertise than implementing other hub solutions.
- *Reliability*—If your network cannot tolerate any down time, consider purchasing a modular hub with redundant power supplies and possibly redundant connections to the backbone as well.

As with NICs, the hub manufacturer's documentation can vary. Appendix A lists popular hub manufacturers and their Web site addresses.

Bridges

Bridges are devices that look like repeaters, in that they have a single input and a single output port, as shown in Figure 6-21. They differ from repeaters in that they can interpret the data they retransmit. Bridging occurs at the Data Link layer of the OSI Model; as you will recall from Chapter 3, this layer encompasses flow control, error handling, and physical addressing. Bridges analyze incoming frames and make decisions about how to direct them to their destination. Specifically, they read the destination (MAC) address information and decide whether to forward (retransmit) the packet to another segment on the network or, if the destination address belongs to the same segment as the source address, filter (discard) it. As nodes transmit data through the bridge, the bridge establishes a **filtering database** (also known as a **forwarding table**) of known MAC addresses and their locations on the network. The bridge uses its filtering database to determine whether a packet should be forwarded or filtered, as illustrated in Figure 6-22.

Figure 6-21 A bridge

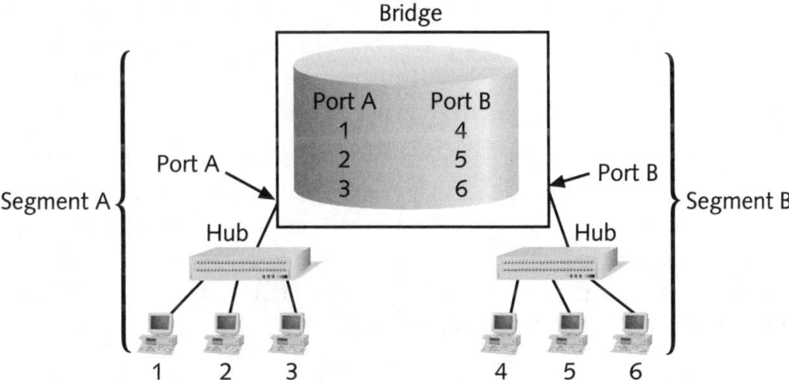

Figure 6-22 A bridge's use of a filtering database

Using Figure 6-22 as an example, imagine that you sit at workstation 1 on segment A of the LAN, and your colleague Abby sits at workstation 2 on segment A. When you attempt to send data to Abby's computer, your transmission will go through your segment's hub and then to the bridge. The bridge will read the MAC address of Abby's computer. It will then search its filtering database to determine whether that MAC address belongs to the same segment you're on or whether it belongs on a different segment. The bridge can determine only that the MAC address of Abby's workstation is associated with its port A. If the MAC address belongs to a different segment, the bridge forwards the data to that segment, whose corresponding port identity is also in the filtering database. In this case, however, your workstation and Abby's workstation reside on the same LAN segment, so the data would be filtered (that is ignored) and your message would be delivered to Abby's workstation through segment A's hub.

Conversely, if you wanted to send data to your supervisor's computer, which is workstation 5 in Figure 6-22, your transmission would first pass through segment A's hub and then on to the bridge. The bridge would read the MAC address for your supervisor's machine (the destination address in your data stream) and search for the port associated with that machine. In this case, the bridge would recognize workstation 5 as being connected to port B, and it would forward the data to that port. Subsequently, the segment B hub would ensure delivery of the data to your supervisor's computer.

A bridge does not arrive on your network already knowing which workstations are associated with its various ports. After its installation, the bridge will poll the network to discover where the destination address for each packet it handles resides. Once it discovers this information, it will record the destination node's MAC address and its associated port in its filtering database. Over time, it will discover all nodes on the network and construct database entries for each.

Because bridges cannot interpret higher-level data, such as Network layer information, they do not distinguish between different protocols. They can forward frames from AppleTalk, TCP/IP, IPX/SPX, and NetBIOS with equal speed and accuracy. This flexibility is a great advantage. Because they are protocol-ignorant, bridges can move data more rapidly than traditional routers, for example, which do care about protocol information (as you will learn later in this chapter). On the other hand, bridges take longer to transmit data than either repeaters or hubs, because bridges actually analyze each packet.

Bridges may follow one of several types of methods for forwarding or filtering packets. A discussion of these methods is beyond the scope of this book, but you should at least be aware of the most popular options. The method used on most Ethernet networks is called **Transparent Bridging**, and the method used on most Token Ring networks is called **Source Route Bridging**. A method of bridging that can connect Token Ring and Ethernet networks is called **Translational Bridging**.

When bridges were first introduced in the early 1980s, they were designed to forward packets between homogenous networks. Since then, however, bridges have evolved to handle data transfer between different types of networks. They have also enjoyed advances in their filtering techniques and transmission speed. Even though sophisticated routers and switches have replaced many network bridges, bridges may still be adequate and appropriate in some situations. The inclusion of bridge on a network enhances the network performance by filtering traffic directed to the various nodes; the nodes therefore spend less time and resources listening for data that may or may not be destined for them. Also, a bridge can detect and discard flawed packets that may create congestion on the network. Perhaps most importantly, bridges extend the maximum distance of a network beyond its previous limits.

Standalone bridges became popular in the 1980s and early 1990s, but they have largely been made obsolete by advanced switching and routing technology. In general, you will rarely work with bridges as standalone devices. Nevertheless, understanding the concept of bridging is essential to understanding how switches work. You will learn more about switches in the next section.

SWITCHES

In recent years, advances in connectivity hardware have blurred the strict distinctions between hubs, switches, routers, and bridges. **Switches** subdivide a network into smaller logical pieces. Unlike hubs, which operate at Layer 1 of the OSI Model, they operate at the Data Link layer (Layer 2) of the OSI Model and can interpret MAC address information. In this sense, switches resemble bridges. In fact, they can be described as multiport bridges. Figure 6-23 illustrates several switches.

By having multiple ports, switches can make better use of limited bandwidth and prove more cost-efficient than bridges. Each port on the switch acts like a bridge, and each device connected to a switch effectively receives its own dedicated channel. In other words, a switch can turn a shared channel into several channels.

Figure 6-23 Examples of LAN switches

From the Ethernet perspective, each dedicated channel represents a collision domain. A **collision domain** is a logically or physically distinct Ethernet network segment on which all participating devices must detect and accommodate data collisions. Because a switch limits the number of devices in a collision domain, it limits the potential for collisions.

Switches have historically been used to replace hubs and ease traffic congestion in LAN workgroups. Introducing a switch on a congested segment is only a temporary solution, however, and arguably not the best use of such a device. More recently, network managers have replaced backbone routers with switches, and switch sales are therefore booming.

The inclusion of switches on a network backbone provides at least two advantages. First, switches are generally very secure because they isolate one device's traffic from other devices' traffic. Second, switches provide separate channels for (potentially) every device. As a result, applications that transfer a large amount of traffic and are sensitive to time delay, such as videoconferencing applications, can make full use of the network's capacity.

Switches have their disadvantages, too. Although they contain buffers to hold incoming data and accommodate bursts of traffic, they can become overwhelmed by continuous, heavy traffic. In that event, the switch cannot prevent data loss. On a shared environment, where many nodes share the same data channel, devices can compensate for collisions; on a fully switched network, where every node uses its own port on the switch and therefore provides a separate data channel, devices cannot detect collisions. Also, although higher-layer protocols, such as TCP, will detect the loss and respond with a timeout, others, such as UDP, will not. For those packets, the number of collisions will mount up, and eventually all network traffic will grind to a halt. For this reason, you should plan placement of switches carefully to match backbone capacity and traffic patterns.

Switches can be classified into a few different categories. One type, a LAN switch, functions on a local area network. LAN switches can be designed for Ethernet or Token Ring networks, although Ethernet LAN switches are more common. LAN switches also differ in the method of switching they use—namely, cut-through mode or store and forward mode. These methods of switching on a LAN are discussed in the next two sections.

Keep in mind that the term *switch* is also sometimes applied to WAN and access server devices. You will learn more about WAN and remote connectivity in Chapter 7.

Cut-Through Mode

A switch running in **cut-through mode** will read a frame's header and decide where to forward the data before it receives the entire packet. Recall from Chapter 5, that the first 14 bytes of a frame constitute its header, which contains the destination MAC address. This information is sufficient for the switch to determine which port should get the frame and begin transmitting the frame (without bothering to hold the data and check its accuracy).

What if the frame becomes corrupt? Because the cut-through mode does not allow the switch to read the Frame Check Sequence before it begins transmitting, it can't verify data integrity in that way. On the other hand, cut-through switches can detect **runts**, or packet fragments. Upon detecting a runt, the switch will wait to transmit that packet until it determines its integrity. It's important to remember, however, that runts are only one type of data flaw. Cut-through switches *cannot* detect corrupt packets; indeed, they may increase the number of errors found on the network by propagating flawed packets.

The most significant advantage of the cut-through mode is its speed. Because it does not stop to read the entire data packet, a cut-through switch can forward information much more rapidly than a store and forward switch can (as described in the next section). The time-saving advantages to cut-through switching become insignificant, however, if the switch is flooded with traffic. In this case, the cut-through switch must buffer (or temporarily hold) data, just like a store and forward switch. Cut-through switches are best suited to small workgroups where speed is important and the relatively low number of devices minimizes the potential for errors.

Store and Forward Mode

In **store and forward mode**, a switch reads the entire data frame into its memory and checks it for accuracy before transmitting the information. Although this method is more time-consuming than the cut-through method, it allows store and forward switches to transmit data more accurately. Store and forward mode switches are more appropriate for larger LAN environments because they do not propagate data errors. In contrast, cut-through mode switches do forward errors, so they may contribute to network congestion if a particular segment is experiencing a number of collisions. In large environments, a failure to check for errors can result in problematic traffic congestion.

Store and forward switches can also transfer data between segments running different transmission speeds. For example, a high-speed network printer that serves 50 students could be attached to a 100 Mbps port on the switch, thereby allowing all of the student workstations to connect to 10 Mbps ports on the same switch. With this scheme, the printer can quickly service multiple jobs. This characteristic makes store and forward mode switches preferable in mixed-speed environments.

Using Switches to Create VLANs

In addition to improving bandwidth usage, switches can create **virtual local area networks (VLANs)** by logically grouping a number of ports into a broadcast domain. A **broadcast domain** is a combination of ports that make up a Layer 2 segment and must be connected by a Layer 3 device, such as a router or Layer 3 switch. The ports do not have to reside on the same switch or even on the same network segment. A VLAN can include servers, workstations, printers, routers, or any other network device you can connect to a switch. Figure 6-24 illustrates a simple VLAN design. Note, however, that one great advantage of VLANs is their ability to link geographically distant users and create small workgroups from large LANs.

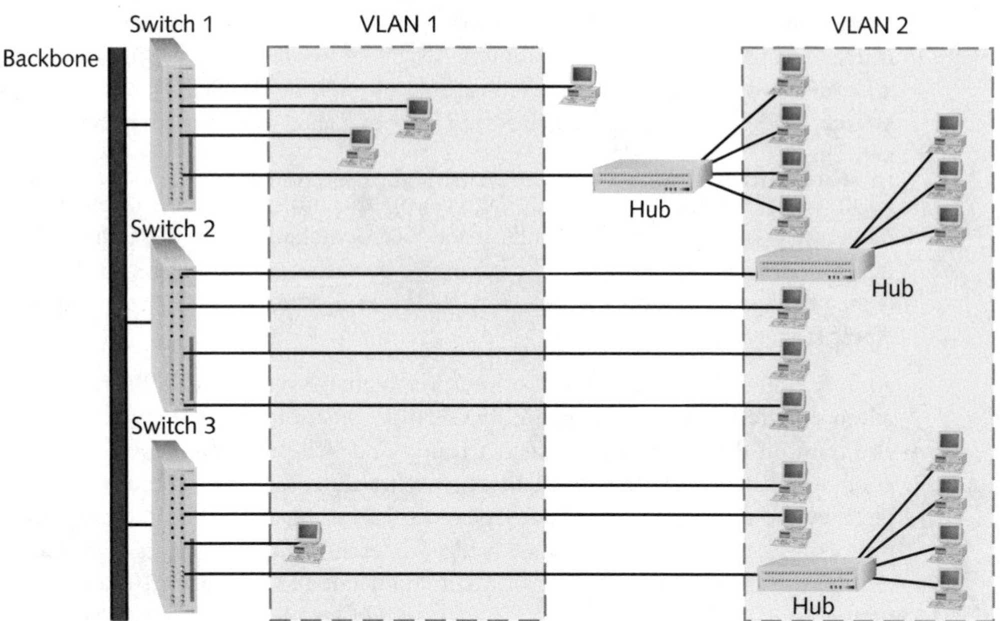

Figure 6-24 A simple VLAN design

To create a VLAN, you must configure the switch properly. In addition to identifying the ports that belong to each logical LAN, you can specify security parameters, filtering instructions (if the switch should not forward any frames from a certain segment, for example), performance requirements for certain users, and network management options. Clearly, switches are very flexible devices.

Describing the variety of ways in which VLANs may be implemented is beyond the scope of this book. If you are charged with designing a network or installing switches, however, you should research VLANs further. Some trade publications (and many switch manufacturers) have touted VLANs as the most advanced approach to networking and the wave of the future. For more information on cutting-edge VLAN technology, refer to Cisco System's white paper on VLANs at http://www.cisco.com/warp/public/538/7.html.

In setting up a VLAN, you are not merely including a certain group of nodes—you are also excluding another group. As a result, you can potentially cut a group off from the rest of the network. VLAN implementation requires careful planning to ensure that all the groups of users who need to communicate can do so after the VLAN is in operation.

Higher-Layer Switches

Earlier in this chapter, you learned that switches operate in Layer 2 (Data Link layer) of the OSI Model, routers operate in Layer 3, and hubs operate in Layer 1. You also learned that the distinctions between hubs, bridges, switches, and routers are blurring. This melding of categories will become more pronounced as switch technology advances. Indeed, manufacturers are already producing switches that can operate at Layer 3 (Network layer) and Layer 4 (Transport layer), making them act more like routers. A switch capable of interpreting Layer 3 data is called a **Layer 3 switch**. Similarly, a switch capable of interpreting Layer 4 data is called a **Layer 4 switch**. These higher-layer switches may also be called **routing switches** or **application switches**.

Competing manufacturers rarely agree on the nomenclature for new technologies. Nevertheless, it is commonly understood that switched traffic is handled entirely by the device's hardware and routed traffic is handled by the device's software. For instance, the same device may act as a Layer 4 switch for IP, a Layer 3 switch for IPX, and a regular router for AppleTalk.

Among other things, the ability to interpret higher-layer data enables switches to perform advanced filtering, statistics keeping, and security functions. Layer 3 and Layer 4 switches may also transmit data more rapidly than a router and will probably remain easier to install and configure than routers. In general, these switches aren't as fully featured as routers. For example, they typically cannot translate between Token Ring and Ethernet networks, encapsulate protocols, or prioritize traffic. These critical differences make switches inappropriate for specific connectivity needs. In other words, if you needed to connect a 10BaseT Ethernet LAN with a 100BaseT Ethernet LAN, a switch would be adequate. If you wanted to connect a Token Ring LAN with an Ethernet LAN, you would have to use a router.

As with other connectivity devices, the features of these Layer 3 and Layer 4 switches vary widely depending on the manufacturer and the price. (This variability is exacerbated by the fact that key players in the networking trade have not agreed on standards for these switches.) Higher-layer switches can cost three times more than Layer 2 switches, and network administrators are only beginning to try them. In general, higher-layer switches are yet another technology you will need to watch closely. One good resource for learning more about switching and internetworking is Cisco System's Designing Switched LAN Internetworks white paper at http://www.cisco.com/warp/public/538/7.html.

ROUTERS

A **router** is a multiport device that can connect dissimilar LANs and WANs running at different transmission speeds and using a variety of protocols. Routers operate at the Network layer (Layer 3) of the OSI Model. Recall from Chapter 2 that the Network layer directs data from one segment or type of network to another. Historically, routers have been slower than switches or bridges because they pay attention to information in Layers 3 and higher, such as protocols and logical addresses. Consequently, unlike bridges and Layer 2 switches, routers are protocol-dependent. They must be designed or configured to recognize a certain protocol before they can forward data transmitted using that protocol.

As is the case with bridges, traditional standalone LAN routers are being slowly replaced by Layer 3 switches that support the routing functions. The concept of routing remains extremely important, however, and everything described in the remainder of this section also applies to Layer 3 switches. Standalone routers are still the technology of choice for connecting remote offices using WAN technology.

Router Features and Functions

A router's strength lies in its intelligence. Routers can not only keep track of the locations of certain nodes are on the network, as switches can, but also determine the shortest, fastest path between two nodes. For this reason, and because they can connect dissimilar network types, routers are powerful, indispensable devices on large LANs and WANs. The Internet, for example, relies on millions of routers across the world.

Routers may use one of two methods for directing data on the network: static or dynamic routing. Static routing is a technique in which a network administrator programs a router to use specific paths between nodes. Since it does not account for occasional network congestion, failed connections, or device moves, static routing is not optimal. Dynamic routing, however, automatically calculates the best path between two nodes and accumulates this information in a routing table. If congestion or failures affect the network, a router using dynamic routing can detect the problems and reroute data through a different path. Most modern networks primarily use dynamic routing, but may include some static routing to indicate a router of last resort, the router that accepts all unroutable packets.

As noted in Chapter 3, some protocols are not routable. Routable protocols include TCP/IP, IPX/SPX, and AppleTalk. Because NetBEUI and SNA are not routable, for example, networks that run these protocols cannot use routers. On the other hand, some routers provide advanced support for Layer 2 bridging that far exceeds what a bridge or switch can accomplish. These bridge-routers (or brouters) are discussed later in this chapter.

A typical router has an internal processor, its own memory and power supply, input and output jacks for different types of network connectors (depending on the network type), and, usually, a management console interface. High-powered, multiprotocol routers may have several slot bays to accommodate multiple network interfaces (RJ-45, BNC, FDDI, and so on). A router with multiple slots that can hold different interface cards or other devices is called a **modular router**.

A router is a very flexible device. Although any one can be specialized for a variety of tasks, all routers can do the following: connect dissimilar networks, interpret Layer 3 information, determine the best path for data to follow from point A to point B, and reroute traffic if a primary path is down but another path is available. In addition to performing these basic functions, routers may perform any of the following options:

- Filter out broadcast transmissions to alleviate network congestion
- Prevent certain types of traffic from getting to a network, enabling customized segregation and security
- Support simultaneous local and remote connectivity
- Provide high network fault tolerance through redundant components such as power supplies or network interfaces
- Monitor network traffic and report statistics to a MIB
- Diagnose internal or other connectivity problems and trigger alarms

Because of their customizability, routers are not simple devices to install. Typically, a technician or engineer must be very familiar with routing technology to figure out how to place and configure a router to best advantage. Figure 6-25 gives you some idea of how routers fit in a LAN environment, although this example is oversimplified. Chapter 7 discusses routers on WANs. If you plan to specialize in network design or router configuration, you should research router technology further. You might begin with Cisco Systems's online documentation at http://www.cisco.com/univercd/home/home.htm. Cisco Systems currently provides the significant majority of networking routers installed in the world.

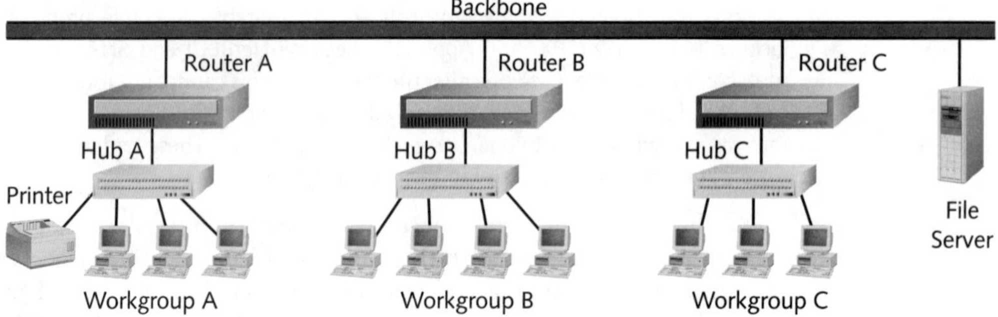

Figure 6-25 The placement of routers on a LAN

In the setup depicted in Figure 6-25, if a workstation in workgroup C wanted to print to a networked printer in workgroup A, it would create a transmission containing the address of the workgroup A printer. Then it would send its packets to hub C. Hub C would simply retransmit the signal to router C. When router C received the transmission, it would temporarily store the packets as it read the Layer 3 information. Upon determining that the packets are destined for a printer in workgroup A, router C would then decide the best way to get the data to the workgroup A printer. In this example, it might send the data directly to router A. Before it forwards the packet, however, router C would increment the number of hops tallied in the packet. (Recall from Chapter 4 that packets can make only so many trips through a router before they are discarded. Each time a packet passes through a router, it has made a hop.) Next, router C would forward the data to router A. Router A would read the packets' destination addresses and forward them to hub A, which would then broadcast the transmission to workgroup A until the printer picked it up.

Routing Protocols: RIP, OSPF, EIGRP, and BGP

Finding the best route for data to take across the network is one of the most valued and sophisticated functions performed by a router. The best path will depend on the number of hops between nodes, the current network activity, the unavailable links, the network transmission speed, and the topology. To determine the best path, routers communicate with each other through **routing protocols**. Keep in mind that routing protocols are *not* identical to routable protocols, such as TCP/IP or IPX/SPX, although they may piggyback on top of routable protocols. Routing protocols are used only to collect data about current network status and contribute to selection of best paths. From these data, routers create routing tables for use with future packet forwarding.

In addition to its ability to find the best path, a routing protocol can be characterized according to its **convergence time,** the time it takes for a router to recognize a best path in the event of a change or outage. Its **bandwidth overhead**, the burden placed on the underlying network to support the routing protocol, is also a distinguishing feature.

Although you do not need to know precisely how routing protocols work, you should be familiar with the most common routing protocols: RIP, OSPF, EIGRP, and BGP. (Several more routing protocols exist, but are not widely used.) These four common routing protocols are described below.

- *RIP (Routing Information Protocol) for IP and IPX*—The oldest routing protocol, RIP, which is still widely used, factors in only the number of hops between nodes when determining a path from one point to another. It does not consider network congestion or link speed, for example. Routers using RIP broadcast their routing tables every 30 seconds to other routers, whether or not the tables have changed. This broadcasting creates excessive network traffic, especially if a large number of routes exists. If the routing tables change, it may take several minutes before the new information propagates to routers at the far reaches of the network; thus the convergence time for RIP is poor. RIP is limited to interpreting a maximum of 16 hops, so it does not work well in very large network environments where data may have to travel through more than 16 routers to reach its destination (for example, on the Internet). Also, compared with other routing protocols, RIP is slower and less secure.
- *OSPF (Open Shortest Path First) for IP*—This routing protocol makes up for some of the limitations of RIP and can coexist with RIP on a network. OSPF uses a more complex algorithm for determining best paths. The term **best path** refers to the most efficient route from one node on a network to another. Under optimal network conditions, the best path comprises the most direct path between two points. If excessive traffic levels or an outage preclude data from following the most direct path, a router may determine that the most efficient path actually

goes through additional routers. Each router maintains a database of the other routers' links, and if notice is received indicating the failure of a given link, the router can rapidly compute an alternate path. This approach requires more memory and CPU power on the routers, but it keeps network bandwidth to a minimum and provides a very fast convergence time, often invisible to the users. OSPF is the second most frequently supported protocol, after RIP.

- *EIGRP (Enhanced Interior Gateway Routing Protocol) for IP, IPX, and AppleTalk*—This routing protocol was developed in the mid-1980s by Cisco Systems. It has a fast convergence time and a low network overhead, but is easier to configure and less CPU-intensive than OSPF. EIGRP also offers the benefits of supporting multiple protocols and limiting unnecessary network traffic between routers. It accommodates very large and heterogeneous networks, but is only supported by Cisco routers.
- *BGP (Border Gateway Protocol) for IP*—BGP is the routing protocol of Internet backbones. The demands on routers created by Internet growth have driven the development of BGP, the most complex of the routing protocols. The developers of BGP had to contend with not only the prospect of 100,000 routes, but also the question of how to route traffic efficiently and fairly through the hundreds of Internet backbones.

Brouters and Routing Switches

By now it should not surprise you that routers, too, can act like other devices. The networking industry has adopted the term **bridge router**, or "brouter," to describe routers that take on some characteristics of bridges. The advantage of crossing a router with a bridge is that you can forward nonroutable protocols, such as NetBEUI, plus connect multiple network types through one device. A bridge router offers support at both Layers 2 and 3 of the OSI Model. It intelligently handles any packets that contain Layer 3 addressing information and simply forwards the rest.

Another router hybrid, a **routing switch**, combines a router and a switch. It can also interpret data from both Layers 2 and 3 of the OSI Model. (*Routing switch* is another term for the higher-layer switches covered earlier in this chapter.) A routing switch is not as fully featured as a true router, and therefore routing switches have not gained wide acceptance from networking professionals.

Gateways

Gateways do not fall neatly into the networking hardware category. In broad terms, they are combinations of networking hardware and software that connect two dissimilar kinds of networks. Specifically, they may connect two systems that use different formatting, communications protocols, or architecture. Unlike the connectivity hardware discussed earlier in this chapter, gateways actually repackage information so that it can be read by another system. To accomplish this task, gateways must operate at multiple layers of the OSI Model. They must communicate with an application, establish and manage sessions, translate encoded data, and interpret logical and physical addressing data.

Gateways can reside on servers, microcomputers, or mainframes. They are more expensive than routers because of their vast capabilities and almost always application-specific. In addition, they transmit data much more slowly than bridges or routers because of the complex translations they conduct. Because they are slow, gateways have the potential to cause extreme network congestion. In certain situations, however, only a gateway will suffice.

During your networking career, you will most likely hear gateways discussed in the context of e-mail systems. Popular types of gateways, including e-mail gateways, are described below.

- *E-mail gateway*—A gateway that translates messages from one type of system to another. For example, an e-mail gateway would allow people who use Eudora e-mail to correspond with people who use GroupWise e-mail.
- *IBM host gateway*—A gateway that establishes and manages communication between a PC and an IBM mainframe computer.
- *Internet gateway*—A gateway that allows and manages access between LANs and the Internet. An Internet gateway can restrict the kind of access LAN users have to the Internet, and vice versa.
- *LAN gateway*—A gateway that allows segments of a LAN running different protocols or different network models to communicate with each other. A router or even a server may act as a LAN gateway. The LAN gateway category might also include remote access servers that allow dial-up connectivity to a LAN.

CHAPTER SUMMARY

- Network interface cards come in a variety of types depending on network transport system (Ethernet versus Token Ring), network transmission speed (for example, 10 Mbps versus 100 Mbps), connector interfaces (for example, BNC versus RJ-45), type of compatible system board or device, and manufacturer.
- Before you order or install a NIC in a network device, you need to know the type of interface required by the device. For a desktop or tower PC, the NIC must match its bus. A bus is the type of circuit used by the system board to transmit data to components. NICs may fit ISA, EISA, MCA, or PCI buses. New computers almost always use PCI buses.
- NICs may connect to interfaces other than a PC's bus. For laptop computers, Personal Computer Memory Card International Association (PCMCIA) slots may be used to connect NICs; older models, parallel ports may serve the same purpose.
- In addition to NICs that interface with network cabling, NICs can be designed for wireless transmission. Typically, a wireless NIC uses an antenna to exchange signals with a base station transceiver. This type of connectivity suits environments where cabling cannot be installed or where roaming clients must be supported.

- Devices other than PCs, such as networked printers, use specialized NICs. Printer NICs also come in a variety of styles suited to different applications. By far, the most popular printer NIC is Hewlett-Packard's JetDirect card.
- On servers and other high-powered computers, you may need to install multiple NICs. For the hardware installation, you can simply repeat the same installation process as used for the first NIC, choosing a different slot. The trick to using multiple NICs on one machine lies in correctly configuring the software for each NIC.
- Firmware combines hardware and software. The hardware component of firmware is a read-only memory (ROM) chip that stores data established at the factory and possibly changed by configuration programs that can write to ROM.
- Installing a NIC involves three steps: installing the hardware, configuring the software, and configuring the firmware. For any of these steps, you should refer to the manufacturer's documentation for help. Because NICs are often the source of connectivity problems, you should know how to install and configure them properly.
- An IRQ is the means by which a device can request attention from the CPU. IRQs are identified by numbers from 0 to 15. The BIOS will attempt to assign free IRQs. Typically, it will assign IRQ 10, 11, 12, or 13, to NICs. If conflicts occur, you must manually set a device's IRQ rather than accept the default suggested by the BIOS.
- Although you can always change IRQ settings in the BIOS, your ability to change them from the operating system software depends on the type of NIC at hand. If you are using a PCI NIC, which requires a PCI bus controller, the PCI controller's settings will dictate whether you can change the NIC's IRQ from the operating system. By default, you cannot.
- To change a NIC's firmware, you will need a bootable floppy disk (DOS version 6.0 or higher) containing the configuration or DOS install utility that shipped with the NIC. To run the utility, you must start the computer with this floppy disk inserted. The NIC configuration utility will not run if an operating system or memory management program is already running.
- NICs come with a variety of features that influence their ease of use, compatibility, and performance. When purchasing a NIC, you should choose one that not only matches your network's type and transmission speed, but also comes with the desired enhancements.
- Repeaters are the connectivity devices that perform the regeneration and amplification of an analog or digital signal. They belong to the Physical layer of the OSI Model; therefore they do not have any means to interpret the data they are retransmitting. For example, they cannot improve or correct a bad or erroneous signal; they can only repeat it.
- At its most primitive, a hub is a multiport repeater containing one port that connects to a network's backbone and multiple ports that connect to a group of workstations (or a patch panel). Hubs typically support a star or hybrid topology on an Ethernet network. On Token Ring networks, hubs are called Multistation Access Units (MAUs).

- In addition to connecting Macintosh and PC workstations, hubs may connect print servers, switches, servers, or other devices to a network. They can support a variety of media and data transmission speeds. Some hubs also allow for multiple media connector types or multiple data transmission speeds.
- Hubs that merely repeat signals are called passive hubs. Like NICs, however, hubs may possess internal processing capabilities. They may perform remote management, filter data, or provide diagnostic information about the network. Hubs that can perform any of these functions are known as intelligent hubs.
- Standalone hubs, as their name implies, serve a workgroup of computers separate from the rest of the network. They may be connected to another hub by a coaxial, fiber-optic, or twisted-pair cable; they are not typically connected in a hierarchical or daisy-chain fashion.
- Stackable hubs are physically designed to be linked with other hubs in a single telecommunications closet. Stackable hubs linked together logically represent one large hub to the network. A great benefit to using this type of hub is that your network or workgroup does not depend on one hub that introduces a single point of failure.
- Modular hubs provide a number of interface options within one chassis, making them more flexible than stackable or standalone hubs. Similar to a PC, a modular hub contains a system board and slots that can accommodate different adapters.
- Intelligent hubs are also called managed hubs, because they can be managed from anywhere on the network. A standalone, stackable, or modular hub may contain processing capabilities and therefore be considered intelligent.
- A MIB (management information base) is a collection of data used by management programs (which may be part of the network operating system or a third-party program) to analyze network performance and problems.
- You will need to analyze the following requirements before selecting a hub for your network: performance, cost, security, reliability, management benefits, and network size and planned growth.
- Bridges resemble repeaters in that they have a single input and a single output port, but they differ from repeaters because they can interpret the data they retransmit. Bridging occurs at the Data Link layer of the OSI Model. Bridges read the destination (MAC) address information and decide whether to forward (retransmit) the packet to another segment on the network or, if the destination address belongs to the same segment as the source address, filter (discard) it.
- As nodes transmit data through the bridge, the bridge establishes a filtering database of known MAC addresses and their locations on the network. The bridge uses its filtering database to determine whether a packet should be forwarded or filtered.
- Switches, like hubs, subdivide a network into smaller logical pieces. Unlike hubs, they operate at the Data Link layer (Layer 2) of the OSI Model and can interpret MAC address information. In this respect, switches resemble bridges. Sometimes switches are described as multiport bridges.

- Switches are finding their way into network backbones. They are generally very secure because they isolate one device's traffic from other traffic devices. Because switches provide separate channels for (potentially) every device, they allow applications that transfer a large amount of traffic and are sensitive to time delay, such as videoconferencing, to make full use of the network's capacity.
- A switch running in cut-through mode will read a frame's header and decide where to forward the data before it receives the entire packet.
- In store and forward mode, switches read the entire data frame into their memory and check it for accuracy before transmitting it. Although this method is more time-consuming than the cut-through method, it allows store and forward switches to transmit data more accurately.
- In addition to improving bandwidth usage, switches can create virtual local area networks (VLANs) by logically grouping several ports into a broadcast domain. The ports do not have to reside on the same switch or even the same network segment.
- Manufacturers are producing switches that can operate at Layer 3 (Network Layer) and Layer 4 (Transport layer) of the OSI Model, making them act more like routers. The ability to interpret higher-layer data enables switches to perform advanced filtering, statistics keeping, and security functions.
- A router is a multiport device that can connect dissimilar LANs and WANs running at different transmission speeds and using a variety of protocols. Routers operate at the Network layer (Layer 3) or higher of the OSI Model. Historically, routers have transmitted data more slowly than switches or bridges because they pay attention to Layer 3 information, such as protocols and logical addresses. Unlike bridges and Layer 2 switches, then, routers are protocol-dependent. They must be designed or configured to recognize a certain protocol before they can forward data transmitted using that protocol.
- Routers can not only keep track of where certain nodes are on the network (as switches can), but also determine the shortest, fastest path between two nodes. For this reason, and because they can connect dissimilar network types, routers are powerful, indispensable devices on large LANs and WANs. The Internet is an example of a network that relies on routers.
- A typical router has an internal processor, its own memory and power supply, input and output jacks for different types of network connectors (depending on the network type), and, usually, a management console interface.
- Finding the best route for data to take across the network is one of the most valued and sophisticated functions performed by a router. The best path will depend on the number of hops between nodes, the current network activity, the unavailable links, the network transmission speed, and the topology. To determine the best path, routers communicate with each other through routing protocols.
- RIP is a routing protocol that simply takes into consideration the number of hops between nodes. It does not consider network congestion or link speed, for example. Routers using RIP broadcast their routing tables every 30 seconds to other routers, whether or not the tables have changed. This broadcasting creates excessive network

traffic. RIP is limited to understanding a maximum of 16 hops, so it does not work well in very large network environments. Compared with other routing protocols, RIP is less effective and less secure.

- OSPF is a routing protocol that compensates for some of the limitations of RIP and can coexist with RIP on a network. OSPF uses a more complex algorithm for determining best paths. With this protocol, routers can dynamically update their routing table information. OSPF is the primary routing protocol used on the Internet. In many instances, it has replaced RIP.
- EIGRP (Enhanced Interior Gateway Routing Protocol), a routing protocol developed in the mid-1980s by Cisco Systems, has a fast convergence time and a low network overhead, but is easier to configure and less CPU-intensive than OSPF. EIGRP also offers the benefits of supporting multiple protocols and limiting unnecessary network traffic between routers.
- BGP (Border Gateway Protocol) is the routing protocol of Internet backbones. The demands on routers created by Internet growth have driven the development of BGP, the most complex of the routing protocols. The developers of BGP had to contend with the prospect of 100,000 routes as well as the goal of routing traffic efficiently and fairly through the hundreds of Internet backbones.
- The networking industry has adopted the term "brouter" to describe routers that take on some characteristics of bridges. Crossing a router with a bridge allows you to forward nonroutable protocols, such as NetBEUI, and to connect multiple network types through one device. A brouter offers support at both Layers 2 and 3 of the OSI Model.
- Gateways are combinations of networking hardware and software that connect two dissimilar kinds of networks. Specifically, they may connect two systems that use different formatting, communications protocols, or architecture. Gateways actually repackage information so that it can be read by another system. To accomplish this task, they must operate at multiple layers of the OSI Model.
- Typically, gateways are used for one of four purposes: as an e-mail gateway, as an IBM host gateway, as an Internet gateway, or as a LAN gateway.

6

KEY TERMS

- **application switch** — Another term for a Layer 3 or Layer 4 switch.
- **bandwidth overhead** — The burden placed on the underlying network to support a routing protocol.
- **base I/O port** — A setting that specifies, in hexadecimal notation, which area of memory will act as a channel for moving data between the NIC and the CPU. Like its IRQ, a device's base I/O port cannot be used by any other device.
- **best path** — The most efficient route from one node on a network to another. Under optimal network conditions, the best path is the most direct path between two points.

- **BIOS (basic input/output system)** — Firmware attached to the system board that controls the computer's communication with its devices, among other things.
- **Border Gateway Protocol (BGP)** — The routing protocol of Internet backbones. The router stress created by Internet growth has driven the development of BGP, the most complex of the routing protocols. The developers of BGP had to contend with the prospect of 100,000 routes as well as the goal of routing traffic efficiently and fairly through the hundreds of Internet backbones.
- **bridge** — A device that looks like a repeater, in that it has a single input and a single output port. A bridge is different from a repeater in that it can interpret the data it retransmits.
- **bridge router (brouter)** — A router capable of providing Layer 2 bridging functions.
- **broadcast domain** — In a virtual local area network, a combination of ports that make up a Layer 2 segment and must be connected by a Layer 3 device, such as a router or Layer 3 switch.
- **bus** — The type of circuit used by the system board to transmit data to components. Most new Pentium computers use buses capable of exchanging 32 or 64 bits of data. As the number of bits of data a bus handles increases, so too does the speed of the device attached to the bus.
- **collision domain** — A portion of a LAN encompassing devices that may cause and detect collisions among their group. Bridges and switches can logically create multiple collision domains.
- **Complementary Metal Oxide Conductor (CMOS)** — Firmware on a PC's system board that enables you to change its devices' configurations.
- **convergence time** — The time it takes for a router to recognize a best path in the event of a change or outage.
- **cut-through mode** — A switching mode in which a switch reads a frame's header and decides where to forward the data before it receives the entire packet. Cut-through mode is faster, but less accurate, than the other switching method, store and forward mode.
- **Enhanced Interior Gateway Routing Protocol (EIGRP)** — A routing protocol developed in the mid-1980s by Cisco Systems that has a fast convergence time and a low network overhead, but is easier to configure and less CPU-intensive than OSPF. EIGRP also offers the benefits of supporting multiple protocols and limiting unnecessary network traffic between routers.
- **erasable programmable read-only memory (EPROM)** — Firmware that belongs on a circuit board and that enables its configuration information to be erased and rewritten. You can write to a NIC's EPROM to change the NIC's default transmission speed, for example.
- **Extended Industry Standard Architecture (EISA)** — A 32-bit bus that is compatible with older ISA devices because it shares the same length and pin configuration as the

ISA bus, but that uses a deeper slot connector to achieve faster throughput. The EISA bus was introduced in the late 1980s to compete with IBM's MCA bus.

- **filtering database** — A collection of data created and used by a bridge that correlates the MAC addresses of connected workstations with their locations. A filtering database is also known as a forwarding table.
- **firmware** — A combination of hardware and software. The hardware component of firmware is a read-only memory (ROM) chip that stores data established at the factory and possibly changed by configuration programs that can write to ROM.
- **forwarding table** — See *filtering database.*
- **gateway** — A combination of networking hardware and software that connects two dissimilar kinds of networks. Gateways perform connectivity, session management, and data translation, so they must operate at multiple layers of the OSI Model.
- **hub** — A multiport repeater containing one port that connects to a network's backbone and multiple ports that connect to a group of workstations. Hubs regenerate digital signals.
- **Industry Standard Architecture (ISA)** — The original PC bus, developed in the early 1980s to support an 8-bit and later 16-bit data transfer capability. Although an older technology, ISA buses are still used to connect serial devices, such as mice or modems, in new PCs.
- **intelligent hub** — A hub that possesses processing capabilities and can therefore monitor network traffic, detect packet errors and collisions, poll connected devices for information, and send the data gathered to a management information base (MIB).
- **IRQ (Interrupt Request Line)** — The means by which a device can request attention from the CPU. IRQs are identified by numbers from 0 to 15, and many PC devices reserve specific numbers for their use alone.
- **Layer 3 switch** — A switch capable of interpreting data at Layer 3 (Network layer) of the OSI Model.
- **Layer 4 switch** — A switch capable of interpreting data at Layer 4 (Transport layer) of the OSI Model.
- **loopback plug** — A connector used for troubleshooting that plugs into a port (for example, a serial or parallel port) and crosses over the transmit line to the receive line, allowing outgoing signals to be redirected back into the computer for testing.
- **managed hub** — See *intelligent hub.*
- **memory range** — A hexadecimal number that indicates the area of memory that the NIC and CPU will use for exchanging, or buffering, data. As with IRQs, some memory ranges are reserved for specific devices—most notably, the system board.
- **MIB (management information base)** — A collection of data used by management programs (which may be part of the network operating system or a third-party program) to analyze network performance and problems.

- **MicroChannel Architecture (MCA)** — IBM's proprietary 32-bit bus for personal computers, introduced in 1987 and later replaced by the more standard EISA and PCI buses.
- **modular hub** — A type of hub that provides a number of interface options within one chassis. Similar to a PC, a modular hub contains a system board and slots accommodating different adapters. These adapters may connect to other types of hubs, routers, WAN links, or to both Token Ring and Ethernet network backbones. They may also connect the modular hub to management workstations or redundant components, such as an extra power supply.
- **modular router** — A router with multiple slots that can hold different interface cards or other devices so as to provide flexible, customizable network interoperability.
- **network adapter** — A synonym for NIC (network interface card). The device that enables a workstation, server, printer, or other node to connect to the network. Network adapters belong to the Physical layer of the OSI Model.
- **open shortest path first (OSPF)** — A routing protocol that makes up for some of the limitations of RIP and can coexist with RIP on a network.
- **passive hub** — A hub that simply amplifies and retransmits signals over the network.
- **PC card** — See *PCMCIA*.
- **PCMCIA** — An interface developed in the early 1990s by the Personal Computer Memory Card International Association to provide a standard interface for connecting any type of device to a portable computer. PCMCIA slots may hold modem cards, network interface cards, external hard disk cards, or CD-ROM cards.
- **Peripheral Component Interconnect (PCI)** — A 32- or 64-bit bus introduced in the 1990s, the PCI bus is the NIC connection type used for nearly all new PCs. It's characterized by a shorter length than ISA, MCA, or EISA cards, but a much faster data transmission capability.
- **repeater** — A connectivity device that regenerates and amplifies an analog or digital signal.
- **router** — A multiport device that can connect dissimilar LANs and WANs running at different transmission speeds and using a variety of protocols. In addition, a router can determine the best path for data transmission and perform advanced management functions. Routers operate at the Network layer (Layer 3) or higher of the OSI Model. They are intelligent, protocol-dependent devices.
- **routing information protocol (RIP)** — The oldest routing protocol that is still widely used. RIP does not work in very large network environments where data may have to travel through more than 16 routers to reach its destination (for example, on the Internet). And, compared to other routing protocols, RIP is slower and less secure.
- **routing protocols** — The means by which routers communicate with each other about network status. Routing protocols determine the best path for data to take between nodes. They are not identical to routable protocols such as TCP/IP or IPX/SPX, although they may piggyback on top of routable protocols.

- **routing switch** — Another term for a Layer 3 or Layer 4 switch. A routing switch comprises a hybrid between a router and a switch and can therefore interpret data from Layer 2 and either Layer 3 or Layer 4.
- **runts** — Packet fragments.
- **Source Route Bridging** — The method of bridging used on most Token Ring networks.
- **stackable hub** — A type of hub designed to be linked with other hubs in a single telecommunications closet. Stackable hubs linked together logically represent one large hub to the network.
- **standalone hub** — A type of hub that serves a workgroup of computers that are separate from the rest of the network. A standalone hub may be connected to another hub by a coaxial, fiber-optic, or twisted-pair cable. Such hubs are not typically connected in a hierarchical or daisy-chain fashion.
- **store and forward mode** — A method of switching in which a switch reads the entire data frame into its memory and checks it for accuracy before transmitting it. While this method is more time consuming that the cut-through method, it allows store and forward switches to transmit data more accurately.
- **switch** — A connectivity device that logically subdivides a network into smaller, individual collision domains. A switch operates at the Data Link layer of the OSI Model and can interpret MAC address information to determine whether to filter (discard) or forward packets it receives.
- **Translational Bridging** — A method of bridging that can connect Token Ring and Ethernet networks.
- **Transparent Bridging** — The method of bridging used on most Ethernet networks.
- **virtual local area network (VLAN)** — The means by which a switch can logically group a number of ports into a broadcast domain. A VLAN can consist of servers, workstations, printers, routers, or any other network device you can connect to a switch.

Review Questions

1. If you purchase a new Pentium desktop computer today, what kind of bus-adapter NIC is it likely to require?
   a. PCI
   b. ISA
   c. EISA
   d. MCA IBM PS/2
2. What does "ISA" stand for?
   a. International Standard Attachment
   b. Industry Standard Architecture

c. Industry Selected Apparatus

d. International Standard Architecture

3. Describe the process for installing a PCMCIA network adapter.

4. When configuring a PCI NIC you have just installed on a desktop computer, where should you change the IRQ number?

   a. in the Computer Properties – Device Properties dialog box

   b. in the CMOS utility

   c. in the NIC setup utility

   d. in the jumper settings for the NIC's dip switches

5. Which two IRQs could you probably assign to a NIC without causing a conflict with other devices?

   a. 4 or 9

   b. 11 or 12

   c. 4 or 5

   d. 1 or 2

6. You can install only one NIC in a computer. True or False?

7. Which of the following could be a symptom of a resource conflict involving the NIC?

   a. The computer won't power on.

   b. The computer beeps three times when it starts up.

   c. The computer presents you with an error message about a video display driver.

   d. The computer alerts you that the NIC is causing data transmission errors.

8. Under what circumstances is it appropriate to use a wireless NIC?

   a. when all of the PC's slots are already in use by other devices

   b. when a PC must be the single member of its own broadcast domain

   c. when a PC would otherwise require expensive, fiber-optic cabling

   d. when a PC needs to be mobile, but still communicate with the network

9. Name three enhancements or features that manufacturers might add to NICs to improve these devices performance.

10. If a workstation locks up when it tries to start, the NIC may be causing an IRQ conflict. True or False?

11. To which layer of the OSI Model do repeaters belong?

   a. Layer 1

   b. Layer 2

   c. Layer 3

   d. Layer 4

12. What is the function of a hub's uplink port?
    a. to connect it to the server on a network
    b. to connect it to the nearest workstation
    c. to connect it to another hub
    d. to connect it to a router
13. Intelligent hubs differ from passive hubs in part because they can perform which of the following functions:
    a. regenerate attenuated signals
    b. provide expansion ports
    c. connect with other hubs in a daisy-chain fashion
    d. provide network management information
14. What kind of hub introduces a single point of failure into a network design?
    a. standalone hub
    b. intelligent hub
    c. switching hub
    d. modular hub
15. What is a MIB?
    a. Management Information Base
    b. Multimode Information Basis
    c. Multimode Integration Base
    d. Multiplexing Indicator Basis
16. If you are designing a network that cannot tolerate any down time, what kind of hub might you suggest using?
    a. standalone hub
    b. intelligent hub
    c. switching hub
    d. modular hub
17. At what layer of the OSI Model do bridges function?
    a. Layer 1
    b. Layer 2 data link
    c. Layer 3
    d. Layer 4
18. Bridges can forward only TCP/IP or IPX/SPX packets. True or False?

19. How do bridges keep track of whether they should forward or filter packets?
    a. They maintain a filtering database that identifies which packets can be filtered and which should be forwarded, based on their destination address.
    b. From each packet they carry, they extract source node addresses; all source node addresses that don't belong to the bridge's broadcast domain are filtered.
    c. They hold each packet until it is requested by the destination node, at which time the bridge forwards the data.
    d. They compare the incoming data's protocol with the previous data's protocol and filter those incoming packets that don't match.
20. Which of the following is an advantage of using switches rather than hubs?
    a. Switches can provide network management information.
    b. Switches can assign dedicated channels to certain nodes, making their transmissions more secure.
    c. Switches can more efficiently transmit data from one segment to another.
    d. Switches can alert the network administrator to high data collision rates.
21. In cut-through switching, which frame field does the switch never read?
    a. start frame delimiter
    b. source address
    c. destination address
    d. Frame Check Sequence
22. Which type of switching is more appropriate for heavily trafficked networks?
    a. Cut-through switching
    b. circuit switching
    c. store and forward switching
    d. message switching
23. Which of the following statements about VLANs is incorrect?
    a. A VLAN can be created using only one switch.
    b. A VLAN may span geographically distant locations.
    c. A VLAN divides groups of devices into separate broadcast domains.
    d. A VLAN may include only servers and workstations.
24. Which of the following is one of a router's primary functions:
    a. determine the best path for forwarding data to its destination
    b. regenerate attenuated signals
    c. separate groups of network devices into broadcast domains
    d. send broadcast signals to all network segments

25. How do routing protocols and routable protocols differ?
    a. Routable protocols contain addressing information and routing protocols do not.
    b. Routable protocols are generated by routers and routing protocols are interpreted by routers.
    c. Routable protocols can be interpreted by routers and routing protocols assist routers in communicating with other routers.
    d. Routable protocols enable communication between routers and routing protocols enable communication between all nodes on a network.
26. OSPF is a more efficient routing protocol than RIP. True or False?
27. Why can't routers forward packets as quickly as bridges can?
    a. Routers operate at Layer 3 of the OSI Model and therefore take more time to interpret logical addressing information.
    b. Routers have smaller data buffers than bridges and therefore can store less traffic at any given time.
    c. Routers wait for acknowledgment from destination devices before sending more packets to those devices.
    d. Routers operate at Layer 4 of the OSI Model and therefore act as the traffic cop for all data, making them slower than bridges, which operate at Layer 3.
28. At which layers of the OSI Model do gateways function?
    a. Layers 1 and 2
    b. Layers 2 and 3
    c. Layers 6 and 7
    d. at all layers
29. EIGRP is a routing protocol that was developed by which company?
    a. Intel
    b. Cisco
    c. Ascend
    d. 3Com
30. What is the function of an e-mail gateway?
    a. It translates e-mail messages from one type of e-mail software package to another.
    b. It translates e-mail messages from one type of operating system to another.
    c. It translates e-mail messages from one type of network transport model to another.
    d. It translates e-mail messages between two or more collision domains.

Hands-on Projects

Project 6-1

In this exercise, you will have the opportunity to install a PCI NIC in a workstation, then properly configure it to connect to the network. For this project and Project 6-2, you will need a new Ethernet PCI NIC, the floppy disk and documentation that came with it, and a Pentium desktop computer with Windows 95 installed. You will also need a Windows 95 installation CD, a Phillips-head screwdriver, and a wrist strap and mat to guard against electrostatic discharge.

1. Before installing the NIC, turn on the PC and note the icons present on the Windows 95 desktop. Do you see a **Network Neighborhood** icon?
2. Right-click the Network Neighborhood icon, then click **Properties** in the shortcut menu. The Network properties dialog box opens.
3. Click the **Configuration** tab, if necessary. Which components are listed as installed?
4. To make certain that you are performing a fresh installation, you will now remove any existing network drivers. If a network adapter is listed as an installed device, remove it from the list of components by highlighting it and then clicking **Remove**. You will be asked whether you want to restart your workstation to allow the changes to take effect. Click **Yes**.
5. Click **Start**, then click **Shutdown**. The Shutdown Windows dialog box opens. Click **Yes** to confirm that you want to shut down the computer. You must always shut down a workstation before installing a card (unless it is a PCMCIA card).
6. Now install the NIC in the PC as described in this chapter, making sure to turn off the power before opening the case. Be sure that the NIC is securely inserted before replacing the computer's cover. If you are unsure about whether the NIC is pushed into the slot far enough, ask your instructor for assistance.
7. Replace the computer's cover, insert the power cable, and turn it on.
8. Does your computer start up without locking up or presenting you with error messages? Either way, proceed to Project 6-2, in which you will have the opportunity to change the NIC's settings in the CMOS utility.

Project 6-2

In this exercise, you will view and, if necessary, change the CMOS settings for your NIC. Note that each computer may have require a different keystroke to invoke the CMOS setup utility while it starts up. Pay attention to the instructions that appear on your screen to find out the correct keystroke or combination of keystrokes.

1. Turn off the computer. Wait at least 8 seconds to allow the hard disk to stop spinning, then turn on the computer again.
2. Watch the screen to find out which key or keys you need to press to enter the setup program, then press those keys.
3. You should now be in the CMOS setup utility. As each CMOS setup utility looks different, you will have to search through the menus to find where the IRQs of PCI devices are listed.
4. Which IRQ has been assigned to your NIC? Do you see any error messages about conflicting devices?
5. Try changing the IRQ assigned to your NIC. Usually, you will want to highlight the current value, then press either the Page Up key, the + key, or Enter to change the value. The key you press will depend on the type of BIOS used by your computer. Read the screen to determine which key or combination of keys you should press.
6. Try changing the NIC's IRQ to 6. Does the BIOS utility prevent you from choosing IRQ 6? If so, what message does it display?
7. Change the IRQ to a number that, according to the BIOS, does not conflict with any other devices.
8. Choose to exit the CMOS setup utility, making sure to save your changes. (Because each CMOS utility uses different keystrokes or combinations of keystrokes, read the screen to find out how to save changed settings.)
9. Upon restarting, does the computer freeze up or display any error messages? If so, try reinstalling the NIC from the beginning. (You may want to enlist your instructor's help with this.) Otherwise, continue to Project 6-3.

Project 6-3

Now that you have installed the network adapter, you need to install the appropriate software so that you can connect to the network. In this exercise, you will use the disk that came with your NIC to install those drivers.

At the end of the Project 6-2, you restarted your computer after installing the NIC. If you have not disabled the plug-and-play technology on your workstation, Windows 95 should recognize the new hardware and prompt you for the device drivers. The first step in this project begins at this point.

1. If Windows 95 prompts you for the device drivers, click **Cancel** to prevent Windows 95 from installing the drivers. If it does not prompt you for the device drivers, continue to Step 2.
2. Click **Start**, point to **Settings**, click **Control Panel**, then double-click the **Network** icon. The Network dialog box opens.
3. Click **Add** under the list of installed components. The Add Components dialog box opens, giving you the choice of installing a Client, Adapter, Protocol, or Service.
4. Double-click **Adapter**. The Select Network Adapter dialog box opens, as shown in Figure 6-27.

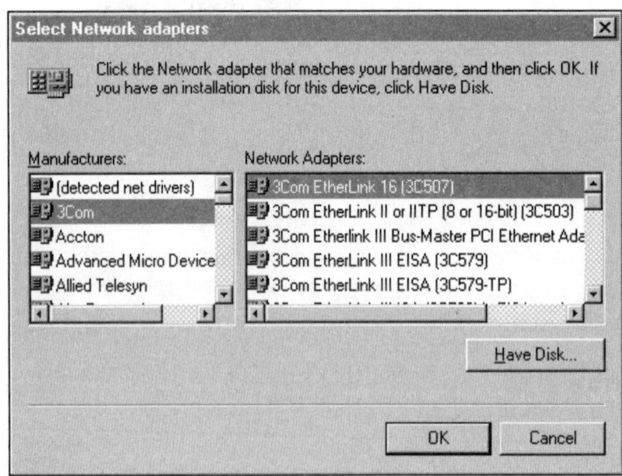

Figure 6-27 Windows 95 Select Network Adapters dialog box

5. Click **Have Disk**. The Install From Disk dialog box opens.
6. Insert the disk that came with the NIC into your floppy disk drive. The default path will be A:\, but you may need to change it, depending on the location of the Windows 95 drivers for your NIC. (Often manufacturers include many different types of drivers on one disk.) If you aren't sure where the Windows 95 drivers are found, you can choose **Browse** to look for them on the disk. Once you have specified the path, click **OK** to continue.
7. Windows 95 copies the drivers to the hard drive and insert references to them in its Registry. During this process, you may be asked to provide some of the Windows 95 system files. In this case, insert the Windows 95 installation CD into the CD-ROM drive, type the correct path, and click **Continue**.
8. When you have finished installing the NIC software, Windows 95 will prompt you to restart the computer. Click **Yes** to confirm that you want to restart the computer.

PROJECT 6-4

In this exercise, you will verify that the NIC you installed and configured in the Projects 6-1, 6-2, and 6-3 works by viewing the device's properties through the operating system and attempting to connect to the network. (Obviously, if Windows 95 displayed error messages pertaining to the NIC after rebooting, it is not installed correctly. You may want to remove it from Network Neighborhood properties, change its driver file in Network Neighborhood properties, or change its settings in the BIOS. Usually, if you can get to the point where Windows recognizes the NIC, but still presents errors pertaining to its use of resources such as its IRQ, you can at least be certain that it is physically installed it correctly.)

1. As long as Windows 95 does not display error messages pertaining to the NIC upon restarting, right-click the **My Computer** icon on your desktop, then click **Properties** in the shortcut menu. The System Properties dialog box opens.
2. Click the **Device Manager** tab.
3. Double-click the **Computer** icon to view all IRQ, base I/O address, and memory range information for the devices. On a piece of paper, write down the NIC's values for these settings. Do the settings appear to conflict with other devices' settings?
4. Click **OK** to close the Computer Resources window, and then click **OK** to close the Device Manager.

PROJECT 6-5

In this exercise, you will use the workstation whose NIC you configured in the previous projects to connect to a server as part of a LAN. You will use a hub to connect the workstation and server to the LAN. If you are working in a classroom setting, your classmates will use the same hub to connect to the network, thus forming a small LAN. This project uses a Windows NT server and, as part of configuring your workstation to connect to this server, you will install Client for Microsoft Networks. You will configure this client so that you and your classmates belong to a Windows NT workgroup (that is, group of devices).

For this project, you will need a working Windows NT server with valid login IDs and a workgroup called CLASS established, a standalone hub, the instruction manual that came with the hub, two or more patch cables that match your NIC and the hub's ports, and the workstation whose NIC you configured in the preceding Hands-On Projects.

1. Set up the hub according to the instruction manual's directions. Usually, summarized directions for installing the hub will appear at the beginning of such a manual. For a small standalone hub, setup should involve little more than connecting it to the wall outlet, making sure it lights up correctly, then connecting it to the server.
2. Connect a patch cable from one of the hub's ports to your NIC, making sure that you do *not* connect to the uplink port.

3. Connect another patch cable from the hub into the NIC of the server.
4. On your workstation, right-click **Network Neighborhood**, then click **Properties**. The Network properties dialog box opens.
5. Under the list of installed components, check to see whether **Client for Microsoft Networks** is installed. If it is not installed, continue to the next step. If it is installed, skip to Step 10.
6. Click **Add**. The Select Network Component Type dialog box opens. In the list of components, double-click **Client**. The Select Network Client dialog box opens.
7. In the list of manufacturers, click **Microsoft**.
8. In the list of network clients, click **Client for Microsoft Networks**.
9. Click **OK**. You return to the Network properties dialog box.
10. In the list of installed components, double-click **Client for Microsoft Networks** to see its properties. Under the Logon Validation, make sure that **Logon to Windows NT domain** is checked. Type **CLASS** (in capital letters) where you are prompted to name the Windows NT domain.
11. Under the Network Logon Options, choose **Quick Logon**.
12. Click **OK**. Click **OK** again at the Network Properties dialog box to save your changes. Click **Yes** to confirm that you want to restart the computer.
13. When Windows 95 starts up again, type the student login ID and password that your instructor has created for you on the server.
14. After some of your classmates have completed Steps 1 through 11, double-click the **Network Neighborhood** icon. What do you see?
15. In Network Neighborhood, double-click the server's icon to open it. Open the **C:\TEMP** directory and begin copying the entire contents of your C:\WINDOWS directory into it. Watch the lights next to the hub's port that connects your workstation.
16. Disconnect your workstation from its port in the hub while the data are being copied. What kind of error messages, if any, appear on your workstation or the server?
17. Wait a minute or more, then reinsert the patch cable. What happens?

Case Projects

1. Evco Insurance, a multimillion-dollar life insurance firm, has asked you to help troubleshoot the network at its corporate headquarters. The network manager admits that he has not kept very close tabs on the network's growth over the last year, and he thinks this omission has something to do with the congestion problems. The marketing department, which is experiencing the worst network response, has added 40 people in the last six months to make a total of 146 people. At some times during the day, the marketing director has complained of waiting 10 minutes before one small e-mail message can get across the wire. He shows you to the telecommunications closet that serves the troubled department. Inside, you find a stack of eight expensive new hubs, blinking away. What are your first thoughts about why these users might be getting such poor response?
2. While you are in the telecommunications closet at Evco Insurance, you notice that one hub has two ports whose collision lights are blinking almost constantly. Being a conscientious network professional, you point out this problem to the network manager. What do you suggest you and he do next?
3. The network manager at Evco Insurance likes the fact that you have helped figure out some of his hub problems. He is especially pleased to know that he does have switching hubs and can reconfigure them to give certain users or groups of users a dedicated channel to the LAN. He thinks he might want to take this approach. The network manager understands the performance benefits that users would gain, but he still isn't sure who should get the benefit of switching. What can you tell him about switching and security that might help him decide which users' nodes should be switched?
4. The network manager at Evco Insurance understands that switches are becoming increasingly more advanced. Evco currently uses routers to connect most of its network segments to the backbone, and it uses routers to connect its 12 satellite offices around town to the corporate headquarters. The network manager asks whether you think he would be wise to replace these routers with switches in the future. What is your response?

CHAPTER 7

广域网 远程访

WANs AND REMOTE CONNECTIVITY

After reading this chapter and completing the exercises, you will be able to:

- Understand the differences between LANs and WANs
- Identify network applications that require WAN technology
- Describe the various WAN transmission methods
- Identify criteria for selecting an appropriate WAN topology, transmission method, and operating system
- Install and configure simple remote connectivity for a telecommuting client

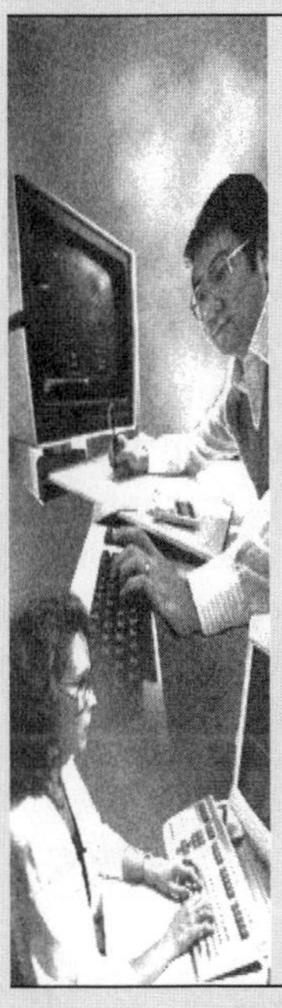

ON THE JOB

As a consultant for a small networking firm, I was thrilled to have the chance to work on the implementation of a WAN for a large West Coast city. The city wanted to connect more than 40 locations, including a sports arena, seniors' center, bus terminal, and maintenance plant, plus its business offices, so as to centrally control all file sharing, messaging, and printing occurring within the city government. It also wanted to provide Internet access for its employees. Some of the locations were located 20 miles from the city center.

Our team of consultants recommended a combination of T1 and ISDN technology. For some locations, such as the city transportation office, we used both a T1 and an ISDN backup to the central connecting point, the city government's headquarters. Although the city didn't want to pay for a full-mesh topology, we did create a partial-mesh WAN by providing alternative routes around critical links. For example, we implemented a 56 KB dial-up link from one government building to another that would carry traffic between the buildings in case one of the T1s failed. We placed all servers at the headquarters, which allowed the city's IT staff to centrally control security and account administration. Finally, we connected the city to an ISP using a fractional T1. As a result, the city government is completely and reliably networked.

James Furness
CSI Networks

Now that you understand the basic transmission media, network models, and networking hardware associated with local area networks (LANs), you need to expand that knowledge to encompass wide area networks (WANs). As you learned in Chapter 1, a WAN is a network that connects two or more geographically distinct LANs. You might assume that WANs are the same as LANs, only bigger. Although a WAN is based on the same principles as a LAN, including the reliance on the OSI Model, its distance requirements affect its entire infrastructure. As a result, nearly everything about a WAN differs from the characteristics of a LAN.

To understand the difference between a LAN and WAN, think of the hallways and stairs of your house as LAN pathways. These interior passages allow you to go from room to room. To reach destinations outside of your house, however, you need to use sidewalks and streets. These public thoroughfares are analogous to WAN pathways—except that WAN pathways are not necessarily public.

This chapter discusses the technical differences between LANs and WANs and describes in detail WAN transmission media and methods. It also notes the potential pitfalls in establishing and maintaining WANs. In addition, it introduces you to remote connectivity for LANs—a technology that, in some cases, can be used to extend a LAN into a WAN. Remote connectivity and WANs are significant concerns for organizations attempting to meet the needs of telecommuting workers, global business partners, and Internet-based commerce. To pass the Net+ certification exam, you must be familiar with the variety of WAN and remote connectivity options. You also need to know how to connect remote users to a LAN.

WAN Essentials

As you know, a WAN traverses a larger geographical area—connecting LANs across the city or across the nation. For example, a WAN might connect the headquarters of an insurance company in New York with its satellite insurance offices in Hartford, Dallas, and San Francisco. The individual geographic locations (Hartford, Dallas, San Francisco) are known as WAN sites. A **WAN link** is a connection between one site (or point) and another site (or point). A WAN link is typically described as **point-to-point**—because it connects one site to only one other site. That is, it does not typically connect one site to several other sites, in the way that LAN hubs or switches connect multiple segments or workstations. Nevertheless, one location may be connected to more than one location by multiple WAN links. Figure 7-1 illustrates the difference between WAN and LAN connectivity.

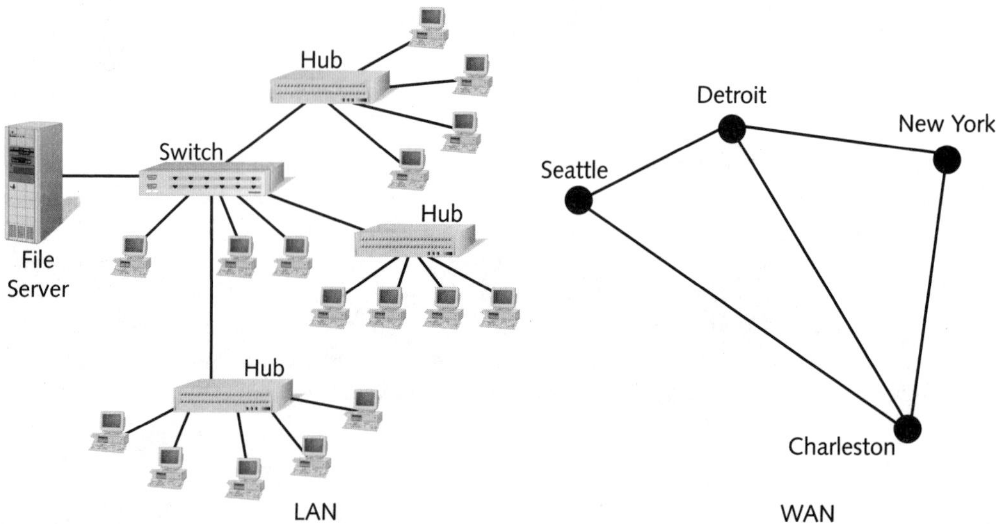

Figure 7-1 Differences in LAN and WAN connectivity

On the one hand, WANs and LANs are similar in some fundamental ways. In general, both can use any of the protocols mentioned in Chapter 3. Also, both primarily carry digital data. Finally, WANs and LANs have a similar function: to enable communications between clients and hosts that are not directly attached to each other.

On the other hand, WANs use different transmission systems, topologies, and sometimes, media, than LANs do. LANs typically use internal cabling, such as coaxial or twisted-pair. In contrast, WANs typically send data over public communications links, such as the telephony backbone provided by local and long distance telephone companies. For better throughput, an organization might lease a continuously available link through another carrier, such as an Internet service provider (ISP). This kind of connection is called a **dedicated line**. Dedicated lines come in a variety of types that are distinguished by their capacity and transmission characteristics. The following section explains how each WAN transmission technology uses the public telecommunications system or dedicated lines.

Chapter 5 introduced the various WAN topologies: star, ring, mesh, partial mesh, and hybrid. In that chapter, you learned that most WANs do not take the form of simple star or ring networks, but more likely employ mesh or partial-mesh configurations. As you know, the Internet is the largest WAN in existence today. Typically, the enterprise-wide WANs of individual organizations are conceived on a much smaller scale. For example, a WAN might begin by connecting only two offices (such as two branches of a bookstore chain that are located at either end of a city). As the organization grows, the WAN might grow to connect more and more sites, located across the city or around the world. Only an organization's information technology budget and aspirations limit the dimensions of its WAN.

Why might an organization need a WAN? Any organization that has multiple sites scattered over a wide geographical area needs a way to exchange data between those sites. Each of the following scenarios demonstrates a need for a WAN:

- A bank with offices around the state needs to connect those offices to gather transaction and account information into a central database.
- A pharmaceutical company's salespeople, who are scattered across the nation, need to dial in their sales figures and receive e-mail from headquarters.
- An insurance company allows parents on family leave to work from home by dialing into the company's network.
- An automobile manufacturer in Detroit contracts its plastic parts manufacturing out to a Delaware-based company. Through WAN links, the auto manufacturer can videoconference with the plastics manufacturer, exchange specification data, and even examine the parts for quality online.
- A technical support technician for the remote pharmaceutical salesperson may need to show the salesperson how to create a macro in an Excel spreadsheet. A remote control program, such as pcANYWHERE, enables the support technician to "take over" the salesperson's PC (over a WAN link) and demonstrate how to create the macro.
- A clothing manufacturer sells its products over the Internet to customers throughout the world.

Though all of these businesses need WANs, they may not need the same kinds of WANs. Depending on the traffic load, budget, and geographical breadth, each might implement a different transmission method. You will learn about the various WAN transmission methods in the next section.

WAN TRANSMISSION METHODS

The WAN transmission methods discussed in this section differ in terms of speed, reliability, cost, distance covered, and security. For every business need, only a few (or possibly only one) appropriate WAN transmission methods may exist. Many WAN technologies can coexist on the same network. As you learn about each technology, pay attention to its characteristics and think about its possible applications. To qualify for Net+ certification, you must be familiar with the variety of WAN transmission methods and able to identify the types of networking environments that each suits best.

PSTN

PSTN, which stands for **Public Switched Telephone Network**, refers to the network of typical telephone lines that service most homes. PSTN may also be called **plain old telephone service (POTS)**. It was originally composed of analog lines and developed to handle voice-based traffic. Now, however, most of the PSTN uses digital transmission through fiber-optic and copper twisted-pair cable, microwave, and satellite connections. This system currently takes care of most dial-up connections to LANs. Indeed, for individuals simply picking up their e-mail or surfing the Web, PSTN is usually adequate. For example, a salesperson traveling to a conference might dial into her office's LAN from her hotel each night to pick up e-mail. So long as she doesn't have to download a significant amount of data, the throughput of her hotel room phone line connection would suffice.

A **dial-up** connection uses a PSTN or other line to access a remote server via modems at both the source (for example, the salesperson's computer) and destination (for example, the office LAN's server). Later in this chapter, you will see how servers can be configured to allow remote access.

The word **modem** is derived from this device's function as a **mod**ulator/**dem**odulator. A modem converts a computer's digital pulses into analog signals for the PSTN (because not all of the PSTN is necessarily capable of handling digital transmission), then converts the analog signals back into digital pulses at the receiving computer's end. Unlike other types of WAN connections, dial-up connections provide a fixed period of access to the network, just as the phone call you make to a friend has a fixed length, determined by when you initiate and terminate the call. Ways to establish dial-up connections and remote connectivity are discussed in detail later in this chapter.

The disadvantage of the PSTN comes from its inability to ensure the quality or throughput required by many WAN applications. The quality of a WAN connection is largely determined by how many data packets that it loses or that become corrupt during transmission, how quickly it can transmit and receive data, and whether it drops the connection altogether. To improve this quality, most data transmission methods employ error-checking techniques. For example, TCP/IP depends on acknowledgments of the data it receives. In addition, many (though not all) PSTN links are now digital, and digital lines are more reliable than the older analog lines. Such digital lines reduce the quality problems that once plagued purely analog PSTN connections.

The more significant limiting factor of the PSTN is its capacity, or throughput. Currently, the most advanced PSTN modems advertise a connection speed of 56 Kbps. The 56 Kbps maximum is actually a *theoretical* threshold that assumes that the connection between the initiator and the receiver is pristine. Splitters, fax machines, or other devices that a modem connection traverses between the sender and receiver will all reduce the actual throughput. In addition, the number of points through which your phone call travels will affect throughput, as described following. Rarely will you ever achieve full 56 Kbps throughput using a modem over the PSTN.

To demonstrate how throughput diminishes over a PSTN connection, it's useful to follow a typical dial-up call from modem to modem, as pictured in Figure 7-2. Imagine you dial into your ISP to surf the Web through a 56 Kbps modem. You first initiate a call through your computer's modem. Your modem converts the digital signal from your computer into an analog signal that travels over the phone line to the local telephone company's **point of presence (POP)**. A POP is the place where the two telephone systems meet—either a long distance carrier with a local telephone company, or a local carrier with an ISP's data center. At the POP, your signal is converted back to digital pulses and transmitted to your ISP's POP through a digital backbone (usually made of fiber-optic cable). The ISP's POP connects to its Internet service provider (the "larger ISP" in the figure) through a digital link, usually a T1 or T3 (discussed later in this chapter). Your request for information enters the Internet, and the transmission process is then reversed to bring you the desired Web page. Each time your transmission travels through a POP, or is converted from analog to digital or digital to analog, it loses a little throughput. By the time the Web page returns to you, the connection may have lost from 5 to 30 Kbps, and your effective throughput might have been reduced to 30 Kbps or less.

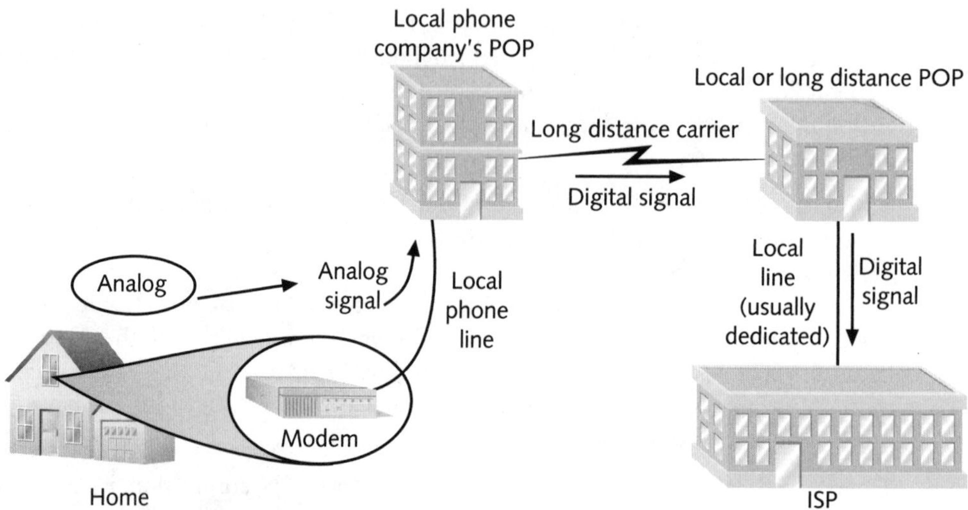

Figure 7-2 A typical PSTN connection to the Internet

"POP" is another network-related acronym that can have two completely different meanings depending on its context. In this discussion of WAN and remote connectivity, a POP refers to a telecommunications service carrier's point of presence. In Chapter 11's in-depth discussion of TCP/IP protocols, POP will refer to the Post Office Protocol, used in e-mail transmission.

The PSTN uses circuit switching. (Recall from Chapter 5 that circuit switching is a means of transmitting data between two nodes with a dedicated point-to-point connection.) You might think that circuit switching makes the PSTN more secure than other types of WAN connections; in fact, the PSTN offers only marginal security. Granted, the PSTN is more secure than some forms of communication, such as cellular communications. Because it is a public network, however, PSTN presents many points at which communications can be intercepted and interpreted on their way from sender to receiver. For example, an eavesdropper could easily tap into the connection where your local telephone company's line enters your house. To make PSTN transmissions more secure, you must encrypt the data before it is sent. Chapter 15 describes data encryption techniques.

ISDN

ISDN (Integrated Services Digital Network) is an international standard, established by the International Telecommunications Union (ITU), for transmitting data over digital lines. ISDN uses the telephone carrier's lines and dial-up connections, like PSTN. It is distinguished from PSTN, however, by the fact that it relies exclusively on digital connections and by the fact that it can carry data and voice simultaneously. ISDN lines may carry as many as two voice calls and one data connection simultaneously. To achieve this feat, however, the ISDN user must have the correct devices to accept all three connections, as described later in this section. Through their ability to transmit voice and data simultaneously, ISDN lines can eliminate the need to pay for separate phone lines to support faxes, modems, and voice calls at one location. Local phone companies began offering ISDN in the mid-1980s, anticipating that the United States would convert to this all-digital system by the turn of the century. ISDN hasn't caught on as quickly as predicted, and other types of digital transmission methods now compete with it to serve customers who require moderate to fast throughput over phone lines.

All ISDN connections are based on two types of channels: B channels and D channels. The **B channel** is the "bearer" channel, employing circuit switching techniques to carry voice, video, audio, and other types of data over the ISDN connection. A single B channel has a maximum throughput of 56 Kbps. As you will learn, the number of B channels in a single ISDN connection may vary. The **D channel** is the "data" channel, employing packet switching techniques to carry information about the call, such as session initiation and termination signals, caller identity, call forwarding, and conference calling signals. A single D channel has a maximum throughput of 16 Kbps. Each ISDN connection uses only one D channel.

In North America, two types of ISDN connections are commonly used: Basic Rate ISDN (BRI) and Primary Rate ISDN (PRI). A third type of ISDN connection, called Broadband ISDN (B-ISDN), was developed by the ITU in the late 1980s to provide more capacity than BRI or PRI. Today, organizations in need of the capacity offered by B-ISDN tend to choose newer, high-capacity lines, such as those using xDSL or T1 technology (both described later in this chapter).

BRI (Basic Rate ISDN) uses two B channels and one D channel, as indicated by the following notation: 2B+D. The two B channels are treated as separate connections by the network and can carry voice and data or two data streams simultaneously and separate from each other. In a process called **bonding**, these two 64 Kbps B channels can be combined to achieve an effective throughput of 128 Kbps—the maximum amount of data traffic that a BRI connection can accommodate. Most consumers who subscribe to ISDN from home use BRI, which is the most economical type of ISDN connection.

Figure 7-3 illustrates how a typical BRI link supplies a home consumer with an ISDN link. (Note that the configuration depicted in Figure 7-3 applies to installations in North America only. Because transmission standards differ in Europe and Asia, different numbers of B channels are used in the standard ISDN connections in those regions.) From the telephone company's lines, the ISDN channels connect to a Network Termination 1 device at the customer's site. The **Network Termination 1 (NT1)** device connects the twisted-pair wiring at the customer's building with the ISDN terminal equipment via RJ-11 (standard telephone) or RJ-45 data jacks. The ISDN **terminal equipment (TE)** may include cards or standalone devices used to connect computers to the ISDN line (similar to a network adapter used on Ethernet or Token Ring networks).

So that the ISDN line can connect to analog equipment, the signal must first pass through a terminal adapter. A **terminal adapter (TA)** converts digital signals into analog signals for use with ISDN phones and other analog devices. (Terminal adapters are sometimes mistakenly called ISDN modems.) Typically, telecommuters who want more throughput than their analog phone line will afford choose BRI as their ISDN connection. For a home user, the terminal adapter would most likely be an ISDN router, such as the 800 series router from

Cisco Systems, while the terminal equipment would be an Ethernet card in the user's workstation plus, perhaps, a phone.

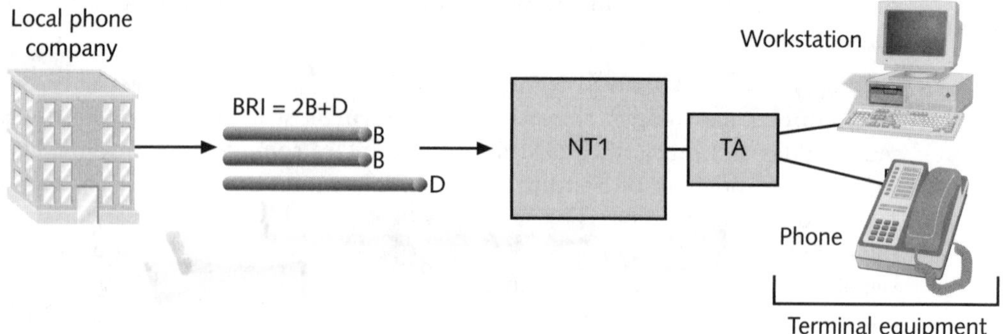

Figure 7-3 A BRI link

PRI (Primary Rate ISDN) uses 23 B channels and one 64 Kbps D channel as represented by the following notation: 23B+D. PRI is less commonly used by individual subscribers than BRI is, but it may be selected by businesses and other organizations that need more throughput. As with BRI, the separate B channels in a PRI link can carry voice and data, independent of each other or bonded together. The maximum potential throughput for a PRI connection is 1.544 Mbps, the same as that for T1; in fact, PRI channels can be carried by T1 trunks.

PRI and BRI connections may be interconnected on a single network. PRI links use the same kind of equipment as BRI links, but require the services of an extra network termination device, called a **Network Termination 2 (NT2)**, to handle the multiple ISDN lines. Figure 7-4 depicts a typical PRI link as it would be installed in North America.

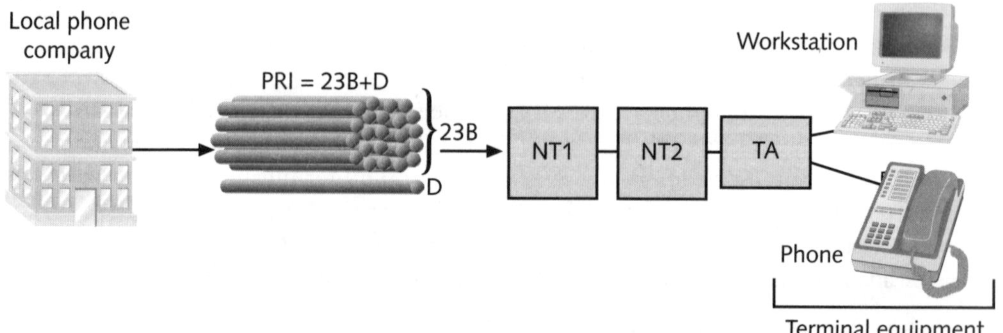

Figure 7-4 A PRI link

Individual customers who need to transmit more data than a typical modem can handle or who want to use a single line for both data and voice commonly use ISDN lines. ISDN, although not available in every location of the United States, can be purchased from most local telephone companies. The cost of using BRI averages $100 to $250 per month, depending on the customer's location. PRI and B-ISDN are significantly more expensive. In some areas, ISDN providers may charge customers additional usage fees based on the total length of time they remain connected.

One disadvantage of ISDN is that it can span a distance of only 18,000 feet before repeater equipment is needed to boost the signal. For this reason, it is only feasible to use for the **local loop** portion of the WAN link—that is, the part of a phone system that connects a customer site with a public carrier's POP.

xDSL

Digital subscriber lines (DSL) is a relatively new transmission technology that competes directly with ISDN. DSL uses advanced data modulation techniques to achieve extraordinary throughput over regular phone lines. In **data modulation**, one signal alters the frequency, phase, or amplitude of another signal.

In Chapter 4, frequency and amplitude were discussed in terms of both digital and analog signals. The term **phase** refers to the progress of a wave through time. An analogy will help to clarify this concept. Imagine you and a friend are walking on the beach, both of you dragging a stick through the sand, swinging it from right to left in a wave pattern. Assume that both of you swing your sticks the same distance to the right and left (amplitude), and also assume that you are walking at the same rate (frequency). If you and your friend begin at the same spot, your waves will have equivalent phases. If, however, your friend starts one foot in front of you, even though she is dragging her stick the same distance to the left and right and walking at the same pace, your waves will not match. That is, their phases will differ. Figure 7-5 illustrates the concept of phase.

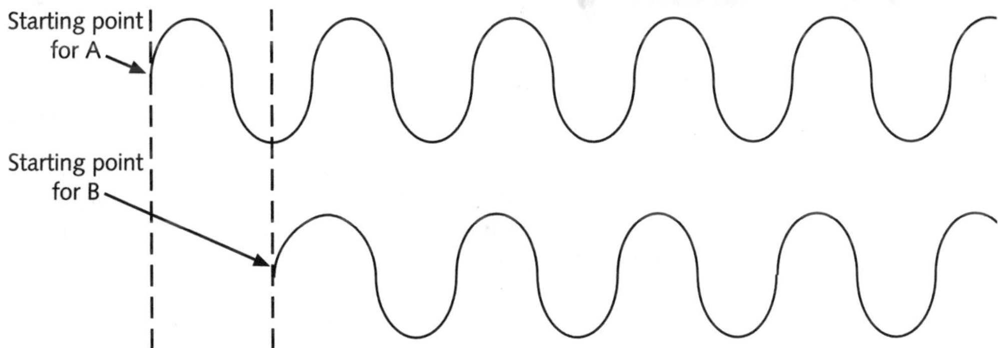

Figure 7-5 Phase differences

Essentially, data modulation ensures that the characteristics (either amplitude, frequency, or phase) of different signals transmitted over the same communications channel differ. Differences in amplitude, frequency, or phase make it possible for multiple signals to traverse the same wiring at the same time without interfering with each other, thus resulting in higher throughput. To ensure that DSL connections can support high throughput over copper wire (the old PSTN), carriers must install new switching equipment. Also, networking hardware manufacturers and standards organizations are currently working to standardize DSL technology. DSL shows promise of stealing some current ISDN and T1 customers, but it is too early to tell whether DSL will become widely adopted.

Like ISDN, DSL can span only limited distances without the help of repeaters and is therefore best suited to the local loop portion of a WAN link. Also, like ISDN, DSL supports multiple data and voice channels over a single line. Unlike (most types of) ISDN, however, DSL uses **dedicated service**, which means that the user does not have to dial up an ISP; the connection is always available. To connect via DSL, the customer must install a DSL modem and the local carrier must have special connectivity equipment that can accommodate the connection.

The term **xDSL** refers to all DSL varieties, of which seven currently exist. The better-known DSL varieties include Asymmetric DSL (ADSL), High Bit-Rate DSL (HDSL), Single-Line DSL (SDSL), and Very High Bit-Rate DSL (VDSL)—the "x" in "xDSL" is replaced by the variety name. DSL types can be divided into two categories: asymmetrical and symmetrical.

To understand the difference between these two categories, you must understand the concept of downstream and upstream data transmission. The term **downstream** refers to data traveling from the carrier's POP to the customer. The term **upstream** refers to data traveling from the customer to the carrier's POP. In some types of DSL, the throughput rates for downstream and upstream traffic differ. That is, if you were connected to the Internet via a DSL link, you might be able to pick up your e-mail messages more rapidly than you could send them. A technology that offers more throughput in one direction than in the other is considered **asymmetrical**. Asymmetrical communication is well suited to users who pull more information off the network than they send to it—for example, people watching videoconferences or people surfing the Web.

Conversely, **symmetrical** technology provides equal capacity for data traveling both upstream and downstream. Symmetrical transmission is suited to users who both upload and download significant amounts of data—for example, a bank's branch office, which sends large volumes of account information to the central server at the bank's headquarters. ADSL and VDSL are examples of asymmetrical DSL; HDSL and SDSL are examples of symmetrical DSL.

The types of DSL also vary in terms of their capacity and maximum line length. A VDSL line that carries as much as 52 Mbps in one direction and as much as 2.3 Mbps in the opposite direction can extend a maximum of 1000 feet between the customer's premises and the carrier's POP. This limitation might suit businesses located close to a telephone company's data center (for example, in the middle of a metropolitan area), but it won't work for most individuals. The most popular form of DSL, ADSL, provides a maximum of 8 Mbps in one direction and a maximum of 1.544 Mbps in the other direction; at its highest speeds, it is limited to a distance of 12,000 feet between the customer's premises and the carrier's POP. This distance (more than 2 miles) renders it suitable for most telecommuters. Table 7-1 compares current specifications for four DSL types.

Table 7-1 Comparison of xDSL Types

xDSL Type	Throughput	Distance Limitations
ADSL	1.5–8 Mbps downstream, maximum of 1.544 Mbps upstream	12,000–18,000 feet
HDSL	1.544 Mbps either way	15,000 feet
SDSL	1.544 Mbps either way	10,000 feet
VDSL	13–52 Mbps downstream, 1.5–2.3 Mbps upstream	1000–4500 feet

As mentioned earlier, standards for xDSL continue to evolve. Service providers and manufacturers are positioning xDSL as competition for T1, ISDN, and cable modem service. The installation, hardware, and monthly access costs for xDSL generally exceed those for ISDN lines but are significantly less than the cost for T1s. Some regional local phone companies are even offering DSL connections at T1 speeds for less than $200 per month. Considering that xDSL technology can provide faster throughput than T1s, it presents a formidable challenge to the T1 industry, especially given that T1s are typically too expensive for home users. DSL's most significant drawbacks are its lack of regulatory standards and, compared with ISDN and T1 technology, its relative newness.

7

To learn more about xDSL technology, standards, and providers, take a look at "The Telechoice Report on xDSL" at http://www.xdsl.com/ or Paradyne's DSL Sourcebook at http://www.paradyne.com/sourcebook_offer/sb_html.html.

CABLE

While local and long distance phone companies race to make xDSL into a standard, cable companies are pushing their own point-to-point connectivity option, based on the cable wiring used for TV signals. Such wiring could theoretically transmit as much as 36 Mbps downstream and as much as 10 Mbps upstream. Thus cable is an asymmetrical technology. Realistically, however, cable will allow approximately 3 to 10 Mbps downstream and 2 Mbps upstream due to its shared nature (described later in this section) as well as bottlenecks that occur either at the Internet carrier's data facilities or on the Internet itself. The asymmetry of cable technology makes it a logical choice for users who want to surf the Web or download data from a network. Some companies are already developing services to deliver music, videoconferencing, and Internet services over cable infrastructure.

Cable connections require that the customer purchase a special cable modem to transmit and receive signals over cable wiring. This cable modem then connects to a NIC in the customer's PC. Before customers can subscribe to cable modem service, however, their local cable company must have the necessary infrastructure.

To provide Internet access through its network, the cable company must upgrade its existing equipment to support bidirectional, digital communications. For starters, the cable company's network wiring must be replaced with **hybrid fiber-coax (HFC)**, a very expensive fiber-optic link that can support high frequencies. The HFC connects the cable company's offices to a node location near the customer. Then, either fiber-optic or coaxial cable may connect the node to the customer's business or residence via a connection known as a **cable drop**. All cable drops for the cable subscribers in the same neighborhood connect to the local node. These nodes then connect to the cable company's central office, which is known as its **head-end**. At the head-end, the cable company can connect to the Internet through a variety of means (often via fiber-optic cable) or it can pick up digital satellite or microwave transmissions. The head-end can transmit data to as many as 1000 subscribers, in a one-to-many communication system. Figure 7-6 illustrates the infrastructure of a cable system.

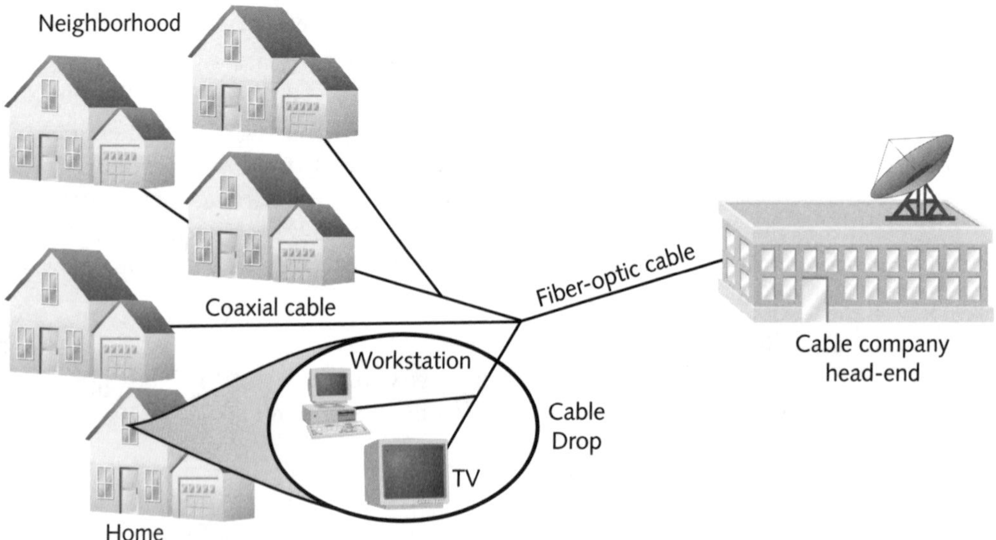

Figure 7-6 Cable infrastructure

One advantage of cable is that, like DSL, it provides a dedicated, or continuous, connection that does not require dialing up a service provider. On the other hand, cable technology requires many subscribers to share the same line, thus raising concerns about security and actual (versus theoretical) throughput. For example, if your cable company supplied you and five of your neighbors with cable access to the Internet, your neighbors could, without much difficulty, capture the data that you transmit to the Internet. Moreover, the throughput of a cable line is fixed. As with any fixed resource, the more one claims, the less that is left for others. In other words, the greater the number of users sharing a single line, the less throughput available to each individual user.

Although cable appears poised to challenge DSL for servicing consumers who demand higher bandwidth than that offered by PSTN or ISDN, it may not be able to keep up with the pace of DSL evolution. Instead, DSL may have the edge because its infrastructure (the PSTN) is already in place, although cable is not ubiquitous. If cable modem technology does become a reality, it will probably be less expensive and easier to install than most DSL services and therefore may prove more attractive to home-based users who are not worried about security. For businesses, cable modems are an impractical technology because of the requirement that several subscribers share a single connection.

To learn more about cable modem technology, standards, and providers, take a look at MIT's Cable Modem Resources page on the Web: http://rpcp.mit.edu/~gingold/cable/.

T-Carriers

Leased lines are permanent dedicated connections established through a public telecommunications carrier and billed to customers on a monthly basis. You have already learned about one type of leased line, xDSL. When networking professionals use the term *leased line,* they are generally referring to T1s, fractional T1s, or T3s—collectively known as **T-carriers.**

AT&T developed T-carrier technology in 1957 in an effort to digitize voice signals, thereby enabling such signals to travel long distances. Before that time, voice signals, which were purely analog, were expensive to transmit over long distances because of the number of connectivity devices needed to keep the signal intelligible. In the 1970s, many businesses installed T1s to obtain more voice throughput per line. With increased data communication needs, such as Internet access, T1s have become almost a necessity for any medium to large business.

T-carrier transmission uses a technology called **multiplexing** to divide a single channel into multiple channels for carrying voice, data, video, or other signals. For example, multiplexing enables a T1 circuit to carry 24 channels, each capable of 64 Kbps throughput; thus a T1 has a maximum capacity of 1.544 Mbps. T-carriers use **time division multiplexing (TDM),** a version of multiplexing that divides the T-carrier into multiple channels and assigns each channel its own time slot to follow.

To understand this concept, imagine a bus in which children are assigned one seat each. When the bus stops at a child's house, the child takes his or her seat. Then the bus picks up another child, who takes his or her assigned seat, and so on. If a child doesn't go to school one day, his or her seat is still reserved, and it stays empty. In TDM, time slots are assigned to channels, and even if a particular channel isn't carrying any data, its time slot remains reserved for its use.

As noted earlier, a total of 24 channels are available for T1s. Devices called **multiplexers** at the sending end of the circuit arrange the data streams into different time slots (multiplexing), and then devices at the receiving end filter them back into separate signals (de-multiplexing). The next section describes the various types of T-carriers, then the chapter moves on to T-carrier connectivity devices.

Types of T-Carriers

A number of T-carrier varieties are available to businesses today, as shown in Table 7-2. The most common T-carrier implementations are T1 and, for higher bandwidth needs, T3. A **T1** circuit can carry the equivalent of 24 voice channels, giving a maximum data throughput of 1.544 Mbps. A **T3** can carry the equivalent of 672 voice channels, giving a maximum data throughput of 44.736 Mbps (its throughput is typically rounded up to 45 Mbps for the purposes of discussion).

The speed of a T-carrier depends on its signal level. The **signal level** refers to the T-carrier's Physical layer electrical signaling characteristics as defined by ANSI standards in the early

1980s. DS0 (which stands for "Data Signals 0") is the equivalent of one data or voice channel. All other signal levels are multiples of DS0.

You may hear signal level and carrier terms used interchangeably—for example, DS1 and T1. Technically, T1 is the North American implementation of the international DS1 standard. In Europe, the DS1 standard is implemented as E1 and offers a slightly higher throughput than T1.

Table 7-2 T-Carrier Specifications

Signal Level	Carrier	Number of T1s	Number of Channels	Throughput (Mbps)
DS0	—	1/24	1	0.064
DS1	T1	1	24	1.544
DS1C	T1C	2	24	3.152
DS2	T2	4	96	6.312
DS3	T3	28	672	44.736
DS4	T4	168	4032	274.176

As a networking professional, you are most likely to work with T1 or T3 lines. In addition to knowing their capacity, you should be familiar with their costs and uses. T1s are commonly used by businesses to connect branch offices or to connect to an ISP. Telephone companies also use T1s to connect their central offices. ISPs typically use one or more T1s to connect their to their Internet carriers.

Because a T3 provides 28 times more throughput than a T1, many organizations may find that a few T1s—rather than a single T3—can accommodate their throughput needs. For example, suppose a university research laboratory needed to transmit molecular images over the Internet to another university, and its peak throughput need (at any given time) was 10 Mbps. The laboratory would require a minimum of seven T1s (10 Mbps divided by 1.544 Mbps equals 6.48 T1s). Leasing seven T1s will prove much less expensive for the university than leasing a single T3.

The cost of T1s varies from region to region. On average, a T1 might cost as much as $4000 to install, plus an additional $1000 to $2000 per month as an access fee. The longer the distance between the provider (such as an ISP or a telephone company) and the subscriber, the higher a T1's monthly charge. Charges for local T1s may be based on mileage, whereas costs for long distance T1s vary on a city-to-city basis. For example, a T1 between Houston and New York will cost more than a T1 between Washington, D.C., and New York. Similarly, a T1 from the western suburbs of Detroit to the city center will cost more than a T1 from the city center to a business three blocks away.

For organizations that do not need constant bandwidth, a dial-up ISDN solution may prove more cost-effective than a T1. For businesses that *do* need a dedicated circuit, but don't always need as much as 1.544 Mbps throughput, a fractional T1 is a better option. A **fractional T1** lease allows organizations to use only some of the channels on a T1 line and be charged according to the number of channels they use. Thus fractional T1 bandwidth can be leased in multiples of 64 Kbps. A fractional T1 is best suited to businesses that expect their traffic to grow and that may require a full T1 eventually, but can't currently justify leasing a full T1.

T3s are very expensive and are used by the most data-intensive businesses—for example, computer consulting firms that provide online data backups and warehousing for a number of other businesses or large long-distance carriers. A T3 is much more expensive than even multiple T1s. It may cost as much as $8000 to install, plus monthly service fees based on usage. For example, for a customer whose monthly usage averages 1.5 Mbps, the monthly T3 charges might be as low as $1200. If the same customer uses 40 Mbps each month, the charges might reach $32,000. Of course, T3 costs will vary depending on the carrier, your location, and the distance covered by the T3. In any event, however, this type of connection is significantly more expensive than a T1. Therefore, only businesses with extraordinary bandwidth requirements should consider using T3s.

T-Carrier Connectivity Devices

The approximate costs mentioned previously include monthly access and installation, but not connectivity hardware. Every T-carrier line requires connectivity hardware at both the customer site and the local carrier's POP. Connectivity hardware may be purchased or leased. If your organization uses an ISP to establish and service your T-carrier line, you will most likely lease the connectivity equipment. If you lease the line directly from the local carrier and you anticipate little change in your connectivity requirements over time, however, you may want to purchase the hardware.

T-carrier lines require specialized connectivity hardware that cannot be used with other WAN transmission methods. In addition, T-carrier lines require different media depending on their throughput. In this section, you will learn about the physical components of a T-carrier connection from the customer site to the local carrier.

Wiring As mentioned earlier, the T-carrier system is based on AT&T's original attempt to digitize existing long distance telephone lines. As a result, T1 technology can use unshielded or shielded twisted-pair copper wiring—in other words, plain telephone wire. Because the digital signals require a cleaner connection (that is, one less susceptible to noise and attenuation), however, shielded twisted-pair is preferable. For T1s using shielded twisted-pair, repeaters must regenerate the signal approximately every 6000 feet. Twisted-pair wiring cannot adequately carry the high throughput of multiple T1s or T3 transmissions. Thus, for multiple T1s, coaxial cable, microwave, or fiber-optic cabling may be used. For T3s, microwave or fiber-optic cabling is necessary.

CSU/DSU (Channel Service Unit/Data Service Unit) Although CSUs (channel service units) and DSUs (data service units) are actually two separate devices, they are typically combined into a single box called a **CSU/DSU**. The CSU/DSU is the connection point for a T1 line at the customer's site. The **CSU** provides termination for the digital signal and ensures connection integrity through error correction and line monitoring. The **DSU** converts the digital signal used by bridges, routers, and multiplexers into the digital signal sent via the cabling. The CSU/DSU box connects the incoming T1 with the multiplexer, as shown in Figure 7-7.

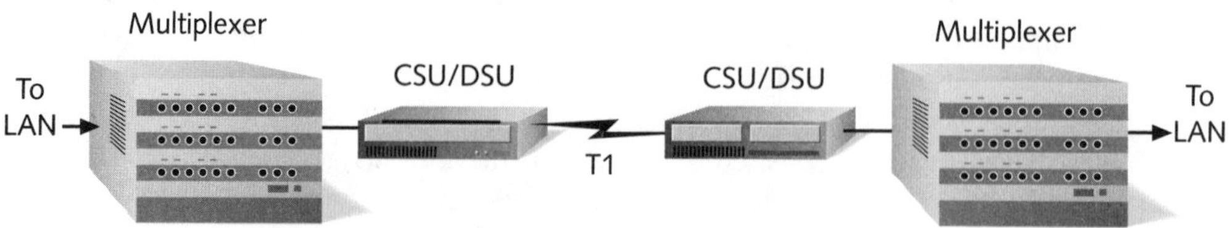

Figure 7-7 A CSU/DSU connecting a T1

Multiplexer As you learned earlier, a multiplexer is a device that combines multiple voice or data channels on one line. The devices that connect to the multiplexer are collectively known as terminal equipment. Multiplexers can take input from a variety of terminal equipment, such as bridges, routers, or telephone exchange devices that accept only voice transmissions (such as a PBX system). Figure 7-8 depicts a typical use of a multiplexer with a T1-connected data network. In some network configurations, the multiplexer is integrated with the CSU/DSU. In the following sections, you will learn how routers and bridges integrate with CSU/DSUs and multiplexers to connect T-carriers to a LAN.

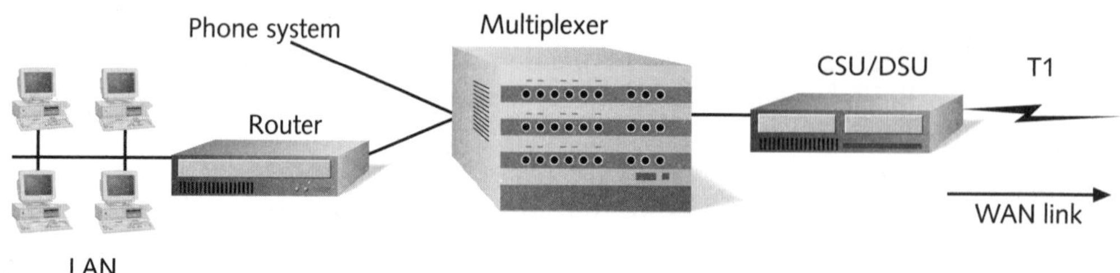

Figure 7-8 Typical use of a multiplexer on a T1-connected data network

Routers and Bridges On a typical T1-connected data network, the terminal equipment will consist of bridges, routers, or a combination of the two. The bridges and routers used in this situation are identical to the bridges and routers you learned about in Chapter 6. With the T1 connection, the bridge or router would typically integrate two types of networks: the Internet and an Ethernet or Token Ring LAN at the customer's site. A router, which can convert TCP/IP to other protocols, is necessary if the internal LAN does not run TCP/IP. Figure 7-9 depicts the use of a router with a T1-connected network.

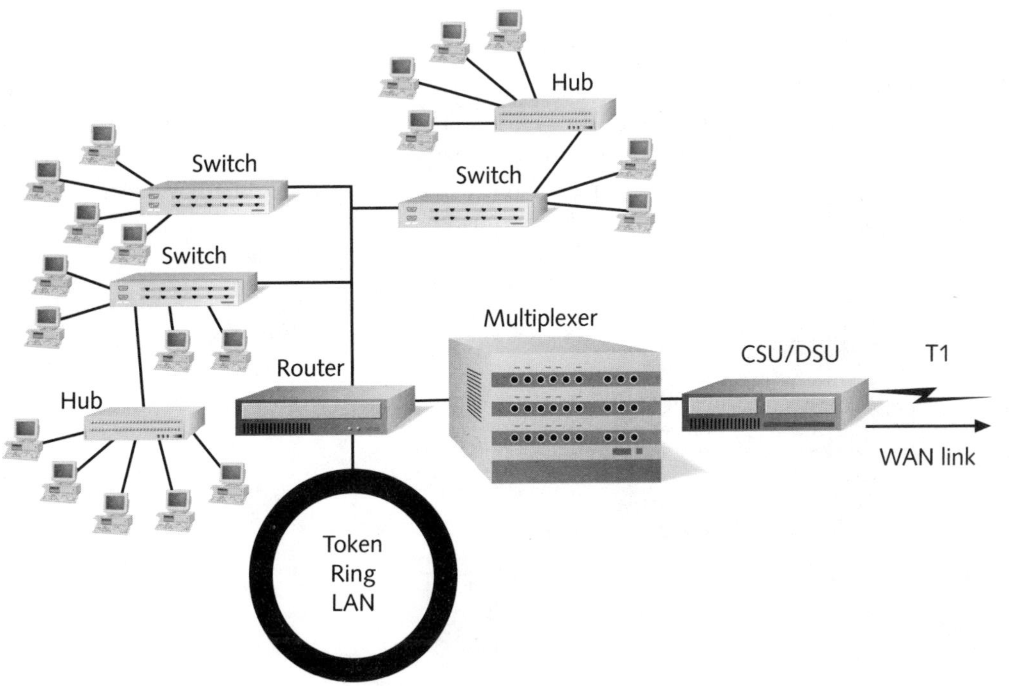

Figure 7-9 A router on a T1-connected network

FDDI (Fiber Distributed Data Interface)

FDDI (Fiber Distributed Data Interface) is a networking standard originally specified by ANSI in the mid-1980s and later refined by ISO. FDDI (pronounced "fiddy") uses a dual fiber-optic ring to transmit data at speeds of 100 Mbps. In fact, FDDI was the first technology to reach the 100 Mbps threshold. For this reason, you will frequently find it supporting network backbones that were installed in the 1980s and early 1990s. Although FDDI isn't exclusively a WAN technology, it is most typically used in these networks.

A popular implementation of FDDI involves connecting LANs located in multiple buildings, such as those on college campuses. FDDI links can span distances as large as 62 miles. Because Ethernet and Token Ring technology have developed faster transmission speeds, FDDI is no longer the much-coveted technology that it was in the 1980s.

Nevertheless, FDDI is a stable technology that offers numerous benefits. Its reliance on fiber-optic cable ensures that FDDI is more reliable and more secure than WAN transmission methods that depend on copper wiring, such as DSL or T1s. Another advantage of FDDI is that it works well with new Ethernet 100BaseTX technology.

One drawback to FDDI technology is its high cost relative to Fast Ethernet (costing 10 times more per switch port than Fast Ethernet). If an organization has FDDI installed, however, it can use the same cabling to upgrade to Fast Ethernet or Gigabit Ethernet, with only minor differences to consider, such as Ethernet's lower maximum segment length.

FDDI resembles a ring network in terms of its topology, as shown in Figure 7-10. It also uses the same token-passing routine that Token Ring networks use. In this routine, a token moves around the network; when a device needs to send data, it grabs the token and adds its data to it, thereby creating a frame. This frame circulates around the network until its destination node picks it up. The destination then dispenses the token so that it is free to circulate the network again (see Chapter 5 for more details). Unlike Token Ring technology, FDDI runs on two complete rings. The primary ring carries data; the secondary ring acts as a backup. This redundancy makes FDDI networks extremely reliable.

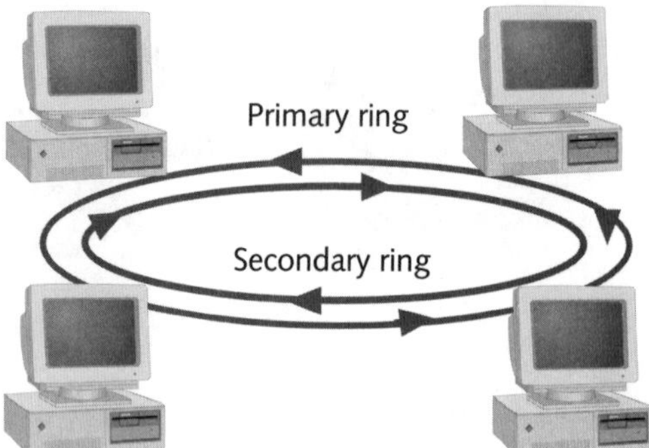

Figure 7-10 A FDDI network

For more information on FDDI technology, take a look at Cisco System's FDDI documentation at http://www.cisco.com/univercd/cc/td/doc/cisintwk/ito_doc/55773.htm.

X.25 and Frame Relay

X.25 is an analog, packet-switched technology designed for long-distance data transmission and standardized by the ITU in the mid-1970s. X.25 can support 56 Kbps throughput. It was originally developed and used to provide communications between mainframe computers and remote terminals. **Frame Relay** is an updated, digital version of X.25 that also relies on packet switching. Because it is digital, Frame Relay supports higher bandwidth than X.25, offering a maximum of 1.544 Mbps throughput.

Recall from Chapter 5 that, in packet switching, packets belonging to the same data stream may follow different, optimal paths to their destination. As a result, packet switching uses bandwidth more efficiently and allows for faster transmission than if each packet in the data stream had to follow the same path, as in circuit switching. Packet switching is also more flexible than circuit switching, because packet sizes may vary.

For almost 20 years, X.25 has been the dominant packet switching technology used on WANs around the world. Only recently has it been replaced by Frame Relay, which was standardized in 1984. In the United States and Canada, Frame Relay is already being replaced by newer, faster technologies. On networking diagrams, packet switched networks such as X.25 and Frame Relay are depicted as clouds, as shown in Figure 7-11, because of the indeterminate nature of their traffic patterns.

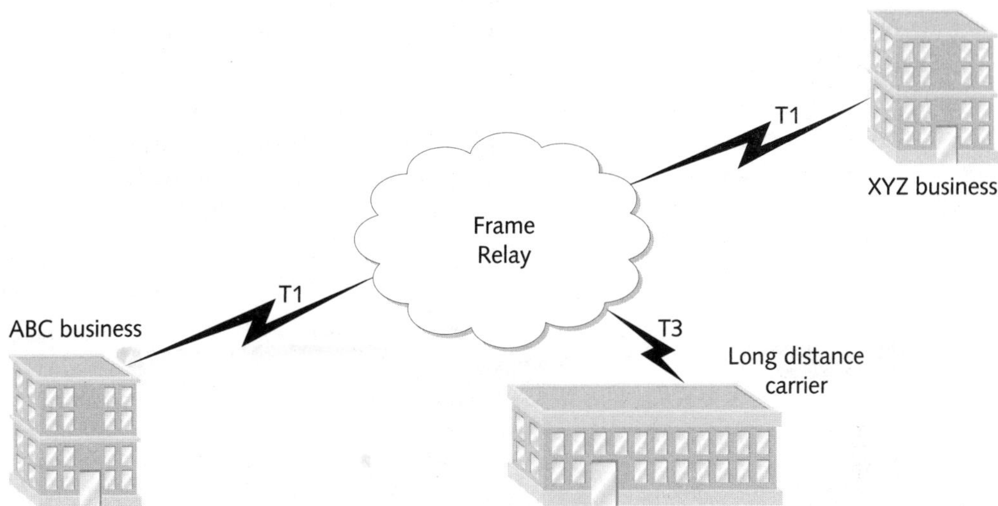

Figure 7-11 A WAN using Frame Relay

Note

You may have seen the Internet depicted as a cloud on networking diagrams as well. In its beginning, the Internet relied largely on X.25 or Frame Relay transmission—hence the similar illustration.

Both X.25 and Frame Relay are configured as permanent virtual circuits (PVCs). **PVCs** are connections over which data may follow any number of different paths to move from point A to point B. For example, a transmission traveling over a PVC from Baltimore to Phoenix might go from Baltimore to Washington, D.C., to Chicago, then to Phoenix; the next transmission over that PVC, however, might go from Baltimore to Boston to Chicago to Kansas City to Phoenix.

PVCs are *not* dedicated like T-carrier services. When you lease an X.25 or Frame Relay circuit from your local carrier, your contract reflects the endpoints you specify and the amount of bandwidth you require between those endpoints. The service provider guarantees a minimum amount of bandwidth, called the **committed information rate (CIR)**. Provisions usually account for bursts of traffic that occasionally exceed the CIR. When you lease a PVC, you share bandwidth with the other X.25 and Frame Relay users on the backbone. Most X.25 and Frame Relay circuits travel over T-carriers.

The advantage to leasing a Frame Relay circuit over leasing a dedicated T1 or T3 is that you pay for only the amount of bandwidth required. Another advantage is that Frame Relay is much less expensive than the newer WAN technologies offered today, such as ATM (discussed later in this chapter). Also, Frame Relay follows an established worldwide standard.

On the other hand, because Frame Relay and X.25 use shared lines, their throughput remains at the mercy of variable traffic patterns. In the middle of the night, data over your Frame Relay network may zip along at 1.544 Mbps; during midday, when everyone is surfing the Web, it may slow down to less than your CIR. In addition, Frame Relay circuits are not as private as dedicated circuits. Nevertheless, because they use the same CSU/DSU and terminal equipment as T-carriers, they can easily be upgraded to T-carrier dedicated lines.

X.25 circuits are not commonly available in North America. Frame Relay circuits, on the other hand, are still useful for some applications—in particular, for businesses that need to communicate overseas. For example, a chemical company might want to connect its plants in Malaysia with its headquarters in Chicago through Frame Relay.

ATM (Asynchronous Transfer Mode)

ATM (Asynchronous Transfer Mode), is a WAN transmission method that relies on a fixed packet size to achieve data transfer rates from 25 to 622 Mbps. It was first conceived by researchers at Bell Labs in 1983, but it took a dozen years before standards organizations could reach an agreement on its specifications.

The fixed packet in ATM, which is called a **cell**, consists of 48 bytes of data plus a 5-byte header. By using a fixed packet size, ATM provides predictable traffic patterns and better control over bandwidth utilization. (As explained in Chapter 5, a smaller packet size requires more overhead.) In fact, ATM's smaller packet size decreases its potential throughput, but the efficiency of using cells compensates for that loss. Compare ATM's maximum throughput of 622 Mbps with Fast Ethernet's maximum throughput of 100 Mbps. Even though an ATM cell is a fraction of the size of an Ethernet frame, ATM's throughput is significantly faster.

Like Frame Relay, ATM relies on virtual circuits. It may use either private virtual circuits (PVCs) or switched virtual circuits (SVCs). **SVCs** are logical point-to-point connections that rely on ATM switches to determine the optimal path between sender and receiver. The ATM switch establishes this path before the network transmits ATM data. In contrast, Ethernet transmits data first and lets the routers and switches down the wire decide how to direct the data. ATM depends on a clean, digital transmission medium, such as fiber-optic cable, to attain its high speed. It may, however, be linked with systems that use other media, such as coaxial cable or twisted-pair, and other transmission methods, such as Ethernet or Frame Relay.

Applications that benefit from ATM technology include those involving time-sensitive data, such as video, audio, imaging, and other extremely large file transfers. For example, a company that wants to use its T1 line between two offices located at opposite sides of a state to carry its voice phone calls might choose ATM. Currently, ATM is very expensive and, due to its cost, is often used as campus-wide WAN technology to interconnect LANs in several buildings located within a relatively short distance from each other. It would also be ideal for long-distance communications because of its high quality of service, load balancing characteristics, speed, and interoperability. The drawbacks to ATM, like those of other emerging technologies, are its expense and its lack of well-defined standards. Gigabit Ethernet—a faster, cheaper, and probably more standard technology—pose a substantial threat to ATM. Indeed, many networking professionals are taking a "wait and see" attitude toward ATM.

SONET (Synchronous Optical Network)

SONET (Synchronous Optical Network) can provide data transfer rates from 64 Kbps to 2.4 Gbps using the same TDM technique used by T-carriers. If X.25 is the Yugo of the WAN transmission technologies, then SONET could be said to be the Rolls Royce. Bell Communications Research developed SONET technology in the 1980s to link different phone systems around the world. SONET has since emerged as the best choice for linking WANs between North America, Europe, and Asia, because it can work directly with the different standards used in different countries. Internationally, SONET is known as **SDH (Synchronous Digital Hierarchy)**. SONET interoperates well with T-carriers, ISDN, and ATM technology, making it a good choice for connecting WANs and LANs over long distances (even within the same country).

SONET depends on fiber-optic transmission media to achieve its extraordinary quality of service and throughput. Like T-carriers, it also uses multiplexers and terminal equipment to connect at the customer's end. A typical SONET network takes the form of a ring topology, similar to FDDI, in which one ring acts as the primary route for data and the other ring acts as a backup. If, for example, a backhoe operator severs one of the rings, SONET technology would automatically reroute traffic along the backup ring. This characteristic, known as **self-healing**, makes SONET very reliable. Companies can lease an entire SONET ring from their local or long distance carrier or they can lease part of a SONET, a circuit that offers T1 throughput, to take advantage of SONET's reliability. Figure 7-12 illustrates a SONET ring and its dual fiber connections.

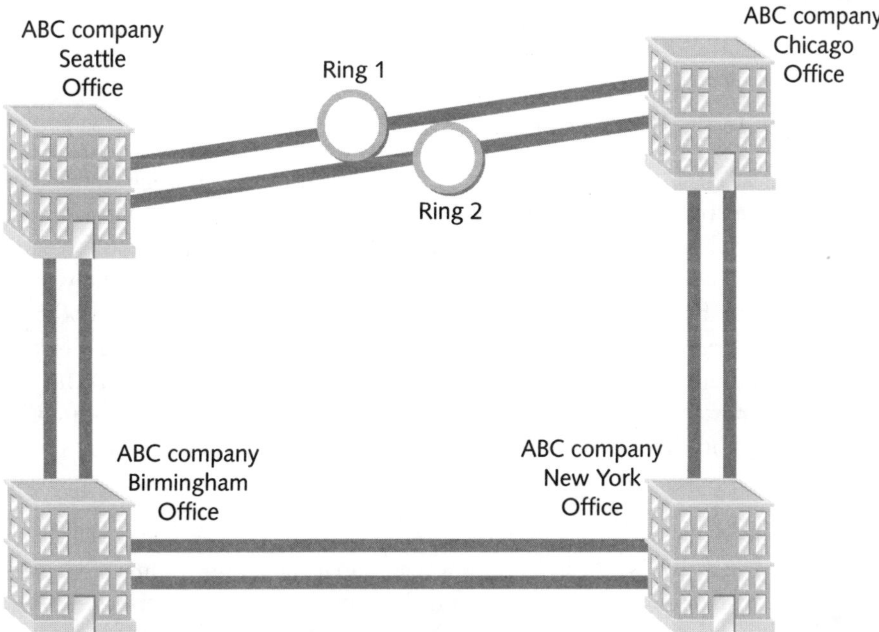

Figure 7-12 A SONET Ring

The data rate of a particular SONET ring is indicated by its Optical Carrier (OC) level, a rating that is internationally recognized by networking professionals and standards organizations. OC levels in SONET are analogous to the digital signal levels of T1s. Table 7-3 lists the OC levels and their maximum throughput. Notice how the different OC levels are used on the WAN depicted in Figure 7-12.

Table 7-3 SONET OC Levels

OC Level	Throughput (Mbps)
OC1	51.84
OC3	155.52
OC12	622
OC24	1244
OC48	2480
OC96	4976
OC192	9952

SONET technology is typically not implemented by small or medium-sized businesses, but rather by large global companies, long distance companies linking metropolitan areas and countries, or ISPs that want to guarantee fast, reliable access to the Internet. Like ATM, SONET is particularly suited to audio, video, and imaging data transmissions. As you can imagine, given its reliance on fiber-optic cable and its redundancy requirements, SONET technology is very expensive to implement.

WAN Implementation

You need to weigh many factors when choosing a WAN for your organization. Among other things, you need to consider how well a WAN solution will integrate with your existing LAN or WAN equipment, what kind of transmission speed is required by your users and applications, what kind of security is necessary, the geographical distance spanned by your WAN, the extent to which the WAN might grow over time and, of course, what kind of technology you can afford. This section compares the WAN technologies mentioned previously on the basis of the most significant and predictable factors: speed, reliability, and security. Although cost is, of course, an important factor, it will vary dramatically depending on your circumstances. For cost estimates, you should contact an ISP or a local or long distance service provider.

Speed

You have learned that WAN links offer a wide range of transmission speeds, from 56 Kbps for a PSTN dial-up connection to potentially 2.48 Gbps for a full-speed SONET connection. Table 7-4 summarizes the speeds offered by each technology discussed in this chapter. Bear in mind that each technology's transmission techniques (for example, switching for Frame Relay versus point-to-point for T1) will affect real throughput, so the maximum transmission speed is a theoretical limit. Actual transmission speeds will vary.

Table 7-4 A Comparison of WAN Technology Transmission Speeds

TWAN Technology	Maximum Transmission Speed
Dial-up over PSTN	56 Kbps
BRI (ISDN)	64–128 Kbps
PRI (ISDN)	1.544 Mbps
xDSL	1.544–52 Mbps
Cable	36 Mbps downstream, 10 Mbps upstream
T1	1.544 Mbps
Fractional T1	*n* times 64 Kbps (where *n* = number of channels leased)
T3	45 Mbps
FDDI	100 Mbps
X.25	56 Kbps
Frame Relay	56 Kbps to 45 Mbps
ATM	25, 45, 155, or 622 Mbps
SONET	51, 155, 622, 1244, or 2480 Mbps

Reliability

Each WAN technology varies in its reliability. A WAN's reliability depends partly on the transmission medium it uses (for example, fiber-optic cable is more reliable than copper wire) and partly on its topology and transmission methods (for example, a fully meshed WAN provides better reliability than a partially meshed WAN, because data have more potential paths open to them should one link fail). WAN technologies can be roughly divided as follows:

- Not very reliable, suited to individual or unimportant transmissions—PSTN dial-up
- Sufficiently reliable, suited for day-to-day transmissions—ISDN, T1, fractional T1, T3, xDSL, cable, X.25, and Frame Relay
- Very reliable, suited to mission-critical applications—FDDI, ATM, and SONET

Although PSTN lines are the least reliable of all WAN technologies, they are adequate for most telecommuting purposes. Their reliability depends on the quality of the local phone connection to a user's residence, which will vary from city to city and from neighborhood to neighborhood. Some connections may be entirely digital; others (particularly in rural areas) may be analog. Some may be subject to more noise than others are. The quality of PSTN dial-up lines also depends on the quality of a user's modem, which will undoubtedly vary from user to user.

For employees picking up e-mail and data files from a business's branch offices across the state, ISDN or T1 lines will usually suffice. Some applications, however, require the highest reliability. For example, if you were transmitting a videoconference of a United Nations meeting in New York to diplomats in Switzerland, you would want to use a very reliable technology such as SONET.

Security

Wise network managers will inspect security at every juncture in their WAN. Although fiber-optic media are the most secure transmission media (as you learned in Chapter 4), it's important to keep in mind that security relies on much more than simply the type of transmission media used. Among other things, you should consider the following issues:

- WAN security depends in part on the encryption measures each carrier provides for its lines. When leasing T1s, Frame Relay circuits, or SONET rings, you should ask a number of providers how they secure information in transit. In addition, you should verify that secure connectivity devices, such as firewalls, are employed at both ends of the connection. (You will learn about firewalls in detail in Chapter 15.)
- Enforce password-based authorization for LAN and WAN access and teach users how to choose difficult-to-decrypt passwords.
- Take the time to develop, publish, and enforce a security policy for users in your organization.
- Maintain restricted access to network equipment rooms and data centers.

All of these factors contribute to the security of your network. In other words, the type of WAN you choose does not affect security as much as the specific security considerations that apply to all networks. Network security is discussed further in Chapter 15.

Virtual Private Networks (VPNs)

Virtual private networks (VPNs) are long-distance networks logically defined over public transmission systems that serve all of an organization's users, but isolate that organization's traffic from other users of the same public lines. They provide a way of constructing a WAN from existing public transmission systems. For example, an organization can carve out a private WAN on the Internet to serve only its offices, while keeping the data secure and isolated from other (public) traffic.

Because VPNs do not entail leasing a full T1 circuit, for example, or paying for a Frame Relay system, they provide inexpensive solutions for creating long-distance WANs. VPNs employ specific protocols and security techniques to ensure that data can be interpreted only at the WAN's nodes. The security techniques used may be purely software-based or they may include hardware such as a firewall.

The software required to establish VPNs is usually inexpensive, in some cases being included with other widely used software. For example, Windows NT Server comes with a remote access utility called RAS that allows you to create a simple VPN. For Novell-based networks, you can use BorderManager, a NetWare add-on product, to construct VPNs. In addition, many other companies offer software that will work with either of these network operating systems to create VPNs. Figure 7-13 depicts one possible implementation of a VPN. The beauty of VPNs is that they are tailored to a customer's distance and bandwidth needs, so, of course, every one is different.

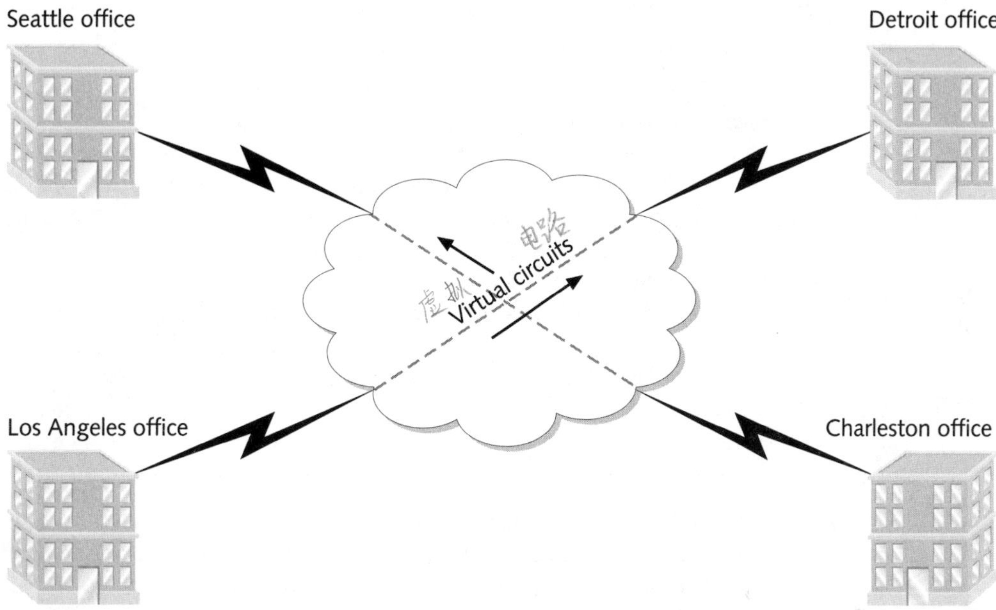

Figure 7-13 An example of a VPN

Do not confuse virtual private networks (VPNs) with the virtual LANs (VLANs) discussed in Chapter 6. VLANs are logically defined LANs created from an organization's existing LAN or WAN infrastructure, usually to serve a particular group of users.

ESTABLISHING REMOTE CONNECTIVITY

You have learned about almost every type of connectivity available for long-distance networking, but you may not know how the average user connects to a WAN. In a large organization with an enterprise-wide network, using a WAN is no different from using a LAN. You might log on to your company's network in Dallas, open Windows Explorer, and choose to view a PowerPoint presentation on a server in Phoenix. Your computer doesn't care about the location of the presentation file, because the WAN link makes it appear to be part of one big network (assuming that the network manager has done his or her job!). If you are at home or on the road, however, connecting to a WAN or LAN is somewhat different. The next two sections describe three methods for accessing a network from a remote location.

REMOTE ACCESS METHODS

As a remote user, you can connect to a LAN in one of three ways: dial directly to the LAN, dial directly to a workstation, or use an Internet connection with a Web interface. Each of these methods offers different advantages and disadvantages, as described following. Bear in mind that the true limiting factor in a remote connection is typically the speed of the modem, PSTN, or ISDN line.

- **Direct dial to the LAN**—The client directly dials a remote access server on the LAN. A **remote access server** (also called a dial-in server) is a combination of software and hardware that provides a central access point for multiple users to dial into a LAN or WAN. The LAN treats the direct-dial remote client like any other client on the LAN; that is, the remote user can perform the same functions he or she could perform while in the office. The computer dialing into the LAN becomes a **remote node** on the network. Although this remote access method is the most complex to configure, especially on the server side, it can provide the best security. Also, the transmission speed of a direct-dial connection does not suffer when the Internet becomes congested. With the proper server hardware and software, this kind of connection can offer multiple users simultaneous remote access to the LAN.
- **Direct dial to a workstation**—The remote user dials into a workstation that is directly attached to the LAN. Software (such as Symantec's pcANYWHERE) running on both the remote user's computer and the LAN computer allows the remote user to "take over" the LAN workstation, a solution known as **remote control**. Remote control is not as difficult to configure and confers the same security and throughput benefits as directly dialing into a remote access server. In addition, this method provides the best performance for processing-intensive applications such as databases, because the data processing can occur on the LAN-attached workstation without having to traverse the slower modem connection to the remote workstation. One disadvantage to this solution is that it allows only one connection to the LAN at any given time.
- **Internet/Web interface**—Through a browser such as Netscape or Internet Explorer, a user at home or on the road connects to a LAN whose files are made visible to the Web through Web server software. This method requires some setup steps on both the client and the server, but it is not usually as complex as a direct-dial configuration. Its security and throughput cannot be controlled as thoroughly as those of the direct-dial solutions, however, because the remote user's connection is not dedicated. Nevertheless, a Web interface is very simple to use and widely available. Also, a nearly unlimited number of remote users can simultaneously access the LAN resources using this method.

Remote connectivity can be established between almost any combination of workstation and operating system, given the appropriate software and hardware configuration. Perhaps the simplest dial-in server is the **Remote Access Service** (**RAS**, pronounced "razz"), which comes with Windows NT Server. Because it is a good example of a remote access server, you should investigate RAS when you work with Windows NT servers. Knowing RAS will help you understand more complex access server technologies.

In addition to Microsoft's remote access methods, networking hardware manufacturers such as Bay Networks, Cisco Systems, and 3Com market their own remote access technologies. In addition, a number of specialized software companies provide programs that run on Windows NT, IntraNetware, or UNIX servers. The method you choose will depend on your requirements for security, throughput, number of connections, and cost and the technical expertise of your users and support staff. If you enable remote access for your network, you will need to be familiar with the process of configuring clients for connection and be able to support those clients. The next section describes how to configure a dial-up networking client.

DIAL-UP NETWORKING

Dial-up networking refers to the process of dialing into a LAN's access server or to an ISP. Dial-up Networking is also the name of the utility that Microsoft provides with its operating systems to achieve this type of connectivity. Most telecommuters use some form of dial-up networking to connect to their LAN. This section describes how to configure a workstation to dial into a server, thereby creating a connection to the Internet. For discussion purposes, the example of a Windows 95's Dial-Up Networking client is used.

To successfully use Dial-Up Networking from a Windows 95 workstation, first make sure that your modem is installed and working properly. Also, verify that you have the Client for Microsoft Networks and that the TCP/IP protocol is installed in your Network properties. Ensure that the Dial-Up Networking utility is installed and bound to TCP/IP and the Client for Microsoft Networks. If Dial-Up Networking is not installed, you can install it from the Windows 95 CD-ROM as described in the following steps.

To install Dial-Up Networking and bind it to your existing protocols and adapters:

1. Insert the Windows 95 CD-ROM into your CD-ROM drive.
2. Click **Start**, point to **Settings**, then click **Control Panel**. The Control Panel window opens.
3. Double-click the **Add/Remove Programs** icon. The Add/Remove Programs dialog box opens.
4. Click the **Windows Setup** tab.
5. In the **Components** list, click **Communications**, then click **Details**. The Communications dialog box opens.
6. Click the check box next to **Dial-Up Networking**.
7. Click **OK**. You are asked to restart your computer.
8. Click **Yes** to confirm that you want to restart your computer.

Once Dial-Up Networking is installed, you will need to create a profile to identify the system into which you will be dialing. If you are dialing into an ISP's server, the ISP should provide its server's telephone number, which is necessary for establishing a Dial-Up Networking profile.

To create a Dial-Up Networking profile:

1. On the Windows 95 desktop, double-click the **My Computer** icon. The My Computer window opens.
2. Double-click the **Dial-Up Networking** icon. The Dial-Up Networking window opens.

If you just installed Dial-Up Networking, the Make New Connection dialog box will pop up automatically.

3. Double-click the **Make New Connection** icon. The Make New Connection wizard opens. This wizard consists of a series of dialog boxes, asking you for the information needed to define a connection, including a name for the system into which you are dialing, modem type, area code, telephone number, and country code.
4. Enter the required information into the appropriate text boxes. You can name the connection anything you want, but preferably something that describes the dial-in server. The name of the connection does not affect its dial-up process.
5. If you have only one modem on your machine and it is installed properly, your modem should be automatically selected, as shown in Figure 7-14. Once you have verified that it is correct, click **Next** to continue.

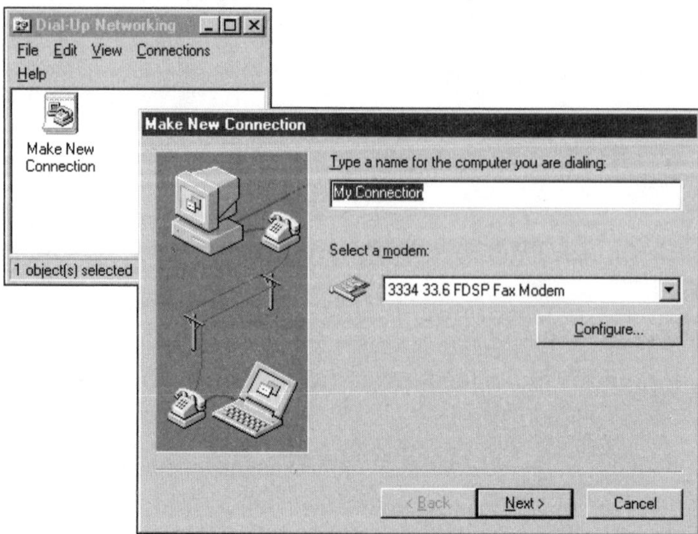

Figure 7-14 Creating a Dial-Up Networking connection

6. In the next dialog box, your area code will appear in the area code box (assuming that you entered it correctly when you installed your modem). In the box next to the area code, type the number of the system you're dialing. You probably will not need to change the country code.
7. Click **Next** to continue. A confirmation dialog box appears.
8. Click **Finish** to save your changes. An icon bearing the name of the connection you created appears in the Dial-Up Networking window.

After creating a new Dial-Up Networking profile, you must configure its connectivity options. Unless you configure it precisely according to the server's parameters, your connection will not work properly. In some cases, if you enter incomplete or incorrect information, you may be able to establish a session between your client and the server, but be unable to send or receive data. If you are dialing into an ISP's server, the ISP must provide all of the information used for this configuration.

To configure a Dial-Up Networking profile:

1. In the Dial-up Networking window, right-click the connection you want to configure. A shortcut menu opens.
2. Click **Properties**. A window titled with the name of your profile opens.
3. Click the **Server Types** tab to display the server properties, including the type of dial-up server, network protocols, and advanced options. Here you have a choice of several different kinds of connections. If you are dialing into an ISP, you will probably use either a PPP or SLIP remote access server. (PPP and SLIP connections are discussed in the next section.)
4. Select the type of server specified by your ISP. If you select the wrong type, you will not be able to connect to the ISP's server.
5. Select any of the following optional parameters: **Log On to Network**, **Enable Software Compression**, or **Require Encrypted Password**. For example, if you want to automatically log on to the server once the dial-up connection is made, select **Log On to Network**.
6. If, as in this example, you are configuring a connection for use with the Internet, you must select at least the TCP/IP protocol from the list of **Allowed Network Protocols**. You may select additional protocols if your dial-up connection supports them. Next, you need to configure the TCP/IP properties for this connection.
7. Click **TCP/IP Settings**. The TCP/IP Settings dialog box opens.

If you have both a modem and a NIC on your PC, changing the TCP/IP properties for the dial-up connection will not affect the TCP/IP properties you have set for your NIC. In Network properties, you will see that TCP/IP is bound to both your NIC and your Dial-Up Adapter and that the properties differ for each TCP/IP binding.

8. Enter the parameters provided by your ISP. Typically, you can leave the **Server Assigned IP Address** option selected, but you will probably need to enter at least one specific name server address.

9. The selection of the last two options, **Use IP Header Compression** and **Use Default Gateway on Remote Network**, depends on your ISP's directions. Usually, they can remain selected.
10. After you have made these required changes, click **OK** to close the TCP/IP Settings dialog box.
11. Click **OK** again to close the Dial-Up Networking properties dialog box.
12. Test your connection to the remote server.

Now that you have become familiar with remote connectivity methods and know how to create and configure a dial-up networking profile, you will learn about the two most common dial-up networking protocols, PPP and SLIP. In order to qualify for Net+ certification, you should understand how to configure these protocols on a Dial-up networking connection; you should also understand the differences between the two protocols.

SERIAL LINE INTERNET PROTOCOL (SLIP) AND POINT-TO-POINT PROTOCOL (PPP)

Serial Line Internet Protocol (SLIP) and **Point-to-Point Protocol (PPP)** are two communications protocols that enable a workstation to connect to a server using a serial connection (in the case of dial-up networking, *serial connection* refers to a modem). Such protocols are necessary to transport Network layer traffic over serial interfaces, which belong to the Data Link layer of the OSI Model. Both SLIP and PPP encapsulate higher-layer networking protocols in their lower-layer data frames. SLIP is a version of the protocol that can carry only IP packets, however, and PPP can carry many different types of Network layer packets, such as IPX or AppleTalk. Another difference between SLIP and PPP is that SLIP supports only asynchronous data transmission and PPP supports both asynchronous and synchronous transmission.

Asynchronous refers to a communications method in which data being transmitted and received by nodes do not have to conform to any timing scheme. In asynchronous communications, a node can transmit at any time and the destination node must accept the transmission as it comes. To ensure that the receiving node knows when it has received a complete frame, asynchronous communications provide start and stop bits for each character transmitted. When the receiving node recognizes a start bit, it begins to accept a new character. When it receives the stop bit for that character, it ceases to look for the end of that character's transmission. Asynchronous data transmission therefore occurs in random stops and starts.

Conversely, **synchronous** refers to a communications method in which data being transmitted and received by nodes must conform to a timing scheme. A clock maintains time for all nodes on a network. A receiving node in synchronous communications recognizes that it should be receiving data by looking at the time on the clock. In synchronous communications, start and stop bits are not necessary, because the clocking indicates where transmission should begin and where it should end. As an analogy, imagine a marathon with 1000 participants, in which each runner starts the race precisely five minutes after the previous runner started. The race's official timekeeper keeps track of when each runner begins, so that when a runner arrives at the finish line, his or her total time can be calculated. Runner B, who starts ten minutes after Runner A, will not be expected to arrive at the finish line at the same time as Runner A. In this analogy, the race official is like the clocking mechanism in synchronous communications.

PPP is the more popular communications protocol for dial-up connections to the Internet, primarily because it does not require as much configuration on the client as SLIP does. When using SLIP, you typically have to specify the IP addresses for both your client and for your server in your dial-up networking profile. PPP, on the other hand, can automatically obtain this information as it connects to the server. Because it is more difficult to configure, SLIP is rarely used.

Chapter Summary

- WANs are distinguished from LANs by the fact that the former networks traverse a wider geographical area. They usually employ point-to-point communications rather than point-to-many communications (where LAN hubs or switches connect multiple segments or workstations). WANs also provide better and faster transmission than LANs.
- WANs typically send data over public communications links, such as the telephony backbone provided by local and long distance telephone companies.
- WAN transmission methods differ in terms of their speed, reliability, cost, distance covered, and security. For every business need, only one or a handful of appropriate WAN transmission methods may exist. Several WAN technologies may be used together on the same network.
- One WAN transmission method, PSTN (Public Switched Telephone Network), relies on the network of telephone lines that typically services homes. The PSTN was originally composed of analog lines but now uses digital transmission over fiber-optic and copper twisted-pair cable, microwave, and satellite connections. PSTN is usually adequate for at-home dial-up LAN or Internet users.
- A remote user can use the PSTN to access a remote server via a dial-up connection. In a dial-up connection, the user's modem converts the computer's digital pulses into analog signals. These signals travel through PSTN to the receiving computer's modem, which then converts the analog signals back into digital pulses. Unlike other types of WAN connections, dial-up connections provide a fixed period of access to the network. (Dial-up connections can also involve other types of transmission methods besides PSTN.)
- Although PSTN dial-up connections may theoretically be capable of a 56 Kbps throughput, in reality throughput is slowed by the number of modems and phone company POPs that the connection must go through.
- Another WAN transmission method, ISDN (Integrated Services Digital Network), is an international standard established by the ITU for transmitting data over digital lines. ISDN uses the telephone carrier's lines and dial-up connections, like PSTN. It differs from PSTN in that it travels exclusively over digital lines and switches.

- ISDN lines may carry voice and data signals simultaneously, but require an ISDN phone to carry voice traffic and an ISDN router and ISDN terminal adapter to carry data. ISDN lines circumvent the need to pay for separate phone lines to support faxes, modems, and voice calls at one location. Local phone companies began offering ISDN in the mid-1980s with the anticipation that the United States would convert to this all-digital system by the turn of the century. In fact, it hasn't caught on as quickly as predicted.
- Two types of ISDN connections are commonly used by consumers in North America: Basic Rate ISDN (BRI) and Primary Rate ISDN (PRI). A third type of ISDN connection, called Broadband ISDN (B-ISDN), was developed by the ITU in the late 1980s to provide more capacity than BRI or PRI. B-ISDN is frequently bypassed in favor of newer, high-capacity lines such as those that use xDSL or T1 technology.
- BRI uses two 64 Kbps circuit-switched bearer channels (or B channels) to transmit and receive data or voice. These two channels carry the traffic from point to point. An additional 16 Kbps channel called a D channel, for "data" channel, carries information about the call, such as session initiation and termination signals, caller identity, call forwarding, and conference calling signals.
- B channels in ISDN lines are treated as separate connections by the network and can carry voice and data or two data streams simultaneously and separate from each other. A process called bonding can combine the throughput of the B channels into a larger effective throughput.
- PRI uses 23 B channels and one 64 Kbps D channel. Individual subscribers rarely use PRI, preferring BRI instead, but PRI may be used by business and other organizations needing more throughput. The maximum potential throughput for a PRI connection is 1.544 Mbps, the same as that for a T1 circuit.
- Individual customers who need to transmit more data than a typical modem can handle or who want to use a single line for both data and voice commonly choose ISDN lines. ISDN, although not available everywhere in the United States, can be purchased from most local telephone companies. Costs for ISDN lines vary depending on your location and bandwidth needs.
- ISDN is feasible only for the local loop portion of the WAN link, or the part of a phone system that connects a customer site with a public carrier's POP.
- Another WAN transmission method is digital subscriber line (DSL). DSL uses advanced data modulation techniques to achieve extraordinary throughput over regular phone lines. Data modulation uses one signal to alter the frequency, phase, or amplitude of another signal. In the case of DSL, multiple high-frequency carrier signals are modulated by modems' data signals, enabling DSL connections to support high throughput over copper wire.
- DSL comes in seven different varieties, each of which is either asymmetrical or symmetrical. In asymmetrical transmission, more data can be sent in one direction than in the other direction. In symmetrical transmission, equal amounts of data can be sent in either direction. The most popular form of DSL is ADSL.

- DSL technology creates a dedicated circuit by using modems at each end of the connection. Although ADSL has the potential to replace ISDN and eclipse cable in the race to provide high bandwidth (as much as 1.544 Mbps) to home users, it is currently hampered by a lack of well-defined standards.
- Cable is another option for WAN transmission. Cable companies are pushing their own point-to-point connectivity option, which relies on the cable wiring used for TV signals. Such wiring could realistically transmit approximately 3 to 10 Mbps downstream and 2 Mbps upstream. The asymmetry of cable technology makes it a logical choice for users who want to surf the Web or download data from a network.
- Cable connections require that the customer purchase a special cable modem to transmit and receive signals over cable wiring. In addition, most cable companies will have to upgrade their existing equipment to support bidirectional, digital communications. Specifically, they will have to replace part of their coaxial cable plant with fiber-optic cable.
- Like DSL, cable provides a dedicated, or continuous, connection that does not require dialing up a service provider. Several cable companies have developed solutions for providing data over their lines, but only recently have they attempted to make their solutions interoperable.
- Other WAN links depend on leased lines. Leased lines are permanent dedicated connections established through a public telecommunications carrier and billed to customers on a monthly basis. When networking professionals use the term *leased line*, they are generally referring to T1s, fractional T1s, or T3s—collectively known as T-carriers.
- T-carrier transmission uses a technology called multiplexing to divide a single channel into multiple channels for carrying voice, data, video, or other signals. More precisely, T-carriers use time division multiplexing (TDM), a version of multiplexing that divides the channel into multiple time slots and assigns each data stream its own time slot to follow. Devices at the sending end arrange the data streams (multiplex), then devices at the receiving end filter them back into separate signals (de-multiplex).
- A number of T-carrier varieties are currently available. The most common T-carrier implementations are T1 and, for higher bandwidth needs, T3. A T1 circuit can carry the equivalent of 24 voice channels, giving a maximum data throughput of 1.544 Mbps. A T3 can carry the equivalent of 672 voice channels, giving a maximum data throughput of 44.736 Mbps.
- The signal level of a T-carrier refers to its Physical layer electrical signaling characteristics, as defined by ANSI standards in the early 1980s. DS0 is the equivalent of one data or voice channel. All other signal levels are multiples of DS0.
- Businesses commonly use T1s to connect branch offices or to connect to an ISP. Telephone companies also use them to connect central offices. ISPs typically take advantage of T1s to connect to their Internet carriers. In fact, they might use multiple T1s. T3s are very expensive and are used only by the most data-intensive businesses.

- A fractional T1 lease allows organizations to use only some channels on a T1 line and pay for only those channels actually used. Thus fractional T1 bandwidth can be leased in multiples of 64 Kbps. A fractional T1 is suited to businesses that expect their traffic to grow and that may require a full T1 eventually, but can't currently justify leasing a full T1.
- T1 technology can use unshielded or shielded twisted-pair copper wiring. Because the digital signals require a cleaner connection, shielded twisted-pair is considered preferable. Twisted-pair wiring cannot adequately carry the high throughput of multiple T1s or T3 transmissions. For multiple T1s, coaxial cable may be used or any of the T3 transmission media—either microwave or fiber-optic cabling.
- The CSU/DSU is the connection point for a T1 line at the customer's site. The CSU provides termination for the digital signal and ensures connection integrity through error correction and line monitoring. The DSU converts the digital signal used by bridges, routers, and multiplexers into the digital signal carried via cabling.
- A multiplexer provides the means of combining multiple voice and/or data channels on one line. Multiplexers can take input from a variety of terminal equipment, such as bridges, routers, or telephone exchange devices, for use with voice.
- The devices that connect to the multiplexer are collectively known as terminal equipment. On a typical T1-connected data network, this equipment consists of bridges and/or routers. A bridge or router would typically integrate two types of networks: the incoming T1 (Internet) and an Ethernet or Token Ring LAN at the customer's site.
- FDDI (Fiber Distributed Data Interface) is a networking standard originally specified by ANSI in the mid-1980s and later refined by ISO. It uses a dual fiber-optic ring to transmit data at speeds of 100 Mbps. In fact, FDDI was the first technology to reach the 100 Mbps threshold; for this reason, it often appears in network backbones installed in the 1980s and early 1990s. Although FDDI isn't exclusively a WAN technology, WANs typically use it.
- FDDI's required fiber-optic cable offers greater reliability and security than twisted-pair copper wire. Also, FDDI works well with the new Ethernet 100BaseTX technology. On the other hand, it is much more expensive than Fast Ethernet. If an organization has FDDI installed, however, it can easily upgrade to Fast Ethernet or Gigabit Ethernet.
- X.25 is an analog packet switched technology optimized for long-distance data transmission and standardized by the ITU in the mid-1970s. It can support 56 Kbps throughput. X.25 was originally developed and used for communications between mainframe computers and remote terminals. Though rare in North America, it remains a WAN standard around the world.
- Frame Relay is an updated, digital version of X.25 that also relies on packet switching. Because it is digital, Frame Relay supports higher bandwidth than X.25, offering a maximum of 1.544 Mbps throughput.
- Both X.25 and Frame Relay are configured as permanent virtual circuits (PVCs). PVCs are point-to-point connections over which data may follow any number of different paths. When you lease an X.25 or Frame Relay circuit from your local carrier, your contract reflects the endpoints you specify and the amount of bandwidth required between those endpoints.

- ATM (Asynchronous Transfer Mode) relies on a fixed packet size to achieve data transfer rates ranging from 25 to 622 Mbps. The fixed packet, called a cell, consists of 48 bytes of data plus a 5-byte header. The fixed packet size allows ATM to provide predictable traffic patterns and better control over bandwidth utilization.
- Like Frame Relay, ATM relies on virtual circuits, although it may use either private virtual circuits (PVCs) or switched virtual circuits (SVCs)—logical point-to-point connections that rely on ATM switches to determine the optimal path between sender and receiver. The ATM switch establishes this path before the network transmits ATM data; in contrast, Ethernet transmits data first and lets the routers and switches down the wire direct the data.
- Applications that benefit from ATM technology include time-sensitive data, such as video, audio, imaging, and other extremely large file transfers. Currently, ATM is very expensive. It would be ideal for long-distance communications because of its high quality of service, load balancing characteristics, speed, and interoperability. One drawback to ATM, as with other emerging technologies, is a lack of well-defined standards.
- SONET can provide data transfer rates from 64 Kbps to 2.4 Gbps using the same TDM technique employed by T-carriers. It is the best choice for linking WANs between North America, Europe, and Asia, because it can link directly with the different standards used in different countries. Internationally, SONET is known as SDH (Synchronous Digital Hierarchy). SONET interoperates well with T-carriers, ISDN, and ATM technology.
- SONET depends on fiber-optic transmission media and uses multiplexers and terminal equipment to connect at the customer's end. A typical SONET network takes the form of a ring topology, similar to FDDI, where one ring acts as the primary route for data and the other ring acts as a backup. If one ring breaks, SONET technology automatically reroutes traffic along the backup ring. This characteristic, known as self-healing, makes SONET very reliable.
- SONET technology is typically not implemented by small or medium-sized businesses, but rather by large global companies, long distance companies linking metropolitan areas and countries, or ISPs that want to guarantee fast, reliable access to the Internet. SONET is particularly suited to audio, video, and imaging data transmissions but is very expensive.
- When implementing a new WAN installation or upgrade, you should consider the following factors: the WAN's ability to integrate with your existing LAN or WAN equipment, the kind of transmission speed required by your users and applications, the kind of security needed, the geographical distance the WAN must span, the extent to which the WAN might grow over time, and, of course, the expense.
- Virtual private networks (VPNs) represent one way to construct a WAN from existing public transmission systems. An organization can carve out a private WAN on the Internet (or over leased lines) to serve only its offices, while keeping the data secure and isolated from other (public) traffic. Because VPNs do not require leasing a full T1, for example, or paying for a Frame Relay system, they provide inexpensive solutions for creating long-distance WANs.

- As a remote user, you can connect to a LAN in one of three ways: direct dial to the LAN, direct dial to a workstation, or use an Internet connection with a Web interface. Each method has different advantages and disadvantages pertaining to its throughput, security, complexity, and number of simultaneous users allowed.
- Serial Line Internet Protocol (SLIP) and Point-to-Point Protocol (PPP) are communications protocols that enable a workstation to connect to a server using a serial connection (in the case of dial-up networking, "serial connection" refers to a modem). Such protocols are necessary to transport Network layer traffic over serial interfaces, which belong to the Data Link layer of the OSI Model. Because it is easier to configure and supports more than one type of Network layer protocol, PPP is preferred over SLIP.

KEY TERMS

- **asymmetrical** — The characteristic of a transmission technology that affords greater bandwidth in one direction (either from the customer to the carrier, or vice versa) than in the other direction.
- **asymmetrical DSL** — A variation of DSL that offers more throughput when data travels downstream—downloading from a local carrier's POP to the customer—than when it travels upstream—uploading from the customer to the local carrier's POP.
- **asynchronous** — A transmission method in which data being transmitted and received by nodes do not have to conform to any timing scheme. In asynchronous communications, a node can transmit at any time and the destination node must accept the transmission as it comes.
- **Asynchronous Transfer Mode (ATM)** — A technology originally conceived in 1983 at Bell Labs, but standardized only in the mid-1990s. It relies on a fixed packet size to achieve data transfer rates ranging from 25 to 622 Mbps. The fixed packet consists of 48 bytes of data plus a 5-byte header. The fixed packet size allows ATM to provide predictable traffic patterns and better control over bandwidth utilization.
- **B channel** — In ISDN, the "bearer" channel, so named because it bears traffic from point to point.
- **bonding** — The process of combining more than one bearer channel of an ISDN line to increase throughput. For example, BRI's two 64 Kbps B channels are bonded to create an effective throughput of 128 Kbps.
- **BRI (Basic Rate ISDN)** — A variety of ISDN that uses two 64 Kbps bearer channels and one 16 Kbps data channel, as summarized by the following notation: 2B+D. BRI is the most common form of ISDN employed by home users.
- **cable drop** — Fiber-optic or coaxial cable that connects a neighborhood cable node to a customer's house.
- **cell** — A packet of a fixed size. In ATM technology, a cell consists of 48 bytes of data plus a 5-byte header.

- **CIR (committed information rate)** — The guaranteed minimum amount of bandwidth selected when leasing a Frame Relay circuit. Frame Relay costs are partially based on CIR.
- **CSU (channel service unit)** — A device used with T-carrier technology that provides termination for the digital signal and ensures connection integrity through error correction and line monitoring.
- **CSU/DSU** — A combination of a CSU (channel service unit) and a DSU (data service unit) that serves as the connection point for a T1 line at the customer's site.
- **data modulation** — A process in which one signal alters the frequency, phase, or amplitude of another signal.
- **D channel** — In ISDN, the "data" channel used to carry information about the call, such as session initiation and termination signals, caller identity, call forwarding, and conference calling signals.
- **dedicated line** — A continuously available link that is leased through another carrier. Examples of dedicated lines include ADSL, T1, and T3.
- **dedicated service** — A type of data connection in which the user does not have to dial-up an ISP; the connection is always available.
- **dial-up** — A type of connection that uses modems at the transmitting and receiving ends and PSTN or other lines to access a network.
- **dial-up networking** — The process of dialing in to a LAN's access server or to an ISP. Dial-up Networking is also the name of the utility that Microsoft provides with its operating systems to achieve this type of connectivity.
- **downstream** — A term used to describe data traffic that flows from a local carrier's POP to the customer. In asymmetrical communications, downstream throughput is usually much higher than upstream throughput. In symmetrical communications, downstream and upstream throughputs are equal.
- **DSL (digital subscriber lines)** — A dedicated remote connectivity or WAN technology that uses advanced data modulation techniques to achieve extraordinary throughput over regular phone lines. DSL currently comes in seven different varieties, the most common of which is Asymmetric DSL (ADSL).
- **DSU (data service unit)** — A device used in T-carrier technology that converts the digital signal used by bridges, routers, and multiplexers into the digital signal used on cabling. Typically, a DSU is combined with a CSU in a single box, a CSU/DSU.
- **FDDI (Fiber Distributed Data Interface)** — A networking standard originally specified by ANSI in the mid-1980s and later refined by ISO. FDDI uses a dual fiber-optic ring to transmit data at speeds of 100 Mbps. It was commonly used as a backbone technology in the 1980s and early 1990s, but lost favor as fast Ethernet technologies emerged in the mid-1990s. FDDI provides excellent reliability and security.
- **fractional T1** — An arrangement that allows organizations to use only some channels on a T1 line and pay for only the channels actually used.

- **Frame Relay** — An updated, digital version of X.25 that relies on packet switching. Because it is digital, Frame Relay supports higher bandwidth than X.25, offering a maximum of 1.544 Mbps throughput. It provides the basis for much of the world's Internet connections. On network diagrams, the Frame Relay system is often depicted as a cloud.
- **head-end** — A cable company's central office, which connects cable wiring to many nodes before it reaches customers' sites.
- **hybrid fiber-coax (HFC)** — A link that consists of fiber cable connecting the cable company's offices to a node location near the customer and coaxial cable connecting the node to the customer's house. HFC upgrades to existing cable wiring are required before current TV cable systems can serve as WAN links.
- **ISDN (Integrated Services Digital Network)** — An international standard, established by the ITU, for transmitting data over digital lines. Like PSTN, ISDN uses the telephone carrier's lines and dial-up connections, but it differs from PSTN in that it exclusively uses digital lines and switches.
- **leased lines** — Permanent dedicated connections established through a public telecommunications carrier and billed to customers on a monthly basis.
- **local loop** — The part of a phone system that connects a customer site with a public carrier's POP. Some WAN transmission methods, such as ISDN, are suitable for only the local loop portion of the network link.
- **modem** — In the context of remote computing, a device that converts a computer's digital pulses into analog signals for the PSTN, then converts the analog signals back into digital pulses at the receiving computer's end.
- **multiplexer** — In the context of T-carrier technology, a device that provides the means of combining multiple voice and/or data channels on one line. Multiplexers can take input from a variety of terminal equipment, such as bridges, routers, or telephone exchange devices, for use with voice traffic.
- **multiplexing** — A technology that divides a single channel into multiple channels for carrying voice, data, video, or other signals.
- **Network Termination 1 (NT1)** — A device used on ISDN networks that connects the incoming twisted-pair wiring with the customer's ISDN terminal equipment.
- **Network Termination 2 (NT2)** — An additional connection device required on PRI to handle the multiple ISDN lines between the customer's network termination connection and the local phone company's wires.
- **phase** — A measurement of a wave's progress through time and compared with other waves.
- **plain old telephone service (POTS)** — See *PSTN*.

- **point of presence (POP)** — The place where the two telephone systems meet—either a long distance carrier with a local telephone company or a local carrier with an ISP's facility.
- **point-to-point** — A link that connects only one site to another site.
- **Point-to-Point Protocol (PPP)** — A communications protocol that enables a workstation to connect to a server using a serial connection. PPP can support multiple Network layer protocols, can use both asynchronous and synchronous communications, and does not require much (if any) configuration on the client workstation.
- **PRI (Primary Rate ISDN)** — A type of ISDN that uses 23 bearer channels and one 64 Kbps data channel as represented by the following notation: 23B+D. PRI is less commonly used by individual subscribers than BRI, but it may be used by businesses and other organizations needing more throughput.
- **PSTN (Public Switched Telephone Network)** — The network of typical telephone lines that has been evolving for 100 years and still services most homes.
- **PVC (private virtual circuit)** — A point-to-point connection over which data may follow any number of different paths, as opposed to a dedicated line that follows a predefined path. X.25, Frame Relay, and some forms of ATM use PVCs.
- **remote access server** — A combination of software and hardware that provides a central access point for multiple users to dial into a LAN or WAN.
- **Remote Access Service (RAS)** — One of the simplest dial-in servers. This software is included with Windows NT Server. Note that "RAS" is pronounced *razz*.
- **remote control** — A remote access solution in which the remote user dials into a workstation that is directly attached to the LAN. Software running on both the remote user's computer and the LAN computer allows the remote user to "take over" the LAN workstation.
- **remote node** — A client that has dialed directly into a LAN's remote access server. The LAN treats a remote node like any other client on the LAN, allowing the remote user to perform the same functions he or she could perform while in the office.
- **SDH (Synchronous Digital Hierarchy)** — The international equivalent of SONET.
- **self-healing** — A characteristic of dual-ring topologies that allows them to automatically reroute traffic along the backup ring if the primary ring becomes severed.
- **Serial Line Internet Protocol (SLIP)** — A communications protocol that enables a workstation to connect to a server using a serial connection. SLIP can support only asynchronous communications and IP traffic and requires some configuration on the client workstation.
- **signal level** — An ANSI standard for T-carrier technology that refers to its Physical layer electrical signaling characteristics. DS0 is the equivalent of one data or voice channel. All other signal levels are multiples of DS0.

- **SONET (Synchronous Optical Network)** — A WAN technology that provides data transfer rates ranging from 64 Kbps to 2.4 Gbps using the same time division multiplexing technique used by T-carriers. SONET is the best choice for linking WANs between North America, Europe, and Asia, because it can link directly with the different standards used in different countries.
- **SVC (switched virtual circuit)** — Logical, point-to-point connections that rely on switches to determine the optimal path between sender and receiver. ATM technology uses SVCs.
- **symmetrical** — A characteristic of transmission technology that provides equal throughput for data traveling both upstream and downstream and is suited to users who both upload and download significant amounts of data.
- **symmetrical DSL** — A variation of DSL that provides equal throughput both upstream and downstream between the customer and the carrier.
- **synchronous** — A transmission method in which data being transmitted and received by nodes must conform to a timing scheme.
- **T1** — A T-carrier technology that provides 1.544 Mbps throughput and 24 channels for voice, data, video, or audio signals. T1s may use shielded or unshielded twisted-pair, coaxial cable, fiber-optic, or microwave links. Businesses commonly use T1s to connect to their ISP, and phone companies typically use at least one T1 to connect their central offices.
- **T3** — A T-carrier technology that can carry the equivalent of 672 channels for voice, data, video, or audio, with a maximum data throughput of 44.736 Mbps (typically rounded up to 45 Mbps for purposes of discussion). T3s require either fiber-optic or microwave transmission media.
- **T-carriers** — The term for any kind of leased line that follows the standards for T1s, fractional T1s, T1Cs, T2s, T3s, or T4s.
- **terminal adapter (TA)** — Devices used to convert digital signals into analog signals for use with ISDN phones and other analog devices. Terminal adapters are sometimes mistakenly called ISDN modems.
- **terminal equipment (TE)** — Devices that connect computers to the ISDN line. Terminal equipment may include standalone devices or cards (similar to the network adapters used on Ethernet and Token Ring networks) or ISDN routers.
- **time division multiplexing (TDM)** — A version of multiplexing that divides the channel into multiple time slots and assigns each data stream its own time slot to follow. Devices at the sending end arrange the data streams (multiplex); devices at the receiving end then filter them back into separate signals (de-multiplex).
- **upstream** — A term used to describe data traffic that flows from a customer's site to the local carrier's POP. In symmetrical communications, upstream throughput is usually much lower than downstream throughput. In symmetrical communications, upstream and downstream throughputs are equal.

- **virtual private network (VPN)** — A logically constructed WAN that uses existing public transmission systems. VPNs can be created through the use of software or combined software and hardware solutions. This type of network allows an organization to carve out a private WAN on the Internet (or, less commonly over leased lines) that serves only its offices, while keeping the data secure and isolated from other (public) traffic.
- **WAN link** — The line that connects one location on a WAN with another location.
- **X.25** — An analog packet switched WAN technology optimized for long-distance data transmission and standardized by the ITU in the mid-1970s. X.25 can support 56 Kbps throughput. It was originally developed and used for communications between mainframe computers and remote terminals.
- **xDSL** — Term used to refer to all varieties of DSL.

Review Questions

1. Name three networking scenarios that would require a WAN.
2. What do WANs and LANs have in common?
   a. They typically use the same protocols.
   b. They typically use the same transmission media.
   c. They typically have the same throughput needs.
   d. They typically have the same topologies.
3. What kind of public links do most dial-up LAN connections use?
   a. DSL
   b. cable lines
   c. PSTN
   d. T1s
4. What type of ISDN line would a traveling sales representative mostly likely use, and what is the maximum throughput of that line?
   a. PRI, 56 Kbps
   b. PRI, 128 Kbps
   c. BRI, 128 Kbps
   d. BRI, 56 Kbps
5. What is the purpose of ISDN's D channel?
   a. to carry call session information
   b. to carry error-checking information
   c. to enable symmetrical transmission
   d. to enable time division multiplexing

6. Which of the following customers would symmetrical DSL best suit?
   a. a home office user who researches technology on the Web
   b. a convention center that provides multiple businesses with videoconferencing facilities
   c. a car manufacturer that obtains specifications from its quality control team across town
   d. a radiology clinic that uploads real-time images to a hospital across town
7. What kinds of companies are in a race with cable companies to service the high-bandwidth home user market?
8. What advantage does DSL have over cable technology?
   a. It is more secure.
   b. It is more affordable.
   c. It is faster.
   d. Its standards are better defined.
9. What's the difference between T1 and fractional T1?
10. DS1 is the same as T1. True or False?
11. What technique does T1 technology use to transmit multiple signals over a single telephone line?
    a. wave division multiplexing
    b. time division multiplexing
    c. amplitude modulation
    d. frequency modulation
12. One T3 is equivalent to how many T1s?
    a. 3
    b. 9
    c. 18
    d. 28
13. How many 64 Kbps channels does a single T1 circuit carry?
    a. 4
    b. 12
    c. 24
    d. 32
14. Why are SONET networks considered "self-healing"?
15. What is the maximum throughput supported by X.25 technology?
    a. 56 Kbps
    b. 128 Kbps

c. 384 Kbps

d. 1.455 Mbps

16. What do Frame Relay and ATM connections have in common?

a. Both rely on the Internet.

b. Both utilize existing PSTN lines.

c. Both rely on virtual circuits.

d. Both are affordable technologies for small businesses.

17. Which of the following may limit a DSL connection's capacity?

a. the number of different customers who share the connection

b. the distance from the customer to the carrier's POP

c. the existence of more than one copper-wire phone line at the customer's location

d. the distance from the carrier's POP to the ISP

18. Which of the following could be part of a T1 customer's terminal equipment?

a. access server

b. hub

c. multiplexer

d. router

19. ATM cannot link with any other networking technology. True or False?

20. Which of the following advantages does ATM's fixed packet size offer?

a. more efficient transmission

b. lower latency

c. better security

d. better integration with other technologies

21. For which of the following WAN applications is ATM uniquely suited?

a. e-mail

b. Web site hosting

c. videoconferencing

d. print services

22. Which of the following WAN technologies is represented in network diagrams by a cloud?

a. X.25

b. T1

c. SONET

d. ATM

23. Internationally, SONET is known as which of the following?
    a. SNS
    b. SDH
    c. STT
    d. SON
24. Name five factors that you should consider when planning a WAN implementation.
25. Which transmission medium does FDDI use?
    a. twisted-pair copper wiring
    b. coaxial cable
    c. microwave
    d. fiber-optic cable
26. Why might a company choose to implement a VPN?
    a. to lower its WAN transmission costs
    b. to avoid using an ISP
    c. to increase its WAN security
    d. to increase the reliability of its WAN
27. If you are configuring a Windows 95 dial-up connection to an ISP, which of the following details must you get from the ISP?
    a. DHCP server address
    b. SNMP server address
    c. name server address
    d. IP number
28. Dial-Up Networking from Windows 95 will work only with Windows NT Remote Access Service (RAS). True or False?
29. For a user running database queries on her office server from home, what kind of access makes sense?
    a. remote access server connection
    b. remote control
    c. Internet access
    d. VPN access
30. Which of the following is the most popular communications protocol for dial-up networking connections?
    a. SLIP
    b. NCP
    c. LDAP
    d. PPP

Hands-on Projects

For these projects, you will need a Windows 95 computer with a working, configured modem and access to a phone line and an ISP account. If TCP/IP and Dial-Up Networking are not installed on your computer, you may need a Windows 95 installation CD-ROM. You will also need a Web browser, such as Internet Explorer or Netscape, installed on your workstation.

Project 7-1

Because you will probably be both a user and technical supporter of Dial-Up Networking, it is important that you know how to make it work. In addition, you should be familiar with the kinds of configuration errors you might encounter. In this exercise, you will install Dial-Up Networking and change some of its parameters to see what happens.

1. Make sure that TCP/IP is installed on your computer. Install it if it isn't (refer to Chapter 3's Hands-on Projects), and accept all of the default properties.
2. If Dial-Up Networking isn't installed on the computer, install it following the steps outlined earlier in this chapter.
3. Using the parameters specified by your ISP, configure Dial-Up Networking according to the steps outlined earlier in this chapter.
4. Dial into your ISP and log on, making sure you have established a connection and can reach the Internet.
5. Log off from your ISP.
6. In the Dial-Up Networking TCP/IP properties for your ISP connection, change the first name server entry to 10.5.78.129, enter the first name server number in the second name server field, and save your changes. Try dialing your ISP. Can you connect? If not, what kind of error message appears?
7. Log off from your ISP if you were able to make a connection in Step 6. Delete the second name server number in the TCP/IP properties of your Dial-Up Networking connection and save your changes. Try dialing your ISP. Can you connect? If not, what kind of error message appears?
8. Change your ISP connection's Dial-Up Networking properties to their correct values, and save your changes.

PROJECT 7-2

In Chapter 8, you will learn more about Internet networking and, in particular, TCP/IP troubleshooting. One TCP/IP utility, called tracert, allows you to view each node that an Internet connection passes through between your station and the destination you are trying to reach. Even if you aren't troubleshooting a TCP/IP connection, using tracert will help you understand the extent of the Internet's WAN links.

1. While connected to the Internet, click **Start**, then click **Run**. The Run dialog box opens.
2. Type **command** then click **OK**. The MS-DOS Prompt window opens.
3. Type **tracert support.novell.com** at the DOS prompt, then press **Enter**.
4. Watch the route that your packets take between your computer and the host you have identified. How many nodes do they pass? Do they ever time out? Can you see the names of long distance carriers in any of the host names that appear in the route—for example, *mci.net*, *att.net*, or *bbnplanet.net?* Do any of the host names contain acronyms that might give you an idea of what kind of WAN technology the node uses—for example, FDDI or ATM?
5. Try the same exercise with different host names, such as http://www.microsoft.com, http://www.amazon.com, http://www.cisco.com, and http://www.npr.org. Do any of your tracert attempts time out? If so, after how many hops?

PROJECT 7-3

If you are asked to recommend software, hardware, or architecture for WAN links, you will definitely need to know the technologies in greater depth than provided by this chapter. Even if you are not in that position, however, you will benefit from staying current on WAN technology developments. One of the most interesting evolving fields in WAN technology is the competition between DSL and cable modems for the home user market. In this project, you will find out more about the current state of this contest.

1. Connect to your ISP and open a new browser window.
2. Point your browser to http://www.zdnet.com.
3. In the Search field, type **DSL WAN** and press **Enter**.
4. How many articles are returned by this search?
5. Choose one article that appears to pertain to DSL technology today and read it. Write a paragraph summarizing its main points.
6. Point your browser to http://www.techweb.com.
7. In the Search field, type **cable modems** and press **Enter**.
8. Choose one article that appears to pertain to the current status of cable modem technology and read it. Write a paragraph summarizing its main points.

CASE PROJECTS

1. A national, nonprofit organization of small business owners called PERKS is holding two simultaneous conferences: one in an Atlanta convention center and one in a Seattle hotel. Both conferences will include speakers, workshops, and exhibit booths showing off new products. The technical manager for PERKS asks for your help in making sure that everything is in order for the conferences. One requirement is having a small LAN established on the exhibit hall floor that will allow visitors to register their names, addresses, and comments. This information needs to be instantly combined with the same registration database of attendees at both the Atlanta and Seattle conferences. What kind of system do you recommend, and why? What additional information might you want to get from the technical manager before you implement anything?

2. A month before the conferences, the technical manager at PERKS decides to add two more hosting locations: Boston and Chicago. The technical manager also wants the keynote speech, which will be delivered at the Boston conference, to be available at the other locations live on computers in the exhibit areas. The technical manager wants each of the 15 computers in each location to play the videoconference. How does this new development change your recommendation? What kind of cautionary advice might you give the technical manager about what he is attempting?
3. You have made the PERKS technical manager a little concerned. Because it is a nonprofit organization, PERKS doesn't have the money to implement the nationwide videoconference solution you proposed. He had no idea how much it would cost. He suggests simply playing the audio portion of the keynote speech on just two computers in each location. From listening to radio broadcasts on the Web, you know that audio files require at least a 56 Kbps connection—but the more throughput, the better. What kind of solution could you implement now?
4. While the technical manager is out of town at the PERKS conference, he needs to dial from his hotel room to his office's server to pick up his e-mail each night. When he discovers that he can't connect to the server, he calls you for help. The error message he receives says something about not being able to establish a dial-up connection. He uses the Windows 95 operating system. What might you suggest that he check, and where can he find those items?

CHAPTER 8

NETWORK OPERATING SYSTEMS AND WINDOWS NT–BASED NETWORKING

After reading this chapter and completing the exercises, you will be able to:

- Define the requirements and characteristics of a Windows NT network environment
- Describe how a Windows NT server fits into an enterprise-wide network
- Perform a simple Windows NT Server installation
- Manage users, groups, and rights under Windows NT Server
- Understand how Windows NT Server integrates with other network operating systems
- Discuss the elements of a network operating system

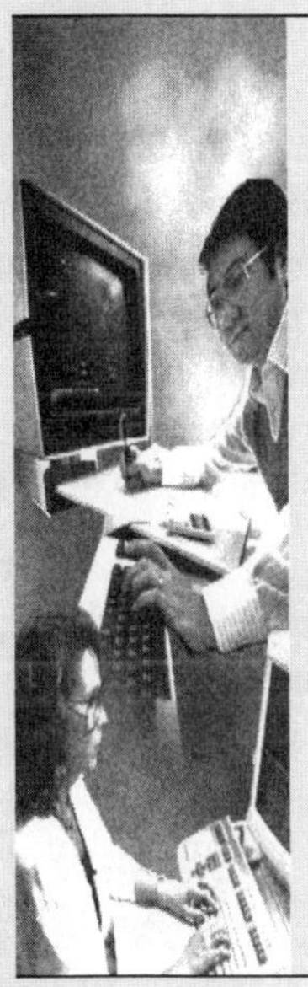

ON THE JOB

In my last job, I was a network administrator for a large electronics manufacturing firm that spanned the globe. The company managed approximately 50,000 workstations for its 60,000 employees and wanted to replace the network operating system it had used for years, LAN Manager. I worked on the committee that helped decide which new network operating system the company should adopt.

One of our significant concerns was scalability. We needed a network operating system that could help us manage the huge volume of users and locations in the company. Windows NT was a natural choice because it allowed us to include as many as 10,000 accounts in each domain, and we could easily organize domains by geography. We also faced the prospect of having redundant user IDs in different locations, which made management of those IDs cumbersome. We wanted to consolidate that management at the company headquarters. Windows NT, with its flexible domain structure, would allow us to accomplish that goal. In addition, we needed a product that would be fully supported by its vendor, unlike LAN Manager. Finally, we needed a network operating system that could support very powerful servers. Windows NT fit the bill because it could support our high-end servers (including the multiple processors we planned to use).

Adam Greissler
New Franklin Investments

Network operating systems enable servers to share file and print functions with clients. They also facilitate other services such as communications, security, and user management. For the most part, network operating systems belong at the uppermost layer of the OSI Model—approximately in the Application layer. Some of their functions, however, occur above the seventh layer (that is, above the top layer) of the OSI Model. In other words, the OSI Model does not usefully describe all aspects of network operating systems.

During your career as a networking professional, you will probably work with more than one network operating system (NOS). At the same time, you may work with several versions of the same network operating system. To qualify for Net+ certification, you must thoroughly understand the inner workings of network operating systems in general. In addition, you must be familiar with the three major network operating systems (Windows NT Server, NetWare, and UNIX) and be able to discuss their similarities and differences. Finally, you must be able to integrate the major operating systems, when necessary.

This chapter introduces the basic concepts related to network operating systems and discusses in detail one of the most popular network operating systems, Windows NT Server. The following two chapters focus on NetWare and UNIX.

INTRODUCTION TO NETWORK OPERATING SYSTEMS

So far you have focused on the foundations of networking—that is, the lower layers of the OSI Model. Specifically, you've learned about the Physical layer up through the middle layers, where protocol addressing, error checking, and session negotiation occur. Now you will tackle the upper layers of the OSI Model, without which you could not control the lower layers.

Some pieces of network operating systems belong to the seventh layer of the OSI Model, the Application layer. This layer allows you to control the transmission of data by taking your requests and translating them into instructions to the lower-layer processes. The pieces of a network operating system that provide the user interface (such as the dialog boxes in Windows NT Server with which you can add users or create groups of users) actually belong *above* the Application layer. Strictly speaking, then, a network operating system does not belong entirely to the Application layer, but rather straddles the Application layer and an eighth layer (which the OSI Model does not address) above the Application layer.

Recall from Chapter 1 that most modern networks are based on a client/server architecture, in which a server enables multiple clients to share resources. Once installed on a server, a network operating system can oversee central data storage, file and print sharing, communications, users and groups, security, and messaging. It may also support many other functions, such as Internet and remote connectivity, network management, and data backup and recovery. Network operating systems are entirely software-based and can run on a number of different hardware platforms and network topologies.

When installing a network operating system, you may accept the default settings or customize your configuration to more closely meet your needs. You may also add special services or enhancements to the basic network operating system. For example, if you install Windows NT Server with only its minimum components, you may later choose to install Internet Information Server (the Microsoft Web server software) to enable your Windows NT server to host Web pages. The components included in each different network operating system and every version of a particular network operating system vary. This variability is just one reason that you should plan your network operating system installation very carefully before beginning the implementation. The myriad ways to install and configure network operating systems are beyond the scope of this book.

In this chapter, the word "server" refers to the hardware on which a network operating system runs. In the field of networking, the word "server" may also refer to an application that runs on this hardware to provide a dedicated service. For example, although you may use a Compaq server as your hardware, you may run the application BorderManager as your proxy server on that hardware.

Although each network operating system discussed in this book supports file and print sharing, plus a host of other services, network operating systems differ in how they achieve those functions, what type of environment they suit, and how they are administered. In the next section, you will learn how to select a network operating system for your network.

SELECTING A NETWORK OPERATING SYSTEM

Realistically, when designing a local area network, you can select from only a handful of network operating systems—specifically, Windows NT Server, NetWare, and UNIX. The only reason not to choose one of these options is if your network is outdated or runs a proprietary, specialized application (for example, a quality control system that measures performance of catalytic converters in a test laboratory) that requires an unusual network operating system (such as Banyan VINES). Many LAN environments include a mix of all three major network operating systems, making interoperability a significant concern.

8

When choosing a network operating system, you should certainly weigh the strengths and weaknesses of the available options before making a choice. Nevertheless, your decision will probably depend largely on the operating systems and applications already running on the LAN. In other words, your choice may be limited by the existing infrastructure. (Infrastructure includes not only other network operating systems, but also LAN topology, protocols, transmission methods, and connectivity hardware.)

For example, suppose that you are the network manager for a community college that uses 150 NetWare 4.11 servers to manage all IDs, security, and file and print sharing for 4000 users. In addition, you oversee five Windows NT servers that provide Web development and backup services. You have been asked to select a network operating system for a new server for the college's Theater department. You probably wouldn't choose Windows NT, because a NetWare server would integrate more seamlessly with your existing network and facilitate administrative tasks, such as adding new users or resources. At another organization, the opposite situation may prevail.

The following list summarizes the questions you should ask when deciding to invest in a network operating system. You need to weigh the importance of each factor in your organization's environment separately. In addition, you should test your network operating system choice in your environment before making a purchase. You can perform such testing on an extra server, using a test group of typical users and applications with specific test criteria in mind. Chapter 16 discusses implementing test (or "pilot") networking systems. Bear in mind that you cannot rely on trade magazine articles or a vendor's marketing information to accurately predict which network operating system will best suit your circumstances.

- Is it compatible with my existing infrastructure?
- Will it provide the security required by my resources?

- Can my technical staff manage it effectively?
- Will my applications run smoothly on it?
- Will it accommodate future growth (that is, is it scalable)?
- Does it support the additional services my users require (for example, remote access, Web site hosting, and messaging)?
- How much does it cost?
- What kind of support can I count on from the vendor?

The importance of these concerns will vary from one network administrator to the next. For example, imagine that you are the network administrator for a multinational chemical company with locations across the globe. Your company's plants and profitability may depend on your network always being available, and your IT budget may be large. In this case, the cost of a network operating system may be less important than its ability to accommodate future growth and the availability of the vendor's technical support. In contrast, if you were the network administrator for a local nonprofit food pantry, your greatest concern may be the cost of the network operating system. In this case, you probably won't care whether the system can easily grow to support hundreds of servers.

Network Operating Systems and Servers

Most networking environments use servers that far exceed the minimum hardware requirements suggested by the software vendor. Every situation will vary, but to determine the optimal hardware for your servers, you should consider the following issues:

- How many clients will connect to the server?
- What kinds of applications will run on the server?
- How much storage space will each user need?
- How much down time is acceptable?
- What can the organization afford?

Perhaps the most important question in this list involves the types of applications to be run by the server. You can purchase an inexpensive, low-end server that runs Windows NT Server adequately, but that will suffice only for file and print sharing. To perform more functions with your network, you would need to invest in a server that can run applications as well. The particular type of server you choose will depend on the applications you want to run. As you can imagine, every application comes with different processor, RAM, and storage requirements. (Consult the application's installation guide for specifics.) In general, you can assume that a database program (such as MS SQL Server) will require more processor and RAM resources than a word-processing application (such as MS Word).

Keep in mind that the particular way an application uses resources may influence your choice of software and hardware. Applications may or may not provide the option of sharing the processing burden between the client and server. For example, you might install a group scheduling and messaging package that requires every client to run executable files from a network drive, thereby almost exclusively using the server's processing resources. Alternatively, you may install the program files on each client workstation and use the server only to distribute messages. The latter solution puts the processing burden on the client.

If your server assumes most of the application processing burden, or if you have a large number of services and clients to support, you will need to add more hardware than the minimum network operating system requirements. For example, you might add multiple processors, as discussed in the next section. You might also install more RAM, multiple NICs, fault-tolerant hard disks, a backup drive, and an uninterruptible power supply. Each of these components will enhance network reliability or performance. (You will learn more about performance and reliability in Chapters 13 and 14.) For now, it suffices to know that you must carefully analyze your current situation and plans for growth before making a hardware purchasing decision. Whereas high-end servers with massive processing and storage resources plus fault-tolerant components can cost as much as $100,000, your department may need only a $2000 server. No matter what your needs, you should ensure that your hardware vendor has a reputation for high quality, dependability, and excellent technical support. Although you may be able to trim your costs on workstation hardware by using generic models, you should spare no expense in purchasing your server. A component failure in a server can cause problems for many people, whereas a workstation problem will probably affect only one person.

MULTIPROCESSING

Some servers and network operating systems can use more than one processor to perform their tasks more quickly. In other words, they may distribute the processing burden among several chips. For example, immediately upon installation, Windows NT Server 4.0 supports the use of four processors; with configuration changes, it can support as many as 32.

The ability to take advantage of several processors at one time is made possible by a technique called **multiprocessing**, which splits tasks among more than one processor to expedite the completion of any single instruction. To understand this concept, think of a busy metropolitan freeway during rush hour. If five lanes are available for traffic, drivers can pick any lane—preferably the fastest lane—to get home as soon as possible. If traffic in one lane slows, drivers may choose another, less congested lane. This ability to move from lane to lane allows all traffic to move faster. If the same amount of traffic had to pass through only one lane, everyone would go slower and get home later. In the same way, multiple processors can handle more instructions more rapidly than a single processor could.

Windows NT Server supports a special type of multiprocessing called **symmetric multiprocessing**, which splits all operations equally among two or more processors. Another type of multiprocessing, **asymmetric multiprocessing**, assigns each subtask to a specific processor. Continuing the freeway analogy, asymmetric multiprocessing would decree that all semi trucks must use the far right lane, all pickup trucks must use the second to the right lane, all compact cars must use the far left lane, and so on. The efficiency of each multiprocessing model is open to debate, but in general symmetric processing completes operations more quickly because the processing load is more evenly distributed.

Multiprocessing offers a great advantage to servers with high CPU utilization—that is, servers that perform numerous tasks simultaneously. If an organization uses its server merely for file and print sharing, however, multiple processors are probably unnecessary. You should carefully assess your processing needs before purchasing a server with multiple processors. Some processing bottlenecks are not actually caused by the processor—but rather by the time it takes to access the server's hard disks or a problem in cabling or a connectivity device. Determining the source of network performance degradation can be an art, and you will learn more about this practice in Chapter 12.

INTRODUCTION TO WINDOWS NT SERVER

Windows NT Server is a popular network operating system known for its intuitive graphical user interface, multitasking capabilities, and compatibility with a huge array of applications. A **Graphical User Interface** (**GUI**; pronounced "gooey") is a pictorial representation of computer functions that, in the case of network operating systems, enables administrators to more easily manage files, users, groups, security, printers, and so on. When Windows NT Server was commercially released in 1993, it was the first network operating system based entirely on a GUI, making network administration easier than ever before. Prior to Windows NT, the only option Microsoft provided for sharing resources between Windows-based workstations was Windows for Workgroups, which employed a peer-to-peer network model.

At the time of this writing, the most recent version of Windows NT was version 4.0. The long-awaited Windows 2000 Server (the next version of Windows NT Server) was still in development, but nearing release. As a consequence, this chapter will focus on Windows NT Server version 4.0.

This chapter gives a broad overview of how Windows NT servers fit into a network environment. It does not attempt to give exhaustive details of the process of installing, maintaining, or optimizing Windows NT networks. For this in-depth knowledge (particularly if you plan to pursue MCSE certification), you should invest in books devoted to Windows NT Server, such as Course Technology's *A Guide to Microsoft NT Server 4.0 in the Enterprise* or *A Guide to Microsoft Windows NT Server 4.0*.

To fully understand Windows NT, you should learn a little about its history. In the late 1980s, Microsoft set out to develop a modular, secure, easy-to-use operating system for shared resources. To achieve the goal of modularity this operating system needed to be built from a series of small programs (in this case, written in the C and C++ languages) that could be easily upgraded, managed, and used with other programs. Once created, the code of this modular operating system would be relatively easy to change, because developers would be able to modify small, discrete parts of the system, rather than one monolithic program.

While developers worked on the first release of Windows NT, Microsoft's Windows 3.0 and 3.1 workstation operating systems won over the desktop market. The Windows desktop GUI became so popular and familiar to users that Microsoft decided to employ the same interface for Windows NT Server 3.0. Today, Windows NT Server 4.0's interface resembles the

Windows 95 operating system interface. In fact, a quick glance may not reveal whether you are looking at a Windows 95 or a Windows NT interface. Figure 8-1 illustrates the similar Windows 95 and Windows NT interfaces. Windows 98 and Windows 2000 Server will also have nearly identical interfaces.

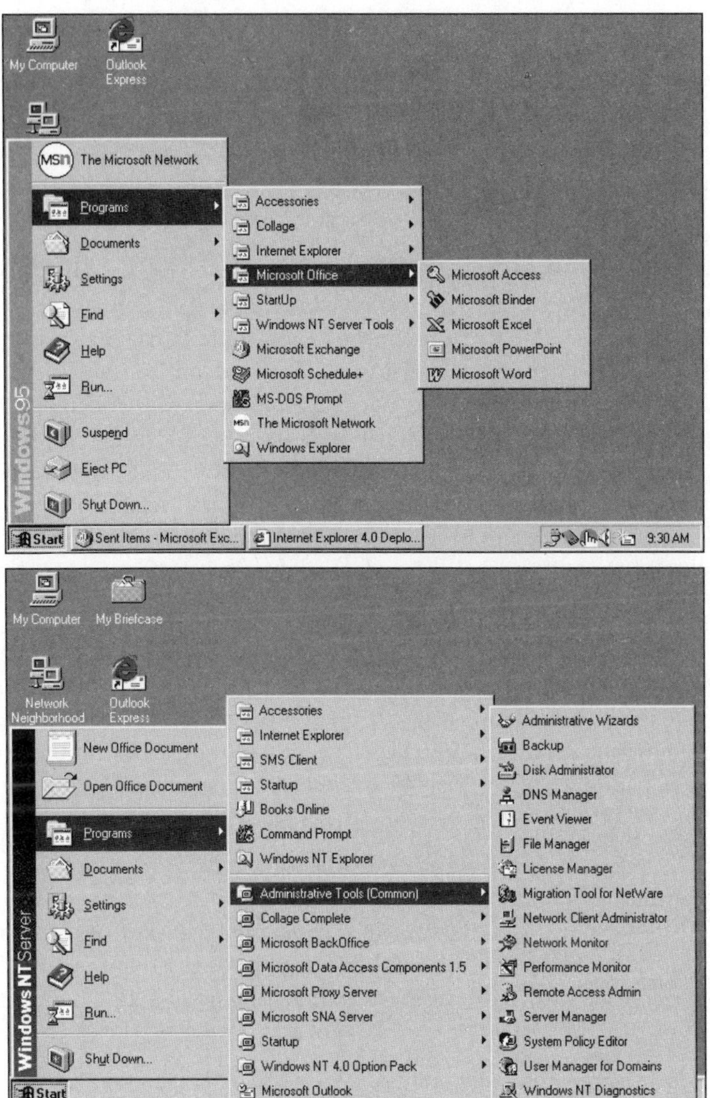

Figure 8-1 Windows 95 interface (top) and Windows NT interface (bottom)

WHY CHOOSE WINDOWS NT SERVER?

Windows NT Server is a popular network operating system because it addresses most of a network administrator's needs very well. Microsoft is, of course, a well-established vendor that leverages its size and influence to ensure that other programs will be compatible with its systems. Its large market share also guarantees that technical support—whether through Microsoft, private developer groups, or third-party newsgroups—will be readily available. If you become MCSE-certified, you will be eligible to receive enhanced support directly from Microsoft. This enhanced support (including a series of CDs) will help you solve problems more quickly and accurately. Because Windows NT is so widely used, you can probably also search newsgroups on the Web and find someone who has encountered and solved a problem like yours.

Windows NT supports any type of topology or protocol that you are likely to run on a LAN. This efficient network operating system takes advantage of multiple processors. Its multitasking capabilities allow server-based processes (for example, retrieving a file, sending a command to a networked printer, or authorizing a user to log on) to share CPU resources. Also, its graphical interface makes Windows NT a simple operating system to administer. Thus technical staff members who are unfamiliar with the system can quickly learn how to perform routine maintenance and operation activities. Windows NT Server also provides excellent security; this feature is highly customizable and easily managed from the server console. In fact, Windows 2000 Server promises to offer significantly enhanced security over that found in version 4.0. Later in this chapter, you will implement file security by assigning resource rights on a Windows NT server.

Despite these assets, Windows NT may not always be the best choice for your network environment. For one thing, network administrators often complain that version 4.0 is not fully scalable. For example, in an enterprise-network that supports many servers, thousands of users, and several geographic locations, Windows NT will require significant administration to optimize it so as to handle resource sharing among multiple servers.

If you have the luxury of designing such a large system from scratch, you may want to consider using a different network operating system. In addition, if your server must run older 16-bit or DOS applications, Windows NT is not a good choice, because it supports only 32-bit programs. Also, Windows NT Server's installation process requires you to know a great deal about your network before you start copying files. This requirement should not concern an experienced network administrator, but it might slow down the installation process for a beginning administrator.

Another potential drawback is that version 4.0 of Windows NT requires you to be physically present at the server console to manage most of its functions. This limitation may pose a minor inconvenience or a major hindrance, depending on the distance between you and your servers. For example, suppose you must help the Marketing department move from the first floor to the third floor of a building that is one of five buildings on the company's campus. The server room resides in the basement of a building on the opposite side of campus. When you enter the Marketing department and start modifying the users' printer settings, you realize that you forgot to give the Marketing group rights to use the third-floor printers. To change these rights, you must run back to the server room (or call a colleague there for help) to do so, unless you have implemented a third-party software solution that is available from every machine (which is unlikely). A more likely scenario is that your feet are sore, the users are in a hurry, and it's five degrees below zero and snowing outside.

Another possible disadvantage to Windows NT Server relates to the fact that any change to the system's configuration requires restarting the server. The restart process takes the server down for at least a matter of minutes; if users are accessing files or using networked printers at that time, they will receive errors. Most client system software can recover well and reconnect automatically when the server restarts, but some users may become confused and call the help desk. Therefore, except in an emergency, you may need to schedule any system changes to a Windows NT server during times when users will not be relying on that server. Some exceptions to this rule exist, which require you to merely stop and start certain processes to activate changes. If you must modify anything in the network operating system, such as the server's IP address, however, you must reboot the machine.

Windows NT Server Hardware

You have learned that servers generally require more processing power, more memory, and more hard disk space than workstation machines do. In addition, servers may contain redundant components for fault tolerance, self-monitoring firmware, multiple processors and NICs, or peripherals other than the common CD-ROM and floppy disk drives. The type of servers you choose for your network will depend partly on your network operating system. As you learned earlier, each network operating system demands specific requirements in terms of server hardware. You can find those requirements on the vendor's Web site or in the installation guide that shipped with the software. Table 8-1 lists Microsoft's minimum server requirements for Windows NT Server 4.0. (Requirements for Windows 2000 Server have not officially been released yet, but are not expected to differ dramatically.)

An important resource for determining what kind of Windows NT hardware to purchase is Microsoft's Hardware Compatibility List. The **Hardware Compatibility List** lists all computer components proven to be compatible with Windows NT Server. The HCL appears on the same CD-ROM as your Windows NT Server software. If you don't find a hardware component on the HCL that shipped with your software, you can look it up on Microsoft's Web site. At the time of this writing, Microsoft's searchable HCL was located at the following Web site: http://www.microsoft.com/isapi/hwtest/hcl.idc. You should always consult this list before buying new hardware. Although hardware that is *not* listed on the HCL may work with Windows NT Server, Microsoft's technical support won't help you solve problems related to such hardware.

Table 8-1 Minimum Hardware Requirements for a Windows NT 4.0 Server

Component	Requirement
Processor	An Intel-compatible 486, Pentium, or RISC-based processor. Out of the box, Windows NT 4.0 can support as many as 4 processors; with additional software, it can support a maximum of 32.
Memory	16 MB RAM (the number should be increased for better performance; 64 MB is recommended).
Hard disk	A hard drive supported by Windows NT (as specified in the HCL), such as an IDE or SCSI, with a minimum of 110 MB free.
NIC	A NIC found on the HCL. More than one NIC can be supported.
CD-ROM	Recommended for all platforms; required for RISC-based processor platforms.
Pointing device	A mouse or other pointing device found on the HCL.
Floppy disk	A 3.5-inch floppy disk drive is required to begin installation of the operating system (and to use emergency floppy disks). Windows NT Server does not support 5.25-inch floppies.

Minimum requirements specify the *least* amount of RAM, hard disk space, and processing power you must have to run the network operating system. Your applications and performance demands, however, may require more resources. Some of the minimum requirements listed in Table 8-1 (for example, the 486 processor) may apply to the smallest test system—not a realistic networking environment. Be sure to calculate the optimal configuration for your network's server based on your environment's needs before you purchase new hardware.

A Closer Look at the Windows NT Operating System

Before you can use the Windows NT Server network operating system, you should understand how it manages its resources (such as files, users, and server memory). This section explains how Windows NT optimizes its use of a server's memory to perform many complex tasks simultaneously. You will learn about the several types of file systems that Windows NT Server can use to allocate space on a server's hard disk. You will also encounter the concept of trust relationships, the means by which multiple Windows NT Servers interconnect to share resources. Finally, you will learn how to use hierarchical structures known as domains to manage multiple Windows NT servers within an organization.

You may be confused about the difference between Windows NT Server and Windows NT Workstation. Windows NT Workstation can act as a central repository for shared resources, but it is not designed to act as a network operating system. For example, Windows NT Workstation can accept only ten simultaneous connections and support only two processors; it does not support redundant hard disks. Its print sharing, Web services, and remote access capabilities are less sophisticated than those of Windows NT Server. In addition, the workstation product doesn't provide interfaces for other operating platforms such as NetWare.

Windows NT Server's Memory Model

Windows NT Server's memory model improves on the old DOS and Windows 3.1 memory model in several ways. First, it uses a 32-bit addressing scheme. To appreciate the advantages of this feature, you may want to review the material on addressing in Chapter 6 (in the discussion of bus-adapter NICs). Essentially, the larger the addressing size, the more efficiently instructions can be processed. The old DOS and Windows 3.1 versions used a 16-bit addressing scheme, half the size of that supported by Windows NT Server 4.0. What's more, Windows 2000 Server will support 64-bit addressing (although many applications will not be able to use this feature immediately).

Another important feature of the Windows NT memory model is that it allows you to install more physical memory on the server, which in turn means that the server can process more instructions faster. The term **physical memory** refers to the chips installed on the computer's system board that provide dedicated memory to that machine. The amount of physical memory required by your server will vary depending on the tasks that it performs. For example, if the Windows NT Server will run applications, Web services, and automatic addressing services, you should install at least 128 MB of physical memory. (When deciding on the appropriate amount of physical memory for your server, remember that the ability to process instructions also depends on processing speed.)

Windows NT Server's memory model also assigns each application (or process) its own 32-bit memory area. This memory area is a logical subdivision of the entire amount of RAM available to the server. Assigning separate areas to processes ensures that the processes become less prone to interfering with each other's operations when they run simultaneously.

Assigning separate memory space to each application is analogous to a company giving each employee a car to commute to work. You can imagine the disadvantage of this approach: It is less efficient than supplying employees with a few commuter vans that can transport ten people to work at the same time. The risk of losing employees to injuries suffered in an accident is less, however, because a commuter van accident affects more employees than an accident involving an individual car driver. Similarly, if each application uses the same memory area, one misbehaving process can take down all applications running in that memory area. On the other hand, if each application uses a separate memory area, each one can harm only itself. As in the car-van scenario, using separate memory spaces for each application is less efficient.

Another way that Windows NT manages memory is through virtual memory—a concept you've probably encountered when working with Windows 95. **Virtual memory** is memory that is logically carved out of space on the hard disk (as opposed to physical memory).

When the currently running programs and processes require more memory than RAM can provide, they can take advantage of virtual memory.

Virtual memory is both a blessing and a curse. On the one hand, if you have extra hard disk space, you can use virtual memory to easily expand the memory available to server applications. This ability is a great advantage when a process temporarily needs more memory than the physical memory can provide. Virtual memory requires no user or administrator intervention and is accessed without the clients' knowledge. As a network administrator, you can define the amount of hard disk space available for virtual memory. On the other hand, using virtual memory slows operations, because accessing a hard disk takes longer than accessing physical memory.

Keep in mind that an excessive reliance on virtual memory will cost you in terms of performance. To find out how much virtual memory your Windows NT server uses, open the Control Panel, double-click the System icon, click the Performance tab, then click the Change button. The Virtual Memory dialog box will appear, as pictured in Figure 8-2. If you suspect that your server's processing is being degraded because it relies on virtual memory too often, you should invest in additional physical memory (RAM).

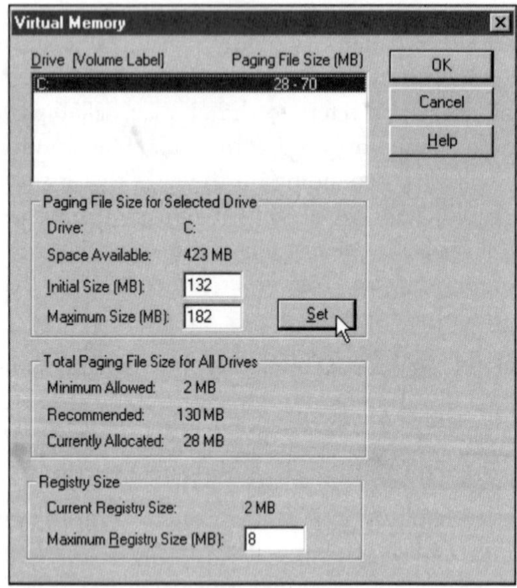

Figure 8-2 Configuring virtual memory

FILE SYSTEMS

The term **file system** refers to an operating system's method of organizing, managing, and accessing its files through logical structures and software routines. Windows NT Server supports the following file systems: HPFS, FAT, NTFS, and CDFS. Each of these file systems is briefly described in the following. You should be familiar with these file systems so as to properly install and manage a Windows NT server.

Before installing Windows NT Server, you should decide which file system (or systems) you will use. In general, you need to worry about only the FAT and NTFS file systems, because HPFS is not native to Windows NT and CDFS is installed automatically. Typically, you will use NTFS unless it is incompatible with your specific server applications. (Later in this chapter, you will have the opportunity to plan and execute a Windows NT server installation.)

You will also need to know which file systems are compatible with each other. The file system type affects issues such as file access, speed, compression, defragmentation, and security. If you completed coursework for the A+ certification, you should already be familiar with the file systems discussed in the following sections.

CDFS (CD-ROM File System)

The **CDFS (CD-ROM File System)** is the read-only file system used to access resources on a CD-ROM disk. (The term *read-only* refers to the fact that CDFS enables you to read from a CD-ROM, but not write to it.) Windows NT supports CDFS so as to allow CD-ROM file sharing. As noted earlier, no intervention is necessary to install or configure the CDFS. Because a CD-ROM is read-only, you cannot assign specific permissions to files through CDFS. You can, however, assign sharing rights to the CD-ROM resource.

FAT (File Allocation Table)

FAT (File Allocation Table) is the original PC file system that was designed in the 1970s to support floppy disks and, later, hard disks. To understand FAT, you must first understand the distribution of data on a disk. Disks are divided into allocation units (also known as clusters). Each allocation unit represents a small portion of the disk's space; depending on your operating system, the allocation unit's size may or may not be customizable. A number of allocation units combine to form a partition. The FAT, a hidden file positioned at the beginning of a partition, keeps track of used and unused allocation units on that partition. The FAT also contains information about the files within each directory, as well as the size of files, their names, and the times that they were created and updated.

When part of a disk uses the FAT method of tracking files, that portion of the disk is called a "FAT partition."

Although FAT has been improved since its introduction, it remains inadequate for most server operating systems because of its partition size limitations, naming limitations, and fragmentation and speed issues. Windows NT Server supports FAT so that one machine can start with either Windows NT or DOS/Windows 3.1. FAT's most significant characteristics include the following:

- A FAT partition or file cannot exceed 4 GB.
- FAT uses 16-bit fields to store file size information.
- FAT (without additional utilities) supports only filenames with a maximum of eight characters in the name and three characters in the extension.

- FAT categorizes files on a disk as Read (a user can read the file), Write (a user can modify or create the file), System (only the operating system can read or write the file), or Hidden (a user cannot see the file on the drive without explicitly searching for hidden files). These identifications constitute file attributes.
- Directories and files on a FAT drive cannot use Windows NT's security.
- A FAT drive stores data in noncontiguous blocks and uses links between fragments to maintain data integrity. This approach is unreliable and inefficient, and it may cause corruption.
- You can convert a FAT drive into an NTFS drive on a Windows NT server, but you cannot convert an NTFS drive into a FAT drive.
- Because of FAT's low overhead, it can write data to a hard disk very quickly.

In general, when given the choice to format a Windows NT server disk as FAT or NTFS, you should choose NTFS because of its better reliability and security. FAT, on the other hand, often is an advantage in that it can be accessed by either HPFS or NTFS partitions.

FAT32

The original FAT file system was enhanced in the mid-1990s to accommodate long filenames and permit faster data access via 32-bit addressing. This version of FAT, called **FAT32**, retains some features of the original FAT, but reduces the maximum size limit on allocation units so that space on a disk is used more efficiently. In some cases, FAT32 can conserve as much as 15% of the space that would be required for the same number of files on a traditional FAT partition. FAT32 can also support larger partitions than FAT (a maximum of 2 terabytes) that can easily be resized without damaging data.

Although FAT32 improves upon the original FAT file system and typically appears on Windows 95 and Windows 98 workstations, it is not optimal for Windows NT servers. Instead, the NTFS file system (explained later) is preferred because it enables a network administrator to take advantage of Windows NT's security and file compression enhancements.

HPFS (High-Performance File System)

HPFS (High-Performance File System) is a file system designed for the OS/2 operating system that offers greater efficiency and reliability than FAT. HPFS organizes data in contiguous blocks, allows data to wait in memory if the processor is too busy to accept it, and assigns information about other data on the disk to each block of data. Collectively, all of these measures enhance HPFS's speed. HPFS also supports extended attributes. In this context, the term **extended attributes** refers to the attributes beyond the basic Read, Write, System, and Hidden attributes supported by FAT. For example, HPFS provides information about file history, the application to which the file belongs, executable code, icons, and files that depend on other files. Because it uses 32-bit fields to store file size information, HPFS can handle larger disk sizes than FAT can. HPFS also supports long filenames.

Despite the many advantages offered by HPFS, you will rarely find it installed on a Windows NT server. One reason is that Windows NT Server versions before 4.0 did not support this file system. Another reason is that HPFS is incompatible with some systems used internationally. Lastly, NTFS provides better security and reliability than HPFS. You would probably want to use HPFS on a Windows NT server only if your server had to start with dual network operating systems or otherwise interact with an OS/2 server.

NTFS (New Technology File System)

Microsoft developed **NTFS (New Technology File System)** expressly for Windows NT Workstation and Windows NT Server. NTFS integrates reliability, compression, the ability to handle massive files, and fast access. You should use NTFS as your file system on all Windows NT servers unless: (1) your server must start with two operating systems, or (2) one of your applications cannot use NTFS. Although you can convert a FAT partition to NTFS after the initial Windows NT Server installation, you should avoid this time-consuming process. To better manage Windows NT Server, familiarize yourself with the following NTFS features:

- NTFS filenames can be a maximum of 256 characters long.
- NTFS stores file size information in 64-bit fields.
- NTFS files or partitions can theoretically be as large as 16 exabytes, (2^{64} bytes).
- NTFS is required for Macintosh connectivity.
- NTFS incorporates sophisticated, customizable compression routines. These compression routines reduce the space taken by files by as much as 40%. A 10 GB database file, for example, could be squeezed into 6 GB of disk space.
- NTFS keeps a log of file system activity to facilitate recovery if a system crash occurs.

One drawback to using an NTFS partition is that it cannot be read by FAT or HPFS partitions (unless you employ a third-party utility). If you plan to specialize in Windows NT–based networks, you should research NTFS and experiment with it on a test server. Doing so will give you a basis for understanding and better maintaining Windows NT servers.

Windows NT Domains

With the release of Windows NT, Microsoft introduced the concept of domains. A **domain** is simply a group of users, servers, and other resources that share account and security information. For example, at a large consulting firm, the Software department might have its own domain, Accounting might belong to another domain, and Marketing to a third domain. Domains are established on a network to facilitate the organization and management of resources and security. The optimum number and structure of domains in a particular organization depend on the organization's needs. For instance, a small, locally based graphics design firm might require only one domain; on the other hand, a large, multinational import/export company might require hundreds of domains. Multiple domains can be organized into several different types of hierarchies, or models. (The various types of domain models are discussed later in this chapter.)

When you install Windows NT Server, you create a domain by assigning a domain controller—the server that keeps track of resources, users, and privileges within a domain—and then assigning resources to that domain. A network that uses multiple Windows NT servers will probably have more than one domain controller, including one that acts as the primary domain controller and at least one that acts as a backup domain controller (see the next section for details).

You will learn more about planning and creating domains later in this section. It's important to plan domains carefully before setting up a Windows NT–based network. Making changes to an existing domain's organization may be time-consuming and confusing—and sometimes even impossible. For example, you cannot change domain names or move a domain controller without reinstalling the entire Windows NT network operating system.

The domain names used in the context of organizing Windows NT servers are entirely different from the domain names used in the context of TCP/IP networking. Chapter 3 introduced TCP/IP features, and you will learn more about TCP/IP domain names in Chapter 11.

Elements of a Domain

Every domain relies on a **primary domain controller (PDC)** to centrally manage its account information and security. Only one PDC can exist for each domain. If the PDC fails, you must rely on a **backup domain controller (BDC)** to assume the management responsibilities. A BDC can also provide authentication of users logging in to the domain. Any number of BDCs per domain is permissible, but you should make sure to have at least one. Because the BDC must be able to read and write to the PDC, you should create a BDC server and add it to the network only after the PDC is running correctly. If the PDC goes down for a significant period of time, the network administrator can promote the BDC to take over the PDC's functions. **Promote** is a Microsoft term that simply means to grant a higher authority to a server.

When the original PDC recovers from a failure, you must demote it to a BDC before it can become part of the domain again. You manage promotion and demotion of domain controllers via the Server Manager's graphical interface. (To open the Server Manager, click Start, click Programs, click Administrative Tools (Common), then click Server Manager.)

Any number of member servers may also belong to a Windows NT domain. A **member server (MS)** is a server that takes no responsibility for managing accounts or security. It is usually devoted to running a particular application, such as MS SQL Server, that requires dedicated processing resources. Using member servers for applications leaves the domain controllers free to "handle account management."

A server in a Windows NT domain must be either a PDC, BDC, or MS; all of these designations are assigned when you install the Windows NT Server operating system. In the next section, you will learn about strategies for combining these three kinds of servers with a single domain.

Trust Relationships

A **trust relationship** (or simply **trust**) is a relationship between domains that makes it possible for users in one domain to access resources in another domain. The domain that grants access to its resources is known as the trusting domain. The domain that accesses the resources is known as the trusted domain. As illustrated in Figure 8-3, a **one-way domain trust relationship** is established when domain A allows the users in domain B to access its resources.

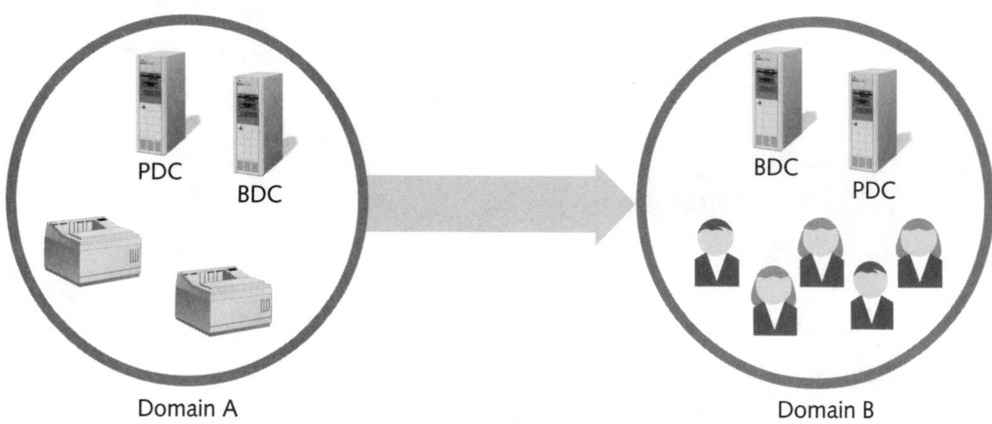

Figure 8-3 One-way domain trust relationship

In a one-way trust relationship, the domain with the resources to share trusts the domain with the users who want to access those resources—not the other way around. An analogous situation would be a man with a fancy sports car, and neighbors who want to borrow the car. Before he would hand over the keys, the car's owner would want to establish a trusting relationship with his neighbors, so he could be sure that they would handle his car safely and return it unharmed. In this case, the man is domain A (the domain with the resource to share), the neighbors are domain B (the domain with users who want to access the resource), and the sports car is the resource.

Networks often make use of several one-way trust relationships. You might use a number of one-way domain trust relationships if you have, for example, one domain for the Internal Auditing department, plus separate domains for Finance, IT, Sales, and Research. In this situation, the Internal Auditing domain would need to access accounting and contract information on servers located in the Finance, IT, Sales, and Research domains. For security reasons, these four domains should not be allowed to access Internal Auditing's domain. In this situation, you would establish several one-way trusts: between Finance and Internal Auditing, between IT and Internal Auditing, between Sales and Internal Auditing, and, between Research and Internal Auditing. Figure 8-4 illustrates this situation.

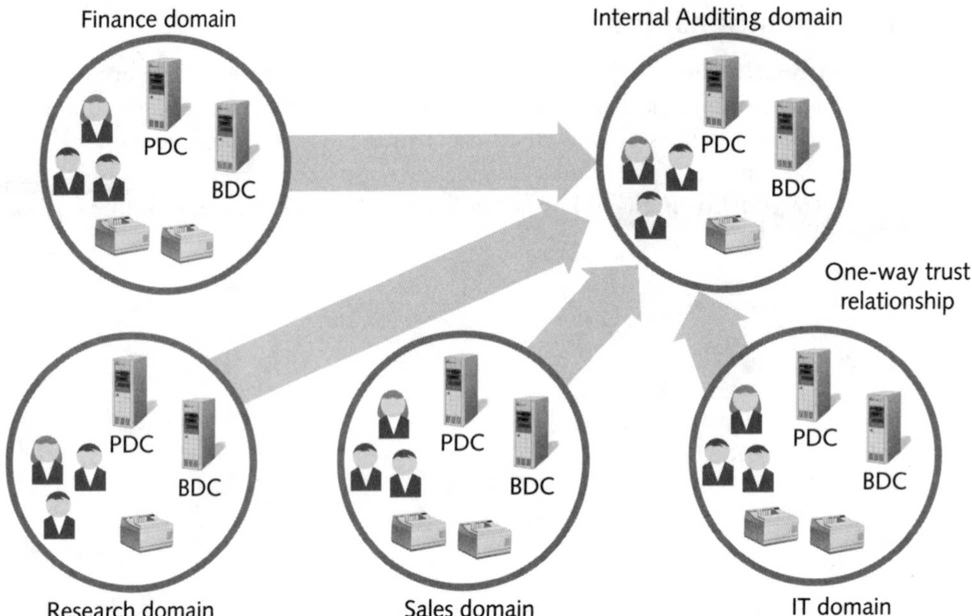

Figure 8-4 Multiple one-way domain trust relationships

If users from domain B should be able to access resources on domain A, and users from domain A should be able to access resources from domain B, you need to establish a **two-way domain trust relationship**, as shown in Figure 8-5. Two-way domain trust relationships are common in WAN situations where two or more locations manage their own domains, but need to share information. For example, a national insurance company might have its headquarters in Reno and maintain regional offices in Portland and Denver. To share information among these three offices, you would need to create two-way domain trust relationships between Reno and Denver, between Reno and Portland, and between Portland and Denver. The complete trust domain model relies on two-way domain trust relationships between every domain on the network.

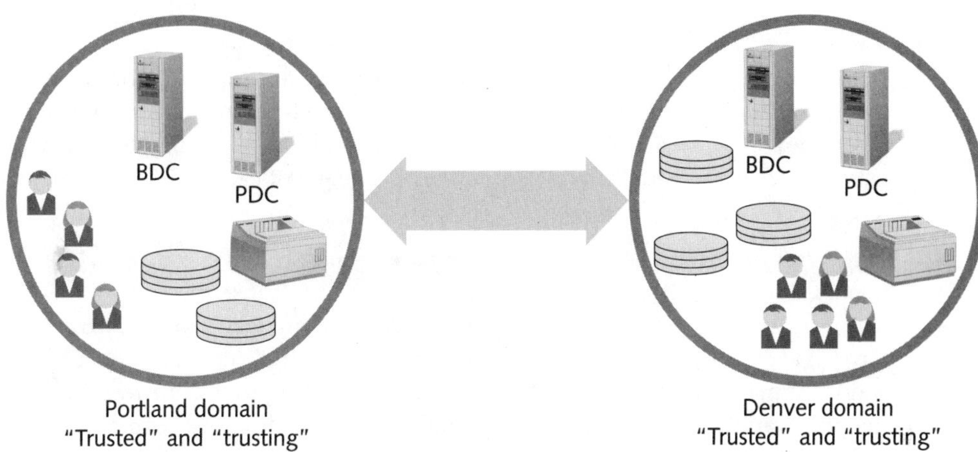

Figure 8-5 A two-way domain trust relationship

Even though trust relationships exist between domains, users and groups within those domains must still be assigned permissions on trusted servers. You assign user and group permissions only after you create trust relationships between servers. For example, if Sally Chen belongs to domain A and can access domain B, it does not automatically mean that she can open a spreadsheet located on domain B's BDC. Without the trust relationship, however, domain B wouldn't even recognize Sally. Note that the need to assign permissions applies to both one-way and two-way domain trust relationships.

To configure trust relationships, you need at least two domains. In addition, you must have administrator rights to the domains. (That is, you must log on to the server either as "Administrator" or an equivalent ID that has rights to modify any parameter associated with the server.) To alter the trust relationships for a particular domain, click **Start**, point to **Programs**, point to **Administrative Tools**, then click **User Manager for Domains**. In the **User Manager for Domains** dialog box, click **Policies** on the menu bar, then click **Trust Relationships**. The Trust Relationship dialog box opens, allowing you to add or remove trust relationships between domains.

Trust relationships can be broken after they have been established. Bear in mind, however, that users may rely on the resources from another domain. Before you remove trust relationships, make sure that no users depend on them. For example, you might have established a trust relationship between the domains of the Accounting and the Internal Auditing departments. The senior accountant, who belongs to the IT domain, may need to edit spreadsheets on the Internal Auditing domain's PDC before closing the books at the end of the fiscal year. If you break the trust relationship between these two domains, the accountant will not be able to access the Internal Auditing department's server—much less modify or create spreadsheet files on that server.

Domain Models

Before you can successfully implement one or more domains in your Windows NT network, you need to understand the suggested methods for organizing domains. Microsoft recommends using one of four domain models: single, master, multiple master, or complete trust. The characteristics, advantages, and disadvantages of each domain model are described in this section.

The **single domain model** is the simplest Windows NT domain model. As its name implies, a single domain model consists of one domain that services every user and resource in an organization. It suits small organizations with few security concerns. For example, a travel agency with six agents in one office might use a single domain model to connect users and share printers. A single Windows NT domain can support as many as 26,000 users, but the practical user limit will depend on the kinds of applications required by the users, the amount of storage space those users require, the frequency with which users access the server, the server's hardware, and other factors. Figure 8-6 illustrates a single domain model.

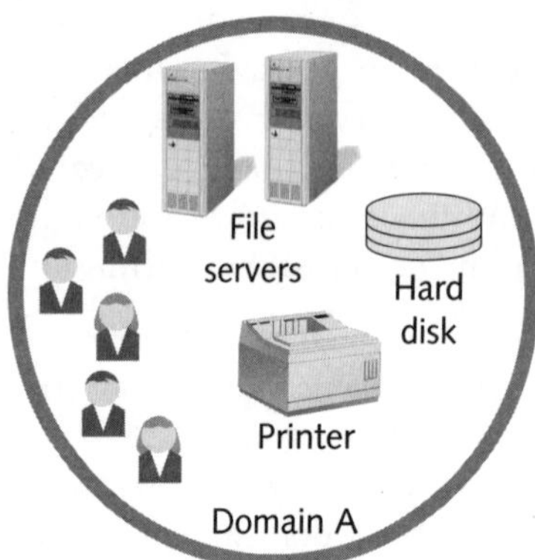

Figure 8-6 A single domain model

The **master domain model** uses a single domain to exert control over user account information, plus separate resource domains to manage resources such as networked printers. This model suits an environment where each department in an organization controls its file and print sharing and a central information technology department manages the user IDs, groups, and relationships between the domains, as shown in Figure 8-7. This arrangement provides a mix of centralized and decentralized control and more flexibility than a single domain model. It also allows resources to be separated by logical group. For instance, a color printer in Advertising might not be available to accountants in Finance, even though Finance and Advertising users log into the same domain. A master domain model can support a maximum of 30,000 users. The actual number supported will depend on the number of servers in the domains and the type of hardware used.

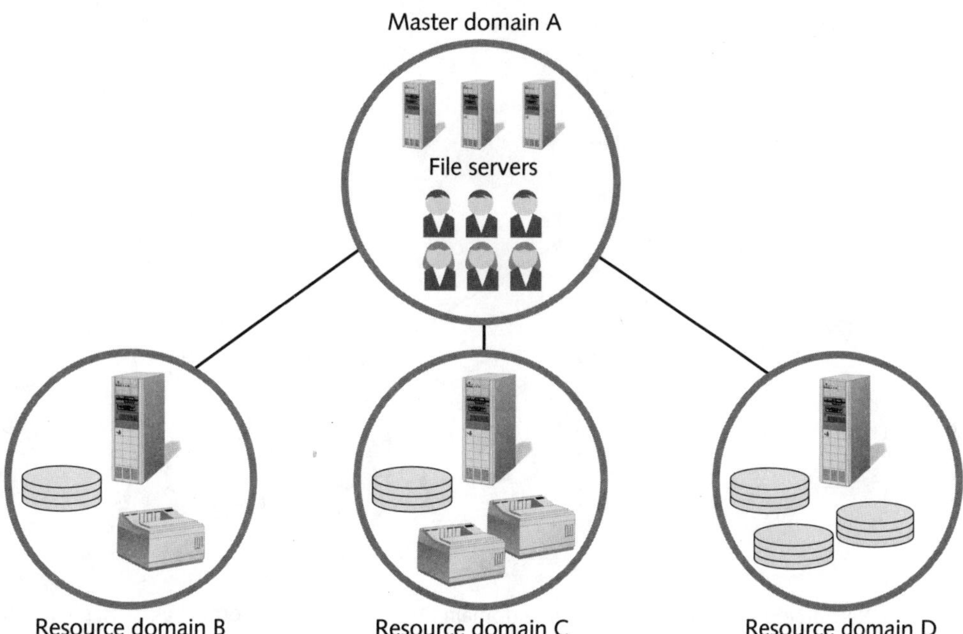

Figure 8-7 A master domain model

The third domain model, the **multiple master domain model**, uses two or more master domains that are joined in two-way trusts to manage many resource domains. As in the master domain model, resource domains consist of separate resources (such as printers) and must have one-way trusts with the master domains. Users in a multiple master domain model can log on to a single master domain and use resources from several different resource domains.

A multiple master domain provides the option of centrally managing all user IDs, groups, and account information, but also allows decentralized administration. In other words, if desired, each separate department could manage its users' access to resource domains from a separate master domain. In addition, a multiple master domain allows users to log in from anywhere on the network, whether on the LAN or on a WAN node. This feature makes resources available to remote users. The multiple master domain model also provides greater redundancy than the previous models because BDCs may be distributed among many different sites on LANs or WANs, thus maintaining account information in several places. The multiple master domain model theoretically supports more than 40,000 users. Figure 8-8 depicts a multiple master domain model.

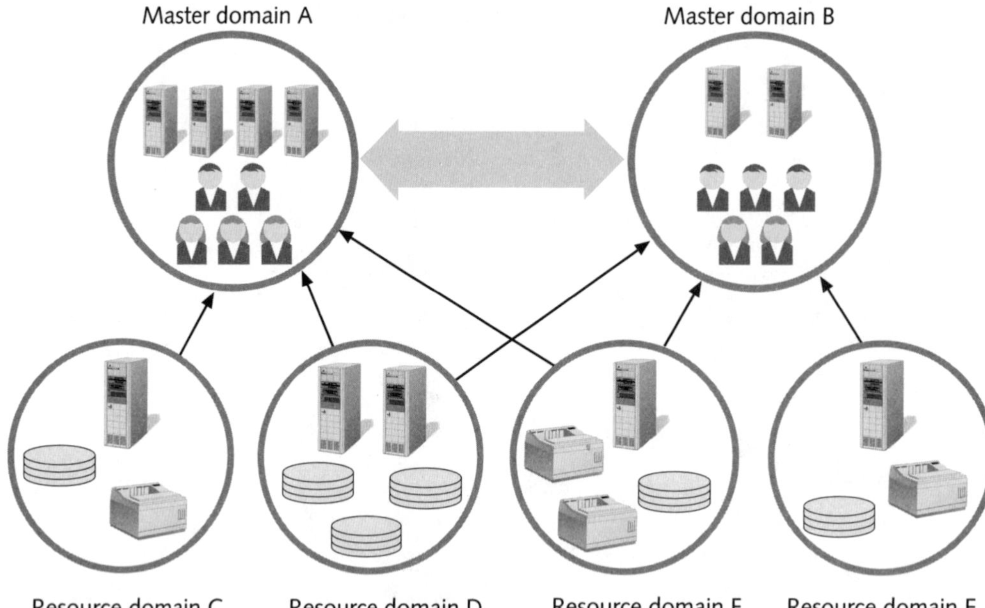

Figure 8-8 A multiple master domain model

The **complete trust domain model** differs from the master domain models in that its administration is completely decentralized. Each domain in this model manages its own user, group, account, and file and print sharing information. To enable domains to communicate with each other, two-way trusts must be established between all domains in the complete trust domain model, as depicted in Figure 8-9. Because each trust relationship requires some configuration and maintenance, this type of model increases the burden on the network administrator. With only 4 domains, 12 trust relationships must be configured. With 12 domains, the number of trust relationships jumps to 132. Use of this model also increases traffic on the network, because each trust relationship generates data-sharing traffic between servers. Nevertheless, companies that have merged or organizations that don't have a clear plan for centralized administration may find this model useful.

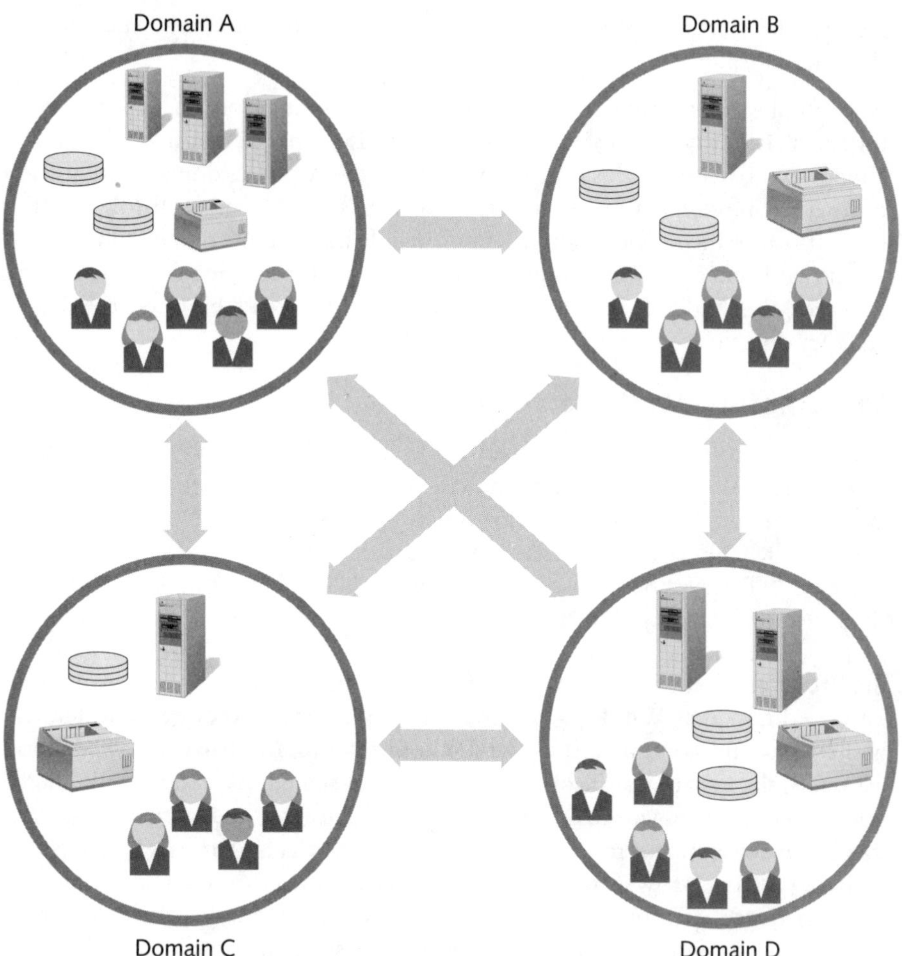

Figure 8-9 A complete trust domain model

The domain model you select will depend on the division of your organization (either by function or geographically), the existing infrastructure, the number of users you support, the site of network administration, and possibly, political pressures from management. One approach to domain building is to assign a domain to each geographical location. Another approach is to create separate domains for each department in a company. If the organization is a small business (fewer than 20 people) a single domain is appropriate. On the other hand, if the organization includes tens of thousands of users, multiple domains will improve performance and ease administration burdens.

In any case, carefully planning your domain structure is essential before you attempt to implement it. Switching an existing network from one domain model to another will require a reevaluation of all trust relationships between domains, including a determination of how users depend on those relationships so as to access resources. Switching domain models can disrupt productivity if vital trust relationships are broken in the process and will undoubtedly create more work for the network administrator, who must fix and attend to all the modifications.

For example, suppose an organization has an Accounting domain that includes servers that store financial information about the company. Also, suppose that since the installation of the Windows NT network, this domain has trusted the Auditing domain. Auditors who belong to the Auditing domain regularly access financial spreadsheets on the Accounting domain's server. If you, as the network administrator, decide that you need to eliminate the Accounting domain and move the Accounting servers into the Operations domain, you risk breaking access for the Auditors that have long relied on the trust between the Accounting and Auditing domains.

Coordinating Multiple Servers

In the previous section, you learned about the different ways in which servers can be arranged in a Windows NT environment. This section provides an overview of how you coordinate multiple servers. Its goal is simply to introduce some basic concepts. If you plan to pursue MCSE certification, however, you will want to invest in a book devoted to Windows NT Server, because questions about domains and trust relationships will appear on MCSE exams. Planning domains and trusts can take a long time to master.

The Browser One important part of any network operating system is the ability to manage shared resources. Windows NT uses a browser service to discover all shared devices on the network and compile a database of those resources. A **browser** is network computer that tracks the location, availability, and identity of shared devices. Several kinds of browsers exist, including a domain master browser, master browser, and backup browser. A **domain master browser** tracks resources for a group of domains. A **master browser** maintains a database (called a **browse list**) of shared resources for its domain. Every time a computer on the network starts, it registers itself with the master browser. In an environment containing two or more domains, each master browser will pass along its browse list to the domain master browser. A **backup browser** keeps a copy of the master browser's browse list in case the master browser goes down. Although every server on a Windows NT network has the potential to act as a browser, by default the PDC is the master browser for its domain. Any BDC, member server, or even Windows NT workstation in the domain can be designated as a backup browser.

The configuration of a browser service should reflect the organization of the network. In a master domain model, for example, the PDC for all domains would be the master domain browser, the BDCs within each domain would serve as master browsers for their domain, and a workstation or member server within each domain would act as a backup browser. Figure 8-10 depicts this logical configuration for a master domain model network.

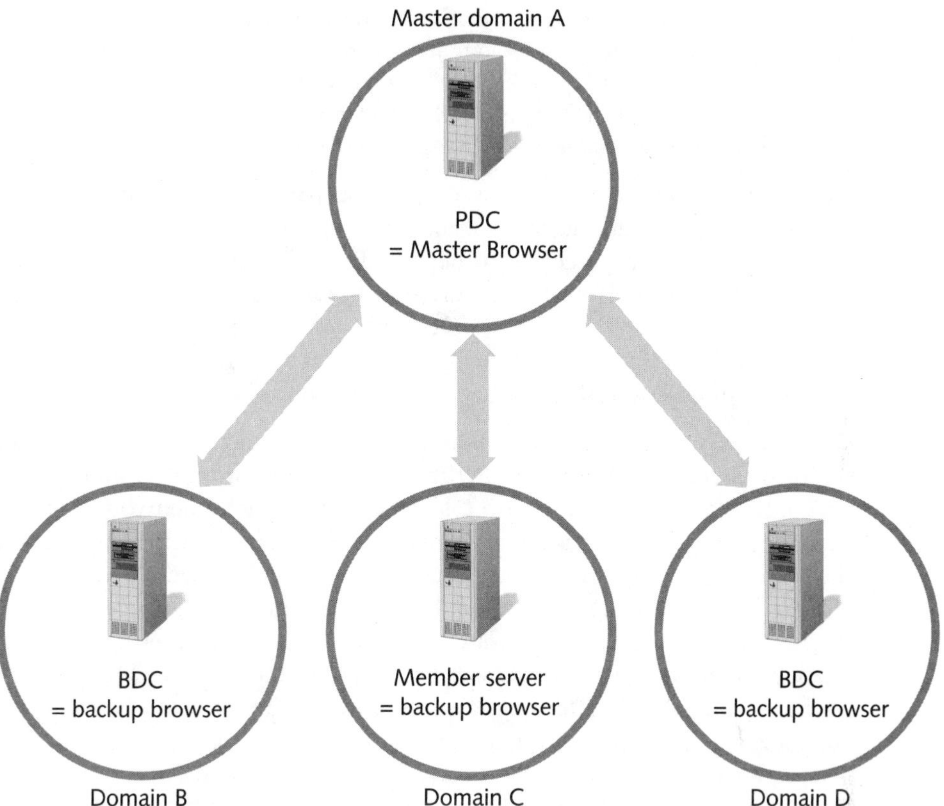

Figure 8-10 Browsers in a master domain model network

Synchronization To keep all computers apprised of current user information on the network, servers must synchronize their user account databases. In **synchronization**, a PDC informs its BDCs that they should request updated user account information. Upon receiving this order, each BDC checks its information against the information held by the PDC. If the BDC detects that its information is outdated, it requests that the PDC send the latest updates, which might include new or changed user passwords, new group memberships, and new or changed user or group IDs. If the BDC and PDC have the same, current information, no information is sent, thereby keeping synchronization traffic to a minimum.

On a large network with several BDCs and frequent administrative changes, synchronization could potentially degrade network performance. To minimize its effect, Windows NT staggers the synchronization requests from the PDC to each BDC. In addition, a network administrator may force synchronization by choosing Server Manager from the Administrative Tools menu on either a PDC or BDC and then selecting one of the synchronize options. You may also customize the synchronization interval by changing parameters in the Windows NT Registry.

You should never edit the Windows NT Registry without fully understanding what kind of changes you plan to make and how to accomplish those changes successfully. Changing the Registry improperly can damage your server's ability to function. Even if you know what you're doing, you should back up the Registry before you make any changes.

Two types of forced synchronizations are possible: partial and full. In a **partial synchronization**, only modifications to user account information are transmitted to the other domain controllers in a domain. In other words, the PDC and BDC look for discrepancies in their databases and resolve them. A **full synchronization** causes the entire user account database to be copied to a BDC. Full synchronization can consume significant bandwidth on the network, depending on the size of the user account database (some can be as large as 40 MB) and the number of domain controllers to be synchronized.

You might wonder why it's ever necessary to force synchronization if the domain controllers synchronize regularly and automatically. Imagine that a user from Accounting complains that he can't access the SQL database you told him he could use when you established his user ID a week ago. This occasion is the first time he's tried to get information from the database, and he needs a payroll report from the database immediately. You discover that you forgot to give him rights to access the database on the server and make the change quickly. Unless you synchronize those changes throughout the domain, however, the user may have to wait until automatic synchronization occurs before he can access the database. Most likely, he'll try to access the database shortly after calling you and will be upset when he still can't get in. In this instance, you should force partial synchronization.

Elections How does a master browser maintain all account information for a domain? You have already learned that each workstation on a network registers itself with the master browser when it logs on to the network. The master browser records that information and synchronizes it with the backup and domain master browsers. If the browsers cannot synchronize the information, or if the clients can't find the master browser, a browser election will take place.

As its name implies, a **browser election** is a vote between computers to determine which one will take responsibility for maintaining the master browse list. An election takes place when a computer that can't find a master browser sends out a broadcast to identify a new master browser. Other computers then respond with their qualifications to become that browser. As in poker, where a king takes precedence over a jack, different types of computers rank higher than others in the browser election. A backup browser takes precedence over a computer that has no current browser role. A Windows NT server takes precedence over a Windows NT workstation. To make sure that a particular machine wins the election, you can "stack the deck" by editing the Windows NT Registry on that computer to identify it as the chosen master browser.

Installing and Configuring a Windows NT Server

The important thing to remember about installing and configuring a network operating system is that before you insert the installation CD, you should have a plan for your server and its place in your network. You need to consider many factors, including organizational structure, server function, applications, number of users, LAN architecture, and optional services (such as remote access) when developing this plan. Once you have installed and configured the network operating system, changing its configuration may prove difficult and cause service disruptions for users. In this section, you will learn about the available options and the decisions you must make when installing and configuring your Windows NT server.

Planning for Installation

The importance of planning for installation cannot be overemphasized. Any seasoned network administrator can probably tell a story about a server operating system installation for which he or she should have prepared better. Poor planning results in more work for the installer, potential down time for users, and headaches for whomever supports the server after installation. The following list summarizes the most critical preinstallation decisions.

- *Will the server be a PDC, BDC, or member (standalone) server?* The server's security role will depend on your overall plan for the organization. If a PDC already exists in a domain, the new server shouldn't be a PDC. If one or more BDCs also exist in the domain, perhaps you shouldn't make the new server a domain controller at all. If the new server will exclusively serve processing-intensive applications to users, you should install it as a member server.

Do not attempt to install a new server as a domain controller when the PDC is down or offline. Doing so will prevent the original PDC from resuming its role once it comes back online.

- *To which domain will the server belong?* Domain names should describe the logical group of servers and users they support. You may use any name including a maximum of 15 alphanumeric characters, but not the following characters into the names: > < [ ] : ; | = , + * " ? Popular schemes for naming domains incorporate geography and function into the names. For example, in a master domain model over WAN links, you might want to name your domains Boston, Chicago, Detroit, Pittsburgh, and so on. In a very large organization, you may want to use a less limiting convention. For example, if your company's business is agricultural genetic engineering, you might want to name your domains Wheat, Corn, Alfalfa, Rice, and so on.

- *What will the server's name be?* You may use any name including a maximum of 15 characters, but not the following characters: > < [ ] : ; | = , + * " ? Choose a practical, descriptive name that distinguishes the server from others. For example, you might use geographical server names, such as Boston or Chicago.

Alternatively, you might name servers according to their function, such as Marketing or Research. If the server is a member of a large domain, you might identify it in relationship to its domain name. For example, the Marketing server in the Pittsburgh domain might be called Pitts_Mktg.

- *How many and what kinds of network adapter cards will the server use?* Before you begin installing Windows NT Server, you should have driver and diagnostics disks on hand for the server's NICs. Also, keep in mind that NIC configuration in Windows NT is trickier than the corresponding process in Windows 95. With the release of Windows 2000 Server, Microsoft promises to include plug-and-play support for devices such as NICs; currently, however, you must configure those devices yourself. For best results, use the configuration and diagnostics programs provided by the NIC manufacturer to establish the NIC's IRQ, shared memory address, and I/O base address before beginning the Windows NT Server installation.
- *Which protocols and network services should the server use?* You need to know which protocols your network requires. Recall from Chapter 3 that an increasing number of networks are moving toward TCP/IP-based transmission because it is flexible, reliable, and widely supported. If your server runs Web services or requires connectivity with UNIX systems, you must install TCP/IP. Even if your server doesn't, you should probably install TCP/IP. Install NetBEUI on your Windows NT server only if you need to communicate with computers running Windows for Workgroups. If your Windows NT server must communicate with a NetWare server, you should also install the NWLink IPX/SPX Compatible Protocol and Gateway Services for NetWare.
- *What kind of disk controllers does my server have?* During the setup process, you will be asked to identify the type of CD-ROM, SCSI, and hard disk controllers required by your server. You may choose to let Windows NT autodetect your hardware and accept the drivers it finds or you may make specific choices from a list of hardware to identify your controllers. Either way, you should know what kind of disk controllers are present on your server (you can find this information in the server's hardware specifications). The Windows NT installation process does not always choose the correct controller by default, and selecting the wrong controller may cause the system to crash.
- *How many, how large, and what kind of partitions will the server require?* Recall from the discussion about Windows NT file systems that the optimal file system for a Windows NT server is NTFS. Choose NTFS unless your system starts with dual operating systems or its applications require a different file system. A simple method of setting partition size is to make the disk into one large partition during installation, then modify partition sizes after installation. Using the Windows NT graphical interface, you can perform partition modification easily and quickly. If you know the number and size of the partitions you need (for example, on a 4 GB hard disk you might want to create a 2 GB system partition and a 2 GB data partition), however, it is best to create them during installation.

- *Will the server support additional services?* This option may determine whether you perform a custom or express setup. In an **express setup**, the most popular installation options are chosen for you. This type of installation goes more rapidly than a **custom setup**, which allows you to determine which services and programs are installed, among other things. The first time you install a Windows NT server (ideally in a test environment), you will probably want to choose express setup to get a feel for how the installation process works. Although it's easiest to include additional services during the original installation, they can be added later as well.
- *Which licensing mode should I choose?* You may choose one of two licensing modes: per seat or per server. The **per server** licensing mode allows a limited number of clients to access the server simultaneously. (The actual number is determined by your Windows NT Server purchase.) In per server mode, any of the clients may be capable of connecting to the server. The number of concurrent connections is restricted. Per server mode is the most popular choice, and if you are unsure of what mode your environment requires, you should choose per server. The **per seat** mode requires a license for every client capable of connecting to the Windows NT server.
- *How can I remember all of this information?* As you make these preinstallation decisions, you should note your choices on a server installation form and keep the form with you during installation. Appendix C offers an example of such a form.

The preceding list highlights only the most significant installation options. You should also be prepared to read and accept the license agreement, identify your name and organization, provide your registration key, select the appropriate time and date, specify display settings, specify an administrator account ID and password, and create an emergency repair disk. (You can use an **emergency repair disk** to restore a Windows NT server to its previous, working hardware configuration if its configuration becomes irreparably botched. It can also repair missing or corrupted system files and fix problems with the Windows NT Registry.) As noted previously, you should also verify that your server's hardware matches hardware on Microsoft's HCL.

THE INSTALLATION PROCESS

Once you have devised a plan for your Windows NT server installation, you can begin the actual installation process. The Windows NT Server package should include three setup floppy disks. You will need these setup disks to start the installation, but you will use the CD as the source for the program files. (You may also install Windows NT Server from floppy disks or a network drive. The former method is cumbersome and the latter causes an inordinate amount of network traffic and shouldn't be performed on a working network.) The most popular method of installing Windows NT is from a CD-ROM drive.

The following summary of the Windows NT Server installation process assumes, for simplicity, that you are using a CD-ROM and choosing the express option. It represents a typical, simple installation. It does not take into consideration any anomalies you might encounter with your server or network environment. As a result, your installation may not proceed so effortlessly.

To install Windows NT Server 4.0 on a server:

1. Verify that the server is turned off.
2. Insert the Setup Disk 1 into the server's floppy disk drive.
3. Boot the server.
4. Insert Setup Disk 2 when prompted, then press **Enter**.
5. Insert the Windows NT Server installation CD into the server's CD-ROM drive.
6. A "Welcome to Setup" message appears. To install Windows NT, press **Enter**.
7. When asked to choose your disk controllers, press **Enter** to allow the setup program to detect your controller devices.
8. When prompted, insert Setup Disk 3, then press **Enter**.
9. A list of found controllers appears. Press **Enter** to accept the list.
10. The license agreement screen should appear. Use the **Page Down** key to read the entire license agreement, and then, when you reach the bottom, press **F8** to continue.
11. Next the setup program will automatically attempt to identify your server's basic hardware configuration. Though the process may choose the wrong devices on occasion, it is usually correct. If you have a special NIC, mouse, keyboard, monitor, etc. for which you want to install specific drivers, you can choose to change the components after the program detects them. For the purposes of this example installation, accept the hardware found by the setup program. To do so, select **The Above List Matches My Computer** and press **Enter**.
12. You are asked to decide what type of partition to install. Assuming you are installing to a test server (and that nothing on the disk drive must be saved), you can select a hard disk area labeled "Unpartitioned Space" and then press **C** to create a partition in that space. (If the server already contains partitions, you will need to delete those.)
13. You are asked to specify a size for the partition. You may select a partition size of between 1 MB up to the maximum drive space available. For this exercise, choose the maximum disk size. (Remember that the Windows NT Server operating system requires at least 110 MB to function.) The setup program will then change the partition label to "New (Unformatted)" and display the partition size.
14. You are asked to select the new partition, then press **Enter** to begin installing Windows NT Server.
15. An informational screen appears. Press **Enter** to continue.
16. To format the partition you created, select **Format partition using the NTFS file system** and then press **Enter**.
17. After the setup program formats the partition, you will be asked to identify the directory to which the Windows NT Server system files will be copied. The

default directory for Windows NT Server 4.0 is \WINNT. Accept this default by pressing **Enter**. (Unless you are running two separate installations of Windows NT Server on one machine, there is no good reason to choose a system directory other than the default.)

18. The setup program attempts to examine your hard disk. This review is a time-consuming process, but you should not bypass it – particularly the first time you install Windows NT Server on a computer. This process detects bad sectors on your hard disk, marks them, and prevents data from being copied to them. Press **Enter** to allow the program to examine your hard disk.
19. After scrutinizing your hard disk, the setup program copies system files from the CD-ROM drive your server's system partition.
20. After the files have been copied, remove any floppy disks and press **Enter** to restart the computer, as prompted. After a minute, if the computer doesn't restart, you can manually restart it.
21. When the server restarts, it shows a graphical interface that walks you through the initial configuration process.

This example installation uses the default selections and simplest methods of configuring the server. In reality, your server installations will probably not be as straightforward.

After completing the preceding steps, you will have copied some files to the server and established its hardware profile. Before it can act as a server, however, you must specify the server's security role, name, licensing mode, program components, and, most importantly, network interfaces. You specify this information during the next part of the setup operation, initial configuration, as described in the following section.

INITIAL CONFIGURATION

The graphical interface portion of the setup process consists of three phases: gathering information about your computer, installing Windows NT networking, and finishing the setup. If you are configuring Windows NT Server version 4.0, this graphical interface will look like a Windows 95 setup program. In Windows 2000 Server (the next release of Windows NT), it will resemble the Windows 98 interface.

In either case, the program will lead you through the final stage of creating your Windows NT server using setup wizards. In Microsoft terminology, a **wizard** is a simple graphical program that assists you in performing complex tasks. If you had to identify a NIC and write its settings to an initialization file without a wizard, you could spend a day or two installing and configuring your server (in fact, in the era before Windows GUIs became available, this requirement was not uncommon).

In the first phase, "gathering information about your computer," you can easily follow the prompts and insert the information you gathered and recorded on your installation form. You will be asked for the server's security role, the administrator account ID and password, whether you want to create an emergency repair disk, and the components you want to install (such as games, communications utilities, and multimedia support). After you select each option, click Next to continue. Ultimately, the setup program will then guide you to the "installing Windows NT networking" phase.

The following steps (which apply to Windows NT Server 4.0) summarize the network setup phase for a simple member server with one NIC. In reality, your network setup will depend on the type and number of NICs found in your server, the protocols used by your network, the network attachment (to a LAN or remotely), and the services that you need to integrate with other systems. Refer to your installation form for these details.

To install Windows NT networking:

1. You are prompted to identify whether the server is directly connected to the LAN or WAN or connects to the network remotely, via a modem, or both. If it is not already selected, select the check box next to "Wired to the Network," and click **Next**.
2. You are asked whether this computer will be used as a server on the Internet. For this exercise, confirm this choice by checking the box that indicates you want to install Microsoft Internet Information Server (IIS). IIS is a fully functional Web and FTP hosting service. Click **Next** to continue.
3. You must choose the brand and model of NIC used by the server. You can either allow the wizard to try to detect your NIC or manually identify your NIC by choosing the "Select From List" button. If you are using a standard NIC (such as one manufactured by SMC, 3Com, IBM, or Intel), the wizard will probably detect it correctly. For this example, click the **Start Search** button to allow the wizard to find the NIC. (If the installation fails at this point, you must begin the entire installation process again.)
4. After identification of the NIC, you must choose the protocols that your server should support. By default, the system installs NWLink IPX/SPX and TCP/IP. You may install as many protocols as you want, but remember: the more protocols you install, the more server resources are consumed. For this example, simply click **Next** to continue.
5. The next window prompts you to install network services. The following services must be installed and you cannot deselect them from the list: Microsoft Internet Information Server, Remote Procedure Calls (RPC), NetBIOS (used to support Microsoft networking naming conventions), Workstation, and Server. Many additional services may be installed by choosing the "Select From List" option. For this example, accept the defaults, then click **Next** to continue.
6. The next configuration dialog boxes that you see will depend on the protocols and services you have installed. Assuming you accepted the default choices for protocols, the next window will prompt you to specify NWLink IPX/SPX properties for the frame type and internal network number. The frame type will depend on the type of NetWare network with which this server must communicate. The internal network number will depend on the IPX naming scheme you devised for

your network. Although it does not have to match the IPX address of the NIC, the internal network number should consist of eight hexadecimal characters. Choose **Auto Frame Type Detection** and enter an internal network number of 0000AAAB. Click **Next** to continue.

7. A dialog box asks you to confirm the bindings for your selected NIC, protocols, and services. Once you have confirmed those bindings, click **Next** to continue.
8. After the configuration and file copying process is complete, the network services will start (if they do not, you probably need to choose the "Back" option and modify your NIC settings). To continue the installation process, click **Next**.
9. You are prompted for the name of the domain you are creating (or, in the case of an additional server, joining). Type the domain name you established during the installation planning, then click **Next**. The startup program will search the network to verify that the domain name you typed is unique.
10. As shown in Figure 8-11, the Windows NT Server Setup dialog box opens, prompting you to finish the setup process.

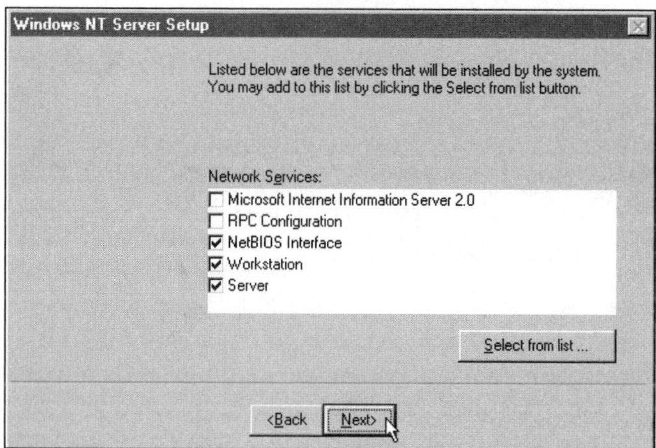

Figure 8-11 Windows NT Server Setup dialog box

In the final phase of the initial configuration "finishing the setup," the wizard guides you through a few last details of configuring your server: selecting date and time properties, selecting display properties, and creating an emergency repair disk (because earlier in the setup process you chose to make one). You should always create an emergency repair disk during installation. After installation, you should create an emergency repair disk whenever the server's system configuration changes. Keep the original disk and the newer disks in a safe place. After creating the emergency repair disk, you can restart the Windows NT server (make sure you remove the emergency disk) and begin its administration.

LOGGING ON TO THE WINDOWS NT SERVER

After your Windows NT server restarts, it will display a logo screen with the instructions to press Ctrl-Alt-Del to log on. Although this key combination in Windows 3.1 and Windows 95 enables you to restart the computer, in Windows NT it brings up a logon box if you are not logged on or a list of system options (including Shutdown) if you are already logged on. If you created a PDC or member server, the administrator account you specified during setup will be the only authorized logon ID for that server. If you created a BDC, you may log on with any authorized ID belonging to the domain. The logon dialog box includes Username, From, and Password fields. Enter the word *Administrator* in the Username field. In the From field, type the domain name for the server.

Next, type the administrator password in the Password field, bearing in mind that Windows NT passwords are case-sensitive. As a result, the password "edelweiss" is not the same as the password "EdelWeiss". If you use capital or small letters in the wrong places in a password, the server will reject your attempt to log on. Passwords in Windows NT cannot exceed 14 characters and may not contain any of the following characters: > < [ ] : ; | = , . + * & " ? \ / { }.

To add users, create groups, modify security, change the identification or role of the server, reconfigure system hardware, or install programs on the server, you must be logged in as the Administrator or as a user with equivalent (administrator) rights.

To enhance security, you should create a new user ID with administrative privileges to perform network administration and disable the Administrator user ID. If you keep the Administrator ID active with full privileges, hackers have half the information they need to break into your system.

ESTABLISHING USERS, GROUPS, AND RIGHTS

In this section, you will learn how to manage users and groups of users so as to keep network resources secure. You will see how to create users and groups and give them rights to files, directories, printers, and remote access resources. You will also learn which tools in Windows NT Server are available to help you manage users and groups. This abbreviated discussion does not thoroughly explore the nuances of managing users and groups in Windows NT Server, but it will point you in the right direction.

You have probably worked with enough computers and networks to know why user IDs are necessary: to grant each user on a network access to files and other shared resources. Imagine that you are the network administrator for a large college campus with 20,000 user IDs. Assigning directory, file, printer, and other resource rights for each user ID would consume all of your time, especially if the user population changes regularly. Instead, you can combine users with similar needs and restrictions into **groups** to more easily manage their access.

Groups form the basis for resource and account management for every type of network operating system, not just Windows NT Server. Many network administrators create groups according to department or, even more specifically, according to job function within a department. They then assign different file or directory access rights to each group. For example, on a high school's network, the administrator may create a group called "students" for the students and a group called "teachers" that contains all teachers' login IDs. The administrator could then easily grant the teachers group rights to view all attendance and grade records on the server, but deny the same access to the students group.

To better understand the nature of groups, first consider their use on a relatively small scale. Suppose you are the network administrator for a public elementary school. You might want to give all teachers and students access to run instructional programs from a network directory called PROGRAMS. In addition, you might want to allow teachers to install their own instructional programs in this same directory. Meanwhile, you need to allow teachers and administrators to record grade information in a central database called GRADES. Of course, students shouldn't read information from this database. Finally, you might want administrators to use a shared drive called STAFF to store performance review information, which should not be accessible to instructors or students. Table 8-2 illustrates how you can provide this security if you separate users into three groups: instructors, students, and administrators.

Table 8-2 Providing Security through Groups

Group	Rights to PROGRAMS	Rights to GRADES	Rights to STAFF
Instructors	Read, change	Full control	No access
Students	Read	No access	No access
Administrators	No access	Read, change	Full control

Plan your groups carefully. Creating a multitude of groups (for example, a separate group for every job classification in your organization) will impose almost as much of an administrative burden as not using any groups. A good approach is to create groups in a hierarchy according to the levels and types of access required by different types of users.

To understand how groups control access to resources, you must first understand the login process. The Windows NT access model is based on the user ID. In other words, before attempting to access any network resources, a user must enter his or her user name and password into the client interface on a Windows NT, Windows 95, Windows 3.1, DOS, Macintosh, or OS/2 workstation. The server then reads the user name and password and authorizes, or accepts, the user. Once it authorizes the user, the server checks the user name against a list of resources and their access restrictions list. If the user name is part of a group with specific access permissions or restrictions, the system will apply those same permissions and restrictions to the user's account.

A user name may contain a maximum of 20 characters and is not case-sensitive. (In other words, the user names RWhite and RWHITE are equivalent.) User names may not contain any of the following characters: > < [ ] : ; | = , . + * & " ? \ / { }. Generally, before you begin adding users to your domain, you should devise a user name policy. For instance, you might decide that all user names should consist of an employee's first initial and last name. Alternatively, you might assign user names according to job function, such as "technician1" or "neuro1."

Creating users in Windows NT is a very simple operation. To create users, click Start, point to Administrative Tools, then click User Manager for Domains. The User Manager window opens. Figure 8-12 shows the options available on the user menu of the User Manager window.

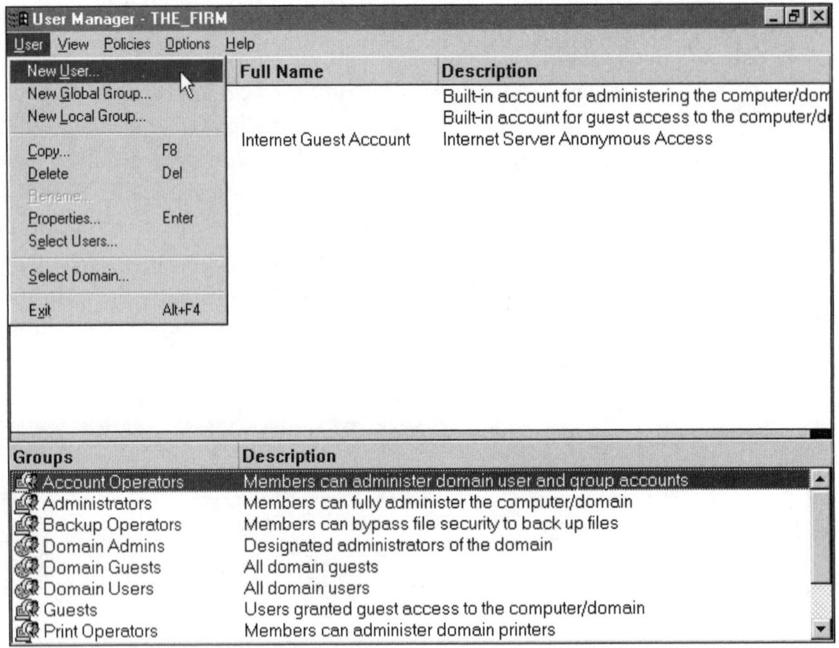

Figure 8-12 User Manager window

Once you have opened the User Manager window, you can add, delete, change, or modify the properties of users (such as their group memberships).

To add a new user:

1. Click **User** on the User Manager for Domains menu bar, then click **New User**. The New User dialog box opens.
2. Type the user name in the Username field.
3. Complete the Full Name and Description fields to identify the new user. These fields are optional, but any information you enter will help in future administration. You may want to establish a policy for entering descriptions—for example, always including the user's room number or phone extension.
4. Enter the user's password. Recall that passwords in Windows NT must not exceed 14 characters and may not contain any of the following characters: > < [ ] : ; | = , . + * & " ? \ / { }. Also remember that, unlike user names, Windows NT passwords *are* case-sensitive.
5. Type the password a second time in the **Confirm Password** field.

6. Below the Confirm Password field, you may select any of four boxes to control the management of a user's password. If it isn't already selected, check the **User Must Change Password at Next Logon** check box to force a user to generate his or her own password (so you, the network administrator, won't know it). Typically, you want to select this option. Check the option **User Cannot Change Password** if you want the password to be controlled from the server. This option might be useful for user accounts that are shared among a few different users. Normally, however, you should *not* prevent users from changing their passwords. Check the **Password Never Expires** option to prevent the user from periodically being prompted to change his or her password. From a security standpoint, allowing users to continue using the same password indefinitely is not wise, but you'll probably find that most users on your network strongly resist having to come up with a new password periodically. Check the **Account Disabled** option to either temporarily disable a currently active user ID or delay making a new user ID active. The network administrator can change any of these options later.
7. Click **Add** to save the new user ID.

Creating groups is as easy as creating users with Windows NT's graphical interface. By default, every new user ID becomes a member of the group called "Everyone," which confers the right to log on to the domain controller. This type of group is called a **global group**, because it can contain users and resources from multiple domains. A group that exists within a single domain is called a **local group**. To create additional groups, begin at the same place you started when creating a user ID, in the User Manager for Domains window.

To create a new group:

1. Click **User** in the User Manager for Domains menu bar, then click **New Global Group**. The New Global Group dialog box opens, as shown in Figure 8-13.

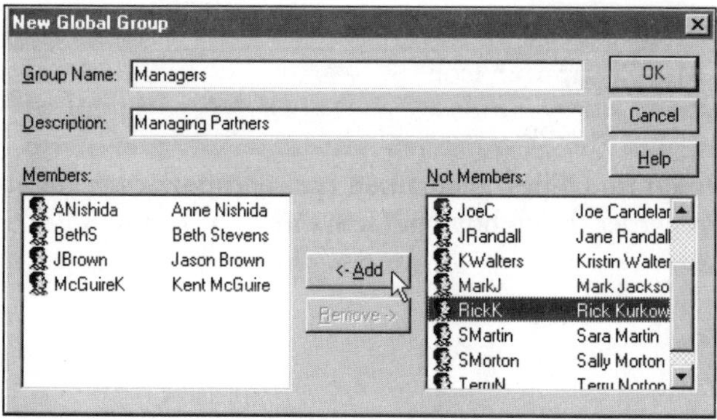

Figure 8-13 New Global Group window

2. Enter a name for the group in the **Group Name** field. This name should bear a natural relationship to the group's purpose. For example, if a group's purpose is to collect all users who need the same rights as an Instructor, you may call the group Instructors. If the group's purpose is to provide access to a tape backup

drive for only certain network administrators, you might want to call the group TAPE_BACKUP.

3. Type a description for the group in the **Description** field. In the case of the TAPE_BACKUP group, you might type a description of "backup administrators."
4. Below the description field appear two columns of user names: members and nonmembers. For a new group, the members list should be empty, because you haven't added any members yet. In the nonmember list, click the user you want to add to the group, then click **Add**.
5. Repeat Step 4 for all users you want to add to the new group.
6. Once you have finished adding users, click **OK** to save the group and its properties.
7. If your new group is to offer any benefit to its users, you need to grant the group privileges to use shared resources. This simple process must be done through the share properties of each resource, as described following.

To modify the properties of the users and groups you have created, you can double-click the group or user name in the listing within the User Manager for Domains window. The user and group dialog boxes will look the same as when you created them, and you can change any of the properties you entered, *except* the group or user name. The name fields identify the user or group and all their properties to the system. To alter the name of a user or group, you must create a new user or group, give it identical properties, and then delete the old user or group.

As mentioned earlier, users and groups are virtually useless unless they have at least minimal rights to the server. You decide to give the group Instructors read and change access to the c:\programs directory on the server.

To modify the rights for a directory:

1. Double-click the **My Computer** icon.
2. Double-click the **C: drive** icon.
3. Right-click the **Programs Files** folder, then click **Properties** in the shortcut menu. The data Properties dialog box opens, as shown in Figure 8-14.

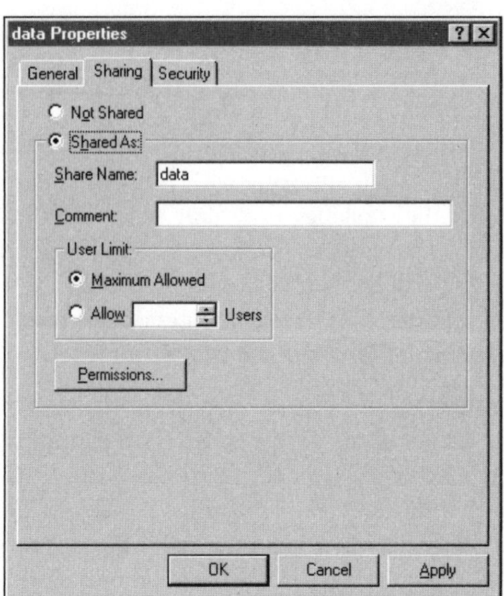

Figure 8-14 Sharing tab of the data Properties dialog box

4. Click the **Sharing** tab.
5. By default, the Not Shared option is selected. Choose the **Shared As** option.
6. In the Share Name field, you can enter a unique share name or accept the default.
7. Click **Permissions**. The Directory Permissions dialog box opens.
8. To grant a user or group rights to this directory, click **Add**.
9. Select the **Instructors** group from the list of users and groups. Click **Add**, then click **OK**.
10. Now you need to select the permissions you want to grant to the group. The permissions options are Read (allows users to view and execute files but not change them in any way), Full Control (allows users to read, modify, and decide who else can read or modify the files), Change (allows users to read, delete, and modify files), and No Access (prevents users from even seeing files). In this example, you should to select **Change**, then click **OK**.
11. Click **OK** to save your changes.

INTERNETWORKING WITH OTHER NETWORK OPERATING SYSTEMS

Windows NT Server can communicate with almost any kind of client, but its ability to communicate with other network operating systems remains somewhat limited. Interoperability is a major concern, as more organizations face the challenge of dealing with mixed networks. In the interest of the consumer, Microsoft and other network operating system vendors have made efforts to close the gap. Most commonly, you will encounter situations in which Windows NT must coexist on the same network with NetWare. This section focuses on Microsoft's solution to the interoperability question. The next chapter discusses the Novell approach.

You might think that establishing communications between two network operating systems is simply a matter of installing the same protocol on both systems. For example, you might think that because both NetWare and Windows NT can run versions of the IPX/SPX protocol, the two should be able to communicate directly. (As you have learned, the NWLink IPX/SPX-compatible protocol is installed by default when you install Windows NT Server. Recall from Chapter 3 that this protocol is required by NetWare versions 3.x and lower and supported by higher versions of NetWare.) In fact, a protocol match is merely one part of the communications equation.

To be fully compatible, operating systems must also run compatible client redirectors. A **client redirector** service is the software required for a client to access a server over a network. Windows NT and NetWare use different client redirector languages that are incompatible. To bridge this gap on a Windows NT server, you must install **Gateway Services for NetWare (GSNW)**, a service that acts as a translator between the different client redirector services. With GSNW installed, a Windows NT server can access files and other shared resources on any NetWare server on the network.

Keep in mind, however, that installing the NWLink IPX/SPX-compatible protocol and GSNW may not suffice to allow your two kinds of servers to communicate. You must be careful to configure the NWLink parameters exactly right. If the two network operating systems still do not communicate, you may need to reconfigure NWLink, paying special attention to the Autodetect Frame Type option. This option may not be detecting the correct frame types. If your NetWare server runs more than one frame type (for example, if it contains a mixed environment of NetWare 3.0 and NetWare 4.11 servers), you cannot use Autodetect for the frame type.

To specify a manual frame type in NWLink:

1. Log on to your Windows NT server as **Administrator**.
2. From the Control Panel, double-click the **Network** icon. The Network Settings dialog box opens.
3. Click the **Protocols** tab.
4. Select the **NWLink** IPX/SPX Compatible Transport protocol, then click **Properties**. The NWLink IPX/SPX Properties dialog box opens, as shown in Figure 8-15.

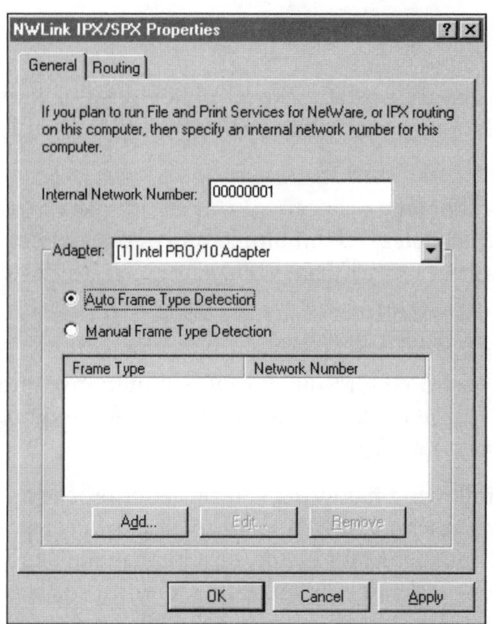

Figure 8-15 NWLink IPX/SPX Properties dialog box

5. If necessary, click the **General** tab, then select the **Manual Frame Type Detection** option.
6. Click **Add** to add a manual frame type. The Manual Frame Type Detection dialog box opens.
7. Choose the appropriate frame type for your network from the drop-down list, then click **Add**. The Manual Frame Type Detection dialog box appears again, with your selected frame type displayed.
8. Click **OK** to save your changes.
9. Choose **Close** to close the Network properties dialog box.
10. You are prompted to restart your server so that the changes can take effect. Choose **Yes** to restart your server.

Windows NT Server also comes with a migration utility, called **NWConv**, which you can use to convert existing NetWare servers to Windows NT servers. This utility allows you to move NetWare user accounts, groups, folders, files, and even servers to the Windows NT platform. To ensure success, you must plan the migration just as carefully as you would plan the creation of a new domain. If you didn't want to use the migration utility, you could manually migrate users from NetWare to Windows NT, by re-creating the NetWare user accounts on the Windows NT server and then copying files from the NetWare server to the Windows NT server.

CHAPTER SUMMARY

- Windows NT Server is a popular network operating system known for its intuitive graphical user interface (GUI), multitasking capabilities, and compatibility with a huge array of applications.
- Windows NT supports any type of topology or protocol you are likely to run on a LAN. This efficient network operating system uses multiple processors and employs multitasking to allow processes on the server to share CPU resources. It's also easy to manage and well supported.
- Drawbacks to Windows NT Server include the fact that it does not natively provide support for remote administration. It also requires significant administrative effort to scale this operating system to a very large enterprise. Windows NT also requires you to restart the server after any significant system change.
- Windows NT Server requires the following hardware: 486 or better processor, 16 MB RAM, CD-ROM, floppy disk drive, at least 110 MB free hard disk space, a pointing device, and a NIC that is included on Microsoft's Hardware Compatibility List (HCL). It supports a maximum of 32 processors on one server with additional software.
- Multiprocessing splits tasks among multiple processors to expedite the completion of any single instruction. It's a great advantage for servers with high CPU utilization. If a server is used merely for file and print sharing, however, multiple processors are probably unnecessary.
- Windows NT Server supports symmetric multiprocessing, which splits all operations equally among two or more processors. In contrast, asymmetric multiprocessing (which is not supported by Windows NT Server) assigns each subtask a specific processor.
- Windows NT Server's memory model improves on the old DOS and Windows 3.1 memory model in two ways: by using a 32-bit addressing scheme and by allowing you to install as much as 4 GB of physical memory on the server.
- Another feature of Windows NT Server's memory model is that it assigns each application its own 32-bit memory area. Although this approach consumes some processing resources, it prevents one misbehaving application from affecting all others.
- Another way that Windows NT Server can manage memory is via virtual memory. Virtual memory is memory that is logically carved out of space on the hard disk (as opposed to physical memory, or RAM). If you have extra hard disk space, virtual memory allows you to easily expand the memory available to server applications. It requires no user or administrator intervention and is accessed without the clients' knowledge. Its use slows operations, however, because accessing a hard disk takes longer than accessing physical memory.
- The term *file system* refers to an operating system's method of organizing, managing, and accessing its files through logical structures and software routines. Windows NT Server supports the following file systems: HPFS, FAT, NTFS, and CDFS. In general, when installing a Windows NT server, you will be concerned with only the FAT, FAT32, and

NTFS file systems; HPFS is not native to Windows NT, and CDFS is automatically installed.

- CDFS (CD-ROM File System) is the read-only file system used to access resources on a CD-ROM disk. Windows NT supports CDFS to allow CD-ROM file sharing. No intervention is necessary to install or configure CDFS.
- FAT (File Allocation Table) is the original PC file system, which was designed in the 1970s to support floppy disks and, later, hard disks. Although FAT has been improved and enhanced over the years, it remains inadequate for most server operating systems because of its partition size limitations, naming limitations, and fragmentation and speed issues.
- FAT uses 16-bit fields to store file size information. FAT (without additional utilities) supports only filenames with a maximum of eight characters in the name and three characters in the extension. Directories and files on a FAT drive cannot take advantage of Windows NT's security features. A FAT drive stores data in noncontiguous blocks and uses links between fragments to maintain data integrity. Although, you can convert a FAT drive into an NTFS drive on a Windows NT Server, you cannot convert an NTFS drive into a FAT drive. Because of FAT's low overhead, it can write data to a hard disk very quickly.
- FAT32 is an enhanced version of FAT that can accommodate long filenames and smaller allocation units. It provides for more efficient use of disk space than the original FAT. Even though FAT32 represents an improvement over FAT and is often used on Windows 95, Windows 98, and Windows NT workstations, it still cannot match the security and file compression advantages that NTFS provides for Windows NT servers.
- HPFS (High Performance File System) is a file system designed for the OS/2 operating system that offers greater efficiency and reliability than FAT. HPFS organizes data in contiguous blocks, allows data to wait in memory if the processor is too busy to accept it, and assigns information about other data on the disk to each block of data. All of these measures enhance HPFS's speed.
- NTFS integrates reliability, compression, the ability to handle massive files, and fast access. Unless the server must start with dual operating systems or one of your applications cannot use NTFS, you should choose NTFS as your file system when installing Windows NT Server.
- NTFS filenames can be a maximum of 256 characters long. NTFS stores file size information in 64-bit fields. NTFS files or partitions can theoretically be as large as 16 exabytes (2^{64} bytes). NTFS is required for Macintosh connectivity. It incorporates sophisticated, customizable compression routines and keeps a log of a volume's data to facilitate recovery in the event of a system crash.
- A domain is a group of users, servers, and other resources that share account and security information.
- Every organization must decide how best to organize its domains. It may require only one domain or several, and it may use a variety of domain hierarchies.

- Every domain relies on a primary domain controller (PDC) to centrally manage its account information and security. Only one PDC can exist for each domain. If the PDC fails, you must rely on a backup domain controller (BDC) to take over the management responsibilities. A BDC can also authenticate users logging into the domain. Any number of BDCs per domain is permissible, but you should definitely have at least one.
- Because the BDC must be able to read and write to the PDC, you should install a BDC only after the PDC is running correctly. If the PDC goes down for a significant period of time, the network administrator can promote the BDC to take over its functions.
- A member server (ms) is a server that takes no responsibility for managing accounts or security. An MS is usually devoted to running a particular application, such as MS SQL Server, that requires dedicated processing resources. Any number of member servers may belong to Windows NT domain.
- Microsoft recommends using one of four domain models: single, master, multiple master, or complete trust. The single domain model—the simplest Windows NT domain model—consists of one domain that services every user and resource in an organization. The master domain model uses a single domain for overall control of user account information, plus separate resource domains that manage resources such as networked printers. The multiple master domain model uses two or more master domains that are joined in a two-way trust to manage many resource domains.
- The complete trust domain model differs from the master domain models, in that its administration is completely decentralized. In this model, each domain manages its own user, group, account, and file and print sharing information. To communicate with each other, domains in the complete trust domain model rely on two-way trusts that are established between all domains.
- A trust relationship, or "trust," enables users from one domain to access resources in another domain. A unique security identifier (SID) identifies each domain, and each domain has its own security database to track rights to files and resources. When domain A trusts domain B, users in domain B can access resources on domain A.
- If users from domain B should be able to access resources on domain A and users from domain A should be able to access resources from domain B, you should establish a two-way domain trust relationship. Two-way domain trust relationships are common in WAN situations where two or more locations manage their own domains, but need to share information.
- Even though trust relationships exist between domains, users and groups within those domains must still be assigned permissions on trusted servers. For example, if Jane Doe belongs to domain A and can access domain B, it does not automatically mean that she can open a spreadsheet located on domain B's BDC.
- Windows NT uses a browser service to discover all shared devices on the network and compile a database of those resources. Several kinds of browsers exist, including domain master browsers, master browsers, and backup browsers. A domain master browser tracks resources for a group of domains. A master browser maintains a database of shared

resources for its domain. A backup browser keeps a copy of the master browser's browse list in case the master browser goes down. Although every server on a Windows NT network has the potential to act as a browser, by default the PDC is the master browser for its domain.

- Each workstation on a network registers itself with the master browser when it logs on to the network. On the server side, the master browser records that information and synchronizes it with the backup and domain master browsers.
- In synchronization, a PDC causes its BDCs to request updated user account information. If a BDC detects then that its information is outdated, it requests that the PDC send changes. The type of information relayed by a PDC during synchronization includes new or changed user passwords, new group memberships, and new or changed user or group IDs. No updates are sent if the BDC and PDC have the same, current information.
- Two types of forced synchronizations are possible: partial and full. In a partial synchronization, only modifications to user account information are transmitted to the other domain controllers in a domain. In other words, the PDC and BDC find discrepancies in their databases and resolve them. In a full synchronization, the entire user account database is copied to a BDC.
- Before you insert the Windows NT Server installation CD, you should develop a plan for your server and its place in your network. You should consider many factors, including organizational structure, server function, applications, number of users, LAN architecture, and optional services (such as remote access), when creating this plan.
- To create a Windows NT server, you need to know the server's security role, NIC type, domain name, server name, licensing mode, number, type, and size of hard disk partitions, protocols, and services that the server should support, type of disk controller, registration key, time zone, and administrator password.
- After you copy the installation files, the Windows NT Server setup program will lead you through the last stage of creating your Windows NT server using setup wizards. A wizard is a simple graphical program that assists you in performing complex tasks.
- You can use an emergency repair disk to restore a Windows NT server to its previous, working hardware configuration if its configuration becomes irreparably damaged. This disk can also repair missing or corrupted system files and fix problems with the Windows NT Registry. You should always create an emergency repair disk during installation. You should also create such a disk whenever you change the server's system configuration. Keep the original disk and the newer disks in a safe place.
- To add users, create groups, modify security, change the identification or role of the server, reconfigure system hardware, or install programs on the server, you must be logged in as the Administrator or as a user with equivalent (administrator) rights. For security reasons, you should create a new user ID with administrative privileges to perform network administration and disable the Administrator user ID. If you keep the Administrator ID active with full privileges, hackers have half the information they need to break into your system.

- Groups form the basis for resource and account management for every type of network operating system, not just Windows NT Server. Many network administrators create groups according to department or, even more specifically, according to job function within a department. Certain groups are granted specific file and other resource rights on the network. Users can belong to more than one group.
- A user name may contain as many as 20 characters and is not case-sensitive. User names may not contain any of the following characters: > < [ ] : ; | = , . + * & " ? \ / { }. Generally, before you begin adding users to your domain, you should devise a user name policy. For instance, you might decide that all user names should consist of an employee's first initial and last name.
- To modify properties of the users and groups you have created, double-click the group or user name in the listing within the User Manager for Domains dialog box. The user and group dialog boxes will look the same as when you created them, and you can change any of the properties you entered, *except* the group or user name. The name fields identify the user or group and all their properties to the system. To change the name of a user or group, you must create a new user or group, give it identical properties, and then delete the old user or group.
- Windows NT comes with a few options to integrate its servers with NetWare servers. To allow these two platforms to communicate over the same network, the Windows NT server must be running the NWLink IPX/SPX protocol (correctly configured) and the Gateway Services for NetWare (GSNW).

KEY TERMS

- **asymmetric multiprocessing** — A method of multiprocessing that assigns each subtask to a specific processor.
- **backup browser** — A server that keeps a copy of the master browser's browse list in case the master browser fails.
- **backup domain controller (BDC)** — A server that backs up the PDC in managing account and security information for a domain. A BDC can also provide authentication for users logging in to the domain. Any number of BDCs per domain is permissible, but at least one should exist. Because the BDC must be able to read and write to the PDC, you should install a BDC only after the PDC is running correctly.
- **browse list** — The list of available resources distributed to specially assigned computers known as browsers.
- **browser** — The service used to discover all shared devices on the network and compile a database of those resources. Also, the server that runs the browser service.
- **browser election** — A vote between computers to determine which one will take over responsibility for maintaining the master browse list.
- **CDFS (CD-ROM File System)** — The read-only file system used to access resources on a CD. Windows NT supports this file system to allow CD-ROM file sharing.

- **client redirector** — The service required for a client to access a server over a network.
- **complete trust domain model** — A way of organizing Windows NT domains in which administration is completely decentralized. In this model, each domain manages its own user, group, account, and file and print sharing information. Each domain also has a two-way trust relationship with every other domain in the network.
- **custom setup** — An option for installing Windows NT Server that allows you to decide which services and programs are installed, among other things. Custom setup generally takes longer than express setup, but it may be necessary if your server uses special hardware or software.
- **domain** — A group of users, servers, and other resources that share account and security information through a Windows NT network operating system.
- **domain master browser** — A server that locates and compiles information about shared resources for a group of domains.
- **emergency repair disk** — A disk that can be used to restore a Windows NT server to its previous, working hardware configuration if its configuration becomes irreparably botched. It can also repair missing or corrupted system files and fix problems with the Windows NT Registry. You should always create an emergency repair disk during installation of the network operating system.
- **express setup** — An option for installing Windows NT Server in which the most popular installation options are chosen for you. Express setup is faster than custom setup.
- **extended attributes** — Attributes beyond the basic Read, Write, System, and Hidden attributes supported by FAT. HPFS supports extended attributes.
- **FAT (File Allocation Table)** — The original PC file system designed in the 1970s to support floppy disks and, later, hard disks. FAT is inadequate for most server operating systems because of its partition size limitations, naming limitations, and fragmentation and speed issues.
- **FAT32** — An enhanced version of FAT that accommodates the use of long filenames and smaller allocation units on a disk. FAT32 makes more efficient use of disk space than the original FAT.
- **file system** — An operating system's method of organizing, managing, and accessing its files through logical structures and software routines.
- **full synchronization** — A process in which the entire user account database is relayed from the PDC to its BDCs. The network administrator can force full synchronization, but it may generate a great deal of network traffic.
- **Gateway Services for NetWare (GSNW)** — A Windows NT service that acts as a translator between the Windows NT and NetWare client redirector services. With GSNW installed, a Windows NT server can access files and other shared resources on any NetWare server on the network.

- **global group** — A group of users and resources that belong to multiple domains.
- **graphical user interface (GUI)** — A pictorial representation of computer functions and elements that, in the case of network operating systems, enables administrators to more easily manage files, users, groups, security, printers, and other issues.
- **group** — A means of collectively managing users' permissions and restrictions to shared resources. Groups form the basis for resource and account management for every type of network operating system, not just Windows NT Server. Many network administrators create groups according to department or, even more specifically, according to job function within a department.
- **Hardware Compatibility List (HCL)** — A list of computer components proven to be compatible with Windows NT Server. The HCL appears on the same CD as your Windows NT Server software and on Microsoft's Web site.
- **HPFS (High-Performance File System)** — A file system designed for the OS/2 operating system that offers greater efficiency and reliability than FAT does. HPFS is rarely used but can be supported by Windows NT servers.
- **local group** — A group of users and resources that belong to one domain.
- **master browser** — A server that locates shared resources for a domain and maintains a database of information about these resources. By default, the PDC acts as the master browser for its domain.
- **master domain model** — A way of organizing Windows NT domains so that a single domain controls all user account information, and separate resource domains manage resources such as networked printers. This model suits an environment in which each department in an organization controls its file and print sharing and a central information technology department manages the user IDs, groups, and relationships between the domains.
- **member server (MS)** — A server that takes no responsibility for managing accounts or security in a Windows NT domain. An MS is usually devoted to running a particular application, such as MS SQL Server, that requires dedicated processing resources.
- **multiple master domain model** — A way of organizing Windows NT domains in which two or more master domains are joined in a two-way trust to manage many resource domains.
- **multiprocessing** — The technique of splitting tasks among multiple processors to expedite the completion of any single instruction.
- **NTFS (New Technology File System)** — A file system developed by Microsoft expressly for Windows NT Workstation and Windows NT Server. NTFS integrates reliability, compression, the ability to handle massive files, and fast access. Most Windows NT Server partitions employ either FAT or NTFS.
- **NWConv** — A utility provided with Windows NT that converts (migrates) an existing NetWare server's user account, file, and other information to a Windows NT server.

- **one-way domain trust relationship** — An arrangement in which one domain allows users in another domain to access its resources; the reverse is not true.
- **partial synchronization** — A type of synchronization in which only modifications to user account information are transmitted between domain controllers in a domain. In other words, the PDC and BDC find discrepancies in their databases and resolve them. Partial synchronization happens automatically.
- **per seat** — A Windows NT Server licensing mode that requires a license for every client capable of connecting to the Windows NT server.
- **per server** — A Windows NT Server licensing mode that allows a limited number of clients to access the server simultaneously. (The number is determined by your Windows NT Server purchase.) The restriction applies to the number of concurrent connections, rather than specific clients. Per server mode is the most popular choice for installing Windows NT Server.
- **physical memory** — The chips installed on the computer's system board that provide dedicated memory to that computer (as opposed to virtual memory).
- **primary domain controller (PDC)** — A computer that centrally manages account information and security for an entire domain. Only one PDC may exist for each domain.
- **promote** — A Microsoft term that refers to the process of granting a server higher authority within the domain. For instance, if a PDC fails, the network administrator may promote the BDC to become a PDC.
- **single domain model** — The simplest Windows NT domain model. It consists of one domain that services every user and resource in an organization.
- **symmetric multiprocessing** — A method of multiprocessing that splits all operations equally among two or more processors. Windows NT Server supports this type of multiprocessing.
- **synchronization** — The process undertaken by a PDC and its BDCs to keep identical user account information in both of their user databases.
- **trust relationship (trust)** — An arrangement that grants users from one domain rights to resources in another domain. A unique security identifier identifies each domain, and each domain has its own security database to track rights to files and resources.
- **two-way domain trust relationship** — An arrangement in which two domains allow each other access to their resources. Two-way domain trust relationships are common in WAN situations where two or more locations manage their own domains, but need to share information.
- **virtual memory** — Memory that is logically carved out of space on the hard disk (as opposed to physical memory).
- **wizard** — A simple graphical program that assists the user in performing complex tasks, such as configuring a NIC on a server.

Review Questions

1. List four factors that you should consider before purchasing a network operating system.
2. Windows NT Server will not support DOS clients. True or False?
3. What is the minimum amount of RAM required to run Windows NT Server, as suggested by Microsoft?
   - a. 16 MB
   - b. 32 MB
   - c. 64 MB
   - d. 128 MB
4. What is the minimum amount of RAM you would recommend for a computer destined to be a Windows NT server?
   - a. 16 MB
   - b. 32 MB
   - c. 64 MB
   - d. 128 MB
5. Why couldn't you use Windows NT Workstation to support a group of 20 clients in a small office?
   - a. Windows NT Workstation can support only 10 clients in a peer-to-peer configuration.
   - b. Windows NT Workstation cannot support the multiprocessing necessary to handle 20 clients.
   - c. Windows NT Workstation cannot use trust relationships, which are necessary to accommodate more than 10 clients.
   - d. Windows NT Workstation cannot support more than 10 clients due to its maximum memory restriction of 64 MB.
6. Where should you look to find out whether a NIC offered for sale on the Web will work in your Windows NT server?
   - a. on the manufacturer's Web site
   - b. in the Microsoft Hardware Compatibility List
   - c. in the vendor's Hardware Compatibility List
   - d. in the Windows NT Server software manual
7. A Windows NT server does not necessarily have to be equipped with a floppy disk drive. True or False?
8. What kind of multiprocessing does Windows NT support?
   - a. symmetric
   - b. asymmetric
   - c. both symmetric and asymmetric
   - d. both symmetric and asymmetric, but only with additional software

9. What is the maximum amount of memory that a Windows NT Server can utilize?
   a. 2 GB
   b. 4 GB
   c. 6 GB
   d. 8 GB
10. What primary advantage does Windows NT gain by assigning each operation its own 32-bit address space?
11. What type of file system allows a Windows NT server to read from CD-ROMs?
   a. CDMS
   b. CDDS
   c. CDFS
   d. CDOS
12. Which file system takes full advantage of Windows NT security?
   a. FAT
   b. FAT32
   c. HPFS
   d. NTFS
13. Which file system is required for Macintosh connectivity?
   a. FAT
   b. FAT32
   c. HPFS
   d. NTFS
14. Why must you plan your organization's domain structure carefully?
15. In a multiple master domain model, what kind of trust relationship must exist between the master domains?
   a. one-way trust
   b. two-way trust
   c. multiple one-way trusts
   d. multiple two-way trusts
16. Which of the following types of organizations is best suited to the single domain model?
   a. a local grocery store
   b. a multinational bank
   c. a regional Internet service provider
   d. a regional blood bank

17. Describe why you might want to use a one-way trust relationship between two domains.

18. What is the longest possible length for a domain name?
    - **a.** 15 characters
    - **b.** 64 characters
    - **c.** 128 characters
    - **d.** 256 characters

19. What is one possible hazard of removing a trust relationship?
    - **a.** ruining links between directories that belong to different domains
    - **b.** preventing users from accessing resources upon which they have come to rely
    - **c.** preventing users from creating new files in their home directories
    - **d.** severing ties between a PDC and its BDC

20. Name six things you need to know before you begin installing the Windows NT Server operating system.

21. When you begin installing Windows NT Server, how do you start the machine?
    - **a.** the Shift-F10 keystroke combination
    - **b.** a CD-ROM
    - **c.** a floppy disk
    - **d.** the Ctrl-Alt-Del keystroke combination

22. What is the default directory for the Windows NT system files?
    - **a.** C:\WINDOWS_NT
    - **b.** C:\WINDOWS
    - **c.** C:\WINNT32
    - **d.** C:\WINNT

23. Which of the following is *not* a valid Windows NT server name?
    - **a.** MKTG+SALES
    - **b.** MKTG-SALES
    - **c.** Mktg^sales
    - **d.** MKTG_and_SALES

24. Describe the purpose of an emergency repair disk.

25. By default, which protocols does the Windows NT Server 4.0 setup program choose?
    - **a.** TCP/IP and IPX/SPX
    - **b.** IPX/SPX and NetBEUI
    - **c.** TCP/IP, NetBEUI, and IPX/SPX
    - **d.** TCP/IP, NetBEUI, IPX/SPX, and AppleTalk

26. When creating a new user, which option should you check to make sure that the user never has to change his or her password?
    - **a.** Password never expires
    - **b.** User may change password
    - **c.** Password must be a minimum of 6 characters long
    - **d.** Password cannot be reused for 90 days

27. If a user has Change rights to a file on a Windows NT server, she cannot delete that file. True or False?

28. Why is it a good idea to disable the Administrator user ID and create a different user name for administrative functions?
    - **a.** The Administrator ID can be used by only one person; thus, if you have multiple network administrators, only one can modify server settings at any given time.
    - **b.** The Administrator ID can be used for only 90 days before its password must be modified, thus making it harder to remember.
    - **c.** The Administrator ID does not have full privileges to modify trust relationships between domains.
    - **d.** The Administrator ID is a well-known ID for all Windows NT Servers, thus providing a potential intruder half the information he or she needs to gain administrative rights to a server.

29. Which services must you install to enable a Windows NT server to communicate with a NetWare server?
    - **a.** NWLink
    - **b.** Gateway Services for NetWare
    - **c.** IPX/SPX
    - **d.** Gateway Services for IPX/SPX

30. What is the name of the utility that allows you to migrate NetWare server account information to a Windows NT server?
    - **a.** NWLink
    - **b.** Gateway Services for NetWare
    - **c.** NWConv
    - **d.** Conversion utility for NetWare

HANDS-ON PROJECTS

For the following projects, you will need a computer with a Pentium processor, at least 24 MB RAM, at least a 1 GB hard disk, a CD-ROM drive, a floppy disk drive, and a NIC. You should have a blank floppy disk to make into an emergency repair disk. You will also need a copy of the Windows NT Server 4.0 software, in the form of the installation CD and the three setup disks. In addition, you should have the configuration and diagnostics disks that came with your NIC. Your computer should not be networked with other computers in the classroom, but all of the computers should be capable of forming a LAN.

PROJECT 8-1

In this project you will install Windows NT Server 4.0.

1. Create an installation checklist that identifies the choices you will need to make during installation of this server. (Appendix C provides an example of an installation checklist.) Plan to make your server act as a PDC.
2. Make sure that your server is not networked with any other computers.
3. Install Windows NT Server according to the steps provided earlier in this chapter, with the following exceptions:
   - Rather than creating one large partition, create two equal-sized partitions: one called **SYS** and one called **DATA**.
   - Use the domain name **CLASSX** and call your server **STUDENTY**, where X is your pair number (assuming the class can divide into pairs) and Y is your seat number.
   - Instead of letting the setup program autodetect your NIC, when prompted, choose **Select From List** and **Have Disk**. Install the drivers from your NIC configuration disk.
4. When asked for the Administrator password, choose a password you believe to be secure.
5. After the installation is complete, restart the computer and log on as the Administrator.

PROJECT 8-2

In this exercise, you will replace the Administrator user with a different user who is authorized to perform administrative tasks.

1. After logging on to your server as the Administrator, click **Start**, point to **Administrative Tools**, then click **User Manager for Domains**. The User Manager for Domains window opens.
2. In the list of users, click the **Administrator** user name to highlight it.
3. Click **User** on the menu bar, then click **Copy User**. The New User dialog box opens.
4. Type a new user name and a secure password, then specify that the password should never expire. Because this new account is a copy of the Administrator account, it will have the same privileges as the Administrator account has. Write down the password you chose.

5. Click **Add**, then **Close** to save your newly created user account. You will return to the User Manager for Domains window.
6. Press **Ctrl-Alt-Del**.
7. Choose to log off.
8. Press **Ctrl-Alt-Del** again and log on with your newly created administrative user name and password.
9. Try adding another account. Did it work? Why or why not?

PROJECT 8-3

Tell the class the name and password that you chose for your new administrative ID. Discuss the elements of a secure password. Explain how you can help users choose more secure passwords and remember them without writing them on a notepad. Why is it also important to pick an unusual user name for the server's administrative account?

PROJECT 8-4

In this exercise, you and a partner will experiment with PDCs and BDCs.

1. Connect your computer to the classroom LAN.
2. If you are not already logged on as the administrative user you created in Project 8-2, log on now.
3. On one computer, click **Start**, point to **Administrative Tools**, then click **Server Manager**. The Server Manager window opens.
4. Highlight your server in the list.
5. Click **Computer** on the menu bar, then click **Demote to Backup Domain Controller**. How long does this process take?
6. On the other computer, click **Start**, point to **Administrative Tools**, then click **Server Manager**.
7. Highlight your server in the list. It should be listed as the PDC.
8. Click **Computer** on the menu bar, then click **Synchronize Entire Domain**. How long does this process take? What circumstances would make it take longer?
9. Continue to experiment with the servers. For example, create share names for directories on both the PDC and the BDC; from the PDC, add a handful of users with different file and directory rights; create groups and assign users to those groups.

Case Projects

1. You have been asked to design a Windows NT domain model for Evergreen Industries, a company that manufactures dolls, doll clothes, and storybooks about each doll. The company's headquarters is located in Chicago, its warehouse is in Nashville, and one of its manufacturing plants is in St. Louis and another in Fargo. Executives at the Chicago headquarters need to pick up reports from each manufacturing plant. The warehouse needs to receive inventory reports from the manufacturing plants and send them to the Accounting department at the headquarters location. The manufacturing plants do not need to receive data from headquarters, but they must communicate with the warehouse. In addition, the company is undergoing a gradual restructuring expected to last for the next two years that will result in many workers being transferred from one location to another. What kind of plan do you suggest that Evergreen implement?
2. The network manager at Evergreen says that she will consider your proposal. Meanwhile, she has a more immediate concern. She has asked for your help in diagnosing a problem with the Windows NT server that the company uses to provide dynamic order forms to its customers on the Web. Since use of the company's Web site has increased, the CPU utilization frequently tops off at 100%. What types of things would you look for on the server?
3. Now that Evergreen's network manager has seen how quickly you can solve problems, she challenges you with another one. One of her technicians told her that it was impossible to connect the small NetWare 4.0 network employed in the Quality Control department with the Windows NT network used by the rest of Evergreen headquarters. The technician indicated that the protocols were incompatible. It's an inconvenience for the people in the Marketing department to copy data onto a floppy disk from the Quality Control workstations and then take the disk back to their offices. What do you suggest to resolve this problem?

CHAPTER 9

NetWare-Based Networking

After reading this chapter and completing the exercises, you will be able to:

- Identify the advantages of using the NetWare network operating system
- Describe NetWare's server hardware requirements
- Describe NetWare's memory, directory structure, and file system architectures
- Plan for and perform a simple NetWare server installation
- Explain how NetWare integrates with other network operating systems

On the Job

A few years ago, I switched from a programming position to a network administrator position. I didn't know much about networks before making the change, but I realized that I wanted to do something other than type code for the rest of my life. One of my first projects was to install a NetWare 4.11 server for a school district. The new server would provide a centralized backup point for all files on the network. I figured the NetWare installation process would be painless, and I worried only about getting the backup software working.

I should have given more thought to the installation! My boss had provided me with an old, but powerful workstation to use for my new server. This workstation still had Windows 95 and a number of applications installed on its hard drive. I knew that I had to reformat the hard disk before installing NetWare. After doing so, I began the installation. Just as I chose the "install in English" option from the installation program, however, the screen went black. I could go no further. I reformatted the hard disk twice, but the same thing happened each time.

Finally I sought the help of a colleague who had many years of experience with NetWare. After I explained my problem, she smiled and confessed that she had once made the same mistake. NetWare's operating system, she told me, cannot be installed over the version of DOS used by Windows. Even though I had erased Windows and the applications from the hard disk, I hadn't erased enough. Instead, I had to install DOS 6.22, format the hard disk, and begin all over. Once I took these steps, the installation worked perfectly.

Rose Suyemoto
Brighton School District

As you learned in Chapter 8, a network operating system is software that resides at the highest layer of the OSI Model and manages resources on a server. In this chapter, you will learn about NetWare, another popular type of LAN and WAN network operating system. Windows NT Server and NetWare share many characteristics, such as their use of groups, file systems, graphical interfaces for management, and processor optimization techniques. Both provide file and print sharing in a client/server networking environment, and both enable you to use additional services such as remote access, Internet connectivity, and network management. As you will see, however, NetWare and Windows NT Server also differ in significant ways.

This chapter will not attempt to cover all of the details of installing, managing, and optimizing a NetWare networking environment. For that type of knowledge, and especially if you intend to pursue CNE certification, you should invest in a book devoted to Novell's NetWare. This chapter merely provides an overview of the requirements, characteristics, and basic structure of Novell's popular network operating system.

INTRODUCTION TO NETWARE

In 1983, Novell introduced its NetWare network operating system. At that time, Windows NT Server had not yet been developed and UNIX was used primarily to make applications available to clients, rather than share resources among clients. NetWare quickly became the operating system of choice for LANs and WANs, providing reliable file and print sharing services to millions of users. In subsequent years, Novell has refined NetWare so that it now includes support for TCP/IP, intranet services, a graphical user interface, and better integration with other operating systems.

Currently, several different versions of NetWare exist. Although versions 3.1 through 3.2 (collectively referred to as **NetWare 3.x**) were introduced in the early 1990s, many network administrators have not replaced their NetWare 3.x installations with newer versions because of the 3.x version's high reliability. You will likely find NetWare 3.x still running in cost-conscious organizations such as schools or nonprofit agencies, because these organizations cannot justify upgrading their network operation systems to a newer version.

Novell introduced NetWare 4.0, 4.1, and 4.11 (collectively known as **NetWare 4.x**) in the mid-1990s. NetWare 4.11 is sometimes referred to as **IntraNetware** because it was the first version of NetWare to support intranet services such as Web server software, IP address management, and FTP hosting. Novell changed the look of its network operating system with NetWare 4.x in an attempt to make this software more user-friendly, replacing most of the old DOS-based commands with a graphical user interface. In fact, many 3.x commands were replaced with new commands in version 4.x. NetWare 4.x also provided much better support for enterprise-wide networks containing multiple servers.

In 1998, Novell released version 5.0 of NetWare. This version not only increases the extent and ease of network management, but also provides a network operating system wholly based on the IP protocol. As you know, the IP protocol is the de facto protocol of the Internet. In addition to being compatible with Windows NT and UNIX operating systems, NetWare 5.0 offers flexibility and easy integration thanks to its use of IP. Another difference between NetWare 5.0 and previous versions of NetWare is that many of its interfaces and services rely on the Java programming language. In addition, NetWare 5.0 contains better printer and file system administration than version 4.x.

You do not need to know the specific differences between versions of NetWare to achieve Net+ certification. As a network administrator or technician, however, you will undoubtedly encounter environments that use one or several NetWare versions. This chapter focuses on the most significant features of NetWare 4.1 and 5.0, which are similar in use and design. Both use Novell Directory Services (NDS) to organize users, groups, servers, and other network resources. (You will learn more about NDS later in this chapter.) Both provide a graphical interface for managing network resources. In addition, both support integration with other network operating systems, Web services, multiple protocols, asset management, migration utilities, and software distribution. Much—but not all—of what you will learn about NetWare 4.1 and 5.0 will apply to NetWare 3.x as well. You can therefore use this chapter as a starting point in your exploration of NetWare.

WHY CHOOSE NETWARE?

As you learned in Chapter 8, you need to answer some basic questions when choosing a network operating system.

- Can it be integrated with my existing infrastructure? (The infrastructure includes not only other network operating systems, but also LAN topology, protocols, transmission methods, and connectivity hardware.)
- Will it provide the security required by my resources?
- Is my technical staff capable of managing it?
- Will my applications run smoothly on it?
- Will it accommodate future growth (that is, is it scalable)?
- Does it support the additional services required by my users (for example, remote access, Web site hosting, and messaging)?
- How much does it cost?
- What kind of support does the vendor offer?

Like Windows NT Server, NetWare offers excellent answers to these questions. In their fierce competition for the network operating system market, NetWare and Windows NT Server have both been forced to address the issues that cause the greatest concern for network administrators: performance, cost, flexibility, interoperability, and support. NetWare has been around for a long time and has a faithful following among network administrators. This popularity arises partly because some veteran networking professionals are more comfortable with NetWare, which was the first network operating system designed for file and print sharing. It also reflects NetWare's efficient processing, reliable services, and strong vendor support.

Like Microsoft, Novell can leverage its size to ensure that network applications are compatible and that support is easily accessible. Novell provides extensive online support from its support Web site, http:\\support.novell.com. From that Web page, you can search Novell's Knowledgebase, a database of technical information documents (TIDs), or join a forum in which networking professionals from around the world share their experiences with Novell products. You can also learn about known bugs in different versions of NetWare and find explanations of common problems at the Novell support site. In addition, the company provides enhanced technical support to Certified NetWare Engineers (CNEs) through CDs and discounted calls to Novell's help desk. As with Microsoft products, you can find a number of third-party discussion groups on the Web as well as technical manuals and books that focus on NetWare products.

As noted earlier, NetWare is flexible, efficient, and secure. One feature contributing to its flexibility is the ability to natively support many different protocols. NetWare 4.x supports IP encapsulated by Novell's native IPX, and NetWare 5.0 supports the use of pure (not encapsulated) IP. Both versions support the AppleTalk, IPX/SPX, and TCP/IP protocols, and both can handle Ethernet or Token Ring networks. Another advantage of NetWare is its ability to run multiple services simultaneously and use as many as 32 internal processors. Its modularity allows the network administrator to isolate some processes from others or change the priority of critical applications. For instance, if your NetWare server runs mail services, file services, and printer services for just one printer, you can make the print service have a lower priority than the mail and file services.

Unlike Windows NT, NetWare does not require you to restart the server whenever you change its configurations. For example, you can change the server's IP address and then simply stop and start a service to implement the change. Suppose you were running the GroupWise mail service on a NetWare server, and you needed to change the name of your Internet gateway within GroupWise. You could stop the GroupWise service, change the gateway name, then restart the GroupWise service, without affecting any other services (such as file retrieval or printing). This "quick change" feature keeps service interruptions brief and limited.

In addition to supporting a number of protocols and permitting quick configuration changes, NetWare offers native interoperability solutions for Macintosh-, Windows-, DOS-, OS/2-, and UNIX-based systems. To improve security, it provides encryption and application-level security measures to prevent intruders from hacking into the server or its resources.

In addition, both NetWare 4.x and 5.0 supply graphical interfaces for managing network resources, including users, printers, groups, profiles, and shared drives. You can use NetWare's graphical interface from any workstation on the network. NetWare 5.0 also provides a graphical server console based on the Java programming language, called ConsoleOne. In addition, version 5.0 provides graphical wizards for part of the server installation. In versions lower than 5.0, you must install and configure NetWare servers entirely through DOS-based commands and menus. This requirement could be considered a drawback for less experienced network administrators.

Like Windows NT Server, however, NetWare does not necessarily suit all organizations. For example, if your organization depends heavily on enterprise-wide Microsoft solutions, such as SQL Server or Internet Information Server, you may want to forego a NetWare purchase. Although NetWare offers graphical interfaces for both management and console functions, one could argue that they are less responsive or intuitive than the Microsoft graphical interfaces. If members of your technical staff prefer a simple graphical interface, Windows NT

Server may therefore be a better choice. On the other hand, if you need to manage hundreds of servers and thousands of users, the scalability of its NDS design means that NetWare will probably make that management easier.

Another difference between NetWare 4.x and Windows NT Server is that NetWare 4.x (and lower versions) cannot support virtual memory. Instead, it can use only the physical memory installed in the machine. Although this feature means that the operating system accesses memory more quickly, it does not allow the operating system to draw on extra hard disk space when physical memory becomes limited. Note, however, that you can use virtual memory with NetWare 5.0.

Ideally, you should test your critical applications (including network management functions such as backup and restore services) on all types of operating systems (NetWare, Windows NT, and UNIX) to determine which will work most efficiently in your environment. Nevertheless, you probably will not have the luxury of designing a network from scratch and being the person who picks the network operating system. As mentioned in Chapter 8, the network operating systems that run on your servers will likely depend on political and technical issues in your environment or current business trends.

NetWare Server Hardware

You have learned that servers generally require more hard disk space, memory, and processing power than do client workstations on the network. Servers may also boast redundant disk drives, NICs, or power supplies or multiple processors. The more components you install on a server, the more expensive the machine. At the same time, however, the machine will likely operate more reliably and quickly with the added components.

Table 9-1 lists the minimum hardware requirements for versions 4.1 and 5.0 of NetWare, as outlined by Novell. If you plan to run applications or certain services on NetWare, such as a Web server or software distribution service (a network management function that was introduced in Chapter 1), your server will need more than these minimum requirements.

Table 9-1 Minimum Hardware Requirements for NetWare 4.x and 5.0 Servers

Component	NetWare 4.x Requirement	NetWare 5.0 Requirement
Processor	An IBM or IBM-compatible PC with a 386sx, 486, or better processor. Out of the box, NetWare 4.x can support as many as 4 processors.	An IBM or IBM-compatible PC with a Pentium processor. Out of the box, NetWare 5.0 can support as many as 32 processors.
Memory	20 MB RAM (the number should be increased for better performance; 64 MB is recommended).	64 MB RAM (the number should be increased for better performance; 128 MB is recommended).
Hard Disk	IDE or SCSI hard disk with at least 15 MB DOS partition and at least 100 MB NetWare partition.	IDE or SCSI hard disk with at least 30 MB DOS partition and at least 550 MB NetWare partition.
NIC	A NIC that supports your network type and for which you have drivers available.	A NIC that supports your network type and for which you have drivers available.
CD-ROM	A model that can read ISO 9660 formatted CDs is recommended.	A model that can read ISO 9660 formatted CDs is recommended.
Pointing device	Optional.	Optional, but necessary if you want to use the GUI console.
Floppy disk	Optional, but a 3.5" floppy disk drive is useful for installing the NetWare operating system license.	Optional, but a 3.5" floppy disk drive is useful for installing the NetWare operating system license.

As you learned in Chapter 8, most networking environments actually require servers that far exceed the minimum hardware requirements suggested by the software vendor. Every situation will vary, but to determine the optimal hardware for your server, you should consider the following:

- How many clients will connect to the server?
- What kinds of applications will run on the server?
- How much storage space will each user need?
- How much down time is acceptable?
- What can your organization afford?

Perhaps the most important question on this list refers to the types of applications that the server will run. As is the case with Windows NT Server hardware, you can purchase an inexpensive server that runs NetWare 4.x, but suffices only for file and print sharing. To accomplish more with your network, you will want to run applications on the server; you will therefore need a more powerful machine. Every application has its own processor, RAM, and storage requirements. Consult the application's installation guide to find out its specific requirements.

When considering the NetWare operating system requirements, you need to keep in mind the number of **NetWare loadable modules (NLMs)** used by each service. NLMs are routines that enable the server to run a range of programs and offer a variety of services, such as protocol support and Web publishing. Each NLM consumes some of the server's memory and processor resources (at least temporarily). For example, when you install NetWare out of the box, your server will run many critical NLMs. If you install Novell's GroupWise e-mail and scheduler software, the server may require another five NLMs. If you install Novell's BorderManager software, the server may require still another five or so NLMs, and so on. The amount of resources consumed by each NLM depends on the NLM's size and complexity.

Novell provides a worksheet to determine how much memory your NetWare server will require. This worksheet, which contains blanks in which you can enter your network's specifications (such as the number of users), can be found in your NetWare documentation or at Novell's Web site. Before you recommend buying or actually purchase memory for your NetWare server, you should consult this worksheet.

As with Windows NT, you can add components to your NetWare server to enhance its fault tolerance and performance. The most popular additional components include multiple processors, extra RAM, multiple NICs, fault-tolerant hard disks, a backup drive, and an uninterruptible power supply. You will learn more about how such components enhance network performance and reliability in Chapters 13 and 14. For now, it suffices to know that you must carefully analyze your current situation and plans for growth before making a hardware purchasing decision. Remember—paying more for a dependable server can be economical if it prevents down time.

A Closer Look at the NetWare Operating System

By now, you have probably noticed many similarities between the major features of NetWare and those of Windows NT. You'll discover even more similarities, as well as some differences, in their operating system details. This section compares and contrasts the various details of the NetWare, Windows NT, and UNIX operating systems.

If you have forgotten any of the concepts discussed in Chapter 8, refer to the key terms from that chapter to refresh your memory.

Multiprocessing

In versions 4.x and higher, NetWare supports the use of as many as 32 processors on one server. Like Windows NT, it takes advantage of symmetric multiprocessing, in which tasks are equally distributed among the processors. As you learned in Chapter 8, multiprocessing increases a server's performance when the server runs several operations simultaneously. For servers performing many processor-intensive activities, having multiple processors is usually worth the investment in the extra hardware. You will learn more analyzing and optimizing network performance in Chapter 13.

To use NetWare 5.0's multiprocessing capabilities, you simply install multiple processors in the server. The operating system will automatically detect and make use of these processors, whether 1 or 32 are present, without additional configuration. In lower versions of NetWare, you must load a symmetric multiprocessing (SMP) module to take advantage of multiple processors.

NetWare's Memory Model

Whereas NetWare 4.x can use only physical memory, NetWare 5.0 can work with both virtual memory and physical memory. Remember that virtual memory is actually hard disk space that can provide temporary memory. NetWare 5.0 needs virtual memory because many of its services use the Java programming language, which has high memory requirements.

NetWare 5.0 can dynamically manage its use of both physical and virtual memory. For example, if a printing service currently resides in physical memory but hasn't been accessed for two hours, NetWare 5.0 can push it into virtual memory so that a critical Java application (such as one needed immediately for file backup services) can use the physical memory. When the contents of virtual memory are required again, NetWare moves the printing service back into physical memory; at the same time, it sends another process from physical memory to virtual memory to open up the desired space.

Since the United States lifted tariffs that had been imposed on memory imported from other countries in the mid-1990s, good-quality memory chips have become very inexpensive. Therefore, you should never force your server to rely on the slower virtual memory to handle its typical processing loads. If the server suffers from too little physical memory and must spend all of its time swapping data to virtual memory, it will have no time to accomplish useful work.

NetWare, like Windows NT, uses 32-bit addressing to provide quick access to the physical memory. It also allows you to run services in a separate memory area from the operating system, which prevents one rogue routine from taking the server down. Assigning a separate memory area to a service is known as running the service in **protected mode**. Protected mode prevents the service and its supporting routines from harming critical server processes.

In NetWare, you can generally customize the extent to which applications are isolated from one another in memory. Many of the core components of the NetWare operating system run in protected mode by default. The only services that cannot run in protected mode are those that must directly access the server hardware. In fact, Novell allows network administrators to adjust the server's use of memory in a number of ways. This flexibility can be both a blessing and a curse, however. If you change a setting in the wrong direction, for example, you may restrict the server's ability to send or transmit data efficiently. Nevertheless, every environment will require some fine-tuning to maximize the use of memory, and every organization's memory needs will vary.

Although you can customize memory on a Novell network, both NetWare 4.x and 5.0 manage physical memory very efficiently right out of the box. One important technique for managing memory is caching. **Caching** is the process of saving frequently used data to an area of the physical memory where it will be readily available for future requests. Caching accelerates the process of accessing the server because the operating system does not have to search for the requested data on the disk.

Conceptually, caching is similar to what goes on at a help desk. If 90% of the time a company's users call the help desk to ask questions about e-mail, the help desk manager might decide to publish a Web site giving answers to frequently asked e-mail questions. This Web site resembles a cache in that it provides commonly required information in an easy-to-access form.

The more physical memory present in your server, the more space the server can use for caching. On the other hand, the more services and applications run by your server, the less space the server will have for caching. As with most other memory settings in NetWare, you can change Cache Read and Write parameters to suit your environment.

THE KERNEL AND CONSOLE OPERATIONS

At the heart of NetWare lies the **kernel**, or the core of the operating system. NetWare's 32-bit kernel is responsible for overseeing all critical server processes. The program SERVER.EXE runs the kernel from a server's DOS partition. Typically, a server will start by activating an AUTOEXEC.BAT file that launches SERVER.EXE; from that point forward, NetWare controls the machine's operations. SERVER.EXE loads the critical NLMs that the kernel needs to run the NetWare operating system. In fact, once an NLM loads into memory, it is considered part of the kernel.

You can envision the kernel as a train with multiple cars. A train may leave Duluth with an engine, two tank cars, and five freight cars. These eight pieces, collectively, make up the train. In St. Paul, the train may pick up four more tank cars and six more freight cars. Now the train contains 18 pieces. If the train stops in Dubuque to deliver (or unload) five cars of iron ore, it does not fundamentally change. It will always need an engine, and no matter how many cars it carries, it remains a train. Much in the same way, NLMs can be loaded and unloaded (either automatically, by a program that requires them, or manually, by a network administrator) based on whether the kernel needs them. Loading and unloading NLMs does not change the kernel, however. The ability to dynamically load and unload NLMs makes the kernel modular and efficient. It also affords network administrators comprehensive control over their network operations.

The network administrator's primary interface to a NetWare server is the **server console**. Unlike in Windows NT, this interface is not entirely graphical. NetWare 4.x employs only text-based server menus at the console. In NetWare 5.0, however, commands can be accessed through either a text-based or graphical menu system. The graphical interface in NetWare 5.0 is called ConsoleOne. Figure 9-1 illustrates a typical DOS-based console screen on a NetWare 4.x server. The NLM depicted in Figure 9-1 is called Monitor. **Monitor** enables the system administrator to view server parameters such as protocols, bindings, system resources, and loaded modules. In any case, it also allows the system administrator to modify these parameters. If you plan to specialize in NetWare administration (no matter which version of NetWare is involved), you should become very familiar with the Monitor NLM.

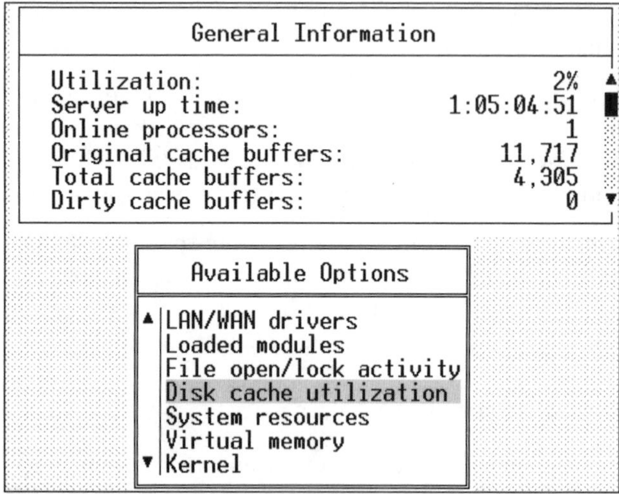

Figure 9-1 A NetWare console screen at the Monitor menu

Hundreds of NLMs are available for the NetWare operating system. In fact, developers can write their own NLMs for special purposes because Novell shares its operating system code. Nevertheless, you probably won't write your own, because most of the NLMs you'll ever need will come with your server software or the additional utilities you install.

You can view the NLMs currently running on your NetWare server by typing *modules* at the NetWare server console. To find out more about a single NLM, type *Help XXX,* where *XXX* is the name of the NLM. For example, to find out more about the Monitor command, type *help monitor* at the console prompt. The server will respond with an explanation of the purpose of the command, its syntax, and its switches.

The NetWare server console prompt is not the same as a DOS prompt (which, among other things, allows you to view, copy, or delete files and directories on a computer). The purpose of the console is not to manage the file system, but rather to manage the server parameters. To manage the file system, you should log in to the server as an administrator from a workstation connected to the network. The next section discusses the NetWare file system in more detail.

THE NETWARE FILE SYSTEM

As you learned in Chapter 8, a file system is an operating system's method of organizing, managing, and accessing its files through logical structures and software routines. NetWare does not allow you to specify the file system types in the same way that Windows NT does, but it offers its own high-performance file system that supports DOS, Macintosh, UNIX,

OS/2, and Windows' long filenames. Whereas the operating system supports DOS filenames by default, achieving support for other filenames requires loading the proper NLMs on the server. Once you have installed the necessary modules, Macintosh, Windows, UNIX, or clients can read from the server as if the server were running the Macintosh, Windows, UNIX, or OS/2 operating system, respectively. Because NetWare uses modules rather than file systems to support access by other operating systems, file/directory size limitations and performance do not vary between NetWare volumes or servers.

Like Windows NT, NetWare uses volumes as the basis for organizing files and directories on the server. When you install NetWare, a volume called SYS is automatically created. At the time of installation, you may choose to create additional volumes such as DATA (for user data) or APPS (for shared applications), as well. (You should make additional volume names short, simple, and descriptive.) You should design the file system so that it meets your performance, security, growth, and data sharing goals. For example, by assigning all user data to its own volume called DATA, separate from the SYS volume that contains system files, you can protect your system files from accidental deletion. Creating a separate DATA volume for data files therefore provides more security than putting all data and system files on one volume.

Plan carefully before establishing a server's volume and directory structure—once established, they are very difficult to change. When installing a NetWare network from scratch, you should consult resources that can guide you through the process of planning the volume and directory structure for your network.

After planning and creating your server's volume(s), you must determine whether the network should take advantage of NetWare's file compression capabilities.

Compression

NetWare 4.x and 5.0 both support file compression, which is performed on a file-by-file basis. In other words, each file is compressed separately; an entire directory or volume is not compressed at the same time. Another feature of NetWare's file compression is that the processes of compression and decompression are transparent to the user. For example, if a directory containing e-mail has been compressed, a user who requests data from that directory will never know that, during the few seconds she waits to pick up the e-mail message, it is being decompressed.

NetWare versions 4.x and 5.0 differ slightly in their default compression services. In both NetWare 4.x and 5.x, unless the network administrator specifically chooses to prevent compression, compression on the server is enabled automatically. The average overall degree of compression attained by a NetWare 5.0 server is 63%. Thus a 4 GB volume with 1 GB of uncompressed data and 3 GB of free space could gain 630 MB of extra free space (for a total of 3.63 GB free space) with normal compression. The compression ratio will vary for each file.

Compression does increase file access time slightly; for this reason, it is not recommended for extremely large files. NetWare will not compress files that exceed 256 MB in size. If you choose to use compression on your server, you'll find that NetWare provides numerous options to optimize disk compression. Among other things, you can instruct the server to wait a specific period of days before first compressing new files, and you can disable compression altogether for some types of files or directories. You can also set a threshold of compression below which the operating system will not compress files. For example, if you specify that a very large database can be compressed by only 10%, it may not be worthwhile to compress it, because it would increase file access time and provide little space savings.

Some applications, such as older DOS-based databases, may not work when compressed on a NetWare server. Although the NetWare operating system can determine which of its own files can be compressed safely, you should verify that other system files and applications will work when compressed.

Block Suballocation

Block suballocation is a technique for using hard disk space more efficiently. To understand block suballocation, you must understand how data are stored on the hard disk. As you learned in Chapter 8's discussion of FAT32, each file on a computer is placed into one or more allocation units, or **blocks**, on the hard disk. (You can configure the standard block size on your server.) Normally, if an entire file does not fit into one block, it will consume as many blocks as required to meet its storage requirements, even if it doesn't use all of the space in every block. For example, suppose your block size is 4 KB. A 17 KB file would require five blocks, or 20 KB of hard disk space, as pictured in the left-hand side of Figure 9-2. This arrangement wastes 3 KB of space.

Suballocation allows you to break blocks into smaller pieces, or suballocation blocks, of 512 Bytes. If a file exceeds a whole number of blocks, it will use parts of additional blocks in increments of 512 Bytes. The 17 KB file in the previous example would therefore use only 4.25 blocks, as shown in the right side of Figure 9-2. Other files can then occupy the remaining 3 KB piece of the fifth block. In this way, block suballocation permits you to use much more of the available space on the server's hard disk.

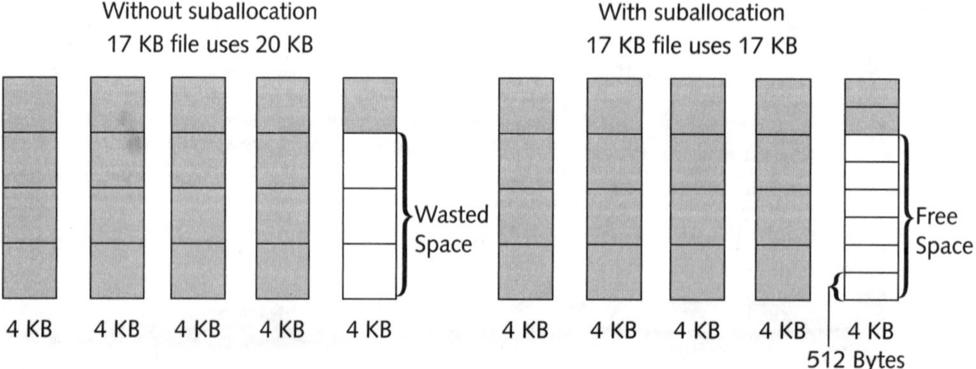

Figure 9-2 Block suballocation

Block suballocation is enabled by default when you install NetWare. To prevent block suballocation, you must deselect this option during a custom installation. Once block suballocation is activated on a volume, you can deactivate it only by reinstalling the server software (that is, NetWare).

NDS

A major development Novell introduced with version 4.0 is NetWare Directory Services. **NetWare Directory Services (NDS)** provides a system for managing multiple servers and their resources, including users, volumes, groups, profiles, printers, and so on. (In NetWare versions *below* 4.0, the Bindery contained this information.) The NDS model is somewhat similar to the concept of domains in Windows NT, but it is more comprehensive in that it centrally organizes not only users, groups, and resources, but also (among other things) security privileges, document libraries, and the use of other Novell programs (such as GroupWise or BorderManager). NDS treats every networked resource as a separate **object** with distinct properties. Each object can then be centrally managed from a single interface.

To understand how NetWare 4.x and 5.0 work, you must first understand NDS. This section introduces the principles of NDS. Although it sounds like a simple concept, NDS can have a very complex implementation in large organizations. For more details on designing and managing NDS structures, you should consult the NetWare documentation or purchase a book devoted to the topic of NetWare administration.

The NetWare installation process for the first server in a network generates the network's initial NDS. When adding servers or other resources to the network, you build upon this original NDS in a hierarchical fashion. Novell uses the analogy of a tree to describe this hierarchical layout. The **NDS tree** is the logical representation of resources in a NetWare enterprise. Unlike a real tree, the NDS tree is upside-down, with a single root at the top and multiple branches at the bottom, as shown Figure 9-3.

The NDS tree can have only one root, which is created during the first NetWare (4.x or higher) server installation on the network. Once created, the root cannot be moved, deleted, or renamed. Consequently, before you begin a NetWare 4.x or 5.0 installation, you should meticulously plan your NDS structure and make sure that all decision makers in your Information Technology department agree on its naming convention.

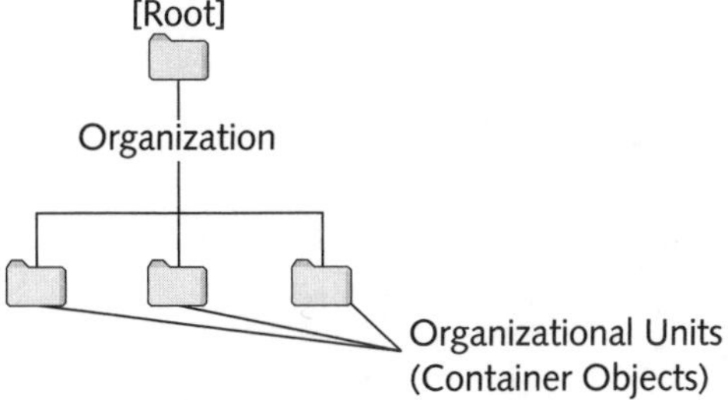

Figure 9-3 A simple NDS tree

The root leads to a hierarchical arrangement of branches. These branches are called **container objects** (or **organizational units**) because their primary purpose is to logically subdivide and hold other objects that belong together, thus simplifying rights assignments, group login scripts, etc.

Container objects may organize users and resources by geographical location, department, professional function, security authorization, or other criteria significant to the particular network. For example, if the root of the Sutkin Manufacturing Company's NDS tree is called "Sutkin," the container objects may be called "Maintenance," "Inventory," "Packing," "Shipping," "Information Services," "Accounting," and so on. On the other hand, if Sutkin Manufacturing is a small company with only a handful of users and other resources in the Maintenance, Inventory, Packing, and Shipping departments, these users and resources may be grouped in a larger branch called "Operations" and departments within the "Operations" container may be distinguished through the use of groups.

Figure 9-4 compares the various ways of grouping objects. For any organization, no single correct way to arrange an NDS tree usually exists. Instead, the organization of resources and container objects is a decision that network administrators must plan carefully.

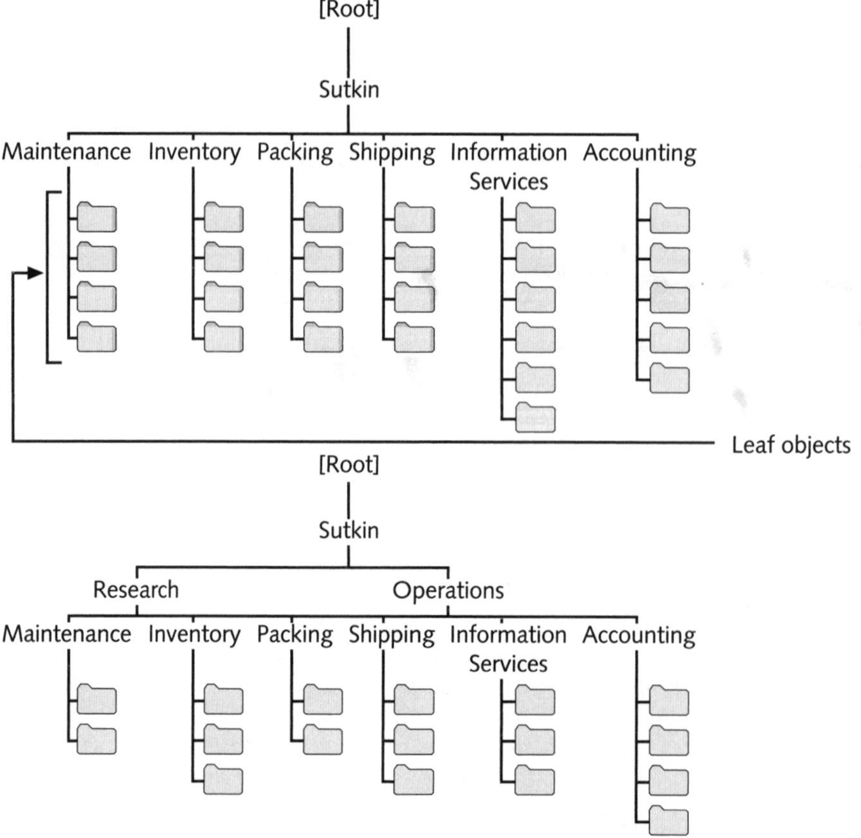

Figure 9-4 Two ways of grouping objects in an NDS tree

Moving away from the root of the tree, branch objects lead to either more branch objects or leaf objects. A **leaf object** is an object in the NDS tree that does not contain other objects. For example, a print queue is a leaf object because it handles only the printer queue. A user is a leaf object because it does not contain or manage any objects other than the network user it represents. Several kinds of leaf objects exist. You will typically deal with user-related leaf objects such as users, groups, profiles, templates, and aliases or printer-related objects such as printers, queues, and print servers. Some Novell packages, such as ManageWise or ZenWorks, introduce other kinds of leaf objects into the tree. Nevertheless, all Novell products integrate with the NDS structure to allow easy, centralized administration. Figure 9-5 depicts a more complex (but still simple compared with the real world) NDS tree with several branch and leaf objects.

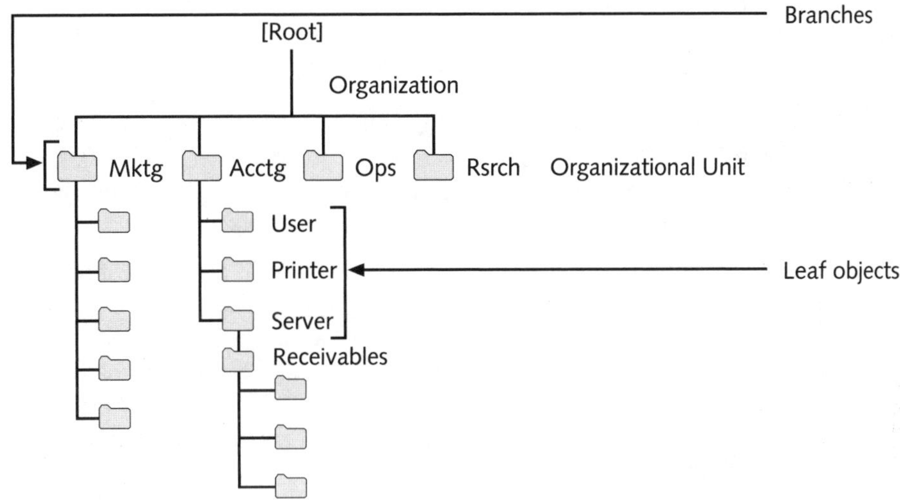

Figure 9-5 A more complex NDS tree

Each object in an NDS tree has a **context** that indicates where that object belongs in the tree. A context consists of an object's organizational unit names, arranged from most specific to most general, plus the organization name. Periods separate the organizational unit names within the context. You can envision the context as a kind of roadmap for locating an object.

Contexts may be expressed in two ways: typeful and typeless. The **typeful** notation is a relatively lengthy way of expressing context that includes identifiers for the organization and organizational units. For example, a user named Phil who works in the Receivables area of the Accounting ("Acctg") department of Sutkin Manufacturing in Figure 9-5 would have a typeful context of OU=Receivables.OU=Acctg.O=Sutkin. In this typeful context "OU" stands for "organizational unit" (another name for a container) and "O" stands for "organization" (which is associated with the root of your tree). A **typeless** notation eliminates the "OU" and "O" designations. In the preceding example, Phil's typeless context would be Receivables.Acctg.Sutkin. Both the typeful and the typeless contexts indicate that Phil is a member of the Receivables organizational unit, which is located in the Acctg organizational unit, which is part of the Sutkin organization.

In a large corporation with a complex NDS tree, a user's context can quickly become very long. Users do not always have to know or provide their context, however. Instead, the workstation support group or network administrator can configure users' client software to assume by default the context and the organization to which each user belongs. Users can then log in to their organization with only a user name. In the preceding example, a user named Phil with the typeful context of OU=Receivables.OU=Acctg.O=Sutkin would simply type "phil" when prompted for his user ID.

Novell has devised an entire lexicon to describe its NDS structure, most of which you can ignore for now. One more NDS term may prove helpful, however: schema. Novell uses the term **schema** to refer to the set of objects (such as user or printer) and their attributes in an NDS tree. The simplest schema is the one that ships with NDS. A network administrator can extend the schema to include additional object classes and attributes. For example, you may want to add a user's fax number as an optional attribute.

Do not confuse NDS with the NetWare file system. The two are completely different entities. The file system pertains to the physical servers and the arrangement and maintenance of the data. NDS refers to the logical organization of servers and resources across an enterprise-wide network.

The NetWare operating system stores NDS information in a database format and distributes the information over several volumes. In larger organizations, NDS information may be distributed over several servers for two reasons: to accommodate its size and ensure its integrity. Conceptually, NDS does not appear to be tied to the server's hard disk. For example, the server does not have a big database file called "NDS.DB" that holds all of the tree and object information. In fact, NetWare keeps NDS information in hidden storage areas across (usually multiple) servers.

Typically, only network administrators have rights that allow them to modify the NDS tree. NDS management can be performed only through NetWare resource management tools, such as the NetWare Administration utility. The **NetWare Administrator utility (NWAdmin)** is a graphical NDS management interface that can be launched from a Windows 95 or Windows NT workstation. Figure 9-6 shows an example of an NWAdmin screen with NDS objects. You will learn more about managing objects through NWAdmin later in this chapter.

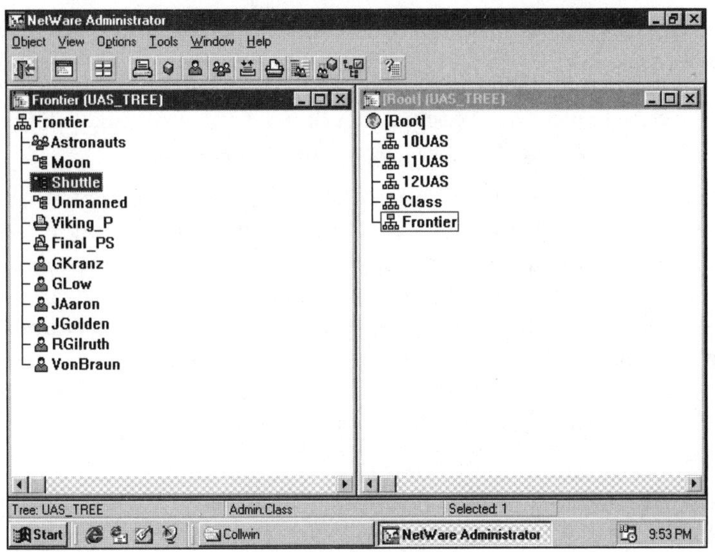

Figure 9-6 An NWAdmin interface

Installing and Configuring a NetWare Server

As with any major installation, you should first draw up a plan before beginning to install NetWare. Before you insert the NetWare CD into your CD-ROM drive, you should consider many factors, including the organization's structure, function of the server, server hardware, applications, number of users, LAN architecture, and optional services (such as Web hosting). As you learned in the discussion of Windows NT Server in Chapter 8, once you have installed and configured the network operating system, changing its configuration may prove difficult and perhaps cause service disruptions for users. This section provides an overview of the decisions you need to make when installing and configuring your NetWare server.

Planning for Installation

The importance of planning for installation cannot be overemphasized. Poor planning results in more work for the installer, potential down time for users, and headaches for whomever supports the server after installation. The following list summarizes the critical preinstallation decisions you should make. As you will see, the list is very similar to the decisions that you must make before installing Windows NT Server; where Windows NT deals in domain models, however, NetWare focuses on the NDS tree.

- *Where does the server fit in the NDS tree?* The place occupied by the server in your network's NDS tree (its context) will depend largely on its function. If this function is merely to allow a group of students to print to a classroom printer, then the server might belong to a small organizational unit for that classroom. If the server will provide network access for all of the math instructors, it may belong in the Math container of your tree. If the server will provide mail services to the entire company, it may have its own organizational unit off the root of the tree called Mail. Clearly, you should develop your organization's tree and its policies for container and leaf objects before you begin installation. The server's place in the NDS tree will affect how easily it can be accessed and managed. Once you have established the server's context, you cannot change it.

- *What name will the server have?* Choose a practical, descriptive name that distinguishes the server from all other servers. You might use geographical server names, such as Boston or Buffalo. Alternatively, you might name servers according to their function, such as Marketing or Research. Bear in mind that the server name can (and usually will) differ from its NDS container's name. For example, the high school Math department server in a school system's NDS structure might be called "MATH_DEPT," but it might belong to the "Math" organizational unit, which might in turn belong to a larger organizational unit called "HS" under the school system's root.
- *How many and what kinds of network adapter cards will the server use?* Before you begin installing NetWare, you should have driver and diagnostics disks on hand for the server's NICs. The NetWare installation process will attempt to find your NIC's driver in its own collection of software, but it may not always be successful in this quest. You should therefore be prepared to supply not only the NIC software, but also the NIC's IRQ, shared memory address, and I/O base address before beginning the server installation.
- *What protocols and network services should the server use?* You need to know which protocols your network requires. As you will recall from Chapter 3, more networks are moving toward TCP/IP-based transmission because this family of protocols is flexible, reliable, and widely supported. If your NetWare server will run Web services or connect to UNIX systems, for example, you must install IP. NetWare 4.x provides support for TCP/IP, whereas NetWare 5.0 runs TCP/IP natively. By default, the NetWare 5.0 installation process selects IP as a protocol that the server will support.
- *What kind of disk controllers does my server have?* NetWare's installation program will attempt to detect what kind of hard disk and CD-ROM drive your server possesses. If the program can correctly identify the hardware, it will install the drivers. Otherwise, it will prompt you to choose drivers from a list or install a driver from a disk. Either way, you should know what kind of disk controllers your server has (you can find this information in the server's hardware specifications). Note that the NetWare installation process does not always choose the right controller by default. NetWare can support SCSI, MicroChannel, IDE, EISA, ISA, AT, and ESDI hard disk controllers.
- *How many, how large, and what kind of volumes will the server require?* NetWare's installation program will ask you to identify the size, number, and names of the server volumes. Initially, the program assigns all free space on the hard disk to its default volume, SYS. To add volumes, you must modify the size of SYS (by subtracting the size of the other volumes you intend to create from SYS's current size).

- *What additional services will the server support?* As in the Windows NT installation, you may choose to perform a custom or simple installation of NetWare, depending on the services and applications that your server will run. In a **simple installation**, the most popular installation options are chosen for you. This type of installation takes place more rapidly than a **custom installation**, which allows you to determine which services and programs should be installed, among other things. The first time you install a NetWare server (ideally, in a test environment), you will probably want to choose a simple setup to see how the installation process works. If you know the exact requirements for your environment and you feel comfortable with the NetWare installation process, you may choose to perform a custom installation. In that case, a list of additional services to install will appear near the end of the installation process. These services include support for Web and FTP hosting, backup utilities, OS/2 utilities, and TCP/IP address management. If you neglect to install a service during this process, you can always install it later.
- *What kind of license do I have?* When you purchased the NetWare operating system, you chose a licensing option for your organization. During the installation of the operating system, you will be prompted for the license diskette (or file, if you've copied it to the server's hard disk) that came with your NetWare software. NetWare licenses vary chiefly in terms of how many concurrent (simultaneously connected) users are supported by the server.
- *How can I remember all of this information?* Once you have made these decisions, you should create a server installation form and keep it with you during installation. Appendix C offers an example of such a form.

The previous list highlighted only the most significant installation options. You should also be prepared to read and accept the license agreement, identify your time zone, and specify an administrator account ID and password.

THE INSTALLATION PROCESS

After you have planned out your installation, you can actually perform it. NetWare can be installed from a CD (the most popular method), floppy disks (not recommended), or another server on the network; the latter process is called an "over-the-wire" installation because the files are copied over the network's wiring. In this section, you can follow the steps to carry out a simple standalone NetWare 4.11 server installation performed from a CD-ROM. The NetWare 5.0 installation differs slightly in that it provides a graphical interface for some stages (making the process somewhat easier). Both installations follow the same pattern and require the same information, as discussed in the previous section. For simplicity's sake, this example uses the default installation options. You should perform a NetWare installation on a server that has a new installation of DOS version 6.22 or higher (do not attempt this installation from a DOS prompt on a server running a Windows operating system or from the DOS version that comes with Windows).

To perform a simple NetWare 4.11 installation:

1. Make sure that the server has a bootable DOS partition at least 15 MB in size and that it has at least 100 MB of free space available. Also, make sure that the drivers for the CD-ROM drive have been loaded.
2. Insert the NetWare 4.11 installation CD into the CD-ROM drive.
3. At the CD-ROM DOS prompt (usually D:), type **install**.
4. You will be prompted to choose the server language. Move your cursor to the line that says **Select this line to install in English**, then press **Enter**.
5. The NetWare terms of use agreement appears. Press any key several times to read this screen and continue.
6. The Select the Type of Installation Desired window appears. Choose **NetWare Server Installation**, then press **Enter**.
7. The program presents you with a list of NetWare 4.11 products to install. Choose **NetWare 4.11**, then press **Enter**.
8. A menu appears asking whether you want to perform a simple or custom installation. Choose **Simple Installation of NetWare 4.11**, then press **Enter**.
9. You are prompted to enter the server's name. For guidance on valid server names, press **F1** to view the Help text. When you are ready to continue, press the **Escape** key to exit the Help text. Type the server name (which you established during your planning process), then press **Enter**.
10. Wait as the installation program copies the server's boot files to the hard disk. If your server contains multiple processors, the install process will detect this configuration and ask whether you want to install symmetrical multiprocessing support. If you receive this prompt, choose **No**.
11. The install program searches for your server's disk controllers and, if it recognizes them, installs the drivers. If the NetWare Installation program does not recognize your hardware, it provides you with a list of drivers to install. In this event, choose the driver from the list that matches your server's disk controllers.
12. You are asked to choose your server's NIC (LAN) driver from a list. Choose the driver that matches your server's NIC, then press **Enter**.
13. You are offered a number of LAN driver setting options, such as the frame types supported by the NCI and the IPX number for the server's network card. Press **Enter** to accept the default values.
14. The NetWare Installation program asks whether you want to install additional LAN drivers. Choose **No** to continue.
15. The program displays the disk controller and LAN drivers it intends to install. Verify that you have at least one driver listed for the hard disk and at least one NIC driver listed and that both are correct. Choose **Continue Installation** from the menu, then press **Enter**.

16. You are asked to create the NetWare disk partition. You can have only one NetWare partition per physical hard disk. Choose to allocate all of the free space (space not used by the bootable DOS partition) to the NetWare partition. If the program asks whether it should delete all nonbootable partitions, select **Yes**, then press **Enter**.
17. Wait while the program copies the preliminary installation files to your server's hard disk. After this process is complete, the NetWare installation program will scan the network for existing NetWare NDS trees.
18. If the program does not find an existing NDS tree, you are prompted to identify whether to identify this server as the first server in the tree or whether it should connect to another server. Highlight **Yes, this is the first server**, then press **Enter**.
19. You are asked to identify your time zone. In the list that appears, highlight the time zone where the server will be installed, then press **Enter**.
20. You are prompted to identify the NDS tree's organization name—that is, the name of your NDS tree. Type the name of your organization, then press **Enter**.
21. A screen appears requesting your administrator password. During a NetWare 4.x or 5.0 installation, the default administrator user ID is ADMIN. For security reasons, you should create a different user with full administrator rights to replace ADMIN (and disable the ADMIN user ID) after the installation ends. If you do not change the administrator ID, a hacker has half the information he or she needs to break into your network. Enter the administrator password, then press **Enter**.

Do not forget the administrator password you choose during this step in the installation process. If you forget the password, you cannot do anything with the server and you must reinstall the NetWare operating system.

22. Enter the password a second time to confirm it, then press **Enter**.
23. The program prompts you to acknowledge the organization name and context you have selected. Press **Enter** to confirm these choices.
24. After directory services are installed on your server's hard disk, you are prompted to provide the license file that came with your NetWare software (usually in diskette form). Insert the diskette that shipped with your software, then press **Enter**.
25. Remove the license diskette and store it in a safe place. If you ever need to reinstall or upgrade the network operating system software or add more NetWare services to the server, you will need this diskette.
26. Wait while the NetWare operating system files are copied to the SYS volume on your server's hard disk.
27. Once all NetWare files have been copied to the SYS volume, a screen appears listing other available installation options. Choose **Continue Installation** from the Other Installation Options menu, then press **Enter**.

28. To exit the installation program and return to the server console, press **Enter**.
29. Restart the server.

In actual practice, your NetWare installation will probably involve more decisions (particularly with regard to volume sizes and names, NDS context, and NetWare services to install) than indicated in this example. You may want to experiment with a simple installation such as this one, however, before you perform installations on your working servers.

After performing a NetWare 4.x installation and restarting the machine, your server should be functional. If you chose the simple installation, the IPX/SPX protocol will be installed and bound to your NIC. To install other protocols at a later date, you must run a configuration utility from the console called inetcfg. On NetWare 5.0 servers, the TCP/IP protocol will be installed and bound to your server's NIC by default. Keep in mind that the method for configuring protocols and NICs (among other things) has changed from NetWare 4.x to NetWare 5.0. In version 5.0, this utility is called nwconfig. Modifying the server's network properties through these commands is beyond the scope of this chapter. If you plan to become a NetWare expert, however, you should study the capabilities of the inetcfg and nwconfig utilities.

After you have installed a NetWare server, verify that you can log on to that server as administrator from a Windows NT or Windows 95 workstation using the Novell Client for NetWare. If this effort fails, you may need to use the configuration commands to verify that the server has network connectivity.

By default, the NetWare installation process (for both version 4.x and 5.0) creates the NDS tree (if one didn't previously exist), a SYS volume, an administrator user called Admin who has supervisory rights to all objects in the NDS tree and all files in the file system, and a group called [Public] that has Browse rights to view all objects in the NDS tree.

Using the NetWare Administrator Utility (NWAdmin)

To make your server functional, you will need to add users and other objects to the NDS tree. After adding objects, you may want to modify their properties or even delete them. This section introduces an important tool in both NetWare 4.x and 5.0 server management, the NetWare Administrator utility (NWAdmin). As explained earlier in this chapter, NWAdmin is a graphical interface that runs from a Windows 95, Windows 98, or Windows NT workstation and enables network administrators to manage NDS objects. Through the use of drop-down menus and toolbars, it simplifies the process of viewing, creating, changing, and deleting objects.

The best way to learn about NWAdmin is to experiment with it on a test server. You will have such an opportunity in the following exercise and in a Hands-on Project at the end of this chapter.

To create objects in the NDS tree:

1. To manage the NDS tree through NWAdmin, you must have administrator rights. Log on to your NetWare 4.x or 5.0 server from a Windows 95, Windows 98, or Windows NT workstation as an administrator.
2. Launch the following executable file from your server's SYS volume: **PUBLIC\WIN32\NWADMN32.EXE.** The NetWare Administrator (NWAdmin) window opens, as shown in Figure 9-7.

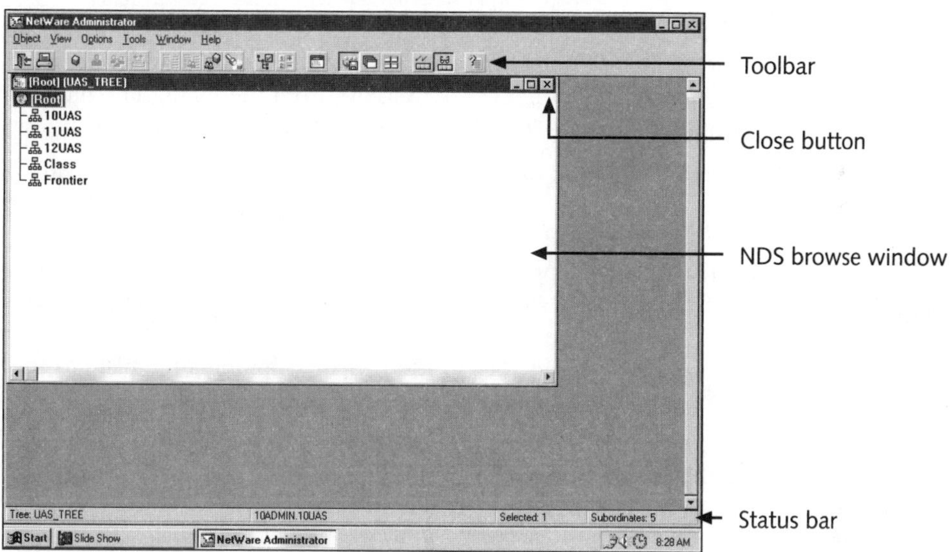

Figure 9-7 NetWare Administrator window

3. If the NWAdmin screen does not display your NDS tree by default, you can specify the tree by choosing **View** on the menu bar, and then choosing **Set Context**. Enter **[Root]** in the context field, then click **OK**.
4. Double-click the root object. Your server's NDS tree will appear, with organizational objects underneath the root and leaf objects (if they exist) underneath the organizational (container) objects. Proceed through the following steps to add objects to your NDS tree.
5. To create an organization, right-click the root object, then choose **Create**.
6. A list of objects appears. Scroll down the list, highlight **Organization**, then click **OK**.
7. The Organization dialog box opens. Enter your Organization name, then click **Create**. The newly created Organization appears in the NDS tree.
8. To create an object inside the Organization, right-click the Organization, then choose **Create** from the menu that appears.

9

9. The program displays a list of objects that you can choose to create within the Organization. Notice how many more options appear in this list than were shown in the list of objects you could create from the Root.
10. To create an Organizational Unit beneath your Organization, select the Organizational Unit object, then click **OK**. The Organizational Unit dialog box opens.
11. Enter the name of the Organizational Unit, then click **Create**. To see the name of the newly created Organizational Unit in the NDS tree, double-click the Organization object.
12. To create a user belonging to your Organizational Unit, right-click the Organizational Unit, then choose **Create** from the menu. The program displays a list of objects you can choose to create within the Organizational Unit.
13. Press **U** to select the User object in the list of objects you can create.
14. Press **Enter** to create a User object.
15. The Create User dialog box appears, as shown in Figure 9-8. You are prompted to enter the user's ID and last name. These two fields are the only fields you must complete to create a user. Often, you will want to choose additional options, such as granting a home directory to the user or assigning a template to the user. Click **OK** after entering the user's ID and last name.

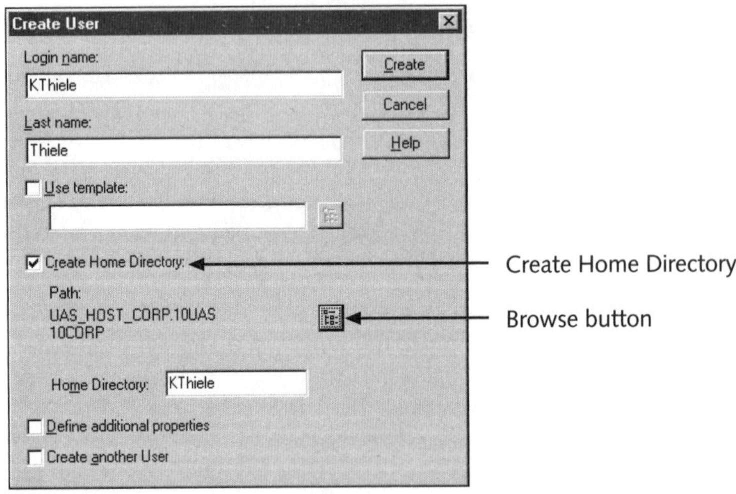

Figure 9-8 Create User dialog box

If you choose to establish a user's home directory when you create the user ID, that user will have all rights to his or her home directory by default. As a result, you do not have to assign Read, Write, Erase, or other rights for the user's home directory later. If you do not create a user's home directory when you create the user ID, and you later decide to grant a home directory to the user, you must manually assign rights before the user can save, change, or delete files in his or her home directory.

After you have created NDS objects, you may want to change their properties. For example, if one of your staff members changes her last name, you will want to change the last name property within her User object. To view or change the properties of any leaf object (such as a printer, user, template, or group), you can right-click the object in the tree, then choose Details from the menu that appears.

To modify the properties of a User object through NWAdmin:

1. Right-click the User object whose properties you want to modify, then choose **Details** from the menu that appears. Alternatively, you can double-click the User object to view its Properties dialog box.
2. The object's Properties dialog box appears. The right side of the properties dialog box contains a number of properties buttons. Click the button whose properties you want to change. For example, if you want to modify the user's password, click the **Password Restrictions** button. The Password Restrictions window appears, as shown in Figure 9-9.

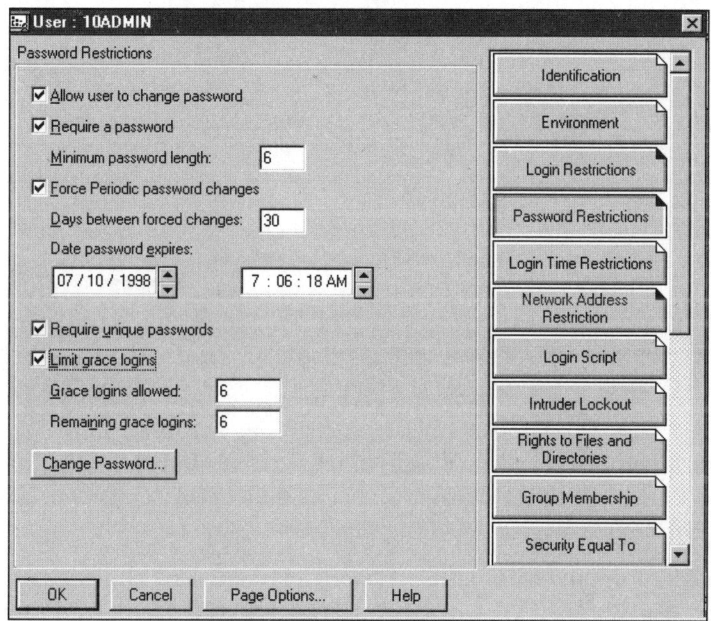

Figure 9-9 Password Restrictions window

3. Change the properties as instructed by the properties dialog box. For example, in the Password Restrictions window, you may choose to force users to change their passwords upon logging in, enforce a minimum length for passwords, or change a user's password.

To delete an NDS object through NWAdmin:

1 Right-click the object, then choose **Delete** from the menu that appears.
2. NWAdmin asks whether you really want to delete the object. Click **Yes** to confirm the deletion.

NWAdmin will not allow you to delete an object that contains leaf objects. If you want to delete a container object, you must delete its subordinate objects first. To do so, highlight the first object in the container to be deleted, hold down the Shift key, then click the last object to be deleted. You should see the objects between the first and the last object highlighted. Press the Delete key. NWAdmin will ask you to confirm that you want to delete the group of objects.

The operations described in this section cover only a small fraction of NWAdmin's capabilities. In real-world day-to-day network operations, you will find that your most frequent use of NWAdmin will consist of viewing, modifying, and creating objects. In addition to carrying out these operations, you may manage other Novell programs, such as NetWare Distributed Printing Services, GroupWise, or ZenWorks from NWAdmin. You may also manage Windows NT resources if Windows NT servers are integrated into your NDS tree. Using NWAdmin, you can search for objects, move objects from one container to another, or assign templates or profiles to objects. In short, NWAdmin is your link to managing your NDS tree.

Internetworking with Other Operating Systems

In Chapter 8, you learned that both Novell and Microsoft have made great strides in enabling their network operating systems to interact. Microsoft has devised one solution (Gateway Services for NetWare), and Novell has created another, called **NDS for NT**. The NDS for NT tool works with the NetWare 4.x and 5.0 operating systems and Windows NT servers to enable Windows NT domains to appear as container objects in NWAdmin. In Novell's terminology, NDS for NT *extends the schema* to include Windows NT resources. Windows NT servers appear as server objects, and groups and users from Windows NT domains appear as NDS group and user objects, respectively. With NDS for NT enabled, users who require services from both Windows NT and NetWare servers can simply log in to the NDS tree, rather than logging in to both types of servers.

NDS for NT provides a simple solution to a network administrator's challenge of integrating Windows NT and NetWare. On Windows NT servers, an NDS for NT client and service must be installed and bound to the network cards. Once this tool is installed, the NT server appears as a container object in the NetWare NDS tree when it connects to the network.

Once the NT server is an NDS object, it can be managed centrally through the NetWare Administrator utility. This ability makes the network administrator's job of managing mixed server environments much easier.

Realistically, you would probably use NDS for NT in a networking environment dominated by NetWare products or in an environment in which the complex structure of servers, users, locations, and so on demands the comprehensive management capabilities of NWAdmin. If most of your servers run Windows NT Server, using Microsoft's Gateway Services for NetWare, as described in Chapter 8, may make more sense.

On the client side, Novell provides client software specifically designed for Windows NT, Windows 95, OS/2, Macintosh, and UNIX clients. These packages come at no extra cost with the NetWare 4.x and 5.0 operating systems, or they can be downloaded from Novell's Web site.

Chapter Summary

- Currently, several versions of NetWare exist. NetWare 3.x includes versions 3.1 through 3.2. Although these versions were introduced in the early 1990s, many have not been replaced with newer versions—a testament to their high reliability. Novell introduced NetWare 4.0, 4.1, and 4.11 (collectively known as NetWare 4.x) in the mid-1990s. NetWare 4.x is more user-friendly and provides much better support for enterprise-wide networks containing multiple servers than NetWare 3.x.
- In 1998, Novell released version 5.0 of NetWare, which not only increases the extent and ease of network management, but also provides a network operating system based on the IP protocol. It uses the programming language Java for many of its interfaces and services. NetWare 5.0 also offers better printer and file system administration than version 4.x does.
- Both NetWare 4.1 and 5.0 use Novell Directory Services (NDS) to organize users, groups, servers, and other network resources. Both versions provide a graphical interface for managing network resources. In addition, both support integration with other network operating systems, Web services, multiple protocols, asset management, migration utilities, and software distribution.
- Novell provides extensive online support from its support Web site. The company also provides enhanced technical support to Certified NetWare Engineers (CNEs) through CDs and discounted calls to its help desk. In addition, a number of third-party discussion groups on the Web focus on NetWare products.
- NetWare is optimal for file and print sharing. It can run multiple services simultaneously and use as many as 32 internal processors. Its modularity allows the network administrator to isolate some processes from others or change the priority of critical applications. NetWare does not require you to restart the server when you change its configurations, keeping service interruptions brief.
- NetWare offers native interoperability solutions for Macintosh-, DOS-, Windows-, OS/2-, and UNIX-based systems.

- NetWare may not suit every organization. If your organization depends heavily on enterprise-wide Microsoft solutions you may want to forego a NetWare purchase. If your technical staff prefers or demands a simple graphical interface, Windows NT Server may be a better choice. Although NetWare offers graphical interfaces for both management and console functions, its interfaces are less responsive or intuitive than Microsoft's graphical interfaces.
- At a minimum, your NetWare 5.0 server should contain a Pentium processor, at least 64 MB RAM, a CD-ROM drive, a floppy disk drive, a hard disk with a DOS partition larger than 30 MB and a NetWare partition larger than 300 MB, a pointing device, and a NIC. In reality, your server will probably require more RAM and hard disk space than the minimum configuration suggested.
- To determine your NetWare server's requirements, you will want to consider the number of NetWare loadable modules (NLMs) used by each service. NLMs are routines that enable the server to run programs and services ranging from protocol support to Web publishing. Each NLM consumes some of the server's memory and processor resources (at least temporarily).
- You can add components to your NetWare server to enhance its fault tolerance and performance. The most popular additional components include multiple processors, more RAM, multiple NICs, fault-tolerant hard disks, a backup drive, and an uninterruptible power supply.
- In versions 4.x and higher, NetWare supports the use of as many as 32 processors on one server and uses symmetric multiprocessing, in which tasks are equally distributed among the processors. Multiprocessing enhances a server's performance when it's running several operations simultaneously. But the advantages of multiprocessing are lessened, when the server is not being utilized very much.
- Whereas NetWare 4.x can use only physical memory, NetWare 5.0 can use both virtual memory and physical memory. Version 5.0 can dynamically manage physical and virtual memory.
- Like Windows NT, NetWare uses 32-bit addressing to provide quick access to the physical memory. NetWare also allows you to run services in a separate memory area from the operating system, which prevents one rogue routine from taking the server down. Assigning a separate memory area to a service is known as running the service in protected mode. In this mode, the service and its supporting routines cannot harm critical server processes.
- Novell allows network administrators to adjust the server's use of memory in a number of ways. This flexibility can be both a blessing and a curse. If you change a setting in the wrong direction you can restrict the server's ability to send or transmit data efficiently. On the other hand, every environment will require some fine-tuning to maximize the use of memory and every organization will have its own memory needs.
- At the heart of NetWare lies the kernel, or the core of the operating system. NetWare's 32-bit kernel is responsible for overseeing all critical server processes. The program SERVER.EXE runs the kernel from a server's DOS partition. Typically, a server will

start from an AUTOEXEC.BAT file that launches SERVER.EXE; from that point forward, NetWare controls the machine's operations.

- The network administrator's primary interface to a NetWare server is the server console. Unlike Windows NT, the NetWare server interface is not entirely graphical. NetWare 4.x uses only text-based server menus at the console. NetWare 5.0, allows you to access commands through either a text-based or graphical menu system. The graphical interface in NetWare 5.0 is called ConsoleOne.
- Hundreds of NLMs are available for the NetWare operating system. In fact, developers can write their own NLMs for special purposes because Novell shares its operating system code. Most of the NLMs you'll ever need, however, will come with your server software or the additional utilities you install.
- NetWare's high-performance file system supports DOS, Macintosh, UNIX, OS/2, and Windows' long filenames. Although DOS filenames are supported by default, you must load the proper NLMs on the server to gain support for other filenames. Once you have installed the necessary modules, Macintosh, Windows, UNIX, or OS/2 clients can read from the server as if the server were speaking their language. Because NetWare uses modules—rather than file systems—to support this type of access, file/directory size limitations and performance do not vary between NetWare volumes or servers.
- Like Windows NT, NetWare uses volumes as the basis for organizing files and directories on the server. When you install NetWare, a volume called SYS is created automatically. At the time of installation, you may also choose to create additional volumes, such as DATA (for user data) or APPS (for shared applications).
- You should design a file system hierarchy that meets your performance, security, growth, and data sharing goals. Keep volume names short, simple, and descriptive. Plan carefully before establishing a server's volume and directory structure—once established, this structure is very difficult to change. If you are installing a NetWare network from scratch, you should consult resources for guidance on planning the volume and directory structure for your network.
- NetWare 4.x and 5.0 both support file compression. Novell's compression is performed on a file-by-file basis, and the compression and decompression operations are transparent to the user. In both NetWare 4.x and 5.x, file compression is enabled by default during installation of the operating system.
- Block suballocation is a technique employed by NetWare for using hard disk space more efficiently. It enables files that don't fit neatly into a whole number of blocks to take up fractions of blocks, leaving the remaining fractions free for use by other data.
- A major development that Novell introduced with version 4.0 is NetWare Directory Services (NDS). NDS is a system of managing multiple servers and their resources, including users, volumes, groups, profiles, and printers. The NDS model is similar to the concept of domains in Windows NT, but more comprehensive. In NDS, every resource is treated as a separate object with distinct properties. All objects can be centrally managed from a single interface.

- The NetWare installation process for the first server in a network generates the network's initial NDS. When adding subsequent servers or other resources to the network, you build upon this original NDS in a hierarchical fashion.
- Novell uses the analogy of a tree when describing this hierarchical layout. The NDS tree is upside-down, with a single root at the top and the leaves at the bottom. The root is created during the first NetWare (4.x or higher) server installation on the network. Once created, the root cannot be moved, deleted, or renamed.
- In the hierarchical NDS structure, the root leads to branches. These branches are called container objects (or organizational units) because their primary purpose is to logically subdivide and hold other objects that belong together. Container objects may organize resources by geographical location, department, professional function, security authorization, or other criteria significant to the particular network.
- Moving away from the root of the tree, branch objects lead to either more branch objects or leaf objects. A leaf object is an object in the NDS tree that does not contain other objects. Several kinds of leaf objects exist. You will typically deal with user-related leaf objects such as users, groups, profiles, templates, and aliases or printer-related objects such as printers, queues, and print servers. The place where an object belongs in an NDS tree is called its context.
- Novell uses the term *schema* to refer to the set of objects, hierarchy rules, and policies (such as security levels) that you establish for your NDS tree. The NDS schema serves as a reference for the logical design of your network, just as an architect's schematic drawing serves as the guiding reference for a building project.
- Before you insert the NetWare CD to begin installation of the operating system, you should consider many factors, including the organization's structure, function of the server, server hardware, applications, number of users, LAN architecture, and optional services (such as Web hosting). Once you have installed and configured the network operating system, changing its configuration may prove difficult and perhaps cause service disruptions for users.
- NWAdmin is a graphical interface that runs from a Windows 95 or Windows NT workstation and enables network administrators to manage NDS objects. Through the use of drop-down menus and toolbars, NWAdmin simplifies the process of viewing, creating, changing, and deleting objects.
- The NDS for NT tool enables Windows NT domains to appear as container objects in NWAdmin. In Novell's terminology, NDS for NT extends the schema to include Windows NT resources. Windows NT servers appear as server objects, and groups and users from Windows NT domains appear as NDS group and user objects, respectively. With NDS for NT enabled, users who require services from both Windows NT and NetWare servers need to log in to only the NDS tree, rather than logging in to both types of servers.

KEY TERMS

- **block** — A unit of disk space and the smallest unit of disk space that can be controlled by the NetWare system. Smaller blocks require more server memory.
- **block suballocation** — A NetWare technique for using hard disk space more efficiently. Files that don't fit neatly into a whole number of blocks can take up fractions of blocks, leaving the remaining fractions free for use by other data.
- **caching** — The process of saving frequently used data to an area of the physical memory so that it becomes more readily available for future requests. Caching accelerates the process of accessing the server because the operating system no longer needs to search for the requested data on the disk.
- **container objects** — Logical subdivisions (or "branches") in NetWare's NDS tree that organize resources by geographical location, department, professional function, security authorization, or other criteria significant to the particular network.
- **context** — A kind of road map for finding an object in an NDS tree. A context is made up of an object's organizational unit names, arranged from most specific to most general, plus the organization name. Periods separate the organizational unit names in context.
- **custom installation** — A NetWare installation option that allows you to determine which services and programs are installed, among other things.
- **IntraNetWare** — Another term for NetWare version 4.11, the version in which support for Internet services was first introduced.
- **kernel** — The core of the NetWare operating system. NetWare's 32-bit kernel is responsible for overseeing all critical server processes. The program SERVER.EXE runs the kernel from a server's DOS partition.
- **leaf object** — A type of NDS object that does not contain other objects. For example, a print queue is a leaf object because it handles only the printer queue.
- **Monitor** — An NLM that enables the system administrator to view server parameters such as protocols, bindings, system resources, and loaded modules. In many cases, it also allows the system administrator to modify these parameters.
- **NDS for NT** — Novell's integration tool for Windows NT networks. It works with the NetWare 4.x and 5.0 operating systems and Windows NT servers to enable the Windows NT domains to appear as container objects in NWAdmin.
- **NDS tree** — A logical representation of how resources are grouped by NetWare in the enterprise.
- **NetWare 3.x** — The group of NetWare versions that includes versions 3.0, 3.1, and 3.2.

- **NetWare 4.x** — The group of NetWare versions that includes versions 4.0, 4.1, and 4.11.
- **NetWare Administrator utility (NWAdmin)** — The graphical NetWare utility that allows administrators to manage objects in the NDS tree from a Windows 95, Windows 98, or Windows NT workstation.
- **NetWare Directory Services (NDS)** — A system of managing multiple servers and their resources, including users, volumes, groups, profiles, and printers. The NDS model is similar to the concept of domains in Windows NT, but more comprehensive. In NDS, every networked resource is treated as a separate object with distinct properties.
- **NetWare loadable modules (NLMs)** — Routines that enable the server to run programs and services. Each NLM consumes some of the server's memory and processor resources (at least temporarily). The kernel requires many NLMs to run NetWare's core operating system.
- **object** — A resource in NetWare's NDS tree. An object may represent a user, group, print queue, server volume, user template, mailbox, and so on. It may or may not contain other objects. All objects can be centrally managed in NDS.
- **organizational unit** — See *container object.*
- **protected mode** — A manner in which NetWare runs services in a separate memory area from the operating system. Running services in protected mode prevents one rogue routine from taking the server down. As a result, the service and its supporting routines cannot harm critical server processes.
- **schema** — The database that defines a set of objects and their attributes for an NDS tree.
- **server console** — The network administrator's primary interface to a NetWare server. Unlike Windows NT, the NetWare server interface is not entirely graphical. NetWare 4.x offers only text-based server menus at the console. NetWare 5.0 allows you to access commands through either a text-based or graphical menu system.
- **simple installation** — A NetWare installation option in which the most popular installation options are chosen for you, and the installation takes less time than if you had chosen a custom installation.
- **typeful** — A way of denoting an object's context in which the Organization and Organizational Unit designators ("O" and "OU," respectively) are included. For example, OU=Inv.OU=Ops.OU=Corp.O=Sutkin.
- **typeless** — A way of denoting an object's context in which the Organization and Organizational Unit designators ("O" and "OU," respectively) are omitted. For example, Inv.Ops.Corp.Sutkin.

Review Questions

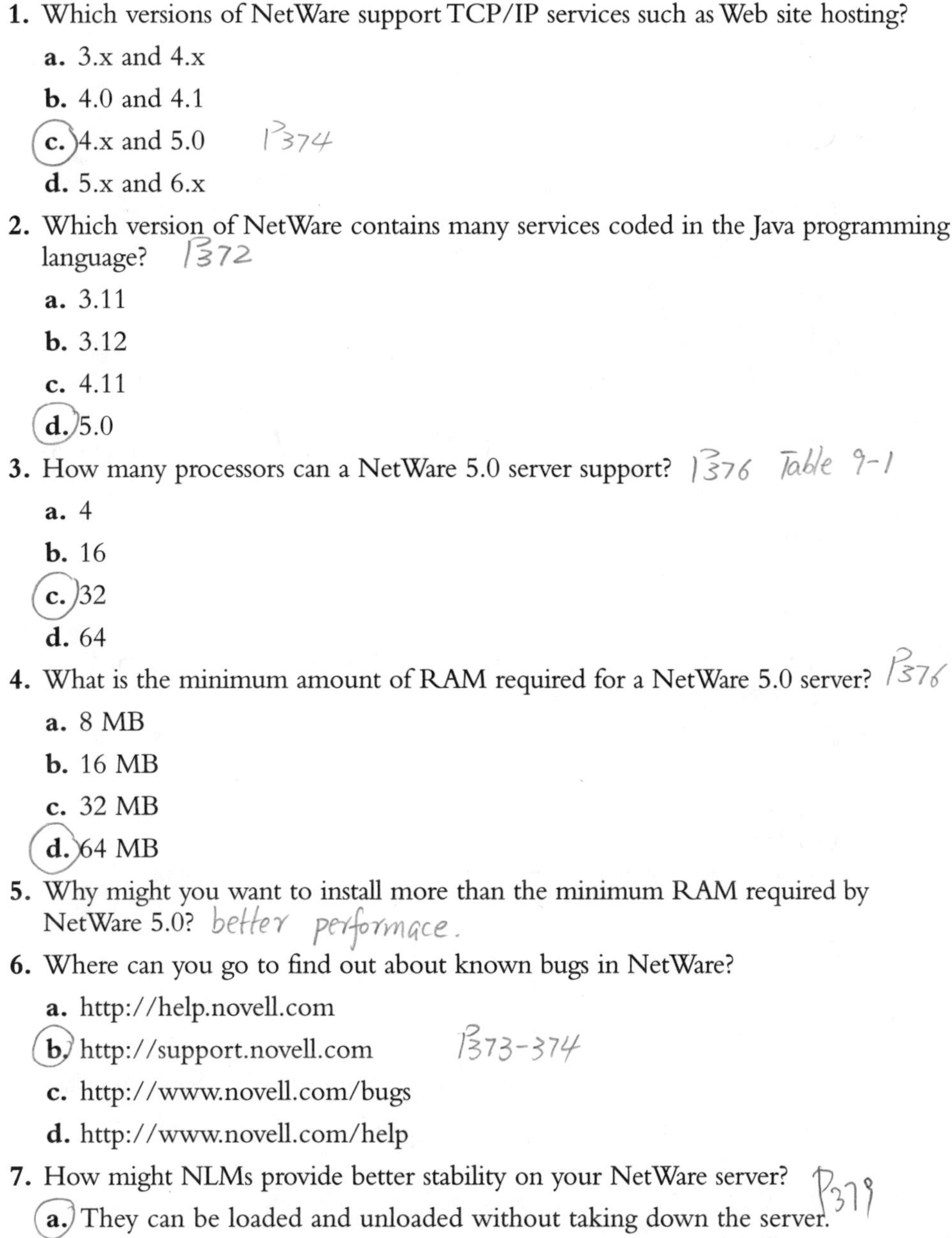

1. Which versions of NetWare support TCP/IP services such as Web site hosting?
   a. 3.x and 4.x
   b. 4.0 and 4.1
   c. 4.x and 5.0
   d. 5.x and 6.x
2. Which version of NetWare contains many services coded in the Java programming language?
   a. 3.11
   b. 3.12
   c. 4.11
   d. 5.0
3. How many processors can a NetWare 5.0 server support?
   a. 4
   b. 16
   c. 32
   d. 64
4. What is the minimum amount of RAM required for a NetWare 5.0 server?
   a. 8 MB
   b. 16 MB
   c. 32 MB
   d. 64 MB
5. Why might you want to install more than the minimum RAM required by NetWare 5.0?
6. Where can you go to find out about known bugs in NetWare?
   a. http://help.novell.com
   b. http://support.novell.com
   c. http://www.novell.com/bugs
   d. http://www.novell.com/help
7. How might NLMs provide better stability on your NetWare server?
   a. They can be loaded and unloaded without taking down the server.
   b. They can use multiple processors.
   c. They can prevent users from tampering with system files.
   d. They can be integrated with intrusion detection devices to recognize security breaches.

8. Which version of NetWare supports the use of virtual memory?
   a. 2.x
   b. 3.x
   c. 4.x
   d. 5.x
9. What stands at the very top of the NDS tree?
   a. root
   b. branch
   c. leaf
   d. trunk
10. If you decide to change the name of your NDS tree after you've installed NetWare, you can rename it through a server console command. True or False?
11. What is the name of the graphical server manager utility in NetWare 5.0?
    a. ServMan
    b. ConsoleOne
    c. NetManager
    d. NetMon
12. Which DOS command loads the NetWare operating system kernel?
    a. INSTALL
    b. LOAD KERNEL
    c. KERNEL.EXE
    d. SERVER.EXE
13. Which of the following file systems does NetWare not support?
    a. DOS
    b. NTFS
    c. UNIX
    d. Macintosh
14. What is the name of the volume created automatically when you install NetWare 4.x or 5.0?
    a. DATA
    b. VOL1
    c. VOL2
    d. SYS
15. File compression is enabled by default during a NetWare 5.0 installation. True or False?

16. Which server resource does block suballocation conserve?
    - a. memory
    - b. CPU
    - c. hard disk space
    - d. power draw
17. What is the purpose of a container object in an NDS tree?
    - a. to logically subdivide objects in the tree
    - b. to logically group users according to security needs
    - c. to logically separate users according to usage patterns
    - d. to logically group subnets
18. A user is an example of what kind of NDS object?
    - a. tree
    - b. root
    - c. leaf
    - d. branch
19. If a user's login ID is "james" and the user belongs to the "marketing" organizational unit, which is in turn part of the "Corporate" organizational unit within the "ABC" Organization, what is this user's context?
    - a. james.marketing.corporate.ABC
    - b. ABC.corporate.marketing
    - c. O_ABC_OU_marketing_OU_corporate_U_james
    - d. marketing.corporate.ABC
20. Which utility allows you to manage NDS objects?
    - a. NDSCON
    - b. NDSadmin
    - c. NWAdmin
    - d. NWManager
21. List five questions that you should answer before beginning a NetWare server installation.
22. After right-clicking an object within NWAdmin, which option should you choose to modify that object's properties?
    - a. Details
    - b. Properties
    - c. More
    - d. Tools

23. In a typeful context notation, how is a user object's container designated?
    a. CXT
    b. CN
    c. OU P385
    d. O
24. Why might you want to create an administrator-equivalent ID that isn't called "Admin"?
    a. for easier management
    b. for security purposes P391
    c. to share administrative rights among many users
    d. to enable remote administration
25. After a simple NetWare 5.0 installation, what rights does the default group called PUBLIC have to the NDS tree? P392
    a. Supervisory
    b. Browse, Modify, Erase
    c. Browse, Modify
    d. Browse
26. In NWAdmin, you can grant users rights to save files in a directory. True or False? P394-395
27. In NetWare version 5.0, which command should you use to access the protocol and NIC configuration utility?
    a. inetcfg P392
    b. ipconfig
    c. netconfig
    d. nwconfig
28. What must the network administrator do in NWAdmin before he or she can delete a container object?
    a. delete all objects within the container P396
    b. rename the container
    c. move the container to the trash
    d. ensure that the container is not part of another container
29. Which Novell utility enables Windows NT servers to appear as objects in the NDS tree?
    a. NetWare Gateway Services
    b. NT-NDS Gateway
    c. NDS for NT P396
    d. NetWare for NT

30. If you use NetWare's integration tool, what type of an object will a Windows NT domain appear as in an NDS tree?
   a. container
   b. group
   c. server
   d. organizational unit

HANDS-ON PROJECTS

PROJECT 9-1

For this project you will need only a pencil and paper.

Before you install your first NetWare server, or even work with objects in an NDS tree, you should have a good understanding of the organization of the NDS tree. This exercise will help you to conceptualize an NDS tree.

1. A city school district has five elementary schools, two middle schools, and one high school running a NetWare 4.11 network. Give the schools and the organization (root of the NDS tree) names.
2. Draw an NDS tree in which each type of school (elementary, middle, and high school) belongs to a separate container object.
3. Add two teacher IDs to one of the containers you created. Based on the names you gave to your containers and tree, write the users' names in typeful context under the user ID you assigned them underneath the users you added (you may want to refer to the examples of typeful context names given in this chapter).

PROJECT 9-2

In this exercise, you will experiment with using commands from the NetWare prompt. With such commands, you can check which modules are running on your server, load new modules, and unload already running modules. For this project you will need a working NetWare 5.0 server installed with no more than the basic operating system.

1. At the NetWare server console prompt, type **modules**. (If your server's screen does not show the prompt, press the **Alt-Esc** key combination until the screen with the prompt appears.) How many modules are loaded on your NetWare server?
2. Sometimes you will want to know whether a module is running, but with hundreds of modules on your server, you may not remember the module's name. In this case, you can simply look for all modules beginning with the same letter. To demonstrate,

type modules c* at the NetWare system prompt. On a piece of paper, write the names of the NLMs running on your server that begin with the letter "c."

3. To view information about how the server is running, type **monitor** at the console prompt. Write down your server's CPU utilization data.
4. Press the **Alt-Esc** key sequence. What happens?
5. At the console prompt, type **nwconfig**. Look at the menu options. Which one will allow you to install an additional NetWare service? Which one will let you manage the protocols bound to the server's NIC(s)?
6. Press the **Alt-Ctrl** key sequence. What happens?
7. Display the monitor screen again.
8. Highlight **Connection Information** in the menu bar, then press **Enter**.
9. How many users are connected to the server?
10. Press **Esc** to return to the main menu.
11. Press **Esc** again, highlight **Exit**, then press **Enter** to confirm that you want to exit the monitor screen.
12. Use the **Alt-Esc** key sequence to return to the nwconfig screen.
13. Press **Esc**. When prompted, confirm that you want to exit the nwconfig screen.
14. At the console prompt, type **volumes**, then press **Enter**. How many volumes are installed on your server? What are their names? What kind of file systems does each volume support?
15. As a network administrator, you will sometimes need to take the server down (for example, to repair a faulty memory module or to install a new NIC). This process can be accomplished by one simple command. To demonstrate, type **down**, then press **Enter**. What kind of message appears? What happens?
16. After all of the processes have stopped running, type **exit**, then press **Enter**. At the DOS prompt, type **dir**. Which directory do you suppose contains the NetWare operating system?
17. Look at the machine's AUTOEXEC.BAT file by typing **type c:\autoexec.bat** at the DOS prompt. What commands are in the server's AUTOEXEC.BAT?
18. To start the NetWare server again, type **server**. Alternatively, you can restart the machine.

PROJECT 9-3

In this exercise, you will experiment with using NetWare Administrator to create users and modify their object properties. For this project, you will need a Windows 95 workstation connected to a NetWare 4.11 or 5.0 network. Your workstation should have (at least) the IPX/SPX protocol and the NetWare client (version 2.2 or higher) installed. You will also need to know the network's administrator-equivalent user ID and password.

1. From your Windows 95 workstation, log in to the server as your administrator-equivalent user.
2. Double-click the **Network Neighborhood** icon.
3. Find your server in the Network Neighborhood list and double-click it.
4. Double-click your server's SYS volume.
5. Open the **PUBLIC** folder on the SYS volume.
6. Open the **Win32** folder.
7. Double-click the **NWADMN32.EXE** file. The NetWare Administrator utility (NWAdmin) loads.
8. Using the steps provided in the chapter as a guide, add two organizational units in the organization of your NDS tree, one called **ACCT** and another called **MKTG**.
9. Add two users to the ACCT container: **Arnold Thomas** and **Faye Bernstein**, making their user IDs be a combination of the first letter of the first name plus the last name. Give the users home directories as you create them.
10. Add two users to the MKTG container: **Debby Chang** and **Matt Winzer**, following the same naming convention you used for the ACCT users. Do not assign these users home directories.
11. Double-click the **AThomas** user icon. The user's Properties dialog box should appear.
12. Make sure that the **Identification** button on the right side of the user's Properties dialog box is selected. Enter the user's first and last name, plus his department, phone number, and location.
13. Click the **Password Restrictions** button from the right side of the user's Properties dialog box. The user's password restrictions properties appear.
14. Click **Change Password**, then type **nw5user** in the new password text box. Type the password again to confirm it.
15. Click **OK** to save your changes. You will return to the user's Properties dialog box.
16. Click **OK** to accept your changes. The user's Properties dialog box will close.
17. In the NWAdmin menu, click **File**, then click **Exit**.
18. Click **Start**, click **Shut Down**, click **Close all programs and log on as different user**, then click **OK**.
19. Log in to the NetWare 5.0 server as **Athomas**, using the password you specified in Step 14.
20. Follow steps 2 through 7 to launch NWAdmin.
21. Double-click the **MKTG** container to see its contents.
22. Right-click the user **DChang**, then choose **Delete** from the menu that appears.
23. What happens? Why?
24. Exit NWAdmin, then log in as your administrator ID again.
25. Try deleting the user called **DChang**.

26. What happens? Why?
27. Close NWAdmin, then log in as **FBernstein**.
28. What kind of password prompt do you receive? Why?
29. Using Network Neighborhood, open the SYS volume of your NetWare server.
30. Double-click the **Users** folder.
31. What do you see? Why?

CASE PROJECTS

1. An office furniture manufacturer called Advanced Ergonomics Solutions (AES) asks you to help the company design a new network. The network managers plan to throw out the obsolete ARCNet system they have used for eight years and install new NetWare 5.0 servers. They do not know how many servers they need or how to organize the servers, users, and groups. AES has two offices in town. The corporate headquarters houses 100 users, including 20 users in Marketing, 20 users in Operations, 40 users in Research, and 20 users in Customer Service. The users in Research save confidential data that no one else in the company is allowed to see. You've been informed that the company plans to increase the headcount at headquarters fourfold within the next 18 months. AES's other office in town is located at a warehouse and includes only 10 shift workers. What recommendations can you provide to the network managers at AES about organizing their network? How many servers will they need? (More than one solution is possible.) Sketch your proposed NDS solution in tree form, beginning with the root object.
2. The network managers at AES have implemented the system that you recommended and they are very pleased. The only problem is that the performance on the Research server seems sluggish compared with the performance of the other servers. The researchers use database files that are nearly 200 MB large to hold their test results, and these files load excruciatingly slowly. The network managers wonder whether they should buy faster servers or change the system somehow. Realizing that you accepted all of the defaults when you installed the NetWare 5.0 operating system, what kinds of things would you check to ensure that performance is at its peak on their servers? What other recommendations can you give?
3. Now the network managers at AES have called you regarding an unrelated problem. One of the company's vendors has developed a chair stress simulation program that can be accessed from a network. AES researchers and customer service personnel are eager to start using it, but the vendor insists that the simulation program can run only on a Windows NT server. AES let the vendor bring in a Windows NT server on a test basis, but now users who want to access the program must log in to the network twice: once for NetWare servers, and once for the Windows NT server. What can you tell the network managers about integration between these two systems that might make sense in their organization?

CHAPTER 10

NETWORKING WITH UNIX

After reading this chapter and completing the exercises, you will be able to:

- Describe the origins and history of the UNIX operating system
- Identify similarities and differences between popular implementations of UNIX
- Understand why you might choose a UNIX server for a corporate network
- Explain and execute basic UNIX commands
- Install Linux on an Intel-based PC
- Use Linux to add groups and users and to change file access permissions
- Explain how UNIX can be internetworked with other network operating systems

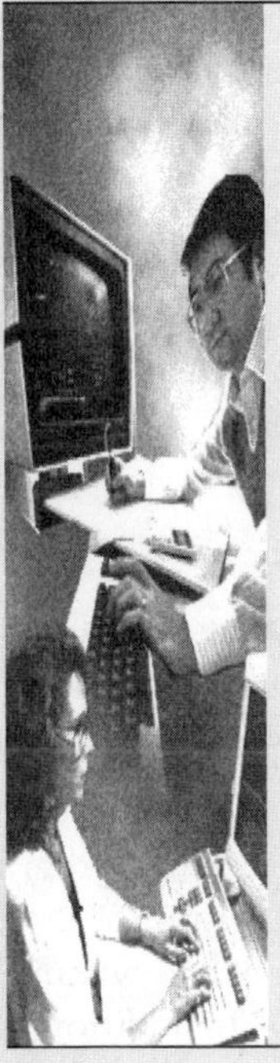

ON THE JOB

I started working with UNIX systems in the early 1980s. I learned UNIX (and the C programming language) at the same time I learned CP/M and MS-DOS, but I tended to prefer the UNIX systems. The most attractive part of UNIX was the incredible power of the command interpreter (or shell). With the UNIX shell, I could create complex new commands out of a few existing commands. I could accomplish things that the programmers of the original commands never imagined. The community of UNIX programmers enjoys thinking about and playing with the system; the result is a system created by programmers.

The other significant facet of the UNIX community is the support that people offer to each other. It's nearly guaranteed that someone else has experienced the problem you're facing at any given time. A simple query posted to the Internet often receives an answer within a few hours. The lack of UNIX-based computer viruses merely illustrates this community's supportive attitude.

Networking with UNIX is simple and straightforward. The UNIX shell is a great place to experiment with networking ideas because it's easy to test those ideas by typing simple commands in the shell and watching the results. With the advent of Linux and other open UNIX-like operating systems, the opportunity to tinker with networking is now readily available to many more people. It's easy for me to understand why UNIX in general and Linux in particular have experienced such explosive growth in the past few years.

David Klann
Berbee Information Networks

Along with Windows NT and Novell NetWare, UNIX is one of the most popular network operating systems. Although all three enable servers to provide resource sharing, UNIX differs in fundamental ways from NetWare and Windows NT. UNIX was developed by researchers at AT&T Bell Laboratories in 1969; thus it is much older than NetWare and Windows NT. In fact, UNIX preceded and led to the development of the TCP/IP protocol suite in the early 1970s. For this reason, it is considered the parent of TCP/IP networking. Today, computers running UNIX account for more than 80% of all Internet servers. Reflecting this operating system's efficiency and ease of use, the number of UNIX systems continues to grow.

You must be familiar with UNIX to set up and maintain most local and wide area networks. Mastering UNIX can be complicated, because it is not controlled and distributed by a single software manufacturer. Instead, numerous vendors sell a number of varieties, such as Solaris from Sun Microsystems, AIX from IBM, and HP-UX from Hewlett-Packard. Although these "flavors" of UNIX follow some accepted, open standards, each vendor distributes a proprietary implementation. In addition, nonproprietary, freely distributed UNIX-like implementations such as Linux, GNU, and FreeBSD are available. Fortunately, the differences between implementations are relatively minor, and with a little effort you can understand them and move from one implementation to another with ease. This chapter introduces the UNIX operating system in general and describes Linux in more detail.

UNIX and Linux share many characteristics, but are subtly and often confusingly different. UNIX is the trademarked name given to the operating system originally developed at Bell Labs. The trademark is owned by a nonprofit industry association named The Open Group. An operating system must pass The Open Group's qualification tests to be called UNIX. Linux grew out of an independent effort to create an operating system that behaves like the trademarked UNIX operating system. This would be equivalent, in the Windows world, to a large group of people getting together and writing a version of Windows NT based on the public specifications. (UNIX, however, has been publicly available for much longer than Windows NT, and Microsoft keeps the specifications to many parts of Windows NT a closely guarded secret.)

A Brief History of UNIX

One of the most enjoyable aspects of dealing with the UNIX operating system is learning about its history. The UNIX system is characterized by a rich tradition and a culture of personal friendships in an era of impersonal disconnectedness that, some would say, the computer itself has fostered.

In the late 1960s, a few programmers grew dissatisfied with the existing programming environments. In particular, they didn't like the cumbersome batch nature of the existing systems. They wanted to work interactively with the programs rather than writing a set of instructions, submitting them all at once, and waiting for the results. In addition, the programmers sought a system that imposed as little structure as possible on the programmer. Two employees at Bell Labs in Murray Hill, New Jersey, Ken Thompson and Dennis Ritchie, decided to overcome these limitations by creating an entirely new programming environment. To properly design this new environment, they decided to start at the lowest level—at the operating system. This environment ultimately evolved into the UNIX operating system.

Antitrust law prohibited AT&T from profiting from the sale of computers and software during the 1970s. Thus, for a nominal licensing fee, anyone could purchase the source code to the work produced at Bell Labs. The word spread rapidly, and researchers in educational institutions and large corporations all over the world soon had this curious new software running on their lab computers. Versions of UNIX that come from the Bell Labs are known as **System V.** Researchers at the University of California at Berkeley were among the first enthusiastic supporters of early versions of UNIX. They added many useful features to the system, including the TCP/IP network subsystem. Berkeley versions of UNIX are known as **BSD (Berkeley Software Distribution)**.

The 1980s saw the breakup of AT&T. This event enabled the company to begin actively marketing the UNIX system to other computer manufacturers. After a number of fits and starts, AT&T eventually sold its rights to the UNIX system. These rights changed hands a number of times during the early 1990s. Today, ownership of the UNIX system is shared by two organizations—The Santa Cruz Operation and The Open Group.

The Santa Cruz Operation, based in California, owns the rights to the UNIX source code. It therefore has the right to distribute copies of the source code—the raw materials for creating a UNIX system. Anyone could write a UNIX operating system, but the effort required to do so is prohibitive. Most organizations choose to start with the existing source code, by obtaining it from The Santa Cruz Operation and then making modifications for their specific computer hardware.

The Open Group, as mentioned earlier, owns the UNIX trademark. After a vendor makes changes to the code licensed from The Santa Cruz Operation, its modified system must pass The Open Group's verification tests before the operating system may be called UNIX. Compaq/Digital, for example, pays source code licensing fees to The Santa Cruz Operation and verification and trademark use fees to The Open Group so that it can call its operating system Tru64 UNIX.

Although many versions of UNIX may be used as network operating systems, all UNIX versions share the following features:

- The ability to support multiple, simultaneously logged in users (a true multiuser system)
- Hierarchical file systems that incorporate demountable volumes
- Consistent interfaces for file, device and interprocess input/output
- The ability to start processes in the background
- Hundreds of subsystems, including dozens of programming languages
- Program source code portability
- User-definable window systems, the most popular of which is the X Window system

You will learn more about the UNIX memory model, file system, processing capabilities, and network integration later in this chapter.

THE CURRENT STATE OF THE MARKET

The UNIX market is huge and highly segmented. As a result, stating its size with precision is difficult. People use UNIX-based systems for everything from running general-purpose workstations to controlling industrial robots and telecommunications equipment. In fact, even some **real-time** implementations of the UNIX system exist, in which the operating system must respond to input immediately. Many rigorous applications use one such implementation, QNX, including a computer vision system for the NASA space shuttle and the international space station.

Proprietary implementations and open source implementations are two of the most significant UNIX market segments, as explained in the following sections.

PROPRIETARY UNIX

Many companies market both hardware and software based on the UNIX operating system. An implementation of UNIX for which the source code is either unavailable or available only by purchasing a licensed copy from The Santa Cruz Operation (costing as much as millions of dollars) is known as **proprietary UNIX.** By most counts, the three most popular vendors of proprietary UNIX are Sun Microsystems, IBM, and Hewlett-Packard. Sun's proprietary version of UNIX, called **Solaris**, runs on the company's proprietary SPARC-based workstations and servers, as well as Intel-based Pentium-class workstations and servers. IBM's proprietary version, **AIX**, runs on its PowerPC-based RS-6000 computers. HP's proprietary version, **HP-UX**, runs on its PA-RISC–based systems. Many other organizations have licensed the UNIX source code and created proprietary UNIX versions that run on highly customized computers (that is, computers that are appropriate for very specific tasks).

Choosing a proprietary UNIX system has several advantages:

- *Accountability and support.* An organization might choose a proprietary UNIX system so that when something doesn't work as expected, it has a resource on which to call for assistance.
- *Optimization of hardware and software.* Workstation vendors who ship proprietary UNIX invest a great deal of time in ensuring that their software runs as well and as fast as possible on their hardware.
- *Predictability and compatibility.* Purveyors of proprietary UNIX systems strive to maintain backward compatibility with new releases. They schedule new releases at somewhat regular, predictable intervals. Customers usually know when and how things will change with proprietary UNIX systems.

One drawback of choosing a proprietary UNIX system, however, relates to the fact that the customer has no access to the system's source code and thus cannot create a custom solution. Open source UNIX solves this problem.

Open Source UNIX

An interesting twist in the UNIX marketplace over the past few years has been the emergence of UNIX-like systems that are not owned by any one company. This software is developed and packaged by a few individuals and made available to anyone without licensing fees. Often referred to as **open source software** or **freely distributable** software, this category includes UNIX-like systems such as **GNU**, **FreeBSD**, and **Linux**. Each of these systems, in turn, comes in a variety of implementations with slightly different features and capabilities. These packages are often referred to as the different **flavors** of the open source software. For example, the different flavors of Linux include RedHat, Caldera, Slackware, and a host of others.

The key difference between freely distributable UNIX and proprietary implementations of UNIX relates to the copyright specification. Open source versions of UNIX include a copyright that *requires* the source code to be made available to anyone receiving the system. As a result, whenever someone improves the software, anyone with a copy of that software has access to the improvement. Another advantage of open source UNIX is that the customer can add functionality not provided by a vendor of proprietary UNIX. A manufacturing company that uses computer-controlled robotic spot welders, for example, might combine open source UNIX with custom software to control its robots. In contrast, it might be very difficult or costly to integrate the robotic control software with a proprietary UNIX system.

Versions of freely distributable UNIX run not only on Intel-based processors, but also on other processor brands such as PowerPC (used in Apple Macintoshes), SPARC (used in Sun Microsystems workstations), and Alpha (used in Compaq/Digital workstations). Although this range of choices is wider than with proprietary UNIX systems, it can also complicate the decision-making process when choosing a network server.

The discussion of UNIX in the remainder of this chapter will focus on one popular open source version, Linux. Linux follows standard UNIX conventions, is highly stable, and is free. It was developed in 1991 by Linus Torvalds, a Finnish scientist. After developing Linux, Torvalds posted it on the Internet and recruited a number of other UNIX aficionados and programmers to help enhance it. Today, Linux is used for file, print, and Web servers across the globe. Its popularity has even convinced large corporations that own proprietary UNIX versions, such as IBM, to publicly embrace Linux.

Why Choose UNIX?

Let's say your supervisor assigns you the task of choosing and installing a new server on your organization's LAN. To make your network as compatible as possible with other networks, you limit your operating system options to the big three: NetWare, Windows NT, and UNIX. Given these options, what considerations might lead you to choose UNIX? The same set of questions posited in Chapters 8 and 9 apply to your consideration of this operating system:

- Can it be integrated with my existing infrastructure?
- Will it provide the security required by my resources?

- Is my technical staff capable of managing it?
- Will my applications run smoothly on it?
- Will it accommodate future growth (that is, is it scalable)?
- Does it support the additional services required by my users (for example, remote access, Web site hosting, and messaging)?
- How much does it cost?
- What kind of support does the vendor offer?

UNIX systems offer a host of features, including the TCP/IP protocol suite and all applications necessary to support the networking infrastructure as a part of the basic operating system. You get the programs necessary to perform operations such as routing, firewalling, domain name service, and automatic IP address assignment when you install the system on your computer. Although Windows NT and NetWare can perform some of these operations, they require separate software packages to carry out certain functions. A UNIX system, however, can provide all of these capabilities without additional software. Furthermore, UNIX supports non-IP protocols such as Novell's IPX/SPX and AppleTalk. Like Windows NT and NetWare, UNIX also supports many different network topologies and physical media, including Ethernet, TokenRing, and FDDI.

UNIX systems can act as file servers to Windows, NetWare, and Macintosh clients. The open source software package called **Samba**, for example, is a complete Windows NT–style file and printer sharing facility. Other proprietary and open source software packages are available that implement the NetWare file and print server facilities as well as Macintosh file and print facilities.

UNIX efficiently and securely handles the growth, change, and stability requirements of today's diverse networks. The source code on which UNIX systems are based is mature, as it has been used and thoroughly debugged for nearly 30 years. Like NetWare, UNIX allows you to change the server's configuration—for example, assigning a different IP address to an interface—without restarting the server. Similarly, you can easily modify a UNIX system while it is running. When you need to access a tape drive, for example, you can enable the tape driver, access the tape, and disable the tape driver without restarting the server. This functionality allows you to use memory on your server very efficiently.

A key difference between UNIX and other network operating systems such as NetWare relates to resource sharing. UNIX was originally developed as a **time-sharing system**—that is, a computing system to which each user must attach directly (usually with a "dumb terminal") to share the resources of that computer. You must log in to a UNIX system and run applications on the system to share its resources.

To understand how this model differs from other client/server resource-sharing methods, consider your company's office environment. You share certain resources: file cabinet space, conference rooms, printers, copiers, and so on. When you are working in your office, you share office resources in the same way that a UNIX system shares its resources. For example, you might walk over to the file cabinet, remove a file, then replace it when you're done with it.

In the NetWare model, in contrast, an intelligent workstation (usually a PC) is attached to the network. When you want to use the server's resources, you simply map a drive to your local computer or send a print job to the server's printer queue. This approach is analogous to a telecommuting situation in which you work at home, but still have access to many of the office's resources. To share your office resources, you can simply call someone at the office and ask to have a paper file sent to your home by courier. Later, the courier can shuttle the file back to the office and replace it in the file cabinet. The disadvantage of this model is that you cannot use some of the office's resources, such as the conference rooms, when you telecommute. Similarly, you can't perform some tasks on a NetWare server because you don't attach directly to the system; instead, you simply use its resources over the LAN.

A real advantage of UNIX is that people have added applications and services that enable sharing of resources in the telecommuter model without eliminating the "drive-to-the-office" model. With UNIX systems, you get the best of both worlds!

UNIX systems also include a robust and mature security model. Some proprietary UNIX systems have even received **Orange Book** certification, which is a rigorous operating system security specification that the U.S. Department of Defense first published in 1985. These characteristics of the UNIX system contribute to its ability to handle networks' growth, change, and stability.

UNIX Server Hardware

UNIX systems may be implemented as workstations or as servers. Unlike Windows NT, in which the server and workstation versions vary considerably, the difference between a UNIX server and a UNIX workstation merely comprises the set of optional packages included during installation. A UNIX system configured as a server has the necessary software to enable sharing of resources such as print queues, file systems, and processor time. Hardware requirements are very similar to those for NetWare and Windows NT servers.

In UNIX, the use of a graphical user interface (GUI) remains optional. Many people see this flexibility as an advantage because you can use the GUI if you like (unlike with NetWare, which relies on a character-based console in all versions except 5.0) or simply work with the command-line interface (unlike with Windows NT, in which you *must* use the GUI for many operations). As servers usually run unattended, it often makes sense to omit the GUI.

The hardware for a UNIX server consists of a base system unit, which must include the following equipment:

- A motherboard with CPU, memory, and I/O control
- A network interface card (NIC)
- A floppy disk drive
- A CD-ROM drive
- One or more fixed disks

Video cards, sound cards, and other I/O devices are optional. Your major decisions in choosing the hardware for a general-purpose UNIX server can be summarized as follows:

- Which applications and services will run on the server?
- How many users will this system serve?
- How much random access memory (RAM) will the server need?
- How much secondary storage (hard disk) will the server need?

Table 10-1 shows the minimum hardware requirements for the various components of a Linux server. You may find more current lists of supported hardware on the **hardware compatibility list (HCL)** at http://metalab.unc.edu/LDP/HOWTO/Hardware-HOWTO.html.

Table 10-1 Minimum Hardware Requirements for a Linux Server

Component	Requirement	Notes
Processor	An Intel-compatible 486, Pentium.	Recent versions of Linux (2.0 and later) include support for as many as 16 Intel processors.
Memory	16 MB RAM.	You should consider more RAM than this minimum for better performance; most network administrators opt for 64 MB or 128 MB of RAM for servers.
Hard disk	A hard drive supported by Linux (as specified in the HCL), such as an IDE or SCSI, with a minimum of 150 MB free space.	Most server implementations require additional hard drive space.
NIC	A NIC found on the HCL.	
CD-ROM	Optional, but recommended. Choose a drive listed on the HCL.	
Floppy disk	Linux installation (and most other UNIX systems) requires one or two 3.5-inch floppy disks to get started. You may create emergency repair disks during installation.	
Pointing device	Optional.	Only necessary if you install the GUI component.

The Linux HCL resembles the NetWare and Windows NT hardware guides in that it recommends *minimum* requirements for simply starting the server. You'll need to add more memory and more disk space based on your applications' requirements. Unfortunately, you sometimes cannot learn the memory requirements of an application until you actually run it on the server. In these instances, it is always better to overestimate your needs than to underestimate them.

No one "right" UNIX server configuration exists. To determine the hardware requirements of your UNIX server, you need to take into account the nature of the work to be performed by the system, the type of software to be run, and the number of users.

A Closer Look at Linux

Linux is the third major network operating system discussed in this book. As you probably realize, both similarities and differences exist among Linux, NetWare, and Windows NT. This section compares Linux with those network operating systems.

Linux Multiprocessing

Any modern network operating system must use the resources of multiple processors in an efficient manner. Linux is truly a modern operating system in this respect. Like NetWare and Windows NT, Linux supports symmetric multiprocessing (SMP). This support for SMP was experimental in version 2.0. However, Linux experts consider SMP to be stable in versions 2.2 (the current version as of this writing) and later. The operating system supports SMP using a maximum of 16 processors per server. The guidelines outlined in the previous chapters for NetWare and Windows NT apply to Linux as well: You must know how your servers will be used, and plan for multiprocessing servers according to your estimated application processing loads.

Default Linux installations prior to version 2.2 leave SMP disabled. You must configure your system so as to enable SMP if you're using version 2.0. Consult the Linux SMP guide at http://www.linux.org.uk/SMP/title.html for details.

The Linux Memory Model

From its inception, Linux was created to use both physical and virtual memory efficiently. (See the "Windows NT Server's Memory Model" section in Chapter 8 for details.) Like Windows NT, Linux allocates a memory area for each application. It attempts to decrease the inefficiency of this practice, however, by sharing memory between programs wherever it can. For example, if five people are using FTP on your Linux server, five instances of the FTP program will run. In reality, only a small part of each FTP program (called the private data region—the part that stores the user name, for example) will receive its own memory space; most of the program will remain in a region of memory shared by all five instances of the program. In this case, rather than using five times the memory required by one instance of the program, Linux sets aside only a little more memory for five FTP users than it does for one FTP user.

Current versions of Linux use a 32-bit addressing scheme that enables programs to access 4 GB of memory. Linux developers are working on a version of the system that uses a 64-bit addressing scheme. Virtual memory in a Linux server can take the form of a disk partition (created with the Windows fdisk command), or it can be in a file (much like the virtual memory file pagefile.sys in Windows NT).

THE LINUX KERNEL

Linux is similar to NetWare in that the core of the system consists of the **kernel**. The Linux kernel is loaded into memory from disk and run when you turn on your computer. Also, as with NetWare, you can add or remove functionality by loading and unloading Linux **kernel modules**, which are analogous to NetWare NLMs. Unlike NetWare, however, Linux does not use loadable modules exclusively to extend the functionality of the system. Rather, you start and stop Linux services and applications by typing commands (much like running commands in a Windows NT command window). Linux offers the best of both worlds: loadable kernel modules to extend the functionality of the Linux kernel (like NetWare), and runnable services and applications to perform most of the work of the server (like Windows NT).

When vendors speak of Linux version numbers, such as 2.0 or 2.2, they are referring to the kernel version. Although vendors (such as Red Hat) may also use their own version numbering scheme (such as Red Hat 5.2), all purveyors of Linux distributions use the same Linux kernel version scheme to identify which kernel is included in the package.

LINUX FILE AND DIRECTORY STRUCTURE

The UNIX system was one of the first operating systems to implement a **hierarchical file system**. This hierarchy somewhat resembles the structure of the NDS inverted tree discussed in Chapter 9. The notion of a file system organized in this way was considered revolutionary at the time of UNIX's inception. Today, most operating systems, including all Microsoft operating systems, NetWare, and even the Apple Macintosh's MacOS, use hierarchical file systems. Figure 10-1 shows a typical Linux file system hierarchy.

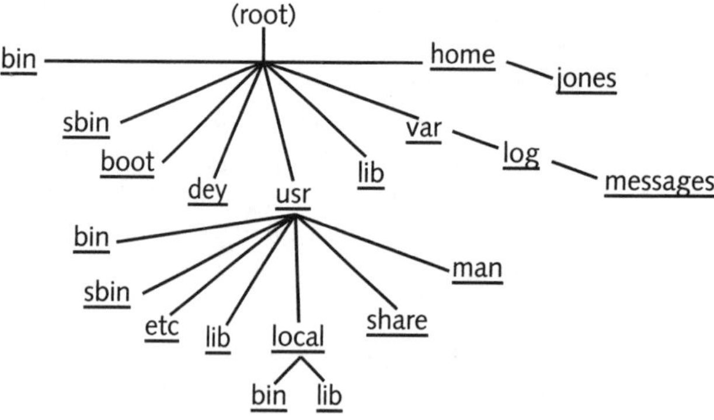

Figure 10-1 Linux file system hierarchy

The */boot* directory contains the Linux kernel and other system initialization files. Linux keeps applications and services in */bin and /sbin* (applications and services in */sbin* support the system initialization process; you'll rarely use these programs). The */var* directory holds variable data (such as log files and print jobs waiting to be printed). The file */var/log/messages*, for example, stores system log messages. Users' login directories appear in */home*. When you create a new user account, the system assigns a directory in */home* to that user. The login (or home) directory matches the account's user name. Thus */home/jones* is the login (or home) directory for the user *jones*.

LINUX FILE SERVICES

In Chapter 8, you learned about the file systems supported by Windows NT. As you will recall, the file system constitutes the operating system's method for organizing, managing, and accessing its files through logical structures and software routines. Linux includes support for multiple types of file systems, including local and remote file systems. The native file system type, called *ext2*, is the "second extended" file system for Linux. Rather than trying to fix some of the problems with the "first extended" file system, the programmers decided to create a new file system from scratch, and named it (creatively) the second extended file system.

Linux allows you to access partitions formatted with the DOS FAT file system as well as the Windows NT NTFS file system (in read-only mode) and the OS/2 HPFS file system. It also supports remote file systems, which are analogous to Windows shares or NetWare network volumes. With Linux, you can both map shared file systems (drives) from Windows or NetWare servers and share local partitions with other users. Sun Microsystems' Network File System (NFS) is the other significant remote file system type supported by Linux. Given how many file system types are accommodated, it's easy to see why Linux has become such a popular server platform in large, diverse networks.

LINUX INTERNET SERVICES

As you learned earlier, UNIX has deep roots in Internet services. For instance, the leading Internet Web server is an open source software application called **Apache** that, until very recently, ran only on UNIX systems. What's more, the original Web tools—including the first browsers and servers—were developed on UNIX-based systems. UNIX-based systems acted as the development platforms for the original ARPAnet and Internet services such as FTP, Telnet, gopher, HTTP, and POP. It should therefore come as no great surprise that current implementations of UNIX include the full range of Internet services as standard components.

This approach differs greatly from that of both Windows NT and NetWare. Windows NT ships with standard Internet client software, such as a Telnet client, an FTP client, and a Web browser. To actually use a Windows NT server as an FTP, Telnet, or Web server, however, you must purchase and install Microsoft's Internet Information Server (IIS) package (or another vendor's Internet services software). In NetWare version 4.x, TCP/IP-based services—such as Internet mail gateways—also required the purchase of an additional package, either from Novell or another vendor. In NetWare version 3.x, some TCP/IP-based services were not even supported. As you have learned, however, NetWare version 5.0 fully integrates the TCP/IP protocol suite and its services. Nevertheless, UNIX, which includes finely tuned support for TCP/IP in everything from the kernel to the applications, enjoys a unique advantage over both of the competing network operating systems.

Linux Processes

Another UNIX innovation is the notion of separate, numbered processes. Each process represents an instance of a running program in memory (RAM). The UNIX kernel allocates separate resources (such as memory space) to each process as it is created. It also manages all programs' access to these resources. This novel approach enables partitioning of processes in memory, thereby preventing one program from disrupting the operation of the entire system. When one program ends unexpectedly on a UNIX system, it doesn't cause the whole computer to crash.

A Linux Command Sampler

The command line is the primary method of interacting with a Linux system. Even when you're running a GUI, the GUI actually executes commands on your behalf in response to your manipulation of the graphical elements on the screen. This section discusses some of the basics of the Linux user interface, interaction with the Linux command line, and some fundamental Linux commands.

The program that accepts your typing and runs the commands for you is called a **command interpreter**. Also known as a **shell**, a command interpreter translates your typed commands into machine instructions that the operating system can understand. Thus it is a program that runs other programs. UNIX command interpreters also perform file globbing (described later) and keep track of the command history (much like the **doskey** command in DOS and Windows NT). The primary UNIX command interpreter is */bin/sh*. It has a similar function to the primary Windows NT command interpreter, *cmd.exe*. The shell enables you to perform tasks, but you really must know which commands to use to accomplish meaningful work on a Linux system.

One especially useful feature of Linux (and UNIX in general) is its online documentation. Linux systems include documentation, known as the Linux **manual pages,** for all commands. You can review the instructions for any command by reading its manual page entry. The Linux manual pages are arranged in eight sections:

- *Section 1* covers the commands that you most typically enter while typing in a command window.
- *Sections 2 through 7* document the programmer's interface to the UNIX system.
- *Section 8* covers the commands used by administrators to manage the system.

You can access manual pages by entering the **man** command in a Linux command window. For example, to read the manual page entry for the **telnet** command, enter **man telnet** in a command window.

Although the Linux manual pages are accurate and complete, Linux newcomers often complain that they can't find the appropriate manual page if they don't know the name of the command they want to use. That's why the **apropos** command exists. It enables you to find possible manual page entries for the command you want to use. For example, you might type **apropos list** to search for a command that lists files. The **apropos** command would then display all commands and programming functions that include the keyword *list* in their manual page entries. Type **man <*command*>** (where <*command*> is a command name displayed by apropos) when you find a command name that looks like it might do what you want.

Commands function in much the same way as sentences in ordinary language. Some sentences are one-word directives to the system requesting that it perform a simple task on your behalf (such as *date* for "tell me the current date and time"). Other sentences are detailed instructions to the system containing the equivalent of nouns, adjectives, and adverbs and creating a precise description of the task you wish the system to perform. For example, to instruct the system to "print all files in the current directory that have been accessed in the past five days," you would type: **find . –type f –atime +5 –print**.

A few rules exist to guide your use of Linux commands and, as you might expect, exceptions to most of the rules also exist. Most commands (though not all) are lowercase alphabetic characters. Using the analogy of a sentence, the command itself would be the verb—that is, the action you want the system to take (for example, *ls* to list information about files). The things on which you want the system to operate (often files) would be the nouns. (So for example, you would type **ls accounts.xls** to list a file named account.xls.) Options to the commands would be adjectives and the adverbs—that is, modifiers that give more specifics about the command. Options are usually specified by typing a dash (-) followed by a letter (such as *ls -a* to list all files, even the "invisible" files in the current directory). You can make commands even more specific by using file **globbing**—the equivalent to using wildcards in Windows and DOS. On a Linux system, this operation is also called filename substitution (for example, **ls –l a*** would produce a detailed listing of all files beginning with the letter "a").

A significant (and perhaps initially confusing) difference between the Linux and Windows NT command-line interfaces relates to the character you use to separate directory names when you type in a command window. The Windows NT separator character is "\" (backslash). The equivalent Linux directory separator character is "/" (forward slash). For example, in a Windows NT command window, you type the *telnet* command as **\winnt\system32\telnet.exe**. The **telnet** command in Linux is **/usr/bin/telnet**.

Windows NT and UNIX share the powerful concept of directing output from one command to the input of another command. A **pipe** (entered as a vertical bar " | ") serves as the connection between two commands. Think of data "flowing" from one command to another. Most commands that display output on the monitor allow you to direct the output to another command. Most commands that accept typing from your keyboard also accept input from other commands. Two or more commands connected by a pipe are called a **pipeline**. UNIX pipes enable you to easily create sequences of commands that might require custom programming on systems without them.

Table 10-2 lists some common Linux commands and provides a brief description of each.

The developers of the original UNIX system worked at AT&T, then the largest public corporation in the world. Two features of communication within large corporations are the tendency to abbreviate words and the reliance on acronyms. The command names in the Linux system reflect this culture in that they drop vowels and syllables (*cp* for *copy*, *cat* for *concatenate*, and so on), and name commands with the "initials" of their intended use (**grep** for *general regular expression parser*, **ftp** for *File Transfer Protocol*). Refer to the relevant manual pages when you encounter command names that you don't understand. The *synopsis* section usually indicates the origin of the command name.

Table 10-2 Commonly Used Linux Commands

Command	Function
`date`	Display the current date and time
`ls -la`	Display all files in the current directory, with details
`ps -ax`	Display details of the current running programs
`find` *dir filename* `-print`	Search for *filename* in the directory *dir* and display the path to the name after finding the file
`cat` *file*	Display the contents of *file*
`cd` */d1/d2/d3*	Change the current directory to *d3*, located in */d1/d2*
`cp` *file1 file2*	Make a copy of *file1* named *file2*
`rm` *file*	Remove (delete) *file*—note that deletion in UNIX is permanent; there is no trashcan or recycle bin from which to recover the deleted file
`mv` *file1 file2*	Move (or rename) *file1* to *file2*
`mkdir` *dir*	Make a new directory named *dir*
`rmdir` *dir*	Remove the directory named *dir*
`who`	Display a list of users who are currently logged in
`vi` *file*	Use the "visual" editor named *vi* to edit *file*
`grep` "*string*" *file*	Search for the string of characters given in *string* in the file named *file*
`sort` *filename*	Sort alphabetically the contents of *filename*
`man` *command*	Display the manual page entry for *command*
`chmod` *rights file*	Change the access rights (the mode) of *file* to *rights*
`telnet` *host*	Start a virtual terminal connection to *host* (where *host* may be an IP address or a host name)
`ftp` *host*	Start an interactive file transfer to (or from) *host* using the FTP protocol (where *host* may be an IP address or a host name)
`startx`	Start the X Window system
`kill` *process*	Attempt to stop a running program with the process ID *process*
`tail` *file*	Display the last 10 lines of *file*
`exit`	Stop the current running command interpreter, and log off the system if it is the initial command interpreter started upon logging in

The most frequently used Linux command is *ls*. By entering *ls*, you learn everything about a file except its contents. Linux systems keep quite a bit of information about each file including:

- The filename
- The file size (in bytes)
- The date and time that the file's i-node (file information node, discussed below) was created
- The date and time that the file was last accessed (viewed or printed)
- The date and time that the file contents were last modified (created, edited, or changed in any way)
- The number of "aliases" or links to the file
- The numeric identifier of the user who owns the file
- The numeric identifier of the group to which the file belongs
- The access rights for the owner, the group, and all others

The system stores this information for each file (except the filename) in a file information node (abbreviated **i-node**). The beginning of each disk partition contains reserved space for all i-nodes on that partition. I-nodes also contain pointers to the actual file contents on the disk. The file's name is stored in the directory that contains the file. To learn about the i-node information, you use the **ls** command. Figure 10-2 shows a sample listing generated with **ls**.

```
% ls -l
total 1278
drwxr-xr-x   2 root     bin          2048 Dec 11 17:05 bin
drwxr-xr-x   2 root     root         1024 Sep 24 01:38 boot
drwxr-xr-x   2 root     root         1024 Feb 26  1998 cdrom
drwxr-xr-x   3 root     root        19456 Jan 16 02:52 dev
drwxr-xr-x   9 root     root         3072 Feb  2 07:27 etc
drwxr-xr-x   2 root     root         1024 May 27  1997 floppy
drwxr-xr-x  78 root     root         2048 Jan 30 11:55 home
drwxrwxr-x   4 root     root         1024 Dec 15 13:12 home2
drwxr-xr-x   3 root     root         1024 Sep 28 13:18 lib
drwxr-xr-x   2 root     root        12288 May 27  1997 lost+found
drwxr-xr-x   2 root     root         1024 Jun 21  1996 mnt
drwxrwxr-x   9 root     root         1024 Jan 16 05:42 nfs
dr-xr-xr-x   5 root     root            0 Jan 15 20:52 proc
drwxr-x--x   6 root     root         1024 Dec 22 05:56 root
drwxr-xr-x   2 root     bin          2048 Jul  7  1998 sbin
drwxr-xr-x   2 root     root         1024 May 27  1997 shlib
drwxrwxrwt  45 root     root        12288 Feb  2 07:56 tmp
drwxrwxr-x  24 root     root         1024 Jan 16 03:54 usr
drwxr-xr-x  17 root     root         1024 Dec 14 08:10 var
-r--------   1 root     root       359327 May 27  1997 vmlinuz-2.0.29
-r--------   1 root     root       468684 May 27  1997 vmlinuz-2.0.29-1
-r--------   1 root     root       404117 Apr  8  1998 vmlinuz-2.0.33
drwxrwxr-x   5 root     binc         1024 Jan 16 05:56 www
%
```

Figure 10-2 Example of output from **ls**

The strings of r's, w's, x's, and so on, in the left column, represent the access permissions for the files. The first character in the access permissions field (on the far left) indicates the file type. Files with a type of "d" are directories. Files whose type is shown with a "-" are regular files such as word processing files or spread sheet files—that is, they simply contain unstructured (to the operating system) data. Other valid file types are as follows:

- "l" for symbolic link files (much like Windows NT shortcuts)
- "b" for block device files (such as disk partitions)
- "c" for character device files (such as serial ports)

Figure 10-3 shows how to interpret the rest of the output of **ls**.

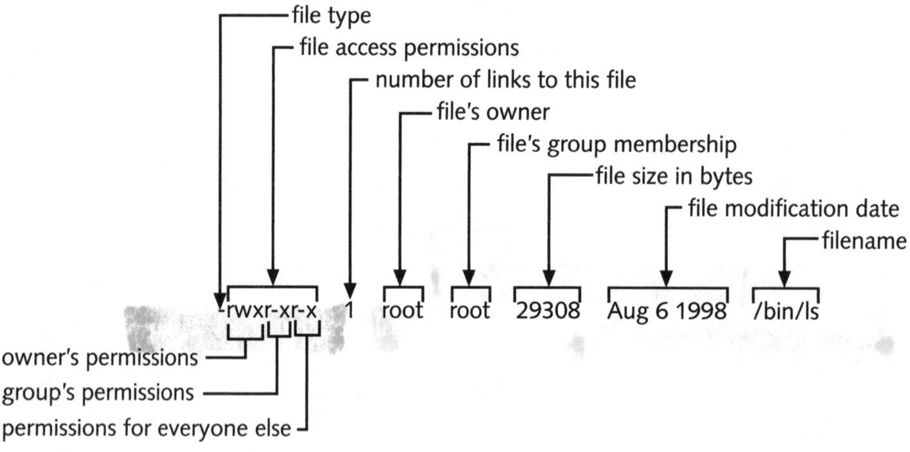

Figure 10-3 Anatomy of **ls** output

INSTALLING AND CONFIGURING A LINUX SERVER

You've had a taste of the Linux system. Now it's time to build one. This section will walk through the installation process for the Intel-based Red Hat Linux. Although you can install Red Hat Linux over a network using **FTP** or **NFS**, this section describes the quickest way—using a CD-ROM.

PREINSTALLATION REQUIREMENTS

In previous chapters, you learned about the importance of thorough planning in the installation of a new server. These considerations apply to Linux as well as to Windows NT and NetWare. Although making changes to the server setup after you install a Linux system is easier and less disruptive than with Windows NT, you should nevertheless plan as carefully as possible to avoid service unavailability after a Linux server is running.

Before installing Linux, you should be prepared to answer the following questions:

- *What is the new server's name?* This name is a less important issue for Linux systems than for Windows NT or NetWare systems, but it's still a good idea to choose it before beginning installation. You can add the server's name to your network name service (DNS, for example) as soon as you choose it. (See Chapter 11 for details about TCP/IP domain names.) You may use any name containing a maximum of 32 alphanumeric characters, not including the following:

> >< [ ] ._: ; | = , + * " ?

- *What is the server's IP address?* You'll need this address to enable the network on the new server. Network administrators usually configure workstations to obtain an IP address automatically while they start up, but they often configure servers with reserved or static IP addresses because some client applications require configuration with a server's IP address rather than a server's name. You'll also need the network mask (see Chapters 3 and 11 for details about TCP/IP addressing), the IP address of the server's primary gateway (in other words, the default gateway), and the IP address of the new server's TCP/IP domain name server.
- *What kind of video card is installed in the server?* The Linux setup process attempts to detect the video card and will install the correct driver if possible. Otherwise, it will prompt you to choose the type of video card from a list. Either way, you should know what kind of video card your server contains.
- *What kind of monitor is attached to the new server?* As yet, an operating system cannot automatically learn this information. You'll need to supply the monitor manufacturer and model number to the Linux setup program.
- *What is the administrative user's password?* Choose a difficult-to-guess password for the Linux administrator account. Chapter 15 provides advice on choosing good passwords.
- *How can I remember all of this information?* Once you have answered these questions, you should create a server installation form and keep the form with you during installation. Appendix C offers an example of such a form.

This list highlights only the most significant installation options. In addition, you should be prepared to identify your keyboard and mouse type, choose a time zone, and specify an administrator account ID.

Although this example involves a standalone Linux system, Linux very peacefully coexists with other operating systems on your primary hard drive. (Read more about multiboot systems at the Linux installation **HOWTO** site:

http://www.linuxhq.com/LDP/HOWTO/Installation-HOWTO.html).

For this installation, you'll need the following:

- A clean PC (one without any operating system installed) that satisfies the Linux hardware requirements detailed previously
- The distribution media for Red Hat version 5.2 (CD-ROM and floppy disk)
- One or two hours of uninterrupted time

THE INSTALLATION PROCESS

The package containing Red Hat version 5.2 of Linux includes a manual, three CD-ROMs, and a bootable floppy disk labeled "Boot Diskette". Place this floppy disk and the first Red Hat CD-ROM near your computer. Turn off your computer before beginning the installation. As you work your way through the installation screens, keep in mind that you can use the arrow keys to highlight desired list items, and the Tab key to select actions. Press Enter (or F12) to proceed from one screen to the next.

To install Red Hat version 5.2 of Linux:

1. Insert the Boot Diskette disk into the server's A: drive.
2. Turn on your computer. The Red Hat welcome screen appears, prompting you to enter a boot command or simply press Enter.
3. Press **Enter**. After loading the image from the floppy, the computer displays the installation welcome screen, as shown in Figure 10-4, and prompts you for basic installation information. Press **Enter** to continue.

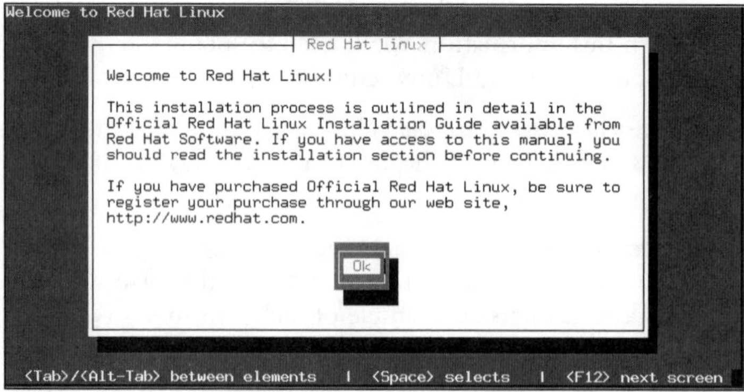

Figure 10-4 Welcome to Red Hat Linux screen

4. The Language Selection screen appears. Choose the language you'll use by pressing the down arrow until the Linux setup highlights your preferred language. Press **Enter** to select your language.
5. The Keyboard Type screen appears. Press the down arrow until **us** is highlighted, then press **Enter** to select it.
6. The setup program may ask you whether you need support for PCMCIA during installation. Choose **No** by repeatedly pressing the Tab key until Linux setup highlights the **No** box. Press **Enter** to continue.
7. The setup program asks you to select the medium from which you'll perform the installation. It highlights Local CD-ROM, the first menu entry. Press **Enter** to choose **Local CD-ROM** and continue.

8. The Installation Path screen appears. Linux setup asks whether you're installing a new system or upgrading an existing system. Choose **Install**, then press **Enter**.
9. The Installation Class screen appears. Select the type of system you're installing by choosing **Server**. Press the arrow key (up or down) until Setup highlights the word "Server," then press **Enter** to continue.
10. Setup may display a *SCSI Configuration* screen. Press **Enter** to indicate that your system does not have any SCSI devices.
11. The Setup Filesystems screen appears. Linux setup formats your server's partitions in this step. You're asked twice to verify that you really do want to perform the formatting. Press **Enter** to proceed with the formatting.
12. The Package Installation screen appears. Red Hat Linux organizes groups of applications, services, and utilities into packages. Behind the scenes, you really chose a set of packages when you selected the "Server" installation class in Step 9. Packages include one or more files: at least one application program, documentation files, and often configuration files. Examples of packages include the Netscape Navigator Web browser, GIMP (a UNIX image manipulation editor similar to Adobe Photoshop), and x3270 (a UNIX terminal emulation program used for accessing IBM mainframes). Linux setup displays the name of each package it's installing and a progress bar showing the percentage of the package installation completed. This setup is the most time-consuming part of the installation and can take as long as 30 or 40 minutes depending on the speed of your system hardware.
13. Once package installation is complete, the Probe Result screen may appear. If so, press **Enter** so that the the Mouse Configuration screen appears, indicating that the system has attempted to detect your mouse type. Your mouse type is highlighted if Linux setup correctly detected it. Use the up and down arrow keys to highlight the proper mouse type if necessary. Press **Tab** once to highlight the **Emulate 3 Buttons** field, then press the spacebar to select that option (Linux setup shows your selection by placing an asterisk in the space between the square brackets). The X Window system uses three-button mice. You simulate the third button by simultaneously clicking both buttons of a two-button mouse. You can change the mouse configuration on your system with **/usr/sbin/mouseconfig** after it's up and running. Press **Tab** and then press **Enter** to continue.
14. Next the PCI Probe screen may appear. This screen will appear only if your configuration includes PCI hardware. Press **Enter** to accept the probe results.
15. The *Xconfigurator* screen appears. *Xconfigurator* asks if you want to probe for your video card. Use **Tab** to indicate that you want Setup to probe for your video card. Press **Enter** to continue. If it is unable to identify your video card, Setup presents you with a series of screens requesting specific video card information including video RAM, clockchip, and video mode. Consult your video hardware manual for the details of your video card installation. This is the most difficult part of the Red Hat 5.2 installation, so you may want to read the *Red Hat 5.2 Installation Guide* for more details. When completing the video hardware configuration screens, you can return to previous screens using the **Back** function. Press

Tab until the word *Back* is highlighted and press **Enter**. After completing the video card setup you'll tell Setup which monitor you're using, as described in the next step.

16. The Monitor Selection screen appears, prompting you to specify your monitor type. As you did in step 13, use the up and down arrow keys to highlight the entry that most closely identifies your monitor brand and model. Press **Tab** and then press **Enter** to continue.
17. Linux setup gives you the option of testing the video driver and monitor type you selected in steps 13 and 14. Press **Enter** to test the driver. A pattern resembling a TV test pattern will appear on the screen if all is well. You can use the **Back** function (by pressing **Tab** until Linux setup highlights the **Back** box, then pressing **Enter**) to return to previous screens and select a different video card or monitor model if the video test pattern looks wrong or doesn't appear. Be sure to read your hardware documentation and the Red Hat Installation Guide (which comes with the Red Hat CD-ROM) if you have problems installing the X Window system.
18. The Boot Protocol screen appears next. Most LAN administrators configure servers with static IP addresses, so this section describes that process. To configure your server to start with a static IP address, press **Enter**.
19. Networking configuration continues with the Configure TCP/IP screen, shown in Figure 10-5. You'll need the information you gathered before starting the installation here. The TCP/IP configuration screen has four fields in which you must type your server's IP address (for example, 10.1.4.10), your server's net-mask (for example, 255.255.255.0), your server's default gateway IP address (for example, 10.1.4.1), and the IP address of your server's primary nameserver (for example, 10.1.1.10). Linux setup guesses the addresses of the last two items, so simply type over them if they are wrong for your network. Press **Tab** to move between fields, and press **Enter** to accept the values and continue with TCP/IP configuration.

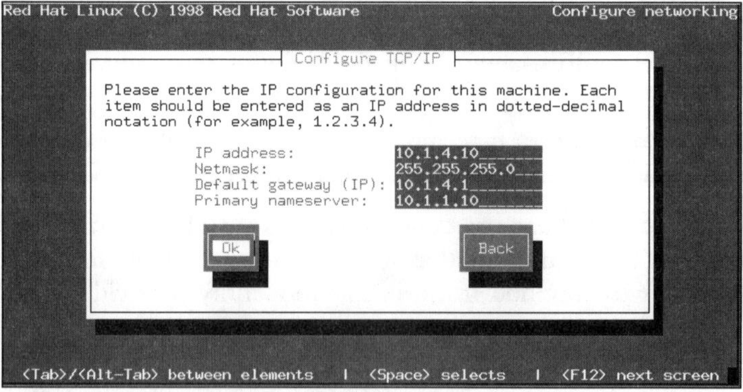

Figure 10-5 Configure TCP/IP screen

20. The Configure Network screen appears, as shown in Figure 10-6. This screen requires you to type your server's domain name (for example, acme.com), your server's host name (for example, host4.redhat.com), (optionally) your server's secondary nameserver (for example, 10.1.2.10), and (optionally) your server's tertiary nameserver. Press **Tab** to move between fields, and press **Enter** to accept the values and complete your server's TCP/IP configuration.

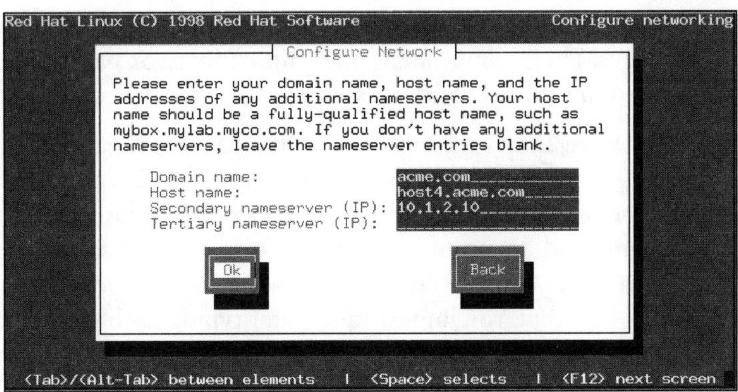

Figure 10-6 Configure Network screen

21. The Configure Timezones screen appears. Choose the time and time zone information as appropriate for your location. Press **Tab** until Linux setup highlights **Hardware clock set to GMT** and ensure that your CMOS clock is properly set to Greenwich Mean Time (check your computer's hardware manual for instructions on setting your CMOS clock). This selection will ensure that your Linux system will properly handle daylight savings time if you are in a location that uses it. Press **Tab** and then press **Enter** to accept your choices.

22. The Root Password screen appears. Enter the password you chose while gathering information prior to installing Linux on your server. Press **Tab** to enter the same password a second time for confirmation. Press **Tab** and then press **Enter** to continue.

23. The Boot Disk Creation screen appears. You use a Linux boot disk primarily in the same way that you use a Windows NT emergency repair disk: to restore your system in the event that it encounters a severe file corruption problem or a catastrophic hard drive failure. Press the spacebar to create the boot disk. A dialog box appears, instructing you to place a blank, formatted disk in your disk drive. Press the spacebar when you're ready to create the boot disk. Remove this disk from the drive when the process is complete and label the disk with a clear title such as "Linux Emergency Boot Disk."

24. The final installation screen appears, reminding you to remove the disk from the disk drive and press Enter to restart your server. Press **Enter**.

25. Log in to your new Linux server as user **root** when the system presents you with the login prompt (using the password you entered in Step 22).

Configuring Linux for Network Administration

A Linux server is little more than a powerful workstation when it has no user accounts. This section introduces you to the setup process for Linux system administration. You'll learn:

- The basics of adding users and groups
- The basics of modifying file access permissions

This section introduces two commands: **groupadd** and **useradd**. Both are documented with their own manual pages. Their names imply their function: **groupadd** enables you to add a new group to the system, and **useradd** enables you to add a new user to the system.

Like Windows NT and NetWare, Linux requires the use of user names and passwords to connect clients to the network. Also like Windows NT, it assigns access rights to groups, and users may be members of multiple groups. For example, the Linux group named *mail* can access the electronic mail programs and electronic mail files. This section assumes that you are logged in to a Linux system as the administrative user ("*root*") and that your system has presented you with a command prompt. You'll press Enter after typing each command to allow Linux to carry out the operation. You may want to reread Table 8-2, which covers security for groups, as that information is relevant here.

Adding Groups and Users

You use the **groupadd** command to add a new group ID to a Linux system. It does not assign users to the new group, but rather makes a new group name available for use. Linux assigns a unique identification number to each group. Note that creating a new group does not automatically assign access rights to that group; you'll learn how to accomplish that task later in this section. You'll use the same school groups and access rights given in Table 8-2 for this section. Creating a new Linux group for instructors is simply a matter of typing the necessary commands. Note that the commands display no information if they successfully complete the operation.

To add group IDs to your Linux system:

1. Log in to your system as user **root** using the password you entered when you installed Linux.
2. Type **groupadd instructors**, then press **Enter** at the command prompt to add the group *instructors*.
3. Type **groupadd students**, then press **Enter** to add the group *students*.
4. Type **groupadd administrators**, then press **Enter** to add the group *administrators*.

You use the **useradd** command to add a new user ID to a Linux system. It creates a new user ID and assigns that user ID to one or more groups. In this example, you'll create a new user, Thomas, and assign that user to the group *instructors*. The new user should be a member of the general users group as well as the group *instructors*. You must use two options when typing the

useradd command: the *–g* option specifies the initial (or primary) group for the user, and the *–G* option specifies the additional groups to which the new user will belong (*instructors,* in this case). Note that **useradd** does not assign a password for the new user ID, so you'll use the **passwd** command to assign a password for *thomas*.

Linux passwords are case-sensitive. You may use any of the characters on the keyboard in your password.

You can use the **passwd** command in one of two ways: while logged on to the system as the administrative user, root, to change another user's password, or while logged on to the system as a normal user to change your own password. As you type the password, notice that the characters do not appear on the screen. This security precaution prevents people from peering over your shoulder and seeing your password as you type it. Read the **passwd** manual page (**man passwd**) to learn more about this command.

To add a new user and assign the user a password:

1. Type **useradd -g users -G instructors thomas**, then press **Enter** to add a new user account named *thomas*.
2. Type **passwd thomas**, then press **Enter**. Linux prompts you to type the new password. After you type the password and press **Enter**, Linux prompts you to retype your password. Enter the same password again; this confirmation helps ensure that you type your new password accurately.

Now that you've added a new group and a new user to the system, you may restrict access to resources owned by the user *thomas* or the group *instructors*.

Changing File Access Permissions

Linux restricts access to resources by comparing user and group IDs with the owner and group membership of files. Every file and directory on a Linux system is owned by exactly one user and is a member of exactly one group. You may assign access permissions for the file's owner, the file's group, and everyone else. Linux assigns new files and directories to the creator's primary group (*users,* in this example). The example from Table 8-2 shows that the directory *PROGRAMS* contains instructional programs. You want to allow teachers to place new programs in *PROGRAMS*. Students should be able to run the programs, but not to add new ones or to delete them.

To create a directory and assign it to a group:

1. To log off your Linux system, type **exit**, then press **Enter**.
2. To log back on to your system as user *thomas,* enter **thomas** at the login prompt.
3. Enter the password you assigned for *thomas*.
4. Linux presents you with a command window and a command prompt. To create the new directory, type the command **mkdir PROGRAMS**, then press **Enter**.
5. List the file with **ls -l**. Notice that the directory belongs to the group *users.*

6. Enter the command **chgrp instructors PROGRAMS** to assign *PROGRAMS* to the group *instructors*.

Now that you've created the directory *PROGRAMS* and assigned it to the group *instructors*, you must limit access to the files. You use the **chmod** command to change the access permissions of files and directories. Read about **chmod** in its manual page (**man chmod**). Your goal is to enable members of the group *instructors* to create new files in and delete files from *PROGRAMS*, and to limit access to all others (specifically, members of the group *students*). To accomplish this task, you must add write permission for the group and remove write permission for all others.

To change the access permissions for the **PROGRAMS** directory:

1. Type **chmod g+w PROGRAMS** to add write access for the *instructors* group to *PROGRAMS*, and then press **Enter.**
2. Type **chmod o-rw PROGRAMS** to remove read and write access by others to *PROGRAMS*, and then press **Enter**.
3. Type **ls -l** to view the access permissions assigned to *PROGRAMS*. You should see a line for *PROGRAMS* that includes permissions of *-rwxrwx-/-x*.

INTERNETWORKING WITH OTHER NETWORK OPERATING SYSTEMS

People have modified the UNIX system over the years to work with other network operating systems and protocols besides TCP/IP. Programmers and network administrators alike have added functionality to the system because they find it so productive. Their changes include the addition of Windows networking, NetWare networking, IBM mainframe terminal emulation, and Windows programming tools. Examples of these tools are described below.

- Samba—The UNIX-based server message block (SMB) and common Internet file system (CIFS) package. This application provides everything needed to make your UNIX system a fully featured Windows file and printer sharing server.
- IPX/SPX—The original Novell networking protocol. It is implemented as a native UNIX protocol in many UNIX versions. Proprietary and open source software solutions, such as Caldera's NetWare for Linux, exist to turn your UNIX server into a NetWare server by including full NDS support.
- AppleTalk—The Apple Macintosh network protocol. Many UNIX system vendors support this protocol and all application programs needed to implement Macintosh file and print servers.
- X3270—An X Window–based 3270 terminal emulator for accessing your mainframe over a TCP/IP connection. This standard application is included with the X Window system for UNIX.

- WABI—The Windows application binary interface package from SunSoft, a Sun Microsystems company. This application provides a complete Windows emulation package. It enables you to run Windows programs on your UNIX system. WABI runs on many UNIX implementations, including Solaris and Linux.
- SoftWindows95—A commercial package that implements a virtual Windows machine. It is another Windows emulation package for UNIX systems.
- WINE—An open source application that implements a Win32 programming subsystem for UNIX, including a Windows emulator. This ongoing project is slowly improving with age as more people begin to use it and contribute changes to the source code.
- Dozens and dozens of command-line utilities that enable you to access the contents of files generated on other systems

CHAPTER SUMMARY

- The UNIX system is a stable, robust network operating system. It forms the basis of much of the Internet. You must be familiar with the operation of UNIX so as to set up and maintain most local and wide area networks. Despite the preponderance of proprietary implementations of UNIX systems, the differences between the various versions are relatively minor. With a little effort, you can understand them and move from one implementation to another with ease.
- The UNIX system is characterized by a rich tradition and a supportive culture. It's history is worth learning to further your understanding of the system. UNIX was born at AT&T's Bell Laboratories, when a few programmers grew dissatisfied with the programming environments available in the late 1960s. Ken Thompson and Dennis Ritchie were the original authors of the system.
- Currently, The Santa Cruz Operation in California owns the rights to the UNIX source code. The Open Group, a nonprofit trade association, owns the UNIX trademark. Every major workstation manufacturer licenses and resells a version of the UNIX system.
- Sun Microsystems, IBM, and Hewlett-Packard sell the three most popular UNIX-based workstations. These products are based on these companies' proprietary implementations of UNIX, which conform to most UNIX standards.
- Recently, nonproprietary implementations of UNIX-like systems have become popular. Often referred to as open source software or freely distributable software, this category includes the UNIX-like systems FreeBSD, GNU, and Linux.
- The key difference between freely distributable UNIX and proprietary implementations is that the copyright on freely distributable implementations requires that anyone purchasing an open source version of UNIX receive access to the source code.
- UNIX systems make great Internet servers. In fact, the leading Internet Web server is an open source software project called Apache. The original Web tools—including browsers and servers—were developed on UNIX-based systems. UNIX systems underlay the

original ARPAnet and Internet services such as FTP, Telnet, gopher, HTTP, and POP. These services are standard with current implementations of UNIX.

- One characteristic of all UNIX systems is a user-definable command interpreter. Its development arose in part because the command line was the primary interface with the system.
- Other characteristics of UNIX systems are as follows: the ability to support multiple, simultaneous users; hierarchical file systems with demountable volumes; a consistent interface for files, devices, and interprocess input/output; hundreds of subsystems and dozens of programming languages; program source code portability between different implementations of the system; and user-definable windowing systems.
- One of the first things you notice about using the UNIX command line is the difference in meaning of the "slash" characters. Windows uses a backslash to separate directories; UNIX uses the forward slash. The backslash character means something completely different to UNIX command interpreters; it instructs the system to delay processing a command until the user presses Enter again.
- UNIX server hardware requirements are roughly equivalent to those of Windows NT and NetWare. You should take into account the nature of the work that the system will perform when you're trying to determine the hardware requirements of your UNIX server. As with any hardware purchase, the type of software and the number of users served are major factors in the buying decision.
- Minimum hardware requirements for a Linux server include an Intel-compatible 80486 processor, 16 MB RAM, 150 MB of hard disk space, a network interface card compatible with the rest of your network, a CD-ROM drive, and a floppy disk drive.
- The UNIX system was among the first operating systems to include a hierarchical file system. This approach led to better organized data and subsystems.
- Each UNIX process represents an instance of a running executable program in core memory (RAM). The UNIX kernel allocates separate resources (such as buffer space, stack space, and open file pointers) to each process as it is created. The kernel manages access to these resources.
- You can liken UNIX commands to ordinary sentences. Some sentences are very short—one-word directives (verbs) to the system requesting it to perform a simple task on your behalf. Other sentences are more detailed—instructions to the system containing the equivalent of nouns, adjectives, and adverbs and creating a precise description of the task that the system should perform. The things on which you want the system to operate are the nouns—often files. Options to the commands are the adjectives and the adverbs.
- A few rules exist to guide your use of UNIX commands. Most commands are lowercase alphabetic characters. Options are usually specified by typing a dash ("-") followed by a letter. The letter is often (but not always) a mnemonic abbreviation for the option (such as "*-l*" for a long file listing).

- Command names are usually acronyms or abbreviations. Consult the command's manual (man) page when you encounter a command name that makes no sense to you. The synopsis usually indicates the origin of the command name.
- The UNIX *ls* command is the most frequently used. It allows you to learn everything about a file except its contents. *ls* reports the filename, the file size, the date and time that the file was created, the date and time that it was last accessed, the date and time that it was last modified, the number of "aliases" or links to the file, the user who owns the file, the group to which the file belongs, and the access rights for the owner, the group, and all others.
- The system uses information nodes (i-nodes) to store everything other than the actual contents of files. I-nodes also contain pointers to file contents on the disk.
- Linux distributions are binary compatible. They differ mainly in the methods they use for installing additional software packages. The Red Hat Linux distribution is one of the most popular.
- Use the useradd command to add new users to your Linux system.
- Use the groupadd command to add new groups to your Linux system.
- The chgrp command assigns a file to a group.
- The chmod command changes file access permissions.
- UNIX systems quite competently interoperate with other network operating systems. You can use them to share files with Windows-based computers and NetWare-based computers, for example. In addition, you can use a UNIX-based computer to access mainframe sessions. You can even run Windows software on UNIX systems with the proper emulation package installed.

Key Terms

- **AIX** — IBM's proprietary implementation of the UNIX system.
- **Apache** — A popular open source software Web server application often used on Linux Internet servers.
- **BSD (Berkeley Software Distribution)** — A UNIX distribution that originated at the University of California at Berkeley. The BSD suffix differentiates these distributions from AT&T distributions. No longer being developed at Berkeley, the last public release of BSD UNIX was version 4.4.
- **command interpreter** — A (usually text-based) program that accepts and executes system programs and applications on behalf of users. Often it includes the ability to execute a series of instructions that are stored in a file.
- **flavor** — Term used to refer to the different implementations of a particular UNIX-like system. For example, the different flavors of Linux include Red Hat, Caldera, and Slackware.

- **FreeBSD** — An open source software implementation of the Berkeley Software Distribution version of the UNIX system.
- **freely distributable** — A term used to describe software with a very liberal copyright. Often associated with open source software.
- **FTP** — File Transfer Protocol. A protocol used on the Internet or intranets for batch or interactive copying of files from one IP-based host to another IP-based host. Can be used to install UNIX.
- **globbing** — A form of file name substitution, similar to the use of wildcards in Windows and DOS.
- **GNU** — The name given to the free software project to implement a complete source code implementation of UNIX; the collection of UNIX-inspired utilities and tools that are included with Linux distributions and other free software UNIX systems. The recursive acronym stands for GNU's Not UNIX.
- **hardware compatibility list (HCL)** — A vendor-maintained list of all hardware that is compatible with a particular operating system. It is usually provided as a document on the vendor's Web site.
- **hierarchical file system** — The organization of files and directories (or folders) on a disk partition in which directories may contain files and other directories. When displayed graphically, this organization resembles a tree-like structure.
- **HOWTO** — A series of brief, highly focused documents giving Linux system details. The people responsible for the Linux Documentation Project centrally coordinate the HOWTO papers (see http://www.linuxhq.com/HOWTO).
- **HP-UX** — Hewlett-Packard's proprietary implementation of the UNIX system.
- **i-node** — A UNIX file system information storage area that holds all details about a file. This information includes the size, access rights, date and time of creation, and a pointer to the actual contents of the file.
- **kernel** — The core of a UNIX system. This part of the operating system is loaded and run when you turn on your computer. It mediates between user programs and the computer hardware.
- **kernel modules** — Portions of the Linux kernel that you can load and unload to add or remove functionality on a running Linux system.
- **Linux** — A freely distributable implementation of the UNIX system. It was originally developed by Finnish computer scientist Linus Torvalds.
- **manual pages** — UNIX online documentation. This documentation describes the use of the commands and the programming interface to the UNIX system.
- **NFS** — Network File System. A client/server application that allows you to view, store and update files on a remote computer as though they were on your own computer. Can be used to install Linux.

- **open source software** — Term used to describe software that is distributed without any restriction and whose source code is freely available. See also "freely distributable".
- **Orange Book** — The security specification for computer operating systems published in 1985 by the U.S. Department of Defense.
- **pipe** — The facility in a UNIX system that enables you to combine commands to form new commands in ways that the authors may never have dreamed. It is one of the most powerful facilities of the UNIX system.
- **pipeline** — A series of two or more UNIX commands connected together with pipe symbols.
- **proprietary UNIX** — Any implementation of UNIX for which the source code is either unavailable or available only by purchasing a licensed copy from The Santa Cruz Operation (costing as much as millions of dollars).
- **real-time** — An operating system that minimally includes two characteristics: an ability to respond to external events (for example, a change in temperature), and an ability to respond to those events deterministically—with predictable response time (for example, turning on a heating element within three microseconds).
- **Samba** — An open source software package that provides complete Windows NT–style file and printer sharing facility.
- **shell** — Another term for command interpreter.
- **Solaris** — Sun Microsystems' proprietary implementation of the UNIX system.
- **System V** — The proprietary version of UNIX, originally developed at AT&T Bell Labs, currently distributed by The Santa Cruz Operation.
- **time-sharing system** — A computing system to which users must attach directly so as to use the shared resources of the computer.

Review Questions

1. In what year did work begin on the UNIX system?

   a. 1990

   b. 1987

   c. 1975

   d. 1969

2. Which of the following are open source software implementations of UNIX-like systems?

   a. Solaris

   b. IRIX

   c. Linux

- **d.** FreeBSD
- **e.** HP-UX

3. Which of the following services might not be appropriate for a UNIX server?

- **a.** Internet services
- **b.** file and print services
- **c.** image database services
- **d.** music on hold service
- **e.** DHCP service

4. It is appropriate to use UNIX systems for network firewalls. True or False?

5. What is the primary method for interacting with the UNIX system?

- **a.** speaking to it through a microphone
- **b.** moving a mouse and clicking on icons
- **c.** typing commands at a command prompt
- **d.** typing commands in a dialog box

6. Which of the following are characteristics common to all UNIX systems?

- **a.** the same font for all windows
- **b.** availability in multiple foreign languages
- **c.** the ability to start processes in the background
- **d.** file systems in which directories cannot contain other directories
- **e.** the availability of Windows emulation programs

7. Which character is used to separate directory names on UNIX systems?

- **a.** backslash
- **b.** colon
- **c.** comma
- **d.** period
- **e.** forward slash

8. Hardware requirements for UNIX servers are roughly equivalent to those of Windows NT or NetWare servers. True or False?

9. Which of the following are stored in a file's i-node?

- **a.** access rights
- **b.** the filename
- **c.** the first 16 bytes of the file
- **d.** the time and date that the file was last printed

10. Which letter does the ls command use to identify a UNIX symbolic link (much like a Windows NT shortcut) in a detailed file listing? P426
    a. L
    b. S
    c. l
    d. y
    e. s
11. Which of the following items are you required to know when installing a Red Hat Linux server? P426–427
    a. your Internet service provider's name
    b. your printer brand and model
    c. the number of buttons on your mouse
    d. the server's IP address
12. The administrative user "root" is subject to which of the following access restrictions, just like any other UNIX system user?
    a. read access
    b. create access
    c. write access
    d. execute access
    e. None of the above.
13. Which open source software application enables UNIX systems to participate in SMB file sharing on a network? P416 or P434
    a. Tango
    b. Samba
    c. Jitterbug
    d. Waltz
14. Which of the following tools might enable you to run Windows programs from your Linux system? P435
    a. SoftWindows
    b. WABI
    c. WINE
    d. Windows NT
15. Which command would you use to create a new directory on a UNIX system? P424 Table 10-2
    a. make
    b. makedir
    c. mkdir
    d. md

16. Which command would you use to remove a directory on a UNIX system?
    a. mkdir
    b. rmdir
    c. deldir
    d. rd
    e. removedir
17. Which option(s) would you use to tell the ls command to display all files in the current directory?
    a. --all
    b. -listall
    c. /a
    d. –a
    e. /all
18. What does grep stands for?
    a. globbing relocation expert processor
    b. general replication executable pointer
    c. generic regular expression pointer
    d. general regular expression parser
    e. None of the above.
19. Which UNIX command might you use to display the last 10 lines of a file?
    a. grep
    b. exit
    c. tail
    d. who
    e. list
20. Under what circumstances would file globbing be useful?
21. If a UNIX command is like a sentence, which part of the command is like the sentence's verb?
    a. the command name
    b. the command options
    c. the Enter key
    d. the filename associated with the command
22. Which part of a UNIX command is like the noun in a sentence?
    a. the command name
    b. the command options
    c. the Enter key
    d. the filename associated with the command

23. How would you learn about a command for which you know the name, but not the purpose?
    a. Ask a friend.
    b. Use the manual command.
    c. Use the man command.
    d. Use the apropos command.
24. What is the full command you would use to revoke write permission for everyone other than yourself for the file named *sent-mail?*
    a. chown root sent-mail
    b. chmod –write sent-mail
    c. chmod og-w sent-mail
    d. chgrp system sent-mail
25. What is the full command you would use to create the directory named *GRADES*?
    a. cp new GRADES
    b. makedir GRADES
    c. mkdir GRADES
    d. make dir GRADES

Hands-on Projects

Project 10-1

In this exercise, you'll learn about some of the basic differences between the Windows (or DOS) command line and the UNIX command line. To complete this project, you'll need a computer system running Linux. If you have not already done so, install Linux by following the steps in this chapter, using a computer that meets at least the minimum hardware requirements, also described in this chapter.

1. Turn on your computer and wait for it to start Linux.
2. Type your user name and password at the login and password prompts.
3. The system presents you with a command-line window (usually called a terminal window or **xterm** window) and a command prompt. Type a slash character (/), then press **Enter**. What happened? The command interpreter was awaiting a command, and you typed a directory name (/).
4. Type a backslash character (\), then press **Enter**. What happened? The backslash character tells the system not to process the command, but to wait for the rest of the command. You can use this feature to enter very long commands on multiple lines and still maintain the readability when you print a copy of the command.

5. Press **Enter** again. What happened this time? The backslash you typed in step 4 instructed the system to wait for more input, but the rest of your input was empty. The system did nothing and displayed the command prompt, awaiting your next command.
6. Press **Ctrl+D**. What happened? Ctrl+D is a special control sequence, signaling to the command interpreter that it should end current processing. As it was sent to your login command interpreter, you signaled to the system that you were logging out.

PROJECT 10-2

In this exercise, you'll get more exposure to the UNIX ls command. Keep the "verbs," "nouns," and rules in mind when trying this exercise, and remember to press Enter after each command. You'll need a running Linux system for this exercise—that is, a computer that meets the minimum hardware requirements with a copy of Linux installed.

1. Turn on your computer and wait for it to start Linux.
2. Log in with your user name and password.
3. Type **ls** at the command-line prompt. What do you see? Don't be alarmed. Linux designers subscribe to the notion that "no news is good news." The fact that running ls generated no output simply means that it found no files to list. This response is quite normal for brand new user accounts.
4. Add the adjective "all" to the verb as follows: **ls –a**. In what way is this command different from that given in step 3? Linux filenames beginning with a period are considered "hidden," much as Windows NT Explorer can hide files with certain extensions.
5. Read the manual page for ls (**man ls**). How does ls sort the output by default? How can you instruct ls to sort the output by the files' timestamps instead?
6. Tell the system you want to see the details of all files in the current directory (**ls –la**). How is this command different from the listing performed in step 4?
7. Produce a detailed listing of all files in the directory */usr/bin,* sorting the listing by file timestamp in reverse date order (**ls -alrt /usr/bin**). Is there a different way to specify the options in this command? Many Linux commands accept both short and long options. You invoke ls with long options by typing two hyphen characters followed by the descriptive option name. The ls manual page documents the long and the short options.

PROJECT 10-3

This project introduces the notion of connected commands. The connection method you'll use is a pipe, the mechanism that directs the output and input of commands. UNIX pipes are used to combine the output of one command with the input of another command; they represent one of the most powerful features of the UNIX system, and a feature that has been mimicked by many other computing systems, including Windows NT. As explained in this chapter, the symbol used for a pipe in the UNIX shell is " | ", the vertical bar, usually located on computer keyboards above the backslash. You type a pipe symbol by pressing **SHIFT** and **backslash**. A UNIX pipeline is simply two or more commands on one command line with a " | " between them. You'll use two commands in this project: **who** and **grep**. The **who** command displays the users who are currently logged on to the system. Running **who** on a busy server might show as many as 100 users logged on. The Linux command **grep** is used to search for strings of characters in files. As in the previous projects, you'll need a running Linux system to complete this exercise. You must be logged in to your lab system at a shell prompt.

1. Type the command **who**, then press **Enter**. You should see a list of all logged-on users (possibly just one).
2. Type **who | grep root**. You should see just one line displayed: the line representing the login information for the user *root*.

CASE PROJECTS

1. Rick Gomez, the director of product development for EarTech, has asked you to investigate setting up a test network for the company's product development team. The network will support the company's new "EarRadio 2000" FM radio cochlear implant. The network should be connected to the company LAN, but only through one system and only for purposes of Internet access. All of the usual services (such as file sharing, printing, and backup) will be handled on the local LAN. Rick suggests that you plan for a maximum of 30 users, 12 of whom might use the network at any given time. After investigating the situation, you learn that the test network will include several kinds of workstations: Windows PCs, Macintoshes, Hewlett-Packard workstations, and Silicon Graphics workstations, plus two networked read-only memory (ROM) programming devices (these look to the users very much like a network printer). Draw a network diagram that includes the following items:
   - The connection to the existing company LAN
   - A few workstations
   - The file server
   - The print server
   - The printer
   - The ROM programming devices

2. After mapping the network, you learn that the users of all three workstation types need to share some common files. Describe how you might set up a single file server that could handle the requirements of the three network file systems. Which facilities of a UNIX server might help to share files three ways?

3. Knowing that UNIX systems provide superior print spooling service as well as file sharing, you decide to streamline the network even more. Describe how you might eliminate a separate print server from the network. Do you think the UNIX file server could be used as a print server as well? Why or why not?

CHAPTER 11

NETWORKING WITH TCP/IP AND THE INTERNET

After reading this chapter and completing the exercises, you will be able to:

- Discuss additional details of TCP/IP addressing and subprotocols
- Understand the purposes and uses of BOOTP, DHCP, WINS, DNS, and host files
- Use TCP/IP protocols for network troubleshooting
- Understand and use TCP/IP applications, such as Internet browsers, e-mail, and e-commerce

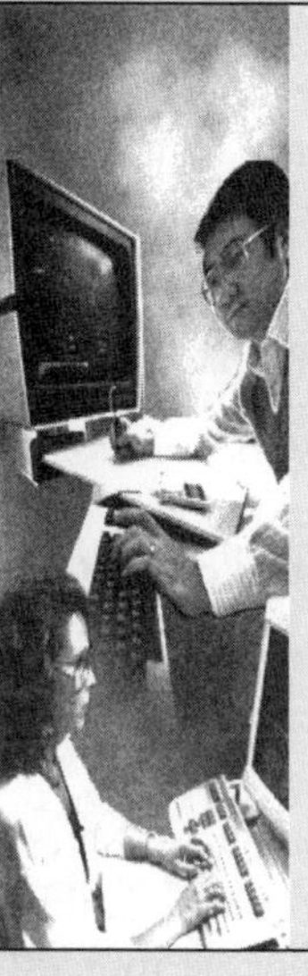

ON THE JOB

My company, which designs custom-made bicycle frames, was one of the first companies on the block to use the Internet for e-mail. It allowed us to economically exchange information with our parts manufacturers and our distributors around the nation. As our company grew, and we opened a second office, we decided it would be great if we could use an Intranet on our internal LAN to share information about orders, schedules, and budgets and to hold forums between staff. This turned out to be a great way to bring staff together.

Still, we felt we could do more with TCP/IP technology. Just last year, with the help of a local consulting company, we made our foray into e-commerce and opened up shop on the Internet. Our Internet sales were slow to begin with, but as word of our site traveled, we began receiving orders from around the world. Now our monthly revenue from Internet sales surpasses sales from all other means (including sale from our storefront).

Because of our success with e-commerce, I plan to steer most of my expenditures in the next fiscal year toward developing and supporting our Web site.

Terry Voss
ZAST, Inc.

The Internet is fast becoming not only a means of communication, but also a means of global commerce, development, and distribution. Industries such as banking, manufacturing, and health care depend on the Internet for daily transactions, record-keeping, and sales. Individuals, too, have become increasingly reliant on the Internet for purchasing and data-gathering operations.

In previous chapters, you learned that the Internet depends on the TCP/IP suite of protocols, as do a number of LAN operating systems. Because of the increasing popularity of the Internet, having TCP/IP expertise can pave the way to a lucrative, challenging, and rewarding career. Even if your organization doesn't connect to the Internet, you will probably need to master TCP/IP to manage your network competently. In Chapter 3, you learned about the basic uses of TCP/IP, as well as TCP/IP subprotocols, routing capabilities, and addressing schemes. You also learned that TCP/IP is a complex and highly customizable protocol. This chapter builds on these basic concepts, examining how TCP/IP networks are managed, maintained, secured, and analyzed. You will start by learning more about TCP/IP addressing.

ADDRESSING AND NAME RESOLUTION

As you learned in Chapter 2, nodes on a network have both logical and physical network addresses (known as MAC addresses). (To refresh your memory about addressing and the OSI Model, it may be helpful to review Chapter 2 now.) The physical address is a unique number that the manufacturer burns into the NIC's circuit board at the factory. It belongs to the Data Link layer of the OSI Model. In contrast, the logical address belongs to the Network layer of the OSI Model and depends on the networking protocol used for data transmission in the Network layer (IP versus IPX, for example). A network administrator must manage logical addresses to ensure that every node on a network can communicate with other nodes, a process known as IP addressing. This section briefly reviews (logical) IP addressing before turning to ways to manage IP addressing that can make data transmission more reliable and your job easier.

IP ADDRESSING

Just as you have a unique street address so as to ensure reliable delivery of your bills and magazines, every device on a TCP/IP-based network has a unique IP address to ensure accurate delivery of data. Without the existence of IP addresses, data could not be routed between networks and devices. Like street addresses, IP addresses must adhere to certain conventions. The following IP addressing characteristics should look familiar:

- An IP address is 32 bits in size.
- Every IP address is grouped into four 8-bit octets.
- Octets are separated by decimal points.
- Valid octet numbers range from 0 to 254 and represent a binary address. For example, an octet with the value of 68 equals 01 00 10 00 in an 8-bit binary pattern.
- Each address consists of two parts: network and host. The network portion is common to all nodes on one network, whereas the host portion is unique to each device. For example, two devices on the same Class C network might have the following IP addresses: 208.133.78.11 and 208.133.78.17. In this example, the network portion of the address for both devices is "208.133.78"; the host portion is ".11" for the first device and ".17" for the second device.

- The network portion of an address indicates whether the device belongs to a Class A, B, C, D, or E network.
- Some octet numbers are reserved for special functions. For example, an address whose bits all equal 1 is a *broadcast address*—that is, an address used to communicate simultaneously with all active nodes on a network. Other reserved addresses include those with a first octet of 127; these addresses are used exclusively for loopback testing.

Given these conventions, an example of a valid IP address for a networked workstation, printer, or other device might be 123.45.67.89.

IP addresses can be assigned manually on each device or automatically for a group of devices by a service called Dynamic Host Configuration Protocol (DHCP). (You will learn more about DHCP later in this chapter.) Typically, a network that supports DHCP uses this protocol for all of its devices, except those such as Web servers, which must have the same IP address at all times so that clients can reliably connect to them. An address that is assigned manually is called a *static address,* because it does not change unless a network technician reconfigures the device. An address that is assigned automatically by a service such as DHCP is called a *dynamic address,* because it can change over time.

Regardless of whether IP addresses are assigned manually or automatically, the network administrator must ensure that IP addresses are assigned consistently according to a plan and within the boundaries of an organization's valid IP address range. Recall from Chapter 3 that InterNIC is the central authority on Internet addresses and names.

Suppose that you are the network administrator for a company of 100 employees located in three separate offices—downtown, east, and west—and that InterNIC has assigned the range of IP addresses from 166.22.120.1 to 166.22.120.254 to your company. In total, you have 255 addresses to manage. If you have fewer than 10 servers, you might choose to assign the numbers 166.22.120.1 through 166.22.120.9 to your servers. If you later analyze your network for performance or errors, you will know that a single digit in the last octet identifies a server node. You might then use DHCP to automatically assign addresses 166.22.120.10 through 166.22.120.99 to devices at the downtown office, 166.22.120.100 through 166.22.120.199 to devices at the east office, and 166.22.120.200 through 166.22.120.254 to devices at the west office. Now whenever you discover errors with a workstation whose last octet begins with a 2, you know that you must examine the west office's network. This example illustrates merely one way that IP addresses can be managed to ease configuration and troubleshooting. Your assignment method will depend largely on the size of your network, its geographic scope, and the availability of competent technical staff.

The IP addresses given in the previous example (for example, 166.22.120.100) were expressed in dotted decimal notation. **Dotted decimal notation**, the most common way of expressing IP addresses, refers to the "shorthand" convention used to represent IP addresses and make them more easily readable by people. In dotted decimal notation, a decimal number between 1 and 254 represents each binary octet. A period, or dot, separates each decimal. An example of a dotted decimal IP address is 10.65.10.18. Each number in the address has a binary equivalent, which is readable by the devices on the network. The binary value for 10.65.10.18, for example, is 00001010 01000001 00001010 00010010. You can calculate the binary value for a dotted decimal IP number by using the binary conversion feature on the calculator that comes with Windows 95, Windows 98, and Windows NT.

Although you will most often use the dotted decimal notation in configuring and troubleshooting networks, to understand TCP/IP design issues such as subnetting (discussed later in this chapter), you must understand the binary foundation of IP addressing. Part of that binary foundation includes the network class to which each IP address belongs.

NETWORK CLASSES

In Chapter 3, you learned that most IP addresses belong to one of three network classes—A, B, or C—and that the network class octets identify the network segment to which a device is attached. For example, your organization might have 20 workstations connected to one hub. All of these workstations would belong to the same network class.

A portion of each IP address contains clues about the network class. For example, an IP address whose first octet is in the range of 1–126 belongs to a Class A network. All IP addresses for devices on a Class A segment share the same first octet, or bits 0 through 7, as shown in Figure 11-1. The second through fourth octets (bits 9 through 31) in a Class A address identify the host.

An IP whose first octet is in the range of 128–191 belongs to a Class B network. All IP addresses for devices on a Class B segment share the first two octets, or bits 0 through 15. The third and fourth octets (bits 16 through 31) on a Class B network identify the host, as shown in Figure 11-1.

An IP address whose first octet is in the range of 192–223 belongs to a Class C network. All IP addresses for devices on a Class C segment share the first three octets, or bits 0 through 23. The fourth octet (bits 23 through 31) on a Class C network identifies the host, as shown in Figure 11-1. If your organization obtains its IP addresses from an Internet service provider (ISP), rather than directly from the InterNIC, you probably use Class C addresses.

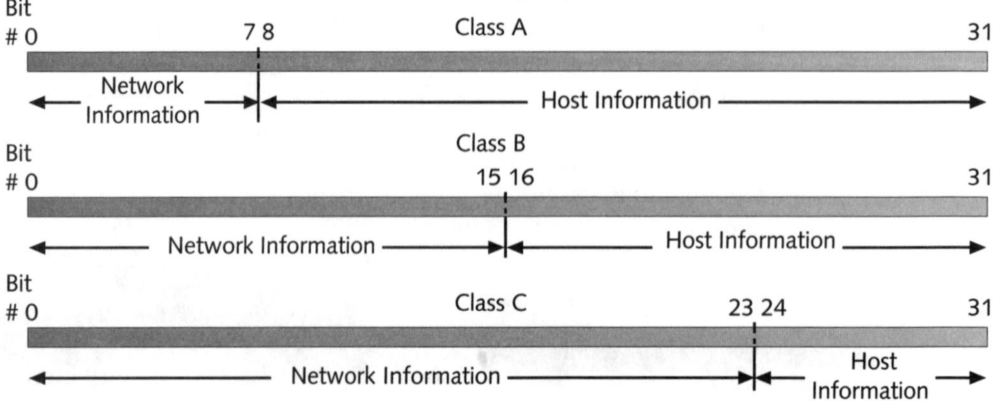

Figure 11-1 IP addresses and their classes

Chapter 3 also explained that each network class has a different number of networks and IP addresses available. For example, because Class A networks must begin with a number between 1 and 126, only 126 Class A networks exist in the world. More host names can be assigned to Class A networks, however, giving a total of more than 16 million possible addresses per network. Table 11-1 reviews what you learned about the number of networks and addresses that belong to each class of network.

Table 11-1 The three commonly used classes of TCP/IP networks

Network Class	Beginning Octet	Number of Networks	Host Addresses per Network
A	1–126	126	16,777,214
B	128–191	>16,000	65,534
C	192–223	>2,000,000	254

In addition to Class A, B, and C networks, Class D and Class E networks also exist, but consumers and companies do not use them. Class D addresses, which begin with an octet whose value is between 224 and 239, are reserved for a special type of transmission called multicasting. **Multicasting** allows one device to send data to a specific group of devices (not the entire network segment). Whereas most data transmission is on a point-to-point basis, multicasting is a point-to-multipoint broadcast method. It can be used for teleconferencing or videoconferencing over the Internet, for example. Class E addresses, which begin with an octet whose value is between 240 and 254, are reserved for experimental use by the Internet Engineering Task Force. You should never use Class D or Class E addresses when configuring your network.

You may think that the use of network classes automatically provides easy organization and a sufficient quantity of IP addresses on the Internet. Although this goal is what the Internet's founders intended, it hasn't necessarily come to pass. In the early days of the Internet, Class A addresses were distributed liberally, with some organizations receiving more reserved addresses than they had devices. Today, many addresses on the Internet go unused, but cannot be reassigned. In addition, although potentially more than 4.3 billion Internet addresses are available, the demand for such addresses grows exponentially every year. The early designers of Internet addressing did not anticipate this kind of growth. To respond to this demand, a new addressing scheme is being developed that can supply the world with enough addresses to last well into the twenty-first century. IP version 6, also known as the next-generation IP, will incorporate this new addressing scheme.

The Web contains a wealth of information about the Internet, including statistics on the number of currently used IP addresses. One example of such a repository is found at http://nw.com/zone/WWW/. Network Wizards, the organization that hosts this site, estimates the number of hosts on the Internet by querying machines worldwide and compiling records of Internet address assignments. It also offers links to graphs that depict the Web's growth over the last decade. Another good site for information on Internet usage, developments, and standards information is hosted by the Internet Sciences Institute at the University of Southern California and can be found at http://info.internet.isi.edu/1/in-notes/.

SUBNETTING

Subnetting is the process of subdividing a single class of network into multiple, smaller networks. Because it results in a more efficient use of IP addresses, subnetting was implemented throughout the Internet in the mid-1980s. Before subnetting, each segment on a network required its own Class A, B, or C network number. With this scheme, if you used a 10Base2 network with a 30-node limitation, once you exceeded 30 devices on your network, you would have needed to request another class of addresses from InterNIC. As you can imagine, this approach was not an efficient use of IP addresses or network managers' time. Not only did a network manager have to apply (and pay) for a new class of addresses, but he or she also needed to change the network's routing tables to accommodate each new network class.

With subnetting, however, a network manager can use one class of addresses for several network segments. This approach becomes possible because one of the address's octets is used to indicate how the network is subdivided, or subnetted. Rather than consisting simply of network and host information, a subnetted address includes network, subnet, and host information, as shown in Figure 11-2. For example, under normal circumstances, if InterNIC granted your organization all of the IP addresses that shared the Class B network ID of 166.144, the last two octets would be available for host information. To better organize your addresses and allow for growth, however, you would be wise to devote the third octet to subnet information. By using the third octet to subdivide the network, you create the functional equivalent of 254 Class C networks (166.144.0.0 through 166.144.254.0) from your single Class B network. As far as InterNIC is concerned, you continue to use a Class B network; within your organization, on the other hand, your LAN is fooled into recognizing several Class C networks.

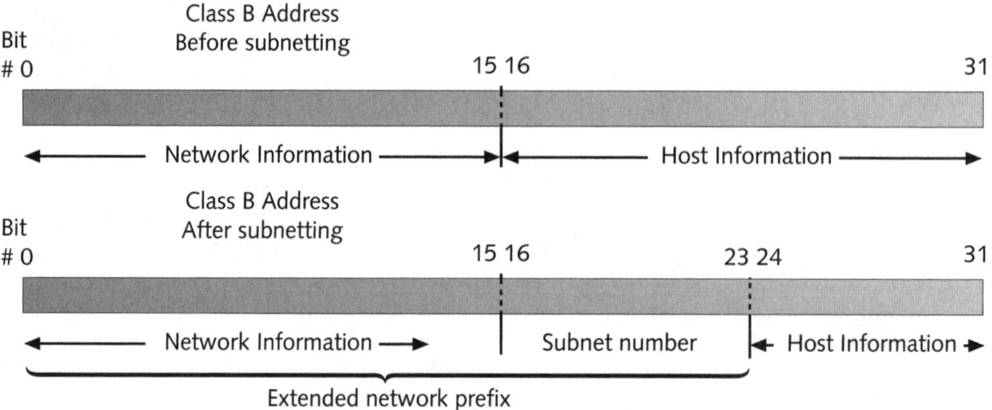

Figure 11-2 IP addresses before and after subnets

The combination of an address's network and subnet information constitutes its **extended network prefix**. By interpreting an address's extended network prefix, a device can determine the subnet to which an address belongs. But how does the device know whether an address is part of a subnet in the first place? After all, the third octet in an IP address could be either a Class B address's subnet number or a part of a Class C address's network information. For example, how can a device tell whether the address 166.144.40.33 belongs to a Class B subnetted network or a Class C network that has not been subnetted?

To make this determination, the device interprets a subnet mask. A **subnet mask** is a special 32-bit number that, when combined with a device's IP address, informs the rest of the network about the network class to which the device is attached. Subnet masks are specified in the same way that IP addresses are specified—either manually, within a device's TCP/IP configuration, or automatically, through a service such as DHCP.

Subnet masks, like IP addresses, are composed of four octets and can be expressed in either binary or dotted decimal notation. An octet of all 1s (using binary notation) in a subnet mask represents part of the extended network prefix in a subnetted IP address that uses that subnet mask. Otherwise, the subnet mask bits are all 0s and the corresponding octets in the subnetted IP address that uses that subnet mask are assumed to represent host information. Thus, for the subnetted IP address 166.144.40.33, the subnet mask would be 11111111 11111111 11111111 00000000 in binary notation or 255.255.255.0 in dotted decimal notation, because the first three octets make up the extended network prefix. Figure 11-3 shows the correlation between an IP address and its subnet mask.

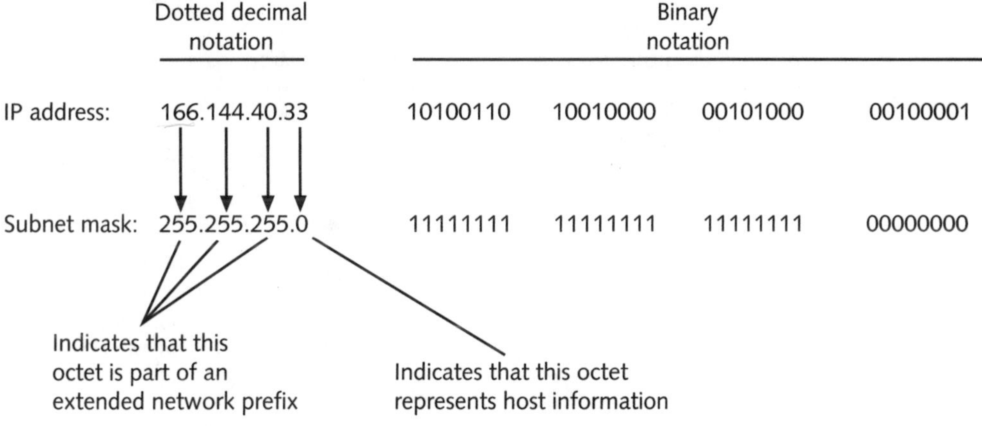

Figure 11-3 A subnetted IP address and its subnet mask

If you do not use subnetting, the extended network prefix will simply equal the network portion of the IP address. You might not want to use subnetting in only three situations: (1) if you have a very small network (as in your home office), (2) if you *never* want to connect to the Internet and so do not have to follow IP addressing standards, or (3) if your organization has more IP addresses than it can ever conceivably use. If you don't specify a subnet mask, the default subnet mask is 255.0.0.0 for a Class A network, 255.255.0.0 for a Class B network, and 255.255.255.0 for a Class C network. To qualify for Net+ certification, you should be familiar with the default subnet masks associated with each network class.

If you use subnetting on your LAN, only your LAN's devices need to interpret your devices' subnetting information. Routers external to your LAN, such as those on the

Internet, pay attention to only the network portion of your devices' IP addresses when transmitting data to them. Recall that the network portions of an organization's addresses are not affected by subnetting and that subnetting modifies only octets that would otherwise be used for host information. As a result, devices external to a subnetted LAN (such as routers on the Internet) can direct data to those LAN devices without interpreting the LAN's subnetting information.

Figure 11-4 illustrates a situation in which a LAN has been granted the Class B range of addresses that begin with 166.144. The network administrator has subnetted this Class B network into at least six smaller networks that begin with the following Class C network prefixes: 166.144.40, 166.144.42, 166.144.56, 166.144.59, 166.144.60, and 166.144.63. When a router on the internal LAN needs to direct data from a machine with the IP address of 166.144.40.12 to a machine with the IP address of 166.144.60.12, its interpretation of the workstations' subnet masks (255.255.255.0) tells the router that they are on different subnets. When a server on the Internet attempts to deliver a Web page to the machine with IP address 166.144.40.12, however, the Internet router does not use the subnet mask information but rather assumes that the machine is on a Class B network. That's all the information it needs to know to reach the organization's router. Once the data enter the organization's LAN, the router then interprets the subnet mask information as if it were transmitting data internally to deliver data to the machine with IP address 166.144.40.12. Because subnetting does not affect how a device is addressed by external networks, a network administrator does not need to inform Internet authorities about new networks created via subnets.

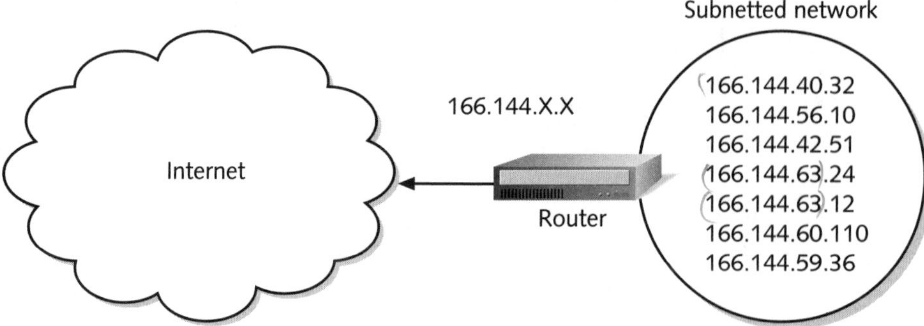

Figure 11-4 A subnetted network connected to the Internet

As you know, routers connect different network segments via their physical interfaces. In the case of subnetting, a router must interpret IP addresses from different subnets and direct data from one subnet to another. Each subnet corresponds to a different interface on the router, and each interface is associated with a default gateway number (described later in this chapter) that ends with "1". Figure 11-5 depicts a network with several subnets connected through a router.

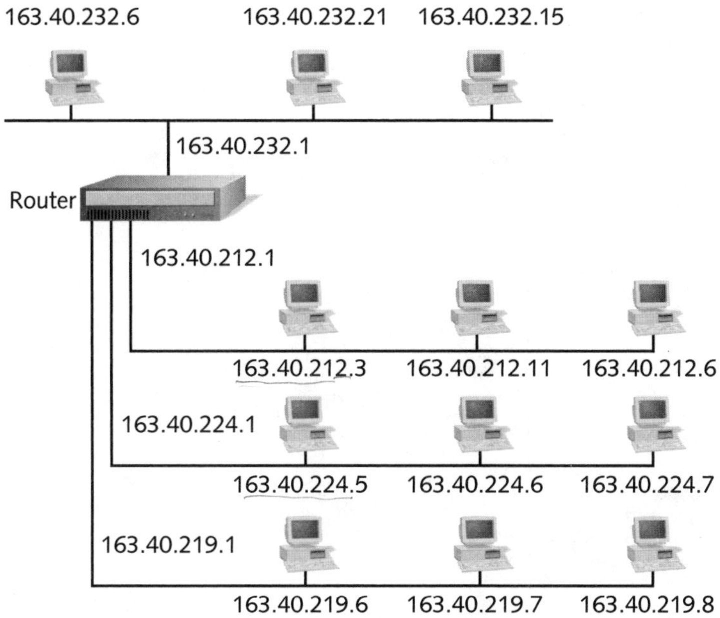

Figure 11-5 A network with several subnets

To understand how subnets and IP addresses work on a network, it's helpful to follow the (simplified) path of data between nodes on different subnets. Imagine you are sitting at the Marketing PC in Figure 11-6. Your colleague has asked you to retrieve a research report from the Internet and then print it for her. The closest printer is located in the IT department, which resides on a different subnet.

First, you connect to the Internet and request the report from the marketing research Web site. Your network's router processes your request, determining that the IP address of the Web site is on the Internet, and passes your request to the Internet routers. The Internet routers forward your request to the marketing research Web site by reading the network information in the destination IP address. The marketing research Web site's server interprets your request for data and sends the report back to the Internet routers, with your IP address in the destination portion of the header. The routers on the Internet read only the network portion of your IP address and forward the data to your router. Your router analyzes the extended network prefix in the destination address to discover your subnet, then uses the host information to send the data to your machine.

When you choose to print the report, your network router interprets your request. It reads the printer's IP address, recognizes that it is a subnetted address, and looks at its extended network prefix to find out the subnet to which it belongs. Then your router forwards the request to the router interface that services the printer's subnet (it may be on the same router or another router). The request proceeds to the printer.

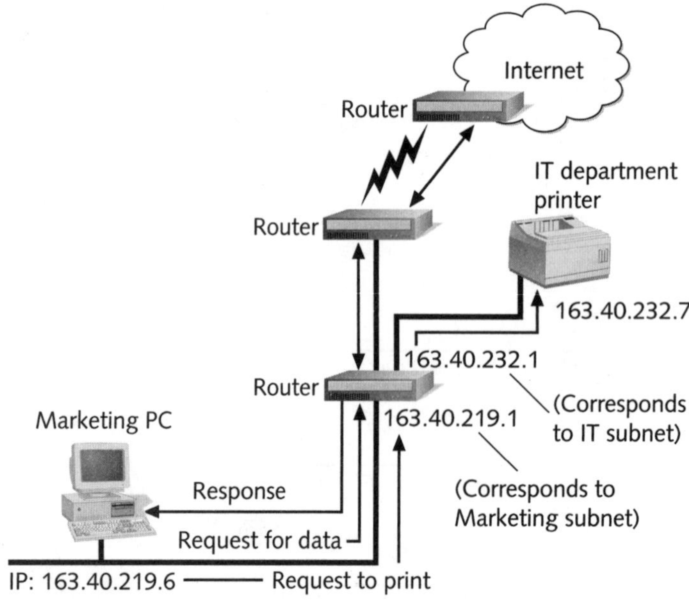

Figure 11-6 Data traveling over subnets

GATEWAYS

In Chapter 6, you learned that **gateways** are a combination of software and hardware that enable two different network segments to exchange data. In the context of IP addressing, a gateway facilitates communication between different subnets. The description of data traveling from one subnet to another in the previous section used routers as gateways. Because one device on the network cannot send data directly to a device on another subnet, a gateway must intercede and hand off the information. Every device has a **default gateway**—that is, the gateway that first interprets its outbound requests and last interprets its inbound requests to and from other subnets.

A gateway is analogous to your local post office. Your post office gathers your outbound mail and decides where to forward it. It also handles your inbound mail just before it heads for your mailbox. Just as a large city has several local post offices, a large organization will have several gateways to route traffic for different groups of devices. Each node on the network can have only one default gateway; that gateway is assigned either manually or automatically (in the latter case, through a service such as DHCP). Of course, if your network includes only one segment and you do not connect to the Internet, your devices would not need a default gateway because no gateways would be used.

Each default gateway (in many cases, an interface on a router) is assigned its own IP address. In Figure 11-7, workstation 10.3.105.23 (workstation A) uses the 10.3.105.1 gateway to process its requests, and workstation 10.3.102.75 (workstation B) uses the 10.3.102.1 gateway for the same purpose.

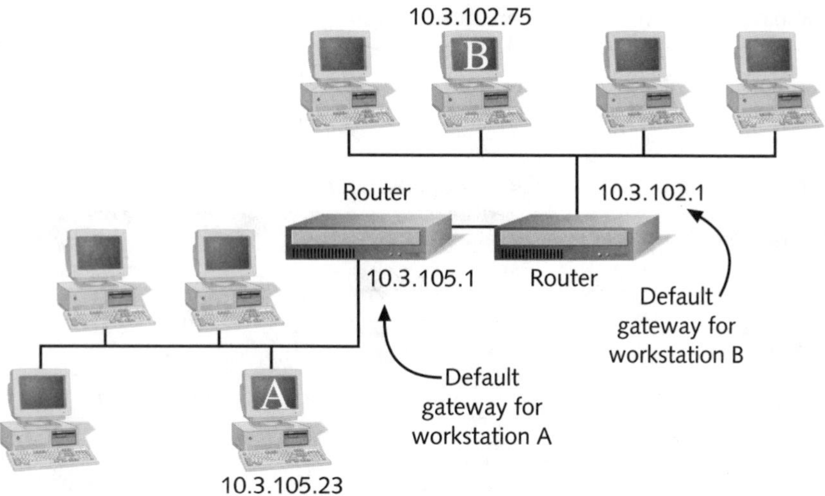

Figure 11-7 The use of default gateways

Default gateways may connect multiple internal networks, or they may connect an internal network with external networks such as WANs or the Internet. As you learned in Chapter 6, routers in an internetwork must maintain a routing table to determine where to forward information. Because gateways are routers (or more specifically, interfaces on routers), they must maintain routing tables as well.

The Internet contains a vast number of routers and gateways. Each gateway would find it too taxing to contain addressing information for every other gateway on the Internet, so each handles only a relatively small amount of addressing information, which it uses to forward data to another gateway that knows more about the data's destination. Like routers on an internal network, Internet gateways maintain default routes to known addresses to expedite data transfer. The gateways that make up the Internet backbone, called **core gateways**, are managed by the Internet Network Operations Center (INOC).

SOCKETS AND PORTS

In Chapter 3, you learned that a **socket** is a logical address assigned to a specific process running on a host computer. It forms a virtual connection between the host and client. The socket's address combines the host computer's IP address with the port number associated with a process. For example, the Telnet service on a Web server with an IP address of 10.43.3.87 might have a socket address of 10.43.3.87:23, where 23 is the standard port number for the Telnet service. In other words, after installation, the Web server software assumes that any requests coming into port number 23 are Telnet requests, unless you configure the software differently. Note that a port number is expressed as a number following a colon after an IP address. The 23 is not considered an additional octet in the socket number, but simply a pointer to that port.

Port numbers can have any value. Some software programs that use TCP/IP (for example, Novell's GroupWise and Hewlett-Packard's Performance Data Alarm Manager) choose their own port numbers by default. The default port numbers for commonly used TCP/IP services generally have values lower than 255, as shown in Table 11-2. Although you do not need to memorize every port number for the Net+ Certification exam, you may be asked about the port numbers associated with common services, such as Telnet, FTP, SNMP, and HTTP. Knowing them will also help you in configuring and troubleshooting TCP/IP network services.

Table 11-2 Commonly used TCP/IP port numbers

Port Number	Process Name	Protocol Used	Description
1	TCPMUX	TCP	TCP port multiplexer service
5	RJE	TCP	Remote job entry
7	ECHO	TCP and UDP	Echo
11	USERS	TCP and UDP	Active users
13	DAYTIME	TCP and UDP	Daytime
17	QUOTE	TCP and UDP	Quote of the day
20	FTP-DATA	TCP	File transfer—data
21	FTP	TCP	File transfer—control
23	TELNET	TCP	Telnet
25	SMTP	TCP	Simple Mail Transfer Protocol
35	PRINTER	TCP and UDP	Any private printer service
37	TIME	TCP and UDP	Time
41	GRAPHICS	TCP and UDP	Graphics
42	NAMESERV	UDP	Host name server
43	NICNAME	TCP	Who is
49	LOGIN	TCP	Login Host Protocol
53	DNS	TCP and UDP	Domain Name Server
67	BOOTPS	UDP	Bootstrap Protocol server
68	BOOTPC	UDP	Bootstrap Protocol client
69	TFTP	UDP	Trivial File Transfer Protocol
79	FINGER	TCP	Finger
80	HTTP	TCP and UDP	World Wide Web HTTP
101	HOSTNAME	TCP and UDP	NIC host name server
105	CSNET-NS	TCP and UDP	Mailbox name server
110	POP3	TCP	Post Office Protocol 3
137	NETBIOS-NS	TCP and UDP	NetBIOS Name Service
138	NETBIOS-DG	TCP and UDP	NetBIOS Datagram Service
139	NETBIOS-SS	TCP and UDP	NetBIOS Session Service

Table 11-2 Commonly used TCP/IP port numbers (continued)

Port Number	Process Name	Protocol Used	Description
161	SNMP	UDP	Simple Network Management Protocol
162	SNMPTRAP	UDP	SNMPTRAP
179	BGP	TCP	Border Gateway Protocol

The use of port numbers simplifies TCP/IP communications. When a client requests communications with a server and specifies port 23, for example, the server knows immediately that the client wants a Telnet session. No extra data exchange is necessary to define the session type, and the server can initiate the Telnet service without delay. The server will connect to the client's Telnet port—by default, port 23—and establish a virtual circuit. Figure 11-8 depicts this process.

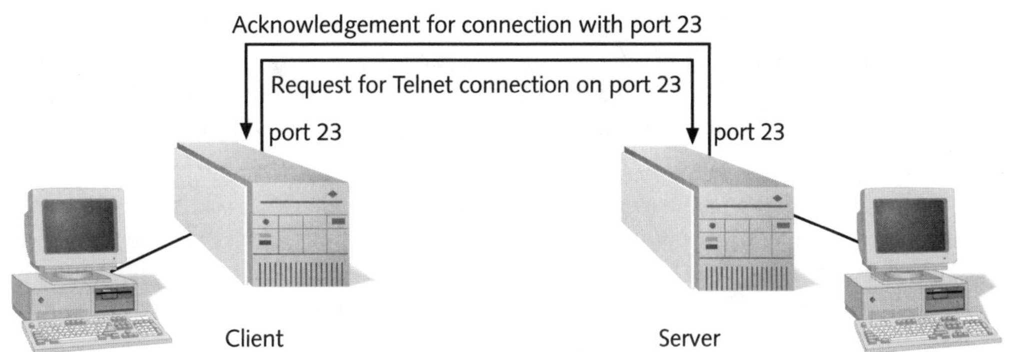

Figure 11-8 A virtual circuit for the Telnet service

As mentioned earlier, you can configure port numbers through software. Most servers maintain an editable, text-based file of port numbers and their associated services. If necessary, you could change the default port number for the Telnet service on your server from 23 to 2330. Changing a default port number is rarely a good idea, however, because it violates the standard. Nevertheless, some network administrators who are preoccupied with security may change their servers' port numbers in an attempt to confuse potential hackers.

Host Names and Domain Name System (DNS)

Most people can remember words better than numbers. Imagine if you had to identify your friends' and families' Social Security numbers whenever you wanted to write a note or talk to them. Communication would be frustrating at the very least, and perhaps even impossible—especially if you're the kind of person who has trouble remembering even your own Social Security number. Similarly, people prefer to associate names with networked devices rather than remember IP addresses. For this reason, the Internet authorities established a naming system for all nodes on the Internet.

As you learned in Chapter 3, every device on the Internet is technically known as a host. Every host can take a **host name**, a name that describes the device. For example, you might name your workstation "PeggySue." If the computer is reserved for a specific purpose, you may want to name it accordingly. For example, a company that offers free software downloads through the FTP service might call its host machine "ftpserver." Generally, when networking professionals refer to a machine's host name, they mean its local host name plus its domain name. The following sections discuss host names and domain names.

Domain Names

Every host is a member of a **domain**, or a group of computers that belong to the same organization and have part of their IP addresses in common. A domain is identified by its **domain name**. Usually, a domain name is associated with a company or other type of organization, such as a university or military unit. For example, IBM's domain name is ibm.com, and the U.S. Library of Congress's domain name is loc.gov. If you worked at the Library of Congress and had named your workstation "PeggySue," your full host name (also known as your **fully qualified host name**) might be "PeggySue.loc.gov."

Although an individual user can name his or her workstation, organizations cannot arbitrarily choose their own domain names. Domain names must be registered with the Internet naming authority, InterNIC. If you use an ISP, your ISP can work with InterNIC to obtain a domain name for you, providing that someone else hasn't already reserved your desired name.

InterNIC has established conventions for domain naming in which certain suffixes apply to every type of organization that uses the Internet. These suffixes are also known as **top-level domains (TLDs)**. Table 11-3 lists common TLDs. In addition, each country has its own domain suffix. For example, Canadian domains end with .ca and Japanese domains end in .jp.

Although domain names may use the international domain suffix, such as .ca for Canada and .jp for Japan, organizations do not necessarily have to use these suffixes. For example, although IBM's headquarters are located in the United States, the company's domain name is www.ibm.com. On the other hand, some U.S. organizations do use the .us suffix. For example, the domain name for the Garden City, New York, public school district is www.gardencity.k12.ny.us.

Table 11-3 Domain Naming Conventions

Domain Suffix	Type of Organization
ARPA	Reverse lookup domain (special Internet function)
COM	Commercial
EDU	Educational
GOV	Government
ORG	Noncommercial organization (such as a nonprofit agency)
NET	Network (such as an ISP)
INT	International treaty organization
MIL	U.S. military organization

Once an organization reserves a domain name, the rest of the world's computers know to associate that domain name with that particular organization, and no other organization can legally use it (as long as the reserving organization pays the required annual registration fee to InterNIC). For example, you might apply for the domain name called "YourName.com"; not only would the rest of the Internet associate that name with your machine, but also no other parties in the world could use "YourName.com" for their machines.

Host names come with some naming restrictions. You can use any alphanumeric combination with a maximum of 63 characters, and you can include hyphens, underscores, or periods in the name, but no other special characters. The interesting part of host and domain naming relates to how all Internet-connected machines in the world know which names belong to which machines. Before tackling the entire world, however, you can start by thinking about how one company might deal with its local host names.

Host Files

The first incarnation of the Internet (called ARPAnet) was used by fewer than 1000 hosts. The entire Internet relied on one text file called HOSTS.TXT to associate names with IP addresses. This file was generically known as a **host file**. The explosive growth of the Internet soon made this simple solution impossible to maintain—the host file would require constant changes, polling one file would strain the Internet's bandwidth capacity, and the entire Internet would fail if the file were accidentally deleted.

Within a company or university, you may still encounter this older system of straightforward ASCII text files that associate internal host names with their IP addresses. Figure 11-9 provides an example of such a file. Notice that each host is matched by one line identifying the host's name and IP address. In addition, a third field, called an **alias**, provides a nickname for the host. An alias allows a user within an organization to address a host by a shorter name than the full host name. Typically, the first line of a host file begins with a pound sign and contains comments about the file's columns. On a UNIX-based computer, this file is called /etc/hosts. On a Windows NT or Windows 95 computer, it is called lmhosts.

```
# IP Address      host name               aliases
132.55.78.109     bingo.games.com         bingo
132.55.78.110     parcheesi.games.com     parcheesi
132.55.78.111     checkers.games.com      checkers
132.55.78.112     darts.games.com         darts
```

Figure 11-9 An example host file

Domain Name System (DNS)

The simple host file can satisfy the needs of one organization, and it can even allow one organization's network to contact hosts on another network. A single host file is no longer sufficient for the Internet, however. Instead, a more automated solution has become mandatory. In the mid-1980s, the Network Information Center (NIC) at Stanford Research Institute devised a hierarchical way of tracking domain names and their addresses, called the **Domain Name System (DNS)**. The DNS database does not rely on one file or even one server, but rather is distributed over several key computers across the Internet to prevent catastrophic failure if one or a few computers go down. DNS is a TCP/IP service that belongs to the Application layer of the OSI Model.

In a simple world, the responsibility for resolving addresses to names might be broken down into national, regional, local, and organizational levels, as depicted in Figure 11-10. In this example, if you worked in the Atlanta office and wanted to exchange data with a machine at another company located in Fairbanks, your organizational DNS server would take your request and pass it off to the local server, which would then pass it off to the regional server, which would in turn pass it off to the national DNS server. The reverse process would occur as the national DNS server passed the request down to the regional, local, and finally organizational servers that know about Fairbanks. This address resolution process assumes that your local DNS server and the Fairbanks local DNS server do not know where to find each other.

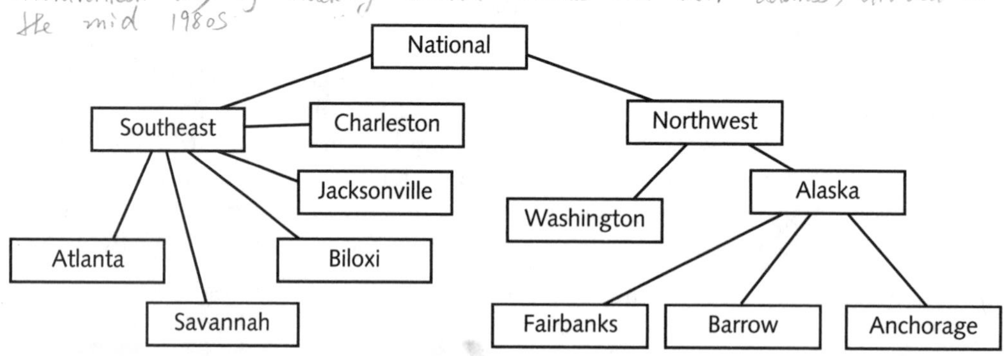

Figure 11-10 DNS server hierarchy by geography

The actual DNS is somewhat more sophisticated than the previous example implies. To route traffic more efficiently, it is divided into three components: resolvers, name servers, and name space. **Resolvers** are any hosts on the Internet that need to look up domain name information. In the example given in the previous paragraph, your machine in Atlanta is a resolver. The resolver client is built into TCP/IP applications such as Telnet, HTTP, and FTP. If you type the command **telnet support.novell.com**, your Telnet client software will kick off the resolver service to find the IP address for support.novell.com. If you have telnetted to the site before, the information may exist in temporary memory and may be retrieved very quickly. Otherwise, the resolver service queries your machine's name server to find the IP address for support.novell.com.

Name servers are servers that contain databases of names and their associated IP addresses. A name server supplies a resolver with the information it requires. If the name server cannot resolve the IP address, the query passes to a higher-level name server. In Figure 11-10, the local, regional, and national servers are all name servers. Each name server manages a group of devices, collectively known as a **zone**; these devices, in turn, distribute naming information. In the example in Figure 11-10, the Southeast name server's zone would include the Atlanta, Savannah, Jacksonville, Biloxi, and Charleston name servers. If the Atlanta server doesn't know the address of a machine in the Savannah area, it can rely on the Southeast name server to supply that information. In a small company, the primary DNS server's zone would include all the computers at the company.

Configuring DNS

Any host that must communicate with other hosts on the Internet needs to know how to find its name server. Although some organizations use only one name server, large organizations often maintain two name servers—a primary and a secondary name server—to help ensure Internet connectivity. If the primary name server experiences a failure, all devices on the network will attempt to use the secondary name server. Each device on the network relies on the name server and therefore must know how to find it. When configuring the TCP/IP properties of a workstation, you need to specify a name server IP address so that the workstation will know which machine to query when it needs to look up a name.

To view or change the name server information on a Windows 95 machine:

1. Right-click the **Network Neighborhood** icon, then click **Properties** in the shortcut menu. The Network Properties dialog box opens.
2. In the list of installed network components, double-click **TCP/IP**. The TCP/IP Properties dialog box opens.
3. Click the **DNS Configuration** tab. The DNS Configuration tab appears, as shown in Figure 11-11.

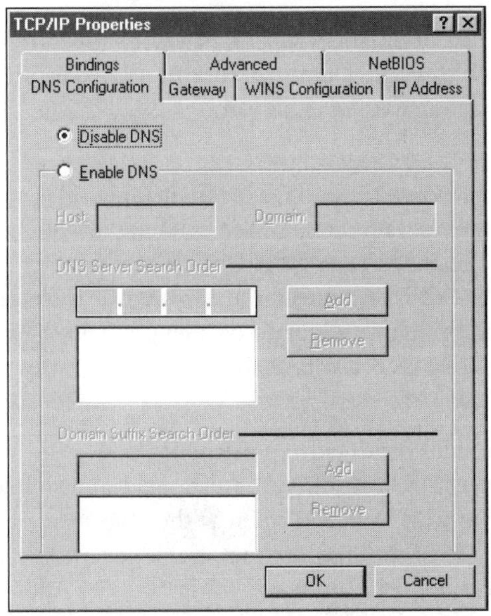

Figure 11-11 DNS Configuration properties tab

4. Make sure that the **Enable DNS** option is selected (unless you are using DHCP or, in some cases, dial-up networking).

5. Type your computer's host name in the Host text box.
6. Type your organization's domain name in the Domain text box.
7. Type your organization's DNS server IP address in the space provided under the heading "DNS Server Search Order."
8. Click **Add** to save the DNS server's IP address.
9. Add as many as two more DNS server IP addresses in the same manner.
10. Click **OK** to save your changes.
11. Click **OK** to close the Network Properties dialog box.
12. Click **Yes** to confirm that you want to restart your computer.

DNS Name Space

As you learned previously, many name servers across the globe cooperate to keep track of IP addresses and their associated domain names. **Name space** refers to the actual database of Internet IP addresses and their associated names. Every name server holds a piece of the DNS name space. At the highest level in the hierarchy sit the root servers. A **root server** is a name server that is maintained by InterNIC and that acts as the ultimate authority on how to contact the top-level domains, such as those ending with .com, .edu, .net, .us, and so on. InterNIC maintains 13 root servers around the world. In Figure 11-10, the national-level name server would actually be a root server for the United States.

Name space is not a database that you can open and view, like a store's inventory database. Rather, this abstract concept describes how the name servers of the world share DNS information. Pieces of it are tangible, however, and are stored on a name server in a **resource record**.

Resource records come in many different types, depending on their function. Each resource record contains a name field to identify the domain name of the machine to which the record refers, a type field to identify the type of resource record involved, a class field to identify the class to which the record belongs (usually "IN" or "Internet"), a time to live field to identify how long the record should be saved in temporary memory, a data length field to identify how much data the record contains, and the actual record data. Approximately 20 types of resource records are currently used.

Each resource record type adheres to specific data field requirements, thus ensuring that any name server across the world can interpret it. For example, the data field of a simple network address record would include only the network address, whereas the data field of a mailbox information record would include the name of the mailbox responsible for error messages and the name of the mailbox responsible for mailing lists. In the following fictitious Address resource record, knight.chess.games.com is the host domain name, IN stands for the Internet record class, A identifies the record type as "address," and 203.99.120.76 is the host's IP address:

```
knight.chess.games.com      IN     A      203.99.120.76
```

This book does not provide in-depth coverage of DNS domains, hierarchy, zones, and databases. If you are interested in Internet server administration, you should investigate host files and DNS in more detail. For Net+ certification, you should know the purpose of DNS and host files, understand the hierarchical nature of DNS, and be able to specify name servers on a client workstation.

BOOTP

To communicate with other devices through TCP/IP, every workstation, printer, or other node on a network requires a unique IP address. On the earliest TCP/IP networks, each device was manually assigned its own number through a local configuration file; that number never changed until someone edited the configuration file. As networks grew larger, however, local configuration files became more difficult to implement. Imagine the arduous task faced by a network administrator who must visit each of 8000 workstations, printers, and hosts on a company's LAN to assign IP addresses and ensure that no single IP address is used twice. Now imagine how much extra work would be required to restructure the company's IP address management system (for example, to implement subnetting) or to move a department's machine to a different network segment.

To facilitate IP address management, a service called the Bootstrap Protocol was developed in the mid-1980s. The **Bootstrap Protocol (BOOTP)** uses a central list of IP addresses and their associated devices' MAC addresses to dynamically assign IP addresses to clients. When a client that relies on BOOTP first connects to the network, it sends a broadcast message to the network asking to be assigned an IP address. This broadcast message includes the MAC address of the client's NIC. The BOOTP server recognizes a BOOTP client's request, looks up the client's MAC address in its BOOTP table, and responds to the client with the following information: the client's IP address, the IP address of the server, the host name of the server, and the IP address of a default router. Figure 11-12 outlines this process. 11

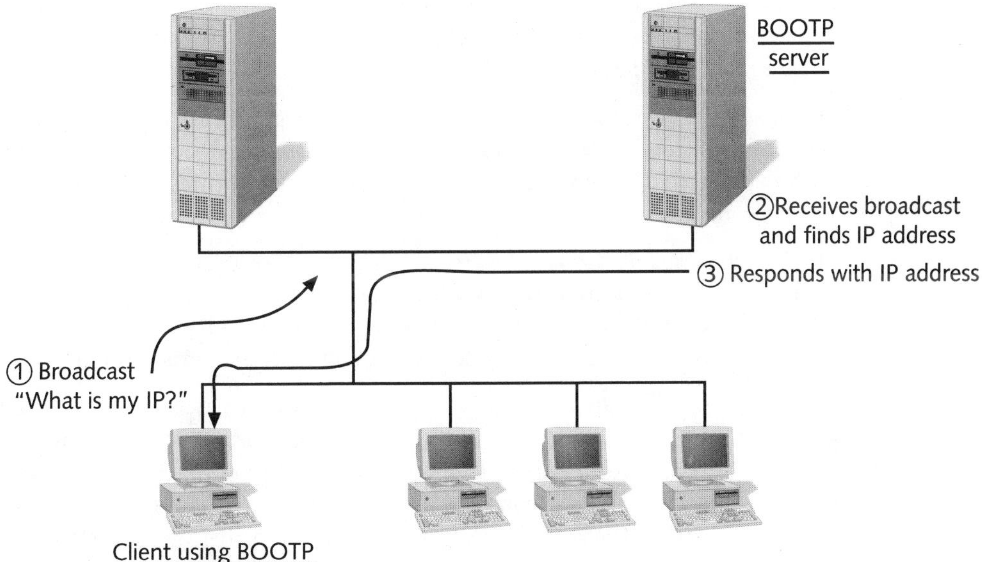

Figure 11-12 The BOOTP process

Thanks to BOOTP, a client does not have to remember its own IP address, and therefore network administrators do not have to go to each workstation on a network in order to manually assign its IP address. This situation is ideal for **diskless workstations**—workstations that do not contain hard disks, but rely on a small amount of read-only memory to get them connected to a network and to pick up their system files.

For other kinds of clients, BOOTP has been surpassed by the more sophisticated IP address management tool, Dynamic Host Configuration Protocol (DHCP). As you will learn in the next section, DHCP requires little intervention, whereas BOOTP requires network administrators to enter every IP and MAC address manually into the BOOTP table. As you can imagine, the BOOTP table can be difficult to maintain on large networks. You may still encounter BOOTP in existing networks, but most likely it will support only diskless workstations (which are sometimes called network computers).

Dynamic Host Configuration Protocol (DHCP)

By now, you have seen several references to DHCP. **Dynamic Host Configuration Protocol (DHCP)** is an automated means of assigning a unique IP address to every device on a network. Reasons for implementing DHCP include the following:

- *To reduce the time and planning spent on IP address management.* Central management of IP addresses eliminates the need for network administrators to edit the TCP/IP configuration on every network workstation, printer, or other device.
- *To reduce the potential for errors in assigning IP addresses.* With DHCP, no possibility exists that a workstation will be assigned an invalid address, and *almost* no possibility exists that two workstations will attempt to use the same IP address and thereby cause network errors (occasionally the DHCP server software may make a mistake). On the other hand, when manually assigning IP addresses on each workstation or even manually editing a BOOTP table, it is easy to type in the wrong address or use the same address twice.
- *To enable users to move their workstations and printers without having to change their TCP/IP configuration.* As long as a workstation is configured to obtain its IP address from a central server, the workstation can be attached anywhere on the network and receive a valid address.
- *To make IP addressing transparent for mobile users.* For example, if a salesperson brought her Windows 95 laptop to your conference room to make an online presentation about Internet commerce, she could attach to your network and receive an IP address without having to change her laptop's configuration.

DHCP was developed by the Internet Engineering Task Force as a replacement for BOOTP. Unlike BOOTP, DHCP does not require the network administrator to maintain a table of IP and MAC addresses on the server. It does, however, require the network administrator in charge of IP address management to install and configure the DHCP service on a server (such as Windows NT, NetWare 4.11 or higher, or UNIX) that can run DHCP.

DHCP Leasing Process

With DHCP, a device borrows, or **leases**, an IP address while it is attached to the network. In other words, it uses the IP address on a temporary basis. When, for example, a client logs off the network, it relinquishes the IP address and the DHCP server can assign it to another device.

Configuring DHCP involves specifying a range of addresses that can be leased to any network device on a particular segment. As a network administrator, you configure the duration of the lease (in the configuration of the DHCP server) to be as short or long as necessary, from a matter of minutes to forever. Once the DHCP server is running, clients can attach to it and receive their unique IP addresses. More specifically, the client and server take the following steps to negotiate the client's first lease (this example applies to a workstation, but devices such as networked printers may also take advantage of DHCP):

1. When the client workstation starts (assuming it has the TCP/IP protocol installed and bound to the NIC), it sends out a DHCP discover packet in broadcast fashion via the UDP protocol to the DHCP/BOOTP server port (by default, port number 67).
2. Every DHCP server that is connected to the same subnet as the client receives the broadcast request. Each DHCP server responds with an available IP address, while simultaneously withholding that address from other clients. The response message includes the available IP address, subnet mask, IP address of the DHCP server, and the lease duration. This message goes out through the DHCP/BOOTP port 68 in broadcast fashion. Because the client doesn't have an IP address, the DHCP server cannot send the information directly to the client.

In some instances, BOOTP and DHCP may appear lumped together under the same category or service. For example, if you are configuring a Hewlett-Packard LaserJet that uses a JetDirect print server card, you can select "BOOTP/DHCP" from the printer's TCP/IP Configuration menu. BOOTP and DHCP are not always distinguished as separate services because they appear the same to the client and use the same server ports to handle their communications to and from the server. The main difference between the two services lies in how the server software distributes IP addresses.

3. The client accepts the first IP address that it receives, responding with a broadcast message that essentially confirms to the DHCP that it wants to accept the address. Because this message is broadcast, all other DHCP servers that might have responded to the client's original query see this confirmation and hence return the IP addresses they had reserved for the client to their pool of available addresses.
4. When the selected DHCP server receives the confirmation, it replies—in a broadcast fashion—with an acknowledgment message. It also provides more information, such as DNS or gateway addresses that the client might have requested.

The preceding steps involve the exchange of only four packets and therefore do not usually increase the time it takes for a client to log on to the network. Figure 11-13 depicts the DHCP leasing process. The client and server do not have to repeat this exchange until the lease is terminated. The IP address will remain in the client's TCP/IP settings even after the device restarts.

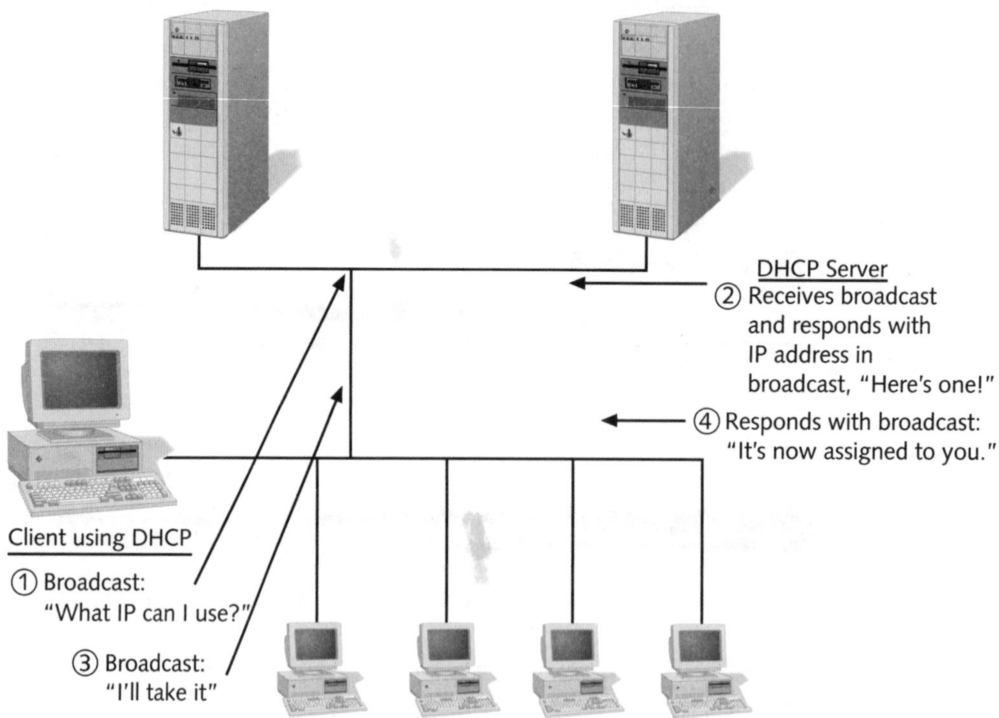

Figure 11-13 The DHCP leasing process

Terminating a DHCP Lease

A DHCP lease may expire based on the period established for it in the server configuration or it may be manually terminated at any time from either the client's TCP/IP configuration or the server's DHCP configuration. In some instances, a user must terminate a lease. Consider what might happen to the previously mentioned salesperson *after* she presents her online demonstration in your conference room. She returns to her office, plugs her laptop network cable into the outlet under her desk, and turns on her machine. Her TCP/IP settings will still contain the IP address and other information (such as DNS server and gateway address) she received from your DHCP server in the conference room. In addition, because the DHCP lease period lasts 30 days, her TCP/IP service will not attempt to pick up a new IP address from her own company's DHCP server. What will happen when the salesperson tries to pick up her e-mail? She will receive an error message, because her IP address will no longer be valid. Unfortunately, the error message will say only that it cannot establish a TCP/IP connection (not that a new IP address is needed). In this situation, the user needs to terminate her lease. In Windows terms, this event is called a **release** of the TCP/IP settings.

To release TCP/IP settings in Windows 95:

1. Click **Start**, then click **Run**. The Run dialog box opens.
2. Type **winipcfg**, then click **OK**. The IP Configuration dialog box opens, displaying the workstation's TCP/IP settings, similar to those shown in Figure 11-14.

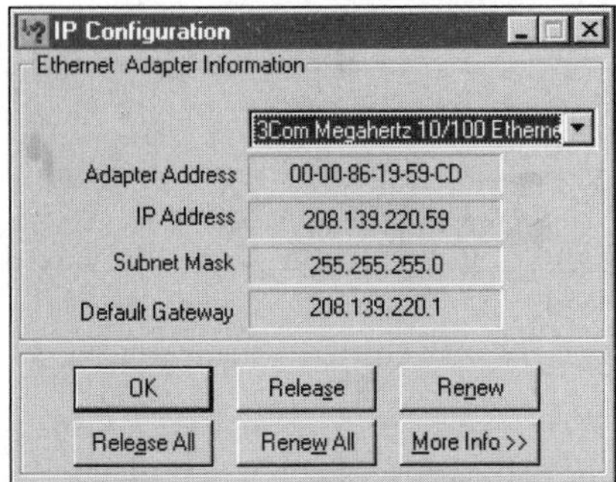

Figure 11-14 IP Configuration window

3. To release the DHCP lease, click **Release All**.
4. Click **OK** to accept the confirmation message that appears. The values for your IP Address, Subnet Mask, and Default Gateway in the IP Configuration dialog box will revert to all zeros.

Releasing old DHCP information is the first step in the process of obtaining a new IP address. In the preceding example, the salesperson would also have to instruct her TCP/IP service to request a new IP address. This task is easily accomplished from most workstations or laptops.

To obtain a new IP address on a Windows 95 workstation:

1. Click **Start**, then click **Run**. The Run dialog box opens.
2. Type **winipcfg**, then click **OK** to display the workstation's TCP/IP settings. The IP Configuration dialog box opens, displaying the workstation's TCP/IP settings.
3. Click **Renew All** to obtain new TCP/IP settings from the DHCP server.
4. Click **OK** to accept the confirmation message that appears. The values for your IP Address, Subnet Mask, and Default Gateway in the IP Configuration dialog box will be appropriate for the subnet to which you are now attached.
5. Click **OK** to close the IP Configuration dialog box.

With TCP/IP becoming the protocol of choice on most networks, you will most certainly have to work with DHCP—either from the client, the server side, or both—at some point in your networking career. As mentioned earlier, DHCP services run on several types of servers. The installation and configurations for each type of server vary; for specifics, you must refer to the DHCP server software's manual. To qualify for Net+ certification, you need not know the intricacies of installing and configuring DHCP server software. You do, however, need to know what DHCP does and how it accomplishes it. You also need to understand the advantages of using DHCP rather than other means of assigning IP addresses.

Windows Internet Naming Service (WINS)

The **Windows Internet Naming Service (WINS)** provides a means of resolving NetBIOS names with IP addresses. Recall from Chapter 3 that NetBIOS is used primarily with Windows-based systems, and that a NetBIOS name is a unique alphanumeric name assigned to each Windows-based workstation on a network. WINS is used exclusively with systems that use NetBIOS—therefore, it usually appears on Windows-based systems.

A computer's NetBIOS name and its TCP/IP host name are different entities. They may or may not be equivalent. Earlier, you learned that DNS provides resolutions of TCP/IP host names and IP addresses. WINS, on the other hand, provides resolution of NetBIOS names and IP addresses. Essentially, WINS has the same relationship to NetBIOS as DNS has to TCP/IP. That is, both WINS and DNS associate names with IP addresses.

Unlike DNS, however, WINS is an automated service that runs on a server. In this sense, it resembles DHCP. WINS may be implemented on servers running Windows NT Server version 3.5 or higher. It maintains a database on the server that accepts requests from Windows or DOS clients to register with a particular NetBIOS name. Note that WINS does not assign names or IP addresses, but merely keeps track of which NetBIOS names are linked to which IP addresses.

WINS offers several advantages:

- *Guarantees that a unique NetBIOS name is used for each computer on a network.* WINS manages which NetBIOS name is associated with each IP address, and it will not allow two machines with the same name to register.
- *Support for DHCP.* WINS can be integrated with the dynamic IP addressing method used by DHCP.
- *Better network performance.* As long as WINS manages the mappings between IP addresses and NetBIOS names, clients do not have to broadcast their NetBIOS names to the rest of the network. The elimination of this broadcast traffic improves network performance.

Every client workstation that needs to register with the WINS server must know how to find the server. Thus the WINS server cannot use a dynamic IP address (such as one assigned by a DHCP server). Instead, a specific IP address must be assigned to it manually.

To configure a Windows 95 workstation to use the WINS service:

1. Right-click the **Network Neighborhood** icon, then click **Properties** in the shortcut menu. The Network Properties dialog box opens.
2. Click the **Configuration** tab.
3. Highlight the **TCP/IP** protocol in the list of installed networking components, then click **Properties**. The TCP/IP Properties dialog box opens.

4. Click the **WINS Configuration** tab.
5. To establish the identity of your WINS server, click **Enable WINS Resolution**.
6. Type the IP address of your WINS server in the spaces provided next to the **Primary WINS Server** text box.
7. If you have a secondary WINS server, type its IP address in the spaces provided next to the **Secondary WINS Server** text box.
8. Click **OK** to save your changes.
9. Click **OK** to exit the Network Properties dialog box.
10. You will be asked whether you want to restart your computer to save your changes. Click **Yes** to confirm that you want to restart it.

As with DNS, a complete discussion of WINS could fill at least an entire chapter. If you plan to specialize in Windows NT networking and clients running NetBIOS, you should investigate this topic further. For Net+ certification, you should be familiar with the purpose and advantages of WINS.

TCP/IP Subprotocols

In Chapter 3, you learned that TCP/IP is not a single protocol, but rather a suite of protocols, commonly called subprotocols, each of which performs a distinct function. That chapter introduced the core subprotocols, including IP, TCP, UDP, ICMP, and ARP, as well as Application layer protocols such as Telnet, FTP, SMTP, and SNMP. This section briefly reviews these subprotocols and introduces several new subprotocols. In addition, it describes in more depth the subprotocols with finite purposes such as SMTP and POP, as opposed to the more general-purpose subprotocols such as TCP and UDP.

In your networking career, you will need to be familiar with all of the subprotocols covered in this book, even if you do not choose to master the fine points of TCP/IP networking. Suppose, for instance, that you are troubleshooting a problem with the e-mail package at your organization. Before you can talk to the vendor's technical support personnel, you must know whether your e-mail software uses POP or IMAP. In troubleshooting and managing a network, you will encounter many situations such as this one that require you to know which TCP/IP subprotocols your network uses and how those subprotocols are implemented.

A Review of TCP/IP Subprotocols

The following list of subprotocols and their functions should look familiar to you. If you do not remember how they fit into the OSI Model or what some of the terms (such as "connectionless") mean, you should review the summary at the end of Chapter 3.

- *Internet Protocol (IP)*—A core protocol in the TCP/IP suite that belongs to the Internet layer of the TCP/IP model and provides information about how and where data should be delivered. IP is the subprotocol that enables TCP/IP to internetwork.

- *Transport Control Protocol (TCP)*—A core protocol of the TCP/IP suite. TCP belongs to the Transport layer and provides reliable data delivery services because it is connection-oriented.
- *User Datagram Protocol (UDP)*—A core protocol in the TCP/IP suite that sits in the Transport layer, between the Internet layer and the Application layer of the TCP/IP model. Unlike TCP, UDP is a connectionless transport service.
- *Internet Control Message Protocol (ICMP)*—A core protocol in the TCP/IP suite that notifies the sender that something has gone wrong in the transmission process and that packets were not delivered.
- *Address Resolution Protocol (ARP)*—A core protocol in the TCP/IP suite that belongs in the Internet layer and obtains the MAC (physical) address of a host, or node, and then creates a local database that maps the MAC address to the host's IP (logical) address.
- *Telnet*—An Application layer terminal emulation protocol used to log on to remote hosts using TCP/IP.
- *File Transfer Protocol (FTP)*—An Application layer protocol used to send and receive files via TCP/IP.
- *Simple Network Management Protocol (SNMP)*—A communication protocol used to manage devices on a TCP/IP network.

Additional and Highlighted Subprotocols

In addition to the subprotocols introduced in Chapter 3, you should understand the subprotocols described in the following sections. Some of these will be new to you, while others (such as POP) will look familiar.

Reverse Address Resolution Protocol

The Address Resolution Protocol (ARP) is a means of obtaining the MAC address of a local host and keeping that information in a local cache. If a device doesn't know its own IP address, however, it can't use ARP, because it cannot issue ARP requests or receive ARP replies. One solution to this problem is to allow the client to send a broadcast message with the MAC address of a device and receive the device's IP address in reply. This process, which is the reverse of ARP, is made possible by the **Reverse Address Resolution Protocol (RARP)**. A RARP server maintains a table of MAC addresses and their associated IP addresses (similar to a BOOTP table). By consulting this table, a RARP server can respond to a client's request for an IP address associated with a particular MAC address. Only a RARP server can provide this service. A network may use more than one RARP server to balance the load caused by RARP requests and responses.

RARP was originally developed as a means for diskless workstations to obtain IP addresses from a server before BOOTP emerged. Figure 11-15 illustrates how RARP can provide an IP address to a diskless workstation.

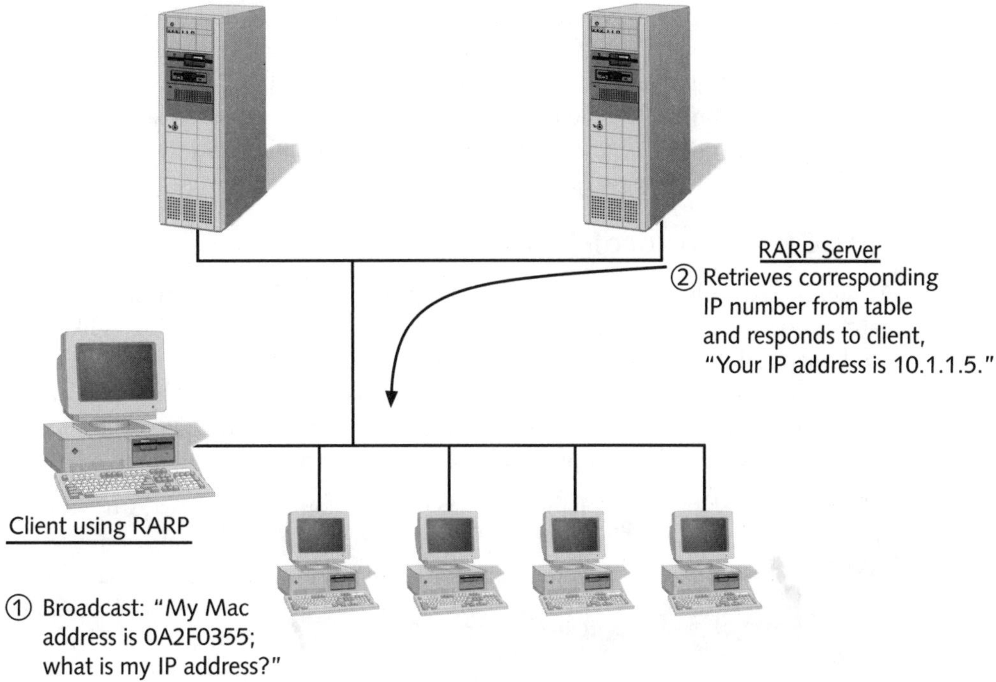
RARP Server
② Retrieves corresponding IP number from table and responds to client, "Your IP address is 10.1.1.5."
Client using RARP
① Broadcast: "My Mac address is 0A2F0355; what is my IP address?"

Figure 11-15 How RARP works

Simple Mail Transfer Protocol (SMTP)

In Chapter 3, you learned that the **Simple Mail Transfer Protocol (SMTP)** is responsible for moving messages from one e-mail server to another over TCP/IP-based networks. SMTP operates from port 25. (That is, requests to receive mail and send mail go through port 25 on the SMTP server.) SMTP, which provides the basis for Internet e-mail service, relies on higher-level programs for its instructions. Although SMTP comes with a set of human-readable commands that you could conceivably use to transport mail from machine to machine, this method would be laborious, slow, and error-prone. Instead, other services, such as the UNIX sendmail software, provide more friendly and sophisticated mail interfaces that rely on SMTP as their means of transport.

SMTP is a simple subprotocol, incapable of doing anything more than transporting mail. In the post office analogy of data communications, SMTP is like the mail carrier who picks up his day's mail load at the post office and delivers it to the homes on his route. The mail carrier does not worry about where the mail is stored overnight or how it gets from another city's post office to his post office. If a piece of mail is undeliverable, he simply holds onto it; the mail carrier does not attempt to figure out what went wrong. In Internet e-mail transmission, higher-level mail protocols such as POP and IMAP, which are discussed in the next two sections, take care of these functions.

When you configure clients to use Internet e-mail, you need to identify the user's SMTP server. (Sometimes this server is called the mail server.) Each e-mail program will specify this setting in a different place, though most commonly in the Mail Preferences section. Assuming your client uses DNS, you do not have to identify the IP address of the SMTP server—only the name. For example, if a user's e-mail address is jdoe@usmail.com, his SMTP server is probably called "usmail.com." You do not have to specify the TCP/IP port number used by SMTP, because both the client workstation and the server will assume that SMTP requests and responses flow through port 25.

Post Office Protocol (POP)

As mentioned earlier, the **Post Office Protocol (POP)** relies on SMTP to provide centralized storage for e-mail messages. In the postal service analogy, POP is like the post office that holds mail until its delivery to customers. A storage mechanism such as POP is necessary because users are not always logged on to the network and available for receiving messages. Both SMTP and a service such as POP are necessary for a mail server to receive, store, and forward messages. These two protocols cannot work without each other.

Users need an SMTP-compliant mail program to connect to their POP server and download mail from storage. POP does not allow users to keep the mail on the server after they retrieve it, which can create a problem for users who move from machine to machine. For example, if three receptionists share a company's front desk PC, each will need a separate area on the hard disk to save mail if the network uses POP. But what happens if someone from the Accounting department needs to fill in at the reception desk one afternoon? The Accounting staff member also wants to read mail while stationed there. With POP, he would have to create yet another area for his mail on the front desk PC. When he returns to his desk in Accounting, however, the mail will not be accessible because it has been saved on a different PC. A few options exist for circumventing this problem (such as keeping users' mail on a LAN server), but a more thorough solution has been provided by a new, more sophisticated e-mail protocol called IMAP, described in the next section.

The "POP" acronym has multiple meanings in the world of networking. In Chapter 7's discussion of remote connectivity, POP stood for a carrier's point of presence. In this chapter's discussion of Internet e-mail, POP stands for Post Office Protocol. Other acronyms also have double meanings in the computer world, so when reading or talking about data communications, you need to understand the particular context. Often the Post Office Protocol will be identified with its version number as well—for example, POP2 or POP3. To make matters more confusing, many networking professionals use POP as a verb, as in the following sentence: "I always POP for mail before I go to lunch."

Internet Mail Access Protocol (IMAP)

The **Internet Mail Access Protocol (IMAP)** is a mail storage and manipulation protocol that also depends on SMTP's transport system. IMAP was developed as a more sophisticated alternative to POP. The most current version of IMAP is version 4 (IMAP4). IMAP4 can (and eventually will) replace POP without the user having to change e-mail programs. The single biggest advantage IMAP4 has over POP relates to the fact that users can store messages on the mail server, rather than always having to download them to the local machine.

This feature benefits users who move from workstation to workstation. In addition, IMAP4 provides the following features:

- Users can retrieve all or only a portion of any mail message. The remainder can be left on the mail server. This feature benefits users who move from machine to machine and users who have slow connections to the network or minimal free hard disk space.
- Users can review their messages and delete them while the messages remain on the server. This feature preserves network bandwidth, especially when the messages are long or contain attached files, because the data need not travel over the wire from the server to the client's workstation. For users with a slow modem connection, deleting messages without having to download them represents a major advantage over POP.
- Users can create sophisticated methods of organizing messages on the server. A user might, for example, build a system of folders to contain messages with similar content. Also, a user might search through all of the messages for only those that contain one particular keyword or subject line.
- Users can share a mailbox in a central location. For example, if several maintenance personnel who use different PCs need to receive the same messages from the Facilities department head but do not need e-mail for any other purpose, they can all log in with the same ID and share the same mailbox on the server. If POP were used in this situation, only one maintenance staff member could read the message; he would then have to forward or copy it to his colleagues.
- IMAP4 can provide better security than POP because it supports authentication. Security is an increasing concern for network managers as more organizations connect to the public Internet.

Although IMAP provides significant advantages over POP, it also comes with a few disadvantages. For instance, IMAP servers require more storage space and usually more processing resources than POP servers do. By extension, network managers must keep a closer watch on IMAP servers to ensure that users are not consuming more than their fair share of space on the server. In addition, if the IMAP server fails, users cannot access the mail left there. (IMAP *does* allow users to download messages to their own PCs, however.)

Until recently, another consideration was that most popular e-mail programs were designed for use with POP servers only. This standard is changing, however, and you should have no difficulty obtaining mail programs that use IMAP4. For example, Eudora Pro, GroupWise, Lotus Notes, Netscape, and Outlook 98 all support IMAP4.

Hypertext Transport Protocol (HTTP)

Hypertext Transport Protocol (HTTP) is the language that Web clients and servers use to communicate. HTTP therefore forms the backbone of the Web. When you type the address of a Web page in your Web browser's address field, HTTP transports the information about your request to the Web server and returns the Web server's information to you in **Hypertext Markup Language (HTML)**, the Web document formatting language. If you access a Web page that contains links to other Web pages, HTTP allows you to connect those links after you click on them. Figure 11-16 outlines this process.

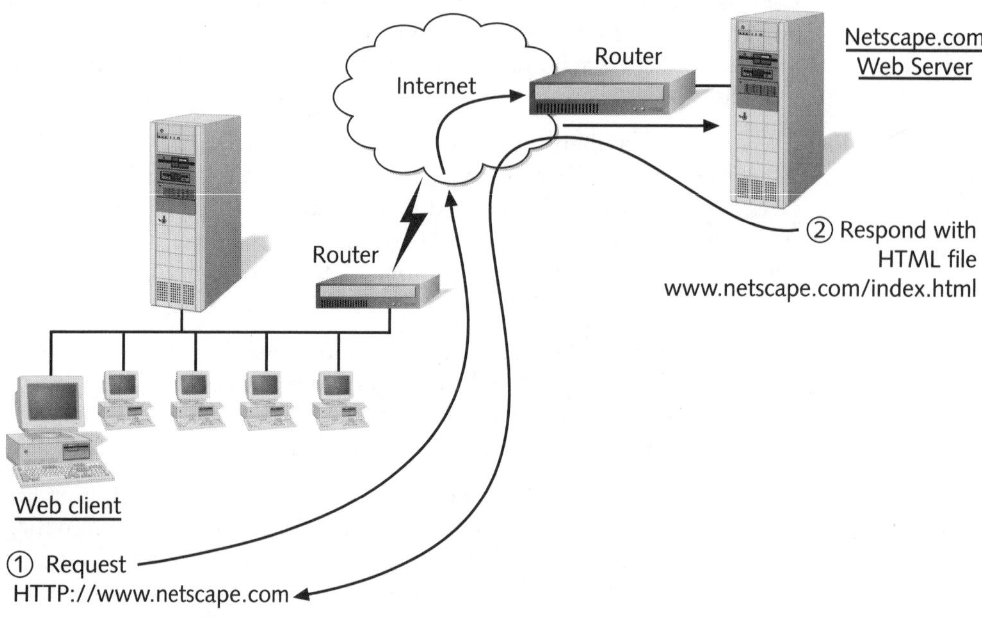

Figure 11-16 Web client/server transmission using HTTP

HTTP/0.9, the original version of HTTP, was released in 1990. This version provided only the simplest means of transferring data over the Internet. Since then, HTTP has been greatly improved to make Web client/server connections more efficient, reliable, and secure. For example, HTTP 1.1, the current version of HTTP, allows servers to transmit multiple objects, such as text and graphics, over a single TCP connection using longer packets. It also allows a client to save Web pages via caching and to compare the saved pages with requested pages. If the two are identical, the Web browser will use the cached copy of the page to save bandwidth and time.

TCP/IP TROUBLESHOOTING

Of all network protocols, TCP/IP carries the highest potential of causing problems because it requires the most planning and post-installation configuration. As with any type of communication, many potential points of failure exist in the TCP/IP transmission process. Fortunately, TCP/IP comes with a complete set of troubleshooting tools that can help you to track down most TCP/IP-related problems without using expensive software or hardware to analyze network traffic. You should be familiar with the use of the following tools and their switches, not only because the Net+ certification exam covers them, but also because you will regularly need these diagnostics in your work with TCP/IP networks. Each of these utilities can be accessed from the command prompt on a server or client running TCP/IP.

PACKET INTERNET GROPER (PING)

The **Packet Internet Groper (PING)** can verify that TCP/IP is installed, bound to the NIC, configured correctly, and communicating with the network. PING uses ICMP to send echo request and echo reply messages that determine the validity of an IP address. These two types of messages work much in the same way that sonar operates. First, a signal, called an **echo request**, is sent out to another computer. The other computer then rebroadcasts the signal, in the form of an **echo reply**, to the sender. The process of sending this signal back and forth is known as **pinging**.

You can ping either an IP address or a host name. By pinging the loopback address, 127.0.0.1, you can determine whether your workstation's TCP/IP services are running. The loopback address automatically transmits a message back to the sending computer—that is, the message "loops back" to the sender. By pinging a host on another subnet, you can determine whether the problem lies with your gateway or DNS server.

For example, suppose that you have recently moved from the Accounting department to the Advertising department and now you cannot access the Web. The first test you should perform is pinging the loopback address. If that test is successful, then you know that your workstation's TCP/IP services are running correctly. Next, you might try pinging your neighbor's machine. If you receive a positive response, you know that your network connection is working. You should then try pinging a machine on another subnet that you know is connected to the network—for example, a computer in the IT department. If this test is unsuccessful, you can safely conclude that you do not have the correct gateway or DNS settings in your TCP/IP configuration or that your organization's gateway is malfunctioning. Figure 11-17 shows the syntax of the PING command. Figure 11-18 gives examples of a successful and an unsuccessful ping.

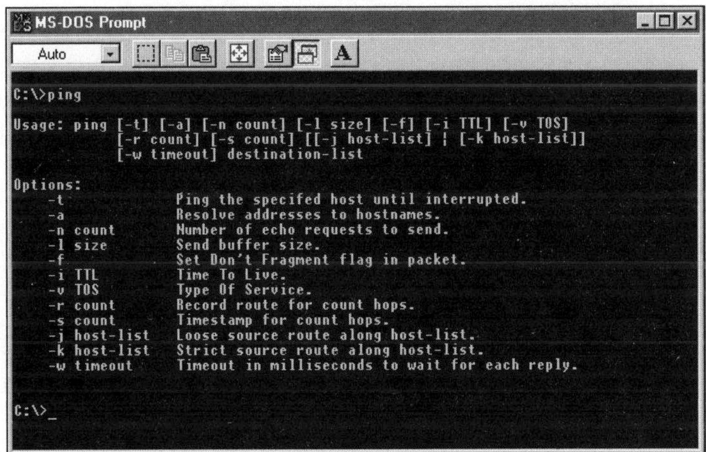

Figure 11-17 Syntax of PING command

```
MS-DOS Prompt
Auto

C:\>ping ftp.netscape.com

Pinging ftp.netscape.com [207.200.72.74] with 32 bytes of data:

Reply from 207.200.72.74: bytes=32 time=171ms TTL=247
Reply from 207.200.72.74: bytes=32 time=177ms TTL=247
Reply from 207.200.72.74: bytes=32 time=170ms TTL=247
Reply from 207.200.72.74: bytes=32 time=164ms TTL=247

C:\>ping www.microsoft.com

Pinging www.microsoft.com [207.46.130.150] with 32 bytes of data:

Request timed out.
Request timed out.
Request timed out.
Request timed out.

C:\>_
```

Figure 11-18 Example of successful and unsuccessful PING

NETSTAT

The **netstat** utility displays TCP/IP statistics and the state of current TCP/IP connections. It also displays ports, which can help you determine whether services are using the correct ports. The `netstat -a` command displays all current TCP and UDP connections from the issuing device to other devices on the network, as well as the source and destination service ports. The `netstat -r` command allows you to post a listing of the routing table on a given machine.

NBTSTAT

The ***nbtstat*** utility provides information about NetBIOS names and their addresses. If you know the NetBIOS name of a workstation, you can use nbtstat to determine its IP address. You also can use the ***`nbtstat -A ip_address`*** command to determine what machine is registered to a given IP address.

NSLOOKUP

The ***nslookup*** utility allows you to look up the DNS host name of a network node by specifying its IP address, or vice versa. This ability is useful for verifying that a host is configured correctly or for troubleshooting DNS resolution problems. The syntax of this command is *`nslookup host name`* or `nslookup` *`ip_address`*, depending on whether you want to determine the host name or IP address of a node. In addition, nslookup reports the DNS server's name.

TRACEROUTE

The **traceroute** command (also known as **tracert** on Windows systems) uses ICMP to trace the path from one networked node to another, identifying all intermediate hops between the two nodes. This utility is useful for determining router or subnet connectivity problems.

To find the route, traceroute transmits a series of UDP datagrams to a specified destination, using either the IP address or the host name to identify the destination. The first three datagrams traceroute transmits have their TTL (time to live) set to 1. Because the TTL determines how many more network hops a datagram can make, datagrams with a TTL of 1 expire as they hit the first router. When they expire, they are returned to the source—in this case, the node that began the traceroute. In this way, traceroute obtains the identity of the first router. After it learns about the first router in the path, traceroute transmits a series of datagrams with a TTL of 2. The process continues for the next router in the path, and then the third, fourth, and so on, until the destination node is reached. Traceroute also returns the amount of time it took for the datagrams to reach each router in the path.

You can infer from traceroute's method and output that this utility can help diagnose network congestion or network failures. Traceroute is not foolproof, however. In fact, its results can be misleading, because traceroute cannot detect routing problems or detect whether a router uses different send and receive interfaces. In addition, routers may not decrement the TTL value correctly at each stop in the path. Therefore, traceroute is best used on a network with which you are already familiar. You can then use your judgment and experience to compare the actual test results with what you anticipate the results should be.

INTERNET SERVICES

By now, you should probably be familiar with Internet services such as the World Wide Web (WWW), FTP, and newsgroups. The following sections discuss how TCP/IP networks provide these services, what protocols each service relies upon, and how these services benefit network administrators who manage and support them. With the growth of Internet commerce and VPNs (discussed in Chapter 7), chances are good that you will install, configure, or support at least one of the services described in the following sections.

WORLD WIDE WEB (WWW)

In the most general sense, the **World Wide Web (WWW**, or **Web)** is a collection of internetworked servers that share resources and exchange information according to specific protocols and formats. On the client side, access to the Web requires the TCP/IP protocol, a unique IP address, a connection to the Internet, and a local interface to the Web called a **browser**. The two most popular browsers in use today are Netscape Navigator (or Communicator) and Microsoft's Internet Explorer. On the server side, a Web site requires the TCP/IP protocol, a connection to DNS servers, routers, Web server software, and remote connections to the Internet.

You have learned that Web servers and clients transmit content through HTTP and HTML. In addition, every Web page is identified by a **Uniform Resource Locator (URL)** that specifies the service it uses, its server's host name, and its HTML page or script name. For example, a valid URL is `http://www.gao.gov/reports.html`, where "http" is the service used by the page, "www.gao.gov" is the server's host name, and "reports.html" is the content page. If a URL does not specify the page name, the Web server displays a default page, called index.html on most systems. On most new versions of browsers, you can type an unqualified host name instead of a fully qualified host name in the browser's URL field. An **unqualified host name** is a host name minus its prefix and suffix. For example, you could type simply "weather" in your browser's URL field, and the browser would automatically add the prefix "www" and the suffix "com" to find the www.weather.com Web site. Not all URLs specify the HTTP protocol. They may also specify Telnet, file, or FTP, as in the following URL: `ftp://ftp.netscape.com/pub`.

As a network administrator, you may be charged with installing and configuring Web server software. You may have to choose from more than 100 Web server software types, and your decision must take into account your operating system, hardware, performance requirements, security requirements, budget, and existing software. Popular Web server software include Apache, AOLServer, Lotus Domino, Microsoft's Internet Information Service, NCSA's HTTPd, and Netscape's FastTrack. Although each program requires a different method of installation and configuration, all contain features for user account management, access (security) management, and content management.

As you can imagine, references for Web protocols, programming, and customization abound on the World Wide Web. If you're searching for more information about the topics covered in this chapter, you might want to start at a site that lists many different Web-related links, such as http://www.webreference.com or http://www.internet.com.

E-MAIL

Through this chapter's discussion of SMTP, POP, and IMAP4, you have learned a great deal about how TCP/IP-based e-mail systems work. Currently, e-mail is the most frequently used and therefore the most relied-upon Internet service you will manage. You therefore need to know how to support and troubleshoot your organization's e-mail package.

Although e-mail packages vary in how they look and, to some degree, how they act, they all work on the same principles. If a user cannot retrieve her e-mail messages from the server, you must verify her TCP/IP settings. If an entire department cannot retrieve or send e-mail, you should investigate possible problems with the department's gateway. Finally, if your entire organization's e-mail system fails, you must troubleshoot your mail server(s) and connection to the Internet.

Supporting and troubleshooting e-mail are no different than supporting and troubleshooting any other networked application. Because so many people depend on this service for their daily business, however, it's critical that you understand how it works.

FILE TRANSFER PROTOCOL (FTP)

In Chapter 3, you learned that the **File Transfer Protocol (FTP)** manages file transfers between TCP/IP hosts. FTP is a simple, yet important part of the TCP/IP suite. Before the WWW provided an easier means of transferring files, FTP commands were regularly used to exchange data between machines. FTP commands will still work without using browser software or special file transfer software based on the FTP protocol. For example, if you do not have a copy of Netscape Navigator, you can FTP to Netscape's server and download the compressed program file to your hard disk.

The FTP service depends on an FTP server that is always waiting for requests. FTP data are exchanged over TCP port 20, and the FTP commands are sent and received through TCP port 21. On the client side, a simple "ftp" command can be issued from the command prompt. For example, to FTP to Netscape's FTP server (ftp.netscape.com), you could type `ftp ftp.netscape.com`, then press Enter to make a connection. To terminate the connection, you simply type `quit`. Of course, you need to know other commands to find and transfer the desired file. To learn about the various FTP commands, you can type `help` after establishing the FTP connection.

As mentioned earlier, the advent of browsers and FTP client software have rendered this command-line method of FTPing files obsolete. Today, many FTP programs provide graphical interfaces for transferring files from a server to a client. Examples of popular, inexpensive (if not free) FTP programs include MacFTP, WS_FTP, CuteFTP, and SmartFTP.

GOPHER

Another Internet service that predates the WWW is gopher. A text-based utility, **gopher** allows you to navigate through a series of menus to find and read specific files. (The program is called "gopher" because it was developed at the University of Minnesota, whose mascot is the gopher.) Gopher is not sophisticated enough to interpret document formatting commands, such as HTML, but it does allow you to transfer files from one host to another by connecting with FTP. In addition, gopher was the first Internet interface to provide links from one host to another that are transparent to the user.

11

This utility requires a local gopher client and a gopher server. In the early 1990s, thousands of gopher servers provided information over the Internet. Gopher is rarely used today, however, because Web servers and browsers have made it obsolete.

NEWSGROUPS

Newsgroups are similar to e-mail, in that they provide a means of conveying messages; they differ from e-mail in that they are distributed to a wide group of users at once rather than from one user to another. Newsgroups have been formed to discuss every conceivable topic, such as political issues, professional affiliations, entertainment interests, or sports clubs. To belong to a newsgroup, a user subscribes to the server that hosts the newsgroup. From that point forward, the user receives all messages that other newsgroup members post with the newsgroup list as their mail-to address.

Newsgroups require news servers and, on the client side, e-mail programs capable of reading newsgroups or special newsgroup reading software. Rather than using SMTP, as e-mail does, newsgroup messages are transported by the **Network News Transfer Protocol (NNTP)**. NNTP supports the process of reading newsgroup messages, posting new messages, and transferring news files between news servers. News servers are organized hierarchically, similar to DNS servers. Your Internet service provider, for example, has a news server that uses a larger carrier's news server to speak with other large carrier news servers.

E-COMMERCE

One of the fastest growing sectors of the Internet is electronic commerce, or e-commerce. The term **e-commerce** refers to a means of conducting business over the Web—be it in retail, banking, stock trading, consulting, or training. Any buying and selling of products or services that occurs over the Internet belongs in the e-commerce category. The first industries to take advantage of e-commerce were retail and finance. You can imagine how convenient and cost-effective shopping can be for both the retailer and the customer when goods can be purchased online.

If you have an interest in Internet technologies, you may want to consider specializing in e-commerce. E-commerce involves customized HTML scripting, software programming, multimedia, graphics, networking, and security skills. Because it currently relies on credit card purchases, security is a significant concern, as you might imagine. Web security is becoming more sophisticated to counter hackers who find new ways to break into systems. Personal identification numbers and file encryption, for example, can no longer guarantee that information cannot be picked up by others in transit. Some day, we may use retinal patterns or fingerprints to provide secure access to Web sites. Chapter 15 discusses network security in more detail.

INTERNET TELEPHONY

Another growing Web-based service is **Internet telephony**, the provision of telephone service over the Internet. Given the Internet's breadth and economy, it seems logical that we would look to the Internet to carry conversations that we currently transmit over the PSTN. With a basic desktop computer equipped with a microphone, speaker, and the appropriate software, you could call anyone else with the same setup, essentially using your IP address as a telephone number. Under this scheme, the cost of a call from New York to Tokyo would be the same as a call across town.

Many companies are seeking to cash in on the prospect of Internet telephony and thereby compete with local telephone companies (which are devising Internet telephony solutions of their own). Nevertheless, significant technical obstacles have prevented Internet telephony from becoming a widespread reality to date. First, more so than data transmissions, voice conversations can easily be distorted by the wire's quality of service. When you talk with your mother, you need to hear her syllables in the order in which she mouthed them, and preferably, without delay. (In contrast, data do not necessarily need to be received in the same order in which they were transmitted, because the destination node will sort the information out when it arrives.) Also, voice transmissions are subject to distortion if the connection becomes too noisy. In general, to prevent delays, disorder, and distortion, a voice connection requires more dedicated bandwidth than a data connection.

Standardization of Internet telephony, or **Voice over IP (VoIP)** as it is sometimes called, has already begun. The U.S. government is taking a hands-off approach in its regulation, letting the vendors and professional organizations sort out its implementation. It's a developing market to watch. You can learn more about Internet telephony at the Enterprise Computer Telephony Forum Web site, http://www.ectf.org, and at the International Multimedia Teleconferencing Consortium Web site, http://www.imtc.org.

CHAPTER SUMMARY

- Every device on a TCP/IP-based network must have a unique IP address to ensure reliable data delivery. Without the correct IP address, data could not be routed between networks and devices.
- Each IP address is a unique 32-bit number, divided into four groups of octets that are themselves separated by periods. An example of a valid IP address is 144.92.43.178. An IP address is typically represented in dotted decimal notation. It contains two types of information: network and host. It may also include subnet information.
- All nodes on a Class A network share the first octet of their IP numbers, a number between 1 and 126. Nodes on a Class B network share the first two octets, and all of their IP addresses begin with a number between 128 and 191. Class C network IP numbers share the first three octets, with their first octet being a number between 192 and 223.
- In addition to Class A, B, and C networks, Class D and Class E networks exist, although consumers and companies do not use them. Class D addresses begin with an octet whose value is between 224 and 239 and are reserved for a special type of transmission called multicasting. Class E addresses begin with an octet whose value is between 240 and 254, and are reserved for experimental use by the Internet Engineering Task Force. Multicasting allows one device to send data to a specific group of devices (not the entire network segment) in a point-to-multipoint fashion.
- To use IP addresses more efficiently, the concept of subnetting was applied to the Internet in the mid-1980s. Subnetting is the process of subdividing a single class of network into multiple, smaller networks.
- With subnetting, a network manager can use one class of addresses for several network segments. Subnetting adds a third type of octet to the standard IP address. Rather than consisting of simply network and host information, a subnetted address includes network, subnet, and host information.
- The combination of an address's network and subnet information is called its extended network prefix. By interpreting an address's extended network prefix, a device can determine to the subnet to which an address belongs.
- To know whether an addresses is part of a subnet in the first place, a device interprets a subnet mask. A subnet mask is a special 32-bit number that, combined with a device's IP address, tells the rest of the network which kind of subnet the device is on. Like IP addresses, subnets contain four octets and use dotted decimal notation. The bits of the subnet mask are set to 1 if the IP address information in the corresponding octets belongs to the extended network prefix. Otherwise, the subnet mask bits are 0 and the corresponding octets are assumed to represent host information.
- Routers external to an organization use only the network portion of the IP address to direct data to devices within that organization. External routers (such as those on the Internet) do not recognize subnets on specific LANs.
- Gateways are a combination of software and hardware that enable two different network segments to exchange data. In the context of IP addressing, a gateway facilitates communication between different subnets. Because one device on the network cannot send

data directly to a device on another subnet, a gateway must intercede and hand off the information.

- Internet gateways maintain default routes to known addresses to expedite data transfer. The gateways that make up the Internet backbone are called core gateways. Core gateways are operated by the Internet Network Operations Center (INOC).
- A socket is a logical address assigned to a specific process running on a host computer. It forms a virtual connection between the host and client. The socket's address represents a combination of the host computer's IP address and the port number associated with a process.
- The use of port numbers simplifies TCP/IP communications. When a client requests communications with a server and specifies port 23, the server knows immediately that the client wants a Telnet session. No extra data exchange is necessary to define the session type, and the server can initiate the Telnet service without delay.
- Every host belongs to a domain; every domain has a name, called the domain name, that identifies it. Usually, a domain name is associated with a company or other type of organization, such as a university or military unit. For example, IBM's domain name is ibm.com, and the U.S. Library of Congress's domain name is loc.gov.
- In the mid-1980s, the Network Information Center (NIC) at Stanford Research Institute devised a hierarchical way of tracking domain names and their addresses, called the Domain Name System (DNS). The DNS database does not rely on one file or even one server, but rather is distributed over several key computers across the Internet to prevent catastrophic failure if one or a few computers go down.
- Resolvers are any hosts on the Internet that need to look up domain name information. The resolver client is built into TCP/IP applications such as Telnet, HTTP, and FTP.
- Name servers are servers that contain databases of names and their associated IP addresses. A name server supplies a resolver with the requested information. If the name server cannot resolve the IP address, the query passes to a higher-level name server. Each name server manages a group of machines called a zone. DNS relies on the hierarchical zones to distribute naming information.
- Any host that must communicate with other hosts on the Internet needs to know how to find its name server. Large organizations often maintain more than one name server—a primary and a secondary name server—to help ensure Internet connectivity. When configuring the TCP/IP properties of a workstation, you need to specify a name server's IP address so that the workstation will know which machine to query when it must look up a name.
- The Name space consists of the actual database of Internet IP addresses and their associated names. Every name server holds a piece of the DNS name space. At the highest level in the hierarchy sit the root servers.
- A root server is a name server maintained by InterNIC that is an authority on how to contact top-level domains, such as those ending with .com, .edu, .net, .us, and so on. InterNIC maintains 13 root servers around the world.

- Name space is not a database that you can open and view, like a store's inventory database. Rather, this abstract concept describes how the name servers of the world share DNS information. Pieces of it are tangible, however. For example, DNS information is stored on a name server in a resource record.
- To communicate with other devices through TCP/IP, every workstation, printer, or other node on a network requires a unique IP address. On the earliest TCP/IP networks, each device was manually assigned its own number through a local configuration file, and the number did not change until someone edited the configuration file. As networks grew larger, however, this scheme became more difficult to implement.
- To ease IP address management, a service called the Bootstrap Protocol (BOOTP) was developed in the mid-1980s. BOOTP uses a central list of IP addresses and their associated devices' MAC addresses to assign IP addresses to clients.
- With BOOTP, a client does not have to remember its own IP address, and therefore network administrators do not have to manage each workstation on a network separately. This situation is ideal for diskless workstations, which do not contain hard disks, but rely on a small amount of read-only memory to get them connected to a network and to pick up their system files.
- DHCP is an automated means of assigning a unique IP address to every device on a network. Reasons for implementing DHCP include the following: to reduce the time and planning spent on IP address management; to reduce the potential for human errors in assigning IP addresses; to enable users to move their workstations and printers without changing their TCP/IP configuration; and to make IP addressing transparent for mobile users.

- DHCP was developed by the Internet Engineering Task Force as a replacement for BOOTP. Unlike BOOTP, DHCP does not require the network administrator to maintain a table of IP and MAC addresses on the server. It does, however, require the network administrator in charge of IP address management to install and configure the DHCP service on a server.
- DHCP configuration involves specifying a range of addresses that can be leased to any network device on a particular segment. The term *lease* identifies how a client borrows a DHCP-assigned IP address.
- The Windows Internet Naming Service (WINS) provides a means of resolving NetBIOS names with IP addresses. WINS is used exclusively with systems that rely on NetBIOS—therefore, it is usually focused on Windows-based systems. A computer's NetBIOS name and its TCP/IP host name are different entities that may or may not be equivalent. DNS provides resolutions of host names and IP addresses, so you can think of WINS being to NetBIOS what DNS is to TCP/IP.
- You should already be familiar with the TCP/IP core subprotocols, including IP, TCP, UDP, ICMP, and ARP, as well as Application layer protocols, including Telnet, FTP, SMTP, and SNMP.
- The Address Resolution Protocol (ARP) is a means of obtaining the MAC address of a local host and keeping that information in a local cache. If a device doesn't know its own IP address, however, it can't use ARP. A solution to this problem is to allow the

client to send a broadcast message with the MAC address of a device and then receive the device's IP address in reply. This process, which is the reverse of ARP, is called the Reverse Address Resolution Protocol (RARP).

- Simple Mail Transfer Protocol (SMTP) is responsible for moving messages from one e-mail server to another over TCP/IP-based networks. SMTP operates through port 25, with requests to receive mail and send mail going through that port on the SMTP server.
- SMTP is a simple subprotocol, incapable of doing anything more than transporting mail. In the post office analogy of data communications, SMTP is like the mail carrier who picks up his day's load of mail at the post office and delivers it to the homes on his route. In Internet e-mail transmission, more sophisticated functions are handled by higher-level mail protocols such as POP and IMAP.
- The Post Office Protocol (POP) runs on top of SMTP and provides centralized storage for e-mail messages. In the postal service analogy, POP is like the post office that holds mail until it can be delivered. A storage mechanism such as POP is necessary because users are not always logged on to the network and available for receiving messages. Both SMTP and a service such as POP are required before a mail server can receive, store, and forward messages.
- The Internet Mail Access Protocol (IMAP), a mail storage and manipulation protocol that depends on SMTP's transport system, was developed as a more sophisticated alternative to POP. The most current version of IMAP is version 4 (IMAP4). IMAP4 can (and eventually will) replace POP without the user having to change e-mail programs. The single biggest advantage IMAP4 has relative to POP is that it allows users to store messages on the mail server, rather than always having to download them to the local machine. This feature benefits users who move from workstation to workstation.
- Hypertext Transport Protocol (HTTP) is the language used by Web clients and servers to communicate with each other. It forms the backbone of the Web. When you type the address of a Web page in your Web browser's address field, HTTP transports the information about your request to the Web server and returns the Web server's information to you in the Hypertext Markup Language (HTML), the Web document formatting language.
- The Packet Internet Groper (PING) can verify that TCP/IP is installed, bound to the NIC, configured correctly, and communicating with the network. PING uses ICMP to send echo request and echo reply messages that determine the validity of an IP address.
- The netstat utility displays TCP/IP statistics and the state of current TCP/IP connections. It also displays ports, which can signal whether services are using the correct ports.
- The nbtstat utility provides information about NetBIOS names and their addresses. If you know the NetBIOS name of a workstation, you can use nbtstat to determine its IP address.
- The nslookup utility allows you to look up the DNS host name of a network node by specifying its IP address, or vice versa. This ability is useful for verifying that a host is configured correctly or for troubleshooting DNS resolution problems.

- The traceroute command, also known as tracert on Windows systems, uses ICMP to trace the path from one networked node to another, identifying all intermediate hops between the two nodes. This utility is useful for determining router or subnet connectivity problems. To find the route, traceroute transmits a series of UDP datagrams to a specified destination. You may use either the IP address or host name to identify the destination.
- The World Wide Web (WWW, or Web) is a collection of internetworked servers that share resources and exchange information according to specific protocols and formats. On the client side, access to the Web requires the TCP/IP protocol, a unique IP address, a connection to the Internet, and a local interface to the Web called a browser.
- Every Web page is identified by a Uniform Resource Locator (URL) that specifies the service used, its server's host name, and its HTML page or script name.
- Currently, e-mail is the most frequently used Internet service you will manage. For this reason, you need to know how to support and troubleshoot your organization's e-mail package. Although e-mail packages vary in how they look and, to some degree, how they act, they all work on the same principles.
- The File Transfer Protocol (FTP) manages file transfers between TCP/IP hosts. FTP is a simple, yet important part of the TCP/IP suite. Before the WWW provided an easier means of transferring files, FTP commands were regularly used to exchange data between machines.
- Gopher is a text-based utility that allows you to navigate through a series of menus to find and read specific files. It is not sophisticated enough to interpret document formatting commands, such as HTML, but it does allow you to transfer files from one host to another by connecting with FTP. Gopher was the first Internet interface to provide links from one host to another that are transparent to the user.
- Newsgroups are similar to e-mail, in that they provide a means of conveying messages; they differ from e-mail, in that they are distributed to a wide group of users at once rather than from one user to another. To belong to a newsgroup, a user subscribes to the server that hosts the newsgroup. From that point forward, the user receives all messages that other newsgroup members post with the newsgroup list as their mail-to address.
- Rather than using SMTP (as e-mail does), newsgroup messages are transported by the Network News Transfer Protocol (NNTP). NNTP supports the process of reading newsgroup messages, posting new messages, and transferring news files between news servers.
- One of the fastest growing sectors of the Internet is electronic commerce, or e-commerce. The term *e-commerce* refers to a means of conducting business over the Web—be it in retail, banking, stock trading, consulting, or training. Any buying and selling of products or services that occurs over the Internet belongs in the e-commerce category. The first industries to take advantage of e-commerce were retail and finance.
- An emerging Web-based service is Internet telephony, the provision of telephone service over the Internet. Given the Internet's breadth and economy, it seems logical that we would look to the Internet to carry our conversations that we currently transmit over the PSTN. With a basic desktop computer equipped with a microphone, speaker, and the appropriate software, you could call anyone else with the same setup, essentially using your IP address as a telephone number.

- Today, significant technical obstacles prevent Internet telephony from becoming a widespread reality. First, voice conversations depend on the wire's quality of service. Also, voice transmissions are subject to distortion if the connection becomes too noisy. Accounting for delays, disorder, and distortion, a voice connection requires more dedicated bandwidth.

KEY TERMS

- **alias** — A nickname for a node's host name. Aliases can be specified in a local host file.
- **Bootstrap Protocol (BOOTP)** — A service that simplifies IP address management. BOOTP maintains a central list of IP addresses and their associated devices' MAC addresses and assigns IP addresses to clients when they request it.
- **browser** — Software that provides clients with a simple, graphical interface to the Web.
- **core gateways** — Gateways that make up the Internet backbone. Core gateways are operated by the Internet Network Operations Center (INOC).
- **default gateway** — The gateway that first interprets a device's outbound requests and last interprets its inbound requests to and from other subnets. In the postal service analogy, the default gateway is similar to a local post office.
- **diskless workstations** — Workstations that do not contain hard disks, but rely on a small amount of read-only memory to connect to a network and to pick up their system files.
- **domain** — A group of computers that belong to the same organization and have at least part of their IP addresses in common.
- **domain name** — The symbolic name that identifies a domain. Usually, a domain name is associated with a company or other type of organization, such as a university or military unit.
- **Domain Name System (DNS)** — A hierarchical way of tracking domain names and their addresses, devised in the mid-1980s. The DNS database does not rely on one file or even one server, but rather is distributed over several key computers across the Internet to prevent catastrophic failure if one or a few computers go down. DNS is a TCP/IP service that belongs to the Application layer of the OSI Model.
- **dotted decimal notation** — The shorthand convention used to represent IP addresses and make them more easily readable by humans. In dotted decimal notation, a decimal number between 1 and 254 represents each binary octet. A period, or dot, separates each decimal.
- **Dynamic Host Configuration Protocol (DHCP)** — An automated means of assigning a unique IP address to every device on a network.
- **echo reply** — The response signal sent by a device after another device pings it.
- **echo request** — The request for a response generated when one device pings another device on the network.

- **e-commerce** — A means of conducting business over the Web—be it in retail, banking, stock trading, consulting, or training. Any buying and selling of products or services that occurs over the Internet belongs in the e-commerce category.
- **extended network prefix** — The combination of an address's network and subnet information. By interpreting an address's extended network prefix, a device can determine the subnet to which an address belongs.
- **File Transfer Protocol (FTP)** — An Application layer TCP/IP protocol that manages file transfers between TCP/IP hosts.
- **fully qualified host name** — The name of a host that includes the full domain name as well as the host name—for example, mymachine.domain.org.
- **gateway** — A combination of hardware and software that enables one type of system to communicate with another type of system.
- **gopher** — A text-based utility that allows you to navigate through a series of menus to find and read specific files.
- **host file** — A text file that associates TCP/IP host names with IP addresses. On Windows 95 and Windows NT platforms, the host file is called "lmhosts."
- **host name** — A symbolic name that describes a TCP/IP device.
- **Hypertext Markup Language (HTML)** — The language that defines formatting standards for Web documents.
- **Hypertext Transport Protocol (HTTP)** — The language that Web clients and servers use to communicate. HTTP forms the backbone of the Web.
- **Internet Mail Access Protocol (IMAP)** — A mail storage and manipulation protocol that depends on SMTP's transport system and improves upon the shortcomings of POP. The most current version of IMAP is version 4 (IMAP4). IMAP4 can (and eventually will) replace POP without the user having to change e-mail programs. The single biggest advantage IMAP4 has relative to POP is that it allows users to store messages on the mail server, rather than always having to download them to the local machine.
- **Internet telephony** — The provision of telephone service over the Internet.
- **lease** — The agreement between a DHCP server and client on how long the client will borrow a DHCP-assigned IP address. As network administrator, you configure the duration of the lease (in the DHCP service) to be as short or long as necessary, from a matter of minutes to forever.
- **multicasting** — A means of transmission in which one device sends data to a specific group of devices (not the entire network segment) in a point-to-multipoint fashion. It can be used for teleconferencing or videoconferencing over the Internet, for example.
- **name server** — A server that contains a database of TCP/IP host names and their associated IP addresses. A name server supplies a resolver with the requested information. If it cannot resolve the IP address, the query passes to a higher-level name server.
- **name space** — The database of Internet IP addresses and their associated names distributed over DNS name servers worldwide.

- **nbtstat** — A TCP/IP troubleshooting utility that provides information about NetBIOS names and their addresses. If you know the NetBIOS name of a workstation, you can use nbtstat to determine its IP address.
- **netstat** — A TCP/IP troubleshooting utility that displays statistics and the state of current TCP/IP connections. It also displays ports, which can signal whether services are using the correct ports.
- **Network News Transfer Protocol (NNTP)** — The protocol that supports the process of reading newsgroup messages, posting new messages, and transferring news files between news servers.
- **newsgroups** — An Internet service similar to e-mail that provides a means of conveying messages, but in which information is distributed to a wide group of users at once rather than from one user to another.
- **nslookup** — A TCP/IP utility that allows you to look up the DNS host name of a network node by specifying its IP address, or vice versa. This ability is useful for verifying that a host is configured correctly or for troubleshooting DNS resolution problems.
- **Packet Internet Groper (PING)** — A TCP/IP troubleshooting utility that can verify that TCP/IP is installed, bound to the NIC, configured correctly, and communicating with the network. PING uses ICMP to send echo request and echo reply messages that determine the validity of an IP address.
- **pinging** — The process of sending an echo request signal from one node on a TCP/IP network to another.
- **Post Office Protocol (POP)** — A TCP/IP subprotocol that provides centralized storage for e-mail messages. In the postal service analogy, POP is like the post office that holds mail until it can be delivered.
- **release** — The act of terminating a DHCP lease.
- **resolver** — Any host on the Internet that needs to look up domain name information.
- **resource record** — The element of a DNS database stored on a name server that contains information about TCP/IP host names and their addresses.
- **Reverse Address Resolution Protocol (RARP)** — The reverse of ARP. RARP allows the client to send a broadcast message with the MAC address of a device and receive the device's IP address in reply.
- **root server** — A DNS server maintained by InterNIC (in North America) that is an authority on how to contact the top-level domains, such as those ending with .com, .edu, .net, .us, and so on. InterNIC maintains 13 root servers around the world.
- **Simple Mail Transfer Protocol (SMTP)** — The TCP/IP subprotocol responsible for moving messages from one e-mail server to another.
- **socket** — A logical address assigned to a specific process running on a host computer. It forms a virtual connection between the host and client.
- **subnet mask** — A special 32-bit number that, when combined with a device's IP address, informs the rest of the network as to what kind of subnet the device is on.

- **subnetting** — The process of subdividing a single class of network into multiple, smaller networks.
- **top-level domain (TLD)** — The highest-level category used to distinguish domain names—for example, .org, .com, .net. A TLD is also known as the domain suffix.
- **traceroute** (or **tracert**) — A TCP/IP troubleshooting utility that uses ICMP to trace the path from one networked node to another, identifying all intermediate hops between the two nodes. Traceroute is useful for determining router or subnet connectivity problems.
- **Uniform Resource Locator (URL)** — A standard means of identifying every Web page, which specifies the service used, its server's host name, and its HTML page or script name.
- **unqualified host name** — A TCP/IP host name minus its prefix and suffix.
- **Voice over IP (VoIP)** — See *Internet telephony*.
- **Windows Internet Naming Service (WINS)** — A service that resolves NetBIOS names with IP addresses. WINS is used exclusively with systems that use NetBIOS—therefore, it is usually found on Windows-based systems.
- **World Wide Web (WWW** or **Web)** — A collection of internetworked servers that share resources and exchange information according to specific protocols and formats.
- **zone** — The group of machines managed by a DNS server.

Review Questions

1. How many octets are used for the network portion of a Class B IP address?
   - **a.** 4
   - **b.** 3
   - **c.** 2
   - **d.** 1
2. Which of the following dotted decimal addresses corresponds to the binary IP address 11111111 11111111 11111111 11111111?
   - **a.** 10.10.10.10
   - **b.** 100.100.100.100
   - **c.** 127.0.0.1
   - **d.** 255.255.255.255
3. What is another term for the address represented by 11111111 11111111 11111111 11111111?
   - **a.** multicast address
   - **b.** broadcast address

c. loopback address

d. RARP address

4. Why would a network manager choose to divide his or her TCP/IP networks into subnets?

a. to conserve router interfaces

b. to minimize traffic between segments on the network

c. to use a limited number of IP addresses more efficiently

d. to reduce the potential for IP addressing conflicts

5. What is the default subnet mask for a Class A network?

a. 255.0.0.0

b. 255.255.0.0

c. 255.255.255.0

d. 255.255.255.255

6. If a client workstation's IP address equals 119.55.60.122, and the network administrator is using subnetting, which of the following is probably the workstation's subnet mask?

a. 255.0.0.0

b. 255.255.0.0

c. 255.255.255.0

d. 255.255.255.255

7. Each node on a TCP/IP network has only one default gateway. True or False?

8. What is the primary advantage to using sockets?

a. They enable clients and servers to communicate more expeditiously.

b. They enable servers to keep a service available at all times.

c. They eliminate the possibility that service requests might become corrupted.

d. They ensure that a connection-oriented protocol is used when requesting services.

9. Which two ports are used in FTP transmission?

a. 23 and 24

b. 21 and 22

c. 20 and 21

d. 22 and 23

10. Which top-level domain would the U.S. Congressional offices use?

a. .loc

b. .con

c. .com

d. .gov

11. What three columns of information would you find in a file called "lmhosts" on a Windows NT workstation?
    - **a.** IP address, domain name, and NetBIOS address
    - **b.** IP address, NetBIOS address, and alias
    - **c.** IP address, domain name, and alias
    - **d.** IP address, host name, and alias
12. How can a resolver quickly find addresses for previously visited sites?
13. An organization may use only one name server. True or False?
14. What is the significant disadvantage to using BOOTP?
    - **a.** It requires two servers to hold the information for a single subnet.
    - **b.** Its tables must be manually updated.
    - **c.** It does not conform to the hierarchical DNS model.
    - **d.** It is unreliable.
15. Although DHCP enables users to move their machines from one location on the network to another without reconfiguring TCP/IP settings, what might a user have to do once she has moved to a new part of the network so as to use TCP/IP applications?
    - **a.** change her primary DNS setting
    - **b.** change her default protocol setting
    - **c.** release and renew her IP address
    - **d.** adjust the time on her DHCP lease
16. When a client needs to obtain an IP address from a DHCP server, what kind of transmission does it send?
    - **a.** broadcast UDP
    - **b.** multicast TCP
    - **c.** broadcast RARP
    - **d.** multicast RARP
17. In total, how many packets are exchanged in the process of a client requesting and obtaining an IP address from a DHCP server?
    - **a.** 2
    - **b.** 4
    - **c.** 6
    - **d.** 8
18. Which of the following is a benefit of using WINS?
    - **a.** It ensures that every device on the network has a unique IP address.
    - **b.** It ensures that every device on the network has a unique host name.
    - **c.** It ensures that every device on the network has a unique NetBIOS name.
    - **d.** It ensures that every device on the network has a unique socket address.

11

19. What is the difference between UDP and TCP?
    a. UDP is a Data Link layer protocol and TCP is a Network layer protocol.
    b. UDP is connectionless and TCP is connection-oriented.
    c. UDP relies on IPX/SPX and TCP relies on TCP/IP.
    d. UDP is more secure than TCP.
20. How could RARP benefit diskless workstations?
21. What is SMTP's primary function?
    a. provide management information about network devices
    b. monitor security breaches at the router interface level
    c. transport mail from one host to another
    d. supply port usage information
22. Where does mail go after it is retrieved by an e-mail program that uses POP?
    a. to the user's mail directory on the mail server
    b. to the user's mail directory on the client workstation
    c. to the root directory on the client workstation
    d. to the recycle bin on the server
23. Which of the following is a benefit of using IMAP4 relative to POP?
    a. It provides mail delivery guarantees.
    b. It allows users to delete mail without downloading it.
    c. It allows users to create mail messages on the server.
    d. It provides better encryption for message attachments.
24. IMAP4 can work without SMTP. True or False?
25. What can you learn by pinging the loopback address?
26. If you know that your boss's TCP/IP host name is JSMITH, and you need to find out what her IP address is, what command (with correct syntax) should you type at your DOS prompt?
    a. nslookup jsmith
    b. netstat jsmith
    c. tracert jsmith
    d. whois jsmith
27. What command might you use to find out whether your ISP's router is especially slow on a particular afternoon?
    a. traceroute
    b. nbtstat
    c. netstat
    d. nslookup

28. How can you view a list of FTP commands once you have connected to an FTP server?

    a. type **commands**

    b. type **show**

    c. type **quit**

    d. type **help**

29. Which protocol is used to transmit and receive messages to and from newsgroups?

    a. NNTP

    b. SNMP

    c. NCP

    d. SMTP

30. Why is security a concern for Web sites that offer e-commerce?

HANDS-ON PROJECTS

PROJECT 11-1

In this exercise, you will set up a Windows 95 workstation with everything it needs to access the Internet. For this project, you will need a Windows 95 workstation that currently has TCP/IP installed and bound to the NIC, but doesn't have any settings specified. You will need to obtain the correct settings for your network from your instructor. In this project, it's important to type the numbers exactly as they are given to you; otherwise, the TCP/IP connection will not work. Each student should use a unique IP address and host name.

1. Obtain the following numbers from your instructor: IP address, subnet mask, DNS primary name server, DNS secondary name server, and domain name.
2. Right-click the **Network Neighborhood** icon, then click **Network properties** in the shortcut menu.
3. Highlight the **TCP/IP protocol** in the list of installed network components, then click **Properties**. The TCP/IP Properties dialog box opens.
4. Click the **IP Address** tab.
5. Select the **Specify an IP Address** check box.
6. Enter your network's IP address in the space provided.
7. Enter your network's subnet mask in the space provided.
8. Click the **DNS Configuration** tab.
9. Select the **Enable DNS** check box.
10. Provide a host name for your machine composed of your first initial and your last name. Do not use any spaces, dashes, or other special characters.

11. Enter your network's domain name in the space provided.
12. Under the "DNS Server Search Order" heading, type the IP address of your primary DNS server, then click **Add**.
13. If you have a secondary DNS server, type it in the same space, then click **Add**.
14. Click **OK** to save your changes to the TCP/IP properties. The dialog box closes.
15. Click **OK** to save the changes to the Network properties. The dialog box closes and you are prompted to restart your computer to save your changes.
16. Click **Yes** to confirm that you want to restart your computer. When your workstation restarts, it will be properly configured for TCP/IP to browse the Web and use TCP/IP applications such as FTP and Telnet.
17. To test whether your change worked, click **Start**, click **Run**, type **telnet locis.loc.gov** in the Open text box, then click **OK**.
18. If you see a text screen titled "LOCIS: Library of Congress Information System," you have successfully modified your TCP/IP properties. If you receive a window titled "Connect Failed!" you either typed the host name incorrectly or need to retrace your steps from the beginning of this exercise to ensure that your TCP/IP properties are correct.

PROJECT 11-2

Computer scientists across the world collaborate to devise Internet protocols and standards. These standards, along with comments and Internet-related meeting notes, are then transformed into Requests for Comments (RFCs). When you want to find the source of an Internet standard, you can look in its RFCs. Some RFCs were written at the genesis of the Internet and have since been revised several times. New RFCs are continually being written. In this exercise, you will use the FTP client to find RFCs at different Internet host sites and explore their content.

For this and subsequent exercises, you will need a PC or UNIX workstation with access to the World Wide Web (a standard TCP/IP installation and an Internet connection such as the one you configured in Project 11-1). Your workstation should also have a Web browser, such as Internet Explorer or Netscape Communicator, installed.

1. Verify that your workstation is connected to the Internet.
2. At the command prompt, type **ftp**, then press **Enter** to begin an FTP session.
3. At the ftp prompt, type **help**, then press **Enter**. How many FTP commands does your FTP client provide? Do any of the commands look familiar?
4. Type **open rs.internic.net**, then press **Enter** to connect to InterNIC's FTP site.
5. Now you need to enter your user name. Because this site allows guests to log in with the user name "anonymous," type **anonymous**, then press **Enter**.

6. Now you need to enter a password. Type your e-mail address as your password, then press **Enter**. If you do not have a valid e-mail address, ask your instructor to provide an address you can use for this purpose.
7. To confirm that you have logged in, the InterNIC FTP server greets you this message: "Guest login ok, access restrictions apply."
8. To change directories to the folder that contains the RFC documents, type **cd rfc** at the ftp prompt, then press **Enter**. This command is case-sensitive, so be sure not to use any capital letters.
9. To show a listing of all RFCs in this directory, type **ls**, then press **Enter**.
10. To copy RFC number 1816 to your hard disk, type **get rfc1816.txt "c:\rfc.txt"** then press **Enter**. Note that "get" is the FTP command for retrieving a file. The name of the file on the FTP server is "fc1816.txt"and "c:\rfc.txt" is the file name you will save it under on your computer.
11. To close the FTP session, type **quit**, then press **Enter**.
12. Open the file c:\rfc.txt using a text editor program (if you are working on a Windows workstation, you may want to use WordPad).
13. Read the header and at least a few paragraphs from this RFC. What is the topic of this RFC? What previously written RFC does it replace? On what date was it published?

PROJECT 11-3

In this exercise, you will use a Web browser to locate an RFC. In addition, you will perform Web searches and use services other than HTTP. To complete this project, you need a workstation with Internet access.

1. Verify that your workstation is connected to the Internet.
2. Go to the following Web site: **http://www.rfc-editor.org/rfcsearch.html**.
3. Under the "Go Directly To" section, in the text box titled "Number", type 1816, then click **Go Direct**.
4. According to this RFC, which domain suffix should local and state agencies use? (Hint: If you are reading the document in a browser window, you can use your browser's search function to look for any instance of the phrase "local and state.")
5. Go to the Internet Engineering Task Force's home page: http://www.ietf.org.
6. To view a list of the IETF's working groups, click the **IETF Working Groups** link.
7. Scroll through the page to get an idea of how many emerging Internet technologies need to be standardized or refined. Under the Operations and Management Area, choose to view more information about the **Remote Network Monitoring** group. What is the purpose of this group? What RFCs have resulted from its work?
8. Go to the following Web site: **ftp://rs.internic.net/rfc/**. Look at the list of text files and directories that appear. It is the same list that you viewed through the FTP command "ls" in Project 11-2.

9. Type **altavista** in your Web browser's address box, press **Enter**, and see whether your browser adds the prefix and suffix to the unqualified host name and finds the appropriate site. If it doesn't, point your browser to the fully qualified host name, **www.altavista.com**.
10. At the AltaVista search engine site, type the following question in the search field: **What is SMTP?** Click **Search**.
11. What kind of response do you get from the search engine?

PROJECT 11-4

In this exercise, you will configure an e-mail program with the correct mail server settings. In a typical LAN environment, users will not know how to specify their mail servers or whether their software uses POP or IMAP4. In addition to knowing this basic information, you should be familiar with any special mail program settings required by your organization, such as whether users are allowed to leave messages on the server and, if so, how long they are allowed to maintain them there.

For this exercise, you will need a Windows 95 or Windows NT workstation with one of the popular e-mail programs, such as Eudora Light, installed. If you do not have the disks to install Eudora Light, you can download the software from Qualcomm's Web site at http://eudora.qualcomm.com/eudoralight/ at no cost. Your instructor can provide the configuration information for your network, such as the mail server name, if you do not already know it.

Although this exercise focuses on the configuration process for the Eudora Light e-mail package, all Internet e-mail packages will require you to enter the same information, if not more. Many e-mail programs share similar menu structures, too. Once you have experience configuring a few popular programs, therefore, you can easily figure out how to configure other e-mail programs.

1. To run the Eudora Light mail program, click **Start**, point to **Programs**, point to **Eudora Light**, then click **Eudora Light**. The Eudora Light window opens.
2. Click **Tools** on the menu bar, then click **Options**. The Options dialog box opens, as shown in Figure 11-19.

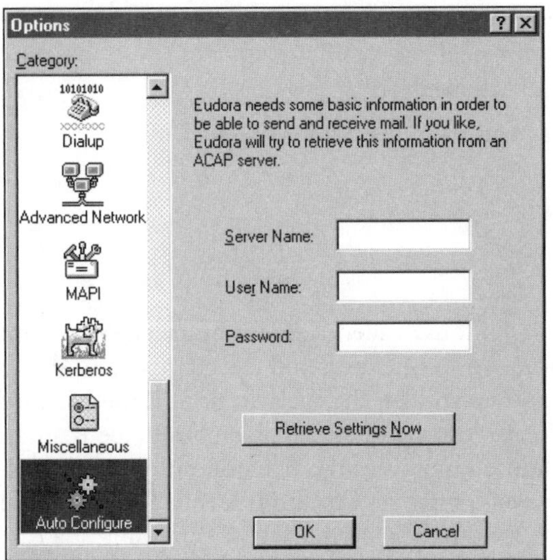

Figure 11-19 Eudora Light Options dialog box

3. Scroll to the top of the **Category** list box, then click the **Getting Started** icon.
4. In the text box under "POP Account," type your full e-mail address.
5. In the text box under "Real Name," type your first and last name.
6. In the text box under "Return Address," type your full e-mail address.
7. In the Category list box, click the **Sending Mail** icon.
8. In the text box under "Domain to Add to Unqualified Addresses" enter your mail server's domain name. For example, if your e-mail address is "jdoe@usa.com," enter "usa.com." This choice enables you to send mail to your friend "usam@usa.com" by typing simply "usam" in the "To:" field of your e-mail message.
9. In the text box under "SMTP Server," enter your SMTP server name.
10. Save your settings by clicking **OK**. You will return to the main Eudora Light window.
11. To test your mail client, click **File** on the menu bar, then click **Check Mail**. Why didn't you have to restart your workstation for these changes to take effect?
12. In the next steps, you will test what happens when a mail server name is spelled incorrectly. To start, click **Tools** on the menu bar, then click **Options**.
13. Click the **Sending Mail** icon. The sending mail options appear.
14. Change one letter in the name of your SMTP server, then click **OK** to save your changes.
15. To create a test message to send to yourself, click **Message** on the menu bar, then click **New Message**. A new message window appears, prompting you to enter the recipient's e-mail address.
16. Type your own e-mail address (correctly) in the To: text box.
17. In the Subject: text box, type **test**.

18. Click the **Send** button. What happens? What kind of error message do you receive when you attempt to retrieve your mail?
19. Follow Steps 13 through 17 again, this time typing in your correct SMTP server name to restore your ability to send e-mail from the Eudora Light client.

CASE PROJECTS

1. Katie Stark, who owns a local greenhouse called Katydid Nursery, knows you from college. She has heard you're a networking expert and calls to ask how she can sell bulbs, seeds, garden tools, and houseplants on the Web. To date, Katie has used computers only to keep her inventories, but she's heard that e-commerce is an easy way to make more money. Her greenhouse employees use five computers, all Pentium 90s. She doesn't think that they are even connected to the Internet. Katie has a limited budget and frankly isn't sure whether having a Web site is something she can afford. If she had a Web site, she tells you, she would call it www.katydids.com. Based on what you know about Internet connections, Web sites, and e-commerce, what kind of connection do you recommend? What advice can you provide about establishing a Web site and preparing her computers to use the Web?
2. Katie told her friend Andy about your skills with computers. Andy knows a bit about computers himself, as he is the sole network technician at a chain of six hardware stores in the Pacific Northwest. His network is connected to the Internet through a dedicated T1 link, and he has registered the address range from 205.38.123.1 through 205.38.123.100 with InterNIC. For the most part, the clients Andy supports use the Internet for e-mail, Web surfing, and exchanging files. The problem with his network is that he's the only employee who knows anything about TCP/IP, and the network is growing faster than he can handle. Andy is constantly visiting one of his users' machines to check their IP address in their TCP/IP properties window, or finding that they've accidentally deleted their gateway setting. How can you help him?
3. Andy's surprised that you know so much about TCP/IP, and he isn't impressed easily. On a day when his connection to the Internet is extremely slow, he challenges you to find out why the performance is so bad. Andy jokes that it might have something to do with the earthquake that just took place in San Jose. What do you do?

CHAPTER 12

TROUBLESHOOTING NETWORK PROBLEMS

After reading this chapter and completing the exercises, you will be able to:

- Describe the elements of an effective troubleshooting methodology
- Discuss practical issues related to troubleshooting
- Use software and hardware tools to diagnose problems

ON THE JOB

Our ISP division hosts Web sites for a number of corporate clients. Each site requires a separate Web server, but multiple Web servers can run on the same machine. Once, at about 3:00 A.M. on a Sunday morning, one of our engineers began upgrading the hardware that supported about 100 of these corporate Web servers. The engineer finished the work on schedule, and everything appeared to be fine. We expected the sites to perform much better with the new hardware installed.

At roughly 6:00 A.M. that morning, I was with a customer working on a network topology conversion project, when the engineer called with bad news. Contrary to our expectations, the Web sites were performing dismally on the new hardware. The exact problem wasn't clear. I made my apologies to the customer (a down condition always takes precedence) and headed back to the office to do some troubleshooting.

Indeed, the performance of the Web sites on the new hardware was awful. I plugged in a Network General Sniffer to our core Ethernet switch and then set the sniffer port to spanning mode so that the sniffer could examine all traffic on the Web server VLAN. I set the sniffer filters such that I was monitoring only packets to the Web server in question. Almost immediately, a problem became apparent. The packets destined for the Web server were plainly seen on the network, but no replies came from the Web server. For some reason, the Web server was not "seeing" the traffic directed to it. A number of causes seemed possible: For example, the wiring to the new Web server might be bad, the Web server might have a defective network interface card (NIC), or, less likely, the switch might have a bad Ethernet port.

I tried the easiest option first, replacing the Category 5 Ethernet cable to the Web server. Sure enough, the problem went away, and the Web pages were quickly served. The sniffer showed normal network protocol behavior.

The company had engaged in discussions about getting a cable tester several times, but never quite got around to making a purchase. After this incident, we ordered a cable tester immediately. We also implemented a policy requiring engineers to test each cable before installing it on the network.

James G. Berbee
Berbee Information Networks, Inc.

By now, you know how networks *should* work. Like other complex systems, however, they don't always work as planned. Many things can go wrong on a network, just as many things can go wrong with your car, house, or a project at work. In fact, a network professional probably spends more time fixing network problems than designing or upgrading a network. Some breakdowns (such as an overtaxed processor) come with plenty of warning, but others (such as a hard disk controller failure) can strike instantly.

As with your car, the best defense against problems is prevention. Just as you should have your car serviced regularly, so you should monitor the health of your network regularly. Of course, even the most well-monitored network will sometimes experience unexpected problems. For example, a utility company could dig a new hole for its cable and accidentally cut your dedicated line to the Internet. In such a situation, your network can go from perfect to disastrous performance in an instant. In this chapter, you learn how to diagnose and solve network problems in a logical, step-by-step fashion, using a variety of tools.

TROUBLESHOOTING METHODOLOGY

Successful troubleshooters proceed logically and methodically. This section introduces a basic troubleshooting methodology, leading you through a series of general problem-solving steps. Bear in mind that experience in your network environment may prompt you to follow the steps in a different order or to skip certain steps entirely. For example, if you know that one segment of your network is poorly cabled, you may try replacing a section of cable in that area to solve a connectivity problem before attempting to verify the physical and logical integrity of the workstation's NIC. In general, however, it is best to follow each step in the order shown. Such a logical approach can save you from undertaking wasteful, time-consuming efforts such as unnecessary software or hardware replacements.

Steps to troubleshooting network problems:

1. Identify the symptoms. Carefully document what you learn from people or systems that alerted you to the problem and keep that documentation handy.
2. Verify user competency. For example, ensure that the user is typing his or her password correctly.
3. Identify the scope of the problem. Is it universal—that is, are all users on the network experiencing the problem at all times? Or is the problem limited to a specific geographic area of the network, to a specific demographic group of users, or to a particular period of time? In other words, is the problem subject to geographic, demographic, or chronological constraints?
4. Recreate the problem, and ensure that you can reproduce it reliably.
5. Verify the physical integrity of the network connection (such as cable connections, NIC installations, and power to devices), starting at the affected nodes and moving outward toward the backbone.

6. Verify the logical integrity of the network connection (such as addressing, protocol bindings, software installations, and so on).
7. Consider recent changes to the network and how those changes might have caused a problem.
8. Implement a solution.
9. Test the solution.

Depending on your findings, you may skip from one step to another step further down in this list, eliminating the need to carry out the intervening steps. For example, if you determine that a NIC has been improperly seated in a workstation's system board, you may skip directly to Step 8 (in this case, reinstall the NIC) without analyzing recent changes to the network. Above all, use common sense in your troubleshooting efforts. As you read through the following sections, you will understand how the suggested troubleshooting steps are interrelated and how answering a question under one step might prompt you to skip to another step.

The flowchart in Figure 12-1 illustrates how these steps are related. Each decision step in the flowchart is discussed in more detail in the following sections, and in some sections the flowchart is expanded to reflect different outcomes based on different findings. The following sections also explain how to narrow down the possible causes for a problem by answering specific questions. In particular, you can question users to get clues about the problem. Finally, the chapter describes ways to test your attempted resolution of a network problem.

In addition to the organized method of troubleshooting described in this section, a good, general rule for troubleshooting can be stated as follows: Pay attention to the obvious! Although some questions may seem too simple to bother asking, don't discount them. You can often save much time by checking cable connections first. Every networking professional can tell a story about spending half a day trying to figure out why a computer wouldn't connect to the network, only to discover that the network cable was not plugged into the wall jack or the device's NIC.

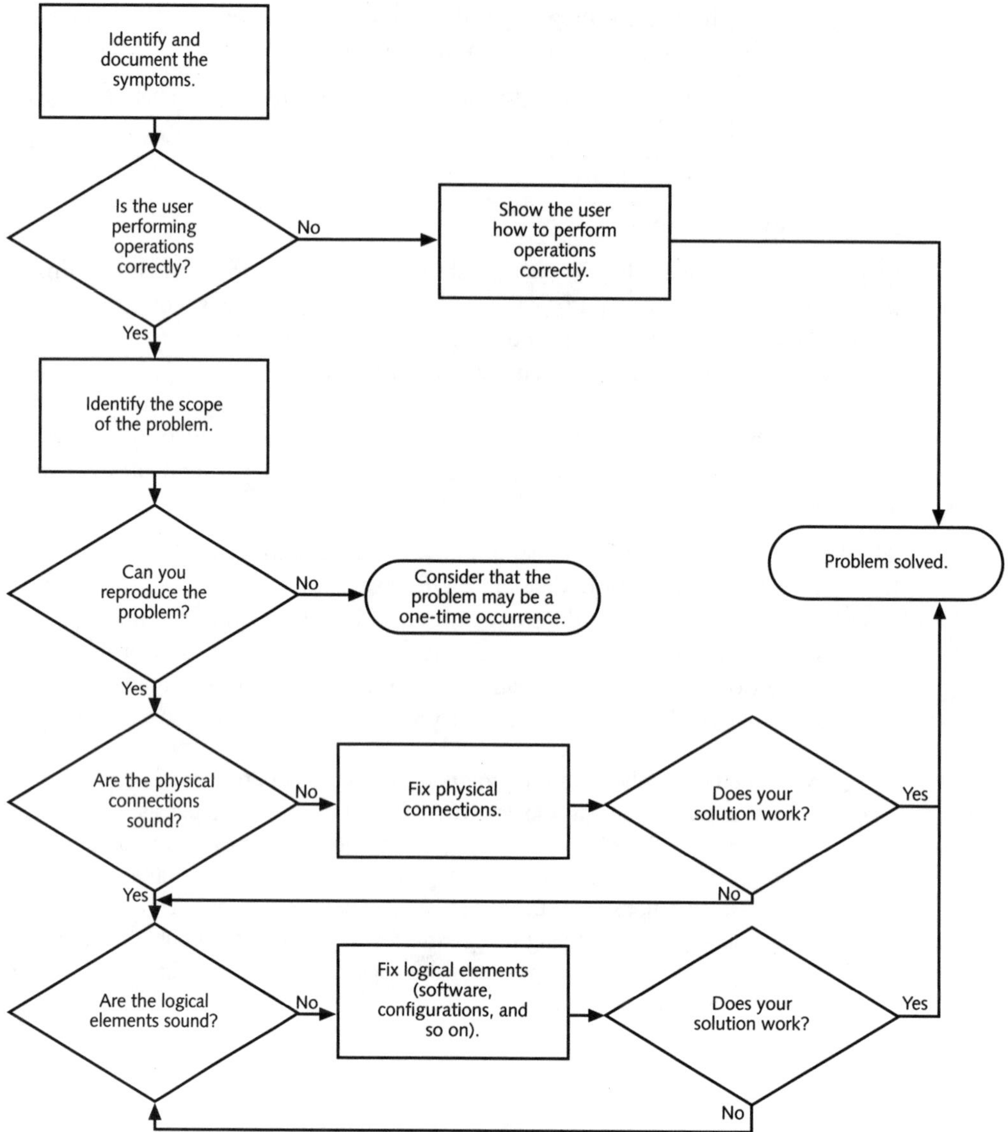

Figure 12-1 A simple flowchart of troubleshooting steps

IDENTIFY THE SYMPTOMS

When troubleshooting a network problem, act like a doctor diagnosing a patient's illness. Your first step should be to identify the specific symptoms of the problem. In a broad sense, this step brings you closer to pinpointing the cause of the problem. For example, identifying a patient's sore throat and headache as symptoms, rules out carpal tunnel syndrome and a host of other ailments. Nevertheless, the problem may still be anything from mononucleosis to allergies.

In a network, symptoms of a single problem might include a user's inability to access a network drive, send e-mail, or print to a specific printer. The problem may be caused by a number of things, including a faulty NIC, faulty cable, faulty hub, faulty router, incorrect client software configuration, server failure, or user error. On the other hand, you can probably rule out a power failure, printer failure, Internet connectivity failure, e-mail server failure, and a host of other problems.

Answering the following questions may help you identify the symptoms of a network problem:

- Is access to the network affected?
- Is network performance affected?
- Are data or programs affected? Or are both affected?
- Are only certain network services (such as printing) affected?
- If programs are affected, does the problem include one local application, one networked application, or multiple networked applications?
- What specific error messages do users report?
- Is one user or multiple users affected?
- Do the symptoms manifest themselves consistently?

One danger in troubleshooting technical problems lies in jumping to conclusions about the symptoms. For example, you might field 12 questions from users one morning about a problem printing to the network printer in the Facilities department. You might have already determined that the problem is an addressing conflict with the printer and be in the last stages of resolving the problem. Minutes later, when a thirteenth caller says, "I'm having problems printing," you might immediately conclude that she is another Facilities staff member and that her inability to print results from the same printer addressing problem. In fact, this user may be in the Administration department, and her inability to print could represent a symptom of a larger network problem.

Take time to pay attention to the users, system and network behaviors, and any error messages. Treat each symptom as unique (but potentially related to others). In this way, you will avoid the risk of ignoring problems or—even worse—causing more problems.

Take note of the error messages reported by users. If you aren't near the users, ask them to read the messages to you directly off their screens or, better yet, print the screens that contain the error messages. (On some computers, pressing the Print Screen button—which is sometimes labeled "Print Scrn" or "Prt Sc"—will perform the Print Screen function. On other computers, you can use the Shift-Print Screen or Alt-Print Screen keystroke combinations.) Keep a record of these error messages along with your other troubleshooting notes for that problem.

Verify User Competency

You have probably experienced a moment in your dealings with computers in which you were certain you were doing everything correctly, but still couldn't access the network or save a file or pick up your e-mail. For example, you may have typed your case-sensitive network password without realizing that the Caps Lock function was turned on. Even though you were certain that you typed the right password, you received a "password incorrect" error message each time you tried to enter your password. All users experience such problems from time to time.

It's natural for humans to make mistakes. Thus, as a troubleshooter, one of your first steps should be to ensure that human error is not the source of the problem. This approach will save you time and worry. In fact, a problem caused by human error is usually simple to solve. It's much quicker and easier to assist a user in remapping a network drive, for example, than to perform diagnostics on the file server.

Often, an inability to log in to the network results from a user error. Users become so accustomed to typing in their passwords every morning and logging on to the network that, if something changes in the login process, they don't know what to do. In fact, some users might never log out, so they don't know how to log in properly. Although these kinds of issues may seem very simple, unless a user receives training in the proper procedures and understands what might go wrong, her or she will never know how to solve a logging-in problem without assistance. Even if the user took a computer class that covered logging on, he or she may not remember what to do in unfamiliar situations.

When diagnosing user errors, your most powerful tool may be patience. The best way to verify that a user is performing network functions correctly is by watching him or her. If this tactic isn't practical, the next best way is to talk with the user by phone while he or she tries to replicate the error. At every step, calmly ask the user to explain what appears on the screen and what, exactly, he or she is doing. After every keystroke or command, ask the user again what appears on the screen. With this methodical approach, you will be certain to catch any user-generated mistakes. At the same time, if the problem does not follow from human error, you will gain important clues for further troubleshooting.

Identify the Scope of the Problem

After you have identified the problem's symptoms and ruled out user error, you should determine the scope of the problem—whether the problem appears only with a certain group of users, with certain areas of the organization, or at certain times. For example, if a problem affects only users on one network segment, you may deduce that the problem lies with that network segment's cabling, configuration, router port, or gateway. On the other hand, if symptoms are limited to one user, you can typically narrow the cause of the problem down to a single cable, workstation (hardware or software) configuration, or user.

In the doctor/patient analogy, this scope identification is similar to the doctor who asks a patient how long his sore throat has lasted and whether anyone else in his family is affected. If the patient answers that the sore throat started yesterday and his twin toddlers both have colds, the doctor might suspect a cold virus. Conversely, if the patient indicates that no one he knows is ill and that his sore throat has lingered for 10 days, the doctor might suspect something other than a simple cold.

Answering the following questions may help you ascertain the scope of a network problem:

- *How many users or network segments are affected?*

  One user or workstation?

  A workgroup?

  A department?

  One location within an organization?

  An entire organization?

- *When did the problem begin?*

  Has the network, server, or workstation *ever* worked properly?

  Did the symptoms appear in the last hour or day?

  Have the symptoms appeared intermittently for a long time?

  Do the symptoms appear only at certain times of the day, week, month, or year?

Like identifying symptoms, narrowing down a problem's scope can eliminate some causes and point to others. In particular, narrowing down the affected groups of users or areas of your organization can help to distinguish workstation (or user) problems from the network problems. If the problem affects only a department or floor of your organization, for example, you will probably need to examine that network segment, its router interface, its cabling, or a server that provides services to those users. If a problem affects users at a remote location, you should examine the WAN link or its router interfaces. If a problem affects all users in all departments and locations, a catastrophic failure has occurred and you should assess critical devices such as central switches and backbone connections.

If a problem is universal—that is, if it affects the entire LAN or WAN—you will naturally want to answer these questions very quickly. In the doctor/patient analogy, this situation would be similar to performing triage in an emergency room.

Usually, network problems are not catastrophic, and you can take a little time to troubleshoot them correctly, by asking specific questions designed to identify their scope. For example, suppose a user complains that his mail program isn't picking up e-mail. You should begin by asking when the problem began, whether it affects only that user or everyone in his department, and what error message (or messages) the user receives when he attempts to pick up mail. In answering your questions, he might say, "The problem began about 10 minutes ago. Both my neighbors are having problems with e-mail, too. And as a matter of fact, a network technician was working on my machine this morning and installed a new graphics program."

As you listen to the user's response, you may need to politely filter out information that is unlikely to be related to the problem. In this situation, the user relayed two significant pieces of information: (1) the scope of the problem includes a group of users, and (2) the problem began 10 minutes ago. With this knowledge, you can then delve further in your troubleshooting. In this example, you would proceed by focusing on the network segment rather than on one workstation.

Discovering the time or frequency with which a problem occurs can reveal more subtle network problems. For example, if multiple users throughout the organization cannot log on to the server at 8:05 A.M., you may deduce that the server needs additional resources to handle the processing burden of accepting so many logins. If a network fails at noon every Tuesday, you may be able to correlate this problem with a test of your building's power system, which causes a power dip that affects the servers, routers, hubs, and other devices.

Identifying the scope of the problem will lead you to your next troubleshooting steps. The path may not always be clear-cut, but as the flowcharts in Figures 12-2 and 12-3 illustrate, some direction can be gained from narrowing both the demographic (or geographic) and chronological scope of a problem. Notice that these flowcharts end with the process of further troubleshooting. In the following sections, you will learn more about these subsequent troubleshooting steps.

The processes of identifying a problem's scope by demographics and by chronology are not mutually exclusive, but rather can be followed simultaneously. For example, you might quickly determine that users in the Software department experience frequent network disconnections, but only during the hours between midnight and 2:00 A.M. Knowing that the only staff members working at that time are Software engineers, you might choose not to continue through the process of narrowing the problem's demographic scope. Instead, you would want to focus on the network activity during those two hours.

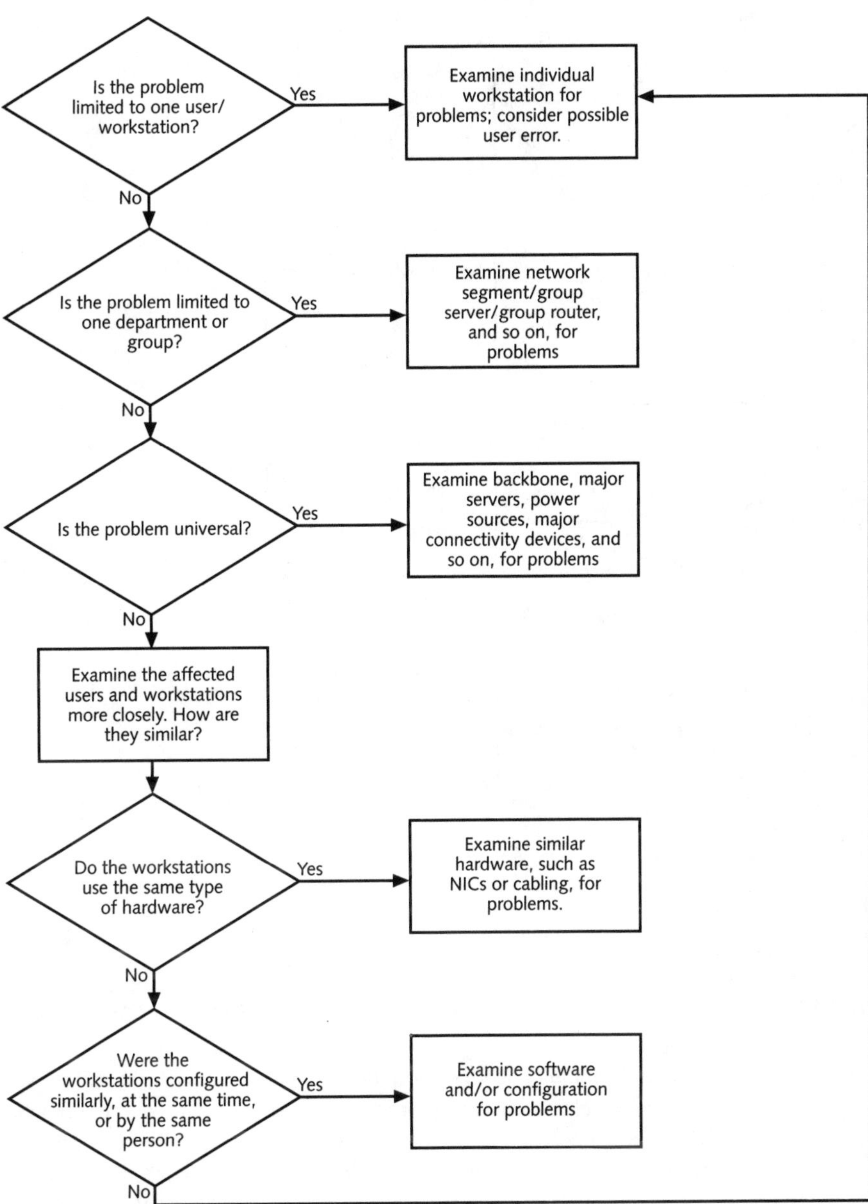

Figure 12-2 Troubleshooting while identifying the demographic scope of a problem

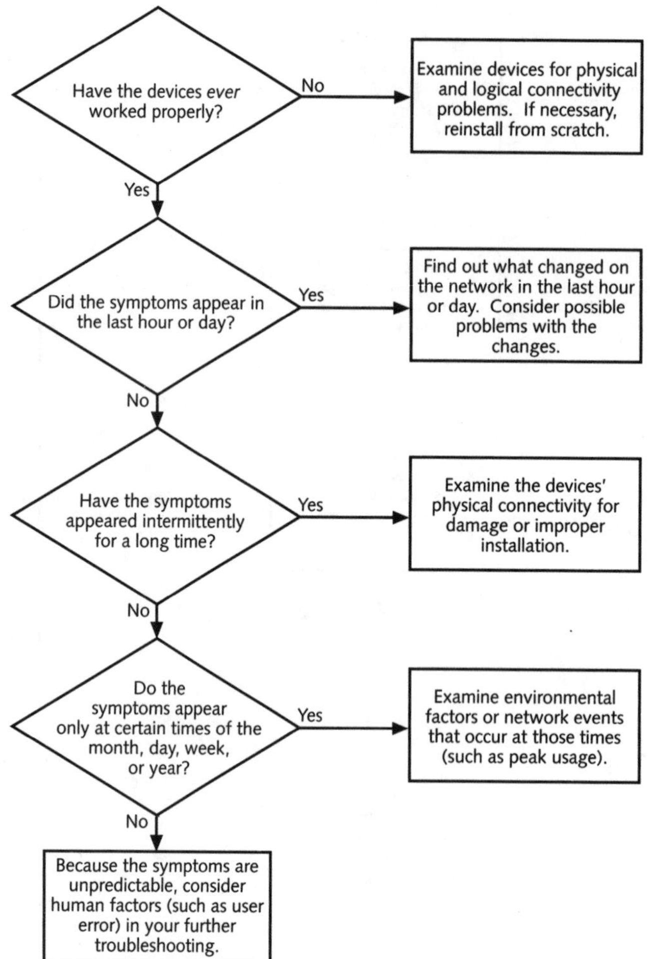

Figure 12-3 Troubleshooting while identifying the chronological scope of a problem

One fascinating example of scope-based (or chronological) troubleshooting was experienced by a wireless networking engineer working on a small metropolitan area network. His spread-spectrum RF network links, which connected businesses to a carrier's POP via a transmitter and receiver on a hospital's roof, worked perfectly all day, but failed when the sun went down each day. When the sun came up the next morning, the wireless links worked again. The engineer confirmed that the equipment was fully operational (as he suspected), then talked with the hospital personnel. The hospital's director informed him that the hospital had installed security cameras on the outside of the building. The cameras used the same RF frequency as the network's wireless links. When the security cameras were activated at sunset, their signals interfered with the wireless network's signals, preventing data from reaching their destination.

RECREATE THE PROBLEM

An excellent way to learn more about the causes of a problem is to try to recreate the symptoms yourself. If you cannot reproduce the symptoms, you may suspect that a problem was a one-time occurrence or that a user performed an operation incorrectly.

You should try to reproduce symptoms both while logged in as the user who reported the problem and while logged in under a privileged account (such as an administrator-equivalent ID). If the symptoms appear only when you're logged in under the user's ID, you may suspect that the problem relates to the user's limited rights on the network. For example, a user may complain that he was able to edit a particular spreadsheet in the Accounting directory on the file server on Friday, but was unable to open the file on Monday. When you visit his workstation, you can verify this sequence of events while logged on with his user name. When you then log in as Administrator, however, you may be able to open and edit the file. The difference in your experiences points to a user rights problem. At that point, you should check the user's privileges—especially whether they have changed since he could last retrieve the file. Perhaps someone removed him from a group that had Read and Modify rights to the Accounting directory.

Answering the following questions may help you determine whether a problem's symptoms are truly reproducible and, if so, to what extent:

- Can you make the symptoms recur every time?
- Can you make the symptoms recur some of the time?
- Do the symptoms happen only under certain circumstances? For instance, if you log in under a different ID or try the operation from a different machine, do the symptoms still appear?
- Do the symptoms *ever* happen when you try to repeat them?

When attempting to reproduce the symptoms of a problem, you should follow the same steps that the person reporting the symptoms followed. As you know, many computer functions can be achieved through different means. For example, in a word-processing program, you might save a file by using the menu bar, using a keystroke combination, or clicking a button on a toolbar. All three methods result in the same outcome. Similarly, you might log on to the network from a command prompt, from a predefined script inside a batch file, or from a window presented by the client software. If you attempt to reproduce a problem by performing different functions than those employed by the user, you may not be able to reproduce a legitimate problem and thus might assume that the symptoms resulted from user error. In fact, you may be missing a crucial clue to solving the problem.

To reproduce a symptom reliably, ask the user precisely what she did before the error appeared. For example, if a user complains that her network connection mysteriously drops when she's in the middle of surfing the Web, you should try to replicate the problem at her workstation; also, find out what else was running on the user's workstation or what kind of Web sites she was surfing.

Use good judgment when attempting to reproduce problems. In some cases, reproducing a problem could wreak havoc on the network, its data, and its devices; you should not attempt to reproduce such a problem. An obvious example involves a power outage in which your backup power source failed to supply power. After your network equipment comes back online, you would not want to try cutting the power again simply to verify that the problem derived from a faulty backup power source.

VERIFY PHYSICAL CONNECTIVITY

After you have reproduced the problem's symptoms, you should examine the most straightforward potential flaw in network communications—the physical connectivity. Physical connectivity may include the cabling from workstation or server to data jack, from data jack to punch-down block, from punch-down block to patch panel, or from patch panel to hub or switch. It may also include the proper physical installation of devices such as NICs, hubs, routers, servers, and switches. As noted earlier, you can save much time by checking the obvious first. Physical connectivity problems can be easy to spot and easy to fix.

Answering the following questions may help you identify a problem pertaining to physical connectivity:

- Is the device turned on?
- Is the NIC properly inserted?
- Is a device's network cable properly (that is, not loosely) connected to both its NIC and the wall jack?
- Do patch cables properly connect punch-down blocks to patch panels and patch panels to hubs or switches?
- Is the hub, router, or switch properly connected to the backbone?
- Are all cables in good condition (without signs of wear or damage)?
- Are all connectors (for example, RJ-45) in good condition and properly seated?
- Do network segment lengths conform to the IEEE 802 specifications?

A first step in verifying the physical integrity of a connection is to follow that connection from one endpoint on the network to the other. For example, if a workstation user cannot log in to the network, and you have verified that he is typing his password correctly, check the physical connectivity from his workstation's NIC and patch cable. Follow his connection all the way through the network to the server that he cannot reach.

Often, physical connectivity problems will be manifested as a continuous or intermittent inability to connect to the network and perform network-related functions. Physical connectivity problems do not typically (but occasionally can) result in application anomalies, the inability to use a single application, poor network performance, protocol errors, software licensing errors, or software usage errors. Some software errors, however, can point to a physical connectivity problem. For example, a user might be able to log on to his file server without problems. When he chooses to run a query on a database, however, his report software might produce an error message indicating that the database is unavailable or not found. If the database resides on a separate server, this symptom could point to a physical connectivity problem with the database server.

In addition to verifying the connections between devices, you must verify the soundness of the hardware used in those connections. A sound connection means that cables are inserted firmly in ports, NICs, and wall jacks; NICs are seated firmly in the system board; connectors are not broken; and cables are not damaged. Damaged or improperly inserted connectivity elements may result in only occasional (and therefore difficult-to-troubleshoot) errors.

For example, you might receive a call from a user who cannot log on to the network in two out of every five attempts. The user might say that she could previously log on to the network without errors and that she thinks the errors have recently become more frequent. Because the error doesn't occur every time, it is probably caused by damaged or improperly installed connectivity hardware or by a segment length that exceeds IEEE 802 specifications. Because the errors are increasing in frequency, they are probably caused by hardware that is sustaining progressively more damage and will eventually fail. Assuming no one else in this user's department is receiving similar errors, you might examine the cable connecting the user's workstation to the wall jack. Quite possibly, this cable could be damaged by a chair rolling over it.

Even if a cable does not show obvious physical damage, it may still have flaws. For example, it might have been poorly manufactured or damaged internally from age or misuse. If you suspect a flawed cable, the easiest and quickest way to test your theory may be to simply replace the cable and note whether the errors disappear. Alternatively, you could use a cable tester to verify the quality of a cable. You will learn more about cable testers later in this chapter.

Other physical components (such as NICs, hubs, or ports on any device) may also have flaws. Often, you can perform diagnostics on the device to determine whether it works correctly. For example, in Chapter 6, you learned that most NIC manufacturers ship a diagnostics program on a floppy disk with the NIC. In some cases, you may need to replace (or "swap out") a part. Later in this chapter, you will learn about the techniques and potential hazards of swapping equipment.

Finally, if symptoms seem to point to a physical connectivity problem, but you cannot find any loose or missing connections or flawed cables, the problem may relate to a network segment whose length exceeds IEEE 802 standards. Recall from Chapter 5 that the different types of networks must adhere to maximum segment lengths. For example, a 10BaseT network segment (the total amount of cabling between the connectivity device and a node) cannot exceed 100 meters. If your segment spans a greater distance, the devices at the end of the segment will experience intermittent connectivity errors or excessive transmission delays. If you have exceeded the maximum segment length, you must rearrange that segment to bring devices closer to the connectivity equipment.

The flowchart in Figure 12-4 illustrates how a logical approach to checking physical connectivity can help you solve a network problem. The steps in this flowchart apply to a typical problem: a user's inability to log in to the network. They assume that you have already ruled out user error and that you have successfully reproduced the problem under both your and the user's login IDs.

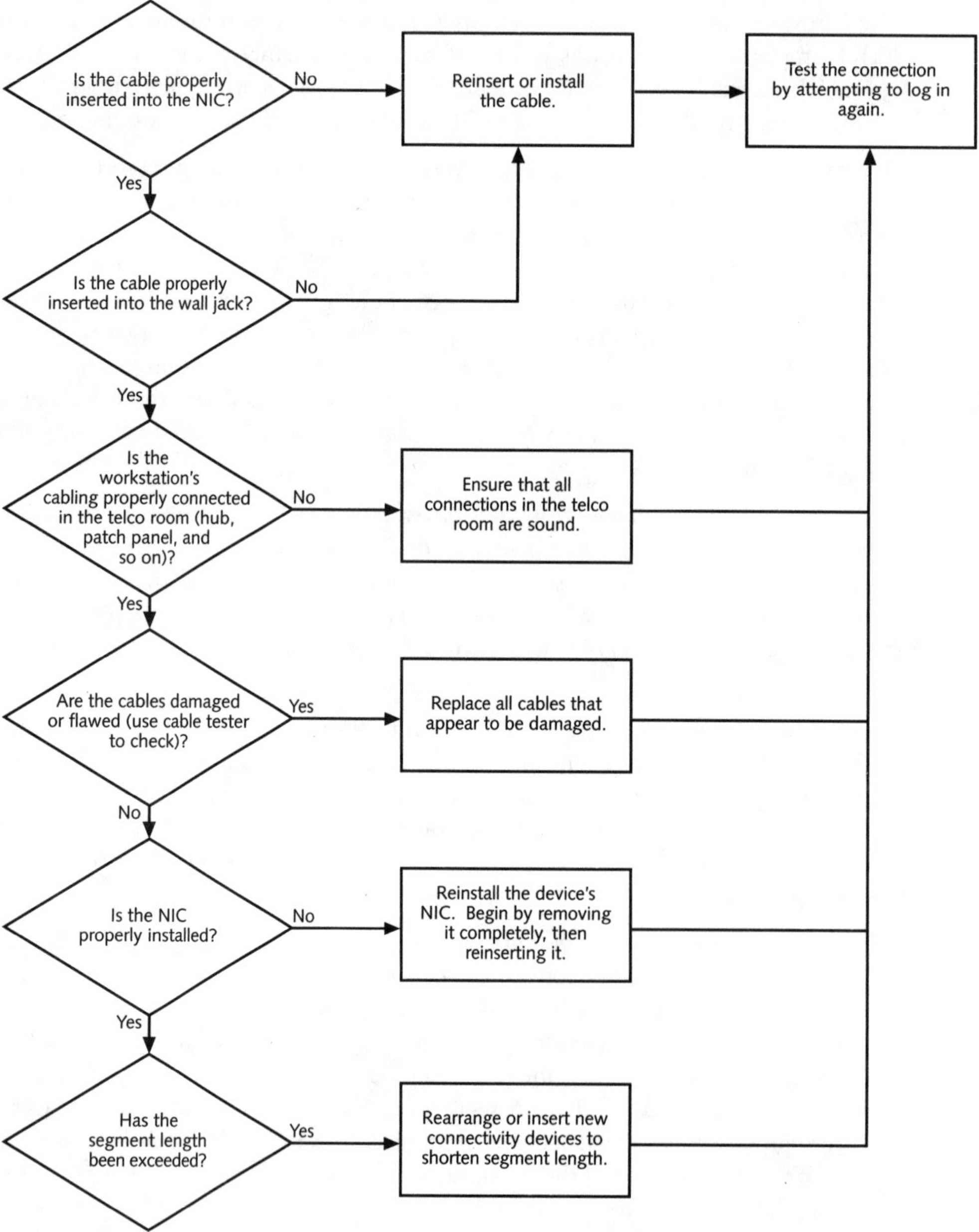

Figure 12-4 Troubleshooting while verifying physical connectivity

As noted in Figure 12-4, physical connectivity errors can frequently be traced to recent changes in the network, such as a replaced hub or a moved server. If you suspect a physical connectivity problem, you should find out whether anything on the network has changed recently. The potential effect of changes on network integrity is covered in detail later in this section. Most modern NICs have at least one LED that flashes green or orange, indicating the NIC's status. Although the meaning and number of these lights may vary according to the NIC model, typically a steady green light indicates that the NIC has successfully connected to the network. The LED will usually blink as the NIC searches for and finds a network connection. A steady blinking orange light generally means that the NIC can't make a network connection. For specific information on your NIC's LEDs, read the NIC's user manual.

VERIFY LOGICAL CONNECTIVITY

Once you have verified the physical connections, you must examine the firmware and software configurations, settings, installations, and privileges. Depending on the type of symptoms, you may need to investigate networked applications, the network operating system, or hardware configurations, such as NIC IRQ settings. All of these elements belong in the category of "logical connectivity."

Answering the following questions may help you identify a problem with logical connectivity:

- Do error messages reference damaged or missing files or device drivers?
- Do error messages reference malfunctioning or insufficient resources (such as memory)?
- Has an operating system, configuration, or application been recently changed, introduced, or deleted?
- Does the problem occur with only one application or a few, similar applications?
- Does the problem happen consistently?
- Does the problem affect a single user or one group of users?

12

Logical connectivity problems often prove more difficult to isolate and resolve than physical connectivity problems, because they can be more complex. For example, a user might complain that she has been unable to connect to the network for the last two hours. After you go to her workstation and find that you can reproduce the symptoms both under her login ID and your own ID, you check the physical connections. Everything seems to be in order. Next, you may ask the user whether anything changed on her machine approximately two hours ago. She tells you that she didn't do a thing to the machine—that it just stopped working.

At this point, you may investigate the workstation's logical connectivity. Some possible software-based causes for a failure to connect to the network include (but are not limited to) the following: resource conflicts with the NIC's configuration, an improperly configured NIC (for example, it may be set to the wrong data rate), improperly installed or configured client software, and improperly installed or configured network protocols or services. In this example, you may take another look at the client login screen and notice that the wrong server is selected as the default. Once you change the default server setting in the user's client software, she will likely be able to log in to the network.

Like many physical connectivity problems, many logical connectivity problems are created by changes to network elements. In the next section, you will learn how to trace the symptoms of a problem to a recent change in the network.

Consider Recent Changes

One could argue that considering recent network changes is not a separate step, but rather a continual and integral part of the troubleshooting process. As you begin troubleshooting, you should be aware of any changes that your network has recently undergone. Changes to the network may include—among other things—introduction of new equipment (cabling, connectivity devices, servers, and so on); repair of existing equipment; removal of equipment; installation of new components on existing equipment; installation of new services or applications on the network; equipment moves; addressing or protocol changes; software configuration changes on servers, connectivity devices, or workstations; and modifications to rights, groups, or users. As you can imagine, such a change can create problems if not planned and implemented carefully.

To ascertain what changes have occurred, you and your colleagues in the IT department should keep complete network change records. You will learn more about maintaining change records in Chapter 13. The more precisely you describe a change, its purpose, and the time and date when it occurred in your records, the easier your troubleshooting will be if the changes subsequently cause problems.

In addition to keeping thorough records, you must make them available to staff members who might need to reference them. For example, you might want to keep a record of changes in a spreadsheet file on a file server, then use a Web-based form to retrieve and submit information from and to the spreadsheet. That way, no matter where a network technician was working in the organization, she could retrieve the information from any Web-enabled workstation. Alternatively, you might keep a simple clipboard in the computer room with notes about changes.

Often, network changes cause unforeseen problems. For example, if you have narrowed down a connectivity problem to a group of six users in the Marketing department, you might refer to your network's change log and find that a hub in the Marketing department's telecommunications closet was recently moved from one end of the closet to another. Reviewing the record of this change can help you more quickly pinpoint the hub as a possible cause of the problem. Perhaps the hub was incorrectly reconnected to the backbone after the move, or perhaps it became damaged in the move or lost its configuration.

The following questions may help you pinpoint a problem that results from a network change:

- Did the operating system or configuration on a server, workstation, or connectivity device change?

- Were new components added to a server, workstation, or connectivity device?
- Were old components removed from a server, workstation, or connectivity device?
- Was a server, workstation, or connectivity device moved from its previous location to a new location?
- Was a server, workstation, or connectivity device replaced?
- Was new software installed on a server, workstation, or connectivity device?
- Was old software removed from a server, workstation, or connectivity device?

If you suspect that a network change has generated a problem, you can address the issue in two ways: you can attempt to correct the problem that resulted from the change, or you can attempt to reverse the change and restore the hardware or software to its previous state. Both options come with hazards. Of the two, reverting back to a previous state is probably less risky and less time-consuming.

Exceptions do occur, however. For example, if you immediately suspect that a change-related problem can be fixed easily, this method may be quicker than reverting back to a previous state. In some cases, it may be impossible to restore a software or hardware configuration to its previous state. In this case, you must solve the problem with the change in place. You will learn more about modifying a network and then reversing this process in Chapter 13.

Before changing a network device or configuration, be certain to develop a plan and gather the proper resources for reversing the change in case things go wrong. For example, if you replace the memory module in a server, you should keep the old memory module handy in case the new one proves to have flaws. In another situation, you might keep a backup of device or application configurations—perhaps by making a copy of the directory that stores the target configuration.

Implement a Solution

At last, after you have found the problem, you can implement a solution. This step may be a very brief process (such as correcting the default server designation in a user's client login screen) or it may take a long time (such as replacing the hard disk of a server). In either event, you should keep a record of your solution in a central location, such as a call tracking database. You will learn more about documenting problems and solutions later in this chapter.

Implementing a solution requires foresight and patience, whether it consists of merely talking a user through a change in a setting in his e-mail program or reconfiguring a router. As with the process of finding the problem, the more methodically and logically you can approach the solution, the more efficient the correction process will be. If a problem is causing catastrophic outages, however, you should expedite your solution as much as practical.

The following steps will help you implement a safe and reliable solution:

1. Collect all documentation you have about a problem's symptoms from your investigation and keep it handy while solving the problem.

2. If you are reinstalling software on a device, make a backup of the device's existing software installation. If you are changing hardware on a device, keep the old parts handy in case the solution doesn't work. If you are changing the configuration of a program or device, take the time to print out the program or device's current configuration. Even if the change seems minor, jot down notes about the original state. For example, if you intend to add a user to a privileged group to allow her to access the Accounting spreadsheets, first write down the groups to which she currently belongs.
3. Perform the change, replacement, move, or add that you believe will solve the problem. Record your actions in detail so that you can later enter the information into a database.
4. Test your solution (see the following section).
5. Before leaving the area in which you were working, clean it up. For instance, if you created a new patch cable for a telco room, remove the debris from splicing the cable.
6. If the solution fixes the problem, record the details you have collected about the symptoms, the problem, and the solution in your organization's call tracking database.
7. If your solution solved a significant change or addressed a significant problem (one that affected more than a few users), revisit the solution a day or two later to verify that the problem has, indeed, been solved and that it hasn't created additional problems.

In the next section, you will learn about one of the most important steps in the troubleshooting process—testing your solution to ensure that it has thoroughly and accurately resolved a problem.

TEST THE SOLUTION

After implementing your solution, you must test it to verify that it works properly. Obviously, the type of testing performed will depend on your solution. For example, if you replaced a patch cable between a hub port and a patch panel, a quick test of your solution would be to determine whether you can connect to the network from the device that relies on that patch cable. If the device does not successfully connect to the network, you may have to try another cable or reconsider whether the problem stems from physical or logical connectivity or some other cause.

Suppose you replaced a switch that served four different departments in an organization. To test your solution, you might not only test connectivity from each department's workstations, but also use a network analysis tool (such as those discussed later in this chapter) to verify that data is being handled correctly by the switch.

It's often a good idea to enlist the user who reported the problem in testing your solution, too. That strategy ensures that you will get an objective assessment of the results. It's possible that you may have been working on the solution so long that you've forgotten the original problem. You might also have enough technical knowledge to circumvent small problems that might flummox the average user. In addition, having the user test your solution will prevent you from leaving a device in a state that is familiar to you, but unfamiliar to the user.

For example, in the process of diagnosing a problem with a user's access to a mail directory, you may have reconfigured his mail settings to log in with your own ID and rule out the possibility of a physical connectivity error. After discovering that the problem was actually due to an IP addressing conflict, you may fix the IP addressing problem but forget that you changed the user's e-mail configuration. Having the user test your solution would reveal this oversight—and prevent you from having to return to the workstation to solve another problem.

You may not be able to test your solution immediately after implementing it. In some cases, you may have to wait days or weeks before you know for *certain* whether it worked. For example, you may have discovered that a server was sometimes running out of processor capacity when handling clients' database queries, causing users to experience unacceptably slow response times. To solve this problem, you might add two processors and reconfigure the server to use symmetric multiprocessing. The timing of the database usage may be unpredictable, however. As a result, you may not find out whether the added processors eliminated the problem until a certain number of users attempt the operations that will push the server to its peak processor usage.

A copy of all questions included in the preceding sections appear on a form in Appendix C, "Examples of Standard Networking Forms." You might want to create your own form based on these questions but tailored to your particular networking environment. Take your form along whenever you set out on a troubleshooting mission. It will help remind you of possibilities that you might otherwise forget to investigate.

PRACTICAL TROUBLESHOOTING

You will acquire much of your troubleshooting expertise through experience, a thorough understanding of your network and its idiosyncrasies, and a trial-and-error process. You can get a head start, however, by learning some practical tips and strategies for troubleshooting. These practical aspects encompass some real-world aspects of network troubleshooting that do not neatly fit into a troubleshooting methodology.

STAFF INVOLVED IN TROUBLESHOOTING

Many staff members may contribute to troubleshooting of a network problem. Often the division of duties is formalized, with a help desk acting as the first, single point of contact for users to call in regarding errors. A help desk is typically staffed with help desk analysts—people proficient in basic (but not usually advanced) workstation and network troubleshooting. Larger organizations may group their help desk analysts into teams based on their expertise. For example, a company that provides users with word-processing, spreadsheet, project planning, scheduling, and graphics software might assign different technical support personnel at the help desk to answer questions pertaining to each application.

The help desk analysts are often considered first-level support, because they provide the first level of troubleshooting. When a user calls with a problem, a help desk analyst typically creates a record for the incident and attempts to diagnose the problem. The help desk analyst may be able to solve a common problem over the phone within minutes by explaining something to the user. On other occasions, the problem may be rare or complex. In such cases, the first-level support analyst will refer the problem to a second-level support analyst. A second-level support analyst is someone who has specialized knowledge in one or more aspects of a network. For example, if a user complains that she can't connect to a server, and the first-level support person narrows the problem down to a failed file server, that first-level support analyst would then refer the problem to the second-level support person. Typically, first-level support analysts stay at the help desk while second-level support analysts are mobile.

In addition to having first- and second-level support analysts, most help desks include a help desk coordinator. The help desk coordinator ensures that analysts are divided in the correct teams, schedules shifts at the help desk, and maintains infrastructure to enable analysts to better perform their jobs.

Most organizations also have an operations manager, who supervises the help desk coordinator. This person knows less about the day-to-day activities of the help desk, but works with the help desk coordinator to determine how to improve customer service and supply analysts with the needed infrastructure. For example, the operations manager may control the budget that provides help desk analysts with office space, call tracking software, a call distribution system, and any additional resources necessary to perform their jobs.

Examples of How to Investigate Problems

The following scenarios illustrate how to narrow down the cause of a network problem. Notice that all questions do not apply in all situations. You should use common sense to decide which questions apply to a particular situation and to interpret the answers you receive. In addition to reviewing the scenarios given here, you will have more opportunities to exercise your investigative and troubleshooting skills in the Case Projects at the end of this chapter.

Scenario 1: Unable to Access the Network

Perhaps one of the most common problems you'll address as a network troubleshooter is an inability to access the network. This problem can be caused by a variety of failures (either hardware or software) and situations (for example, user error or changes in the network infrastructure). If you receive notice of the problem from a user, rather than from your automated network monitoring system or a fellow computer professional, the initial information you receive may not be very helpful. Your conversation with the user might go something like this:

USER: I can't log on to the network.

YOU: When did the problem begin?

USER: Just this morning. I came into work and I couldn't log on. I really have to get my invoices done now, because they're due to my boss by 10:00 A.M.

YOU: As far as you know, are you the only person in your area who's having this problem?

USER: I think so.

YOU: And what kind of error message do you receive when you try to log on?

USER: It says something about the network being unavailable.

YOU: Let's check to make sure your network cable hasn't accidentally been pulled out or loosened.

USER: I checked it already, and I'm sure it's all right.

YOU: Well, humor me a little. I just want to rule out any possibility of a connection problem. Sometimes the janitors accidentally jar a connection loose when they clean the floors.

USER: OK. (Checks the connections according to your guidance.) Nope, they seem to be plugged in just fine.

YOU: All right, thanks for checking. Has anything changed on your computer in the last day? For example, did you have to add any programs, or did a PC technician work on your machine?

USER: Yeah, someone was in here last night trying to get my sound card working.

YOU: Let's take a look at the configuration for the sound card . . .

By following this set of questions, you have narrowed the scope of the problem to only one workstation, verified that the physical connections work correctly, and discovered that a configuration change on the workstation might have caused the problem. At this point, you can probably assume that whoever worked on the user's sound card created a resource conflict between the sound card and the NIC, preventing the NIC from making a connection to the network. If you feel comfortable talking the user through checking the device settings, you could proceed with that approach. If not, you could visit the workstation yourself and fix the problem.

Scenario 2: A Misbehaving Network Printer

Network printers cause as many problems as network workstations (although they are usually less critical than servers). Typically, a malfunctioning network printer affects everyone who tries to use it. Although user input may prove helpful in solving network printer problems, you will probably get more information faster by checking the printer yourself. Following are some logical steps you might take to assess a network printer problem:

1. Try to narrow down the scope of the problem by determining whether everyone who normally uses the printer is having problems printing, or the inability to print is isolated to one or a few users.

2. Try to replicate the error yourself. First, try to print to the printer from your machine (which is properly connected to the network and has the printer device drivers properly installed) to discover whether the problem might derive from workstation configurations. If you receive an error, note the exact wording of the error. If you do not receive an error, the symptoms are not network-wide, and the problem may be caused by either a user error or an incorrect printer device configuration on one workstation.

3. If you cannot replicate the problem from your computer, go to the workstations that have problems and try to replicate the error from them.
4. If the error occurs on only one workstation, the problem may be caused by physical connectivity problems or logical connectivity problems with that workstation. Check that workstation's network cable and NIC, then check its printer device drivers and settings. Reinstall the device drivers if necessary.
5. If the error occurs on multiple workstations, the problem probably has to do with the printer itself. Visit the printer and verify its physical and logical connectivity. Make sure that the printer is turned on. Verify that the printer is properly connected to the network. Also, verify that the printer is ready to print—that is, it is online and has no internal errors.
6. If the printer is connected and ready to print, print a test page to view the printer's configuration. From this test page, you can determine whether the printer is connecting to the correct server, is receiving protocols correctly, and has a properly set-up network configuration (for example, if it's on an Ethernet network and using IPX/SPX, make sure it has the correct frame type setting).

This logical sequence of steps allows you to zero in on the possible causes of the problem. Once you have determined that multiple workstations are experiencing the problem, that the problem is repeatable, that the device drivers are installed correctly on every workstation, and that the printer is properly physically connected to the network, you can turn your attention to the printer's network configuration. By process of elimination, this configuration is probably the source of the fault.

Scenario 3: Unable to Connect to the Internet

If your organization depends on e-mail and other Internet-related services, such as Web databases or e-commerce, an inability to connect to the Internet can quickly hamper productivity and perhaps affect the organization's profitability. At the least, being disconnected from the Internet is an inconvenience. An inability to connect to the Internet, like many network problems, may be caused by errors at a number of different points in the system. In the following scenario, a large group of users is affected by an Internet-related problem. The following steps suggest a way to troubleshoot the problem:

1. A user calls and complains that he can't pick up his e-mail. At the same time, the other two network administrators in your department are fielding similar calls. When you finish your phone calls and compare notes, you realize that the users who called are all located in your company's Finance department.
2. You call your company's help desk and tell the first-level support analysts that the Finance department has lost Internet access. You ask the analysts to let you know whether any other departments report the same problem.
3. You attempt to reproduce the problem by trying to access the Internet from your workstation.

4. If you fail to connect to the Internet, you would use the PING utility to see whether you could contact your TCP/IP gateway.
5. In this example, let's assume that you can reach the Internet. You therefore know that the problem must be isolated to other areas of the company, which include the Finance department.
6. Still at your desk, you try pinging the Finance department's default gateway address. A positive response indicates that physical connectivity to that gateway is sound. A negative response tells you that the gateway may be physically disconnected or otherwise incapacitated.
7. If you receive a positive response from the default gateway PING, your next step is to go to a Finance department workstation and attempt to ping a host on another subnet (perhaps your own workstation, as you know that its TCP/IP resources are functional). A positive response from this test indicates that the workstation can communicate with and through the Finance department's gateway. Thus the Finance gateway may not be incapacitated, but rather something else in the network (such as cabling from the router to the backbone) may not be working.
8. In this example, let's assume that you receive a negative response from the default gateway PING, which suggests either workstation or subnet connectivity problems from that node. Your next step is to try pinging the loopback address. A positive response to the loopback PING indicates that the workstation's TCP/IP services are installed and operating properly. Thus you have narrowed the problem down to the subnet that includes the Finance department.
9. A help desk analyst pages you with a message that the Accounting and Human Resources departments are experiencing the same problems. You know that these departments are on the same subnet as Finance.

With the information you have gathered, you can conclude that the TCP/IP connectivity fault lies somewhere on the subnet that serves those three departments. You leave the Finance department and begin analyzing the network to find out whether the problem lies in the subnet's router or cabling.

SWAPPING EQUIPMENT

If you suspect a problem lies with a network component, one of the easiest ways to test your theory is to exchange that component for a functional one. In many cases, such a swap will resolve the problem very quickly, so you should consider trying this tactic early in your troubleshooting process. It won't always work, of course, but with experience you will learn what types of problems are most likely due to component failure.

For example, if a user cannot connect to the network, as in Scenario 1 in the "Examples of How to Investigate Problems" section, and even after entering the correct user ID and password still can't log in, you might consider swapping the user's network cable with a functional one. As you learned in Chapter 4, network cables must meet specific standards to operate properly. If one becomes damaged (for example, by a chair repeatedly rolling over it), it will prevent a user from connecting to the network. Swapping an old network cable with a new one is a quick test that may save you further troubleshooting.

In addition to swapping network cables, you might need to change a patch cable from one port in a hub or switch to another, or from one data jack to another. Ports and data jacks can be operational one day and faulty the next. You might also swap a NIC from one machine to another or try installing a new NIC, making sure it's precisely the same make and model as the original. It's more difficult to swap a switch or router because of the number of nodes serviced by these components and the potentially significant configuration they require; if network connectivity has failed, however, this approach may provide a quicker answer than attempting to troubleshoot the faulty device.

A better alternative to swapping parts is to have redundancy built into your network. For example, you might have a server that contains two NICs, allowing one NIC to take over for the other if one NIC should fail. If properly installed and configured, this arrangement results in no down time; in contrast, swapping parts requires at least a few minutes of service disruption. In the case of swapping a router, the down time might last for several hours.

Before swapping any network component, make sure that the replacement has exactly the same specifications as the original part. By installing a component that doesn't match the original device, you risk thwarting your troubleshooting efforts, because the new component might not work in the environment. In the worst case, you may damage existing equipment by installing a component that isn't rated for it.

Using Vendor Information

Some networking professionals pride themselves in being able to install, configure, and troubleshoot devices without reading the instructions—or at least exhausting all possibilities before they submit to reading a manual. Although some manufacturers clearly write better documentation than others, you have nothing to lose by referring to the manual, except a little time. Chances are you will find exactly what you need—jumper settings for a NIC, configuration commands and their arguments for a router, troubleshooting tips for a network operating system function.

In addition to the booklets that ship with the networking component (which are often lost in a network manager's pile of documentation and miscellaneous equipment), most network software and hardware vendors provide free online troubleshooting information. For example, both Microsoft and Novell offer searchable databases in which you can type your error message or a description of your problem and receive lists of possible solutions. Reputable equipment manufacturers, such as 3Com, Cisco, Intel, and Hewlett-Packard, also offer sophisticated Web interfaces for troubleshooting their equipment. If you cannot find the documentation for a networking component, you should try looking for information on the Web.

Bear in mind that some vendors require you to register for online support, and occasionally you may have to pay for this service. Nevertheless, most vendors provide a significant amount of information (including entire manuals) free of charge from their Web sites. Table 12-1 lists links to technical support Web sites for popular networking vendors. (Note that these URLs were verified at the time of this writing, but may change without notice.)

Table 12-1 Links for Troubleshooting Resources on the Web

Vendor	Technical Support Web Site Address
3Com	http://support.3com.com
Ascend	http://aos.ascend.com
Cisco	http://www.cisco.com/univercd/home/home.htm
Compaq/Digital	http://www.service.digital.com
Dell	http://www.dell.com/support/index.htm
Hewlett-Packard	http://www.hp.com/ghp/services.html
IBM	http://app-01.www.ibm.com/support
Intel	http://www-cs.intel.com
Microsoft	http://support.microsoft.com
Nortel/Bay	http://www.nortel.com/home/training.html
Novell	http://support.novell.com
Oracle	http://www.oracle.com/support
SMC	http://www.smc.com/Support_Index.html
Sun	http://docs.sun.com:80/ab2

Call the vendor's technical support phone number only after you have read the manual and searched the vendor's Web page. In some cases, you may wait a long time before getting an answer when you call. With some manufacturers, you can talk to a technical support agent only if you have established and paid for a support agreement. With others, you must pay per phone call. Each vendor has a different pricing structure for technical support, so before you agree to pay for technical support, you should find out whether the vendor charges on a per-hour or per-problem basis.

Keep a list handy (preferably online, either on a Web page or in a shared file on the network) of the hardware and software vendors for your networking equipment; the list should include not only the company's name, but also its technical support phone number, a contact name (if available), its technical support Web site address, policies for technical support, and the type of agreement you currently have with the vendor. You can find an example of such a form in Appendix C, "Examples of Standard Networking Forms." Make sure the list is updated regularly and available to all Information Services personnel who might need it.

TROUBLESHOOTING FOLLOW-UP

After fixing a problem on your network, you should take steps to communicate your solution to your colleagues and to prevent further problems. This section outlines some procedures that will decrease your likelihood of wrestling with the same problem twice—or at least decrease the time you spend troubleshooting it.

Document Problems and Solutions

Whether you are a one-person network support team or one of a hundred network technicians at your organization, you should always write down the symptoms of a problem and your solution for it. Given the volume of problems you and other analysts will troubleshoot, it will be impossible to remember the circumstances of each incident. In addition, networking personnel frequently change jobs, and everyone will appreciate clear, thorough documentation. An optimal way of documenting problems and solutions is in a centrally located database to which all networking personnel have online access.

Some organizations use a software program for documenting problems, known as a **call tracking system** (also informally known as help desk software). Examples of popular call tracking systems include Clientele, Expert Advisor, Professional Help Desk, Remedy, and Vantive. These programs provide user-friendly graphical interfaces that prompt the user for every piece of information associated with the problem. They assign unique identifying numbers to each problem, in addition to identifying the caller, the nature of the problem, the time necessary to resolve it, and the nature of the resolution.

Most call tracking systems are highly customizable, so you can tailor the form fields to your particular computing environment. For example, if you work for an oil refinery, you might add fields for identifying problems with the plant's flow-control software. In addition, most call tracking systems allow you to type in free-form text explanations of problems and solutions. Some also offer Web-based interfaces.

If your organization does not have a call tracking system, you should at least keep records in a simple electronic form. You can find an example of a network problem record in Appendix C, "Examples of Standard Networking Forms." A typical problem record form should include at least the following fields:

- The originator's (the person who first noticed the problem) name, department, and phone number
- Information regarding whether the problem is software- or hardware-related
- If the problem is software-related, the package to which it pertains; if the problem is hardware-related, the device or component to which it pertains
- Symptoms of the problem, including when it was first noticed
- The name and telephone number of the network support contact
- The amount of time spent troubleshooting the problem
- The resolution of the problem

As discussed earlier in this chapter, many organizations operate a help desk staffed with personnel who have only basic troubleshooting expertise and who record problems called in by users. To effectively field network questions, an organization's help desk staff must maintain current and accurate records for network support personnel. Your department should take responsibility for managing a supported services list that help desk personnel can use as a reference. A **supported services list** is a document (preferably online) that lists every service and software package supported within an organization, plus the names of first- and second-level support contacts for those services or software packages. Anything else you or your department can do to increase communication and availability of support information will expedite troubleshooting.

In addition to communicating problems and solutions with your peers whenever you work on a network problem, you should follow up with the user who reported the problem. Make sure that the client understands how or why the problem occurred, what you did to resolve the problem, and who to contact should the problem recur. This type of education will not only help your clients make better decisions about the type of support or training they need, but will also improve their understanding of and respect for your department.

Notify Others of Changes

After solving a particularly thorny network problem, you should not only record its resolution in your call tracking system, but also notify others of your solution and what, if anything, you needed to change to fix the problem. This communication serves two purposes: (1) it alerts others about the problem and its solution, and (2) it notifies others of network changes you made, in case they affect other services.

The importance of recording changes cannot be overemphasized. Imagine that you are the network manager for a group of 5 network technicians who support a WAN consisting of 3 different offices and 150 users. One day the company's CEO travels from headquarters to a branch office for a meeting with an important client. At the branch office, she needs to print out a financial statement, but encounters a printing problem. Your network technician discovers that her login ID does not have rights to that office's printer, because users on your WAN do not have rights to printers outside the office to which they belong. The network technician quickly takes care of the problem by granting all users rights to all printers across the WAN. What are the implications of this change? If your technician tells no one about this change, at best users may incorrectly print to a printer in Duluth from the St. Paul office. In a worst-case scenario, a "guest" user account may gain rights to a networked printer, potentially creating a security hole in your network.

Large organizations often implement change management systems to methodically track changes on the network. A **change management system** is a process or program that provides support personnel with a centralized means of documenting changes to the network. In smaller organizations, a change management system may be as simple as one document on the network to which networking personnel continually add entries to mark their changes. In larger organizations, it may consist of a database package complete with graphical interfaces and customizable fields tailored to the computing environment. Whatever form your change management system takes, the most important element is participation. If networking personnel do not record their changes, even the most sophisticated software is useless.

The types of changes that network personnel should record in a change management system include the following:

- Adding or upgrading software on network servers or other devices
- Adding or upgrading hardware components on network servers or other devices
- Adding new hardware on the network (for example, a new server)
- Changing the network properties of a network device (for example, changing the IP address or NetBIOS name of a server)
- Increasing or decreasing rights for a group of users
- Physically moving networked devices
- Moving user IDs and their files/directories from one server to another
- Making changes in processes (for example, a new backup schedule or a new contact for DNS support)
- Making changes in vendor policies or relationships (for example, a new hard disk supplier)

It is not necessary to record minor modifications, such as changing a user's password, creating a new group for users, creating new directories, or changing a network drive mapping for a user. Each organization will have unique requirements for its change management system, and analysts who record change information should clearly understand these requirements.

Preventing Future Problems

If you review the list of questions and the troubleshooting scenarios given at the beginning of this chapter, you can predict how some network problems can be averted by network maintenance, documentation, security, or upgrades. Although not all network problems are preventable, many can be avoided. Just as with your body's health, the best prescription for network health is prevention.

For example, to avoid problems with users' access levels to network resources, you can comprehensively assess users' needs, set policies for groups, use a variety of groups, and communicate to others who support the network why those groups exist. To prevent overutilization of network segments, you should perform regular network health checks—perhaps even continual network monitoring—and ensure that you have the means to either redesign the network to distribute traffic or purchase additional bandwidth well before utilization reaches critical levels. With experience, you will be able to add more suggestions for network problem prevention. When planning or upgrading a network, you should consciously think about how good network designs and policies can prevent later problems—not to mention, make your job easier and more fun.

TROUBLESHOOTING TOOLS

So far, this chapter has focused on the easiest, quickest, and most practical ways of troubleshooting network problems. In the real world, however, these common sense techniques may lead nowhere or take too much time. In some cases, the most efficient approach is to use a tool specifically designed to analyze and isolate network problems. Several such tools are available, ranging from simple cable testers that indicate whether a cable is faulty, to sophisticated protocol analyzers that capture and interpret all types of data traveling over the network. The type of tool you choose will depend on the particular problem you need to investigate and the characteristics of your network.

The following sections describe a variety of network troubleshooting tools, their functions, and their relative costs. In the Hands-On Projects at the end of this chapter, you will have the opportunity to try some of these network troubleshooting tools.

CABLE TESTING TOOLS

Cable testing tools are essential for both cable installers and network troubleshooters. Symptoms of cabling problems can be as elusive as occasional lost packets or as obvious as a break in network connectivity. By some estimates, more than 50% of all network problems derive from defective or improper wiring. You can easily test cables for faults with specialized tools. This section describes two categories of cable testing tools: cable checkers, which perform a simple pass/fail test on a cable, and cable testers, which perform more sophisticated tests, such as measuring the signal loss along the length of the cable.

Cable Checkers

Basic **cable checkers** simply determine whether your cabling can provide connectivity. To accomplish this task, they apply a small voltage to each conductor at one end of the cable, then check whether that voltage is detectable at the other end. They may also check whether voltage cannot be detected on other conductors in the cable. Figure 12-5 depicts a typical simple cable checker.

Most cable checkers provide a series of lights that signal pass/fail. Some also indicate a cable pass/fail with an audible tone. A pass/fail test provides a simple indicator of whether a component can perform its stated function.

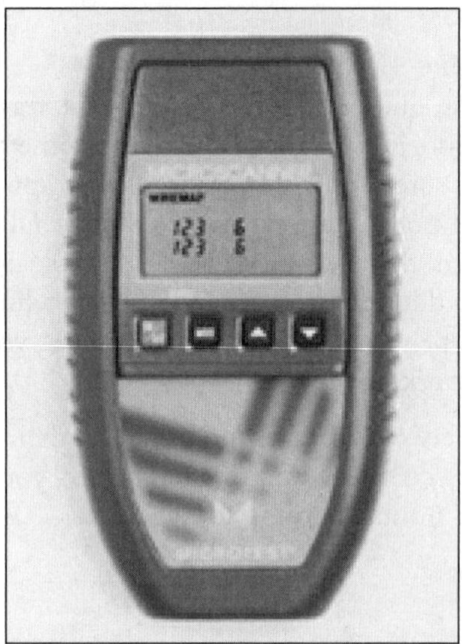

Figure 12-5 A basic cable checker

In addition to checking cable continuity, a good cable checker will verify that the wires are paired correctly and that they are not shorted, exposed, or crossed. Recall from Chapter 4 that different network models use specific wire pairings and follow cabling standards set forth in TIA-568. Make sure that the cable checker you purchase can test the type of network you use—for example, 10BaseT Ethernet, Ethernet 100BaseTX, or Token Ring.

When you make your own cables, it is especially important to verify their integrity with at least a cable checker (better yet, a cable tester). Even if you purchase cabling from a reputable vendor, you should make sure that it meets your network's required standards. Just because a cable is labeled "CAT5" does not necessarily mean that it will live up to that standard. Testing cabling before installing it may save many hours of troubleshooting after the network is in place.

Cable checkers cannot test the continuity of fiber-optic cabling, because fiber cable uses light rather than voltage to transmit data. To test fiber-optic cabling, you need a specialized fiber cable tester.

Do not use a cable checker on a live network cable. Disconnect the cable from the network, then test its continuity.

For convenience, most cable checkers are portable and lightweight and typically use one 9-volt battery. A basic cable checker will cost between $100 and $300, but it may save many hours of work. Popular cable checker manufacturers include Belkin, Fluke, Microtest, and Paladin.

Cable Testers

The difference between cable checkers and cable testers lies in their sophistication and price. A **cable tester** performs the same continuity and fault tests as a cable checker, but also provides the following functions:

- Ensures that the cable is not too long
- Measures the distance to a cable fault
- Measures attenuation along a cable
- Measures near-end crosstalk between wires
- Measures termination resistance and impedance for Thinnet cabling
- Issues pass/fail ratings for CAT3, CAT5, CAT6, or even CAT7 standards
- Stores and prints cable testing results

Some cable testers may provide even more features—for example, a graphical output depicting a cable's attenuation and crosstalk characteristics over the length of the cable. Because of their sophistication, cable testers cost significantly more than cable checkers. A high-end unit may cost from $5000 to $8000, and a low-end unit may cost between $1000 and $4000. Popular cable tester manufacturers include Fluke and Microtest. Figure 12-6 shows an example of a high-end cable tester.

When choosing a cable tester for twisted-pair networks, make sure to purchase one that performs attenuation and crosstalk testing for the frequency range used by your network. For example, if you want to test a 100BaseT Ethernet network, purchase a cable tester capable of testing up to 100 MHz.

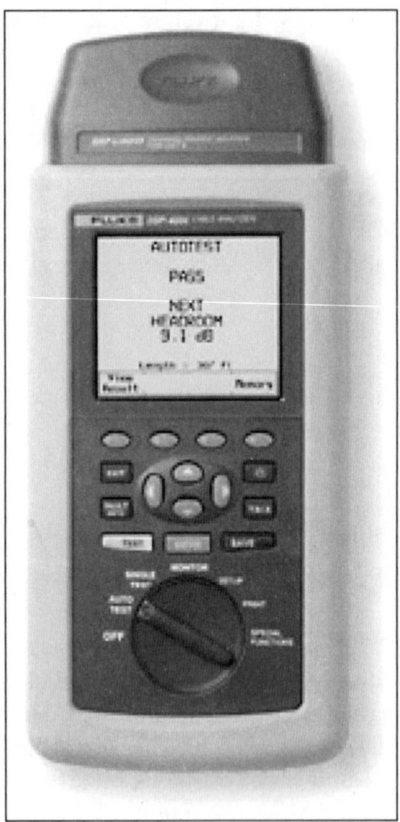

Figure 12-6 A high-end cable tester

To better appreciate how many problems a good cable tester can diagnose, recall from Chapter 4 that network segments must adhere to strict length limits to ensure that data reach their destinations on time and error-free. If one room of workstations continually experiences intermittent problems logging in to the network or very slow connections, you could use a cable tester to discover whether those workstations are situated beyond their maximum distance from the network hub. If another group of workstations frequently experiences slow responses from the network, a cable tester might reveal the presence of too many stations between the sending and receiving nodes, which causes excessive signal attenuation.

Another significant factor in data transmission is near-end crosstalk. Recall from Chapter 4 that crosstalk occurs when the signals on one wire interfere with signals on an adjacent wire. The result is interference, much in the same way that the voices from two conversations in a loud room interfere with each other and prevent listeners from understanding the words. Crosstalk often arises when wires are crushed or crossed at the connector end of a cable. For this reason, you can accurately test for crosstalk only after installation of a cable, and you should perform the test at both ends of the wire.

NETWORK MONITORS AND ANALYZERS

As noted earlier, once you have ruled out user error and physical connectivity problems (including faulty cabling) in your troubleshooting, a more in-depth analysis of the network may be necessary. Tools that enable you to analyze network traffic include network monitors and network analyzers. Both capture and interpret data on the network.

A **network monitor** is usually a software-based tool that continually monitors traffic on the network from a server or workstation attached to the network. Network monitors typically can interpret up to Layer 3 of the OSI Model. They can determine the protocols passed by each packet, but can't interpret the data inside the packet.

A **network analyzer** is a portable, hardware-based tool that a network manager connects to the network expressly to determine the nature of network problems. Network analyzers can typically interpret data up to Layer 7 of the OSI Model. For example, they can identify that a packet uses TCP/IP and, more specifically, that it is an ARP request from one particular workstation to a server. Analyzers can also interpret the payload portion of packets, translating from binary or hexadecimal code to human-readable form. As a result, network analyzers can capture passwords going over the network, if their transmission is not encrypted. Some network analyzer software packages can run on a standard PC, but others require PCs equipped with special NICs and operating system software.

Network monitoring tools are generally less expensive than network analyzers and may be included in your network operating system software. In the following sections, you will learn about two tools that can be part of your network operating system: Microsoft's Network Monitor (which ships with Windows NT Server version 4.0) and Novell's LANalyzer agent (which is bundled with Novell's ManageWise software package). These packages actually blur the distinction between network monitors and network analyzers, because they provide some of the same functionality as high-end protocol analyzers. In addition, you will learn about network analyzers, such as Network Associates' NetXRay, and sniffer products. Once you have worked with one network monitoring or analyzing tool, you will find that other products work in much the same way. Most even use very similar graphical interfaces.

12

To take advantage of software-based network monitoring and analyzing tools, the NIC installed in your machine must support promiscuous mode. In **promiscuous mode,** a device driver directs the network adapter card to pick up all frames that pass over the network—not just those destined for the node served by the card. You can determine whether your NIC supports promiscuous mode by reading its manual or checking with the manufacturer. Some network monitoring software vendors may even suggest which NICs to use with their software.

Before adopting a network monitor or analyzer, you should be familiar with some of the data errors that these tools can distinguish. The following list defines some commonly used terms for abnormal data patterns and packets, along with their characteristics:

- **Local collisions**—Collisions that occur when two or more stations are transmitting simultaneously. Excessively high collision rates within the network usually result from cable or routing problems.

- **Late collisions**—Collisions that take place outside the window of time in which they would normally be detected by the network and redressed. Late collisions are usually caused by one of two problems: (1) a defective station (for example, a card or transceiver) that is transmitting without first verifying line status, or (2) failure to observe the configuration guidelines for cable length, which results in collisions being recognized too late.
- **Runts**—Packets that are smaller than the medium's minimum packet size. For instance, any Ethernet packet that is smaller than 64 bytes is considered a runt.
- **Giants**—Packets that exceed the medium's maximum packet size. For example, any Ethernet packet that is larger than 1518 bytes is considered a giant.
- **Jabber**—A device that handles electrical signals improperly, usually affecting the rest of the network. A network analyzer will detect a jabber as a device that is always retransmitting, effectively bringing the network to a halt. A jabber usually results from a bad NIC. Occasionally, it can be caused by outside electrical interference.
- **Negative frame sequence checks**—The result of the Cyclic Redundancy Checksum (CRC) generated by the originating node not matching the checksum calculated from the data received. It usually indicates noise or transmission problems on the LAN interface or cabling. A high number of negative CRCs usually results from excessive collisions or a station transmitting bad data.
- **Ghosts**—Frames that are not actually data frames, but aberrations caused by a repeater misinterpreting stray voltage on the wire. Unlike true data frames, ghosts have no starting delimiter.

Microsoft's Network Monitor (NetMon)

Network Monitor (NetMon) is a software-based network monitoring tool that comes with Windows NT Server 4.0 or Microsoft's Systems Management Server (SMS) suite of tools (for earlier versions of Windows NT Server). It offers the following capabilities:

- Capturing network data traveling from one or many segments
- Capturing frames sent by or to a specified node
- Reproducing network conditions by transmitting a selected amount and type of data
- Detecting any other running copies of NetMon on the network (depending on the placement and configuration of routers)
- Generating statistics about network activity

Probably NetMon's most useful capability is capturing data as it travels across the network. As with hardware-based network analyzers, you can instruct NetMon to pay attention to the network for a period of time and to capture all data that travel across the particular segment. (Because NetMon takes advantage of promiscuous mode, it captures all data—not just data to or from the NetMon console.)

How can capturing data help you solve a problem? Imagine that traffic on a segment of the network you administer suddenly grinds to a halt one morning at about 8:00. You no sooner step in the door than everyone from the help desk calls to tell you how slowly the network is running. Nothing has changed on the network since last night, when it ran normally, so you can think of no obvious reasons for problems. You suspect a faulty NIC on one workstation is using network bandwidth by continually transmitting bad packets.

At the workstation where you have previously installed NetMon, you capture all data transmissions for approximately five minutes. You can then sort out the erroneous frames in NetMon, arranging the nodes in order based on how many bad packets each has generated. If your suspicion is correct, the workstation at the top of the list will be the culprit, generating significantly more bad data transmissions than any other node.

Novell's LANalyzer

Novell provides a network monitoring tool that is similar to Microsoft's Network Monitor, called the **LANalyzer** agent. It can act as a standalone program on a Windows 95 or Windows 98 workstation or as part of the ManageWise suite of network management tools on a NetWare server. LANalyzer performs the following functions:

- Initially discovering all network nodes on a segment
- Continuously monitoring network traffic
- Tripping alarms when traffic conditions meet preconfigured thresholds (for example, if utilization exceeds 70%)
- Capturing traffic to and from all or selected nodes

Like Network Monitor, LANalyzer enables you to capture traffic, identify data errors by node, and generate traffic statistics by segment. In addition, as part of the ManageWise suite, the LANalyzer agent can poll the network to find all nodes on a particular segment. It can use this data to build a network management system that can gather more than simple traffic information—for example, discovering how many times a user has logged in at a certain workstation or noting what kind of programs a workstation typically requests from the server.

LANalyzer can also provide real-time network statistics and send alert messages and/or sound alarms when network thresholds are reached. For example, to make sure that average network traffic never exceeds 50% of your network's capacity, you could configure LANalyzer to warn you when the average reaches 49%. If this warning occurs frequently on one segment of your network, you can take steps to redistribute the traffic or reinforce your network's capacity. Note that an average utilization means that LANalyzer would have to measure a 49% reading more than a single time; a single reading represents a **spike**. You can also customize the sensitivity of the triggers.

Network Analyzers

In addition to using the software that comes with the network operating system, you can purchase network analyzing software from vendors that specialize in products for network management. One popular example is Network Associates' **NetXRay**, network analyzer software that provides data capture and analysis, node discovery, traffic trending, history, alarm tripping, and utilization prediction. Essentially, NetXRay has the same features as Network Monitor and LANalyzer, plus a few extras. It can also generate traffic in an attempt to reproduce a network problem and monitor multiple network segments simultaneously. Its graphical interface makes this product very easy to use, readily revealing the traffic flow across the network. In addition, NetXRay supports a multitude of protocols and network topologies. Figure 12-7 depicts a NetXRay traffic map, which shows in real time which nodes are conversing on the network.

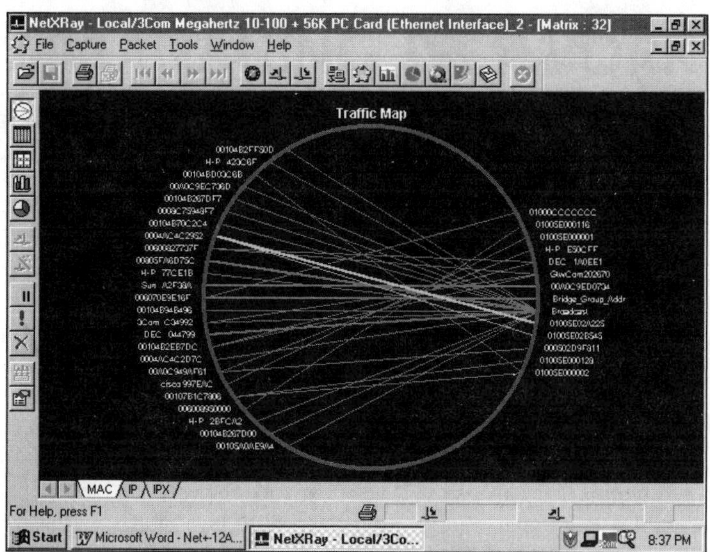

Figure 12-7 A NETXRay traffic map

One advantage to using a network monitor or analyzer that is not part of the network operating system relates to mobility. With NetXRay installed on your laptop, for instance, you can roam from one network segment to another, analyzing traffic without having to install multiple network monitoring consoles. Hardware-based network analyzers, such as the sniffers discussed below, also offer the advantage of mobility.

Network Associates has also led the way in developing hardware-based network analyzers, known as sniffers. **Sniffers** are usually regular laptops equipped with a special NIC and network analysis software. The sole job of a sniffer is to analyze network problems. Unlike laptops that may have a network monitoring tool installed, sniffers typically cannot be used for other purposes, because they don't depend on an operating system such as Windows. They have their own, proprietary operating system (developed by Network Associates, for example). Because they do not rely on a desktop operating system such as Windows, hardware-based network analyzers have an advantage over network monitoring software. As they do not rely on Windows device drivers (for the NIC), for example, they can capture information that the NIC would automatically discard, such as runt packets.

Sniffers offer a great deal of versatility in the type and depth of information they can reveal. The danger in using this type of tool is that it may collect more information than you or the machine can reasonably process, thus rendering your exercise futile. To avoid this problem, you should set filters on the data gathered. For example, if you suspect that a certain workstation is causing a traffic problem, you should filter the data collection to accept only packets to or from that workstation's MAC address. If you suspect that you have a gateway-related TCP/IP problem, you would set a filter to capture only TCP/IP packets and to ignore other protocols from the gateway's MAC address.

Sniffers are complex and powerful tools. To learn more about using them, you may want to take a class, such as those offered by Network Associates through its Sniffer University program.

Sniffers are tailored to a particular type of network. For example, one sniffer may be able to analyze both Ethernet and Token Ring networks, but another sniffer may be necessary to analyze fiber or ATM networks. A sniffer represents a significant investment, with costs ranging from $10,000 to $30,000.

Recall from Chapter 6 that using a switch logically separates a network into several segments. If a network is fully switched (that is, if every node is connected to its own switch port), your network analyzer can capture only broadcast packets and packets destined for the node on which you're running the software, because those packets are the only ones that will travel through a switched environment. The increasing use of switches has made network monitoring more difficult, but not impossible. One solution to this problem is to reconfigure the switch to reroute the traffic so that your network analyzer can pick up all traffic. Obviously, you would want to weigh the disruptive effects of this reconfiguration against the potential benefits from being able to analyze the network traffic and solve a problem.

CHAPTER SUMMARY

- Before you can resolve a network problem, you need to ascertain its cause. The key to solving network problems is to approach them methodically and logically, using your experience to inform your decisions and knowing when to ask for someone else's help.
- When assessing a network problem, act like a doctor diagnosing a patient. First, ask a series of standard questions in a logical order to ascertain the problem's symptoms. Never ignore the obvious! Although some questions may sound too simple to bother asking, don't discount them.
- Early in the troubleshooting process, you should ensure that the user is performing all functions correctly. It's easy for a user to make mistakes and assume that something is wrong with the network.
- After ruling out user error, you should identify the scope of the problem. In general, a network problem may be limited by the number of users, departments, or areas it affects or by what times of day or week it occurs.
- Once you have determined the scope of the problem, attempt to reproduce the problem's symptoms. If possible, go to the location where the problem is occurring and try to repeat the steps precisely. Note also whether a problem is repeatable only under specific circumstances.
- After ensuring that the problem is reproducible, check whether the affected device(s) have sound connections to the network, from workstation to backbone. Physical connectivity may be impaired by poorly or incorrectly installed cabling, NICs, or connectivity devices; flawed or damaged components; or excessive segment length.

- If you find no physical connectivity problems, determine whether the affected device(s) have properly configured software, including applications, hardware configurations, operating system software, and client software.
- At each point in the troubleshooting process, stop to consider what kind of changes have occurred on the network that might have created a problem. Changes pertaining to hardware may include the addition of a new device, the removal of an old device, a component upgrade, a cabling upgrade, or an equipment move. Changes pertaining to software may include an operating system upgrade, device driver upgrade, new application, or changed configuration.
- Only after undertaking the previous steps, should you implement your solution. If this solution involves a change to hardware or software, make sure to have a plan and the necessary resources for reversing the change if necessary. Also, make sure to document your solution and record it in a call tracking system along with the problem and its symptoms.
- After implementing your solution, you must test it to ensure that it works correctly. The type of testing you perform will depend on your solution. Enlist the help of users to test the solution. If the solution required significant network changes, revisit the solution a day or two after you implement it to verify that it has truly worked and not caused additional problems.
- Most organizations operate a help desk staffed with first-level support personnel who field user questions, perform initial problem diagnosis, and record problems in a call tracking database. Help desks also use second-level support personnel, who are experts in some aspect in a specific area of computing. In addition, help desk coordinators maintain help desk schedules and ensure that help desk staff members have the resources necessary to perform their jobs. An operations manager typically supervises the help desk coordinator and approves the help desk's budget.
- If you suspect a problem lies with a network component, one of the easiest ways to test your theory is to exchange that component for a functional one. In many cases, this tactic will resolve the problem very quickly, so you should consider trying it early in your troubleshooting process.
- Before swapping any network component, make sure that the replacement has exactly the same specifications as the original part. By installing a component that doesn't match the original device, you risk thwarting your troubleshooting efforts, because the new component might not work in the environment. In the worst case, you may damage existing equipment by installing a component that isn't rated for it.
- Although some manufacturers clearly write better documentation than others, you have nothing to lose by referring to the manual. Chances are you will find exactly what you need—jumper settings for a NIC, configuration commands and their arguments for a router, troubleshooting tips for a network operating system function. In addition to the booklets that ship with the networking component, most network software and hardware vendors provide free online troubleshooting information.

- Keep a list (preferably online, either on a Web page or in a shared file on the network) of the hardware and software vendors for your networking equipment. This list should include not only the company's name, but also its technical support phone number, a contact name (if available), its technical support Web site address, its policies for technical support, and the type of agreement that you currently have with the vendor.
- Call the vendor's technical support phone number only after you have read the manual and searched the vendor's Web page. In some cases, you may wait a long time before getting an answer when you call. With some manufacturers, you can talk to a technical support agent only if you have established and paid for a support agreement. With others, you must pay per phone call.
- Some organizations use a software program for documenting problems, known as a call tracking system (informally known as help desk software). These programs provide a user-friendly graphical interface that prompts the user for every piece of information associated with the problem.
- Whether you use a formal call tracking system or a simple form, you should record the following details about a problem: the originator's (the person who first noticed the problem) name, department, and phone number; information regarding whether the problem is software- or hardware-related; if the problem is software-related, the package to which it pertains; if the problem is hardware-related, the device or component to which it pertains; symptoms of the problem, including when it was first noticed; the name and telephone number of the network support contact; the amount of time spent troubleshooting the problem; and the resolution of the problem.
- Your department should maintain a supported services list that help desk personnel can use as a reference. A supported services list is a document (preferably online) that lists every service and software package supported within an organization, plus the names of first- and second-level support contacts for those services or software packages.
- In addition to communicating problems and solutions to your peers whenever you work on a network problem, you should follow up with the person who reported the problem. Make sure that the client understands how or why the problem occurred, what you did to resolve the problem, and who to contact should it recur.
- Organizations often implement change management systems to methodically track changes on the network. A change management system is a process or program that provides support personnel with a centralized means of documenting changes to the network. In smaller organizations, a change management system may be as simple as a document to which networking personnel continually add entries to mark their changes; in large organizations, it may be an enterprise-wide software package.
- Network personnel should record the following types of changes in a change management system: adding or upgrading software on network servers or other devices; adding or upgrading hardware components on network servers or other devices; adding new hardware on the network (for example, a new server); changing the network properties of a network device (for example, changing the IP address or NetBIOS name of a server); increasing or decreasing rights for a group of users; physically moving networked devices; moving user IDs and their files/directories from one server to another; making

changes in processes (for example, a new backup schedule or a new contact for DNS support); and making changes in vendor policies or relationships (for example, a new hard disk supplier).

- Although not all network problems are preventable, many can be avoided. Just as with your body's health, the best prescription for network health is prevention. When planning or upgrading a network, you should consciously think about how good network designs and policies can prevent later problems—not to mention, make your job easier and more fun.
- Basic cable checkers determine whether your cabling can provide connectivity. To accomplish this task, they apply a small voltage to each conductor at one end of the cable, then check whether that voltage is detectable at the other end. They may also verify that voltage cannot be detected on other conductors in the cable. In addition to checking cable continuity, a good cable checker will verify that the wires are paired correctly and that they are not shorted, exposed, or crossed.
- For convenience, most cable checkers are portable and lightweight and typically use one 9-volt battery. A basic cable checker costs between $100 and $300, but may save several hours of work.
- A cable tester performs the same continuity and fault tests as a cable checker, but also ensures that the cable length is not too long, measures the distance to a cable fault, measures attenuation along a cable, measures near-end crosstalk between wires, measures termination resistance and impedance for Thinnet cabling, issues pass/fail ratings for CAT3, CAT5, CAT6, or even CAT7 standards, and stores and prints cable testing results. Some cable testers provide even more features—for example, a graphical output depicting a cable's attenuation and crosstalk characteristics over the length of the cable.
- Because of their sophistication, cable testers cost significantly more than cable checkers. A high-end unit may cost from $5000 to $8000, and a low-end unit may cost between $1000 and $4000.
- A network monitor is usually a software-based tool that continually monitors traffic on the network from a server or workstation attached to the network. Network monitors typically can interpret up to Layer 3 of the OSI Model. They can determine the protocols passed by each packet, but can't interpret the data inside the packet.
- A network analyzer is a portable, hardware-based tool that a network manager connects to the network expressly to determine the nature of network problems. Network analyzers can typically interpret data up to Layer 7 of the OSI Model. They can also interpret the payload portion of packets, translating from binary or hexadecimal code to human-readable form.
- Before adopting a network monitor or analyzer, you should be familiar with some of the data errors that these tools can distinguish, such as runts, late collisions, jabber, and negative frame sequence checks.
- To take advantage of software-based network monitoring and analyzing tools, the NIC installed in your machine must support promiscuous mode. Promiscuous mode means that a device driver directs the network adapter card to pick up all frames that pass over the network—not just those destined for the node served by the card.

- Microsoft's Network Monitor (NetMon) is a software-based network monitoring tool that comes with Windows NT Server 4.0 or with Microsoft's Server Management System (SMS) suite of tools (for earlier versions of Windows NT Server).
- Novell provides a similar network monitoring tool to Network Monitor, called the LANalyzer agent. It can act as a standalone program on a Windows 95 or Windows 98 workstation or as part of the ManageWise suite of network management tools on a NetWare server. Like Network Monitor, LANalyzer can capture traffic, identify data errors by node, and generate traffic statistics by segment. In addition, as part of the ManageWise suite, it can poll the network to find all nodes located on a particular segment.
- In addition to using software that comes with the network operating system, you may choose to purchase network analyzing software from vendors that specialize in products for network management. One popular example is Network Associates' NetXRay, network analyzer software that provides data capture and analysis, node discovery, traffic trending, history, alarm tripping, and utilization prediction. Essentially, NetXRay has the same features as Network Monitor and LANalyzer, plus a few extras.
- Network Associates has also led the way in hardware-based network analyzers, known as sniffers. Sniffers are usually regular laptops equipped with a special NIC and network analysis software and dedicated to network analysis. Unlike laptops that may have a network monitoring tool installed, they typically cannot be used for other purposes, because they don't depend on an operating system such as Windows.
- Sniffers are tailored to a particular type of network. For example, one sniffer may be able to analyze both Ethernet and Token Ring networks, but another sniffer may be necessary to analyze fiber or ATM networks. The cost of sniffers can range from $10,000 to $30,000.

KEY TERMS

- **cable checker** — A simple handheld device that determines whether cabling can provide connectivity. To accomplish this task, a cable checker applies a small voltage to each conductor at one end of the cable, then checks whether that voltage is detectable at the other end. It may also verify that voltage cannot be detected on other conductors in the cable.
- **cable tester** — A handheld device that not only checks for cable continuity, but also ensures that the cable length is not excessive, measures the distance to a cable fault, measures attenuation along a cable, measures near-end crosstalk between wires, measures termination resistance and impedance for Thinnet cabling, issues pass/fail ratings for wiring standards, and stores and prints cable testing results.
- **call tracking system** — A software program used to document problems (also known as *help desk software*). Examples of popular call tracking systems include Clientele, Expert Advisor, Professional Help Desk, Remedy, and Vantive.
- **change management system** — A process or program that provides support personnel with a centralized means of documenting changes to the network. In smaller organizations, a change management system may be as simple as one document on the network

to which networking personnel continually add entries to mark their changes. In larger organizations, it may consist of a database package complete with graphical interfaces and customizable fields tailored to the particular computing environment.

- **ghosts** — Frames that are not actually data frames, but rather aberrations caused by a repeater misinterpreting stray voltage on the wire. Unlike true data frames, ghosts have no starting delimiter.
- **giants** — Packets that exceed the medium's maximum packet size. For example, any Ethernet packet that is larger than 1518 bytes is considered a giant.
- **jabber** — A device that handles electrical signals improperly, usually affecting the rest of the network. A network analyzer will detect a jabber as a device that is always retransmitting, effectively bringing the network to a halt. A jabber usually results from a bad NIC. Occasionally, it can be caused by outside electrical interference.
- **LANalyzer** — Novell's network monitoring software package. LANalyzer can act as a standalone program on a Windows 95 or Windows 98 workstation or as part of the ManageWise suite of network management tools on a NetWare server. LANalyzer offers the following capabilities: discovery of all network nodes on a segment; continuous monitoring of network traffic; tripping alarms when traffic conditions meet preconfigured thresholds (for example, if utilization exceeds 70%); and capturing traffic to and from all or selected nodes.
- **late collisions** — Collisions that take place outside the normal window in which collisions are detected and redressed. Late collisions are usually caused by a defective station (such as a card, or transceiver) that is transmitting without first verifying line status or by failure to observe the configuration guidelines for cable length, which results in collisions being recognized too late.
- **local collisions** — Collisions that occur when two or more stations are transmitting simultaneously. Excessively high collision rates within the network can usually be traced to cable or routing problems.
- **negative frame sequence checks** — The result of the Cyclic Redundancy Checksum (CRC) generated by the originating node not matching the checksum calculated from the data received. It usually indicates noise or transmission problems on the LAN interface or cabling. A high number of CRCs usually results from excessive collisions or a station transmitting bad data.
- **network analyzer** — A portable, hardware-based tool that a network manager connects to the network expressly to determine the nature of network problems. Network analyzers can typically interpret data up to Layer 7 of the OSI Model.
- **network monitor** — A software-based tool that continually monitors traffic on the network from a server or workstation attached to the network. Network monitors typically can interpret up to Layer 3 of the OSI Model.
- **Network Monitor (NetMon)** — A software-based network monitoring tool that comes with Windows NT Server 4.0 or with Microsoft's Server Management System (SMS) suite of tools (for earlier versions of Windows NT Server). Its capabilities include

capturing network data traveling from one or many segments; capturing frames sent by or to a specified node; reproducing network conditions by transmitting a selected amount and type of data; detecting any other running copies of NetMon; and generating statistics about network activity.

- **NetXRay** — Network analyzer software from Network Associates that provides data capture and analysis, node discovery, traffic trending, history, alarm tripping, and utilization prediction.
- **promiscuous mode** — The feature of a network adapter card that allows a device driver to direct it to pick up all frames that pass over the network—not just those destined for the node served by the card.
- **runts** — Packets that are smaller than the medium's minimum packet size. For instance, any Ethernet packet that is smaller than 64 bytes is considered a runt.
- **sniffer** — A laptop equipped with a special NIC and network analysis software that performs network analysis. Unlike laptops that may have a network monitoring tool installed, sniffers typically cannot be used for other purposes, because they don't depend on an operating system such as Windows.
- **spike** — A single (or short-lived) jump in a measure of network performance, such as utilization.
- **supported services list** — A document (preferably online) that lists every service and software package supported within an organization, plus the names of first- and second-level support contacts for those services or software packages.

Review Questions

1. If you cannot reproduce symptoms of a problem, what might you suspect as the cause of the problem?
   - **a.** user error
   - **b.** faulty cabling
   - **c.** incorrect software configuration
   - **d.** incompatible protocols
2. Which of the following symptoms probably points to a physical connectivity problem?
   - **a.** a group of users consistently experiences delays on the network
   - **b.** a user always loses his drive mappings to file server directories
   - **c.** a group of users complain that they cannot log on to the network
   - **d.** a user can send e-mail but can't pick it up

3. Which part of the network should you examine if a network problem affects a single workstation?
   a. the segment's router interface
   b. the workstation's NIC and cabling
   c. the workgroup's hub
   d. the cabling between the switch and the backbone
4. When troubleshooting a network problem, it's a good policy to try the obvious solution first. True or False?
5. Answering which of the following questions may help you identify the demographic scope of a problem?
   a. When did the problem first occur?
   b. How frequently does the problem occur?
   c. Are the cables properly inserted into the hub, wall jack, and device NIC?
   d. Do the symptoms appear on all workstations in one department?
6. Which of the following is a characteristic symptom of a gateway failure?
   a. All workstations on a segment are unable to perform networked functions at all times.
   b. All workstations on a segment are intermittently prevented from connecting to the network.
   c. All workstations on a segment lose their IP addresses.
   d. Only one workstation is unable to log in to the network.
7. Under what circumstances should you try swapping equipment?
8. Which of the following is an example of a network change that could cause a group of workstations to lose connectivity to one file server?
   a. The server is renamed.
   b. The dedicated line to the Internet fails.
   c. One of the server's two NICs fails.
   d. The server's backup device fails.
9. If a user reports that she receives an error message each time she attempts to access a networked drive, what should you suggest she do to document the problem?
   a. Click Cancel.
   b. Press the keystroke combination to print the error message, then bring the printout to you.
   c. Write down the error, then bring the note to you.
   d. Take a snapshot of her screen, then save it to the file server.

10. Which member of the IT department staff is usually the first to receive notice of a network problem?
    a. help desk analyst
    b. IT director
    c. network administrator
    d. help desk supervisor
11. If you don't have the manual for your 3Com NIC, how can you find out whether it supports promiscuous mode?
    a. Read its label.
    b. Look up the information on 3Com's Web site.
    c. Attach it to a network protocol analyzer.
    d. Attempt to flood it with traffic and gauge its response.
12. What kind of tool would you use to verify that your new cable meets CAT5 standards?
    a. cable tester
    b. cable checker
    c. cable monitor
    d. cable gauge
13. Which TCP/IP command can you use to find out whether a workstation's TCP/IP stack is operating properly?
    a. netstat
    b. nbtstat
    c. ftp
    d. ping
14. What is near-end crosstalk, and where is it most likely to occur?
15. Which tool can help you determine whether your Thinnet connection has the proper amount of impedance at each end?
    a. protocol analyzer
    b. cable tester
    c. cable gauge
    d. repeater
16. Which of the following frequently causes negative frame sequence checks?
    a. noise
    b. excessive nodes on a segment
    c. excessive segment length
    d. incorrect protocol configuration

17. Which of the following frequently causes a jabber?
    a. near-end crosstalk
    b. faulty cabling
    c. faulty NIC
    d. noise
18. With what operating system does NetMon work?
    a. UNIX
    b. NetWare
    c. Linux
    d. Windows NT
19. The LANalyzer agent can help you determine when network traffic exceeds 50%. True or False?
20. If you wanted to determine the average daily traffic on your network's backbone, what type of tool would you use?
    a. network analyzer
    b. cable tester
    c. UPS
    d. network monitor
21. Name two advantages of using a sniffer over using NetMon or LANalyzer.
22. Which of the following functions can both network monitors and network analyzers perform?
    a. capture and analyze data traveling from one node to another
    b. identify a faulty cable
    c. trend traffic data from a switch port
    d. capture and interpret unencrypted passwords on the network
23. How do switches affect network analyzers?
    a. They prevent network analyzers from working.
    b. They limit the amount of the traffic that a network analyzer can capture.
    c. They cause interference that can skew the data captured by a network analyzer.
    d. They generate excessive numbers of bad packets, thereby flooding the network analyzer with data.
24. You can typically use the same sniffer for your Token Ring and ATM networks. True or False?

25. Which of the following is a network change that does not need to be recorded in the change management system?
    a. adding a new disk drive to a server
    b. moving a hub from one closet to another
    c. replacing the NIC in a router
    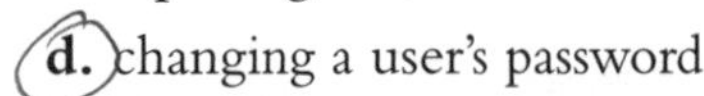
    d. changing a user's password

Hands-on Projects

Until you use a network troubleshooting tool, such as Network Monitor, it's difficult to understand how these programs work. The following Projects offer you a chance to try out cable testers and network monitors. In a real networking environment, you will probably use a number of different tools, depending on your network environment. They are similar enough, however, so that if you master one you can easily master another.

For the following exercises, you will need the cable you created during the Projects in Chapter 4, a cable tester (such as the Fluke DSP-4000 CableAnalyzer), a penknife (or scissors), and a Windows NT 4.0 server with several clients connected to it.

Project 12-1

In this project, you will find out how a cable tester detects and reports a damaged cable.

1. In the Projects in Chapter 4, you created a CAT5 cable with two RJ-45 connectors. Retrieve that cable (or make a new one), and use the cable tester to find out whether it meets CAT5 standards.
2. If your cable does not meet CAT5 standards, cut off both connectors and recrimp it according to the standard. Test it again.
3. If your cable does meet CAT5 standards, use a penknife to slice about one-fourth of the way through the cable, making sure to pass the housing and at least nick one of the twisted pairs.
4. Try testing the cable again with your cable tester. What kind of message (or messages) do you receive?

Project 12-2

In this exercise, you will use Network Monitor from a Windows NT 4.0 server to capture data on the network.

1. With at least five clients connected to your Windows NT 4.0 server, open Network Monitor as follows: Click **Start**, point to **Programs**, point to **Administrative Tools (Common)**, then click **Network Monitor**.

2. Maximize one or both Network Monitor screens, if necessary.
3. Click **Capture** on the menu bar, then click **Start**. Network Monitor begins capturing frames.
4. Go to (or have one of your classmates go to) one of the clients connected to the Windows NT server and start an application from the server. Exit to a DOS prompt, and then ping the server's IP address. Have someone log in to the server from a different client on the network.
5. After you have generated a few minutes of network traffic, click **Capture** on the menu bar, then click **Stop** or **Pause**, then click **Stop**.
6. To view more detail on the captured data, click **Capture** on the menu bar, then click **Display Captured Data**.
7. Use the scroll bars on each of the four windows to view the captured data, including network utilization, statistics, and address information.
8. In the bottom window, click a network address to view its data frames in more detail. What kind of protocols do the frames use? If the network is based on Ethernet, what version are you using? What is your server's MAC address?
9. Find the frames that pertain to the login process mentioned in step 4. Can you read the person's password in ASCII form?

PROJECT 12-3

In this project, you will use the troubleshooting methodology discussed in this chapter to solve a network problem of your own creation. (If you are in a classroom setting and can work in pairs, it may be more fun to have a partner create a connectivity problem with your workstation, and then troubleshoot the problem.) For this exercise, you will use one of the clients from Project 12-2, in addition to the Windows NT 4.0 server.

1. Turn off your workstation and remove the cover, as you learned to do when installing NICs in Chapter 6.
2. Find the NIC and loosen it from its slot until approximately half of the pins are above the slot connector. (Depending on how far you remove the NIC, you may experience different types of symptoms.)
3. Close your workstation's cover and turn on the workstation, making sure that the network cable is properly connected to the NIC and data jack.
4. Follow the steps in the troubleshooting methodology described at the beginning of this chapter, answering all questions under each step. Keep your answers on a separate sheet of paper.
5. Once you have followed the troubleshooting steps, summarize how the problem manifested itself. At step 3 of the troubleshooting process, to how many different types of problems could your symptoms have applied? How many at step 5?

6. Resolve the problem.
7. After you have resolved the problem, create a method for testing the problem to verify that your solution worked. Did it work? How can you be sure?

CASE PROJECTS

1. You are a network support technician for a college with 4000 users scattered over five locations. A group of users from the downtown location has called your help desk, complaining that they cannot send or receive messages from the Internet, although they can receive messages on the college's internal GroupWise system. List the steps you will take to troubleshoot this problem and describe why each step is necessary.
2. While you're downtown fixing the first problem, a fellow network technician asks you to look at the library's server. She informs you that it's "flaky." Sometimes it doesn't allow users to log in; other times, it works perfectly. Sometimes it responds so slowly to requests for programs or files that users think it's frozen, but after several minutes it does finally respond. How would you troubleshoot this problem in the most efficient manner? Explain why you chose the steps you propose and how each might save you time.
3. You're in high demand because the word has gotten around the college that you can fix problems quickly. A small satellite campus requests that you visit and examine a group of workstations in a computer lab that often—but not always—have problems connecting to a server. Your contact is a new instructor who teaches Interior Design in the lab. The workstations worked perfectly until the beginning of the semester, and no hardware or software changes have been made to the machines. Explain how you would troubleshoot this problem and why you chose the steps you propose.
4. Suggest ways that the problems in Case Projects 12-1, 12-2, and 12-3 might have been prevented.
5. Your friend Joseph, who works as a network technician for a global long-distance firm with 300 networked locations along the Eastern seaboard, calls you for help. Usually, five other technicians are on duty to help him handle technical problems. Today, two of his co-workers are out sick, one is away on jury duty, and another has not shown up for work yet. That leaves Joseph and one other technician to solve all of the problems that have occurred on this particular morning, including the following:

   - A WAN link is down between the Washington and New York locations, causing traffic to be rerouted from Washington to Boston, then to New York. As a result, customers are complaining about slow performance.
   - The Albany, New York, location's network appears to have suffered a catastrophic failure. This failure has caused outages for thousands of customers in the upstate New York region.

- Three executive users at Joseph's corporate headquarters in Baltimore cannot pick up their e-mail, and they are calling every five minutes to ask when the problem will be fixed.
- A networked printer that provides services to the Accounting group at the Baltimore headquarters is not accepting any print jobs. The users have asked Joseph to troubleshoot the printer. They need to send invoices out to customers by noon.
- Half of the workstations in the Advertising department seem to be infected with a virus, and Joseph is worried that these users will copy the virus to the network, thus risking widespread data damage.

Joseph asks for advice about the order in which he and his other colleague should address the problems (or which ones simultaneously) and why you would place them in that order. What do you tell him?

6. Joseph is very grateful for your assistance and calls you at the end of the day to tell you how things turned out. One problem was particularly difficult to diagnose, because he didn't get all of the details until well into the troubleshooting process. As it turned out, the three executives—Sal, Martha, and Gabe—who couldn't pick up their e-mail messages were all sitting in a conference room with another two executives, Barb and Darrel. Barb and Darrel were vice-presidents in the Operations group and had scheduled the meeting in a conference room down the hall from their offices. Sal, Martha, and Gabe, on the other hand, were vice-presidents of Marketing, Engineering, and Research. They had to travel from other buildings on the headquarters' grounds to reach the conference room. Although Barb and Darrel could pick up their e-mail before the meeting started, the other three executives couldn't. He asks you to guess what the problem was. What do you tell him? 12
7. Joseph tells you that he first received the call for help from Sal at 7:54 A.M. and finally solved the executives problem by 10:00 A.M. Write a sample tracking record for the incident described in Case Project 6. Include all pertinent details that will help future troubleshooters more quickly diagnose the same kind of problem and that will enable you to give the executives thorough, clear answers in case they call to ask why the problem took so long to fix.

CHAPTER 13

MAINTAINING AND UPGRADING A NETWORK

After reading this chapter and completing the exercises, you will be able to:

- Perform a baseline analysis to determine the state of your network
- Plan and follow regular hardware and software maintenance routines
- Describe the steps involved in upgrading network operating system software
- Describe the steps involved in adding or upgrading network hardware
- Address the potential pitfalls of making changes to the network
- Research networking trends to plan future network upgrades

ON THE JOB

I once worked in the computer services department of a world-class opera house and theater. Two years ago it became clear that our needs had outgrown our network. Users experienced slow responses and frequent down time, and the networking professionals found it difficult to support the outdated equipment. It was time for an upgrade.

We found the financing to completely overhaul our network, from backbone to desktop. We enlisted a consulting firm to help us plan this undertaking. Because the project was so large (affecting every bit of our operation, from Marketing to Payroll), the consultants recommended dividing the conversion into phases that would be less disruptive: backbone upgrade, LAN cabling, network device migration, desktop migration, and documentation and maintenance. One of the most difficult tasks was recabling our facility—a building that didn't resemble your average office building. Nevertheless, over a period of six months, and with help from several contractors, we completed the entire project.

The new network allows the theater's staff to work more efficiently. The network handles data more quickly and almost never suffers down time. And I now work for the consulting company that performed the upgrade!

Sophie Harris
Sage Systems

A network, like any other complex system, is in a constant state of flux. Whether the changes are due to internal factors, such as increased demand on the server's processor, or external factors, such as the obsolescence of a certain model of hub, you should count on spending a significant amount of time investigating, performing, and troubleshooting changes to your network. In Chapter 12, you learned how to find and resolve problems on a network. Some of the solutions discussed there required changes to software or hardware. In this chapter, you will build on this knowledge to learn about changes dictated by immediate needs as well as those needed to enhance the network's functionality, growth, performance, or security.

Ideally, you will plan and budget for all changes to your network. In reality, however, many network changes result from sudden, unexpected requirements. For example, a security breach at your organization might prompt the Vice President of IT to declare that all firewall operating systems must be upgraded and that all system access permissions must be scrutinized. To accomplish these quick changes, you must possess excellent technical skills, understand your network thoroughly, and think fast. Upgrading firewalls is one small example of a network enhancement that you need to properly plan and test. In this chapter, you will learn about a variety of ways to maintain and upgrade your network so as to make it more secure, reliable, and responsive.

KEEPING TRACK

As you learned in Chapter 12, keeping accurate and updated documentation on every aspect of your network will facilitate troubleshooting and help you manage your network more effectively. With network maintenance tasks, you should track all changes and upgrades you perform. You should also note the state of the network before and after you implement any modifications. The first topic in this section, baselining, suggests how to begin this process of documentation.

BASELINING

The first step in properly maintaining your network is to identify its current state. You cannot predict how a network will perform in the future until you have analyzed its past performance. The practice of measuring and recording a network's current state of operation is called **baselining**. Baselining measurements may include the utilization rate for your network backbone, number of users logged on per day or per hour, number of protocols that run on your network, statistics about errors (such as runts, collisions, jabbers, or giants, described in Chapter 12), frequency with which networked applications are used, or information regarding which users take up the most bandwidth. Figure 13-1 shows a graph that provides a baseline for daily network traffic over a six-week period.

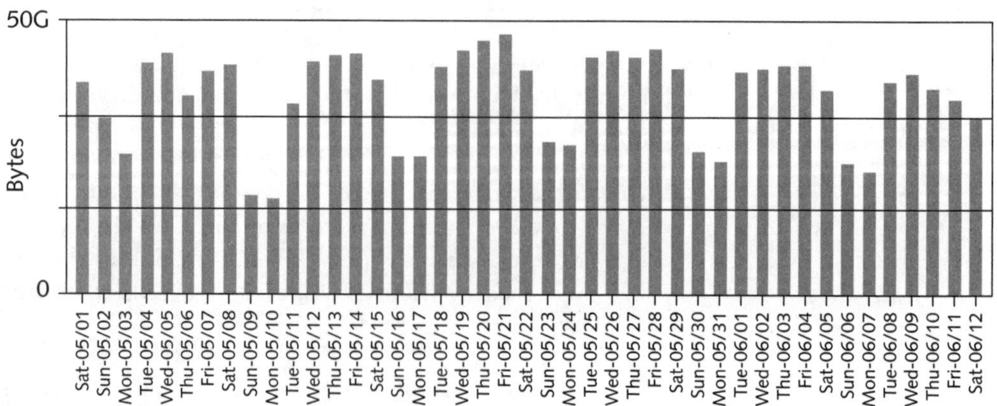

Figure 13-1 Baseline of daily network traffic

Each network will require its own baselining approach. The elements you measure will depend on which functions are most critical to your network and its users. If your staff members run the Lotus Notes application from their local hard disks, for example, but need to post the data they generate through queries to the Internet, you will probably be most concerned about the utilization rate of your gateway, rather than that of your server.

Baseline measurements allow you to compare future performance increases or decreases caused by network changes with past network performance. Baselining is the only way to know for certain whether your upgrades or changes help or harm your level of service.

For example, imagine that you have just added a new switch for the shared workstations in your organization's Customer Service department. Your manager wants you to prove that the switch is really worth the money she paid for it. If you have previously baselined the Customer Service department's network segment in terms of utilization and response time, you can measure the same characteristics after you install the switch and demonstrate how much more rapidly the users receive their data off the network. If the response time becomes worse, you will know that you probably configured or installed the switch improperly.

In another example, suppose that a group of users from the corporate headquarters complains about slow response time over the WAN. If you have baselined the characteristics of that WAN link, you can determine whether their slow response reflects higher-than-normal traffic or whether traffic is excessive and possibly caused by a network error.

In addition, baselining can help you predict the impact of a significant network change. When you are planning system upgrades, it provides the best way to predict your needs. For instance, suppose that your network currently serves 500 users and that your backbone traffic exceeds 50% at 10:00 A.M. and 2:00 P.M. each business day. That pattern constitutes your baseline. Now suppose that your company decides to add 200 users who perform the same types of functions on the network. The added number of users equals 40% of the current number of users (200/500). Therefore, you can predict that your backbone's capacity should increase by approximately 40% to maintain your current service levels.

Network traffic patterns are notoriously difficult to forecast, because you cannot predict users' habits, the effects of new technology, or changes in demand for resources over a given period of time. For instance, the preceding example assumed that all new users would share the same network usage habits as the current users. In fact, however, the new users may generate a great deal more, or a great deal less, network traffic.

Baselining may help you decide how to accommodate capacity increases. For example, determining which, if any, groups of users generate the most network traffic can help you decide whether to upgrade the network from 10 Mbps to 100 Mbps Ethernet, whether to upgrade only certain segments of the network, or whether to manage the increase by adding switches and further subnetting the network.

You may wonder about the difference between network monitoring (described in Chapter 12) and baselining. One significant difference is that a baselined characteristic can be used as a gauge for future reference, whereas network monitoring provides a continual check on problems on the network. These tools work well together, but they are not identical.

How do you gather baseline data on your network? Although you could theoretically use a network monitor or network analyzer and record its output at regular intervals, several programs can perform the baselining for you. These programs range from freeware available on the Internet to expensive, customizable hardware and software combination products.

Before choosing a network baselining tool, you should determine how you will use it. If you manage a small network that provides only one critical application to users, an inexpensive tool may suffice. If you work on a WAN with several critical links, however, you should investigate purchasing a more comprehensive program. Look for a program with a familiar and easy-to-use interface, preferably one that provides templates and wizards to enable you to set your measurement parameters quickly. Make sure that the tool can be integrated with your operating system environment and that it supports the networking hardware used by your organization.

The baselining tool should also be capable of measuring the statistics needed. For example, only a sophisticated baselining tool can measure traffic generated by each node on a network, filter traffic according to types of protocols and errors, and simultaneously measure statistics from several different network segments.

In most cases, baselining tools record the information they collect in common database formats that enable you to generate reports and graphs depicting the health of your network. Examples of popular baselining tools include Concord Communications' Network Health, NetScout Systems' NetScout Manager Plus, and Wandel and Goltermann's WG Wizard.

Once you have identified the network statistics critical for your organization, chosen a baselining tool, and completed the initial baselining, you should set a regular schedule for reevaluating your network. You may want to perform baselining after any major network change or according to dates on the calendar. Regardless of which option you choose, regularly repeating the baseline measurements is the only way to establish a history of your network's performance. By creating such a history, you can identify trends and predict future needs.

ASSET MANAGEMENT

Another key component in the evaluation of your network is identifying and tracking the hardware and software on your network, a process called **asset management**. The first step in asset management is to take an inventory of each node on the network. This inventory should include not only the total number of components on the network, but also each device's configuration files, model number, serial number, location on the network, and a technical contact for support. In addition, you will want to keep records of every piece of software purchased by your organization, its version number, vendor, and technical support contact.

As with a baselining tool, the asset management tool you choose will depend on your organization's needs. You may purchase a program that can automatically discover all devices on the network and then save that information in a database, or you may use a simple spreadsheet to save the data. In either case, your asset management records should be comprehensive and accessible to all personnel who may become involved in maintaining or troubleshooting the network. In addition, you should ensure that the asset management database is regularly updated, either manually or automatically, as changes to network hardware and software occur. The information you retain is useful only while it is current.

Asset management simplifies maintaining and upgrading the network chiefly because you know what the system includes. For example, if you discover that a router purchased two years ago requires an upgrade to its operating system software to fix a security flaw, you need to know how many routers are installed, where they are installed, and whether any have already received the software upgrade. An up-to-date asset management system allows you to avoid searching through old invoices and troubleshooting records to answer these questions.

In addition, asset management provides network administrators with information about the costs and benefits of certain types of hardware or software. For example, if you conclude that 50% of your staff's troubleshooting time is spent on one flawed brand of NIC, an asset management system can reveal how many NICs you would need to replace if you chose to replace those cards, and whether it would make sense to replace the entire installed base. In addition, some asset management programs can track the length of equipment leases and alert network managers when leases will expire.

The term "asset management" originally referred to an organization's system for keeping tabs on every piece of equipment it owned. This function was usually handled through the Accounting department. Some of the accounting-related tasks included under the original definition for asset management, such as managing the depreciation on network equipment or tracking the expiration of leases, apply to asset management in networking as well.

CHANGE MANAGEMENT

In Chapter 12, you learned about using a change management system to track every modification you make while troubleshooting a network problem. You should also use your change management system to record any changes resulting from network maintenance or upgrades. In general, updating your change management system regularly will alert your colleagues of changes you've made and help you remember when you instituted them. This type of system will also enable you to correlate additions, removals, or changes in network components with differences in the network's performance. This benefit may simplify the process of taking baseline and network performance measurements.

Like asset management systems, change management systems are useful only if they are kept current. Unlike asset management records, however, change management records cannot be created by a program that automatically discovers hardware and software on the network. Instead, you (or your fellow network administrators) must supply information regarding when, why, and how changes occur.

SOFTWARE CHANGES

If you have ever supported desktop computers professionally or even maintained your own computer at home, you know that an important part of keeping a system running optimally is upgrading its software.

You are most likely to implement the following types of software changes on your network: patches (improvements or enhancements to a particular piece of a software program), upgrades (major changes to the existing code), or revisions (a general term for minor or major changes to the existing code). Although the specifics vary for each type of software change, the general steps involved can be summarized as follows:

1. Determine whether the change (whether it be a patch, revision, or upgrade) is necessary.
2. Research the purpose of the change and its potential effects on other programs.
3. Determine whether the change should apply to some or all users and whether it will be distributed centrally or machine-by-machine.
4. If you decide to implement the change, notify system administrators, help desk personnel, and users. Schedule the change for completion during off-hours (unless it is an emergency).
5. Back up the current system or software before making any modifications.
6. Prevent users from accessing the system or part of the system being altered (for example, disable logins).
7. Keep the upgrade instructions handy and follow them during installation of the patch or revision.
8. Make the change.
9. Test the system fully after the change, preferably exercising the software as a typical user would. Note any unintended or unanticipated consequences of the modification.
10. If the change was successful, reenable access to the system. If it was unsuccessful, revert to the previous version of the software.
11. Inform system administrators, help desk personnel, and users when the change is complete. If you had to reverse it, explain why.
12. Record your change in the change management system.

As a general rule, upgrading or patching software according to a vendor's recommendations is a good idea and can often prevent network problems. For example, a vendor may issue an alert to its customers regarding a security flaw in its Web browser product. To fix this flaw, it may supply a patch. At other times, you may have to search for product upgrades on your own. Whatever your means of finding patches and upgrades, you should take responsibility for this task and make the necessary changes to your network's software. Bear in mind, however, that such changes can sometimes create even more trouble on your system. You should therefore be prepared to reverse software upgrades or patches, just in case.

In the following sections, you will learn about the types of software changes associated with sensible network maintenance. You will also see the best way to approach these changes.

PATCHES

As mentioned earlier, a **patch** is an improvement or enhancement to a particular piece of a software program. It differs from a revision or software upgrade in that it changes only part of a software program, leaving most of the code untouched. Patches are often distributed at no charge by software vendors in an attempt to fix a bug in their code or to add slightly more functionality.

You'll encounter patches in all areas of routine networking maintenance. Among other things, network maintenance sometimes requires patching the server's network operating system. For example, if your server runs NetWare 4.11, you may need to patch it to resolve a UNIX printer compatibility issue or to ensure that it works properly after the year 2000. A Windows NT server might require similar patches or perhaps something quite different.

Microsoft calls its significant patches for Windows NT Server "**service packs**." You may see them abbreviated as "SP3" and "SP4" for Service Pack 3 and Service Pack 4, respectively.

Keep in mind that a patch is not a replacement for an entire software package; instead, a patch is installed on top of the existing software. Patches apply to more than just network operating system software. For example, you might have to patch the software on your Cisco switch to allow it to handle IP multicasts over a Token Ring network. Alternatively, you might patch the program that allows you to centrally control your printers across the network.

If you install new hardware on a Windows NT server after installing a service pack, you will be prompted to insert your original Windows NT installation CD to obtain the device driver and support files for that hardware. By doing so, however, you may overwrite some of the files that were updated by the service pack. Therefore, it is a good idea to upgrade your server's hardware *before* applying service packs. If you do upgrade the server's hardware after installing a service pack, you will have to implement the service pack a second time.

Patch installations are no more difficult than installations of new software programs. The patch itself should come with installation instructions and a description of its purpose, at the very least, in the form of a text file. As with any significant system change, you should back up the system before installing a patch. Although patches ought to be fully tested by the vendor before release, you cannot assume that they will work flawlessly on your system. This consideration is especially important when you are patching network operating system software. Although some patch programs will automatically make a backup of the system before installation begins, you should not rely on this method. Always make sure you have a way to reverse a software change if it does more harm than good.

In addition, try to perform software patches during a time when users cannot and will not attempt to access the network. Even if you suspect that a patch can be implemented quickly and without adverse effects on current users, don't take a chance by applying it during normal business hours. If the patch does create problems, you will need extra time to reverse the process. Depending on how complicated or comprehensive the patch is, you may want to alert users to stay off the system for only a few hours or perhaps overnight.

After applying the patch, test the system to verify that its desired enhancements have taken effect. At this time, you should review the vendor's documentation to ensure that you have correctly understood the patch's purpose and installed it correctly. For some patches to take effect, you will have to change system configuration files and restart the system. Test the software to verify that the patch hasn't caused any unintentional, undesired effects. Once you are certain that the patch worked successfully, you can allow users to access the system again.

To stay apprised of patches released by your vendors, you should regularly check the vendor's technical support Web site or subscribe to its mailing list. Manufacturers will usually attempt to bundle a number of bug fixes into one large patch; if you're a registered user, they will alert you about the release of significant patches. News about patches from vendors as large as Novell and Microsoft will also probably appear in trade magazines. Smaller vendors may need to release a patch that fixes a single problem with their program only occasionally.

Make it a policy to keep informed about patches to your network software, whether it involves the operating system, an application, or a client program. If you work in a large organization with several servers, routers, and other devices, you may want to assign one network administrator to manage patches for the servers, one to manage patches for the printers, and so on.

CLIENT UPGRADES

As you are probably aware, a software **upgrade** is a major change to the existing code, which may or may not be offered free from a vendor and may or may not be comprehensive enough to substitute for the original program. An upgrade to the client program replaces the existing client program. In general, upgrades are designed to add functionality and fix bugs in the previous version of the client. For example, Microsoft's technical support site offers an upgrade for the Windows 95 Dial-Up Networking client that automatically adjusts the IP packet size depending on the speed of your dial-up connection, among other things. On a Novell client, you might perform an upgrade that enables local support for Novell's Z.E.N. Works centralized desktop management program. The scope and purpose of client upgrades vary widely, depending on whether the upgrade is a redesign or simply a bug fix.

The term **bug** is frequently used to describe a flaw in a software program that causes some part of the program to malfunction. Less frequently, this term may also be used to describe a hardware defect. Legend has it that the term originated when a moth became trapped inside the electrical workings of the first digital computer.

Before upgrading client software, carefully read the instructions accompanying the upgrade. It should reveal how to best install the software, whether the upgrade requires you to first install any previous upgrades, whether the upgrade requires any special preparation, and how its changes will affect users.

A client upgrade may be transparent to users, or it may completely change the appearance of the network logon interface. Client upgrades typically overwrite some system files (such as .dll files) on the workstation, so their installation may affect other programs adversely. They may even prevent other programs from working as they did in the past. For example, a user who receives an upgrade to his or her Windows 95 Dial-Up Networking client may later experience problems with an older version of AOL software that worked perfectly for the last two years. In this case, the best solution may be to upgrade the AOL software as well.

As with all upgrades, you should test a client upgrade on a single workstation before distributing it to all users. Also, you should prepare a way to reverse the process. Because most client upgrades do not back up the previous version automatically, you should keep the old client software close at hand, either on the network or on disk, in case you need to reinstall it.

You may either perform client upgrades on a workstation-by-workstation basis or use a software distribution program such as Microsoft's Systems Management Server to upgrade multiple workstations simultaneously from the network. Although the latter approach is more efficient, it may not be appropriate in all situations. Consider a network of 500 users who have different software, hardware, and usage requirements. Can you be certain that the client upgrade will be compatible with each workstation's hardware and software? Can you be certain that the client upgrade will not adversely affect any user's current software setup? Can you be certain that every user will log in to the network to receive his or her upgrade? (For instance, what happens if many users are mobile?)

In general, you need to plan carefully and become familiar with your client characteristics before allowing a software distribution program to upgrade client software. In addition, you should notify clients about the upgrade and explain how their workstation might change as a result. If you don't, users may become alarmed at the changes and flood the help desk with questions.

APPLICATION UPGRADES

Like client upgrades, application upgrades represent modifications to all or part of a program that are designed to enhance functionality or fix problems related to software. Application upgrades, however, apply to software shared by clients on the network. Bear in mind that changes to shared applications will affect all users at once. You should therefore take extra precautions to ensure that the application upgrade does not cause unanticipated problems. It's essential to test it fully before allowing users to access the new version.

The principles underlying the modification of shared applications on the network are the same as those for the modification of client software. Before applying the change, you should determine the need for it and it potential effects. You should also back up the current software before upgrading it, prevent users from accessing the software during the implementation process, and keep users and system administrators informed of all changes.

Unlike client or system software upgrades, application upgrades are not usually designed to fix problems in the software, but rather to enhance the program's functionality. For this reason, an application upgrade may be more a matter of convenience than necessity. Therefore, the time, cost, and effort involved in application upgrades should be weighed against the necessity of performing operating system or client upgrades. This consideration is especially important if a networking professional's time is limited (as it usually is). For example, users may urge a network administrator to upgrade the company's version of WordPerfect. If the only advantage in doing so is to allow users to print watermarks on their labels, the upgrade may be a waste of time and money. On the other hand, if the application upgrade will add a necessary feature, such as integration with the company's messaging system, it may be well worth the effort.

For a significant application upgrade, you may also need to provide (or suggest classes for) user training. If you choose to refer your users to an outside training facility, make sure they will learn about the particulars of the application in your networking environment. For instance, if you make it a policy never to install the sample spreadsheets for a Lotus 1-2-3 program, make sure your users know about this constraint. Likewise, if you have limited the functionality of a program (for example, preventing users from posting the Web pages they create in Microsoft FrontPage to the server), you should publicize this policy. The better you prepare and inform your users, the fewer support calls your help desk will have to field.

NETWORK OPERATING SYSTEM UPGRADES

Perhaps the most critical type of software upgrade you'll perform is an upgrade to your network operating system. It usually involves significant, potentially drastic, changes to the way your servers and clients operate. As such, it requires plenty of forethought, product research, and rigorous testing before you implement it. In fact, for any network with more than a few users, you should create and follow a project plan for this undertaking. This plan should include all of the precautions typically associated with other software upgrades. In addition, you should consider the following in your project plan:

- How will the upgrade affect user IDs, groups, rights, and policies?
- How will the upgrade affect file, printer, and directory access on the server?
- How will the upgrade affect applications or client interactions on the server?
- How will the upgrade affect configuration files, protocols, and services running on the server?
- How will the upgrade affect the server's interaction with other devices on the network?
- How accurately can you test the upgrade software in a simulated environment?
- How can you take advantage of the new operating system to make your system more efficient?

- What is your technical support arrangement with the operating system's manufacturer if you need help in the midst of the upgrade?
- Have you allotted enough time to perform the upgrade (for example, would it be more appropriate to do it over a weekend rather than overnight?)?
- Have you ensured that the users, help desk personnel, and system administrators understand how the upgrade will affect their daily operations and support burdens?

The preceding items are only some of the critical questions you need to ask before embarking on a network operating system upgrade. Your networking environment may warrant additional considerations. For example, suppose that you are the network administrator for a company that is merging with a second company. Your two companies may use dissimilar network operating systems, and the IT Director may ask you to upgrade your network's operating system to match the other company's version. In this situation, you would have not only the previous list of questions to consider, but also a list of questions pertaining to the other company's operating system. For instance, how are its domains (or NDS tree) organized? By addressing these questions before you upgrade your own network operating system, you will ensure that the merger of the two networks goes more smoothly.

A network operating system upgrade is a complex and far-reaching change. It should not be undertaken with severe budgetary, resource, or time constraints. The following scenario illustrates how careful planning and a methodical process can help you accomplish a network operating system upgrade. In this scenario, a network administrator performs an exemplary network operating system upgrade.

Tom is the network administrator for an accounting firm that employs 400 full-time staff members and uses three NetWare 3.12 servers. Tom is considering upgrading the servers to NetWare 5.0. He has read about the benefits of NetWare 5.0 and thinks his organization may be outgrowing its NetWare 3.12 servers. In addition, his colleagues and a few of his knowledgeable users have been asking when the servers will be upgraded. Tom decides to make the upgrade one of his priorities. He delegates some of his other tasks to co-workers and gets to work.

1. Research—Tom gathers the trade magazine articles he's seen about NetWare 5.0. Because he knows that trade magazine articles can be inaccurate or biased, he also searches Novell newsgroups on the Internet to find out what network administrators who have performed a similar upgrade report about their experiences. He calls a trusted local consultant to ask her advice. In addition, Tom searches through Novell's Web site to see if the features provided by NetWare 5.0 are needed for his network and users. Finally, he finds out how much the software will cost. Once he has collected this information, Tom summarizes it in an outline form, just as if he were writing a term paper. In his outline, he lists the benefits and risks involved in embarking on this network operating system upgrade.
2. Proposal—Tom's initial research indicates that installing NetWare 5.0 would solve a number of technical problems, not to mention enabling his desktop support group to centrally manage their company's 400 computers. Based on his research outline, Tom writes a proposal to evaluate the product, including a plan to pur-

chase and implement NetWare 5.0 if his proposal is accepted. His proposal includes the following elements:

- Questions to answer during evaluation (for example, "Can NetWare 5.0 work with my current network monitoring software?")
- Names of personnel who will assist with evaluation and final approval
- A rough timeline and plan for implementing the change if it is approved
- A rough project plan for implementing the change if it is approved
- Cost considerations
- A review of the short- and long-term benefits of the upgrade
- A review of the risks involved in the upgrade
- A recommendation for or against performing the operating system upgrade
- A plan for purchasing the software and implementing the change

3. Evaluation—Assuming that Tom's proposal concluded that his firm should proceed with an upgrade and that his superiors approved his recommendation, Tom is ready to begin the evaluation phase. He orders a demonstration copy of NetWare 5.0 from his Novell sales representative. He installs the software on an old server that is currently unused, but whose hardware is similar to the hardware of his three production servers (making sure that his servers meet Novell's recommended hardware requirements). On this system, he creates several mock user IDs and groups to simulate the real network environment. Tom also installs all of the applications and services that the server will support if it goes into production.

   Tom distributes updated client software to his team of engineers and asks them to use the mock IDs and groups to test the system. Over a given time period, they exercise the system and keep notes on how the system meets the requirements specified in Tom's proposal. The engineers pay particular attention to the new user interface for clients, the way in which their company's critical applications operate, the system's response time, and any new features provided by the upgrade. Tom and the engineers meet regularly during the evaluation period to discuss and compare their experiences. In addition, Tom asks the engineers (or a consultant, if the engineers don't have the appropriate knowledge) to double-check his work in installing NetWare 5.0. This approach ensures that the test provides a fair trial of the software.

4. Training—Judging by the results from the initial stages of evaluation, Tom predicts that his company will purchase the upgrade. To prepare for this event, he sends the networking engineers to NetWare 5.0 training. He also recommends training for the help desk personnel. In addition, Tom discusses possibilities for user training with the company's computer training manager. Most importantly, he signs up for NetWare 5.0 training himself, because he will actually perform the upgrade. He schedules his training to take place only a few weeks before the anticipated implementation date so that his new skills will be fresh when he begins the conversion.

5. Pre-implementation—As the first step of implementation, Tom expands on the rough timeline and plan that he created in his proposal. The result is a full-fledged project plan for the upgrade. He plans the transfer of the IDs, groups, and their rights to the new system. He decides how to organize the NetWare NDS tree and what types of volumes to create. In addition, Tom reviews the existing servers to determine which applications, files, and directories should be transferred and which can be archived. He plans to upgrade the operating system on only one server at a time.

   Two weeks before upgrading the first server, Tom informs users, help desk personnel, and other networking staff of the timeline and explains what changes to expect. He recommends to users that they clean up their data directories on the server and discard any unnecessary files. Similarly, he asks networking staff to remove any unnecessary applications or services they have installed on the server. If necessary, he and his staff arrange to upgrade the client software on all workstations that will be affected by the operating system upgrade. A few days before the upgrade, he issues a final warning to staff specifying how long he will have the server down to accomplish the upgrade.

6. Implementation—Tom decides to implement the upgrade over a weekend. Before beginning the process, he gathers the software documentation and his plan, along with the software CDs and a bootable disk for the server (making certain that the CD-ROM device driver is on the bootable disk). At 7:00 P.M. on Saturday, he sends a broadcast warning to all users on the network that the server will be going down in five minutes. Five minutes later, he disables all logins to the network. He then backs up the entire server to a tape drive. When the backup is complete, he uses his backup software to verify that critical files were successfully copied.

   Once he's certain that the backup worked, Tom starts the server with DOS and follows Novell's instructions for upgrading from NetWare version 3.12 to version 5.0. This process may take an hour or more. After the upgrade finishes, Tom configures the server according to Novell's instructions and his network's specifications (for example, setting the TCP/IP parameters). Once he has added all services and configured the server properly, he enables himself (but no other users) to log in and test the server's functionality. Tom also tests the critical applications on the server as well as the server's connectivity with the rest of the systems and devices on the network. Not only does he test the network using his (privileged) ID, but Tom also tests it using an average client's ID.

7. Post-implementation—After he is satisfied that the network operating system upgrade was successful, Tom reenables logins to the network and informs all staff that the system is running again. He and his staff review the upgrade process to see if they learned any lessons that could make the other server upgrades more efficient and less troublesome. They work with the help desk personnel to understand the kinds of support calls generated by the upgrade. They also continue testing the new operating system, fine-tuning when necessary, to fix problems or find errors before they become problems for users.

Unfortunately, the careful process of evaluation, planning, and then implementation described in these steps rarely reflects reality. Most network administrators are too busy to perform all of these functions themselves. With some foresight, however, they can strive to perform most of these steps and save themselves the consequences of poor planning during or after the operating system is upgraded.

Reversing a Software Upgrade

If the software upgrade you perform creates problems in your existing system, you should be prepared to reverse the process. The process of reverting to a previous version of software after attempting to upgrade it is known as **backleveling**. Every network professional has been forced to backlevel at some point in his or her career. The steps that constitute this process differ depending on the complexity of the upgrade and the network environment involved.

Although no hard and fast rules for backleveling exist, Table 13-1 summarizes some basic suggestions. Bear in mind that you must always refer to the software vendor's documentation to reverse an upgrade. If you must backlevel a network operating system upgrade, you should also consult with experienced professionals about the best approach for your network environment.

Table 13-1 Reversing a Software Upgrade

Type of Upgrade	Options for Reversing
Operating system patch	Use the patch's automatic uninstall utility
Client software upgrade	Use the upgrade's automatic uninstall utility or reinstall previous version of the client on top of the upgrade
Application upgrade	Use the application's automatic uninstall utility or maintain complete copy of the previous installation of the application and reinstall it over the upgrade
Operating system upgrade	Prior to the upgrade, make a complete backup of the system; to backlevel, restore entire system from the backup; uninstall an operating system upgrade only as a last resort

Hardware and Physical Plant Changes

Hardware and physical plant changes may be required when a network component fails or malfunctions, but more often they are performed as part of an upgrade to increase capacity, improve performance, or add functionality to the network. In this section, you will learn about the simplest and most popular form of hardware change—adding more of what you already use, such as adding four more switches to the backbone or adding 10 new networked printers. You will also learn about more complex hardware changes, such as replacing the entire network backbone with a more robust system.

Many of the same issues apply to hardware changes as apply to software changes. In particular, proper planning is the key to a successful upgrade. When considering a change to your network hardware, use the following steps as a guide:

1. Determine whether the change is necessary.
2. Research the upgrade's potential effects on other devices, functions, and users.
3. If you decide to implement the change, notify system administrators, help desk personnel, and users and schedule it during off-hours (unless it is an emergency).
4. If possible, back up the current hardware's configuration. Most hardware (for example, routers, switches, and servers) has a configuration that you can easily copy to a disk. In other cases (for example, networked printers), you may have to print out the hardware's configuration.
5. Prevent users from accessing the system or the part of the system that you are changing.
6. Keep the installation instructions and hardware documentation handy.
7. Implement the change.
8. Test the hardware fully after the change, preferably putting a higher load on the device than it would incur during normal use in your organization. Note any unintended or unanticipated consequences of the change.
9. If the change was successful, reenable access to the device. If it was unsuccessful, isolate the device or reinsert the old device, if possible.
10. Inform system administrators, help desk personnel, and users when the change is complete. If it was not successful, explain why.
11. Record your change in the change management system.

Adding or Upgrading Equipment

The difficulty involved in adding or upgrading hardware on your network will depend largely on whether or not you have used the hardware in the past. For instance, if your organization always uses Intel hubs, adding one more Intel hub to your second-floor telecommunications closet may take only a few minutes and cause absolutely no disruption of service to your users. On the other hand, even if your company uses Intel hubs, adding an Intel router to your network may be an entirely new experience. You should research, evaluate, and test any unfamiliar piece of equipment that you intend to add or upgrade on your network, even if it is manufactured by a vendor that supplies much of your other hardware.

With the rapid changes in the hardware industry, you may not be able to purchase identical hardware even from one quarter to the next. If consistency is a concern—for example, if your technical staff is familiar with only one brand and model of printer, and you do not have the time or money to retrain personnel—you would be wise to purchase as much hardware as possible in a single order. If this approach is not feasible, purchase equipment from vendors with familiar products and solid reputations.

Each type of device that you add or upgrade on the network will have different preparation and implementation requirements. Knowing exactly how to handle the changes will require not only a close reading of the manufacturer's instructions, but also some experience with the type of networking equipment at hand. The following list provides a very general overview of how you might approach adding or upgrading devices on the network, from the least disruptive to the most complex types of equipment. The devices at the bottom of the list are not only the most disruptive and complex to add or upgrade, but also the most difficult to remove or backlevel.

- *Networked workstation*—A networked workstation is perhaps the simplest device to add. It directly affects only a few users but does not alter network access for anyone else. If your organization has a standard networked workstation configuration (for example, a disk image—a compressed snapshot of the workstation's contents—on the server), adding a networked workstation will be a quick operation as well. You can successfully add a networked workstation without notifying users or support staff and without worrying about down time.
- *Networked printer*—A networked printer is easy to add to your network, too. Adding this equipment is slightly more complex than adding a networked workstation, however, because of its unique configuration process and because it is shared. Although it affects multiple users, a networked printer does not typically perform a mission-critical function in an organization, so the length of time required to install one does not affect productivity. Thus, although you should notify the affected users of a networked printer addition, you do not need to notify all users and support staff. Likewise, you do not need to restrict access to the network or worry about down time in this instance.
- *Hub*—As you learned in Chapter 6, a single hub may service as few as 4 or as many as 64 users. You do not have to worry about down time or notifying users when adding a new hub, however, because it cannot affect anyone until it is actually in use. If you are upgrading or swapping out an existing hub, you must notify the affected users. The upgrade or swap will create down time; you may have to perform the operation during off-hours. In addition, you must consider the traffic and addressing implications of adding or upgrading a hub. For example, if you need to expand the capacity of a TCP/IP-based network segment from 24 users to 60 users, you can easily enough swap your 24-port hub with a 64-port hub. Before doing so, make sure that the segment has enough free IP addresses to service 60 users; otherwise, these users will not be able to access the network.
- *Server*—A server addition or upgrade can be tricky. Typically, this type of change (unless it is the replacement of a minor component) requires a great deal of foresight and planning. Before installing a new server, you need to consider the hardware and connectivity implications of the change, as well as issues relating to the network operating system. Even if you are adding a server that will not be used immediately, you still need to plan for its installation. Preferably, you should add the server while network traffic is low. You should also restrict access to the servers; otherwise, one of your users could find the server while browsing the network and try to save files to it or run an application from it.

Upgrading the hardware (such as a NIC or memory) on an existing server requires almost the same amount of planning as adding an entirely new server. You should schedule upgrades to an existing server for off-hours, so that you can shut down the server without inconveniencing any users who rely on it.

- *Switches and routers*—Switches and routers are the most complex type of additions or changes to a network design for several reasons. First, they can be physically disruptive—that is, they often require the installation of new racks or other support frames in your telecommunications room. Second, they affect many users—perhaps all users—on the network. For instance, if you must replace the Internet gateway for your organization's headquarters, you will cut every user's access to the Internet in the process (unless you have redundant gateways, which is the optimal setup if you rely on the Internet for mission-critical services). You should notify all users on the network about the impending change, even if you don't think that they will be affected—sometimes a router or switch may have unintended effects on segments of the network other than the one it services. In addition, you should plan at least weeks in advance for switch or router changes and expect at least several hours of down time. Because routers and switches are expensive, you should take extraordinary care when handling and configuring the equipment. Also, because switches and routers serve different purposes, rely on the manufacturer's documentation to guide you through the installation process.

The best way to safely gain experience with adding, upgrading, or repairing devices is to experiment with devices that are not currently used on a network. If you are taking a networking class, ask your instructor whether you can spend extra time in the computer lab polishing your skills with the equipment. Work with a partner, if possible, so you can question each other about what you are doing and why.

Bear in mind that adding a new processor to a server, a new NIC to a router, or more memory to a printer may affect your service or warranty agreement with the manufacturer. Before purchasing any components to add or replace in your network devices, check your agreement for stipulations that might apply. You may be allowed to add only components made by the same manufacturer or risk losing all support from that manufacturer.

Above all, keep safety in mind when you upgrade or install hardware on a network. Never tinker with the insides of a device that is plugged in or turned on. Make sure that all cords and devices are stowed safely out of the way and cannot cause trips or falls. Avoid wearing jewelry, scarves, or very loose clothing when you work on equipment; if you have long hair, tie it back. Not only will you prevent injury this way, but you will also be less distracted. By removing metal jewelry, you may prevent damage to the equipment caused by a short if the metal touches a circuit. If the equipment is heavy (such as a large switch or server), do not try to lift it by yourself. Finally, to protect the equipment from damage, follow the manufacturer's temperature, ventilation, antistatic, and moisture guidelines.

Cabling Upgrades

Cabling upgrades (unless they involve the replacement of a single faulty patch cable) may require significant planning and time to implement, depending on the size of your network. Remember from Chapter 12 that troubleshooting cabling problems is difficult because the cable layout may be undocumented and poorly planned, particularly if it was installed years before and survived intact despite building changes and network growth. For the same reason, cabling is rarely simple to upgrade. The best way to ensure that future upgrades go smoothly is to carefully document the existing cable *before* making any upgrades. If this assessment is not possible, you may have to compile your documentation as you upgrade the existing cabling.

Because a change of this magnitude will affect all users on the network, you should upgrade the network in phases. Perhaps you can schedule an upgrade of the first-floor east wing of your building one weekend, then the first-floor west wing of your building the next, and so on. Weigh the importance of the upgrade against its potential for disruption. For example, if the Payroll department is processing end-of-month checks and having no difficulties other than somewhat slow response time, it is not critical to take away its access to install CAT5 wiring. On the other hand, if the building maintenance staff needs a 100 Mbps connection to run a new HVAC controls system, you will probably make it a priority to take down this access temporarily and replace the wiring. In this case, not only will you have to replace the wiring, but you may also need to replace hubs and NICs.

For the most part, only organizations that run very small networks upgrade or install their own network cabling. Most other organizations rely on contractors who specialize in this service. Nevertheless, as a networking professional you should know how to run a cable across a room, either under a raised floor or through a ceiling, to connect a device to the network.

Backbone Upgrades

The most comprehensive and complex upgrade involving network hardware is a backbone upgrade. Recall from Chapter 5 that the network backbone represents the main conduit for data on LANs and WANs, connecting major routers, servers, and/or switches. A backbone upgrade requires not only a great deal of planning, but also the efforts of several personnel (and possibly contractors) and a significant investment. You may upgrade parts of the backbone—a NIC in a router or a section of cabling, for example—at any time, but upgrading the entire backbone changes the whole network.

Examples of backbone upgrades include migrating from Token Ring to Ethernet, migrating from Ethernet to ATM, migrating from a slower technology to a faster one, and replacing all routers with switches (to make use of VLANs, for example). Such upgrades may satisfy a variety of needs: a need for faster throughput, a physical move or renovation, a more reliable network, greater security, more consistent standards, support of a new application, or greater cost-effectiveness. For example, switching from Token Ring to Ethernet may make a LAN less expensive to maintain because Ethernet's components are more economical and technical support may be easier to find. The need for faster throughput may prompt an upgrade from an older Ethernet technology to Gigabit Ethernet. Likewise, the need to support videoconferencing may require a backbone upgrade from CAT5 to fiber and from Ethernet to ATM.

If you recall from Chapter 6 the cabling and hardware required for the different networking technologies, you will get an idea of how far-reaching a backbone upgrade can be. For example, to convert from Token Ring to Ethernet, you must replace or upgrade connectivity equipment such as hubs and routers. In addition, you must replace the NIC in every workstation and printer on the network and change the configuration for each device so that it works with Ethernet rather than Token Ring. For a small network, this effort may not be more than a weekend's work. For a network of thousands of users, such an upgrade requires the services of a dedicated team.

Because backbone upgrades are expensive and time-consuming, the first step in approaching such a project is to justify it. Will the benefits outweigh the costs? Can the upgrade wait a year or more? If so, you might be wise to wait and find out whether a cheaper or better technical solution will become available later. Don't try to wait until the technology "settles down," because networking progress never stands still. On the other hand, do wait to implement brand-new technology until you can find out how it has worked on other networks similar to your own or until the manufacturer eliminates most of the bugs.

The second step is to determine which kind of backbone design to implement. To make this decision, you must analyze the future capacity needs of your network, decide whether you want a distributed or collapsed backbone, discover whether you want to rely on switches or routers, decide whether to use subnetting and to what extent, and so on. Although some of these predictions will be guesswork, you can minimize the variables by examining the history of your organization's growth and needs. This effort is where your baselining proves valuable.

For example, if you work with a retailer that opened 15 new stores across the country this year and predicts a growth rate of 30% over the next 5 years, you can predict that your WAN will grow by approximately 20 nodes next year and approximately 27 nodes the following year. You should plan a network upgrade that can accommodate that growth: one that uses a reliable service provider, an addressing scheme that can be expanded, and connectivity devices that can be upgraded easily.

After designing your backbone upgrade, you should develop a project plan to accomplish the upgrade. Given that you don't upgrade your backbone every day, you might want to contract this work to a firm that specializes in network design and upgrades. In that case, you will draft a request for proposal (RFP) to specify what that contractor should do. (Drafting an RFP is just one step in managing a large networking project. You will learn more about this process in Chapter 16, "Managing Network Design and Implementation.")

Regardless of whether you employ specialists, your project plan should include a logical process for upgrading the backbone one section at a time (if possible). Because this process will cause network outages, determine how best to proceed based on users' needs. If you are lucky, you will choose a time when usage is low (such as over a holiday) to perform your upgrade.

Reversing Hardware Changes

As with software changes, you should provide a way to reverse the hardware upgrade and reinstall the old hardware if necessary. If you are replacing a faulty component or device, this restoration will, of course, not be possible. If you are upgrading a component in a device, on the other hand, you should keep the old component safe (for example, keep network interface cards in static-resistant containers) and nearby. Not only might you need to put it back in the device, but you might also need to refer to it for information. For example, if you have not documented the necessary jumper settings for an interface card in a switch, the old card might indicate the jumper settings needed on your new card. Even if the device seems to be operating well with the new component, keep the old component for a while, especially if it is the only one of its kind at your organization.

Managing Growth and Change

One of the most challenging and exciting aspects of being a networking professional is keeping up with the myriad changes in the industry. Technology trends come and go, as do software and hardware suppliers. Because no one can predict the future, you must learn to do the next best thing—prepare for the future. You will not always make the right decisions, but understanding the history of networking trends and researching possibilities for the future ensure that you can make well-reasoned decisions. The following sections will help you decide how to manage your organization's networking needs.

Trends in Networking Technology

You have probably recognized trends in networking technology while reading this book (for example, the debate over cable modem versus DSL technology for low-cost, high-bandwidth WAN connections mentioned in Chapter 7) or while working in an IT department. Switches are becoming more like routers. Older transmission media such as Thicknet and Thinnet Ethernet are being replaced by twisted-pair cabling. TCP/IP is becoming the protocol of choice on many networks. These trends have been developing for a long time, however. The more interesting question is, What can we learn from these trends that will help us predict new trends over the next decade?

Each of the networking trends evident today provides users with at least one of the following advantages: faster data processing and transmission, more comprehensive integration, open standards, greater accessibility for a more diverse population, or smarter devices (which facilitates more automation of tasks, usually saving time and money). Consider how each of these factors might influence currently developing trends:

- Faster data processing and transmission will bring network access to more people in less time. If you apply this trend to the Internet, you can imagine how commerce, education, and entertainment can be easily carried worldwide over the Web. Will it replace your TV or phone? Or will your TV rely on the Web?

- More comprehensive integration means that more products sold by different vendors will work well together. This compatibility not only makes your job as a networking professional easier (because you have fewer systems to master), but also merges industries. Think of how the roles of telephone companies and Internet service providers are converging. ISPs are now selling voice over IP services, whereas telephone companies are trying to provide Internet access over their networks.
- Open standards will make networking careers less specialized and probably more interesting. With TCP/IP networking skills, for example, you could just as easily get a job with a large aerospace firm as you could with a small nonprofit agency.
- Greater accessibility will bring technology to more users. In the 1950s, computers were used only by elite computer scientists and didn't even fit into one room. Today, the majority of U.S. households own a computer, and millions of users are connected around the world through the Internet. How might this trend affect the global economy? How might it affect cultures and political systems around the world?
- Smarter devices will contribute to each of the trends mentioned above, enabling the development of faster, more open standards and providing greater accessibility. For example, advanced wireless devices will enable users to pick up their e-mail from handheld devices while sipping coffee at an outdoor café.

Notice that lower cost is not necessarily a driving factor in networking technology trends. It doesn't have to be, because the trend toward smarter, faster, and more standardized devices also implies lower costs. Because networking equipment develops so rapidly, today's expensive and powerful devices become tomorrow's inexpensive commodities.

Some of the current trends will bring a greater concern for security. As systems adopt the same (open) standards, they become more vulnerable to hackers who can easily figure out the code after mastering similar systems. As accessibility increases, security threats also increase, because the network offers more entry opportunities for hackers. In Chapter 15, you will learn about protecting data from the unintended consequences of business's increasing reliance on the networking trends discussed above.

Researching Networking Trends

If you are charged with purchasing or planning decisions in your IT department, you will need to research networking technology trends before making any choices. Often you will hear about new technologies from colleagues, classmates, or trade magazine articles, but you cannot rely on the accuracy of everything you hear. The best way to evaluate networking technology is to test it in your organization. That way you can find out how it operates in your networking environment—with your equipment, applications, and users. During the testing, you can note what you like or don't like and decide whether you even need the technology.

On the other hand, many networking trends require such drastic or expensive upgrades that you cannot afford to test them first. In this case, you must rely on someone else who has experience with the technology. A good option is to discuss your needs with a reputable consulting firm that has implemented the same technology at other organizations. Discuss the project not only with the consultants who performed the upgrade work, but also with the customer that is currently using the new technology. If possible, visit facilities that have already adopted the technology.

Newsgroups on the Web can provide valuable information, too. After a new technology has been marketed for a month or more, you should be able to find comments from other networking professionals regarding their experience with the technology. Post a message to the newsgroup inquiring about the technology's pros and cons. Most technicians will happily share their experiences. If the technology works as promised, they will undoubtedly want to spread the good news. If it causes more problems than it solves, they will want to warn others. As you read the postings on a newsgroup, one message will come through loud and clear: Don't rely on the manufacturer's claims regarding the merits of a particular product or service. Instead, test the technology yourself, or at least discuss it with someone who has tested it.

Chapter Summary

- In every aspect of networking, keeping accurate and updated documentation will reduce troubleshooting time and help you manage the network more effectively. When maintaining the network, you should track all changes and upgrades that you perform, as well as the state of the network before and after the changes were implemented.
- The practice of measuring and recording your network's current state of operation is called baselining. Baselining measurements may include the utilization rate on your network backbone, the number of users per day or per hour, the number of protocols run on your network, statistics about errors (such as runts, collisions, jabbers, or giants), the frequency with which networked applications are used, or the identification of those users who take up the most bandwidth.
- Baseline measurements allow you to compare future performance increases or decreases due to network changes with past network performance. Baselining offers the only way to discern whether your upgrades or changes really helped or harmed the level of service.
- Baselining can also help you predict the effect of a significant network change. When you are planning system upgrades, baselining provides the best way to predict your needs.
- Baselining differs from network monitoring. A baselined characteristic can be used as a gauge for future reference, whereas network monitoring provides a continual check for problems on the network. These tools work well together, but they are not identical.
- An asset management system includes an inventory of the total number of components on the network as well as each device's configuration files, model number, serial number, location on the network, and a technical contact for support. In addition, it records every piece of software purchased by your organization, its version number, vendor, and technical support contact.

- You should document any changes to a network as the result of maintenance or upgrades in a change management system. This information will alert your colleagues to changes made and help you remember when you implemented them. It will also assist in baselining and network performance measurement, because you will know exactly when a network component was added, removed, or changed, and can correlate this information with performance data.
- No matter what type of software upgrade you perform, you should generally follow the same process. First, determine whether the change (whether it be a patch, revision, or upgrade) is necessary. Next, research the upgrade's purpose and potential effects on other programs. Determine whether the change should apply to all or only some users and whether it will be distributed centrally or machine-by-machine. If you decide to implement the change, notify system administrators, help desk personnel, and users and schedule the upgrade during off-hours (unless it is an emergency). Back up the current system or software before making any changes. Prevent users from accessing the system or part of the system affected (for example, disable logins). Keep the upgrade instructions handy and follow them during installation of the patch or revision. Make the change. Test the system fully after the change, noting any unintended or unanticipated consequences. If the change was successful, reenable access to the system. If it was unsuccessful, revert to the previous version of the software. Inform system administrators, help desk personnel, and users when the change is complete, or if you had to reverse it, explain why. Record your change in the change management system.
- A patch is an enhancement or improvement to a part of a software program, often distributed at no charge by software vendors to fix a bug in their code or to add slightly more functionality. Patches differ from revisions and software upgrades because they change only part of the software program, leaving most of the code untouched.
- Make it a policy to keep informed about patches to your network software, whether they involve the operating system, an application, or a client program. If you work in a large organization with several servers, routers, and other devices, you may want to assign one network administrator to manage patches for the servers, another to manage patches for the printers, and so on.
- A software upgrade represents a major change to the existing code, which may or may not be offered free from a vendor and may or may not be comprehensive enough to substitute for the original program. An upgrade to the client program replaces the existing client program so as to add functionality and fix bugs found in the previous version.
- Before upgrading client software, carefully read the instructions that accompany the upgrade to find out how best to apply it, whether it depends on any previous upgrades, whether it requires any special preparation, and how its changes will affect users. Client upgrades typically overwrite some system files (such as .dll files) on the workstation, so their installation may affect other programs adversely.
- Like client upgrades, application upgrades consist of modifications to all or part of a program that are designed to enhance functionality or fix problems with the software. Application upgrades, however, affect software programs shared by clients on the network.

- Perhaps the most critical type of software upgrade you'll perform comprises an upgrade to your network operating system. This effort usually involves significant, potentially drastic, changes to the operation of your servers and clients. As such, it requires plenty of forethought, product research, and rigorous testing before you implement it. In fact, for any network with more than a few users, you should create and follow a project plan for this undertaking.
- The process of upgrading a network operating system should include research, proposal, evaluation, training, pre-implementation, implementation, and post-implementation phases.
- If the software upgrade you perform causes problems to your existing system(s), you should know how to reverse the process. The restoration of a previous version of software after an attempted upgrade is known as backleveling.
- Hardware and physical plant changes may be required when your network has problems. More often, however, they are performed as part of a move to increase capacity, improve performance, or add functionality to the network.
- Research, evaluate, and test any unfamiliar piece of equipment you intend to add or upgrade on your network, even if it is manufactured by a vendor that supplies much of your other hardware. The process of implementing a hardware upgrade is very similar to that of carrying out a software upgrade, including notifying users and preparing to bring the system down during the change.
- Each type of device you add or upgrade on the network will have its own preparation and implementation requirements. Knowing exactly how to handle the changes will require a close read of the manufacturer's instructions as well as some experience with the type of networking equipment to be installed.
- A networked workstation is perhaps the simplest device to add. It directly affects only one or a few users but does not alter network access for anyone else.
- A networked printer is easily added to your network. Adding one is slightly more complex than adding a networked workstation because of its unique configuration process and because it is shared. Although it affects multiple users, a networked printer does not typically perform a mission-critical function in an organization, so the length of time required for its installation does not affect productivity.
- If you are adding a new hub, you do not have to worry about down time or notification of users. If you are upgrading or swapping out an existing hub, you must notify the affected users. The upgrade or swap will cause down time and may require that you perform it during off-hours. In addition, you must consider the traffic and addressing implications of adding or upgrading a hub.
- Installing a new server will require that you consider not only the hardware and connectivity but also the network operating system implications of the new server. Even if you are adding a server that will not be used immediately, you need to plan for its addition and preferably install it while the network has little traffic. Typically, a server addition or upgrade (unless it is the replacement of a minor component) requires a great deal of foresight and planning.

- Switches and routers are the most complex type of additions or changes to a network design for several reasons. First, they can be physically disruptive, often requiring the installation of new racks or other support frames in your telecommunications room. Second, they affect many users—perhaps all users—on a network. You should notify all users on the network about the impending change, even if you don't think that they will be affected. A router or switch can have unintended effects on segments of the network other than the one it services. In addition, you should plan at least weeks in advance for switch or router changes and expect at least several hours of down time.
- Cabling upgrades (unless they involve the replacement of a single faulty patch cable) may require significant planning and time to implement, depending on the size of your network. Because an upgrade of this magnitude will affect all users on the network, you should upgrade the network in phases.
- The most comprehensive and complex upgrade involving network hardware is a backbone upgrade. The network backbone serves as the main conduit for data on LANs and WANs, connecting major routers, servers, and/or switches. A backbone upgrade not only requires a great deal of time to plan, but also the efforts of several staff members (and possibly contractors) and a significant investment.
- A variety of needs may drive backbone upgrades: for faster throughput, a physical move or renovation, a more reliable network, greater security, more consistent standards, support of a new application, or greater cost-effectiveness.
- Because backbone upgrades are expensive and time-consuming, the first step in approaching such a project is to justify it. The next step is to determine what kind of backbone design to implement. To make this decision, you must analyze the future capacity needs of your network, determine whether you want a distributed or collapsed backbone, decide whether you need to rely on switches or routers, decide whether to use subnetting and to what extent, and so on. After you have designed your backbone upgrade, you should develop a project plan to accomplish it.
- You should provide a way to reverse the hardware upgrade and replace it with the old hardware. If you are upgrading a component in a device, keep the old component safe (for example, keep NICs in static-resistant containers) and nearby. Not only might you need to put it back in the device, but you might also need to refer to it for information.
- Each of the networking trends observed today provides users at least one of the following advantages: faster data processing and transmission, more comprehensive integration, open standards, greater accessibility for a more diverse population, or smarter devices (which increases the automation of tasks, usually saving time and money).
- Some of the current trends will raise greater concerns for security. As systems adopt the same (open) standards, they become more vulnerable to hackers who can easily figure out the code after mastering similar systems. As accessibility increases, security threats also increase, because the network offers more entry opportunities for hackers.
- The best way to evaluate networking technology is to test it in your organization. That way you can find out how it operates in your networking environment—with your equipment, applications, and users. Another good option is to discuss your needs with a

reputable consulting firm that has implemented the same technology at other organizations. Discuss the project not only with the consultants who performed the upgrade work, but also with the customer that is currently using the new technology. If possible, visit facilities that have already adopted the technology.

Key Terms

- **asset management** — A system for identifying and tracking the hardware and software on a network.
- **backleveling** — The process of reverting to a previous version of a software program after attempting to upgrade it.
- **baselining** — The practice of measuring and recording a network's current state of operation.
- **bug** — A flaw in software or hardware that causes it to malfunction.
- **patch** — An upgrade to a part of a software program, often distributed at no charge by software vendors to fix a bug in their code or to add slightly more functionality.
- **service pack** — A significant patch to Windows NT Server software.
- **upgrade** — A major change to the existing code in a software program, which may or may not be offered free from a vendor and may or may not be comprehensive enough to substitute for the original program.

Review Questions

1. Which of the following is *not* a benefit of a baselining tool?
   - **a.** It helps predict the impact of future device additions.
   - **b.** It helps predict bandwidth needs.
   - **c.** It helps determine how much traffic currently travels over the network.
   - **d.** It helps determine where additional WAN nodes ought to be located.
2. Name three network characteristics that might belong in a baseline measurement.
3. If you were planning to purchase a baselining tool for your network, which of the following is one factor you would *not* use to evaluate your options?
   - **a.** interoperability with word-processing applications
   - **b.** compatibility with network hardware and software
   - **c.** measurement of data critical to your network's performance
   - **d.** ease of use
4. What hardware-related data might you record in an asset management system and why?
5. Some asset management programs can automatically discover all devices on a network. True or False?

6. Which of the following times would be the best time to install a patch to your network operating system?
   a. 7:00 A.M. on Monday
   b. 6:00 P.M. on Wednesday
   c. 1:00 A.M. on Sunday
   d. 2:00 P.M. on Friday
7. How does a software patch differ from an upgrade?
   a. A patch is more comprehensive.
   b. A patch is more current.
   c. A patch fixes bugs.
   d. A patch replaces only some of the software files.
8. Under what circumstances should network administrators inform users of software changes?
   a. always
   b. when the change might affect applications or utilities relied on by the users
   c. when the change might result in the addition of an application
   d. when the change might affect how users are added to the system
9. Name five considerations that you should address before undertaking a network operating system upgrade.
10. When considering a major upgrade, such as a network operating system or backbone upgrade, you should depend on a manufacturer's Web site materials to determine whether the upgrade is necessary and useful. True or False?
11. What is another name for reversing a software upgrade?
    a. uninstalling
    b. backleveling
    c. reverting
    d. undoing
12. Which of the following is the best way to reverse a network operating system upgrade?
    a. Reinstall the previous version of the operating system.
    b. Uninstall the upgrade.
    c. Remove the upgrade software folder from the server.
    d. Restore the server's software and configuration from a backup.
13. Name three reasons to perform a hardware upgrade on a network.

14. Which of the following changes probably requires the most planning?
    a. modifying a router's access list
    b. upgrading the network client on a department's workstations
    c. replacing a router with a switch
    d. applying a patch to a networked application
15. If you use hardware from only one manufacturer, you can assume that its switches are installed similarly to how its hubs are installed. True or False?
16. Why are cabling and backbone upgrades often implemented in phases?
17. What is the first step in a backbone upgrade?
    a. Justify it.
    b. Create a project plan.
    c. Determine its effect on users.
    d. Determine its effect on routing traffic.
18. Name two good reasons to perform a backbone upgrade.
19. Which of the following networking trends makes security a greater concern for network managers?
    a. greater network accessibility
    b. faster devices
    c. smarter devices
    d. increased use of wireless technology
20. Which of the following is the best way to research a new networking technology you are considering adapting?
    a. Ask friends about it.
    b. Read articles about it.
    c. Test it in your organization.
    d. Based on what you read, create a hypothetical scenario for the technology in your environment.

HANDS-ON PROJECTS

Even though you may not be in a position to upgrade your company's entire network backbone, you will probably have to upgrade software and hardware components on a regular basis. From these smaller upgrades and the troubles you encounter in their implementation, you can learn about more complex types of upgrades. In the next three Projects, you will perform minor software and hardware upgrades and use the information you learn to prepare for a hypothetical major network upgrade. For these exercises, you will need a Windows 95 or Windows 98 computer with Web access that is connected to Windows NT Server 4.0.

You will need administrator-equivalent rights on the server. The server should not have Service Pack 4 installed, but you should have CDs containing these patches. You should also have a Windows NT Server 4.0 CD and a blank floppy disk. For the hardware upgrade exercise (Project 13-2), you should have a memory chip compatible with your server's hardware and space in your server to accept additional memory.

PROJECT 13-1

In this exercise, you will install Service Pack 4 (SP4) to a working Windows NT server, paying attention to the patch's effects on users and applications.

1. Before you install SP4 on your Windows NT server, you need to find out what it does and how it will change your system. Search Microsoft's Web site to find the features of SP4. On a separate piece of paper, list five changes made by this patch. What types of improvements do the changes entail?
2. Now that you know what SP4 is supposed to achieve, research it a little more to find out whether it will be truly beneficial to your network. One idea is to search through technical trade magazine articles to find out what others have said about SP4. Point your browser to these URLs: http://www.techweb.com/search/advsearch.html and www.zdnet.com. Perform searches on the term **service pack 4** at both sites. If you have the option, search the magazine sites for the term according to its relevance in the article, rather than according to the date of the article (for example, at the Techweb site, deselect the **Sort results by date** option). Note that you may have to sift through the articles to find one that concentrates on SP4. Does anything in the articles you find make you skeptical about performing the upgrade? Why?
3. Log in to your Windows NT server as an administrator equivalent and insert the SP4 CD.
4. Find the instructions for installing the service pack on the CD (in the readme.txt file) and study them before beginning the installation.
5. Close all applications currently running on the server.
6. To disable all logins to the Windows NT server, click **Start**, click **Settings**, **Control Panel,** then double-click the – **Services** icon. Stop the NT Server service.
7. In this step you will create an emergency repair disk to ensure that you have a good copy of the server's configuration in case the software installation (or later backleveling) causes problems. To create an emergency repair disk, click **Start,** point to **Programs,** click **Command Prompt,** type **rdisk** at the DOS prompt, then press **Enter**.
8. The Repair Disk Utility dialog box opens. Click **Update Repair Info** to update the Emergency Repair Directory on your hard drive. (If you have previously created an emergency repair disk, a dialog box will appear informing you that the information from the last repairs will be deleted, and asking you if you want to continue. In this case, click **Yes** to confirm that you want to replace the old information.)
9. You are asked if you want to create an emergency repair disk. Click **Yes**.

10. You are prompted to insert a blank disk. Insert your floppy disk, then click **OK** to continue.
11. Once the configuration files are copied to your floppy disk, click **Exit** to close the Repair Disk Utility. After closing the Repair Disk Utility, type **Exit** at the DOS prompt to exit the command prompt window. Now that you have a good copy of your server's configuration, you can install SP4 by following the instructions that came with it.
12. When the installation program asks whether you want to create an uninstall folder, choose **Yes**. You should always create an uninstall folder when you install service packs. In the case of SP4, you need 80 MB of space to create the uninstall folder.
13. After the service pack has finished installing, restart the Windows NT server and remove the service pack CD from the CD-ROM drive. The Windows NT server service will restart to enable users to log in.
14. Log on to the server as the administrator. Do you receive any messages notifying you that the service pack was installed or that certain features have changed?

PROJECT 13-2

In this exercise, you will add memory to your Windows NT Server 4.0. If you are familiar with PC technology, you know that each machine has its own physical memory requirements. Figure 13-2 shows some popular types of memory modules (or chips).

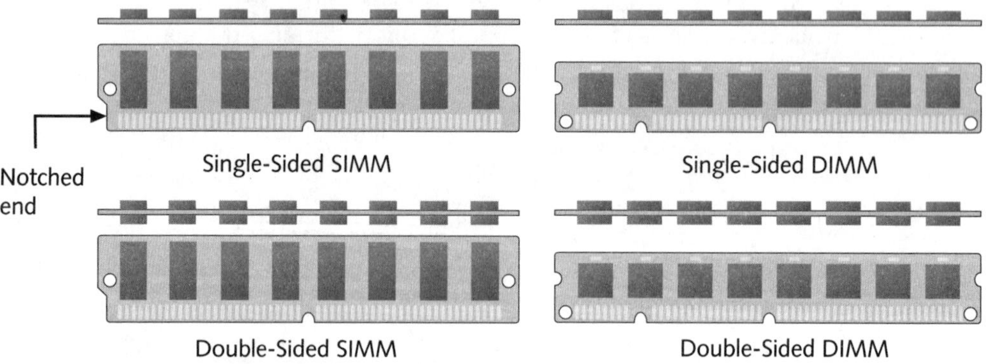

Figure 13-2 Popular memory chips

1. Log on to the Windows NT server as the administrator.
2. Click **Start**, point to **Programs**, point to **Administrative Tools**, then click **Windows NT Diagnostics**. The Windows NT Diagnostics window opens.
3. Click the **Memory** tab to see how much memory your Windows NT Server contains.

4. Before taking down the server to perform a memory upgrade, you must ensure that no users are currently connected. To find out which users are logged in, click **Start**, point to **Programs**, point to **Administrative Tools**, then click **Server Manager**. To see the **Properties for Server** window, click **Computer** on the menu bar, then click **Properties**. The Properties for Server window opens. Click the **Users** button to see which users are currently logged on to your system. Assuming that no users are connected you can shut down the server. Otherwise, you could use the **Alerts** button to send the connected users a message about the server being taken down for upgrades.
5. Click **Start,** then click – **Shutdown** to shut down the server.
6. Turn off the server and unplug it. Detach all cables, including the monitor, network, mouse, and keyboard connectors.
7. Wear a static-dissipating wristband and use static guard mat while you open the server's casing. Because each computer is different, you should consult with your instructor to find out how to remove the casing.
8. Once you have opened the computer, insert the new memory chip by following your instructor's instructions.
9. When you have successfully installed the chip, reattach the server's cover and reconnect the power, keyboard, network, mouse, and monitor cables.
10. Turn the server on.
11. When prompted, log on to Windows NT as the administrator.
12. Repeat steps 2 and 3 to find out how much memory the server now has.

PROJECT 13-3

In this exercise, you will reverse, or uninstall, the service pack that you installed in Project 13-1. Because it is not uncommon to have to uninstall a service pack, you should always create an uninstall folder. Note that you should never attempt to uninstall software (especially on a Windows-based system) by deleting the new software from the system (for example, by dragging the software's folder to the trash). Instead, you must follow proper uninstall procedures to ensure that the software's removal will not cause harm.

1. Log on to your Windows NT server as an administrator (if you aren't already).
2. Click **Start,** point to **Settings,** click **Control Panel,** then double-click the–**Add/Remove Programs** icon.
3. Select **Windows NT 4.0 Service Pack 4**, then click **Add/Remove**. Click **Yes** to confirm the uninstall.
4. After the removal is complete, you will be prompted to restart the server to make the changes effective. Choose **Yes**.

After removing the service pack, you will have returned all applications and services to their previous state, for better or for worse. Note that the uninstall process will not remove the newer security files installed by SP4. If you want to reinstall SP4 in the future, you will need to create another uninstall folder.

PROJECT 13-4

In this project, you will investigate one of the most popular network baselining tools—Concord Communications' Network Health. Rather than installing the program (which is expensive), you can view Concord Communications' online demo for its product. This demo includes graphs of network performance for an imaginary LAN/WAN environment. This exercise requires a workstation with Internet access and a Web browser.

1. Point your browser to the following URL: http://www.concord.com/webdemo /web_demo/mainmenu.htm
2. The Concord Communications' Network Health demo page opens. Under the introductory text, a list of report options appears. Click the **Health** icon to view a number of LAN/WAN health reports.
3. In the list of network health reports, click the **Daily Lan health report** option.
4. Notice that this page has four frames. In the upper-right frame under the Concord logo, notice that a baseline time period of 6 weeks is specified. In the upper-left frame, click the **Network Summary** option.
5. A number of graphs summarizing the network's health appear in the main (lower-right) frame. Scroll through that frame to see how the network traffic and problem data are presented. At what hour of the day is traffic volume highest? At what hour of the day is the network experiencing the most collisions and Ethernet errors?
6. Click your browser's **Back** button three times to return to the demo page.
7. Click the **Traffic Accountant** icon to view statistics on the type and volume of traffic on the network.
8. Notice that you may choose to view several reports. Click the report titled **What is my WWW traffic pattern?**
9. Continue to investigate the Network Health demo. While doing so, consider the advantages and disadvantages of having so much information available to network administrators. Also, consider what types of reports would be important to a company that uses its network for e-commerce versus a company that uses a WAN to perform videoconferencing.

CASE PROJECTS

1. You work as one of five networking engineers in a large insurance company with 500 small offices located across the United States. The headquarters, where you work, relies on 10 Windows NT 3.51 servers with 64 MB RAM, Pentium 166 processors, and redundant disk arrays; roughly half of these disk arrays provide remote access for field users, and the other half provide applications to headquarters. You have been migrating most of your routers to switches this year, and you run an Ethernet 100 Mbps LAN at headquarters. All of the 500 field offices have their own Windows NT servers, but the remote users often complain of poor support and slow or unreliable access to headquarters. Managers are also concerned about security and a need to update the company's intranet. Your manager is currently developing next year's budget. She tells you that she has more than $500,000 to spend on networking upgrades, both hardware and software. She asks your opinion about which items to include in the budget. How would you research your recommendations? What factors would influence you? What additional information should you gather? What kinds of immediate upgrades would you suggest, and which ones are optional or could wait another year?
2. Because one of your suggestions was to upgrade the server hardware, you have been asked to work with a database programmer to develop a customized asset management tool. This tool should track not only the basic facts about your hardware, but also the lease periods and the maintenance needs. Write a one-page request for proposal that will enable a developer to understand your needs. Explain the project's goals and indicate why you included the requirements, time frames, and necessary tasks that you did. Also, describe how the developer and you can make this tool easy to use and adaptable to future needs.
3. You have worked with a friend to upgrade the network operating system on a NetWare 4.11 server to NetWare 5.0 at his small auto repair office. His LAN consists of 1 server and 15 users who rely on the server for billing, customer service, word processing, and Internet access. You helped your friend follow the correct procedure of researching the upgrade, informing the users, creating a backup, and implementing the upgrade. You and he work from 6:00 P.M. to midnight performing the upgrade. When you start your testing at midnight, it looks as though the billing system doesn't work with the new operating system. The staff will begin coming to work at 5:00 A.M. What do you do, how do you do it, and why?

CHAPTER 14

ENSURING INTEGRITY AND AVAILABILITY

After reading this chapter and completing the exercises, you will be able to:

- Identify the characteristics of a network that keep data safe from loss or damage
- Protect an enterprise-wide network from viruses
- Explain network- and system-level fault-tolerance techniques
- Discuss issues related to network backup and recovery strategies
- Describe the components of a useful disaster recovery plan

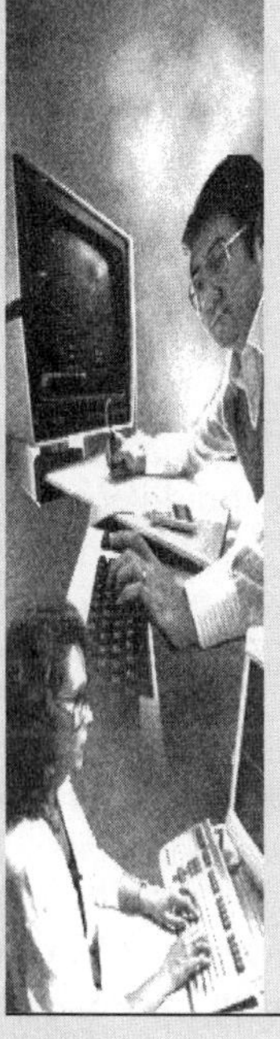

ON THE JOB

I run a very small network for a technical writing firm. (It's my wife's company, and I'm a CNA—Certified NetWare Administrator—so by default I'm the IT manager.) Every evening before leaving the office, my wife religiously starts the network backup.

One morning, I got a "panic" page from my wife: "The server went down last night and won't come back up. Some error about 'unable to mount volume sys'!" I left a client's site for my wife's office. Sure enough, the server had a failed hard drive. "No problem," I confidently announced, "I'll just copy last night's backup to a workstation and you can run in workgroup mode until I replace the drive."

I started the backup software and clicked "Restore." The program responded with an "Error reading tape" message. No matter how furiously I clicked the Restore button, no data streamed forth from any of the backup tapes—not last night's, not last week's, not even last month's. The tapes contained filenames, and a full directory structure existed. Nevertheless, all of the files were the same size: zero. The tape drive had apparently failed some months ago and was dutifully backing up file and directory names, but no actual data.

The moral of this story is that setting a schedule for backups and running backups regularly are not enough. You must consistently test and verify the integrity of your backups to ensure that your data are protected.

Steve Trunk
Manual Labour

As networks take on more of the burden of transporting and storing a day's work, you need to pay increasing attention to the risks involved. You can never assume that data are safe on the network until you have taken explicit measures to protect the information. In this book, you have learned about the architecture of a robust enterprise-wide network as well as hardware, network operating systems, and network troubleshooting. But all the best equipment and software cannot ensure that server hard drives will never fail or that a malicious employee won't sabotage your network.

The topic of protecting data covers a lot of ground, from fault-tolerant servers to security cameras in the computer room. This chapter provides a broad overview of measures that you can take to ensure that your data remain safe. Undoubtedly, these issues will continue to evolve quickly as networks become more open and ubiquitous. If you are interested in specializing in fault tolerance, for example, you can read entire books on the topic. The far-reaching topic of network security is covered in the next chapter.

WHAT ARE INTEGRITY AND AVAILABILITY?

Before learning how to ensure integrity and availability, you should fully understand what these terms mean. **Integrity** refers to the soundness of a network's programs, data, services, devices, and connections. To ensure a network's integrity, you must protect it from anything that might render it unusable. Closely related to the concept of integrity is availability. **Availability** of a file or system refers to how consistently and reliably it can be accessed by authorized personnel. For example, a server that allows staff to log on and use its programs and data 99.99% of the time is considered to be highly available. To ensure availability, you need not only a well-planned and well-configured network, but also data backups, redundant devices, and protection from malicious intruders who could potentially immobilize the network.

A number of phenomena may compromise both integrity and availability, including security breaches, natural disasters (such as tornadoes, floods, hurricanes, and ice storms), malicious intruders, power flaws, and human error. Every network administrator should consider these possibilities when designing a sound network. You can readily imagine the importance of integrity and availability of data in a hospital, for example, where the network not only stores patient records but also provides quick medical reference material, video displays for surgical cameras, and perhaps even control of critical care monitors.

Even if you don't have sophisticated hardware and software to address availability and integrity, as network administrator you can and should take several precautions. This section will remind you of common-sense approaches to data integrity and availability, such as properly restricting file access and developing an enterprise-wide security policy. Later in this chapter, you will learn about more specific or formal (and potentially more expensive) approaches to data protection.

If you have ever supported computer users, you know that they sometimes unintentionally harm their own data, applications, software configurations, or even hardware. Networks may also be intentionally harmed by users unless network administrators take precautionary measures and pay regular, close attention to systems and networks so as to protect them. Although you can't predict every type of vulnerability, you can take measures to guard against most damaging events. Following are some general guidelines for protecting your network:

- *Prevent anyone other than a network administrator from opening or changing the system files.* Pay attention to the rights assigned to regular users (including the groups "users" or "everyone"). The use of rights to restrict network access to servers will be discussed in depth in Chapter 15. For now, bear in mind that the worst consequence of applying overly stringent file restrictions is a temporary inconvenience to a few users. In contrast, the worst consequence of applying overly lenient file restrictions could be a network disaster.

- *Monitor the network for unauthorized access or changes.* You can install programs that routinely check whether and when the files you've specified (for example, autoexec.ncf on a NetWare server) have changed. Such monitoring programs are typically inexpensive and easy to customize. They may even enable the system to page or e-mail you when a system file changes. In addition, you can monitor the network for unauthorized access to devices such as routers or switches. This practice, called **intrusion detection**, is described in more detail later in this chapter.
- *Record authorized system changes in a change management system.* In Chapters 12 and 13, you learned about the importance of change management. Recording system changes in a change management system will enable you and your colleagues to understand what's happening to your network and protect it from harm. For example, suppose that a Windows NT server hangs up when you attempt to restart it. Before launching into troubleshooting techniques that may create more problems and reduce the availability of the system, you could review the change management log. It might indicate that a colleague recently installed a new service pack. With this information in hand, you could focus on the service pack as the probable source of the problem.
- *Install redundant components.* The term **redundancy** refers to a situation in which more than one component is installed and ready to use for storing, processing, or transporting data. To maintain high availability, you should ensure that critical network elements, such as your WAN connection to the Internet or your single file server's hard disk, are redundant. Some types of redundancy require large investments, so your organization should weigh the risks of losing connectivity or data against the cost of adding expensive duplicate components such as data links or high-end servers.
- *Perform regular health checks on the network.* Prevention is the best weapon against network down time. By implementing a network monitoring program such as those discussed in Chapter 13, you can anticipate problems before they affect availability or integrity. For example, if your network monitor alerts you to rapidly rising utilization on a critical network segment, you can analyze the network to discover where the problem lies and perhaps fix it before it takes down the segment.
- *Monitor system performance, error logs, and the system log book regularly.* By keeping track of system errors and trends in performance, you have a better chance of correcting problems before they cause a hard disk failure and potentially damage your system files. By default, all network operating systems keep error logs. It's important that you know where these error logs reside on your server and understand how to interpret them.
- *Keep backups, boot disks, and emergency repair disks current and available.* If your file system or critical boot files become corrupted by a system crash, you can use the emergency or boot disks to recover the system. Otherwise, you may need to reinstall the software before you will be able to start the system. If you ever face the

prospect of recovering from a system loss or disaster, you will need to recover in the quickest manner possible. For this effort, you will need not only backup devices, but also a backup strategy tailored to your environment.

- *Implement and enforce security and disaster recovery policies.* Everyone in your organization should know what he or she is allowed to do on the network. For example, if you decide that it's too risky for employees to download games off the Internet because of the potential for virus infection, you may inform them of a ban on downloading games. You might enforce this policy by restricting users' ability to create or change files (such as executable files) that are copied to the workstation during the downloading of games. Making such decisions and communicating them to staff should be part of your security policy. Likewise, everyone in your organization should be familiar with your disaster recovery plan, which should detail your strategy for bringing the network back to functionality in case of an unexpected failure. Although such policies take time to develop and may be difficult to enforce, they can directly affect your network's availability and integrity.

These measures are merely first steps to ensuring network integrity and availability, but they are essential. The following sections describe what types of policies, hardware, and software you can implement to achieve these goals.

VIRUSES

Strictly speaking, a **virus** is a program that replicates itself so as to infect more computers, either through network connections or through floppy disks passed among users. A virus may damage files or systems, or it may simply annoy users by flashing messages or pictures on the screen or by causing the keyboard to beep. In fact, some viruses cause no harm and can remain unnoticed on a system forever.

Many other unwanted and potentially destructive programs are mistakenly called viruses. For example, a program that disguises itself as something useful but actually harms your system is called a **Trojan horse**, after the famous wooden horse in which soldiers were hidden. Because Trojan horses do not replicate themselves, they are not technically viruses. An example of a Trojan horse is an executable file that someone sends you over the Internet, promising that the executable will install a great new game, when in fact it reformats your hard disk.

In this section, you will learn about the different types of viruses and other malicious programs that may infect your network, their methods of distribution, and, most importantly, protection against them. Viruses can infect computers running any type of operating system—Macintosh, NetWare, Windows, or UNIX—at any time. As a network administrator, you must take measures to guard against them.

TYPES OF VIRUSES

Many thousands of viruses exist, although only a relatively small number cause the majority of virus-related damage. Viruses can be classified into different categories based on where they reside on a computer and how they propagate themselves. Often, creators of viruses apply slight variations to their original viruses to make them undetectable by antivirus programs. The result is a host of related, albeit different viruses. The makers of antivirus software must then update their checking programs to recognize the new variations, and the virus creators may again alter their viruses to render them undetectable. This cycle continues, ad infinitum. No matter what their variation, all viruses belong to one of the categories described below:

- *Boot sector viruses*—The most common types of viruses, **boot sector viruses** reside on the boot sector of a floppy disk and become transferred to the partition sector or the DOS boot sector on a hard disk. The only way to infect a computer with a boot sector virus is to attempt to start the computer from an infected floppy disk. This event may happen unintentionally if a floppy disk is left in the drive when a machine starts.

  For example, one afternoon a colleague may give you a floppy disk with a spreadsheet that you need to edit and return to him. You put the floppy into your disk drive and open the spreadsheet file. So far, the virus in the floppy disk's boot sector has gone unnoticed. You begin to edit the spreadsheet, but get sidetracked by a critical file server problem. It's six o'clock by the time you have fixed the file server, and you're late for your evening cooking class, so you close all programs, turn off your machine, and rush out the door. The next morning, you switch on your machine and walk away to refill your coffee cup. Because you left the floppy disk in your disk drive, your computer attempts to start from the floppy disk drive. It loads the first sector into memory and executes it (normally, this sector contains a program written by Microsoft to load DOS or, if it can't find DOS on the disk, to tell you so). Because the floppy drive is infected with a boot sector virus, however, it executes the virus program instead. The virus installs itself on your computer's hard disk, replacing the hard disk's boot sector record. Until you disinfect your computer, the virus will propagate to every floppy disk to which you write information.

  Boot sector viruses are very common in part because most users don't understand how they work, and because floppy disks are frequently passed from user to user without any virus checking. Examples of boot sector viruses include "Stoned," "Boot-437," "Goldbug," "Lilith," "Crazy Eddie," and "Peak." The Stoned virus, for example, originated in New Zealand in 1988; since then, a multitude of variations on it have been distributed under different names. Its main symptom of infection is a message that appears upon starting the computer, announcing that "This PC is now stoned." In addition, typical of boot sector viruses, at least some of the workstation's files will be unreachable by the file system as a result of infection.

- *Macro viruses*—**Macro viruses** are newer types of viruses that take the form of a word-processing or spreadsheet program macro, which may be executed as the user works with a word-processing or spreadsheet program. Macro viruses were the first type of virus to infect data files rather than executable files. Because data files are more apt to be shared among users, and because macro viruses are typically easier to write than executable viruses, macro viruses have quickly become prevalent. Although the earliest versions of macro viruses proved annoying but not harmful, currently circulating macro viruses may threaten data files.

Because macro viruses work under different applications, they can travel between computers that use different operating systems. For example, you might send a Microsoft Word document as an attachment to an e-mail message, or give it to someone on a floppy disk. If that document contains a macro virus, when the recipient opens the document, the macro runs, and all future documents created or saved by that program will be infected. Examples of macro viruses include "Groov," "Laroux," "Trasher," "Caligula," and "Jedi." Symptoms of macro virus infection vary widely but may include missing options from application menus; damaged, changed, or missing data files; or strange pop-up messages that appear when you use an application such as Microsoft's Word or Excel.

- *File-infected viruses*—**File-infected viruses** attach themselves to executable files. When the infected executable file runs, the virus copies itself to memory. Later, the virus will attach itself to other executable files. Some file-infected viruses can attach themselves to other programs even while their "host" executable runs a process in the background, such as a printer service or screen saver program. Because they stay in memory while you continue to work on your computer, these viruses can have devastating consequences, infecting numerous programs and requiring you to not only disinfect your computer, but also reinstall virtually all software. Examples of file-infected viruses include "Tequila," "Harry," "Anxiety," "Tentacle," and "Cabanas." Symptoms of a virus infection may include damaged program files, inexplicable file size increases, changed icons for programs, strange messages that appear when you attempt to run a program, or the inability to run a program.
- *Network viruses*—**Network viruses** propagate themselves via network protocols, commands, messaging programs, and data links. Although all viruses could theoretically travel across network connections, network viruses are specially designed to take advantage of network vulnerabilities. For example, a network virus may attach itself to FTP transactions to and from your Web server. Another type of network virus may spread through Microsoft Exchange messages only.

  Because network access has become more sophisticated over the last decade, few network viruses have had the opportunity to thrive. Examples of network viruses include "Homer" and "ShareFun." Because network viruses are characterized by their transmission method, their symptoms may include almost any type of anomaly, ranging from strange pop-up messages to file damage.
- *Worms*—**Worms** are not technically viruses, but rather programs that run independently and travel between computers and across networks. They may be transmitted by any type of file transfer, including e-mail. Worms do not alter other programs in the same way that viruses do, but they may carry viruses. Because they can transport (and hide) viruses, you should be concerned about picking up worms when you exchange files from the Internet or through floppy disks. Examples of worms include "Acoragil," "Simpsalapim, "W32/Ska," and "TME.643." Symptoms of worm infection may include almost any type of anomaly, ranging from strange pop-up messages to file damage.

- *Trojan horse*—As mentioned earlier, a Trojan horse (sometimes simply called a "Trojan") is not actually a virus, but rather a program that claims to do something useful but instead harms the computer or system. Trojan horses range from being nuisances to causing significant system destruction. Most virus-checking programs will recognize known Trojan horses and eradicate them. The best way to guard against Trojan horses, however, is to refrain from downloading an executable file whose origins you can't confirm.

  Suppose, for example, that you needed to download a new driver for a NIC on your network. Rather than going to a generic "network support site" on the Internet, you should download the file from the NIC manufacturer's Web site. Most importantly, never run an executable file that has been sent to you over the Internet as an attachment to a mail message whose sender or origins you cannot verify.

  Examples of Trojan horses include "Coke," "On4ever," "Steroid Trojan," and "Telefoon." One Trojan horse program, "Antigen," disguises itself as an antivirus program; when executed, it scans the computer's hard disk for personal information such as network IDs, passwords, and telephone numbers. It then compiles this information and mails it to a specific e-mail address.

Virus Characteristics

Viruses that belong to any of the preceding categories may have additional characteristics that make them harder to detect and eliminate. Some of these characteristics are discussed below:

- **Encryption**—Some viruses are encrypted to prevent detection. As you will learn in the following section, most virus-scanning software searches files for a recognizable string of characters that identify the virus. If the virus is encrypted, it will thwart the antivirus program's attempts to detect it.
- **Stealth**— Some viruses hide themselves to prevent detection. Typically, stealth viruses disguise themselves as legitimate programs or replace part of a legitimate program's code with their destructive code.
- **Polymorphism**—Polymorphic viruses change their characteristics (such as the arrangement of their bytes, size, and internal instructions) every time they are transferred to a new system, making them harder to identify. Some polymorphic viruses use complicated algorithms and incorporate nonsensical commands to achieve their changes. Polymorphic viruses are considered to be the most sophisticated and potentially dangerous type of virus.
- **Time-dependence**—Time-dependent viruses are programmed to activate on a particular date. These types of viruses, also known as "time bombs," can remain dormant and harmless until their activation date arrives. Like any other type of virus, time-dependent viruses may have destructive effects or may cause some innocuous event periodically. For example, viruses in the "Time" family cause a PC's speaker to beep approximately once per hour.

Hundreds of new viruses are unleashed on the world's computers each month. Although it is impossible to keep abreast of every virus in circulation, you should at least know where you can find out more information about viruses. Some excellent resources for learning about new viruses, their characteristics, and ways to get rid of them are McAfee's Virus Information Library at http://vil.mcafee.com/villib/query.asp and Dr. Solomon's Virus Central at http://www.drsolomon.com/vircen/index.cfm.

VIRUS PROTECTION

Now that you know about the different types of viruses, you may think that you can simply install a virus-scanning program on your network and move on to the next issue. In fact, virus protection involves more than just installing antivirus software. It requires choosing the most appropriate antivirus program for your environment, monitoring the network, continually updating the antivirus program, and educating users. In addition, you should draft and enforce an antivirus policy for your organization.

Antivirus Software

Even if a user doesn't immediately notice a virus on his or her system, the virus will generally leave evidence of itself, whether by changing the operation of the machine or by announcing its signature characteristics in the virus code. Although the latter can be detected only via antivirus software, users can typically detect the former changes without any special software. For example, you may suspect a virus on your system if any of the following symptoms appear:

- Unexplained increases in file sizes
- Programs (such as Microsoft Word) launching, running, or exiting more slowly than usual
- Unusual error messages appearing without probable cause
- Significant, unexpected loss of system memory
- Fluctuations in display quality

Often, however, you will not notice a virus until it has already damaged your files.

Although virus programmers have become more sophisticated in disguising their viruses (for example, using encryption and polymorphism), antivirus software programmers have kept pace with them. The antivirus software you choose for your network should at least perform the following functions:

- It should detect viruses through **signature scanning**, a comparison of a file's content with known virus signatures (that is, the unique identifying characteristics in the code) in a signature database. This signature database must be frequently updated so that the software can detect new viruses as they emerge. Updates can usually be downloaded from the antivirus software vendor's Web site.
- It should detect viruses through **integrity checking**, a method of comparing current characteristics of files and disks against an archived version of these characteristics to discover any changes. The most common example of integrity

checking involves the use of a checksum, though this tactic may not prove effective against viruses with stealth capabilities.

- It should detect viruses by monitoring unexpected file changes or virus-like behaviors.
- It should receive regular updates and modifications from a centralized network console. The vendor should provide free upgrades on a regular (at least monthly) basis, plus technical support.
- It should consistently report only valid viruses, rather than reporting "false alarms." Scanning techniques that attempt to identify viruses by discovering "virus-like" behavior, also known as **heuristic scanning**, are the most fallible and most likely to emit false alarms. As you might imagine, using an antivirus package that detects more viruses than are actually present can be not only annoying, but also a waste of time.

Occasionally, shrink-wrapped, off-the-shelf software will ship with viruses on its disks. Therefore, it is always a good idea to scan authorized software from known sources just as you would scan software from unknown sources.

Your implementation of antivirus software will depend on your computing environment's needs. For example, you may use a desktop security program on every computer on the network that prevents users from copying executable files to their hard disks or to network drives. In this case, it may be unnecessary to implement a program that continually scans each machine; in fact, this approach may be undesirable because the continual scanning may adversely impact performance. On the other hand, if you are the network administrator for a student computer lab where potentially thousands of different users will bring their own disks for use on the computers, you will want to scan the machines thoroughly at least once a day and perhaps more often.

When installing antivirus software on a network, one of your most important decisions is where to put it. If you install antivirus software only on every desktop, you have addressed the most likely point of entry, but ignored the most important files that might be infected—those on the server. If the antivirus software resides on the server and checks every file and transaction, you will protect important files but slow your network performance considerably. Likewise, if you put antivirus software on firewalls and routers, your network will experience performance problems, bringing all network communication to a crawl. How can you find a balance between sufficient protection and minimal impact on performance? Depending on your network infrastructure, you may want to implement antivirus software that scans each desktop once daily, as well as scans new files on the e-mail server, as those locations are the most likely places for viruses to enter. You should also ensure that file servers are scanned regularly, although continual may be unnecessary.

Obviously, the antivirus package you choose should be compatible with your network and desktop operating systems. Popular antivirus packages include McAfee's Virus Scan, Dr. Solomon's Virex, Computer Associates' NetShield, ThunderByte's Virus Control, and Norton's AntiVirus.

In addition to using specialized antivirus software to guard against virus infection, you may find that your applications can help identify viruses. Microsoft's Word and Excel programs, for example, will warn you when you attempt to open a file that contains macros. You then have the option of disabling the macros (thereby preventing any macro viruses from working when you open the file) or allowing the macros to remain usable. In general, it's a good idea to disable the macros in a file that you have received from someone else, at least until after you have checked the file for viruses with your virus scanning software.

Antivirus Policies

Antivirus software alone will not keep your network safe from viruses. You also need to implement policies that limit the potential for users to introduce viruses to their workstations and to the network. The importance of these policies will increase as a network grows larger and more accessible and therefore becomes more susceptible to viruses.

To understand why, think of a day-care center attended by only 2 children with 1 adult supervising. These 3 people will bring and share whatever germs they have encountered outside the day-care center; any one person could catch the germs of the other two. If the day-care center houses 20 children and 7 adults, however, the number of germs that people may pass to each other multiplies. Now any single person could catch the germs of 26 others. Similarly, a network with 1,000 users, each of whom might bring floppy disks from home and download files off the Web, inherently carries a greater risk of virus infection than a network serving only 10 users.

Because most computer viruses can be prevented by the application of a little technology and a little intelligence, it's important that all network users understand how to prevent viruses. An antivirus policy should provide rules for using antivirus software and policies for installing programs, sharing files, and using floppy disks. Furthermore, it should be authorized and supported by the organization's management, and sanctions should by outlined for disobeying the policy. Some good, general guidelines for an antivirus policy are as follows:

- Every computer in an organization should be equipped with virus detection and cleaning software that regularly scans for viruses. This software should be centrally distributed and updated to stay current with newly released viruses.
- Users should not be allowed to alter or disable the antivirus software.
- Users should know what to do in case their antivirus program detects a virus. For example, you might recommend that the user not continue working on his or her computer, but instead call the help desk and receive assistance in disinfecting the system.
- Every organization should have an antivirus team that focuses on maintaining the antivirus measures in place. This team would be responsible for choosing antivirus software, keeping the software updated, educating users, and responding in case of a significant virus outbreak.
- Users should be prohibited from installing any unauthorized software on their systems. This edict may seem extreme, but in fact users bringing programs (especially games) on disk from home are the most common source of viruses. If your

organization permits game playing, you might institute a policy in which every game must be first checked for viruses and then installed on a user's system by a technician.

- Organizations should impose penalties on users who do not follow the antivirus policy.

When drafting an antivirus policy, bear in mind that these measures are not meant to restrict users' freedom, but rather to protect the network from serious damage and expensive down time. Explain to users that the antivirus policy protects their own data as well as critical system files. If possible, automate the antivirus software installation and operation so that users barely notice its presence. Do not rely on users to run their antivirus software each time they insert a disk or download a new program, because they will quickly forget to do so.

VIRUS HOAXES

As in any other community, rumors sometimes spread through the Internet user community. One type of rumor consists of a false alert about a dangerous, new virus that could cause serious damage to your workstation. Such an alert is known as a **virus hoax**. Virus hoaxes usually have no realistic basis and should be ignored, as they merely attempt to create panic. Sometimes the origins of virus hoaxes can be traced (for example, the famous virus hoax, "GoodTimes," was traced to students at Swarthmore College), but often their sources remain anonymous.

A typical example of a virus hoax is one called "It Takes Guts to Say 'Jesus'," in which the body of the message says the following:

> VIRUS WARNING !!!!!!!
> If you receive an e-mail titled "It Takes Guts to Say 'Jesus'," DO NOT open it. It will erase everything on your hard drive. Forward this letter to as many people as you can. This is a new, very malicious virus and not many people know about it. This information was announced yesterday morning from IBM; please share it with people who might access the Internet.

Notice that the hoax warns that the virus will erase everything on your hard drive. In fact, no current virus can erase your hard drive when you merely open an infected e-mail message. Only an executable file, such as a Trojan horse, can accomplish this damage. Virus hoaxes also typically demand that you pass the alert to everyone in your Internet address book, thus propagating the rumor.

Virtually the only way to decide whether a message that warns about a virus is a hoax is to look it up on a Web page that lists virus hoaxes. A good resource for verifying virus hoaxes is http://www.icsa.net/services/consortia/anti-virus/alerthoax.shtml. This Web site also allows you to learn more about the phenomenon of virus hoaxes.

If you or your colleagues receive a virus hoax, simply ignore it. Educate your colleagues to do the same, explaining why virus hoaxes should not cause alarm. Remember, however, that even a virus hoax message could potentially contain an *attached* file that does cause damage if executed. Once again, the best policy is to refrain from running any program whose origins you cannot verify.

FAULT TOLERANCE

Fault tolerance is the capacity for a system to continue performing despite an unexpected hardware or software malfunction. Before you can understand the issues related to fault tolerance, you must recognize the difference between failures and faults as they apply to networks. In broad terms, a **failure** is a deviation from a specified level of system performance for a given period of time. In other words, a failure occurs when something doesn't work as promised or as planned. For example, if your car breaks down on the highway, you can consider the breakdown to be a failure. A **fault**, on the other hand, involves the malfunction of one component of a system. A fault can result in a failure. For example, the fault that caused your car to break down might be a leaking water pump. The goal of fault-tolerant systems is to prevent faults from progressing to failures.

Fault tolerance can be achieved in varying degrees, with the optimal level of fault tolerance for a system depending on how critical its services and files are to productivity. At the highest level of fault tolerance, a system would remain unaffected by a drastic problem, such as a power failure. For example, an uninterruptible power supply (UPS) or a gas-powered generator that supplies electricity to a server despite a city-wide power failure provides high fault tolerance.

In addition to using alternative power sources, fault tolerance can be achieved through mirroring. When two servers mirror each other, they can quickly take over for their partner if it should fail. The process of one component immediately assuming the duties of an identical component is known as automatic **fail-over**. Even if one server's NIC fails, for example, failover ensures that the other server can automatically handle the first server's responsibilities. In highly fault-tolerant schemes, network users will not even recognize that a problem has occurred. In a moderately fault-tolerant system, on the other hand, users may have to endure brief service outages. An example of a moderately fault-tolerant system is one in which two servers mirror each other's data, but require a network administrator to intervene and switch users from one server to the other.

An excellent way to achieve fault tolerance is to provide duplicate, or redundant, elements to compensate for faults in critical components. You can implement redundancy for servers, cabling, routers, hubs, gateways, NICs, hard disks, power supplies, and other components. The most common type of network redundancy is data backup. **Hard disk redundancy**, called **RAID** (for **Redundant Array of Inexpensive Disks**), represents a sophisticated means for dynamically replicating data over several physical hard drives. These and other fault-tolerant techniques are discussed in more depth in later sections, which are ordered according to the layer of the OSI Model to which they correspond, from the Physical layer to the Application layer.

To assess the fault tolerance of your network, you must identify any **single point of failure**—that is, a point on the network where, if a fault occurs, the transfer of data may break down without possibility of an automatic recovery. For instance, if a LAN in your home consists of three PCs, each of which is connected to a hub and a file server in the basement, your LAN has several single points of failure: the connection between the hub and the file server; the hub itself; each of the hub's ports; the electrical connection that powers the hub; the electrical connection that powers the file server; the file server's NIC, fan, hard disk, memory, and processor; and—depending on the criticality of each PC—potentially all of their connections and components.

Redundancy is intended to eliminate single points of failure. If your network cannot tolerate any down time, you must consider redundancy for power, cabling, hard disks, NICs, data links, and any other components that might halt operations if they suffer a fault. As you can imagine, complete redundancy is expensive. Therefore, you must understand not only where your network's single points of failure exist, but also how their malfunctioning might affect the network.

ENVIRONMENT

As you consider sophisticated fault-tolerance techniques for servers, routers, and WAN links, remember to analyze the physical environment in which your devices operate. Part of your data protection plan involves protecting your network from excessive heat or moisture, break-ins, and natural disasters. In the case of natural disasters, the best approach is to store data backups in a location other than where your servers reside.

In addition, you should make sure that your telecommunications closets and equipment rooms are air-conditioned and maintained at a constant humidity, according to the hardware manufacturer's recommendations. You can purchase temperature and humidity monitors that trip alarms if specified limits are exceeded. These monitors can prove very useful because the temperature can rise rapidly in a room full of equipment, causing overheated equipment to fail.

POWER

No matter where you live, you have probably experienced a complete loss of power (a blackout) or a temporary dimming of lights (a brownout). Such fluctuations in power are frequently caused by forces of nature such as hurricanes, tornadoes, or ice storms. They may also occur when a utility company performs maintenance or construction tasks. The following section describes the types of power fluctuations for which network administrators should prepare. The next two sections describe alternative power sources, such as a UPS (uninterruptible power supply) or electrical generator, that can compensate for these flaws.

Power Flaws

Whatever the cause, networks cannot tolerate power loss or less than optimal power. The following list describes power flaws that can damage your equipment:

- ***Surge***—A momentary increase in voltage due to distant lightning strikes or electrical problems. Surges may last only a few thousandths of a second, but several surges can degrade a computer's power supply. Surges are common. Indeed, without a surge protector, systems will be subjected to multiple surges each year.
- ***Line noise***—A fluctuation in voltage levels caused by other devices on the network or electromagnetic interference. Some line noise is unavoidable, but excessive line noise may cause a power supply to malfunction, immediately corrupting program or data files and gradually damaging motherboards and other computer

circuits. When you turn on fluorescent lights or a laser printer and the lights dim, you have probably introduced noise into the electrical system. If you continue working on your computer during a lightning storm, your computer will be subject to line noise. Some UPSs guard against line noise, and any critical system should have this type of protection.

- ***Brownout***—A momentary decrease in voltage; also known as a **sag**. An overtaxed electrical system may cause brownouts, which you may recognize in your home as a dimming of the lights. Such decreases in voltage can cause significant problems for computer devices. Most UPSs guard against brownouts.
- ***Blackout***—A complete power loss. A blackout may or may not cause significant damage to your network. If you are performing a network operating system upgrade when a blackout occurs and you have not protected the server, its network operating system may be damaged so completely that the server will not restart and its operating system must be reinstalled from scratch. If the file server is idle when a blackout occurs, however, it may recover very easily. All UPSs are designed to compensate for blackouts, but how quickly and completely and for how long will depend on the particular unit. To handle extended blackouts or to support a building full of computers, you will need something more powerful than a UPS, such as a gas- or diesel-powered electrical generator.

Each of these power problems can adversely affect network devices and their availability. Not surprisingly then, network administrators must spend a great deal of money and time ensuring that power remains available and problem-free. The following sections describe devices and ways of dealing with unstable power.

Uninterruptible Power Supply (UPS)

A popular way to ensure that a network device does not lose power is to install an **uninterruptible power supply (UPS)**. A UPS is a battery-operated power source directly attached to one or more devices and to a power supply (such as a wall outlet), which prevents undesired features of the wall outlet's A/C power from harming the device or interrupting its services.

UPSs vary widely in the type of power aberrations they can rectify, the length of time for which they can provide power, and the number of devices they can support. Of course, they also vary widely in price. Some UPSs are intended for home use, designed to merely keep your PC running long enough for you to properly shut it down in case of a blackout. Other UPSs perform sophisticated operations such as line conditioning, power supply monitoring, and error notification. The type of UPS you choose will depend on your budget, the number and size of your systems, and the critical nature of those systems.

UPSs are classified into two general categories: standby and online. A **standby UPS** provides continuous voltage to a device by switching instantaneously to the battery when it detects a loss of power from the wall outlet. Upon restoration of the power, the standby UPS switches the device back to using A/C power again. One problem exists with standby UPSs: in the time that it takes the UPS to discover that power from the wall outlet has faltered, a sensitive device (such as a server) may have already detected the power loss and shut down or restarted. This time gap may last from two to four seconds. Technically, a standby UPS doesn't provide continuous power; for this reason, it is sometimes called an "offline" UPS. Nevertheless, standby UPSs may prove adequate even for critical network devices such as servers, routers, and gateways. They cost significantly less than online UPSs. Figure 14-1 depicts a standby UPS.

Figure 14-1 Standby UPSs

An **online UPS** uses the A/C power from the wall outlet to continuously charge its battery, while providing power to a network device through its battery. In other words, a server connected to an online UPS always relies on the UPS battery for its electricity. An online UPS offers the best kind of power redundancy available. Because the server never needs to switch from the wall outlet's power to the UPS's power, there is no risk of momentarily losing service. Also, because the UPS always provides the power, it can deal with noise, surges, and sags before the power reaches the attached device. As you can imagine, online UPSs are much more expensive than standby UPSs. Figure 14-2 shows an online UPS.

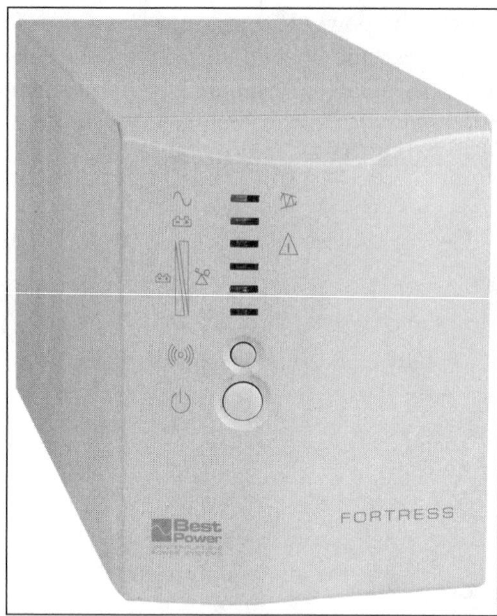

Figure 14-2 An online UPS

How do you decide which UPS is right for your network? You must consider a number of factors:

- *Amount of power needed*—The more power required by your device, the more powerful the UPS needed. Suppose that your organization decides to cut costs and purchase a UPS that cannot supply the amount of power required by a device. If the power to your building ever fails, this UPS will not support your device—you might as well have not installed any UPS.

  Electrical power is measured in volt-amps. A **volt-amp (VA)** is the product of the voltage and current (measured in amps) of the electricity on a line. To determine approximately how many VAs your device requires, you can use the following conversion: 1.4 volt-amps = 1 watt (W). A desktop computer, for example, may use a 200 W power supply and therefore require a UPS capable of at least 280 VA to keep the CPU running in case of a blackout. If you want backup power for your entire home office, however, you must account for the power needs for your monitor and any peripherals, such as printers, when purchasing a UPS. A medium-sized server with a monitor and external tape drive may use 402 W, thus requiring a UPS capable of providing at least 562 VA power. Determining your power needs can prove a challenge. Not only do you have to account for your existing equipment, but you should also consider how you might upgrade the supported device over the next several years. For example, you may purchase a server with only 4 GB of hard disk space, but plan to add 24 GB next year. When you upgrade the hard disk, you may also need to upgrade the UPS. Before you spend thousands of dollars on a UPS, consult with your equipment manufacturer to obtain its recommendations on power needs.

- *Period of time to keep a device running*—Most UPSs are rated to support a device for 15 to 20 minutes. The longer you anticipate needing a UPS to power your device, the more powerful your UPS must be. For example, the medium-sized server that could rely on a 574 VA UPS to remain functional for 20 minutes would need a 1100 VA server to remain functional for 90 minutes. To determine how long your device might require power from a UPS, consider the length of your typical power outages. If you live in an area that frequently suffers severe thunderstorms, you might want to purchase a higher-capacity UPS to cover longer outages.
- *Line conditioning*—Any UPS used on a network device should also offer surge suppression to protect against surges and line conditioning, or filtering, to guard against line noise. Line conditioners and UPS units include special noise filters that remove line noise. The manufacturer's technical specifications should indicate the amount of filtration required for each UPS. Noise suppression is expressed in decibel levels (dB) at a specific frequency (KHz or MHz). The higher the decibel level, the greater the protection.
- *Cost*—Prices for good UPSs vary widely, depending on the unit's size and extra features. A relatively small UPS that can power one server for 5 to 10 minutes might cost between $50 and $300. A large UPS that can power a sophisticated router for 10 to 20 minutes might cost between $200 and $3,000. On a critical system, however, you should not try to cut costs by buying an off-brand, potentially unreliable, or weak UPS.

As with other large purchases, you should research several UPS manufacturers and their products before reaching a decision. Also ensure that the manufacturer provides a warranty and lets you test the UPS with your equipment. It's important to try out the UPS with your equipment to ensure that it will satisfy your needs. Popular UPS manufacturers are APC, Best, Deltec, MGE, and Tripp Lite.

Generators

If your organization cannot withstand a power loss of any duration, either because of its computer services or other electrical needs, you might consider investing in an electrical generator for your building. Generators can be powered by diesel, liquid propane gas, natural gas, or steam. Although they do not provide surge protection, generators do provide clean (free from noise) electricity.

As when choosing a UPS, you should calculate your organization's crucial electrical demands to determine what size of generator you need. You should also estimate how long the generator may be required to power your building. Gas or diesel generators may cost between $10,000 and $3,000,000 (for the largest industrial types). Alternatively, you can rent electrical generators. To find out more about options for renting or purchasing generators in your area, contact your local electrical utility.

TOPOLOGY

You have read about topology and architecture fault tolerance in previous chapters of this book. In Chapter 5, you learned about a variety of physical network topologies: star, ring, bus, mesh, and hybrid. Recall that each of these topologies inherently assumes certain advantages and disadvantages, and you need to assess your network's needs before designing your data links.

A mesh topology offers the best fault tolerance. To refresh your memory, a mesh network is one in which nodes are connected either directly or indirectly by multiple pathways. Figure 14-3 depicts a fully meshed network.

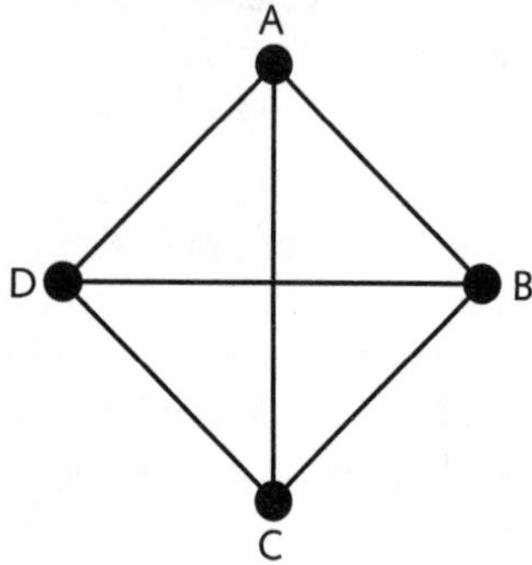

Figure 14-3 A fully meshed network

In a mesh topology, data can travel over multiple paths from any one point to another. For example, if the direct link between point A and point B in Figure 14-3 becomes severed, data can be rerouted automatically from point A to point C and then to point B. Alternatively, it may be rerouted from point A to point D to point B, and so on. You can see that a fully meshed network provides multiple redundancies and therefore greater fault tolerance than a network with a single redundancy.

Figure 14-4 illustrates a network that contains single redundancy. In this example, if one link between point A and point B becomes severed, data can automatically be rerouted over the second link. If the link between point A and point B and the link between point A and point C are both severed, however, the network will suffer a failure.

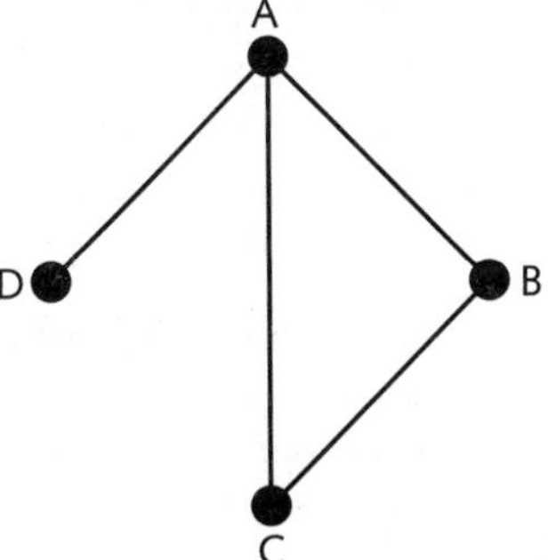

Figure 14-4 A network with one redundant connection

The physical media you use may also offer redundancy. Recall from Chapter 7 that a FDDI or SONET ring can easily recover from a fault in one of its links because it forms a ring, as pictured in Figure 14-5. In this example, if the outer SONET link between point A and point B becomes severed, data can circumvent the fault to move between the two points.

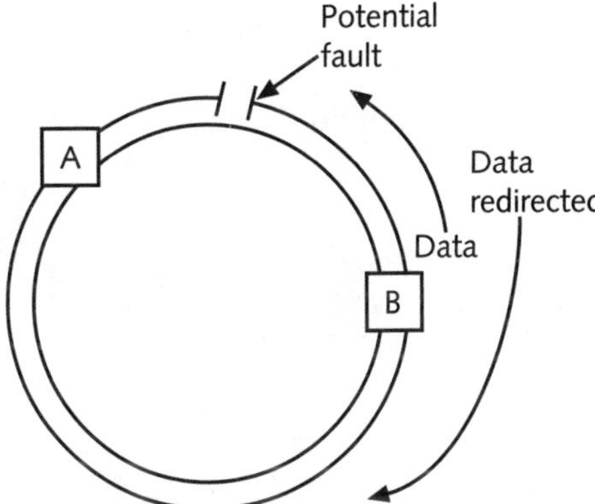

Figure 14-5 A self-healing SONET ring

Mesh topologies and SONET rings are good choices for highly available LANs and WANs. But what about connections to the Internet? Or data backup connections? You may need to establish more than one of these types of links.

As an example, imagine that you work for a data services firm called PayNTime that processes payroll checks for a large oil company in the Houston area. Every day you receive updated payroll information over a T1 link from your client, and every Thursday PayNTime compiles this information and then cuts 2,000 checks that you ship overnight to the client's headquarters. What would happen if the T1 link between PayNTime and the oil company suffered damage in a flood and became unusable on a Thursday morning? How would you ensure that the employees received their pay? If no redundant link to the oil company existed, you would probably need to gather and input the data into your system at least partially by hand. Even then, chances are that you wouldn't process the payroll checks in time to be shipped overnight.

In this type of situation, you would want a duplicate connection between PayNTime and the oil company's site. You might contract with two different service carriers to ensure the redundancy. Alternatively, you might arrange with one service carrier to provide two redundant routes. However you provide redundancy in your network topology, you should make sure that the critical data transactions can follow more than one possible path from source to target.

Redundancy in your network offers the advantage of reducing the risk of losing functionality, and potentially profits, from a network fault. As you might guess, however, the disadvantage of redundancy is its cost. If you subscribed with two different service providers for two T1 links in the PayNTime example, you would probably double your monthly leasing costs of approximately $1,000. Multiply that amount times 12 months, and then times the number of clients for which you need to provide redundancy—and the extra layers of protection quickly become expensive. Redundancy is like a homeowner's insurance policy: you may never need to use it, but if you don't get it, the cost can be much higher than your premiums. As a general rule, you should invest in connection redundancies where they are absolutely necessary.

Now suppose that PayNTime provides services not only to the oil company, but also to a temporary agency in the Houston area. Both links are critical because both companies need their payroll checks cut each week. With links to two customers, you may be able to take advantage of a T1 connection between the customers' sites to create a partially meshed network, as pictured in Figure 14-6. Now if the link between PayNTime and the oil firm suffers a fault, data can theoretically be rerouted through the temporary agency's connection.

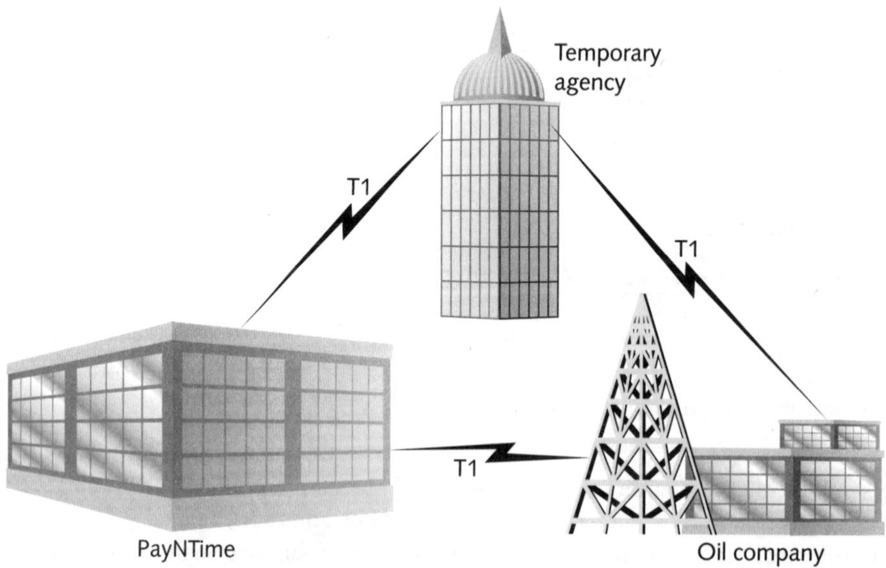

Figure 14-6 Redundancy between a firm and two customers

You may notice a problem with this scenario, however. What if the temporary agency doesn't want the oil company's transactions using its bandwidth, even in case of emergency? And what happens when the third and fourth customers are added to the network? To address concerns of capacity and scalability, you may want to consider partnering with an ISP and establishing secure VPNs with your clients. With a VPN, PayNTime could shift the costs of redundancy and network design to the service provider and concentrate on the task it does best—processing payroll. Figure 14-7 illustrates this type of arrangement.

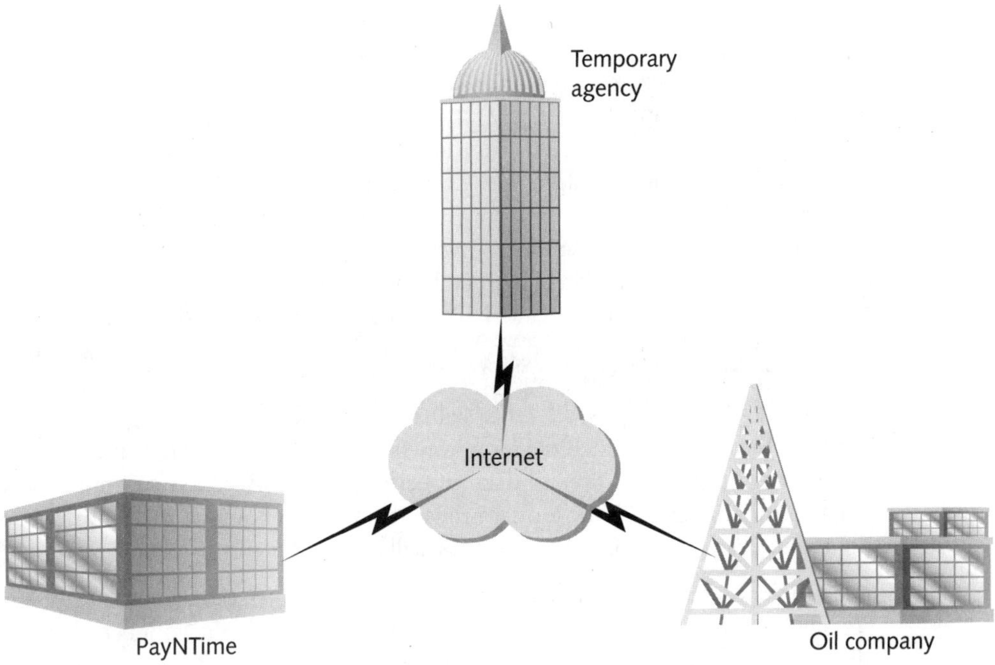

Figure 14-7 VPNs linking multiple customers

CONNECTIVITY

In the previous section, you learned the basics about providing fault tolerance in a LAN or WAN topology. But what about the devices that connect one segment of a LAN or WAN to another? What happens when they experience a fault? In Chapter 6, you learned how routers, bridges, hubs, and switches work. In Chapter 7, you saw how dedicated lines terminate at a customer's premises and in a service provider's data center. In this section, you will consider how to fundamentally increase the fault tolerance of connectivity devices and a LAN's or WAN's connecting links.

To understand how to increase the fault tolerance of not just the topology, but also the network's connectivity, let's return to the example of PayNTime. Suppose that the company's network administrator decides to establish a VPN agreement with a national ISP. PayNTime's bandwidth analysis indicates that a T1 link will be sufficient to transport the data of five customers from the ISP's office to PayNTime's data room. Figure 14-8 provides a detailed representation of this arrangement.

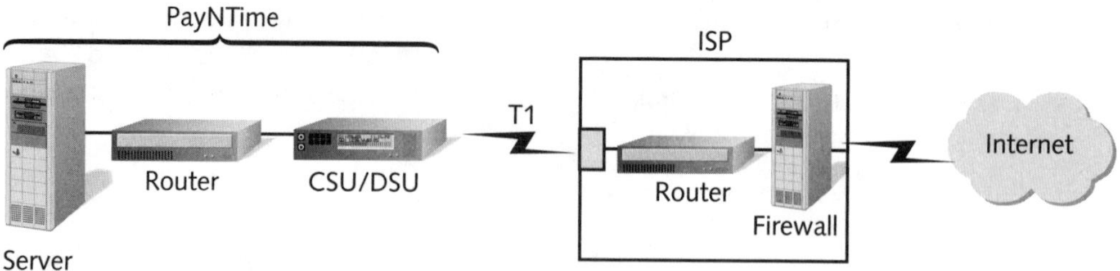

Figure 14-8 ISP connectivity

Notice the single points of failure in the arrangement depicted in Figure 14-8. As mentioned earlier, the T1 connection could incur a fault. In addition, any one of the routers, CSU/DSUs, or firewalls might suffer faults in their power supplies, NICs, or circuit boards. In a critical component such as a router or switch, high fault tolerance necessitates the use of redundant power supplies, cooling fans, interfaces, and I/O modules, all of which should ideally be hot swappable. The term **hot swappable** refers to identical components that automatically assume the functions of their counterpart if one suffers a fault. In a sense, hot swappable components work like your kidneys. If one fails, the other will automatically assume all responsibility for filtering waste from the blood. In much the same way, if a router's processor fails, the redundant processor will automatically take over all data-processing functions. When you purchase switches or routers to support critical links, look for those that contain hot swappable components. As with other redundancy provisions, these features will add to the cost of your device purchase.

Purchasing connectivity devices does not address all faults that may occur on a WAN. In fact, faults may also affect the connecting links. For example, if you connect two offices with a dedicated T1 connection and the T1 fails, it doesn't matter whether your router has redundant NICs. The connection will still be down. Because a fault in the T1 link has the same effect as a bad T1 interface in a router, a fully redundant system might be a better option. Such a system is depicted in Figure 14-9.

Figure 14-9 A fully redundant system

The preceding scenario utilizes the most expensive and reliable option for providing network redundancy for PayNTime. In addition, this solution allows for **load balancing**, or an automatic distribution of traffic over multiple links or processors to optimize response. Load balancing would maximize the throughput between PayNTime and its ISP because the aggregate traffic flowing between the two points could move over either T1 link, avoiding potential bottlenecks on a single T1 connection. Although one company might be willing to pay for such complete redundancy, another might prefer a less expensive solution. A less expensive redundancy option might be to use a dial-back WAN link. For example, a company that depends on a Frame Relay WAN might have an access server with an ISDN or 56 KB modem link that automatically dials the remote site when it detects a failure of the primary link.

SERVERS

As with other devices, you can make servers more fault-tolerant by supplying them with redundant components. Critical servers (such as those that perform user authentication for an entire LAN, or those that run important, enterprise-wide applications such as an electronic catalog in a library) often contain redundant NICs, processors, and hard disks. These redundant components provide assurance that if one item fails, the entire system won't fail; at the same time, they enable load balancing.

For example, a server with two 100 Mbps NICs, such as the one pictured in Figure 14-10, may be receiving and transmitting traffic at a rate of 46 Mbps during a busy time of the day. With additional software provided by either the NIC manufacturer or a third party, the redundant NICs can work in tandem to distribute the load, ensuring that approximately half the data travels through the first NIC and half through the second. This approach improves response time for users accessing the server. If one NIC fails, the other NIC will automatically assume full responsibility for receiving and transmitting all data to and from the server. Although load balancing does not technically fall under the category of fault tolerance, it helps to justify the purchase of redundant components that do contribute to fault tolerance.

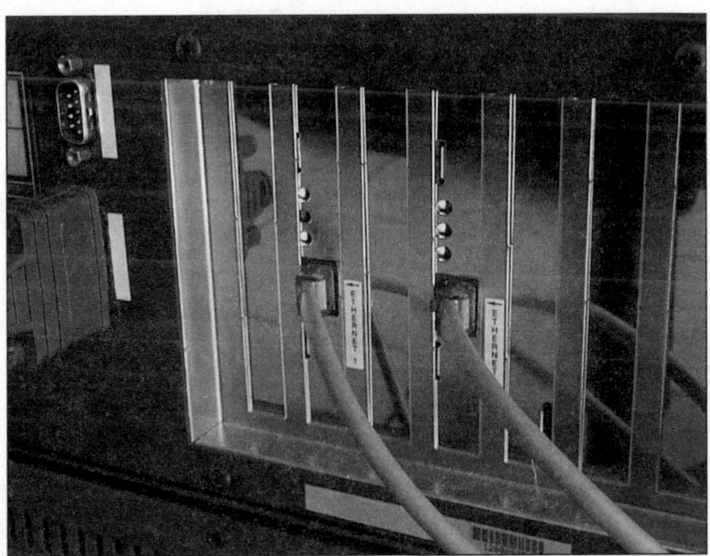

Figure 14-10 A server with redundant NICs

The following sections describe more sophisticated ways of providing server fault tolerance, beginning with RAID.

Redundant Array of Inexpensive Disks (RAID)

Another important server redundancy feature is a **Redundant Array of Inexpensive Disks (RAID)**. A group of hard disks is called a disk **array** (or a drive). The collection of disks that work together in a RAID configuration is often referred to as the "RAID drive." To the system, the multiple disks in a RAID drive appear as a single logical drive. The advantage of using RAID is that a single disk failure will not cause a catastrophic loss of data.

Although RAID comes in many different forms (or levels), all types use shared, multiple physical or logical hard disks to ensure data integrity and availability. Some RAID designs also increase storage capacity and improve performance. RAID is typically used on servers, but not on workstations because of its cost. It's important to keep in mind that RAID relies on a combination of software and hardware. The software may be a third-party package, or it may exist as part of the network operating system. On a Windows NT server, for example, RAID drives are configured through the Disk Administrator program.

To obtain Net+ certification, you should thoroughly understand RAID technology and be familiar with the most common levels currently used in systems: RAID Levels 0, 1, 3, and 5, as described below.

RAID Level 0 – Disk Striping **RAID Level 0** (otherwise known as **disk striping**) is a very simple implementation of RAID in which data are written in 64 KB blocks equally across all disks in the array. Disk striping is not a fault-tolerant method because if one disk fails, the data contained in it will be inaccessible. Thus RAID Level 0 does not provide true redundancy. Nevertheless, it does use multiple disk partitions effectively, and it improves performance by utilizing multiple disk controllers. The multiple disk controllers allow several instructions to be sent to the disks simultaneously.

Figure 14-11 illustrates how data are written to multiple disks in RAID Level 0. Notice how each 64 KB piece of data is written to one discreet area of the disk array. For example, if you were saving a 128 KB file, the file would be separated into two pieces and saved in different areas of the drive. Although RAID Level 0 is easy to implement, it should not be used on mission-critical servers because of its lack of fault tolerance.

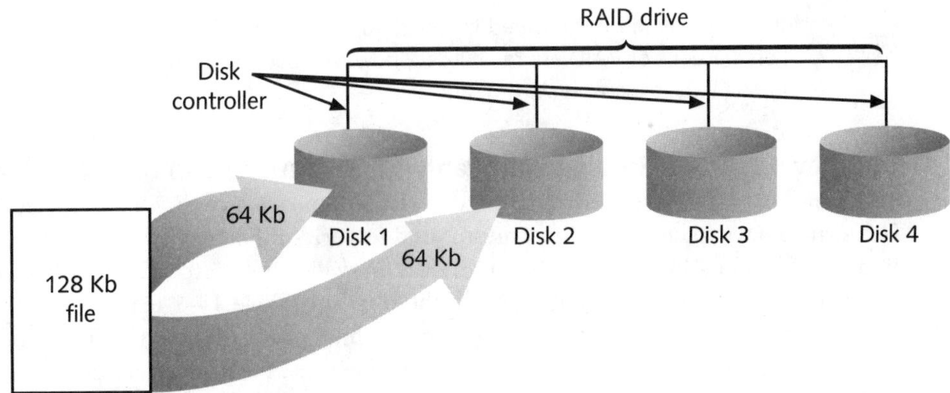

Figure 14-11 RAID Level 0 — disk striping

RAID Level 1 – Disk Mirroring **RAID Level 1** provides redundancy through a process called **disk mirroring**, in which data from one disk are copied to another disk automatically as the information is written. Because data are continually saved to multiple locations, disk mirroring provides a dynamic data backup. If one disk in the array fails, the disk array controller will automatically switch to the disk that was mirroring the failed disk. Users will not even notice the failure. After repairing the failed disk, the network administrator must perform a resynchronization to return it to the array. As the disk's twin has been saving all of its data while it was out of service, this task is rarely difficult.

The advantages of RAID Level 1 derive from its simplicity and its automatic and complete data redundancy. On the other hand, because it requires two identical disks instead of just one, RAID Level 1 is somewhat costly. In addition, it is not the most efficient means of protecting data, as it usually relies on system software to perform the mirroring, which taxes CPU resources. Figure 14-12 depicts a 128 KB file being written to a disk array using RAID Level 1.

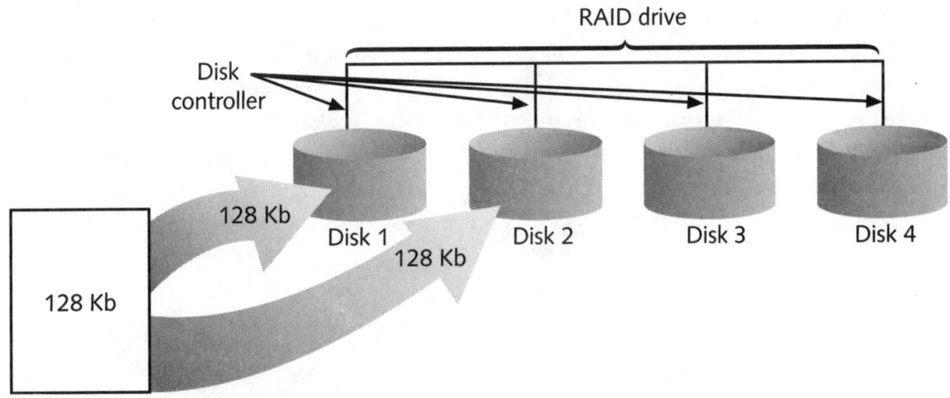

Figure 14-12 RAID Level 1 — disk mirroring

Although they are not covered in this chapter, RAID levels 2 and 4 also exist. These versions of RAID are rarely used, however, because they are less reliable or less efficient than Levels 1, 3, and 5.

RAID Level 3 – Disk Striping with Parity ECC **RAID Level 3** involves disk striping with a special type of error correction code (ECC) known as parity error correction code. The term **parity** refers to the mechanism used to verify the integrity of data by making the number of bits in a byte sum to either an odd or even number. To accomplish parity, a parity bit (equal to either 0 or 1) is added to the bits' sum. Table 14-1 expresses how the sums of many bits achieve even parity through a parity bit. Notice that the numbers in the fourth column are all even. If the summed numbers in the fourth column were odd, an odd parity would be used. A system may use either even parity or odd parity, but not both.

Table 14-1 The use of parity bits to achieve parity

Original Data	Sum of Data Bits	Parity Bit	Sum of Data Plus Parity Bits
01110010	4	0	4
00100010	2	0	2
00111101	5	1	6
10010100	3	1	4

Parity tracks the integrity of data on a disk. It does not reflect the data type, protocol, transmission method, or file size. A parity bit is assigned to each data byte when it is transmitted or written to a disk. When data are later read from the disk, the data's bits plus the parity bit are summed again. If the parity does not match (for example, if the end sum is odd but the system uses even parity), then the system assumes that the data have suffered some type of damage. The process of comparing the parity of data read from disk with the type of parity used by the system is known as **parity error checking**.

In RAID Level 3, parity error checking takes place when data are written across the disk array. If the parity error checking indicates an error, the RAID Level 3 system can automatically correct it. The advantage of using RAID 3 is that it provides a high data transfer rate when reading from or writing to the disks. This quality makes RAID 3 particularly well suited to applications that require high speed in data transfers, such as video editing. A disadvantage of RAID 3 is that the parity information appears on a single disk, which represents a potential single point of failure in the system. Figure 14-13 illustrates how RAID Level 3 works.

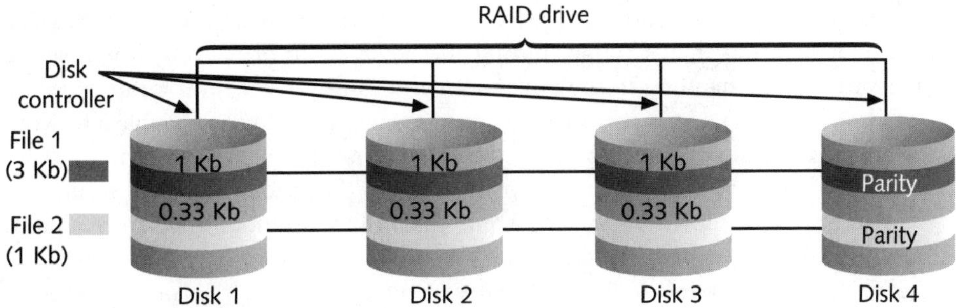

Figure 14-13 RAID Level 3 — disk striping with parity ECC

RAID Level 5 – Disk Striping with Distributed Parity **RAID Level 5** is the most popular, highly fault-tolerant, data storage technique in use today. In RAID Level 5, data are written in small blocks across several disks. At the same time, parity error checking information is distributed among the disks, as pictured in Figure 14-14.

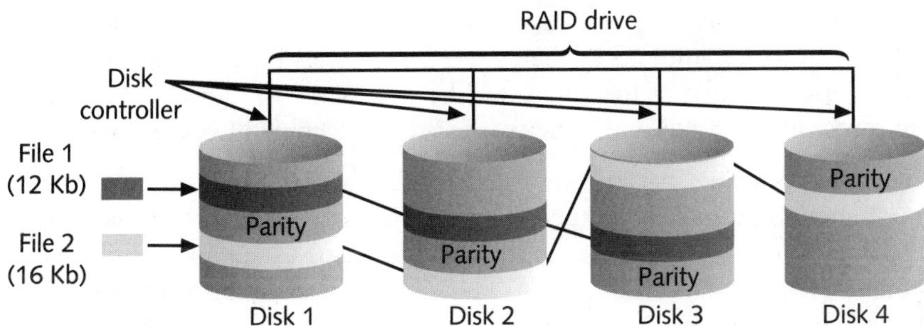

Figure 14-14 RAID Level 5 — disk striping with distributed parity

14

RAID Level 5 is similar to, but has several advantages over, RAID Level 3. First, it can write data more rapidly because the parity information can be written by any one of the several disk controllers in the array. Unlike RAID Level 3, RAID Level 5 uses several disks for parity information, making it more fault-tolerant. Also, RAID Level 5 allows you to replace failed disks with good ones without any interruption of service.

Server Mirroring

Server mirroring is a fault-tolerance technique in which one server duplicates the transactions and data storage of another. The servers involved must be identical machines using identical components. As you would expect, mirroring requires a link between the servers. It also entails software running on both servers that allows them to synchronize their actions continually and, in case of a failure, that permits one server to take over for the other.

To illustrate the concept of mirroring, suppose that you give a presentation to a large group of people, with the audience being allowed to interrupt you to ask questions at any time. You might talk for two minutes, then wait while someone asked a question, then answer the question, then begin lecturing again, take another question, and so on. In this sense, you act like a primary server, busily transmitting and receiving information. Now imagine that your identical twin is standing in the next room and can hear you over a loudspeaker. Your twin was instructed to say exactly what you were saying as quickly as possible after you speak, but to an empty room containing only a tape recorder. Of course, your twin must listen to you before imitating you. It takes time for the twin to digest all that you're saying and repeat it, so you must slow down your lecture and your room's question-and-answer process. A mirrored server acts in much the same way. The time it takes to duplicate the incoming and outgoing data will detrimentally affect network performance if the network handles a heavy traffic load. But if you should faint during your lecture, for example, your twin can step into your room and take over for you in very short order. The mirrored server also stands ready to assume the responsibilities of its counterpart.

One advantage to mirroring is that the servers involved can stand side by side or be positioned in geographically side-by-side locations—perhaps in two different buildings of a company's headquarters, or possibly even on opposites sides of a continent. One potential disadvantage to mirroring, however, is the time it takes for a mirrored server to assume the functionality of the failed server. This delay may last 15 to 90 seconds. Obviously, this down time makes mirroring imperfect; when a server fails, users lose network service and any data in transit at the moment of the failure will be susceptible to corruption. Another disadvantage to mirroring is its toll on the network as data are copied between sites.

Examples of mirroring software include Vinca's Standby Server and Fulltime's Octopus. Although such software can be expensive, the hardware costs of mirroring are even more significant because one server is devoted to simply acting as a "tape recorder" for all data in case the other server fails. Depending on the potential cost of losing a server's functionality for any period of time, however, the expense involved may be justifiable.

You may be familiar with the term "mirroring" as it refers to Web sites on the Internet. Mirrored Web sites are locations on the Internet that dynamically duplicate other locations on the Internet, to ensure their continual availability. They are similar to, but not necessarily the same as, mirrored servers.

Server Clustering

Server clustering is a fault-tolerance technique that links multiple servers together to act as a single server. In this configuration, clustered servers share processing duties and appear as a single server to users. If one server in the cluster fails, the other servers in the cluster will automatically take over its data transaction and storage responsibilities. Because multiple servers can perform services independently of other servers, as well as ensure fault tolerance, clustering is more cost-effective than mirroring.

To understand the concept of clustering, imagine that you and several colleagues (who are not exactly like you) are giving separate talks in different rooms in the same conference center simultaneously. All of your colleagues are constantly aware of your lecture, and vice versa. If you should faint during your lecture, one of your colleagues can immediately jump into your spot and pick up where you left off, without the audience ever noticing. (At the same time, your colleague must continue to present his own lecture, which means that he will have to split his time between these two tasks.)

To detect failures, clustered servers regularly poll each other on the network, essentially asking, "Are you still there?" They then wait a specified period of time before again asking, "Are you still there?" If they don't receive a response from one of their counterparts, the clustering software initiates the fail-over. This process may take anywhere from a few seconds to a minute, because all information about a failed server's shared resources must be gathered by the cluster. Unlike with mirroring, users will not notice the switch. Later, when the other servers in the cluster detect that the missing server has been replaced, they will automatically relinquish that server's responsibilities. The fail-over and recovery processes are transparent to network users.

One disadvantage to clustering is that the clustered servers must be geographically close—although the exact distance depends on the clustering software employed. Typically, clustering is implemented among servers located in the same data room. Some clusters can contain servers as far as a mile apart, but clustering software manufacturers recommend a closer proximity. Before implementing a server cluster, you should determine your organization's fault-tolerance needs and fully research the options available on your servers' platforms.

Despite its geographic limitations, clustering offers many advantages over mirroring. Each server in the cluster can perform its own data processing; at the same time, it is always ready to take over for a failed server if necessary. Not only does this ability to perform multiple functions reduce the cost of ownership for a cluster of servers, but it also improves performance.

Like mirroring, clustering is implemented through a combination of software and hardware. Microsoft's WolfPack is just one example of a clustering software package. In fact, clustering has been part of the UNIX operating system since the early 1990s.

DATA BACKUP

You have probably heard or even spoken the axiom, "Make regular backups!" A **backup** is a copy of data or program files created for archiving or safekeeping purposes. Without backing up your data, you risk losing everything through a hard disk fault, fire, flood, or malicious or accidental erasure or corruption. No matter how reliable and fault-tolerant you believe your server's hard disk (or disks) to be, you still risk losing everything unless you make backups on separate media and store them off-site.

To fully appreciate the importance of backups, imagine coming to work one morning to find that everything disappeared from the server: programs, configurations, data files, user IDs, passwords, and the network operating system. It doesn't matter how it happened. What matters at this point is how long it will take to reinstall the network operating systems; how long it will take to duplicate the previous configuration; and how long it will take to figure out which IDs should reside on the server, which groups they should belong in, and which rights each group should have. What will you say to your colleagues when they learn that all of the data that they have worked on for the last year is irretrievably lost? When you think about this scenario, you will quickly realize that you can't afford *not* to perform regular backups.

Some network administrators don't pay enough attention to backups because they find the process confusing or difficult to track. True, many different options exist for making backups. They can be performed by different types of software and hardware combinations, including via network operating system utilities. In this section, you will learn about the most common methods of performing data backup, ways to schedule them, and methods for determining what you need to back up. Backup methods unsuitable for large systems, such as floppy disks or other removable storage media, are not covered in this section. Note that backing up workstations and backing up servers and other host systems are different operations. To qualify for Net+ certification, you should focus on making server backups.

Tape Backups

Currently, the most popular method for backing up networked systems is tape backup, because this method is simple and relatively economical. Tape backups require the use of a tape drive connected to the network (via a system such as a file server or dedicated, networked workstation), software to manage and perform backups, and, of course, backup media. The tapes used for tape backups resemble small cassette tapes, but they are of a higher quality, specially made to reliably store data. Figure 14-15 depicts two types of backup tape media: 4 mm and 8 mm.

On a relatively small network, standalone tape drives may be attached to each server. On a large network, one large, centralized tape backup device may manage all of the subsystems' backups. This tape backup device will usually be connected to a computer other than a busy file server to reduce the possibility that backups might cause traffic bottlenecks. Extremely large environments (for example, global manufacturers with several terabytes of inventory and product information to safeguard) may require robots to retrieve and circulate tapes from a tape storage library (or **vault**) that may be as large as a warehouse. Figure 14-16 illustrates how tape drives typically fit into a medium or large network.

Figure 14-15 Examples of backup tape media

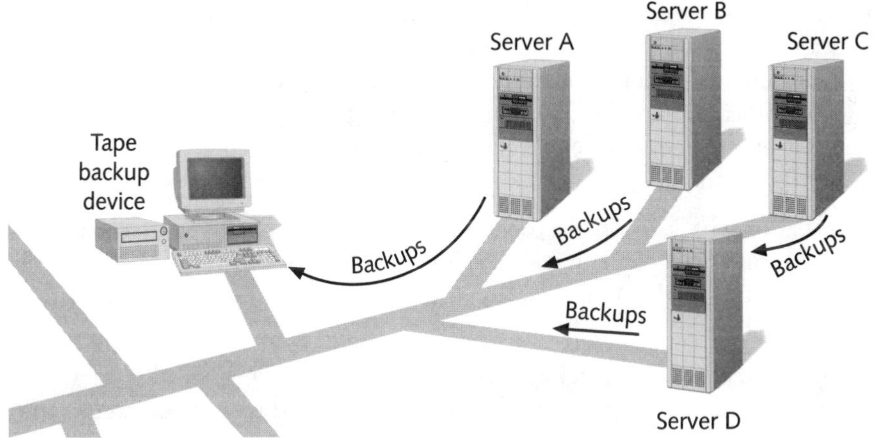

Figure 14-16 A tape drive on a medium or large network

To select the appropriate tape backup solution for your network, you should consider the following questions:

- Does the backup drive and/or media provide sufficient storage capacity?
- Are the backup software and hardware proven to be reliable?
- Does the backup software use data error checking techniques?

- Is the system quick enough to complete the backup process before daily operations resume?
- How much do the tape drive, software, and media cost?
- Will the backup hardware and software be compatible with existing network hardware and software?
- Does the backup system require frequent manual intervention? (For example, will staff members need to become involved in tape rotation?)
- Will the backup hardware, software, and media accommodate your network's growth?

Examples of tape backup software include Computer Associates' ARCserve, Dantz's Retrospect, Hewlett-Packard's Colorado and OmniBack, IBM's ADSM, Legato's NetWorker, and Seagate's Backup Exec. Popular tape drive manufacturers include Exabyte, Hewlett-Packard, IBM, Quantum, Seagate, and Sony. You will need to consult the software and hardware specifications to determine whether a particular backup system is compatible with your network.

Online Backups

Many companies on the Internet now offer to back up data over the Internet—that is, to perform **online backups**. Usually, online backup providers require you to install their client software. You also need a connection to the Internet. Online backups implement strict security measures to protect the data in transit, as the information must traverse public carrier links. Most online backup providers allow you to retrieve your data at any time of day or night, without calling a technical support number. Both the backup and restoration processes are entirely automated. In case of a disaster, the online backup company may offer to create CD-ROMs containing your servers' data.

A potential drawback to online backups is that the cost of this service can vary widely. In addition, despite strict security controls, it may be difficult to verify that your data has been backed up successfully. Online backup providers include @Backup, Atrieva, Connected, HotWired, and Safeguard.

When evaluating an online backup provider, you should test its speed, accuracy, security, and, of course, the ease with which you can recover the backed up data. Be certain to test the service before you commit to a long-term contract for online backups.

Backup Strategy

After selecting the appropriate tool for performing your servers' data backups, you should devise a backup strategy to guide you and your colleagues in performing reliable backups that provide maximum data protection. This strategy should be documented in a common area (for example, on a Web site accessible to all IT staff) and should address at least the following questions:

- What kind of rotation schedule will backups follow?
- At what time of day or night will the backups occur?
- How will you verify the accuracy of the backups?
- Where will backup media be stored?
- Who will take responsibility for ensuring that backups occurred?
- How long will you save backups?
- Where will backup and recovery documentation be stored?

Different backup methods provide varying levels of certainty and corresponding labor and cost. The various methods are described below:

- ***Full backup***—All data on all servers are copied to a storage medium, regardless of whether the data are new or changed.
- ***Incremental backup***—Only data that have changed since the last backup are copied to a storage medium.
- ***Differential backup***—Only data that have changed since the last backup are copied to a storage medium, and that information is then marked for subsequent backup, regardless of whether it has changed.

When managing network backups, you need to determine the best possible **backup rotation scheme**, which specifies when and how often backups will occur. The aim of a good backup rotation scheme is to provide excellent data reliability without overtaxing your network or requiring a lot of intervention. For example, you might think that backing up your entire network's data every night is the best policy because it ensures that everything is completely safe. But what if your network contains 50 GB of data and is growing by 10 GB per month? Would the backups even finish by morning? How many tapes would you have to purchase? Also, why should you bother backing up files that haven't changed in three weeks? How much time will you and your staff need to devote to managing the tapes? How would the transfer of all of the data affect your network's performance? All of these considerations point to a better alternative than the "tape-a-day" solution—that is, an option that promises to maximize data protection but reduce the time and cost associated with backups.

When planning your backup strategy, you can choose from several standard backup rotation schemes. The most popular of these schemes, called "**grandfather-father-son**," uses daily (son), weekly (father), and monthly (grandfather) backup sets. As depicted in Figure 14-17, in the grandfather-father-son scheme, three types of backups are performed each month: daily incremental (every Monday through Thursday), weekly full (every Friday), and monthly full backups (last day of the month).

In this scheme, backup tapes are reused regularly. For example, week 1's Monday tape would also serve as week 2's and week 3's Monday tape. One day each week, a full backup, called "father," is recorded in place of an incremental one and labeled for the week to which it corresponds—for example, "week 1," "week 2," and so on. This "father" tape is reused monthly—for example, October's week 1 tape would be reused for November's week 1 tape. The final set of media is labeled "month 1," "month 2," and so on, according to which month of the quarter the tapes will be used. This "grandfather" medium records full backups on the last business day of each month and is reused quarterly. Each of these media may consist of a single tape or a set of tapes, depending on the amount of data involved. A total of 12 media sets are required for this basic rotation scheme, allowing for a history of two to three months.

	Monday	Tuesday	Wednesday	Thursday	Friday
Week 1	A	A	A	A	B
Week 2	A	A	A	A	B
Week 3	A	A	A	A	B
Week 4	A	A	A	A	B
Week 5	A	A	C		

One month of backups

A = Incremental "son" backup (daily)
B = Full "father" backup (weekly)
C = Full "grandfather" backup (monthly)

Figure 14-17 The "grandfather-father-son" backup rotation scheme

Once you have determined your backup rotation scheme, you should ensure that backup activity is recorded in a backup log. Information that belongs in a backup log include the backup date, tape identification (day of week or type), type of data backed up (for example, accounting department spreadsheets or a day's worth of catalog orders), type of the backup (full, incremental, or differential), files that were backed up, and site at which the tape is stored. Having this information available in case of a server failure will greatly simplify data recovery.

Finally, once you begin to back up network data, you should establish a regular schedule of verification. In other words, from time to time (depending on how often your data change and how critical the information is), you should attempt to recover some critical files from your backup media. Many network administrators can attest that the darkest hour of their career was when they were asked to retrieve critical files from a backup tape and found that no backup data existed because their backup system never worked in the first place!

DISASTER RECOVERY

Disaster recovery is the process of restoring your critical functionality and data after an enterprise-wide outage that affects more than a single system or a limited group of users. Disaster recovery must take into account the possible extremes, rather than relatively minor outages, failures, security breaches, or data corruption. In a disaster recovery plan, you should consider the worst-case scenarios, from a far-reaching hurricane to a military attack. You should also consider what might happen if your typical networking staff isn't available. The plan should outline multiple contingencies, in case your best options don't pan out. Although you must attend to all of the protection methods discussed in this chapter, disaster recovery also requires a comprehensive strategy for restoring functionality and data after things go terribly awry.

Every organization should have a disaster recovery team (with an appointed coordinator) and a disaster recovery plan. This plan should address not only computer systems, but also power, telephony, and paper-based files. When writing the sections of the plan related to computer systems, your team should specifically address the following issues:

- Contact names for emergency coordinators who will execute the disaster recovery response in case of disaster, as well as roles and responsibilities of other staff.
- Details on which data and servers are being backed up, how frequently backups occur, where backups are kept (off-site), and, most importantly, how backed up data can be recovered in full.
- Details on network topology, redundancy, and agreements with national service carriers, in case local or regional vendors fall prey to the same disaster.
- Regular strategies for testing the disaster recovery plan.
- A plan for managing the crisis, including regular communications with employees and customers. Consider the possibility that regular communications modes (such as phone lines) might be unavailable.

Having a comprehensive disaster recovery plan not only lessens the risk of losing critical data in case of extreme situations, but also makes potential customers and your insurance providers look more favorably on your organization.

CHAPTER SUMMARY

- Integrity refers to the soundness of your network's files, systems, and connections. To ensure their integrity, you must protect them from anything that might render them unusable, such as corruption, tampering, natural disasters, and viruses. Availability of a file or system refers to how consistently and reliably it can be accessed by authorized personnel.
- Security breaches, natural disasters, and human error can compromise both integrity and availability. Every network administrator should consider these possibilities when trying to design a sound network.

- Several basic measures can be employed to protect data and systems on a network: (1) prevent anyone other than a network administrator from opening or changing the system files; (2) monitor the network for unauthorized access or changes; (3) record authorized system changes in a change management system; (4) install redundant components; (5) perform regular health checks on the network; (6) monitor system performance, error logs, and the system log book regularly; (7) keep backups, boot disks, and emergency repair disks current and available; and (8) implement and enforce security and disaster recovery policies.
- A virus is a program that replicates itself so as to infect more computers, either through network connections or through floppy disks passed among users. Viruses may damage files or systems or simply annoy users by flashing messages or pictures on the screen or by causing the keyboard to beep.
- Many other unwanted and potentially destructive programs are mistakenly called viruses. For example, a program that disguises itself as something useful but actually harms your system is called a Trojan horse. An example of a Trojan horse is an executable file sent to you over the Internet that purportedly installs a new game, but actually reformats your hard disk.
- Boot sector viruses are the most common types of viruses. They reside on the boot sector of a floppy disk and become transferred to the partition sector or the DOS boot sector on a hard disk. The only way a boot sector virus can move from a floppy to a hard disk is if the floppy disk is left in the drive when the machine starts up.
- Macro viruses are a newer type of virus that take the form of a word-processing or spreadsheet program macro, which may be executed when you use the word-processing or spreadsheet program. Macro viruses were the first type of virus to infect data files rather than executable files. Because data files are more apt to be shared among users and because macro viruses are typically easier to write than executable viruses, these viruses have quickly become widespread.
- File-infected viruses attach themselves to executable files. When the infected executable file runs, the virus copies itself to memory. Later, the virus will attach itself to other executable files.
- Network viruses take advantage of network protocols, commands, messaging programs, and data links to propagate themselves. Although all viruses could theoretically travel across network connections, network viruses are specially designed to take advantage of network vulnerabilities.
- Worms are not technically viruses, but rather programs that run independently and travel between computers and across networks. Although they do not alter other programs as viruses do, worms may carry viruses.
- Any type of virus may have additional characteristics that make it harder to detect and eliminate. These characteristics may be encrypted, stealth, polymorphic, or time-dependent.

- Encrypted viruses are altered so as to prevent their detection. Most virus-scanning software searches files for a recognizable string of characters that identify the virus. If the virus is encrypted, it will thwart the antivirus program's attempts to detect it.
- Stealth viruses hide themselves to prevent detection. Typically, they disguise themselves as legitimate programs or replace part of a legitimate program's code with their destructive code.
- Polymorphic viruses change their characteristics (such as the arrangement of their bytes, size, and internal instructions) every time they move to a new system, making them harder to identify. Some polymorphic viruses use complicated algorithms and incorporate nonsensical commands to achieve their changes. These viruses can be considered the most sophisticated and potentially dangerous type of virus.
- Time-dependent viruses are programmed to become activated on a particular date. These types of viruses, which are also known as "time bombs," can remain dormant and harmless forever until their activation date arrives.
- Although a well-written virus attempts to avoid detection, you may suspect the presence of a virus on your system if you notice any of the following symptoms: unexplained increases in file sizes; programs (such as Microsoft Word) launching, running, or exiting more slowly than usual; unusual error messages appearing without probable cause; significant, unexpected loss of system memory; or fluctuations in display quality.
- A good antivirus program should be able to detect viruses through signature scanning, integrity checking, and heuristic checking. It should also be compatible with your network environment, centrally manageable, easy to use (transparent to users), and not prone to false alarms.
- Antivirus software is merely one piece of the puzzle in protecting your network from viruses. An antivirus policy is another essential component. It should provide rules for using antivirus software and policies for installing programs, sharing files, and using floppy disks. Furthermore, it should be authorized and supported by the organization's management and should include sanctions for disobeying the policy.
- A virus hoax is a false alert about a dangerous, new virus that could seriously damage your workstation. Virus hoaxes usually have no realistic basis and should be ignored. They merely attempt to create panic.
- In broad terms, a failure is a deviation from a specified level of system performance for a given period of time. In other words, a failure occurs when something doesn't work as promised or as planned. A fault, on the other hand, is the malfunction of one component of a system. A fault can result in a failure. The goal of fault-tolerant systems is to prevent faults from progressing to failures.
- Fault tolerance is a system's capacity to continue performing despite an unexpected hardware or software malfunction. It can be achieved in varying degrees, with the optimal level of fault tolerance for a system depending on how critical its services and files are to productivity. At the highest level of fault tolerance, a system will be unaffected by a drastic problem, such as a power failure.

- An excellent way to achieve fault tolerance is to provide duplicate elements to compensate for faults in critical components, a practice known as redundancy. You can implement redundancy for servers, cabling, routers, hubs, gateways, NICs, hard disks, power supplies, and other components.
- To assess the fault tolerance of your network you must look for single points of failure—places on the network where, if a fault occurs, the transfer of data may break down without possibility of an automatic recovery.
- As you consider sophisticated fault-tolerance techniques for servers, routers, and WAN links, remember to address the environment in which your devices operate. Protecting your data also involves protecting your network from excessive heat or moisture, break-ins, and natural disasters.
- Networks cannot tolerate power loss or less than optimal power. You will have to guard against the following power flaws: blackouts, brownouts (sags), surges, and line noise.
- A UPS is a battery-operated power source directly attached to one or more devices and to a power supply (such as a wall outlet), which prevents undesired features of the power source from harming the device or interrupting its services. UPSs vary widely in the type of power aberrations they can rectify, the length of time they can provide power, and the number of devices they can support.
- A standby UPS provides continuous voltage to a device by switching instantaneously to the battery when it detects a loss of power from the wall outlet. Upon restoration of the power, the standby UPS switches the device to use A/C power again. A standby UPS requires a brief service outage when it detects that A/C power has stopped; in this time, a sensitive device (such as a server) may have already detected the power loss and shut down or restarted.
- An online UPS uses the A/C power from the wall outlet to continuously charge its battery, while providing power to a network device through its battery. In other words, a server connected to an online UPS always relies on the UPS battery for its electricity. An online UPS provides the best kind of power redundancy available. Because the server never needs to switch from the wall outlet's power to the UPS's power, no risk of momentarily losing service exists.
- To choose the best UPS for your network, you must consider a number of factors: the amount of power needed, the period of time in which you must keep a device running, line conditioning, and cost.
- If your organization cannot withstand a power loss, either because of its computer services or other electrical needs, you might consider investing in an electrical generator for your building. Generators can be powered by diesel, liquid propane gas, natural gas, or steam. They do not provide surge protection, but they do provide clean (free from noise) electricity.
- The type of network topology that offers the best fault tolerance is a mesh topology. In a mesh network, nodes are connected either directly or indirectly by multiple pathways. In a mesh topology, data can travel over these multiple paths from any one point to another.

- The physical media you use may also offer redundancy. An FDDI or SONET ring, for example, can easily recover from a fault in one of its links because it forms a self-healing ring.
- The advantage of having redundancy in your network is little risk of losing functionality, and potentially profits, from a network fault. Its disadvantage relates to its cost.
- When components are hot swappable, they have identical functions and can automatically assume the functions of their counterpart if it suffers a fault.
- The use of multiple components enables load balancing, or an automatic distribution of traffic or processing to optimize response.
- As with other devices, you can make servers more fault-tolerant by supplying them with redundant components. Critical servers often contain redundant NICs, processors, and/or hard disks. These redundant components provide assurance that if one fails, the whole system won't fail, and they enable load balancing.
- An important server redundancy feature is a Redundant Array of Inexpensive Disks (RAID). All types of RAID use shared, multiple physical or logical hard disks to ensure data integrity and availability; some designs also increase storage capacity and improve performance. RAID is typically used on servers, but not on workstations because of its added cost. RAID is accomplished through a combination of both software and hardware.
- RAID Level 0 is a very simple implementation of RAID in which data are written in 64 KB blocks equally across all of the disks in the array, a technique known as disk striping. Disk striping is not a fault-tolerant method because if one disk fails, the data contained in it will be inaccessible. Thus RAID Level 0 does not provide true redundancy.
- RAID Level 1 provides redundancy through a process called disk mirroring, in which data from one disk are automatically copied to another disk as the information is written. This option can be considered a dynamic data backup. If one disk in the array fails, the disk array controller will automatically switch to the disk that was mirroring the failed disk.
- RAID Level 3 involves disk striping with parity error correction code. Parity refers to the integrity of the data as expressed in the number of 1s contained in each group of correctly transmitted bits. In RAID Level 3, parity error checking takes place when the data are written across the disk array.
- RAID Level 5 is the most popular, highly fault-tolerant, data storage technique in use today. In RAID Level 5, data are written in small blocks across several disks; parity error checking information is also distributed among the disks.
- A fault-tolerance technique that involves utilizing a second, identical server to duplicate the transactions and data storage of one server is called server mirroring. Mirroring can take place between servers that are either geographically side by side or distant. Mirroring requires not only a link between the servers, but also software running on both servers to enable the servers to continually synchronize their actions and to permit one to take over in case the other fails.

- Server clustering is a fault-tolerance technique that links multiple servers together to act as a single server. In this configuration, clustered servers share processing duties and appear as a single server to users. If one server in the cluster fails, the other servers in the cluster will automatically take over its data transaction and storage responsibilities.
- A backup is a copy of data or program files created for archiving or safekeeping purposes. If you do not back up your data, you risk losing everything through a hard disk fault, fire, flood, or malicious or accidental erasure or corruption. No matter how reliable and fault-tolerant you believe your server's hard disk(s) to be, you still risk losing everything unless you make backups on separate media and store them off-site.
- Currently, the most popular method for backing up networked systems is tape backup, because it is simple and relatively economical. Tape backups require a tape drive connected to the network (via a system such as a file server or dedicated, networked workstation), software to manage and perform backups, and backup media.
- To select the appropriate tape backup solution for your network, you should consider the following issues: storage capacity; proven reliability; data error checking techniques; speed; cost of the tape drive, software, and media; compatibility with existing network hardware and software; and extent of automation.
- Many companies on the Internet now offer to back up data over the Internet—that is, to perform online backups. Usually, online backup providers require that you have their client software in addition to a connection to the Internet. They implement strict security measures to protect the data in transit, because the information must traverse public carrier links. Most online backup providers allow you to retrieve your data at any time of day or night, without calling a technical support number. Both the backup and restore processes are entirely automated.
- A good backup strategy should be well documented and should address at least the following questions: What kind of rotation schedule will backups follow? At what time of day or night will the backups occur? How will you verify the accuracy of backups? Where will backup media be stored? Who will take responsibility for ensuring that backups occurred? How long will you save backups? Where will backup and recovery documentation be stored?
- Different backup methods provide varying levels of certainty and corresponding labor and cost. A full backup copies all data on all servers to a storage medium, regardless of whether the data are new or changed. An incremental backup copies only data that have changed since the last backup A differential backup copies only data that have changed since the last backup, and that information is marked for subsequent backup, regardless of whether it has changed.
- If you are responsible for the network's backups, your most important decision will relate to when and how often backups will occur—that is, the backup rotation scheme. Several standard backup rotation schemes have been devised for centralized data backup. The aim of a good backup rotation scheme is to provide excellent data reliability but not to overtax your network or require much intervention.
- The most popular backup rotation scheme is called "grandfather-father-son." This scheme uses daily (son), weekly (father), and monthly (grandfather) backup sets.

- Once you have determined your backup rotation scheme, you should ensure that backup activity is recorded in a backup log. Information that belongs in a backup log include the following: when the backup took place; which tape was used (day of week or type); which data were backed up; whether the backup was full, incremental, or differential; which files were backed up; and where the tape is stored. Having this information available in case of a server failure will greatly simplify data recovery.
- Disaster recovery is the process of restoring your critical functionality and data after an enterprise-wide outage that affects more than a single system or a limited group of users. It must account for the possible extremes, rather than relatively minor outages, failures, security breaches, or data corruption. In a disaster recovery plan, you should consider the worst-case scenarios, from a hurricane to a military attack.
- Every organization should have a disaster recovery team (with an appointed coordinator) and a disaster recovery plan. The plan should address not only computer systems, but also power, telephony, and paper-based files.

Key Terms

- **array** — A group of hard disks.
- **availability** — How consistently and reliably a file, device, or connection can be accessed by authorized personnel.
- **backup** — A copy of data or program files created for archiving or safekeeping purposes.
- **backup rotation scheme** — A plan for when and how often backups occur, and which backups are full, incremental, or differential.
- **blackout** — A complete power loss.
- **boot sector virus** — A virus that resides on the boot sector of a floppy disk and is transferred to the partition sector or the DOS boot sector on a hard disk. A boot sector virus can move from a floppy to a hard disk only if the floppy disk is left in the drive when the machine starts up.
- **brownout** — A momentary decrease in voltage, also known as a *sag*. An overtaxed electrical system may cause brownouts, recognizable as a dimming of the lights.
- **disaster recovery** — The process of restoring critical functionality and data to a network after an enterprise-wide outage that affects more than a single system or a limited group of users.
- **differential backup** — A backup method in which only data that have changed since the last backup are copied to a storage medium, and that information is marked for subsequent backup, regardless of whether it has changed.
- **disk mirroring** — A RAID technique in which data from one disk are automatically copied to another disk as the information is written.
- **disk striping** — A simple implementation of RAID in which data are written in 64 KB blocks equally across all disks in the array.

- **encrypted virus** — A virus that is encrypted to prevent detection.
- **fail-over** — The capability for one component (such as a NIC or server) to assume another component's responsibilities without manual intervention.
- **failure** — A deviation from a specified level of system performance for a given period of time. A failure occurs when something doesn't work as promised or as planned.
- **fault** — The malfunction of one component of a system. A fault can result in a failure.
- **fault tolerance** — The capacity for a system to continue performing despite an unexpected hardware or software malfunction.
- **file-infected virus** — A virus that attaches itself to executable files. When the infected executable file runs, the virus copies itself to memory. Later, the virus will attach itself to other executable files.
- **full backup** — A backup in which all data on all servers are copied to a storage medium, regardless of whether the data are new or changed.
- **grandfather-father-son** — A backup rotation scheme that uses daily (son), weekly (father), and monthly (grandfather) backup sets.
- **hard disk redundancy** — See *Redundant Array of Inexpensive Disks (RAID).*
- **heuristic scanning** — A type of virus scanning that attempts to identify viruses by discovering "virus-like" behavior.
- **hot swappable** — A characteristic that enables identical components to automatically assume the functions of their counterpart if it suffers a fault.
- **incremental backup** — A backup in which only data that have changed since the last backup are copied to a storage medium.
- **integrity** — The soundness of a network's files, systems, and connections. To ensure integrity, you must protect your network from anything that might render it unusable, such as corruption, tampering, natural disasters, and viruses.
- **integrity checking** — A method of comparing the current characteristics of files and disks against an archived version of these characteristics to discover any changes. The most common example of integrity checking involves a checksum.
- **intrusion detection** — The process of monitoring the network for unauthorized access to its devices.
- **line noise** — Fluctuations in voltage levels caused by other devices on the network or by electromagnetic interference.
- **load balancing** — An automatic distribution of traffic over multiple links, hard disks, or processors intended to optimize responses.
- **macro viruses** — A newer type of virus that takes the form of a word-processing or spreadsheet program macro, which may execute when a word-processing or spreadsheet program is in use.

- **network virus** — A type of virus that takes advantage of network protocols, commands, messaging programs, and data links to propagate itself. Although all viruses could theoretically travel across network connections, network viruses are specially designed to attack network vulnerabilities.
- **online backup** — A technique in which data are backed up to a central location over the Internet.
- **online UPS** — A power supply that uses the A/C power from the wall outlet to continuously charge its battery, while providing power to a network device through its battery.
- **parity** — The mechanism used to verify the integrity of data by making the number of bits in a byte sum to either an odd or even number.
- **parity error checking** — The process of comparing the parity of data read from a disk with the type of parity used by the system.
- **polymorphic virus** — A type of virus that changes its characteristics (such as the arrangement of its bytes, size, and internal instructions) every time it is transferred to a new system, making it harder to identify.
- **RAID Level 0** — An implementation of RAID in which data are written in 64 KB blocks equally across all disks in the array.
- **RAID Level 1** — An implementation of RAID that provides redundancy through disk mirroring, in which data from one disk are automatically copied to another disk as the information is written.
- **RAID Level 3** — An implementation of RAID that uses disk striping for data and parity error correction code on a separate parity disk.
- **RAID Level 5** — The most popular, highly fault-tolerant, data storage technique in use today, RAID Level 5 writes data in small blocks across several disks. At the same time, it writes parity error checking information among several disks.
- **redundancy** — The use of more than one identical component for storing, processing, or transporting data.
- **Redundant Array of Inexpensive Disks (RAID)** — A server redundancy measure that uses shared, multiple physical or logical hard disks to ensure data integrity and availability. Some RAID designs also increase storage capacity and improve performance. See also *disk striping,* and *disk mirroring.*
- **sag** — See *brownout.*
- **server clustering** — A fault-tolerance technique that links multiple servers together to act as a single server. In this configuration, clustered servers share processing duties and appear as a single server to users. If one server in the cluster fails, the other servers in the cluster will automatically take over its data transaction and storage responsibilities.
- **server mirroring** — A fault-tolerance technique in which one server duplicates the transactions and data storage of another, identical server. Server mirroring requires a link between the servers and software running on both servers so that the servers can continually synchronize their actions and take over in case the other fails.

- **signature scanning** — The comparison of a file's content with known virus signatures (unique identifying characteristics in the code) in a signature database to determine whether the file is a virus.
- **single point of failure** — A place on the network where, if a fault occurs, the transfer of data may break down without possibility of an automatic recovery.
- **standby UPS** — A power supply that provides continuous voltage to a device by switching instantaneously to the battery when it detects a loss of power from the wall outlet. Upon restoration of the power, the standby UPS switches the device to use A/C power again.
- **stealth virus** — A type of virus that hides itself to prevent detection. Typically, stealth viruses disguise themselves as legitimate programs or replace part of a legitimate program's code with their destructive code.
- **surge** — A momentary increase in voltage due to distant lightning strikes or electrical problems.
- **time-dependent virus** — A virus programmed to activate on a particular date. This type of virus, also known as a "time bomb," can remain dormant and harmless until its activation date arrives.
- **Trojan horse** — A program that disguises itself as something useful but actually harms to your system.
- **uninterruptible power supply (UPS)** — A battery-operated power source directly attached to one or more devices and to a power supply (such as a wall outlet), which prevents undesired features of the power source from harming the device or interrupting its services.
- **vault** — A large tape storage library.
- **virus** — A program that replicates itself so as to infect more computers, either through network connections or through floppy disks passed among users. Viruses may damage files or systems or simply annoy users by flashing messages or pictures on the screen or by causing the keyboard to beep.
- **virus hoax** — A rumor, or false alert, about a dangerous, new virus that could supposedly cause serious damage to your workstation.
- **volt-amp (VA)** — A measure of electrical power. A volt-amp is the product of the voltage and current (measured in amps) of the electricity on a line.
- **worm** — An unwanted program that travels between computers and across networks. Although worms do not alter other programs as viruses do, they may carry viruses.

REVIEW QUESTIONS

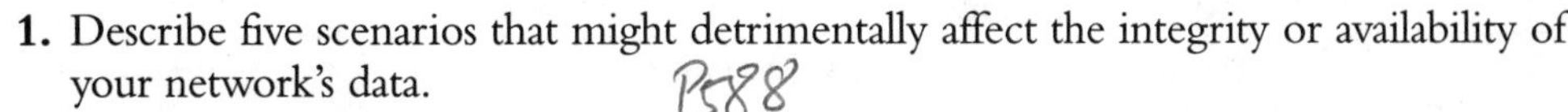

1. Describe five scenarios that might detrimentally affect the integrity or availability of your network's data.
2. Which of the following percentages represents the highest availability for a network?
   a. 0.10%
   b. 0.01%
   c. 99%
   d. 99.99%
3. To ensure that a system change does not detrimentally affect integrity and availability, what information should you record about the change?
   a. who performed the change and why it was necessary
   b. when the change occurred, why it was necessary, who performed the change, and what the change involved
   c. what the change involved and when it occurred
   d. when the change occurred and how to reverse it
4. Which of the following symptoms might make you suspect that your workstation is infected with a macro virus?
   a. Your computer takes a long time to start up.
   b. While in Microsoft Word, you receive a message that says, "WXYC rules the roost."
   c. While navigating through folders, your icons suddenly switch from pictures of folders to pictures of pineapples.
   d. You can no longer save word-processing files to your hard disk.
5. Why are stealth viruses difficult to detect?
   a. They attach themselves to legitimate programs.
   b. They frequently change their file size characteristics.
   c. They disguise themselves as legitimate programs.
   d. They destroy the file allocation table to prevent directory scanning.
6. Name three key components of an enterprise-wide antivirus policy.
7. Which of the following is a popular antivirus program?
   a. Norton VirusPro
   b. Scandisk
   c. Norton AntiVirus
   d. McAfee Virex
8. A worm is a type of polymorphic virus. True or False?

9. How does a Trojan horse disguise itself?
   a. It frequently changes its code characteristics.
   b. It disguises itself as a useful program.
   c. It prevents the user from performing directory scans.
   d. It does not appear in a directory listing.
10. Which of the following techniques does a polymorphic virus employ to make itself more difficult to detect?
   a. It frequently changes its code characteristics.
   b. It disguises itself as a useful program.
   c. It damages the file allocation table to prevent directory scanning.
   d. It moves from one location to another on the hard disk.
11. If your antivirus software uses signature scanning, what must you do to keep its virus-fighting capabilities current?
   a. Purchase new virus signature scanning software every three months.
   b. Reinstall the virus scanning software each month.
   c. Manually edit the signature scanning file.
   d. Regularly update the antivirus software's signature database.
12. What might you tell a user who receives what seems to be a virus hoax message?
   a. Ignore and delete the message.
   b. Open the message to verify that it is indeed a hoax.
   c. Send the message to the help desk.
   d. Save the message for you to review.
13. Describe the main difference between a fault and a failure.
14. Fail-over is a technique used in highly fault-tolerant systems. True or False?
15. What makes two components hot swappable?
   a. Both are similar and installed in the same device.
   b. Both are similar and one can be quickly swapped in for the other in case of a fault.
   c. Both are identical, both are installed in the same device, and one can instantly take over from the other in case of a fault.
   d. Both are identical and one can be quickly swapped in for the other in case of a fault.
16. Over time, what might electrical line noise do to your system?
   a. wear down the power switch
   b. damage the internal circuit boards
   c. increase the system board's response time
   d. cause more frequent outages

17. How long will an online UPS take to switch its attached devices to battery power?
    - a. 15 seconds
    - b. 10 seconds
    - c. 5 seconds
    - d. no time
18. Which of the following is the most highly fault-tolerant network topology?
    - a. bus
    - b. ring
    - c. partial mesh
    - d. full mesh
19. Which characteristic of SONET rings makes them highly fault-tolerant?
    - a. They are self-healing.
    - b. They are geographically diverse.
    - c. They are made of fiber-optic cable.
    - d. They share traffic over many lines.
20. Describe how load balancing between redundant NICs works.
21. Why is simple disk striping not fault-tolerant?
    - a. It can be performed only on a single disk drive.
    - b. If one disk fails, data contained on that disk are unavailable.
    - c. It does not keep a dynamic record of where data are striped.
    - d. It relies on a single disk controller.
22. Why is RAID Level 5 superior to RAID Level 3?
23. Which of the following can be considered an advantage of server clustering over server mirroring?
    - a. Clustering does not affect network performance.
    - b. Clustering fail-over takes place more rapidly.
    - c. Clustering has no geographical distance limitations.
    - d. Clustering keeps a more complete copy of a disk's data.
24. What is currently the greatest disadvantage to using server clustering?
    - a. It's expensive.
    - b. It detrimentally affects performance.
    - c. It requires that servers in a cluster be geographically close.
    - d. It is difficult to maintain.
25. List four considerations that you should weigh when deciding on a data backup solution.

26. Which factor must you consider when using online backups that you don't typically have to consider when backing up to a LAN tape drive? P618
    a. reliability
    b. geographical distance
    c. security
    d. time to recover
27. In a "grandfather-father-son" backup scheme, the October–week 1–Thursday backup tape would contain what types of files? P619
    a. files changed since last Thursday
    b. files changed since a month ago Thursday
    c. files changed since Wednesday
    d. files changed since a week ago Wednesday
28. Which of the following is a major disadvantage to performing full system backups on a daily basis?
    a. They would take too long to perform.
    b. They would take too long to restore.
    c. They would be less reliable than incremental backups.
    d. They would require manual intervention.
29. How can you verify the accuracy of tape backups?
30. Name four components of a smart disaster recovery plan.

HANDS-ON PROJECTS

In the following Hands-on Projects, you will have a chance to experiment with some fault-tolerance measures. Bear in mind that solutions will vary with each network environment.

PROJECT 14-1

For this project, you will need a NetWare 4.x or higher server with a Windows 95 or Windows 98 client workstation attached. The server should contain at least a Pentium processor in addition to the NetWare operating system and its connection to the network. The client workstation should contain at least a Pentium processor and a CD-ROM drive, and you should be able to connect to the Internet from that workstation. You will also need a copy of Norton AntiVirus software for NetWare.

To install Norton AntiVirus on a NetWare server:

1. Log on to the server as an administrator from a Windows workstation attached to your NetWare server.

2. Map a drive to the server's **SYS** volume.
3. Insert the Norton AntiVirus CD into your workstation's CD-ROM drive. If the CD menu does not automatically open, open **My Computer**, double-click the CD-ROM drive, then double-click on the **setup.exe** file to begin the installation process.
4. The program may ask permission to restart the workstation so as to perform virus checks on it before installing to the network. Click **OK**. After restarting, the installation program will scan memory, the master boot record, and system files for viruses.
5. If a virus is found on your workstation, do not continue with the installation. Instead, use the Norton AntiVirus software for Windows workstations to disinfect the machine.
6. The software registration dialog box opens. Enter your name and your institution's name in the Name and Company text boxes, then click **OK** to continue.
7. Select **Automatic Installation**, then click **OK**.
8. Accept the default installation path for the Norton AntiVirus Network Loadable Module (NAV NLM), **SYSTEM\NAVNLM**.
9. Accept the default installation path for the Windows configuration program, **C:\NAVNLM**.
10. After the NLM and the configuration program are installed, you have the option to update the AUTOEXEC.NCF file. Select **Let Install Make the Changes** to accept this option.
11. Now that you have installed the software on the server, you will need to initialize it. At the server console, type **load navnlm** to start the Norton AntiVirus program. After the NLM has loaded, you can use Norton AntiVirus on your NetWare server to detect viruses.
12. At the Windows workstation, experiment with the NAV program to immediately scan servers, change configuration options, and set a regularly scheduled server scan.

Project 14-2

Because the Norton AntiVirus software uses signature scanning as one of its antivirus measures, you will have to update the signature database on a regular schedule. In this exercise, you will update the software you installed on your NetWare server in Project 14-1.

1. Open your Web browser and go to http://www.sarc.com/avcenter/download.html, the Norton Download AntiVirus Updates page.
2. Click the **Product** list arrow, then select **NAV for NetWare**.
3. Click the **Language** list arrow, then select **English – US** (if it is not already selected).
4. Click **Next** to continue.

5. You will be prompted to choose the version of Norton AntiVirus for which you want to download an updated file. Click **Norton AntiVirus 5.0 for Windows 95/98**.
6. The pointer will be positioned at the beginning of the list of downloadable files for that version of Norton AntiVirus. Underneath, a filename and its creation date, release date, and file size will be listed. Click on a self-extracting executable file name to download that file.
7. The Save As dialog box opens. Save the file to your **C:\TEMP** directory. Click **Save** to begin the download.
8. If you aren't already logged in as Administrator, log on to the network from your workstation as an administrator. Run the file you just downloaded, supplying the location of your NAV NLM.
9. Follow instructions on the screen to ensure that your antivirus signature database was updated.

PROJECT 14-3

In this exercise, you will use an online UPS capacity tool to determine the UPS needed for an imaginary network server. UPS vendors such as APC supply these online tools so that you do not have to calculate by hand the VA necessary for your network. To complete this project, you will need a workstation with access to the Internet.

1. From the networked workstation, launch the Web browser and go to http://www.apcc.com/template/size/apc/. This Size UPS Web site provides a UPS sizing utility that you can use to determine your UPS capacity needs. In this case, you want to determine the needs of your server.
2. Click the **Server** icon on the menu bar. A new page opens, containing a drop-down list from which you can select your server model.
3. Click the drop-down arrow, click **Compaq Proliant 6000**, then click **Submit**. A new page opens, allowing you to specify a number of options that characterize your server.
4. To the default specifications, add a 17-inch monitor, one attached tape drive, and four external hard drives.
5. Click **Add this unit to configuration**. A new page opens, allowing you to set more parameters for your server.
6. Click **Continue to Preferences**.
7. Note the defaults, including a 20-minute run time.
8. Click **Get Recommendations**. A new page opens, containing the recommendations for the type of server that you specified.

9. Scroll to the bottom of the page to view your configuration. How many volts did the utility estimate your configuration would require? How many watts and VA would the UPS have to supply to keep the server, monitor, tape drive, and external hard disks running for 20 minutes?
10. Click the **Back** button on your browser to return to the last set of parameters you specified.
11. Click the **Start Over** button to begin a new configuration.
12. Repeat steps 2 through 8, this time selecting an IBM Netfinity 7000 server. How many volts would this configuration require? How many watts and VA would the UPS have to supply to keep the Netfinity server running for 20 minutes?

CASE PROJECTS

1. You have been asked to help a local hospital improve its network's fault tolerance. The hospital's network carries critical patient care data in real time from both a mainframe host and several servers to PCs in operating rooms, doctors' offices, the billing office, teaching labs, and remote clinics located across the region. Of course, all of the data transferred is highly confidential and must not be lost or accessed by unauthorized personnel. Specifically, the network consists of the following:

   - Six hundred PCs are connected to 5 shared servers that run Novell NetWare 4.11. Fifty of these PCs serve as training PCs in medical school classrooms. Two hundred PCs sit in doctors' offices and are used to view and update patient records, submit accounting information, and so on. Twenty PCs are used in operating rooms to perform imaging and for accessing data in real time. The remaining PCs are used by administrative staff.
   - The PCs are connected in a mostly switched, star-wired bus network using Ethernet 100BaseT technology. Where switches are not used, some hubs serve smaller workgroups of administrative and physician staff.
   - An Internet gateway supports e-mail, online medical searches, and VPN communications with four remote clinics. The Internet connection is a single T1 link to a local Internet service provider.
   - A firewall prevents unauthorized access from the T1 connection into the hospital's network.

   The hospital's IS director has asked you to identify the critical points of failure in her network and to suggest how she might eliminate them. On a sheet of paper, draw a logical diagram of the network and identify the single points of failure, then recommend which points of failure should be addressed to increase availability and how to achieve this goal. For each fault-tolerant component or method you recommend, find manufacturers' data available on the Web to identify its cost.

2. Unfortunately, the solution you provided for the hospital was rejected by the board of directors because it was too expensive. How would you go determine where to cut costs in the proposal? What questions should you ask the IS director? What points of failure do you suggest absolutely must be addressed with redundancy?
3. Your second proposal, with its reduced cost, was accepted by the board of directors. Now the hospital's IS director has asked you to outline a disaster recovery plan. Based on what you have learned about the hospital's topology, usage patterns, and current fault-tolerance measures, develop a disaster recovery plan for the hospital that specifically addresses how functionality and data will be restored.
4. After you submitted your outline of the hospital's disaster recovery plan, the IS director takes you aside and confesses that she isn't sure whether her network administrator is doing the right thing with the hospital's antivirus software and policy. Currently, the antivirus software is installed on each workstation in the hospital and scans each workstation's memory and hard disk once per week. She asks whether you have a solution for a better antivirus implementation and whether she should ask users to scan their hard disks more frequently than once per week. How do you respond?

C H A P T E R 15

NETWORK SECURITY

After reading this chapter and completing the exercises, you will be able to:

- Identify security risks in LANs and WANs
- Explain how physical security contributes to network security
- Discuss hardware- and design-based security techniques
- Use network operating system techniques to provide basic security
- Implement enhanced security through specialized software
- Describe the elements of an effective security policy

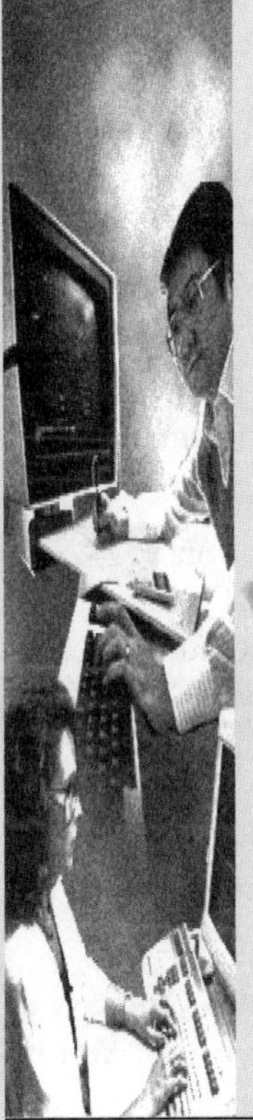

ON THE JOB

With few exceptions, today's commercial computer networks are vulnerable to break-ins. As a network security assessor, I've seen even the most secure commercial networks breached within a few days' time.

Commercial state-of-the-art network security includes such technical solutions as public key encryption, one-time passwords, over 1024-bit strong encryption, fingerprint verification, and even retinal scanning. But the reality remains that an intruder can access secured systems by finding "convenient short cuts" installed by system and network administrators.

The most common method for gaining access to a presumed-secure network system is finding these short cuts and taking advantage of them. During network security assessments, for example, we often find a trusted relationship between two or more hosts. One of the hosts is usually less secure than the others. When we gain access to one system, the others dutifully allow us right in.

In one instance, a firewall-protected network appeared very secure. However, when we scanned the TCP port ranges, we found the signature of a popular commercial mail server. We ran a mail client, attached to the server, and tried a couple of generic user IDs. Incredibly, we were able to gain access to the network manager's mailbox—without a password! Even better, sensitive mail was not encrypted. One message included the complete set of configuration statements for some remote office network routers. Without firewalls, these routers were connected to the Internet and had trusted relationships with the home office. On gaining access to one of the remote office routers, we immediately logged in to the organization's home office router. From there, it was a short time before we found and gained access to a number of UNIX and Windows NT servers—the backbone of the organization's network.

Two small "conveniences" enabled us to circumvent the highly secured firewall and breach the organization's network within a couple of hours!

David Klann
Berbee Information Networks, Inc.

In the early days of computing, when secured mainframes acted as central hosts and data repositories that were accessed only by dumb terminals with limited rights, network security was all but certain. As networks have become more geographically distributed and heterogeneous, however, the risk of their misuse has also increased. Consider the largest, most heterogeneous network in existence: the Internet. Because it contains millions of points of entry, millions of servers, and millions of miles of cabling, it is vulnerable to millions of break-ins. Because so many networks connect to the Internet, the threat of an outsider accessing an organization's network via the Internet, and then stealing or destroying data, is very real. In this chapter, you will learn how to assess your network's risks, how to manage those risks, and, perhaps most importantly, how to convey the importance of network security to the rest of your organization through an effective security policy.

TERMINOLOGY

Before delving into network security issues, you should have a clear understanding of terminology frequently used in this field. First, you should understand the difference between a hacker and a cracker. A **hacker** is someone who masters the inner workings of operating systems and utilities in an effort to better understand them. A **cracker** is someone who uses his or her knowledge of operating systems and utilities to intentionally damage or destroy data or systems. The primary difference between hackers and crackers is that hackers do not conduct their experimentation with malicious intent. In fact, hackers may be commissioned to break into networks as part of security audits, in an effort to test whether a cracker could do the same. This chapter will focus on network security in terms of how it protects against crackers.

Another frequently used term related to network security is "root." In general, **root** refers to a highly privileged user ID that has all rights to create, delete, modify, move, read, write, or execute files on a system. Specifically, it may mean the administrator on a UNIX-based network. Getting the root ID and password on one system often allows crackers to gain access to attached systems, which is typically their goal. For this reason, information about root accounts should be carefully guarded.

Every network operating system requires that users provide authentication. **Authentication** is the process of verifying a user's validity and authority on a system; it generally takes place during the login process. Different systems use different credentials to authenticate users as they log in. You are probably most familiar with the user ID and password combination. Some systems, however, may also base authentication on digital signatures, IP addresses, session IDs, or a combination of these methods. Generally, the more information required for authentication, the more secure the system, and the stronger the authentication. If a protocol or system uses little information to verify an attempt to access its data, the protocol or system is considered to have weak authentication.

Authentication usually occurs at the Application layer of the OSI Model. One way of breaking into a network from the outside is to falsify authentication information. You will learn more about authentication later in this chapter.

SECURITY AUDITS

Before spending time and money on network security, you should examine your network's security risks. As you learn about each risk facing your network, you should consider the effect that a loss of data, programs, or access would have on your network. The more serious the potential consequences, the more attention you will want to pay to the security of your network. In general, deciding how much to invest in network security is similar to buying life insurance. If you are unmarried with no dependents, no debts, and very few assets, you might not care much about life insurance coverage; you might therefore choose not to invest in monthly premiums. If you have 6 children and you run a business that employs 200 people, however, you will want to ensure that your loved ones and your business will be protected in case of your death.

Much in the same way, different types of organizations have variable levels of network security risk. For example, if you work for a large savings and loan institution, and your clients have the choice of viewing their current loan status online, you have a number of risks associated with data and access. If someone obtained unauthorized access to your network, all of your customers' personal financial data would be at risk. On the other hand, if you work for a local greenhouse that is not connected to the Internet and uses its internal LAN only to track plant inventory and sales, you may not be concerned if someone gains access to your network, because you have little to lose and nothing is very private. Just as you learned in Chapter 14, the key question is, "What will I lose if my system goes down?" In addition, when considering security risks, you should ask, "How much of the information that I store, transmit, and receive is confidential?"

Every organization should assess its security risks by conducting a **security audit**, at least annually and preferably quarterly. For each threat listed in the following sections, your security audit should rate the severity of its potential effects, as well as its likelihood. A threat's consequences may be severe, potentially resulting in a network outage or the dispersal of top-secret information, or it may be mild, potentially resulting in a lack of access for one user or the dispersal of a relatively insignificant piece of corporate data. The more devastating a threat's effects and the more likely it is to happen, the more rigorously your security measures should address it. Appendix C, "Examples of Standard Networking Forms," provides an example of a checklist you can use to perform a fundamental security audit.

A qualified consulting company can also conduct security audits for your network. The advantage of having an objective third party, such as a consultant, analyze your network is that he or she might find risks that you overlooked because of your familiarity with your environment. Third-party audits may seem expensive, but if your network hosts confidential and critical data, they will be well worth their cost.

After identifying your network's vulnerabilities, you should examine how each security risk might detrimentally affect your data and systems. In the next section, you will learn about risks associated with people, hardware, software, and Internet access.

Security Risks

Now that you understand the basic terms associated with network security, you are ready to learn about the types of risks facing most networks. The following sections describe these risks. Later in this chapter, you will learn how to protect against each type of threat.

As you learned in Chapter 14, natural disasters, viruses, and power faults can damage a network's data, programs, and hardware. A security breach, however, can harm a network just as easily and quickly. To understand how to manage network security, you should first recognize the types of threats that your network may suffer. Not all security breaches result from a manipulation of network technology. Instead, some occur when staff members purposely, or inadvertently reveal their passwords; others result from undeveloped security policies.

As you read about each security threat, think about how it could be prevented, whether it applies to *your* network (and if so, how damaging it might be), and how it relates to other security threats. Keep in mind that malicious and determined intruders may use one technique to bring them to a second technique, which allows them to use a third technique, and so on. For example, a cracker might discover a user's ID by watching her log on to the network; the cracker might then use a password-cracking program to access the network, where he might plant a program to generate a denial-of-service attack.

RISKS ASSOCIATED WITH PEOPLE

By some estimates, human errors, ignorance, or omissions cause more than half of all security breaches sustained by networks. One of the most common methods for an intruder to gain access to a network is to simply ask a user for his or her password. For example, the intruder might pose as a technical support analyst who needs to know the password to troubleshoot a problem, or the password might be learned through a casual conversation about passwords. This strategy is commonly called **social engineering**, because it involves manipulating social relationships to gain access. This and other risks associated with people are listed below. Many people-related risks can be addressed through a clear, simple, and strictly enforced enterprise-wide security policy. You will learn how to develop an effective security policy later in this chapter.

Risks associated with people include the following:

- Intruders or attackers using social engineering or snooping to obtain user passwords
- An administrator incorrectly creating or configuring user IDs, groups, and their associated rights on a file server, resulting in file and login access vulnerabilities
- Network administrators overlooking security flaws in topology or hardware configuration
- Network administrators overlooking security flaws in operating system or application configuration
- Lack of proper documentation and communication of security policies leading to deliberate or inadvertent misuse of files or network access
- Dishonest or disgruntled employees abusing their file and access rights
- An unused computer or terminal being left logged into the network, thereby providing an entry point for an intruder
- Users or administrators choosing easy-to-guess passwords
- Authorized staff leaving computer room doors open or unlocked, allowing unauthorized individuals to enter
- Staff discarding disks or backup tapes in public waste containers
- Administrators neglecting to remove access and file rights for employees who have left the organization

Human errors account for so many security breaches because taking advantage of them is the easiest way to circumvent network security. Imagine a man named Kyle, who was recently fired from his job at a local bank. Because Kyle felt he was unfairly treated, he wants to take revenge on his employer. He still has a few friends at the bank. Even though the bank's network administrator was wise enough to deactivate Kyle's network login ID and rights upon his termination, and even though the bank has a policy prohibiting employees from sharing their passwords, Kyle knows his friends' IDs and passwords. Nevertheless, the bank's policy prevents former employees from walking into its offices.

How might Kyle attain his goal of deleting a month's worth of client account activity statements? In this scenario, although the bank has a network security policy, employees such as Kyle's friends probably don't pay much attention to it. Kyle could most likely walk into the bank's offices, ostensibly to meet one of his friends for lunch. While in the offices, Kyle could either sit down at a machine where his friend was still logged in or log in as his friend because he knows his friend's password. Once in the system, he could locate the account activity statements and delete them. Although this example may be an oversimplification of the process, it isn't far from reality.

Risks Associated with Hardware and Network Design

This section describes security risks inherent in (roughly) Layers 1 and 2 of the OSI Model—the Physical and Data layers. Recall that the transmission media, NICs, hubs, network methods (for example, Ethernet), and topologies reside at these layers. This section will also discuss security risks in higher-level hardware, such as routers. At these levels, security breaches require more technical sophistication than those that take advantage of human errors. For instance, to eavesdrop on transmissions passing over CAT5 cabling, an intruder must use a device such as a sniffer. In the middle layers of the OSI Model, it becomes somewhat difficult to distinguish between hardware and software techniques. For example, because a router acts to connect one type of network to another, an intruder might take advantage of the router's security flaws by sending a flood of TCP/IP transmissions to the box, thereby disabling it from carrying legitimate traffic. You will learn about software-related risks in the following section. 15

The following risks are inherent in network hardware and design:

- Wireless transmissions can typically be intercepted (whereas fiber-based transmissions cannot).
- Networks that use leased lines, such as VPNs over the Internet, are vulnerable to eavesdropping.
- Repeater hubs broadcast traffic over the entire segment, thus making transmissions more widely vulnerable to sniffing. (By contrast, switches provide logical point-to-point communications, which limit the availability of data transmissions to the sending and receiving nodes.)

- Unused hub, router, or server ports can be exploited and accessed by crackers if they are not disabled. A router's configuration port, accessible by Telnet, may not be adequately secured.
- If routers are not properly configured to mask internal subnets, users on outside networks (such as the Internet) can read the private addresses.
- Modems attached to network devices may be configured to accept incoming calls, thus opening security holes if they are not properly protected.
- Dial-in access servers used by telecommuting or remote staff may not be carefully secured and monitored.
- Computers hosting very sensitive data may coexist on the same subnet with computers open to the general public.

Even though security breaches occur less frequently at the lower layers of the OSI Model, they can arise and can prove equally, if not more, damaging. Imagine that a cracker wants to bring a university library's database and mail servers to a halt. Suppose also that the library's database is public and can be searched by anyone on the Web. The cracker might begin by scanning ports on the database server to determine which have no protection. If she found an open port on the database server, the cracker might connect to the system and deposit a program that would, a few days later, damage operating system files or cause a flurry of traffic that disables the machine from functioning. She might also use her newly discovered access to determine the root password on the system, gain access to other systems, and launch a similar attack on the library's mail server, which is attached to the database server. In this way, even a single mistake (not protecting an open port) on one server can lead to failures of multiple systems.

Risks Associated with Protocols and Software

Like hardware, networked software is only as secure as you configure it to be. This section describes risks inherent in the higher layers of the OSI Model, such as the Transport, Session, Presentation, and Application layers. As noted earlier, the distinctions between hardware and software risks are somewhat blurry because protocol and hardware risks operate in tandem. For example, if a router has not been properly configured, a cracker may exploit the openness of TCP/IP to gain access to a network. Network operating systems and application software present different risks. In most cases, their security is compromised by a poor understanding of file access rights or simple negligence in configuring the software. Remember—even the best encryption, computer room door locks, security policies, and password rules make no difference if you grant access to the wrong users to critical data and programs on the network.

The following are some risks pertaining to networking protocols and software:

- TCP/IP contains several security flaws. For example, IP addresses can be falsified easily, checksums can be deceived, UDP requires no authentication, and TCP requires only weak authentication.
- Trust between one server and another may allow a cracker to access the entire network because of a single flaw.

- Network operating system software typically contains "backdoors" or security flaws. Unless the network administrator performs regular updates, a cracker may exploit these flaws.
- If the network operating system allows server operators to exit to a DOS prompt, intruders could run destructive command-line programs.
- Administrators might accept the default security options after installing an operating system or application. Often, defaults are not optimal. For example, the default user ID that enables someone to modify anything on or about the system in Windows NT Server is called "Administrator." Because this default is well known, if you leave the default ID as "Administrator," you have given a cracker half the information he or she needs to access your system and obtain full rights.
- Transactions that take place between applications, such as databases and Web-based forms, may be left open to interception.

To understand the risks that arise when an administrator accepts the default settings associated with a software program, consider the following scenario. Imagine that you have invited a large group of computer science students to tour your IT department. While you're in the computer room talking about subnetting, a bored student standing next to a Windows NT workstation decides to find out which programs are installed on the workstation. He discovers that this workstation has the SQL Server administrator software installed. Your organization uses a SQL database to hold all of your employees' salaries, addresses, and other confidential information. The student knows a little about SQL, including the facts that the default administrator user ID is called "sa," and that, by default, no password is created for this ID when someone installs SQL Server. He tries connecting to your SQL database with the "sa" user ID and no password. Because you accepted the defaults for the program during its installation, within seconds the student is able to gain access to your employees' information. He could then change, delete, or steal any of the data.

Risks Associated with Internet Access

Although the Internet has brought computer crime, such as cracking, to the public's attention, network security is more often compromised "from the inside" than from external sources. Nevertheless, the threat of outside intruders is very real, and it will only grow as more people gain access to the Internet.

At the same time, users need to be careful when they connect to the Internet. Even the most popular Web browsers sometimes contain bugs in their releases that permit rogue Internet scripts to access your system while you're connected, potentially for the purpose of causing damage. And be careful what information you provide while browsing the Web. Some sites will capture that information to use when attempting to break into systems. Bear in mind that crackers are creative and typically revel in devising new ways of breaking into systems; new Internet-related security threats arise frequently. By keeping your software current and designing your Internet access wisely, you can prevent most of these threats. Common Internet-related security breaches include the following:

- A firewall may not be adequate protection, if it is configured improperly. For example, it may allow outsiders to obtain internal IP addresses, then use those addresses to pretend that they have authority to access your internal network from the Internet—a process called **IP spoofing**. Alternatively, a firewall may not be configured correctly to perform even its simplest function—preventing unauthorized packets from entering the LAN from outside. (You will learn more about firewalls later in this chapter.) Correctly configuring a firewall is one of the best means to protect your internal LAN from Internet-based attacks.
- When a user Telnets or FTPs to your site over the Internet, his or her user ID and password will be transmitted in plain text—that is, unencrypted. Anyone monitoring the network can pick up the user ID and password and use it to gain access to the system.
- Crackers may obtain information about your user ID from newsgroups, mailing lists, or forms you have filled out on the Web (for example, to register to win a new car on a promotional site).
- While users remain logged on to Internet chat sessions, they may be vulnerable to other Internet users who might send commands to their machines that cause the screen to fill with garbage characters and require them to terminate their chat sessions. This type of attack is called **flashing**.
- After gaining access to your system through the Internet, a cracker may launch denial-of-service attacks. A **denial-of-service attack** occurs when a system becomes unable to function because it has been deluged with messages or otherwise disrupted. This incursion is a relatively simple attack to launch (for example, a cracker could create a looping program that sent thousands of e-mail messages to your system per minute). The easiest resolution of this problem is to bring down the attacked server, then reconfigure the firewall to deny service (in return) to the attacking machine. Denial-of-service attacks may also result from malfunctioning software. In Chapter 13, you learned how to apply patches to your server's operating system and utilities and research vendors' update alerts. Regularly performing these upgrades is essential to maintaining network security.

ADDRESSING RISKS ASSOCIATED WITH PEOPLE

As you have learned, most network security breaches occur from within an organization, and many take advantage of human errors. This section describes how to minimize the risk of break-ins by communicating with and managing the users in your organization via a thoroughly planned security policy. Before any hardware or software measures can offer effective protection, a security policy must be implemented that tells users how to set secure passwords and that makes critical data accessible only to authorized personnel.

AN EFFECTIVE SECURITY POLICY

The first step in securing your network is devising and implementing a security policy. This document identifies your security goals, risks, levels of authority, designated security coordinator and team members, responsibilities for each team member, and responsibilities for each employee. In addition, it specifies how to address security breaches. It should *not* state exactly which hardware, software, architecture, or protocols will be used to ensure security, nor how hardware or software will be installed and configured. These details will change from time to time and should be shared only with authorized network administrators or managers.

Security Policy Goals

Before drafting a security policy, you should understand why the security policy is necessary and how it will serve your organization. Typical goals for security policies are as follows:

- Ensuring that authorized users have appropriate access to the resources they need
- Preventing unauthorized users from gaining access to the network, systems, programs, or data
- Protecting sensitive data from unauthorized access, both from within and from outside the organization
- Preventing accidental damage to hardware or software
- Preventing intentional damage to hardware or software
- Creating an environment where the network and systems can withstand and, if necessary, quickly recover from any type of threat
- Communicating each employee's responsibilities with respect to maintaining data integrity

A company's security policy may also include content that does not pertain to computers or networks. For example, it might state that each employee should shred paper files that contain sensitive data or that each employee is responsible for signing in their visitors at the front desk and obtaining a temporary badge for them. Non-computer-related aspects of security policies are beyond the scope of this chapter, however.

15

After defining the goals of your security policy, you can devise a strategy to attain them. First, you might form a committee composed of managers and interested parties from a variety of departments, in addition to your network administrators. The more decision-making people you can involve, the more supported and effective your policy can be. This committee can assign a security coordinator, who will then drive the creation of a security policy.

To make your security policy more accepted in your organization, tie security measures to business needs and clearly communicate the potential effects of security breaches. For example, if your company sells clothes over the Internet and a two-hour outage (as could be caused by a cracker who uses IP spoofing to gain control of your systems) could cost the company $1 million in lost sales, make certain that users and managers understand this fact. If they do, they will be more likely to embrace the security policy.

A security policy must address an organization's specific risks. To understand your risks, you should conduct a security audit that identifies vulnerabilities and rates both the severity of each threat and its likelihood of occurring, as described earlier in this chapter. Once risks are identified, the security coordinator should assign one person the responsibility for addressing that threat.

For example, imagine that you are the network administrator for a nonprofit organization that collects blood donations from the public and arranges to ship them to victims of disasters across the country. Your LAN contains not only your organization's financial and personnel data, but also databases listing all blood donors in your area and the last date that they gave blood. In addition, your network contains records of the people whom your organization has assisted during the last five years. Your network is connected through the Internet to other, similar organizations, so that you can share your resources with them and they can help you with your needs. What security risks exist in this system, and how should you manage them?

First, your servers hold a great deal of potentially sensitive information—not only financial information, but also health and community data. To prevent unauthorized access to this information, one person should be assigned the task of protecting it. Second, your network presumably has a number of workstations attached to it. At least one person should be given the responsibility of making sure that PCs do not hold sensitive data on their hard disks and that PC users understand and adhere to security policies. Third, your network has a link to the Internet. One person should therefore be assigned the task of verifying that the Internet connection does not permit crackers to access your internal network.

Security Policy Content

After your risks are identified and responsibilities for managing them are assigned, the policy's outline should be generated with those risks in mind. Some subheadings for the policy might include the following: Password policy; Software installation policy; Confidential and sensitive data policy; Network access policy; E-mail use policy; Internet use policy; Modem use policy; Remote access policy; Policies for connecting to remote locations, the Internet, and customers' and vendors' networks; Policies for use of laptops and loaner machines; and Computer room access policy. Although compiling all of this information might seem like a daunting task, the process will ensure that everyone understands the organization's stance on security and the reasons why it is so important.

The security policy should clearly explain to users what they can and cannot do and how these measures protect the network's security. Clear and regular communication about security policies will make them more acceptable and better understood. One idea for making security policies more sustainable is to distribute a "security newsletter" that keeps security issues fresh in everyone's mind. Perhaps the newsletter could highlight industry statistics about significant security breaches and their effort on the victimized organizations. You might also hold a contest for guessing a password, thereby demonstrating how unsafe passwords threaten security.

Another tactic is to create a separate section of the policy that applies only to users. Within the users' section, divide security rules according to the particular function or part of the network to which they apply. This approach will make the policy easier for users to read and understand; it will also prevent them from having to read through the entire document. An abridged example of a section organized in this way is provided below.

3.2.1 Passwords
Users may not share passwords with friends or relatives.
Users must choose passwords that exceed six characters and are composed of both letters and numbers.
Users should choose passwords that bear no resemblance to a spouse's name, pet's name, a birth date, anniversary, or other widely available information.
Users must change their passwords every 90 days.
Users may not use the same password until one year after its expiration.
Users may not write down their passwords or send them in e-mail correspondence.

3.2.2 Networks
Users must ensure that confidential data transmitted over the network are encrypted.
Users should be aware that most e-mail programs allow administrators to read any messages that are sent from or received by the system.
Users may not have modems attached to their machines unless they have received authorization from their supervisor.
Users may not install software obtained from the Internet or other outside sources.

Notice that this example policy asks users to encrypt confidential data when transmitting such information over the network. But how will users know what type of information is confidential? Your security policy should define what "confidential" means to your organization. In general, information is confidential if it could be used by other parties to impair your organization's functioning, decrease your customers' confidence, cause a financial loss, damage your organization's status, or give a significant advantage to a competitor. If you work in an environment such as a hospital, where most data are sensitive or confidential, however, your security policy should classify information in degrees of sensitivity that correspond to how strictly its access is regulated. For example, "top secret" data may be accessible only by the organization's CEO and Vice Presidents, whereas "confidential" data may be accessible only to those who must modify or create it (for example, doctors or accountants in a hospital).

15

Response Policy

Finally, a security policy should provide for a planned response in the event of a security breach. The response policy should identify the members of a response team, all of whom should clearly understand the security policy, risks, and measures in place. Each team member should be assigned a role and responsibilities. Like a disaster recovery response team, the security response team should regularly rehearse their defense by participating in a security threat drill. Some suggestions for team roles are listed below:

- *Dispatcher*—This team member is the person on call who first notices or is alerted to the problem. The dispatcher notifies the lead technical support specialist and then the manager. He or she opens a record on the incident, detailing the time it began, its symptoms, and any other pertinent information about the situation. The dispatcher remains available to answer calls from clients or employees or to assist the manager.

- *Manager*—This team member coordinates the resources necessary to solve the problem. If in-house technicians cannot handle the break-in, the manager should find outside assistance. The manager also ensures that the security policy is followed and that everyone within the organization is aware of the situation. As the response ensues, the manager continues to monitor events and communicate with the public relations specialist. After the incident has been resolved, the manager should hold a postmortem meeting to discuss how the breach happened, how the problem was resolved, and what measures are being taken to prevent a recurrence.
- *Technical support specialist*—This team member focuses on only one thing: solving the problem as quickly as possible. After the situation has been resolved, the technical support specialist describes in detail what happened and assists the manager in finding ways to avert such an incident in the future. Depending on the size of the organization and the severity of the incident, this role may be filled by more than one person.
- *Public relations specialist*—If necessary, this team member learns about the situation and the response, then acts as official spokesperson for the organization to the public.

After resolving a problem, you need to review what happened, determine how it might have been prevented, then implement those measures to prevent future problems. Better than having to learn from your own mistakes, though, is learning from others' mistakes. By searching the Web, you can find many examples of security breaches that cost businesses millions of dollars in lost revenue either because their systems failed or because they lost valuable trade secrets.

PASSWORDS

Choosing a secure password is one of the easiest and least expensive ways to guard against unauthorized access. Unfortunately, too many people prefer to use an easy-to-remember password. If your password is obvious to you, however, it may also be easy for a cracker to figure out. The following guidelines for selecting passwords should be part of your organization's security policy. It is especially important for network administrators not only to choose difficult passwords, but also to keep passwords confidential and to change them frequently.

Tips for making and keeping passwords secure include the following:

- Do not use the familiar types of passwords, such as your birth date, anniversary, pet's name, child's name, spouse's name, own name or nickname, user ID, phone number, address, or any other words or numbers that others might associate with you.
- Do not use any word that might appear in a dictionary. Crackers can use programs that try a combination of your user ID and every word in a dictionary to gain access to the network.

- Make the password longer than six characters—the longer, the better.
- Choose a combination of letters and numbers; add special characters, such as exclamation marks or hyphens, if allowed.
- Do not write down your password or share it with others.
- Change your password at least every 90 days. If you are a network administrator, establish controls through the network operating system to force users to change their passwords every 90 days. If you have access to sensitive data, change your password even more frequently.

Password guidelines should be clearly communicated to everyone in your organization through your security policy. Although users may grumble about having to choose a combination of letters and numbers and change their passwords frequently, you can assure them that the company's financial and personnel data will be safer as a result. No matter how much your colleagues protest, do not back down from your password requirements. Many companies mistakenly require employees only to use a password, without helping them choose a good one. This apathy increases the risk of security breaches.

PHYSICAL SECURITY

Another important element in network security is the restriction of physical access to its components. At the very least, only authorized networking personnel should have access to computer rooms. If computer rooms are not locked, intruders may easily steal equipment or sabotage software and hardware. For example, a malicious visitor could slip into an unsecured computer room and take control of a NetWare server console where an administrator is logged in, then shut down the machine or—worse—reformat its hard disk. Although a security policy may define who has access to the computer room, locking the computer room is necessary to keep unauthorized individuals out.

It isn't only the computer room that must be secured. Think of all the points at which your systems or data could be compromised: hubs or switches in a wiring closet, a workstation at someone's desk, a telecommunications closet where your leased line to the Internet terminates, a storage room for archived data and backup tapes. If a wiring closet is left unlocked, for example, a prankster could enter, grab a handful of wires, and pull them out of the patch panels.

Locks may be either physical or electronic. Many large organizations require authorized employees to wear electronic access badges. These badges can be programmed to allow their owner access to some, but not all, rooms in a building. Figure 15-1 depicts a typical badge access security system.

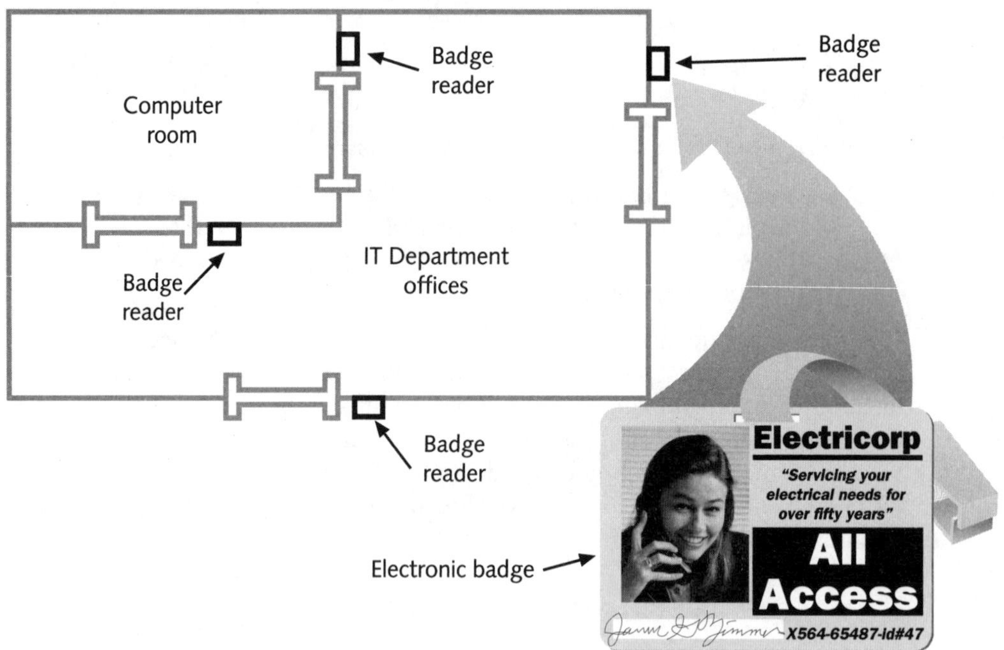

Figure 15-1 A badge access security system

A less expensive alternative to the electronic badge access system consists of locks that require entrants to punch a numeric code to gain access. For added security, these electronic locks can be combined with key locks. A more expensive solution involves **bio-recognition access**, in which a device scans an individual's unique physical characteristics, such as the color patterns in her eye's iris or whorls in her handprint, to verify her identity. On a larger scale, organizations may regulate entrance through physical barriers to their campuses, such as gates, fences, walls, or landscaping.

Many IT departments also use closed-circuit TV systems to monitor activity in secured rooms. Surveillance cameras may be placed in computer rooms, telco rooms, supply rooms, and data storage areas, as well as facility entrances. A central security office may display several camera views at once, or it may switch from camera to camera. The footage generated from these cameras is usually saved for a time in case it's needed in a security breach investigation or prosecution.

As with other security measures, the most important way to ensure physical security is to plan for it. You can begin your planning by asking questions related to physical security checks in your security audit. Relevant questions include the following:

- Which rooms contain critical systems or data and need to be secured?
- Through what means might intruders gain access to the facility, computer room, telecommunications room, wiring closet, or data storage areas (including not only doors, but also windows, adjacent rooms, ceilings, temporary walls, hallways, and so on)?

- How and to what extent are authorized personnel granted entry? (Do they undergo background or reference checks? Is their need for access clearly justified? Are their hours of access restricted? Who ensures that lost keys are reported?)
- Are employees instructed to ensure security after entering or leaving secured areas (for example, by not propping open doors)?
- Are authentication methods (such as ID badges) difficult to forge or circumvent?
- Do supervisors or security personnel make periodic physical security checks?
- Are all combinations, codes, or other access means to computer facilities protected at all times, and are these combinations changed frequently?
- Does a plan exist for documenting and responding to physical security breaches?

Addressing Risks Associated with Hardware and Design

Addressing the risks associated with people is just one part of a comprehensive security approach. Even if you restrict access to computer rooms, teach employees how to select secure passwords, and enforce a security policy, breaches may still occur due to poor LAN or WAN design. In this section, you will learn how to address some security risks via intelligent networking hardware and design.

Of course, the optimal way to prevent external security breaches from affecting your LAN is to not connect your LAN to the outside world at all. This option is impractical in today's business environment, however. The next best protection is to restrict access at every point where your LAN connects to the rest of the world. This principle forms the basis of hardware- and design-based security.

Much of the information covered in this section builds upon material discussed in Chapter 7, such as WAN design, VPNs, and remote connectivity. It may be helpful to review Chapter 7 before reading this section.

Firewalls

A **firewall** is a specialized device (typically a router, but possibly only a PC running special software) that selectively filters or blocks traffic between networks. A firewall typically involves a combination of hardware and software (for example, the router's operating system and configuration). It may reside between two interconnected private networks or, more typically, between a private network and a public network (such as the Internet), as shown in Figure 15-2. Many types of firewalls exist, and a detailed discussion of each is beyond the scope of this book. To understand secure network design and to qualify for Net+ certification, however, you should recognize which functions firewalls can provide, where they can appear on a network, and how to decide what you need in a firewall.

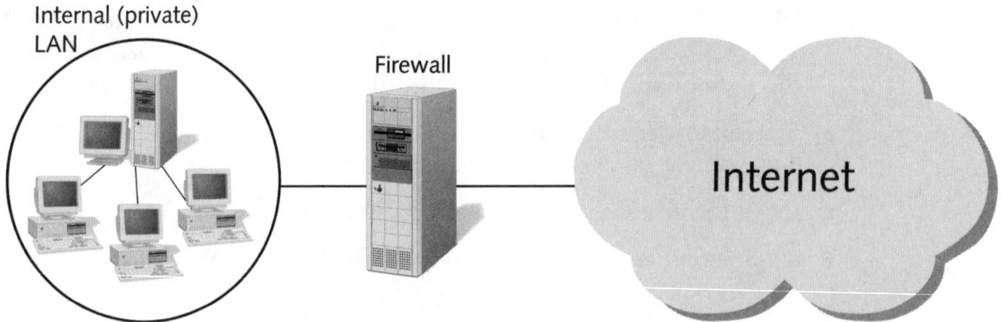

Figure 15-2 Placement of a firewall between a private network and the Internet

The term "firewall" is derived from the physical "wall" installed in automobiles to help prevent engine fires from spreading to the passenger area.

The simplest and most common form of a firewall is a **packet-filtering firewall**, which is a router that operates at the Data Link and Transport layers of the OSI Model. It examines the header of every packet of data that it receives to determine whether that type of packet is authorized to continue to its destination. Packet-filtering firewalls are also called **screening firewalls**. An example of a popular packet-filtering firewall is the Cisco 2503 router, pictured in Figure 15-3.

These types of firewalls require a great deal of custom configuration to be effective; that is, the network administrator must configure the firewall to accept or deny certain types of traffic. Some of the criteria that a firewall might use to accept or deny data include the following:

- Source and destination IP addresses
- Source and destination ports (for example, ports that supply TCP/UDP connections, FTP, Telnet, SNMP, RealAudio, and so on)
- The TCP, UDP, or ICMP protocols
- A packet's status as the first packet in a new data stream or a subsequent packet
- A packet's status as inbound or outbound to or from your private network
- A packet's status as originating from or being destined for an application on your private network

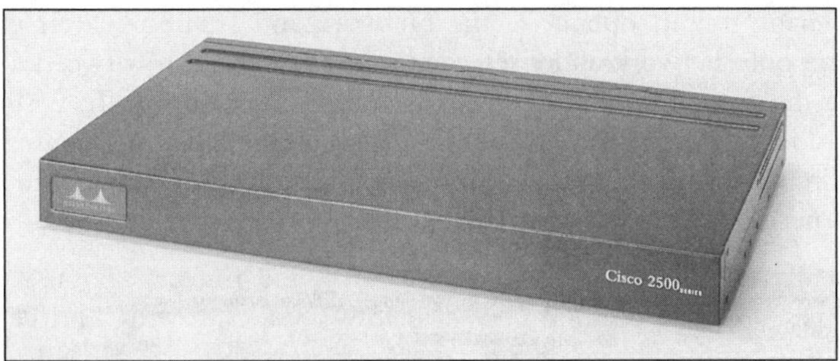

Figure 15-3 A packet-filtering firewall

You will recognize examples of firewall placement in most VPN architectures. For example, you might design a VPN that uses the Internet to connect your Milwaukee office with your Dubuque office. To ensure that only traffic from Milwaukee can access your Dubuque LAN, you could install a packet-filtering firewall between the Dubuque LAN and the Internet that accepts incoming traffic only from IP addresses that match the IP addresses on your Milwaukee LAN. In a way, the firewall acts like a bouncer at a private club who checks everyone's ID and ensures that only club members enter through the door. In the case of the Milwaukee-Dubuque VPN, the firewall will discard any data packets that arrive at the Dubuque firewall and do not contain source IP addresses that match those of Milwaukee's LAN.

In another example, suppose your network in Dubuque hosts a server that stores confidential employee information, such as payroll and health benefits, which only the Dubuque-based human resources manager should be able to access. In this situation, you could add a filter in the firewall to block all external traffic (from the Internet as well as the Milwaukee LAN) from reaching the destination address of that server.

Because you must tailor a firewall to your network's needs, you cannot simply purchase one, install it between your private LAN and the Internet, and expect it to offer much security. Instead, you must first consider what type of traffic you want to filter, then configure the firewall accordingly. It may take weeks to achieve the best configuration—not so strict that it prevents authorized users from transmitting and receiving necessary data, and not so lenient that you risk security breaches. Further complicating the matter is that you may need to create exceptions to the rules. For example, suppose that your human resources manager is working out of the Milwaukee office while recruiting new employees and needs to access the Dubuque server that stores payroll information. In this instance, the Dubuque network administrator might create an exception to allow transmissions from the human resources manager's workstation's IP address to reach that server. In the networking profession, creating an exception to the filtering rules is called "punching a hole" in the firewall.

Because packet-filtering routers operate at the Network and Transport layers of the OSI Model and examine only network addresses, they cannot distinguish between a user who is trying to breach the firewall and a user who is authorized to do so. To ensure that an unauthorized user does not simply sit down at the workstation belonging to an authorized user and try to circumvent the firewall, a more sophisticated technique—such as user authentication—is necessary.

One approach to enhancing the security of the Network and Transport layers provided by firewalls is to combine a packet-filtering firewall (hardware device) with a proxy service. A **proxy service** is a software application on a network host that acts as an intermediary between the external and internal networks, screening all incoming and outgoing traffic. The network host that runs the proxy service is known as a **proxy server** or **gateway**. Proxy servers manage security at the Application layer of the OSI Model. To understand how they work, think of the secure data on a server as the president of a country, and the proxy server as the secretary of state. Rather than having the president risk his or her safety by leaving the country, the representative travels abroad, speaking for the president and bringing information back to the president. In fact, foreign leaders may never actually meet the dignitary. Instead, the representative acts as his or her proxy.

Although a proxy server appears to the outside world as an internal network server, in reality it is merely another filtering device for the internal LAN. Among other things, it prevents the outside world from discovering the addresses of the internal network. For example, your LAN uses a proxy server, and you want to send an e-mail message from your workstation to your mother via the Internet, your message would first go to the proxy server (depending on the configuration of your network, you may or may not have to log in separately to the proxy server first). The proxy server would repackage the data frames that make up the message so that, rather than your workstation's IP address being the source, the proxy server would insert its own IP address as the source. Next, the proxy server would pass your repackaged data to the packet-filtering firewall. The firewall would verify that the source IP address in your packets is valid (that it came from the proxy server) and then send your message to the Internet. Examples of proxy server software include Novell's BorderManager and Microsoft's Proxy Server, an optional service for Windows NT servers. Figure 15-4 depicts how a proxy server might fit into a WAN design.

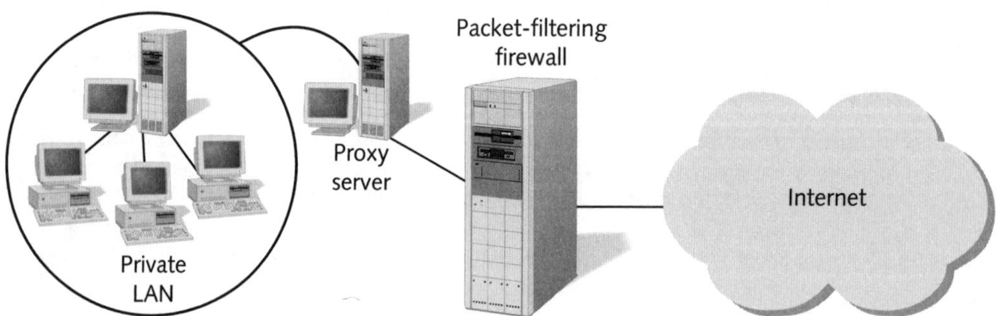

Figure 15-4 A proxy server used on a WAN

Many more sophisticated firewalls—both hardware- and software-based—exist. Choosing the appropriate firewall for your network can be a difficult task. Among the factors you will want to consider in your decision are the following:

- Does the firewall support encryption? (You will learn more about encryption later in this chapter.)
- Does the firewall support user authentication?
- Does the firewall allow you to manage it centrally and through a standard interface (such as one that uses SNMP)?
- How easily can you establish rules for access to and from the firewall?
- Does the firewall support filtering at the highest layers of the OSI Model, not just at the Data Link and Transport layers?
- Does the firewall provide logging and auditing capabilities, or alert you to possible intrusions?
- Does the firewall protect the identity of your internal LAN's addresses from the outside world?

REMOTE ACCESS

As you learned in Chapter 7, many companies supply traveling employees, telecommuters, or distant vendors with access to their private LANs or WANs. This type of access is often referred to as **remote access.** When working with remote access, you must remember that any entry point to a LAN or WAN creates a potential security risk. In other words, if an employee can get to your network in New York from his hotel room in Rome, a smart cracker can likely do the same. You can, however, take advantage of techniques designed to minimize the possibility of such unauthorized remote access. For example, firewalls can prevent certain addresses and users from gaining access to your LAN from the outside. In this section, you will learn about other security measures tailored to remote access solutions, such as remote control and dial-up networking.

Remote Control

Recall from Chapter 7 that remote control systems enable a user to connect to a host system on a network from a distance and use that system's resources as if the user were sitting in front of it. This type of access can have benefits for employees who work at home or who travel frequently. Although such remote control systems can be convenient, they can also present serious security risks. Most remote control software programs (for example, Symantec's pcANYWHERE or Avalan Technology's Remotely Possible) offer features that increase the security of remote control. If you intend to allow remote control access to a host on your LAN, you should investigate these security features and know how to implement them correctly. Important security features that you should seek in a remote control program include the following:

- A login ID and password requirement for gaining access to the host system.

- The ability for the host system to call back. This feature enables a remote user to dial into the network, enter a user ID, and hang up. The host system then calls the user back at a predetermined number (the authorized user's modem number), thus preventing a cracker from taking over a system even if he or she obtains the correct user ID and password for the host system.
- Support for data encryption on transmissions between the remote user and the system.
- The ability to leave the host system's screen blank while a remote user works on it. This feature prevents people walking by from seeing (potentially confidential) data that the remote user is accessing.
- The ability to disable the host system's keyboard and mouse. Essentially, this feature turns the host system into a terminal that responds to only remote users.
- The ability to restart the host system when a remote user disconnects from the system. This feature prevents anyone from reviewing what happened during the remote user's session or gaining access if the session was accidentally terminated before the remote user could properly log off.

Dial-up Networking

In Chapter 7, you learned about different ways for remote users to log in to a network. One method involved having users dial into a remote access server attached to the network, also known as dial-up networking. Like other remote access solutions, this approach presents security risks. In this section, you will learn how to make dial-up networking more secure.

Dial-up networking differs from remote control in that it effectively turns a remote workstation into a node on the network, through a remote access server. When choosing a remote access software package, you should evaluate its security. A secure remote access server package will include at least the following features:

- Login ID and password authentication
- The ability to log all dial-up connections, their sources, and their connection times
- The ability to perform callbacks to users who initiate connections
- Centralized management of dial-up users and their rights on the network

In environments where more than a few dozen simultaneous dial-up connections must be supported and their user IDs and passwords managed, a special kind of server known as a **Remote Authentication Dial-In User Service (RADIUS)** may be implemented to offer authentication services to the network's access server (which may run Windows NT's RAS or Novell's NAS, for example). RADIUS provides a single, centralized point of authentication for dial-in users. It is highly scalable, as it can attach to pools containing hundreds of modems. In addition, RADIUS is also more secure than using a simple remote access solution because its method of authentication prevents users' IDs and passwords from traveling across the phone line in clear text format.

Many Internet service providers use a RADIUS server to allow their subscribers access to the Internet through their modem pools. Other organizations employ it as a central authentication point for mobile or remote users. Figure 15-5 illustrates these two methods for allowing remote users to connect using RADIUS authentication.

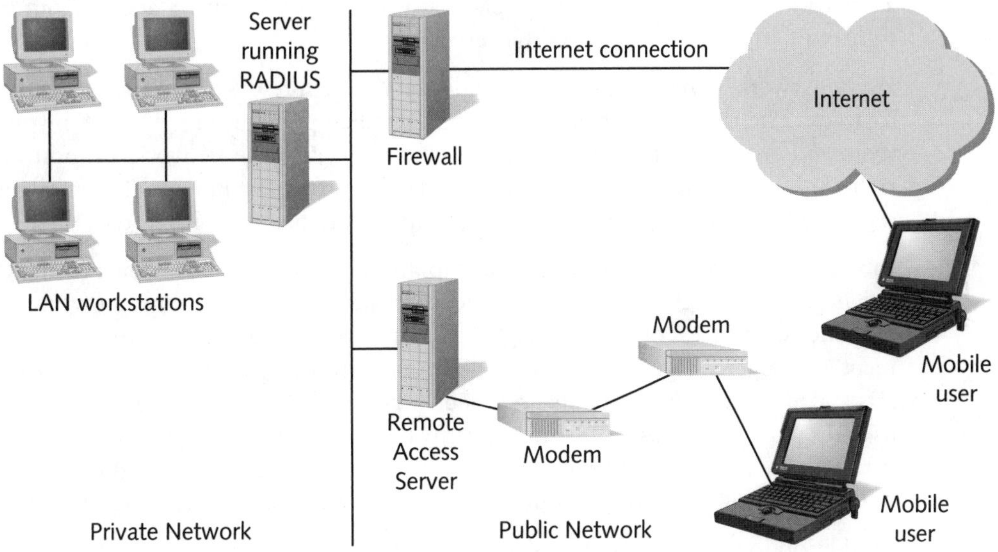

Figure 15-5 A RADIUS server providing central authentication

RADIUS may run on UNIX-, Windows NT–, or Novell-based networks. A similar, but earlier version of a centralized authentication system is **Terminal Access Controller Access Control System (TACACS)**.

As you learned in Chapter 7, dial-up networking depends on special protocols—for example, PPP or SLIP. Later in this chapter, you will learn about additional protocols that make dial-up networking part of a secure virtual private network.

Addressing Risks Associated with Software

Now that you have learned how to design a more secure network, it's time to examine the software tools that can help you protect your network against unauthorized access. Be sure to remember that all of these security techniques complement one another. No single technique is more important than any other, and if you neglect a technique, you may put your network at risk.

One of the simplest ways to protect your organization's data, programs, and access is to use the tools that come with your network operating system. In this section, you will learn the basics of restricting access through this software. You will also learn about a more advanced software-level security technique—encryption.

SECURITY PROVIDED BY THE NETWORK OPERATING SYSTEM

Regardless of whether you run your network on a Novell, Microsoft, or UNIX operating system, you can implement basic security by restricting what users are authorized to do on a network. This section reiterates what you learned in Chapters 8 and 9 about establishing rights to files and directories on the server.

Every network administrator should understand which resources on the server all users need to access. The rights conferred to all users are called public rights, because anyone can have them and exercising them presents no security threat to the network. In most cases, public rights are very limited. They may include privileges to view and execute programs from the server and to read, create, modify, delete, and execute files in a shared data directory.

In addition, network administrators need to group users according to their security levels and assign additional rights that meet the needs of those groups. As you know, creating groups simplifies the process of granting rights to users. For example, if you work in the IT department at a large college, you will most likely need more than one person to create new user IDs and passwords for students and faculty. Naturally, the staff in charge of creating new user IDs and passwords need the rights to perform this task. You could assign the appropriate rights to each staff member individually, but a more efficient approach is to put all of the personnel in a group, and then assign the appropriate rights to the group as a whole.

In addition to restricting users' access to files and directories on the server, a network administrator can constrain the ways in which users can access the server and its resources. The following is a list of additional restrictions that network administrators can use to strengthen the security of their networks:

- Time of day. Some user IDs may be valid only during specific hours—for example, between 8:00 A.M. and 5:00 P.M. Specifying valid hours for an ID can increase security by preventing any ID from being used by unauthorized personnel after hours.
- Total time logged in. Some user IDs may be restricted to a specific number of hours per day of logged-in time. Restricting total hours in this way can increase security in the case of temporary IDs. For example, suppose that your organization offers a WordPerfect training class to a group of high school students one afternoon, and the WordPerfect program and training files resided on your staff server. You might create IDs that could log in for only four hours that day.
- Source address. You can specify that user IDs can log in only from certain workstations or certain areas of the network (that is, domains or segments). This restriction can prevent unauthorized use of login IDs from workstations outside the network.
- Unsuccessful login attempts. Crackers may repeatedly attempt to log in under a valid ID for which they do not know the password. As the network administrator, you can set a limit on how many subsequent unsuccessful login attempts from a single user ID the server will accept before blocking that ID from even attempting to log in.

ENCRYPTION

Encryption is the use of an algorithm to scramble data into a format that can be read only by reversing the algorithm—that is, decrypting the data—so as to keep the information private. Many forms of encryption exist, with some being more secure than others. Even as new forms of encryption are developed, new ways of cracking their codes emerge, too.

The most popular kind of encryption algorithm weaves a **key** (some random string of characters) into the original data's bits—sometimes several times in different sequences—to generate a unique data block. The longer the key, the less easily the encrypted data can be decrypted by an unauthorized system. For example, a 512-bit key is considered secure, whereas a data block generated with a 16-bit key could be cracked in no time. Key encryption is similar to what happens when you finish a card game and place your five-card hand into the deck, then shuffle the deck numerous times. After shuffling, it might take you a while to retrieve your hand. As you can imagine, if you shuffled your five cards into four decks of cards at once, it would be even more difficult to find your original hand. In encryption, theoretically only the computer that systematically shuffled the data knows how to unshuffle it and retrieve the original sequence of data.

The following are some types of encryption with which you should be familiar:

- **Pretty Good Privacy (PGP)**—Pretty Good Privacy is a key-based encryption system for e-mail that uses a two-step verification process.
- **Digital certificates**—A digital certificate is a password-protected and encrypted file that holds an individual's identification information, including a public key and a private key. The individual's public key is used to verify the sender's digital signature, and the private key allows the individual to log on to a third-party authority that administers digital certificates.
- **Secure Sockets Layer (SSL)**—Secure Sockets Layer is a method of encrypting Web pages (or HTTP transmissions) en route. If you trade stocks or purchase goods on the Web, you are most likely using SSL to transmit your order information. The most recent versions of Netscape and Internet Explorer support SSL.
- **IP Security Protocol (IPSec)**—IPSec defines encryption, authentication, and key management for the upcoming IPv6 (mentioned in Chapter 11). It operates at the Network layer (Layer 3) of the OSI Model, adding security information to the header of all IP packets.

VIRTUAL PRIVATE NETWORKS (VPNs)

Loosely defined, virtual private networks (VPNs) are private networks that use public channels to connect clients and servers. Often VPNs integrate a wide variety of clients, from dial-up users at home to networked workstations in offices to Web servers at an ISP. The mix of client types, transmission methods, and services used by VPNs adds to their design complexity, as well as to the complexity of their security needs. Security considerations must be woven into both hardware/design and software for VPNs. These types of networks are so varied and potentially complicated that fully describing their nuances is beyond the scope of this book. In this section, however, you will learn about the significant security techniques particular to VPNs.

VPNs typically use the Internet to connect multiple sites; as the Internet is the largest public network in the world, its use presents obvious security hazards. VPNs often take advantage of firewalls and special protocols that encrypt the data transmitted over public connections. The following paragraphs describe some of the special protocols used in VPN connectivity.

As you learned in Chapter 7, PPP is a dial-in protocol that belongs in the Data Link layer (Layer 2) of the OSI Model and provides datagram transport services over serial and digital communications lines for the TCP/IP, NetBEUI, and IPX/SPX protocols. PPP originated for use with direct dial-in connections to Windows NT RAS servers. The **Point-to-Point Tunneling Protocol (PPTP)** expands on PPP by encapsulating it so that any type of PPP data can traverse the Internet masked as pure IP transmissions. PPTP supports the encryption, authentication, and LAN access services provided by RAS. Instead of users having to dial directly into an access server, however, they can dial into their ISP using PPTP and thereby gain access to their corporate LAN over the Internet.

The process of encapsulating one protocol to make it appear as another type of protocol is known as **tunneling**. Essentially, tunneling makes a protocol fit a type of network that it wouldn't normally match. PPTP is easy to install, is available at no extra cost with Microsoft networking services, and supports multiple kinds of protocols. For these reasons, it is the most popular VPN tunneling protocol in use today.

PPTP is available with Windows NT Server 4.0 and Windows NT Workstation 4.0 as part of RAS. You can purchase an upgrade from Microsoft to enable PPTP to work with the Windows 95 Dial-up Networking client. PPTP support is included automatically in the Windows 98 operating system.

Layer 2 Forwarding (L2F) is similar to PPTP in that it is a Layer 2 protocol that provides tunneling for other protocols and can work with the authentication methods used by PPP. The difference between PPTP and L2F lies in the type of encryption that each supports, and the fact that PPTP was developed by Microsoft, and L2F was developed by Cisco Systems. One disadvantage of L2F compared to PPTP is that the former protocol requires special hardware on the host system end, whereas PPTP will work with any Windows NT server. On the other hand, L2F can encapsulate protocols to fit more than just the IP format, unlike PPTP.

Both PPTP and L2F, however, will gradually be replaced by a third type of tunneling protocol called **Layer 2 Tunneling Protocol (L2TP).** This Layer 2 tunneling protocol was developed by a number of industry consortia. L2TP is an enhanced version of L2F that, like L2F, supports multiple protocols. Unlike L2F, however, L2TP does not require costly hardware upgrades to implement. It is also optimized to work with the next generation of IP (IPv6) and IPSec (the Layer 3 IP encryption protocol).

CHAPTER SUMMARY

- A hacker is someone who masters the inner workings of operating systems and utilities in an effort to better understand them. A cracker is someone who uses his or her knowledge of operating systems and utilities to intentionally damage or destroy data or systems.
- The root is a highly privileged user ID that has all rights to create, delete, modify, move, read, write, or execute files on a system. This term may specifically refer to the administrator on a UNIX-based network. Getting the root ID and password on one system often allows crackers to gain access to attached systems (which is typically their goal).
- Authentication is the process of verifying a user's validity and authority on a system. Different systems use different credentials to verify users. You are probably most familiar with the user ID and password combination. Systems may also base authentication on digital signatures, IP addresses, session IDs, or a combination of these methods. Generally, the more information required for authentication, the more secure the system.
- Every organization should assess its security risks by conducting a security audit, at least annually and preferably quarterly. For each threat, your security audit should rate the severity of its potential consequences, as well as its likelihood. A threat's effects may be severe, potentially resulting in a network outage or the dispersal of top-secret information, or they may be mild, potentially resulting in a lack of access for one user or the dispersal of a relatively insignificant piece of corporate data.
- By some estimates, human errors, ignorance, or omissions cause more than half the security breaches sustained by networks. One of the most common methods for an intruder to gain access to a network is to simply ask a user for his or her password. This strategy is commonly called social engineering, because it involves manipulating social relationships to gain access.
- Security risks associated with people include the following: intruders or attackers using social engineering to obtain user passwords; an administrator incorrectly creating or configuring user IDs, groups, and their associated rights on a file server; network administrators overlooking security flaws in topology or hardware configuration; network administrators overlooking security flaws in operating system or application configuration; lack of proper documentation and communication of security policies; dishonest or disgruntled employees abusing their file and access rights; a computer or terminal being left logged into the network while its operator is away; users or even administrators choosing easy-to-guess passwords; authorized staff leaving computer room doors propped open or unlocked, thereby allowing unauthorized individuals to enter; and administrators neglecting to remove access and file rights for employees who have left the organization.
- Risks inherent in network hardware and design include the following: twisted-pair cabling that emits electromagnetic radiation; wireless transmissions, which can typically be intercepted (transmissions over fiber-based networks cannot); networks that use leased lines, such as VPNs over the Internet, which are subject to eavesdropping; repeater hubs that broadcast traffic over the entire segment (whereas switches, for

example, provide logical point-to-point communications), thus making transmissions more widely vulnerable to sniffing; unused hub, router, or server ports that can be exploited and accessed by crackers if not disabled; a router's configuration port, accessible by Telnet, that may not be adequately secured; routers that may not be properly configured to mask internal subnets; modems attached to network devices that may be configured to accept incoming calls; dial-in access servers used by telecommuting or remote staff that may not be carefully secured and monitored; and computers hosting very sensitive data that may coexist on the same subnet with computers open to the general public.

- Some risks pertaining to networking protocols and software include the following: TCP/IP security flaws; trust between one server and another; network operating system software "backdoors" or security flaws; a network operating system that allows server operators to exit to a DOS prompt; administrators who accept default operating system security; and transactions that take place between applications left open to interception.

- Crackers may obtain information about your user ID from newsgroups, mailing lists, or forms that you fill out on the Web (for example, to register to win a new car on a promotional site).

- While users remain logged on to Internet chat sessions, they may be vulnerable to other Internet users who might send commands to their machines that cause the screen to fill with garbage characters and require the users to terminate their chat sessions. This type of attack is called flashing.

- A denial-of-service attack occurs when a system becomes dysfunctional because it is deluged with traffic. It is a relatively simple attack to launch, and the easiest resolution is to bring down the attacked server. Denial-of-service attacks may also be caused by malfunctioning software. For this reason, you should keep your server's operating system and utilities patched with the latest code and watch for bug reports.

- The first step in securing your network should be to devise and implement an enterprise-wide security policy. This document identifies your security goals, risks, levels of authority, designated security coordinator and team members, responsibilities for each team member, responsibilities for each employee, and strategies for addressing security breaches. It should *not* include specific information on what hardware, software, architecture, or protocols will be used to ensure security, nor should it indicate how hardware or software will be installed and configured. These details will change occasionally and should be shared only with authorized network administrators or managers.

- Goals for an effective security policy should include the following: ensuring that authorized users have appropriate access to the resources they need; preventing unauthorized users from gaining access to the network, systems, programs, or data; protecting sensitive data from unauthorized access, both from within and without the organization; preventing accidental damage to hardware or software; preventing intentional damage to hardware or software; creating an environment where the network and systems can withstand and, if necessary, quickly recover from any type of threat; and communicating each employee's responsibilities with respect to maintaining data integrity.

- The security policy should clearly explain to users what they can and cannot do and indicate how these measures protect the network's security. Clear and regular communication about security policies will make them more acceptable and better understood.
- The security policy should provide for a planned response in the event of a security breach. The response policy should identify members of a response team who clearly understand the security policy, risks, and measures in place. Each team member should be assigned a role and responsibilities. Like a disaster recovery response team, the security response team should regularly rehearse their defense in a security threat drill.
- Choosing a secure password is one of the easiest and least expensive ways to guard against unauthorized access. If your password is obvious to you, it will likely be easy for a cracker to figure out as well. The following guidelines for selecting passwords should be part of your organization's security policy: do not use the familiar types of passwords such as your birth date, anniversary, pet's name, child's name, spouse's name, own name or nickname, user ID, phone number, address, or any other words or numbers that others might associate with you; do not use any word that can be found in a dictionary; make the password longer than six characters; choose a combination of letters and numbers; add special characters, such as exclamation marks or hyphens, if allowed; do not write down your password or share it with others; change your password at least every 90 days; and, if you are a network administrator, establish controls through the network operating system to force users to change their passwords at least every 90 days.
- Another element in securing a network comprises restricting physical access to its components. At the very least, computer rooms should allow access only to authorized networking personnel. If computer rooms remain unlocked, intruders may easily enter and steal equipment, or sabotage software and hardware.
- Places other than the computer room should also be secured. Think about the many places where your systems or data could be compromised—hubs or switches in a wiring closet, a workstation at someone's desk, a telecommunications closet where your leased line to the Internet terminates, a storage room for archived data and backup tapes.
- Ask the following questions as part of a security audit that addresses your organization's physical security: Which rooms contain critical systems or data and need to be secured? Through what means might intruders gain access to the facility, computer room, telecommunications room, wiring closet, or data storage areas? How and to what extent are authorized personnel given entry? Are employees instructed to ensure security after entering or leaving secured areas (that is, not to prop open doors)? Are authentication methods difficult to forge or circumvent? Do supervisors or security personnel make periodic physical security checks? Do all combinations, codes, or other access means to computer facilities remain protected at all times, and are these combinations changed periodically? Is a plan in place for documenting and responding to physical security breaches?
- A firewall is a specialized device (typically a router, but possibly only a PC running special software) that selectively filters or blocks traffic between networks. It may be placed between two interconnected private networks or, more typically, between a private network and a public network (such as the Internet).

- The simplest and most common form of firewall is a packet-filtering firewall. This router operates at the Data Link and Transport layers of the OSI Model, examining the header of every packet of data that it receives to determine whether that type of packet is authorized to continue to its destination. Packet-filtering firewalls are also called screening firewalls.
- A firewall may not be adequate protection if it is not configured properly. Alternatively, a firewall may not be configured to filter unauthorized packets from entering the LAN from outside—the simplest function that firewalls perform. Correctly configuring a firewall is one of the best methods for protecting your internal LAN from Internet-based attacks.
- A more sophisticated security technique is necessary to perform user authentication. One approach is to combine a packet-filtering firewall (hardware device) with a proxy service—a software application on a network host that acts as an intermediary between the external and internal networks, screening all incoming and outgoing traffic.
- The network host that runs the proxy service is known as a proxy server or gateway. Although a proxy server appears to the outside world as an internal network server, in reality it is merely another filtering device for the internal LAN. Among other things, it prevents the outside world from discovering the addresses of the internal network.
- Remote control systems enable a user to connect to a host system on a network from a distance and use that system's resources as if he or she were sitting in front of it. This type of access can prove useful for employees who work at home or those who travel. Although remote control systems can be convenient, they can also present serious security risks.
- Important security features that you should seek in a remote control program include the following: a login ID and password requirement to gain access to the host system; the ability for the host system to call back; support for data encryption on transmissions between the remote user and the system; the ability to leave the host system's screen blank while a remote user works on it; the ability to disable the host system's keyboard and mouse; and the ability to restart the host system when a remote user disconnects from the system.
- Dial-up networking differs from remote control in that it effectively turns a remote workstation into a node on the network through a remote access server. When choosing a remote access software package, you should evaluate its security. A secure remote access server package will include at least the following features: login ID and password authentication; the ability to log all dial-up connections, their sources, and their connection times; the ability to perform callbacks to users who initiate connections; and centralized management of dial-up users and their rights on the network.
- In environments where more than a few dozen simultaneous dial-up connections must be supported and their user IDs and passwords managed, a special kind of server known as a Remote Authentication Dial-In User Service (RADIUS) may be implemented to offer authentication services to the network's access server. RADIUS provides a single, centralized point of authentication for dial-in users. It is highly scalable, as it can attach to pools containing hundreds of modems.

- Every network operating system provides at least some security by allowing you to limit users' access to files and directories on the network. In addition, network administrators can constrain how user IDs can use the network by setting restrictions on, for example, time of day, total time logged in, source address, and number of unsuccessful login attempts.
- Encryption is the use of an algorithm to scramble data into a format that can be read only by reversing the algorithm—or decrypting the data—to keep the information private. Many forms of encryption exist, with some being more secure than others. Even as new forms of encryption are developed, new ways of cracking their codes emerge, too.
- The most popular kind of encryption algorithm weaves a key (a random string of characters) into the original data's bits, sometimes several times in different sequences, to generate a unique data block. The longer the key, the less easily the encrypted data can be decrypted by an unauthorized system. You should be familiar with at least the following types of encryption: Pretty Good Privacy (PGP), digital certificates, Secure Sockets Layer (SSL), and IP Security Protocol (IPSec).
- Virtual private networks (VPNs) are private networks that use public channels to connect clients and servers. Often they integrate a wide variety of clients, from dial-up users at home to networked workstations in offices to Web servers at an ISP. The mix of client types, transmission methods, and services used by VPNs adds to their design complexity, as well as to the complexity of their security needs. Security considerations must be woven into both hardware/design and software for VPNs.
- The Point-to-Point Tunneling Protocol (PPTP) expands on PPP by encapsulating it so that any type of PPP data can traverse the Internet masked as pure IP transmissions. PPTP supports the encryption, authentication, and LAN access services provided by RAS. Instead of users having to dial directly into an access server, they can dial into their ISP using PPTP and gain access to their corporate LAN over the Internet.
- Layer 2 Forwarding (L2F) is similar to PPTP. PPTP and L2F differ in the type of encryption supported by each, and the fact that PPTP was developed by Microsoft and L2F was developed by Cisco Systems. One disadvantage to L2F compared to PPTP is that the former protocol requires special hardware on the host system end, whereas PPTP will work with any Windows NT server. On the other hand, L2F can encapsulate protocols to fit more than just the IP format, unlike PPTP.
- Layer 2 Tunneling Protocol (L2TP) is a Layer 2 tunneling protocol developed by a number of industry consortia. This enhanced version of L2F supports multiple protocols, like L2F; unlike L2F, however, L2TP does not require costly hardware upgrades to implement. L2TP is also optimized to work with the next generation of IP (IPv6) and IPSec (the Layer 3 IP encryption protocol).

KEY TERMS

- **authentication** — The process of verifying a user's validity and authority on a system. Different systems use different credentials to authenticate users.
- **bio-recognition access** — A method of authentication in which a device scans an individual's unique physical characteristics (such as the color patterns in his or her eye's iris or whorls in his or her handprint) to verify the user's identity.
- **cracker** — A person who uses his or her knowledge of operating systems and utilities to intentionally damage or destroy data or systems.
- **denial-of-service attack** — A security attack caused by a deluge of traffic that disables the victimized system.
- **digital certificate** — A password-protected and encrypted file that holds an individual's identification information, including a public key and a private key. The individual's public key is used to verify the sender's digital signature, and the private key allows the individual to log on to a third-party authority who administers digital certificates.
- **encryption** — The use of an algorithm to scramble data into a format that can be read only by reversing the algorithm—or decrypting the data—to keep the information private. The most popular kind of encryption algorithm weaves a key into the original data's bits, sometimes several times in different sequences, to generate a unique data block.
- **firewall** — A specialized device (typically a router, but possibly only a PC running special software) that selectively filters or blocks traffic between networks. A firewall may be strictly hardware-based, or it may involve a combination of hardware and software.
- **flashing** — A security attack in which an Internet user sends commands to another Internet user's machine that cause the screen to fill with garbage characters. A flashing attack will cause the user to terminate his or her session.
- **gateway** — See *proxy server.*
- **hacker** — A person who masters the inner workings of operating systems and utilities in an effort to better understand them.
- **IP Security Protocol (IPSec)** — A Layer 3 protocol that defines encryption, authentication, and key management for the new version of the TCP/IP protocol suite, IPv6. IPSec adds security information to the header of all IP packets.
- **IP spoofing** — A security attack in which an outsider obtains internal IP addresses, then uses those addresses to pretend that he or she has authority to access a private network from the Internet.
- **key** — A series of characters used in many encryption schemes to make decrypting the data more difficult.
- **Layer 2 Forwarding (L2F)** — A Layer 2 protocol similar to PPTP that provides tunneling for other protocols and can work with the authentication methods used by PPP. L2F was developed by Cisco Systems and requires special hardware on the host system end. It can encapsulate protocols to fit more than just the IP format, unlike PPTP.

- **Layer 2 Tunneling Protocol (L2TP)** — A Layer 2 tunneling protocol developed by a number of industry consortia. L2TP is an enhanced version of L2F. Like L2F, it supports multiple protocols; unlike L2F, it does not require costly hardware upgrades to implement. L2TP is optimized to work with the next generation of IP (IPv6) and IPSec (the Layer 3 IP encryption protocol).
- **packet-filtering firewall** — A router that operates at the Data Link and Transport layers of the OSI Model, examining the header of every packet of data that it receives to determine whether that type of packet is authorized to continue to its destination. Packet-filtering firewalls are also called *screening firewalls.*
- **Point-to-Point Tunneling Protocol (PPTP)** — A Layer 2 protocol developed by Microsoft that encapsulates PPP so that any type of data can traverse the Internet masked as pure IP transmissions. PPTP supports the encryption, authentication, and LAN access services provided by RAS. Instead of users having to dial directly into an access server, they can dial into their ISP using PPTP and gain access to their corporate LAN over the Internet.
- **Pretty Good Privacy (PGP)** — A key-based encryption system for e-mail that uses a two-step verification process.
- **proxy server** — A network host that runs a proxy service. Proxy servers may also be called *gateways.*
- **proxy service** — A software application on a network host that acts as an intermediary between the external and internal networks, screening all incoming and outgoing traffic and providing one address to the outside world, instead of revealing the addresses of internal LAN devices.
- **remote access** — The capability for traveling employees, telecommuters, or distant vendors to access an organization's private LAN or WAN through specialized remote access servers.
- **Remote Authentication Dial-In User Service (RADIUS)** — A server that offers authentication services to the network's access server (which may run Windows NT's RAS or Novell's NAS, for example). RADIUS provides a single, centralized point of authentication for dial-in users and is often used by ISPs.
- **root** — A highly privileged user ID that has all rights to create, delete, modify, move, read, write, or execute files on a system. This term may specifically refer to the administrator on a UNIX-based network.
- **screening firewall** — See *packet-filtering firewall.*
- **Secure Sockets Layer (SSL)** — A method of encrypting Web pages (or HTTP transmissions) as they travel over the Internet.
- **security audit** — An assessment of an organization's security vulnerabilities. A security audit should be performed at least annually and preferably quarterly. For each risk found, it should rate the severity of a potential breach, as well as its likelihood.

- **social engineering** — Manipulating relationships to circumvent network security measures and gain access to a system.
- **Terminal Access Controller Access Control System (TACACS)** — A centralized authentication system for remote access servers that is similar to RADIUS.
- **tunneling** — The process of encapsulating one protocol to make it appear as another type of protocol.

Review Questions

1. If you have root privileges on a system, you could delete user IDs from that system. True or False? P640
2. What do you call manipulating people to get them to reveal confidential information, such as their passwords? P642
   - **a.** social engineering
   - **b.** social manipulation
   - **c.** social coercion
   - **d.** social affectation
3. Which of the following is the most secure password? P649
   - **a.** 123
   - **b.** dolphins
   - **c.** !tz0g557x
   - **d.** password
4. Which of the following would not typically be used for authenticating to a system? P640
   - **a.** IP address
   - **b.** user ID
   - **c.** password
   - **d.** last name
5. Name three different security risks associated with people. P642
6. What is the most likely way that a network's security will be compromised? P646
   - **a.** from within the organization
   - **b.** from a cracker on the Internet
   - **c.** from a cracker posing as a contractor
   - **d.** from a cracker using IP spoofing over a modem connection

7. Which device could a cracker use to intercept and interpret transmissions on the network?
   a. router
   b. hub
   c. switch
   d. sniffer
8. Accepting the default options for security on a server-based application is usually a good policy. True or False?
9. If someone obtains one of your LAN's internal IP addresses and uses it to gain access through your firewall from the Internet, what method of security attack is he or she using?
   a. flashing
   b. IP spoofing
   c. denial of service
   d. framing
10. The UDP protocol is more secure than the TCP protocol. True or False?
11. If someone floods your LAN's router with excessive traffic so that your legitimate traffic cannot go out or come in, what method of security attack is he or she using?
    a. flashing
    b. IP spoofing
    c. denial of service
    d. framing
12. Which of the following is not typically addressed in a security policy?
    a. preventing accidental damage to network software and hardware
    b. ensuring that authorized users have appropriate access to the resources they need
    c. communicating each employee's responsibilities with respect to maintaining data integrity
    d. specifying what model and make of firewall is appropriate for the network
13. What is the primary purpose for establishing a security response team?
    a. to demonstrate to users the security risks they face
    b. to train users to respond to security threats as they happen
    c. to devise a coordinated response to security breaches while or after they occur
    d. to comprehensively audit the security of the network

14. What should an organization do to assess its potential security risks?
    a. perform a security audit
    b. freeze any new user ID creation
    c. question users about odd behavior on their workstations
    d. train users to watch for suspicious activity
15. Name four questions that should be addressed in a security audit.
16. What's the simplest way to stop a denial-of-service attack?
    a. shut down the victimized server
    b. shut down the firewall between your LAN and the Internet
    c. turn on TCP and UDP filtering
    d. restart your central switch to clear traffic
17. Which of the following transmission media is the most secure?
    a. UTP
    b. STP
    c. coaxial cable
    d. fiber-optic cable
18. It's more important to secure the computer room than the tape backup storage room. True or False?
19. Which of the following doesn't contribute to a network's physical security?
    a. closed-circuit TV
    b. badge access systems
    c. door locks
    d. digital certificates
20. Which of the following network operating system restrictions is most likely to stop a cracker who is attempting to discover someone's password?
    a. number of unsuccessful login attempts
    b. time of day
    c. total time logged in
    d. source address
21. Name four criteria that a packet-filtering firewall might use for filtering traffic.
22. At which two layers of the OSI Model does a packet-filtering firewall operate?
    a. Transport and Network layers
    b. Network and Data Link layers
    c. Data Link and Transport layers
    d. Session and Transport layers

23. Before a firewall can effectively filter unwanted traffic, it must be:
    - **a.** placed between a private and public network
    - **b.** configured according to an organization's security needs
    - **c.** combined with a proxy server
    - **d.** attached to a switch on the internal LAN
24. Which of the following best describes the function of a proxy server?
    - **a.** to deny LAN access to specific IP addresses
    - **b.** to filter inappropriate content traveling from the Internet to an internal LAN
    - **c.** to encapsulate protocols in the IP format
    - **d.** to act as a gateway between an internal LAN and the outside world, masking the IP addresses of private LAN devices
25. Which of the following security risks does using the callback feature on a remote control system address?
    - **a.** the possibility for passersby to take over the host system that is being controlled remotely
    - **b.** the possibility for unauthorized users to take over the host system after they have discovered its phone number and login ID
    - **c.** the possibility for unauthorized users to scan a host system's ports and discover its phone number
    - **d.** the possibility for passersby to shut down the system in mid-session
26. If a company wants to save leasing costs and allow 50 of its employees to work at home, what type of arrangement would be the most secure, practical, and economical for granting home workers access to the LAN?
    - **a.** create exceptions in the firewall filtering rules to accept incoming traffic from each home worker's workstation
    - **b.** set up a VPN that uses a RADIUS server to centrally authenticate and grant LAN access to dial-in users
    - **c.** establish a Windows NT RAS server with direct PPP dial-in capability
    - **d.** program Web front ends for the applications used by home workers and employ SSL to transmit their work over the Internet
27. What service does PPTP provide?
    - **a.** It encapsulates protocols so they can run on IP-based networks such as the Internet.
    - **b.** It authenticates dial-up users according to their source address.
    - **c.** It ensures that remote control callback mechanisms are secure.
    - **d.** It encrypts data using the IPv6 protocol.

28. Which company developed the L2F protocol?
    a. IBM
    b. Microsoft
    c. Cisco
    d. Oracle
29. In general, the longer the key, the more secure the encryption. True or False?
30. PGP is frequently used for what type of network communication?
    a. e-mail
    b. FTP
    c. HTTP
    d. Telnet

Hands-on Projects

Project 15-1

For a networking professional, it's important to stay abreast of new security threats and learn how to address them. In fact, in a large organization, a team of professionals might be devoted to network security, with one team member responsible for researching new security threats. In this project, you will look at some Web resources that can help you find out about vulnerabilities on your network. For this project, you will need a workstation with Internet connectivity and a Web browser.

1. Connect to the Internet and point your browser to the following URL: http://www.microsoft.com/security/bulletins/current.asp. The Microsoft Security Advisor page should appear. Notice that security risks associated with Microsoft software and patches to fix them are listed according to the date they were discovered.
2. Scroll through the list and click **MS99-008, "Patch available for Windows NT Screensaver Vulnerability" (March 12, 1999)**.
3. Read the description of the problem and how Microsoft has addressed it. Think of examples of how Windows NT might be used that would allow someone to exploit this vulnerability.
4. Click the **Back** button on your browser and browse more Microsoft security bulletins.
5. Now point your browser to the URL http://developer.novell.com/research/appnotes/1997/november/a6frame.htm to read about security measures you should use with NetWare-based networks.

6. According to what you read in the NetWare security document, why isn't it a good idea to use RCONSOLE (unless it's absolutely necessary)? On a NetWare server, what is the default setting for allowing clients to use unencrypted passwords—yes or no? What command can you use on a NetWare network to find out who has rights that are equivalent to yours?
7. One organization that provides an updated list of many types of security risks is CERT, a clearinghouse for security risks established by the Carnegie Mellon Software Engineering Institute. To view its current alerts, point your browser to the following URL: http://www.cert.org/advisories/. Notice that the alerts are organized by the date they were released.
8. View information about a denial of service alert by clicking on the bulletin titled "**CA 98-13-tcp-denial-of-service**."
9. Read through the advisory. What type of router configuration change does CERT recommend network administrators make to defend against this attack?
10. Press the **Back** button on your browser to return to the list of advisories. Browse through the most recent alerts. To what types of software or systems do most of the alerts pertain?

PROJECT 15-2

As you have learned, enforcing user password restrictions, such as the length of passwords, is an important part of securing a network. In this project, you will work on a Windows NT Server 4.0 to establish the default password requirements for all users. You will need a Windows NT Server 4.0 and the capability to log on as Administrator to that server.

1. Log on to the server, click **Start**, point to **Programs**, then point to **Administrative Tools (Common)**.
2. Click **User Manager for Domains**.
3. Click **Policies** on the menu bar, then click **Account**. The Account Policy dialog box opens, offering options that you can use to set password security and account lockout policies, as shown in Figure 15-6.

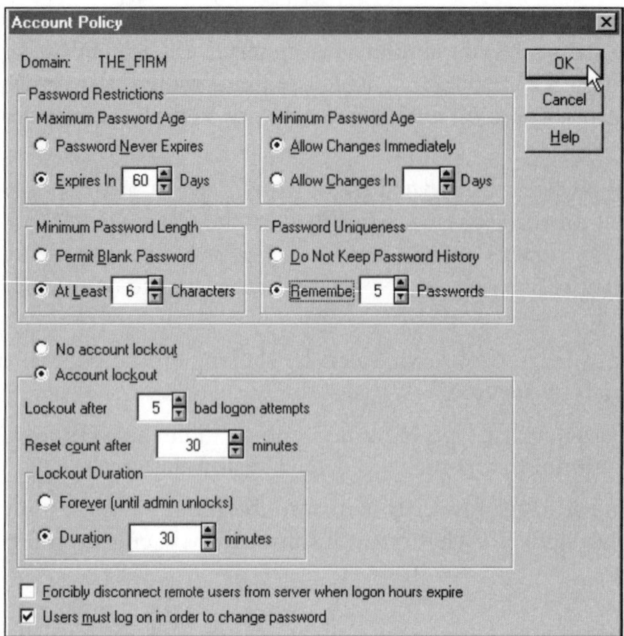

Figure 15-6 Account Policy dialog box

4. Under Maximum Password Age, click **Expires In** ________________ **Days** and type **60.** This setting requires each user to change his or her password every 60 days.
5. Under Minimum Password Age, click **Allow Changes Immediately**. This setting allows users to use their new password the next time they log on.
6. Under Minimum Password Length, click **At Least** ________________ **Characters** and type **6.** This setting forces users to choose a password that is six characters or more in length.
7. Under the Password Uniqueness, click **Remember** ________________ **Passwords** and type **5**. This setting prevents users from reusing their last five passwords.
8. Click the **Account lockout** option button.
9. Select **5** in the **Lockout after** ________________ **bad logon attempts** scroll box. This setting means that the account cannot be accessed after someone enters the wrong password five times.
10. Select **30** in the **Reset counter after** ________________ **minutes** scroll box. This setting means that if five bad logon attempts occur within 30 minutes, the account will be locked, allowing no access until the account is "unlocked" by an administrator.
11. Under Lockout Duration, click **Duration** ________________ **minutes** and type **30** again. This setting specifies the number of minutes that the account will remain locked until it can be accessed again.

12. At the bottom of the screen, select the **Users must log on in order to change password** checkbox. This setting means that a user must be able to log on to change a password. If the user waits to change his or her password until after the expiration date, then he or she will have to ask the network administrator to change it.
13. Click **OK** to confirm the settings, then exit the Account Policy dialog box.
14. Close User Manager for Domains.

PROJECT 15-3

Another important principle of protecting network data from security breaches is assigning the proper rights to each individual or group that has access to your network's servers. In this project, you will assign appropriate rights for five groups of users on a Windows NT server. You will need a Windows NT Server 4.0 with a Windows 95 or Windows 98 client workstation attached and the capability to log in to the server. You should have Administrator rights on the server. Before beginning this exercise, you should delete the Everyone group from the server. The Windows NT server should contain the following user IDs: Bob, Patrick, Mary, Errol, Sally, Chris, Inez, Richard, Dave, and Cory. Each ID should be associated with the same password, "3ntxx09", and users should have no modifications to their default file access rights. The server should also contain the following directories:

```
C:\DATA\BUDGET
C:\DATA\SAMPLES
C:\DATA\CONTRACTS
C:\DATA\PAYABLES
C:\DATA\RECEIVABLES
```

The users should belong to groups as follows:

15

Users	Group
Bob, Patrick, Mary, Errol, Sally, Chris, Inez, Richard, Dave, Cory	Accounting
Mary, Patrick, Sally	Accounts Payable
Bob, Chris, Cory	Accounts Receivable
Inez, Richard, Chris	Finance
Errol, Patrick, Dave, Inez	Managers

1. Log on to the server from the client workstation as **Patrick**, using the password **3ntxx09**.
2. Attempt to open the directory C:\DATA\CONTRACTS on the server. What message do you see?

3. Now you will give group rights to each directory. Begin by logging into the Windows NT server as **Administrator**.
4. Double-click the **My Computer** icon to see a list of drives on the server.
5. Double-click the **C:** drive to view its contents.
6. Double-click the **DATA** directory to view its subdirectories.
7. Right-click the C:\DATA\BUDGET folder, then click **Properties**. The C:\DATA\BUDGET Properties dialog box opens.
8. Click the **Security** tab.
9. Click **Permissions**. The Directory Permissions dialog box opens.
10. Click **Add**. The Add Users and Groups dialog box opens.
11. Click the **Accounting** group. In the Type of Access drop-down list, choose **Add & Read**. This setting gives the Accounting group permission to create (or add) new files and execute program files, but not to modify existing files.
12. Click **OK** in the Add Users and Groups dialog box.
13. Click **OK** in the Directory Permissions dialog box.
14. Click **OK** in the C:\DATA\BUDGET Properties dialog box.
15. Repeat steps 7 through 13 using the directory names and their respective privileges as shown below:

Directory	Group	Permissions
C:\DATA\SAMPLES	All groups	Change
C:\DATA\CONTRACTS	Managers	Full control
C:\DATA\CONTRACTS	Accounts Receivable	Read
C:\DATA\CONTRACTS	Accounts Payable	Read
C:\DATA\PAYABLES	Accounts Payable	Change
C:\DATA\RECEIVABLES	Accounts Receivable	Change

Case Projects

1. As an experienced networking professional, you have been asked by the local teacher's credit union to conduct a security audit on their network. The union currently has two locations, a headquarters office downtown and a branch office on the east side of town. The headquarters has the following equipment:

   - 20 Windows NT workstations, connected to a Windows NT server
   - 1 Windows NT RAS server for home workers to access after hours
   - 1 Windows NT server for record keeping

- 1 UNIX database server
- 1 UNIX Web server for members to check their account balances online
- 1 firewall where the network connects to the union's ISP via a T1 dedicated link

The east-side office has five Windows NT workstations, connected to the headquarters office Windows NT server through a dedicated ISDN link.

All tape backups are housed in a secure room in the headquarters office, with copies being kept in a file cabinet at the east-side office. At the headquarters, the servers reside in a locked room that admits authorized users with an electronic badge access system. Both locations have numerous security cameras, including cameras in the computer room and backup tape storage vault at the headquarters. The manager also tells you that the credit union has a security policy that all employees are required to read and sign when they begin work. He believes that the network is very secure, and asks you if he could do anything else to ensure that the network is safe from security breaches. In response, create a checklist of items on this network that should be evaluated for security. Describe any access points or situations that constitute potential security risks. In addition, explain how the credit union manager could better train his employees to understand network security.

2. As part of your security audit, you have recommended credit union employees change their passwords to be more secure, and that the IT department enforce password changes every 60 days, because of the confidential nature of the data on their workstations and servers. The credit union employees are not enthusiastic about this change, and they complain that they already have too many things to remember. How might you convince them that choosing secure passwords and changing their passwords frequently are in their own best interest and for the good of their employer?

3. The credit union is experiencing tremendous growth and needs to either open another branch office on the west side of town or allow their auditors and loan processing staff to work from home. It asks you to compare the security requirements of opening a new branch office versus implementing a dial-VPN solution (using the Internet) for work-at-home employees. As part of your comparison, list the costs associated with these security requirements. For an expansion of 10 users, which solution do you recommend?

CHAPTER 16

MANAGING NETWORK DESIGN AND IMPLEMENTATION

After reading this chapter and completing the exercises, you will be able to:

- Describe the elements and benefits of project management
- Analyze the current status of a network
- Perform a needs assessment and recommend changes based on your findings
- Manage a network implementation project
- Design and test a pilot network

ON THE JOB

I'm a network manager at a packaging company. A year ago we decided to change our network from Token Ring to Ethernet (partly because Token Ring devices are so much more expensive than their Ethernet counterparts). That project began a year ago and it's still going on. We ran into numerous obstacles that we just didn't expect.

One significant problem was staffing the project. Many of my staff are highly skilled engineers who are happy designing networks but aren't enthused about installing new NICs in PCs. We found some temporary staff to help us, but then we spent a lot of time training the staff. The time spent training them caused our project timelines to slip.

Another problem was explaining the change to the rest of our company, who didn't know what Token Ring or Ethernet meant. They only knew that we would be taking down the network and taking over their machines from time to time. Halfway into the project we decided to hold user meetings, in which we would describe the changes and their consequences and field questions from users. These meetings helped users understand what was going on and bolstered our staff's reputation.

While we couldn't have foreseen everything, better planning would have made this project easier and maybe less costly from the start. For my next large project, I'm hiring a professional project manager to help.

Joe Witkowski
M-Star Industries

In preceding chapters, you learned about the various elements that make up networks. In this chapter, you will learn how to put those elements together to improve an existing network or plan a network from start to finish. One of the first steps in implementing a network is devising a plan. Before you can create such a plan, however, you must learn some project management fundamentals. Project management is a broad term that refers to the process of managing timelines, resources, budgets, and personnel so as to reach a specific goal. Each of us regularly embarks on projects—whether the project involves writing a term paper or fixing a car's engine. Rarely do we devise project plans for our own projects. For projects that affect many people, require significant capital outlay, or influence a company's profitability, project management is essential to ensure the project's success. This chapter will discuss not only project management, but also techniques for approaching typical network implementation projects.

Introduction to Project Management

Project Management is the practice of managing resources, staff, budget, timelines, and other variables so as to achieve a specific goal within given bounds. For example, if you were a Web site development consultant, you might implement project management to establish an online store for a national furniture retailer. The project may be constrained by time (for example, you may aim to establish the e-commerce site before November 1 so as to cater to holiday shoppers), money, or the number of developers who can help you with the project. In the networking field, you might employ the basic principles of project management in the process of replacing the CAT3 wiring in your organization's building with CAT5 wiring.

Every project begins with identifying a need (although, of course, identifying a need may not result in a project). As you will learn later in this chapter, you can conduct a feasibility study to determine whether a particular need warrants a full-fledged project. If the feasibility study confirms that a project is necessary, you must appoint a project manager and begin planning the project. As discussed in the following section, the project manager's first step is to conduct a needs assessment and establish the project goals. Only then can the project manager create a project plan.

The other elements of a full-scale project include participants, funding, a specific means of communication, definitive processes, contingency plans, and a testing and evaluation phase. The following sections describe these elements in more detail.

The Web offers many valuable resources for project managers. A good place to start is at the Project Management Institute's Web site for project managers at http://www.pmi.org/.

The Project Plan

A **project plan** is the way in which details of a managed project (for example, the timeline and the significant tasks) are organized. Plans for small projects may take the form of a simple text or spreadsheet document (in fact, they may begin as notes scribbled on a piece of paper). For larger projects, however, you will typically take advantage of project management software (such as Microsoft Project, PlanView, or PrimaVera Project Planner). Project management software facilitates project planning by providing a framework for inputting tasks, timelines, resource assignments, completion dates, and so on. Such software is also highly customizable, so you can use only a small portion or all of its features, depending on the scope of your project and your project management skills. Figure 16-1 shows a list of tasks as they might appear in Microsoft Project.

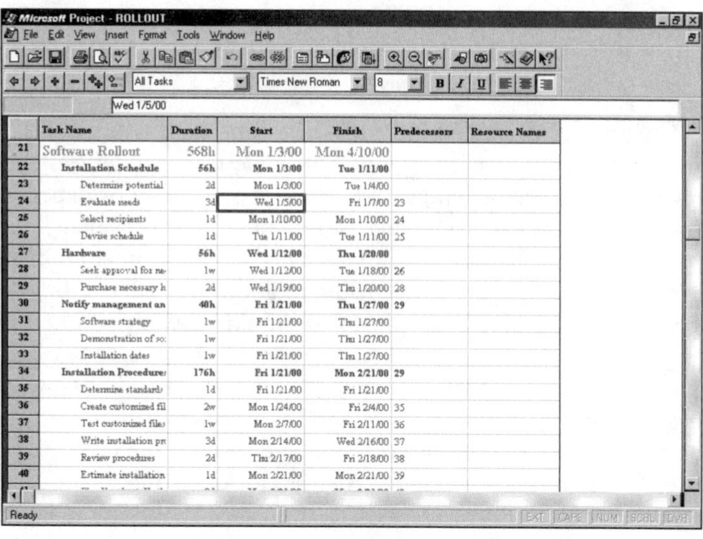

Figure 16-1 A view of a project in Microsoft Project

No matter how large or small the project, its project plan will contain some common elements, as described below:

- *Task breakdown*—A project should be divided into specific tasks. Larger tasks are then broken into even smaller subtasks. For example, establishing an e-commerce Web site and server at an Internet service provider's data center represents a large task with numerous subtasks: obtaining racks for the equipment, ensuring backup and bandwidth capacity, obtaining software and hardware, installing equipment and software, configuring the hardware, testing the software, and so on.

You may find it tricky to separate a project into meaningful, discrete tasks that are specific enough to measure progress and guide participants, but not so narrow that they lose meaning. As you gain project planning experience, you will better be able to gauge how to best separate tasks into smaller but significant subtasks.

16

- *Dependencies*—The project plan specifies which tasks depend on the completion of previous tasks before you can begin them. In some project management software, the tasks that must be completed before other tasks can begin are called **predecessors**. In the example of establishing an e-commerce server, you would have to determine which type of server you want to purchase before ordering the equipment racks. This ordering of tasks is necessary because racks come in different widths and depths. Thus the task of obtaining the racks constitutes a predecessor of the task of determining the type of server needed. It's critical to examine potential dependencies in a project plan, because a dependency means that part of the project depends on another part. If you neglect to consider a dependency at the beginning of a project, stopping to address it during the project may delay the schedule and impose unnecessary stress on team members, who must later rush to complete their tasks. Careful planning will reveal any dependencies that might affect the project's timeline and success.

- *Timeline*—The project plan should identify how long each task will take (with start and finish dates), which tasks take priority (due to dependencies), and how the timeline might change depending on resource availability or dependencies. Timelines are not always easy to predict. Seasoned professionals may be able to gauge how long a particular task might take based on their previous experience with similar tasks. Every project may entail conditions that affect a timeline differently, however. When creating a timeline, you should allow extra time for any especially significant tasks. For instance, in the e-commerce server example, the manufacturer might tell you that obtaining the equipment racks will take one week. If you plan for delivery in a week, and the installation of the Web site depends on this task, your entire project will be delayed if the racks don't arrive for two weeks. A **Gantt chart** is a popular method for depicting when projects begin and end along a horizontal timeline. Figure 16-2 illustrates a simple Gantt chart.

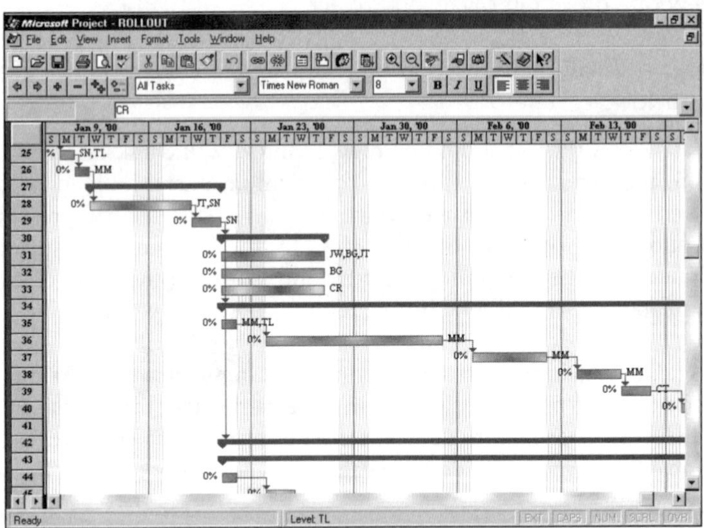

Figure 16-2 A simple Gantt chart

You may be asked to plan a project with seemingly impossible deadlines. One technique for making the project fit into a tight time frame is to work backward to create the timeline. In other words, begin at the project's predetermined endpoint and move toward the beginning of the project, allowing the normal time requirements for tasks. This method will highlight which tasks may delay the project and therefore need to be dropped or modified, at least temporarily.

- *Resources*—All projects require the staffing, materials, and money that are collectively known as **resources**. A project plan can specify all resources needed for each task or group of tasks. At the very least, it should identify who is responsible for tasks, whether it is a committee, consultant, manager, or technical person. This person is the **owner** of the task. The owner does not necessarily have to perform the work himself or herself, but nevertheless must ensure that it is completed on time and within budgetary guidelines.

- *Milestones*—Every project has significant accomplishments that mark specific steps in their progress. In project planning, a **milestone** is a reference point that marks the completion of a major task or group of tasks in the project and contributes to measuring the project's progress. For example, if you were in charge of the e-commerce server project, you might designate the completion of the software installation on your server as being a milestone. Milestones are particularly useful in large projects that have high visibility within the organization. They provide a quick indication of a project's relative success or failure.

In addition to these elements, project plans may provide information on task priority, the amount of flexibility in the timeline, task successors, links to other project plans, and so on. With most project planning software, you can add your own columns to the plan and insert any type of information you deem appropriate. For example, if you are managing a very large network design project, you might create a Web site with links to documentation for each phase of the project. In the project plan, you might include a column to list the URLs of the documents for each task or group of tasks.

During the course of a project, the project plan will likely undergo several changes. Some changes may result from unforeseen circumstances; others may reflect milestone evaluations and adjustments. Later in this section, you will learn more about these contingencies and how to plan for them.

PROJECT PARTICIPANTS

As mentioned previously, each project depends on many resources. The human resources involved in a project may be employees from your department or other departments within the organization, outside consultants, vendor representatives, or employees from other organizations. Usually, human resources from various factions work together in teams. Although a single person may handle some project tasks (such as ordering a server, updating a document, or configuring a router), larger tasks should be accomplished by teams. For example, as the project manager for a network redesign, you might assign the task of determining how to upgrade the backbone to a team consisting of a cabling vendor, a network technician, a facilities architect, and an IT manager. In an organization with limited staff members, some project participants may belong to more than one team.

As a project manager, you probably won't supervise everyone involved in the project. Therefore, you need managers who agree with the project's goals and will strive to help you achieve them. These authority figures are called project **sponsors**. Although sponsors rarely participate in project tasks and do not necessarily supervise the project manager, they can lobby for budget increases necessary to complete the project, appeal to a group of managers to extend a project's deadline, assist with negotiating vendor contracts, and so on.

A sponsor may be the person who originated the idea for the project. For example, suppose users in your organization complain about slow network response time, particularly when they try to pick up their e-mail. As a network administrator, you respond to these complaints by finding out the source of the poor network performance. You determine that the problem lies in the fact that the network uses routers and a 10 Mbps transmission rate. To solve the problem, you would like to upgrade the network to be fully switched and to run at 100 Mbps. You write a proposal for the change and bring it to the director of IT. She agrees with your research and your proposal, so she offers to become the project's sponsor. She will take your proposal to your company's executive board and attempt to obtain approval for the resources necessary to complete the project.

Another important group of project participants comprises the stakeholders. A **stakeholder** is any person who may be affected by the project, for better or for worse. In the example of upgrading a network to a fully switched, 100 Mbps environment, the stakeholders will include users (who will benefit from faster network access), executives (not only because they are network users, but also because they have responsibility for the budget), IT managers (who will ultimately determine the success or failure of the project), and project team members. Typically, the stakeholders are the people to whom the project teams must answer. At the beginning of a project, it is wise to communicate the project's goals, timelines, affects, and contingencies to project stakeholders. As you'll learn in the next section, it is also advisable to maintain regular communication with stakeholders about the project's progress.

FUNDING

Every project—whether it entails a simple hardware upgrade or an entire network redesign—requires funding. A project budget is usually set at the beginning of a project and approved by a hierarchy of managers whose staff participate in the project. Of course, a project's budget will depend on its breadth and complexity. As a project manager, you may have little control over the project's budget after it is established. For this reason, you should estimate your costs generously in the initial proposal for the project. It is always preferable to complete a project under budget than to continually appeal for more funding.

In some cases, the amount of funding available to your project can help to make other resources available. Naturally, if managers allocated $200,000 to your project rather than $20,000, you will have 10 times more money to spend on staffing, tools that might make your teams more efficient, or state-of-the-art hardware and software. Sometimes, however, no matter how much funding is available to your project, other constraints may block your progress. For example, your project of upgrading the company's customer service database may depend on the highly specialized knowledge of just two programmers who originally developed the system. Even a budget allocation of $2,000,000 for contractors or new staff wouldn't help you obtain qualified staff, because only these two programmers truly understand how the application works. In addition, the software they're creating might be constrained by functional limits on how many people can change the code at any given time. Thus your project is forced to rely on the efficiency of those two programmers.

Communications

Even if a project has sufficient funding, technical staff, and support from sponsors, it will falter if communication methods are not well defined and carefully followed. Communications are critical for several purposes:

- To ensure that a project's goals are understood by participants, stakeholders, and sponsors
- To keep a project's timeline and budget on track
- To encourage teamwork among participants
- To allow you to learn from previous mistakes
- To prevent fingerpointing if a task is not completed correctly or on time
- To avoid duplication of efforts
- To prepare stakeholders for the effects of the change

At the beginning of a project, the project manager should take responsibility for establishing the methods of communication. Suggested methods include weekly status meetings, daily status briefings for each team, weekly messages to stakeholders about the project's progress, monthly reports that compare a project's *anticipated* spending and timeline with its *actual* spending and timeline, distribution lists for each project team to share e-mail correspondence, and a Web page containing an archive of meeting minutes and other important documents pertaining to the project. Be creative—you might find other effective ways to communicate within your team. Whatever methods you choose, keep in mind that carefully fostered teamwork will contribute to the success of your project.

Processes

In almost everything you do, you follow a process: buying groceries, reading a book, building a deck. When you perform these tasks alone, you can do them whichever way you prefer. When a team of individuals must perform tasks together, however, agreeing on a process beforehand will help to ensure that the task is completed efficiently and that the team's efforts result in a desirable, high-quality outcome.

Process management consists of planning for and handling the steps needed to accomplish a goal in a systematic way. The processes you might manage during a project's implementation include change, support, training, transitioning, delegation, and problem resolution. If you've never managed processes before, it may be difficult to envision this endeavor without concrete examples. Consider how process management can help in the following scenarios:

- You and your colleagues decide to upgrade the network operating system on one of your file servers. You are responsible for ensuring that the change works correctly. Before performing the upgrade, you may want to define a change process. The change process could include notifying potentially affected users at least five business days before you make the modification, documenting exactly what the change will involve and who will make it, backing up the server prior to making the change, and providing a plan for reversing the operation should it cause problems on the server.

- A new network administrator is hired to shoulder some of the responsibilities previously assigned to an existing network administrator. The current network administrator plans to go on a two-week vacation on a remote island only seven days after the new network administrator starts. Before the new employee arrives, you may want to establish a training process. Part of this process could include asking the existing network administrator to identify recently completed tasks, outlining a training plan for the new employee, and identifying other employees who can act as resources for the new employee in different subject areas.
- You manage the 7 days a week, 24 hours a day support team for a corporate LAN. If serious problems arise during the night or on weekends, you may need to help with problem resolution. Having a problem management process in place will make your job and the jobs of the support analysts easier. Part of your problem management process may include notification of all affected customers if the problem hasn't been resolved within 30 minutes, maintenance of a list of second-level support contacts, instructions for how to record the problem in a call-tracking system, and procedures for contacting vendors required to troubleshoot hardware or software.

For any endeavor that requires the cooperation of several team members, process management is a wise investment of time. Creating a process will not be sufficient, however, unless everyone understands the process. You must ensure that the process is communicated to all participants. Begin by proposing the need for a process at a meeting and ask for participants' input. After drafting the process, distribute it as a memo or post it on a Web page where everyone can find it. During the course of a project, urge colleagues to follow the agreed-upon processes.

Processes help you manage unusual or troublesome situations. In the next section, you will learn about another element of project management that can guide participants when things go seriously awry.

CONTINGENCY PLANNING

Even the most meticulously planned project may be derailed by unforeseen circumstances. For instance, a key team participant may quit, your budget may be unexpectedly cut, or a software package may not work as promised. Each of these conditions may threaten to delay your project's completion. To prepare for such circumstances, you must create a contingency plan at the beginning of the project. **Contingency planning** is the process of identifying steps that will minimize the risk of unforeseen events that endanger the quality or timeliness of the project's goals.

Although you cannot predict all possible pitfalls in a project, you should at least plan for the most likely hazards. To identify potential threats to the success of your project, you should analyze your organization's history. For instance, you may work for a company that is notorious for pulling team participants into new projects after they're already committed to an existing project. In that case, you may want to increase the number of people working on the project initially, so that losing one or two participants will not detrimentally affect your project's success. Alternatively, you may want to budget for subcontractors to step in when or if your organization's staff members become unavailable. In another organization, you may have experience with programmers who chronically underestimate the time needed to customize programs for your users. In this case, you should add time to the customization tasks to plan for the possibility that the programming will take longer than the programmers suggest.

In a networking project, taking some of the following measures in the beginning can prevent you from having to scramble during the project's implementation:

- Order more hardware components than you think you need.
- Ensure that your hardware and software vendors have extra components on hand and that they will respond to your requests.
- Document each piece of hardware and software that you order for the project. Also, keep a tally of supplies as they are received.
- Rely on a pilot network to test your project's goals (for example, to determine whether choosing switches over routers will improve your network's performance), in addition to testing the hardware and software components (for example, each switch that you purchase) that you will use.
- If the technology required to implement the project is new to project participants, ask a local consulting company with expertise in that technology to be available for questions in case you need help.

The amount of preparation you perform for each contingency should be commensurate with the potential effects of that possibility. For example, if you were planning a demonstration of your application to a very high-profile client who was considering purchasing the application for $5,000,000, you would want to plan a backup for everything that could possibly go wrong with your presentation. On the other hand, if you were planning a demonstration of the same program to your colleagues, you may not spend much time wondering what to do in case the splash screen containing your company logo doesn't appear.

Another way to help ensure your project's success is to perform regular testing and evaluation, as discussed in the following section.

TESTING AND EVALUATION

Once you have reached a project milestone, you will want to verify that you are on the right path. One way of accomplishing this goal is through testing. For instance, if you were managing a project to upgrade a building's LAN from 10 Mbps to 100 Mbps, you might want to tackle one small segment of the network first. Before moving to the next segment, you should ensure that all workstation and switch or router configurations on the first segment work correctly. By confirming this fact, you can potentially prevent future down time or troubleshooting.

To successfully test your implementation, you must establish a testing plan that includes relevant methods and criteria. For example, your method of testing the network performance may be to use the Windows NT Server Network Monitor program from a server. For each performance test you perform, you will want to replicate this arrangement, so that you can compare your results across the various tests. In this case, the criteria you use to measure network performance may be the number of bytes that travel from one particular workstation to the server every five minutes.

Once you have devised a testing plan, emphasize to all project participants how vital it is to adhere to the plan. If participants ignore the testing plan for a backbone upgrade, for example, they might be tempted to quickly set up a workstation on a new network segment and assume that if they reach the network login prompt, the change is a success. Unfortunately, this approach may overlook protocol or transmission speed issues that can cause problems later. To provide an accurate assessment, a test plan should address at least the following questions:

- Was the change nominally successful? (For example, if the change comprised a backbone upgrade, can a client on the new backbone connect to the server?)
- Did the change fully accomplish its purpose? (For example, if the change comprised a backbone upgrade, did it result in a performance improvement?)
- If the change did not fully accomplish its purpose, did it partially accomplish its goal?
- Did the change result in unexpected consequences?
- Did the change point to a need for additional changes? (For example, if the change comprised a backbone upgrade, did testing reveal that new cabling was required for a segment whose cabling was initially thought to be adequate?)

For testing to be useful, project participants should clearly define the change's purpose before testing commences. For example, network technicians may suggest that a backbone upgrade will result in at least a 25% increase in performance for users on their company's WAN. This figure should be based on technical calculations of expected performance increases (rather than assumptions).

Accurately measuring such increases in performance depends on keeping a baseline of the network's performance before the change occurred. Performance baselines will aggregate network response data from different times of day and different places on the network. After the change is instituted, performance measurement should likewise be conducted at different nodes on the WAN and at different times of day (preferably using a network management software package). The testing team should then compare the new measurements to the baseline to determine whether the change accomplished its goal of increasing network performance by at least 25%.

In addition to developing test criteria, testing large-scale changes will require defining a test period, testing methods, and evaluation methods. In some cases, the testing may be straightforward. For example, if you installed a database software package on the server, you might ask users to attempt to log in and perform a simple query one afternoon to verify that the software works correctly. If all users perform their tasks successfully, then you can assume that the change was successful. Otherwise, you should consider the installation unsuccessful.

In other cases, test results may be more subjective. For example, you may have upgraded a database software package to improve the security of the database. In this case, testing may involve asking skilled security engineers or programmers to attempt to break into the database after implementation of the change. If they quickly break into the entire database, your testing reveals that the change was unsuccessful. If it takes a week for them to obtain only insignificant database information, however, your testing may reveal that the change worked as planned.

No matter whether your testing will be straightforward or subjective, the project manager should assign a leader to take charge of the testing team. This team leader will develop testing criteria, recruit testing volunteers, identify ways of gathering test data, compile test data, and, based on the testing results, pass conclusions to the project manager about the success of the change.

In addition to testing the project's changes and processes, you should test every piece of equipment required by the project as soon as it arrives. By verifying basic hardware functionality immediately, you will avoid later project delays caused by faulty components.

Now that you have been introduced to project management techniques, you are ready to learn about aspects of project management of particular interest to networking professionals.

Managing Network Implementation

Although numerous professions perform project management, information technology presents some unique challenges to successfully deploying changes. For example, although an architect must consider issues such as obtaining the proper building permits in her project plan, a network administrator needs to consider much more complicated issues, such as the compatibility of protocols and connectivity devices. In the previous section, you learned about project management elements that apply to any project. This section describes some project management techniques that apply specifically to network and other technology implementations.

Implementation Steps

This section presents a list of typical steps involved in implementing a network change after stakeholders and participants have identified some kind of unmet need. This outline is meant to be a guide to planning, not an actual project plan. You may find that not every step applies to your network or situation. In that case, you can move to the next step or modify the step to be more appropriate. The most significant steps in this process are described in more detail in the following sections.

1. Determine whether the proposed change is feasible, given the time, resource, and budgetary constraints. Compare proposed costs to proposed benefits.
2. If a change is deemed feasible and desirable, identify specific goals for a project. Break larger, vague goals into smaller, concrete goals.

3. Assess the current state of the network, including physical and logical topology, protocols, applications, operating systems, and number, type, and location of devices. Keep this documentation in a centrally accessible location.
4. Assess the requirements as expressed by stakeholders, including users, technical staff, and managers.
5. Create a project plan that includes tasks and subtasks, dependencies, resource allocation, timelines, and milestones. Specify necessary hardware and software purchases, in addition to desired contributions from contractors or vendors.
6. If possible, build a pilot network—a small-scale replica of your changed network—based on your recommendations. Define testing criteria for the small-scale network and evaluate your results against your needs.
7. If the pilot network shows promise, begin to implement the changes on a larger scale. At this stage, you may have to purchase hardware or software, coordinate with vendors, install or remove wiring, hardware, or software, or reconfigure hardware or software. Before you begin, make sure that you have all of the necessary tools and components.
8. If possible (if the changes are not on a global scale and can be effected in stages), release the changes to a hand-picked group of users who will evaluate the success of your network changes, using predefined criteria.
9. If the evaluation indicates that the changes were successful, release the changes to all users.
10. Update your network baseline documentation to reflect the changes.

Determining Project Feasibility

The first decision to make about any proposed project is whether spending time and resources on this project makes sense—that is, whether it's feasible. Often, and especially in technology-based companies, staff become so enamored with gadgetry and the desire for faster network access that they are willing to push a project through without realistically assessing its costs and benefits. For example, a network manager may attend a week-long conference on IP telephony, then return and announce to his staff that they should replace the entire phone system with a voice-over-data system. This project may be completed, despite the fact that the existing phone system works perfectly well, and despite the fact that spending money on a voice-over-data scheme may be less of a priority than purchasing redundant file servers.

To formalize the process of determining whether a proposed project makes sense, you can conduct a feasibility study. A **feasibility study** outlines the costs and benefits of the project and attempts to predict whether it will result in a favorable outcome (for example, whether it will achieve its goals without imposing excessive cost or time requirements on the organization). You can think of a feasibility study as a "pre-project plan." A feasibility study should be performed for any large-scale project before resources are committed to that project.

Often, organizations hire business consultants to help them develop a feasibility study. The advantage to outsourcing this work is that consultants will not make the same assumptions that internal staff might make when weighing the costs and benefits of a proposed project.

SETTING PROJECT GOALS

Once a project is deemed feasible, you and the project team should define the project's goals. One technique for setting project goals is to begin with a broad goal, then narrow it down into specific goals that will contribute to the larger goal. For example, if your organization's board of directors has accepted a consultant's recommendation to redesign your WAN so as to improve communications between offices and enable better Internet access, these two goals may equate to the overarching project goals. Beneath those goals, you may insert several smaller goals, such as partnering with a nationwide ISP, increasing WAN performance by 40% between the Chicago and San Diego offices, building an infrastructure that will enable growth into the East Asian market, and so on.

In addition to being specific, project goals should be attainable. The feasibility study should help determine whether you can achieve the project goals within the given time, budgetary, and resource constraints. If project goals are not attainable from the outset, you risk losing backing from both project sponsors and participants. And if you lose backing, chances are good that the project will fail.

Projects without clear goals will suffer from inefficiencies. That is, a lack of well-defined goals can result in misunderstandings between project participants, sponsors, and stakeholders; lack of focus among team members; lack of proper resource allocation; and an uncertainty about whether the project's outcomes constituted success. Before developing the project plan, work with project participants and sponsors to clearly define the project's goals.

BASELINING

In Chapter 13, you learned that baselining is the practice of measuring and recording a network's current state of operation. As described in that chapter, baselining includes keeping a history of performance measurements, such as response times and number of collisions. It also involves tracking the physical topology, logical topology, number of devices on the network, operating systems and protocols in use, and number and type of applications in use. In other words, this effort provides a complete picture of the network's current state. Baselining is critical to network implementations because it provides the basis not only for determining which changes may improve the network, but also for later evaluating how successful those improvements were.

16

The following list details the questions you need to answer as part of a baseline assessment. Bear in mind that your network may use several types of topologies, operating systems, devices, transmission speeds, applications, and so on.

- *Physical topology*—Which types of LAN and WAN topologies does your network use: bus, star, ring, hybrid, mesh, or a combination of these? Which type of backbone does your network use—collapsed, distributed, parallel, serial, or a combination of these? Which type and grade of cabling does your network use?

- *Logical topology*—Which transmission method does your network use—Ethernet or Token Ring? What transmission speed does it provide? Which switching methods does it apply?
- *Protocols*—Which protocols are used by servers, nodes, and connectivity devices?
- *Devices*—How many of the following devices are connected to your network—switches, routers, hubs, gateways, firewalls, servers, UPSs, printers, backup devices, and clients? Where are they (physically) located? What are their model numbers and vendors?
- *Operating systems*—Which network and desktop operating systems appear on the network? Which versions of these operating systems are used by each device? Which type and version of operating systems are used by connectivity devices such as routers?
- *Applications*—Which applications are used by clients and servers? Where do you store the applications? From where do they run?

If you have not already collected and centrally stored this information, it may take the efforts of several people and several weeks to compile it, depending on the size and complexity of your network. This evaluation will involve visits to the telecommunications and equipment rooms, an examination of servers and desktops, a review of receipts for software and hardware purchases, and potentially use of a sniffer or network monitoring software package. A baseline assessment may take a great deal of time and effort to complete, but it promises to save work in the future. Once you have compiled the information, organize it into a format (such as a database) that can be easily updated, allowing your staff to keep the baseline current.

Assessing Needs and Requirements

Everyone in your department might agree that your current e-mail system is too slow and needs to be replaced, or numerous users might complain that the connection between their office and the headquarters' LAN is unreliable. Often a network change project begins with a group of people (or one person in a position of authority) identifying a need. Before you concur with popular opinion about what must be changed and how the change must occur, as a responsible network administrator you should perform a thorough, objective needs assessment. A **needs assessment** is the process of clarifying the reasons and objectives underlying a proposed change. It involves interviewing users and other stakeholders and comparing perceptions to factual data. It may also involve analyzing network baseline data. Your goal in performing a needs assessment is to decide whether the change is worthwhile and necessary; you should also determine the appropriate scope and nature of the change.

A needs assessment may address the following questions:

- Is the expressed need valid, or does it mask a different need?
- Can the need be resolved?

- Is the need important enough to allocate resources to its resolution?
- If fulfilled, will the need result in additional needs? Will fulfilling the need satisfy other needs?
- Do users affected by the need agree that change is a good answer? What kind of resolution will satisfy them?

In the following sections, you will learn how to investigate needs and requirements driven by users, network performance, availability, scalability, integration, and security. Although only one or a few of these needs may constitute driving forces for your project, you should consider each aspect before drafting a project plan. A project based solely on user requirements may result in unforeseen, negative consequences on network performance, if performance needs are not considered as well.

User Requirements

If you have worked as a computer support technician, you know that customers express their needs in a variety of ways. They may regularly call the help desk and ask why they can't access the company's accounting system, they may appeal to their supervisors for access, or they may simply complain to their friends about their unmet need. Each of these methods makes public a need. Unfortunately, none of these methods clearly details the need. To clarify user requirements, you must undertake a more rigorous investigation.

A good technique for beginning to clarify user requirements is user interviews. Just as if you were a reporter, you should ask pointed questions. If the answer is not complete or sufficiently specific, you should follow up your original question with additional questions. The more narrowly focused the answers, the easier it will be to suggest how a project might address those needs. The questions you ask will depend on the type of need involved as well as the user's knowledge and attitude. You may begin your questioning with the following queries:

- What do you need?
- What makes you think this need should be addressed?
- How quickly do you think this need must be addressed?
- Can you suggest at least three ways we can meet this need?
- What kind of priority would you place on this need?
- Are you willing to ignore other needs to have this need met?

Your aim in interviewing users should not be to interrogate them, but rather to guide them to a better articulation of their need. Users often aren't sure about what they want. You can help by drawing out answers and then restating those answers to verify that you have heard and understood them correctly.

During the interview process, be certain not to impose your own opinions on what the user is saying. By doing so, you might miss the point entirely or make the user feel as if you don't truly want to understand his or her needs. Like a reporter, be as objective as you possibly can.

In the process of interviewing users, you may recognize that not all users have the same needs. In fact, the needs of one group of users may conflict with the needs of another group. In such cases, you will have to sort out which needs have a greater priority, which needs were expressed by the majority of users, whether the expressed needs have anything in common, and how to address needs that do not fall into the majority.

After you have interviewed users and collected the results of those interviews, you should be better able to articulate the nature and scope of their needs. The next step is to return to the users (perhaps in a group meeting) and reiterate what you think they were saying. Give users an opportunity to dispute or refine your conclusions. The more time you spend clarifying users' needs, the less time you will have to spend later explaining the project to users and attempting to win their approval for your efforts.

Performance Requirements

Another reason for changing a network may be to improve performance. In an ideal world, the IT department would recognize these impending needs before customers even notice them. For example, if the network administrator is tracking the network's performance and notices that it has been degrading very slightly for the last six months, he may initiate a discussion about how to improve the network performance before users experience noticeable slowdowns.

Although you might think that performance needs are easily quantifiable and therefore easily agreed upon, in fact several engineers and technicians will likely have differing opinions about the nature of the needs and the best tactics for addressing them. Having technical staff answer the following questions will help you identify performance requirements:

- Where do current performance bottlenecks exist? Why do they exist there?
- What kind of performance is optimal?
- Compared with other projects, what priority would you assign to improving performance?
- What measures can bring current performance levels to your recommended level?
- How will performance improvements affect access, availability, customer needs, security, and scalability?
- How will you ensure that measures taken to improve performance are successful?

Take the same approach in interviewing technical staff about performance as you would when interviewing users about their needs: be objective, ask follow-up questions to ensure that you understand the needs they express, and try to guide the staff into defining the needs as specifically as possible. After conducting these interviews, draw conclusions based on the opinions of the majority of participants. Reiterate your conclusions to technical staff to verify that you correctly understood the needs they articulated.

Availability Requirements

Recall from Chapter 14 that "availability" describes how consistently and reliably a file, device, or connection can be accessed by authorized personnel. A number of factors can affect a network's or system's availability, including policies, security, use of redundant components (such as dual power supplies in a critical router), use of redundancy techniques (such as RAID on a server), and connectivity bottlenecks. The need for higher availability may represent the impetus for a network change.

To best determine availability requirements, you should interview both technical and management staff. Technical staff will provide insight about how availability can best be achieved and where the network currently falls short of availability goals. Management staff will provide insight into what types of availability are most important and why.

For example, you may be asked to identify the availability requirements of your organization's new online catalog, which is hosted on a Windows NT server in your equipment room. You interview technical staff to determine what type of availability is currently in place and how it might be improved. You also interview management staff to determine how much down time is acceptable, based on their educated guesses regarding how down time will affect sales. If that prediction points to millions of dollars of lost sales for every hour that the server fails, management may be willing to invest hundreds of thousands of dollars to provide entirely redundant server systems to ensure that the online catalog remains continuously available.

Asking the following questions of technical staff will help you clarify their availability requirements:

- Where do current availability flaws or vulnerabilities exist? Where are the network's single points of failure?
- What kind of availability is acceptable (for example, is 99.5% satisfactory, or must the network be available 99.99% of the time)?
- Compared with other projects, what priority would you assign to improving availability?
- What measures can boost current availability to your recommended percentage?
- How will availability improvements affect access, performance, customer needs, security, and scalability?

Asking the following questions of management staff will help you clarify their availability requirements:

- What is the cost of one hour of down time during business hours?
- What is the cost of one hour of down time during off-hours?
- What is your ideal availability percentage?
- What part of the application or access is most important to keep available?

- Compared with other projects, what priority would you assign to improving availability?
- How much are you willing to spend to ensure that the network or system remains available for your ideal percentage of time?

If managers do not have a networking or systems background, they may not realize the costs associated with high availability. Although achieving 99.5% availability may be feasible given their budgetary constraints, increasing the availability to 99.99% may bring exorbitant costs (for example, rather than simply purchasing one switch with dual NICs and dual power supplies, you may need to purchase two identical switches; this component alone could cost more than $50,000). Use your interview as an opportunity to educate members of management, as well as determining their requirements. It's important to emphasize that 100% availability is not possible and that accomplishing 99.99% availability is very expensive.

Integration and Scalability Requirements

With each network change project, you must consider how the proposed change might affect the network's integration and ability to grow and adapt to future changes. In fact, integration and scalability needs may drive network changes, although they are less likely to represent the primary reason for changes than are customer, performance, or security needs.

Because integration and scalability require input from both technical and management staff (perhaps in the form of interviews focused on availability), you should conduct interviews emphasizing these issues with both groups. Asking technical staff to answer the following questions will help you clarify scalability and integration needs:

- How and where is the network's growth currently limited?
- What needs to change to accommodate growth or new hardware/software?
- In what ways (for example, number of users, number of applications, geographical breadth, speed) do you expect the network to grow over the next two years?
- How will improving scalability and integration affect customers, performance, security, and availability?
- How would you prioritize your suggested measures for accommodating growth?

To learn more about scalability and integration needs, you should ask management staff to answer the following questions:

- In what ways do you expect the network (and the organization) to grow over the next one to five years (for example, number of users, number of applications, geographical breadth, speed)?
- Which of these growth directions is your top priority?
- What type of hardware and software do you expect to adopt in coming months and years?
- How much are you willing to spend to optimally position the network and systems for growth?

- Would you place a higher priority on positioning the network and systems for growth or on improving network security, availability, usability, or performance?
- Would you place a higher priority on facilitating better network and systems integration or on improving network security, availability, usability, or performance?

Asking both technical and management staff to delineate their priorities is particularly important in assessing integration and scalability needs. In most cases, positioning the network for growth and better integration will not be as important to either group as other requirements, such as security (discussed in the following section).

Security Requirements

Some projects result from a need to improve network security rather than an attempt to address user or performance needs. Security needs are typically identified by the technical staff—either network administrators or managers. Examples of projects driven by security needs include installation of firewalls at WAN locations, modifications to firewall or router configurations or operating systems, implementation of intrusion detection systems, or a company-wide effort to enforce security policies, such as good password selection. As you can imagine, the scope and cost of security-related projects can vary dramatically.

No matter what their nature, security needs—like user or performance needs—must be clearly defined before a project commences. Ask management staff how they would prioritize security improvements and how much they would be willing to pay to improve network or systems security. In addition, ask technical staff to answer the following questions to help you identify which needs should be addressed so as to improve your network's security:

- What type of security must be improved (hardware, software, user, facilities)?
- Why does security need to be improved?
- Based on the reasons underlying the need for improved security, to what extent does security need to be improved?
- Will the improvement require extra staff, hardware, software, or consulting services?
- Compared with other needs, what is the priority of security improvements?
- How will security improvements affect network access, performance, or scalability?

As with analyzing user requirements, assessing security requirements may reveal conflicting needs. For example, one faction of network technicians may believe that simply upgrading the version of a server's operating system will address a security flaw, whereas another group of technicians may insist that the security flaw can be resolved only by installing an expensive firewall upgrade. You may find it helpful to gather technical personnel to debate their points of view and reach a consensus. Alternatively, based on the priority assigned to security improvements, you may conclude that a stronger security measure—such as intrusion detection—is warranted at any cost.

For example, suppose you are the network manager for a growing investment firm that currently uses firewalls at each of its WAN locations and has an effective security policy. Even with these firewalls in place, you may experience an IP spoofing attack that brings down your network. Quantifying the cost of this outage may prove difficult, but you might recognize that you lost potentially hundreds of customers and perhaps millions of dollars in sales. As a result of this breach, you may identify a few critical security needs—for example, the need for better firewall configuration and the need for a mechanism (such as intrusion detection) to stop attacks as they begin. You can assume that if you do nothing, another security breach will occur; the next attack might even be worse (perhaps resulting in stolen or damaged data). Therefore, implementing an expensive intrusion detection system may be well worth its cost.

Using a Pilot Network

As you learned in Chapter 13, one of the best ways to evaluate new technology is to test it in your environment. Similarly, the best way of evaluating a large-scale network or systems implementation is to first test it on a small scale. A small-scale network that stands in for the larger network is sometimes called a **pilot network**. Although a pilot network will be much smaller than the enterprise-wide network, it should be similar enough to closely mimic the larger network's hardware, software, connectivity, unique configurations, and load. If possible, you should establish the pilot network in the same location or environment in which the final network will exist.

The following tips will help you create a more realistic and useful pilot network:

- Include at least one of each type of device (whether a critical router or a client workstation) that might be affected by the change.
- Use the same transmission methods and speeds as employed on your network.
- Try to emulate the number of segments, protocols, and addressing schemes in your network.
- Always implement the same server and client software and configurations on your pilot network as found in your current network.
- Once you have established the pilot network, test it for at least two weeks to verify that its performance, security, availability, or other characteristics meet your criteria.

As the pilot network is intended for testing only, do not connect the pilot network to your live network. By keeping the two networks separate, you will ensure that you do not inadvertently harm your functioning network by making (experimental) changes to it.

The pilot network offers you opportunities to both educate yourself and test your implementation goals. Use your time with the pilot network to become familiar with any new features in the hardware or software. Be certain to document what you learn about the new technology's features and idiosyncrasies. As you evaluate your results against your predefined test criteria, note where your results show success or failure. All of this documentation will provide valuable information for your final implementation and for future baselining.

PREPARING USERS

No matter how small and insignificant your network change appears, if it could potentially affect the way that users accomplish their daily work, you must prepare them for the change. In some cases, the likelihood of a change affecting users will be plainly evident. For example, if you upgrade the version of NetWare used by your file servers and therefore must upgrade the Novell networking client version used by clients, every user will see a slightly different screen when he or she starts up the computer and logs into the network. If you replace a segment of CAT3 cabling with CAT5 cabling, however, users may never notice the difference.

In almost every instance, you are well advised to notify users of impending changes. That way, if something goes wrong with a change that shouldn't have affected users, creating problems when users try to access the network, these employees will not be caught off guard. For example, you and your staff may install additional RAM in all of your servers over the weekend. Normally, no reason exists to notify users of such an upgrade, assuming it is not performed during business hours. If one of the new memory chips causes problems for a server, however, the change will affect users. In this situation, you might prepare users by announcing that the servers will receive memory upgrades over the weekend and that this change should not cause any changes or problems for client access. Inform users that any type of change represents a possibility for problems to arise, however.

For a major network change, you definitely must inform users. As soon as you have firm details about the nature and timeline of the change, let everyone know about it. Among other things, you should explain to users:

- How their access to the network will be affected
- How their data will be protected during the change. (Even if you are confident that the data will remain unaffected by the change, you should explain how the protection works.)
- Whether you will provide any means for users to access the network during the change
- Whether the change will require users to learn new skills

Although providing all of this information may seem burdensome, it will lessen the possibility that your project might be stymied by negative public reaction. To minimize the amount of time spent communicating with users, you might convene company-wide meetings or send mass e-mail distributions. If a network implementation has the potential to drastically change the way that users perform their work, you might want to form a committee of user representatives who can attend project meetings and provide input from the users' point of view.

Chapter Summary

- Project management is the practice of managing resources, staff, budget, timelines, and other variables so as to complete a specific goal within given bounds. The person who designs the project plan and oversees the project is the project manager. A project needs not only a plan, but also participants, funding, a specific means of communication, definitive processes, contingency plans, and a testing and evaluation phase.
- A project plan describes how the details of a managed project (for example, the timeline and the significant tasks) are organized. Project plans may take the form of a simple text or spreadsheet document for small projects. Larger projects, however, often require the use of project management software (such as Microsoft Project, PlanView, or PrimaVera Project Planner).
- No matter how large or small the project, its project plan will contain some common elements—tasks and subtasks, timelines, dependencies, resources, and milestones. In addition, project plans may provide information on task priority, flexibility provided in the timeline, task successors, links to other project plans, and so on.
- Every project depends on many resources. The human resources involved in a project may include employees from your department or other departments within the organization, outside consultants, vendor representatives, or employees from other organizations.
- People involved in a project may include project participants, task owners, stakeholders, and sponsors. Stakeholders are people affected by a proposed implementation and the ones to whom the project teams must answer. Sponsors are typically managers or executives who believe in the concept of the project and agree to help obtain support and resources for it.
- Every project, whether it entails a simple hardware upgrade or an entire network redesign, requires funding. A project budget is usually determined as a project begins and approved by a hierarchy of managers whose staff are involved in the project. A project's budget will depend on its breadth and complexity.
- Communications among project participants, stakeholders, and sponsors are critical for several reasons: to ensure that a project's goals are understood by participants, stakeholders, and sponsors; to keep a project's timeline and budget on track; to encourage teamwork among participants; to learn from previous mistakes; to prevent fingerpointing if a task is not completed correctly or on time; to prevent duplication of efforts; and to ensure that stakeholders are prepared for the effects of change.
- Process management involves planning for and handling the steps required to accomplish a goal in a systematic way. The processes you might manage during a project's implementation include change, support, training, transitioning, delegation, and problem resolution.
- For any endeavor that requires the cooperation of several team members, process management is a wise investment of time. Creating a process is not sufficient, however, unless everyone understands the process. You must ensure that the process is communicated to all participants.

- Contingency planning involves identifying steps that will minimize the risk of unforeseen circumstances endangering the quality or timeliness of the project's goals. In other words, it provides a plan for recovering after things go wrong. It's important to spend time planning for contingencies that have a reasonable chance of occurring during the project.
- Once you have reached a project milestone, you will want to verify that you are on the right path. You can accomplish this goal through testing. For testing to be useful, project participants should clearly define the change's purpose before the testing phase commences. To successfully test your implementation, you must establish a testing plan that includes methods and criteria.
- The first decision to make about any proposed project is whether spending the time and resources on this project makes sense—that is, whether it's feasible. To formalize the process of determining whether a proposed project makes sense, you may conduct a feasibility study. A feasibility study outlines the costs and benefits of the project and attempts to predict whether it will produce a favorable outcome (for example, whether it will achieve its goals without imposing excessive cost or time requirements on the organization).
- Once a project is deemed feasible, you and the project team should define the project's goals. One technique for setting project goals is to begin with a broad goal, then create narrower, more specific goals that will contribute to the larger goal.
- In addition to being specific, project goals should be attainable. If project goals are not feasible from the outset, you risk losing backing from both project sponsors and participants. If you lose their support, the project will most likely fail.
- Baselining includes keeping a history of network performance, the physical topology, logical topology, number of devices on the network, operating systems and protocols in use, and number and type of applications in use. In other words, it provides a complete picture of the network's current state. Baselining is critical to network implementations because it provides the basis not only for determining what types of changes might improve the network, but also for later evaluating how successful the improvements were.
- If you have not already collected and centrally stored baseline information, it may take the work of several people and several weeks to compile it, depending on the size and complexity of your network. This evaluation will involve visits to the telecommunications and equipment rooms, an examination of servers and desktops, a review of receipts for software and hardware purchases, and potentially the use of a sniffer or network monitoring software package.
- Needs assessment is the process of clarifying the reasons and objectives for proposed change. It involves interviewing users and other stakeholders and comparing their perceptions to factual data. In addition, it may involve analyzing network baseline data. Your goal in performing a needs assessment is to decide whether the change is worthwhile and necessary and to determine the appropriate scope and nature of the change.
- A good technique for beginning to clarify user requirements involves user interviews. Just as if you were a reporter, you should ask pointed questions. The more specific the answers provided, the easier it will be to suggest how a project might address those

needs. Users often are unsure about what they want. You can help by drawing out answers and then restating those responses to verify that you have heard and understood the users correctly.

- In the process of interviewing users, you may recognize that not all share the same needs. In fact, the needs of one group of users may conflict with the needs of another group. In such cases, you must sort out which needs have a higher priority, which needs were expressed by the majority of users, whether the expressed needs have any common suggestions, and how to address needs that do not fall into the majority.
- Although you might think that performance needs are easily quantifiable and therefore readily agreed upon, several engineers and technicians will more likely have differing opinions about the nature of the needs and ways to satisfy them. Have technical staff answer a number of questions to clarify performance requirements.
- To best determine availability requirements, you should interview both technical and management staff. Technical staff will provide insight about how availability can best be accomplished and where the network currently falls short of availability goals. Management staff will provide insight into what types of availability are most important and why.
- If managers do not have a networking or systems background, they may not realize the costs associated with high availability. Although achieving 99.5% availability may be feasible given their budgetary constraints, increasing the availability to 99.99% may bring exorbitant costs. Use your interview as an opportunity to educate managers, as well as to determine their requirements.
- Integration and scalability needs may drive network changes, although they are less likely to be the primary reason for changes than are customer, performance, or security needs. Asking both technical and management staff to outline their priorities is particularly important in assessing integration and scalability needs. In most cases, positioning the network for growth and better integration will not be as important to either group as satisfying other requirements.
- Some projects result from a need to improve network security rather than addressing user or performance needs. Security needs are typically identified by the technical staff—either network administrators or managers.
- Like user or performance needs, security needs must be clearly defined before a project commences. Ask management staff how they would prioritize security improvements and how much they would be willing to pay to improve network or system security. In addition, have technical staff answer a number of questions about how best to improve security.
- The best way of evaluating a large-scale network or systems implementation is to first test it on a small scale. A small-scale network that stands in for the larger network is sometimes called a pilot network. Although a pilot network will differ from the enterprise-wide network, it should mimic it closely enough to represent the larger network's hardware, software, connectivity, unique configurations, and load.

- In almost every instance, it is advisable to notify users of changes. You should share at least the following information: how users' access to the network will be affected; for how long their access to the network will be affected; how their data will be protected during the change; whether you will provide any means for users to access the network during the change; and whether the change will require them to learn new skills.

Key Terms

- **contingency planning** — The process of identifying steps that will minimize the risk of unforeseen circumstances endangering the quality or timeliness of the project's goals.
- **feasibility study** — A study that determines the costs and benefits of a project and attempts to predict whether the project will result in a favorable outcome (for example, whether it will achieve its goal without imposing excessive cost or time burdens on the organization).
- **Gantt chart** — A popular method of depicting when projects begin and end along a horizontal timeline.
- **milestone** — A reference point that marks the completion of a major task or group of tasks in a project and contributes to measuring the project's progress.
- **needs assessment** — The process of clarifying the reasons and objectives for a proposed change so as to determine whether the change is worthwhile and necessary and to elucidate the scope and nature of the proposed change.
- **owner** — The person who takes responsibility for ensuring that project tasks are completed on time and within budgetary guidelines.
- **pilot network** — A small-scale network that stands in for the larger network. A pilot network may be used to evaluate the effects of network changes or additions.
- **predecessors** — Tasks in a project that must be completed before other tasks can begin.
- **process management** — Planning for and handling the steps involved in accomplishing a goal in a systematic way. Processes that might be managed during a project's implementation include change, support, training, transitioning, delegation, and problem resolution.
- **project management** — The practice of managing resources, staff, budget, timelines, and other variables so as to complete a specific goal within given bounds.
- **project plan** — The way in which details of a managed project (for example, the timeline and the significant tasks) are organized. Some project plans are created via special project planning software, such as Microsoft Project.
- **resources** — In project management, a term used to refer to staffing, materials, and money.

- **sponsors** — People in positions of authority who supports a project and who can lobby for budget increases necessary to complete the project, appeal to a group of managers to extend a project's deadline, assist with negotiating vendor contracts, and so on.
- **stakeholder** — Any person who may be affected by a project, for better or for worse. A stakeholder may be a project participant, user, manager, or vendor.

Review Questions

1. What type of chart is used in project management to express how tasks will occur over a horizontal timeline?
   - **a.** Pert
   - **b.** Gantt
   - **c.** Stuelt
   - **d.** Ager
2. What do you call a task that must be completed before another task can begin?
   - **a.** decessor
   - **b.** successor
   - **c.** predecessor
   - **d.** subsessor
3. What is the purpose of a milestone?
   - **a.** to mark the beginning of a major task
   - **b.** to mark the completion of a subtask within a major task
   - **c.** to mark the completion of a major task or group of tasks
   - **d.** to mark the completion of the project
4. Who would be a likely sponsor for a network backbone upgrade?
   - **a.** help desk technician
   - **b.** network technician
   - **c.** Vice President of Operations
   - **d.** IT Director
5. In a project to upgrade the version of Microsoft Exchange on the network, a receptionist who uses Exchange is an example of a project stakeholder. True or False?
6. In what type of situation might additional funding have no effect on an enterprise's ability to complete a project more quickly?
   - **a.** when the project depends on a limited number of highly specialized staff members
   - **b.** when the IT department's budget is fixed
   - **c.** when customers' needs aren't clearly defined
   - **d.** when resource costs exceed the initial estimate

7. Name four benefits of effective communication among project participants.
8. What type of process can be managed to improve the efficiency of how modifications to a project plan are handled?
   a. problem
   b. change
   c. support
   d. training
9. Which predefined process can help you recover when a project suffers a setback?
   a. contingency planning
   b. transition planning
   c. budget reevaluation
   d. feasibility study
10. Which of the following implementation steps should come first?
    a. find vendors for necessary hardware additions
    b. determine the feasibility of the proposed project
    c. evaluate how users' needs might conflict
    d. identify the need for a project
11. Which step in the implementation of network projects should precede the final release of changes to all users?
    a. update the documentation to reflect changes on the network
    b. reinstall client software on older workstations
    c. release the change to a group of test users who will evaluate it
    d. suggest ways to improve the network's availability after the change
12. What is the last step in a network implementation project?
13. Why is it sometimes advisable to hire external consultants to perform a feasibility study?
14. Which of the following is a good example of test criteria that can be used to evaluate the success of a network backbone upgrade?
    a. Did the change improve network performance?
    b. Are 50% of the customers more satisfied with the network's performance?
    c. As a result of the change, are customers receiving e-mail more quickly?
    d. Did the change result in a 30% reduction in the time that it takes for data to travel from the router in building A to the router in building B?
15. Baselining will help you determine how long a project should take. True or False?

16. What can you do if your needs assessment interviews indicate that two groups of customers have conflicting needs?
    a. reinterview customers with the aim of reaching consensus
    b. gather customers with conflicting views in one room and ask them to debate the merits of their positions
    c. determine the costs of addressing each conflicting need and make a decision based on the lowest-cost solution
    d. compile the results of your interviews and determine which needs are better justified and expressed by the majority of users
17. Why does it cost significantly more to achieve 99.99% availability than it does to achieve 99.5% availability?
18. Which of the following questions should you ask your organization's management staff so as to better determine scalability needs?
    a. How much are you willing to spend to optimally position the network and systems for growth?
    b. Where is the network currently inhibited from accommodating new devices?
    c. In what ways can the WAN be expanded to integrate new locations easily?
    d. How will increasing the network's capacity for growth affect its performance?
19. Give two examples of projects that might be driven by security concerns.
20. If you were planning to replace all 25 routers in your enterprise-wide network with switches, what kind of pilot network might you design to test whether the switches will work as planned?

Hands-on Projects

Project 16-1

To familiarize yourself with project management, you may find it helpful to experiment with project management software, such as Microsoft Project for Windows 95. As this software is the most popular project management package, this exercise will use it to demonstrate the creation of a project plan. You will identify tasks, subtasks, timelines, and resources for a sample networking project. For this exercise, you will need a computer with Microsoft Project for Windows 95 installed.

1. To launch Microsoft Project, click **Start**, point to **Programs**, then click **Microsoft Project**.
2. Unless you have disabled it, the Welcome! dialog box opens. Click **Work on Your Own** to begin adding tasks to the project plan.

3. The main Microsoft Project window appears, with a frame for task listings on the left side of the screen and a blank timeline on the right side of the screen. Click on **row 1** of the task list. To add the first task, type **Upgrade Network**.
4. Click and drag the vertical bar that separates the task list from the timeline to the right so that you can view all columns above the task list. By default, you should see the columns Task Name, Duration, Start, Finish, Predecessors, and Resource Names, as shown in Figure 16-3.

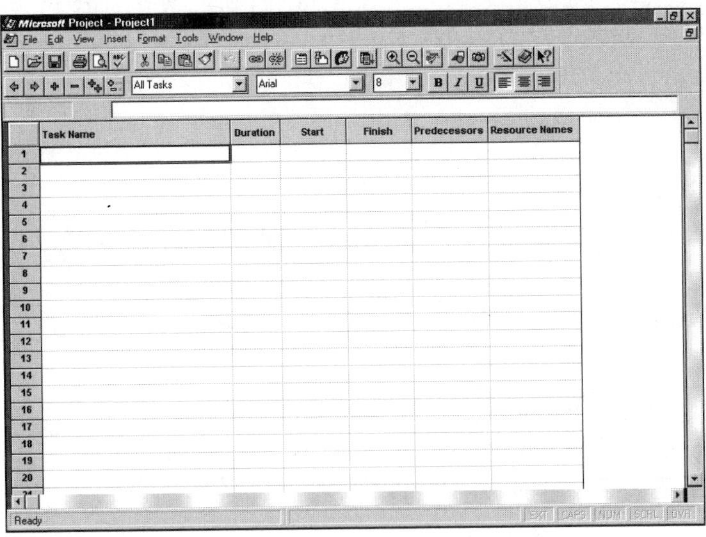

Figure 16-3 Default columns in Microsoft Project

5. Now you will enter some subtasks that make up the larger task you just created. Insert the following tasks in rows 2, 3, 4, and 5 respectively: **Assess Users' Needs**, **Purchase Hardware and Software**, **Implement Pilot Network**, **Implement Backbone Changes**.
6. To identify these five tasks as subtasks belonging to the "Upgrade Network" task, highlight each of them, then click the right arrow button on the formatting toolbar to indent the task. Notice that "Upgrade Network" becomes bolded.

7. Click the Duration cell next to the task name "Perform Network Baseline," then enter a duration of **10** (days).
8. Enter durations for the remaining four subtasks, based on how long you guess they might take. As you add these durations, the duration for the "Upgrade Network" task changes to reflect the length of its subtasks' durations.
9. By default, the project's Start date for the subtasks will be set to today's date. Change the Start date for "Perform Network Baseline" to **1/3/2000**. Notice that the Finish date changes, based on the duration that you entered in step 7.

10. In the Predecessors column for "Purchase Hardware and Software," enter **2** to indicate that this task is dependent on the second task, "Perform Network Baseline." What happens to this task's Start and Finish dates? Why?
11. Change the Start date for "Assess User Needs" to **12/15/1999**.
12. Now you can insert predecessors for the remaining tasks. Make "Purchase Hardware and Software" dependent on task 3, "Implement Pilot Network" dependent on task 4, and "Implement Backbone Changes" dependent on task 5.

Now you have created the skeletal beginnings of a project plan, with start and finish dates and predecessors. In the following exercises, you will expand on this simple plan.

PROJECT 16-2

Earlier in this chapter, you were introduced to the concept of a Gantt chart, which offers a way to depict project timelines. In this exercise, you will view and modify a Gantt chart that is based on the simple project plan that you created in Project 16-1. For this project, you will require the computer with Microsoft Project for Windows 95 installed that you used in the previous project.

1. View the project plan that you began in Hands-on Project 16-1.
2. Click **Format** on the menu bar, then click **GanttChartWizard**. The GanttChartWizard - Step 1 dialog box appears.
3. Click **Next** to continue.
4. The GanttChartWizard - Step 2 dialog box opens, prompting you to identify what kind of information you want to include in your Gantt chart. The default selection is **Standard**. Keep this selection, clicking **Next** to continue.
5. The GanttChartWizard - Step 9 dialog box opens. (Because you accepted the standard settings in the previous step, the wizard skipped from Step 2 to Step 9.) Here you can identify what kind of task information should appear in your Gantt chart. Select **Dates**, then click **Next** to continue.
6. The GanttChartWizard - Step 13 dialog box opens. (Again, based on your selection in the previous step, the wizard skips ahead to Step 13.) Here you can specify whether the chart should show link lines between dependent tasks. Keep the default selection of **Yes, please**, then click **Next** to continue.
7. The GanttChartWizard - Step 14 dialog box opens, announcing that the wizard is ready to format your Gantt chart. Click **Format It** to continue.
8. Click **Exit Wizard** to close the wizard and return to the project plan
9. To view the Gantt chart, click and drag the vertical bar that separates your task list from the timeline to the left. The Gantt chart will appear on the right side of the screen. Use the scroll bar at the bottom of the screen to view the entire chart.

PROJECT 16-3

In this project, you will elaborate on the plan that you began in Project 16-1 by assigning resources and adding milestones. This exercise requires the same computer and Microsoft Project file that you used in the two previous exercises.

1. Drag the vertical separator bar to the right to hide the Gantt chart and reveal the list of tasks on the left side of the Microsoft Project screen.
2. Click on the Resource Names cell for the "Perform Network Baseline" task. Enter **RG, BT** to indicate that Reggie Gibson and Brett Turrel will handle this task.
3. Assign resources to the remaining subtasks. In the Resource Names cell for "Assess Users' Needs," enter **KR, SN**. In the Resource Names cell for "Purchase Hardware and Software," enter **SS**. In the Resource Names cell for "Implement Pilot Network," enter **RG, BT, MM, MG**. In the Resource Names cell for "Implement Backbone Changes," enter **BT, MM, SS, AV**.
4. As the task of implementing a pilot network is a significant part of the project, its completion should mark a milestone. To identify this task as a milestone, double-click the task name. The Task Information window appears. The General tab is selected by default, as shown in Figure 16-4.

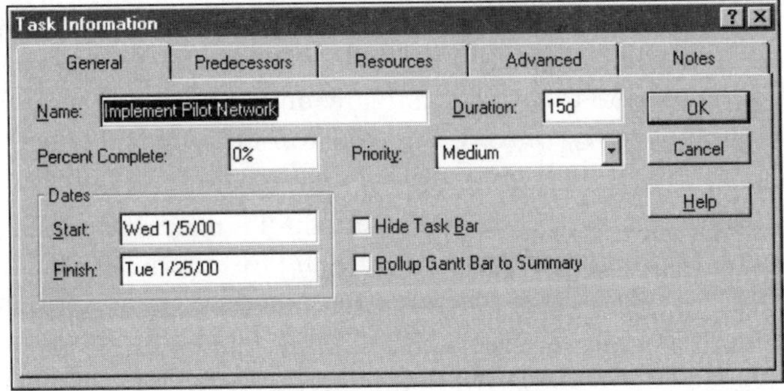

Figure 16-4 Task Information window

5. Click the **Advanced** tab to view additional information about the task. On that tab, check the box next to **Mark Task as Milestone**.
6. Click **OK** to save your changes.

Case Projects

1. Your colleagues in the IT department are considering migrating your organization's network from 4 Mbps Token Ring to 100 Mbps Ethernet. They posit that the change will provide users with better performance and position your network for easier growth in the future. Your organization's network consists of the following items:

   - 5 file- and print-sharing servers running Novell NetWare 4.11
   - 1 backup server
   - 1 Internet gateway and mail server
   - 350 users in two buildings located across the street from each other and connected via a T1 link

   Each user in your organization depends on the network for e-mail, file storage, printing, and office applications (including word-processing, spreadsheet, and database programs).

   The IT Director has asked you to list the ways in which this change could improve network performance. In addition, list ways that this change could affect users, support, maintenance, profitability, scalability, integration, and security.

2. Your company's project to migrate from Token Ring to Ethernet has been deemed feasible by an independent consultant. As this change represents a major network overhaul, the IT Director decides it might also be time to make smaller changes to accommodate users' needs. He assigns you the task of determining the needs of the 350 users. Draft a questionnaire that you will follow during your user interviews. When writing the questionnaire, consider how you will measure and tally the responses and what you might do if users' needs conflict with one another.

3. As a result of your thorough user needs assessment, the IT management staff has decided that, although the migration from Token Ring to Ethernet is important, a more pressing need is to upgrade the version of the NetWare client on each desktop. The IT Director assigns you to manage the project. Draft a project plan outline that will serve as a roadmap for accomplishing this wholesale client upgrade. Include estimated timelines, dependencies, and milestones.

4. Because the company-wide client upgrade will change the way that every user accesses the network, you want to apprise every user of the change and explain how it might affect him or her. Write a memo to users that communicates this information.

5. While you are conducting the client upgrades across the network, one of your colleagues is planning for the larger project of changing the network from Token Ring to Ethernet. She asks your help in setting up a test lab to use for the pilot network. List every item that should be in the test lab so as to adequately test the change plan.

APPENDIX A

Resources for More Information on Networking Software and Hardware

Throughout this book, you have read about many different networking hardware and software products. This appendix provides contact information for vendors that manufacture such products, including each vendor's address, home page URL, technical Web site URL, and phone number. Manufacturers that supply networking hardware are listed first, followed by those that supply networking software.

Resources for Hardware Manufacturers

3Com

Products:	Network interface cards, hubs, bridges, routers
Home page:	http://www.3com.com
Technical support page:	http://www.support.3com.com
Address:	5400 Bayfront Plaza Santa Clara, CA 95052
Phone:	(408) 326-5000 (408) 326-5001

American Power Conversion (APC)

Products:	UPSs, surge suppressors
Home page:	http://www.apcc.com
Technical support page:	http://www.apcc.com/english/svice
Address:	132 Fairgrounds Road West Kingston, RI 02892
Phone:	(800) 800-4272

Anixter

Products:	Structured cabling systems, wire, cable
Home page:	http://www.anixter.com
Technical support page:	http://www.anixter.com
Address:	6400 Shafer Court, Suite 350 Rosemont, IL 60018
Phone:	(800) 264-9837

Ascend Communications

Products:	Routers, multiplexors
Home page:	http://www.ascend.com
Technical support page:	http://aos.ascend.com/aos:/index.html
Address:	1701 Harbor Bay Parkway Alameda, CA 94502-3002
Phone:	(510) 769-6001
Fax:	(510) 747-2300

Belkin Components

Products:	Computer cables, surge protectors, peripheral-sharing devices
Home page:	http://www.belkin.com
Technical support page:	http://www.belkin.com/support/index.html
Address:	501 West Walnut Street Compton, CA 90220
Phone:	(800) 223-5546

Best Power

Products:	UPSs
Home page:	http://www.bestpower.com
Technical support page:	http://www.bestpower.com
Address:	P O Box 280 Necedah, WI 54646
Phone:	(800) 356-5737

Cabletron Systems

Products:	Hubs, routers, bridges
Home page:	http://www.ctron.com
Technical support page:	http://www.ctron.com/support
Address:	35 Industrial Way Rochester, NH 03867
Phone:	(603) 332-9400

Cisco Systems

Products:	Routers, switches, access servers, firewalls, intrusion detection devices
Home page:	http://www.cisco.com
Technical support page:	http://www.cisco.com/support
Address:	170 West Tasman Drive San Jose, CA 95134
Phone:	(800) 553-6387

Compaq/Digital

Products:	PCs, workstations, servers
Home page:	http://www.digital.com
Technical support page:	http://www.compaq.com/support
Address:	20555 SH 249 Houston, TX 77070-2698
Phone:	(281) 370-0670

Dell Computer Corporation

Products:	PCs, workstations, servers, fiber-channel storage, storage hardware
Home page:	http://www.dell.com
Technical support page:	http://www.dell.com/support/index.htm
Address:	One Dell Way Round Rock, TX 78682
Phone:	(888) 560-8324

Deltec Electronics

Products: UPSs
Home page: http://www.deltecpower.com
Technical support page: http://www.deltecpower.com
Address: 2727 Kurtz Street
San Diego, CA 92110
Phone: (800) 854-2658

Digitan Systems Inc.

Products: Routers, hubs, modems, NICs, system boards
Home page: http://www.digitan.com
Technical support page: http://www.digiclick.com
Address: 2363 Bering Drive
San Jose, CA 95131
Phone: (408) 954-8270

D-Link Systems

Products: PCMCIA cards, NICs, hubs, switches, bridges, routers
Home page: http://www.dlink.com
Technical support page: http://www.dlink.com/tech
Address: 53 Discovery Drive
Irvine, CA 92618
Phone: (949) 788-0805

Exabyte Corporation

Products: Tape backup units
Home page: http://www2.exabyte.com
Technical support page: http://www2.exabyte.com/home/suppserv.html
Address: 1685 38th Street
Boulder, CO 80301
Phone: (800) 445-7736

Fluke Corporation

Products: Electronic test tools
Home page: http://www.fluke.com
Technical support page: http://www.fluke.com/service/default.htm
Address: 6920 Seaway Boulevard
Everett, WA 98203
Phone: (425) 347-6100

FORE Systems

Products: Switches
Home page: http://www.fore.com
Technical support page: http://www.fore.com/support
Address: 1000 Fore Drive
Warrendale, PA 15086
Phone: (888) 404-0444

Frontline Test Equipment

Products: Protocol analyzers
Home page: http://www.fte.com
Technical support page: http://www.fte.com/techsupp/techarea.htm
Address: P.O. Box 7507
Charlottesville, VA 22906
Phone: (800) 359-8570

Fuji Photo Film USA

Products: Data storage media
Home page: http://www.fujifilm.com
Technical support page: http://www.fujifilm.com/home/service/info.htm
Address: 400 Commerce Boulevard
Carlstadt, NJ 07072
Phone: (800) 488-3854

Fujitsu Business Communication Systems

Products: ATM switches
Home page: http://www.fbcs.fujitsu.com
Technical support page: http://www.fbcs.fujitsu.com/service
Address: 3190 Miraloma Avenue
Anaheim, CA 92806
Phone: (800) 553-3263

Hayes Microcomputer Products

Products: Remote access servers, modems
Home page: http://www.hayes.com
Technical support page: http://www.hayes.com/support
Address: P.O. Box 105203
Atlanta, GA 30348-5203
Phone: (800) 429-3739

Hewlett-Packard

Products: PCs, workstations, servers, printers, scanners
Home page: http://www.hp.com
Technical support page: http://www.hp.com/ghp/services.html
Address: 3000 Hanover Street
Palo Alto, CA 94304-1185
Phone: (650) 857-1501

IBM

Products: PCs, workstations, servers, mainframes
Home page: http://www.ibm.com/products
Technical support page: http://www.ibm.com/support
Address: New Orchard Road
Armonk, NY 10504
Phone: (800) 426-4968

Intel Corporation

Products: Microprocessors
Home page: http://www.intel.com
Technical support page: http://www.intel.com/sites/support/index.htm
Address: 2200 Mission College Boulevard
Santa Clara, CA 95052-8119
Phone: (408) 765-8080

LanOptics

Products: Switches, firewall hardware and software
Home page: http://www.lanoptics.com
Technical support page: http://www2.lanoptic.com/html/in_sup.html
Address: 2445 Midway Road, Building # 2
Carrollton, TX 75006
Phone: (800) 533-8439

Lantronix

Products: Hubs, switches
Home page: http://www.lantronix.com
Technical support page: http://www.lantronix.com
Address: 15353 Barranca Parkway
Irvine, CA 92618
Phone: (800) 422-7055

Linksys

Products: NICs, hubs, modems
Home page: http://www.linksys.com
Technical support page: http://www.linksys.com/scripts/support.asp
Address: 17401 Armstrong Avenue
Irvine, CA 92614
Phone: (800) 546-5797

LSI Logic Storage Systems, Inc.

Products: Storage devices
Home page: http://www.lsilogic.com
Technical support page: http://www.lsilogic.com/products/unit5_ts.html
Address: 3718 North Rock Road
Wichita, KS 67226
Phone: (800) 862-7729

Lucent Technologies

Products: Switches, UPSs, firewalls, remote access servers, wireless LAN equipment
Home page: http://www.lucent.com
Technical support page: http://www.lucent.com/dns/services
Address: 300 Baker Avenue
Concord, MA 01742
Phone: (800) 286-9526

Madge Networks

Products: NICs, switches
Home page: http://www.madge.com
Technical support page: http://www.madge.com/Support/SupportHome.asp
Address: 2314 North First Street, Suite 100
San Jose, CA 95131-1011
Phone: (800) 876-2343

MGE UPS Systems

Products: UPSs
Home page: http://www.mgeups.com
Technical support page: http://www.mgeups.com/products/pdt120/service/service.htm
Address: 1660 Scenic Avenue
Costa Mesa, CA 92626
Phone: (800) 523 0142

Microtest

Products: Cable testers
Home page: http://www.microteStreetcom
Technical support page: http://www.microteStreetcom/support
Address: 4747 North 22nd Street
Phoenix, AZ 85016-4708
Phone: (800) 638-3497

Motorola

Products: 56 Kbps modems, Frame Relay access devices, ISDN BRI terminal adapters, small ISDN routers
Home page: http://www.motorola.com/networking
Technical support page: http://www.motorola.com/MIMS/ISG/mailform.html
Address: 20 Cabot Boulevard
Mansfield, MA 02048-1193
Phone: (800) 544-0062

Multi-Tech Systems

Products: Modems
Home page: http://www.multitech.com
Technical support page: http://www.multitech.com/support
Address: 2205 Woodale Drive
Mounds View, MN 55112
Phone: (800) 328-9717

NEC America – Corporate Networks Group

Products: ATM switches, servers
Home page: http://www.cng.nec.com
Technical support page: http://www.cng.nec.com/html/support
Address: 1555 West Walnut Hill Lane
Irving, TX 75038
Phone: (800) 832-6632

Network Appliance

Products: Multiprotocol servers
Home page: http://www.netapp.com
Technical support page: http://www.netapp.com/support
Address: 2770 San Tomas Expressway
Santa Clara, CA 95051
Phone: (800) 443-4537

Network Associates

Products:	Sniffers
Home page:	http://www.nai.com
Technical support page:	http://www.nai.com/services/support
Address:	3965 Freedom Circle Santa Clara, CA 95054
Phone:	(800) 764-3337

Nortel Networks / Bay Networks

Products:	Switches, routers, access servers, computer telephony integration
Home page:	http://www.nortelnetworks.com
Technical support page:	http://www.nortelnetworks.com/servsup
Address:	One Brunswick Square, Atrium, Suite 100 Street John, NB E2L 4V1, Canada
Phone:	(800) 466-7835

Olicom

Products:	Ethernet and Token Ring NICs, ATM adapters, switches, hubs, routers
Home page:	http://www.olicom.com
Technical support page:	http://www.olicom.com/middle.asp?item=897
Address:	1680 North Prospect Drive Richardson, TX 75081
Phone:	(972) 907-4600

Oracle Corporation

Products:	Web server software, Java development tools
Home page:	http://www.oracle.com
Technical support page:	http://www.oracle.com/support
Address:	500 Oracle Parkway Redwood Shores, CA 94065
Phone:	(800) 672-2531

Paladin

Products:	Cable testers, crimpers, tools
Home page:	http://www.paladin-tools.com
Technical support page:	http://www.paladin-tools.com/contact.htm
Address:	10446 Lakeridge Parkway Ashland, VA 23005-8124
Phone:	(800) 272-8665

Powerware

Products: UPSs
Home page: http://www.powerware.com
Technical support page: http://www.powerware.com
Address: Forum III
8609 Six Forks Road
Raleigh, NC, 27615
Phone: (800) 554-3448

Quantum Corporation

Products: Tape backup devices, disk drives
Home page: http://www.quantum.com
Technical support page: http://service.quantum.com
Address: 500 McCarthy Boulevard
Milpitas, CA 95035
Phone: (408) 894-4000

Racal-Datacom

Products: Frame Relay access devices, ISDN BRI terminal adapters
Home page: http://www.racal.com/rdg
Technical support page: http://www.milgo.com/rdg/solserv/solserv.htm
Address: 1601 North Harrison Parkway
Fort Lauderdale, FL 33340-7044
Phone: (800) 722-2555

RadioLAN

Products: Wireless LAN
Home page: http://www.radiolan.com
Technical support page: http://www.radiolan.com/technical.html
Address: 455 DeGuigne Drive
Sunnyvale, CA 94086
Phone: (888) 272-3465

Raytheon Wireless Solutions

Products: Wireless LANs
Home page: http://www.raylink.com
Technical support page: http://www.raylink.com/micro/raylink/sc.htm
Address: 362 Lowell Street
Andover, MA 01810
Phone: (800) 457-6811

Samsung Networks

Products: Switches
Home page: http://www.samsungnetworks.com
Technical support page: http://www.samsungnetworks.com/needhelp
Address: 1130 East Arapaho Road
Richardson, TX 75081
Phone: (888) 987-4356

Seagate Technology

Products: Tape backup devices, disk drives
Home page: http://www.seagate.com
Technical support page: http://www.seagate.com/support
Address: 920 Disc Drive
Scotts Valley, CA 95066
Phone: (831) 438-6550

SMC

Products: Microprocessors, NICs
Home page: http://www.smc.com
Technical support page: http://www.smc.com/Support_Index.html
Address: 6 Hughes
Irvine, CA 92618
Phone: (800) 762-4968

Sharp Electronics Corporation

Products: Network printers
Home page: http://www.sharp-usa.com
Technical support page: http://www.sharp-usa.com/c.asp
Address: Sharp Plaza
Mahwah, NJ 07430-2135
Phone: (800) BE-SHARP

Sony Recording Media and Energy Group

Products: Data storage media
Home page: http://www.sel.sony.com/SEL/rmeg
Technical support page: http://www.sel.sony.com/SEL/rmeg/support
Address: 680 Kinderkamack Road
Oradell, NJ 07649
Phone: (888) 206-4973

Sun Microsystems

Products:	Servers, workstations, storage devices
Home page:	http://www.sun.com
Technical support page:	http://wwwwswest2.sun.com/service
Address:	901 San Antonio Road Palo Alto, CA 94303
Phone:	(650) 960-1300

Tektronix

Products:	Network printers, test devices, network computers
Home page:	http://www.tektronix.com
Technical support page:	http://www.tek.com/home/support.html
Address:	26600 Southwest Parkway Avenue Wilsonville, OR 97070-1000
Phone:	(800) 835-6100

Telebyte

Products:	ISDN routers, ISDN terminal adapters, protocol analyzers
Home page:	http://www.telebyteusa.com
Technical support page:	http://www.abc.com/tech.htm
Address:	270 Pulaski Road Greenlawn, NY 11740
Phone:	(800) 835-3298

Toshiba

Products:	Servers, desktop computers
Home page:	http://www.toshiba.com
Technical support page:	http://www.toshiba.com/support/index.htm
Address:	13131 West Little York Road Houston, TX 77041
Phone:	(800) 231-1412

Tripp Lite Worldwide

Products:	UPSs
Home page:	http://www.tripplite.com
Technical support page:	http://www.tripplite.com/contacts
Address:	1111 West 35th Street Chicago IL 60609
Phone:	(773) 869-1111

UNISYS

Products:	Servers
Home page:	http://www.unisys.com
Technical support page:	http://www.service.unisys.com
Address:	Towship Line and Union Meeting Roads Blue Bell, PA 19424
Phone:	(800) 586-4797

Wyse Technologies

Products:	Network computers
Home page:	http://www.wyse.com
Technical support page:	http://www.wyse.com/service/support
Address:	3471 North First Street San Jose, CA 95134
Phone:	(800) 438-9973

Xerox

Products:	Network printers
Home page:	http://www.xerox.com
Technical support page:	http://www.xerox.com/go/xrx/support/Support.jsp?trk=/ Support
Address:	800 Phillips Road 111-01X Webster, NY 14580
Phone:	(800) 349-3769

Xircom

Products:	PCMCIA cards, NICs
Home page:	http://www.xircom.com
Technical support page:	http://www.xircom.com/suprtset.html
Address:	2300 Corporate Center Drive Thousand Oaks, CA 91320-1420
Phone:	(805) 376-9300

Xylan

Products:	Switches, firewalls
Home page:	http://www.xylan.com
Technical support page:	http://www.xylan.com/support/index.html
Address:	26707 West Agoura Road. Calabasas, CA 91302
Phone:	(800) 999-9526

Zoom Telephonics

Products:	Modems, ISDN routers
Home page:	http://www.zoomtel.com
Technical support page:	http://www.zoomtel.com/techsupport.html
Address:	207 South Street Boston, MA 02111
Phone:	(800) 666-6191

Resources for Software Manufacturers

@Backup

Products:	Online backups
Home page:	http://www.atbackup.com
Technical support page:	http://www.atbackup.com
Address:	3550 General Atomics Court San Diego, CA 92109
Phone:	(800) 344-2000

Atrieva Corporation

Products:	Online backups
Home page:	http://www.atrieva.com
Technical support page:	http://www.atrieva.com/support
Address:	600 University Street, Suite 911 Seattle, WA 98101
Phone:	(888) 640-2908

Citrix Systems

Products:	Remote computing software
Home page:	http://www.citrix.com
Technical support page:	http://www.citrix.com/support
Address:	6400 Northwest 6th Way Fort Lauderdale, FL 33309
Phone:	(954) 267-3000

Computer Associates

Products:	Enterprise backup software
Home page:	http://www.cai.com
Technical support page:	http://support.cai.com
Address:	One Computer Associates Plaza Islandia, NY 11788
Phone:	(800) 225-5224

Concord Communications

Products: Network performance trending
Home page: http://www.concord.com
Technical support page: http://www.concord.com/support.htm
Address: 33 Boston Post Road West
Marlboro, MA 01752
Phone: (800) 851-8725

Connected Corporation

Products: Online backups
Home page: http://www.connected.com
Technical support page: http://www.connected.com/support/Default.htm
Address: 63 Fountain Street
Framingham, MA 01702
Phone: (888) 922-2587

CyberGuard Corporation

Products: Firewall, VPN, encryption software
Home page: http://www.cyberguard.com
Technical support page: http://www.cybg.com/support/service.html
Address: 2000 W. Commercial Boulevard, Suite 200
Fort Lauderdale, FL 33309
Phone: (800) 666-4273

Dantz Development Corporation

Products: Enterprise backup software
Home page: http://www.dantz.com
Technical support page: http://www.dantz.com/tech_support.html
Address: 4 Orinda Way, Building C
Orinda, CA 94563
Phone: (925) 253-3000

Dr Solomon's Software

Products: Antivirus software
Home page: http://www.drsolomon.com
Technical support page: http://www.drsolomon.com/support
Address: 3965 Freedom Circle
Santa Clara, CA 94588
Phone: (801) 492-2600

Hot Wire Data Security

Products:	Online backup
Home page:	http://www.backup.net
Technical support page:	http://www.backup.net/support
Address:	1227 Liberty Street Allentown, PA 18102
Phone:	(888) 468-9473

Hummingbird Communications

Products:	Remote access software, Windows NT NFS clients and servers
Home page:	http://www.hummingbird.com
Technical support page:	http://www.hummingbird.com/support
Address:	1 Sparks Avenue North York, ON M2H 2W1 Canada
Phone:	(416) 496-2200

Informix Software

Products:	Web middleware
Home page:	http://www.informix.com
Technical support page:	http://www.informix.com/informix/services/techinfo
Address:	4100 Bohannon Drive Menlo Park, CA 94025
Phone:	(800) 374-0304

Legato Systems

Products:	Enterprise backup software
Home page:	http://www.legato.com
Technical support page:	http://www.legato.com/support
Address:	3210 Porter Drive Palo Alto, CA 94304
Phone:	(650) 812-6000

Lotus Development Corporation

Products:	Software applications
Home page:	http://www.lotus.com/
Technical support page:	http://support.lotus.com
Address:	55 Cambridge Parkway Cambridge, MA 02142
Phone:	(800) 553-4270

McAfee.com

Products:	Antivirus software
Home page:	http://www.mcafee.com
Technical support page:	http://support.mcafee.com
Address:	3965 Freedom Circle Santa Clara, CA 95054
Phone:	(408) 988-3832

Microsoft

Products:	Windows NT, Windows 95/98, applications
Home page:	http://www.microsoft.com
Technical support page:	http://www.microsoft.com/support
Address:	One Microsoft Way Redmond, WA 98052
Phone:	(425) 882-8080

Netscape

Products:	Internet browsers
Home page:	http://home.netscape.com/products
Technical support page:	http://help.netscape.com/index.html
Address:	501 East Middlefield Road Mountain View, CA 94043
Phone:	(650) 254-1900 (650) 528-4124

Novell

Products:	Networks, e-mail, groupware, document management
Home page:	http://www.novell.com
Technical support page:	http://support.novell.com
Address:	122 East 1700 South Provo, UT 84606
Phone:	(888) 321-4272

Octopus (Fulltime Software)

Products:	High-availability and data protection software
Home page:	http://www.qualix.com/java/index.html
Technical support page:	http://www.qualix.com/java/service-support/index.html
Address:	177 Bovet Road, 2nd Floor San Mateo, CA 94402
Phone:	(800) 245-8649

Oracle

Products:	Databases, client/server connectivity, applications
Home page:	http://www.oracle.com
Technical support page:	http://www.oracle.com/support
Address:	500 Oracle Parkway Redwood City, CA 94065
Phone:	(650) 551-8900

PLATINUM technology

Products:	Backup software, Web middleware, Web-to-database connectivity
Home page:	http://www.platinum.com
Technical support page:	http://support.platinum.com
Address:	1815 South Meyers Road Oakbrook Terrace, IL 60181-5241
Phone:	(800) 890-7528

Safeguard Interactive

Products:	Online backups
Home page:	http://www.sgii.com
Technical support page:	http://www.sgii.com/support.html
Address:	115 Evergreen Heights Drive Pittsburgh, PA 15229-1346
Phone:	(412) 415-5200

Shiva Corporation

Products:	Remote access and firewall software, VPN gateways
Home page:	http://www.shiva.com
Technical support page:	http://www.shiva.com/prod
Address:	28 Crosby Drive Bedford, MA 01730-1437
Phone:	(800) 977-4482

Silicon Graphics

Products:	Video and Internet server software
Home page:	http://www.sgi.com
Technical support page:	http://www.sgi.com/support/support_help.html
Address:	2011 North Shoreline Boulevard Mountain View, CA 94043
Phone:	(800) 800-7441

Sybase

Products:	Client/server connectivity, database products
Home page:	http://www.sybase.com
Technical support page:	http://mysupport.sybase.com
Address:	6475 Christie Avenue Emeryville, CA 94608-105
Phone:	(800) 8-SYBASE

Symantec

Products:	Antivirus software
Home page:	http://www.symantec.com
Technical support page:	http://www.symantec.com/techsupp
Address:	10201 Torre Avenue Cupertino, CA 95014
Phone:	(800) 441-7234

Veritas

Products:	Enterprise backup software, storage management
Home page:	http://www.veritas.com
Technical support page:	http:// www.veritas.com/services/supSer/support.html
Address:	1600 Plymouth Street Mountain View, CA 94043
Phone:	(650) 335-8000

Vinca Corporation

Products:	Server mirroring software
Home page:	http://www.vinca.com
Technical support page:	http://www.vinca.com/support
Address:	1201 North 800 East Orem, UT 84097
Phone:	(888) 808-4622

Wall Data

Products:	Remote computing software
Home page:	http://www.walldata.com
Technical support page:	http://www.walldata.com
Address:	11332 122nd Way, N.E. Kirkland, WA 98034-6931
Phone:	(800) 755-9255

Appendix B

A Networking Professional's Toolkit

Throughout this book, you have learned about the many tools you may use while implementing, analyzing, and troubleshooting a network. Although information on networking devices or software packages is readily available, it is not always easy to find details about the tools used by networking professionals. This appendix provides pictures of networking tools, some familiar and some probably unfamiliar, along with their proper names and uses. You can often find these tools together in toolkits with carrying cases. Toolkit providers include Aven Tools, Black Box, Curtis, Paladin, and Siemon.

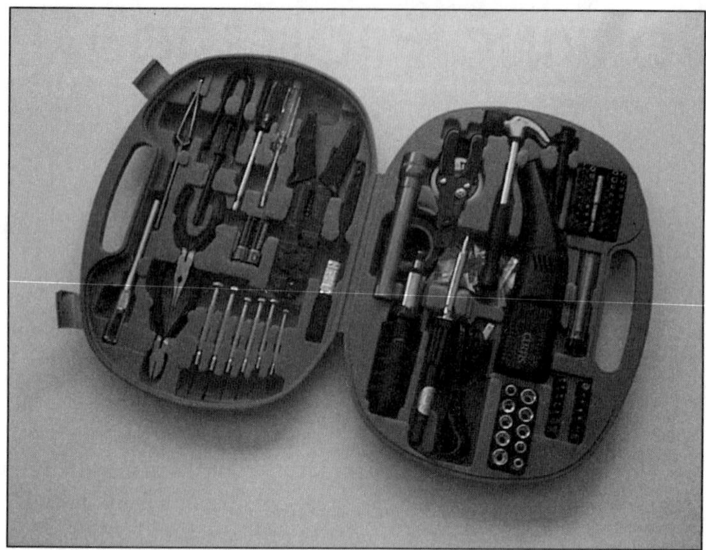

Figure B-1 A networking professional's toolkit

Many of the tools used by networking professionals are similar or identical to tools used by electricians. Tools pictured in the following figures fall into this category.

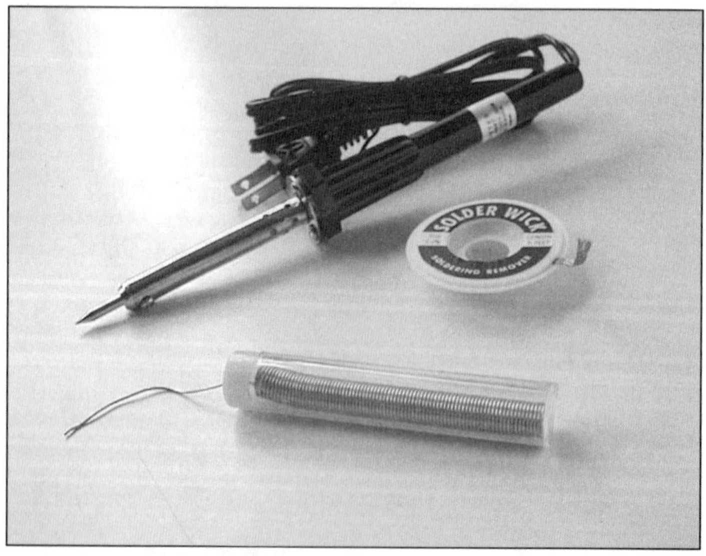

Figure B-2 Soldering iron, solder, and solder wick; used for repairing connections

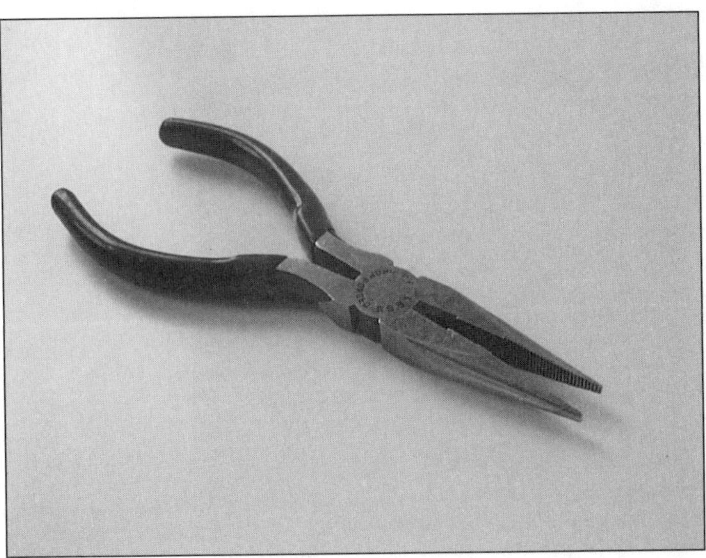

Figure B-3 Pliers; used for bending cable or components or working in tight spaces

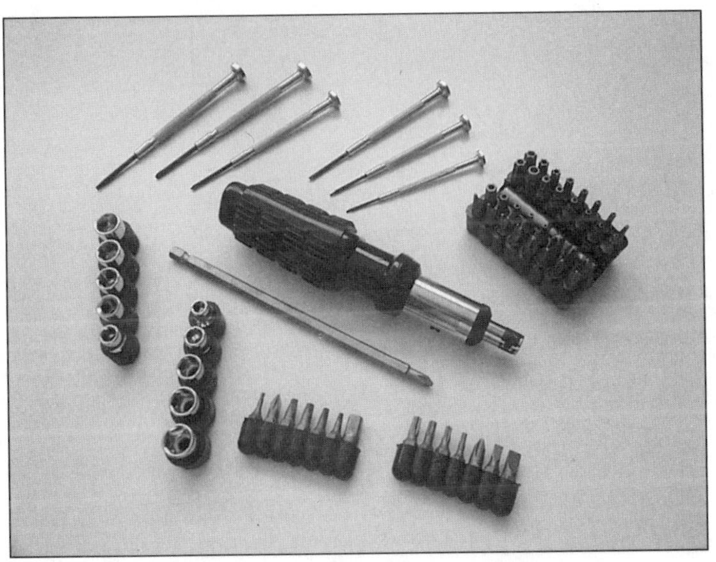

Figure B-4 Screwdriver with several different head types; used for installing and uninstalling components

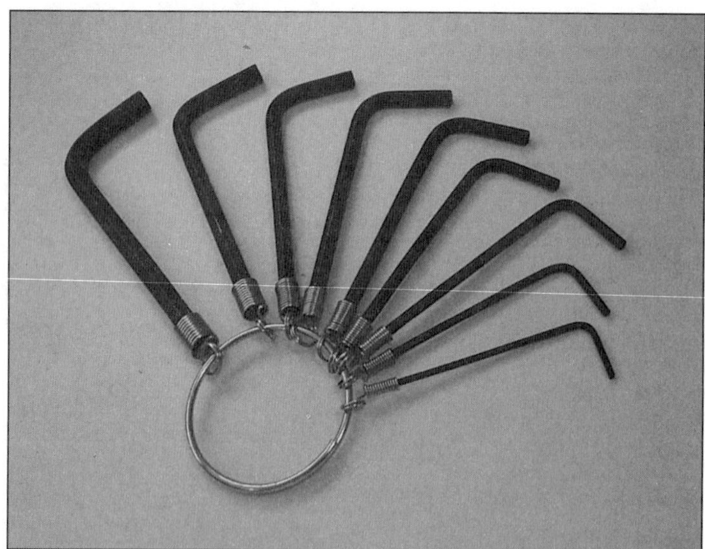

Figure B-5 Hex keyset; used for removing computer covers or components

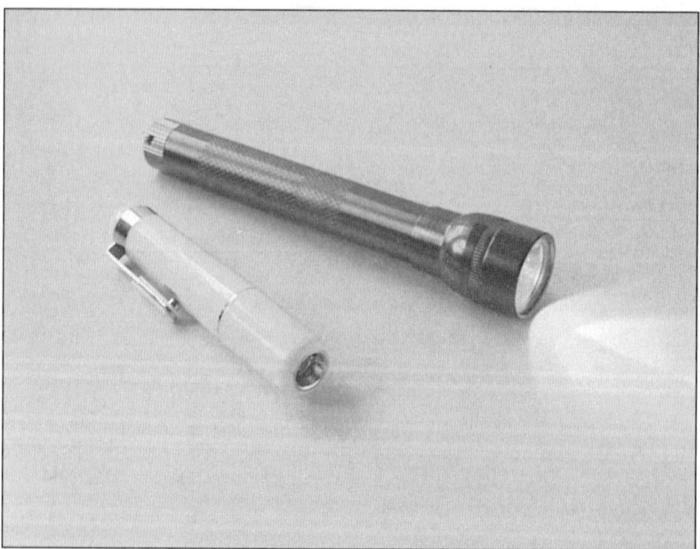

Figure B-6 Pocket flashlights; used to illuminate the interior of devices

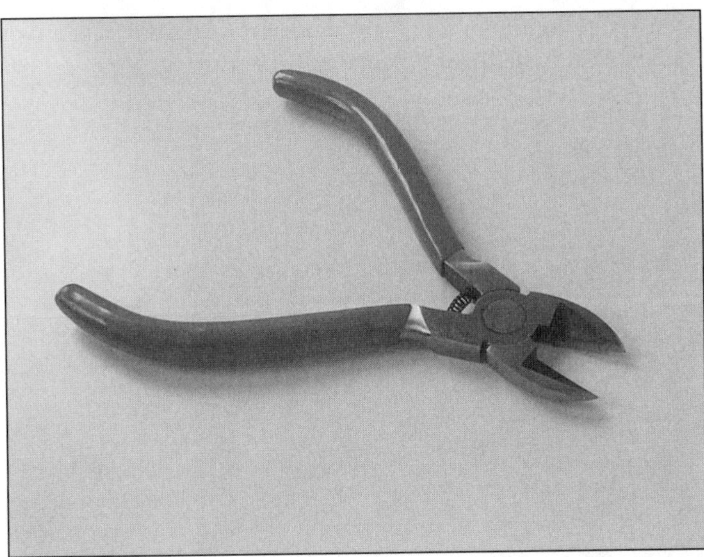

Figure B-7 Wire cutters

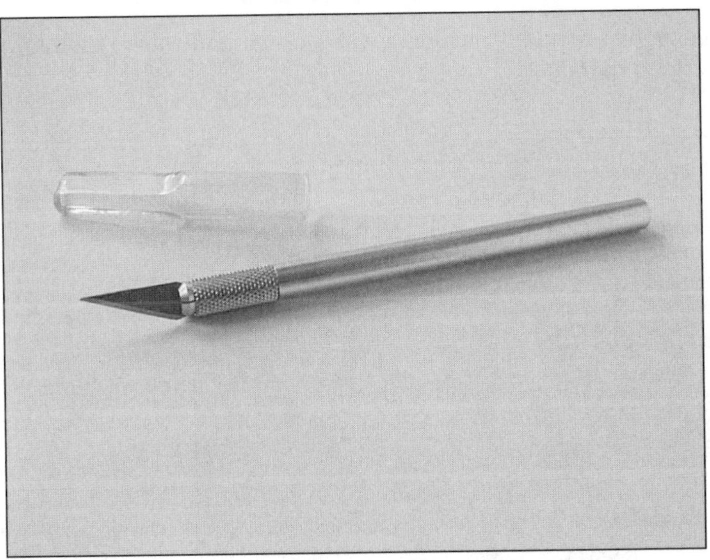

Figure B-8 Precision knife

Other tools used by networking professionals are unique to computer repair or telephony technicians. Tools pictured in the following figures fall into this category.

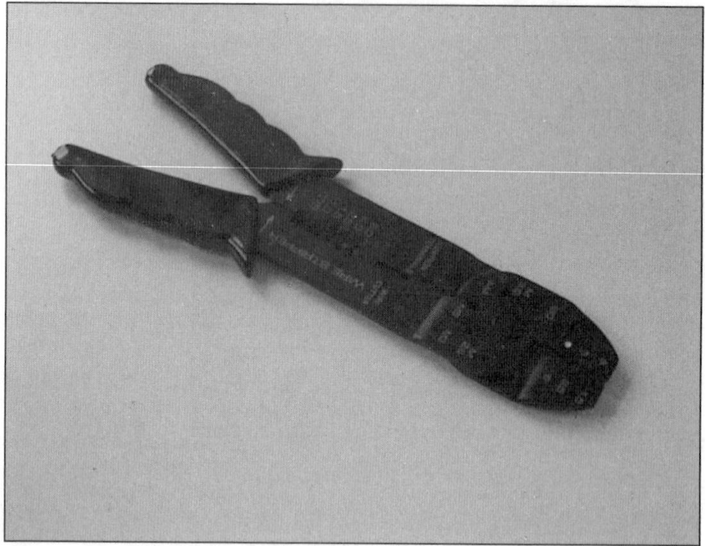

Figure B-9 Cable preparation tool, including wire stripper and cutter; used for preparing cable for termination

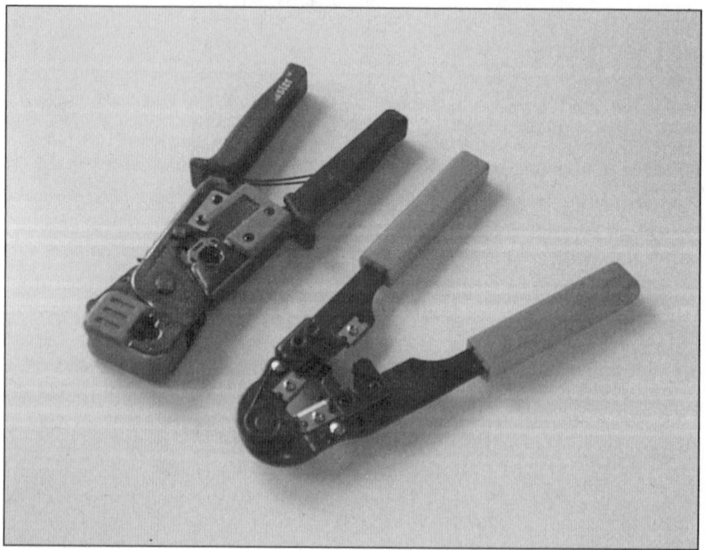

Figure B-10 Crimp tool; used for crimping wires into terminators

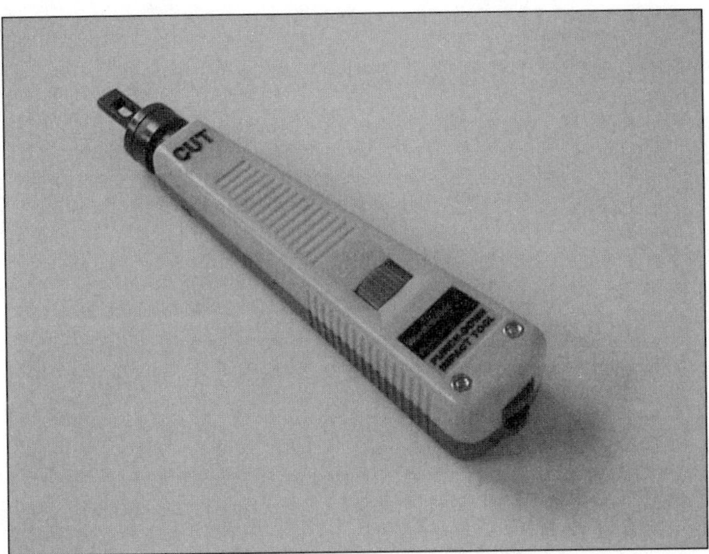

Figure B-11 Punchdown block tool; used for crimping wires into punch-down blocks

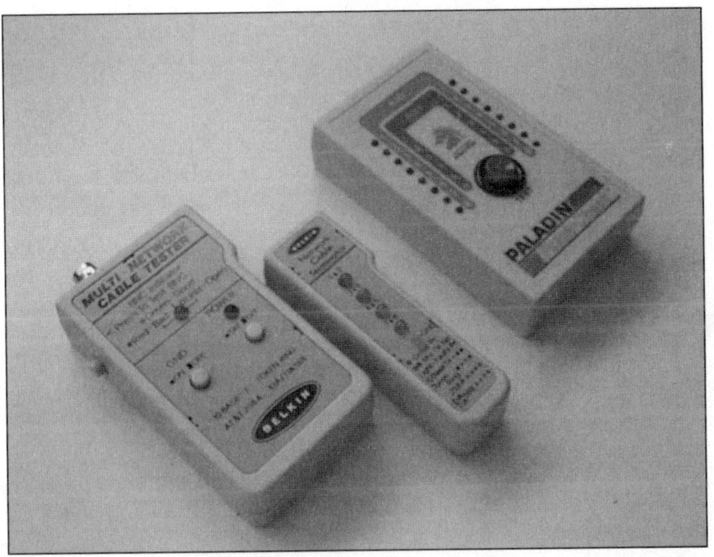

Figure B-12 Cable testing tools; used for verifying cable integrity

Figure B-13 Cable ties; used for holding bundles of cables together

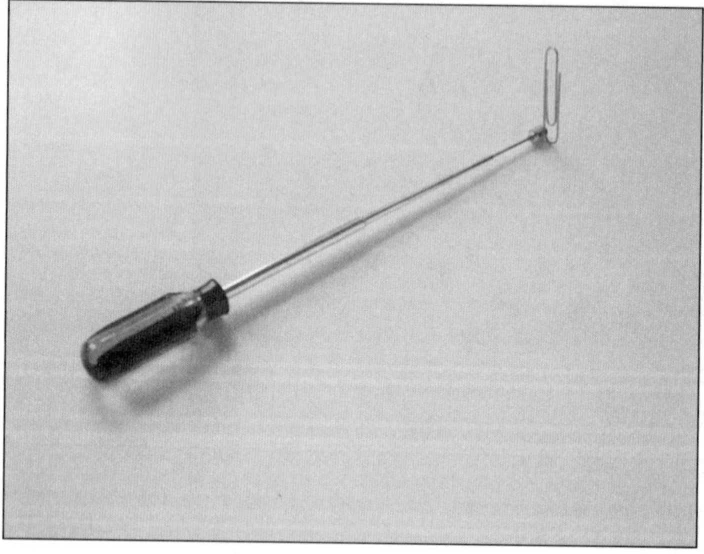

Figure B-14 Magnetic extractor; used for retrieving small components

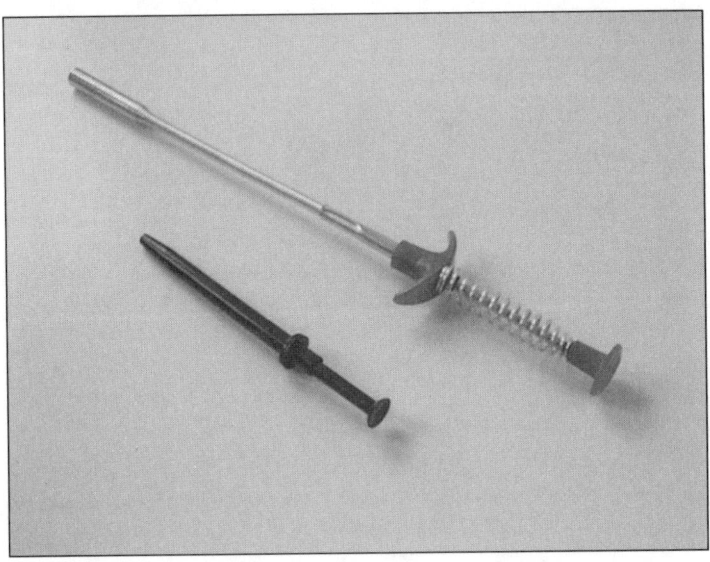

Figure B-15 Extractors; used for retrieving small components

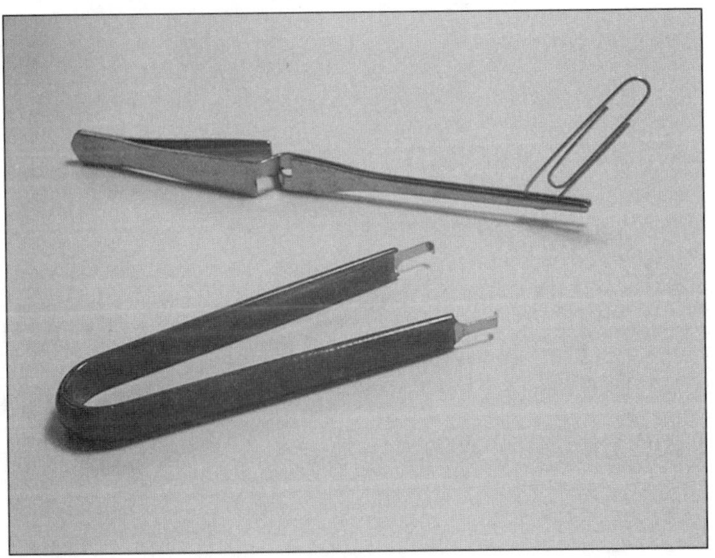

Figure B-16 Tweezers; used for holding and maneuvering small components

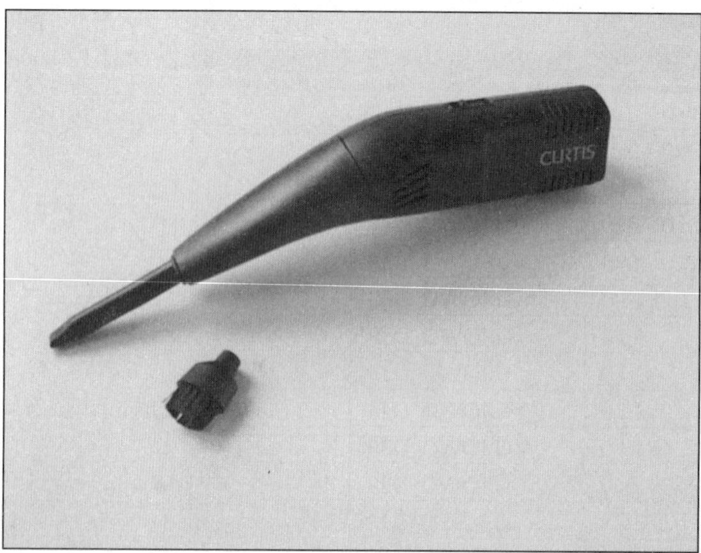

Figure B-17 Anti-static vacuum; used for cleaning electronic devices

STANDARD NETWORKING FORMS

Throughout this book, you have learned about various operating procedures and policies that can help your IT operations, upgrades, and installations run more smoothly. This appendix offers examples of forms you can use when planning and maintaining a network. You may need to change the forms slightly to suit your environment, but having a form template can help you remember steps that you might otherwise have forgotten.

This appendix provides the following forms:

- Server Installation Checklist – Windows NT
- Server Installation Checklist – NetWare
- Server Installation Checklist – Red Hat Linux
- User Account Creation Form
- Technical Support Contacts Form
- Incident Report Form
- Network Security Checklist

Server Installation Form – Windows NT

Installer: ______________________ Date:________________

Model and Serial Number: ________________________________

RAM: ______________ Processor: ________ Hard Disk: __________

Server is a: ❑ PDC ❑ BDC ❑ Member Server

Server Name: ______________________________

Domain Name: ______________________________

NIC 1 Type: __________ IRQ:________ Base I/O: ________ DMA: ______

NIC 2 Type: __________ IRQ:________ Base I/O: ________ DMA: ______

Protocols:

❑ NetBEUI

❑ NWLink IPS/SPX-Compatible Protocol

❑ Other: ________________

❑ TCP/IP

IP Address: __________

Gateway: __________

DNS Server: __________

Disk Controller Type(s): ________________________________

Partitions:

	Type:	Size:	Name:
1:			
2:			
3:			
4:			

Registration Key: ________________________________

Licensing Mode: ❑ Per Server ❑ Per Seat

Server Installation Checklist – NetWare

Installer: ______________________ Date: ______________

Model and Serial Number: ________________________________

RAM: ______________ Processor: ________ Hard Disk: __________

Server Name: ________________________

Install symmetrical multiprocessing support? ❑ Yes ❑ No

Disk Controller Type(s): ____________________________

NIC 1 Type: ________ IRQ: ________ Base I/O: ________ DMA: ________

NIC 2 Type: ________ IRQ: ________ Base I/O: ________ DMA: ________

Partitions:

1: Type: Size: Name:

2: Type: Size: Name:

3: Type: Size: Name:

4: Type: Size: Name:

NDS Tree: __________________ NDS Container: ____________

License Number: ________

Protocols:

❑ NetBEUI

❑ NWLink IPX/SPX-Compatible Protocol

❑ Other: ________________

❑ TCP/IP

IP Address: ________

Gateway: ________

DNS Server: ________

Server Installation Checklist – Red Hat Linux

Installer: ______________________________ Date:______________________

Model and Serial Number: ____

RAM: ___________________ Processor: _________ Hard Disk: ___________

Keyboard Type: __________________ Monitor: ________________________

PCMCIA Support ❑ Yes ❑ No

Packages to Install: ____

____

Mouse Type: ____________________________________

Video Card Type: __________________________________

TCP/IP Settings:

IP Address: ________ Net Mask: ________________

Default Gateway: _________ Primary Name Server __________

Domain Name: _________ Host Name: _____________

User Account Creation Form

User Name: ______________________________________

Department/Location: ________________ Phone: ______________

Created by: _________________ Date: ____________________

Requested by: _________________________

Approved by: _________________________

User ID: ________________________

Context (NetWare) or Domain (Windows NT): _____________________

Group Memberships: ____

Home Directory: ___________________________

Password Restrictions:

Minimum password length: _____ Require unique passwords?: ❑ Yes ❑ No

Days before password expires: ______ Grace logins: _____

Login Restrictions:

Valid login times: _______ Maximum connections: ___________

Address restrictions: ______ Location restrictions: ____________

Technical Support Contacts Form

Vendor Name: ______________________________

Address: ______________________________

General Phone Number: __________ Tech. Support Phone Number: ________

General Web Page: ______________ Tech. Support Web Page: __________

Contact Name: ______________________________

Products Supported:

Product name: __________ Product license number: __________

Product name: __________ Product license number: __________

Product name: __________ Product license number: __________

Product name: __________ Product license number: __________

Support Agreement Specifics:

Support Experiences with Vendor:

Date:	Reason for call:	Resolution:
Date:	Reason for call:	Resolution:
Date:	Reason for call:	Resolution:
Date:	Reason for call:	Resolution:
Date:	Reason for call:	Resolution:

Incident Report Form

User Name: ______________________________

User ID: ____________________

Location: ________________ Phone: ______________

Date: _____________ Time: __________

Received by: __________________________

Nature of the Problem:

Resolution:

Date: _______ By: _________________

Notes:

Follow-up Call:

Date: __________ By: ______________

Notes:

Network Security Checklist

- ❑ Write and enforce security policy
- ❑ Communicate security policy to all employees
- ❑ Identify vulnerabilities
- ❑ Enforce use of passwords
- ❑ Require minimum password length
- ❑ Require frequent password changes
- ❑ Disable Administrator user on servers (use another ID with equivalent privileges)
- ❑ Implement virus scanning on servers and workstations
- ❑ Implement firewalls between private and public networks
- ❑ Properly configure firewall and router access
- ❑ Review remote access links for security threats
- ❑ Implement enterprise-wide intrusion detection
- ❑ Restrict logins to TCP/IP ports
- ❑ Encrypt sensitive data in transit (e.g., use digital certificates)
- ❑ Implement automated, enterprise-wide virus detection
- ❑ Implement badge access for equipment and telecommunications rooms
- ❑ Use security cameras to monitor entrances and equipment rooms
- ❑ Perform background checks on prospective employees
- ❑ Plan for security breaches by having a trained response team

GLOSSARY

1 Gigabit Ethernet A new version of high-speed Ethernet specified by IEEE's 802.3z project. 1 Gigabit Ethernet runs at 1000 Mbps and usually relies on fiber-optic cable, although it can run on short segments of unshielded twisted-pair wiring.

10Base2 An Ethernet adaptation that, according to IEEE 802.3 standards, uses thin coaxial cable and a simple bus topology. 10Base2 is also called Thinnet or Thin Ethernet. Its name derives from the fact that it can transmit data at 10 Mbps (thus the "10Base") and its maximum segment length is 185, or approximately 200, meters (thus the "2"). See *Thinnet.*

10Base5 The original cabling standard for Ethernet; it uses a bus topology and thick coaxial cable. It is also known as Thicknet or Thick Ethernet. Its name derives from the fact that it can transmit data at 10 Mbps (thus the "10Base") and its maximum segment length is 500 meters (thus the "5"). See *Thicknet.*

10BaseT An Ethernet version that uses twisted-pair cabling and a star-bus or hierarchical hybrid topology to transmit data at 10 Mbps. Its name derives from the fact that it can transmit data at 10 Mbps (thus the "10Base") and it requires twisted-pair wiring (thus the "T").

100BaseT An Ethernet version specified in the IEEE 802.3u standard that enables LANs to run a 100 Mbps data transfer rate, without requiring significant investment in new infrastructure. 100BaseT uses baseband transmission in a star-bus or hierarchical hybrid topology, like 10BaseT. Also like 10BaseT, the "T" in 100BaseT refers to the fact that it uses twisted-pair cabling.

100BaseT4 A type of 100BaseT technology that achieves its speed by breaking the 100 Mbps data stream into three streams of 33 Mbps each. These three streams are sent over three pairs of unshielded twisted-pair wiring. The fourth pair is used for collision detection. 100BaseT4 uses lower-cost Category 3 wiring.

100BaseTX A type of 100BaseT technology that achieves its speed by sending the signal 10 times faster and condensing the time between digital pulses and the time a station is required to wait and listen in CSMA/CD. It requires Category 5 unshielded twisted-pair cabling.

100BaseVG A network transport model that can transmit data at 100 Mbps. Unlike Ethernet, 100BaseVG uses a demand priority access method rather than CSMA/CD. Like 100BaseTX, 100BaseVG uses all four wire pairs in a twisted-pair cable. The "VG" in its name refers to the fact that it can be used for "voice grade" communications (i.e., to carry audio or video signals).

802.3 The IEEE standard for Ethernet networking devices and data handling.

802.5 The IEEE standard for Token Ring networking devices and data handling.

A

A+ Professional certification established by CompTIA that verifies knowledge about PC operation, repair, and management.

ACK (acknowledgment) A response generated at the Transport layer of the OSI Model that confirms to a sender that its frame was received.

active monitor On a Token Ring network, the workstation that maintains timing for token passing, monitors token and frame transmission, detects lost tokens, and corrects problems when a timing error or other disruption occurs. Only one workstation on the ring can act as the active monitor at any given time.

active topology A topology in which each workstation participates in transmitting data over the network.

address A number that uniquely identifies each workstation and device on a network. Without unique addresses, computers on the network could not reliably communicate.

address management Centrally administering a finite number of network addresses for an entire LAN. Usually this task can be accomplished without touching the client workstations.

Address Resolution Protocol (ARP) A core protocol in the TCP/IP suite that belongs in the Internet layer. It obtains the MAC (physical) address of a host, or node, and then creates a local database that maps the MAC address to the host's IP (logical) address.

addressing The scheme for assigning a unique identifying number to every workstation and device on the network. The type of addressing used on a network depends on its protocols and network operating system.

AIX IBM's proprietary implementation of the UNIX system.

alias A nickname for a node's host name. Aliases can be specified in a local host file.

alien crosstalk A type of interference that occurs when signals from adjacent cables interfere with another cable's transmission.

amplitude A measure of a signal's strength.

ANSI (American National Standards Institute) An organization composed of more than 1000 representatives from industry and government who together determine standards for the electronics industry in addition to other fields, such as chemical and nuclear engineering, health and safety, and construction.

analog A signal that uses variable voltage to create continuous waves, resulting in an inexact transmission.

API (application programming interface) A routine (or set of instructions) that allows a program to interact with the operating system. APIs belong to the Application layer of the OSI Model.

Apache A popular open source software Web server application often used on Linux Internet servers.

AppleTalk The protocol suite used to interconnect Macintosh computers. Although AppleTalk was originally designed to support peer-to-peer networking among Macintoshes, it can now be routed between network segments and integrated with NetWare- or Microsoft-based networks.

AppleTalk network number A unique 16-bit number that identifies the network to which an AppleTalk node is connected.

AppleTalk node ID A unique 8-bit or 16-bit (if you are using extended networking, in which a network can have multiple addresses and support multiple zones) number that identifies a computer on an AppleTalk network.

AppleTalk zone Logical groups of computers defined on an AppleTalk network.

Application layer The seventh layer of the OSI Model. The Application layer provides interfaces to the software that enable programs to use network services.

application switch Another term for a Layer 3 or Layer 4 switch.

array A group of hard disks.

asset management Collecting and storing data on the number and types of software and hardware assets in an organization's network. The data collection is automated by electronically examining each network client from a server.

asymmetric multiprocessing A method of multiprocessing that assigns each subtask to a specific processor.

asymmetrical The characteristic of a transmission technology that affords greater bandwidth in one direction (either from the customer to the carrier, or vice versa) than in the other direction.

asymmetrical DSL A variation of DSL that offers more throughput when data travels downstream—downloading from a local carrier's POP to the customer—than when it travels upstream—uploading from the customer to the local carrier's POP.

asynchronous A transmission method in which data being transmitted and received by nodes do not have to conform to any timing scheme. In asynchronous communications, a node can transmit at any time and the destination node must accept the transmission as it comes.

Asynchronous Transfer Mode (ATM) A technology originally conceived in 1983 at Bell Labs, but standardized only in the mid-1990s. It relies on a fixed packet size to achieve data transfer rates ranging from 25 to 622 Mbps. The fixed packet consists of 48 bytes of data plus a 5-byte header. The fixed packet size allows ATM to provide predictable traffic patterns and better control over bandwidth utilization.

attenuate To lose signal strength as a transmission travels farther away from its source.

attenuation The amount of signal loss over a given distance.

authentication The process of verifying a user's validity and authority on a system. Different systems use different credentials to authenticate users.

autosense A feature of modern NICs that enables a NIC to automatically sense what types of frames are running on a network and set itself to that specification.

availability How consistently and reliably a file, device, or connection can be accessed by authorized personnel.

B

B channel In ISDN, the "bearer" channel, so named because it bears traffic from point to point.

backbone The cabling that connects each connectivity device, or the different levels of a hierarchy of connectivity devices.

backleveling The process of reverting to a previous version of a software program after attempting to upgrade it.

backup A copy of data or program files created for archiving or safekeeping purposes.

backup browser A server that keeps a copy of the master browser's browse list in case the master browser fails.

backup domain controller (BDC) A server that backs up the PDC in managing account and security information for a domain. A BDC can also provide authentication for users logging in to the domain. Any number of BDCs per domain is permissible, but at least one should exist. Because the BDC must be able to read and write to the PDC, you should install a BDC only after the PDC is running correctly.

backup rotation scheme A plan for when and how often backups occur, and which backups are full, incremental, or differential.

bandwidth A measure of the difference between the highest and lowest frequencies that a media can transmit.

bandwidth overhead The burden placed on the underlying network to support a routing protocol.

base I/O port A setting that specifies, in hexadecimal notation, which area of memory will act as a channel for moving data between the NIC and the CPU. Like its IRQ, a device's base I/O port cannot be used by any other device.

baseband A form of transmission in which digital signals are sent through direct current pulses applied to the wire. This direct current requires exclusive use of the wire's capacity, so baseband systems can transmit only one signal, or one channel, at a time. Every device on a baseband system shares a single channel.

baselining The practice of measuring and recording a network's current state of operation.

bend radius The radius of the maximum arc into which you can loop a cable before you will cause data transmission errors. Generally, a cable's bend radius is less than four times the diameter of the cable.

best path The most efficient route from one node on a network to another. Under optimal network conditions, the best path is the most direct path between two points.

binary A system founded on using 1s and 0s to encode information.

binding The process of assigning one network component to work with another.

bio-recognition access A method of authentication in which a device scans an individual's unique physical characteristics (such as the color patterns in his or her eye's iris or whorls in his or her handprint) to verify the user's identity.

BIOS (basic input/output system) Firmware attached to the system board that controls the computer's communication with its devices, among other things.

bit Short for binary digit. A bit equals a single pulse in the digital encoding system. It may have only one of two values: 0 or 1.

blackout A complete power loss.

block A unit of disk space and the smallest unit of disk space that can be controlled by the NetWare system. Smaller blocks require more server memory.

Block ID The first set of six characters that make up the MAC address and that are unique to a particular vendor.

block suballocation A NetWare technique for using hard disk space more efficiently. Files that don't fit neatly into a whole number of blocks can take up fractions of blocks, leaving the remaining fractions free for use by other data.

BNC T connectors Connectors used by nodes on a Thinnet (Ethernet 10Base2) cabling technology to tap into the network.

bonding The process of combining more than one bearer channel of an ISDN line to increase throughput. For example, BRI's two 64 Kbps B channels are bonded to create an effective throughput of 128 Kbps.

boot sector virus A virus that resides on the boot sector of a floppy disk and is transferred to the partition sector or the DOS boot sector on a hard disk. A boot sector virus can move from a floppy to a hard disk only if the floppy disk is left in the drive when the machine starts up.

Bootstrap Protocol (BOOTP) A service that simplifies IP address management. BOOTP maintains a central list of IP addresses and their associated devices' MAC addresses and assigns IP addresses to clients when they request it.

Border Gateway Protocol (BGP) The routing protocol of Internet backbones. The router stress created by Internet growth has driven the development of BGP, the most complex of the routing protocols. The developers of BGP had to contend with the prospect of 100,000 routes as well as the goal of routing traffic efficiently and fairly through the hundreds of Internet backbones.

braiding A braided metal shielding used to insulate some types of coaxial cable.

BRI (Basic Rate ISDN) A variety of ISDN that uses two 64 Kbps bearer channels and one 16 Kbps data channel, as summarized by the following notation: 2B+D. BRI is the most common form of ISDN employed by home users.

bridge A device that looks like a repeater, in that it has a single input and a single output port. A bridge is different from a repeater in that it can interpret the data it retransmits.

bridge router (brouter) A router capable of providing Layer 2 bridging functions.

broadband A form of transmission in which signals are modulated as radio frequency analog pulses that use different frequency ranges. Unlike baseband, broadband technology does not use binary encoding. The use of multiple frequencies enables a broadband system to use several channels and therefore carry much more data than a baseband system.

broadcast A transmission to all stations on a network.

broadcast domain In a virtual local area network, a combination of ports that make up a Layer 2 segment and must be connected by a Layer 3 device, such as a router or Layer 3 switch.

brownout A momentary decrease in voltage, also known as a *sag*. An overtaxed electrical system may cause brownouts, recognizable as a dimming of the lights.

browse list The list of available resources distributed to specially assigned computers known as browsers.

browser The service used to discover all shared devices on the network and compile a database of those resources. Also, the server that runs the browser service.

browser election A vote between computers to determine which one will take over responsibility for maintaining the master browse list.

BSD (Berkeley Software Distribution) A UNIX distribution that originated at the University of California at Berkeley. The BSD suffix differentiates these distributions from AT&T distributions. No longer being developed at Berkeley, the last public release of BSD UNIX was version 4.4.

bug A flaw in software or hardware that causes it to malfunction.

bus The type of circuit used by the system board to transmit data to components. Most new Pentium computers use buses capable of exchanging 32 or 64 bits of data. As the number of bits of data a bus handles increases, so too does the speed of the device attached to the bus.

bus topology A topology in which a single cable connects all nodes on a network without intervening connectivity devices.

byte Eight bits of information. In a digital signaling system, one byte carries one piece of information.

C

cable checker A simple handheld device that determines whether cabling can provide connectivity. To accomplish this task, a cable checker applies a small voltage to each conductor at one end of the cable, then checks whether that voltage is detectable at the other end. It may also verify that voltage cannot be detected on other conductors in the cable.

cable drop Fiber-optic or coaxial cable that connects a neighborhood cable node to a customer's house.

cable plant The hardware that constitutes the enterprise-wide cabling system.

cable tester A handheld device that not only checks for cable continuity, but also ensures that the cable length is not excessive, measures the distance to a cable fault, measures attenuation along a cable, measures near-end crosstalk between wires, measures termination resistance and impedance for Thinnet cabling, issues pass/fail ratings for wiring standards, and stores and prints cable testing results.

caching The process of saving frequently used data to an area of the physical memory so that it becomes more readily available for future requests. Caching accelerates the process of accessing the server because the operating system no longer needs to search for the requested data on the disk.

call tracking system A software program used to document problems (also known as *help desk software*). Examples of popular call tracking systems include Clientele, Expert Advisor, Professional Help Desk, Remedy, and Vantive.

capacity see *throughput*.

Carrier Sense Multiple Access with Collision Detection (CSMA/CD) Rules for communication used by shared Ethernet networks. In CSMA/CD each node waits its turn before transmitting data, to avoid interfering with other nodes' transmissions.

Category 1 (CAT1) A form of UTP that contains two wire pairs. CAT1 is suitable for voice communications, but not for data. At most, it can carry only 20 Kbps of data.

Category 2 (CAT2) A form of UTP that contains four wire pairs and can carry up to 4 Mbps of data. CAT2 is rarely found on modern networks, because most require higher throughput.

Category 3 (CAT3) A form of UTP that contains four wire pairs and can carry up to 10 Mbps with a possible bandwidth of 16MHz. CAT3 has typically been used for 10 Mbps Ethernet or 4 Mbps Token Ring networks. Network administrators are gradually replacing CAT3 cabling with CAT5 to accommodate higher throughput. CAT3 is less expensive than CAT5.

Category 4 (CAT4) A form of UTP that contains four wire pairs and can support up to 16 Mbps throughput. CAT4 may be used for 16 Mbps Token Ring or 10 Mbps Ethernet networks. It is guaranteed for data transmission up to 20 MHz and provides more protection against crosstalk and attenuation than CAT1, CAT2, or CAT3.

Category 5 (CAT5) The most popular form of UTP for new network installations and upgrades to Fast Ethernet. CAT5 contains four wire pairs and supports up to 100 Mbps throughput and a 100 MHz signal rate. In addition to 100 Mbps Ethernet, CAT5 wiring can support other fast networking technologies, such as Asynchronous Transfer Mode (ATM) and Fiber Distributed Data Interface (FDDI).

Category 6 (CAT6) A twisted-pair cable that contains four wire pairs, each wrapped in foil insulation. Additional foil insulation covers the bundle of wire pairs, and a fire-resistant plastic sheath covers the second foil layer. The foil insulation provides excellent resistance to crosstalk and enables CAT6 to support at least six times the throughput supported by regular CAT5.

CDFS (CD-ROM File System) The read-only file system used to access resources on a CD. Windows NT supports this file system to allow CD-ROM file sharing.

cell A packet of a fixed size. In ATM technology, a cell consists of 48 bytes of data plus a 5-byte header.

certification The process of mastering material pertaining to a particular hardware system, operating system, programming language, or other software program, then proving your mastery by passing a series of exams.

Certified Network Engineer (CNE) Professional certification established by Novell that demonstrates an in-depth understanding of Novell's networking software, including NetWare.

change management system A process or program that provides support personnel with a centralized means of documenting changes to the network. In smaller organizations, a change management system may be as simple as one document on the network to which networking personnel continually add entries to mark their changes. In larger organizations, it may consist of a database package complete with graphical interfaces and customizable fields tailored to the particular computing environment.

CIR (committed information rate) The guaranteed minimum amount of bandwidth selected when leasing a Frame Relay circuit. Frame Relay costs are partially based on CIR.

circuit switching A type of switching in which a connection is established between two network nodes before they begin transmitting data. Bandwidth is dedicated to this connection and remains available until users terminate the communication between the two nodes.

cladding The glass shield around the fiber core of a fiber-optic cable. Cladding acts as a mirror, reflecting light back to the core in patterns that vary depending on the transmission mode. This reflection allows fiber to bend around corners without losing the integrity of the light-based signal.

client A computer on the network that requests resources or services from another computer on a network. In some cases, a client could also act as a server. The term "client" may also refer to the user of a client workstation.

client redirector The service required for a client to access a server over a network.

client/server architecture The model of networking in which clients (typically desktop PCs) use a central file server to share applications and data.

coaxial cable A type of cable that consists of a central copper core surrounded by an insulator, a braided metal shielding, called braiding, and an outer cover, called the sheath or jacket. Coaxial cable, called "coax" for short, was the foundation for Ethernet networks in the 1980s and remained a popular transmission medium for many years.

collapsed backbone A type of enterprise-wide backbone that uses a router or switch as the single central connection point for multiple subnetworks.

collision domain A portion of a LAN encompassing devices that may cause and detect collisions among their group. Bridges and switches can logically create multiple collision domains.

command interpreter A (usually text-based) program that accepts and executes system programs and applications on behalf of users. Often it includes the ability to execute a series of instructions that are stored in a file.

communications server A server that runs communications services such as Windows NT's RAS or NetWare's NAS, also known as an "access server."

Complementary Metal Oxide Conductor (CMOS) Firmware on a PC's system board that enables you to change its devices' configurations.

complete trust domain model A way of organizing Windows NT domains in which administration is completely decentralized. In this model, each domain manages its own user, group, account, and file and print sharing information. Each domain also has a two-way trust relationship with every other domain in the network.

Computing Technology Industry Association (CompTIA) An association of computer resellers, manufacturers, and training companies that sets industry-wide standards for computer professionals. CompTIA established and sponsors the A+ and Network+ (Net+) certifications.

conduit Pipeline used to contain and protect the cabling. Conduit is usually made from metal.

connection-oriented A feature of some protocols that requires the establishment of a connection between communicating nodes before the protocol will transmit data.

connectionless A feature of some protocols that allows the protocol to service a request without requiring a verified session and without guaranteeing delivery of data.

connectors The pieces of hardware that connect the wire to the network device, be it a file server, workstation, switch, or printer.

container objects Logical subdivisions (or "branches") in NetWare's NDS tree that organize resources by geographical location, department, professional function, security authorization, or other criteria significant to the particular network.

context A kind of road map for finding an object in an NDS tree. A context is made up of an object's organizational unit names, arranged from most specific to most general, plus the organization name. Periods separate the organizational unit names in context.

contingency planning The process of identifying steps that will minimize the risk of unforeseen circumstances endangering the quality or timeliness of the project's goals.

convergence time The time it takes for a router to recognize a best path in the event of a change or outage.

core The central component of a fiber-optic cable that consists of one or several pure glass fibers.

core gateways Gateways that make up the Internet backbone. Core gateways are operated by the Internet Network Operations Center (INOC).

cracker A person who uses his or her knowledge of operating systems and utilities to intentionally damage or destroy data or systems.

CRC (Cyclic Redundancy Check) An algorithm used to verify the accuracy of data contained in a data frame.

crosstalk A type of interference caused by signals traveling on nearby wire pairs infringing on another pair's signal.

CSU (channel service unit) A device used with T-carrier technology that provides termination for the digital signal and ensures connection integrity through error correction and line monitoring.

CSU/DSU A combination of a CSU (channel service unit) and a DSU (data service unit) that serves as the connection point for a T1 line at the customer's site.

custom installation A NetWare installation option that allows you to determine which services and programs are installed, among other things.

custom setup An option for installing Windows NT Server that allows you to decide which services and programs are installed, among other things. Custom setup generally takes longer than express setup, but it may be necessary if your server uses special hardware or software.

cut-through mode A switching mode in which a switch reads a frame's header and decides where to forward the data before it receives the entire packet. Cut-through mode is faster, but less accurate, than the other switching method, store and forward mode.

Cyclical Redundancy Check (CRC) An algorithm used by the FCS field in Ethernet frames. CRC takes the values of all preceding fields in the frame and generates a unique 4-byte number, the FCS. When the destination node receives the frame, it unscrambles the FCS via CRC and makes sure that the frame's fields match their original organization. If this comparison fails, the receiving node assumes that the frame has been damaged in transit and requests the source node retransmit the data.

D

D channel In ISDN, the "data" channel used to carry information about the call, such as session initiation and termination signals, caller identity, call forwarding, and conference calling signals.

daisy-chain A linked series of devices.

Data Link layer The second layer in the OSI Model. The Data Link layer bridges the networking media with the Network layer. Its primary function is to divide the data it receives from the Network layer into frames that can then be transmitted by the Physical layer.

Data Link layer address See MAC address.

data modulation A process in which one signal alters the frequency, phase, or amplitude of another signal.

data packet A discreet unit of information sent from one computer on a network to another.

dedicated circuits Continuous physical or logical connections between two access points that are leased from a communications provider, such as an ISP or local phone company.

dedicated line A continuously available link that is leased through another carrier. Examples of dedicated lines include ADSL, T1, and T3.

dedicated service A type of data connection in which the user does not have to dial-up an ISP; the connection is always available.

default gateway The gateway that first interprets a device's outbound requests and last interprets its inbound requests to and from other subnets. In the postal service analogy, the default gateway is similar to a local post office.

demand priority A method for data transmission used by 100BaseVG Ethernet networks. Each device on a star or hierarchical network sends a request to transmit to the central hub, which grants the requests one at a time. The hub examines incoming data packets, determines the destination node, and forwards the packets to that destination. Because demand priority runs on a star topology, no workstations except the source and destination can "see" the data. Data travel from one device to the hub, then to another device.

denial-of-service attack A security attack caused by a deluge of traffic that disables the victimized system.

Device ID The second set of six characters that make up a network device's MAC address. The Device ID, which is added at the factory, is based on the device's model and manufacture date.

dial-up A type of connection that uses modems at the transmitting and receiving ends and PSTN or other lines to access a network.

dial-up networking The process of dialing in to a LAN's access server or to an ISP. Dial-up Networking is also the name of the utility that Microsoft provides with its operating systems to achieve this type of connectivity.

differential backup A backup method in which only data that have changed since the last backup are copied to a storage medium, and that information is marked for subsequent backup, regardless of whether it has changed.

digital As opposed to analog signals, digital signals are composed of pulses that can have a value of only 1 or 0.

digital certificate A password-protected and encrypted file that holds an individual's identification information, including a public key and a private key. The individual's public key is used to verify the sender's digital signature, and the private key allows the individual to log on to a third-party authority who administers digital certificates.

direct infrared transmission A type of infrared transmission that depends on the transmitter and receiver being within the line of sight of each other.

disaster recovery The process of restoring critical functionality and data to a network after an enterprise-wide outage that affects more than a single system or a limited group of users.

disk mirroring A RAID technique in which data from one disk are automatically copied to another disk as the information is written.

disk striping A simple implementation of RAID in which data are written in 64 KB blocks equally across all disks in the array.

diskless workstations Workstations that do not contain hard disks, but rely on a small amount of read-only memory to connect to a network and to pick up their system files.

distributed backbone A type of enterprise-wide backbone that consists of a number of hubs connected to a series of central hubs or routers in a hierarchy.

domain A group of users, servers, and other resources that share account and security information through a Windows NT network operating system.

domain master browser A server that locates and compiles information about shared resources for a group of domains.

domain name The symbolic name that identifies a domain. Usually, a domain name is associated with a company or other type of organization, such as a university or military unit.

Domain Name System (DNS) A hierarchical way of tracking domain names and their addresses, devised in the mid-1980s. The DNS database does not rely on one file or even one server, but rather is distributed over several key computers across the Internet to prevent catastrophic failure if one or a few computers go down. DNS is a TCP/IP service that belongs to the Application layer of the OSI Model.

dotted decimal notation The shorthand convention used to represent IP addresses and make them more easily readable by humans. In dotted decimal notation, a decimal number between 1 and 254 represents each binary octet. A period, or dot, separates each decimal.

downstream A term used to describe data traffic that flows from a local carrier's POP to the customer. In asymmetrical communications, downstream throughput is usually much higher than upstream throughput. In symmetrical communications, downstream and upstream throughputs are equal.

DSL (digital subscriber lines) A dedicated remote connectivity or WAN technology that uses advanced data modulation techniques to achieve extraordinary throughput over regular phone lines. DSL currently comes in seven different varieties, the most common of which is Asymmetric DSL (ADSL).

DSU (data service unit) A device used in T-carrier technology that converts the digital signal used by bridges, routers, and multiplexers into the digital signal used on cabling. Typically, a DSU is combined with a CSU in a single box, a CSU/DSU.

Dynamic Host Configuration Protocol (DHCP) An Application layer protocol in the TCP/IP suite that manages the dynamic distribution of IP addresses on a network. Using a DHCP to assign IP addresses can nearly eliminate duplicate-addressing problems.

E

e-commerce A means of conducting business over the Web—be it in retail, banking, stock trading, consulting, or training. Any buying and selling of products or services that occurs over the Internet belongs in the e-commerce category.

echo reply The response signal sent by a device after another device pings it.

echo request The request for a response generated when one device pings another device on the network.

EIA (Electronics Industry Alliance) A trade organization composed of representatives from electronics manufacturing firms across the United States.

electromagnetic interference (EMI) A type of interference that may be caused by motors, power lines, televisions, copiers, fluorescent lights, or other sources of electrical activity.

emergency repair disk A disk that can be used to restore a Windows NT server to its previous, working hardware configuration if its configuration becomes irreparably botched. It can also repair missing or corrupted system files and fix problems with the Windows NT Registry. You should always create an emergency repair disk during installation of the network operating system.

encrypted virus A virus that is encrypted to prevent detection.

encryption The use of an algorithm to scramble data into a format that can be read only by reversing the algorithm—or decrypting the data—to keep the information private. The most popular kind of encryption algorithm weaves a key into the original data's bits, sometimes several times in different sequences, to generate a unique data block.

enhanced CAT5 A higher-grade version of CAT5 wiring that contains high-quality copper, offers a high twist ratio, and uses advanced methods for reducing crosstalk. Enhanced CAT5 can support a signaling rate of up to 200 MHz, double the capability of regular CAT5.

Enhanced Interior Gateway Routing Protocol (EIGRP) A routing protocol developed in the mid-1980s by Cisco Systems that has a fast convergence time and a low network overhead, but is easier to configure and less CPU-intensive than OSPF. EIGRP also offers the benefits of supporting multiple protocols and limiting unnecessary network traffic between routers.

enterprise An entire organization, including local and remote offices, a mixture of computer systems, and a number of departments. Enterprise-wide computing takes into account the breadth and diversity of a large organization's computer needs.

erasable programmable read-only memory (EPROM) Firmware that belongs on a circuit board and that enables its configuration information to be erased and rewritten. You can write to a NIC's EPROM to change the NIC's default transmission speed, for example.

Ethernet A networking technology originally developed at Xerox in 1970 and improved by Digital Equipment Corporation, Intel, and Xerox. Today, four types of Ethernet technology are used on LANs, with each type being governed by a set of IEEE standards.

Ethernet 802.2 The default frame type for Novell's IntraNetware network operating system. It supports the IPX/SPX protocol. The defining characteristics of its data portion are the source and destination service access points that belong to the Logical Link Control layer, a sublayer of the Data Link layer.

Ethernet 802.3 The original NetWare Ethernet frame type and the default frame type for networks running NetWare versions lower than 3.12. It supports only the IPX/SPX protocol. Ethernet 802.3 is sometimes called 802.3 "raw," because its data portion contains no control bits.

Ethernet II The original Ethernet frame type developed by Digital, Intel, and Xerox, before the IEEE began to standardize Ethernet. Ethernet II lacks Logical Link Control layer information but contains a 2-byte type field to identify the upper-layer protocol contained in the frame.

Ethernet SNAP An adaptation of Ethernet 802.2 and Ethernet II. SNAP stands for Sub-Network Access Protocol. The SNAP portion of the frame contains the three Logical Link Control fields (DSAP, SSAP, and control). An additional field, the Organization ID (OUI), provides a method of identifying the type of network on which the frame is running. In addition, Ethernet SNAP frames carry Ethernet type information, just as an Ethernet II frame does.

express setup An option for installing Windows NT Server in which the most popular installation options are chosen for you. Express setup is faster than custom setup.

extended attributes Attributes beyond the basic Read, Write, System, and Hidden attributes supported by FAT. HPFS supports extended attributes.

Extended Industry Standard Architecture (EISA) A 32-bit bus that is compatible with older ISA devices because it shares the same length and pin configuration as the ISA bus, but that uses a deeper slot connector to achieve faster throughput. The EISA bus was introduced in the late 1980s to compete with IBM's MCA bus.

extended network prefix The combination of an address's network and subnet information. By interpreting an address's extended network prefix, a device can determine the subnet to which an address belongs.

external network number Another term for the network address portion of an IPX/SPX address.

F

fail-over The capability for one component (such as a NIC or server) to assume another component's responsibilities without manual intervention.

failure A deviation from a specified level of system performance for a given period of time. A failure occurs when something doesn't work as promised or as planned.

Fast Ethernet See 100BaseT.

FAT (File Allocation Table) The original PC file system designed in the 1970s to support floppy disks and, later, hard disks. FAT is inadequate for most server operating systems because of its partition size limitations, naming limitations, and fragmentation and speed issues.

FAT32 An enhanced version of FAT that accommodates the use of long filenames and smaller allocation units on a disk. FAT32 makes more efficient use of disk space than the original FAT.

fault The malfunction of one component of a system. A fault can result in a failure.

fault tolerance The capacity for a system to continue performing despite an unexpected hardware or software malfunction.

FDDI (Fiber Distributed Data Interface) A networking standard originally specified by ANSI in the mid-1980s and later refined by ISO. FDDI uses a dual fiber-optic ring to transmit data at speeds of 100 Mbps. It was commonly used as a backbone technology in the 1980s and early 1990s, but lost favor as fast

Ethernet technologies emerged in the mid-1990s. FDDI provides excellent reliability and security.

feasibility study A study that determines the costs and benefits of a project and attempts to predict whether the project will result in a favorable outcome (for example, whether it will achieve its goal without imposing excessive cost or time burdens on the organization).

fiber-optic cable A form of cable that contains one or several glass fibers in its core. Data are transmitted via pulsing light sent from a laser or light-emitting diode through the central fiber(s). Outside the fiber(s), a layer of glass called cladding acts as a mirror, reflecting light back to the core in patterns that vary depending on the transmission mode. Outside the cladding, a layer of plastic and a braiding of Kevlar protect the inner core. A plastic jacket covers the braiding

file-infected virus A virus that attaches itself to executable files. When the infected executable file runs, the virus copies itself to memory. Later, the virus will attach itself to other executable files.

file server A computer that runs the network operating system and enables workstations connected to the network to share resources.

file services The function of a file server that allows users to share data files, applications, and storage areas.

file system An operating system's method of organizing, managing, and accessing its files through logical structures and software routines.

File Transfer Protocol (FTP) An Application layer TCP/IP protocol that manages file transfers between TCP/IP hosts.

filtering database A collection of data created and used by a bridge that correlates the MAC addresses of connected workstations with their locations. A filtering database is also known as a forwarding table.

firewall A specialized device (typically a router, but possibly only a PC running special software) that selectively filters or blocks traffic between networks. A firewall may be strictly hardware-based, or it may involve a combination of hardware and software.

firmware A combination of hardware and software. The hardware component of firmware is a read-only memory (ROM) chip that stores data established at the factory and possibly changed by configuration programs that can write to ROM.

flashing A security attack in which an Internet user sends commands to another Internet user's machine that cause the screen to fill with garbage characters. A flashing attack will cause the user to terminate his or her session.

flavor Term used to refer to the different implementations of a particular UNIX-like system. For example, the different flavors of Linux include Red Hat, Caldera, and Slackware.

flow control A method of gauging the appropriate rate of data transmission based on how fast the recipient can accept data.

forwarding table See *filtering database*.

fractional T1 An arrangement that allows organizations to use only some channels on a T1 line and pay for only the channels actually used.

frame A package for data that includes not only the raw data, or "payload," but also the sender's and receiver's network addresses and control information.

Frame Check Sequence (FCS) The field in a frame responsible for ensuring that data carried by the frame arrives intact. It uses an algorithm, such as CRC, to accomplish this verification.

Frame Relay An updated, digital version of X.25 that relies on packet switching. Because it is digital, Frame Relay supports higher bandwidth than X.25, offering a maximum of 1.544 Mbps throughput. It provides the basis for much of the world's Internet connections. On network diagrams, the Frame Relay system is often depicted as a cloud.

FreeBSD An open source software implementation of the Berkeley Software Distribution version of the UNIX system.

freely distributable A term used to describe software with a very liberal copyright. Often associated with open source software.

frequency The number of times that a signal's amplitude changes over a fixed period of time, expressed in cycles per second, or Hertz (Hz).

full backup A backup in which all data on all servers are copied to a storage medium, regardless of whether the data are new or changed.

full duplexing An enhancement that allows simultaneous two-way transmission between nodes on a network while eliminating collisions. Full duplexing can potentially double a network's bandwidth.

full synchronization A process in which the entire user account database is relayed from the PDC to its BDCs. The network administrator can force full synchronization, but it may generate a great deal of network traffic.

fully qualified host name The name of a host that includes the full domain name as well as the host name—for example, mymachine.domain.org.

G

Gantt chart A popular method of depicting when projects begin and end along a horizontal timeline.

gateway A combination of networking hardware and software that connects two dissimilar kinds of networks. Gateways perform connectivity, session management, and data translation, so they must operate at multiple layers of the OSI Model. See *proxy server.*

Gateway Services for NetWare (GSNW) A Windows NT service that acts as a translator between the Windows NT and NetWare client redirector services. With GSNW installed, a Windows NT server can access files and other shared resources on any NetWare server on the network.

ghosts Frames that are not actually data frames, but rather aberrations caused by a repeater misinterpreting stray voltage on the wire. Unlike true data frames, ghosts have no starting delimiter.

giants Packets that exceed the medium's maximum packet size. For example, any Ethernet packet that is larger than 1518 bytes is considered a giant.

global group A group of users and resources that belong to multiple domains.

globbing A form of file name substitution, similar to the use of wildcards in Windows and DOS.

GNU The name given to the free software project to implement a complete source code implementation of UNIX; the collection of UNIX-inspired utilities and tools that are included with Linux distributions and other free software UNIX systems. The recursive acronym stands for GNU's Not UNIX.

gopher A text-based utility that allows you to navigate through a series of menus to find and read specific files.

grandfather-father-son A backup rotation scheme that uses daily (son), weekly (father), and monthly (grandfather) backup sets.

graphical user interface (GUI) A pictorial representation of computer functions and elements that, in the case of network operating systems, enables administrators to more easily manage files, users, groups, security, printers, and other issues.

group A means of collectively managing users' permissions and restrictions to shared resources. Groups form the basis for resource and account management for every type of network operating system, not just Windows NT Server. Many network administrators create groups according to department or, even more specifically, according to job function within a department.

H

hacker A person who masters the inner workings of operating systems and utilities in an effort to better understand them.

hard disk redundancy See *Redundant Array of Inexpensive Disks (RAID)*.

Hardware Compatibility List (HCL) A list of computer components proven to be compatible with Windows NT Server. The HCL appears on the same CD as your Windows NT Server software and on Microsoft's Web site.

head-end A cable company's central office, which connects cable wiring to many nodes before it reaches customers' sites.

Hertz (Hz) A measure of frequency equivalent to the number of amplitude cycles per second.

heuristic scanning A type of virus scanning that attempts to identify viruses by discovering "virus-like" behavior.

hierarchical file system The organization of files and directories (or folders) on a disk partition in which directories may contain files and other directories. When displayed graphically, this organization resembles a tree-like structure.

hierarchical hybrid topology A network topology that uses layers to separate devices by their priority or function.

host A computer connected to a network that uses the TCP/IP protocol.

host file A text file that associates TCP/IP host names with IP addresses. On Windows 95 and Windows NT platforms, the host file is called "lmhosts."

host name A symbolic name that describes a TCP/IP device.

hot swappable A characteristic that enables identical components to automatically assume the functions of their counterpart if it suffers a fault.

HOWTO A series of brief, highly focused documents giving Linux system details. The people responsible for the Linux Documentation Project centrally coordinate the HOWTO papers (see http://www.linuxhq.com/HOWTO).

HP-UX Hewlett-Packard's proprietary implementation of the UNIX system.

HPFS (High-Performance File System) A file system designed for the OS/2 operating system that offers greater efficiency and reliability than FAT does. HPFS is rarely used but can be supported by Windows NT servers.

hub A multiport repeater containing one port that connects to a network's backbone and multiple ports that connect to a group of workstations. Hubs regenerate digital signals.

hybrid fiber-coax (HFC) A link that consists of fiber cable connecting the cable company's offices to a node location near the customer and coaxial cable connecting the node to the customer's house. HFC upgrades to existing cable wiring are required before current TV cable systems can serve as WAN links.

hybrid topology A complex combination of the simple physical topologies.

Hypertext Markup Language (HTML) The language that defines formatting standards for Web documents.

Hypertext Transport Protocol (HTTP) The language that Web clients and servers use to communicate. HTTP forms the backbone of the Web.

I

i-node A UNIX file system information storage area that holds all details about a file. This information includes the size, access rights, date and time of creation, and a pointer to the actual contents of the file.

IEEE (Institute of Electrical and Electronic Engineers) An international society composed of engineering professionals. Its goals are to promote development and education in the electrical engineering and computer science fields.

incremental backup A backup in which only data that have changed since the last backup are copied to a storage medium.

indirect infrared transmission A type of infrared transmission in which signals bounce off walls, ceilings, and any other objects in their path. Because indirect infrared signals are not confined to a specific pathway, this means of transmitting data is not very secure.

Industry Standard Architecture (ISA) The original PC bus, developed in the early 1980s to support an 8-bit and later 16-bit data transfer capability. Although an older technology, ISA buses are still used to connect serial devices, such as mice or modems, in new PCs.

infrared A type of data transmission that uses infrared light signals to transmit data through space, similar to the way a television remote control sends signals across the room. Networks may use two types of infrared transmission: direct or indirect.

integrity The soundness of a network's files, systems, and connections. To ensure integrity, you must protect your network from anything that might render it unusable, such as corruption, tampering, natural disasters, and viruses.

integrity checking A method of comparing the current characteristics of files and disks against an archived version of these characteristics to discover any changes. The most common example of integrity checking involves a checksum.

intelligent hub A hub that, rather than simply regenerating signals, can manage transmissions by dictating which nodes can send and receive data at every instant.

Internet A complex WAN that connects LANs around the globe.

Internet Control Message Protocol (ICMP) A core protocol in the TCP/IP suite that notifies the sender that something has gone wrong in the transmission process and that packets were not delivered.

Internet Mail Access Protocol (IMAP) A mail storage and manipulation protocol that depends on SMTP's transport system and improves upon the shortcomings of POP. The most current version of IMAP is version 4 (IMAP4). IMAP4 can (and eventually will) replace POP without the user having to change e-mail programs. The single biggest advantage IMAP4 has relative to POP is that it allows users to store messages on the mail server, rather than always having to download them to the local machine.

Internet Protocol (IP) A core protocol in the TCP/IP suite that belongs to the Internet layer of the TCP/IP model and provides information about how and where data should be delivered. IP is the subprotocol that enables TCP/IP to internetwork.

Internet services Services that enable a network to communicate with the Internet, including World Wide Web servers and browsers, file transfer capabilities, Internet addressing schemes, security filters, and a means for directly logging in to other computers.

Internet telephony The provision of telephone service over the Internet.

internetwork To traverse more than one LAN segment and more than one type of network through a router.

Internetwork Packet Exchange (IPX) A core protocol of the IPX/SPX suite that operates at the Network layer of the OSI Model and provides routing and internetwork services, similar to IP in the TCP/IP suite.

Internetwork Packet Exchange/Sequenced Packet Exchange (IPX/SPX) A protocol originally developed by Xerox, then modified and adopted by Novell in the 1980s for the NetWare network operating system.

InterNIC The authority for Internet IP addressing and domain name registration. Also known as *Network Solutions*.

IntraNetWare Another term for NetWare version 4.11, the version in which support for Internet services was first introduced.

intrusion detection The process of monitoring the network for unauthorized access to its devices.

IP address A logical address used in TCP/IP networking. This unique 32-bit number is divided into four groups of octets, or 8-bit bytes, that are separated by periods.

IP datagram The IP portion of a TCP/IP frame that acts as an envelope for data, holding information necessary for routers to transfer data between subnets.

IP Security Protocol (IPSec) A Layer 3 protocol that defines encryption, authentication, and key management for the new version of the TCP/IP protocol suite, IPv6. IPSec adds security information to the header of all IP packets.

IP spoofing A security attack in which an outsider obtains internal IP addresses, then uses those addresses to pretend that he or she has authority to access a private network from the Internet.

IPX address An address assigned to a device on an IPX/SPX network.

IRQ (Interrupt Request Line) The means by which a device can request attention from the CPU. IRQs are identified by numbers from 0 to 15, and many PC devices reserve specific numbers for their use alone.

ISDN (Integrated Services Digital Network) An international standard, established by the ITU, for transmitting data over digital lines. Like PSTN, ISDN uses the telephone carrier's lines and dial-up connections, but it differs from PSTN in that it exclusively uses digital lines and switches.

ISO (International Organization for Standardization) A collection of standards organizations representing 130 countries with headquarters located in Geneva, Switzerland. Its goal is to establish international technological standards to facilitate the global exchange of information and barrier-free trade.

ITU (International Telecommunications Union) A United Nations agency that regulates international telecommunications, including radio and TV frequencies, satellite and telephony specifications, networking infrastructure, and tariffs applied to global communication. It also provides developing countries with technical expertise and equipment to advance these nations' technological bases.

J

jabber A device that handles electrical signals improperly, usually affecting the rest of the network. A network analyzer will detect a jabber as a device that is always retransmitting, effectively bringing the network to a halt. A jabber usually results from a bad NIC. Occasionally, it can be caused by outside electrical interference.

jamming The process by which a station's NIC will first propagate a collision throughout the network so no other station attempts to transmit; after propagating the collision, the NIC will remain silent for a period of time.

K

kernel The core of an operating system. NetWare's 32-bit kernel is responsible for overseeing all critical server processes. The program SERVER.EXE runs the kernel from a server's DOS partition.

kernel modules Portions of the Linux kernel that you can load and unload to add or remove functionality on a running Linux system.

key A series of characters used in many encryption schemes to make decrypting the data more difficult.

L

LAN topology The physical layout of a local area network (LAN).

LANalyzer Novell's network monitoring software package. LANalyzer can act as a standalone program on a Windows 95 or Windows 98 workstation or as part of the ManageWise suite of network management tools on a NetWare server. LANalyzer offers the following capabilities: discovery of all network nodes on a segment; continuous monitoring of network traffic; tripping alarms when traffic conditions meet preconfigured thresholds (for example, if utilization exceeds 70%); and capturing traffic to and from all or selected nodes.

late collisions Collisions that take place outside the normal window in which collisions are detected and redressed. Late collisions are usually caused by a defective station (such as a card, or transceiver) that is transmitting without first verifying line status or by failure to observe the configuration guidelines for cable length, which results in collisions being recognized too late.

latency The delay between the transmission of a signal and its receipt.

layer A logical division between devices on a network.

Layer 2 Forwarding (L2F) A Layer 2 protocol similar to PPTP that provides tunneling for other protocols and can work with the authentication methods used by PPP. L2F was developed by Cisco Systems and requires special hardware on the host system end. It can encapsulate protocols to fit more than just the IP format, unlike PPTP.

Layer 2 Tunneling Protocol (L2TP) A Layer 2 tunneling protocol developed by a number of industry consortia. L2TP is an enhanced version of L2F. Like L2F, it supports multiple protocols; unlike L2F, it does not require costly hardware upgrades to implement. L2TP is optimized to work with the next generation of IP (IPv6) and IPSec (the Layer 3 IP encryption protocol).

Layer 3 switch A switch capable of interpreting data at Layer 3 (Network layer) of the OSI Model.

Layer 4 switch A switch capable of interpreting data at Layer 4 (Transport layer) of the OSI Model.

leaf object A type of NDS object that does not contain other objects. For example, a print queue is a leaf object because it handles only the printer queue.

lease The agreement between a DHCP server and client on how long the client will borrow a DHCP-assigned IP address. As network administrator, you configure the duration of the lease (in the DHCP service) to be as short or long as necessary, from a matter of minutes to forever.

leased lines Permanent dedicated connections established through a public telecommunications carrier and billed to customers on a monthly basis.

license tracking Determining how many copies of a single application are currently in use on the network.

line noise Fluctuations in voltage levels caused by other devices on the network or by electromagnetic interference.

Linux A freely distributable implementation of the UNIX system. It was originally developed by Finnish computer scientist Linus Torvalds.

load balancing An automatic distribution of traffic over multiple links, hard disks, or processors intended to optimize responses.

local area network (LAN) A network of computers and other devices that is confined to a relatively small space, such as one building or even one office.

local collisions Collisions that occur when two or more stations are transmitting simultaneously. Excessively high collision rates within the network can usually be traced to cable or routing problems.

local computer The computer on which you are actually working (as opposed to a remote computer).

local group A group of users and resources that belong to one domain.

local loop The part of a phone system that connects a customer site with a public carrier's POP. Some WAN transmission methods, such as ISDN, are suitable for only the local loop portion of the network link.

Logical Link Control (LLC) sublayer The upper sublayer in the Data Link layer. The LLC provides a common interface and supplies reliability and flow control services.

logical topology The data transmission characteristics of a network design, such as its network transport model.

loopback address An IP address reserved for communicating from a node to itself (used mostly for testing purposes). The value of the loopback address is always 127.0.0.1.

loopback plug A connector used for troubleshooting that plugs into a port (for example, a serial or parallel port) and crosses over the transmit line to the receive line, allowing outgoing signals to be redirected back into the computer for testing.

M

MAC address A number that uniquely identifies a network node. The manufacturer hard-codes the MAC address on the NIC. This address is composed of the block ID and device ID.

macro viruses A newer type of virus that takes the form of a wordprocessing or spreadsheet program macro, which may execute when a word-processing or spreadsheet program is in use.

mail services Network services that manage the storage and transfer of e-mail between users on a network. In addition to sending, receiving, and storing mail, mail services can include intelligent e-mail routing capabilities, notification, scheduling, indexing, document libraries, and gateways to other mail servers.

managed hub See *intelligent hub.*

management services Network services that centrally administer and simplify complicated management tasks on the network. Examples of management services include license tracking, security auditing, asset management, addressing management, software distribution, traffic monitoring, load balancing, and hardware diagnosis.

manual pages UNIX online documentation. This documentation describes the use of the commands and the programming interface to the UNIX system.

master browser A server that locates shared resources for a domain and maintains a database of information about these resources. By default, the PDC acts as the master browser for its domain.

master domain model A way of organizing Windows NT domains so that a single domain controls all user account information, and separate resource domains manage resources such as networked printers. This model suits an environment in which each department in an organization controls its file and print sharing and a central information technology department manages the user IDs, groups, and relationships between the domains.

Media Access Control (MAC) sublayer The lower sublayer of the Data Link layer. The MAC appends the physical address of the destination computer onto the frame.

Megabits per second (Mbps) A measure of how much data a network can optimally transmit, based on its physical characteristics.

member server (MS) A server that takes no responsibility for managing accounts or security in a Windows NT domain. An MS is usually devoted to running a particular application, such as MS SQL Server, that requires dedicated processing resources.

memory range A hexadecimal number that indicates the area of memory that the NIC and CPU will use for exchanging, or buffering, data. As with IRQs, some memory ranges are reserved for specific devices—most notably, the system board.

mesh network An enterprise-wide topology in which routers are interconnected with other routers so that at least two pathways connect each node.

mesh WAN topology A WAN topology that consists of many directly interconnected locations forming a complex mesh.

message switching A type of switching in which a connection is established between two devices in the connection path; one device transfers data to the second device, then breaks the connection. The information is stored and forwarded from the second device once a connection between that device and a third device on the path is established.

MIB (management information base) A collection of data used by management programs (which may be part of the network operating system or a third-party program) to analyze network performance and problems.

MicroChannel Architecture (MCA) IBM's proprietary 32-bit bus for personal computers, introduced in 1987 and later replaced by the more standard EISA and PCI buses.

Microsoft Certified Systems Engineer (MCSE) A professional certification established by Microsoft that demonstrates in-depth knowledge about Microsoft's products, including Windows 98 and Windows NT.

Microsoft Message Queueing (MSMQ) An API used in a network environment. MSMQ stores messages sent between nodes in queues then forwards them to their destination based on when the link to the recipient is available.

milestone A reference point that marks the completion of a major task or group of tasks in a project and contributes to measuring the project's progress.

modem A device that modulates analog signals into digital signals at the transmitting end for transmission over telephone lines, and demodulates digital signals into analog signals at the receiving end.

modular hub A type of hub that provides a number of interface options within one chassis. Similar to a PC, a modular hub contains a system board and slots accommodating different adapters. These adapters may connect to other types of hubs, routers, WAN links, or to both Token Ring and Ethernet network backbones. They may also connect the modular hub to management workstations or redundant components, such as an extra power supply.

modular router A router with multiple slots that can hold different interface cards or other devices so as to provide flexible, customizable network interoperability.

Monitor An NLM that enables the system administrator to view server parameters such as protocols, bindings, system resources, and loaded modules. In many cases, it also allows the system administrator to modify these parameters.

multicasting A means of transmission in which one device sends data to a specific group of devices (not the entire network segment) in a point-to-multipoint fashion. It can be used for teleconferencing or videoconferencing over the Internet, for example.

multimode fiber A type of fiber-optic cable that carries several frequencies of light simultaneously over a single fiber or over multiple fibers. It is the type of fiber-optic system typically used by data networks. Multimode fiber is less expensive than single-mode fiber.

multiple master domain model A way of organizing Windows NT domains in which two or more master domains are joined in a two-way trust to manage many resource domains.

multiplexer In the context of T-carrier technology, a device that provides the means of combining multiple voice and/or data channels on one line. Multiplexers can take input from a variety of terminal equipment, such as bridges, routers, or telephone exchange devices, for use with voice traffic.

multiplexing A technology that divides a single channel into multiple channels for carrying voice, data, video, or other signals.

multiprocessing The technique of splitting tasks among multiple processors to expedite the completion of any single instruction.

multiprotocol network A network that uses more than one protocol.

Multistation Access Unit (MAU) A device on a Token Ring network that regenerates signals; equivalent to a hub.

N

name server A server that contains a database of TCP/IP host names and their associated IP addresses. A name server supplies a resolver with the requested information. If it cannot resolve the IP address, the query passes to a higher-level name server.

name space The database of Internet IP addresses and their associated names distributed over DNS name servers worldwide.

narrowband A type of radio frequency transmission in which signals travel over a single frequency. The same method is used by radio and TV broadcasting stations, and signals can be easily intercepted and decoded.

nbtstat A TCP/IP troubleshooting utility that provides information about NetBIOS names and their addresses. If you know the NetBIOS name of a workstation, you can use nbtstat to determine its IP address.

NDS for NT Novell's integration tool for Windows NT networks. It works with the NetWare 4.x and 5.0 operating systems and Windows NT servers to enable the Windows NT domains to appear as container objects in NWAdmin.

NDS tree A logical representation of how resources are grouped by NetWare in the enterprise.

needs assessment The process of clarifying the reasons and objectives for a proposed change so as to determine whether the change is worthwhile and necessary and to elucidate the scope and nature of the proposed change.

negative frame sequence checks The result of the Cyclic Redundancy Checksum (CRC) generated by the originating node not matching the checksum calculated from the data received. It usually indicates noise or transmission problems on the LAN interface or cabling. A high number of CRCs usually results from excessive collisions or a station transmitting bad data.

NetBEUI (NetBIOS Enhanced User Interface) Microsoft's adaptation of IBM's NetBIOS protocol. NetBEUI expands on NetBIOS by adding an Application layer component. NetBEUI is a fast and efficient protocol that consumes few network resources, provides excellent error correction and requires little configuration.

netstat A TCP/IP troubleshooting utility that displays statistics and the state of current TCP/IP connections. It also displays ports, which can signal whether services are using the correct ports.

NetWare 3.x The group of NetWare versions that includes versions 3.0, 3.1, and 3.2.

NetWare 4.x The group of NetWare versions that includes versions 4.0, 4.1, and 4.11.

NetWare Administrator utility (NWAdmin) The graphical NetWare utility that allows administrators to manage objects in the NDS tree from a Windows 95, Windows 98, or Windows NT workstation.

NetWare Core Protocol (NCP) One of the core protocols of the IPX/SPX suite. NCP handles requests for services, such as printing and file access, between clients and servers.

NetWare Directory Services (NDS) A system of managing multiple servers and their resources, including users, volumes, groups, profiles, and printers. The NDS model is similar to the concept of domains in Windows NT, but more comprehensive. In NDS, every networked resource is treated as a separate object with distinct properties.

NetWare loadable modules (NLMs) Routines that enable the server to run programs and services. Each NLM consumes some of the server's memory and processor resources (at least temporarily). The kernel requires many NLMs to run NetWare's core operating system.

network A group of computers and other devices (such as printers) that are connected by some type of transmission media, usually wire or cable.

Network+ (Net+) Professional certification established by CompTIA that verifies broad networking technology skills such as an understanding of protocols, topologies, networking hardware, and network troubleshooting.

network adapter A synonym for NIC (network interface card). The device that enables a workstation, server, printer, or other node to connect to the network. Network adapters belong to the Physical layer of the OSI Model.

network analyzer A portable, hardware-based tool that a network manager connects to the network expressly to determine the nature of network problems. Network analyzers can typically interpret data up to Layer 7 of the OSI Model.

network architect A professional who designs networks, performing tasks that range from choosing basic components (such as cabling type) to figuring out how to make those components work together (by, for example, choosing the correct protocols).

network interface card (NIC) The device that enables a workstation to connect to the network and communicate with other computers. NICs are manufactured by several different companies and come with a variety of specifications that are tailored to the workstation's and the network's requirements.

Network layer The third layer in the OSI Model. The **Network layer** translates network addresses into their physical counterparts and decides how to route data from the sender to the receiver.

Network layer addresses Addresses that reside at the Network level of the OSI Model, follow a hierarchical addressing scheme, and can be assigned through operating system software.

network monitor A software-based tool that continually monitors traffic on the network from a server or workstation attached to the network. Network monitors typically can interpret up to Layer 3 of the OSI Model.

Network Monitor (NetMon) A software-based network monitoring tool that comes with Windows NT Server 4.0 or with Microsoft's Server Management System (SMS) suite of tools (for earlier versions of Windows NT Server). Its capabilities include capturing network data traveling from one or many segments;

capturing frames sent by or to a specified node; reproducing network conditions by transmitting a selected amount and type of data; detecting any other running copies of NetMon; and generating statistics about network activity.

Network News Transfer Protocol (NNTP) The protocol that supports the process of reading newsgroup messages, posting new messages, and transferring news files between news servers.

network operating system (NOS) The software that runs on a file server and enables the server to manage data, users, groups, security, applications, and other networking functions. The most popular network operating systems are Microsoft's Windows NT and Novell's NetWare.

Network Termination 1 (NT1) A device used on ISDN networks that connects the incoming twisted-pair wiring with the customer's ISDN terminal equipment.

Network Termination 2 (NT2) An additional connection device required on PRI to handle the multiple ISDN lines between the customer's network termination connection and the local phone company's wires.

network transport systems A set of rules specifying which data are packaged and transmitted over network media.

network virus A type of virus that takes advantage of network protocols, commands, messaging programs, and data links to propagate itself. Although all viruses could theoretically travel across network connections, network viruses are specially designed to attack network vulnerabilities.

NetXRay Network analyzer software from Network Associates that provides data capture and analysis, node discovery, traffic trending, history, alarm tripping, and utilization prediction.

newsgroups An Internet service similar to e-mail that provides a means of conveying messages, but in which information is distributed to a wide group of users at once rather than from one user to another.

NFS Network File System. A client/server application that allows you to view, store and update files on a remote computer as though they were on your own computer. Can be used to install Linux.

node Any computer or other device connected to a network.

noise Unwanted signals, or interference, from sources near network cabling, such as electrical motors, power lines and radar.

nslookup A TCP/IP utility that allows you to look up the DNS host name of a network node by specifying its IP address, or vice versa. This ability is useful for verifying that a host is configured correctly or for troubleshooting DNS resolution problems.

NTFS (New Technology File System) A file system developed by Microsoft expressly for Windows NT Workstation and Windows NT Server. NTFS integrates reliability, compression, the ability to handle massive files, and fast access. Most Windows NT Server partitions employ either FAT or NTFS.

NWConv A utility provided with Windows NT that converts (migrates) an existing NetWare server's user account, file, and other information to a Windows NT server.

O

object A resource in NetWare's NDS tree. An object may represent a user, group, print queue, server volume, user template, mailbox, and so on. It may or may not contain other objects. All objects can be centrally managed in NDS.

octet One of the four 8-bit bytes that are separated by periods and together make up an IP address.

one-way domain trust relationship An arrangement in which one domain allows users in another domain to access its resources; the reverse is not true.

online backup A technique in which data are backed up to a central location over the Internet.

online UPS A power supply that uses the A/C power from the wall outlet to continuously charge its battery, while providing power to a network device through its battery.

open shortest path first (OSPF) A routing protocol that makes up for some of the limitations of RIP and can coexist with RIP on a network.

open source software Term used to describe software that is distributed without any restriction and whose source code is freely available. See also "freely distributable".

Open Systems Interconnection (OSI) Model A model for understanding and developing computer-to-computer communication developed in the 1980s by ISO. It divides networking architecture into seven layers: Physical, Data Link, Network, Transport, Session, Presentation, and Application.

Orange Book The security specification for computer operating systems published in 1985 by the U.S. Department of Defense.

organizational unit See *container object.*

owner The person who takes responsibility for ensuring that project tasks are completed on time and within budgetary guidelines.

P

Packet Internet Groper (PING) A TCP/IP troubleshooting utility that can verify that TCP/IP is installed, bound to the NIC, configured correctly, and communicating with the network. PING uses ICMP to send echo request and echo reply messages that determine the validity of an IP address.

packet-filtering firewall A router that operates at the Data Link and Transport layers of the OSI Model, examining the header of every packet of data that it receives to determine whether that type of packet is authorized to continue to its destination. Packet-filtering firewalls are also called *screening firewalls.*

packet switching A type of switching in which data are broken into packets before they are transported. In packet switching, packets can travel any path on the network to their destination, because each packet contains a destination address and sequencing information.

parallel backbone The most robust enterprise-wide topology. This variation on the collapsed backbone arrangement consists of more than one connection from the central router or switch to each network segment.

parity The mechanism used to verify the integrity of data by making the number of bits in a byte sum to either an odd or even number.

parity error checking The process of comparing the parity of data read from a disk with the type of parity used by the system.

partial synchronization A type of synchronization in which only modifications to user account information are transmitted between domain controllers in a domain. In other words, the PDC and BDC find discrepancies in their databases and resolve them. Partial synchronization happens automatically.

passive hub A hub that simply amplifies and retransmits signals over the network.

patch An upgrade to a part of a software program, often distributed at no charge by software vendors to fix a bug in their code or to add slightly more functionality.

patch cable A relatively short section (usually between 3 and 50 feet) of twisted-pair cabling with connectors on both ends that connects network devices to data outlets.

patch panel A wall-mounted panel of data receptors into which cross-connect patch cables from the punch-down block are inserted.

PC card See *PCMCIA*.

PCMCIA An interface developed in the early 1990s by the Personal Computer Memory Card International Association to provide a standard interface for connecting any type of device to a portable computer. PCMCIA slots may hold modem cards, network interface cards, external hard disk cards, or CD-ROM cards.

peer-to-peer communication A simple means of networking computers using a single cable. In peer-to-peer communication, no single computer has more authority than another and each computer can share files with other computers.

peer-to-peer topology A WAN with single interconnection points for each location.

per seat A Windows NT Server licensing mode that requires a license for every client capable of connecting to the Windows NT server.

per server A Windows NT Server licensing mode that allows a limited number of clients to access the server simultaneously. (The number is determined by your Windows NT Server purchase.) The restriction applies to the number of concurrent connections, rather than specific clients. Per server mode is the most popular choice for installing Windows NT Server.

Peripheral Component Interconnect (PCI) A 32- or 64-bit bus introduced in the 1990s, the PCI bus is the NIC connection type used for nearly all new PCs. It's characterized by a shorter length than ISA, MCA, or EISA cards, but a much faster data transmission capability.

phase A measurement of a wave's progress through time and compared with other waves.

Physical layer The lowest, or first, layer of the OSI Model. The Physical layer contains the physical networking media, such as cabling and connectors.

physical memory The chips installed on the computer's system board that provide dedicated memory to that computer (as opposed to virtual memory).

physical topology The physical layout of a network. A physical topology depicts a network in broad scope; it does not specify devices, connectivity methods, or addresses on the network. Physical topologies are categorized into three fundamental geometric shapes: bus, ring, and star. These shapes can be mixed to create hybrid topologies.

pilot network A small-scale network that stands in for the larger network. A pilot network may be used to evaluate the effects of network changes or additions.

pinging The process of sending an echo request signal from one node on a TCP/IP network to another.

pipe The facility in a UNIX system that enables you to combine commands to form new commands in ways that the authors may never have dreamed. It is one of the most powerful facilities of the UNIX system.

pipeline A series of two or more UNIX commands connected together with pipe symbols.

plain old telephone service (POTS) See *PSTN*.

plenum The area above the ceiling tile or below the subfloor in a building.

point of presence (POP) The place where the two telephone systems meet—either a long distance carrier with a local telephone company or a local carrier with an ISP's facility.

point-to-point A link that connects only one site to another site.

Point-to-Point Protocol (PPP) A communications protocol that enables a workstation to connect to a server using a serial connection. PPP can support multiple Network layer protocols, can use both asynchronous and synchronous communications, and does not require much (if any) configuration on the client workstation.

Point-to-Point Tunneling Protocol (PPTP) A Layer 2 protocol developed by Microsoft that encapsulates PPP so that any type of data can traverse the Internet masked as pure IP transmissions. PPTP supports the encryption, authentication, and LAN access services provided by RAS. Instead of users having to dial directly into an access server, they can dial into their ISP using PPTP and gain access to their corporate LAN over the Internet.

polymorphic virus A type of virus that changes its characteristics (such as the arrangement of its bytes, size, and internal instructions) every time it is transferred to a new system, making it harder to identify.

port The address on a host where an application makes itself available to incoming data.

Post Office Protocol (POP) A TCP/IP subprotocol that provides centralized storage for e-mail messages. In the postal service analogy, POP is like the post office that holds mail until it can be delivered.

predecessors Tasks in a project that must be completed before other tasks can begin.

Presentation layer The sixth layer of the OSI Model. The Presentation layer serves as a translator between the application and the network. Here data are formatted in a schema that the network can understand, with the format varying according to the type of network used. The Presentation layer also manages data encryption and decryption, such as the scrambling of system passwords.

Pretty Good Privacy (PGP) A key-based encryption system for e-mail that uses a two-step verification process.

PRI (Primary Rate ISDN) A type of ISDN that uses 23 bearer channels and one 64 Kbps data channel as represented by the following notation: 23B+D. PRI is less commonly used by individual subscribers than BRI, but it may be used by businesses and other organizations needing more throughput.

primary domain controller (PDC) A computer that centrally manages account information and security for an entire domain. Only one PDC may exist for each domain.

print services The network service that allows printers to be shared by several users on a network.

process management Planning for and handling the steps involved in accomplishing a goal in a systematic way. Processes that might be managed during a project's implementation include change, support, training, transitioning, delegation, and problem resolution.

project management The practice of managing resources, staff, budget, timelines, and other variables so as to complete a specific goal within given bounds.

project plan The way in which details of a managed project (for example, the timeline and the significant tasks) are organized. Some project plans are created via special project planning software, such as Microsoft Project.

promiscuous mode The feature of a network adapter card that allows a device driver to direct it to pick up all frames that pass over the network—not just those destined for the node served by the card.

promote A Microsoft term that refers to the process of granting a server higher authority within the domain. For instance, if a PDC fails, the network administrator may promote the BDC to become a PDC.

proprietary UNIX Any implementation of UNIX for which the source code is either unavailable or available only by purchasing a licensed copy from The Santa Cruz Operation (costing as much as millions of dollars).

protected mode A manner in which NetWare runs services in a separate memory area from the operating system. Running services in protected mode prevents one rogue routine from taking the server down. As a result, the service and its supporting routines cannot harm critical server processes.

protocol The rules that the network uses to transfer data. Protocols ensure that data are transferred whole, in sequence, and without error from one node on the network to another.

proxy server A network host that runs a proxy service. Proxy servers may also be called *gateways*.

proxy service A software application on a network host that acts as an intermediary between the external and internal networks, screening all incoming and outgoing traffic and providing one address to the outside world, instead of revealing the addresses of internal LAN devices.

PSTN (Public Switched Telephone Network) The network of typical telephone lines that has been evolving for 100 years and still services most homes.

punch-down block A panel of data receptors into which horizontal cabling from the workstations is inserted.

PVC (private virtual circuit) A point-to-point connection over which data may follow any number of different paths, as opposed to a dedicated line that follows a predefined path. X.25, Frame Relay, and some forms of ATM use PVCs.

R

radio frequency (RF) A type of transmission that relies on signals broadcast over specific frequencies, in the same manner as radio and TV broadcasts. RF may use narrowband or spread spectrum technology.

radio frequency interference (RFI) A kind of interference that may be generated by motors, power lines, televisions, copiers, fluorescent lights, or broadcast signals from radio or TV towers.

RAID Level 0 An implementation of RAID in which data are written in 64 KB blocks equally across all disks in the array.

RAID Level 1 An implementation of RAID that provides redundancy through disk mirroring, in which data from one disk are automatically copied to another disk as the information is written.

RAID Level 3 An implementation of RAID that uses disk striping for data and parity error correction code on a separate parity disk.

RAID Level 5 The most popular, highly fault-tolerant, data storage technique in use today, RAID Level 5 writes data in small blocks across several disks. At the same time, it writes parity error checking information among several disks.

real-time An operating system that minimally includes two characteristics: an ability to respond to external events (for example, a change in temperature), and an ability to respond to those events deterministically—with predictable response time (for example, turning on a heating element within three microseconds).

reassembly The process of reconstructing data units that have been segmented.

redundancy The use of more than one identical component for storing, processing, or transporting data.

Redundant Array of Inexpensive Disks (RAID) A server redundancy measure that uses shared, multiple physical or logical hard disks to ensure data integrity and availability. Some RAID designs also increase storage capacity and improve performance. See also *disk striping,* and *disk mirroring*.

regeneration The process of retransmitting a digital signal. Regeneration, unlike amplification, repeats the pure signal, with none of the noise it has accumulated.

release The act of terminating a DHCP lease.

remote access The capability for traveling employees, telecommuters, or distant vendors to access an organization's private LAN or WAN through specialized remote access servers.

remote access server A combination of software and hardware that provides a central access point for multiple users to dial into a LAN or WAN.

Remote Access Service (RAS) One of the simplest dial-in servers. This software is included with Windows NT Server. Note that "RAS" is pronounced *razz*.

Remote Authentication Dial-In User Service (RADIUS) A server that offers authentication services to the network's access server (which may run Windows NT's RAS or Novell's NAS, for example). RADIUS provides a single, centralized point of authentication for dial-in users and is often used by ISPs.

remote computer The computer that you are controlling or working on via a network connection.

remote control A remote access solution in which the remote user dials into a workstation that is directly attached to the LAN. Software running on both the remote user's computer and the LAN computer allows the remote user to "take over" the LAN workstation.

remote node A client that has dialed directly into a LAN's remote access server. The LAN treats a remote node like any other client on the LAN, allowing the remote user to perform the same functions he or she could perform while in the office.

remote user A person working on a computer in a different geographical location from the LAN's server.

repeater A connectivity device that regenerates and amplifies an analog or digital signal.

resolver Any host on the Internet that needs to look up domain name information.

resource record The element of a DNS database stored on a name server that contains information about TCP/IP host names and their addresses.

resources The devices and data provided by a computer, whether standalone or shared.

restore The process of retrieving files from a backup if the original files are lost or deleted.

Reverse Address Resolution Protocol (RARP) The reverse of ARP. RARP allows the client to send a broadcast message with the MAC address of a device and receive the device's IP address in reply.

ring topology A network layout in which each node is connected to the two nearest nodes so that the entire network forms a circle. Data are transmitted unidirectionally around the ring. Each workstation accepts and responds to packets addressed to it, then forwards the other packets to the next workstation in the ring.

ring WAN topology A WAN topology in which each site is connected to two other sites so that the entire WAN forms a ring pattern. This architecture is similar to the LAN ring topology, except a WAN ring topology connects locations rather than local nodes.

risers The backbone cabling that provides vertical connections between floors of a building.

root A highly privileged user ID that has all rights to create, delete, modify, move, read, write, or execute files on a system. This term may specifically refer to the administrator on a UNIX-based network.

root server A DNS server maintained by InterNIC (in North America) that is an authority on how to contact the top-level domains, such as those ending with .com, .edu, .net, .us, and so on. InterNIC maintains 13 root servers around the world.

routable Protocols that can span more than one LAN segment because they carry Network layer and addressing information that can be interpreted by a router.

route To direct data between networks based on addressing, patterns of usage, and availability of network segments.

router A multiport device that can connect dissimilar LANs and WANs running at different transmission speeds and using a variety of protocols. In addition, a router can determine the best path for data transmission and perform advanced management functions. Routers operate at the Network layer (Layer 3) or higher of the OSI Model. They are intelligent, protocol-dependent devices.

routers Devices that connect network segments and intelligently direct data based on information contained in the data frame.

routing information protocol (RIP) The oldest routing protocol that is still widely used. RIP does not work in very large network environments where data may have to travel through more than 16 routers to reach its destination (for example, on the Internet). And, compared to other routing protocols, RIP is slower and less secure.

routing protocols The means by which routers communicate with each other about network status. Routing protocols determine the best path for data to take between nodes. They are not identical to routable protocols such as TCP/IP or IPX/SPX, although they may piggyback on top of routable protocols.

routing switch Another term for a Layer 3 or Layer 4 switch. A routing switch comprises a hybrid between a router and a switch and can therefore interpret data from Layer 2 and either Layer 3 or Layer 4.

runts Packets that are smaller than the medium's minimum packet size. For instance, any Ethernet packet that is smaller than 64 bytes is considered a runt.

S

sag See *brownout*.

Samba An open source software package that provides complete Windows NT–style file and printer sharing facility.

schema The database that defines a set of objects and their attributes for an NDS tree.

screening firewall See *packet-filtering firewall.*

SDH (Synchronous Digital Hierarchy) The international equivalent of SONET.

Secure Sockets Layer (SSL) A method of encrypting Web pages (or HTTP transmissions) as they travel over the Internet.

security audit An assessment of an organization's security vulnerabilities. A security audit should be performed at least annually and preferably quarterly. For each risk found, it should rate the severity of a potential breach, as well as its likelihood.

security auditing Evaluating security measures currently in place on a network and notifying the network administrator if a security breach occurs.

segment A part of a LAN that is separated from other parts of the LAN and that shares a fixed amount of traffic capacity.

segmentation The process of decreasing the size of data units when moving data from a network segment that can handle larger data units to a network segment that can handle only smaller data units.

self-healing A characteristic of dual-ring topologies that allows them to automatically reroute traffic along the backup ring if the primary ring becomes severed.

Sequence Packet Exchange (SPX) One of the core protocols in the IPX/SPX suite. SPX belongs to the Transport layer of the OSI Model and works in tandem with IPX to ensure that data are received whole, in sequence, and error free.

sequencing The process of assigning a placeholder to each piece of a data block to allow the receiving node's Transport layer to reassemble the data in the correct order.

serial backbone The simplest kind of backbone, consisting of two or more hubs connected to each other by a single cable.

Serial Line Internet Protocol (SLIP) A communications protocol that enables a workstation to connect to a server using a serial connection. SLIP can support only asynchronous communications and IP traffic and requires some configuration on the client workstation.

server A computer on the network that manages shared resources. Servers usually have more processing power, memory, and hard disk space than clients. They run network operating software that can manage not only data, but also users, groups, security, and applications on the network.

server-based network A network that uses special computers, known as file servers, to process data for and facilitate communication between the other computers on the network.

server clustering A fault-tolerance technique that links multiple servers together to act as a single server. In this configuration, clustered servers share processing duties and appear as a single server to users. If one server in the cluster fails, the other servers in the cluster will automatically take over its data transaction and storage responsibilities.

server console The network administrator's primary interface to a NetWare server. Unlike Windows NT, the NetWare server interface is not entirely graphical. NetWare 4.x offers only text-based server menus at the console. NetWare 5.0 allows you to access commands through either a text-based or graphical menu system.

server mirroring A fault-tolerance technique in which one server duplicates the transactions and data storage of another, identical server. Server mirroring requires a link between the servers and software running on both servers so that the servers can continually synchronize their actions and take over in case the other fails.

Service Access Point (SAP) A feature of Ethernet networks that identifies a node or internal process that uses the LLC protocol. Each process between a source and destination node on the network may have a unique SAP.

Service Advertising Protocol (SAP) A core protocol in the IPX/SPX suite that works in the Application, Presentation, Session, and Transport layers of the OSI Model and runs directly over IPX. NetWare servers and routers use SAP to advertise to the entire network which services they can provide.

service pack A significant patch to Windows NT Server software.

services The features provided by a network.

session A connection for data exchange between two parties. The term "session" is most often used in the context of terminal and mainframe communications.

Session layer The fifth layer in the OSI Model. The Session layer establishes and maintains communication between two nodes on the network. It can be considered the "traffic cop" for network communications.

sheath The outer cover, or jacket, of a cable.

shell Another term for command interpreter.

shielded twisted-pair (STP) A type of cable containing twisted wire pairs that are not only individually insulated, but also surrounded by a shielding made of a metallic substance such as foil. The shielding acts as an antenna, converting the noise into current (assuming that the wire is properly grounded). This current induces an equal, yet opposite current in the twisted pairs it surrounds. The noise on the shielding mirrors the noise on the twisted pairs, and the two cancel each other out.

signal bounce A phenomenon in which signals travel endlessly between the two ends of a bus network. Using 50-ohm resistors at either end of the network prevents signal bounce.

signal level An ANSI standard for T-carrier technology that refers to its Physical layer electrical signaling characteristics. DS0 is the equivalent of one data or voice channel. All other signal levels are multiples of DS0.

signature scanning The comparison of a file's content with known virus signatures (unique identifying characteristics in the code) in a signature database to determine whether the file is a virus.

simple installation A NetWare installation option in which the most popular installation options are chosen for you, and the installation takes less time than if you had chosen a custom installation.

Simple Mail Transfer Protocol (SMTP) The TCP/IP subprotocol responsible for moving messages from one e-mail server to another.

Simple Network Management Protocol (SNMP) A communication protocol used to manage devices on a TCP/IP network.

single domain model The simplest Windows NT domain model. It consists of one domain that services every user and resource in an organization.

single-mode fiber A type of fiber-optic cable that carries a single frequency of light to transmit data from one end of the cable to the other end. Data can be transmitted faster and for longer distances on single-mode fiber than on multimode fiber. Single-mode fiber is extremely expensive.

single point of failure A place on the network where, if a fault occurs, the transfer of data may break down without possibility of an automatic recovery.

sneakernet The only means of exchanging data without using a network. Sneakernet requires that data be copied from a computer to a floppy disk, carried (presumably by someone wearing sneakers) to another computer, then copied from the floppy disk onto the second computer.

sniffer A laptop equipped with a special NIC and network analysis software that performs network analysis. Unlike laptops that may have a network monitoring tool installed, sniffers typically cannot be used for other purposes, because they don't depend on an operating system such as Windows.

social engineering Manipulating relationships to circumvent network security measures and gain access to a system.

socket A logical address assigned to a specific process running on a host computer. It forms a virtual connection between the host and client.

soft skills Skills such as customer relations, leadership ability, and dependability, which are not easily measured, but are nevertheless important in a networking career.

software distribution The process of automatically transferring a data file or program from the server to a client on the network.

Solaris Sun Microsystems' proprietary implementation of the UNIX system.

SONET (Synchronous Optical Network) A WAN technology that provides data transfer rates ranging from 64 Kbps to 2.4 Gbps using the same time division multiplexing technique used by T-carriers. SONET is the best choice for linking WANs between North America, Europe, and Asia, because it can link directly with the different standards used in different countries.

Source Route Bridging The method of bridging used on most Token Ring networks.

spike A single (or short-lived) jump in a measure of network performance, such as utilization.

sponsors People in positions of authority who supports a project and who can lobby for budget increases necessary to complete the project, appeal to a group of managers to extend a project's deadline, assist with negotiating vendor contracts, and so on.

spread spectrum A type of radio frequency transmission that uses lower-level signals distributed over several frequencies simultaneously. Spread spectrum RF is more secure than narrowband RF.

stackable hub A type of hub designed to be linked with other hubs in a single telecommunications closet. Stackable hubs linked together logically represent one large hub to the network.

stakeholder Any person who may be affected by a project, for better or for worse. A stakeholder may be a project participant, user, manager, or vendor.

standalone computer A computer that uses programs and data only from its local disks and that is not connected to a network.

standalone hub A type of hub that serves a workgroup of computers that are separate from the rest of the network. A standalone hub may be connected to another hub by a coaxial, fiber-optic, or twisted-pair cable. Such hubs are not typically connected in a hierarchical or daisy-chain fashion.

standards Documented agreements containing technical specifications or other precise criteria that are used as guidelines to ensure that materials, products, processes, and services suit their intended purpose.

standby UPS A power supply that provides continuous voltage to a device by switching instantaneously to the battery when it detects a loss of power from the wall outlet. Upon restoration of the power, the standby UPS switches the device to use A/C power again.

star topology A physical topology in which every node on the network is connected through a central device, such as a hub. Any single physical wire on a star network connects only two devices, so a cabling problem will affect only two nodes. Nodes transmit data to the hub, which then retransmits the data to the rest of the network segment where the destination node can pick it up.

star WAN topology A WAN topology that mimics the arrangement of star LANs. A single site acts as the central connection point for several other locations.

star-wired bus topology A hybrid topology in which groups of workstations are connected in a star fashion to hubs that are networked via a single bus.

star-wired ring topology A hybrid topology that uses the physical layout of a star and the token-passing data transmission method.

static IP address An IP address that is manually assigned to a device.

stealth virus A type of virus that hides itself to prevent detection. Typically, stealth viruses disguise themselves as legitimate programs or replace part of a legitimate program's code with their destructive code.

store and forward mode A method of switching in which a switch reads the entire data frame into its memory and checks it for accuracy before transmitting it. While this method is more time consuming that the cut-through method, it allows store and forward switches to transmit data more accurately.

structured cabling A method for uniform, enterprise-wide, multivendor cabling systems specified by the TIA/EIA 568 Commercial Building Wiring Standard. Structured cabling is based on a hierarchical design using a high-speed backbone.

subnet mask A special 32-bit number that, when combined with a device's IP address, informs the rest of the network as to what kind of subnet the device is on.

subnets In an internetwork, the individual networks that are joined together by routers.

subnetting The process of subdividing a single class of network into multiple, smaller networks.

subprotocols Small, specialized protocols that work together and belong to a protocol suite.

supported services list A document (preferably online) that lists every service and software package supported within an organization, plus the names of first- and second-level support contacts for those services or software packages.

surge A momentary increase in voltage due to distant lightning strikes or electrical problems.

SVC (switched virtual circuit) Logical, point-to-point connections that rely on switches to determine the optimal path between sender and receiver. ATM technology uses SVCs.

switch The hardware that manages network switching; used to separate a network segment into smaller segments, with each segment being independent of the others, and supporting its own traffic.

Switched Ethernet A newer Ethernet model that enables multiple nodes to simultaneously transmit and receive data and individually take advantage of more bandwidth because they are assigned separate logical network segments through switching.

switching A component of a network's logical topology that manages how packets are filtered and forwarded between nodes on the network.

symmetric multiprocessing A method of multiprocessing that splits all operations equally among two or more processors. Windows NT Server supports this type of multiprocessing.

symmetrical A characteristic of transmission technology that provides equal throughput for data traveling both upstream and downstream and is suited to users who both upload and download significant amounts of data.

symmetrical DSL A variation of DSL that provides equal throughput both upstream and downstream between the customer and the carrier.

synchronization The process undertaken by a PDC and its BDCs to keep identical user account information in both of their user databases.

synchronous A transmission method in which data being transmitted and received by nodes must conform to a timing scheme.

System V The proprietary version of UNIX, originally developed at AT&T Bell Labs, currently distributed by The Santa Cruz Operation.

T

T-carriers The term for any kind of leased line that follows the standards for T1s, fractional T1s, T1Cs, T2s, T3s, or T4s.

T1 A T-carrier technology that provides 1.544 Mbps throughput and 24 channels for voice, data, video, or audio signals. T1s may use shielded or unshielded twisted-pair, coaxial cable, fiber-optic, or microwave links. Businesses commonly use T1s to connect to their ISP, and phone companies typically use at least one T1 to connect their central offices.

T3 A T-carrier technology that can carry the equivalent of 672 channels for voice, data, video, or audio, with a maximum data throughput of 44.736 Mbps (typically rounded up to 45 Mbps for purposes of discussion). T3s require either fiber-optic or microwave transmission media.

TCP segment The portion of a TCP/IP packet that holds TCP data fields and becomes encapsulated by the IP datagram.

TCP/IP core protocols The subprotocols of the TCP/IP suite.

Telnet A terminal emulation protocol used to log on to remote hosts using the TCP/IP protocol. Telnet resides in the Application layer of the TCP/IP suite.

terminal A device with little (if any) of its own processing or disk capacity that depends on a host to supply it with applications and data-processing services.

Terminal Access Controller Access Control System (TACACS) A centralized authentication system for remote access servers that is similar to RADIUS.

terminal adapter (TA) Devices used to convert digital signals into analog signals for use with ISDN phones and other analog devices. Terminal adapters are sometimes mistakenly called ISDN modems.

terminal equipment (TE) Devices that connect computers to the ISDN line. Terminal equipment may include standalone devices or cards (similar to the network adapters used on Ethernet and Token Ring networks) or ISDN routers.

terminator A resistor at the end of a bus network used to stop signals after they have reached their destination.

Thicknet A type of coaxial cable, also known as thickwire Ethernet, that is a rigid cable approximately 1 cm thick. Thicknet was used for the original Ethernet networks. Because it is often covered with a yellow sheath, Thicknet is also called "yellow Ethernet." IEEE has designated Thicknet as 10Base5 Ethernet, with the "10" representing its throughput of 10 Mbps, the "Base" standing for baseband transmission, and the "5" representing the maximum segment length of a Thicknet cable, 500 m.

Thinnet A type of coaxial cable, also known as Thin Ethernet, that was the most popular medium for Ethernet LANs in the 1980s. Like Thicknet, Thinnet is rarely used on modern networks.

IEEE has designated Thinnet as 10Base2 Ethernet, with the "10" representing its data transmission rate of 10 Mbps, the "Base" representing the fact that it uses baseband transmission, and the "2" roughly representing its maximum segment length of 185 m.

throughput The amount of data that a medium can transmit during a given period of time. Throughput is usually measured in megabits (1,000,000 bits) per second, or Mbps. The physical nature of every transmission media determines its potential throughput.

tiered WAN topology A WAN topology in which sites are connected in star or ring formations and interconnected at different levels with the interconnection points organized into layers.

time-dependent virus A virus programmed to activate on a particular date. This type of virus, also known as a "time bomb," can remain dormant and harmless until its activation date arrives.

time division multiplexing (TDM) A version of multiplexing that divides the channel into multiple time slots and assigns each data stream its own time slot to follow. Devices at the sending end arrange the data streams (multiplex); devices at the receiving end then filter them back into separate signals (de-multiplex).

time-sharing system A computing system to which users must attach directly so as to use the shared resources of the computer.

token A special control frame that indicates to the rest of the network that a particular node has the right to transmit data.

token passing A means of data transmission in which a 3-byte packet, called a token, is passed around the network in a round-robin fashion.

Token Ring A networking technology developed by IBM in the 1980s. It relies upon direct links between nodes and a ring topology, using tokens to allow nodes to transmit data.

top-level domain (TLD) The highest-level category used to distinguish domain names—for example, .org, .com, .net. A TLD is also known as the domain suffix.

topology The physical layout of a computer network.

traceroute (or **tracert**) A TCP/IP troubleshooting utility that uses ICMP to trace the path from one networked node to another, identifying all intermediate hops between the two nodes. Traceroute is useful for determining router or subnet connectivity problems.

traffic The data transmission and processing activity taking place on a computer network at any given time.

traffic monitoring Determining how much processing activity is taking place on a network or network segment and notifying administrators when a segment becomes overloaded.

Translational Bridging A method of bridging that can connect Token Ring and Ethernet networks.

transmission media The means through which data are transmitted and received. Transmission media may be physical, such as wire or cable, or atmospheric (wireless), such as radio waves.

Transparent Bridging The method of bridging used on most Ethernet networks.

Transport Control Protocol (TCP) A core protocol of the TCP/IP suite. TCP belongs to the Transport layer and provides reliable data delivery services.

Transport layer The fourth layer of the OSI Model. The Transport layer is primarily responsible for ensuring that data are transferred from point A to point B (which may or may not be on the same network segment) reliably and without errors.

Trojan horse A program that disguises itself as something useful but actually harms to your system.

trust relationship (**trust**) An arrangement that grants users from one domain rights to resources in another domain. A unique security identifier identifies each domain, and each domain has its own security database to track rights to files and resources.

tunneling The process of encapsulating one protocol to make it appear as another type of protocol.

twist ratio The number of twists per meter or foot in a twisted-pair cable.

twisted-pair (TP) A type of cable similar to telephone wiring that consists of color-coded pairs of insulated copper wires, each with a diameter of 0.4 to 0.8 mm, twisted around each other and encased in plastic coating.

twisted-pair cable The least expensive LAN cabling, consisting of four sets of two insulated wires twisted around each other. The two insulated wires form the "pair." One wire in each pair carries signal information, and the other is grounded and absorbs interference.

two-way domain trust relationship An arrangement in which two domains allow each other access to their resources. Two-way domain trust relationships are common in WAN situations where two or more locations manage their own domains, but need to share information.

typeful A way of denoting an object's context in which the Organization and Organizational Unit designators ("O" and "OU," respectively) are included. For example, OU=Inv.OU=Ops.OU=Corp.O=Sutkin.

typeless A way of denoting an object's context in which the Organization and Organizational Unit designators ("O" and "OU," respectively) are omitted. For example, Inv.Ops.Corp.Sutkin.

U

Uniform Resource Locator (URL) A standard means of identifying every Web page, which specifies the service used, its server's host name, and its HTML page or script name.

uninterruptible power supply (UPS) A battery-operated power source directly attached to one or more devices and to a power supply (such as a wall outlet), which prevents undesired features of the power source from harming the device or interrupting its services.

unqualified host name A TCP/IP host name minus its prefix and suffix.

unshielded twisted-pair (UTP) A type of cabling that consists of one or more insulated wire pairs encased in a plastic sheath. As its name implies, UTP does not contain additional shielding for the twisted pairs. As a result, UTP is both less expensive and less resistant to noise than STP.

upgrade A major change to the existing code in a software program, which may or may not be offered free from a vendor and may or may not be comprehensive enough to substitute for the original program.

upstream A term used to describe data traffic that flows from a customer's site to the local carrier's POP. In symmetrical communications, upstream throughput is usually much lower than downstream throughput. In symmetrical communications, upstream and downstream throughputs are equal.

User Datagram Protocol (UDP) A core protocol in the TCP/IP suite that sits in the Transport layer, between the Internet layer and the Application layer of the TCP/IP model. UDP is a connectionless transport service.

user A person who uses a computer.

V

vault A large tape storage library.

virtual local area network (VLAN) The means by which a switch can logically group a number of ports into a broadcast domain. A VLAN can consist of servers, workstations, printers, routers, or any other network device you can connect to a switch.

virtual memory Memory that is logically carved out of space on the hard disk (as opposed to physical memory).

virtual private network (VPN) A logically constructed WAN that uses existing public transmission systems. VPNs can be created through the use of software or combined software and hardware solutions. This type of network allows an organization to carve out a private WAN on the Internet (or, less commonly over leased lines) that serves only its offices, while keeping the data secure and isolated from other (public) traffic.

virus A program that replicates itself so as to infect more computers, either through network connections or through floppy disks passed among users. Viruses may damage files or systems or simply annoy users by flashing messages or pictures on the screen or by causing the keyboard to beep.

virus hoax A rumor, or false alert, about a dangerous, new virus that could supposedly cause serious damage to your workstation.

Voice over IP (VoIP) See *Internet telephony*.

volt-amp (VA) A measure of electrical power. A volt-amp is the product of the voltage and current (measured in amps) of the electricity on a line.

W

WAN link The line that connects one location on a WAN with another location.

WAN topology The physical layout of a WAN.

wide area network (WAN) A network connecting geographically distinct locations, which may or may not belong to the same organization.

Windows Internet Naming Service (WINS) A service that resolves NetBIOS names with IP addresses. WINS is used exclusively with systems that use NetBIOS—therefore, it is usually found on Windows-based systems.

wireless Networks that transmit signals through the atmosphere via infrared or RF signaling.

wizard A simple graphical program that assists the user in performing complex tasks, such as configuring a NIC on a server.

workstation A computer that typically runs a desktop operating system and connects to a network.

World Wide Web (WWW or **Web)** A collection of internetworked servers that share resources and exchange information according to specific protocols and formats.

worm An unwanted program that travels between computers and across networks. Although worms do not alter other programs as viruses do, they may carry viruses.

X

X.25 An analog packet switched WAN technology optimized for long-distance data transmission and standardized by the ITU in the mid-1970s. X.25 can support 56 Kbps throughput. It was originally developed and used for communications between mainframe computers and remote terminals.

xDSL Term used to refer to all varieties of DSL.

Z

zone The group of machines managed by a DNS server.

INDEX

A

B

C

D

E

F

G

H

I

J

K

L

M

O

R

S

T

U

V

W